I wholeheartedly recommend it
- Jancis Robinson

The de facto Bible of
South African wine
- Sunday Times

As eagerly awaited as the start of a new pressing season
- Cape Argus

One of the most successful titles
in SA book publishing
- Cape Times

An icon of the industry
- Beeld

There is no wine area in the world
so well-served by such a minutely
detailed and all-encompassing
annual guide
Tom Cannavan's wine-pages

Unquestionably the nation's
best and most useful wine
tasting resource
- The Wine Lovers' Page

Compact, clear and concise
- Prix du Champagne Lanson award citation

John Platter
SOUTH AFRICAN
WINES
2 0 0 7

THE GUIDE TO CELLARS, VINEYARDS

WINEMAKERS, RESTAURANTS

AND ACCOMMODATION

The John Platter SA Wine Guide (Pty) Ltd
www.platteronline.com

Publisher
Andrew McDowall

Editor
Philip van Zyl

Tasters
Michael Fridjhon, Angela Lloyd; Master of Wine Cathy van Zyl; Cape Wine Masters Tim James, Clive Torr, Irina von Holdt & Christine Rudman; honorary member of the Institute of Cape Wine Masters Dave Hughes; Jabulani Ntshangase, Dave Swingler, Mzokhona Mvemve, Ingrid Motteux & Meryl Weaver. 2006 Guide: Neil Pendock & Jörg Pfützner

Associate editors
Tim James, Lindsaye McGregor, Cathy van Zyl & Jos Baker

Contributors
Lindsaye McGregor, Lynne Kloot, Wendy Toerien, Pippa de Bruyn, Ingrid Motteux, Fran Botha, Lynn Bolin, Joanne Simon, Ginette de Fleuriot CWM & Leonie Joubert

Co-ordinators
Anneke Potgieter, Ina de Villiers & Meryl Weaver

Maps & typesetting
Gawie du Toit

Photography
Dennis Gordon

Advertising
Linda Ransome   T 021·438·6161
Young Media   T 011·648·3869

Sales
Alison Worrall   T 083·530·9761

© The John Platter SA Wine Guide (Pty) Ltd 2006
PO Box 1466 Hermanus 7200

Tel: 082 490·1820
Fax: 021 851·7980

winebook@mweb.co.za
www.platteronline.com

ISBN 0-9584506-5-X

Contents

Widespread and disruptive early-season power cuts in 2006 did little to dampen winegrowers' spirits as they brought in one of the healthiest and most promising harvests in recent years. We highlight some of the personalities and events which made this a vintage to remember.

How to Use This Guide

All wines rated 4 stars or more are set in red type

✓ Good value

Visitable wineries in the A-Z are open on public holidays unless noted

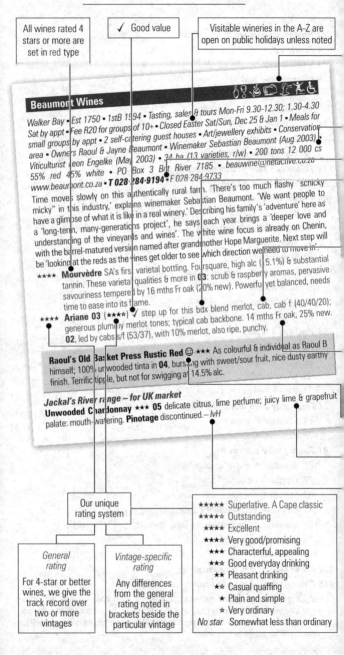

Beaumont Wines

Walker Bay ▪ Est 1750 ▪ 1stB 1994 ▪ Tasting, sales & tours Mon-Fri 9.30-12.30; 1.30-4.30 Sat by appt ▪ Fee R20 for groups of 10+ ▪ Closed Easter Sat/Sun, Dec 25 & Jan 1 ▪ Meals for small groups by appt ▪ 2 self-catering guest houses ▪ Art/jewellery exhibits ▪ Conservation area ▪ Owners Raoul & Jayne Beaumont ▪ Winemaker Sebastian Beaumont (Aug 2003) ▪ Viticulturist Leon Engelke (May 2003) ▪ 34 ha (13 varieties, r/w) ▪ 200 tons 12 000 cs 55% red 45% white ▪ PO Box 3 Bot River 7185 ▪ beauwine@netactive.co.za ▪ www.beaumont.co.za ▪ **T 028·284·9194** ▪ F 028·284·9733

Time moves slowly on this authentically rural farm. 'There's too much flashy "schicky micky" in this industry,' explains winemaker Sebastian Beaumont. 'We want people to have a glimpse of what it is like in a real winery.' Describing his family's 'adventure' here as a 'long-term, many-generations project', he says each year brings a 'deeper love and understanding of the vineyards and wines'. The white wine focus is already on Chenin, with the barrel-matured version named after grandmother Hope Marguerite. Next step will be 'looking at the reds as the vines get older to see which direction we need to move in'.

★★★★ **Mourvèdre** SA's first varietal bottling. Foursquare, high alc (15.1%) & substantial tannin. These varietal qualities & more in 03: scrub & raspberry aromas, pervasive savouriness tempered by 16 mths Fr oak (20% new). Powerful yet balanced, needs time to ease into its flame.

★★★★ **Ariane 03 (★★★★)** ✓ step up for this bdx blend merlot, cab, cab f (40/40/20); generous plummy merlot tones; typical cab backbone. 14 mths Fr oak, 25% new. **02**, led by cabs s/f (53/37), with 10% merlot, also ripe, punchy.

Raoul's Old Basket Press Rustic Red ☺ ★★★ As colourful & individual as Raoul B himself; 100% unwooded tinta in 04, bursting with sweet/sour fruit, nice dusty earthy finish. Terrific tipple, but not for swigging at 14.5% alc.

Jackal's River range – for UK market
Unwooded Chardonnay ★★★ 05 delicate citrus, lime perfume; juicy lime & grapefruit palate: mouth-watering. **Pinotage** discontinued.— *IvH*

Our unique rating system

General rating	Vintage-specific rating
For 4-star or better wines, we give the track record over two or more vintages	Any differences from the general rating noted in brackets beside the particular vintage

★★★★★ Superlative. A Cape classic
★★★★☆ Outstanding
★★★★ Excellent
★★★★ Very good/promising
★★★ Characterful, appealing
★★★ Good everyday drinking
★★ Pleasant drinking
★★ Casual quaffing
★ Plain and simple
★ Very ordinary
No star Somewhat less than ordinary

Symbols

- Ö Bottles own wine on property
- Ŷ Open for tasting (no tasting fee unless noted)
- 🔥 Restaurant/refreshments
- 🛏 Accommodation
- ♬ Other tourist attractions/amenities on the property
- 🍴 Bring your own (BYO) picnic
- 🏃 Child friendly
- ♿ Wheelchair friendly

Case = 12 × 750 ml bottles

T = Telephone number
F = Fax number

cabernet/cab = cabernet sauvignon
pinot = pinot noir
chenin = chenin blanc
sauvignon = sauvignon blanc
riesling = Rhine/weisser riesling
touriga = touriga nacional
tinta = tinta barocca
tinta r = tinta roriz
tinta f = tinta franca

Unless noted, red wines wooded (in 225/300ℓ French oak barrels); Fr = French Am = American oak; whites unoaked

☺ Exceptionally drinkable and well priced

All wines dry unless noted

Taster's initials

Abbreviations

% alc	Percentage alcohol by volume
1stB	First bottled vintage
BYO	Bring your own (wine, picnic)
Bdx	Bordeaux
Cs	Cases
CWG	Cape Winemakers Guild
CWT	Classic Wine Trophy
Est	Date established
EW	Estate wine
g/ℓ	Grams per litre
IWC	International Wine Challenge
IWSC	International Wine & Spirit Competition
JCWCA	Juliet Cullinan Wine Connoisseur's Award
LBV	Late Bottled Vintage
Malo	Malolactic fermentation
MCC	Méthode cap classique
MIWA	Michelangelo Int. Wine Awards
NE	Non-estate wine
NLH	Noble Late Harvest
NV	Non-vintage. Year of harvest not stated on label
RS	Residual sugar
SAA	South African Airways (selected for First or Premium Class)
SAYWS	SA Young Wine Show
SLH	Special Late Harvest
Swiss	Swiss Int. Air Lines Wine Awards
TWS	Trophy Wine Show
Veritas	SA National Bottled Wine Show
VG	Veritas gold medal
VDG	Veritas double-gold medal
Wine	*Wine* magazine
WO	Wine of Origin
WOM	Wine of the Month Club
WS	*Wine Spectator*

Foreword

The release of Nelson Mandela from political incarceration in 1990 and the democratisation process which followed opened up new opportunities for the wine industry, both locally and internationally. The lifting of sanctions saw our wines once more available and accepted worldwide (though in certain instances, I suspect, it may have had rather less to do with the quality of the wines and more the novelty of drinking a wine from 'Mandela's country').

At the same time, just as our wines were making their way to other countries, winelands abroad too began to see South Africa as a new market for their products. While this impacted on the wine industry in term of competition, it also forced more producers to start focusing on quality rather than relying in any way on being a South African product. Increasingly sophisticated consumers, on the other hand, saw this as an opportunity to access international wines, some of them at extremely competitive prices given the stronger rand.

Important as it was to gain entry into the international arena, expanding the market at home became paramount since the greater volume of wine was still sold locally – and without the exorbitant transport costs and vagaries of fluctuating exchange rates associated with export. Any expansion at home would not, however, succeed without taking real steps to ensure effective participation of marginalised groups – black people and women – as owners, winemakers and consumers.

While there is still a long way to go before we can say the industry is fully transformed and inclusive, steps have been taken to address the issues. We have seen an increase in the number of black players who are involved in the industry, as owners, co-owners, winemakers and cellar managers. We have also seen a growth in the number of black people – and increasingly women of all ethnic groups – who appreciate a glass or two from time to time.

Wine shows have been held in areas such as Khayelitsha and Soweto, thereby taking the wine to the townships. (Interestingly, taking wine to Soweto first happened more than 20 years ago when a few winemakers met with about 60 black enthusiasts at a hall at Baragwanath Hospital for a winetasting.) Unfortunately, this opening into a vast untapped market has not yet been taken up to the fullest by the industry. This needs to be addressed to ensure that shebeens, too, offer wine either by the glass or bottle. For this to become a reality, investment in marketing and fostering relations between shebeen owners and winegrowers will be required.

Wine enjoyment is as much the function of promotion, education and those who sell it knowing about the product as it is a personal journey. This is very important when it comes to tourists. We need to expose more foreigners to our wines when they visit our country, regardless of which province they may be in. Visitors exposed to good South African wines are more likely to seek out these wines once back home.

This guide plays an important role in the promotion of wine. Even the most knowledgeable wine enthusiast always looks forward to the next edition to read not only about those wines which got the highest rankings but about general trends in the industry, the farms, the winemakers, how the wines were made, their ageing potential and, above all, to refer to its comprehensive tasting notes, a wonderful way to track to what extent we who are novices can identify the aromas and flavours as outlined. It is simply one of those books which any winelover, seasoned or not, should have to hand at their home or cellar.

I commend it to all who, like me, are still learning about wine. After all, the enjoyment of wine is not about how much you know about it but more about what wine you enjoy at what time of the day and with whom. Ultimately, wine is all about lifestyle and making new friends.

Mbhazima Shilowa
Gauteng Premier

Editor's Note

For this, the 27th annual edition, our aims and approach remain the same: to taste, rate and describe as many of the wines available during the currency of the book, both locally and overseas, as possible. The record number included in these pages – some 6000 individual wines – is a testament both to the growth of the industry and the need to market increased volumes off a total vineyard area which has expanded significantly in recent years. A continuing paradox is the relatively high quantities of unsold stocks, the result of steadily declining local consumption and the generally higher value of the rand, impacting negatively upon export sales. For the guide, the combination of more products and slower sales (plus a tight deadline) meant that we were unable to retaste and re-rate wines which had been submitted previously yet will still be available for sale during the book's currency. Only wines which last year were reviewed as tank or barrel samples, and thus rated provisionally (or considered too young and unformed to rate), were revisited for the current book. New, previously untasted vintages were of course reviewed as normal.

While the number of wine brands and producers burgeoned unabated, wine prices increased much less swiftly, if at all, and we were able to maintain the last two years' value for money parameters. We therefore feel that wines flagged with either the good-value symbol (✓), indicating wines of 3½-star quality or better, or the super-quaffing icon (☺), identifying best buys at 3 stars and below, continue to represent outstanding value in the present market.

Talking of which, the introduction last edition of the guide's first 'Superquaffer of the Year' – the wine which, in the opinion of our tasting team, represents the best value and drinkability of all the entry-level wines scrutinised – was very well received. Accordingly, we continued this year to focus on identifying ultra-easy-drinkers, and are pleased to publish the results of our tastings in the relevant section under the Wines of the Year heading (see p 9). Also listed there are the top-ranked wines for 2006 (the Five Stars and Highly Recommended wines), plus a selection of wines to lay down for future enjoyment.

Our unique star-rating and -notation system, which, for the more ambitious wines (4 stars and more) includes the 'track record' of the particular wine over a minimum of two vintages, is the subject of ongoing debate and enquiry. We have revamped and expanded both the 'How to use the Guide' and 'How to use the A-Z' sections in the hope that these will now better illuminate the star rating system, as well as provide a better guide to the voluminous information contained in the A-Z.

How do we arrive at our star ratings? Each year towards the end of June we mobilise our team of internationally experienced tasters to assess the wines on sale locally and overseas. (Unavoidably examples slip past us, and of course we try to incorporate these and any new releases in the next edition.) The results of their tastings are reflected in the A-Z section, along with news about the wineries and winemakers, general information about products, vinification facilities, vineyards, amenities available to visitors and more. (The ratings for all the wines in the A-Z are also conveniently listed separately in the section now named 'This Year's Ratings Summarised'.)

In line with heightened international interest in SA wine, we continue to highlight names of brands and alternative labels used by local producers for overseas markets (these are also cross-referenced for convenience). Also featured in the A-Z are general style indicators and technical details (note that alcohol, acid, sugar levels, time in wood etc are provided only where they are useful in giving clues to the character of the wine).

For visitors in search of wine-route information, the maps have again been fully updated, along with the accompanying tables which provide additional information about the wineries of the particular region, such as whether or not they are open on weekends and public holidays, offer meals or refreshments, specifically cater for children, and are disabled-friendly.

Staying with disabled-friendliness for a moment: a highlight of this edition for us is the resumption of our earlier initiative to provide professionally conducted audits of winetasting areas, cellar tours and other visitor facilities in the winelands. This programme was launched in 2001 but then had to be shelved for practical reasons. Now it is on track again; read more on page 114.

Also of interest to tourists and wine-ramblers is the Eat-out and Stay-over sections, featuring hotels, B&Bs, restaurants, delis and a plethora of other fine-dining and -reclining venues among the vines. Edited this time by well-seasoned and -travelled Jos Baker. See page 82.

Our wine ranking system remains the same as last year. We cover the full spectrum, from wines we consider 'somewhat less than ordinary' (and award 0 stars) to 'superlative Cape classics', worthy of a full 5 stars. Wines rated ★★★★ or higher are usually listed first in each entry, and set in red type. Vintages deviating from the general rating are individually starred in the text. Very good/promising wines and more modest examples (★★★★ or fewer) are included in the 'run-on' listings at the end of entries. For easy identification, the quaffing best-buys are both boxed together and individually labelled with the wallet-cordial ☺ sign. See also the above-mentioned sections 'How to use the Guide' and 'How to use the A-Z'.

Because of deadlines, many wines in the guide are tasted freshly bottled or as works-in-progress; any considered unrateable as a result are noted as such in the text. It's worth mentioning that we taste from the end of June to early August. Except for the bottlings assessed for five stars (see the preamble to the Wines of the Year), all wines are tasted 'sighted' (with labels exposed), necessarily so, given the high number of unfinished wines submitted for rating. Because of the subjective element associated with wine assessment, we strongly recommend you view our rankings as adjuncts to the tasting notes rather than as oracular pronouncements. For this purpose we include the results of other professional tastings and competitions in both the A-Z and the Top Performers table.

Wines featured in the guide were assessed by our tasting team whose professionalism and unflagging enthusiasm we again gratefully acknowledge. Their names and, now, potted biographies appear in the Credits section (page 3) and the end-papers at the back of the book. Note that tasters' initials appear below the wines they tasted.

Warm thanks to the rest of the splendid and much enlarged team (see Credits). Special thanks to new wine coordinator Anneke Potgieter and her team of Elves; my assistant Ina de Villiers; Sean de Kock for IT magic; Mark White and XtraSmile; Johan Enslin for the icons; Hanneli Smit & co at VinLAB; Ryk Taljaard for the WO maps; the ever helpful SAWIS. And to Gauteng Premier Mbhazima Shilowa for the enthused and inspiring Foreword.

Special thanks to indefatigable wife Cathy, still merrily Trekking, and son Luke, who's disconcertingly morphed (with aid and abetting from mum) into a fan of flamboyant rock singer Meat Loaf!

And last but certainly not least, sincere thanks to SA's wine producers, without whose support the book could not be produced. And the usual invitation to visit our website, www.platteronline.com, plus an invitation to check out the new version of the guide for Windows Mobile based handheld computers at selected retail stockists.

Wines of the Year

In the course of tasting and rating close to 6 000 wines for this edition, the members of our team individually identified a limited number of bottlings showing exceptional quality. These were entered into a second round of tasting, open only to finished/bottled wines, available during the currency of the book. The short-listed wines were retasted 'blind' (without sight of the label) by an assembled panel, and those regarded as superlative in an SA context awarded the guide's highest grading — five stars. These stand-outs are listed below under the heading 'Five Stars'. The highest scoring five-star wines were subjected to a further evaluation to determine the overall top scorer. The wine which emerged from this stringent selection represents the pinnacle of SA winemaking and is the recipient of the guide's highest accolade: Wine of the Year.

The wines which did not make the five-star selection, but which are extremely fine and collectible in their own right, are listed immediately below the Five Stars under the heading 'Highly Recommended'. Implicit in wines of this calibre is the potential to improve with further bottle-maturation — say 8-10 years, perhaps more, in the case of the reds and fortifieds, and around 6-8 years for the whites. (Proper storage is, of course, vital for sound maturation.) During the cycle of tasting, our tasters identified a number of bottlings, over and above the candidate five-stars, which show particular potential for cellaring. These ageworthy wines are listed separately under the heading 'Buy Now, Drink Later'.

Also listed are a selection of entry-level wines offering exceptional drinkability at budget prices. The 'Superquaffer of the Year' provides the best overall value and quaffability in this category.

Further details about all releases listed in this section will be found under the names of the relevant producers in the A-Z directory. The five-star tasting is audited by PKF (Cpt) Inc.

▮ Wine of the year

White blends
- Vergelegen White

▮ Five stars

Cabernet sauvignon
- Boekenhoutskloof 2004
- Rudera 2003
- Neil Ellis Vineyard Selection 2004

Chardonnay
- Hamilton Russell Vineyards 2005
- Waterford 2005

Chenin blanc
- De Morgenzon 2005
- Rudera Robusto 2005
- Spier Private Collection 2005

Dessert wine unfortified
- Ken Forrester 'T' Noble Late Harvest 2005
- Paul Cluver Weisser Riesling NLH 2005
- Signal Hill Eszencia NV

Pinot noir
- Bouchard Finlayson Tête de Cuvée Galpin Peak 2003

Port
- Boplaas Vintage Reserve 2004
- Boplaas Cape Tawny Vintner's Reserve 1980
- De Krans Vintage Reserve 2004
- JP Bredell Wines Cape Vintage Reserve 2001

■ Five Stars *(continued)*

Red blends
- Ernie Els Ernie Els 2004

Sauvignon blanc
- Cape Point Vineyards (Woolworths) Limited Release 2006

Shiraz
- Boekenhoutskloof Syrah 2004
- Fairview Solitude 2004
- Hartenberg The Stork 2004
- Raka Biography 2004
- Saxenburg Select 2003

White blends
- Cape Point Vineyards Isliedh 2005

■ Highly Recommended

Cabernet franc
- Raats Family 2004

Cabernet sauvignon
- Glen Carlou Gravel Quarry 2004
- Rustenberg Peter Barlow 2004
- Springfield Whole Berry 2004
- Thelema 2004

Chardonnay
- Jordan Winery Nine Yards Reserve 2005
- Nederburg Private Bin D270 2005
- Springfield Méthode Ancienne 2004
- Uva Mira 2005
- Vergelegen Lower Schaapenberg 2005

Chenin blanc
- Jean Daneel Signature 2005
- Ken Forrester The FMC 2004
- Spice Route 2005

Dessert wine unfortified
- Hazendal The Last Straw 2005

Merlot
- Hartenberg 2004

Pinot noir
- Hamilton Russell Vineyards 2005

Pinotage
- De Waal Top of the Hill 2004
- Simonsig Redhill 2004

Port
- Axe Hill Cape Vintage Port 2004
- Boplaas Cape Tawny NV
- De Krans Cape Tawny NV

Red blends
- Boekenhoutskloof Chocolate Block 2005
- Camberley Philosopher's Stone 2004
- De Trafford Elevation 393 2004
- Hartenberg The MacKenzie 2004
- Havana Hills Kobus 2003
- Kaapzicht Steytler Vision 2003
- Kanonkop Paul Sauer 2003

Red blends *(continued)*
- Post House Penny Black 2004
- Rustenberg John X Merriman 2004
- The Winery of Good Hope Black Rock 2005
- Waterford CWG Auction Reserve 2004
- Yonder Hill Inanda 2004

Sauvignon blanc
- Groote Post (Woolworths) Reserve 2006
- Oak Valley Mountain Reserve 2005
- Springfield Special Cuvée 2006
- Steenberg Reserve 2006
- The Company of Wine People Kumkani 2006
- Tokara White 2005

Semillon
- Cape Point Vineyards 2005

Shiraz
- Cloof Crucible 2004
- Flagstone CWG Auction Reserve 'Love Handles' 2004
- Gilga Wines Syrah 2004
- Glen Carlou Syrah 2005
- Muratie 2004
- Ridgeback Wines 2004
- Sadie Family Columella 2004
- Saxenburg Private Collection 2003
- The Observatory Cellars Syrah 2004

White blends
- Sadie Family Palladius 2005
- The Company of Wine People Kumkani Chardonnay-Viognier 2005

■ Buy Now, Drink Later

Cabernet franc
- Plaisir de Merle 2004
- Cabernet sauvignon
- Alto 2004
- Anura Reserve 2004
- Boschendal Reserve Collection 2003
- Buitenverwachting 2002
- Grangehurst Reserve 2003
- Hartenberg 2004
- Le Riche Reserve 2003
- Paul Cluver 2003
- Saxenburg 2003
- Stark-Condé Wines Condé 2004
- Vergelegen 2004
- Zorgvliet 2004
- Zorgvliet Richelle 2004

Chardonnay
- Ataraxia 2005
- Thelema 2005

Dessert wine unfortified
- Klein Constantia Vin de Constance 2001
- Klein Constantia Sauvignon Blanc Noble Late Harvest 2005
- Tulbagh Mountain Vineyards TMV Vin Pi One NV
- Vergelegen Weisser Riesling NLH 2005

Merlot
- Asara 2001
- Plaisir de Merle 2003
- Vergelegen 2004

Méthode cap classique
- Graham Beck Blanc de Blancs 2002

Petit verdot
- Zorgvliet 2005

Pinot noir
- Chamonix 2005
- Oak Valley 2005
- Paul Cluver 2004

Pinotage
- Ashbourne Ashbourne 2004
- Grangehurst 2001
- Kanonkop 2004
- Scali 2004
- Southern Right 2005

Red blends
- Adoro Red 2004
- Asara Bell Tower Collection Estate Wine 1999
- Ataraxia 'Ataraxia' 2005

Red blends (continued)
- Buitenverwachting Christine 2002
- Chamonix Troika 2004
- Diemersfontein Heaven's Eye 2004
- Eikendal Classique 2003
- Fryer's Cove Richard Fryer 2004
- Glen Carlou Grand Classique 2003
- Grangehurst Nikela 2001
- Grangehurst Cabernet Sauvignon-Merlot 2001
- Grangehurst Shiraz-Cabernet Sauvignon Reserve 2003
- Havana Hills Du Plessis Reserve 'Du Plessis' 2004
- Jean Daneel Signature Cabernet Sauvignon-Merlot 2002
- Ken Forrester Gypsy 2003
- Klein Constantia Marlbrook 2005
- Klein Gustrouw Cabernet Sauvignon-Merlot 2004
- La Motte Shiraz-Viognier 2004
- Lammershoek Roulette 2004
- Le Bonheur Prima 2003
- Meerlust Rubicon 2003
- Meinert Synchronicity 2004
- Newton Johnson Shiraz-Mourvèdre 2005
- Oak Valley The Oak Valley Blend 2004
- Plaisir de Merle Grand Plaisir 2004
- Remhoogte Estate Wine 2004
- Rupert & Rothschild Baron Edmund 2003
- Simonsig Frans Malan 2004
- Tulbagh Mountain Vineyards Syrah-Mourvèdre 2004
- Tulbagh Mountain Vineyards TMV Viktoria 2005
- Vriesenhof Kallista 2003
- Warwick Trilogy 2004

Riesling
- Klein Constantia Rhine Riesling 2006

Shiraz
- Asara 2003
- Cederberg CWG Auction Teen die Hoog Shiraz 2004
- Domaine Finlayson-Edgebaston First Release 2004
- La Motte 2004

▪ Buy Now, Drink Later *(continued)*

Shiraz *(continued)*
- Plaisir de Merle 2003
- Rudi Schultz Syrah 2005
- Scali Syrah 2004
- Simonsig Tiara 2004
- Simonsig Merindol Syrah 2004
- Simonsig Auction Reserve 2004
- Stark-Condé Wines Syrah 2004
- The Cheviot Winery Syrah 2004
- Tulbagh Mountain Vineyards TMV Swartland Syrah 2005
- Vins D'Orrance Syrah 'Cuvée Ameena' 2004

White blends
- Adoro Naudé White Blend 2006
- De Grendel Winifred 2006
- Klein Constantia Madame Marlbrook 2005
- The Observatory Cellars Chenin Blanc-Chardonnay 2005

▪ Superquaffer of the Year

Merlot
- Yonder Hill 'Y' 2006

Exceptionally Drinkable & Well Priced
Chenin blanc
- Perdeberg Winery Chenin Blanc (Dry) 2006
- Zidela 2006

Dessert wine unfortified
- Roodezandt Special Late Harvest 2005

Gewürztraminer
- Koelenhof Winery Koelnektar 2006

Red blends
- Botha Wine Cellar Dassie's Rood 2005
- Craighall Cabernet Sauvignon-Merlot 2005
- De Krans Relishing Red NV
- De Meye Little River Blend 2004
- Dominion Sugarbush Ridge Cabernet Sauvignon-Merlot 2005
- Jason's Hill Jason's Creek Classic Red 2004
- Knorhoek Two Cubs Cape Blend 2005

Shiraz
- Roodezandt 2005

This Year's Ratings Summarised

Here we summarise all wines featured in the A–Z section, with their ratings, sorted first by wine style, in alphabetical order, and then by producer or brand New wines in **bolder** type. **NS** = no star; **NT** = not tasted; **NR** = tasted but not rated; **D** = discontinued. Where wineries produce more than one version of a particular style, the number of versions is indicated in brackets after the name.

Barbera
★★★☆ Fairvw ★★★ Altyd, Riverstn ★★★ Hofstraat ★★ Lndzicht

Blanc de noir
★★★ Bein, Btnvrwchtng, **Nthlingshof** ★★★ Bschndal, **Dmrsdal**, Grt Cnstntia, Hzndal, Klein Parys, Lndskrn, Louiesnhf, Lynx, Swrtland, Wlworths ★★ Aan de Drns, Boplaas, Goudini, Jonkhr, KWV, Van Lvren ★★ Country C (Low alc), Klawer, Montpllr, Oranje, Oude Kaap, Van Lvren ★★ Cltzdorp, Du T'kloof, **Freedom Hill**, Oude Wllngton, **Rietrvr NT** Clmborg, Picardi **D** Ashton

Bukettraube
★★★ Cedrbrg ★★★ Du T'kloof, Smnsvlei ★★ Swrtland ★★ Citrus

Cabernet franc
★★★★★ Raats Fam

★★★★ Bellnghm, Ekndal, High C, Plaisir, Warwick, Zrgvliet

★★★☆ Avndale, Avntuur, Cpe Grace, **Hpietrsfntein**, Lournsfd, Ndrburg, Rainbow, Whlhaven, Zrgvliet ★★★ Môreson, Nthlingshof ★★★ Weening Barge ★★ My Wyn , **NT** Philip J **NR** Signal H

Cabernet sauvignon
★★★★★ Bknhtskloof, Neil E, Rudera

★★★★☆ Asara, Blue Creek, Carisbrke, De Traf, **Glen C**, Katbakkies, KWV, Le Riche (2), Mischa, Mrgnhof, Rstnberg, Rudera, Sprgfield (2), Stark-C, Stony B, Thelema (3), Verglgn (2), Waterfd

★★★★ Alto, Annandale, Anura, Avndale, Bellnghm, Bilton, Bloemndal, Blwklppn, Boland, Bon Cap (organic), Bon Crge, Bschndal, Btnvrwchtng, Cedrbrg (2), Cloof, Crows Nest, Darling C, Daview, Delaire, Delheim, Dmrsfntn, **Ernie Els**, Fairvw, Fleur dC (2), Flgstone (2), G Beck, Goede H, Goedvrwcht, Gracelnd, Grnde Prvnce, Grnghurst, Hidden V, Hrtnberg, Jordan, JP Bredell, Kaapzicht (2), Kleine Z, Kloovnbrg, Knrhoek, KWV (2), L'Avenir, La Couronne, Le Riche, Linton P, Lndskrn (2), L'Ormarins, L'rdge, Makro, Manley, Marklew, Mischa, Mnt Rozier, Mooipls, Muratie, Ndrburg, Neil E, Nitida, Nthlingshof, Olsen, Olyvenbosch, Ovrgaauw, Paul C, Plaisir, Rbtson, Rhbsklf, Rijk's, Rmhoogte, Seidel, Signal H, Spier, Stellky, **Sterhuis**, **Stnberg**, Stnwall, Stony B, Sxnburg, The Winery, Tokara, **Usana**, Vriesenhof, Vruchtbaar, Waverley Hills (organic), Wbrsburg, Wlworths, Zrgvliet

★★★☆ Afrcn Pride, Allesvlrn, Alluvia, Alter Ego, **Babylon's Pk**, Bergsig, Bernheim, Black Pearl, Blue Crane, Bodraai, Bon Crge, Bonfoi, Bonnivle Cllrs, Boplaas, Bottlry Int, **Bovlei**, BWC, Chamnx, Cilandia, Clmborg, Cls Mlvrne, Darling C, Dbn Hills, De Meye, De Wetsh, Dieu D, Dmrsdal, Domaine B, Drmrshire, Du T'kloof, Eaglevlei, Eikehof, Ekndal, **F'hoek Vyds**, Fredine Wines, G Beck, **Galleon**, Gehot Bosch, Grnghurst, **Groenld**, Grt Cnstntia, Hildenb (2), Hofstraat, Hpnbrg, Jacobsdal, Jonkhr, K Constantia, Kleine Z, Knonkp, KWV (2), La Motte, La Petite F, Laborie, Laibach, Lanzerac, Ldrsburg, Le Bonh, Linde, Linton P, Lndhorst, Lournsfd (2), Lynx, Mdlvlei, Meerend, Môreson, Mrgnhof, **Ndrburg** (3), Neil E Meyer N, Ntvbij, Oewerzicht, Oracle, Ormonde, Oude Cmpgnies, Post Hse, **Rbtson** (3), Rdezandt (2), Rickety, Ridgeback, **Rietvallei** (2), Royle Fam, Rstnberg, Rtrsvlei, Rust en V, Savanha, S'bosch Hills, Shoprite, Smnsig, Smnsvlei, Stark-C, Stellnzcht, **Stettyn**, **Sthrn Sky**, Swrtland, Sylvnvle, Terroir, The Co of Wne (2), **Thelema**, Uitkyk, **Upland** (organic) (2), Van Lvren, Villiera, Vljsdrift, Vrgnoegd, Warwick, Welbedcht, Western (2),

Zevnwacht, Zonneblm, **Zrgvliet** (3) ★★★ Afrcn Terroir (2), Altyd, Ashanti, Ashton, Assegai, **Audacia** (2), Avntuur, **Ayama**, Bartinney, Bcksbrg, **Beau Joubert**, Bianco, Bknhtskloof, Boland, **Bosman Fam**, Botha, Bottlry Int, Bovlei, Bscheim, Bschklf, **Bucks Rdg**, Cameradi, Cilliers, Clairvx, Clovelly, Conradie, Cowlin, **Cpe First** (2), Cru, Daview, De Krans, De Meye, Devon H, Dispore Kamma, Dmrsfntn, Domein Drnkraal, Doolhof, Douglas G, Drknsig, **Du Preez**, Eaglevlei, Ernst Co, Exclsor (2), Freedom Hill, Goedvertw, Groenld, High C, **Jacques Smit**, **Janéza**, Jason's, Klein Parys (2), Kleine Z (2), Klnvallei, Krnskop, KWV, Libertas, Long Mntn (2), Lushof, Lyngrove, MAN Vintners, **Marianne**, McGreg, Mellasat, Mnt Rochelle, Mntn Ridge, **Môreson**, My Wyn, Napier, Nelson, New Begin, New Cape, Niel J, Nthlingshof, Nuy, Obikwa, Opstal, Oude Kaap, Pick's Pick, Pulpit Rock, **R Suter**, Rainbow, Riebeek, Rooibrg, Rtrsvlei, Rusticus, Savanha, Slaley, Slnghoek, Smnsvlei (2), Smrbsch, Spier, Stellar (organic), Stellndrft (2), Sthrn Cape Vyds, Sthrn Sky, Stony B, Table Mtn, The Co of Wne (2), Tulbagh, Vinus Via, Welgegund, **Welgevallen**, Wine Source SA, **Withington**, Wlworths, Wndmeul, Yonder, Zndbrg, Zrgvliet ★★★ Afrcn Pride, Afrcn Terroir, Agterplaas, Bergwater, Botha, Cloof, **Cltzdorp**, Cpe Hutton, Cru, De Villiers, **Elberti**, **Eshkl Kshr**, FirstCpe, Furstnbrg, **Goudini**, Hippo, Jonkhr, Kango (2), Kln Draken (Kosher), La Providnce, Lategnskp, Le Grand Chass, Lindiwe, Linton P, Lngvrwacht, Major's Hill, Mellasat, Mns Ruber (2), **Mnt Vernon**, Mntn River, Montpllr, **Mooi Bly**, Oranje, **Origin**, Pulpit Rock, Riebeek, Riverstn, Schlkbnbsch, Seidel (2), Shoprite, **Slow Wine**, Stellar, Swrtland, Tulbagh (2), Wamaker (2), Welgelee, Westcrp Int, Wlington, **Wlworths** (2) (organic) ★★ Afrcn Terroir (2) (organic), Belbon Hills, Boplaas, **Brndvlei**, Cpe Coastal, **Devonvale Golf**, Drknsig, Drostdy, Du T'kloof, F'hoek Vyds, Grt Eilnd, Jacaranda, **Jacques Smit**, Keukenhof, **Le Mnoir Brndel**, Leopard's, **Long Mntn**, Ltzvlle, Mostrtsdrift, **Natte Valleij**, Onderklf, **Org de Rac** (organic), **Ovrhex Int**, Rooibrg, Stellar (organic), Tulbagh, Under Oaks, Vlrsdorp, Wandsbeck, Wlington, Wndmeul ★★ Citrus, De Zoete (2), Du T'kloof, Makro, Oranje, Origin (organic), Stellrust, Tall Horse, Wlworths ★ Lndzicht ✩ Oude Wllington, Rose Garden, Welvenpas **NT** Anthill, Belfield, **Blue Cove** (2), Blwklppn, Bodega, Bonnivle Cllrs, De Doorns, Drostdy, Eshkl Kshr, Fairseat, Fort S, Hrtswater, Huguenot, Kingsrivier, Klnhof, Koningsrvr, La Bri, Mouton, Mrhof, Old Brdge (2), Prmium Cpe Wnes, Prospect (2), Schoonberg, Stnberg, Stormhoek, Uitvlucht, Ultra Liq, Waverly TBS (2), Wine Concepts, Wldekrans, **Zandrft NR** Arabella, Coleraine, Elgin Vntnrs, Hemlzcht, **Org de Rac** (organic), Oudeklf **D** Assegai, Bcksbrg (2), Bschndal, Cpe Coastal, De Compagnie, Dieu D, Ekndal, Havana, Hldrkruin, Kanu, L'Avenir, L'rdge, Newton J, Perdebrg (2), Ridder's, The Co of Wne, Thorn, Vendôme, Havana

Cabernet-based blends

★★★★✩ Anwilka, Cls Mlvrne, De Traf, Ernie Els, Flgstone, Ingwe, KWV, Ndrburg, Nthlingshof

★★★★ Alto, Bonfoi, **Bschklf**, **Cameradi**, Carisbrke, Cloof, Cls Mlvrne, Cmbrly, De Meye, Dmrsfntn, Ernie Els, Gracelnd, **Heron Rdg**, Joostnbrg, L'Avenir, Le Riche, Lournsfd, **Mooipls**, Mulderb, Rijk's, Rmhoogte, Rust en V, Uva Mira, Waterfd, Zonneblm

★★★☆ Allee B, Avndale, Bodraai, Bschndal, Cls Mlvrne, Cpe Bay, **Cpe Point**, **Croydon**, Doolhof (2), Douglas G, Flgstone, Hrtnberg, Jordan, Kaapzicht, KWV, Lushof, Nabyglgn, Ndrburg, Oude Cmpgnies, **Pick's Pick**, **R Suter**, Rstnberg, Slaley, Smrbsch, Stormhoek, **Swrtland**, Uitkyk, Vrdnheim, Vrgin Erth, **Wlington**, Wlworths, Wstbrdge, Zndvliet ★★★ 32 South, Asara, **Bergwater**, Boland, Cabrière, **Cloof** (2), **Cpe Grace**, De Trafford, Dieu D, Dmrsdal, **Dornier**, Flgstone, Glen C, Goede H, Grte Pst, **Herold**, Hill & Dale, **Jacques Smit**, Klnvallei, Le Grand Chass, Lmrshoek, Lndhorst, Lvland, Lynx, Mnt du Toit, Mntn Range, Mooitsg, Opstal, **Origin** (2), Rbtson, Seven Oaks, **Skilpadvlei**, Smook, Stellndrft, Sxnburg, Van Lvren, Vrede en Lust (2), **Vrgin Erth** ★★☆ Agterplaas, Bon Crge, Bonnivle Cllrs, Chamnx, Delheim, Janéza, Kango, **La Petite F**, **Montagu**, Oranje, **Origin**, Padda, Rietvallei, Smnsig, **Sthrn Sky**, Western, Wlworths ★★ Ch Lib, Fairvw, Olsen, Schlkbnbsch, Slaley, Tassenbrg ★☆ Bottlry Int, Origin, Tangara **NT** Boland, Drostdy, **Du T'kloof**, Eshkl Kshr, Seven Oaks **NR** **Devonvale Golf D** Bonnivle Cllrs, Bschndal, Cordoba, Cpe Coastal, De Zoete, La Couronne, Lvland

Cape 'Bordeaux' (cab sauv with: cab f, merlot, malbec and/or petit verdot)

✮✮✮✮✮ Ernie Els

✮✮✮✮✩ Asara, Btnvrwchtng, Byrskloof, Capaia, Cmbrly, Cordoba, Dalla Cia, Dbn Hills, De Toren, Dornier, Grnghurst, Havana (2), High C, Horse Mtn, Hrtnberg, Ingwe, Jordan (2), Kln Gustrw, Knonkp, Meinert, Mrgnhof, Mrgnster, Mrlust, Muratie, Ovrgaauw, R&R, Rstnberg, Sprgfield, Stellky, Tokara, Veenwdn, Verglgn (2), Vilafonte (2), Von O, Vrgnoegd, Warwick, **Wlworths**, Yonder, Zrgvliet

✮✮✮✮ Adler, Avntuur, Bcksbrg, Bellevue, **Bilton**, Blwklppn, Bschklf, Bschndal, Chamnx, Cloof, Cls Mlvrne, Cmbrly, Con Uitsig, Conspirare, Daview (2), De Toren, Delaire, Delheim, Ekndal, Flgstone, Fryer, G Beck, Glen C, Goede H, Goedvrwcht, Grt Cnstntia, **High Road**, Hillcrest, Idiom, Jean D, **Joostnbrg**, JP Bredell, K Constantia, Kanu, La Motte, Laibach, Le Bonh, Lynx, L'Ormarins, M Mossop Wines, Makro (2), Meerend, **Mnt Destin**, Mrgnster, Mrlust, Mulderb, Môreson, Nabyglgn, Ndrburg (2), Neil E, Nitida, **Oak Valley**, Old Vines, Plaisir, Raka, Ridgeback, Rijk's, Seidel, Smnsig, Spier, Stellnzcht, Stnwall, Stony B, S'bonga, **The Goats**, Veenwdn, Villiera, Vljsdrift, Von O, Vriesenhof, **Vuurberg**, **Warwick**, Wbrsburg, Welbedcht, Welgemnd (2), Wlworths (organic), Zrgvliet

✮✮✮✩ Allee B, Amani, **Anura**, **Armarjaro**, Beaumnt, **Bergsig**, **Black Oyster**, **Blank Bottle**, Blouvlei, Bovlei, Btnvrwchtng, Bwland, **Bwland**, Capaia, Cloof, Cmbrly, Cowlin, Delaire, Dmrsdal, Gusto, **Haskell**, **High Road**, Iona, **J Schaal**, Jean D, Jonkhr, Jordan, K Constantia, **Kleinfntn**, **Kloovnbrg**, La Bri, Laborie, Laibach (2) (organic), Lanzerac, Ldrsburg, **Leopard Frog**, Lndskrn, **Louiesnhf**, Lyngrove, Makro, Mnt Rochelle, Mntn River, Mrgnster, **Mvemve Raats**, Môreson, Napier, Nick Forti's, Nico V, Nthlingshof, Ormonde, Paul C, R&R, Reyneke, Saronsbrg, **Ses'Fikile**, Slaley, Smnsvlei, Stellrust, Swrtland, S'bosch Hills, The Co of Wne (3), Two Oceans, Uva Mira, **Vendôme**, Verglgn, **Vrede en Lust**, Vriesenhof (2), Vuurberg, Welgemnd, **Wlworths** (2), **Ziggurat** ✮✮✮ Agterplaas, Audacia, Avntuur, Avntuur, Bellnghm, Blouvlei, Bonnivle Cllrs, Bottlry Int, Cls Mlvrne, Coleraine, Cordoba, Cpe Bay, **Cpe First** (2), Crghall, Crows Nest, Detendu, Dominion, **Doolhof**, **Freedom Hill**, G Beck, Joubert-T, KWV, **La Couronne**, Louisvle, Lyngrove, MAN Vintners, **Mnt du Bleu**, Mnterosso, New Cape, **Niel J**, Oude Kaap, Rickety, Romond, Rooibrg, **Rtrsvlei** (2), Seidel, **Seven Oaks**, Shoprite, Smnsig, The Winery, Van Z'hof, Vaughan J, **Vlrsdorp**, Vrede en Lust, Wlworths, W'drift ✮✮✩ B Gould, Bergwater, Bovlei, **Cherry Hill**, Citrus, Cpe Vyds, Cru, Daschbsch, Dispore Kamma, Domein Drnkraal, Dreamview, El Dorado, FirstCpe, Grnde Prvnce, Hzndal, Jacaranda, Kln Draken (Kosher), **La Couronne**, Leopard's, **Liquor Wrld**, **Marianne**, Mooitsg, Ovrhex Int, Perdebrg, Rhbsklf, Schlkbnbsch (2), Seidel, **Skilpadvlei**, Swrtland, Tangara, **The Co of Wne**, The Winery, Wine Source SA, Wldekrans (2), Wlworths ✮✮ McGreg, Nuy, Slnghoek, Stellndrft, Wlworths, Wndmeul, Alter Ego, Bernheim, Cellr-Vie, **Juno Co**, **Origin**, Tangara, **Van Lvren**, Zidela ✮✩ Ashton, Cpe Coastal, Du T'kloof, **Origin**, Waverly TBS, Westcrp Int ✩ Dominion **NT** Avndvrde (2), Bonnivle Cllrs, Bottlry Hills, Brnthrst, **Elgin Vntnrs**, Koningsrvr, Old Brdge, Rainbow, Rozendal, Thabani, Umkhulu, Wedderwill **NR** Shoprite **D** Cpe First, Cpe Grace, De Compagnie, De Toren, Dieu D, Dominion, Du T'kloof, Hegewisch, Hldrkruin (2), Horse Mtn, Krnskop, Makro, Malan, Raka, Smrbsch, Sthrn Sky, The Co of Wne, Tulbagh Mtn Vyds, Vendôme, Wlworths (2)

Carignan

✮✮✮✮ Fairvw

✮✮✮✮ Welgegund

Chardonnay, unwooded

✮✮✮✮ Con Uitsig, De Wetsh, Sprgfield, Wlworths (2), Zrgvliet

✮✮✮✩ Bchrd-F, Bcksbrg (organic), Cloverfld, De Wetsh (2), Grt Parys, Grte Pst, Jordan, La Couronne, Mostrtsdrift, Nthlingshof, Rstnberg, Stnberg, Von O, Wlworths ✮✮✮ Agulhas Wines, Asara, Avndale, Beaumnt, Darling C, De Krans, De Meye, Dieu D, Doolhof, G Beck, **Glnwood**, Goedvertw, Hillcrest, Kleine Z, Louisvle, **Lournsfd**, Main Str, Millstrm, My Wyn, Rietvallei, The Winery, Vinus Via, Wamaker, Wltvrede, Wlworths ✮✮✩ Bon Crge, Cpe Bay, Delaire, G Beck, Goudini, Hildenb, **J van Zyl**, Janéza, Jonkhr (2), Juno Co,

Kaapzicht, Leopard's, Linton P, Louiesnhf, McGreg, Mnt Rochelle, Smrbsch, Terroir, Tulbagh, Van Z'hof, Vlrsdorp, **Vukani**, Wlworths, Zndvliet ★★ **Afrcn Terroir** (2), Boplaas, Botha, Cloof, **Dominion**, Du T'kloof, F'hoek Vyds, New Cape, Oude Wllngton, Padda, Rhbsklf, Seidel, **Ses'Fikile**, Tall Horse, Wlworths, Zidela ★★ Afrcn Terroir (2), Ashton, Bartinney, Citrus, Cpe Coastal, Ltzvlle, Mns Ruber (2), Shoprite, Tulbagh ★ **Headbutt**, **Kango**, Urbane **NT** Bloupunt, Hrtswater, Montagu, Uitvlucht, Vriesenhof **NR** Môreson **D** La Petite F, Mntn Ridge, Ridder's, The Co of Wne, Vendôme, Yonder

Chardonnay, wooded

★★★★★ HRV, Waterfd

★★★★☆ **Ataraxia**, Avntuur, Btnvrwchtng, Chamnx, Dbn Hills, Glen C (2), Glnwood, Jordan (2), Ndrburg, **Oak Valley**, Paul C, Sprgfield, Sumardg, The Winery, Uva Mira, Veenwdn, Verglgn, **Wlworths**

★★★★ **Alvi's Drift**, **Amani** (2), Asara, **Bchrd-F** (3), Bcksbrg, Beaumnt, Btnvrwchtng, Cloverfld, Con Uitsig, Cpe First, De Meye, De Wetsh, Delaire, Delheim, Dmrsdal, Doolhof, Ekndal, Fleur dC, Fort S, G Beck, Glen C, Grt Cnstntia, **Grt Parys**, Grte Pst, Haskell, Hrtnberg (2), Ht Espoir, **J Schaal**, Jordan, K Constantia, Kleine Z, Kloovnbrg, Koelfntn, KWV, La Motte, Louisvle, L'rdge, MC Square, Mntn Oaks (organic), Môreson, Mrgnhof, Mrlust, Mulderb, Muratie, Neil E (3), Nelson, Newton J, Ovrgaauw, Quoin, R&R, Rbtson, Rhbsklf, Riebeek, **Riverstn**, Rstnberg (2), Saronsbrg, **Smnsig**, Sterhuis, Thelema (2), Tokara, Verglgn, Vins d'Orrance, Von O, Warwick, **Waterklf**, Wltvrede (3), Wlworths (2), Zndvliet

★★★☆ Afrcn Pride, Amani, Anthill, Anura, Arendsig, **Babylon's Pk**, Badsberg, Bellnghm, Bergsig, Bon Crge, Bonfoi, Bonnivle Cllrs, Bschklf, Bschndal, Chamnx, Conradie, Cordoba, Cpe Point, Crows Nest, De Wetsh (2), Dieu D, Dmrsdal, Dominion (2), Eikehof, Ernst Co, Fat B, F'hoek Vyds, **Fort S**, G Beck, Goede H, Grnde Prvnce, Havana, Hildenb, Hillcrest, Hpnbrg, Jack & Knox, Jonkhr, Joubert-T, Kanu, KWV (2), L'Avenir, La Bri, La Petite F, Laibach, Lanzerac, Le Bonh, Linton P, Long Beach, Louisvle, Lyngrove (2), Marklew, Meerend, Mulderb, Ndrburg, Nelson, Nitida, **Nthlingshof**, Ormonde, **Pick's Pick**, Plaisir, Pulpit Rock (2), Rbtson, Rdezandt, Rhbsklf, Rietvallei (2), S'bosch Hills, Slaley, Smnsig, Smook, StllnHills (2), Stony B, Sxnburg, The Co of Wne (3), **The Goats**, Tokara, Western, Whlhaven ★★★ Ashton, Avndale, Bcksbrg, Bellnghm, Cpe Classics, Cpe Grace, Cru, Dalla Cia, Daschbsch, Dbn Hills, De Zoete, **Deetlefs**, Delheim, **Die Huis van Anje**, Du Preez, Ekndal, Fairvw, Fleur dC, Goedvrwcht, Grt Cnstntia, Hpnbrg, Hzndal, Klnvallei, Krnskop, KWV (2), La Chaumiere, La Couronne, Laborie, Libertas, Lngvrwacht, Long Mntn, Lorraine, Lournsfd, Makro, MAN Vintners, McGreg, Mdlvlei, Napier, Ndrburg, New Begin, New Cape, Nuy, Oaklnds Exprtrs, Obikwa, Onderklf, Opstal, Oracle, Ormonde, Rickety, Riebeek, Rijk's, Rooibrg, Rtrsvlei, Savanna, Seidel, Smnsvlei, Spier (2), Stellnzcht, **Stettyn**, Stnwall, Table Mtn, **The Stables**, Tulbagh, Uitkyk, Waverly TBS, Western, **Withington**, Wlworths (organic), Wm Everson, **Ziggurat** ★★★ Afrcn Pride, **Afrcn Terroir** (2), Altyd, **Beau Joubert**, Clovelly, Cltzdorp, Cpe Vyds, De Villiers, Deetlefs, Detendu, Douglas G, **False Bay**, **FirstCpe**, Hill & Dale, J van Zyl, Jonkhr, **Kanu**, Klawer, Klein Parys, KWV, Le Grand Chass, Lyngrove, **Major's Hill** (2), Mnt Rozier, Mntn River, Mooi Bly, **Mooitsg**, **Origin** (2), Rooibrg, Rose Garden, Slnghoek, Smook, **Stellar** (organic), Sthrn Cape Vyds, Thorn, Two Oceans, Van Z'hof, Vljsdrift, Vrede en Lust, Waverly TBS, Welbedcht, Zonneblm ★★ Bcksbrg (Kosher), Boland, Bonnivle Cllrs, Bovlei, Clairvv, Clmborg, Cpe First, Cpe Vyds (2), Drostdy, Du T'kloof (2), Exclsor, Furstnbrg, Grt Eilnd, Jason's, Klein Parys, Kln Draken (Kosher), Lindiwe, Lndskrn, **Long Mntn** (2), Lushof, **Mrhof**, Olsen, Oude Kaap, **Rbtson** (2), Riebeek, Sthrn Cape Vyds, Swrtland, Van Lvren, Western ★★ Afrcn Terroir (organic), Bovlei, Brndvlei, Country C, Cpe Coastal, Cpe Vyds, Niel J, Oranje, Origin (2), Van Lvren ★ De Wet, Kango, Lndzicht, **Mntn River**, Montpllr, **Mrhof NT** Bloupunt, Boland, Bonnivle Cllrs, Bottlry Int, Breelnd, De Doorns, De Wetsh, Eshkl Kshr, Fairseat, FBW, F'hoek Vyds, Hippo, Kln DasBsch, Klnhof, Prospect, Ultra Liq, Vriesenhof, W'drift, Wldekrans **NR Bon Cap** (organic), **Eaglevlei**, Hemlzcht, **Le Riche**, Lvland, Mnt Rochelle, Tangara **D** Assegai, Avntuur, Bcksbrg, Bonnivle Cllrs, Bschndal, Cpe

Coastal, Daview, Fairvw, F'hoek Vyds, Goudini, Hegewisch, Hldrkruin, L'Ormarins, Malan, Mntn Ridge, Ovrhex Int, Perdebrg, Signal H, Umkhulu, Waverly TBS

Chardonnay-based blends, unwooded
★★★★ Cabrière, KWV, Wlworths ★★★ Bschndal, Cowlin, Cpe Grace, FirstCpe, The Co of Wne, Wlworths ★★★ Ashanti, Bellnghm, Crghall, Mooitsg, Waverly TBS, Zndvliet ★★ Clairvx, Domein Drnkraal, Mntn Range, Nelson, Ntvbij, Ovrhex Int, Rhbsklf, Sthrn Cape Vyds, Westcrp Int ★★ Sthrn Cape Vyds **NT** Eshkl Kshr, S/SW

Chardonnay-based blends, wooded
★★★★★ Flgstone
★★★★ Bschndal, Chamnx ★★★ Drostdy ★★ Western

Chenin blanc, unwooded, dry
★★★★ Mnterosso, Old Vines, Raats Fam
★★★★ Avndale, **Blue Cove** (2), Cedrbrg, Cloverfld, Kleine Z, L'Avenir, Mnt Destin, Mntn Oaks (organic), **Mooipls**, **Môreson**, Napier, **The Co of Wne**, **Tierhoek**, Vuurberg, Waterfd ★★★ Altyd, Anura, **Arabella**, Blue Crane, Bovlei, Bwland, Carolinahve, **De Meye**, Flgstone, Grte Pst, Hrtnberg, Hzndal, Jason's, Kleine Z, Laibach, **Lazanou**, Lournsfd, MAN Vintners, Mhudi, Mnt Vernon, Nuy, Ormonde, Perdebrg, **Sagila**, **Ses'Fikile**, Seven Oaks, Shoprite, Smnsvlei, Teddy Hall, Terroir, The Winery, **Welbedcht**, Wlworths, Wndmeul, **Wrcester Wnlnds**, **Zidela** (2), ★★★ Anura, Assegai, **Ayama**, Bottlry Int, **Conradie**, Cru, De Krans, De Villiers, Du Preez, Du T'kloof, Eshkl Kshr, Grt Parys, Knrhoek, KWV, Leopard's, Libertas, Main Str, Mntn River, Môreson, New Cape, Nwedrift, **Oaklnds Exprtrs**, Obikwa, Onderklf, Oude Kaap, **Rbtson** (3), Riebeek (2), Seidel, Table Mtn, The Co of Wne, Van Z'hof, Vlrsdorp, Vrdnheim, Wlington ★★ 32 South, **Babylon's Pk**, Badsberg, Bergsig, Boland, Citrus, Cpe Bay, Cru, **Daschbsch**, **De Wet**, Drostdy (2), Du T'kloof, **Ernst Co**, Fair Valley, F'hoek Vyds, FirstCpe, Grt Eilnd (2), Jacaranda, Jonkhr, Kaapzicht, Klein Parys, **La Couronne**, Lindiwe, Lndskrn, Lngvrwacht, McGreg, Millstrm, Mnt Rozier, Mntn River, Mooi Bly, Niel J, Opstal, Oudeklf, Rooibrg, Rose Garden, Seidel, Slnghoek, Smrbsch, **Spier**, **Stettyn**, Swrtland, Uitvlucht, Vaughan J, Vinus Via, Vljsdrift, Wamaker (2), Waverly TBS, Wlworths ★★ **Aan de Drns**, Bergsig, Bernheim, Brndvlei, Clmborg, Klawer, Long Mntn, Montpllr, Rickety, Smnsvlei, Stellar (organic), Text, Tulbagh, Under Oaks ★ Afrcn Terroir, **Ashton**, **Mntn Ridge**, Montagu, Mostrtsdrift, Origin, Tulbagh (organic), Wandsbeck ★ Kango, Mellasat, Welvenpas **NT** Alvi's Drift, Belbon Hills, Breelnd, **Crossrds**, De Doorns, Drostdy (2), McGreg, Montpllr Sud, Old Brdge (2), **The Stables**, Tulbagh, Wlworths (organic), Wnklshk **NR** Eaglevlei, Pulpit Rock **D** Assegai, Bonnivle Cllrs, Deetlefs, Du T'kloof, Hldrkruin, L'rdge, Rhbsklf, Swrtland, Thorn, Winecorp

Chenin blanc, unwooded, off-dry/semi-sweet
★★★★ Bschndal, Kanu ★★★ Cpe First, Ken F, Lndskrn, Old Vines, Perdebrg, S'bosch Hills, Swrtland, **Vrgn Erth** ★★★ Bcksbrg, Glnview, Hzndal, **JP Bredell**, Klein Parys, KWV, Mike's Ktchn, Old Vines, Origin, Rtrsvlei, Smnsig, **Sthrn Sky**, **Weening Barge**, Wlworths ★★ **Angora**, Botha, Brndvlei, Cloof, **Cpe Coastal**, **Die Huis van Anje**, **Du T'kloof**, Goudini, Grt Eilnd, Oranje, Rhbsklf, Rtrsvlei, **Stellrust**, **Wamaker**, Wlworths ★★ Lndzicht, Ltzvlle (2), Oranje, Smnsvlei (2), **Van Lvren** ★ Leopard's **NT** Grndheim, Huguenot, Prmium Cpe Wnes **D** Bonnivle Cllrs

Chenin blanc, wooded
★★★★★ De Morgenzon, Rudera, Spier
★★★★★ Jean D, Ken F, Post Hse, Spice R, Sprngfntein
★★★★ Beaumnt (2), Bellnghm, Cedrbrg, De Traf, Fleur dC, Hzndal, Katbakkies, Ken F, Mntn Oaks (organic), Mrgnhof, Mulderb, Old Vines, Raats Fam, Rijk's, Rudera, Smnsig, The Winery, Tierhoek, Villiera
★★★★ Barton, Cpe Classics, **Darling C**, Domaine B, **Dornier**, Ekndal, Fort S (2), **Grt Parys**, Hildenb, Jordan, Kanu, Kleine Z, Lmrshoek, Perdebrg, Signal H, Smrbsch, **Sterhuis**, Stormhoek, Tokara, Villiera, Wlworths ★★★ Bucks Rdg, Cpe Coastal, **False Bay**, Fredine Wines, **Hidden V**, **Jason's**, Klnhof, Nabyglgn, **Saltare**, **Stormhoek**, Sylvnvle, Tukulu, Tulbagh, Welbedcht, Zevnwacht ★★★ Cpe Vyds, KWV, Stbosch Cntry Est, Waverly TBS,

Wlington ★★ Bernheim, Wldekrans (2) **NT** Alvi's Drift **NR** B Gould, Lazanou **D** Assegai, Avntuur, Glen C, Tulbagh Mtn Vyds

Chenin blanc-based blends, unwooded

★★★★☆ Adoro, Dornier
★★★★ The Observatory
★★★★ Bschndal, Mike's Ktchn, Old Vines, Ridgeback ★★★ **Afrcn Pride**, **Ernst Co**, Hidden V, Jason's, Jordan, Knrhoek, La Chataigne, **Mia Cara**, Mrgnhof, Nabyglgn, S'bonga, **Slow Wine**, Vrede en Lust, Winecorp ★★★ Afrcn Pride, Bonnivle Cllrs, Clmborg, Cpe First, Darling C, Dellrust, **Du Preez**, Ernst Co, Kleine Z, KWV, Leopard's, Mnt Rozier, Mntn Oaks (organic), Mystery, Ndrburg, Nuy, **Origin**, Spier, Sthrn Cape Vyds, Swrtland, Sxnburg, Two Oceans (2), Wine Source SA, Zevnwacht, Zonneblm ★★ Citrus, Country C, Deetlefs, **Dominion**, Douglas, Du Preez, Du T'kloof, Grünb, Makro, Nelson, Ntvbij, **Oranje**, Origin (3), **The Co of Wne** (2), Tulbagh (2), Western (2), Wlworths (2) ★★ Afrcn Terroir, Cellr Csk, Douglas, Mntn Ridge, Origin (3), Ovrhex Int, Rooibrg, Stellar (organic), Stellndrft, Tulbagh, Westcrp Int, Wldekrans ★ Westcrp Int (3) (Low alc) **NT** Belbon Hills, Boland, Hrtswater, Huguenot, Prmium Cpe Wnes **D** Cellr Csk, Cpe First, Lvland, Sthrn Sky, Swrtland

Cinsaut

★★★ Perdebrg ★★★ Lndskrn ★★ Welgegund ★☆ Clmborg **D** Wamaker

Colombard

★★★ Bon Crge, Goedvrwcht, Nuy (2) ★★★ Lngvrwacht, McGreg, Origin, Rbtson ★★ Ashton, Botha, Origin (organic), Van Lvren ★★ Montagu, Oranje ★☆ Aan de Drns, Oranje **NT** De Doorns, Stellar (organic) **D** Aan de Drns, Wltvrede ★★ **Conradie** ★☆ Rooibrg **NT** Jonkhr **D** Wlworths

Fernão pires

★★ Van Lvren ★★ Swrtland (Low alc) **D** Nuy

Fortified   see Hanepoot, Jerepigo, Morio, Muscadel, Muscat, Non-muscat, Port

Gamay noir

★★★ Kleine Z

Gewürztraminer

★★★★★ Paul C, Wlworths
★★★★ Smnsig, Zevnwacht
★★★★ Btnvrwchtng, Delheim, Ndrburg, Nthlingshof, Villiera, Wltvrede ★★★ 32 South, Altyd, Bergsig, Klnhof, Oude Wllngton ★★☆ Lndzicht, **Wlworths D** Wlworths

Grenache blanc

★★★★ Signal H

Grenache noir

★★★★ Signal H ★★★ Tierhoek ★★★ J van Zyl

Hanepoot/Muscat d'Alexandrie, fortified

★★★★ Badsberg, Deetlefs, Du Preez, Du T'kloof
★★★★ Brndvlei, Citrus, Cltzdorp, **Deetlefs**, Goudini, Kaapzicht, SoetKaroo, Sthrn Cape Vyds, **Vriesenhof** ★★★ Aan de Drns, Boplaas, Bottlry Int, Grt Eilnd, Klnhof, Mns Ruber, Mooitsg, Muratie, Opstal, Padda, Slnghoek, Smnsvlei, Swrtland, Vlrsdorp ★★★ **Belbon Hills**, Botha, Lndzicht, Oranje, Westcrp Int, Wlington ★★ Kango, Mooitsg, Rietrvr **NT** De Doorns, Huguenot, Klawer **D** Daschbsch, De Wet, Rooibrg, Wamaker

Icewine

★★★★ Signal H

Italian varieties, blends with

★★★★ Bchrd-F, Bcksbrg, Ndrburg, **Stellky**
★★★★ Fairvw, Flat Roof ★★★ Havana **D** Wlworths, Stormhoek

Jerepigo red, fortified

★★★☆ Badsberg, Grndheim, Tulbagh ★★★ Citrus, Lmrshoek ★★★ Mns Ruber, Sdgwick's, Smnsvlei ★★ Botha, Douglas, Kango, Riebeek, Ship Shry ★☆ Dellrust, Lndzicht, Oranje, Swrtland ★ Mooitsg **NT** BWC, Hrtswater, Huguenot, Slnghoek **D** Alter Ego, Rooibrg

Jerepigo white, fortified

★★★☆ Cabrière, Feiteiras ★★★ Tulbagh ★★★ Grndheim, Kango ★★ Jacaranda, Mns Ruber, Swrtland ★☆ Cltzdorp **NT** Domein Drnkraal, Huguenot, Klnhof **NR** Tulbagh **D** De Krans, Mooitsg

Late harvest

★★★ Boplaas, Delheim ★★★ De Zoete, Drostdy, Westcrp Int ★★ Wlworths ★☆ Mooitsg, Ovrmeer, Pick 'n P, Rbtson, Wlworths ★☆ Ashton, Carnival, Oranje ★ K'prinz **NT** De Doorns, Hrtswater, Huguenot (2), Picardi, Swrtland, Wnklshk **D** Cellr Csk, Wlworths, Wndmeul ★★★ KWV ★★★ Wlington ★★ Citrus, Cltzdorp, Country C, Montagu, Smnsvlei ★☆ Bernheim, Riebeek, Rvnswood ★ McGreg, Rietrvr, Tulbagh **NT** Douglas, Grndheim, Jonkhr, Klawer, Swrtland, Vlrsdorp **D** Du T'kloof

Light & low-alcohol

★★★ Twee JG ★★ Fleur dC, Rbtson, Wlworths ★☆ Wlworths ★ Country C, Smnsvlei, Tulbagh ☆ Drostdy, Oranje, Riebeek, Van Lvren **NT** Rbtson, Swrtland

Malbec

★★★★ Bellevue, High C, Paul W, Signal H, Wlworths
★★★☆ Anura, Ashanti, Bellevue, Dmrsfntn, Hildenb, KWV, Ndrburg, Spier ★★★ Umkhulu ★★ Cpe Vyds

Merlot

★★★★★ Avndale, Bilton, Hrtnberg, L'rdge, Quoin, Slaley, Stnberg, Thelema, Veenwdn, Verglgn

★★★★ Akkerdal, Amani, Anura, Asara, Bein, Bellnghm, Btnvrwchtng, Cmbrly, Coleraine, Cordoba, Dbn Hills (2), De Traf, Delaire, DeWaal, Dornier, Du Preez, Ekndal, Grt Cnstntia, Jordan, Kanu, Kleine Z, KWV (2), Laibach, Linton P, Main Str, Meinert, Mrgnhof, Mrlust, Ndrburg, Neil E Meyer N, Org de Rac (organic), Oude Cmpgnies, Ovrgaauw, Plaisir, Raka, Ridgeback, Rmhoogte, Rust en V, Spice R, Spier, Sumardg, Sxnburg, The Winery, Thelema, Villiera, Von O, Waterklf, Wlworths (2), Yonder

★★★☆ Altyd, Anura, Audacia, Avntuur, Beau Joubert, Bellnghm, Bknhtskloof, Bloemndal, Blubrry Hill, Blwklppn (2), Boland, Bottlry Int, Bovlei, Cowlin, Daview, De Grendel, Dmrsdal, Dmrsfntn, Douglas G, Du Preez, Ernie Els, F'hoek Vyds, Fleur dC, Fraai U, Freedom Hill, Glnwood, Gracelnd, Grt Cnstntia, Grte Pst, Hillcrest, Hofstraat, Hpnbrg, Hzndal, JP Bredell, Kaapzicht, Kleine Z, Koelfntn, L'Avenir, La Couronne, La Petite F, Laborie, Lindiwe, Lndhorst, Lournsfd, L'rdge, Makro, Manley, Marianne, Marklew, Maske, Meerend, Mischa, Mnt Rozier, Mooipls, Môreson, Mrgnhof, Muratie, Nthlingshof, Ormonde, Post Hse, Rbtson (2), Rooibrg, Ross G, Savanha (2), Seidel, Slaley, Spier, Stark-C, Stellky, Stellnzcht, Sterhuis, Sthrn Cape Vyds, Stellrust, Stony B, Usana, Vooruitsg, Vrgnoegd, Wlworths, Zonneblm ★★★ 32 South, Ashanti, Ayama, Badsberg, Bcksbrg, Bein, Blank Bottle (2), Blue Crane, Bonfoi, Bschklf, Clovelly, Cpe Classics, Cpe Grace, Darling C, Daview, Dbn Hills, De Zoete, Deetlefs, Delheim, Dellrust, DeWaal, Dmrsfntn, Doolhof, Drknsig (2), Drostdy (2), Du T'kloof, Eaglevlei, Eikehof, Elberti, Ernst Co, Exclsor, Fairvw, Fleur dC, Flgstone, Fort S (2), G Beck, Goedvrwcht, Goudini, Jacaranda, Janéza, Jonkhr, Ken F, Kleinfntn, Kloovnbrg, Krnskop, KWV (2), Lanzerac, Le Riche, Libertas, Linton P (2), Lournsfd, Mike's Ktchn, Mischa, Mrgnhof, Ndrburg, Nelson, Nico vdM, Ntvbij, Obikwa, Olyvenbosch, Pulpit Rock, Rickety, Riebeek, Rijk's, Rusticus, S'bosch Hills, Shoprite, Slow Wine, Smnsvlei, Stellar (organic), Table Mtn, The Co of Wne, Villiera, Wamaker, Welbedcht, Welgegund, Westcrp Int, Whlhaven, Wine Source SA, Withington, Wlington, Wlworths (organic), Yonder, Zevnwacht ★★☆ Arabella, Assegai, Bergwater, Boland, Boplaas, Cherry Hill, Clmborg, Cpe First, Cru, Du T'kloof, Ernst Co, FirstCpe, Flat Roof, Hill & Dale, Jason's, Jonkhr, Liquor Wrld, Lndskrn, Lushof, Major's Hill, Miravel, Mnt Rochelle, Origin (organic), Pick's Pick, Rietrvr, Seidel,

Smrbsch, **Spier**, Swrtland, The Co of Wne, **The Marais Fam**, Tulbagh, Uitvlucht, Van Lvren, **Vlrsdorp**, Waverly TBS, Western, Wlworths ★★ Afrcn Terroir (2), Botha, Bovlei, Cltzdorp, Cpe Coastal, Dieu D, **Dispore Kamma**, **Du Preez**, Eshkl Kshr, F'hoek Vyds, Freedom Hill, Glnview, Grt Eilnd, Hippo, Kango, Klawer, Le Mnoir Brndel, Lyngrove, Makro, Mntn River, **Mrhof**, **Natte Valleij**, Niel J, **Oaklnds Exprtrs**, Pulpit Rock, Rtrsvlei, Shoprite, Slnghoek, Teubes, Thorn, Umkhulu, Wamaker, Westcrp Int, Wldekrans, Wlworths, Wndmeul, **Zidela** ★★ Afrcn Terroir (2) (organic), Botha, Domeln Drnkraal, Keukenhof Lndzicht, Montpllr, Urigin, Rhbsklf, Riebeek, Rietrvr, Rooibrg, Rtrsvlei, Seidel, Stellar (2) (organic), Stellndrft, Tall Horse, Tulbagh ★ Du T'kloof, **Headbutt**, Origin, Wlworths **NS** Rose Garden **NT** Avndvrde, Bloupunt, **Blue Cove** (2), Bodega, **Elgin Vntnrs**, Eshkl Kshr, Excelsious, Fairseat, FBW, Kln DasBsch, Klnhof, La Bri, Ltzvlle, Montpllr Sud, Norton, Old Brdge (3), Oubenhm, Rose Garden, Thabani, Ultra Liq, Waverly TBS **NR** Devon H, **Lomond**, **Org de Rac** (organic), Wstbrdge **D** Assegai, Bschndal, Dominion, Hldrkruin (2), Krnskop, L'Ormarins (2), Mnt Rozier, Perdebrg, Signal H, Wlworths, Havana (2)

Merlot, blends with

★★★★☆ Post Hse
★★★★ **Adoro**, Devon H, **Oude Cmpgnies**, Rmhoogte, Stnberg, The Winery
★★★☆ Amani, Annandale, Avndale, Doolhof, Du Preez, Joostnbrg, Kaapzicht, KWV, Mnt Rochelle, Nico vdM, Raka, Stellrust, Stony B, Vljsdrift, Whlhaven ★★★ **Afrcn Pride**, Bknhtskloof, Coleraine, DeWaal, Fort S, Hrtnberg, Jonkhr, JP Bredell, Knrhoek, La Chataigne, Lournsfd, **Marianne**, Mrgnhof, Origin, Sxnburg, Two Oceans, **Villiera**, Wltvrede, **Wlworths** ★★☆ Audacia, Bellevue, Boplaas, Bovlei, De Krans, Ekndal, Long Mntn, **Mnt Vernon**, Stellndrft, Whlhaven ★★ Aan de Drns, Dmrsfntn, Domein Drnkraal, **Feiteiras**, Montagu, Nelson, Origin, **Skilpadvlei**, Umkhulu, Westcrp Int, Western ★☆ **Welvenpas** ★ **Welvenpas NT** Blwklppn **D** Assegai, Fort S, Hill & Dale, Vuurberg, Wlworths

Méthode cap classique see Sparkling

Mon-muscat, red, fortified

★★★★ Domein Drnkraal, Laborie
★★★ Boplaas ★★★ Perdebrg ★★ **Daschbsch**, Louiesnhf ★★ Mooitsg

Morio muscat, fortified

★★★☆ Lndskrn

Mourvèdre

★★★★ Beaumnt
★★★☆ Spice R ★★★ Fairvw

Muscadel, red, fortified

★★★★★ Boplaas, Monis, Rietvallei
★★★★ Avndale, Badsberg, Du T'kloof, Grt Cnstntia, Jonkhr, KWV (2), Nuy, Rietvallei, Rooibrg
★★★☆ Bon Crge, De Wet, Kango, Montagu, Riverstn, Sthrn Cape Vyds, Van Lvren, Wltvrede ★★★ Grndheim, Klawer, McGreg, Mns Ruber, Ovrhex Int, Rdezandt, Rietrvr, Seidel, **The Marais Fam**, W'drift, Westcrp Int ★★☆ Aan de Drns, Uitvlucht ★ Ashton, Douglas, **Excelsr Vlkteplaas**, **Ldrsburg**, Mooitsg, Oranje, Slnghoek ★★ Wandsbeck ★ Lndzicht **NT** Boland, De Doorns **D** Bonnivle Cllrs

Muscadel, white, fortified

★★★★★ Alvi's Drift
★★★★ Avndale, Bon Crge, De Krans, De Wetsh, G Beck, Jonkhr (2), KWV, Nuy, Sthrn Cape Vyds
★★★☆ Ashton, Boplaas, Citrus, De Krans, Mns Ruber (2), Saronsbrg, Thelema ★★★ Clairvx, Cltzdorp, Domein Drnkraal, Mns Ruber, Twee JG, Westcrp Int ★★☆ Boplaas, Kango, Klawer, Lndzicht, Ltzvlle, McGreg, Mooitsg, Oranje, Uitvlucht, Wltvrede, Yonder ★★ **Excelsr Vlkteplaas**, Grndheim, Montagu, Ovrhex Int, Rietrvr **NT** Boland, Rdezandt **D** Bonnivle Cllrs

Muscat d'Alexandrie/Hanepoot, unfortified
★★☆ Bianco ★★ Ovrhex Int ★☆ Bianco, Waverly TBS

Muscat de Frontignan, unfortified
★★★★ Ndrburg
★★★ Grt Cnstntia, Thelema, Uitvlucht

Muscat de Hambourg, fortified
★★★★ S'bosch Hills

Muscat Ottonel
★★★ Villiera

Natural sweet, red
★★ Van Lvren ★☆ Rooibrg **NT** Prmium Cpe Wnes, **Rbtson D** Allee B

Natural sweet, rosé
★★★ Ntvbij ★★★ Rbtson (2) (Low alc) ★★ Boplaas, **Cpe Coastal** (Low alc), **Jonkhr**, Rbtson, Smnsvlei, Tulbagh (Low alc) ★☆ Citrus, Grünb (Low alc), Lndzicht (Low alc), Rooibrg, Van Lvren ★ Clairvx, Darling C, **Mntn Ridge**, Riebeek (Low alc), Rietrvr, Rose Garden **NT** Prmium Cpe Wnes, Rose Garden

Natural sweet, white
★★★★★☆ K Constantia
★★★★ Nabyglgn, Sylvnvle
★★★★ Bon Crge, Btnvrwchtng, L'Avenir, Laibach, Quoin, Rstnberg, Zevnwacht ★★★ Goudini, Kaapzicht, Mrgnhof, Slnghoek, Thnskraal, Twee JG (Low alc), Wltvrede ★★☆ Ashanti, De Krans, Sxnburg ★★ Rbtson (2) (Low alc), The Saints (Low alc), Vrdnheim ★☆ Darling C, Grünb (Low alc), Lndzicht (Low alc), Van Lvren ★ Riebeek (Low alc), Rooibrg ★ My Wyn **NT** Bloemndal, Domein Drnkraal, Lvland, Meerend, Prmium Cpe Wnes (2), Rbtson

Nebbiolo
★★★★ Stnberg ★★ Bianco

Noble late harvest
★★★★★ Ken F, Paul C, Rbtson, **Signal H**
★★★★☆ Asara, Bon Crge, Darling C (2), **Hillcrest**, Joostnbrg, Kanu, Nthlingshof, Rudera (2), Smnsig
★★★★ Btnvrwchtng, Cpe Point, De Wetsh, **Deetlefs**, Delheim, Fleur dC, Jordan, K Constantia, Lournsfd, Ndrburg (4), Rbtson, Rstnberg, Signal H (3), **Slaley**, Verglgn, Villiera (2), Waterfd, Wlworths
★★★☆ Afrcn Terroir, Badsberg, Beaumnt, Dieu D, Du T'kloof, Ekndal, **Hildenb**, Jason's, **L'illa**, Mrgnhof, Nuy ★★★ 32 South, Dmrsdal, Slnghoek, Stony B, Twee JG, **Van Lvren NT** Bergsig, Bknhtskloof **NR** Ridgeback **D** Spier, Waverly TBS

Non-muscat, white, fortified
★★★★ Daschbsch ★★★ Bcksbrg

Nouvelle
★★★ Boland

Organic
Afrcn Terroir, Bcksbrg, Bon Cap, Laibach, Lords, Mntn Oaks, Org de Rac, Origin, Sadie Fam, Stellar, Upland, Waverley Hills, Western, Wlworths

Perlé wines
★★★ De Wet (Low alc) ★★ Autumn Hvst, Du T'kloof, Grünb, Jonkhr, Riebeek (Low alc) ★☆ Ashton, Carnival, **Conradie** ★ Du T'kloof **D** Zidela

Petit verdot
★★★★ Du Preez, Ndrburg, Signal H, Zrgvliet
★★★☆ Anura, Bellevue ★★★ F'hoek Vyds, **My Wyn**

Pinot gris/Pinot grigio

★★★☆ L'Ormarins ★★★ Flat Roof, Stormhoek ★★ Van Lvren **NT** Louiesnhf, Wlworths

Pinot noir

★★★★★ Bchrd-F

★★★★☆ Bchrd-F, Cabrière, Chamnx, HRV

★★★★ BWC, De Traf, **Flgstone**, Glen C, Herold, **Oak Valley**, Paul C, Vriesenhof, Weening Barge, Whlhaven, **Wlworths**

★★★☆ **Bon Crge**, De Wetsh, Kln Optnhrst, Makro, Minke, Muratie, Newton J, Signal H, **The Winery** (2), Topaz, Wlworths ★★★ Bellevue, Btnvrwchtng, Cpe First, Elgin Vntnrs, Flgstone, Goedvertw, Grte Pst, Hpnbrg, K Constantia, Mrlust, Rusticus, Sthrn Cape Vyds, The Co of Wne (2), **Vriesenhof** ★★☆ Rose Garden ★★ Avntuur ★☆ Sumardg ★ Montpllr **NT** Lemberg, Montpllr Sud, **Zrgvliet NR** Fryer **D** Ashton

Pinotage

★★★★☆ Ashbourne, Bellevue, Byrskloof, Cmbrly, DeWaal, Dmrsfntn, Fairvw, Kaapzicht, Knonkp, **L'Avenir**, Smnsig, Sthrn Rght, Umkhulu

★★★★ Avntuur, Beaumnt, Bellevue, Bellnghm, Boplaas, Cls Mlvrne, Darling C, Deetlefs, DeWaal, Dmrsfntn, Domaine B, Flgstone, G Beck, Grnghurst, Hidden V, Horse Mtn, Jacobsdal, Kaapzicht, Ktzenbrg, KWV, L'Avenir, Laibach, L'rdge, Lyngrove, Mntn Oaks (organic), Mooipls, Ndrburg, Nelson, Nthlingshof, Rbtson, Reyneke, Rooibrg, S'bonga, Scali, Slaley, Stanfrd Hills, Sxnburg, Tukulu, Vljsdrift, Wstbrdge

★★★☆ Allee B, Altyd, Anura, Assegai, Bon Cap (organic), Botha, Bottlry Int, Byrskloof, Darling C, Deetlefs, DeWaal, Dmrsdal, Doolhof, **Dornier**, Douglas G, Fairvw, Freedom Hill, G Beck, Goede H, Goudini, Grt Cnstntia, Hrtnberg, Hzndal (2), Jonkhr, Kleine Z, Knrhoek, KWV, Laborie, Lanzerac, Ldrsburg, Lmrshoek, Lournsfd, Manley, **Marianne**, Mdlvlei, Meerend, Môreson, Neil E, Nitida, Ntvbij, Onderklf, Oracle, Oude Cmpgnies, Perdebrg (2), Pulpit Rock, Raka, Rbtson, Riebeek (2), Rijk's, Signal H, Smnsig, Spice R, Spier, Sprngfntein, **Sthrn Sky**, Sylvnvle, Tempel, The Co of Wne, **The Stables**, Thelema, Wamaker, Warwick, Western, Wldekrans, **Wlworths** (4) (organic), Wstbrdge, Zevnwacht ★★★ Afrcn Terroir, Ashanti, Bellnghm, Bergsig, **Boland**, Bon Crge, Botha, Cilandia, Clmborg, Cloof, Cls Mlvrne, Cpe Bay, Cpe Classics, Cpe Vyds (2), Dbn Hills, De Krans, De Zoete, Delheim, Dellrust, Dieu D, Du T'kloof, Eaglevlei, FirstCpe, Fleur dC, Fort S, G Beck, Jason's, Jonkhr, Ken F, Klein Parys, Kleine Z, Klnvallei, KWV, La Petite F, Lndskrn, L'rdge, Lyngrove, Major's Hill, McGreg, Mhudi, Môreson, Ndrburg, New Begin, **New Cape**, Olsen, Rhbsklf, Riebeek, Rusticus, Seidel (2), Ses'Fikile, Smnsvlei, Smook, Smrbsch, Spier, Stellnzcht, Stettyn, Sthrn Cape Vyds, **Stormhoek**, Sumardg, Terroir, The Co of Wne, **The Stables**, **The Winery**, Tulbagh, Villiera, Vrdnheim, **Vrgin Erth**, **Welbedcht**, Wine Source SA, Wldekrans, Wlington, Zonneblm ★★☆ Aan de Drns, Afrcn Terroir (3), Avndale, Avntuur, Bcksbrg, Bergheim, Bernheim, Bianco, Bon Cap (organic), Boplaas, Chamnx, Cloof, **Conradie**, **Cpe First**, Cru, De Villiers, De Wet, Detendu, Devon Rocks, Drknsig, Hill & Dale, Libertas, Lndhorst, Louiesnhf, Main Str, Mellasat, **Mia Cara**, Mntn Ridge, Mntn River, Mrgnhof, Nelson, Obikwa, Oranje, Origin, Rooibrg, Rtrsvlei, S'bosch Hills, Seidel, Shoprite, Slaley, Slnghoek, Smnsvlei, Sthrn Cape Vyds, **The Stables**, Uitvlucht, Van Lvren, Wamaker, Western ★★ Afrcn Terroir (organic), Bcksbrg (Kosher), Bovlei, **Cherry Hill**, Citrus, Cpe Coastal, Devon H, Dominion, Drknsig, **Du T'kloof**, F'hoek Vyds, Fort S, J van Zyl, Klein Parys, Le Grand Chass, Le Mnoir Brndel, **Liquor Wrld**, Long Mntn, Ltzvlle, MAN Vintners, Mnt Rozier, **Mntn River** (2), Niel J, Nthlingshof, Oude Kaap, Pulpit Rock, Rietrvr, Stellar (2) (organic), Swrtland, Tulbagh (2), Two Oceans, **Van Lvren**, Waverly TBS, Westcrp Int, Wlworths ★★ Boland, Daschbsch, Drostdy, Fair Valley, Grt Eilnd, **Headbutt**, Hippo, Kango, Klawer, Kln Draken (Kosher), Lindiwe, Millstrm, Origin, **Ridder's**, Rose Garden, Stellndrft, Tulbagh, Wlington, Wndmeul ★ **Kango**, Origin, Shoprite ★ Welvenpas **NS** Lndzicht, **Môrewag NT** Anthill, Badsberg, Belbon Hills, Bodega, Bottlry Int, Eshkl Kshr (2), Fairseat, Huguenot, Klnhof, Lemberg, Mdlpos, Mrhof, Old Brdge (2), Oubenhm, **Pick's Pick**, Rose Garden, Stbosch Cntry Est, Ultra Liq, Vriesenhof, Waverly TBS, **Welgegund**, Windfall **NR** Avndale,

L'Auberge, Shoprite, Swrtland **D** Assegai, Goede H, Hldrkruin (2), Hpnbrg, L'Avenir, Lyngrove, Makro, Malan, Mrgnhof, Smrbsch, Stony B, Thorn, Winecorp

Pinotage, blends with

✰✰✰✰✰ Byrskloof, Darling C, DeWaal, G Beck, Grnghurst (2), Kaapzicht, Meinert, Vriesenhof

✰✰✰✰ Asara, Ashanti, Cls Mlvrne, Dellrust, Flgstone, Kaapzicht, Nthlingshof, Smnsig, The Observatory, Warwick

✰✰✰✫ Alvi's Drift, Babylon's Pk, Cedrbrg, Cloof, Cls Mlvrne, **Croydon**, Devon H, Domaine B, Du Preez, Fairvw, Freedom Hill, Knonkp, KWV, Leopard's, Mdlvlei, **Post Hse**, Stellky, Sylvnvle, Umkhulu (2), Welgemnd ✰✰✰ 32 South, **Afrcn Terroir** (2), Allee B, Ashanti, Bellevue, Blwklppn, Byrskloof, Clairvx, Cloof, Cls Mlvrne, Cpe Grace, De Krans, Deetlefs, Domaine B, Flgstone, Goedvertw, Goudini, Leopard's, Lorraine, Makro, **Mia Cara**, Rhbsklf, Rmhoogte, **Spier** (2), Stellnzcht, The Winery, Villiera, **Vruchtbaar**, Wldekrans ✰✰✰ Ashton, Bianco, **Bonnivle Cllrs**, Carolinahve, Cloof, Cpe Bay, Cru, Drostdy (2), Kleine Z, Malan, Mntn River, Ndrburg, Ntvbij, Origin (2), Oudeklf, Padda, Slaley, The Co of Wne, Tulbagh, Two Oceans, Western, Winecorp ✰✰ Cru, Domein Drnkraal, Douglas G, Du T'kloof (3), Hrtswater, Klein Parys, L'Avenir, Mntn Ridge, Mooitsg (2), Origin, Ovrhex Int, Ovrmeer, S'bosch Hills, Tulbagh, Wamaker, Waverly TBS, Western (3), Wlworths ✰✫ **Dominion**, Du T'kloof, **Mntn River**, **Origin** (4), Rietrvr (2), ★ Origin **NT** Belbon Hills, Bonnivle Cllrs, Bottlry Hills, Drostdy, Huguenot, Klnhof, **Lemberg**, S/SW **D** Afrcn Terroir, Hidden V, Lournsfd, Wlworths

Port, red, fortified

✰✰✰✰✰ Boplaas (2), De Krans, JP Bredell

✰✰✰✰✫ Allesvlrn, Axe Hill, Boplaas (3), De Krans, JP Bredell

✰✰✰✰ Bergsig (2), Boplaas (2), De Krans (2), Domein Drnkraal, JP Bredell, KWV (2), Lndskrn, Makro, Monis, Muratie, Ovrgaauw, P Bayly, **Pick's Pick**

✰✰✰✫ Annandale, Bcksbrg, Botha, Byrskloof, Cltzdorp, De Wet, Du T'kloof, **Feiteiras**, Flgstone, Goudini, Grt Cnstntia, Kango, KWV, L'Avenir, Louiesnhf, Mrgnhof (2), Rtrsvlei, Villiera, Vljsdrift ✰✰✰ Beaumnt, Bon Crge, Cltzdorp, **Jacques Smit**, Jean D, L'Ormarins, McGreg, Mns Ruber, Muratie, **Ntvbij**, Rbtson, Riebeek, Rstnberg, Slnghoek, Smrbsch, Sthrn Cape Vyds, Swrtland, Tulbagh, **Upland** (organic), Van Lvren, Vrgnoegd, Withoek, Wndmeul ✰✰✰ Grndheim, Lmrshoek, Padda, Rooibrg, Tulbagh, Vlrsdorp ✰✰ Aan de Drns, Ashton, Badsberg, Bonnivle Cllrs, Bovlei, De Zoete, Kango, Mooitsg, Oranje, Rietrvr ✰✫ Citrus, Dellrust ★ Clairvx, Linton P, Montpllr, Swrtland, Uitvlucht **NT** Boland, Domein Drnkraal, Douglas G, Grndheim, Hrtswater, Huguenot (2), Klawer, Klnhof, Major's Hill, **The Stables**

Port, white, fortified

✰✰✰✰ Axe Hill

✰✰✰✫ Asara ✰✰✰ Boplaas, De Krans **NT** Domein Drnkraal **D** Mooitsg

Primitivo see Zinfandel

Red blends, other

✰✰✰✰✰ Makro, Raka, The Observatory

✰✰✰✰ Ataraxia, Boplaas, De Krans, Fairvw, Lmrshoek, Makro, Mnt du Toit (2),

✰✰✰✫ Afrcn Pride, Akkerdal, Marklew, Mnt du Toit, Signal H, Stellky, Veenwdn, Vrgnoegd ✰✰✰ Babylon's Pk, Beaumnt, Botha, Bottlry Int, Cpe Vyds, Darling C, Du Preez, Goudini, H Boom, Kaapzicht, KWV, Lategnskp, Lndskrn, Main Str, **Mia Cara**, **Micu Narunsky**, Perdebrg, Rdezandt, Rose Garden, Schlkbnbsch, Smnsvlei, The Co of Wne, Thnskraal, Withoek, Wlington ✰✰✰ Anura, Assegai, Bcksbrg, Bergsig, Blwklppn, Brndvlei, Carnival, Citrus, Dellrust, **Hpietrsfntein**, KWV, Leopard's, Millstrm, Mostrtsdrift, **Origin**, Oude Kaap, Perdebrg, Rbtson, Sthrn Cape Vyds (2), The Co of Wne, The Saints, Uitvlucht, Vaughan J, **Weening Barge**, Western, Wlworths (2), Zndvliet ✰✰ 32 South, Afrcn Terroir, **Brndvlei**, Citrus, Clmborg, Country C, Drostdy, Grt Eilnd, Hippo, KWV, Pick 'n P, Rbtson, Rvnswood, Slnghoek, Swrtland, Text, **Weening Barge**, Wlworths ✰✫ Crows Nest, Origin, Ridder's, Riebeek, Rooibrg, Schlkbnbsch, Smnsvlei (2) ★ Douglas **NT**

Aufwaerts, Bottlry Hills, **Crossrds**, Crows Nest, De Doorns, Douglas, Eshkl Kshr, Fairseat, Fredine Wines, Grndheim, **Kaapzicht**, Montagu, Picardi, Prmium Cpe Wnes, **Rbtson**, **Sterhuis**, Swrtland, Ultra Liq (2), Waverly TBS (2), Windfall, Wine Vllge, Wnklshk (2) **D** Assegai, Cellr Csk, Mnt Rozier, Mrhof, Ndrburg, Winecorp, Wlworths

Riesling (Cape or SA)

★★★ Bon Crge ★★ De Villiers, Du T'kloof, KWV, Ndrburg, Thnskraal ★★ Van Lvren **D** Boland, Do Wot

Riesling (Rhine or weisser)

★★★★ Hrtnberg, K Constantia, Paul C, Wltvrede, Wlworths

★★★★ Btnvrwchtng, De Wetsh, **Deetlefs** (2), Jack & Knox, Ndrburg, Thelema, Villiera, Wlworths ★★★ Bergsig, Jordan, Lvland ★★★ **Mrhof**, Rietvallei ★★ **Rhbsklf** **NT** Delheim, Montpllr Sud **D** Rooibrg

Rosé, dry

★★★★ Solms-Delta

★★★★ **Andy Mtchell**, High C, Newton J, Signal H, **Stonehill**, The Goats, **Ziggurat** ★★★ Allee B, Asara, Avntuur, Byrskloof, Cabrière, Darling C, De Meye, **Delaire**, Fairvw, Goedvrwcht, Hildenb, Ht Espoir, Ldrsburg, Origin, Raka, **Rstnberg**, Stony B, Stormhoek, Sylvnvle, Villiera, **Waterklf** ★★★ Anura, Ashanti, Bcksbrg, Bergsig, Cpe Grace, Drmrshire, Flgstone, Fort S, Horse Mtn, L'Avenir, Lournsfd, Mnt Vernon, Mrgnhof, New Cape, **Oaklnds Exprtrs**, Rietvallei, Rooibrg, Slaley, **The Co of Wne** (3), Vrede en Lust, Zrgvliet ★★ Afrcn Terroir, Bernheim, Bloemndal, Bottlry Int, Cloof, Crghall, **De Villiers**, Deetlefs, Drostdy, **FirstCpe** (2), Hill & Dale, **Hpietrsfntein**, **Kloovnbrg**, Lmrshoek, Mnt du Bleu, Môreson, Nelson, **Niel J**, Org de Rac (organic), Origin, **Rdezandt**, Sumardg, **Van Lvren**, **Wlworths**, **Woodhill** ★★ Mntn River (2), **Origin** (2), Schlkbnbsch, Stellar (organic), Weening Barge ★ Leopard's ★ Westcrp Int (Low alc), Wlworths **NT** Bknhtskloof, **Blue Cove** (2), Jason's, **Louiesnhf**, Mrhof, Prmium Cpe Wnes, Vljsdrift, Waverly TBS, Welgegund **NR** Tangara **D** Dominion, Zrgvliet

Rosé, off-dry/semi-sweet

★★★★ **Mulderb** ★★★ Beaumnt, De Krans, **Herold**, KWV, **Nuy**, **Thokozani**, Wlington ★★★ Angora, Bcksbrg, **Bergwater**, **Bon Cap** (organic), **Bschndal**, Carnival, Chamnx, Country C, Delheim, Dellrust, Dieu D, **Ekndal**, Exclsor, G Beck, Grnde Prvnce, Kanu, **Knrhoek**, KWV, L'Avenir, Le Grand Chass, Millstrm, Ndrburg, **Slow Wine**, Sylvnvle, Two Oceans, Vrdnheim, **Western**, Whlhaven, Wlworths, Zndvliet ★★ Ashton, **Avndale** (2), Bellnghm, Bovlei, Clmborg, Cru, **Daschbsch**, **Du T'kloof** (2), Graça, Klnhof, La Chataigne, **Ltzvlle**, Ovrhex Int, Riebeek, Rtrsvlei, Seidel, Shoprite, **Skilpadvlei**, Slnghoek, **Spier**, Swrtland, The Saints (Low alc), Thnskraal, Vlrsdorp, **Wamaker**, Winecorp ★★ Cellr Csk, Grt Eilnd, Mystery, **Pick 'n P**, Riebeek, Rvnswood, Seidel, Smnsvlei, Tulbagh, Uitvlucht, Van Lvren, Wlworths ★ Badsberg, Blwklppn, **De Zoete** (2), **Eaglevlei**, Ltzvlle, Mooitsg, Sthrn Cape Vyds, Westcrp Int, **Zidela** ★ Douglas (Low alc) **NT** Eshkl Kshr, Hrtswater, Lanzerac, Montagu, Swrtland, Ultra Liq **NR** Mnt du Bleu **D** Bonnivle Cllrs, Du T'kloof, Riebeek

Roussanne

★★★★ Rstnberg

Ruby cabernet

★★★ Goudini, Rbtson, **Riverstn** ★★★ Lngvrwacht, Ltzvlle, McGreg, Oude Wllngton, Rbtson ★★ Long Mntn, Oude Wllngton, Sthrn Cape Vyds, Wandsbeck ★★ **Kango**, Oude Kaap, Rusticus ★ Oranje **NT** Fairseat, Hrtswater, Kingsrivier, McGreg, Windfall **D** Daschbsch, Mnt Rozier, Zndvliet

Sacramental wines

★★ Citrus, Mooitsg **NT** Eshkl Kshr, Huguenot, Kln Draken (Kosher)

Sangiovese

★★★★ Anura, Fairvw, Idiom, **Klein Parys** ★★★ L'Ormarins, Mnterosso, **Raka**

Sauvignon blanc, unwooded

★★★★★ Wlworths

★★★★☆ Con Glen, **Dbn Hills** (2), Fort S, Fryer, **Hpietrsfntein**, Iona, Jordan, K Constantia, La Motte, Mulderb, Neil E, Newton J, Nitida, Oak Valley (2), Rbtson, Sprgfield, Stnberg, The Co of Wne, Verglgn, **Wlworths**

★★★★ Adler, **Adoro**, Agulhas Wines, Alluvia, **Amani**, Ataraxia, **Black Oyster**, Bloemndal, Boplaas, **Bschndal**, Btnvrwchtng (2), Cedrbrg, Con Uitsig, Cpe Point, **Dbn Hills**, De Grendel, **Dmrsdal** (2), Fairvw, Fleur dC, **Flgstone** (2), G Beck, Grnde Prvnce, Grt Cnstntia, Herold, **Hidden V**, High C, Hillcrest, **Hpietrsfntein** (2), K Constantia, Kleine Z, KWV, L'Avenir, **La Vierge**, Lomond, L'Ormarins, **L'rdge**, Lushof, Meerend, Mnt Rochelle, **Ndrburg** (4), Nitida, Oracle, Ormonde, Paul C, Plaisir, Quando, Quoin, Raka, Ross G, Saronsbrg, **South Hill**, Spier, Sprgfield, Sthrn Rght, Stnberg, Sxnburg (2), The Co of Wne, Thelema (2), Tokara (2), Usana, Verglgn, Villiera, Waterfd, Western, Wltvrede, Wlworths, Zrgvliet (2)

★★★☆ **Afrcn Pride**, Allee B, Altyd, Amani, **Armarjaro**, Avndale, Bchrd-F, Bellevue, Blue Crane, Bonfoi, Bschndal, BWC, Capaia, Chamnx, Clouds, Cls Mlvrne, Dalla Cia, Darling C (2), De Wetsh, Delaire, Dellrust, DeWaal, **Die Huis van Anje**, Doolhof, Du Preez, Elgin Vntnrs, Ernst Co, Fat B, Fleur dC, Flgstone, G Beck, Glnwood, Goede H, Grte Pst, Havana, Hemlzcht, **Hidden V**, Hillcrest, Hpnbrg, Hrtnberg, Hzndal, Kanu, Kleine Z, Knrhoek, KWV (2), La Chataigne, La Motte, Lanzerac, Lmrshoek, Lomond, Lournsfd, Main Str, Meerend, Mnt Rochelle, Mntn River, Mooipls, Ndrburg, New Cape, Nthlingshof, Ntvbij, Onderklf, Ovrgaauw, Perdebrg, Ridgeback, Rietvallei, Ross G, Rstnberg, Savanha, Smnsvlei, Smrbsch, Spice R, **Spier**, Sterhuis, Stony B, Sumardg, Tierhoek, **Uitkyk** (2), Uva Mira, Villiera, Von O, **Vukani**, Warwick, **Waterfd**, **Waterklf** (2), Waverly TBS, Wlworths, Zevnwacht, **Ziggurat**, Zoetendal, Zonneblm, Zrgvliet ★★★ **Anatu**, Anura, Asara, Avntuur, Badsberg, **Beau Joubert**, Beaumnt, Bellnghm, Bknhtskloof, **Blue Cove** (2), **Blwklppn** (2), Bottlry Int, Cloverfld, Cpe Bay, Cpe Classics, Cpe Coastal, (2) Cpe First, Crows Nest, Cru, Daschbsch, Dbn Hills, Delheim, Dmrsdal, Drknsig, **Eaglevlei**, Ekndal, Exclsor, FirstCpe, Fleur dC, Flgstone, Gallop Hill, Goedvertw, **Grnde Prvnce**, Haskell, Hill & Dale, Kaapzicht, Ken F, Klein Parys, Kloovnbrg, KWV, Laborie, Laibach, Ldrsburg, Le Bonh, Libertas, **Lndhorst**, Long Beach, Louiesnhf, **Lournsfd** (2), Lvland, Major's Hill, Mhudi, **Miravel**, Mnt Rozier, Môreson, Mrgnhof, Obikwa, **Origin**, Ormonde, Rbtson (2), Rijk's, Ross G, **Sagila**, Savanha, S'bosch Hills, **Ses'Fikile**, Slaley, Smnsig, Spier, Stellnzcht, Sthrn Cape Vyds, Table Mtn, Terroir, Vljsdrift, Vlrsdorp, Vrgin Erth, Vruchtbaar, Wedderwill, Wlworths (2) (organic), Zndvliet ★★☆ ACJ Fine Wines, Afrcn Pride, Agterplaas, Bcksbrg, Bergsig, Boland, Bon Cap, Bon Crge, Bonnivle Cllrs, Bottlry Int, Clairvx, Cowlin, **Cpe First** (2), Cpe Vyds, De Villiers, De Wet, Devon H, Dieu D, Du T'kloof, **False Bay**, F'hoek Vyds, **Freedom Hill**, Goedvrwcht, Goudini, Gusto, Jason's, Kanu, KWV, La Couronne, La Petite F, Langeberg, Lategnskp, Ldrsburg, Leopard's, Lindiwe, Lndskrn, Long Mntn, **Lords** (2) (organic), Lyngrove, MAN Vintners, McGreg, Mnt Rozier, Mnterosso, Nabyglgn, Nelson, New Cape, Nuy, Opstal, Origin, **Pick's Pick**, Rdezandt, Rhbsklf, Rickety, Rietvallei, Riverstn, Schlkbnbsch, Shoprite, **Skilpadvlei**, Smnsvlei, **Stellar** (organic), **Stellrust**, Stettyn, Stormhoek, Swrtland, The Co of Wne, The Marais Fam, The Winery, Tulbagh, Two Oceans, Under Oaks, W'drift, Wldekrans, Wlington, **Wlworths** (2), Zidela (2) ★★ **Aan de Drns**, Afrcn Terroir, **Arabella**, Ashton, Assegai, Belbon Hills, Blouvlei, Boplaas, Botha, **Conradie**, Cpe Bay, **Deetlefs**, Du Preez, **Elberti**, Goudini, Grt Eilnd, Janéza, Jonkhr, Le Grand Chass, Linton P, **Long Mntn**, **Longbarn**, Lorraine, **Marianne**, McGreg, Mnt Rozier (2), Mntn Ridge, Mntn River, **Mooitsg**, Môreson, Mostrtsdrift, Ovrhex Int, Riebeek, Rooibrg, Seidel, **Spier**, Stellar (organic), Swrtland, Thorn, Tulbagh, Van Z'hof, Wamaker, Western, Wlworths, Wndmeul, **Wrcester Wnlnds** ★☆ Afrcn Terroir (2) (organic), **Bergwater**, Bovlei (2), Brndvlei, Citrus, Clmborg, **Dominion** (4), Drostdy, Du T'kloof, Fair Valley, **Headbutt**, **Juno Co**, Kango, Klawer, Kln Draken (Kosher), **Mia Cara**, Mostrtsdrift, Niel J, Origin, Padda, Ridder's, Van Lvren, Wandsbeck, Westcrp Int ★ Afrcn Terroir (2), Cltzdorp, Hippo, Le Mnoir Brndel, Ltzvlle, Mystery, Origin, Rietrvr, Slnghoek, Tulbagh, Urbane ☆ Country C **NS** Bracken **NT** Alvi's Drift, Amavara, Boland, Bonnivle Cllrs, Bottlry

Hills, Cpe Coastal, Cru, Douglas G, Drostdy, Du T'kloof, Excelsious, Fairseat, FBW, Fort S, Ht Espoir, Klnhof (2), Lemberg, Mntn River, Oaklnds Exprtrs, Old Brdge (2), Prmium Cpe Wnes, Prospect, Rtrsvlei, Sthrn Sky, Stnberg, Thabani, The Stables (2), Ultra Liq, Umkhulu, Waverly TBS **NR** Bartinney, **Bilton**, Crghall, **Eaglevlei**, **Lomond D** Assegai, Bonnivle Cllrs, Bschndal, Daview, Hldrkruin, Land's E, Landau, L'rdge, Malan, Manley, The Co of Wne (2)

Sauvignon blanc, wooded

★★★★☆ Chamnx, Cpe Point, Neil E, Tokara, Verglgn

★★★★ **Babylon**, Black Oyster, Jordan, Stnberg

★★★☆ Bcksbrg, Bschndal, Delaire, Flgstone ★★★ De Wetsh, Drmrshire, La Petite F, Reyneke, Smnsig **NR** Reyneke **D** Fort S, L'Ormarins

Sauvignon blanc-based blends, unwooded

★★★★ Grte Pst

★★★☆ Asara, Btnvrwchtng, Jordan, **Vendôme** ★★★ Allee B, Delheim, Dmrsdal, **FirstCpe**, Glen C, Grte Pst, **Hpietrsfntein**, Jean D, La Couronne, Smnsig, The Co of Wne (2), **Villiera** (2) ★★☆ Bellnghm, Cpe Grace, Ekndal, **Lournsfd**, Rietvallei, **Rijk's**, S'bosch Hills, Schlkbnbsch, Western, Wltvrede, **Wlworths** (2) ★★ **Afrcn Terroir**, Deetlefs, DeWaal, Kaapzicht, **Origin**, The Saints, Tulbagh, Western ★★ Horse Mtn, Schlkbnbsch ★ **De Zoete NT** Bottlry Hills, Drostdy, Fort S, **Kaapzicht**, Mooitsg **D** De Wetsh, Malan, Seidel, Sthrn Sky

Sauvignon blanc-based blends, wooded

★★★★★ Cpe Point

★★★★☆ Ingwe, Stnberg

★★★★ Ashbourne, Flgstone, Ndrburg (2), Newton J

★★★☆ Nico V, Nico vdM ★★★ Ndrburg ★★★ Le Grand Chass

Semillon, unwooded

★★★ Alter Ego ★★ Aan de Drns **NT** Breelnd

Semillon, wooded

★★★★★ Verglgn

★★★★☆ Bknhtskloof, Black Oyster, Con Uitsig, Cpe Point, Stnberg

★★★★ Btnvrwchtng, **Deetlefs**, Ekndal, Fairvw, Fleur dC, Jack & Knox, **La Bourgogne**, Landau, Nitida, Rijk's, Stony B, Verglgn

★★★☆ **Armarjaro**, Flat Roof, Hildenb, K Constantia, Ndrburg, Stellnzcht, Stormhoek, Wldekrans, Wlworths ★★★ Bloemndal, Eikehof, F'hoek Vyds, La Petite F, Rickety ★★☆ Deetlefs, Ht Espoir ★★ Slnghoek ★ My Wyn **D** Zrgvliet

Semillon-based blends, unwooded

★★★☆ Grt Cnstntia ★★★ The Winery, Thnskraal ★★★ Leopard's, Long Mntn, **Smrbsch** ★★ Wlworths **D** Glnwood, Raka

Semillon-based blends, wooded

★★★★★ Verglgn

★★★★☆ K Constantia, Verglgn

★★★★ Allee B, Con Uitsig

★★★☆ **Waverley Hills**, Zrgvliet ★★★ Jason's ★★★ **Origin** ★★ Two Oceans **D** Stettyn

Shiraz/Syrah

★★★★★ Bknhtskloof, Fairvw, Hrtnberg, Raka, Sxnburg

★★★★☆ Annandale, Anthony de J, Asara, Avndale, Bknhtskloof, **Cedrbrg**, Cloof, Cmbrly, De Traf, Delheim, DeWaal, Fairvw, **Flgstone**, G Beck, Gilga, Glen C, Horse Mtn, Hrtnberg (2), Kleine Z, Kloovnbrg, KWV, La Motte, Luddite, Muratie, Neil E, Quoin, Rbtson, Reyneke, Rickety, Ridgeback, **Rijk's**, Rudi S, Sadie Fam (organic), Signal H, Smnsig (2), Stark-C, Stellnzcht, Sxnburg, The Co of Wne, The Foundry, The Observatory, Tulbagh Mtn Vyds, Verglgn, Waterfd

★★★★ Akkerdal, Alto, Anatu, **Anthill**, Avndale, Beaumnt, Bellnghm (2), Bilton, Bknhtskloof, Black Pearl, Boland, Bon Crge, Bonfoi, **Boplaas**, Bschklf, **Bschndal** (2),

C Marshall, Cedrbrg, Cloof, Coleraine, Cowlin, Darling C (2), De Meye, **De Toren**, **De Traf** (2), Delheim, DeWaal, Dmrsfntn (2), **Domaine F**, Drknsig, **Ernie Els**, Fairvw (2), Fat B, Flgstone, For My Frnds, Freedom Hill, G Beck, Grnde Prvnce, Havana, Heron Rdg, Hildenb, Hzndal, Jack & Knox, JP Bredell (2), Kaapzicht, KWV, La Couronne, Laborie, Linton P (2), Lmrshoek, Lndhorst, Luddite, Main Str, **Makro**, Manley, Mdlvlei, **Metzer**, Mischa, Mnt Destin, Mnt Rochelle, **Ndrburg** (2), Neil E, Nghton's Flght, Nitida, Nthlingshof, Plaisir, Post Hse, Rbtson, Rstnberg, Rudera, Sanctum, Saronsbrg, Scali, Slaley, **Solms-Delta**, **Spice R** (2), Spier, Stark-C, Stnberg, Stony B, **The Cheviot**, The Mason's (2), The Winery, Thelema, Tokara, Topaz, **Tukulu**, Veenwdn, Vins d'Orrance, Vrgnoegd, Weening Barge, Western, Wlworths, Zevnwacht, **Ziggurat**, Zndvliet (4)

★★★☆ Afrcn Pride, Allesvlrn, Altyd, **Amani**, Andy Mtchell, Angora, **Anura**, Arendsig, Avntuur, Babylon's Pk, **Bergsig**, Bernheim, **Black Oyster**, **Blank Bottle**, Bloemndal, Blwklppn, Bon Cap (organic), Bon Crge, Boplaas, Bottlry Int, Bovlei, Bschndal, Bschrivier, Bucks Rdg, Cilandia, Cloof, Cls Mlvrne, Cpe Classics, Daview, Dbn Hills, De Grendel, Dmrsdal, **Domaine F**, Drmrshire, Du T'kloof, Ekndal, **Elgin Vntnrs**, Ernie Els, Ernst Co, Flgstone, G Beck, Glnwood, Goede H, Goedvrwcht, Gracelnd, **Groenendal**, **Groenld**, Grte Pst, Havana, Heron Rdg, Hidden V, Hpnbrg, Iona, **J Schaal**, **Jacques Smit**, Jordan, Joubert-T, **K Constantia** (2), Kanu, Katbakkies, **Keisseskrl**, Kleine Z, Kleinood, Klnhof, Knrhoek, **Koelfntn**, KWV, **La Chaumiere**, Lanzerac, Ldrsburg, Lndskrn, Lournsfd, L'rdge, Lvland, Lyngrove, Lynx, MAN Vintners, **Marianne**, Mellasat, **Mia Cara**, Mischa, Mnt Rozier, Mntn Ridge, Mooipls, **Mortons**, Mulderb, My Wyn, Ndrburg, Nelson (2), Nick Forti's, Nico vdM, Oracle, **Org de Rac** (organic), Oude Cmpgnies, Pella, Perdebrg, Rainbow, **Rbtson** (3), Riebeek (2), **Rietvallei**, Rooibrg, Ross G, Rust en V, Saltare, **Ses'Fikile** (2), **Shoprite**, Signal H, Slaley, Smnsig, Smook (2), Stellar (organic), **Sthrn Sky**, Stony B, Sumardg, Swrtland, Terroir, The Co of Wne, **The Stables**, Thelema, Tulbagh Mtn Vyds, Twee JG, Uitkyk, Umkhulu, Villiera, Vljsdrift, Wedderwill, Welgelee, Western, Wldekrans, Wltvrede, Wm Everson, Wndmeul, Zoetendal, Zonneblm, Zrgvliet ★★★ Afrcn Pride, **Afrcn Terroir** (2), Agulhas Wines, Allee B, Anura, **Arabella**, Ashanti, Ashton, Audacia, Avndale (2), **Ayama**, Bcksbrg, Bellevue, Bianco, Blue Crane, Blyde, Boland, Bonnivle Cllrs, Boplaas, Bottlry Int, Cameradi, Cloverfld, **Cpe First**, Cpe Vyds, Crows Nest, De Meye, De Zoete, Deetlefs, **Deetlefs**, Dennebm, Devon H (2), Dieu D, Dispore Kamma, Domaine B, Douglas G, Drknsig, **Drmrshire**, Drostdy, **Eaglevlei**, Eikehof, **FirstCpe**, Fleur dC, Fort S, Goudini, **Groenendal**, Groenld, Grt Cnstntia (2), Herold, **Hidden V**, Hofstraat, Jordan, Klein Parys, Krnskop, KWV, La Petite F, Laborie, Linde, Lndskrn, Lorraine, **Lournsfd**, Major's Hill, MAN Vintners, McGreg, Mnt Rozier, Ndrburg, New Cape (2), Niel J, **Nuy**, Obikwa, **Origin** (2), Oudeklf, PAX Vrbtm, Perdebrg, Pulpit Rock, **R Suter**, Rdezandt, Rietrvr, Rietvallei, Riverstn, Rooibrg, Royle Fam, Rtrsvlei (2), Savanha (2), S'bosch Hills, Schlkbnbsch, Seidel, Smnsvlei (2), Smrbsch, Spier, Stellar (organic), Stellnzcht, Stellrust, Stoney Crft, Swrtland, Terroir, The Co of Wne, The Winery, Thorn, Tulbagh, Van Lvren, Vaughan J, Vrdnheim, Wamaker, Waverley Hills (organic), Waverly TBS, Wederom, **Welbedcht**, Westcrp Int, Wine Source SA, Wlworths (2) (organic), Yonder, Zidela, Zrgvliet (2) ★★★ ACJ Fine Wines, Afrcn Terroir (3), Assegai, Bergwater, Bonnivle Cllrs, Botha (2), Bovlei, Buthelezi, Citrus, Clairvx, Cltzdorp, Cpe Coastal, Cru, De Villiers, **De Wet**, Detendu (2), Eshkl Kshr, **Exclsor** (2), F'hoek Vyds, FirstCpe, Grt Eilnd, **Haskell**, Jason's, Juno Co, **Kango**, Klawer, Klein Parys, Le Mnoir Brndel, Leopard's, Lngvrwacht, Lushof, Meerend, Migliarina, Nwedrift, Onderklf, Oranje, Origin (2) (organic), Oude Dboom, Ovrhex Int, **Pick's Pick**, Rhbsklf, Ridder's, Rietrvr, Rusticus, Seidel, Shoprite, Slnghoek, **Sthrn Cape Vyds**, Stormhoek, Sylvnvle, Terroir, The Co of Wne, Tulbagh (3), Two Oceans, Vinus Via, **Vukani**, Wamaker, **Westcrp Int** (2), Wlington, Wlworths, **Wrcester Wnlnds**, Wstbrdge, Zidela, Zrgvliet ★★ Afrcn Terroir (organic), **Bergheim**, Cpe Coastal (2), Cru, **Daschbsch**, Du Preez (2), **Du T'kloof**, **Glnview**, Hippo, **Kango**, Le Grand Chass, Lindiwe, Linton P, **Long Mntn**, Ltzvlle, Lyngrove, **Malan de V**, Matzikama, **Mntn River** (2), **Mrhof** (2), Oude Wllngton, Pulpit Rock, Riebeek, Rose Garden, Seidel, Sthrn Cape Vyds, Urbane, Wlington, **Wlworths** ★☆ Afrcn Terroir, Belbon Hills, Bergwater,

Dominion, Lndzicht, Stellar (organic), Tall Horse, Uitvlucht, **Versailles, Vlrsdorp,** Waterhof, Wndmeul ★ Rusticus, Stellar (organic), Teubes, Wandsbeck ☆ Kln Draken (Kosher) Montpllr **NS** Rose Garden **NT** Badsberg, **Blue Cove, Bonnivle Cllrs,** Bottlry Hills, **Crossrds,** Drostdy, Excelsious, Fairseat, False Bay, Ht Espoir, Kingsrivier, Koningsrvr, **Lady Auret,** Oaklnds Exprtrs, Old Brdge (3), Oubenhm, Rose Garden, Stbosch Cntry Est, Thabani, Wlworths (2), **Zandrft NR** Blue Cove, **Lomond** (2), **Nthlingshof, Org de Rac** (organic) **D** Assegai, Bonnivle Cllrs, BWC, Dominion (2), Hldrkruin (2), Land's E, Makro, The Co of Wne (2), Waverly TBS, Wlworths, Zndvliet

Shiraz-based blends

★★★★☆ Bilton, Bknhtskloof, **Grnghurst,** Ken F, La Motte, Nico vdM, Spice R, The Winery, Waterfd

★★★★ Avndale, Barton, Black Pearl, **Bovlei,** Dmrsfntn, Freedom Hill, Gilga, Hzndal, **La Bri,** Lmrshoek, Ndrburg, Newton J, Saronsbrg, Sequillo, Solms-Delta, Sxnburg, **The Co of Wne, The Goats** (2), **The Stables,** Tulbagh Mtn Vyds (2), **Wlworths,** Yonder (2)

★★★☆ Akkerdal, Anura (2), Black Pearl, Blyde, **Boplaas,** Bscheim, **Bschndal,** Cpe Coastal, Doolhof, Ernie Els, **F'hoek Vyds, Flat Roof,** G Beck, **Groenld,** Havana, Idiom, Karusa, Ken F, Klein Parys, Knrhoek, Lndhorst, Lndskrn, Long Mntn, **Lournsfd, Makro** (2), Mnt Destin, Ovrgaauw, Quoin, Ridgeback, Riebeek, Spier, StllnHills, Stonehill, Swrtland, The Co of Wne, The Goats (2), Western, Wlworths, Zevnwacht ★★★ **Armarjaro, Bon Cap** (organic), **Bschndal,** Cowlin, **Cpe Rock,** De Meye, G Beck, Gallop Hill, Groenld, **Hex River Crssng,** Kanu, KWV, Leopard Frog, Lyngrove, Makro, Muratie, Mystery, New Cape, Oaklnds Exprtrs, Old Vines, Rickety, Ridgeback, Riebeek, **Rijk's,** Stettyn, Terroir, The Co of Wne (2), **Thokozani,** Van Lvren, **Vukani, Withington** ★★☆ Afrcn Pride, Country C, De Wet, **FirstCpe** (2), Grt Cnstntia, Kanu, Klein Parys, Kleine Z, Mellasat, My Wyn, **Oranje, Origin,** Riebeek, Rtrsvlei, Seidel, Sthrn Cape Vyds, Tulbagh, Van Lvren ★★ Douglas, **Elberti, Mnt Rozier,** Ovrhex Int (2), Smrbsch, Swrtland, Westcrp Int (2), Zidela ★☆ Ltzvlle ★ Westcrp Int (Low alc) **NT** Doolhof, Klawer, Maiden, Mrhof, Onderklf, Swrtland, Wndmeul **D** Afrcn Terroir, Bonnivle Cllrs, Cpe First, Riverstn, Sthrn Sky, Tulbagh Mtn Vyds, Wlworths, Wlworths

Sparkling, méthode cap classique, red

★★★ Nitida

Sparkling, méthode cap classique, rosé

★★★★ Ambeloui, Cabrière, G Beck, JC le R, **Ross G,** Twee JG, Villiera

★★★★☆ Smnsig, Wlworths

Sparkling, méthode cap classique, white

★★★★☆ Cabrière (2), G Beck, JC le R, Smnsig, Villiera, Wlworths

★★★★ Ambeloui, Avntuur, Bon Crge (2), Bschndal, Cabrière, Chamnx (2), G Beck, High C, Hzndal, JC le R (2), Jean D, Laborie, L'rdge, Mrgnhof, Old Vines, Saltare, Silverthorn, Smnsig (2), Stnberg, Twee JG, Villiera, Wlworths

★★★☆ Bschndal, Btnvrwchtng, Cabrière, Dieu D, Grt Cnstntia, Môreson, Pongracz (2), Villiera, Wltvrede, Wlworths ★★★ De Zoete, JC le R, Le Grand Chass, Long Mntn, Môreson, My Wyn, Sxnburg, The Co of Wne (2), **Villiera** ★★☆ Bramon ★★ Bloemndal, Montpllr, **Rhbsklf,** Wldekrans (2) **NT** Montpllr Sud, Rtrsvlei **D** Rstnberg

Sparkling, non-MCC, red

★★★ JC le R

Sparkling, non-MCC, rosé, dry

★★★ Byrskloof, Laborie, Twee JG ★★ Boplaas ★ Westcrp Int (Low alc)

Sparkling, non-MCC, rosé, off-dry/semi-sweet

★★★ Le Grand Chass ★★ Bon Crge, Cold Duck (Low alc), Domein Drnkraal, Wlworths ★☆ **Aan de Drns,** Van Lvren **NT** Klnhof **D** Rooibrg

Sparkling, non-MCC, white, dry

★★★ Lyngrove, Riverstn, Westcrp Int ★★☆ Bergsig, Botha, Citrus, Du T'kloof, Ekndal, Goudini, **Headbutt,** JC le R, Klein Parys, Ndrburg, Oranje, Swrtland, **Westcrp Int** (Low alc) ★★ Cru, KWV, Makro, Riebeek, Rooibrg, Van Lvren, Wlworths ★★ Bonnivle Cllrs, Dominion, Origin **NT** Bon Cap (organic), Delheim, Fairseat, Mooitsg, SInghoek

Sparkling, non-MCC, white, off-dry/semi-sweet

★★★ Badsberg, **Goedvrwcht**, Kango ★★☆ Afrcn Terroir, Citrus, JC le R, Montagu, Nuy, Ovrhex Int, SInghoek, Van Lvren, Vrdnheim ★★ Afrcn Terroir, Boplaas, Botha, JC le R, Klawer, KWV (2), **Lindiwe**, Makro (2), Oranje, Rhbsklf, Rooibrg, Swrtland, Westcrp Int (2) (Low alc), Wlworths ★☆ Capnheimr, **De Zoete**, Grand Msx, Ovrhex Int, Uitvlucht (2) ★ Rietrvr **NT Daschbsch**, De Doorns, Douglas, Hrtswater, Klnhof, Lndzicht, Mooitsg **NR** Wamaker **D** Afrcn Terroir

Special late harvest

★★★☆ Bon Crge, **Fairvw**, Ndrburg ★★★ Rbtson, Rhbsklf ★★☆ Badsberg, Du T'kloof, Rdezandt, SInghoek ★★ De Wet, Drostdy ★☆ Ashton, Botha, Oranje **NT** Bergsig, Douglas, Hrtswater, Klawer **NR** Van Lvren

Sweet red

★★★★ Sylvnvle

★★★★ Asara

★★★ Fairvw ★★☆ **Goudini** ★★ Hrtswater, The Saints, Wlworths ★☆ Cellr Csk, Rbtson, Taverna **NT** Prmium Cpe Wnes **D** Avntuur

Sylvaner

★★★☆ Ovrgaauw

Syrah see Shiraz

Tempranillo

NR De Krans

Tinta barocca

★★★☆ Allesvlrn, De Krans, Lmrshoek, **Riebeek** ★★★ Louiesnhf, Swrtland ★★☆ Boplaas

Touriga nacional

★★★★ Bergsig

★★★☆ **Axe Hill**, De Krans, Jonkhr ★★★ Allesvlrn, Boplaas ★★☆ Cltzdorp

Vin de paille

★★★★☆ De Traf, Fairvw, Hzndal, Stellar, **Tulbagh Mtn Vyds**

★★★★ Fairvw, Rstnberg

★★★☆ Lmrshoek, Signal H ★★★ Stettyn ★ Mellasat

Viognier

★★★★ Bellnghm, Fairvw, G Beck, **Hex River Crssng**, Lournsfd, Riverstn, Smnsig, Spice R, The Co of Wne, The Foundry, **The Winery**

★★★☆ Adler, **Afrcn Pride**, Bcksbrg, Bon Cap (organic), **Cpe Coastal**, Dmrsfntn, **Eagle's Nest**, Fleur dC, Idiom, Katbakkies, Mischa, Ndrburg, New Cape, Perdebrg, Ridgeback, Royle Fam, Rstnberg, Spier, **Zrgvliet** ★★★ Babylon's Pk, Blue Cove (2), Coleraine, DeWaal, Exclsor, My Wyn, **New Cape**, Rbtson, Signal H ★★☆ Schlkbnbsch, Seidel, Wamaker ★★ **Arabella**, Niel J **NT** Sthrn Cape Vyds, Wlworths

Viognier, blends with

★★★★☆ Sadie Fam (organic), The Co of Wne

★★★★ Bschklf, De Grendel, Fleur dC, Joostnbrg (3), Lmrshoek, M Mossop Wines, Rstnberg, Scali, Solms-Delta, The Winery, **Tulbagh Mtn Vyds**

★★★☆ Akkerdal, **Armarjaro** (2), Bchrd-F, **Cpe Grace**, G Beck, Ndrburg (2), Pick's Pick, Quoin, Raka, Spier, The Co of Wne, The Goats, Veenwdn, Whlhaven, Zevnwacht ★★★ Akkerdal, Bon Cap, Drostdy, **FirstCpe**, **Lournsfd**, Leopard's, **Pick's Pick**, Sxnburg, The Goats, **Thokozani** ★★☆ Boplaas, **Ndrburg**, Origin (2), **Weening Barge** ★★ Blwklppn, Rhbsklf **D** Bschndal, Riverstn, Wlworths

White blends, other, unwooded dry

★★★☆ **Makro** ★★★ Flgstone, H Boom, Twee JG ★★★ Bon Crge, Douglas G, FirstCpe, Grt Eilnd, Lngvrwacht, **Mnt du Bleu**, Rbtson, **Skilpadvlei**, Slnghoek, Van Lvren, Vaughan J, **Vlrsdorp**, Wlworths, Zonneblm ★★ Bellnghm, Bonnivle Cllrs, Carnival, Country C, Goudini (2), **La Petite F**, McGreg, Ndrburg, Oranje, Pick 'n P (Low alc), Rbtson (Low alc), Ridder's, Rietrvr, Rvnswood (Low alc), Swrtland, Twee JG, Vljsdrift, Wlworths ★★ Country C, De Villiers, Drostdy, Hippo, KWV, **Ltzvlle**, **Origin** (2), Ovrmeer, Pick 'n P, Rbtson (Low alc), Rvnswood, Smnsvlei, Stellar (organic), Umkhulu, Van Lvren (3), Vaughan J, Westcrp Int ★ Botha, Oude Kaap, Ovrhex Int, Riebeek ✩ Domein Drnkraal **NT** ACJ Fine Wines, Ashton, Aufwaerts, Bonnivle Cllrs, **Crossrds**, Douglas, Fairseat, Hrtswater, Huguenot, Picardi, Rbtson, Swrtland (3), Uitvlucht, Wine Vllge, Wndmeul, Wnklshk **D** F'hoek Vyds, Wlworths

White blends, other, unwooded, off-dry/semi-sweet

★★★☆ Onderklf, Verglgn ★★★ Altyd, Bschndal, Kln Draken, L'Avenir, Ndrburg (2), Zevnwacht ★★★ Cpe Bay, De Wet, Grnde Prvnce, Malan, Mooitsg (2), Mystery, **Rbtson** (2), Smnsig (2), Spier, Zndvliet ★★ Bellnghm, Blwklppn, Clairvx, Country C, Drostdy, Graça, Kupfer, Mooitsg, Oranje, Rdezandt, Rietrvr, Rtrsvlei (2), Rvnswood, Seidel (2), Slnghoek, The Saints, Tulbagh, Westcrp Int (3) ★★ Bonnivle Cllrs, Bovlei, Grt Eilnd, KWV, Lndzicht, **Ltzvlle**, **Mnt du Bleu**, Oude Kaap, Ovrhex Int, Pick 'n P, Rbtson, Riebeek, Rvnswood, Smnsvlei (2), Wlworths ★ Carnival, Kango, **Ltzvlle** ✩ Oom T, Virginia **NT** Bergsig, Douglas, Huguenot, Montagu, Picardi, Swrtland (3), Ultra Liq (2), Wnklshk **D** Cellr Csk, F'hoek Vyds, Spier, Wlworths

White blends, other, wooded, dry

★★★★ Quoin

★★★☆ Flgstone ★★★ Western ★★ Aan de Drns, Western (organic) ★✩ Origin **NT** Stellar (organic) **NR** Solms-Delta **D** Bschndal

Zinfandel/Primitivo

★★★★ Zevnwacht

★★★☆ Blwklppn, Glen C, Idiom

Top Performers 2005–6

The following are SA's top wines as measured by their showing in selected wine competitions, challenges and professional tastings in 2005/6, as well as in the 2006 edition of this guide. The listing covers the following results (see also section on SA wine competitions for more details): Veritas 2005 – we indicate double-gold medals; Trophy Wine Show (TWS) 2006 – trophies & gold medals; Michelangelo International Wine Awards (MIWA) 2005 – trophies & double-gold medals (Grand d'Or); SA *Wine* magazine (www.winemag.co.za) – 4-5 stars Jun 2005-06; UK *Decanter* magazine (www.decanter.com) – 4-5 stars Jun 2005-06 and World Wine Awards 2006 – trophies & gold medals; US *Wine Spectator* magazine (WS, www.winespectator.com) – 90-100 points Jun 2005-06; International Wine Challenge 2006 (IWC, www.wineint.com) – gold medals; and International Wine & Spirit Competition 2006 (IWSC, www.iwsc.net) – gold medals. Our own 4½ and 5 star ratings for the 2006 edition are also shown. The results below, as well as rankings in other local and international competitions are included in the A-Z section under the relevant producers and brands. Be aware that some wineries do not enter competitions and might not be represented here.

	Vintage	Platter	Veritas	Wine	TWS	Michelangelo	Decanter	Wine Spectator	IWC	IWSC
Cabernet Franc										
Eikendal	03			4						
Plaisir de Merle	03	4½								
Raats Family	03	4½		4						
Raats Family	04			4						
Whalehaven	04		DG							
Cabernet Sauvignon										
Asara	98	4½								
Beyerskloof	03			4						
Blue Creek	04	4½								
Boekenhoutskloof	03	4½		4				90		
Boland Kelder No 1 Reserve	03		DG	4						
Bon Courage Inkará	03		DG	4½						
Boschendal	03			4						
Buitenverwachting	01	4½								
Carisbrooke	01	4½								
Cederberg V Generations	03	4½								
Cederberg	03						4			
Delaire Botmaskop	02	4½								
De Trafford	02							90		
De Trafford	03							91		
De Trafford	04	4½								
Devon Hill	03			4						
DeWaal	02			4½						
Diemersfontein Carpe Diem	03			4						
Flagstone The Music Room	03					4				
Goedverwacht Maxim Limited Release	03		DG							
Graceland	03			4						
Graham Beck The Coffeestone	03			4						

	Vintage	Platter	Veritas	Wine	TWS	Michelangelo	Decanter	Wine Spectator	IWC	IWSC
Havana Hills Du Plessis Reserve	00		DG							
Kanu	01	4½								
Kathakkies	03	4½								
KWV Cathedral Cellar	02	4½								
Landskroon	03						4			
L'Avenir CWG Auction Reserve	03	4½								
Le Riche	01	4½								
Mischa	03	4½								
Morgenhof Reserve	01	4½								
Mount Rozier Cuvée Burr	03			4						
Mount Rozier Cuvée Burr	04								G	
Nederburg Private Bin	03			4½						
Nederburg Private Bin R163	03	4½								
Neil Ellis Stellenbosch	03	4½								
Neil Ellis Vineyard Selection	03	4½		4						
Overgaauw	03	4½								
Rijk's	02	5		4			4			
Rudera	01	4½								
Rudera	03							90		
Rudera CWG Auction Reserve	02	4½								
Rustenberg Brampton	04				T		4			
Rustenberg Peter Barlow	02						4			
Rustenberg Peter Barlow	03	4½		4						
Saxenburg Private Collection	03									G
Seidelberg Roland's Reserve	03						4			
Spier Private Collection	03			4						
Springfield Méthode Ancienne	99	4½								
Springfield Whole Berry	03	4½								
Stark-Condé 'Condé'	03	4½		4						
Steenberg	03			4½						
Stellekaya	03								G	
Thelema	03	4½		4				91		
Thelema CWG Auction Reserve	03	4½								
Thelema The Mint	04								G	
Vergelegen	01							90		
Vergelegen	03	4½								G
Vergelegen 'V'	03	4½								
Waterford	03	4½								
Chardonnay										
Anura	04					DG				
Avontuur Luna de Miel	01			4						
Avontuur Luna de Miel	04	4½								
Bergsig	04		DG							
Buitenverwachting Husseys Vlei	04	4½								
Cape Chamonix Reserve	03	4½								
Cape First Makana	04			4		DG				

A GOOD WINE IS LIKE A GOOD BOOK: GOOD BOOK:

IT DESERVES
TO BE SHARED.

Fancy a cool crisp white? A bold deep red?
Or blush-blush, does pink take your fancy?
Share good times with good wines...
at good prices, from your Pick 'n Pay
Supermarket. Meant to be savoured,
down to the last page.

	Vintage	Platter	Veritas	Wine	TWS	Michelangelo	Decanter	Wine Spectator	IWC	IWSC
Cape Point	04			4						
Durbanville Hills Rhinofields	03	4½								
Fleur du Cap Unfiltered	04			4						
Glen Carlou Quartz Stone	05				G					
Glen Carlou Reserve	02	4½								
Glen Carlou Reserve Black Label	04	4½								
GlenWood Vigneron's Selection	05				G					
Groote Post	04			4						
Hamilton Russell	04	4½								
Hartenberg Reserve	03	4½					T			
Haut Espoir Reserve	04		DG			DG				
Jordan	04		DG							G
Jordan CWG Auction Reserve	04	4½								
Jordan Nine Yards Reserve	04	4½								
KWV Cathedral Cellar	03						T			
Lanzerac	04			4						
Longridge	04	4½		4						
Meerlust	03							90		
Mount Rozier Rozier Bay	04		DG							
Mulderbosch Barrel Fermented	01			4						
Mulderbosch Barrel Fermented	04			4						
Neethlingshof	02	4½								
Pulpit Rock	04					DG				
Rijk's	03					DG				
Rijk's	04			4						
Rupert & Rothschild Baroness Nadine	03	4½								
Rupert & Rothschild Baroness Nadine	04			4						
Rustenberg Five Soldiers	03							91		
Rustenberg Stellenbosch	03						4			
Rustenberg Stellenbosch	04			4						
Springfield Méthode Ancienne	02	4½								
Springfield Wild Yeast	03	4½								
Sterhuis Barrel Selection	04			4½						
Sterhuis Barrel Selection	04	4½								
Sumaridge	05	4½								
The Winery of Good Hope Radford Dale	04	4½								
Thelema	04								G	
Tokara	04							90		
Uva Mira Vineyard Selection	04									G
Veenwouden Special Reserve	04	4½								
Vergelegen Reserve	04	4½								
Viljoensdrift River Grandeur	04			4½		DG				
Weltevrede Poet's Prayer	03	4½								
Chenin Blanc										
Anura	04			4½						
Bellingham The Maverick	04		DG	4½			T			G

	Vintage	Platter	Veritas	Wine	TWS	Michelangelo	Decanter	Wine Spectator	IWC	IWSC
De Morgenzon	05			4						
De Trafford	04							90		
Fort Simon Fortress Hill	05			4						
Jordan	04				T					
Kanu Wooded	04			4						
Katbakkies	04	4½								
Ken Forrester	05			4½						
Ken Forrester The FMC	03	4½					4	90		G
Ken Forrester The FMC	04			4½					G	
Kleine Zalze Barrel Fermented	04						G			
Kleine Zalze Barrel Fermented	05			4						
Kleine Zalze Bush Vines	04						T			
Kleine Zalze Bush Vines	05			4						
KWV Val du Chêne	04			4						
Mont Destin	05			4						
Old Vines	04	4½								
Post House	04	4½								
Raats Family	04							91		
Rudera Robusto	01			4						
Rudera Robusto	03	4½								
Rudera	03							5		
Simonsig	02	DG								
Simonsig Avec Chêne	04			4						
Spice Route	04	4½		4						
Spier Private Collection	04	4½		4½						
Springfontein Jil's Dune	04	4½								
Tokara Zondernaam	04		DG							
Tokara Zondernaam	05			4						
Fortified Dessert										
Alvi's Drift Muscat de Frontignan	04	4½								
Boplaas Red Muscadel Vintners Reserve	75	4½								
De Wet Red Muscadel	03		DG							
Monis Muscadel	92	4½								
Rietvallei Muscadel 1908	03	4½								
Seidelberg De Leuwen Jagt Muscadel	NV					DG				
SoetKaroo Red Muscat d'Alexandrie	04					DG				
Gewürztraminer										
Neethlingshof	04			4						
Paul Cluver	04	4½								
Merlot										
Avondale	00	4½								
Blaauwklippen Vineyard Selection	04			4						
Hartenberg	04			4						
Jordan	96			4						
KWV Cathedral Cellar	02	4½								
Laibach	03			4½						

	Vintage	Platter	Veritas	Wine	TWS	Michelangelo	Decanter	Wine Spectator	IWC	IWSC
Linton Park	01	4½								
Longridge	03	4½								
Marklew	03			4						
Meerendal	04				T					
Morgenhof Reserve	01	4½								
Overgaauw	03	4½								
Post House	03			4						
Quoin Rock	02	4						4		
Quoin Rock	03	4½								
Sentinel	03			4						
Slaley Reserve	99	4½								
Spier Private Collection	03			4						
Steenberg	04	4½								
Sumaridge	03			4						
Thelema Reserve	03	5								
Veenwouden	03	4½								
Vergelegen	03	4½								
Thelema	02							90		
Méthode Cap Classique										
Bon Courage Jacques Bruére Brut Reserve Blanc de Blanc	00	4½								
Cabrière Blanc de Blancs	NV	4½								
Dieu Donné Maingard Brut Blanc de Blancs	02			4						
Graham Beck Brut Blanc de Blancs	00	4½								
Graham Beck Brut Blanc de Blancs	99			4						
Graham Beck Brut	94			4						
High Constantia Clos André	03	4½								
JC le Roux Desiderius Pongrácz	98			4						
JC le Roux Pinot Noir	97	4½								
Laborie Blanc de Blanc	00		4½							
Villiera Brut Natural	03	4½								
Villiera Monro	99			4						
Villiera Tradition Brut Rosé	NV			4						
Weltevrede Philip Jonker Brut	00			4						
Woolworths (Villiera) Blanc de Blanc Chardonnay Brut	02			4						
Woolworths (Villiera) Brut	98			4						
Pinot Noir										
Bouchard Finlayson Galpin Peak	03	4½								
Bouchard Finlayson Tête de Cuvée Galpin Peak	01	5								
Hamilton Russell	04	4½		4						
Muratie	03			4						
Sumaridge	04			4						
Vriesenhof	04	4½								
Pinotage										
Allée Bleue	04					T				

	Vintage	Platter	Veritas	Wine	TWS	Michelangelo	Decanter	Wine Spectator	IWC	IWSC
Ashbourne	04	4½								
Bellevue PK Morkel	04	4½								
Beyerskloof Reserve	03	4½								
Bon Cap Organic	04					T				
Camberley	04	4½	DG							
DeWaal Top of the Hill	03	4½								
Diemersfontein Carpe Diem	04	4½								
Dornier	04			4						
Fairview Primo	04	4½								
Kaapzicht Steytler	02	4½								
Kanonkop	03	4½								
L'Avenir	04		DG							
L'Avenir CWG Auction Reserve	04	4½								
Manley	04			4						
Môreson	04		DG							
Neethlingshof Lord Neethling	01			4						
Pulpit Rock	04		DG	4						
Simonsig Redhill	03	4½	DG							
Simonsig Redhill	04			4						
Southern Right	01	4½		4						
Spier Private Collection	03								G	
The Company of Wine People Kumkani	04	4½								
Umkhulu	03	4½								
Wamakersvallei La Cave	04			4						
Port										
Allesverloren Port	99	4½								
Axe Hill Cape Vintage Port	03	5								
Beyerskloof Lagare Cape Vintage Port	04			4						
Boplaas Cape Tawny Port	NV		DG		T					
Boplaas Cape Vintage CWG	03	4½								
Boplaas Cape Vintage Port	04			4						
Boplaas Cape Vintage Reserve Port	03		DG							
Boplaas Cape Vintage Reserve Port	04			4	T					
Boplaas Vintners Rsrv Selection Cape Tawny	NV			4						
Boplaas Vintners Vintage Rsrv Selection Port	03		DG							
De Krans Vintage Reserve Port	03	5								
JP Bredell Cape Vintage Reserve Port	00	4½								
JP Bredell Cape Vintage Reserve Port	97				T					
JP Bredell CWG Auction Reserve Port	03	4½								
Overgaauw Cape Vintage	97	5								
Red Blends										
Assegai Ineva	03	4½								
Avondale Graham Reserve	01		DG							
Babylon's Peak Basson Stephan's Blend	04			4						
Beyerskloof Beyerskloof	96			4½						
Beyerskloof Beyerskloof	02	4½								

	Vintage	Platter	Veritas	Wine	TWS	Michelangelo	Decanter	Wine Spectator	IWC	IWSC
Beyerskloof Synergy Reserve	02	4½	DG							
Blyde Bona Dea	02			4						
Boekenhoutskloof The Chocolate Block	04	4½								
Boschendal Grand Reserve	01	4½								
Boschkloof Reserve	01	4½								
Buitenverwachting Christine	96			4						
Buitenverwachting Christine	01	4½								
Camberley Philosophers Stone	02	4½								
Capaia 'Capaia'	04	4½								
Chamonix Troika	03				T					
Cloof Cab Franc-Cab Sauvignon-Merlot	03			4						
Clos Malverne Auret Cape Blend Ltd Release	01	4½								
Cordoba Crescendo	03	4½								
Dalla Cia Giorgio	02						4			
Darling Cellars Kroon	02	4½								
De Toren Fusion V	02						4			
De Toren Fusion V	03	4½						91		
De Trafford Elevation 393	01							90		
De Trafford Elevation 393	03	4½								
DeWaal Cape Blend	03	4½								
Ernie Els Engelbrecht-Els Proprietor's Blend	03	4½								
Ernie Els 'Ernie Els'	02			4						
Ernie Els 'Ernie Els'	03	4½						92		
Ernie Els Guardian Peak Frontier	04				T					
Fairview Formosa Peak Cab Sauv-Shiraz	03			4						
Flagstone CWG Black South Easter	03	4½								
Flagstone Mary Le Bow	03	4½								
Glen Carlou Grand Classique	02	4½	DG	4						
Graham Beck The William	03	4½								
Grangehurst Cabernet Sauvignon-Merlot	00	4½								
Grangehurst CWG Cape Blend	03	4½								
Grangehurst Nikela	00	4½								
Hartenberg The Mackenzie	03									G
Havana Hills Du Plessis Reserve Du Plessis	03	4½								
High Constantia Sebastiaan	01	4½					4			
Horse Mountain Michele	04	4½								
Idiom Shiraz-Mourvèdre-Viognier	04		DG	4						
Ingwe Amehlo	03	4½								
Ingwe Ingwe	03	4½								
Jean Daneel Signature Cab-Merlot	01	4½								
Jordan Cobblers Hill	02			4						
Jordan Cobblers Hill	03	4½								G
Jordan Sophia CWG Auction Reserve	03	4½								
Kaapzicht Bin 3	03					DG	4			
Kaapzicht Steytler Vision	02	5		4						
Kanonkop CWG Auction Reserve	01	4½								

	Vintage	Platter	Veritas	Wine	TWS	Michelangelo	Decanter	Wine Spectator	IWC	IWSC
Kanonkop Paul Sauer	96			4						
Kanonkop Paul Sauer	02	4½					5			
Ken Forrester Gypsy	02	4½								
Klein Gustrouw Cabernet Sauvignon-Merlot	03	4½								
KWV Cathedral Cellar Triptych	01	4½								
Lanzerac Classic	02									G
Lourensford Seventeen Hundred	03					DG				
Makro (Overgaauw) Touriga Nacnl-Cab Sauv	03	4½								
Meerlust Red	02			4						
Meerlust Rubicon	01	4½								G
Meinert Synchronicity	00						4			
Meinert Synchronicity	03	4½						90		
Miles Mossop Max	04				G					
Mont du Toit Le Sommet	02	4½			4½					
Morgenhof Première Sélection	01	4½								
Morgenster Lourens River Valley	02	4½								
Morgenster 'Morgenster'	01						4			
Morgenster 'Morgenster'	03	4½								
Muratie Ansela van de Caab	03	4½		4						
Napier Red Medallion	00				G					
Neethlingshof Lord Neethling Laurentius	01	4½								
Neil Ellis Stellenbosch Cab-Merlot	03	4½								
Nick & Forti's Epicentre	04				G					
Nico van der Merwe Mas Nicolas	02	4½								
Overgaauw Tria Corda	03	4½								
Overgaauw Tria Corda	04			4						
Raka Figurehead	04					DG				
Raka Quinary	03	DG								
Rustenberg John X Merriman	03	4½					5			
Rust en Vrede Estate Blend	02			4				90		
Saronsberg Full Circle	04	DG								
Saxenburg Shiraz-Cabernet-Merlot	03			4						
Simonsig Frans Malan	03	DG		4						
Spice Route Malabar	03	4½		4						
Spier Vntg Slctn Malbec-Cab Franc-Petit Verdot	03	DG								
Spier Vntg Slctn Shiraz-Mourvèdre-Viognier	03			4						
Springfield The Work of Time	02	4½								
Stellekaya Orion	03	4½								
The Observatory Syrah-Carignan	03	4½								
The Winery of Good Hope Black Rock	04	4½								
The Winery of Good Hope Radford Dale Gravity	04	4½								
Tokara Red	03	DG		4			4	90		
Veenwouden Classic	03	4½								
Vergelegen CWG Auction Rsv 'Vergelegen'	02	4½								
Vergelegen 'Vergelegen'	01	5						5		
Vergelegen 'Vergelegen'	03	4½								G

	Vintage	Platter	Veritas	Wine	TWS	Michelangelo	Decanter	Wine Spectator	IWC	IWSC
Vilafonté Series C	03	4½							G	
Vilafonté Series M	03	4½								
Vriesenhof Enthopio	02	4½								
Vriesenhof Kallista	02	4½								
Warwick Trilogy/Estate Blend	03	4½					4			
Waterford CWG Auction Reserve	03	4½								
Yonder Hill Shiraz-Merlot	03			4						
Zonnebloem Lauréat	03			4						
Zonnebloem Lauréat	04								G	G
Zorgvliet Silver Myn Merlot-Cabernet Franc	03		DG							
Riesling										
Weltevrede Rhine Riesling	01			4						
Sauvignon Blanc										
Amarava	05			4						
Bartho Eksteen Premier Choix	03	4½								
Bloemendal Suider Terras	05			4						
Cape Chamonix Reserve	04	4½								
Cape Point	04	4½		4½						
Cape Point Isliedh	04			4½	T					
Cederberg	05			4						
Constantia Glen	05	4½		4						
Delaire	05							90		
Durbanville Hills Biesjes Craal	05	4½								
Fleur du Cap Unfiltered	05			4		DG				
Fleur Du Cap Unfiltered Limited Release	05	4½	DG							
Fryer's Cove	05	4½		5						
Graham Beck Pheasants' Run	05		DG			DG				
Groote Post	05					DG				
Klein Constantia Perdeblokke	05	4½		4½						
Kleine Zalze Family Reserve	05			4						
Lomond Sugarbush	05								G	
Mulderbosch	05	4½						90		
Neil Ellis Groenekloof	05	4½								
Neil Ellis Vineyard Selection	04	4½								
Nitida Club Select	04	4½								
Oak Valley	05	4½								
Ormonde Alexanderfontein	05			4						
Robertson Winery Retreat	05			4						
Spice Route	05			4						
Spier Private Collection	05	4½								
Springfield Special Cuvée	04			4½						
Steenberg Reserve	04			4½						
Steenberg Reserve	05	5		4						G
Sterhuis	04			4						
Sterhuis	05			4						
The Co of Wine People Credo	04						T			

	Vintage	Platter	Veritas	Wine	TWS	Michelangelo	Decanter	Wine Spectator	IWC	IWSC
The Co of Wine People Kumkani	05	4½								
The Co of Wine People Kumkani Lanner Hill	05	4½	DG	4						
Tokara White	04	4½					4			
Vergelegen Schaapenberg	04	4½								
Warwick Professor Black	05								G	
Zorgvliet	05	4½								
Semillon										
Boekenhoutskloof	04	4½								
Buitenverwachting	03				G					
Cape Point	03	5								
Constantia Uitsig Reserve	04	4½								
Fairview Oom Pagal	04	4½								
Fleur du Cap Unfiltered	04									G
Jack & Knox Green on Green	04			4						
Landau du Val	04				T					
Steenberg	05	5		4						
Stellenzicht Reserve	01			4						
Stony Brook	04			4						
Vergelegen CWG Auction Reserve	03	4½								
Shiraz										
Akkerdal Syrah	03			4						
Alto	01						T			
Annandale	01	4½								
Anthony de Jager	04	4½								
Anthony Smook Reserve	03		DG							
Avondale Les Pleurs Syrah	02	4½								
Avondale Syrah	03		DG							
Boekenhoutskloof CWG Auction Syrah	03	4½								
Boekenhoutskloof Syrah	02							91		
Boekenhoutskloof Syrah	03	4½						91		
Bon Courage	03			4						
Bonfoi	03			4						
Boschendal Reserve	02			4						
Boschendal Syrah	03	4½								
Boschkloof Syrah	04							90		
Boschrivier	03			4½						
Camberley	03	4½								
Cederberg	04			4						
Cloof Crucible	03	4½				T	G			
Cloof Crucible	04		DG							
Coleraine Culraithin Syrah	02	4½								
Crow's Nest Marcel de Reuck	03					DG				
De Trafford	02							92		
De Trafford	03							94		
De Trafford	04	4½								
De Trafford Blueprint	03			4				91		

	Vintage	Platter	Veritas	Wine	TWS	Michelangelo	Decanter	Wine Spectator	IWC	IWSC
Delheim Vera Cruz Estate	03	4½								
DeWaal	02	4½								
Diemersfontein Carpe Diem	03			4						
Ernie Els Cirrus Syrah	03			4½						
Ernie Els Cirrus Syrah	04				G					
Fairview The Beacon	03	4½								
Fairview Jakkalsfontein	03							91		
Fairview Solitude	03	4½						91		
Fairview The Beacon	04									G
Flagstone Dark Horse	03		DG	4						
Flagstone Fiona Syrah	02			4½						
Gilga Syrah	03	4½								
Glen Carlou Syrah	04	5				DG	G	90		
Graceland	03			4						
Graham Beck The Joshua	03		DG							
Graham Beck The Ridge Syrah	03	4½								
Groenendal Andreas	04			4		T				
Groote Post	03			4½						
Hartenberg	03	4½		4½						
Hartenberg CWG Auction Reserve Gravel Hill	03	4½								
Havana Hills Du Plessis Reserve	03		DG							
Horse Mountain	04	4½								
Jack & Knox The Outsider	04			4						
Kleine Zalze Family Reserve	03			5						
Kleine Zalze Family Reserve	04	4½		4						
Kloovenburg	04	4½								
Koelfontein	04			4						
KWV Cathedral Cellar	02	4½								
La Motte	03					DG				
Lievland	03			4						
Luddite	03	4½								
Mischa	04					DG				
Muratie	04				G					
Neil Ellis Vineyard Selection Syrah	03	4½								
Quoin Rock Syrah	03	4½					4			
Raka Biography	04		DG		T					
Rickety Bridge	03	4½								
Ridgeback	03	4½								
Rijk's	02	4½		4						
Robertson Winery No 1 Constitution Road	03	4½								
Rudi Schultz Syrah	03							90		
Rudi Schultz Syrah	04	4½								
Rustenberg Brampton	04								G	
Sadie Family Columella	03	4½		4						
Sanctum	03							91		
Saronsberg	04		DG	4½		DG				

	Vintage	Platter	Veritas	Wine	TWS	Michelangelo	Decanter	Wine Spectator	IWC	IWSC
Saxenburg Select (SSS)	02	4½								
Scali Syrah	03	4½						90		
Sentinel	03			4						
Simonsig CWG Auction Reserve	03	4½								
Simonsig Merindol Syrah	03	4½								
Spice Route Flagship Syrah	02			4						
Spice Route Flagship Syrah	03							90		
Spier Private Collection	03									G
Stellenzicht Syrah	01				G					
Stellenzicht Syrah	02	4½								
Stellenzicht Syrah	03			4						
The Foundry Syrah	03	4½						91		
The Observatory Syrah	02	4½								
The Winery of Good Hope Radford Dale	04	4½								
Thelema	03							91		
Tokara Zondernaam	03	4½								
Tulbagh Mountain Vyds TMV Swartland Syrah	04	4½								
Vergelegen	03	4½								
Vierlanden	04			4						
Waterford Kevin Arnold	03	4½		4				91		
Unfortified Dessert										
Asara NLH	03	4½		4						
Bon Courage NLH	04	4½								
Darling Cellars NLH	02	4½								
Darling Cellars NLH Barrel Selection	02	4½								
De Trafford Straw Wine	03			4				92		
De Trafford Straw Wine	04	4½								
Fairview La Beryl Blanc	04	4½		4						
Hazendal The Last Straw Straw Wine	03			4½						
Joostenberg Chenin Blanc NLH	04			4						
Jordan Mellifera NLH	05	4½								
Kanu Kia-Ora NLH	03			4			90			
Kanu Kia-Ora NLH	04	4½								
Ken Forrester 'T' NLH Chenin Blanc	03	4½		4						
Klein Constantia Vin de Constance	00	5								
Nederburg Edelkeur NLH	04	4½								G
Nederburg NLH	04	4½								
Nederburg NLH	05									G
Nederburg Pvt Bin S316 Weisser Riesling NLH	04									G
Neethlingshof Weisser Riesling NLH	04	4½								
Paul Cluver Weisser Riesling NLH	03						T	91		
Paul Cluver Weisser Riesling NLH	04	4½								
Robertson Winery Wide River Reserve NLH	01	4½								
Rudera Chenin Blanc NLH	05	4½								
Rudera CWG Auction Rsv Chenin Blanc NLH	03	4½								
Simonsig Vin de Liza	04	4½								

	Vintage	Platter	Veritas	Wine	TWS	Michelangelo	Decanter	Wine Spectator	IWC	IWSC
Spier Private Collection NLH	04	4½								
Stellar Heaven on Earth Vin de Paille	03	4½								
SylvanVale Jewel of the Valley Natural Sweet	NV			4						
Vergelegen Semillon NLH	00	4½								
White Blends										
Allée Bleue L'amour Toujours	04		DG							
Boschendal Jean le Long Chardonnay-Chenin Blanc-Viognier	05			4						
Cape Point Isliedh	05				T					
Constantia Uitsig Constantia White	03			4						
Constantia Uitsig Constantia White	04	4½								
Miles Mossop Saskia	04			4						
Newton Johnson Pour Mes Amis	05			4						
Sadie Family Palladius	04	5								
Steenberg CWG Auction Reserve Barrel Fermented Sauvignon Blanc-Semillon	05	4½								
Vergelegen CWG Auction Reserve White	04	4½								
Vergelegen White	04	5								

The South African Wine Industry

■ The industry in brief

South Africa in 2003 (latest available year) retained its ranking as the world's 9th largest wine producer, its ±885m litres representing 3.3% of global production. France, with 17.4%, and Italy, with 16.5%, again were 1 and 2. Newest official SA statistics (for 2005) show a continuing decline in grape growers, from 4 406 in 2004 to 4 360, yet a sustained rise in wine cellars crushing grapes (561 vs 581). There are now 495 private cellars, 65 co-operatives ('producer cellars' in officialese) and 21 producing wholesalers. More than half (51%) of all cellars crush fewer than 100 tons – further evidence of the importance of micro-wineries and *garagistes*.

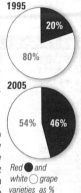

1995
20%
80%

2005
54% 46%

Red ● *and white* ○ *grape varieties as % of total area*

The vineyards

New white-wine planting continues to outstrip red, by 2 706ha to 945ha, according to the latest data. The grape most enthusiastically planted remains chenin (679ha added), still closely followed by chardonnay (667ha). Sauvignon (618ha), 3rd, has bumped shiraz (246ha) into 6th most-planted spot, with colombard (438ha) 4th and 'king' cab (266ha) now a fairly lowly 5th. Chenin, historically the staple of the industry, remains 1st in terms of hectarage (±19% of the total 101 607ha). Chenin, by a wide margin, also remains the most uprooted variety. Overall, the proportion of young, scarcely productive vines continues to decline. Some 14% of vines are under 4 years, while roughly 42% are 4–10 years and ±16% older than 20.

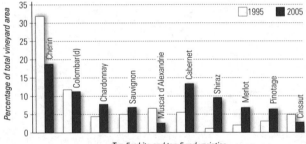

Top 5 white and top 5 red varieties

Exports

Exports of Cape wine remain buoyant despite global over-supply and the relative strength of the rand (see graph). Interestingly, the latest (2005) data show a surge in exports of pinotage, to almost 16m litres (bottled & bulk), placing the controversial variety ahead of sauvignon and cab. Chenin and chardonnay remain the most-exported varietal wines. The top five markets for SA bottled wine are, in descending order, the UK, Netherlands, Sweden, Germany and the US.

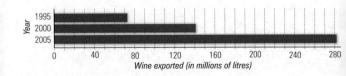

Wine exported (in millions of litres)

South African Wine Industry – Ten-year Overview

	1996	1997	1998	1999	2000	2001	2002	2003	2004	2005
Number of wineries	298	295	315	337	355	388	428	505	561	581
Total vine area (excl sultana) (hectares)	85 176	87 301	89 935	92 601	93 656	94 412	96 233	98 605	100 207	101 607
Producing area 4 yrs & older (excl sultana) (hectares)	75 218	76 025	76 895	75 892	74 335	76 071	79 073	82 719	85 331	87 284
Avg yield (tons/hectare)	15.26	14.74	13.54	15.46	14.77	12.85	13.66	14.91	15.38	13.42
Avg grape price – producer cellars/co-ops (R/ton) (2004/2005 est)	NOT AVAILABLE		796	934	966	1136	1333	1624	1439	1307
Avg grape price – excl producer cellars/co-ops (R/ton)	1551	2115	2641	2845	3278	3640	3953	4041	4133	3593
Grapes crushed (millions of tons)	1.15	1.12	1.04	1.17	1.10	0.98	1.08	1.23	1.31	1.17
Total production (millions of litres)	899.3	880.9	815.6	914.1	837.2	746.5	834.2	956	1015.7	905.2
Domestic sales (millions of litres)	405.7	401.6	384.6	390.9	389.2	390.2	388.4	348.7	350.9	345.0
Consumption per capita (litres SA wine)	9.4	9.8	9.2	9.2	9.0	9.0	8.9	7.9	7.7	7.4
Export volume (millions of litres)	99.9	110.6	118.4	129.1	141.0	177.3	217.7	239.4	267.7	281.8
Stock (millions of litres)	219.8	221.3	250.2	315.6	290.5	242.3	209.3	336.8	363.7	339.4
Stock : sales ratio	0.43:1	0.43:1	0.50:1	0.61:1	0.55:1	0.43:1	0.35:1	0.57:1	0.59:1	0.54:1

Local wine consumption

While SA wine exports have soared, domestic per-capita consumption has slumped to a new low of 7.37ℓ. This has seen SA slide further in the world rankings, to 35, behind the increasingly bibulous US. Luxembourg, at more than 66ℓ/liver, still convincingly tops the order. Of natural wine sold locally, about 43% is in glass – a steadily rising proportion – and close to 60% is in the standard 750ml bottle.

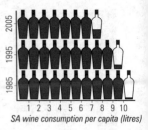

SA wine consumption per capita (litres)

Note

Statistical data used above and elsewhere in this guide are kindly provided by SA Wine Industry Information & Systems (see below).

■ Wine industry organisations

ARC Infruitec-Nietvoorbij Research & technology manager: Dr Johan van Zyl ▪ PR: Daleen Bosman ▪ **T** 021·809·3018 ▪ F 021·809·3002 ▪ bosmand@arc.agric.za ▪ www. arc.agric.za ▪ www.heritagegarden-stellenbosch.com

Internationally-regarded one-stop research institute, generating advanced technology for deciduous fruit- and grape-growers and related processors.

Biodiversity & Wine Initiative (BWI) Manager: Joan Isham ▪ bwi@sawb.co.za ▪ www.bwi.co.za ▪ **T** 021·886·8428 ▪ F 021·882·9510

Pioneering partnership between the wine industry and conservation sector to minimise loss of threatened natural vegetation and foster sustainable production through biodiversity guidelines. Under BWI auspices, producers have set aside over 17 000ha of pristine vegetation for future generations. BWI is communicated through Wines of South Africa's diversity positioning, producers' biodiversity stories and the biodiversity wine routes. See also Integrated Production of Wine.

Cape Estate Wine Producers' Association (CEWPA) Chair: Braam van Velden ▪ **T** 021·881·3815 ▪ F 021·881·3436 ▪ info@overgaauw.co.za ▪ Manager: Pierre Loubser **T** 021·855·1128 ▪ F 021·855·4351 ▪ pierre.l@mweb.co.za

Units registered for the production of estate wine (total: 123; pvsly 109)

Akkerdal, Frhoek
Allesverloren, Swtlnd
Alto, Stbosch
Altydgedacht, Dbnvlle
Ardein, Rbtsn
Asara, Stbosch
Avontuur, Stbosch
Bellevue, Stbosch
Bergsig, Wrcstr
Bloemendal, Dbnvlle
Bon Courage, Rbtsn
Bonfoi, Stbosch
Boschendal, Grt Drknstn
Cabrière, Frhoek
David Frost, Paarl
De Compagnie, Paarl
De Heuvel, Tbgh
De Wetshof, Rbtsn
De Zoete Inval, Paarl
Deetlefs, Wrcstr
Devonvale, Stbosch

Diemersdal, Dbnvlle
Doolhof, Wellngtn
Dormershire, Stbosch
Du Preez, Wrcstr
EagleVlei, Stbosch
Elsenburg, Stbosch
Excelsior, Rbtsn
Fort Simon, Stbosch
Goede Hoop, Stbosch
Goedvertrouw, Bot R
Goedverwacht, Rbtsn
Goudveld
Graham Beck Wines,
   Frhoek & Rbtsn
Grande Provence
   (BoweJoubert), Stbosch
Groot Constantia, Constia
Hamilton Russell, W Bay
Hartenberg, Stbosch
Hildenbrand, Wellngtn
Hillcrest, Dbnvlle

Jacaranda, Paarl
Jacobsdal, Stbosch
Jasonsfontein (Jason's
   Hill), Wrcstr
Johann Graue
   (Nederburg), Paarl
Joubert, Stbosch
Kaapzicht, Stbosch
Kanonkop, Stbosch
Keerweder, Frhoek
Kingsriver, Rbtsn
Klawervlei, Stbosch
Klein Constantia, Constia
Klein Gustrouw, Stbosch
Kloofzicht, Tbgh
Kranskop, Rbtsn
La Chaumiere, Frhoek
L'Avenir, Stbosch
Le Bonheur, Stbosch
Le Grand, Rbtsn
Lemberg, Tbgh

Lievland, Stbosch
Loopspruit, Mpumalanga
Lushof, Stbosch
Major's Hill, Rbtsn
Manley, Tbgh
Marianne, Stbosch
Meerendal, Dbnvlle
Meerlust, Stbosch
Middelvlei, Stbosch
Mischa, Wellngtn
Mon Don, Rbtsn
Mons Ruber, L Karoo
Mont Blois, Rbtsn
Monterosso, Stbosch
Mooiplaas, Stbosch
Morgenhof, Stbosch
Morgenster, Stbosch
Mount Rozier, Stbosch
Muratie, Stbosch
Neethlingshof, Stbosch
Nelson, Paarl

Nicholaas L Jonker (Jonkheer), Rbtsn
Niel Joubert, Paarl
Nieuwedrift, Swtlnd
Olyvenbosch, Wellngtn
Onverwacht, Wellngtn
Opstal, Wrcstr
Org de Rac, Swtlnd
Oubenheim, Olfnts R
Oude Nektar, Stbosch
Oude Wellington, Wellngtn
Overgaauw, Stbosch
Paul Cluver, Elgin
Quoin Rock, Stbosch
Rainbow's End, Stbosch
Remhoogte, Stbosch
Rhenosterkop, Paarl
Rico Suter, Wrcstr
Rietvallei, Rbtsn
Rozenburg, Paarl
Rust en Vrede, Stbosch
Schalkenbosch, Tbgh

Seidelberg, Paarl
Simonsig, Stbosch
Slaley, Stbosch
Springfontein, W Bay
Springfield, Rbtsn
Theuniskraal, Tbgh
Tulbagh Mntn Vyds, Tbgh
Twee Jonge Gezellen, Tbgh
Uiterwyk, Stbosch
Uitkyk, Stbosch
Upland, Wellngtn
Van Zylshof, Rbtsn
Vera Cruz, Stbosch
Vergenoegd, Stbosch
Warwick, Stbosch
Waterford, Stbosch
Welgemeend, Paarl
Weltevrede, Rbtsn
Wildekrans, W Bay
Wonderfontein, Rbtsn
Zandvliet, Rbtsn

Cape Winemakers Guild (CWG) See separate entry in A-Z section

Chenin Blanc Association (CBA) Chair: Irina von Holdt ▪ **T** 021·685·6428/ 083·459·4433 ▪ F 021·685·6446 ▪ irina@oldvines.co.za ▪ Manager: Wilmari Borel-Saladin **T** 021·872·9779/082·770·8001 ▪ F 021·871·1619 ▪ wilmaribs@mweb.co.za ▪ www. chenin.co.za

Fairtrade South Africa Chair: Werner Piek ▪ werner.piek@gmail.com ▪ **T** 082·465·0377 ▪ Secretariat: Sandra Kruger, sandrakruger@fairtrade.org.za ▪ **T** 076·150·5259 ▪ info@ fairtrade.org.za, www.fairtrade.org.za

Garagiste Movement Coordinator: Tanja Beutler ▪ **T** 021·855·4275 ▪ F 021·855·5086 ▪ tanja@topazwines.co.za ▪ www.garagiste.co.za

Institute of Cape Wine Masters Chair: Margaret Fry ▪ **T** 083·628·6511 ▪ F 086·686·3412 ▪ capewinemasters@gmail.com ▪ www.capewinemasters.co.za Successful completion of examinations set since 1983 by the Cape Wine & Spirit Education Trust and, latterly, the Cape Wine Academy, have qualified 57 Cape Wine Masters. Their Institute holds seminars, runs tasting workshops, charts trends and names a Wine Personality of the Year. Current members are (new inductees in bold): Chris Bargmann (UK) ▪ Berenice Barker ▪ Margie Barker ▪ FC 'Duimpie' Bayly ▪ Paul Benade ▪ Cathy Brewer ▪ Marietjie Brown (Aus) ▪ Robin Brown (US) ▪ Sue Brown (Aus) ▪ Michael Claasens ▪ Marilyn Cooper ▪ Henry Davel ▪ Dick Davidson ▪ Greg de Bruyn ▪ Ginette de Fleuriot (Ger) ▪ Heidi Rosenthal Duminy ▪ Stephan du Toit ▪ Pieter Esbach (UK) ▪ Margie Fallon ▪ Margaret Fry ▪ **Vashti Galpin** ▪ Peter Gebler (Ger) ▪ **Brad Gold** ▪ Penny Gold ▪ **Karen Green** ▪ Jeff Grier ▪ Bennie Howard ▪ Dave Johnson ▪ Val Kartsounis ▪ Peter Koff (US) ▪ **Hymli Krige** ▪ Gerald Ludwinski ▪ Alf Mauff ▪ Allan Mullins ▪ Boets Nel ▪ Carel Nel ▪ Elsie Pells ▪ Jenny Ratcliffe ▪ Christine Rudman ▪ Lynne Sheriff (UK) ▪ Caroline Snyman ▪ Cornel Spies ▪ **De Bruyn Steenkamp** (UK) ▪ Clive Torr ▪ Charl van Teijlingen ▪ Sue van Wyk (Aus) ▪ Junel Vermeulen ▪ Irina von Holdt ▪ Cathy White ▪ Geoff Willis ▪ Honorary members: Colin Frith, Phyllis Hands and Dave Hughes.

Integrated Production of Wine (IPW) Manager: Andries Tromp ▪ trompa@arc.agric.za ▪ **T** 021·809·3143 ▪ F 021·809·3113 Innovative, widely supported initiative aimed at producing wine in an environmentally sustainable, profitable way by means of guidelines for both farm and cellar, embracing all aspects of grape production, winemaking and, now, biodiversity conservation. See also Biodiversity & Wine Initiative.

Méthode Cap Classique Producers' Association Chair: Jeff Grier ▪ **T 021·865·2002** ▪ F 021·865·2314 ▪ wine@villiera.com

Muscadel Association Chair: Swepie le Roux ▪ **T 044·241·2556** ▪ F 044·241·2548 ▪ swepie@odn.co.za ▪ Vice-chair: Henri Swiegers **T 023·344·3021** ▪ winemaker@badsberg.co.za

Pinotage Association Chair: Beyers Truter ▪ **T 021·865·1235** ▪ F 021·865·2683 ▪ beyers@beyerskloof.co.za ▪ Manager: Pierre Loubser **T 021·855·1128** ▪ F 021·855·4351 ▪ info@pinotage.co.za ▪ www.pinotage.co.za

Shiraz Association Chair: Jacques Borman ▪ **T 021·881·3268** ▪ F 021·881·3032 ▪ jborman@adept.co.za

South African Port Producers' Association (SAPPA) Chair: Carel Nel ▪ **T 044·213·3326** ▪ F 044·213·3750 ▪ boplaas@mweb.co.za

South African Society for Enology & Viticulture (SASEV) President: Ilse Trautmann ▪ **T 021·809·3123** ▪ F 021·809·6335 ▪ sasev@arc.agric.za
Disseminates the latest scientific knowledge and technology locally and world-wide, to improve the quality of grapes, wines and related products.

South African Vintners Alliance Chair: Vivian Kleynhans ▪ **T/F 021·982·2200** ▪ miacara.wines@incapetown.com
Recently formed association, furthering the interests of the growing number of Black Economic Empowerment (BEE) wineries.

South African Wine Industry Council CEO: Johan van Rooyen ▪ **T 021·886·8992** ▪ F 021·882·9510 ▪ johan@sawb.co.za or lcoetzee@sawb.co.za ▪ www.sawb.co.za
Recently renamed (from South African Wine & Brandy Company) and restructured non-profit body aimed at fast-tracking important issues (including transformation), promoting industry growth, and streamlining relations among all stakeholders to stimulate competitiveness and development locally and abroad.

South African Wine Industry Information & Systems (SAWIS) Executive manager: Yvette van der Merwe ▪ **T 021·807·5703** ▪ F 021·807·6000 ▪ info@sawis.co.za
Company not for gain, collects, processes and disseminates industry information, and administers the Wine of Origin (WO) system.

South African Wine Industry Trust (SAWIT) Chair: Charles Erasmus ▪ **T 021·889·8101** ▪ F 021·889·5900 ▪ charles@sawit.co.za ▪ Administration: **T 021·889·8101** ▪ F 021·889·5900 ▪ sawit@infruit.agric.za ▪ www.sawit.co.za
Aims to transform the wine industry through its Section 21 companies: BUSCO (Wine Industry Business Support Company), concentrating on research, development and technology transfer as well as generic local/export marketing; DEVCO (Wine Industry Development Company), focusing on establishing new wine farmers from previously disadvantaged groups, support/upliftment of farm workers and communities, and black economic empowerment within the wine industry; and WEF (Wine Education Fund).

Wine & Spirit Board Chair: Njabulo Nduli ▪ Secretary: Hugo van der Merwe ▪ **T 021·889·6555** ▪ F 021·889·5823 ▪ vdmerweh@arc.agric.za
Mainly administers the Wine of Origin, estate brandy and Integrated Production of Wine (IPW) schemes.

Wine Industry Ethical Trade Association (WIETA) CEO: Peter Lewis ▪ **T 021·447·5660** ▪ F 021·447·5662 ▪ pete@wieta.org.za ▪ www.wieta.org.za
Non-profit, voluntary organisation established in 2002 to promote ethical trade in the wine industry. WIETA has adopted a code of labour standards for the industry, and its main task is to conduct ethical audits to assess members' compliance with the code.

Wines of South Africa (WOSA) Chair: Paul Cluver Snr ▪ **T/F 021·844·0605** ▪ drcluver@cluver.co.za ▪ CEO: Su Birch **T 021·883·3860** ▪ F 021·883·3861 ▪ info@wosa.co.za ▪ www.wosa.co.za
Generic marketing organisation, responsible for raising the profile of SA wine in key export markets. See also Biodiversity & Wine Initiative.

Wine Industry Network of Expertise & Technology (WINETECH) Executive manager: Jan Booysen ▪ **T 021·807·3324** ▪ F 021·807·3385 ▪ booysenj@winetech.co.za

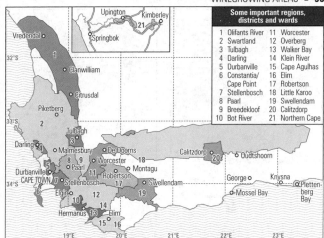

Some important regions, districts and wards	
1 Olifants River	11 Worcester
2 Swartland	12 Overberg
3 Tulbagh	13 Walker Bay
4 Darling	14 Klein River
5 Durbanville	15 Cape Agulhas
6 Constantia/	16 Elim
Cape Point	17 Robertson
7 Stellenbosch	18 Little Karoo
8 Paarl	19 Swellendam
9 Breedekloof	20 Calitzdorp
10 Bot River	21 Northern Cape

Coordinates the research, training and technology transfer programmes of participating institutions and individuals, to improve the competitiveness of the wine industry.

◼ Winegrowing areas

From modest beginnings in the Dutch East India Company's gardens below Table Mountain, SA's vineyards now cover 101 607 ha and more than 60 official appellations. Recent changes to the Wine of Origin (WO) scheme of 1972/3 saw 'geographical units' incorporated into the WO classification alongside 'regions', 'districts' and 'wards' (the latter have the smallest footprint of the WO areas, following earlier amendments to the 'estate' legislation). Below are brief notes on the most important grape cultivation zones. Figures are supplied by SA Wine Industry Information & Systems (SAWIS), and reflect latest available data (2005) for the WO areas. *Note:* Area maps are not to the same scale.

Cape Point Small (26ha), cool district on mainly western slopes of the Cape Peninsula. Recognised for sauvignon and semillon; the first red-wine vineyards recently came on-stream. Major varieties (ha): sauvignon (11), cab (6), shiraz (4) and chardonnay (3).

Constantia Premier viticultural ward on the eastern flank of the Cape Peninsula, summer-cooled by south-easterly sea breezes. Recognised for whites generally, notably sauvignon, semillon and muscat. Sauvignon (138), cab (60), chardonnay (60), merlot (45), shiraz (29).

Darling District around the eponymous town, best known for the wines from its higher-lying ward, Groenekloof, long the source of top-class sauvignon; also showing promise with reds such as shiraz. Groenekloof: cab (546), shiraz (347), sauvignon (248), pinotage (242), chenin (213).

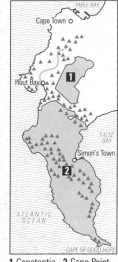

1 Constantia 2 Cape Point

1 Swartland **3** Philadelphia
2 Darling **4** Durbanville

1 Lutzville Valley **4** Citrusdal Mntn
2 Bamboes Bay **5** Citrusdal Valley
3 Olifants River **6** Piekenierskloof

Durbanville Ward within the Tygerberg district, with solid reputation for striking merlot and sauvignon. The latter (337) is now the dominant variety, followed by cab (305), merlot (228), shiraz (224) and pinotage (95).

Elgin Cool upland ward within the Overberg district, yielding exciting aromatic whites and elegant reds. Sauvignon (184), cab (61), merlot (47), shiraz (44), pinot (40).

Elim Small, promising maritime ward within the Cape Agulhas district, its 114ha of vineyards are arrayed around the old mission village of Elim near Africa's most southerly point. Sauvignon (53), cab (16), shiraz (15), semillon (10), pinot (10).

Little Karoo Scrubby semi-arid region, ideal for ostrich farming but something of a challenge for viticulture, which is reliant on irrigation. Similarities (in climate, if not soil) with Portugal's Douro Valley have inspired some local growers, chiefly around Calitzdorp, to apply their talents to 'port', with results that impress even the Portuguese. Interesting stirrings in the tiny (47ha) Upper-Langkloof ward. Region also recognised for fortifieds generally.

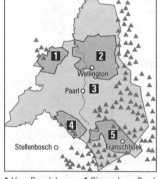

1 Voor Paardeberg **4** Simonsberg-Paarl
2 Wellington **5** Franschhoek
3 Paarl

1 Bottelary **5** Simonsberg-
2 Devon Valley Stellenbosch
3 Papegaaiberg **6** Jonkershoek Valley
4 Stellenbosch **7** Banghoek

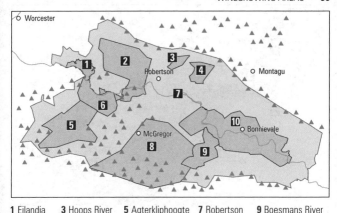

1 Eilandia **3** Hoops River **5** Agterkliphoogte **7** Robertson **9** Boesmans River
2 Vink River **4** Klaasvoogds **6** Le Chasseur **8** McGregor **10** Bonnievale

Calitzdorp district: hanepoot (110), colombard (44), cab (26), palomino (18), chardonnay (17). Tradouw ward: colombard (27), chardonnay (23) merlot (15), shiraz (12), cab (12).

Lower Orange This ward along the Orange River (Gariep) is a production zone within the Northern Cape Geographical Unit. Overwhelmingly a white-grape area but red plantings are increasing. Sultana (9 321), colombard (2 360), chenin (791), hanepoot (243), ruby cab (46), palomino (45).

Northern Cape See Lower Orange.

Olifants River Quality moves are afoot in this north-westerly Cape grape-growing region, particularly in the Bamboes Bay 'micro-ward' (just 6ha) and Lutzville Valley district nearer the coast, as well as the cool upland wards of Cederberg and Piekenierskloof. Further inland, a climate conducive to organic cultivation is now beginning to be exploited to that end. Koekenaap ward (Lutzville Valley): chenin (194), colombard (166), sauvignon (111), cab (69), chardonnay (48). Cederberg: merlot (13), shiraz (12), chenin, pinotage & sauvignon (all 9). Piekenierskloof: palomino (84), cab (77), pinotage (66), chenin (55), sauvignon (45).

Paarl This district has many mesoclimates, soils and aspects, and thus succeeds with a variety of styles and grapes. Paarl proper is recognised for shiraz and, more recently, viognier and mourvèdre grown on warmer slopes. Chenin (1 708), cab (1 318), shiraz (946), cinsaut (556); pinotage (551). The following are all wards: Wellington shows promise, especially with shiraz and gutsy red blends generally. Chenin (1 127), cab (883), shiraz (495), cinsaut (440), merlot (366). Franschhoek, founded by 17th-century French Huguenots and now a millionaire's playground, recognised for cab and semillon. Sauvignon (220), cab (187), chardonnay (157), shiraz (141), merlot (137). Simonsberg-Paarl, on the warmer slopes of the Simonsberg, recognised for red blends, shiraz and chardonnay. Cab (349), chardonnay (222), shiraz (175), merlot (151), sauvignon (145). Voor Paardeberg, long an uncredited source of top-quality grapes, now becoming a star in own right. Cab (419), shiraz (282), chenin (227), merlot (212), pinotage (187).

Philadelphia A ward of Tygerberg, cooled by the Atlantic air and noted for cab, merlot and bordeaux-style reds. Cab (100), sauvignon (70), merlot (29), chardonnay (18), shiraz (15).

Robertson Traditionally a white-wine district, increasingly recognised for shiraz and cab. Chardonnay, sauvignon and sparkling remain stand-outs. Chardonnay (2 100), colombard (2 079), chenin (1 726), cab (1 423), sauvignon (1 095).

Stellenbosch To many, this intensively farmed district is the wine capital of SA. Key contributors to quality are the cooler mountain slopes, varied soil types and breezes off False

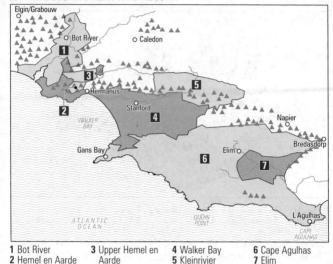

1 Bot River **3** Upper Hemel en **4** Walker Bay **6** Cape Agulhas
2 Hemel en Aarde   Aarde **5** Kleinrivier **7** Elim

Bay which moderate summer temperatures. Jonkershoek Valley, a ward east of Stellenbosch town, is recognised for cab and cab blends. Cab (63), merlot (27), chardonnay (20), sauvignon (20), shiraz (16). Simonsberg-Stellenbosch, in the south-western foothills of the Simonsberg mountain, is especially recognised for cab, cab blends, pinotage and reds generally. Cab (352), sauvignon (173), merlot (173), shiraz (151), chardonnay (118). North-west of Stellenbosch town are three adjoining wards: Bottelary, noted for pinotage, shiraz and warm-blooded blends – chenin (508), cab (420), sauvignon (343), shiraz (299), pinotage (260); Devon Valley, recognised mainly for red blends – merlot (187), cab (167), shiraz (111), sauvignon (93), pinotage (67); and Papegaaiberg – chardonnay (25), sauvignon (23), chenin (23), cab (14), pinotage (13). Banghoek, the mountain amphitheatre above the village of Pniel, in 2006 was declared a sixth ward – cab (91), shiraz (44), sauvignon (41), merlot (35), chardonnay (29). The remainder of the

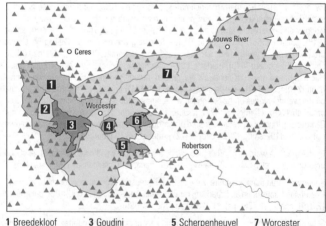

1 Breedekloof **3** Goudini **5** Scherpenheuvel **7** Worcester
2 Slanghoek **4** Aan-de-Doorns **6** Nuy

district, as yet unappellated, includes Stellenboschberg/kloof, Helderberg and Faure, recognised for red blends, chenin and sauvignon. Cab (2 186), shiraz (1 351), merlot (1 164), sauvignon (1 124), chenin (914).

Swartland Traditionally associated with beefy reds, especially pinotage and shiraz, this sunny district north of Cape Town has two wards, Malmesbury and Riebeekberg, plus a large appellated area. Riebeekberg: chenin (248), shiraz (183), cab (172), chardonnay (164), pinotage (158). Malmesbury: cab (781), chenin (616), shiraz (517), pinotage (436), merlot (287). 'Swartland': chenin (2 597), cab (939), pinotage (895), shiraz (756), chardonnay (410).

Tulbagh This inland district, traditionally known for sparkling and lightish whites, is rapidly moving towards quality reds. Major varieties: chenin (570), colombard (324), cab (192), shiraz (167), chardonnay (129).

Walker Bay Highly regarded maritime district south-east of Cape Town, recognised for pinot, aromatic pinotage, sauvignon and chardonnay. Sauvignon (92), shiraz (50), cab (49), chardonnay (46), merlot (42). A Bot River ward under consideration at press time.

Worcester Still the largest winegrowing district, measured by number of vines (more than 65m, over 20% of the total), producing chiefly for the brandy industry and merchant trade, but small quantities bottled under own labels often represent good quality/value. Recognised for everyday reds/whites and fortifieds. Chenin (4 107), colombard (2 461), chardonnay (1 591), cab (1 200), hanepoot (1 033).

Wine of Origin-defined production areas
(New appellations in **bold**.)

Region	District	Ward
Breede River Valley	**Breedekloof**	Goudini
		Slanghoek
	Robertson	Agterkliphoogte
		Boesmansrivier
		Bonnievale
		Eilandia
		Hoopsrivier
		Klaasvoogds
		Le Chasseur
		McGregor
		Vinkrivier
	Swellendam	Buffeljags
		Stormsvlei
	Worcester	Aan-de-Doorns
		Nuy
		Scherpenheuvel
Coastal	Cape Point	–
	–	Constantia
	Darling	Groenekloof
	Paarl	Franschhoek Valley
		Simonsberg-Paarl
		Voor Paardeberg
		Wellington
	Tygerberg	Durbanville
		Philadelphia
	Stellenbosch	**Banghoek**
		Bottelary
		Devon Valley
		Jonkershoek Valley
		Papegaaiberg
		Simonsberg-Stellenbosch
	Swartland	Malmesbury
		Riebeekberg
	Tulbagh	–

Region	District	Ward
Little Karoo	Calitzdorp	—
	—	Montagu
	—	Outeniqua
	—	Tradouw
	—	Upper Langkloof
Olifants River	—	Bamboes Bay
	Citrusdal Mountain	Piekenierskloof
	Citrusdal Valley	
	Lutzville Valley	Koekenaap
	—	Spruitdrift
	—	Vredendal
—	**Bot River**	
—	Cape Agulhas	Elim
—	Douglas*	—
—	Overberg	Elgin
—		Kleinrivier
—	**Plettenberg Bay**	—
—	Walker Bay	**Upper Hemel-en-Aarde**
		Hemel-en-Aarde
—	—	Cederberg
—	—	Ceres
—	—	Hartswater*
—	—	Herbertsdale
—	—	Lower Orange*
—	—	Prince Albert Valley
—	—	Rietrivier (Free State)*
—	—	Ruiterbosch
—	—	Swartberg
Boberg (fortified wines from Paarl & Tulbagh)		

*Production zones within the officially designated Northern Cape Geographical Unit (GU); all other areas above are part of the Western Cape GU. A third GU, KwaZulu-Natal, was gazetted last year. Source: SAWIS

▪ Grape varieties

Though vines have been grown in SA for almost 350 years, Old World-style regional specialisation such riesling in the Moselle Valley or nebbiolo in the Langhe Hills hardly exists here, and where it does, it is of fairly recent origin (Constantia muscat is a notable exception). Cabernet is acknowledged to do exceptionally well in the Simonsberg foothills, but it is also a feature of most other vineyard areas. Less forgiving varieties, such as merlot, are cultivated from Cape Point to the Kalahari. Recent years have brought a greater understanding of, and emphasis on, the importance of selecting the most suitable sites for any given variety, based on the evidence of scientific investigation and accumulated experience. International exposure has given the present generation of vinegrowers fresh perspectives and possibilities, suggesting that trial and experimentation with grapes and

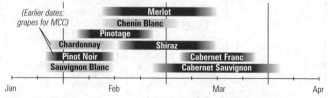

Approximate ripening dates in the Stellenbosch area for some important grape varieties

terroirs will continue to be a key feature of SA viticulture well into the future. Below are brief notes on the main grape varieties in SA today, and their contribution to the national vineyard (statistics from SA Wine Industry Information & Systems — SAWIS). See under Winegrowing Areas for details of the most widely planted and best-performing varieties in the major vine cultivation zones.

Red-wine varieties

Cabernet sauvignon Adaptable and internationally planted black grape making some of the world's finest and longest-lasting wines. And retaining some of its inherent qualities even when overcropped in less suitable soils and climates. Can stand alone triumphantly, but frequently blended with a wide range of other varieties: traditionally, as in Bordeaux, with cab franc, merlot and a few minor others, but also in SA sometimes partnering varieties such as shiraz and pinotage. Number of different clones, with differing characteristics. A steady ±13% of total vineyard area.

Cabernet franc Like its descendant cabernet sauvignon, with which it is often partnered, a classic part of the Bordeaux blend, but in SA and elsewhere also used for varietal wines — particularly in the Loire. Tiny vineyard area (1%), increasing.

Carignan Hugely planted in the south of France, where it is not much respected. But there, as in SA, older, low-yielding vines can produce pleasant surprises. Insignificant vineyard area.

Cinsaut (noir) 'Cinsault' in France. Another of the mass, undistinguished plantings of southern France, which only occasionally comes up trumps. Used to be known locally as hermitage, the name reflected in its offspring (with pinot noir), pinotage. Less than 3% of vineyard area, decreasing.

Gamay noir Although it produces some serious long-lived wines in Beaujolais, its use for (mainly) early- and easy-drinking 'nouveau' wines there, often using carbonic maceration, is the model mostly copied in SA. Insignificant vineyard area.

Grenache (noir) The international (ie French) name for the Spanish grape garnacha. Widespread in Spain and southern France, generally used in blends (as in Rioja and Châteauneuf), but occasionally solo. A favourite for rosés. When vigour restrained, capable of greatness, but this is rare. Tiny plantings here. (White/pink versions also occur.)

Malbec Once a significant part of Bordeaux's blend, now most important in Cahors in western France (where it is known as cot), and as Argentina's signature variety. In SA a few varietal and blended examples; very small plantings.

Merlot Classic blending partner (as in Bordeaux) for cabernet, fashionable around the world, where it tends to be seen as an 'easier' version of cab — although this is perhaps because it is often made in a less ambitious manner. Merlot varietal wines increasingly common in SA too. A steady ±7% of vineyard area.

Mourvèdre Internationally known by its French name, though originally Spanish (monastrell). In Australia and California also called mataro. Particularly successful in some serious southern French blends, and increasingly modish internationally. Minuscule plantings here.

Nebbiolo Perhaps the greatest red grape to have scarcely ventured from its home — Piedmont in this case, where it makes massive, tannic, long-lived wines. Minute plantings here.

Petit verdot Use of this excellent variety in the Médoc limited by its late ripening. Now appearing in some local blends, and a few varietals. Tiny but increasing quantities.

Pinotage A 1920s cross between pinot noir and cinsaut ('hermitage'). Made in a range of styles, from simply fruity to ambitious, well-oaked examples. 6.4% of vineyard area, decreasing (7.3% at zenith in 2001).

Pinot noir Notoriously difficult grape to succeed with outside its native Burgundy, but SA, along with the rest of the New World, now producing some excellent examples, especially as use of BK5 'champagne' clone wanes. Usually matured in wood; seldom at a bargain price. Still very small proportion of the vineyard (0.5%).

Ruby cabernet US cross between cabernet sauvignon and carignan, designed for heat tolerance. Rather rustic, used mostly in cheaper blends. 2.6% of vineyard area.

Shiraz Better known as syrah outside SA and Australia (and on some local labels too). Internationally increasing in popularity, with northern Rhône and now also Australia as its major domiciles. Clearly happy in warmer climates, shiraz is seen by many as the great hope for SA wine. Made here in a variety of styles – generally wooded, often with American oak. 9.6% of vineyard area, steadily increasing.

Tinta barocca Elsewhere spelt 'barroca'. One of the important Portuguese port-making grapes, which is now its primary role in SA, usually blended. Also used for some varietal unfortified wines, and namelessly in some 'dry reds'. Insignificant vineyard area.

Touriga nacional Important Portuguese port-making grape, now usefully grown here for similar ends, along with tinta franca, tinta roriz (tempranillo) and souzão. Tiny plantings.

Zinfandel The quintessential Californian grape (of European origin, and the same as Italy's primitivo), used here in a small way for some big wines. Tiny plantings.

White wine varieties

Chardonnay In the Cape, as elsewhere, many new vineyards of this grape have come on-stream in recent years, with wines showing a wide range of styles, quality and price. Generally used varietally, but also in blends. Often heavily wooded in more ambitious wines. 7.8% of vineyard area, increasing slowly.

Chenin blanc SA has more chenin (locally also called steen) than even France's Loire Valley, the variety's home. Used here for everything from generic 'dry whites' to ambitious sweet wines, to brandy. Some notable table-wine successes in recent years, in a sea of overcropped mediocrity. 18.8% of vineyard area, still declining.

Colombar(d) One of the mainstays of brandy production in the Cape, colombard (usually without the 'd' in SA) also used for numerous varietal and blended wines, ranging from dry to sweet – seldom wooded. 11.3% of vineyard area, marginally inclining.

Gewürztraminer Readily identifiable from its rose-petal fragrance, best known in its Alsatian guise. In the Cape usually made in sweeter styles. Insignificant vineyard area.

Hanepoot Traditional Afrikaans name for muscat d'Alexandrie, the Cape's most planted muscat variety (see also muscadel below). 2.6% of vineyard area (some for raisins and table grapes), slowly declining.

Muscadel Name used here for both muscat de Frontignan and muscat blanc à petits grains (both red and white versions). The grape associated with the famous Constantia dessert wines of the 18th century today is used chiefly for dessert and fortified wines and for touching up blends. Red and white versions total ±1% of vineyard area.

Muscat See Hanepoot and Muscadel.

Riesling The name a source of confusion to consumers, and of distress to the producers of what is known in its great homeland, Germany, simply as riesling and here officially as Rhine or weisser riesling. In SA, standing alone, 'riesling' usually, and officially, refers to Cape riesling (sometimes called SA riesling), a much inferior grape properly known as crouchen blanc, mostly used here anonymously in blends, and sometimes varietally. Rhine/weisser riesling frequently in off-dry style here, in blends or varietally, some noteworthy botrytised dessert examples – and developing terpene character much earlier in SA than in cooler climates. Cape riesling: 1.1% of vineyard area, decreasing; Rhine: stable at a miniscule 0.3%. Note: in this guide 'riesling' without qualification refers to the latter.

Sauvignon blanc Prestigious vine most associated with eastern Loire regions, Bordeaux and, increasingly, New Zealand – whose wines have helped restore fashionability to the grape. The Cape version no longer a poor relation of these. Usually dry, but some sweet wines; sometimes wooded, more often not (former sometimes called fumé blanc/blanc fumé). 7.5% of vineyard area, increasing.

Semillon Spelt sémillon in French. The present small hectarage devoted to semillon in SA is a far cry from the early 19th century, when the grape, also known as 'groen' (green), a reference to its bright foliage, represented 93% of all Cape vines. Now only ±1%. Sometimes heavily wooded.

Viognier Increasingly fashionable variety internationally, spreading out from its home in the northern Rhône, now showing promise here. Usually wooded. Still tiny plantings.

■ SA wine competitions, challenges & awards

An increasing number of wine competitions, awards and challenges are run by liquor industry bodies, independent companies, publishing houses and individuals. Below are the main national events:

ABSA Top Ten Pinotage Competition Run annually by the Pinotage Association and a major financial institution to help set international quality targets for growers of pinotage. Local judges. See under Industry Organisations for contact details.

Calyon Trophy Bordeaux Blend Challenge New competition lauding the best blends of at least two of the 'Bordeaux reds', cabernets sauvignon and franc, merlot, malbec and petit verdot. Local/overseas judges. ▪ alex@outsorceress.co.za ▪ T 011·482·5936 ▪ F 011·482·2272

Classic Wine Trophy Staged under rules of the Office Internationale de la Vigne et du Vin (OIV), recognising ageworthy, Old World-inclined SA wines. Overseas judges. ▪ info@winemaker.co.za or ridon@iafrica.com ▪ T 083·675·0280 (Jean-Vincent Ridon)

Diners Club Winemaker of the Year Inaugurated 1981, this prestigious competition features a different category each year. Local panel with some overseas representation. ▪ celiag@rsp.co.za ▪ www.winemag.co.za ▪ T 021·530·3145 ▪ F 021·531·2212

Juliet Cullinan Wine Connoisseur's Award National competition organised by local wine-entrepreneur Juliet Cullinan and judged by a panel of Cape Wine Masters. julietcullinan@tiscali.co.za ▪ T 011·447·1885/083·255·9430 ▪ F 011·219·7064

Landbouweekblad Woman Winemaker of the Year Launched 2004 to acknowledge the role and skills of women winemakers, and highlight the special qualities they bring to their craft. ▪ lorman@yebo.co.za ▪ www.sawinewoman.co.za ▪ T 039·314·9913/5 or 082·556·8679 ▪ F 039·314·9914

Old Mutual Trophy Wine Show See Trophy Wine Show

Michelangelo International Wine Awards Well-established event (1997) featuring international panel and one local judge. Aims to identify SA wines which will appeal to foreign palates. ▪ lorman@yebo.co.za ▪ www.michelangeloawards.com ▪ T 039·314·9913/5 or 082·556·8679 ▪ F 039·314·9914

Muscadel Award for Excellence Annual competition aimed at raising consumer awareness and recognising quality in the creation, packaging and promotion of SA's muscadel wines. Local judges. ▪ swepie@odn.co.za ▪ T 044·241·2556 ▪ F 044·241·2548

Peter Schulz Excellence Awards for Port Sponsored by importer-wholesaler NMK Schulz, and organised by the SA Port Producers' Association with the assistance of SA *Wine*, to select the best wine in each of the various port categories, and an overall winner. Local judges. ▪ boplaas@mweb.co.za ▪ www.sappa.co.za ▪ T 044·213·3326 ▪ F 044·213·3750

South African Airways (SAA) Wine Awards Annual selection of wines to fly with the national carrier (drinkability in flight conditions an important consideration). The top red, white, bubbly and port each receive a trophy. Local & overseas palates. ▪ Mpho Omotola ▪ mphoomotola@flysaa.com ▪ www.flysaa.com ▪ **T 011·978·3311** ▪ F 011·978·3115

SA Young Wine Show Inaugurated 1975 to gauge the quality of embryo wines, prior to finishing and bottling, thereby also recognising wineries which sell their products in bulk. The grand champion receives the General Smuts Trophy. Local judges. ▪ ferreira@vinpro.co.za ▪ www.youngwineshow.co.za ▪ T 021·807·3104 ▪ F 021·863·2079

Swiss International Air Lines Wine Awards Annual competition, judged by international/local wine buyers and Cape Wine Masters. Selected award winners fly with Swiss Business/1st Class. ▪ info@gourmetsa.com ▪ www.gourmetsa.com ▪ T 021·797·4500 ▪ F 021·797·4179

Terroir Wine Awards A new (2006) competition, rewarding the best wines from SA's officially recognised winegrowing areas. Local judges. ▪ mlab@iafrica.com ▪ www.novare.co.za ▪ T 021·975·8166 ▪ F 021·979·0867

Trophy Wine Show Launched in 2002 as Fairbairn Capital TWS, now sponsored by Old Mutual. Identifies the best wines in SA and awards trophies to the top wines in each of the major classes, as well as the top producer overall. Local and international judges. ▪ celiag@rsp.co.za ▪ www.trophywineshow.co.za ▪ T 021·530·3145 ▪ F 021·531·2212

Veritas SA's biggest competition for market-ready wines, awarding double-gold, gold, silver and bronze medals across a wide range of categories. Local palates with some overseas input. ferreira@vinpro.co.za ▪ www.veritas.co.za ▪ **T 021·807·3104** ▪ F 021·863·2079

Wine Magazine Amorim Cork Cap Classique Challenge Annual competition to anoint SA's top bottle-fermented sparkling wines. Local judges. ▪ celiag@rsp.co.za ▪ www.winemag.co.za ▪ T 021·530·3145 ▪ F 021·531·2212

Wine Magazine Value Awards SA judges gather annually to select the best value wines based on quality vs price. Results published in *Wine*'s *Best Value Wine Guide*. ▪ celiag@rsp.co.za ▪ www.winemag.co.za ▪ T 021·530·3145 ▪ F 021·531·2212

Wine Magazine Tops at Spar Chenin Blanc Challenge Annual event in which wooded and unwooded chenins in the drier spectrum (max 20g/ℓ sugar) are assessed by a mostly SA panel. ▪ celiag@rsp.co.za ▪ www.winemag.co.za ▪ T 021·530·3145 ▪ F 021·531·2212

Wine Magazine Tops at Spar Shiraz Challenge Another SA *Wine*/Tops at Spar collaboration, uncovering benchmark SA wines made from shiraz/syrah. Local judges. ▪ celiag@rsp.co.za ▪ www.winemag.co.za ▪ T 021·530·3145 ▪ F 021·531·2212

Wine Magazine Tops at Spar Value for Money Pinotage Awards Reconfigured Pinotage Champion of the Year competition, now dedicated to showcase the best-value pinotages of a given vintage. SA judges. ▪ celiag@rsp.co.za ▪ www.winemag.co.za ▪ T 021·530·3145 ▪ F 021·531·2212

Winemakers' Choice Now in its 2nd year, this 'peer review' is conducted by a panel of top winemakers. Diamond Awards go to the winning wines, and trophies to the best red and white on show. ▪ info@winemakerschoice.co.za ▪ www.winemakerschoice.co.za ▪ T/F 021·889·8479

> **Note:** For a list of wines rated highest in selected professional tastings and competitions in the past year, plus our own 4½ and 5-star ratings, see Top Performers.

■ Wine education

Cape Wine Academy Long-established (1979) general wine education body. Based in Stellenbosch and Johannesburg with satellites in Durban, Pretoria, Windhoek and Harare. Runs wine theory and tasting courses with examinations at several levels, from Introduction to SA Wine to Cape Wine Master, as well as skills workshops for front-of-house sales staff. The MD is Marilyn Cooper.

Stellenbosch **T 021·889·8844** ▪ F 021·889·7391 ▪ info@cwa.org.za ▪ Johannesburg T 011·783·4585 ▪ F 011·883·2356 ▪ busi.cwa@iafrica.com ▪ Durban T/F 031·564·5067 ▪ Pretoria T/F 012·333·1978 ▪ www.capewineacademy.co.za

The Wine Ambassador thewineambassador@telkomsa.net ▪ www.thewineambassador.co.za ▪ **T 021·975·3906/ 084·499·6014**

■ Selected wine shops

The following retail outlets stock a wide range of fine-wines and/or provide specialised services to the wine-consuming public. 'Bricks-and-mortar' shops are listed first, by area, followed by on-line emporia.

Eastern Cape

Da Vino's (Port Elizabeth) ▪ T 041·583·2166 ▪ F 041·583·6220

Makro Port Elizabeth ▪ T 041·397·8000 ▪ F 041·397·8058

Picardi Rebel Fine Wines & Liquors Port Elizabeth (Walmer) ▪ T 041·368·2840 ▪ F 041·368·2420

Picardi Rebel Fine Wines & Liquors Port Elizabeth (Fig Tree Park) ▪ T/F 041·581·3177

Prestons (Walmer) ▪ T/F 041·581·1993

Spargs Liquor Mart (East London) ▪ T 043·748·1383 ▪ F 043·748·5059

Ultra Liquors East London ▪ T 043·743·5174/722·3476 ▪ F 043·743·4283

Ultra Liquors Newton Park ▪ T 041·364·1103 ▪ F 041·364·2277

Vintage Liquors (Port Alfred) ▪ T 046·624·3120 ▪ F 046·624·4419

Free State

Liquor City Bloemfontein ▪ T 051·448·6222

Liquor World Bloemfontein T 051·434·1292 ▪ F 051·435·3074

Ultra Liquors Bloemfontein ▪ T 051·447·3328 ▪ F 051·447·3600

Garden Route

Picardi Rebel Fine Wines & Liquors George ▪ T 044·887·0053 ▪ F 044·887·0054

Picardi Rebel Fine Wines & Liquors Knysna ▪ T 044·382·3318 ▪ F 044·382·3319

Picardi Rebel Fine Wines & Liquors Plettenberg Bay (Beacon Isle) ▪ T/F 044·533·1225

Picardi Rebel Fine Wines & Liquors Plettenberg Bay (Main Str) ▪ T 044·533·1340 ▪ F 044·533·0574

The Lagoon Wine Shop (Plettenberg Bay) ▪ T 044·533·2440 ▪ F 044·533·2442

34° South Wine Shop (Knysna) ▪ T/ F 044·382·7331

Ultra Liquors George ▪ T 044·874·5514 ▪ F 044·874·5511

Gauteng

Alberts Liquors (Pretoria) ▪ T 012·543·0813

Alpha Liquor Store (Roodepoort) ▪ T 011·763·8740 ▪ F 011·763·8741

Bamboo-WINE+ (Melville) ▪ T 011·482·1020 ▪ F 011·482·5958

Bootleggers Liquor Specialist ▪ Booysens: T 011·493·2536 ▪ Fourways Crossing: T 011·465·9777 ▪ Glenanda: T 011·432·3570 ▪ Glenvista: T 011·432·3093 ▪ Irene: T 012·667·1907 ▪ Lombardy: T 011·882·6252

Cellar d'Or ▪ T 0861·235·527 ▪ F 011·465·9744

Central Liquors @ The Square (Boksburg) ▪ T 011·826·5070 ▪ F 011·826·7151

Glenfair Wine & Liquor (Pretoria) ▪ T 012·361·4509/4563 ▪ F 012·361·4509

John Wilson Sandton City ▪ T 011·783·7035 ▪ F 011·783·7036

Liquor City Bassonia ▪ T 011·432·0457/71

Liquor City Beyers Naudé (Northcliff) ▪ T 011·888·9374

Liquor City Boksburg ▪ T 011·917·0866

Liquor City Boksburg West ▪ T 011·826·2336

Liquor City Brackengate (Alberton) ▪ T 011·900·4493

Liquor City Brixton ▪ T 011·837·7079

Liquor City Broadacres (Randburg) ▪ T 011·465·3795

Liquor City Cleo's (Boksburg) ▪ T 011·916·2358

Liquor City Cornwall View (Pretoria) ▪ T 012·345·5198

Liquor City Crystal Park (Benoni) ▪ T 011·969·3700

Liquor City Dawnpark (Boksburg) ▪ T 011·862·2044

Liquor City Eden Meadows (Edenvale) ▪ T 011·452·1993

Liquor City Fourways ▪ T 011·465·6910
Liquor City Geduld (Springs) ▪ T 011·811·5869
Liquor City Glen Marais Hyper (Kempton Park) ▪ T 011·391·7819
Liquor City Glen Marais (Kempton Park) ▪ T 011·391·6005
Liquor City Glen Nerine (Douglas Dale) ▪ T 011·658·1706
Liquor City Heidelberg ▪ T 016·349·2512
Liquor City Highlands Shop(Centurion) ▪ T 012·664·3424
Liquor City Jean·Len (Centurion) ▪ T 012·663·9389
Liquor City Lambton (Germiston) ▪ T 011·827·4566
Liquor City Leondale ▪ T 011·865·1690
Liquor City Lonehill ▪ T 011·467·9887
Liquor City Montana (Pretoria) ▪ T 012·548·7780
Liquor City Moreleta (Pretoria) ▪ T 012·993·0201
Liquor City Mount Dev (Northcliff) ▪ T 011·782·6485/4
Liquor City Northpoint (Boksburg) ▪ T 011·864·1672
Liquor City Pretoria North ▪ T 012·546·8839
Liquor City Princess Crossing (Roodepoort) ▪ T 011·768·6813
Liquor City Radiokop (Roodepoort) ▪ T 011·675·0493
Liquor City Rooihuiskraal (Pretoria) ▪ T 011·958·2453
Liquor City Ruimsig (Roodepoort) ▪ T 011·958·2453
Liquor City Ryngate (Benoni) ▪ T 011·969·1559
Liquor City Satelite (Boksburg North) ▪ T 011·917·0791
Liquor City Selcourt ▪ T 011·818·2961
Liquor City Silverton ▪ T 012·810·0090
Liquor City Towers (Boksburg North) ▪ T 011·823·5221
Liquor City Triomf ▪ T 011·673·1893
Liquor City V.C.(Brakpan) ▪ T 011·744·0776
Liquor City Waverley (Pretoria) ▪ T 012·332·0535
Liquor City Westwood (Boksburg) ▪ T 011·894·6567
Liquor City Woodhill (Garsfontein) ▪ T 012·993·5042
Liquor Inn Heidelberg ▪ T 016·341·2343
Liquor World Camaro Square (Oakdene) ▪ T 011·436·1776
Liquor World Denver ▪ T 011·622·9494 ▪ F 011·622·4301
Liquor World East Rand (Boksburg) ▪ T 011·826·1420 ▪ F 011·826·1462
Liquor World Hillfox(Weltevreden Park) ▪ T 011·679·5670 ▪ F 011·475·5139
Liquor World Pretoria (Roseville) ▪ T 012·379·6050 ▪ F 012·379·7388
Liquor World Pretoria East ▪ T 012·809·0800 ▪ F 012·809·0985
Liquor World Springs ▪ T 011·817·1133 ▪ F 011·817·4702
Lynnridge Wine & Liquor (Lynnridge Mall) ▪ T/F 012·348·3456
Makro Centurion ▪ T 012·673·3734 ▪ F 012·665·1125
Makro Crown Mines ▪ T 011·309·1108 ▪ F 011·309·1089
Makro Germiston ▪ T 011·372·0313 ▪ F 011·453·1698
Makro Strubens Valley (Roodepoort) ▪ T 011·671·8422 ▪ F 011·671·8480
Makro Wonderboom (Annlin West) ▪ T 012·567·9158 ▪ F 012·567·9038
Makro Woodmead ▪ T 011·208·9152 ▪ F 011·208·9092
Manuka Wine Boutique Killarney Mall (Jhb) ▪ T 011·646·9600 ▪ F 011·646·9607
Manuka Wine Boutique Woodhill (Pretoria East) ▪ T 012·97·4669 ▪ F 012·997·1480
Morara Wines & Spirits Emporium (Soweto) ▪ T 011·982·2290 ▪ F 011·982·3734
Norman Goodfellow's Hyde Park ▪ T 011·325·6462 ▪ F 011·325·5450
Norman Goodfellow's (Johannesburg) ▪ T 011·788·4814 ▪ F 011·442·8868
Picardi Rebel Fine Wines & Liquors Bedfordview ▪ T 011·615·9160 ▪ F 011·622·2475
Picardi Rebel Fine Wines & Liquors Blackheath ▪ T 011·678·6817 ▪ F 011·678·5017
Picardi Rebel Fine Wines & Liquors Fourways ▪ T 011·465·6921 ▪ F 011·465·6922
Picardi Rebel Fine Wines & Liquors Honeydew ▪ T 011·475·4658 ▪ F 011·675·6404
Picardi Rebel Fine Wines & Liquors Morning Glen (Gallo Manor) ▪ T 011·802·0964 ▪
F 011·802·0965

Picardi Rebel Fine Wines & Liquors Northmead • T 011·849·5392 • F 011·849·7332
Picardi Rebel Fine Wines & Liquors Sandton • T 011·884·2151 • F 011· 884·1067
Rivonia Cellars • T 011·803·6121/2 • F 011·803·7600
Ultra Liquors Corlett Drive • T 011·887·1001/2/3 • F 011·887·4947
Vintages – The Wine Seller (Sandton) • T 011·784·8676/7 • F 011·784·8674
Wine Direct (Midrand) • T 011·315·3088 • F 011·315·3098

KwaZulu-Natal
Blue Bottles Wine Cellar (Shelly Beach) • T 039·315·1336
Buxtons La Cave Liquors • F 031·572·2619 • Umhlanga: T 031·561·6792 • La Lucia
Mall: T 031·572·6073
Liberty Liquors (Durban) • T 031·303·9857 • F 031·303·9864
Liquor World Durban • T 031·902·8144/912·3730 • F 031·912·3730
Liquor World Mt Edgecombe • T 031·502·5380 • F 031·502·6555
Makro Pietermaritzburg • T 033·846·3600 • F 033·386·8120
Makro Rossburgh • T 031·480·7096 • F 031·480·7060
Makro Springfield • T 031·203·2827 • F 031·203·5905
Marriot Gardens Liquor Store (Greyville) • T 031·309·2079 • F 031·309·2097
Parklane Cellars (Pietermaritzburg) • T 033·342·3487 • F 033·342·6413
The Village Vineyard (Kloof Village Mall) • T 031·764·6679 • F 031·764·7196
The Wine Cellar (Rosetta) • T/F 033·267·7044
Ultra Liquors New Germany • T 031·705·3777 • F 031·705·6640
Ultra Liquors Tollgate (Mayville) • T 031·261·2233/67 • F 031·261·7980
Ultra Liquors Westville • T 031·266·4364/60 • F 031·266·4300

Limpopo
Liquor World Polokwane (Magnesiet Str) • T 015·298·8800 • F 015·298·8468
Liquor World Polokwane (Nikkel Str) • T 015·292·2354 • F 015·292·2352
Liquor World Tzaneen • T 015·307·1254 • F 015·307·1767

Mpumalanga
Big M Liquor Store (Delmas) • T 013·665·2461
Hi-Octane Store (Secunda) • T 017·634·7033
Liquor City Nelspruit • T 013·752·2034
Liquor City White River • T 013·750·2184
Liquor City Witbank • T 013·690·2855
Liquor World Nelspruit • T 013·753·2146 • T 013·752·2915
Liquor World Hazyview • T 013·737·6314 • T 013·737·6315
Windmill Wine Shop (R536 between Hazyview & Sabie) • T 013·737·8175 •
F 013·737·8966

Northern Cape
Liquor World Kimberley • T 053·832·0878 • T 053·832·0902
Zebrani Liquor City (Upington) • T 054·331·2831 • F 054·332·7928

North West
De Wijnwinkel & Deli (Wolmaransstad) • T 083·262·0387 • F 018·596·2890
Liquor City Bushveld (Warmbaths) • T 014·736·3215
Liquor City Euronooi (Mooinooi, Brits) • T 014·574·3060
Liquor City Geelhout (Rustenburg) • T 014·594·1768
Liquor City Mafikeng • T 018·381·2326/7
Liquor City Rustenburg Square (Rustenburg) • T 014·594·2531
Liquor City Safari Tuine (Rustenburg) • T 014·533·3467

Western Cape
Aroma Fine Wine Centres Constantia (Aroma Alphen Cellars): • T 021·794·8693 •
Canal Walk: T 021·551·7511 • Somerset West (Central): T 021·852·755 • Somerset
West (Waterstone Village): T 021·850·0603

Bergkelder Vinoteque Wine Bank (Stellenbosch) ▪ T 021·809·8283 ▪ F 021·883·9533

Caroline's Fine Wine Cellar ▪ City Bowl: T 021·419·8984 ▪ F 021·419·8985 ▪ V&A Waterfront: T 021·425·5701 ▪ F 021·425·5702

Cellar in the City @ Cape Town Tourism (Cape Town) ▪ T 021·426·2295 ▪ Kalk Bay: T 021·788·9116 M 072·431·4100

Chapmans Peak Wine & Spirits (Hout Bay) ▪ T 021·790·1088 ▪ F 021·790·1089

Darling Wine & Art Shop (Darling) ▪ T 022·492·3740 ▪ F 022·492·3524

De Oude Paarl Wijn Boutique (Paarl) ▪ T 021·872·1002 ▪ F 021·872·1003

De Wijngarten Boetiek (Bonnievale) ▪ T 023·616·2367 ▪ F 023·616·3160

Donvino, The Wine Merchant (Bellville) ▪ T 021·914·6952 ▪ F 086·684·7107

Gehot Bosch Wine Boutique & Winery See A–Z section for details

Grand World of Wines (Cape Town) ▪ T 021·412·9302 ▪ F 021·412·9305

Harbour Road Wines (Kleinmond) ▪ T 028·271·5151 ▪ F 086·620·5251

I Love Wine (Paarl) ▪ See A–Z section for details

La Cotte Inn Wine Sales (Franschhoek) ▪ T 021·876·3775 ▪ F 021·876·3036

Liquor World Cape Town (Milnerton) ▪ T 021·551·9080 ▪ F 021·555·0223

Liquor World Cape Gate (Brackenfell) ▪ T 021·908·8000 ▪ F 021·981·0098

Liquor World George ▪ T 044·874·1370 ▪ F 044·874·1377

Main Ingredient (Cape Town) ▪ T 021·439 5169 ▪ F 021·439·5169

Makro Milnerton ▪ T 021·550·6348 ▪ F 021·550·6362

Makro Ottery ▪ T 021·703·6852 ▪ F 021·703·2508

Manuka Wine Boutique (Noordhoek) ▪ T 021·789·0898 ▪ F 086·684·2635

Manuka Wine Boutique (Somerset West) ▪ T 021·851·6060 ▪ F 021·851·9145

Manuka Wine Boutique (Stellenbosch) ▪ T 083·657·6958

Manuka Wines Boutique (Tokai) ▪ T 021·701·2046 ▪ F 021·701·0386

Manuka Wine Boutique (Tygervalley) ▪ T 021·914·7242 ▪ F 021·914·9561

Mooiberge (Stellenbosch) ▪ T/F 021·881·3222

Picardi Rebel Fine Wines & Liquors Cape Town ▪ T 021·425·1639/425·1664 ▪ F 021·421·5841

Picardi Rebel Fine Wines & Liquors Claremont (Main Rd) ▪ T 021·671·9918/671·9611 ▪ F 021·683·9025

Picardi Rebel Fine Wines & Liquors Durbanville ▪ T 021·976·5318 ▪ F 021·976·5341

Picardi Rebel Fine Wines & Liquors Longbeach Mall (Noordhoek) ▪ T 021·785·3323 ▪ F 021·785·3318

Picardi Rebel Fine Wines & Liquors Parklands ▪ T 021·556·2675 ▪ F 021·556·2680

Picardi Rebel Fine Wines & Liquors Rosmead (Claremont) ▪ T 021·683·1406 ▪ F 021·674·2094

Picardi Rebel Fine Wines & Liquors Somerset West ▪ T 021·852·2580 ▪ F 021·852·3519

Picardi Rebel Fine Wines & Liquors Sun Valley ▪ T 021·785·2149 ▪ F 021·785·2942

Picardi Rebel Fine Wines & Liquors Tokai ▪ T 021·712·5082/712·5032 ▪ F 021·712·2536

Picardi Rebel Fine Wines & Liquors Tygervalley ▪ T 021·914·1649/914·1650 ▪ F 021·914·2420

Riedel@Aroma (Constantia) ▪ T 021·794·8693 ▪ F 021·794·8694

Rubin's Liquors (Cape Town) ▪ T 021·425·4692 ▪ F 021·419·9405

Spier Wine Centre (Stellenbosch) ▪ T 021·809·1143 ▪ F 021·809·1144

Stellenbosch Wine Export Centre ▪ T/F 021·883·3814

Steven Rom Wine Merchants & Exporters ▪ Cape Town: Sea Point T 021·439·6043 ▪ F 021·434·0401 ▪ Three Anchor Bay T 021·434·0001 ▪ Kloof Street T 021·424·8476 ▪ Stellenbosch (The Cape Grape & Wine Co): T 0860·10·30·34 / 021·905·0290 ▪ F 021·905·0293

The Cape Grape & Wine Company See Steven Rom Wine Merchants & Exporters

The Vineyard Connection (Muldersvlei) ▪ T 021·884·4360 ▪ F 021·884·4361
The Wine Shop at Constantia Uitsig (Constantia) ▪ T 021·794·1810 ▪ F 021·794·1812
Ultra Liquors Goodwood ▪ T 021·591·5581 ▪ F 021·591·8492
Ultra Liquors Greenpoint ▪ T 021·434·4847/4302/4838 ▪ F 021·434·7548
Ultra Liquors Parow ▪ T 021·930·2415/6 ▪ F 021·930·4007
Ultra Liquors Wynberg ▪ T 021·762·5885/1473 ▪ F 021·761·6005
Vaughan Johnson's Wine & Cigar Shop See A-Z section for details
Vino Pronto (Cape Town) ▪ T 021·424·5587 ▪ F 021·423·5707
Wine Cellar (incl insulated/secure maturation cellars; Cape Town) ▪ T 021·448·4105
Wine & Company (Hermanus) ▪ T 028·313·2047 ▪ F 028·312·4029
Wine Concepts ▪ Newlands: T 021·671·9030 ▪ F 021·671·9031 Gardens:
T 021·426·4401 ▪ F 021·426·4402
Wines@Oude Libertas (Stellenbosch) ▪ T 021·886·7404 ▪ F 021·886·7405
Wine Village Hermanus ▪ T 028·316·3988 ▪ F 028·316·3989

Online Wine Shops
Cybercellar.com ▪ www.cybercellar.com
eWine ▪ www.ewine.co.za
Getwine ▪ www.getwine.co.za
I Love Wine ▪ www.ilovewine.co.za
Manuka Wine Exports ▪ www.manuka.co.za
Michelangelo International Wine Awards Wine Shop ▪ www.michelangeloawards.
com
SA Wines ▪ www.sawines.com
WineClub ▪ www.wineclub.co.za
Wine Direct ▪ www.winedirectonline.co.za
WINEmag.co.za Online Auctions ▪ www.winemag.co.za/auction
Wineseller-Fine Wine On-Line ▪ www.wineseller.co.za
Wine Village Hermanus ▪ www.wine-village.co.za
Wine Web ▪ www.wineweb.co.za
Wine with Personality ▪ www.winewithpersonality.co.za

■ A-Code Numbers & Certification Codes

Many wines appear on the market under brand names, with, at first glance, no reference to their producers or purveyors. However, consumers need not buy 'blind', and may trace a wine's provenance by checking the official 'A-number' which appears on the bottle or pack. This identity code tells you either who has produced the wine, or who has acquired it. In the latter case, an enquiry to the purveyor should elicit the source. The list keeps growing and being revised, and is too lengthy to reproduce in this guide. It is administered by Marian Honing, Department of Agriculture, Directorate Plant Health & Quality, Pvt Bag   X5015, Stellenbosch, 7599; marianh@nda.agric.za; T 021·809·1687; F 021·887·6396/2. Via the online SAWIS portal (**www.sawis.co.za**), it is possible to search the list of A-codes, as well as the certification codes issued for each wine by the Wine & Spirit Board, for details about the production area, variety and vintage. Navigate to Statistics, Searches, and see under Wine Seal and Label 'A' Number.

Vintages & Styles

■ Recent Cape vintages

SA wines do not exhibit the major vintage variations seen in cooler northern climes. There are, nevertheless, perceptible differences from year to year. Dry, hot summers are the norm but a variety of factors make generalisations difficult and dangerous.

2006 Excellent and largely problem free (though complicated by Western Cape power cuts). Perhaps the best white-wine vintage in a decade - particularly expressive sauvignons and chenins. Fleshy, mild-tannined reds, with lower alcohols all round.

2005 Short, early and particularly challenging. Bone-dry winter followed by early-season rains, sparking disease and excessive plant vigour; then prolonged heatwaves. Concentrated if alcoholic reds; whites mostly average, some stellar exceptions.

2004 Long and late, bedevilled by uneven berry-set and an early aroma-stripping heatwave. Yet cooler dry conditions yielded healthy, elegant, often ageworthy wines with lower alcs and yielding tannins. Chardonnay, merlot and shiraz especially promising.

2003 Outstanding, especially for reds - concentrated and structured, and, on current evidence, slow to show their best. General euphoria tempered by some difficulties with late-ripening varieties in certain areas.

2002 Challenging and patchy, marred by disease and high harvest temperatures. Generally, individual producers' track record rather than variety or terroir should guide the purchase/cellaring decision.

2001 Hot, dry, largely disease-free vintage; some excellent reds - fruity and concentrated, possibly long-lived. White-wine producers who picked between heatwaves delivered flavourful if alcoholic wines.

2000 Another hot year with predictably powerful, concentrated reds, sometimes with big tannins. The best should keep very well. Whites, by contrast, generally less stellar and not for long ageing.

1999 Near-perfect ripening conditions meant fat, alcoholic reds with ripe fruit for earlier drinking. Some attractive, fruity chardonnay, semillon and chenin, but generally not too much excitement.

1998 Excellent vintage. Deep, lusty (sometimes tannic) reds with enough fruit for extended cellaring. Whites somewhat less sexy; some good fuller-bodied versions but even these not for keeping.

■ Older vintages

1997 Among coolest, latest on record. Supple, elegant reds; some excellent, stylish whites. **1996** Generally awkward reds, not for keeping; whites, except for top NLHs, best drunk up. **1995** For many, vintage of the 90s. Ripe, fruity, concentrated reds, maturing spectacularly. **1994** Hottest, driest vintage in decades; variable quality; new-clone cabs, early ripening reds fared well. **1993** Without serious mishaps; some excellent sauvignons; above-average reds. **1992** Coolish, favouring whites, especially sauvignon; reds (especially pinotage) very good to outstanding; **1991** Dry, warm to hot, favouring early to mid-season ripeners; some concentrated, long-lasting reds. **1990** Uneven year, alternately cool, warm; average whites; middling reds with some very characterful examples. The **1980s**: even years (82, 84, 86) usually more favourable for reds; uneven years, marginally cooler, favoured whites, but 'white' years 87 and, especially, 89 produced remarkable reds. The **1970s**: again, even years generally favoured reds. The best of the 70s was undoubtedly 74; but top wines from some other vintages are still delicious. The **1960s** and earlier yielded some astonishingly long-lived wines, prompting a new generation to look at the traditional 'dikvoet' winemaking style with fresh eyes.

■ SA wine styles

Blanc de blancs White wine made from white grapes only; also used for champagne and méthode cap classique.

Blanc fumé or **fumé blanc** Dry white from sauvignon, not necessarily finished in wood (nor smoked, smoky).

Blanc de noir A pink wine (shades range from off-white through peach to pink) made from red grapes. May be labelled 'vin gris'.

Blend See Varietal wine and Cape blend

Brut See sugar or sweetness, sparkling wine.

Cap classique See Méthode cap classique.

Cape blend Evolving term, increasingly used to denote a (red) blend with pinotage, the 'local' grape making up 30%-70% of the assemblage; sometimes simply a blend showing a distinct 'Cape' character.

Carbonated See Sparkling wine.

Cultivar Grape variety (a contraction of 'cultivated variety').

Cuvée French term for the blend of a wine.

Demi-sec See Sugar or sweetness.

Dessert wine A sweet wine, often to accompany the dessert but sometimes pleasurably prior, as in the famous Sauternes/foie gras combo.

Dry to sweet See sugar or sweetness.

Estate wine Term now reserved for wine originating from an officially registered 'unit for the production of estate wine' (see under Industry Organisations for complete list). Fruit and, with some historical exceptions, vinification, maturation and bottling must from/on the 'estate' in question.

Fortified wines Increased in alcoholic strength by the addition of spirit, by SA law to minimum 15% alcohol by volume.

Grand cru See Premier Grand Cru

Jerepiko or **jerepigo** Red or white wine, produced without fermentation; grape juice is fortified with grape spirit, preventing fermentation; very sweet with considerable unfermented grape flavours.

Kosher See Winemaking terms section

Late Harvest Sweet wine from late -harvested and therefore sweeter grapes. See Sugar or sweetness.

Méthode cap classique (MCC) See Sparkling wine.

Noble Late Harvest (NLH) Sweet dessert wine (still, perlé or sparkling) exhibiting a noble rot (botrytis) character, from grapes infected by the *botrytis cinerea* fungus. This mould, in warm, misty autumn weather, attacks the skins of ripe grapes, causing much of the juice to evaporate. As the berries wither, their sweetness and flavour become powerfully concentrated. SA law dictates that grapes for NLH must be harvested at a minimum of 28° Balling and residual sugar must exceed 50g/ℓ.

Nouveau Term originated in Beaujolais for fruity young and light red, usually from gamay and made by the carbonic maceration method. Bottled a few weeks after vintage to capture the youthful, fresh flavour of fruit and yeasty fermentation.

Perlant, perlé, pétillant Lightly sparkling, carbonated wine.

Port Fortified dessert with improving quality record in Cape since late 1980s, partly through efforts of SA Port Producers' Association which recommends use of word 'Cape' to identify the local product. Following are SAPPA-defined styles: **Cape White**: non-muscat grapes, wood-aged min 6 mths, any size vessel; **Cape Ruby**: blended, fruity, components aged min 6 mths, up to 3 years depending on size of vessel. Average age min 1 year. **Cape Vintage**: fruit of one harvest; dark, full-bodied, vat-aged (any size); **Cape Vintage Reserve**: fruit of one harvest in year of 'recognised quality'. Preferably aged min 1 year, vats of any size, sold only in glass; **Cape Late Bottled Vintage** (LBV): fruit of single 'year of quality', full-bodied, slightly tawny colour, aged 3-6 years (of which min 2 years in oak); **Cape Tawny**: wood-matured, amber-orange (tawny) colour, smooth, slightly nutty taste (white grapes not permitted); **Cape Dated Tawny**: single-vintage tawny.

Premier Grand Cru Unlike in France, not a quality rating in SA — usually an austerely dry white.

Residual sugar See Sugar or sweetness.

Rosé Pink wine, made from red or a blend of red and white grapes. The red grape skins are removed before the wine takes up too much colouring.

Single vineyard wine A new classification for wines from officially registered vineyards, no larger than 6ha in size and planted with a single variety.

Sparkling wine Bubbly, or 'champagne', usually white but sometimes rosé and even red, given its effervescence by carbon dioxide — allowed to escape in the normal winemaking process. **Champagne** undergoes its second fermentation in the bottle. Under an agreement with France, SA does not use the term which describes the sparkling wines from the Champagne area. Instead, **méthode cap classique** (MCC) is the SA term to describe sparkling wines made by the classic method. **Charmat** undergoes its second, bubble-forming fermentation in a tank and is bottled under pressure. **Carbonated** sparklers are made by the injection of carbon dioxide bubbles (as in fizzy soft drinks). See also Sugar or sweetness.

Special Late Harvest (SLH) SA designation for a lighter dessert style wine. There is no longer a legal stipulation for residual sugar content, but if the RS is below 20g/ℓ, the label must state 'extra dry', 'dry', 'semi-dry' or 'sweet', as the case may be. The minimum alcohol content has been raised from 10% to 11% by volume.

Stein Semi-sweet white wine, usually a blend and often confused with steen, a grape variety (chenin blanc), though most steins are made partly from steen grapes.

Sugar or sweetness In still wines: extra-dry or bone-dry wines have less than 2.5g/ℓ residual sugar, undetectable to the taster. A wine legally is dry up to 5g/ℓ. Taste buds will begin picking up a slight sweetness, or softness, in a wine — depending on its acidity — at about 6g/ℓ, when it is still off-dry. By about 8–9g/ℓ a definite sweetness can usually be noticed. However, an acidity of 8–9g/ℓ can render a sweet wine fairly crisp even with a sugar content of 20g/ℓ plus. Official sweetness levels in SA wine are:

Still wines	Sugar (g/ℓ)	Sparkling wines	Sugar (g/ℓ)
Extra dry	≤ 2.5	Extra dry/brut	≤ 15
Dry	≤ 5	Dry/sec	15–35
Semi-dry	5 ≤ 12	Semi-sweet/demi-sec	35–50
Semi-sweet	< 5 < 30	Sweet/doux	50
Late Harvest	≥ 20		
Special Late Harvest (SLH)	—		
Natural Sweet (or Sweet Natural)	> 20		
Noble Late Harvest	> 50		
Naturally dried grape wine (straw wine)	> 30		

Varietal wine From single variety of grape. Recently amended legislation requires the presence in the wine of 85% of the stated variety or vintage (previously 75% if for local market, 85% if exported). Blends may name component parts only if those components were vinified separately, prior to blending; then they are listed with the larger contributor(s) named first. If any one of the blend partners is less than 20%, percentages for all the varieties must be given. Proposed amendments will allow the blending of wines vinified separately in any recognised WO area (previously WO 'districts' only). Component areas may be named, as above (except the threshold is 30%).

Vintage In SA primarily used to denote year of harvest. Not a substantive quality classification (a 'vintage' port in Europe means one from an officially declared great port grape year).

■ Wine & food partners

Here are some recommendations on matching cuisine and wine:

Artichokes Make most wines taste metallic. Drink water or squeeze lemon onto the chokes, which seems to tone down the tinny edges, and team with a high-acid, fresh dry white.

Asparagus A difficult customer. A dry white with lots of flavour like fresh sauvignon.

Avocado Riesling, white port.

Barbecue See Braai below.

Beef Roast: Cape Bdx blend, cab, cab franc, merlot, pinot; just about any serious red. Cold roast beef: room for a bit of light here, reds that can take a spot of chilling, pinot; also rosé, blanc de noir, sparkling dry rosé. See also Stews below.

Biltong (savoury air-dried meat snack, usually sliced) Not usually partnered with wine, but try robust shiraz (or beer).

Bobotie (spicy ground-meat, usually lamb) Many possible wine-partners: try dry sparkling, fresh young chenin, riesling, pinotage or other fruity, easy-drinking reds.

Bouillabaisse Fresh young white, sauvignon, dry rosé.

Braai (the traditional barbecue, a national institution) Depends on what's being braaied, but whether meat, fish or fowl, choose a wine with character and muscle, not a fragile little thing that would be overwhelmed by the smoke for a start.

Carpaccio Meat: Just about any red. Fish: chardonnay, MCC.

Charcuterie Simple fresh reds.

Cheese A good cheddar can be excellent with an elegant red or ruby port. Cream cheese is better with full-bodied whites – try semillon or chardonnay. Goat's cheese: full-bodied white or dry red. Blue cheese: as long as it's not too powerful, good with rich dessert whites such as NLH and port.

Chicken Roast: best red or white. Pie: try light to medium shiraz or young pinotage.

Chinese MCC, dry (or dryish) white with flavour; riesling.

Chocolate Difficult. Demi-sec bubbly, fruity dry red, red muscadel, Cape Pineau des Charentes. Or wait and have a glass of dry bubbly after the choc mousse.

Crudités Simple dry white.

Curry Fish curry: wooded chardonnay is good, especially when coconut milk is an ingredient. A cheerful, slightly off-dry (and slightly pétillant) chenin blend is fine too. Also blanc de noir. Sweetish Cape Malay curries: try matching the spice with gewürz or young riesling, or contrasting with sauvignon.

Desserts See Chocolate above.

Duck Fruity young red, champagne, shiraz, off-dry riesling, pinot.

Eggs Not great for or with any wine, but a simple omelette calls for a simple glass of red.

Foie gras Sweet white, NLH/SLH, MCC, merlot.

Fruit MCC, sweet sparkling wine, Late or Special Late Harvest, hanepoot jerepiko or rosé. Strawberries: with cream: NLH; without cream: light red.

Game birds Rosé, pinot or Cape Bdx blend. Remember, the darker the meat, the darker/stronger the wine. Guinea fowl: pinot, merlot or powerful oaked chenin.

Ham Young pinot; fresh, juicy red.

Hamburgers Dry, simple red.

Ice-cream (If not too sweet) Good bubbly.

Kidneys Full red, riesling, chardonnay.

Lamb and **mutton** Roast: best red (cabernet, merlot etc). Chops: shiraz or young cab. Try to avoid mint sauce – it distorts the taste of even minty, new-clone contenders. Stews: light red.

Liver Fruity, forceful young red such as pinotage.

Mushrooms Pinot or just about any well-aged red.

Mustard sauce Light red, pinotage.

Nuts Port after a meal; sherry before; nutty desserts: MCC.

Oxtail Shiraz, zinfandel.

Pasta Seafood: sauvignon, un/lightly-wooded chardonnay; cream, cheese, egg, meat, tomato sauces: sturdy red.

Pastries and **cakes** SLH.

Pâté Champagne, gewürz, riesling, pinot.

Phutu or mealie meal (SA equivalent of **polenta**) Sturdy red.

Pizza Depends on ingredients, but also see pasta above.

Pork Off-dry white, fruity red, rosé, zinfandel. Pinotage with spare ribs. In Portugal, roast sucking pig is often teamed with bubbly.

Quiche Full fruity white, riesling, gewürz, sylvaner.

Rabbit Depends on how it's cooked, and the ingredients. Anything from great to simple, red or white.

Ratatouille Light, fruity red, rosé, blanc de noir.

Risotto Fish: medium-bodied dry white; mushrooms: pinot.

Salads Go easy on the vinaigrette — vinegar affects wine. A prickly fresh white or rosé with a salade niçoise. Chardonnay with a grand shellfish salad. Or something non-serious like a blanc de noir. Or top up one's water table.

Seafood

- **Fish** Dry sparkling, MCC or dry white (sauvignon or chardonnay, or a chardonnay blend) are safe choices for saltwater; more delicate white or MCC for freshwater. Grilled: sauvignon; cream sauce: chardonnay, chardonnay blend. With red-wine sauce: red used in recipe or pinot. Smoked: crisp aromatic white, sauvignon, full-bodied (wooded) chardonnay, gewürz or riesling, dry or with a touch of sugar. Sushi: a not-too-grand (or too rich) chardonnay, brut sparkling.
- **Shellfish** Grilled, boiled, steamed or cold (with mayonnaise): sauvignon, crisp young chenin or off-dry riesling. Rich sauce: MCC or chardonnay-semillon blend. Piri-piri: this spicy/hot sauce calls for a light pétillant white.
- **Calamari** (squid) Sauvignon, dry white blend or light red.
- **Cape salmon** (geelbek) Racy sauvignon.
- **Caviar** MCC.
- **Crab** Riesling or off-dry chenin.
- **Crayfish** (Cape rock lobster or *kreef*) Sauvignon or chardonnay.
- **Elf** (shad) Chardonnay, dry chenin or Cape riesling.
- **Galjoen** Sauvignon, chardonnay or full-flavoured blanc de noir.
- **Kingklip** Chardonnay or wood-matured white.
- **Langoustine** (deep-sea, from SA's East Coast) MCC, chardonnay.
- **Mussels** Sauvignon or chenin. Smoked: wooded chardonnay
- **Oysters** MCC, sauvignon, lightly wooded or unwooded chardonnay.
- **Perlemoen** (abalone) Chardonnay or sauvignon.
- **Prawns** Chardonnay or sauvignon.
- **Salmon** Chardonnay or fruity non-tannic young red.
- **Sardines** (grilled) Crisp pétillant white, young red.
- **Smoorvis** (braised fish, usually lightly spicy) Frisky (off-dry) chenin, chardonnay or young pinotage.
- **Snoek** Assertive dry white, young red or pinotage.
- **Sole** Grilled: sauvignon or Cape riesling. Sauced: chardonnay.
- **Trout** Young riesling

Snacks Of the canapé sort: aperitif white, fruity, dry to off-dry, kir, sparkling white/rosé, blanc de noir, dry sherry.

Snails Chardonnay, pinot, dry riesling.

Sosaties Local version of the south-east Asian satay; as for curry.

Soufflés Cheese: red; fish: white; dessert: dessert white.

Steak Red wine: cab, merlot, shiraz — take your pick. Pepper steak: somehow smoothes tannins, so doesn't need a mellow old bottle.

Stews and **bredies** Hearty red. Fish casserole: fresh young white, sauvignon or dry rosé. Waterblommetjie bredie: sauvignon, chardonnay, young pinotage or merlot.

Sweetbreads Chardonnay, fine claret, pinot.

Thai Draughts of cool fresh dry white for the chilli-hot dishes. Lemongrass, coconut milk and good (wooded) chardonnay go surprisingly well together. A chilled nouveau style could hold its own. Or riesling.

Tongue Gently dry white, fruity red.

Tripe Hearty red, simple dry white or dry rosé. With tomato: dry red. With onions or white sauce: off-dry chenin or chenin-blend.

Turkey Zinfandel, dry rosé, pinot.

Veal Take your pick, depending on preparation. With vitello tonnato try a chilled, light red.

Vegetables Sauvignon, probably.

Venison Powerful pinot, pinotage, shiraz or mature Cape bdx-style blend.

Frequently Used Words & Phrases

■ Winetasting terms

Short of a ready description? Here are a few frequently-used words, phrases and explanations that may be helpful. See also Winemaking terms; SA wine styles.

Accessible, approachable Flavours and feel of the wine are harmonious, easily recognised; it is ready to drink.

Aftertaste The lingering flavours and impressions of a wine; its persistence — the longer, the better.

Alcoholic 'Hot' or, in excess, burning character caused by imbalanced or excessive alcohol. Also simply spiritous.

Astringent Mouth-puckering sensation in the mouth, associated with high tannin (and sometimes acid); also bitter, sharp.

Aroma Smells in the bouquet, or nose, especially the odours associated with the grape rather than the winemaking process.

Attack First sensations on palate/nose — pungent, aggressive, quiet etc.

Austere Usually meaning unyielding, sometimes harsh. Sometimes, more favourably, to imply a notable restraint/refinement.

Backbone The wine is well formed, firm, not flabby or insipid.

Baked 'Hot', earthy quality. Usually from scorched/shrivelled grapes which have been exposed too long to the sun, or from too warm a barrel fermentation, especially in some whites.

Balance Desirable attribute. The wine's chief constituents — alcohol, acid, tannin, fruit and wood (where used) — are in harmony.

Bead Bubbles in sparkling wine; a fine, long-lasting bead is the most desirable. See also Mousse.

Big Expansive in the mouth, weighty, full-bodied, as a result of high alcohol or fruit concentration.

Bite or **grip** Imparted by tannins and acids (and alcohol in fortified wines); important in young wines designed for ageing. If overdone can impart undesirable bitterness, harshness or spirity 'glow'.

Bitter Sensation perceived mainly on the back of the tongue, and in the finish of the wine. Usually unpleasant, though an accepted if not immediately admired character of certain Italian wines. Sometimes more positively associated with the taste of a specific fruit or nut, such as cherry-kernel or almond.

Body Fullness on the palate.

Botrytis/ed Exhibits a noble rot/botrytis character, from grapes infected by the *botrytis cinerea* fungus.

Bottle age Negative or positive, depending on context. Positively describes development of aromas/flavours (ie complexity) as wine moves from youth to maturity. Much-prized attribute in fine whites and reds. Negatively, bottle age results in a wine with stale, empty or even off odours.

Buttery Flavour and texture associated with barrel-fermented white wines, especially chardonnays; rich, creamy smoothness.

Charming Usually used in the context of lighter, simpler wines. Sometimes synonymous with 'sweet' (both as in 'sugary' and 'dear').

Claret Another name for a dry red bordeaux or bordeaux-like red

Classic Showing characteristics of the classics of Bordeaux, Burgundy etc; usually implying balance, elegance, subtlety.

Coarse Rough, unbalanced tannins, acid, alcohol or oak.

Complexity Strong recommendation. A complex wine has several layers of flavour, usually developing with age/maturation. See Bottle age.

Concentration See Intensity.

Confected Over-elaborately constructed, artificial, forced; also overly sweet.

Corked Wine is faulty; its flavours have been tainted by yeast, fungal or bacterial infections, often but not necessarily from the cork. It smells damp and mouldy in its worst stages – but sometimes it's barely detectable. In a restaurant, a corked wine should be rejected and returned immediately; producers are honour-bound to replace corked wine.

Creamy Not literally creamy, of course; more a silky, buttery feel and texture.

Crisp Refers to acidity. Positively, means fresh, clean; negatively, too tart, sharp.

Deep and depth Having many layers; intense; also descriptive of a serious wine.

Dense Well-padded texture, flavour-packed.

Deposits (also sediment or crust) Tasteless and harmless tartrates, acid crystals or tannin in older red wines. Evidence that wine has not been harshly fined, filtered or cold-stabilised.

Dried out Bereft of fruit, harder constituents remaining; tired.

Earthy Usually positive, wine showing its origins from soil, minerally, damp leaves, mushrooms etc.

Easy Undemanding (and hopefully inexpensive).

Elegant Stylish, refined, 'classic'.

Esters Scents and smells usually generated by alcohols and acids in wine. A wine may be 'estery' when these characteristics are prominent.

Extract An indication of the 'substance' of a wine, expressed as sugar-free or total extract (which would include some sugars). 18g/ℓ would be low, light; anything much above 23g/ℓ in whites is significant; the corresponding threshold for reds is around 30g/ℓ.

Fat Big, full, ample in the mouth.

Finesse Graceful, polished. Nothing excessive.

Finish The residual sensations – tastes and textures – after swallowing. Should be pleasant (crisp, lively) and enduring, not short, dull or flat. See also Length.

Firm Compact, has good backbone.

Flabby Usually, lacking backbone, especially acid.

Flat Characterless, unexciting, lacks acid. Or bubbly which has lost its fizz.

Fleshy Very positive, meaning a wine is well fleshed out with texture and grape flavours.

Flowery Floral, flower-like (i.e. the smell of rose, honeysuckle, jasmine etc). Distinct from 'fruity' (ie smell/taste of papaya, cantaloupe, grape! etc)

Forward rather than shy; advancing in age too; mature.

Fresh Lively, youthful, invigorating. Closely related to the amount of acid in the wine and absence of oxidative character: a big, intensely sweet dessert without a backbone of acidity will taste flat and sickly; enough acid and the taste is fresh and uncloying.

Fruity See Flowery.

Full High in alcohol and extract.

Gamey Overripe, decadent; not universally unattractive.

Gravel/ly With suggestions of minerally, earthy quality; also firm texture.

Green Usually unripe, sour; sometimes simply youthful.

Grip Often almost literally gripping, firm on palate, in finish. Acid, tannin, alcohol are contributors.

Heady Usually refers to the smell of a wine. High in alcohol; intense, high-toned.

Herbaceous Grassy, hay-like, heathery; can also indicate under-ripeness.

Hollow Lacking substance, flavours.

Honey or **honeyed** Sometimes literally a honey/beeswax taste or flavour; a sign of developing maturity in some varieties or more generally a sign of bottle age.

Hot Burning sensation of alcohol in finish.

Intensity No flab, plenty of driving flavour; also deep colour.

Lean Thin, mean, lacking charm of ample fruit; also, more positively, compact, sinewy.

Lees/leesy Taste-imparting dead yeast cells (with grape skins and other solid matter) remaining with wine in tank/barrel (or bottle in the case of *méthode champenoise* sparkling wines) after fermentation. The longer the wine is 'on its lees' (sur lie) the more richness and flavour it should absorb.

Light/lite Officially wines under 10% alcohol by volume, also light in body (and often short on taste); a health-conscious trend in both reds and whites.

Lively Bouncy, fresh flavours.

Long or **length** Enduring; wine's flavours reverberate in the palate long after swallowing.

Maderised Oxidised and flat; colour is often brownish. Over-mature.

Meaty Sometimes suggesting a general savouriness; but also literally the aroma of meat – raw, smoked etc.

Mousse Fizz in sparkling wines; usually refers also to quality, size and effervescence of the bubbles. See also Bead.

Mouthfeel, mouthfilling Texture, feel; racy, crispness (fine with appropriate dishes) or generous, supple, smooth.

Neutral What it says, neither here nor there.

New World Generally implies accessible, bold, often extrovert (in terms of fruit and use of oak). **Old World** embraces terms like subtle, complex, less oaky, more varied and generally more vinous (than fruity). See also Classic.

Oaky Having exaggerated oak aromas/flavours (vanilla, spice, char, woodsmoke etc). Oak balanced by fruit in young wines may lessen with age, but over-oaked young wines (where fruit is not in balance) will become over-oaked old wines.

Palate Combination of flavour, taste and texture of a wine.

Pebbly See Gravelly.

Perfumed or **scented** Strong fragrances (fruity, flowery, animal etc)

Plump Well fleshed in a charming, cherubic way.

Porty Heavy, over-ripe, stewed; a negative in unfortified wine.

Rich Flavourful, intense, generous. Not necessarily sweet.

Robust Strapping, full-bodied (but not aggressive).

Rough Bull-in-a-china-shop wine, or throat sand-papering quality.

Round Well balanced, without gawkiness or jagged edges.

Sharp or **tart** All about acid, usually unbalanced. But occasionally sharpish, fresh wine is right for the occasion.

Short or **quick** Insubstantial wine, leaving little impression.

Simple One-dimensional or no flavour excitement.

Stalky Unripe, bitter, stemmy.

Stewed Over-ripe, cooked, soft, soggy fruit.

Structure Vague word, usually refers to the wine's make up (acid, tannin, alcohol) in relation to its ageing ability; if a wine is deemed to have 'the structure to age' it suggests these principal preservatives are in place.

Stylish Classy, distinguished; also voguish.

Supple Very desirable (not necessarily subtle), yielding, refined texture and flavours. See also Mouthfeel.

Tannic Tannins are prominent in the wine, imparting, positively, a mouth-puckering, grippy, tangy quality; negatively, a harsh, unyielding character.

Tension Racy, nervous fruity-acid play on the palate.

Terpene(s)/terpenoid Strong, floral compounds influencing the aromas of especially riesling, gewürztraminer and the muscats; with bottle-age, terpenes often develop a pungent resinous oiliness.

Texture Tactile 'feel' in the mouth: hard, acidic, coarse and alcoholic; or, smooth, velvety, 'warm'.

Toasty Often used for barrel-fermented and aged wines showing a pleasant biscuity, charry character.

Vegetal Grassy, leafy, herby – in contrast to fruity, flowery, oaky. Overdone, a no-no.

Yeasty Warm bakery smells, often evident in barrel-fermented whites and *méthode champenoise* sparkling wines, where yeasts stay in contact with the wine after fermentation.

■ Winemaking terms

A few brief reference explanations. See also sections Winetasting terms, SA wine styles.

Acid and **acidity** The fresh – or, in excess, sharp or tart – taste of wine. Too little acid and the wine tastes dull and flat. In SA, winemakers are permitted to adjust acidity either by adding acid – at any stage before bottling – or by lowering the acid level with a de-acidifier. See also Volatile acid and Malolactic.

Alcohol Essential component of wine, providing fullness, richness and, at higher levels, sometimes an impression of sweetness. Also a preservative, helping keep wines in good condition. Produced by yeasts fermenting the sugars in the grape. Measured by volume of the total liquid. Most unfortified table wines in SA have between 11% and 14.5% alc by vol; fortifieds range from ±16% to 21%. A variation of up to 1% between the strength stated on the label and the laboratory analysis is permitted by local law. Various techniques (such as reverse osmosis and 'spinning cone', also the addition of water) exist to address the increasingly important issue of high alcohol levels in wine, and some have recently been legalised in SA (though not for export to, eg, Europe).

Barrels (**barrel-aged**; **barrel-fermented**) Wines are transferred into barrels to age, pick up oaky flavours etc. When must or fermenting must is put into barrels, the resulting wine is called barrel-fermented. A barrel or cask is generally a 225-500ℓ oak container; *barrique* is a French word for a 225ℓ barrel; a pipe, adapted from the Portuguese *pipa*, usually indicates a vessel of 530-630ℓ; vat is a term generally used for larger (2 000-5 000ℓ) wooden vessels.

Batonnage See Lees.

Biodynamic See Organic.

Blend A wine made from two or more different grape varieties, vintages, vineyards or containers. Some of the world's finest wines are blends.

Bottles While the 750ml (75cl) bottle is now the most widely used size of container for wine, it is by no means the only one. Smaller bottles (375 & 500ml) are popular with restaurants and airlines, and larger sizes are prized by collectors because of their novelty value and/or their tendency to promote slower wine ageing. The following are the larger bottle sizes (note: some no longer in production):

Capacity		Bordeaux	Champagne/Burgundy
litres	*bottles*		
1.5	2	magnum	magnum
3	4	double magnum	Jéroboam
4.5	6	Jéroboam	Rehoboam
6	8	Impériale	Methuselah
9	12	–	Salmanazar
12	16	–	Balthazar
15	20	–	Nebuchadnezzar

Brettanomyces or **'brett'** Currently much-focused-on naturally occurring yeast, usually associated with red wine and regarded as a spoilage factor, because its growth triggers the formation of volatile acids, phenols and other compounds which, in sufficient concentration, impart a range of unpleasant characters, from barnyard to sweat to cheese.

Carbonic maceration or **maceration carbonique** Method of fermenting wine without first crushing the grapes. Whole clusters with stalks etc are put into closed vat; intracellular fermentation occurs within the grape berries, which then burst.

Chaptalisation Originally French term for the addition of sugar to grape must to raise the alcohol of a wine. Selectively legal in northern Europe, where acid adjustments are not allowed as they are in SA. Winemakers in both hemispheres bend the rules.

Charmat Method of making sparkling wine in a sealed tank (*cuvée close*) under pressure. Easier, cheaper than méthode champenoise.

Chips See Oak chips

Cold ferment 'Cold' is a relative term; applied to fermentation of mainly white wines in temperature-controlled tanks, it refers to a temperature around usually 13-16°C. The benefits, especially important in a warm country, include conserving the primary fruit aromas and ensuring fermentation is carried out steadily and thoroughly.

Cold soak or **cold maceration**. Red winemaking method carried out prior to fermentation. Skins and juice are held, usually for a few days, at a sufficiently cool temperature to prevent fermentation. The theory is that this extracts more favourable colour and aromas than after fermentation.

Cold stabilisation Keeping a wine at about -4°C for a week or more to precipitate tartaric acid and 'clean up' the wine, preventing later formation of (harmless) tartrate crystals in bottle. Some winemakers believe this process damages flavour and prefer to avoid it.

Disgorgement (*dégorgement* in French) Important stage in the production of traditionally fermented sparkling where accumulated sediment (or lees), which could cloud the finished wine, is removed from the neck of the bottle.

Dosage The sugar added to sparkling wine after the second fermentation.

Fermentation The conversion of sugar in grapes into alcohol and carbon dioxide, a function of enzymes secreted by yeasts. Wild yeasts occur in vineyards and wineries, but in modern Cape winemaking cultured yeasts are normally added to secure the process. Beyond about 15% of alcohol, yeasts are overwhelmed and fermentation ceases, although it usually is stopped (for instance by cooling, filtration or the addition of alcohol) before this stage. See also Malolactic.

Filtration Removes last impurities including **yeast** cells. Done excessively, can thin a wine. Some traditionalists bottle without cold- or protein-stabilisation or filtration.

Fining and **protein stabilisation** Fining is ridding wine of suspended particles by adding substances that attract and draw the particles from the wine.

Flash-pasteurisation See Kosher

Free run After grapes have been de-stalked and crushed, juice runs freely.

Garage wine Generic term for wine made in minuscule quantities, sometimes literally in a garage; grower of such wine sometimes called a *garagiste*.

Glycerol Minor product of alcoholic fermentation; from the Greek for sweet. Has an apparent sweetening effect on even dry wines and also gives a viscous, mouthfilling character.

Icewine Sweet, concentrated wine from grapes picked and pressed while frozen. Not a recognised category for SA wine production.

Kosher Wine made 'correctly', i.e. under rabbinical supervision, to be suitable for use by religious Jews. Vinification and any initial movement of the wine must be done by an observant Jew. Flash-pasteurisation, increasingly by means of new flavour-preserving processes such as Thermoflash, renders the resulting *meshuval* (literally 'boiled' or 'cooked') wine fit for handling by non-Jews.

Leafroll virus Virus (or complex of viruses), widespread throughout the winegrowing world, which causes the vine to perform below its potential and thereby produce wine which is lower in colour, body and flavour than that derived from virus-free or 'cleaned-up' plants.

Lees Spent yeast cells and other matter which collect at the bottom of any container in winemaking. Yeast autolysis, or decomposition, can impart richness and flavour to a wine, sometimes referred to as leesy. Lees stirring or *batonnage* involves mixing the bed of lees in a barrel or tank through the wine, which is said to be sur lie; it is employed primarily on barrel-fermented white wines. The main effects of mixing lees and wine are to prevent off-odours developing from lack of oxygen, to limit the amount of wood tannin and flavour extracted, and to increase flavour.

Malolactic fermentation (malo) Occurs when bacteria convert malic into lactic acids. This reduces the acidity of a wine, a normal and healthy process, especially in reds — provided, of course, it occurs before bottling.

Maturation Ageing properties are closely related to tannin and/or fixed acid content of a wine. A relatively full red wine with tannin has lasting power. With age, it may develop complexity, subtlety and smooth mellowness. Lighter wines with lower tannins are drinkable sooner but probably will not reach the same level of complexity. A number of Cape whites, especially chardonnays and rieslings, now mature well over several years, but most are best drunk in their fruity youth, up to 18 months.

Méthode champenoise Classic method of making champagne by inducing secondary fermentation in the bottle and producing fine bubbles. Due to French restrictions on terminology, Cape sparkling wines made in this way are called méthode cap classique (MCC).

Micro-oxygenation Relatively new (1990) technique enabling introduction of precise, controlled doses of oxygen to must/wine. Advocates claim softer tannins, more stable colours and other advantages.

Oak chips, either in older barrels or stainless steel tanks, are used increasingly in SA, as are oak **staves**. Still frowned on by some purists, the 'additives' approximate the flavour effects of a new barrel, far more cheaply, more easily handled.

Oak-matured See Barrels.

Organic viticulture/winemaking Increasingly popular alternative to 'conventional' or 'industrialised' winegrowing, emphasising natural and sustainable farming methods and cellar techniques. A variant is biodynamic viticulture, influenced by anthroposophy, focused on improving wine quality through harmony with nature and its rhythms.

Oxidation Change (usually for the worse) due to exposure to air, in whites often producing dark yellow or yellowish colour (called maderisation), altering, 'ageing' the taste. Controlled aeration is used to introduce acceptable and desirable development in wine.

Pasteurisation See Kosher

pH A chemical notation, used in winemaking and evaluation. The pH of a wine is its effective, active acidity — not in volume but by strength or degree. The reading provides a guide to a wine's keepability. The optimum pH in a wine is somewhere between 3.1 and 3.4 — which significantly improves a wine's protection from bacterial spoilage, so permitting it to mature and develop if properly stored.

Racking Drawing or pumping wine off from one cask or tank to another, to leave behind the deposit or lees.

Reductive Wine in an unevolved, unoxidised state is said to be 'reductive'; usually with a tight, sometimes unyielding character. The absence of air (in a bottled wine) or the presence of substantial sulphur dioxide (anti-oxidant) levels, will inhibit both oxidation and reduction processes, which are linked and complementary.

Reverse osmosis A specialised filtration technique, now permitted in SA for various purposes, including the removal of water from wine. See also Alcohol

Skin contact After crushing and de-stemming, white grapes may be left for a period with the juice, remaining in contact with skins (before being moved into the press, from which the grape juice is squeezed). Some winemakers believe the colours and flavours in and under the grape skins should be maximised in this way; others believe extended (or any) contact can lead to coarseness, even bitterness.

Spinning cone See Alcohol.

Sulphur dioxide (SO$_2$) Sterilising agent and preservative, near-ubiquitous in winemaking since antiquity, now strictly controlled. In SA, max total SO$_2$ levels for dry wines is 150-160mg/ℓ; for wines with 5+ g/ℓ sugar it is 200mg/ℓ; and botrytis-style wines 300 mg/ℓ. Any wine with more than 10mg/ℓ total SO$_2$ must carry the warning 'Contains sulphites' (or 'sulfites') on the label.

Sur lie See Lees.

Tannin Vital preservative in wine, which derives primarily from the grape skins. Necessary for a red wine's longevity. A young wine's raw tannin can give it a harshness, but no red wine matures into a great one without tannin, which itself undergoes change, combines with other substances and mellows. Tannin leaves a mouth-puckering dryness about the gums, gives 'grip' to a wine. A wooded wine will also contain some wood tannin. Various types or qualities of tannin are increasingly commented on.

Tartrates Harmless crystals formed by tartaric acid precipitating in non-cold-stabilised wine. Because of lack of public acceptance, usually avoided through cold stabilisation.

Terroir Important, controversial (and in SA over-used) French term embracing soil, climate, topography and other elements which constitute the natural environment of a vineyard site and give it a unique character.

Thermovinification/Thermoflash See Kosher.

Unfiltered See Filtration.

Virus or **virused** See Leafroll.

Volatile acid (VA) The part of the acidity which can become volatile. A high reading indicates a wine is prone to spoilage. Recognised at high levels by a sharp, 'hot', vinegary smell. In SA, most wines must by law be below 1.2g/ℓ of VA; in practice, the majority are well below 1g/ℓ.

Whole-bunch pressing or **cluster pressing** Some SA cellars use this age-old process of placing whole bunches directly in the press and gently squeezing. The more usual method is to de-stem and crush the grapes before pressing. Whole-bunch pressing is said to yield fresher, cleaner must, and wine lower in polyphenols which, in excess, tend to age wines faster and render them coarser.

Wood-fermented/matured See Barrels.

Yeasts Micro-organisms that secrete enzymes which convert or ferment sugar into alcohol. See fermentation.

Touring Wine Country

■ Wine routes, trusts & associations

For localised information about regional official wine routes and wineries, contact these organisations:

Breedekloof Wine and Tourism ▪ T 023·349·1791 ▪ F 023·349·1720
info@breedekloof.com ▪ www.breedekloof.com

Calitzdorp Wine Route ▪ T 044·213·3775 ▪ F 044·213·3302
calitzdorpinfo@kannaland.co.za ▪ www.calitzdorp.co.za

Constantia Wine Route ▪ T 021·794·5190 (Lars Maack) ▪ F 021·794·1351
lars@buitenverwachting.co.za

The Darling Wine Route ▪ T 022·492·3430 (Shaun Mc Laughlin) ▪ F 022·492·2935
mclaughlin@worldonline.co.za ▪ www.darlingtourism.co.za

Durbanville Wine Valley Association ▪ T 083·310·1228 ▪ F 021·976·1467 ▪ info@durbanvillewine.co.za ▪ www.durbanvillewine.co.za

Elim Winegrowers ▪ T 028·482·1717 (Janine Steyn), ▪ F 028·482·1720 ▪ zoetendal@telkomsa.net

Franschhoek See Vignerons de Franschhoek

Green Mountain Eco Route (Elgin/Bot River) ▪ T 021·859·3596 ▪ F 021·859·7451 ▪ info@villaexner.com ▪ www.villaexner.com

Helderberg See Stellenbosch

Little/Klein Karoo Wine Route ▪ T/F 028·572·1284 (Ellen Marais)
info@kleinkaroowines.co.za ▪ www.kleinkaroowines.co.za

Northern Cape Wine Association ▪ T 054·337·8800 (Herman Cruywagen) ▪ F 054·332·4408
marketing@owk.co.za

Olifants River Vodacom Wine Route ▪ T/F 027·213·3126/082·611·3999
wineroute@matzikamamun.co.za ▪ www.olifantsriverwineroute.com

Orange River Wine Route See Northern Cape Wine Association

Outeniqua Wine Route ▪ T/F 044·873·4212/072·833·8223
harpie@xsinet.co.za

Paarl Vintners ▪ T 021·863·4886 ▪ F 021·863·4883
paarl@wine.co.za ▪ www.paarlwine.co.za

Rawsonville Wine Route See Breedekloof Wine & Tourism

Robertson Wine Valley ▪ T 023·626·3167/083·701·5404 ▪ F 023·626·1054
manager@robertsonwinevalley.com ▪ www.robertsonwinevalley.com

Stellenbosch American Express Wine Routes ▪ T 021·886·4310 ▪ F 021·886·4330
info@wineroute.co.za ▪ www.wineroute.co.za ▪ Helderberg office: T 021·852·6166 ▪ F 021·852·6168 ▪ hwr@mweb.co.za ▪ www.helderbergwineroute.co.za

Swartland Wine Route ▪ T 022·487·1133 ▪ F 022·487·2063
swartlandinfo@westc.co.za ▪ www.swartlandwineroute.co.za

Tulbagh Wine Route ▪ T/F 023·230·1348
info@tulbaghwineroute.com ▪ www.tulbaghwineroute.com

Vignerons de Franschhoek ▪ T 021·876·3062 ▪ F 021·876·2964
franschhoek@wine.co.za ▪ www.franschhoekwines.co.za

Walker Bay Wine Wander ▪ T 028·316·3988 ▪ F 028·316·3989
wine@hermanus.co.za

Wellington Wine Route ▪ T 021·873·4604 ▪ F 021·873·4607
welltour@mweb.co.za ▪ www.wellington.co.za

Worcester Winelands ▪ T 023·342·8710/20 ▪ F 023·342·2294
manager@worcesterwinelands.co.za ▪ www.worcesterwinelands.co.za

■ Winelands tourism offices

For additional accommodation options, brochures and local advice, contact the information offices and/or publicity associations of the wine areas you plan to visit.

Franschhoek Wine Valley Tourist Association ▪ T 021·876·3603 ▪ F 021·876·2768
info@franschhoek.org.za ▪ www.franschhoek.org.za

Helderberg Tourism ▪ T 021·851·4022 ▪ F 021·851·1497
info@helderbergtourism.co.za www.helderbergtourism.co.za

Hermanus Tourism Bureau ▪ T 028·312·2629 ▪ F 028·313·0305
infoburo@hermanus.co.za ▪ www.hermanus.co.za www.tourismhermanus.co.za

McGregor Tourism ▪ T 023·625·1954 ▪ F 086·612·9636
info@tourismmcgregor.co.za ▪ www.tourismmcgregor.co.za

Northern Cape Tourism ▪ T 053·832·2657 ▪ F 053·831·2937
tourism@northerncape.org.za ▪ www.northerncape.org.za

Paarl Tourism Association ▪ T 021·863·4937 ▪ F 021·863·4883
info@paarlonline.com ▪ www.paarlonline.com

Robertson Tourism Association ▪ T 023·626·4437 ▪ F 023·626·4290
info@robertson.org.za ▪ www.robertsonr62.com

Route 62 ▪ T 023·616·3563 ▪ F 023·616·3422 ▪ info@route62.co.za ▪ www.route62.co.za

Stellenbosch Tourism Info Bureau ▪ I 021·883·3584 ▪ F 021·883·8017
info@stellenboschtourism.co.za ▪ www.stellenboschtourism.co.za

Wellington Tourism Bureau ▪ T 021·873·4604 ▪ F 021·873·4607
welltour@mweb.co.za ▪ www.wellington.co.za

West Coast Peninsula Tourism Bureau ▪ T 022·714·2088 ▪ F 022·714·4240
bureau@kingsley.co.za

Worcester Tourism Bureau ▪ T 023·342·8710/20 ▪ F 023·342·2294
assistant@worcestertourism.com ▪ www.worcestertourism.com

■ Specialist wine tours

Adamastor & Bacchus ▪ johnford@iafrica.com ▪ T 439·5169/083·229·1172 ▪
F 439·5169

African Wonder Tours ▪ info@africanwonder.co.za ▪www.africanwonder.co.za ▪
T 082·325·1485

Amber Wine Tours ▪ ambertours@wol.co.za ▪ www.ambertours.co.za ▪
T 083·448·7016

Exclusively African Tours ▪ ian@exclusively-african.com ▪ www.exclusively-african.
com ▪ T 021·852·0278/082·309·9991

Gourmet Wine Tours ▪ sflesch@iafrica.com ▪ www.gourmetwinetours.co.za ▪
T 705·4317/083·229·3581 ▪ F 706·0766

Gudrun Grünewald ▪ happyholiday@adept.co.za ▪ www.happyholiday.co.za ▪
T 082·699·3098

It Just Did! Wine Tourism ▪ info@itjustdid.com ▪ www.itjustdid.com ▪
T 082·390·6092

Judy's Tours ▪ judyk@zsd.co.za ▪ T 084·500·1941/851·7009

Ocean & Vine Tours ▪ wayne@wine.co.za ▪ T 082·900·6999

Redwood Tours ▪ rwt@adept.co.za ▪ www.redwoodtours.co.za ▪
T 886·8138/082·443·6480

Southern Destinations ▪ info@southerndestinations.com ▪ www.
southerndestinations.com ▪ T 671·3090 ▪ F 674·7481

Tri Active Events Management (Green Mountain Eco Route) ▪ info@triactive.co.
za ▪ www.triactive.co.za ▪ T 859·4250 ▪ F 859·4230

Vineyard Ventures ▪ vinven@iafrica.com ▪ www.vineyardventures.co.za ▪
T 434·8888/082·920·2825 ▪ F 434·9999

Vintage Cape Tours Paarl ▪ www.vintagecape.co.za ▪
T 872·9252/082·553·8928/082·656·3994 ▪ F 862·1484

Vintour ▪ helmut@vintour.co.za ▪ T/F 976·5709/083·626·0029
Walker Bay Wine Destination ▪ wine@hermanus.co.za ▪ T 028·316·3988
Wanderer Wines ▪ wines@wanderer.co.za ▪ www.wanderer.co.za ▪
 T·021·788·6850/082·878·1176
Wellington Wine Walk ▪ judy@winescapetours.co.za ▪ T 083·313·8383 ▪
 F 461·5555
Window on Cape Wine ▪ mvweaver@iafrica.com ▪ T/F 866·1002/082·782·5198
Wine Desk at the Waterfront ▪ winedesk@tourcapetown.com; ligia@winedesk.co.
 za ▪ www.winedeskwaterfront.co.za ▪ T 405·4550/082·822·6127 **Wine Walks** ▪
 info@winewalks.co.za ▪ www.winewalks.co.za ▪ T 851·2785/083·631·5944

■ Eat-outs in the winelands and Cape Town

Below are some dining out options in Cape Town and the winelands. For more eat-outs
among the vines, consult the A-Z section of the guide for wineries which offer light
lunches, picnics etc. Look for the 🐌 symbol beside the individual entries. Unless stated
to the contrary, all allow you to bring your own (BYO) wine — the corkage fee is indicated
at the start of each entry. Any claims to disabled-friendliness are unverified by the publishers of the guide. The eat-outs featured here supplied information on their culinary
styles, menus and attractions, which was edited by Jos Baker.

Index of eat-outs
Listed alphabetically, with region.

onewaterfront . . . . Cape Town
On the Terrace @
  Lindhorst-Wines . . . . . . Paarl
Peddlars on the Bend . . . Constantia
Pier Café & Bistro . . . . . . Cape Town
Red Indigo . . . . Gansbaai
Reuben's Restaurant &
  Bar . . . . Franschhoek
Rhebokskloof Restaurant . Paarl
Sand at The Plettenberg . Plettenberg Bay
Savoy Cabbage
  Restaurant &
  Champagne Bar . . . . Cape Town
Schulphoek Seafront
  Guesthouse Restaurant . Hermanus
Seafood at The Marine . . Hermanus
Seasons at Diemers-
  fontein Wine and
  Country Estate . . . . Wellington
Societi Bistro . . . . Cape Town

Sommelier Restaurant at
  Santé Winelands . . . . . . Paarl
Terroir Restaurant . . . . . . Stellenbosch
The Cape Malay
  Restaurant . . . . Constantia
The French Connection
  Bistro Restaurant . . . . . Franschhoek
The Goatshed . . . . Paarl
The Greenhouse
  Restaurant . . . . Constantia
The Guinea Fowl
  Restaurant . . . . Kuils River
The Nose Restaurant &
  Wine Bar . . . . Cape Town
The Pavilion . . . . Hermanus
The River Café . . . . Constantia
theshowroom . . . . Cape Town
Veranda Restaurant . . . . . Cape Town
Zachary's Restaurant . . . Knysna
Zevenwacht Restaurant . Stellenbosch

Cape Town

Aubergine Restaurant 39 Barnet Street, Gardens, Cape Town ■ Continental cuisine with Asian influences ■ Lunch Wed-Fri; 'Cinq à Sept' Mon-Sat 17:00-19:00 & dinner Mon-Sat ■ Closed Sun ■ Booking advised ■ Children welcome ■ Major credit cards accepted ■ Corkage R50 ■ Owner Harald Bresselschmidt ■ aubergin@mweb.co.za ■ www. aubergine.co.za ■ **T** 021·465·4909 ■ F 021·461·3781

A consistently delicious destination, now with a winter garden to enhance the inviting terrace. Gourmet delights include an East meets West Cape sea harvest and springbok and smoked kudu parfait with glazed fresh prunes. Go degustation with accompanying wines, or à la carte with matured wine from the well-selected winelist. The sommelier will help match food and wine for a complete dining experience.

Balducci's Shop 6162, Victoria Wharf, V&A Waterfront, Cape Town ■ Cal-Med cuisine ■ Open daily 9 am till late ■ Booking advised ■ Children welcome (but no under 12 at night) ■ Wheelchair-friendly ■ Major credit cards accepted ■ No BYO ■ Owners Ian Halfon & Doron Duveen ■ info@slickrestaurants.com ■ www.balduccis.co.za ■ **T** 021·421·6002/3 ■ F 021·421·6010

The place for crowd-watching over coffee in the V&A Waterfront. Overlooking the harbour, the stylish, award-winning international café-restaurant is equally popular for luxury breakfasts, healthy or hearty lunches, leisurely dinners, or a pre-movie bite. The menu is wide (try the wood-fired pizzas), helpings are generous and service attentive. The adjacent Balducci's Royal Sushi Bar is internationally acclaimed and regarded as one of the best around.

Bascule Whisky Bar and Wine Cellar Cape Grace, West Quay Road, V&A Waterfront, Cape Town ■ Modern classical cuisine ■ Open daily 12:00-late ■ Wheelchair-friendly ■ Major credit cards accepted ■ Corkage R40 ■ Owner Meikles Africa ■ bascule@ capegrace.com ■ www.bascule.co.za ■ **T** 021·410·7082 ■ F 021·419·7622

This stylish water's edge bar maintains a collection of over 450 single malts and blends — one of the largest in the southern hemisphere. A whisky sommelier is on hand, and tastings for up to 25 people can be arranged. A tempting cocktail menu and excellent winelist make sundowners on the quayside, overlooking an international yacht marina, Signal Hill and Table Mountain, a popular option. (See also Stay-over section.)

Belthazar Restaurant & Wine Bar Shop 153, Victoria Wharf, V&A Waterfront, Cape Town ■ Grill & seafood ■ Open daily 12:00-late ■ Booking advised ■ Children 12+ welcome ■ Wheelchair-friendly ■ Major credit cards accepted ■ No BYO ■ Owners Ian Halfon, Doron Duveen & Jonathan Steyn ■ info@slickrestaurants.com ■ www.belthazar.co.za ■ T 021·421·3753/6 ■ F 021·421·3748

Indulge your palate at the world's biggest wine-by-the-glass bar, where sommeliers serve 178 of the Cape's finest wines by the glass and offer advice on a 600-choice winelist. Pair sought-after vintages with specialities from butter-tender aged Karan beef to game and the freshest South African and Mozambican export quality seafood. Voted Best Steakhouse Greater Cape Town 2004 and elevated to best in South Africa 2005.

Café Bascule   Cape Grace, West Quay Road, V&A Waterfront, Cape Town ▪ Open daily 07:30–16:00 ▪ Children welcome ▪ Wheelchair-friendly ▪ Major credit cards accepted ▪ Owner Meikles Africa ▪ bascule@capegrace.com ▪ www.bascule.co.za/cafebascule ▪ **T 021·410·7100** ▪ F 021·419·7622

Great news for addicts! The comfortable café extension of the popular Bascule Whisky Bar and Wine Cellar offers multi-facetted coffees from a blend of international beans unique to Bascule. Teas range from green, leaf and herbal to a SA Rooibos first: Red Espresso and Red Cappuccino. The mouthwatering light menu invites indulgence in an ambience that draws in the harbour, yachts and view of Table Mountain. (See also Stay-over section.)

Caroline's Cape Kitchen   Caroline's Fine Wine Cellar, 15 Long Street, Cape Town ▪ Modern Cape cuisine ▪ Lunch Mon–Fri 12:00–14:30, evening functions by prior arrangement ▪ Closed Sat & Sun, public holidays ▪ Booking advised ▪ Wheelchair-friendly ▪ Major credit cards accepted ▪ No BYO ▪ Owner Caroline Rillema ▪ carowine@mweb.co.za ▪ **T 021·419·8984** ▪ F 021·419·8985

Enjoy lunch surrounded by the finest Cape wines. Caroline Rillema, experienced, hands-on proprietor of a specialist wine shop in the Cape Town CBD, has converted the large wine cellar into a convivial restaurant where lunches (try *Cape Malay* curry) are prepared in an open kitchen and six different wines can be tasted by the glass. Special tastings (R50 per person) offered before lunch. Booking essential.

Catharina's Restaurant   see under Constantia

Den Anker Restaurant   Pierhead, V&A Waterfront, Cape Town ▪ French/Belgian cuisine ▪ Open daily 11:00–16:00 & 18:00–22:30 (kitchen); 11:00–24:00 (bar) ▪ Booking advised ▪ Children welcome ▪ Wheelchair-friendly ▪ Major credit cards accepted ▪ No BYO ▪ Owner L De Visscher ▪ denanker@mweb.co.za ▪ www.denanker.com ▪ **T 021·419·0249** ▪ F 021·419·0251

Visit Den Anker at lunchtime for its prime water's edge position: seals bask and gulls swoop against the backdrop of Table Mountain mothering her city. A V&A 'pioneer', the restaurant celebrated its 12th birthday with a subtle facelift. Signature mussels and frites are still a best-seller, but try delights like *foie gras*, seared tuna, and sinful Belgian chocolate mousse. Excellent winelist and Belgian beers.

Dine at the Andros   Andros Boutique Hotel, cnr Newlands & Phyllis Roads, Claremont, Cape Town ▪ Open daily 07:00–23:00 ▪ Booking advised ▪ Children 12+ welcome ▪ Wheelchair-friendly ▪ Major credit cards accepted ▪ Corkage R30 ▪ Owners The Barrow Family ▪ info@andros.co.za ▪ www.andros.co.za ▪ **T 021·797·9777** ▪ F 021·797·0300

This intimate 35-seater restaurant in a boutique hotel offers a straightforward yet sensual dining experience. Seasonal French-style menus from Chef Nicolene Barrow (who trained under Michel Roux Jr at London's Le Gavroche) include favourites like beef fillet with marrow bone, braised shoulder of spring lamb and poached pear brûlée. Enjoy dinner beside the fire in winter and in summer relax on the veranda overlooking park-like gardens. (See also Stay-over section.)

onewaterfront   Cape Grace, West Quay Road, V&A Waterfront, Cape Town ▪ Modern Classical cuisine ▪ Open daily for breakfast, lunch & dinner ▪ Booking advised ▪ Children welcome ▪ Wheelchair-friendly ▪ Major credit cards accepted ▪ Corkage R40 ▪ Owner Meikles Africa ▪ onewaterfront@capegrace.com ▪ www.onewaterfront.co.za ▪ **T 021·410·7080** ▪ F 021·419·7622

Inspired by a country as rich in heritage as creativity, award-winning onewaterfront restaurant at Cape Grace is a vibrant combination of friendly, seamless service, relaxed atmosphere and adventurous culinary flair. Savour bold tastes and traditional flavours paired with award-winning wines that pay tribute to the world class winemakers of the Western Cape. (See also Stay-over section.)

Pier Café & Bistro   Pier Place, Adderley Street, Foreshore, Cape Town ▪ Continental/contemporary South African cuisine ▪ Open Mon–Fri 06:30–16:30 ▪ Closed Sat & Sun, public holidays ▪ Children welcome ▪ Wheelchair-friendly ▪ Major credit cards accepted ▪ Corkage R15 ▪ Owners Philip & Sandra Engelen ▪ **T/F 021·418·5676**

After hosting patrons for 14 years in Greyton, Philip and Sandra are now in a tree-shaded square in the city – just two minutes walk from the CTICC. The mood is relaxed, the ambience contemporary and the winelist innovative. Specialities are steaks, char-grilled to your specifications, mouthwatering gourmet sandwiches made to order, wraps and Sandra's signature dessert, crunchy topped crème brûlée.

Savoy Cabbage Restaurant & Champagne Bar   101 Hout Street, Cape Town ▪ Contemporary cuisine ▪ Lunch Mon–Fri 12:00–14:30, dinner Mon–Sat 19:00–22:30 ▪ Closed Sun ▪ Booking essential ▪ Major credit cards accepted ▪ Air-conditioned ▪ Smoking section ▪ Secure night-time parking ▪ Corkage R20 ▪ Owner Caroline Bagley ▪ savoycab@iafrica. com ▪ **T 021·424·2626** ▪ F 021·424·3366

Winner of a string of accolades, including CNN's only 'Hot Spot' for Cape Town, and highly praised by *The New York Times* restaurant critic Frank Bruni, this city-centre venue with high ceilings, exposed brick and open staircase, is consistently satisfying. Daily changing menus revolve around the freshest seasonal produce (try the port-soaked figs with chicken liver parfait), game, offal and appetising vegetarian dishes. Boutique winelist.

Societi Bistro   Shop 6155, V&A Waterfront (next to Exclusive Books), Cape Town ▪ French Provençal/Countryside Bistro ▪ Open daily for breakfast 09:00–12:00, lunch & dinner 12:00–23:00 ▪ Booking advised ▪ Children welcome ▪ Wheelchair-friendly ▪ Major credit cards accepted ▪ Corkage R30 ▪ Owners Tammy Botbyl & Peter Weetman ▪ info@ societi.co.za ▪ www.dining-out.co.za ▪ **T 021·418·9483** ▪ F 021·418·8495

A slice of the Old World in the heart of the new. In Cape Town's cosmopolitan V&A Waterfront, Societi Bistro's rustic ambience and hearty fare offers a restful respite. The ambience embodies comfort, pleasure and timeless ritual, inspired by a love of the Italian countryside and Provençal food. Sample specialities like wood-fired shellfish from the wood burning oven, or classics like *fillet au poivre*.

The Nose Restaurant & Wine Bar   Cape Quarter, Dixon Street, Green Point, Cape Town ▪ Contemporary home-styled cuisine ▪ Open daily 09:00–late ▪ Closed Christmas & New Year's days ▪ Booking advised ▪ Children welcome daytime & early evening ▪ Wheelchair-friendly ▪ Major credit cards accepted ▪ No BYO ▪ Owners Cathy & Kevin Marston ▪ info@thenose.co.za ▪ www.thenose.co.za ▪ **T 021·425·2200** ▪ F 021·425·2210

Discover Cape wine by picking The Nose! This laidback, friendly venue on a piazza in trendy De Waterkant offers over 40 wines by the glass, many more by the bottle. First releases and unusual grape varieties marry signature Cape Malay curry, gourmet bangers 'n' mash, char-grilled steaks or tasty finger food platters. Wine-tasting flights and full bar always available, plus introductory wine courses and food and wine-matching evenings.

theshowroom   10 Hospital Street, Harbour Edge, Green Point, Cape Town ▪ Modern flavours ▪ Lunch Mon–Fri 12:00–15:00, dinner Mon–Sat 19:00–22:30 ▪ Closed Sun ▪ Booking essential ▪ Wheelchair-friendly ▪ Major credit cards accepted ▪ Corkage R50 ▪ Chef/Owner Bruce Robertson ▪ reservations@theshowroomrestaurant.co.za ▪ www.theshowroomrestaurant.co.za ▪ **T 021·421·4682** ▪ F 021·421·3858

Expect glass, class and panache. And a Lamborghini on the menu: Bruce Robertson's new slick city restaurant (with secure parking) adjoins the Bloomsbury showroom at Harbouredge. Simplicity rules in minimalist Melbournesque décor and graphic presentation. Delectable dishes; unique mop-your-plate sauce selection and informed wine pairing, by the bottle or glass. The award-winning chef is on view 'in action' in the open plan kitchen.

Veranda Restaurant   Metropole Hotel, 38 Long Street, Cape Town ▪ Continental cuisine ▪ Open Mon–Sun 07:00–23:00 for breakfast, lunch & dinner ▪ Booking advised ▪ Children welcome ▪ Wheelchair-friendly ▪ Major credit cards accepted ▪ Corkage R35 ▪

Owners Steve van der Merwe & Jens Merbt ▪ reservations@metropolehotel.co.za ▪ www.metropolehotel.co.za ▪ **T 021·424·7247** ▪ F 021·424·7248

The first-floor restaurant of the hip, refurbished Metropole Hotel has uninterrupted views of Long Street. Aptly, the menu offers 'city cuisine'. Dishes have an urban edginess: seared prawns come with watermelon and chilli; blue cheese and green onion spring rolls take cranberry syrup; and lime aioli seasons beer-battered hake and chips. Portions are generous, presentation eye-catching and the wide choice will suit all tastes. (See also Stay-over section.)

Constantia

Buitenverwachting Restaurant & Café Petit Buitenverwachting, Klein Constantia Road, Constantia ▪ European contemporary cuisine ▪ Restaurant — open Tue-Sat (Apr-Sep) & Mon-Sat (Oct-Mar) for lunch & dinner ▪ Café Petit — open Tue-Sat (Apr-Sep) for lunch only & Mon-Sat (Oct-Mar) for lunch & dinner ▪ Closed Sun, some public holidays & Jul to mid-Aug ▪ Booking advised ▪ Children 12+ welcome ▪ Wheelchair-friendly ▪ Major credit cards accepted ▪ Corkage R35 ▪ Owners Lars Maack/Edgar Osojnik (partner) ▪ restaurant@buitenverwachting. com ▪ www.buitenverwachting.co.za ▪ **T 021·794·3522** ▪ F 021·794·1351

Spectacular views over vineyards to the Constantiaberg match award-winning food. Ambience is relaxed and the constantly changing, multi-layered menu is as exotic as it is continental — using only the freshest local ingredients. Linger over chef Edgar Osojnik's original take on the classics and end indulgently with the chocolate variation. Buitenverwachting wines make a perfect partner, by the bottle or glass. (See also A-Z section.)

Catharina's Restaurant Steenberg Estate, cnr Steenberg & Tokai Road, Tokai ▪ Contemporary South African cuisine ▪ Open daily 7:00-22:00 ▪ Booking advised ▪ Children welcome ▪ Wheelchair-friendly ▪ Major credit cards accepted ▪ Corkage R30 ▪ Owner Graham Joshua Beck ▪ info@steenberghotel.com ▪ www.steenberghotel.com ▪ **T 021·713·2222** ▪ F 021·713·2251

Named after Catharina, feisty first owner of the estate, this Cape-style restaurant occupies the original wine cellar, extending onto an oak-shaded patio. Host is Garth Almazan, Cape Town-born exec chef, who emerges from the kitchen to greet guests and discuss the menu. Tempting choices include signature dishes with a Cape slant — speciality is butter-tender venison — and don't miss the picture-perfect, five-flavour crème brûlée. (See also Stay-over & A-Z sections.)

Constantia Uitsig Restaurant Constantia Uitsig, Spaanschemat River Road, Constantia ▪ Mediterranean with a strong Italian influence ▪ Open daily for lunch 12:30-14:30, dinner 19:30-21:30 ▪ Closed for lunch 31 Dec, New Year's day ▪ Booking advised ▪ Children welcome ▪ Wheelchair-friendly ▪ Major credit cards accepted ▪ Corkage R30 ▪ frank@uitsig.co.za ▪ www.uitsig.co.za ▪ **T 021·794·4480** ▪ F 021·794·3105

Constantia Uitsig wines take centre stage at this inviting restaurant, backed by those from the Constantia Valley, and an impressive selection of the best SA has to offer. (Check the Wine Specials for price-friendly offers.) Match your choice to all-time favourites: *beef carpaccio con rucola, abacchio alla Toscana, spaghetti vareggina*. Were they removed from the menu, regulars would riot. (See also Stay-over & A-Z sections.)

Jonkershuis Bar and Eatery Groot Constantia Wine Estate, Groot Constantia Road, Constantia ▪ Bistro style cuisine with Cape Malay influence ▪ Open daily for breakfast 09:00-12:00 & lunch 12:00-17:00, Mon-Sat dinner till 22:00 ▪ Booking advised ▪ Children welcome ▪ Wheelchair-friendly ▪ Major credit cards accepted ▪ Corkage R25 ▪ Owners Tammy Botbyl & Chris Coetzee ▪ info@jonkershuisconstantia.co.za ▪ **T 021·794·6255** ▪ F 021·794·4813

Sample Cape Malay cuisine at the all-new Jonkershuis at the heart of Groot Constantia wine estate. Now a wine bar and bistro, the reinvented restaurant is adjacent to the historic manor house and surrounded by ancient oaks and the legendary Groot Constantia vineyards. Specialities are four Malay curries: vegetarian, chicken, lamb and seafood, and over 100 wines are listed — 44 by the glass. (See also A-Z section.)

La Colombe Constantia Uitsig, Spaanschemat River Road, Constantia ▪ Southern French cuisine ▪ Open daily for lunch 12:30-14:30, dinner 19:30-21:30 ▪ Closed Sun eve (winter) & New Year's day lunch ▪ Booking advised ▪ Children welcome ▪ Wheelchair-friendly ▪ Major credit cards accepted ▪ Corkage R30 ▪ lc@uitsig.co.za ▪ www.lacolombe.co.za ▪ **T (021) 794·2390** ▪ F 021·794·7914

Chosen as one of the top 50 restaurants in the world by UK *Restaurant* magazine. Varied wine varieties and unusual finds on the 'spoilt for choice' winelist enhance an epicurean experience in an airy, contemporary garden setting. Enticing menus feature seasonal gourmet treats like tian of avocado and aubergine with basil, and grilled springbok medallions with butternut and Bokaap spices. Wine Stewards are on hand to recommend complementary wines. (See also Stay-over & A–Z sections.)

Peddlars on the Bend 3 Spaanschemat River Road, Constantia ▪ Cosmopolitan cuisine ▪ Open daily 11:00–23:00 (bar), 12:00–23:00 (kitchen) ▪ Closed Christmas & New Year's days ▪ Booking advised ▪ Children welcome ▪ Wheelchair-friendly ▪ Major credit cards accepted ▪ Corkage R15 from 2nd bottle ▪ peddlars@mweb.co.za ▪ **T 021·794·7747/50** ▪ F 021·794·2730

Hospitable country restaurant (the kitchen's open all day), specialising in steaks, seafood and hearty country-style dishes, with a pub menu for popular garden and bar areas. The award-winning winelist showcases local producers and a good selection of cognac, malt whisky, cigars and liqueurs. The bar draws an eclectic crowd who mix well and know how to party. Plenty of free parking.

The Cape Malay Restaurant The Cellars-Hohenort Hotel, 93 Brommersvlei Road, Constantia ▪ Cape Malay cuisine ▪ Open Mon-Sat 19:00–21:30 ▪ Closed Mon (low season) & Sun ▪ Booking advised ▪ Children 12+ welcome ▪ Major credit cards accepted ▪ Corkage R50 ▪ Owner Liz McGrath ▪ reservations@collectionmcgrath.com ▪ www.collection· mcgrath.com ▪ **T 021·794·2137** ▪ F 021·794·2149

Be adventurous: go local and introduce your palate to a choice of traditional taste treats. This welcoming restaurant offers authentic Cape Malay food, from *Smoorsnoek* and beef *bobotie* to *koeksisters* or chef Martha Williams' famous Malva pudding. Spicy, rustic colours create a soothing Eastern ambience and warm, friendly service enriches the dining experience. Excellent winelist, chosen to complement the aromatic dishes. (See also Stay-over section.)

The Greenhouse Restaurant The Cellars-Hohenort Hotel, 93 Brommersvlei Road, Constantia ▪ Contemporary French cuisine ▪ Open daily for breakfast 7:00–10:30, lunch 12:00–14:30 & dinner 19:00–21:30 ▪ Booking advised ▪ Children 12+ welcome ▪ Wheelchair-friendly ▪ Major credit cards accepted ▪ Corkage R50 ▪ Owner Liz McGrath ▪ reservations@collectionmcgrath.com ▪ www.collectionmcgrath.com ▪ **T 021·794·2137** ▪ F 021·794·2149

This stylish restaurant opens off a light-filled lounge where 152 Martini's are offered at The Martini (making this one of the world's longest martini lists). Unparalleled garden vistas from the airy interior or sun-drenched terrace, friendly but unobtrusive service, an informed sommelier and excellent winelist. Focus is on contemporary French cuisine, infused with flavours of Africa, with signature dishes slow-roasted crispy duck, and classic orange and Grand Marnier soufflé. (See also Stay-over section.)

The River Café Constantia Uitsig, Spaanschemat River Road, Constantia ▪ Healthy and wholesome cuisine ▪ Open daily 8:30–17:00 ▪ Closed Good Friday, Christmas, Boxing & New Year's days ▪ Booking advised ▪ Children welcome ▪ Wheelchair-friendly ▪ Major credit cards accepted ▪ Corkage R15 ▪ therivercafe@uitsig.co.za ▪ www.uitsig.co.za ▪ **T (021) 794·3010** ▪ F 021·794·1812

Convivial café where breakfasts in the lavender-scented courtyard (try eggs Benedict), coffee (with chocolate brownies) and lunches (feast on outsize organic salads or open sandwiches) vie in appeal. While Constantia Uitsig wines take prime position, the compact winelist provides a choice of South Africa's top performers and some emerging estates. Wine tastings also offered at The Wine Shop next door. (See also Stay-over & A–Z sections.)

Darling

Groote Post Restaurant Groote Post Farm, Darling Hills Road, Darling ▪ Modern country cuisine ▪ Open for lunch Wed-Sat, dinners/functions by arrangement ▪ Closed Sun-Tue & July ▪ Booking advised ▪ Children welcome ▪ Wheelchair-friendly ▪ Major credit cards accepted (excl Amex) ▪ No BYO ▪ Owner Shaun Mc Laughlin ▪ mclaughlin@worldonline. co.za ▪ www.grootepost.com ▪ **T 022·492·2825** ▪ F 022·492·2693

Enjoy wine, history and fresh farm produce. Lunch at the restaurant in the historic manor house on Groote Post wine farm (just outside Darling) complements award-winning wines from the farm — at cellar prices. Chef Debbie Mc Laughlin uses only the freshest ingredients for her tasty interpretation of modern country cooking. A perfect venue for country weddings, small conferences and birthday parties. (See also A-Z section.)

Durbanville

Durbanville Hills M13, Durbanville ▪ Contemporary cuisine ▪ Lunch Tue-Sun 12:00–15:00; dinner Wed-Sat 19:00-22:00 (Aug-Apr) ▪ Closed Mon, religious & public holidays ▪ Booking advised ▪ Children welcome ▪ Wheelchair-friendly ▪ Major credit cards accepted ▪ No BYO ▪ Owners Natasha Jewaskiewitz, Marike Roggen & Marleen Brynard ▪ info@durbanvillehills.co. za ▪ www.durbanvillehills.co.za ▪ **T 021·558·1300** ▪ F 021·559·8169

The view is a sweeping panorama of Table Bay, Table Mountain, the Atlantic Ocean and Durbanville Hills vineyards. Match it to regional food, lightened with Mediterranean nuances, and presented in seasonal menus designed to complement the cellar's award-winning wines. Specialities range from smoked kudu salad, biltong and blue cheese soup, and lamb neck in red wine sauce, to popular sago pudding. (See also A-Z section.)

Meerendal Restaurants Meerendal Wine Estate, Vissershok Road, Durbanville ▪ Bistro, deli & fine dining cuisine ▪ **Wheatfields** lunch & dinner Tue-Sat; **The Deli & Bistro** breakfast & lunch daily 08:00-17:00; **The Barn & Lawn** Sun lunch 'The Cape Table' from 12:30 ▪ Children welcome ▪ Wheelchair-friendly ▪ Booking advised for Wheatfields ▪ Major credit cards accepted ▪ Corkage R30 ▪ Chefs David Higgs, Wade van der Merwe & Stephan Fraser ▪ info@meerendal.co.za ▪ www.meerendal.co.za ▪ **T/F 021·975·1655/072·856·6298**

A spectrum of eating options on a historic wine estate: pick the venue to please your palate. All three restaurants are in the hands of a talented culinary triumvirate: chefs David Higgs, Wade van der Merwe and newcomer Stephan Fraser. Though venues differ in ambience, style (and price) priorities remain constant — menus change to highlight fresh ingredients, and all complement Meerendal wines. The **Deli & Bistro** provides satisfying breakfasts, hearty lunches, scones, cakes, coffees and teas. The **Barn & Lawn,** rich in winelands views, presents an appetising 'Cape Table' Sunday lunch buffet. (With a lawn where a marquee can accommodate up to 600, it's also an ideal venue for weddings and corporate functions). At **Wheatfields**, in the Meerendal manor house, the emphasis is on fine dining, showcasing the skills of the award-winning chefs. Delight in innovative combinations of texture, colour, foams and flavour in picture-perfect plating. (See also A-Z section.)

Franschhoek & Environs

Backsberg Restaurant Backsberg Estate Cellars, Klapmuts/Simondium Road ▪ South African/Continental cuisine ▪ Open Tue-Sun 11:00-17:00 ▪ Closed Mondays — except if public holiday, Good Friday ▪ Booking advised ▪ Children welcome ▪ Wheelchair-friendly ▪ Visa & MasterCard accepted ▪ No BYO ▪ Owner Backsberg Estate Cellars ▪ deon@ backsberg.co.za ▪ www.backsberg.co.za ▪ **T 021·875·5952** ▪ F 021·875·5144

Family friendly venue that makes fine wine and food an everyday pleasure. Beautiful mountain views and large lawns for relaxed al fresco lunching; a warming fire indoors on cold days. Lamb on the spit daily with roast potatoes; platters of meats and cheeses, and chocolate *roulade* as dessert speciality. To enjoy with Backsberg wines by the bottle or glass. Live music on Sundays. (See also A-Z section.)

Bread & Wine Restaurant – Farm Grocer Môreson Farm, Happy Valley Road, Franschhoek ▪ Rustic Mediterranean ▪ Open Wed-Sun & public holidays 12:00-15:00, daily from 20 Dec-7 Jan, Tue-Sun 10 Jan-4 Mar ▪ Closed Mon & Tue, winter closing from

17 Jul–16 Aug ▪ Booking advised ▪ Children welcome ▪ Major credit cards accepted ▪ No BYO ▪ Owner Richard Friedman ▪ breadandwine@moreson.co.za ▪ www.moreson.co.za ▪ **T 021·876·3692** ▪ F (021) 876-3105

Bread & Wine — Farm Grocer, the perfect pit stop for wine routers intent on a rustic taste of the Winelands. Courtyard seating under umbrellas provides a relaxed setting for enjoyment of freshly baked artisan breads and moreish hand-crafted charcuterie. Innovative dishes, beautifully presented, highlight Neil Jewell's culinary talent. Môreson wines are served by the glass or bottle. (See also Le Quartier Français – 'iCi', Le Quartier Français 'The Tasting Room' & A–Z section for Môreson.)

Café Allée Bleue   T-Junction R45 & R310, Groot Drakenstein ▪ Fusion ▪ Open daily 08:00–17:00 ▪ Closed 25 Dec ▪ Booking advised ▪ Children welcome ▪ Wheelchair-friendly ▪ Major credit cards accepted ▪ Corkage R25 ▪ Owners Elke & Wilfred Dauphin ▪ madelain@alleebleue.com ▪ www.alleebleue.com ▪ **T 021·874·1886** ▪ F 021·874·1850

Approached through an avenue of eucalyptus trees, this appealing blue and white venue encourages relaxation over light dishes with authentic flavours. Fresh ingredients are sourced locally and menus showcase produce from the fertile farm garden. Treat yourself to Allée Bleue wine and cheese tasting platters — tantalizing selections from Gorgonzola, Asiago and smoked Mozzerella to Dalewood Porcini Brie and red pepper Boerenkaas.

Chamonix Restaurant   Chamonix Wine Estate, Uitkyk Street, Franschhoek ▪ Contemporary fusion cuisine ▪ Open for lunch Mon-Sun 12:00–16:00, dinner Fri & Sat 18:30 till late ▪ Booking advised ▪ Children welcome ▪ Wheelchair-friendly ▪ Major credit cards accepted ▪ No BYO ▪ Owners Don & Dane Newton ▪ dnewton@mweb.co.za ▪ www.chamonix-restaurant.co.za ▪ **T 021·876·2393** ▪ F 021·876·4950

'French contemporary fusion cuisine'. That's owner Don Newton's description of the fare at The Old Cape Dutch restaurant on the mountainside, where the executive chef (his son Dane), excites tastebuds with specialities like orange and soya-glazed fresh Franschhoek salmon trout, and quail stuffed with chicken and sage, with caramelized apple risotto and coffee-chocolate jus. Complimentary tastings of Chamonix award-winning wines offered. (See also A–Z section.)

Grande Provence — The Restaurant   Grande Provence Estate, Main Road, Franschhoek ▪ Global contemporary cuisine ▪ Open daily for lunch & dinner ▪ Booking advised ▪ Children welcome ▪ Wheelchair-friendly ▪ Major credit cards accepted ▪ Corkage R30 ▪ Owner Grande Provence ▪ restaurant@grandeprovence.co.za ▪ www.grandeprovence.co.za ▪ **T 021·876·8600** ▪ F 021·876·8601

While the 300 year-old estate and Owner's Cottage reflect their Huguenot heritage, The Restaurant at Grande Provence projects a chic industrial presence with steel joinery, galvanised metals and skylights. Durban-born chef Vanie Padayachee injects her fresh, seasonal food with authentic home touches: springbok shank is slow-braised with biryani spice. Dishes range from simple (try seared salmon trout) to decadent chocolate fondant with peanut butter ice-cream. (See also Stay-over & A–Z sections.)

Haute Cabrière Cellar Restaurant   Pass Road, Franschhoek ▪ Global fine dining ▪ Summer: lunch & dinner daily; Winter: lunch daily, dinner Fri & Sat ▪ Booking advised ▪ Children welcome ▪ Wheelchair-friendly ▪ Major credit cards accepted ▪ No BYO ▪ Owners Matthew, Nicky & Penny Gordon ▪ hautecab@iafrica.com ▪ www.hautecabriere.com ▪ **T 021·876·3688** ▪ F 021·876·3691

Two unique talents, cellarmaster Achim von Arnim and chef-patron Matthew Gordon, reinvent the eating out experience. It's an epicurean adventure, with menus created to complement Haute Cabrière wines and Pierre Jourdan Cap Classiques. No starters or mains, but a variety of tastebud-titillating dishes (like butternut and parmesan soufflé, or scallop and prawn tempura with crayfish sauce) in full and half portions to pair with the wines. (See also A–Z section for Cabrière Estate.)

La Couronne Restaurant   see Mange Tout & Mont Rochelle Restaurant

La Petite Ferme Restaurant   La Petite Ferme, Pass Road, Franschhoek ▪ Contemporary, rustic cuisine ▪ Lunch daily from 12:00–16:00 ▪ Closed 25 Dec & 1 Jan ▪ Booking advised ▪ Children welcome ▪ Wheelchair-friendly ▪ Major credit cards accepted ▪ Corkage R25 ▪ Owners Mark & Josephine Dendy Young ▪ restaurant@lapetiteferme.co.za ▪ www.lapetiteferme.co.za ▪ **T 021·876·3016** ▪ F 021·876·3624

A magnificent view, fresh, flavourful cuisine from local produce and warm hospitality. That's the winning recipe from this three-generation family restaurant (with Mark Dendy Young concentrating on increased wine production). Wines are made with the food in mind, and are all available by the glass. Succulent specialities from the all-girl kitchen team include home-smoked Franschhoek rainbow trout, slow-roasted lamb, and warthog bresaola. (See also Stay-over & A-Z sections.)

Le Manoir de Brendel Spa, Wine & Guest Estate R45 Main Road to Franschhoek ▪ Cosmopolitan cuisine ▪ Open daily 12:00-15:00 ▪ Booking advised ▪ Children welcome ▪ Wheelchair-friendly ▪ Major credit cards accepted ▪ No BYO ▪ Owner Christian Brendel ▪ lemanoir@brendel.co.za ▪ www.le-manoir-de-brendel.com ▪ **T 021·876·4525** ▪ F 021·876·4524

Relax in a restaurant with idyllic setting and country-fresh cosmopolitan cuisine, prepared with French flair. Appetising choices include tomato and blue cheese brochette with anchovy butter; spiced venison medallions, crispy bacon and rocket pesto; and wine-poached pears with three-cheese compote. Be tempted to linger: walk through the vineyards, be soothed at the spa or work out at the gym. Wedding and conference facilities available. (See also Stay-over & A-Z sections.)

Le Quartier Français — 'iCi' 16 Huguenot Street, Franschhoek ▪ Contemporary cuisine ▪ Open Mon-Sun 12:00-22:00 ▪ Booking advised ▪ Children welcome ▪ Major credit cards accepted ▪ No BYO ▪ Chef Margot Janse ▪ restaurant@lqf.co.za ▪ www.lequartier.co.za ▪ **T 021·876·2151** ▪ F 021·876·3105

Fun, funky décor as a backdrop to contemporary food cooked in a wood-burning oven from the finest seasonal produce. Each ingredient is distinct and the flavour combinations perfectly judged. An excellent winelist to complement the food. (See also Bread & Wine and Le Quartier Français 'The Tasting Room'.)

Le Quartier Français 'The Tasting Room' 16 Huguenot Street, Franschhoek ▪ Contemporary cuisine ▪ Open Mon-Sun for dinner only ▪ Booking advised ▪ Children 12+ welcome ▪ Major credit cards accepted ▪ No BYO ▪ Chef Margot Janse ▪ restaurant@lqf.co.za ▪ www.lequartier.co.za ▪ **T 021·876·2151** ▪ F 021·876·3105

A cutting edge experience. This is innovative cuisine that enchants the palate. Choose four or six courses off an à la carte menu or indulge in an eight-course Gourmand version with or without wines. (With enhances the experience). Voted 'Best Restaurant in Africa and the Middle East — 2005' and 'One of the Top 50 Restaurants in the World — 2006' by *Restaurant* magazine. (See also Bread & Wine and Le Quartier Français — iCi.)

Mange Tout & Mont Rochelle Restaurant Mont Rochelle Hotel & Mountain Vineyards, Dassenberg Road, Franschhoek ▪ Two restaurants — fine dining or al fresco Mediterranean ▪ Open daily for breakfast, lunch & dinner ▪ Booking advised ▪ Children welcome ▪ Wheelchair-friendly ▪ Major credit cards accepted ▪ No BYO ▪ Owners Erwin Schnitzler & Miko Rwayitare ▪ res@montrochelle.co.za ▪ www.montrochelle.co.za ▪ **T 021·876·2770** ▪ F 021·876·3788

Dine fine or alfresco — or opt for a picnic basket. The rebuilt, revamped Mont Rochelle Hotel and Vineyards boasts two restaurants: a relaxed venue offering a smorgasbord of fresh dishes and delicacies at the wine tasting room, and a cosmopolitan feast at elegant Mange Tout in the hotel's main wing. Check the wrap-round view — and yes, pianist Alfio is back at a new white baby piano. (See also Stay-over & A-Z sections).

Monneaux Restaurant at the Franschhoek Country House Main Road, Franschhoek ▪ Contemporary cuisine ▪ Open 7 days a week for breakfast, lunch & dinner ▪ Booking advised ▪ Children welcome ▪ Wheelchair-friendly ▪ Major credit cards accepted ▪ Corkage R30 ▪ info@fch.co.za ▪ www.fch.co.za ▪ **T 021·876·3386** ▪ F 021·876·2744

Voted as one of South Africa's top restaurants, with a reputation for innovative modern French cuisine, prepared with fresh, well-sourced ingredients and exquisitely presented. Lunch à la carte on the magnificent fountain terrace; dine in the understated, elegant dining room or enclosed veranda. The winelist centres round local wines, which can also be enjoyed by the glass in the cosy wine bar or underground cellar. (See also Stay-over section.)

Reuben's Restaurant & Bar   19 Huguenot Street, Franschhoek ▪ Global cuisine ▪ Open daily for breakfast, lunch & dinner ▪ Closed New Year's day ▪ Booking advised ▪ Children welcome ▪ Wheelchair-friendly ▪ Major credit cards accepted ▪ Corkage R30 (excl. big functions) ▪ Owners Reuben Riffel, Marc Kent & Tim Rands ▪ reubens@mweb.co.za ▪ www.reubens.co.za ▪ **T 021·876·3772** ▪ F 021·876·4464

A byword for simply prepared, fresh and unintimidating food (a sauce is never termed a jus), extensive winelist and fine selection of wines by the glass. Ambience is warm (so is the sunny courtyard for alfresco meals) and the uncluttered interior extends into a smoking bar. Menu musts include Indian prawn risotto and avo cream, and roast duck salad with honey-chilli dressing, mizuna and mint.

The French Connection Bistro Restaurant   48 Huguenot Street, Franschhoek ▪ French bistro ▪ Open daily for lunch 12:00–15:30, light lunch 15:30–18:00 & dinner 18:30–22:00 ▪ Closed Christmas eve ▪ Booking advised ▪ Children welcome ▪ Wheelchair-friendly ▪ Major credit cards accepted ▪ BYO discouraged — corkage R20 ▪ Owners Matthew Gordon & Trevor Kirsten ▪ french@worldonline.co.za ▪ **T 021·876·4056** ▪ F 021·876·4036

Experience that true '*La Provence*' feeling. Watch the activity in the glass-fronted, typical French countryside kitchen or relax on the terraced veranda with local wine. Chef-patron Matthew Gordon pampers your palate with carefully selected ingredients and simple but delicious fare. Savour specialities like slow roasted crispy duck with raspberry vinegar jus, or juicy steaks with a selection of home-made sauces.

Gansbaai

Red Indigo   Grootbos Private Nature Reserve, off the R43, between Stanford & Gansbaai ▪ New World cuisine ▪ Open daily for lunch 12:00–14:00 & dinner 18:30–21:00 ▪ Booking advised ▪ Wheelchair-friendly ▪ Major credit cards accepted ▪ Corkage R55 ▪ Owners Michael & Tertius Lutzeyer ▪ info@grootbos.co.za ▪ www.grootbos.com ▪ **T 028·384·8000** ▪ F 028·384·8100

A team of young and energetic chefs creates refreshingly modern 'New World' fare that matches the setting, bringing eye-appeal and simplicity to dishes. Fresh seafood is a speciality: the restaurant is within sight and sound of the sea. The winelist highlights award-winning wines from local wine farms and the private cellar is just big enough for a private dinner party or candle-lit dinner for two. (See Stay-over section.)

Hermanus

La Vierge Champagne Veranda and Restaurant   La Vierge Winery, Hemel en Aarde Valley Road (R320), Hemel en Aarde Valley, Hermanus ▪ French cuisine ▪ Open Tue-Sun for lunch & dinner ▪ Booking advised ▪ Children welcome ▪ Wheelchair-friendly ▪ Major credit cards accepted ▪ Corkage R40 ▪ Owner Babylon Wines (Pty) Ltd ▪ info@lavierge.co.za ▪ www.lavierge.co.za ▪ **T 028·312·4631** ▪ F 028·312·1388

Feast on seafood in the restaurant atop the recently revamped La Vierge Winery and sip sparkling wines at the Champagne bar on the Champagne veranda. Architecture is stunning; views a 270° vineyard panorama to the sea, and the menu specialises in local and exotic fish, shellfish and mouth-watering daily delicacies. Complemented by a carefully selected local winelist with emphasis on valley wines, Champagne and Methode Cap Classique. (See also A–Z section.)

Schulphoek Seafront Guesthouse Restaurant   44 Marine Drive (entrance at Piet Retief Crescent), Sandbaai, Hermanus ▪ Global cuisine ▪ **Restaurant is limited to stay-over guests** ▪ Open 7 days a week ▪ Closed month of June ▪ Booking advised ▪ Children welcome ▪ Limited wheelchair access ▪ Major credit cards accepted (excl Amex) ▪ No BYO ▪ Owners Wehrner & Janet Gutstadt ▪ Interactive hosts Petro & Mannes van Zyl ▪ schulphoek@hermanus.co.za ▪ www.schulphoek.co.za ▪ **T 028·316·2626** ▪ F 028·316·2627

Stay over at this seven-roomed guesthouse on a beautiful bay 5km from Hermanus centre and enjoy a four-course menu du jour (specialities are seafood, fresh fish and venison), complemented by over 7 000 bottles of SA wine. Book 24 hours in advance, and dinner on the first night is complimentary. Spacious double en-suite accommodation from garden bedrooms to a luxurious first floor room with spectacular sea views. (See also Stay-over section.)

Seafood at The Marine   The Marine Hotel, cnr Marine Drive & Main Road, Hermanus ▪ Contemporary Seafood ▪ Open daily for lunch 12:00–14:30 & dinner 19:00–21:30 ▪ Booking advised ▪ Children 12+ welcome ▪ Major credit cards accepted ▪ Corkage R50 ▪ Owner Liz McGrath ▪ reservations@collectionmcgrath.com ▪ www.collectionmcgrath.com ▪ **T 028·313·1000** ▪ F 028·313·0160

Culinary theatre in action. The busy open kitchen forms the focal point of this informal, bustling restaurant – the only sea view is on your plate! Opt for the freshest fish from Walker Bay; Marine seafood soup, or crisply battered 'rich man's fish and chips' with the crunchy chips served in a business page cone. End indulgently with a chocolate brownie. (See also Stay-over section.)

The Pavilion   The Marine Hotel, cnr Marine Drive & Main Road, Hermanus ▪ International cuisine with a strong South African influence ▪ Open daily for breakfast 07:00–10:30 & Tue-Sat 19:00–21:30 for dinner ▪ Closed May to mid-Aug ▪ Booking advised ▪ Children 12+ welcome ▪ Major credit cards accepted ▪ Corkage R50 ▪ Owner Liz McGrath ▪ reservations@collectionmcgrath.com ▪ www.collectionmcgrath.com ▪ **T 028·313·1000** ▪ F 028·313·0160

Perched on the Hermanus cliffs overlooking the ocean, this uncluttered, elegantly relaxed restaurant places the focus firmly on food from a creative culinary team: delicacies like abalone, sea-fresh fish, crispy slow-roasted duck and featherlight soufflés from the pastry kitchen. Wines, showcased in a well-stocked, 'floating cellar' in the centre of the restaurant, are integral to the dining experience. (See also Stay-over section.)

Knysna

Zachary's Restaurant   Pezula Resort Hotel & Spa, Lagoonview Drive, Knysna ▪ Contemporary classic cuisine ▪ Open daily for breakfast 07:00–10:30, lunch 12:00–14:30 & dinner 18:00–22:00 ▪ Booking advised ▪ Children welcome ▪ Wheelchair-friendly ▪ Major credit cards accepted ▪ Corkage R25 ▪ Owner The Pezula Group ▪ reservations@pezula.com ▪ www.pezula.com ▪ **T 044·302·3333** ▪ F 044·302·3303

Sweeping views of the Pezula Championship Course and Knysna Lagoon are matched by classic yet contemporary cuisine – with a Menu Gourmand on Friday nights. Ambience is elegant by day and intimate at night; the food embodies New York-born chef Geoffrey Murray's culinary ethic of 'fresh local organic ingredients with a global influence'. The impressive cellar includes many of South Africa's rare boutique wines. (See also Stay-over section.)

Kuils River

The Guinea Fowl Restaurant   Saxenburg Wine Farm, Polkadraai Road (M12), Kuils River ▪ Continental cuisine ▪ Lunch Wed-Mon, dinner Wed-Sat ▪ Closed Tue, Jun-Jul ▪ Booking advised ▪ Children welcome ▪ Wheelchair-friendly ▪ Major credit cards accepted ▪ Corkage R20 ▪ Owners Adrian & Birgit Bührer ▪ restaurant@saxenburg.com ▪ www.saxenburg.co.za ▪ **T 021·906·5232** ▪ F 021·906·0489

Relaxed country venue in the capable hands of experienced restaurateur Leo Romer, with guinea fowl (naturally) a signature dish. The fowl also appear on the farm's wine labels – look no further for perfect food and wine pairing. Eating options from a garden lapa for snacks and light meals, to a view-rich terrace and intimate dinners indoors. Awarded a Chaine des Rotisseurs Blazon for culinary excellence. (See also A-Z section.)

Zevenwacht Restaurant   see under Stellenbosch

Montagu

Mimosa Lodge Restaurant   Church Street, Montagu ▪ French Continental cuisine ▪ Open daily 19:30–21:30 ▪ Booking advised ▪ Children by prior arrangement ▪ Wheelchair-friendly ▪ Major credit cards accepted ▪ Corkage R25 ▪ Owners Bernhard & Fida Hess ▪ mimosa@lando.co.za ▪ www.mimosa.co.za ▪ **T 023·614·2351** ▪ F 023·614·2418

Discover Swiss-trained culinary skill in a country village at the heart of Route 62. Swiss owner-chef Bernhard Hess (ex Ma Cuisine in Parktown North) deserted the city for country life – and now picks fresh ingredients in his guest house garden. His creative cuisine blends colour and texture in dishes that combine country flavours with sophisticated presentation. Don't miss the veal or confit of duck. (See also Stay-over section.)

Paarl & Environs

Backsberg Restaurant   see under Franschhoek

Bistro Allegro   Grande Roche Hotel, Plantasie Street, Paarl ▪ International casual dining experience ▪ Open daily from 11:00-close ▪ Closed mid-May to 31 Jul inclusive ▪ Booking advised ▪ Children welcome ▪ Wheelchair-friendly ▪ Major credit cards accepted ▪ No BYO ▪ General Manager Garnet Basson ▪ reserve@granderoche.co.za ▪ www.granderoche. com ▪ **T** 021·863·5100 ▪ F 021·863·2220

A relaxed dining experience, with light repertoire catering for both savoury and sweet palates – at very competitive prices. Whether a seafood tagliatelle with Riesling sauce, tantalizing vegetarian option, cheese platter or club sandwich, dishes receive the same care from the Grande Roche professional chefs. Well-chosen winelist offers first and second labels, half bottles, or wine by the glass to complement your meal. (See also Stay-over section.)

Bosman's Restaurant   Grande Roche Hotel, Plantasie Street, Paarl ▪ Global cuisine ▪ Breakfast 7:00-10:30, lunch 12:00-13:45 & dinner 19:00-21:00 ▪ Closed mid-May to 31 Jul inclusive ▪ Booking advised ▪ Children welcome (4+ for dinner) ▪ Wheelchair-friendly ▪ Major credit cards accepted ▪ No BYO ▪ General Manager Garnet Basson ▪ reserve@ granderoche.co.za ▪ www.granderoche.com ▪ **T** 021·863·5100 ▪ F 021·863·2220

World-class consistency. The first and only hotel-restaurant on the African continent to achieve Relais Gourmand status, and four-time winner of the Business Day Restaurant of the Year award, Bosman's offers a global gourmet experience in a gracious manor house. The breakfast buffet (with oysters) is extensive; lunches informal and dinners elegant, with array of contemporary menus complemented by wines from the superbly stocked cellar (a regular Diner's Club Winelist Diamond Award winner). Expect masterly flavour combinations like bread dumpling wrapped springbok loin, complemented by red cabbage and black peppercorn jus, or oven-roasted kingklip on ostrich neck ragoût with Chardonnay foam. (See also Stay-over section.)

Cadeaux at Santé Winelands   Simonsvlei Road, Simondium, Paarl-Franschhoek Valley ▪ Organic cuisine ▪ Open for lunch Mon-Sun 12:00-15:00 and dinner Tue-Sat 19:00-22:00 ▪ Booking advised ▪ Children welcome ▪ Wheelchair-friendly ▪ Major credit cards accepted ▪ Corkage R25 ▪ Owner Fidentia Holdings Pty Ltd ▪ info@santewellness. co.za ▪ www.santewellness.co.za ▪ **T** 021·875·8100 ▪ F 021·875·8111

A spa with delectable lunch buffet? Yes – at SA's first organic wellness restaurant at a five-star hotel, in a stunning winelands setting. Drink smoothies and organic wines and feast (healthily) on crunchy-fresh salads, paprika roasted sweet potato, organic meats, fresh Franschhoek trout, herb and Verjus risotto with grapes and grilled prawn – some of the innovative spa dishes at Santé Winelands Hotel & Wellness Centre. Rated as one of the top three spas in the world by *Conde Nast Traveller* UK, Jan 2006. (See also Stay-over section.)

Joostenberg Bistro   see under Stellenbosch

Knorhoek Lapa Restaurant   see under Stellenbosch

Marc's Mediterranean Cuisine & Garden   129 Main Street, Paarl ▪ Mediterranean cuisine ▪ Open daily for breakfast, lunch & dinner ▪ Closed Sun night, July (yearly holiday) ▪ Booking advised ▪ Children welcome ▪ Wheelchair-friendly ▪ Major credit cards accepted ▪ Corkage R30 ▪ Owner Marc Friederich ▪ chezmarc@mweb.co.za ▪ **T** 021·863·3980 ▪ F 021·863·3990

Marc Friederich, owner, award-winning sommelier and chef, has extensive experience in top restaurants in Europe and SA. Share his belief that a great eating-out experience depends on the perfect combination of good food, good wine, atmosphere and company.

The restaurant extends on to a lavender-scented garden, and there's a new private dining room for tastings, dinners and small functions. The Mediterranean mezze is a must.

On the Terrace@Lindhorst Wines Lindhorst Wines, R45, Southern Paarl ▪ Country cuisine ▪ Open Wed-Sun 12:00-16:00, book for evening functions ▪ Closed Mon & Tue, Aug ▪ Booking advised ▪ Children welcome ▪ Wheelchair-friendly ▪ Major credit cards accepted ▪ Corkage R15 ▪ Owners BEE project & Lindhorst Wines ▪ belinda@lindhorstwines.com ▪ www.lindhorstwines.com ▪ **T** 021·863·0199 ▪ F 021·863·3694

Hearty, home-style helpings to enjoy overlooking a vista of vines, or indoors, warmed by a fire in winter. This BEE project is powered by local women whose friendliness permeates the premises. Crusty pies, savoury pancakes, signature lasagne, soups and country fresh salads to pair with award-winning Lindhorst wines — and a sure to appeal basket for kids with gift to entertain them over lunch. (See also Stay-over & A-Z sections.)

Rhebokskloof Restaurant Rhebokskloof, Wine Route No 8, Agter-Paarl Road, Paarl ▪ Global cuisine ▪ Open daily for tea & lunch, dinner Thu-Mon (Sep-May), dinner Fri-Sun (Jun-Aug) ▪ Booking advised ▪ Children welcome ▪ Wheelchair-friendly ▪ Major credit cards accepted ▪ No BYO ▪ Owner Rhebokskloof Wines ▪ restaurant@rhebokskloof.co.za ▪ www.rhebokskloof.co.za ▪ **T** 021·869·8606 ▪ F 021·869·8906

A superb setting. Enjoy a journey of the senses overlooking manicured lawns and a bird-rich lake. Savour wines from a list highlighting the Rhebokskloof range, complemented by innovative global cuisine. Best-sellers are tasty trios: a combination of springbok with red wine, kudu with rosemary, and impala with balsamic; and for dessert, three different, equally tempting white and dark chocolate delights. (See also A-Z section.)

Seasons at Diemersfontein Wine and Country Estate see under Wellington

Sommelier Restaurant at Santé Winelands Simonsvlei Road, Simondium, Paarl-Franschhoek Valley ▪ Contemporary cuisine ▪ Open daily for breakfast 06:00-11:00, lunch 12:30-15:00 and dinner 19:00 till late ▪ Booking advised ▪ Wheelchair-friendly ▪ Major credit cards accepted ▪ Corkage R25 ▪ Owner Fidentia Holdings Pty Ltd ▪ info@santewellness.co.za ▪ www.santewellness.co.za ▪ **T** 021·875·8100 ▪ F 021·875·8111

Fine dining and gourmet fare for epicures in a spectacular winelands' setting. The seasonal menu changes daily, and includes specialities like *crepinet* of lamb loin served with *brunoise* roasted root vegetables, red wine jus and five-spice angel hair. Winner Diners Club Winelist Award of Excellence 2005. Santé Winelands Hotel & Wellness Centre was rated as one of the top three spas in the world by *Conde Nast Traveller* UK, Jan 2006. (See also Stay-over section.)

The Goatshed Fairview Farm, Suid-Agter Paarl Road, Suider Paarl ▪ Country Mediterranean cuisine ▪ Open daily from 09:00-17:00 (kitchen closes 16:30) ▪ Closed Good Friday, 25 Dec & 1 Jan ▪ Booking advised ▪ Wheelchair-friendly ▪ Major credit cards accepted ▪ No BYO ▪ Owner Charles Back ▪ info@fairview.co.za ▪ www.fairview.co.za ▪ **T** 021·863·3609 ▪ F 021·863·2591

Fairview's welcoming and relaxed farm eatery offers gourmet cheese platters, meat platters, home-made preserves and seasonal specials, as well as a wide and moreish range of breads, baked daily on the premises. With over 40 wines available, as well as excellent coffees (enjoy the aroma), the eclectic, informal ambience and open-air terrace offer a wonderful way to while away Cape afternoons. (See also A-Z section.)

Plettenberg Bay

Sand at The Plettenberg The Plettenberg Hotel, 40 Church Street, Plettenberg Bay ▪ Modern South African cuisine with strong international flavours ▪ Open daily 07:00-21:30 ▪ Booking advised ▪ Children 12+ welcome ▪ Major credit cards accepted ▪ Corkage R50 ▪ Owner Liz McGrath ▪ reservations@collectionmcgrath.com ▪ www.collectionmcgrath.com ▪ **T** 044·533·2030 ▪ F 044·533·2074

A happy marriage of fresh local produce with Platinum award-winning winelist, served in a sophisticated seafront setting. Décor is a subtle blend of cool creams and off-white tones, and a glassed-in terrace enhances magnificent views of ocean and mountains. Culinary temptations include Bitou Bay seafood bisque with a salad of prawns, mussels and calamari, fragrant Karoo lamb and signature vanilla crème brûlée. (See also Stay-over section.)

Robertson

Fraai Uitzicht 1798 Klaas Voogds East, on Route 62 between Robertson & Montagu ■ Sophisticated country cuisine ■ Open Mon-Sun from 08:30 ■ Closed Jun-Aug, 1 Jan ■ Booking advised ■ Children welcome ■ Wheelchair-friendly ■ Major credit cards accepted ■ No BYO ■ Owner Karl Papesch ■ info@fraaiuitzicht.com ■ www.fraaiuitzicht.com ■ **T 023·626·6156** ■ F 023·626·5265

Enjoy a real vineyard experience on a historic wine and guest farm: the cellar's a step up from the award-winning restaurant. Hosts are attentive and the ambiance friendly; sophisticated country cuisine, prepared with personal attention, makes the most of fresh produce from the vegetable and herb garden. Menus are complemented by a selection of the best wines from the Robertson 'valley of wine and roses'. (See also Stay-over & A-Z sections.)

Somerset West & Environs

96 Winery Road Restaurant Zandberg Farm, Winery Road, off the R44 between Somerset West & Stellenbosch ■ Country, global cuisine ■ Lunch daily from 12:00, dinner Mon-Sat from 19:00 ■ Closed Sun eve ■ Booking advised ■ Children welcome ■ Wheelchair-friendly ■ Major credit cards accepted ■ Corkage R30 ■ Owners Ken Forrester, Martin Meinert, Allan Forrester & Natasha Wray ■ wineryrd@mweb.co.za ■ www.96wineryroad.co.za ■ **T (021) 842·2020** ■ F 021·842·2050

Warm, relaxing venue — unofficial HQ for local and international wine luminaries — celebrating over a decade of fresh, colourful, uncomplicated and generous food. (Speciality is well-hung beef, aged on the premises). Menus change frequently according to the whim and creativity of chef Craig Backhouse and Mother Nature. The extensive award-winning winelist is the first SA list to win a Grand Award in *Wine Spectator*.

Stanford

Red Indigo see under Gansbaai

Stellenbosch & Environs

@ Jakarta Rijsttafel Restaurant La Provence Road, Stellenbosch (behind Polkadraai farm stall on the M12 Stellenbosch-Kuils River) ■ Asian, authentic Indonesian food & some Dutch snacks ■ Open daily for breakfast, lunch & dinner Mon-Sat till late ■ Closed Sun dinner, New Year's day ■ Booking advised ■ Children welcome ■ Wheelchair-friendly ■ Major credit cards accepted ■ Corkage R15 ■ Owner Duncan Fransz (a Dutchman born in Djakarta) ■ sunhillf@iafrica.com ■ www.M12Djakarta.co.za ■ **T 021·881·3243** ■ F 021·881·3299

The only restaurant in SA serving authentic Rijsttafel — with local wines at pocket-friendly prices. Seating in a rose garden setting and oak-shaded terrace, or on an oriental-style sundeck, also suitable for functions. Inside, dine warmed by a log fire amid antiques and art — everything you see is for sale, except the staff! Courtesy transport (book in advance) to/from guest houses/hotels in Stellenbosch) in London taxi or Rolls Royce. (See also Stay-over section for Sunhill Farm Self-contained Cottages.)

De Oewer Aan de Wagen Road (next to De Volkskombuis), Stellenbosch ■ Global contemporary cuisine ■ Lunch 7 days a week 12:00-15:00, dinner Mon-Sat 18:30-22:00 & Sun (Nov-Mar) ■ Closed Good Friday, Jun-Aug ■ Booking advised ■ Children welcome ■ Wheelchair-friendly ■ Major credit cards accepted ■ Corkage R20 ■ Owners Dawid & Christelle Kriel ■ mail@volkskombuis.co.za ■ www.deoewer.co.za ■ **T 021·886·5431** ■ F 021·883·3413

With a delightfully relaxed setting on the banks of the Eerste River under venerable oaks, this friendly restaurant is well-known for alfresco-style lunches and dinners. An appetising array of Mediterranean dishes and extensive winelist will ensure your enjoyment of the occasion. Ideal for functions.

De Volkskombuis Aan de Wagen Road, Stellenbosch ■ SA cuisine ■ Lunch 7 days a week 12:00-15:00, dinner Mon-Sat 18:30-22:00 & Sun (Nov-Mar) ■ Closed Good Friday ■ Booking advised ■ Children welcome ■ Wheelchair-friendly ■ Major credit cards accepted ■

Corkage R20 ▪ Owners Dawid & Christelle Kriel ▪ mail@volkskombuis.co.za ▪ www. volkskombuis.co.za ▪ **T** 021·887·2121 ▪ F 021·883·3413

A specialist in traditional fare for over a quarter-century, serving favourites like baked Karoo lamb rib, honey-roast duck, oxtail and a 'Cape country sampler'. Dawid and Christelle Kriel took over the family business in 2001, and their passion for food, wine, people and personal touch, have enhanced the restaurant's reputation for meals in good company, seven days a week. Diners Club '02 Platinum award-winning winelist.

Fishmonger Stellenbosch NPK Building, cnr Ryneveld & Plein Streets, Stellenbosch ▪ Mediterranean – seafood ▪ Mon-Sat 12:00–22:00, Sun & public holidays 12:00–21:00 ▪ Closed Christmas, New Year & Good Friday ▪ Booking advised ▪ Children welcome ▪ Wheelchair-friendly ▪ Major credit cards accepted ▪ Corkage R10 (if on winelist or more than 1 bottle per 2 pax) ▪ Owners André Viljoen, Craig Seaman & Nico Strydom ▪ fish-monger@adept.co.za ▪ **T** 021·887·7835 ▪ F 021·887·7834

A bustling Mediterranean-style alfresco taverna in the heart of the winelands, where patrons enjoy the best and freshest linefish and seafood (sushi is an added attraction), with service to match. The winelist showcases local producers and changes seasonally. Good food, good service and good wine are the watchwords here.

Flavours Restaurant Devon Valley Hotel, Devon Valley Road, Stellenbosch ▪ Contemporary Cape cuisine ▪ Open daily for breakfast 07:00–11:00, lunch & dinner 11:00–22:00 ▪ Booking advised ▪ Children welcome ▪ Wheelchair-friendly ▪ Major credit cards accepted ▪ Corkage R20 ▪ Owner LGI Hotels & Vineyards ▪ info@devonvalleyhotel.com ▪ www. devonvalleyhotel.com ▪ **T** 021·865·2012 ▪ F 021·865·2610

Authentic, contemporary Cape cuisine, with an award-winning winelist to complement a pleasurable, relaxed dining experience in a vineyard setting. Focus is on bold flavours, classic, uncomplicated dishes and fresh, clean tastes. Leisurely summer light lunches on the terrace (admire the view) and cosy fireside dinners in winter are firm local favourites. (See also Stay-over section & A-Z for SylvanVale.)

Herenhuis Restaurant Zorgvliet Wine Estate, Banhoek Valley, Helshoogte Pass, Stellenbosch ▪ Fine dining cuisine ▪ Open daily for lunch, dinner Mon-Sat ▪ Booking advised ▪ Children welcome ▪ Wheelchair-friendly ▪ Major credit cards accepted ▪ No BYO ▪ Owners Mac & Marietjie van der Merwe ▪ herenhuis@zorgvliet.com ▪ www.zorgvliet. com ▪ **T** 021·885·2580 ▪ F 021·885·2581

Relive the nostalgia of yesteryear in the renovated manor house, dating back to 1692 and relishing a new lease of life as a popular restaurant. Savour traditional Cape cooking with a surprisingly modern twist, while enjoying the elegant surroundings and award-winning Zorgvliet wines. (See also Stay-over & A-Z sections.)

Joostenberg Bistro Klein Joostenberg Farm, R304, Muldersvlei ▪ French bistro ▪ Open Tue-Sun 08:00–17:00 ▪ Closed Mon ▪ Booking advised ▪ Children welcome ▪ Wheelchair-friendly ▪ Major credit cards accepted ▪ Corkage R15 ▪ Owners Susan Dehosse, Christophe Dehosse & Philip Myburgh ▪ bistro@joostenberg.co.za ▪ **T** 021·884·4208 ▪ F 021·884·4135

Friendly family-run bistro offering traditional French cooking – with fresh bread and filled omelettes to start your day. Joostenberg wines and pork from the farm are showcased (try braised cheeks with mashed potatoes and carrot puree). Enquire about book-ahead wine and food matching lunches, available to parties over four. Ambience is relaxed, with a cosy fire in winter, and shady stoep in summer. Families welcomed. (See also A-Z section.)

Knorhoek Lapa Restaurant Knorhoek Farm, off R44 (Klapmuts to Stellenbosch Road), Stellenbosch ▪ South African fusion ▪ Open Tue-Sun for lunch 12:00–15:00, functions 08:30-late ▪ Closed Mon, Jun, Jul & Aug (only functions) ▪ Booking advised ▪ Children welcome ▪ Wheelchair-friendly ▪ Major credit cards accepted ▪ No BYO ▪ Owner Van Niekerk Trust ▪ anita.prop@yebo.co.za ▪ www.knorhoek.co.za ▪ **T/F** 021·865·2958

Be part of nature in summer, and snuggle up to a log fire in winter, at one of Stellenbosch's most beautiful, tranquil and child-friendly settings for lunch, private functions and wedding receptions. The rustic thatch-roofed restaurant, framed by sweeping lawns, nestles in the bend of a mountain stream. Cuisine is traditional Cape, with aromatic Karoo lamb from a spitbraai, complemented by Knorhoek Wines. (See also Stay-over & A-Z sections.)

Morgenhof Restaurant Klapmuts Road, Stellenbosch ■ A la carte, country cuisine ■ Open Mon-Sun 12:00-14:30 ■ Closed Good Friday, Christmas & New Year's days ■ Booking advised ■ Children welcome ■ Wheelchair-friendly ■ Major credit cards accepted ■ No BYO ■ Owner Anne Cointreau ■ info@morgenhof.com ■ www.morgenhof.com ■ **T 021·889·2024** ■ F 021·889·5266

Enjoy light lunches or hearty meals with Morgenhof's award-winning wines, by the bottle or glass — or in dishes: Norwegian salmon is poached in white wine; chocolate marquise drizzled with port wine reduction. Eat al fresco under a centuries-old oak in summer; in winter, relish comfort food in the fire-warmed Gazebo restaurant, or soak up winter sun under a canopy of vines. Breakfast by reservation only. (See also A-Z section.)

Olivello Restaurant Marianne Wine Estate, Valley Road, off R44, between Klapmuts & Stellenbosch ■ Cape Mediterranean ■ Seasonal opening times, generally closed Mon & Tue ■ Booking advised ■ Children welcome ■ Wheelchair-friendly ■ German, Italian & French spoken ■ Visa & MasterCard accepted ■ Corkage R35 ■ Owners Laurille Krug & Lynne Aberdeen ■ restaurant@olivello.co.za ■ www.olivello.co.za ■ **T 021·875·5443** ■ F 021·875·5483

Ex Café Paradiso partners Laurille and Lynne put their passion to work in picturesque surroundings, ensuring that friendly service, delicious food and a lake setting provide a feast for the senses. Sunday speciality is a Mediterranean Table, presented buffet-style in the kitchen. Relax, play boules, row the boat or just laze on the lawns. Ideal for weddings, birthdays or corporate events. (See also Stay-over & A-Z sections.)

Terroir Restaurant Kleine Zalze Wine Farm, Techno Park turn-off, Strand Road (R44), Stellenbosch ■ Classic French Provençal restaurant ■ Open for lunch Tue-Sun from 12:30, dinner Tue-Sat from 19:00 ■ Closed Mon ■ Booking advised ■ Children welcome ■ Wheelchair-friendly ■ Major credit cards accepted ■ No BYO ■ Owners Michael Broughton & Nic van Wyk ■ terroir@kleinezalze.co.za ■ www.terroir.co.za ■ **T 021·880·8167** ■ F 021·880·0862

Bistro-style destination that's attracting awards and wooing foodies with a constantly changing, flavourful menu of Provençal-inspired classics — and a wood-fired oven for an authentic touch. Chefs Michael Broughton and Nic van Wyk conjure up winners like roasted pork belly with shallot puree, confit duck pancakes with fresh fig jam or seafood risotto with pea and truffle puree, each dish complemented by Kleine Zalze wines.

Zevenwacht Restaurant Zevenwacht Wine Farm, Langverwacht Road, Kuils River ■ Global cuisine ■ Open 365 days per year for breakfast, lunch & dinner ■ Booking advised ■ Children welcome ■ Wheelchair-friendly ■ Major credit cards accepted ■ No BYO ■ Owner Manie Wolmarans ■ restaurant@zevenwacht.co.za ■ www.zevenwacht.co.za ■ **T 021·903·5123** ■ F 021·903·5257

Surrounded by lush gardens overlooking a lake, the restaurant in the Cape Dutch manor house offers seasonal menus that blend traditional South African and global cuisines. Specialties like ostrich fillet and red currant sauce, platters of Zevenwacht cheeses and the signature Zevenwacht Merlot, Tin Mine and orange sorbet trio, provide a mouthwatering experience. Popular estate picnic baskets can be enjoyed in the gardens. (See also Stay-over & A-Z sections.)

Wellington

Carolinahoeve Italian Restaurant Carolinahoeve Boutique Wine Estate, Malanstasie Road 172 (turnoff Malanstasie Road on R44 to Hermon), Wellington ■ Italian Country cuisine ■ Open daily 11:00-late (kitchen closes at 21:30) ■ Booking advised ■ Debit-, Visa & Mastercard accepted ■ Corkage R20 ■ Owners Lee-Ann Millin & Carolina Dagevos-Millin ■ info@carolinahoeve.com ■ www.carolinahoeve.com ■ **T 021·873·0741** ■ F 021·873·0742

According to an Italian born and raised in Naples, the pizzas are 'the best in the world'. This authentic Italian restaurant (with wood-fired oven) offers à la carte country cuisine — from a range of tasty, traditional pasta dishes to salads and home-made desserts — in a relaxing rural setting. Fresh ingredients are paramount, including milk and cream from the farm's own cows. (See also A-Z section.)

Seasons at Diemersfontein Wine and Country Estate Jan van Riebeeck Drive (R301), Wellington ▪ Country cuisine ▪ Open daily 8:00–late (if no bookings received by 19:00 the restaurant closes) ▪ Booking advised ▪ Children welcome ▪ Wheelchair-friendly ▪ Major credit cards accepted ▪ Corkage R20 ▪ Owners David & Sue Sonnenberg ▪ restaurant@diemersfontein.co.za; hospitality@diemersfontein.co.za ▪ www.diemersfontein.co.za ▪ **T 021·864·5050** ▪ F 021·864·2095

Overlooking pastures and farm dam, this welcoming restaurant offers à la carte country cuisine, lightened by a sophisticated touch. The appropriately seasonal menu is strong in specials, highlighting fresh, locally-sourced ingredients and devised with Diemersfontein wine in mind. (Enquire about wine and food matching events.) 'Side attractions' for visitors wanting a snack, and gourmet picnics, complete with rug and basket, also available. (See also Stay-over & A-Z sections.)

■ Stay-overs in the winelands and Cape Town

Featured below are some guest lodges, hotels, country inns, B&Bs and self-catering cottages in the winelands, many of them on wine farms (look for the 🛏 symbol beside the individual entries in the A-Z section of this guide). Unless stated to the contrary, all speak English and Afrikaans, have parking and gardens/terraces. Rates are for standard double rooms unless otherwise specified – for example per person (pp) or breakfast included (B&B). Tourism Grading Council of South Africa (TGCSA) ratings where provided. The stay-overs featured here supplied information on their attractions, which was edited by Jos Baker.

Index of stay-overs
Listed alphabetically, with region.

Mont Rochelle Hotel . . . . Franschhoek
Natte Valleij Farm . . . . . . Stellenbosch
Oak Tree Lodge . . . . Paarl
Ons Genot Country Lodge . Stellenbosch
Pat Busch Private Nature
   Reserve. . . . . Robertson
Pezula Resort Hotel & Spa . Knysna
Rosenhof Country House . Oudtshoorn
Sanddrif Holiday Resort. . Clanwilliam
Santé Winelands Hotel &
   Wellness Centre . . . . . . Paarl
Schulphoek Seafront
   Guesthouse. . . . . Hermanus
Sonop Guesthouse . . . . . Paarl
Steenberg Hotel . . . . Constantia
Sunhill Farm Self-
   contained Cottages. . . . Stellenbosch
The Cellars-Hohenort
   Hotel . . . . Constantia
The Marine Hotel. . . . . . . Hermanus

The Mews Flat at La
   Providence . . . . Franschhoek
The Old Wine House
   Guest Cottage. . . . . Wellington
The Plettenberg Hotel . . . Plettenberg Bay
The Retreat at
   Groenfontein . . . . Calitzdorp
The Westridge. . . . . Constantia
Tierhoek Cottages . . . . . . Robertson
Villa Exner – Exclusive
   Country Manor . . . . Elgin Valley
WB Winery Guest Villa . . Somerset West
Whale Cottage Camps
   Bay   . . . . Cape Town
Whale Cottage
   Franschhoek   . . Franschhoek
Whale Cottage Hermanus
   . . . . Hermanus
Zevenwacht Country Inn . Stellenbosch
Zorgvliet Suites & Spa . . . Stellenbosch

Calitzdorp

Calitzdorp Country House Calitz Street, Calitzdorp ▪ TGCSA 5-star guest house ▪ Single from R750 B&B, double from R600 pp sharing B&B ▪ Visa & MasterCard accepted ▪ Dinner ▪ Pool ▪ TV ▪ Air-conditioning ▪ Ceiling fans ▪ Under-floor heating ▪ Owners Lyn & Allan Fabig ▪ calchouse@mweb.co.za ▪ www.cchouse.co.za ▪ **T 044·213·3760** ▪ Mobile 082·339·1554

   In a spectacular setting, with views across a fertile valley of vineyards and orchards to the majestic Swartberg mountains, Calitzdorp Country House lies at the heart of the Klein Karoo's world-class tourist attractions. Furnished with antiques, Persian rugs and original art, the House captures the style of a gentleman's country residence – down to the well-stocked wine cellar. Escape with that special someone.

The Retreat at Groenfontein Groenfontein Farm, District Calitzdorp ▪ TGCSA 4-star guest house ▪ R520–R690 pp sharing DB&B, single & winter rates on request ▪ Visa & MasterCard accepted ▪ Pool ▪ French, German, Italian & Swedish spoken ▪ Owners Grant & Marie Burton ▪ groenfon@iafrica.com ▪ www.groenfontein.com ▪ **T/F 044·213·3880**

   A consistent award-winner (AA Accommodation Award 03, 04 & 05, Hall of Fame 2006), this three- and four-star graded Victorian farmhouse offers both standard and luxury rooms. The inviting lounge and dining room overlook sweeping lawns and the majestic Swartberg, and you'll be pampered with hearty breakfasts and tasty dinners. Enjoy leisurely walks, challenging trails, or simply relax at the pool and let the silence soak into your soul.

Cape Town

Andros Boutique Hotel cnr Newlands & Phyllis Roads, Claremont, Cape Town ▪ TGCSA 5-star ▪ May-Sep: single R1 050 B&B, double/twin R1 590 per room B&B, suite R1 900 per suite B&B; Oct – Apr: single R1 400 B&B, double/twin R2 100 per room B&B, suite R2 900 per suite B&B ▪ Major credit cards accepted ▪ Dine at the Andros restaurant ▪ Children 12+ welcome ▪ Facilities for conferences, exclusive corporate and private functions & elegant weddings ▪ Pool ▪ TV ▪ Air-conditioning ▪ Gym ▪ Sauna ▪ Beauty clinic ▪ Owners The Barrow Family ▪ info@andros.co.za ▪ www.andros.co.za ▪ **T 021·797·9777** ▪ F 021·797·0300

   This gracious Herbert Baker-designed homestead in leafy Claremont, one of Cape Town's beautiful southern suburbs, has been lovingly restored and updated, preserving its old-world charm. Gourmet breakfasts are served on the terrace overlooking vast gardens and pool; candle-lit dinners on the patio or in the intimate restaurant, Dine. Less than 10 minutes from the city and Waterfront; 20 minutes from the airport. (See also Eat-out section.)

Cape Grace West Quay Road, V&A Waterfront, Cape Town ▪ TGCSA & SATOUR 5-star luxury hotel ▪ Single from R3 550–R14 510 B&B, double from R3 690–R14 510 per room B&B ▪ Major credit cards accepted ▪ onewaterfront Restaurant ▪ Bascule Whisky Bar and Wine Cellar ▪ Café Bascule ▪ Pool ▪ Satellite TV ▪ Air-conditioning ▪ Spa ▪ German, French,

Swedish, Xhosa, Spanish, Italian, Czech, Danish, Russian, Norwegian, Slovak, Portuguese, Greek, Maltese spoken ▪ Owner Meikles Africa ▪ info@capegrace.com ▪ www.capegrace.com ▪ **T** 021·410·7100 ▪ F 021·419·7622

Luxury hotel with a cluster of international awards and award-winning restaurant. A series of comfortable spaces, all guest rooms and suites feature exquisite furniture, luxurious fabric and intriguing detail, providing an immediate sense of place. Double-glazed French doors open onto beautiful views of the International yacht marina, Table Mountain and Waterfront Harbour. 122 rooms. (See also Eat-out section.)

Dunkley House   3B Gordon Street, Gardens, Cape Town ▪ TGCSA 4-star guest house ▪ Single from R500–R650 B&B, double from R700–R900 per room B&B ▪ Visa, MasterCard & Diners Club accepted ▪ Pool ▪ TV ▪ Air-conditioning ▪ German & French spoken ▪ Owner Sharon Scudamore ▪ reservations@dunkleyhouse.com ▪ www.dunkleyhouse.com ▪ **T 021·462·7650** ▪ F 021·462·7649

Retreat to an in-city oasis of luxury, friendly service and welcoming ambience. Sip sundowners at the courtyard pool and chill out under the shade of banana palms. Set in a turn-of-the-century Dutch-colonial house in a private, tropical garden, Dunkley House offers spacious, individually decorated en-suite rooms with all creature comforts. Sumptuous breakfasts with homemade breads and muffins (there's a full-time chef) add to your pleasure.

Metropole Hotel   38 Long Street, Cape Town ▪ SATOUR 4-star ▪ High season: double from R1 290 B&B, single from R890 B&B ▪ Major credit cards accepted ▪ Veranda Restaurant ▪ Conference facilities ▪ TV ▪ Air-conditioning ▪ German & French spoken ▪ Owners Steve van der Merwe & Jens Merbt ▪ reservations@metropolehotel.co.za ▪ www.metropolehotel.co.za ▪ **T 021·424·7247** ▪ F 021·424·7248

New meets old in Cape Town's hottest luxury boutique hotel. Described as 'the coolest kid on the block', the historic venue in the heart of the city has been revamped as a hip hotel with modern appeal. The renovated 29-room building is stylish, luxurious and fun. Includes the cosmopolitan Veranda Restaurant (see Eat-out section), sexy M-Bar & Lounge, M Café and a small boardroom.

Steenberg Hotel   see under Constantia

Whale Cottage Camps Bay   57 Camps Bay Drive, Camps Bay ▪ TGCSA 4-star guest house ▪ Out of season: R300 pp B&B, in season: R500–R640 pp B&B ▪ Major credit cards accepted ▪ Pool ▪ TV ▪ Air-conditioning ▪ German spoken ▪ Owner Chris von Ulmenstein ▪ campsbay@whalecottage.com ▪ www.whalecottage.com ▪ **T 021·438·3840** ▪ F 021·438·4388

Welcome to a whale of a stay at Whale Cottage Camps Bay, a beach villa with magnificent views over the Atlantic ocean. Just 500 meters from Camps Bay beach and 25 restaurants (a safe walk) and a 10 minute drive from Table Mountain cableway. Secure parking, sparkling pool and free wireless internet. Proudly South African.

Clanwilliam

Bushmans Kloof Wilderness Reserve and Retreat   Cederberg Mountains near Clanwilliam, West Coast, Western Cape ▪ TGCSA 5-star ▪ Luxury rooms: single from R2 050–R3 000, double from R1 500–R2 100 pp sharing; Deluxe rooms: single from R2 550–R3 850, double from R1 750–R2 600 pp sharing; Suites: single from R3 310–R5 100, double from R2 250–R3 500 pp sharing — Rates include all meals, laundry & valet, early morning guided rock art excursion, evening drive with sundowner drinks & snacks ▪ Major credit cards accepted ▪ Restaurant — various venues ▪ Conference facilities ▪ Spa & fitness centre ▪ Library ▪ 4 Pools ▪ TV in lounge area ▪ Air-conditioning ▪ Ceiling fans ▪ Owner Tollman family ▪ info@bushmanskloof.co.za ▪ www.bushmanskloof.co.za ▪ **T 021·685·2598** ▪ F 021·685·5210

Ultimate pampering. This award-winning 5-star retreat, 270km from Cape Town, is a sanctuary for indigenous plants and animals, with 130 rock art sites providing a unique wilderness experience. Sixteen rooms and suites, special conference packages and facilities. Exhilarating outdoor activities include nature drives, garden tours, hiking, mountain biking, canoeing and fly-fishing. Award-winning cuisine and soothing spa treatments complete the Relais & Châteaux experience.

Sanddrif Holiday Resort Sanddrif, Dwarsrivier Farm, off the N7, Cederberg, Clanwilliam ▪ Self-catering ▪ R400 per cottage – up to four people ▪ Visa & MasterCard accepted ▪ Mountain pool ▪ Owner Gebrs Nieuwoudt ▪ sanddrif@cederbergwine.com ▪ www.cederbergwine.com ▪ **T 027·482·2825** ▪ F 027·482·1188

Paradise for star gazers, mountain bikers, 4X4 enthusiasts, mountain climbers, hikers and bird watchers, this get-away-from-it-all retreat offers 14 well equipped self-catering houses. Enjoy the pleasures nature can offer: swim in clear mountain pools, discover rock formations, watch black eagles in flight and admire breathtaking sunsets. For more 'civilized' moments, there are wine tastings and cellar tours. (See also A-Z section for Cederberg Private Cellar.)

Citrusdal
Sanddrif Holiday Resort see under Clanwilliam

Constantia
Constantia Uitsig Hotel and Spa Constantia Uitsig, Spaanschemat River Road, Constantia ▪ SATOUR 5-star ▪ Single from R1 100–R1 600 B&B, double from R1 650–R2 400 per room B&B ▪ Major credit cards accepted ▪ Three Restaurants ▪ Pool ▪ TV ▪ Air-conditioning ▪ Ceiling fans ▪ reservations@uitsig.co.za ▪ www.uitsig.co.za ▪ **T 021·794·6500** ▪ F 021·794·7605

Relax among vineyards a mere 20 minutes from Cape Town's Waterfront. This peaceful hotel, set on a private wine estate on the Constantia Wine Route, has 16 garden rooms, each with sweeping views of the Constantia Valley. (A spa is due for completion in early 2007). La Colombe, one of three world-renowned restaurants on the property, was recently voted 28th Best Restaurant in the World. (See also Eat-out section for Constantia Uitsig Restaurant, La Colombe & The River Café, & A-Z section.)

Hampshire House 10 Willow Road, Constantia ▪ TGCSA 4-star guest house ▪ Single from R395–R595 B&B, double from R295–R395 pp sharing B&B ▪ Major credit cards accepted ▪ Pool ▪ TV ▪ Air-conditioning ▪ Ceiling fans ▪ Owners Ricky & Carole Chapman ▪ stay@hampshirehouse.co.za ▪ www.hampshirehouse.co.za ▪ **T 021·794·6288** ▪ F 021·794·2934

The ideal base for exploring the Cape Peninsula. Set in the Costantia wine valley, this 4-star guesthouse (runner up – highly commended – in the AA Accommodation Awards 'Guest House of the Year' 2006) offers easy motorway access to Table Mountain, the Waterfront, winelands, beaches and local restaurants. Five individually decorated en-suite bedrooms. English and continental buffet breakfasts; swimming pool and secure off-street parking.

Steenberg Hotel Steenberg Estate, cnr Steenberg & Tokai Road, Tokai ▪ TGCSA 5-star ▪ Rates on request ▪ Major credit cards accepted ▪ Catharina's Restaurant ▪ Conference facilities ▪ Spa ▪ 2 Pools ▪ Satellite TV ▪ Air-conditioning ▪ German & French spoken ▪ Owner Graham Joshua Beck ▪ info@steenberghotel.com ▪ www.steenberghotel.com ▪ **T 021·713·2222** ▪ F 021·713·2251

Experience Cape hospitality in a national monument dating back to 1682, sensitively restored and converted into a luxury hotel with top-rated restaurant. Past elegance blends seamlessly with contemporary comforts – including a chic pool bar and luxurious spa. Sheltered by the Steenberg mountains and set in manicured vineyards with award-winning winery, and 18-hole championship golf course, the hotel is an ideal base for exploring the Cape. AA Accommodation Awards – Gold – Superieur. (See also Eat-out & A-Z sections.)

The Cellars-Hohenort Hotel 93 Brommersvlei Road, Constantia ▪ SATOUR 5-star Relais & Chateaux Boutique Hotel ▪ Low season: single R1 200 per room B&B, double R1 600 per room B&B; high season: single R1 800 per room B&B, double R3 000 per room B&B ▪ Major credit cards accepted ▪ The Cape Malay Restaurant, The Greenhouse Restaurant & The Martini ▪ Conference facilities ▪ 3 Pools (one heated) ▪ Tennis court ▪ Golf green ▪ Gym ▪ Spa ▪ Hair salon ▪ TV ▪ Air-conditioning ▪ Creole, French, Italian, German, Swahili,

Xhosa & Zulu spoken ▪ Owner Liz McGrath ▪ reservations@collectionmcgrath.com ▪ www.collectionmcgrath.com ▪ **T 021·794·2137** ▪ F 021·794·2149

A tranquil haven in the heart of the Constantia valley, The Cellars-Hohenort marries two great traditions: the magnificent restoration of the 18th century Klaasenbosch wine cellars and the splendid Hohenort manor house. Combining understated elegance with charm, the 5-star hotel boasts 53 luxury rooms and suites, with breathtaking views across nine acres of world-renowned gardens and vineyard. A member of the International Relais & Chateaux Association. (See also Eat-out section.)

The Westridge   5 Westridge Close, Constantia Hill ▪ Single R400, double R600 per room — luxurious self-catering ▪ Major credit cards accepted ▪ Owner Peter Weetman ▪ gerhard@societi.co.za ▪ www.capestay.co.za/thewestridge ▪ **T 072·392·9556** ▪ F 086·650·9942

Escape everyday stress, relax in total privacy and enjoy the beauty of the Cape. These stylish, architecturally designed and fully serviced en-suite rooms have no TV or telephones to disturb your peace. All feature white 100% cotton linen and towels, underfloor heated bathrooms, equipped kitchenette, and open onto balconies looking over bridle paths into Tokai forest, against the backdrop of Steenberg mountains.

Whale Cottage Camps Bay   see under Cape Town

Darling

Darling Lodge   22 Pastorie Street, Darling ▪ TGCSA 4-star B&B ▪ Single from R360–R400 B&B, double from R270–R320 pp B&B ▪ Visa & MasterCard accepted ▪ Wedding/private function/conference facilities ▪ Pool ▪ TV ▪ Ceiling fans ▪ Dutch, French & German spoken ▪ Owner Mathe Hettasch ▪ info@darlinglodge.co.za ▪ www.darlinglodge.co.za ▪ **T 022·492·3062** ▪ F 022·492·3665

Stylish, beautifully restored Victorian home in the gentle Darling valley offers a harmonious blend of old and new in an environment of vineyards, pastures, wheat fields and spectacular wild flower displays. Enjoy the area's award-winning wines and olives in a delightful garden with inviting pool. Dinner by arrangement only. An hour from Cape Town and minutes from the Atlantic Ocean. Winelands, beaches, golf, whale watching nearby.

Elgin Valley

Glen Stuart Cottages   114 The Valley Road, Elgin ▪ One night rate R800 per cottage (sleeps 4 @ R200 pp), weekend rate R1 200 per cottage ▪ Self-catering, breakfast by arrangement ▪ Visa & MasterCard accepted ▪ German spoken ▪ Owner Gower family ▪ rossgowerwines@worldonline.co.za ▪ **T/F 021·844·0197**

Four newly-renovated and individually decorated cottages on a family-owned wine farm, each with two en-suite double bedrooms and large lounge/diningroom with fireplace. Well equipped kitchenettes (and Weber braais) make self-catering a pleasure; meals and picnic lunches available by prior arrangement. Magnificent views of surrounding vineyards and the neighbouring Kogelberg Biosphere from each cottage. On the Elgin wine route, centrally situated between Somerset West/Franschhoek/Hermanus. (See also A–Z for Ross Gower Wines.)

Villa Exner – Exclusive Country Manor   11 Essenhout Avenue, Klipkop, Grabouw/Elgin Valley ▪ TGCSA 5-star country house ▪ May-Sep: Single from R490 B&B, double from R350 pp sharing B&B; Oct-Apr: Single from R840 B&B, double from R600 pp sharing B&B ▪ Major credit cards accepted ▪ Restaurant ▪ Conferences ▪ Weddings ▪ Pool ▪ TV ▪ Air-conditioning ▪ German, French & Russian spoken ▪ Owner Sascha Sulliman-Exner ▪ info@villaexner.com ▪ http://www.villaexner.com ▪ **T 021·859·3596** ▪ F 021·859·7451

Relax and rejuvenate at this tranquil haven and registered birder-friendly venue, less than an hour's drive from Cape Town. The inviting main house, rich in modern pieces and personally chosen art, is set among smooth lawns and lush private gardens with mountain views. Close to the Green Mountain Eco-Route, the world's first biodiversity wine route and the protected Kogelberg Biosphere, the Cape's floral kingdom.

Franschhoek & Environs

Akademie Street Guesthouses 5 Akademie Street, Franschhoek ▪ TGCSA 5-star ▪ From R700–R1 100 B&B (low season) to R1 400–R2 200 B&B (high season) per guest-house ▪ Major credit cards accepted ▪ Pool ▪ TV ▪ Air-conditioning ▪ Ceiling fans ▪ Xhosa spoken ▪ Owners Arthur & Katherine Mc William Smith ▪ info@aka.co.za ▪ www.aka.co.za ▪ **T 021·876·3027** ▪ F 021·876·3293

A choice of three five-star guesthouses within easy, safe walking distance of the village: a two-bedroomed, restored 1860s cottage sleeping three; intimate garden suite with wide balconies and mountain views, and spacious double-storey villa (each sleeping two). All have a private garden and pool and are linked by garden paths to a Cape Dutch home where breakfasts are served on a vine-covered patio. Voted 'Best small guesthouse in South Africa' in the 2006 Automobile Association Awards.

Akkerdal Guest House Akkerdal Estate, R45, Franschhoek ▪ Single R450 per room, double R750 per room ▪ Self-catering ▪ Major credit cards accepted ▪ TV ▪ Owner Pieter Hanekom ▪ wine@akkerdal.co.za ▪ www.akkerdal.co.za ▪ **T 021·876·3481; 082·442·1746** ▪ F 021·876·3189

Accept an invitation 'to share and enjoy the perfected bottled art and poetry of Akkerdal Estate' in the picturesque Franschhoek Valley. The friendly artisan winery provides accommodation ideal for family or friends: two double rooms, shared bathroom, fully equipped Oregon pine kitchen, covered braai, bookings arranged at Franschhoek restaurants. Relax overlooking vineyards — and enjoy sundowners beside the Berg River as the sun sets behind the Simonsberg. (See also A–Z section.)

Burgundy Bourgogne Manor House & Cottages Burgundy Bourgogne Farm, Excelsior Road, Franschhoek ▪ TGCSA 4-star self-catering ▪ R570–R684 pp sharing (1–2 people), R456–R570 pp sharing (3–4 people) ▪ Visa & MasterCard accepted ▪ Pool ▪ TV ▪ Air-conditioning ▪ Ceiling fans ▪ Fly-fishing ▪ Owner Trevor Kirsten ▪ burgundybourgogne@ saol.com ▪ www.burgundybourgogne.co.za ▪ **T 021·876·4623** ▪ F 021·876·3817

Recapture the style and atmosphere of life on a 17th-century Huguenot wine farm. Set amidst olive orchards, vines and centuries-old oaks, Burgundy Bourgogne Farm offers luxury self-catering accommodation in the historic manor house and fully equipped cottages.

Franschhoek Country House & Villas Main Road, Franschhoek ▪ TGCSA 4 & 5-star country house ▪ Low season: single from R862 B&B, double from R575 pp sharing B&B; High season: Single from R1 042 B&B, double from R695 pp sharing B&B ▪ Major credit cards accepted ▪ Monneaux Restaurant ▪ Conference facilities ▪ Beauty Salon ▪ 2 Pools ▪ TV ▪ Air-conditioning ▪ Ceiling fans ▪ info@fch.co.za ▪ www.fch.co.za ▪ **T 021·876·3386** ▪ F 021·876·2744

Space combined with luxury: all 14 rooms and 12 new villa suites (each 100m^2) provide the features and facilities expected of a first-class hotel. Laze at the pools (one heated), admire the mountain vistas, visit the area's boutique wine farms, or explore the charming village founded by the French Huguenots. Conference facilities for up to 45 delegates available in the fully-equipped new elegant club room. (See also Eat-out section.)

Grande Provence – The Owner's Cottage Grande Provence Estate, Main Road, Franschhoek ▪ Rates on request ▪ Major credit cards accepted ▪ Restaurant ▪ Conference facilities ▪ Pool ▪ TV ▪ Air-conditioning ▪ Art Gallery ▪ Owner Grande Provence ▪ owners-cottage@grandeprovence.co.za ▪ www.grandeprovence.co.za ▪ **T 021·876·8600** ▪ F 021·876·8601

Relish the sumptuous comfort of contemporary luxury in the idyllic setting of a 300 year-old estate. The superbly-appointed cottage comprises five rooms, including a honeymoon suite, conservatory, lounge and jacuzzi pool area. Understated in a palette of charcoal slate and white linen, the rooms promise an indulgent experience and intimate repose. Harmony pervades, from tranquil lake to private pool lounging areas, where deck chairs invite relaxation. (See also Eat-out & A–Z sections.)

La Couronne Hotel   see Mont Rochelle Hotel

La Fontaine Guest House 21 Dirkie Uys Street, Franschhoek ▪ TGCSA 4-star guest house ▪ Single from R450–R600 B&B, double from R350–R395 pp sharing B&B ▪ Major credit cards accepted ▪ Children 12+ welcome, under 12 by arrangement ▪ Pool ▪ TV ▪ Air-conditioning ▪ Ceiling fans ▪ Owner Linquenda Guest House cc ▪ lafontaine@wam.co.za ▪ www.lafontainefranschhoek.co.za ▪ **T/F 021·876·2112**

Experience country hospitality in this gracious home in the heart of Franschhoek, within walking distance of restaurants, galleries and shops. Spectacular mountain views from 12 spacious en-suite double rooms (including three garden rooms with fireplace, TV, fridge, separate entrance and patio, and one family suite in tranquil garden). Generous buffet breakfasts served indoors or under vine-covered pergola. Wheelchair-friendly and secure off-street parking. AA Quality Assured program 'Superior' rating.

La Maison Bleue Self-catering Guest Accommodation 30 Uitkyk Street, Franschhoek ▪ From R300–R350 pp self-catering — minimum 3 nights ▪ Major credit cards accepted ▪ Pool ▪ TV ▪ Fans ▪ German & Dutch spoken ▪ Owners Richard & Rebekah Kelley ▪ Contact Rosemary Beetge ▪ rosemary_beetge@absamail.co.za ▪ www.rlmproperty.co.za ▪ **T/F 021·876·3849; 083·456·9371**

SA home of Platter Guide contributor and Master of Wine Richard Kelley, La Maison Bleue is located in a quiet area on the edge of Franschhoek village. The house has an extensive living area with three bedrooms (two doubles, one twin), well-equipped kitchen and garden with mountain views, terrace, pool and *petanque piste*. Long- or short-term lets.

La Petite Ferme Guest Suites La Petite Ferme, Pass Road, Franschhoek ▪ TGCSA 5-star B&B ▪ R650–R1 200 pp sharing B&B ▪ Major credit cards accepted ▪ Restaurant ▪ Plunge pool per suite ▪ TV ▪ Air-conditioning ▪ Ceiling fans ▪ Owners Mark & Josephine Dendy Young ▪ info@lapetiteferme.co.za ▪ www.lapetiteferme.co.za ▪ **T 021·876·3016** ▪ F 021·876·3624

Privacy, elegance and breathtaking views on a boutique wine farm. Nestled into the Middagkrans mountain high above Franschhoek, overlooking vineyards and the lush valley below. Luxury, elegance and comfort are paramount, with five individually decorated suites set among vineyards. Each free-standing suite features a private patio and plunge pool. The spacious interiors have a fireplace, TV, mini bar, air-conditioning and en-suite bathroom. (See also Eat-out & A-Z sections.)

La Petite Providence at La Providence La Providence, Middagkrans Road, Franschhoek ▪ TGCSA 5-star & AA Superior luxury cottage ▪ Two double-bedroomed cottage: R2 500 per night, two persons sharing; R4 000 per night, three or four persons — minimum two night stay ▪ Continental breakfast included ▪ Visa/MasterCard accepted ▪ Private swimming pool ▪ Use of tennis court ▪ Satellite TV ▪ Internet facilities ▪ Air-conditioning ▪ Ceiling fans ▪ Secure off-road parking ▪ Owners Andy & Ana Higgins ▪ info@laprovidence.co.za ▪ www.laprovidence.co.za ▪ **T 021·876·4790** ▪ F 021·876·4898

Enjoy 5-star graded luxury accommodation on a boutique wine farm and within walking distance of Franschhoek village with its many restaurants, shops and cafés. (See also A-Z section.)

Le Manoir de Brendel Spa, Wine & Guest Estate R45 Main Road to Franschhoek ▪ TGCSA 5-star guest house ▪ Rates on request ▪ Major credit cards accepted ▪ Restaurant ▪ Conference facilities ▪ Chapel ▪ Spa ▪ Gym ▪ Pool ▪ Tennis court ▪ TV ▪ Air-conditioning ▪ Ceiling fans ▪ German spoken ▪ Owner Christian Brendel ▪ lemanoir@brendel.co.za ▪ www.le-manoir-de-brendel.com ▪ T 021·876·4525 ▪ F 021·876·4524

Five-star accommodation, with multiple attractions. For energetic guests, there's a gym, tennis court and walking trail through the vineyards. For relaxation and rejuvenation, pamper yourself at the luxurious spa or browse at the curio shop. Then please your palate at the restaurant and enjoy the estate wines in the 'leather bar'. A chapel and conference facility are ideal venues for weddings and functions. (See also Eat-out & A-Z sections.)

Mont Rochelle Hotel Mont Rochelle Hotel & Mountain Vineyards, Dassenberg Road, Franschhoek ▪ TGCSA 5-star boutique hotel ▪ R2 250–R5 500 per room B&B ▪ Major credit cards accepted ▪ Two restaurants ▪ Boardroom ▪ Pool ▪ TV ▪ Air-conditioning ▪ Wellness centre ▪

German, Xhosa & Zulu spoken ▪ Owners Erwin Schnitzler & Miko Rwayitare ▪ res@montrochelle.co.za ▪ www.montrochelle.co.za ▪ **T 021·876·2770** ▪ F 021·876·3788

Phoenix-like, the former La Couronne Hotel has risen from the ashes of last year's devastating fire and reinvented itself as Mont Rochelle Hotel and Mountain Vineyards. The setting on a 33ha wine farm is superb. The individually decorated 16 bedrooms and six suites (two with designer splash pools) match the spectacular view. Fine or alfresco dining at two restaurants; a wellness centre, cellar tours and fine wines. (See also Eat-out & A-Z sections).

The Mews Flat at La Providence La Providence, Middagkrans Road, Franschhoek ▪ R1 500 per night, maximum two persons ▪ Continental breakfast included ▪ Visa/MasterCard accepted ▪ Use of tennis court ▪ TV ▪ Internet facilities ▪ Secure off-road parking ▪ Owners Andy & Ana Higgins ▪ info@laprovidence.co.za ▪ www.laprovidence.co.za ▪ **T 021·876·4790** ▪ F 021·876·4898

A first floor superior mews flat with enticing king-sized four poster bed, and outside terrace overlooking beautiful gardens on a boutique wine farm. Within walking distance of Franschhoek village, with its many restaurants, shops and cafés. (See also A-Z section.)

Whale Cottage Franschhoek   11 Akademie Street, Franschhoek ▪ TGCSA 4-star guest house ▪ Out of season: R250 pp B&B, in season: R400-R500 pp B&B ▪ Major credit cards accepted ▪ Pool ▪ TV ▪ Air-conditioning ▪ German spoken ▪ Owner Chris von Ulmenstein ▪ winelands@whalecottage.com ▪ www.whalecottage.com ▪ **T 021·876·3929** ▪ F 021·438·4388

Welcome to a whale of a stay at Whale Cottage Franschhoek, a country house with a delightful garden and babbling brook, located in the heart of South Africa's gourmet capital. Top restaurants Reubens and Le Quartier Français are 200 meters away. Beautiful mountain views. Sparkling swimming pool. Secure parking. Free wireless internet. Luxury honeymoon suite. Wir sprechen Deutsch. Proudly South African.

Gansbaai

Grootbos Private Nature Reserve Off the R43, between Stanford & Gansbaai ▪ TGCSA 5-star lodge ▪ Single from R2 570-R3 410 B&B, double from R1 840-R2 500 pp sharing B&B ▪ Major credit cards accepted ▪ Red Indigo Restaurant ▪ Conference facilities ▪ Pool ▪ TV ▪ Air-conditioning ▪ German spoken ▪ Owners Michael & Tertius Lutzeyer ▪ info@grootbos.co.za ▪ www.grootbos.com ▪ **T 028·384·8000** ▪ F 028·384·8100

Less than two hours from Cape Town, set in 4 000 acres of fynbos, with panoramic views of beautiful Walker Bay. Spacious luxury suites in the forest offer privacy, with wooden decks, generous bathrooms, outdoor shower, mini bar and hospitality tray. Dedicated conservationists accompany guests on daily botanical tours, 4X4 drives, horse riding and boat tours to view seals, penguins, sharks and Southern Right whales. (See also Eat-out section.)

Grabouw

Villa Exner – Exclusive Country Manor see under Elgin Valley

Hermanus

Schulphoek Seafront Guesthouse 44 Marine Drive (entrance at Piet Retief Crescent), Sandbaai, Hermanus ▪ TGCSA 5-star guesthouse ▪ Superior, luxury & standard rooms ▪ Low season: R544-R850 pp sharing B&B; high season: R731-R1 254 pp sharing B&B (includes complimentary 4-course dinner on first night); single supplement + 50% to pp rate ▪ Major credit cards accepted (excl Amex) ▪ Restaurant ▪ Body therapy (by appointment) ▪ Heated pool ▪ Owners Wehrner & Janet Gutstadt ▪ Interactive hosts Petro & Mannes van Zyl ▪ schulphoek@hermanus.co.za ▪ www.schulphoek.co.za ▪ www.schulphoek.co.za ▪ **T 028·316·2626** ▪ F 028·316·2627

Overlooking beautiful Schulphoek bay (5km from Hermanus centre), the guesthouse boasts seven spacious, individually decorated en-suite double rooms, from garden bedrooms with private entrances to a luxurious first floor room with spectacular sea views. Book 24 hours in advance for a complimentary dinner on the first night: four-course *menus du jour* in the seafront dining room are complemented by a collection of over 7 000 bottles of SA wine. (See also Eat-out section.)

The Marine Hotel Cnr Marine Drive & Main Road, Hermanus ▪ SATOUR 5-star Relais & Chateaux Boutique Hotel ▪ Low season: single R1 200 per room B&B, double R1 600 per room B&B; high season: single R1 800 per room B&B, double R3 000 per room B&B ▪ Major credit cards accepted ▪ Seafood at The Marine & The Pavilion restaurants ▪ Conference facilities ▪ Heated salt water pool & tidal pool ▪ Beauty spa ▪ TV ▪ Air-conditioning ▪ German, Xhosa & Zulu spoken ▪ Owner Liz McGrath ▪ reservations@collectionmcgrath.com ▪ www.collectionmcgrath.com ▪ **T** 028·313·1000 ▪ F 028·313·0160

Unique in its position, the Marine is perched atop the cliffs in one of the most beautiful natural landscapes in Africa. Wrapped in understated luxury and sophisticated décor, the hotel boasts 43 luxury rooms and suites. Bedroom windows overlook an ocean edged by a crescent of white sand, and during whale season offer some of the best land-based whale watching in the world. A Relais & Chateaux boutique hotel. (See also Eat-out section.)

Whale Cottage Hermanus 38 Westcliff Drive, Hermanus ▪ TGCSA 4-star guest house ▪ Out of season: R250 pp B&B, in season: R400-R500 pp B&B ▪ Major credit cards accepted ▪ Pool ▪ TV ▪ Air-conditioning ▪ German spoken ▪ Owner Chris von Ulmenstein ▪ hermanus@whalecottage.com ▪ www.whalecottage.com ▪ **T** 028·313·0929 ▪ F 021·438·4388

You'll have a whale of a stay at Whale Cottage Hermanus, a marine-themed beach house with magnificent views over Walker Bay, and of whales B & B (breaching and blowing). Hermanus is the whale capital of South Africa, and offers the best land-based whale watching in the world. Just a 1km walk to village centre and craft market. Sparkling pool. Secure parking. Proudly South African.

Knysna

Pezula Resort Hotel & Spa Lagoonview Drive, Knysna ▪ Single suites from R3 490-R5 060, double from R3 700-R5 270; Mufaro & Kufara suites from R9 495-R11 100 ▪ Major credit cards accepted ▪ Zachary's Restaurant ▪ Conference facilities ▪ Pool ▪ TV ▪ Air-conditioning ▪ Spa & Gym ▪ Jacuzzi ▪ Sauna ▪ 4 Tennis courts ▪ Golf course ▪ Owner The Pezula Group ▪ reservations@pezula.com ▪ www.pezula.com ▪ **T** 044·302·3333 ▪ F 044·302·3303

A whole new world of luxury in an elegant African style. Set on the Eastern Head of Knysna, the hotel has sweeping views of the Pezula Championship Golf Course, Indian Ocean and Knysna Lagoon. Dine at Zachary's gourmet restaurant, be pampered at the award-winning spa, hike through forests, follow nature trails, picnic on the secluded Noetzie beach, horse-ride through the fynbos … the choice is endless. (See also Eat-out section.)

Kuils River

Zevenwacht Country Inn see under Stellenbosch

Montagu

Mimosa Lodge Church Street, Montagu ▪ TGCSA 4-star guest house ▪ Single from R400-R580 B&B, double from R310-R425 pp sharing B&B ▪ Major credit cards accepted ▪ Restaurant ▪ Pool ▪ Ceiling fans ▪ German & Swiss-German spoken ▪ Owners Bernhard & Fida Hess ▪ mimosa@lando.co.za ▪ www.mimosa.co.za ▪ **T** 023·614·2351 ▪ F 023·614·2418

Perfectly placed as a stay-over between Cape Town and the Garden Route. You're ensured of a warm welcome at this Swiss-owned, carefully renovated historic house in the village. Explore the wine route, go bird-watching, hiking and climbing — or simply relax at the pool in the magnificent garden. Allow time to enjoy the lodge's creative cuisine, highly acclaimed both nationally and internationally. (See also Eat-out section.)

Oudtshoorn

Rosenhof Country House 264 Baron van Reede Street, Oudtshoorn ▪ TGCSA 5-star ▪ Low season: single R1 110 B&B, double R1 664 per room B&B; High season: single R1 413 B&B, double R2 119 per room B&B ▪ Major credit cards accepted ▪ Restaurant ▪ Conference facilities ▪ Pool ▪ TV ▪ Air-conditioning ▪ Gym ▪ Jacuzzi ▪ Beauty clinic ▪ Owners NJ Barrow & FR Barrow ▪ rosenhof@xsinet.co.za ▪ www.rosenhof.co.za ▪ **T** 044·272·2232 ▪ F 044·272·3021

The beautiful rose gardens, which gave Rosenhof its name, lead to stylishly decorated bedrooms with two totally private suites, each with its own lounge and swimming pool. The award-winning restaurant serves traditional country cuisine and an extensive wine collection is available from the private cellar. The Wellness Centre offers a fully equipped gym, jacuzzi, sauna and beauty clinic.

Paarl & Environs

Diemersfontein Wine and Country Estate Guest House   see under Wellington

Grande Roche Hotel   Plantasie Street, Paarl ■ SATOUR 5-star silver ■ Low season: R1 720 per room B&B; High season: from R2 480–R5 200 (honeymoon suite) per room B&B ■ Major credit cards accepted ■ Bosman's Restaurant & Bistro Allegro ■ Conference facilities ■ TV ■ Air-conditioning ■ 2 Pools (1 heated) ■ Sauna ■ Fitness centre ■ 2 Tennis courts (floodlit) ■ German, Swedish & French spoken ■ General Manager Garnet Basson ■ reserve@granderoche.co.za ■ www.granderoche.com ■ **T 021·863·5100** F 021·863·2220

Overlooking vineyards and rugged mountains, this award-winning, all-suite estate hotel is the ideal 5-star base from which to explore the Cape. Member of the Relais Chateaux Association, it is a byword for 'incredible attention to detail, impeccable grounds, excellent food and superb levels of luxury'. Relax at the swimming pools, go biking, play tennis, visit the fitness centre or the hotel's private masseur. (See also Eat-out section for Bosman's Restaurant – the first and only hotel-restaurant on the African continent to achieve Relais Gourmand status – & Bistro Allegro.)

Landskroon Self-catering Cottage   Landskroon   Wines,   Suid-Agter-Paarl   Road, Suider-Paarl ■ From R500–R550 per cottage – ideal for 2 adults + 2 children ■ Picnic lunches on request Oct-Apr ■ Major credit cards accepted ■ landskroon@mweb.co.za ■ www.landskroonwines.com ■ **T 021·863·1039** ■ F 021·863·2810

Fully equipped, self-catering cottage on a working wine farm in the heart of the Cape winelands. Drink in spectacular views from the southern slopes of Paarl Mountain, and enjoy your meals with the farm's own wine. Serviced daily, carport, TV and security. (See also A-Z section.)

Lindhorst Wines Vineyard Cottage   Lindhorst Wines, R45, Southern Paarl ■ R600 per cottage, plus R100 pp over 2 persons – self catering ■ Major credit cards accepted ■ Restaurant – lunch only ■ TV ■ Ceiling fans ■ Fireplace ■ Owners Belinda & Mark Lindhorst ■ belinda@lindhorstwines.com ■ www.lindhorstwines.com ■ **T 021·863·0990** ■ F 021·863·3694

Self-catering luxury cottage with 360° views, at the edge of the merlot vineyards on a working wine and fruit farm. Spacious double-volume living areas, two bedrooms and two bathrooms sleep four comfortably. Alternatively, this is an ideal cosy romantic getaway and convenient springboard for exploring the winelands. Well equipped for meals/braais at home (with Lindhorst wines) and close to fine restaurants. (See also Eat-out & A-Z sections.)

Marianne Wine Estate Guest Apartments   see under Stellenbosch

Oak Tree Lodge   32 Main Street, Paarl ■ TGCSA 3-star guest house ■ Single from R395 B&B, double from R275 pp sharing B&B ■ Major credit cards accepted ■ Conference facilities ■ Pool ■ TV ■ Air-conditioning ■ German spoken ■ Owners Yvette & Gerd Baudewig ■ info@oaktreelodge.co.za ■ www.oaktreelodge.co.za ■ **T 021·863·2631** ■ F 021·863·2607

Centrally located in the historic winelands town of Paarl. Spacious en-suite bedrooms offer TV with satellite and German satellite channels, telephone, air-conditioning, underfloor heating, bar fridge, hairdryer and tea trays. Choose between standard rooms or recently built luxury garden rooms next to the pool, with superb vineyard and mountain views. Restaurants and wine tastings within walking distance.

Santé Winelands Hotel & Wellness Centre   Simonsvlei Road, Simondium, Paarl-Franschhoek Valley ■ SATOUR 5-star ■ Single from R1 680–R2 295 B&B, double from R2 450–R3 040 per room B&B ■ Major credit cards accepted ■ 2 Restaurants ■ Conference facilities ■ Pool ■ TV ■ Air-conditioning ■ German & Netherlands spoken ■ Owner Fidentia Holdings Pty Ltd ■ info@santewellness.co.za ■ www.santewellness.co.za ■ **T 021·875·8100** ■ F 021·875·8111

One of the top three spas in the world (*Conde Nast Traveller* UK, Jan 2006) is to be found on a wine estate in the Paarl- Franschhoek valley. Luxury accommodation includes manor rooms, spa suites and vineyard villas. Two restaurants, an award-winning wellness centre designed to touch all the senses (vinotherapy is a signature treatment) and conference facilities for 140 guests complete the holistic wellness experience. (See also Eat-out section for Cadeaux SA's first organic wellness restaurant at a five star hotel and Sommelier.)

Sonop Guesthouse   Sonop Wine Farm, Windmeul, Voor-Paardeberg, Paarl ▪ TGCSA 3-star B&B ▪ From R180–R250 pp B&B ▪ Major credit cards accepted ▪ Conference facilities ▪ Pool ▪ TV ▪ Owner Jacques Germanier ▪ office@african-terroir.co.za ▪ www.african-terroir.co.za ▪ **T** 021·869·8534 ▪ F 086·510·4551

Live in harmony with nature, experiencing farm life in the comfort of a 3-star guest-house. Sonop is cuddled at the foot of the Paardeberg Mountains, offering spectacular views of the Paarl Valley. All who live and work on the farm will surround you with warm hospitality and personal attention, promising to 'awaken your senses' with delicious meals and Sonop organic wines. (See also A–Z section for African Terroir.)

Plettenberg Bay

The Plettenberg Hotel   40 Church Street, Plettenberg Bay ▪ SATOUR 5-star Relais & Chateaux Boutique Hotel ▪ Low season: single R1 200 per room B&B, double R1 600 per room B&B; high season: single R1 800 per room B&B, double R3 000 per room B&B ▪ Major credit cards accepted ▪ Sand at The Plettenberg restaurant ▪ Conference facilities ▪ Pool ▪ Beauty spa ▪ Air-conditioning ▪ French, German & Xhosa spoken ▪ Owner Liz McGrath ▪ reservations@collectionmcgrath.com ▪ www.collectionmcgrath.com ▪ **T** 044·533·2030 ▪ F 044·533·2074

Built on a rocky headland with breathtaking vistas of sea, mountains and golden sand, The Plettenberg boasts a prime position in one of the most spectacular resorts in Africa — Plettenberg Bay. Décor is stylish contemporary, the mood relaxed and the experience delight-fully idyllic and indulgent. In whale season, watch dolphins and whales from sea-facing rooms and the hotel terrace. A Relais & Chateaux boutique hotel. (See also Eat-out section.)

Robertson

Ballinderry, The Robertson Guest House   8 Le Roux Street, Robertson ▪ TGCSA 4-star ▪ Single from R330–R465 B&B low season to R330–R495 B&B high season, double from R290–R350 pp sharing B&B low season to R330–R390 pp sharing B&B high season ▪ Major credit cards accepted ▪ Pool ▪ TV ▪ Ceiling fans ▪ Flemish, French & German spoken ▪ Owners Luc & Hilde Uyttenhove ▪ info@ballinderryguesthouse.com ▪ www.ballinderry-guesthouse.com ▪ **T** 023·626·5365 ▪ F 023·626·6305

Luxury accommodation in a charming contemporary thatched villa (with 5 double rooms and one single), set in a large and tranquil tropical garden in the heart of Robertson. Hands-on Belgian owners Luc and Hilde provide personal service and champagne breakfasts: Hilde's fine cooking fuses French, Italian and South African cuisines. Near the region's best-known wineries, with a golf course only five minutes away. AA Superior Accommodation.

Fraai Uitzicht 1798   Klaas Voogds East, on Route 62 between Robertson & Montagu ▪ TGCSA 4-star guest house ▪ Single from R630 B&B, double from R420 pp sharing B&B ▪ Major credit cards accepted ▪ Restaurant ▪ Pool ▪ TV (in cottages) ▪ Game drives in Private Nature Reserve ▪ German, Xhosa & Italian spoken ▪ Owner Karl Papesch ▪ info@fraai-uitzicht.com ▪ www.fraaiuitzicht.com ▪ **T** 023·626·6156 ▪ F 023·626·5265

Unwind in this tranquil retreat, balm for the soul and the perfect place for a relaxing, comfortable and culinary few days. Nestling among the Langeberg hills, the historic wine and guest farm provides the real vineyard experience. Stylishly appointed guest cottages and suites, set amid vineyards and orchards, offer luxurious comfort with spectacular views. Attentive hosts ensure fine dining in the award-winning restaurant. (See also Eat-out & A–Z sections.)

Jan Harmsgat Country House   On the R60, between Ashton (20 kms) and Swellendam (25 kms) ▪ TGCSA 4-star guest house ▪ Low season from R375–R550 pp sharing B&B, high season from R450-R850 pp sharing B&B ▪ Major credit cards accepted ▪ Restaurant ▪ Pool ▪ Air-conditioning ▪ Ceiling fans ▪ German spoken ▪ Owners Brin & Judi Rebstein ▪ brinreb@iafrica.com ▪ www.jhghouse.com ▪ **T 023·616·3407/023·616·3311** ▪ F 023·616·3201

Experience true Cape hospitality at a genuine country house (four-star graded) set among pecan nut, almond and fruit orchards on a working farm, renowned for cheeses and preserves. Accommodation adds luxury to tradition, cuisine is delectable and the wine collection superb. Multiple award-winner for outstanding service in the development and inclusion of local communities in tourism. Awarded Fair Trade in Tourism Trademark 2005. Two hours from Cape Town between Swellendam and Ashton on the Robertson wine route.

Pat Busch Private Nature Reserve Klaas Voogds West, Robertson ▪ Single from R150-R300, double from R110-R300 pp sharing ▪ Self-catering – breakfast optional ▪ Major credit cards accepted ▪ Conference facilities ▪ Fans ▪ Hammocks ▪ Indoor fireplaces ▪ Guided game drives ▪ Mountain dam ▪ German spoken ▪ Owner Busch family ▪ patbusch@intekom.co.za ▪ www.patbusch.co.za ▪ **T 023·626·2033** ▪ F 023·626·1277

Shed city stress at a private nature reserve surrounded by mountains. Standard or exclusive self-catering cottages (all with indoor fireplaces) sleep between 45 and 50. Indoor and outdoor showers with sweeping views. Exclusive access to hiking trails, plus swimming and fishing in selected freshwater dams. Guided game drives through the Klaas Voogds Game Reserve. Cellar tours and wine tastings at Rusticus Vintage Cellar (see A-Z section).

Tierhoek Cottages Tierhoek Farm, Noree Valley, Robertson ▪ Single R200, double R400 per room – breakfast R45 pp ▪ No credit card facilities ▪ Pool ▪ TV (in 2 cottages) ▪ Ceiling fans ▪ Owners Bruce & Alison Gilson ▪ gilson@barvallei.co.za ▪ www.tierhoekcottages.co.za ▪ **T/F 023·626·1191**

Take time out on a working organic fruit and vine farm. Pepper Tree, Lucky Bean and Tierhoek House are private, self-catering cottages, elegantly furnished, well equipped, with open fireplaces, private verandas and braai areas. Use of own private pools. Enjoy spectacular scenery with walks in the mountains and an abundance of birds and wildlife. Breakfast and dinner 'baskets' on request.

Somerset West & Environs
Dankbaarheid Guest House see under Stellenbosch

WB Winery Guest Villa Weening & Barge Winery, Ridgemor Farm, R102 Kuilsrivier Road, Firgrove, Somerset West ▪ From R2 700-R3 000 per apartment B&B (fully equipped kitchen) ▪ Pool ▪ Jacuzzi ▪ TV ▪ Air-conditioning ▪ Dutch, French, Polish & German spoken ▪ Owner Veronique Weening ▪ info@weeningbarge.com ▪ **T 021·842·2255** ▪ F 021·842·3393

Prepare to be pampered by staff dedicated to your enjoyment. Surrounded by vineyards, this exclusive guest villa on a fully secure wine farm offers luxurious accommodation and a warm, personalized ambience. The villa can be rented as a whole or as two separate units, each with private entrance and carport. Jacuzzi, braai facilities and, on request, a private chef, massage and personalized shopping (excluding goods). Wine tastings offered. (See also A-Z section.)

Stanford
Grootbos Private Nature Reserve see under Gansbaai

Stellenbosch & Environs
33 Stellenbosch Vlottenburg Road (off R310), Vlottenburg, 5 km from Stellenbosch ▪ TGCSA 4-star ▪ From R350 pp sharing B&B, single from R500 B&B ▪ Major credit cards accepted ▪ Pool ▪ TV ▪ Air-conditioning ▪ Internet access ▪ Home cinema & conference centre ▪ French & German spoken ▪ Owners Simon & Louise Lavarack ▪ info@33.co.za ▪ www.33.co.za ▪ **T 021·881·3792** ▪ F 021·881·3177

Built in 1903, and immaculately restored, this homestead in the heart of the Stellenbosch winelands is known for its gracious hospitality and fine country living. Four luxury bedrooms overlooking distant mountains or a piazza-styled courtyard and fountain, two smaller bedrooms downstairs with separate showers, and a wheelchair-friendly en-suite bedroom. Relax at the pool while you plan your day of golfing, sightseeing and wine tasting. AA Quality Assured, 4-Star TGCSA.

Alluvia Wine Estate Glen Arum Road, Helshoogte Pass, Banhoek Valley, Stellenbosch ▪ TGCSA 4-star guest house, 5-star self-catering ▪ Apartments: single from R700–R1 450 B&B, double from R550–R1 300 pp sharing B&B ▪ Major credit cards accepted ▪ Restaurant ▪ Pool ▪ Spa ▪ DSTV ▪ Mountain bikes ▪ Fly-fishing ▪ Winelands & peninsula scenic flights ▪ Owners Delarey & Sandie Brugman ▪ info@alluvia.co.za ▪ www.alluvia.co.za ▪ **T 021·885·1661** ▪ F 021·885·2064

A carefree 'vineyard lifestyle' is captured in this luxury rural retreat on an active wine estate in the Stellenbosch mountains. Five ultra-premium private suites, each with spectacular views over the estate and valley below, ensure that the rest of the world goes by unnoticed. PGA Golf green, golf carts to roam the estate and picnics at the dam. Custodians of the 'Give me a chance trustfund'. (See also A-Z section.)

Auberge Rozendal Rozendal Farm, Omega Street, Stellenbosch ▪ Single R590, double R945 per room ▪ Major credit cards accepted ▪ Restaurant ▪ Conference facilities ▪ Pool ▪ German, Xhosa & Zulu spoken ▪ Owners Ammann family ▪ rozendal@mweb.co.za ▪ www.rozendal.co.za ▪ **T 021·809·2600** ▪ F 021·809·2640

Taste the tranquility of country life on a working organic farm with the convenience of close proximity to Stellenbosch. Located at the gateway of the Jonkershoek Valley, the auberge offers rooms set between the vineyards with majestic views of the surrounding mountains (walks are an added attraction). The cuisine is wholesome, healthy and always fresh, complemented by the wines from Rozendal farm and surrounds. Stellenbosch Tourism & Information Association Grading — Oak Leaf 3. (See also A-Z section.)

Batavia Boutique Hotel 12 Louw Street, Stellenbosch ▪ TGCSA 5-star ▪ Single from R525–R1 125 B&B, double from R350–R750 pp sharing B&B, ▪ Major credit cards accepted ▪ Pool ▪ TV ▪ Air-conditioning ▪ General Manager Elana van Niekerk ▪ batavia@mweb.co.za ▪ www.bataviahouse.co.za ▪ **T 021·887·2914** ▪ F 021·887·2915

Experience genuine hospitality backed by personal, first-class service and hands-on attention to detail, at this luxurious boutique hotel. (AA Accommodation Awards Winner — Best Boutique Hotel 2005 & 2006.) Offering five en-suite bedrooms and a garden cottage, Batavia is conveniently located off Dorp Street, the historic main street and centre of Stellenbosch, close to restaurants and with easy access to wine farms.

Caledon Villa Guest House 7 Neethling Street, Stellenbosch ▪ TGCSA 4-star ▪ National monument ▪ From R350 pp sharing (in season), R300 pp sharing (out of season) ▪ 15 rooms — suite, luxury, honeymoon, standard or family ▪ Major credit cards accepted ▪ Large pool ▪ Secure off-street parking ▪ Library ▪ Children by appointment ▪ German spoken ▪ Owners Johan & Ode Krige ▪ info@caledonvilla.co.za ▪ www.caledonvilla.co.za ▪ **T/ F 021·883·8912**

Discover the winelands from this splendid Art Nouveau-style Edwardian guesthouse in the historic core of Stellenbosch. Owners Johan and Ode share their passion for the arts and love of wine, grown from the Krige family's 300-year involvement in wine farming and their historical links with well-known wine estates. Within walking distance of restaurants, shops and sports facilities, with easy access to golf courses and wineries.

Clouds Villa Guesthouse Clouds Vineyards, Helshoogte Road, Stellenbosch ▪ AA Superior ▪ Double from R800–R1 200 per room B&B (out of season) to R1 200–R1 600 per room B&B (in season), single less 40% ▪ Major credit cards accepted ▪ Dinners/functions by arrangement ▪ Piazza: wedding venue for 70-100 guests, chapel seat up to 120 persons, conferences up to 70 persons ▪ Pool ▪ TV ▪ Air-conditioning ▪ Ceiling fans ▪ Owners Bernard & Petro Immelman ▪ info@cloudsguesthouse.com ▪ www.cloudsestate.com ▪ **T 021·885·1819** ▪ Mobile 082·444·5215

The new Clouds Villa on a boutique wine farm at the top of the Helshoogte Pass, 6 km from Stellenbosch, overlooks one of the most photographed views in the Cape. 'Mediterranean' in style, with architectural features borrowed from favourite places visited over the years, it offers 5 luxurious air-conditioned double suites, all with full bathroom, satellite TV, coffee/tea station and honesty bar, private entrance and covered patio. (See also A–Z section.)

Clouds Village Self-catering Cottages   Clouds Vineyards, Helshoogte Road, Stellenbosch ▪ AA Superior self-catering ▪ Double from R500-R600 per room (out of season) to R800-R1 000 per room (in season), single less 40% ▪ Major credit cards accepted ▪ Dinners/functions by arrangement ▪ Piazza: wedding venue for 70-100 guests, chapel seat up to 120 persons, conferences up to 70 persons ▪ Pool ▪ TV ▪ Air-conditioning ▪ Ceiling fans ▪ Owners Bernard & Petro Immelman ▪ info@cloudsguesthouse.com ▪ www. cloudsestate.com ▪ **T 021·885·1819** ▪ Mobile 082·444·5215

Four charming self-catering cottages, each with double bedroom, full bathroom, lounge with double sleeper couch, fully fitted kitchenette, fireplace, quality linen, air-conditioning, ceiling fan, wall heaters, satellite TV. Covered patios with BBQ facility and magnificent views. Sunbathe at the swimming pool, walk, cycle, go horse-riding or play golf — easily accessible to many golf courses. See the website for details. (See also A–Z section.)

Dankbaarheid Guest House   Eikendal Road, off R44 between Stellenbosch & Somerset West ▪ TGCSA 3-star self-catering ▪ Price per unit from R300 (studio) to R810 (luxury apartment) ▪ No credit card facilities ▪ TV ▪ German & French spoken ▪ Owners Kristo & Tita Truter ▪ dankbaar@adept.co.za ▪ www.dankbaar.co.za ▪ **T/F 021·855·4907**

Voted one of South Africa's best farm stays and 3-star graded, Dankbaarheid wine farm is set in the 'golden triangle' wine area of Stellenbosch, offering four comfortable self-catering apartments (sleeping 2-5) with quality fixtures, automatic shutters, braai, private patios, secure parking, views — and more. Resident owners and hosts Kristo and Tita give their guests personal attention and tourist advice.

Devon Valley Hotel   Devon Valley Road, Stellenbosch ▪ TGCSA 4-star ▪ R585 pp sharing B&B, single R795 B&B ▪ Major credit cards accepted ▪ Flavours Restaurant ▪ Pool ▪ TV & DSTV ▪ Air-conditioning ▪ German spoken ▪ Owner LGI Hotels & Vineyards ▪ info@devonvalleyhotel. com ▪ www.devonvalleyhotel.com ▪ **T 021·865·2012** ▪ F 021·865·2610

This much-loved and recently rejuvenated Stellenbosch landmark (which celebrates its 60th birthday in 2007), offers spectacular views, 38 stylish rooms, innovative contemporary Cape cuisine, an award-winning winelist and one of the most definitive collections of single malt whiskies in the country. Enjoy garden and vineyard walks, two swimming pools, or just sit on the terrace and savour their award-winning SylvanVale wines. Winner of The Great Wine Capitals Best of Wine Tourism Award for accommodation. (See also Eat-out section & A–Z for SylvanVale.)

Kleine Zalze Lodges   Kleine Zalze Wine Farm, Technopark Road, off R44, Stellenbosch ▪ From R398 pp sharing, single from R690 ▪ Breakfast R65 pp ▪ Major credit cards accepted ▪ Terroir Restaurant ▪ Pool ▪ Satellite TV ▪ Air-conditioning ▪ Conference/wedding venue (120 pax) ▪ De Zalze Golf Course ▪ Owner Kleine Zalze Lodges (Pty) Ltd ▪ accommodation@ kleinezalze.co.za ▪ www.kleinezalze.com ▪ **T 021·880·0740** ▪ F 021·880·2215

Just 3km from Stellenbosch, these stylish 47-roomed lodges on a working wine farm are surrounded by vineyards, the magnificent Stellenbosch mountains and De Zalze golf course. Taste award-winning wines from the farm and please your palate at Terroir, a restaurant specializing in fresh Provençale-style fare. Other facilities include an 18-hole golf course, 17-metre swimming pool, mountain biking and vineyard walks. (See also Eat-out & A–Z sections.)

Knorhoek Guest House and Wines   Knorhoek Farm, Knorhoek Road, off R44 (between Stellenbosch & Klapmuts/N1), Stellenbosch ▪ TGCSA 3-star guest house ▪ From R310-R380 pp sharing B&B, single supplement R100 ▪ Major credit cards accepted ▪ Summer restaurant ▪ Pool ▪ TV ▪ Owners Carol & Ingrid van Niekerk ▪ guesthouse@ knorhoek.co.za ▪ www.knorhoek.co.za ▪ **T 021·865·2114/5** ▪ F 021·865·2627

Shaded by oaks and flanked by vineyards and Simonsberg mountain, Knorhoek offers the unique combination of old world charm and modern comfort, with a working wine cellar at the end of the garden. Eight individually decorated en-suite bedrooms, each with a patio or balcony. Your hosts, fourth-generation owners, invite you to relax and enjoy vineyard walks, tennis, wine tasting and bird watching (there are resident owls). AA travel guide – highly recommended. (See also Eat-out & A-Z sections.)

L'Avenir Guest House Klapmuts Road (R44), Stellenbosch ▪ TGCSA 4-star luxury accommodation ▪ Single R400-R1 125 B&B, double R500-R1 500 per room B&B ▪ Major credit cards accepted ▪ Pool ▪ TV with DSTV ▪ Air-conditioning ▪ Ceiling fans ▪ Owner Michel Laroche ▪ guesthouse@lavenir.co.za ▪ www.lavenir.co.za ▪ **T** 021·889·5001 ▪ F 021·889·5258

Colonial charm and comfort in the foothills of the Simonsberg. You'll be assured of warm hospitality and personalized service. The guest house, with 11 guest suites, is surrounded by 70 hectares of well-tended vineyards. Picnics, bird-watching and olives from the farm. Close to golf courses, 20 minutes from picturesque Franschhoek and 5 minutes from the historic town of Stellenbosch. (See also A-Z section.)

Marianne Wine Estate Guest Apartments Marianne Wine Estate, Valley Road, off R44, between Klapmuts & Stellenbosch ▪ TGCSA 4-star B&B ▪ Single from R290-R525 B&B, double from R480-R690 per room B&B ▪ Visa & MasterCard accepted ▪ Olivello Restaurant ▪ Pool ▪ TV ▪ German spoken ▪ Owner Dauriac family ▪ info@mariannewinefarm.co.za ▪ www.mariannewinefarm.co.za ▪ **T** 021·875·5040/875·5672 ▪ F 021·875·5036

Relax on the foothills of the Simonsberg in spacious, comfortable apartments, uniquely African in style, surrounded by citrus orchards and vineyards. Enjoy scenic walks, laze at the swimming pool, taste the estate wines on large terraces with a picture-postcard view of Table Mountain. Breakfast is served at the nearby lakeside restaurant – Olivello – offering Cape comfort food enhanced by delicious Mediterranean flavours. Children welcome. Secure parking. (See also Eat-out & A-Z sections.)

Natte Valleij Farm Natte Valleij, Klapmuts Road (R44), between Stellenbosch and Paarl ▪ TGCSA 3-star B&B & self-catering ▪ 2 Cottages – both private with patio and bbq – Vineyard cottage (sleeps 6) & Cellar cottage (sleeps 2 adults + 2 children) ▪ R250 pp B&B, self-catering from R160 pp ▪ Owners Charles & Charlene Milner ▪ milner@intekom.co.za ▪ www.nattevalleij.co.za ▪ **T** 021·875·5171

This historic farm, in the prime wine making 'Muldersvlei bowl' area, with a magnificent Cape Dutch homestead, was the original land grant of the area. There is a secluded pool set in the large garden. Wonderful walking either through vineyards or through the neighbouring game reserve where one can see wildebeest, gemsbok, zebra, springbok, bontebok and eland. (See also A-Z section.)

Ons Genot Country Lodge Bottelary Road, Stellenbosch ▪ TGCSA 4-star guest house ▪ Single from R390-R620 B&B, double from R320-R490 pp sharing B&B ▪ Major credit cards accepted ▪ Restaurant ▪ Conference facilities ▪ Tennis court ▪ Pool ▪ TV ▪ Air-conditioning ▪ Ceiling fans ▪ Dutch, French & German spoken ▪ Owners Eric & Marleen Bovijn ▪ info@onsgenot.com ▪ www.onsgenot.com ▪ **T** 021·865·2233 ▪ F 021·865·2250

Exclusive 4-star country retreat on the outskirts of historic Stellenbosch and a finalist in the AA Accommodation Awards 02, 03 & 04. Features include luxury en-suite air-conditioned rooms with private terrace and attractive garden, television, mini-bar, wall safe, phone, bathroom with bath and shower – and a private jacuzzi in the honeymoon suite. Conference room for 20 people.

Sunhill Farm Self-contained Cottages La Provence Road, Stellenbosch (behind Polkadraai farm stall on the M12 Stellenbosch-Kuils River) ▪ From R250-R300 per cottage B&B ▪ Major credit cards accepted ▪ @ Jakarta Rijsttafel Restaurant ▪ Small conference facilities (booking essential) ▪ 24/7 'boltproof' powerstation ▪ Pool ▪ TV ▪ Dutch spoken ▪ Owners Duncan & Veronica Fransz ▪ sunhillf@iafrica.com ▪ www.M12Djakarta.co.za ▪ **T** 021·881·3243 ▪ F 021·881·3299

Modestly billed as 'probably Stellenbosch's most unpretentious self-contained cottages, but very cosy and romantic', these two comfortable cottages sleep two, and are fully equipped for self-catering. Outside braai facilities and wide verandas make the most of the spreading vineyard view. Fishing and pottery classes available. (See also Eat-out section.)

Zevenwacht Country Inn   Zevenwacht Wine Farm, Langverwacht Road, Kuils River ▪ TGCSA 4-star ▪ Low season: single from R380 B&B, double from R260 pp sharing B&B; High season: single from R510 B&B, double from R350 pp sharing B&B ▪ Major credit cards accepted ▪ Restaurant ▪ Conference facilities ▪ Pool ▪ TV ▪ Air-conditioning ▪ Sauna ▪ Tennis court ▪ German spoken ▪ Owner Harold & Denise Johnson ▪ reservations@ zevenwacht.co.za ▪ www.zevenwacht.co.za ▪ **T 021·903·5123** ▪ F 021·906·1570

Multi-faceted Zevenwacht wine farm offers accommodation from luxury suites in the Country Inn to vineyard cottages and a self-catering chalet. Spectacular views of Table Bay and False Bay. Restaurant in the historic manor house open daily for breakfast, lunch & dinner; garden picnics also available. Pool and floodlit tennis court. Facilities for weddings, launches and conferences, cheesery, wine tasting centre, gift shop, chef school, and African Day Spa. (See also Eat-out & A-Z sections.)

Zorgvliet Suites & Spa   Le Pommier, Banhoek Valley, Helshoogte Pass, Stellenbosch ▪ TGCSA 5-star B&B ▪ Single from R995–R1 415 B&B, double from R1 680–R2 200 per room B&B ▪ Major credit cards accepted ▪ Herenhuis Restaurant ▪ Conference facilities ▪ Pool ▪ TV ▪ Air-conditioning ▪ Owners Mac & Marietjie van der Merwe ▪ suite@zorgvliet.com ▪ www.zorgvliet.com ▪ **T 021·885·2483** ▪ F 021·885·2485

Relax on a working wine farm in the beautiful Banhoek Valley, where 18 luxurious suites provide spectacular views over the vineyards and surrounding mountains, and the spa soothes guests with *TheraVINE* treatments. Two restaurants, the Herenhuis (take sundowners on the stoep before your meal) and the more casual Le Pommier, braais (barbecues) high in the mountains, wine tasting and cellar tours. (See also Eat-out & A-Z sections.)

Swellendam
Jan Harmsgat Country House   see under Robertson

Tulbagh
Lemberg Wine Estate and Guest House   Off the R46 near Nuwekloof Pass, Straatskerk Road, 4 km west of Tulbagh ▪ R300 pp sharing B&B ▪ Major credit cards accepted ▪ German spoken ▪ Owner Klaus Schindler ▪ schindler@lando.co.za ▪ www.kapstadt. de/lemberg ▪ **T 023·230·0659** ▪ Mobile 083·270·3449 ▪ F 023·230·0661

Set in the lush garden of this boutique wine estate, a stylish, spacious rondavel overlooking a bird-friendly lake offers up to four guests a peaceful retreat. Mountain views enrich delicious breakfasts in the garden, though self-catering is also an option. Owner Klaus (a professional hunter) offers day or longer hunting trips to nearby hunting farms. (See also A-Z section.)

Wellington
Diemersfontein Wine and Country Estate Guest House   Jan van Riebeeck Drive (R301), Wellington ▪ From R380 pp sharing B&B ▪ Major credit cards accepted ▪ Seasons at Diemersfontein restaurant ▪ Conference facilities ▪ Pool ▪ TV in lounges ▪ Air-conditioning (some rooms) ▪ Ceiling fans ▪ Owners David & Sue Sonnenberg ▪ hospitality@ diemersfontein.co.za ▪ www.diemersfontein.co.za ▪ **T 021·864·5050** ▪ F 021·864·2095

Gorgeous gardens provide a colourful backdrop to beautifully appointed garden rooms and vineyard cottages offering 18 double rooms, 16 en suite. (Centrally situated Tulani Cottage boasts lounge, TV room, honesty bar and veranda.) Swimming, horse riding, walks, hikes, and gourmet picnics in summer. Winter weekend packages allow guests to shed city stress and enjoy log fires, great wine and food in breathtaking surroundings. (See also Eat-out section & A-Z sections.)

Fisantekuil Guest Farm   Fisantekuil Farm, Upland Organic Estate, Blouvlei Road, Wellington ▪ R110 pp — self catering ▪ Pool ▪ German spoken ▪ Owner Edmund Oettle ▪ edmund@oettle.com ▪ www.organicwine.co.za ▪ **T 021·864·1184** ▪ F 021·873·5724

Two rustic, secluded self-catering cottages on an organic fruit and nut farm offer an idyllic private holiday or weekend retreat. Enjoy walks, hiking trails, bird watching, fishing, swimming, warming log fires, and organic farm produce. Cottage crafts are also available. Only an hour's drive from Cape Town, Fisantekuil is close to Wellington, beautiful Bain's Kloof and Paarl. (See also A-Z section for Upland Organic Estate.)

The Old Wine House Guest Cottage   Doolhof Wine Estate, Bovlei Road, Wellington ▪ R650 per cottage – self-catering ▪ Visa & MasterCard accepted ▪ Pool ▪ TV ▪ Air-conditioning ▪ MD Dennis Kerrison ▪ wine@doolhof.com ▪ www.doolhof.com ▪ **T 021·873·6911** ▪ F 021·864·2321

Relish the charm and tranquility of a lovingly restored and air-conditioned thatched stone cottage nestling between the Groenberg and Bain's Kloof in the unspoiled Doolhof 'labyrinth valley'. Hike through the fynbos and vineyards, try your hand at clay pigeon shooting, and taste the Doolhof wines. Fully equipped for self-catering, the luxury accommodation comprises a spacious living area, large double bedroom, kitchen and shower. (See also A-Z section.)

■ Disabled access in SA wineries

Current market research indicates that there are more than 340 million disabled individuals who travel abroad during any given year, and in the process spend tens of billions on accommodation, activities and the like. Many have no children and therefore are free to travel when they please, thereby representing a significant a-seasonal market, and perhaps one-third make their travel arrangements without the aid of an agent, and are therefore 'targetable' directly. Their average stay, research indicates, is a relatively lengthy 10-14 days.

Given the size of the total South African population, the estimated number (there are no accurate figures) of wheelchair users in SA is surprisingly large: between 150 000 and 200 000. Add ambulant but frail or elderly people, and foreign tourists, and it is clear that the disabled community is sizeable and economically powerful, and that it represents an important growth market for wine and wine tourism.

In early 2001, this guide commissioned the first comprehensive audit of wine estates and farms in the Western and Northern Cape, aimed at verifying that venues which are open to the public at set times, and claim to be disabled friendly, are in fact accessible - not only for wheelchairs but for all types of disability. (Wineries open only by appointment were excluded, as it was felt that in these cases visitors could ascertain their individual requirements when making an appointment.)

The access audit was carried out in stages, and the results incorporated into guides 2002-04. The intention was to continue to visit and assess new and upgraded venues, but for practical reasons the project had to be placed on hold. However, we are pleased to say the issues have been overcome and the initiative restarted.

Since the last audit many new visitor centers have opened, and a number of previously assessed venues have undertaken renovations and improvements which, the owners believe, have rendered them wheelchair accessible. As a first step, therefore, our disability consultants Andrew Stodel and Guy Davies focused their attention on the new and recently upgraded properties, and the results of their evaluations are set out in the table below as well as being incorporated, into the relevant producer entries in the A-Z section of this book in the form of universally recognisable 'wheelchair' icons.

Of the venues visited in the current round, special recognition is due to three: Graham Beck, Cowlin and Lindhorst. All have excellent facilities, are fully accessible and - importantly - display an eagerness to attend to the particular needs of disabled visitors.

In general, venues interested in becoming wheelchair friendly should pay special attention to road surfaces and pathways, as cobbled or rough brick paving can be very hazardous. It's worth seeking the advice of a recognised disability consultant, as accessibility is often relatively easy and inexpensive to achieve. And, as we remarked in a previous edition, good accessibility is not exclusive, and usually benefits many people who are often not viewed as 'disabled'.

This introduces an important point to consider when using the results of the current audit as reflected in the A-Z: there we followed past practice of focusing on the tasting room - i.e. if this area is deemed accessible by our consultants, we consider the venue worthy of a wheelchair icon. It may be argued, however, that a property cannot be considered truly accessible unless the parking area and approach are also laid out in a conducive manner. Not just prospective travellers, but also winery owners contemplating new visitor facilities or upgrading existing ones should consider this important factor.

We would like to extend our appreciation and thanks to Andrew and Guy, and invite readers to contact them either through the guide's offices or directly with any comments or suggestions. Andrew's email address is andrews@rsp.co.za; Guy can be reached at guy@disabilitysolutions.co.za.

In closing, it is important to stress that wineries which are not included below or in the A-Z do not necessarily have deficient or non-existent disabled facilities; it merely means we are not yet in a position to be able to comment on them. Going forward, the intention is to not only continue but if possible expand our coverage of disabled facilities in the winelands, and we welcome any input on how this might be achieved in a user-friendly manner.

Area	Estate	Parking	Tasting	Toilet	Tour
Bot River	Gehot Bosch Winery	N	N	N	
	Keisseskraal Vineyards	N	N		
Breedekloof	Daschbosch Wine Cellar	Y	Y	Y	
	Deetlefs Estate	Y	Y	Y	
Cape Town	Wine Concepts	Y	N	N	n/a
Darling	Ormonde Private Cellar	Y	Y	N	
Durbanville	Bloemendal Estate	N	Y	N	
	Hillcrest Estate	N	N	N	
Elgin	Iona Vineyards	N	N	N	
	Oak Valley Wines	N	N	N	
	Agulhas Wines	N	N	N	
	Zoetendal Wines	N	N	N	Y
Franschhoek	Allée Bleue	Y	Y	N	n/a
	Graham Beck Wines	Y	Y	Y	Y
	La Bri	Y	N	N	Y
	Le Manoir de Brendel	N	N	N	
	Lynx Wines	N	Y	N	Y
Klein River	Raka	N	N	Y	
Paarl	African Terroir	N	Y	Y	Y
	Cowlin Wines	Y	Y	Y	Y
	Domaine Brahms Wineries	Y	N	N	n/a
	Drakensig Wines	N	N	N	
	Freedom Hill Wines	N	Y	Y	N
	I love Wine	N	Y	N	N
	Joostenberg Wines	Y	Y	N	n/a
	Klein Parys Vineyards	Y			
	Klompzicht	N	Y	Y	N
	Lindhorst Wines	Y	Y	Y	Y
	Ridgeback Wines	Y	Y	Y	N
	Vrede en Lust Wine Farm	N	Y	Y	N
	Windmeul Cooperative Cellar	Y	Y	Y	N
	Ziggurat Vineyards	N	N	N	Y
Piketberg	Winkelshoek Wine Cellar	Y	Y	N	
Robertson	Bon Cap Organic Winery	N	Y	N	
	Graham Beck Wines	Y	Y	Y	Y

Area	Estate	Parking	Tasting	Toilet	Tour
	Wederom	N	N	n/a	N
Simondium	Rupert & Rothschild Vignerons	Y	Y	N	
Slanghoek	Jason's Hill Private Cellar	N	N	N	
Stellenbosch/ Helderberg	Asara Estate	N	Y	N	N
	De Trafford Wines	N	N	N	
	Dombeya	Y	N	N	
	Dornier Wines	N	Y	Y	N
	Ernie Els Wines	N	Y	Y	Y
	Flagstone Winery	Y	N	N	
	Goede Hoop Estate	Y	N	N	
	Grangehurst Winery	N	Y	N	n/a
	Groenland	N	Y	N	
	Haskell Vineyards	Y	N	N	
	Helderberg Winery/The Company of Wine People	Y	Y	N	n/a
	Le Riche Wines	Y	N	N	
	Lourensford	N	N	N	Y
	Lushof Estate	N	N		n/a
	Monterosso Estate	N	N	N	
	Morgenster Estate	N	N	N	n/a
	Post House Cellar	Y	Y	N	Y
	Stellekaya Winery	N	Y	N	
	Stellenbosch Hills	N	N	Y	
	Stellenrust	Y	Y	N	Y
	Stellenzicht Vineyards	N	N	N	
	Sterhuis	N	Y	N	N
	Uva Mira Vineyards	N	Y	Y	Y
	Wedderwill Estate Wines	Y	Y	N	Y
	Westbridge Vineyards	Y	N	N	
	Yonder Hill Wine Farm	Y	Y	N	n/a
	Zorgvliet Wines	N	Y	Y	N
Swartland	Allesverloren Estate	Y	N	N	
	Kloovenburg Vineyards	Y	N	N	
	Lammershoek Winery	N	N	N	
	Org de Rac Domain	Y	N	N	
	Porterville Cellars (Tulbagh Wineries Co-op)	Y	N	N	
	Pulpit Rock Winery	Y	N	Y	
	Riebeek Cellars	Y	N	N	
Tulbagh	Manley Private Cellar	N	N	?	
	Montpellier	N	N	N	N
	Saronsberg Cellar	N	N	N	N
	Schalkenbosch Wines	Y	N	N	
	Tulbagh Wineries Co-op	Y	N	N	
Walker Bay	Feiteiras Vineyards	N	N	N	N
	Wildekrans Estate	N	N	N	N
Wellington	Carolinahoeve	N	N	N	n/a
	Doolhof Estate	N	N	N	Y

Area	Estate	Parking	Tasting	Toilet	Tour
	Eshkol Kosher Winery	Y	N	N	n/a
	Maze Valley	N	N	N	Y
	Wamakersvallei Winery	N	Y	Y	N
	Welbedacht Wines	N	Y	N	N
	Wellington Cooperative Cellar	Y	Y	N	n/a
	Welvanpas	N	N	N	n/a
Wolseley	Mountain Ridge Wines (Romansrivier)	Y	N	N	
Worcester	Bergsig	Y	N	N	
	Conradie Family Vineyards	N	N	N	N
	De Doorns Winery	N	N	N	
	Lateganskop Winery	N	Y	N	
	New Cape Wines	N	Y	N	

Winelands Maps

The maps in this section show locales where wine is available for tasting/sale either at set times or by appointment. The larger-scale map below shows the areas covered by the maps, and the table starting on the next page lists some details for prospective visitors.

Areas covered by the maps

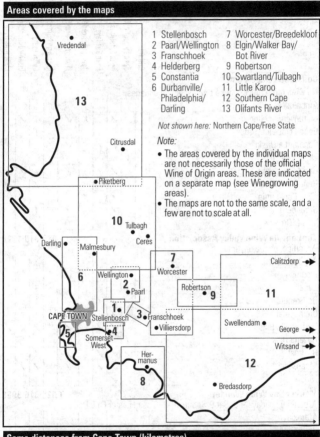

1 Stellenbosch
2 Paarl/Wellington
3 Franschhoek
4 Helderberg
5 Constantia
6 Durbanville/
   Philadelphia/
   Darling
7 Worcester/Breedekloof
8 Elgin/Walker Bay/
   Bot River
9 Robertson
10 Swartland/Tulbagh
11 Little Karoo
12 Southern Cape
13 Olifants River

Not shown here: Northern Cape/Free State

Note:
- The areas covered by the individual maps are not necessarily those of the official Wine of Origin areas. These are indicated on a separate map (see Winegrowing areas).
- The maps are not to the same scale, and a few are not to scale at all.

Some distances from Cape Town (kilometres)

Calitzdorp	370	Paarl	60	Tulbagh	120
Franschhoek	75	Robertson	160	Vredendal	300
Hermanus	120	Stellenbosch	45	Worcester	110

Key for maps

═══ Main access roads   R62 R60 = Road numbers
─── Roads   ⬤ Towns
····· Gravel roads

Details of locales shown on maps

The table below summarises the following details by region: map grid-reference, if applicable; whether open by appointment only (T), open on Saturdays, Sundays (✓ = at set times; T = by appointment), public holidays (✗ = closed all public holidays; otherwise assume open all or some holidays); availability of meals/refreshments (BYO = bring your own picnic; S = seasonal), accommodation, cellar tours, facilities for children; and disabled friendliness, as audited by our disability consultant. For detailed information, particularly items marked with an asterisk, see the A-Z and Eat-out/Stay-over sections.

	Grid ref	Open by appt only	Open Saturdays	Open Sundays	Open pub. holidays	Meals/refreshments	Accommodation	Cellar tours	Disabled friendly	Child friendly
Constantia/Cape Point										
No wine route office. Phone the respective wineries.										
Ambeloui		T						T		
Buitenverwachting			✓		✗	✓		T	✓	
Cape Point Vineyards		T						T		
Constantia Uitsig			✓	✓		✓	✓			
Eagle's Nest		T								
Groot Constantia			✓	✓		✓		✓	✓	
High Constantia			✓	✓				✓		
Klein Constantia			✓		✗				✓	
Steenberg			✓			✓	✓	T	✓	
Vins D'Orrance		T								
Durbanville Wine Valley Association								T 083·310·1228		
No office, phone anytime										
Altydgedacht			✓					T		
Bloemendal			✓	✓		✓				
Capaia		T						T		
De Grendel			✓					T		
Diemersdal			✓			✓/BYO		T		
Durbanville Hills			✓	✓		✓		✓	✓	✓
Havana Hills		T								
Hillcrest			✓	✓		✓		T		
Meerendal			✓	✓		✓		✓	✓	
Nitida			✓					T	✓	
Walker Bay Wine Wander								T 028·316·3988		
Mon-Fri & holidays 9-6 Sat 9-5 Sun 10-3 Closed Easter Fri & Dec 25										
Ataraxia		T								
Barry Gould		T								
Barton		T*						✓		
Beaumont			✓				T	✓	✓	✓
Boschrivier		T								
Bouchard Finlayson			✓		✗				✓	
Dispore Kamma		T								
Elgin Vintners		T								
Feiteiras Vineyards		T						✓		
Gehot Bosch			✓	✓				✓		

	Grid ref	Open by appt only	Open Saturdays	Open Sundays	Open pub. holidays	Meals/refreshments	Accommodation	Cellar tours	Disabled friendly	Child friendly
Goedvertrouw		T				T	T			✓
Hamilton Russell Vineyards			✓			BYO*		T		
Hemelzicht			✓		X					
Hermanuspietersfontein (Bartho Eksteen)			✓	✓*		T			✓	
Iona						BYO	✓	✓		
Keisseskraal			T	T		BYO*				
La Vierge			✓			✓		✓		
Luddite		T								
Newton Johnson/Cape Bay			✓*		X		✓			
Oak Valley										
Paul Cluver			✓			BYO	✓		✓	
Raka			✓			BYO		T		
Ross Gower Wines			T		T	✓	✓	T		
South Hill		T				BYO	✓			
Southern Right			✓			T		T		
Springfontein		T				BYO	✓	T		✓
Stanford Hills		T					✓			
Sumaridge			✓	✓		✓	✓			
Whalehaven/Idiom			✓	✓*		BYO		T		
Wildekrans (Farm cellar)					X*	T	✓	T		✓
Wildekrans (Orchard Farmstall)			✓	✓		✓				✓

Vignerons de Franschhoek   T 021·876·3062
Mon-Fri 9-6 (Oct-Apr); 9-5 (May-Sep) Sat 10-5 Sun & holidays 10-4
Closed Good Fri and Dec 25

	Grid ref	Open by appt only	Open Saturdays	Open Sundays	Open pub. holidays	Meals/refreshments	Accommodation	Cellar tours	Disabled friendly	Child friendly
Akkerdal		T			X		✓			
Allée Bleue			✓	✓		✓				
Blueberry Hill		T					✓			
Boekenhoutskloof										
Boschendal			✓	✓		✓		T	✓	
Cabrière			✓			✓		✓	✓	
Cape Chamonix			✓	✓		✓	✓	T	✓	✓
Colmant			✓	T				T		
Dieu Donné			✓	✓		✓		T		
Eikehof		T						T		
Franschhoek Vineyards			✓	✓		✓				
GlenWood			✓*	✓*				✓		
Graham Beck			✓					T		
Grande Provence			✓	✓		✓	✓	✓	✓	
Haut Espoir		T						T		
La Bourgogne		T					✓			
La Bri					X					
La Chaumiere		T						T		
La Chataigne		T					✓			
La Couronne			✓		X	✓		T		✓
La Motte			✓			✓*			✓	

	Grid ref	Open by appt only	Open Saturdays	Open Sundays	Open pub. holidays	Meals/refreshments	Accommodation	Cellar tours	Disabled friendly	Child friendly
La Petite Ferme			✓	✓		✓	✓			
Landau du Val		T								
Le Manoir de Brendel			✓	✓		✓	✓			
L'Ormarins			✓							
Lynx Wines			✓	T				✓		
Mont Rochelle			✓	✓		✓	✓	✓		
Môreson			✓	✓		✓		T	✓	
Plaisir de Merle			✓					T		
Rickety Bridge			✓			BYO	✓	T		
Solms-Delta			✓	✓		✓		✓		
Stony Brook			✓							
Von Ortloff		T								

Stellenbosch American Express Wine Routes (Hldrbrg office)   T 021·852·6166
Phone for information

	Grid ref	Open by appt only	Open Saturdays	Open Sundays	Open pub. holidays	Meals/refreshments	Accommodation	Cellar tours	Disabled friendly	Child friendly
Agterplaas		T						T		
Assegai		T					✓			
Avontuur			✓	✓		✓		T	✓	
Conspirare		T								
Cordoba		T			✗					
Croydon		T								
Dellrust			✓		✗			T	✓	✓
Dreamview Hill			✓*	✓*		✓				
Eikendal			✓	✓		✓	✓	✓	✓	✓
Elberti		T								
Flagstone/Ses'Fikile			✓	T				T		
Grangehurst			✓	✓*			✓			
Helderberg/Thandi/The Co of Wine People			✓			✓				✓
Heron Ridge		T								
Ingwe										
JP Bredell			✓					T		
Ken Forrester/Meinert/Zandberg (96 Wnry Rd)			✓	✓		✓	✓	T	✓	
L'Auberge du Paysan						✓			✓	
Lourensford			✓	✓				✓		
Lushof			T		✗			T		
Lyngrove		T					✓			
Miravel		T					✓			
Morgenster			✓	✓				T		
Mount Rozier		T			✗			T		
Onderkloof		T				T		T		
Post House			T					✓		
Romond		T								
Somerbosch			✓	✓		✓		T	✓	✓
Stonewall		T								
The Winery of Good Hope		T								
Vergelegen			✓	✓		✓		✓	✓	

	Grid ref	Open by appt only	Open Saturdays	Open Sundays	Open pub. holidays	Meals/refreshments	Accommodation	Cellar tours	Disabled friendly	Child friendly
Waterhof		T				✓		T		
Wedderwill		T	T			BYO		T		
Weening & Barge							✓			
Yonder Hill					✗			✓		

Little/Klein Karoo Wine Route				**T 028·572·1284**
Phone Ellen Marais Mon-Fri 9-5				
Calitzdorp Wine Route				**T 044·213·3775**
Open daily 9-5				
Outeniqua Wine Route		**T 072·833·8223/044·873·4212**
Phone Vivien Harpur		

	Grid ref	Open by appt only	Open Saturdays	Open Sundays	Open pub. holidays	Meals/refreshments	Accommodation	Cellar tours	Disabled friendly	Child friendly
Axe Hill		T								
Barrydale			✓			BYO		T		
Bergwater										
Boplaas			✓*					T		
Calitzdorp			✓			BYO		T		
De Krans			✓			✓/BYO*		T	✓	
Domein Doornkraal			✓			✓		T		
Excelsior Vlakteplaas										
Grundheim			✓							
Herold		T								
Joubert-Tradauw			✓			✓	✓	T		✓
Kango			✓			✓/BYO		T		
Ladismith					✗*	BYO		T		
Schoonberg		T								
Mons Ruber			✓				✓			
Montagu			✓		✗	BYO			✓	
Peter Bayly		T								
Rietrivier			✓		✗	✓/BYO		T		
Uitvlucht			✓	✓*					✓	
Virgin Earth/Pendoorn		T								
Withoek							✓	T		

Northern Cape Wine Association				**T 054·337·8800**
Mon-Fri 7.30-5				

	Grid ref	Open by appt only	Open Saturdays	Open Sundays	Open pub. holidays	Meals/refreshments	Accommodation	Cellar tours	Disabled friendly	Child friendly
Douglas Cellar					✗	BYO				
Iin0 Goudveld			T					✓		
Groblershoop			✓	✗				✓		
Grootdrink			✓	✗				✓		
Hartswater			T			✓		T		
Kakamas			✓	✗				✓		
Keimoes			✓	✗				✓		
Landzicht			✓	✗		T/BYO		T		✓
Oranjerivier/Upington			✓	✗				✓	✓	

Olifants River Vodacom Wine Route			
Mon-Fri 8-5 Sat 8-1 Closed Good Fri & Dec 25			

	Grid ref	Open by appt only	Open Saturdays	Open Sundays	Open pub. holidays	Meals/refreshments	Accommodation	Cellar tours	Disabled friendly	Child friendly
Cape Rock		T				BYO		T		
Cederberg			✓			BYO	✓	✓		

	Grid ref	Open by appt only	Open Saturdays	Open Sundays	Open pub. holidays	Meals/refreshments	Accommodation	Cellar tours	Disabled friendly	Child friendly
Citrusdal Cellars			✓			BYO	✓	T	✓	
Johan van Zyl Wines		T								
Keukenhof		T						T		✓
Klawer			✓		✗*	BYO			✓	
Lutzville			✓			✓		T	✓	
Stellar Winery								T		
Stoumann's (pvsly Excelsious)			✓							
Teubes Family		T			✗		✓			
WestCorp/Vredendal			✓		✗	T/BYO		✓*	✓	
Paarl Vintners T 021·863·4886 Mon-Fri 8-5			**Wellington Wine Route T 021·873·4604** Mon-Fri 8-5 Sat 9-2 Closed Christian holidays							
African Terroir	C1					T/BYO	✓	T		
Anura	C7		✓	✓		✓		T		
Armajaro	C1	T								
Avondale	F6		✓					T	✓	
Avondvrede	C8	T				T		T		
Backsberg	D8		✓	✓*		✓		✓	✓	✓
Bergheim	E5		✓							
Bernheim	E3		✓					T	✓	
Black Pearl	D5	T						T		
Blyde Wines	E5		✓					T		
Boland Kelder	E4		✓					T		
Bosman Family Vineyards	G1	T								
Bovlei/Headbutt	G2		✓						✓	
Carolinahoeve	E1		✓	✓		✓				
Coleraine	D6		✓					T		
Cowlin	D8		✓			T		T		✓
Crows Nest/De Reuck	D3		✓	✓		✓		✓		✓
Cru Wines	D7		✓			✓				
David Frost Wines	D1							T		
De Compagnie	H1	T				T		T		
De Zoete Inval	E6	T*						T	✓	
Détendu	C1	T						T		
De Villiers Wines	E6	T								
Diemersfontein/Thokozani	F2		✓	✓		✓	✓	T		
Domaine Brahms	C3		T					T		
Doolhof	H1		T				✓	✓		
Drakensig	D8		✓*							
Eshkol	F1	T				T*		T		
Fairview/Spice Route/Goats/Fairvalley	D6		✓	✓		✓			✓	
Freedom Hill	F7		✓		✗	BYO				
Gallop Hill	D4	T				✓	✓			
Glen Carlou	D7		✓					T	✓	
Groenendal	G1	T			✗			T		
Groot Parys	E5	T								

	Grid ref	Open by appt only	Open Saturdays	Open Sundays	Open pub. holidays	Meals/refreshments	Accommodation	Cellar tours	Disabled friendly	Child friendly
Hildenbrand	G2		✓	✓		✓	✓	T		
Horse Mountain	D1	T				BYO		T		
I Love Wine	E6		✓			✓				
Jacaranda	F1		✓			BYO	✓	✓		
Jacques Smit	F2		✓							✓
Joostenberg	A8		✓	✓		✓		T		
Juno	E5		✓		✗*					
Kleine Draken	D6				✗	BYO		T	✓	
Klein Parys	E5		✓			✓		T		
Kleinvallei	F4	T								
KWV	E6		✓	✓		✓		✓	✓	
Laborie	E6		✓	✓*		✓		T*	✓	
Landskroon	D6		✓			BYO*	✓	T		✓
Lindhorst	D7		✓	✓		✓	✓	T		✓
Linton Park	G1	T				T		T		
Longbarn	F1	T						T		
Main Street	E5	T						T		
Marianne	C8		✓					✓	T	
Maske Wines	G2	T								
Mellasat	G5	T*						T		
Mischa	F1	T			✗	T		T		
Mont Destin	C8	T								
Mont du Toit/Blouvlei	G2	T								
Mooi Bly	F4	T					✓			
Mount Vernon	C7	T				BYO		T		
Nabygelegen	H1		✓			BYO		T		
Napier	G2		✓	T			✓	T		
Natte Valleij	F1	T								
Nederburg	F5		✓	✓		T		T	✓	
Nelson/New Beginnings	D3		✓	T		T		✓*	✓	✓
Niel Joubert/Klein Simonsvlei	D8	T								
Olsen Wines	G5	T				T		T		
Oude Denneboom	C2	T								
Oude Wellington	G2	T				✓	✓			✓
Perdeberg	B2		✓					T		
Rhebokskloof	D3		✓	✓		✓		T	✓	✓
Ridgeback	D3		✓	✓*		✓	✓*	T		✓
Rose Garden Vineyards	C3	T				T/BYO		T		
Ruitersvlei	D6		✓	✓				T	✓	✓
Rupert & Rothschild	D8	T								
Scali	C1	T					✓			
Seidelberg	D6		✓	✓		✓		✓		✓
Simonsvlei	D7		✓	✓		✓		T	✓	✓
Smook Wines	C1	T	✓*					T		
The Mason's Winery	E5	T	✓*					T		

	Grid ref	Open by appt only	Open Saturdays	Open Sundays	Open pub. holidays	Meals/refreshments	Accommodation	Cellar tours	Disabled friendly	Child friendly
Under Oaks	D3	T								
Upland	G2	T					✓	T		
Veenwouden	E2	T*			✗			T		
Vendôme	E6		✓		✗			T	✓	
Vrede en Lust	D8		✓	✓		✓	✓	T		✓
Wamakersvallei	E2		✓		✗*	BYO		T		
Welbedacht Wines	F1		✓	T		T/BYO*		✓		✓
Welgegund	G2	T					✓			
Welgeleë	D7		✓							
Welgemeend	C7		✓		✗				✓	
Wellington	E2									
Welvanpas	H1		✓							
William Everson Wines	E6	T				BYO		T		
Withington	E5	T								
Windmeul	D3		✓		✗			T		
Ziggurat	D3		✓				✓	T		
Robertson Wine Valley Mon-Fri 8-5 Sat & Sun 9-2						**T 023·626·3167/084·701·5404**				
Angora		T			✗					
Arabella/Blue Cove			✓					T		
Arendsig		T						T		
Ashton			✓		✗	BYO		T		
Bon Cap			✓	✓		✓	✓	T		✓
Bon Courage			✓			✓			✓	✓
Bonnievale			✓						✓	
Bushmanspad			✓	✓		BYO	✓	✓		
Cilandia		T						T		
Clairvaux			✓			BYO		T	✓	
Cloverfield			✓							
De Wetshof			✓					T		
Fraai Uitzicht			✓	✓		✓	✓	T		
Goedverwacht			✓			BYO		T		
Graham Beck			✓					T		
Janéza		T				T				
Jonkheer		T			✗					
Karusa		T								
Kingsriver (pvsly Jewel of the Breede River)		T*		✓						
Koningsrivier		T						T		
Kranskop			✓			T		✓	✓	✓
Langverwacht					✗			T	✓	
Le Grand Chasseur			✓			✓*	✓	T		
Lord's		T				BYO		T		
Major's Hill			✓					T		✓
McGregor			✓						✓	
Mooiuitsig							✓	T		

	Grid ref	Open by appt only	Open Saturdays	Open Sundays	Open pub. holidays	Meals/refreshments	Accommodation	Cellar tours	Disabled friendly	Child friendly
Nordale					X	BYO		T		
Quando			T					T		
Rietvallei				✓		✓BYO				✓
Robertson Winery				✓	✓	BYO		T		
Roodezandt				✓				T	✓	
Rooiberg				✓		✓		T	✓	✓
Rusticus				✓		BYO		✓		
Springfield				✓		BYO				
The Marais Family				✓		BYO				
Van Loveren				✓		✓*		✓	✓	
Van Zylshof				✓				T		
Viljoensdrift				✓	✓*	✓		T		
Vruchtbaar			T			BYO	✓	T		
Wandsbeck								T	✓	
Wederom				✓		T				✓
Weltevrede				✓		✓	✓	T		
Wolvendrift				✓		BYO		T	✓	
Zandvliet				✓		BYO			✓	
Agulhas Wines						BYO	✓	T		
Andy Mitchell			T							
Black Oystercatcher			T							
Jean Daneel			T*			T*				
Oewerzicht							✓			
Zoetendal				✓		T/BYO		✓		

Stellenbosch American Express Wine Routes   T 021·886-4310

Mon-Fri 8.30-5 Sat, Sun & holidays: enq Tourism Office, Closed Good Fri, Dec 25 & Jan 1

	Grid ref	Open by appt only	Open Saturdays	Open Sundays	Open pub. holidays	Meals/refreshments	Accommodation	Cellar tours	Disabled friendly	Child friendly
Alluvia	H5	T*					✓	T		✓
Alto	E8		✓							
Amani	B6		✓		X			T	✓	
Anatu	E5	T								
Annandale	E8		✓					T	✓	
Asara	D6		✓			BYO*	✓*	T		
Audacia	E7		✓					T	✓	
Beau Joubert	B6	T					✓			
Bein	B6	T								
Bellevue	C3		✓							
Bergkelder	E5		✓			T*		T	✓	
Beyerskloof/Bouwland	E3		✓			✓			✓	
Bilton	E8		✓			✓*			✓	
Blaauwklippen	E6		✓	✓		✓		T	✓	
Blue Creek	E7		✓	✓						
Bonfoi	C5		✓		X	BYO			✓	
Boschheim	E5	T								
Boschkloof	C6	T						T		
Bottelary	D3		✓			✓		T		

	Grid ref	Open by appt only	Open Saturdays	Open Sundays	Open pub. holidays	Meals/refreshments	Accommodation	Cellar tours	Disabled friendly	Child friendly
Camberley	H5		✓	T*			✓	T		
Cape First	E7	T								
Cape Hutton	E7	T						T		
Carisbrooke	C6		✓*							
Clos Malverne	D4		✓			BYO		T		
Clouds	G5	T				T	✓			
Clovelly	D3	T						T		
Dalla Cia (phone for details)	E5									
De Meye	E1		✓							
De Toren	B6	T						T		
De Trafford	G8		✓					✓		
Delaire	G5		✓	✓				T	✓	
Delheim	F2		✓	✓*		✓		✓	✓	
Devon Hill	D4		T		✗			T	✓	
Devon Rocks	D3	T					✓	T		
Devonvale	D3	T								
DeWaal/Uiterwyk	C5		✓*							
Dormershire	A5		✓					✓		
Dornier Wines	F7		✓	✓*		✓*		T		
Ernie Els	F8		✓			✓*				
Ernst & Co	E1	T								
EagleVlei	E1		✓	✓		✓		✓		✓
Fort Simon	C4		✓		✗	T		T	✓	
Gilga	D6	T						T		
Goede Hoop	C3					T/BYO		T		
Graceland	E7				✗		✓			
Groenland	B3		✓			T		T		
Hartenberg	D3		✓	✓*		✓		T*		
Haskell	E8		✓*			✓		✓		
Hazendal	B3		✓	✓		✓		✓		
Hidden Valley	F8		✓	✓				✓		
Hoopenburg	E1		✓*			BYO		T		
Jacobsdal	B6	T								
JC le Roux	D4		✓	✓*					✓	
Jordan	C5		✓	✓		BYO		T	✓	
Kaapzicht	B4		✓			T/BYO	✓	T		
Kanonkop	F2		✓			T/BYO			✓	
Kanu	C6		✓*		✗					
Klawervlei	D1	T						T	✓	
Klein DasBosch	F7	T								
Klein Gustrouw	G6	T						T		
Kleine Zalze	E6		✓	✓		✓	✓	T	✓	✓
Kleinood	F7	T						T		
Knorhoek/Fryer's Cove	F3		✓	✓		✓*	✓		✓	✓
Koelenhof	D1		✓			BYO			✓	✓

	Grid ref	Open by appt only	Open Saturdays	Open Sundays	Open pub. holidays	Meals/refreshments	Accommodation	Cellar tours	Disabled friendly	Child friendly
L'Avenir	E3		✓			✓	✓	T		
Laibach	F1		✓*					T		
Lanzerac	G5		✓	✓		✓	✓	✓	✓	
Le Bonheur	F1		✓							
Le Riche	G6		T				✓			
Lievland	F1		✓	✓		T		T	✓	
Louiesenhof	E4		✓	✓*		✓*			✓	✓
in0Louisvale	D4							T	✓	
Marklew	F1	T						T		
Meerlust	B8	T			✗					
Middelvlei	E5		✓					✓	✓	
Mitre's Edge	F1	T								
Monterosso	E4		✓					T		
Mooiplaas	B4		✓			BYO				
Morgenhof	F3		✓	✓		✓			✓	
Morton Wines	G4	T								
Mostertsdrift	E4	T				T		T		
Mulderbosch	E3	T								
Muratie	F3		✓	✓		T	✓	T		
Natte Valleij		T					✓	T		
Neethlingshof	D5		✓	✓		✓		T	✓	✓
Niel Ellis/Meyer-Näkel	G6		✓							
Nietvoorbij	F4		T		✗					
Overgaauw	D6		✓					T	✓	
Quoin	F3		✓	✓*		✓		T		
Raats Family/Mvemve Raats	B6	T								
Rainbow's End	H5							T		
Remhoogte	F3		T*					T		
Reyneke	B6	T					✓			
Rozendal	G5	T				✓	✓	T		
Rust en Vrede	E8		✓							
Rustenberg	G4		✓						✓	
Saxenburg	A6		✓	✓		✓				
Simonsig	E2		✓			✓ BYO		✓	✓	✓
Skilpadvlei	C6		✓	✓		✓	✓			✓
Slaley	E2		✓					T		
Spier/Savanha	C7		✓	✓		✓	✓		✓	✓
Stark-Condé	G6		✓							
Stellekaya/Anatu	E5		✓		✗	T				
Stellenbosch Hills	D6		✓			✓*			✓	
Stellendrift/Cilliers Cellars	D6		✓	✓		✓			✓	
Stellenrust/JJ Wines	C3		✓		✗*	✓ BYO		✓		
Stellenzicht	E7		✓	✓						
Sterhuis	C4	T								✓
Stonehill	D4	T								

	Grid ref	Open by appt only	Open Saturdays	Open Sundays	Open pub. holidays	Meals/refreshments	Accommodation	Cellar tours	Disabled friendly	Child friendly
SylvanVale (Devon Valley Hotel)	D4		✓	✓		✓	✓	T	✓	✓
The Cheviot Winery	F5	T								
The Foundry	B8	T						T		
Thelema	H4		✓	✓*	✗	BYO			✓	
Tokara	G4		✓	✓		✓			✓	
Uitkyk	F2		✓	✓		✓*			✓	
Uva Mira	F8		✓							
Vergenoegd	B8		✓	✓*		✓		T	✓	
Vilafonté	E5		✓	✓		✓		T		
Villiera/M'hudi	D1		✓			BYO*		✓*	✓	
Vredenheim	D6		✓			✓			✓	
Vriesenhof	F7		✓			T		T		
Vuurberg Vyds	H4	T								
Warwick	F1		✓	✓		T/BYO		T		
Waterford	F7		✓							✓
Webersburg	E8	T			✗		✓			
Welgevallen	F5	T								
Welmoed/Thandi/The Co of Wine People	C7		✓	✓		✓				✓
Westbridge	E1		✓*				✓			
Zevenwacht	A5		✓	✓		✓	✓	✓	✓	
Zorgvliet/Le Pommier	H4		✓	✓		✓	✓	T		✓

Swartland Wine Route   T 022·487·1133
Mon-Fri 8-5 Sat & holidays 8.30-12 Closed Good Fri, Dec 25 & Jan 1
The Darling Wine Route   T 022·492·3430
Mon-Fri 9-4.50 Sat 9-2.30 Closed Easter Fri-Mon, Dec 25 & Jan 1

	Grid ref	Open by appt only	Open Saturdays	Open Sundays	Open pub. holidays	Meals/refreshments	Accommodation	Cellar tours	Disabled friendly	Child friendly
Allesverloren				✓		✓/BYO		T		✓
Babylon's Peak		T					✓	T		
Cloof				✓		✓*			✓	
Darling Cellars				✓		BYO		T	✓	
Groote Post				✓		✓/BYO			✓	
Hofstraat		T						T		
Kloovenburg				✓		BYO		T		
Lammershoek			T	T		T/BYO		T		
Meerhof				✓		T/BYO		T		
Nieuwedrift				✓	T	T	✓			✓
Org de Rac				✓				✓		
Ormonde				✓		T/BYO		T		✓
Porterville/Tulbagh Wineries				✓		T/BYO		T		
Pulpit Rock				✓		BYO		T		
Riebeek				✓		BYO		T		
Sadie Family		T								
Sequillo		T								
Swartland Winery				✓		BYO		T		✓
The Observatory		T								
Winkelshoek				✓						

	Grid ref	Open by appt only	Open Saturdays	Open Sundays	Open pub. holidays	Meals/refreshments	Accommodation	Cellar tours	Disabled friendly	Child friendly
Tulbagh Wine Route							T 023·230·1348			
Mon-Fri 9-5 Sat & holidays 10-4 Sun 11-4 Closed: Good Fri, Dec 25 & Jan 1										
Blue Crane	T									
Bianco			✓					✓		
Buck's Ridge	T						✓			
Drostdy-Hof			✓							
Lemberg			✓	✓		T	✓	✓		
Manley			✓	✓			✓	✓		
Montpellier			✓	✓			✓	✓		✓
Montpellier du Sud/Constantia de Tulbagh	T									
Oude Compagnies Post	T									
Paddagang			✓	✓		✓	✓			
Rijk's			✓			✓/BYO	✓	✓	✓	
Saronsberg			✓			BYO		T		
Schalkenbosch			✓	✓		T	T	T		
Theuniskraal			✓			BYO			✓	
Tulbagh Wineries Co-op			✓						✓	
Tulbagh Mountain Vineyards	T							T		
Twee Jonge Gezellen			✓					✓		
Waverley Hills	T							T		
Worcester Winelands							T 023·342·8710			
Mon-Fri 8-5 Sat 9-4 Sun & holidays: 10-3										
Breedekloof Wine & Tourism							T 023·349·1791			
Mon-Fri 8.30-4.30 Sat 9-4 Sun 10-4 Closed Good Fri & Dec 25										
Aan de Doorns					✗			T*	✓	
Alvi's Drift		T				BYO		T		
Aufwaerts		T								
Badsberg			✓		✗	BYO		T*		✓
Bergsig			✓			✓		T		
Botha			✓			BYO		T		✓
Brandvlei					✗			T		
Conradie Family			✓	✓		✓	✓	✓		
Daschbosch			✓			BYO				✓
De Doorns			✓							
Deetlefs			✓			T/BYO*		✓		
De Wet			✓		✗	BYO			✓	
Die Huis van Anjé		T				BYO				
Du Preez/Rockfield			✓		✗	BYO		T	✓	✓
Du Toitskloof/Lost Horizons			✓	✓*		BYO		T	✓	
Goudini			✓			✓				
Groot Eiland							✓	T	✓	
Hex River Crossing		T				T				
Jason's Hill			✓	T		T				✓
Lateganskop								T		
Lorraine		T				BYO		T		

	Grid ref	Open by appt only	Open Saturdays	Open Sundays	Open pub. holidays	Meals/refreshments	Accommodation	Cellar tours	Disabled friendly	Child friendly
Mountain Oaks			✓	✓	✗	T	✓	✓		
Mountain Ridge			✓			BYO		T		
New Cape Wines			✓			✓*	✓*	✓		
Nuy			✓			✓*			✓	
Opstal			✓			✓		T		
Overhex					✗	BYO		T	✓	
Rico Suter		T				BYO	✓*	T		
Riverstone/Merwida			✓				✓		✓	
Slanghoek			✓		✗	BYO		T	✓	
Stettyn			✓			BYO		T	✓	
Villiersdorp Cellar/Slowine			✓	✓		✓			✓	
Waboomsrivier			✓		✗	BYO		T	✓	
Worcester Winelands			✓			✓/BYO	✓			

Constantia/Cape Point

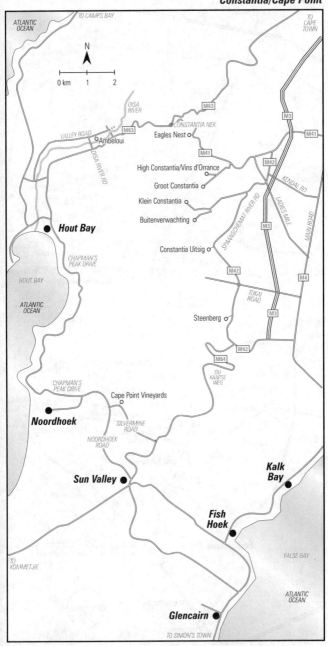

ATLANTIC
OCEAN

TO CAMPS BAY

TO CAPE TOWN

N

0 km   1   2

DISA RIVER

M63

CONSTANTIA NEK

M3

M41

VALLEY ROAD

M63

Eagles Nest ○

Ambeloui ○

M41

M42

DISA RIVER RD

High Constantia/Vins d'Orrance ○

KENDAL RD

Groot Constantia ○

Hout Bay ●

Klein Constantia ○

Buitenverwachting ○

LADIES MILE

MAIN ROAD

CHAPMAN'S PEAK DRIVE

SPAANSCHEMAT RIVER RD

M3

Constantia Uitsig ○

HOUT BAY

M42

M4

ATLANTIC
OCEAN

TOKAI ROAD

M3

Steenberg ○

M42

M64

OU KAAPSE WEG

CHAPMAN'S PEAK DRIVE

Cape Point Vineyards ○

SILVERMINE ROAD

Noordhoek ●

NOORDHOEK ROAD

Kalk Bay ●

Sun Valley ●

Fish Hoek ●

TO KOMMETJIE

FALSE BAY

ATLANTIC
OCEAN

Glencairn ●

TO SIMON'S TOWN

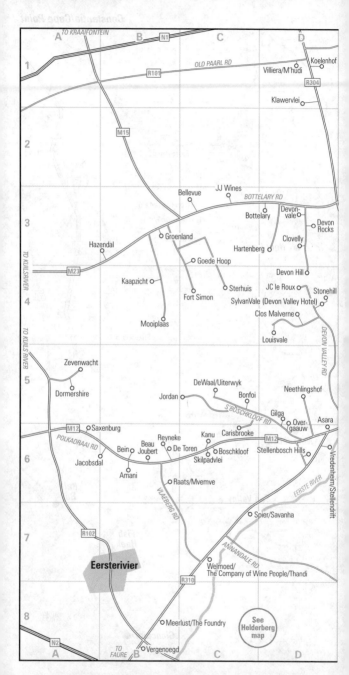

Stellenbosch

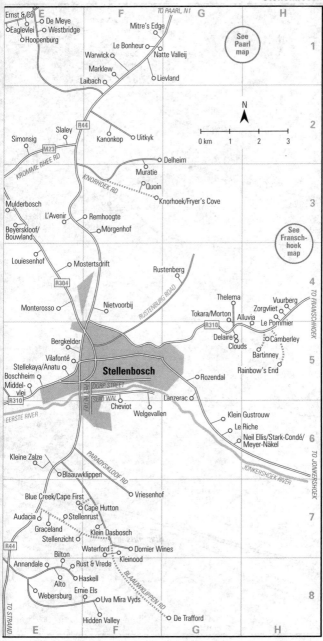

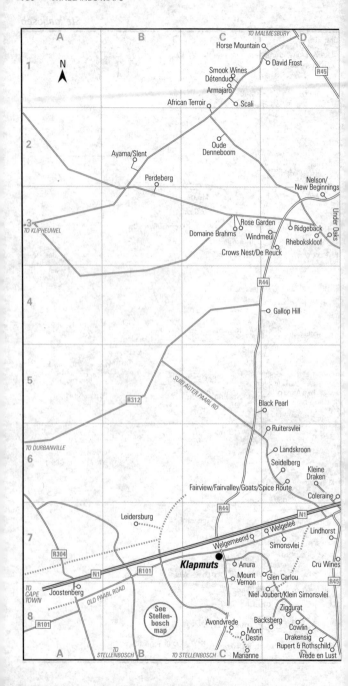

Paarl & Wellington

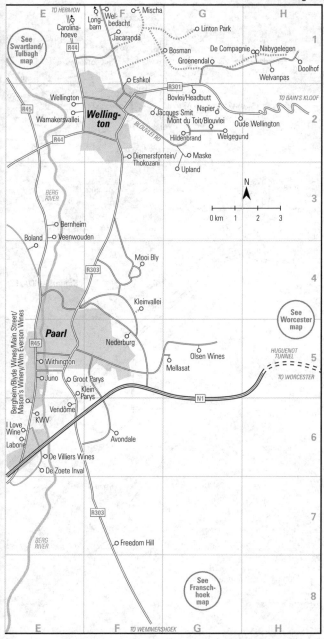

See Swartland/Tulbagh map

TO HERMON

Carolina-hoeve

Long-barn

Wel-bedacht

Mischa

Linton Park

R44

Jacaranda

Bosman

De Compagnie Nabygelegen

Groenendal

Doolhof

Eshkol

Welvanpas

R301

Bovlei/Headbutt

Wellington

TO BAIN'S KLOOF

Wamakersvallei

Welling-ton

Jacques Smit Napier

R45

Mont du Toit/Blouvlei Oude Wellington

R44

Hildenbrand Welgegund

BLOUVLEI RD

Diemersfontein/Thokozani

Maske

Upland

N

0 km 1 2 3

BERG RIVER

Bernheim

Veenwouden

Boland

Mooi Bly

R303

Kleinvallei

See Worcester map

Paarl

Nederburg

R45

Olsen Wines

HUGUENOT TUNNEL

Withington

Mellasat

Juno

Groot Parys

N1

TO WORCESTER

Klein Parys

Bergheim/Blyde Wines/Main Street/Mason's Winery/Wm Everson Wines

Vendôme

KWV

I Love Wine

Avondale

Laborie

De Villiers Wines

De Zoete Inval

R303

BERG RIVER

Freedom Hill

See Franschhoek map

TO WEMMERSHOEK

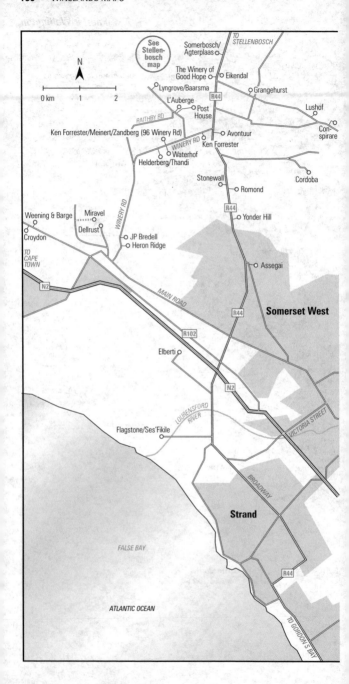

See Stellenbosch map

N

0 km   1   2

TO STELLENBOSCH

Somerbosch/
Agterplaas

The Winery of
Good Hope ○ Eikendal

Lyngrove/Baarsma ○ Grangehurst

L'Auberge ○ Post House   R44

Lushof

RAITHBY RD

Ken Forrester/Meinert/Zandberg (96 Winery Rd)   WINERY RD   ○ Avontuur

Con-
spirare

○ Waterhof   Ken Forrester

Helderberg/Thandi

Stonewall

○ Romond   Cordoba

Weening & Barge   Miravel   R44

Croydon   Dellrust   ○ Yonder Hill

TO CAPE TOWN

JP Bredell
○ Heron Ridge

N2

WINERY RD

MAIN ROAD   ● Assegai

Somerset West

R44

R102

Elberti ○

N2

LOURENSFORD RIVER

VICTORIA STREET

Flagstone/Ses'Fikile

BROADWAY

Strand

FALSE BAY

R44

ATLANTIC OCEAN

TO GORDON'S BAY

Helderberg

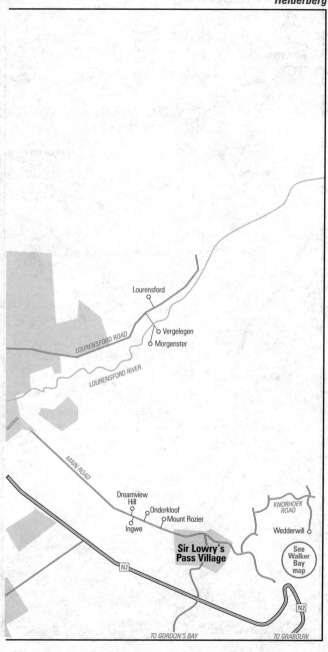

Lourensford

Vergelegen
Morgenster

LOURENSFORD ROAD

LOURENSFORD RIVER

MAIN ROAD

Dreamview
Hill
Onderkloof
Mount Rozier
Ingwe

KNORHOEK
ROAD

Wedderwill

See
Walker
Bay
map

**Sir Lowry's
Pass Village**

N2

N2

TO GORDON'S BAY

TO GRABOUW

Durbanville/Philadelphia/Darling

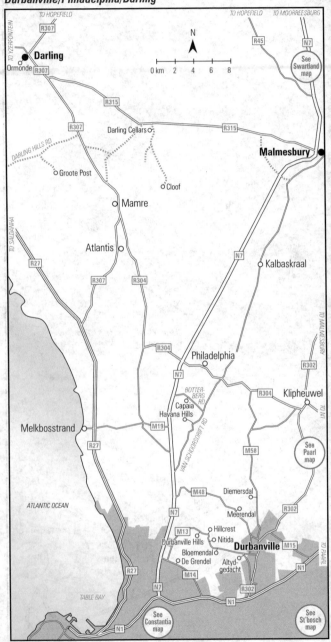

Franschhoek

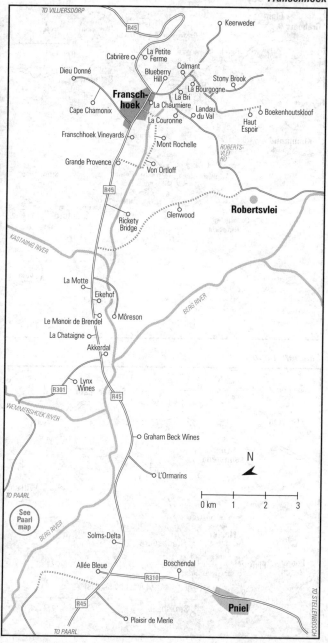

Elgin/Walker Bay

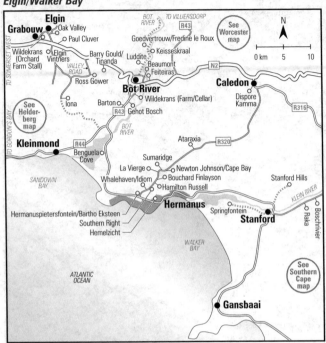

Southern Cape

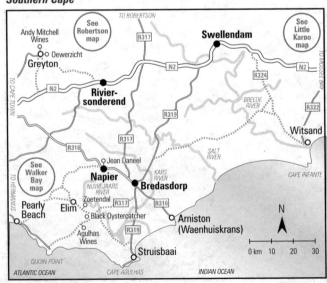

Worcester, Breedekloof & Villiersdorp

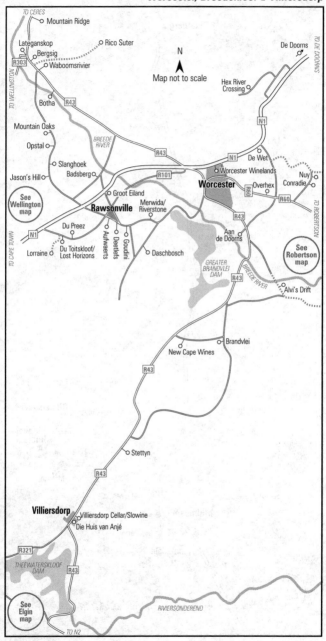

TO CERES

Mountain Ridge

Lateganskop
Bergsig
R303
Waboomsrivier

Rico Suter

De Doorns

TO WELLINGTON

Botha
R43

N

Map not to scale

TO DE DOORNS

Hex River
Crossing

N1

Mountain Oaks

Opstal

BREEDE
RIVER

R43

N1

De Wet

Slanghoek
Badsberg

R101

Worcester Winelands

Jason's Hill

Groot Eiland

Worcester

Nuy
Conradie

R60

Overhex

R60

See
Wellington
map

Rawsonville

Merwida/
Riverstone

R43

TO ROBERTSON

TO CAPE TOWN

N1

Du Preez

Lorraine

Du Toitskloof/
Lost Horizons

Aufwaerts
Deetlefs
Goudini

Daschbosch

Aan
de Doorns

BREEDE RIVER

See
Robertson
map

GREATER
BRANDVLEI
DAM

R43

Alvi's Drift

Brandvlei

New Cape Wines

R43

Stettyn

R43

Villiersdorp
Villiersdorp Cellar/Slowine
Die Huis van Anjé

R321

THEEWATERSKLOOF
DAM

R43

See
Elgin
map

RIVIERSONDEREND

TO N2

Swartland

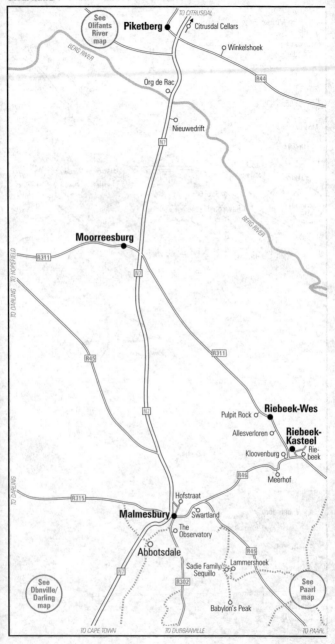

Tulbagh

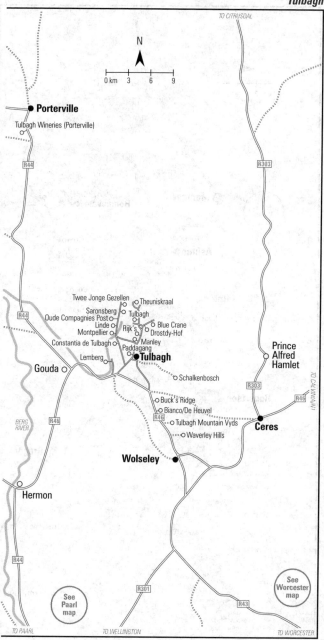

Robertson

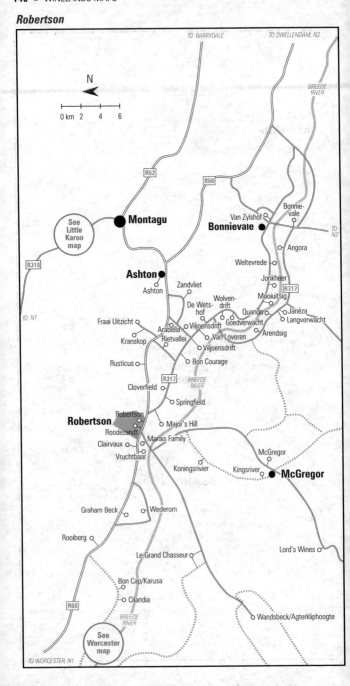

N

0 km 2   4   6

TO BARRYDALE

TO SWELLENDAM, N2

BREEDE RIVER

R62

R60

See Little Karoo map

R318

TO N1

Montagu

Van Zylshof

Bonnie-vale

Bonnievale

TO N2

Angora

Weltevrede

Ashton

Ashton

Zandvliet

Jonkheer

R317

Mooiuitsig

Wolven-drift

Quando

Janéza

De Wets-hof

Goedverwacht

Langverwacht

Fraai Uitzicht

Arabella

Viljoensdrift

Van Loveren

Arendsig

Kranskop

Rietvallei

Viljoensdrift

Rusticus

Bon Courage

R317

BREEDE RIVER

Cloverfield

Springfield

Robertson

Robertson

Major's Hill

Roodezandt

Marais Family

Clairvaux

Vruchtbaar

Koningsrivier

McGregor

Kingsriver

McGregor

Graham Beck

Wederom

Rooiberg

Lord's Wines

Le Grand Chasseur

Bon Cap/Karusa

Cilandia

R60

BREEDE RIVER

See Worcester map

Wandsbeck/Agterkliphoogte

TO WORCESTER N1

Olifants River

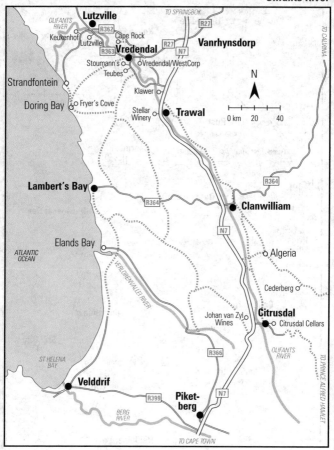

Little Karoo

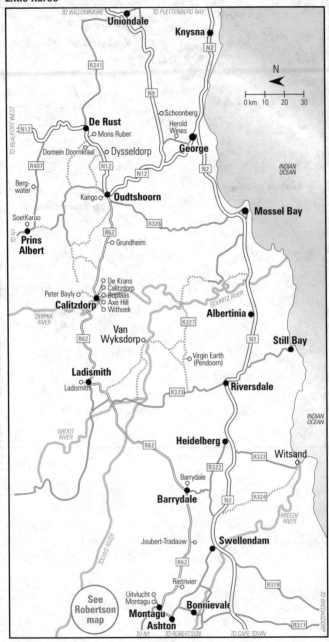

Northern Cape, Free State, North West

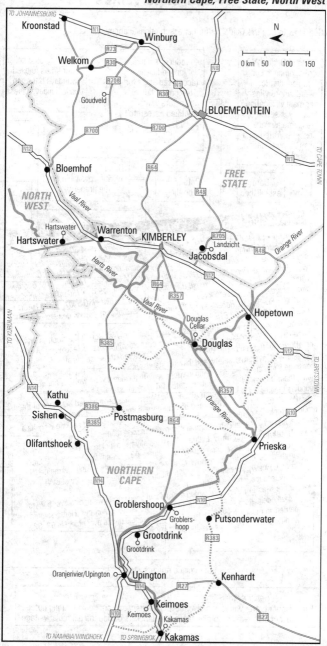

A-Z of Cape Wines

See 'How to Use this Guide' for further assumptions & abbreviations.

Wine of Origin (WO) geographical unit, region, district or ward where winery or main vinification facility is situated; assume all wines described/rated bear this WO certification, unless noted

Producer's name (only officially recognised 'units for the production of estate wine' identified as 'estate')

See Maps section for location

Tasting, sales & cellar tour times (closed Sundays but open public holidays unless noted)

Date established

Date of first bottling

Other attractions or activities available on the property

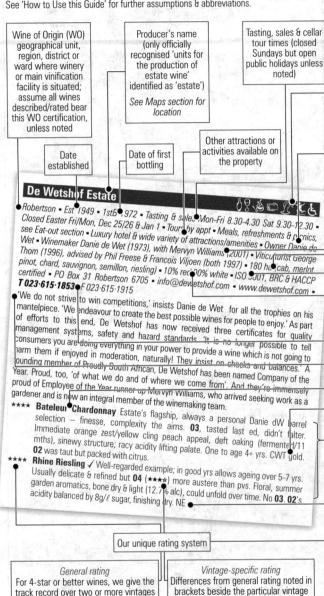

De Wetshof Estate

Robertson • Est 1949 • 1st 1972 • Tasting & sales Mon-Fri 8.30-4.30 Sat 9.30-12.30 Closed Easter Fri/Mon, Dec 25/26 & Jan 1 • Tour by appt • Meals, refreshments & picnics, see Eat-out section • Luxury hotel & wide variety of attractions/amenities • Owner Danie de Wet • Winemaker Danie de Wet (1973), with Mervyn Williams (1996), advised by Phil Freese & Francois Viljoen (both 1997) • Viticulturist George Thom (1996) • 180 ha • cab, merlot pinot, chard, sauvignon, semillon, riesling • 10% red 90% white • ISO 9001, BRC & HACCP certified • PO Box 31 Robertson 6705 • info@dewetshof.com • www.dewetshof.com • *T* 023-615-1853 • *F* 023-615-1915

'We do not strive to win competitions,' insists Danie de Wet for all the trophies on his mantelpiece. 'We endeavour to create the best possible wines for people to enjoy.' As part of efforts to this end, De Wetshof has now received three certificates for quality management systems, safety and hazard standards. 'It is no longer possible to tell consumers you are doing everything in your power to provide a wine which is not going to harm them if enjoyed in moderation, naturally! They insist on checks and balances.' A founding member of Proudly South African, De Wetshof has been named Company of the Year. Proud, too, 'of what we do and of where we come from'. And they're immensely proud of Employee of the Year runner-up Mervyn Williams, who arrived seeking work as a gardener and is now an integral member of the winemaking team.

★★★★ Bateleur Chardonnay Estate's flagship, always a personal Danie dW barrel selection — finesse, complexity the aims. **03**, tasted last ed, didn't falter. Immediate orange zest/yellow cling peach appeal, deft oaking (fermented/11 mths), sinewy structure; racy acidity lifting palate. One to age 4+ yrs. CWT gold. **02** was taut but packed with citrus.

★★★★ Rhine Riesling ✓ Well-regarded example; in good yrs allows ageing over 5-7 yrs. Usually delicate & refined but **04 (★★★½)** more austere than pvs. Floral, summer garden aromatics, bone dry & light (12.7% alc), could unfold over time. No **03**. **02**'s acidity balanced by 8g/ℓ sugar, finishing dry. NE

Our unique rating system

General rating
For 4-star or better wines, we give the track record over two or more vintages

Vintage-specific rating
Differences from general rating noted in brackets beside the particular vintage

Symbols

☺ Bottles own wine on property

☺ Open at set hours or by appointment

☺ Meals & refreshments

☺ Accommodation

☺ Bring your own (BYO) picnic

☺ Other attractions (eg festivals, function venues, walks, permanent exhibits)

☺ Child friendly

☺ Audited by our independent disability consultants & deemed disabled friendly

Name of owner

Name of winemaker, viticulturist & consultant(s); year/month of appointment in brackets

Hectares under vine (not necessarily in production); main varieties planted

Compliance, where applicable, with internationally recognised quality assurance & food safety standards, eg ISO (International Standards Organisation), HACCP (Hazard Analysis & Critical Control Point) and BRC (British Retail Consortium)

Production, in tons and/or 12-bottle cases (cs) and red:white ratio

Postal & email address, website, phone & fax number

Brief introduction/news update

Wine name, vintage, colour & style

Selected recent awards; see also Top Performers section

Listings of wines available during the currency of the book

Grape variety/ies & fruit-source; assume own vineyards unless stated; bottlings certified as 'estate wine' flagged as 'EW'; bottlings made by registered 'units for the production of estate wine' but not certified as estate-made, are noted as 'NE'

★★★★★ Superlative. A Cape classic
★★★★☆ Outstanding
★★★★ Excellent
★★★ Very good/promising
★★☆ Characterful, appealing
★★ Good everyday drinking

★★ Pleasant drinking
★☆ Casual quaffing
★ Plain and simple
☆ Very ordinary
No star Somewhat less than ordinary

Aan de Doorns Co-operative Winery

Worcester · Est 1954 · Tasting & sales Mon–Fri 8–5 · Closed pub hols · Tours during harvest by appt · Owners 57 members · Cellarmaster Johan Morkel (Nov 1993) · Winemakers Gert van Deventer (Sept 1997) & Derick Koegelenberg (Dec 2005) · 1 370 ha (pinotage, chard, chenin, colombard) · 20 400 tons 8 300 cs own label · PO Box 235 Worcester 6849 · info@ aandedoorns.co.za · T 023·347·2301 · F 023·347·4629

A flurry of new deals and ventures has seen this winery join forces with FirstCape Wines and looking to increase bulk wine sales to the price-sensitive UK and Dutch markets. Cellarmaster Johan Morkel is also eyeing markets in Scandinavia and the US. Strong growth over the past year, however, has put pressure on both supply and capacity, hence substantial investment in cellar and maturation space. Implementation of BRC and HACCP standards has also seen concrete tanks and asbestos roofing eliminated.

Pinotage ☺ ★★★ Much improved on pvs; 05 smartly oaked (with staves, yr); green banana & savoury whiffs, ripe fruit reins in dry tannins. **Muscat d'Alexandrie** ☺ ★★★ Fortified dessert with delightful raisin & honeysuckle bouquet on 05; rich yet uncloying despite 219g/ℓ sugar. **Red Muscadel** ☺ ★★★ 06 back on form with succulent blackcurrant flavour, spot-on balance of spirit, acid & sugar. Try this, Muscat d'A above, over crushed ice.

Doornroodt ★★ Merlot & ruby cab in gutsy *vin ordinaire*. 04's robust tannins punctuate smoky/ savoury fruit. Yr Am oak. **Blanc de Noir** Out of stock. **Chenin Blanc** new ★★ Softly perfumed quaffer, 06 little varietal character but pleasant enough. **Sauvignon Blanc** new ★★ Well crafted, crisply dry 06, light bodied, with muted artichoke & asparagus notes. **Semillon** new ★★ 06 eminently drinkable; grassy, fresh & dry. Sample tasted of this & next wine. **Colombar-Chardonnay** ★★ 06 zesty, unashamedly fruity 50/50 blend; fermentation of chard on Am chips gives pleasantly understated oak character. **Colombar Semi-Sweet** ★ 06 light, gently sweet peach-scented tipple. **Sparkling** ★★ Light bodied demi-sec style bubbly from colombard, dash ruby cab gives coral glints & fragrant berry aroma. Carbonated, **NV**. **Cape Ruby** ★★ Equal portions classic port varieties tinta, touriga (but still old-style low fortification & relatively high sugar); 05 smoky, raisined fruitcake tones, sweet finish. **Colombar** discontinued. — *CT*

ACJ Fine Wines

Durbanville · Est/1stB 2004 · Closed to public · Owner Billy Martin · ±9 200 cs own label · Brand for customer: Cattle Baron Group · 33% red 66% white · PO Box 3546 Tyger Valley 7536 · cwacj@telkomsa.net · T/F 021·919·6731

Negociant Billy Martin sources his Bryde wines, named after the whale species, from vineyards across the Western Cape. He also supplies The Cattle Baron eateries with house and own-brand wines, and represents selected local cellars here and overseas (currently Canada and the US).

No new vintages in sight for following: **Bryde Shiraz**★★★04 shy woodsmoke & choc nose, flavours; smooth, rounded for early drinking. Unoaked. Ex-Slnghoek vyds. **Sauvignon Blanc 05** & **Colombard-Chenin Blanc 04** not tasted. — *AL*

Adler

Wellington · Est/1stB 2004 · Closed to public · Owners/winemakers Oliver Meckler & Hans J Mamsell · 1 100 cs 55% red 45% white · adler@olimeck.co.za · www.olimeck.co.za/adler · PO Box 104 Linbro Park 2065 · T 011·579·1980 · F 011·579·1981

Geisenheim-trained Oliver Meckler and close friend Hans Mamsell make their wines at Mischa Estate in Wellington using fruit they select from the estate's well-tended vineyards.

★★★★ **Modus M** Bdx blend of equal cab & merlot, dollop petit v (10%) in 05; another beauty: the usual ringing mineral tone, fine complexity, bit more concentration; ample build (±15% alc) hidden behind veil of ripe tannin, elegant acidity. Super now, doubtless better in another yr/2. Yr Fr/Hngrian/Am oak.

Sauvignon Blanc 05 unstabilised sample last ed too unformed to rate, so full-fledged 06 (★★★★ ✓) a delicious surprise. Packed with ripe gooseberry, riveting acidity, great length — all best attributes of variety, well & clearly expressed. Bunch-pressed. **Viognier** ★★★☆ Attractive aperitif style; fruity/savoury **06** has a rather fascinating bouquet of peach pip & prosciutto; very (too?) soft, ideal for those less keen on the 'savage' white above. All NE. — *CR*

■ *Admiralty House* see Cape Bay

Adoro Wines   new

Stellenbosch ▪ 1stB 2004 ▪ Closed to public ▪ Owner Aspen Freight ▪ Winemaker Ian Naudé (May 2005) ▪ Viticulturist Lucas de Kock (Aug 2005) ▪ 50% red 50% white ▪ PO Box 982 Stellenbosch 7599 ▪ info@adorowines.co.za ▪ www.adorowines.co.za

Being the partner of a Scotch whisky distillery, Ben Riach, in Speyside lends a whole new perspective to the wine business, smiles winemaker Ian Naudé. He and viticulturist Lucas de Kock believe it's important to begin at the end — with a mental picture of the quality, price and even the 'table setting' of the finished wine. Then they select from top vineyards around the winelands for their 'building blocks'. If the results have lots of character, interesting layers and get the imbiber talking, that's part of their vision too.

★★★★ **Red** Elegant merlot-led blend (62%), dollop shiraz (25%) for mid-palate weight, equal proportions mourvèdre/grenache for Old World spice. **04** winsome plum, white pepper & cardamom bouquet; long juicy flavours focused by ultra-fine, expertly massaged tannins. 2 yrs 1st/2nd fill Fr; 14.5% alc folded away. Structure to improve gd few yrs.

★★★★★ **Naudé White Blend** Stellar debut; **06** mainly chenin, semillon (54/37) with dash Elim sauvignon. Intense tropical & thatch/fynbos scents, honeyed hint, semillon waxiness lifted by elegant chenin acidity. 3 mths new Fr oak gives mid-palate weight, grip to tail. Poised now, shd improve with few yrs ageing. 13% alc. Expect bar to raise as team tweak fruit sources, vinification.

★★★★ **Sauvignon Blanc** With quintet quality sauvignon areas represented, **06** achieves Naudé goal of 'SA character' (& more). A changeling: Dbnvlle dust one minute, Stbosch tropical fruit the next; pervasive cool zest via Elgin, Darling, Elim. Gd persistence, flavour, incl Loire-like hint blackcurrant. Drinks well now, shd gain complexity over next few yrs. — *CvZ*

■ *A Few Good Men* see Riebeek Cellars
■ *Affinity* see African Terroir, La Bri
■ *African Collection* see Rooiberg
■ *African Dawn* see Rooiberg
■ *African Gold* see Old Bridge
■ *African Horizon* see Origin Wine

African Pride Wines

Constantia ▪ Est/1stB 2002 ▪ Closed to public ▪ Owner Afrifresh Holdings ▪ Winemaker Mike Graham (May 2002) ▪ 60% red 40% white ▪ PO Box 518 Constantia 7848 ▪ info@africanpridewines. co.za ▪ www.africanpridewines.co.za ▪ T 021·794·0323 ▪ F 021·794·0344

Mike Graham and team are flying high — that's the message as far as their chardonnays are concerned, with listings on both SAA and Singapore Airlines business class. Not that this happened on a wing and a prayer. Hard work has also seen the Footprint range make great strides in the US market and scoop a prestigious listing on Royal Caribbean Cruise Lines. Judging by foreign buyer demand, new reserve range Footprint Impression has made one too.

Lady Anne Barnard range

Cabernet Sauvignon ★★★☆ Elegant & understated **02**, hints wet heath & leafy footpath to red-berried ripeness; tannins supple but structured to age few yrs. 18 mths Fr oak. **Syrah** ★★★☆ **02** creamy mulberry aroma, lively, juicy palate features ripe Hldrberg fruit, well expressed. 16 mths oak, new/2nd fill. **Chardonnay** ★★★★ Statement wine with big oak presence; **03** flavours of lemon, lime & buttered toast. Fermented/9 mths new Fr oak, portion native yeasts. Above not retasted, notes from earlier ed. **Sauvignon Blanc** new ★★★☆ Lovely grassy, herbal notes on **05**, with a green edge that pervades, gives character & interest. Long, tangy, lime-infused finish. Delicious. These WO Sbosch, all below W Cape or Coastal.

Footprint Impression range `new`

Petit Verdot-Shiraz ★★★☆ With white pepper & prosciutto notes on a bed of dark fruit, **05** has nicely judged oaking, enough to add structure, definition without interfering with appetite appeal. Dry finish, perfect for food. **Viognier** ★★★☆ Not boastful but has a lot going for it, a gd example of the variety. **05** offers appealing peach (fruit & pip) styling, some floral notes; rounded, almost fleshy mouthfeel, long finish.

Footprint range

> **Chenin Blanc-Semillon** `new` ☺ ★★★ Cool-grown fruit, early picking (11.5% alc) has given **06** a leafy delicacy that charms while it refreshes. Nothing overdone but perfect quaffing fare. Equal blend.

Cabernet Sauvignon ★★★ Appealing early-drinking style; **04** last ed showed a fresh red-fruit profile, toasty dry finish from 20% barrelled portion. **Shiraz** ★★★ Juicy mulberries, plums, given firm oak treatment, adding a touch of seriousness to **05**. Still accessible, but to accompany prime beef or rich stews rather than casual drinking. Dab viognier. **Merlot-Pinotage** `new` ★★★ Fruit dominates **05**, plums & full-ripe berries, some smoky spice, but it's more than a pretty face; some palate stiffening holds everything in place. Not for long keeping. **Chardonnay** ★★★ **06** has peach & floral perfumes, flavours, light textured drinkability. **Sauvignon Blanc** ★★★ **05** shows a lot of ripeness, stewed apple, despite modest alc. Palate is approachable, with gd clean finish.

Cape MacLear range

Shiraz-Cabernet Sauvignon ★★★ **04** identical blend to pvs (66/33), unwooded; shiraz nose, cab active on palate, which slightly firmer than last though still accessible. **Chenin Blanc-Chardonnay** ★★★ **04** offered fruit salad aromas, rounded peach flavours in lively & juicy 60/40 blend. No new vintages tasted. — *CR*

■ *African Sky see* Drostdy

African Terroir

Paarl ▪ Est 1991 ▪ 1stB 1991 ▪ Visits Mon-Fri 9-5 (phone ahead) ▪ Fee R15 refunded on purchase of 2+ btls ▪ Closed Dec 25/26 & Jan 1 ▪ Picnic baskets, platters & beverages by appt; or BYO ▪ Guest house (see Stay-over section) ▪ Tour groups ▪ Conferencing ▪ Owner Jacques Germanier ▪ Operations manager Heiko Huber ▪ Head winemaker Mathieu Labaki (Jan 2003) ▪ Winemakers Lizette Steyn-James & Johnnie Loubser (both Nov 2005) ▪ Viticulturist Francois Brink (Dec 2002) ▪ 75 ha (own vyds: cab, shiraz) ▪ 400 tons ▪ BRC, HACCP & ISO 9001:2000 accredited ▪ Ranges for customers: Indaba, Mooiberge, Unity & Affinity ▪ PO Box 2029 Windmeul 7630 ▪ office@african-terroir.co.za ▪ www.african-terroir.co.za ▪ T 021·869·8103 ▪ F 021·869·8104

Now heading up the production team is operations manager Heiko Huber, with chief winemaker Mathieu Labaki assisted by Lizette Steyn-James, settled after a brief stint at Bianco, and Johnnie Loubser, post a season in France. Plans are to develop the local market to its full potential and, export-wise, expand further into Eastern Europe. The winery has had a fair amount of TV exposure of late: it was among producers selected by Fairtrade for a documentary for Belgian and French audiences, and its Sonop winery, a worker-empowerment project, was filmed last year by students from Vienna.

Azania range

Listed intermittently in the guide. **Cabernet Sauvignon** ★★★ **05** ripe-fruited though quite stern, plenty of tannins showing on the finish. **Merlot** ★★ **05** subtly oaked, so berry fruit to the fore; juicy, tasty, good food accompaniment. **Pinotage** ★★★ Warm, spicy Xmas pudding whiffs on **05**, well packed with ripe fruit, gd firm tannins. **Shiraz** ★★★ Balanced, appealing **05**, salad of red & black berries; lovely fruit & freshness makes it fun to drink. **Chardonnay** ★★★ Briefly oaked **06** has gd flesh, character & peachy flavour; attractively light 13% alc. **Sauvignon Blanc** ★ **06** lightish, simple dry white with a baked-fruit character.

Big Five range

Another intermittently listed line-up. **Cabernet Sauvignon** ★★★ Wine fits lion pictured on front label, though **05** growls rather than roars: typical cab cedary fruit, firm tannins, pleasant grip to finish. **Pinotage** ★★★ Well built, flavoursome **05**; generous in fruit department; juicy & fresh. **Shiraz** ★★★ 'Hot' baked-fruit character shows warm **05** vintage; juicy plum fruit in balance with soft dry tannins. **Chardonnay** ★★ **06** starts well & attractively with buttered toast tone (though unwooded, say winemakers) then disappears rather suddenly. **Sauvignon Blanc** ★★ **06** light, undemanding quaffer with lemon-drop & earthy notes, mild acidity.

Diemersdal range

Cabernet Sauvignon, **Merlot**, **Pinotage**, **Shiraz**, **Harmony**, **Chardonnay**, **Sauvignon Blanc** all discontinued.

Elixir range

Sauvignon Blanc Noble Late Harvest ★★★★ Soft, silky **00** still available; when last tasted fairly developed aromas, dried apricot whiffs & good botrytis dusting, clean fruity acids. Grapes ex-Dbnville, yr barrel aged.

Milton Grove range

Shiraz ★★ **05** has almost nothing of pvs's plummy character; very ripe, fat, with volatile touch & bitter finish. **Chardonnay** ★★★ new **06** recognisably chard; orange marmalade flavours, soft fruity entry followed by brisk acidic twist.

Out of Africa range

Cabernet Sauvignon ★★ **05** ungenerous dry red with light, stalky/green tone. **Merlot** ★★ Not a lot to report on **05** except big dry tannins overriding fruit. **Pinotage** ★★★ Again drinkable & fun; **05** bright red-cherry fruit, soft juicy tannins which slip down smoothly. **Shiraz** ★★★ **05** some crushed red-berry flavours, fairly sinewy, with quick dry finish. Fr oak influenced. **Rosé** new ★★ From cab; **06** dry, slightly savoury red-fruit flavours with satisfying weight. **Chardonnay** ★★ **06** similar to pvs's friendly, sunny style; faint dried-peach whiffs, gentle fruit, low acidity. **Sauvignon Blanc** ★ Featherweight **06** usual water-white transparency & pear-drop aroma, otherwise very little character. **Pinotage-Shiraz** discontinued.

Sonop Organic range

Merlot ★★ A less ripe & generous version this yr; **06** muted fruit, stalky tones, lots of freshness needing food. Following trio of **05**s not revisited: **Cabernet Sauvignon** ★★ Hot climate feel, raisined & porty, with soft acidity. **Pinotage** ★★ Unshowy, almost delicate red-berried appeal, easy to drink if quick finishing. **Shiraz** ★★ Smoky entry to this gentle, softly plummy version; lower alc (13.7%) than pvs, less tight tannin. **Chardonnay** ★★ **06** firmer, less flesh & padding than pvs; lemon-biscuit flavours with touch tannin on exit. **Sauvignon Blanc** ★★ Herby/minty touch to **06**'s gooseberry fruit; dry, very light (12.4% alc), notch up on pvs.

Tribal Spear range

Replaces Tribal Winemakers Collection. **Cabernet Sauvignon** ★★★ Ripe, well textured **05**; warm blackberry jam flavours, ripe cedary tannins, balanced & moreish. **Merlot** ★★ Inviting mulberry intro to **05**; light bodied but ripe & lively; suitable for lightly chilling in summer. **Pinotage** ★★★ Any & all edges smoothed in **05**; creamy fruit, red berry juiciness, balanced tannins & uplifting cranberry tang. **Shiraz** ★★★ Vintage's ripeness apparent on **05**, touch porty, sweet-warm fruit yet manages a proper dry finish. **Chardonnay** ★★ **06** vinous rather than fruity; suggestion of citrus; light, with v firm acidity. **Chenin Blanc** ★ **06** soft, completely undemanding dry white with modest pear-drop flavour.

Tribal range

Following all unwooded. **Dry Red** ★★ ('African Red' pvs ed.) Compote of baked plum & raisin on light bodied **NV** from ruby cab, cab & shiraz; contrasting dry gripping tannins. **Rosé** ★★ Light bodied summer refresher from cab; **06** understated varietal character, some weight, lingering properly dry finish. **Sauvignon Blanc-Colombard** new ★★ 06 fresh, sprightly dry white, light & effortlessly pleasant. **Dry White** ★★ ('African White' pvs ed.) **NV** from blancs chenin & sauvignon plus colombard; soft, easy, guava toned quick-quaff. Following bubblies **NV**: **Sparkling White Off-Dry** ★★★ Light sweetish fizz from hanepoot, with brisk, even elegant bubbles & soft citrus tone. **Sparkling Semi-Sweet** ★★ Less refined version of above; appreciably sweet with lemon sherbet character. **African White Semi Sweet** discontinued.

Winds of Change range

Fairtrade Organic Shiraz new ★★★ Pleasantly plump 06; clean-cut red & dark cherry fruit; nice flick of dry tannin in tail. **Pinotage-Cabernet Sauvignon** ★★★ Slightly different proportions this yr (60/40 blend), same approachability & generous flavours; **05** attractive easy-drinker. **Pinotage-Shiraz** new ★★★ Compatible 60/40 mix, unwooded; **05** clean uncluttered feel; lots of berry & plum, balancing tannin & freshness. **Fairtrade Chardonnay** new ★★ Well made quaffer. 06 juicy & padded with surprisingly persistent peach & baked-pear fruit. **Sauvignon Blanc** new ★★ Airy 06, ultra-soft & easy, with modest sauvignon grassiness & hint of capsicum. **Shiraz-Merlot** discontinued. Fruit for above ranges sourced widely: all WO W Cape. — *IvH*

■ *African Treasure* see Vin-X-Port
■ *African Wine Adventure* see Mooiuitsig

African Wines & Spirits

*Cape Town • Est 1999 • Closed to public • Owners Edward Snell & Co • Directors DV Hooper & CC Weeden • 40% red 60% white • PO Box 318 Paarden Eiland • **T** 021·506·2600 F 021·510·4560*

This wholesaling and marketing company is owned by Edward Snell & Co, and has the Craighall range made to spec by The Company of Wine People in Stellenbosch. Other brands in the stable include Cinzano sparkling, now bottled in Italy and imported.

■ *Agterkliphoogte* see Wandsbeck

Agterplaas Wines

*Stellenbosch (see Helderberg map) • Est/1stB 2003 • Visits by appt • Owner/winemaker James Basson • PO Box 863 Stellenbosch 7599 • 4.5 tons 250 cs • agterplaas@webmail.co. za • **T/F** 021·855·3483*

'Backyard' is the Afrikaans name of this micro winery, because the Cape Town northern suburbs home of cellar designer James Basson is where it all happens — and a corner of his friends' Somerbosch cellar near Stellenbosch. This ed we tasted the Cab-Merlot alluded to last year, but the 'stunning' bordeaux-style 05 red mentioned earlier by Basson remains a deferred pleasure for now.

Cabernet Sauvignon-Merlot ★★★ Powerful Aussie style menthol/eucalyptus lead-in to **04**, forward fruited, smooth textured mouthful, hearty 14% alc neatly in check. 60/40 blend, 18 mths oak, 50% new. No newer releases tasted for: **Cabernet Sauvignon** ★★★ Appealing 03 maiden from Hldrberg vines; mulberry & sweet/sour fruit flavours, firm yet friendly wood tannins from 18 mths 3rd fill Fr oak. **Mike's Red** ★★★ Old-Cape style blend cab, cinsaut (79/21), **03** cool cedar notes, softish tannins & fresh acidity. 8 mths used Fr oak. **Sauvignon Blanc** ★★★ 04 assertive, lean & bone-dry, with rapier-direct acid. — *CT/IvH*

Agulhas Wines

*Elim • Est 2002 • 1stB 2003 • Tasting & sales Mon-Fri 8-5 • BYO picnic • 2 self-catering guest cottages • Tours by appt • Tour groups by arrangement • Walks • Owners Strandveld Vineyards & Rietfontein Trust • Winemaker/viticulturist Conrad Vlok (Dec 2004) • 67 ha (pinot, shiraz, chardonnay, sauvignon, semillon) • 120 tons 8 600 cs 45% red 55% white • Export brands: Strandveld & First Sighting • PO Box 10 Elim 7284 • info@agulhaswines.com • www. firstsighting.co.za • **T/F** 028·482·1902/6*

Part of newly established Elim Winegrowers, with its 'real people making a real difference' credo, Agulhas winemaker Conrad Vlok's current reality is juggling increasing volumes. The 2006 harvest, up by 33% to 120 tons, is expected to double this year. The Sauvignon from Africa's southernmost vineyards at Uintjieskuil – one of the coolest winegrowing areas – has met with a warm reception, having been selected as one of top 10 for Bartho Eksteen's annual Sauvignon Blanc Celebration. Expect the release of a maiden Pinot this year under the Strandveld label.

First Sighting Range

Shiraz ★★★ Full bodied but elegant **04**; quiet mocha/red fruits nose, initial spicy oomph on palate blurred by hint sweet oak (Fr, 14 mths). Incl tiny portion maiden home-grown shiraz/cab, bal Darling. WO Coastal, as is… **Chardonnay** ★★★ **05** unwooded to play up generous pineapple, grapefruit zest flavours. Creamy, with good acid spine; rounded finish. Perfect partner for Asian or other spicy food. **Sauvignon Blanc** Gooseberry, passion-fruit, tangerine peel pungency leaps from glass on previewed **06** (★★★★). Sufficient weight to balance overall lively minerality; pure, elegant 'sauvage' flavours, rousing length. More concentrated than maiden **05** (★★★☆). Incl 12% semillon. —AL

Akkerdal Estate

Franschhoek ▪ Est 2000 ▪ 1stB 2001 ▪ Tasting & sales by appt Mon-Fri 8-5 Sat 9-1 ▪ Sales also at Franschhoek Vineyards (see A-Z entry) & La Cotte Inn Wine Sales (see Wine shops section) ▪ Closed pub hols ▪ Self-catering guest house (see Stay-over section) ▪ Owner/winemaker/viti-culturist Pieter Hanekom, advised by Eben Archer & Dawid Saayman ▪ 18 ha (malbec, merlot, mourvèdre, petit v, pinotage, shiraz, chard, sauvignon, semillon, viognier) ▪ ±3 000 cs own label 95% red 5% white ▪ ISO certification in progress ▪ PO Box 36 La Motte 7691 ▪ wine@akkerdal.co.za ▪ www.akkerdal.co.za ▪ T 021·876·3481/082·442·1746 ▪ F 021·876·3189

Franschhoek winegrower Pieter Hanekom rates 2006 great for winemaking but under incredibly difficult circumstances. One of several pre-season Cape winelands veldfires raced through the valley straight into Akkerdal's premium sauvignon vineyards. With 16 precious rows lost, vines were cut down and immediately started shooting, auguring well for next vintage. Firefighters Hanekom and his workers, all suffering the after-effects, made it through the harvest. Positives include a new Kallie's Dream bottling and a successful overseas marketing trip.

★★★★ **Merlot 04** toasty oak combines with racy yet ripe fruit to deliver rich, rounded, lingering mouthful, structure for development over 3-5 yrs. 14 mths mainly 1st fill oak. **03** (★★★★) had savoury notes, dry herbaceous finish from 18 mths older barrels.

Syrah With perfect ripeness, balance, powerful & ripe tannic punch, **03** (★★★★) step up on **02** (★★★★). Scrub & liquorice wafts, concentrated berry fruit softened with drop viognier & dollop mourvèdre. Barrels as above, 18 mths. **Wild Boar** ★★★ Unconventional blend excites the tastebuds – malbec, mourvèdre, petit v, tempranillo, roobernet, barbera & cab f (we did ask!). Juicy, smooth; accessible but with tannins to carry ± 5 yrs. Oaking as for Syrah. **Passion Red** ★★★★ **04** rings the changes: to blend: (now shiraz led) & to quality level: (up). Shiraz pepper dominates wild/mulberry nose; mourvèdre, malbec & pinotage add spice & zest. Robust, muscled tannins great with steak. 14 mths combo Fr/Am/Hungarian oak. **Passion White** ★★★★ **04** unoaked blend equal (almost) portions chardonnay, sauvignon, semillon & viognier; balanced with waxy roundness, pleasing, dry finish; complex with citrus fruit/floral fragrances/favours. **Kallie's Dream** ★★★ Oaked dinner table companion; viognier/sauvignon (35/30) lead chardonnay/semillion (23/12). Nuanced bouquet of buttered toast, lime, earth; palate rich & smooth. None above retasted this ed. —CT

■ *Alexanderfontein see Ormonde*

Allée Bleue

Franschhoek ▪ Est 1690 ▪ 1stB 2001 ▪ Tasting & sales daily 9-5 ▪ Café Allée Bleue daily 9-5 (see Eat-out section) ▪ Other attractions see intro ▪ Tours by appt ▪ Tour groups ▪ Owners DAUPHIN Entwicklungs-und Beteiligungs GMH (Germany) ▪ Winemaker Gerda Willers (Dec 2001) ▪ Viti-culturist Douw Willemse ▪ Consultant Rob Meihuizen (2001) ▪ 13 ha (cab, merlot, pinotage,

shiraz, sauvignon) ▪ *80% red 18% white 2% rosé* ▪ *PO Box 100 Groot Drakenstein 7680* ▪ *info@alleebleue.com* ▪ *www.alleebleue.com* ▪ **T** *021·874·1021* ▪ F *021·874·1850*

No effort's been spared to allure visitors (and keep them entertained). Among new attractions are a deli, selling home-grown olives and their maiden vintage oils, fields of rosemary and lavender for fragrant strolling, a banqueting area with a 1 000-year-old wild olive tree the pivotal feature of its courtyard, and a corporate winetasting venue. But the key facility is a new cellar, brought into use for the fist time last year. 'No, no, not hi-tech,' laughs winemaker Gerda Willers, 'just a practical working cellar.' First out was a maiden Starlette Blanc, the second-tier white blend, and a Sauvignon.

★★★★ **Isabeau** Fine wooded semillon/chard blend; **05** honeyed waxy notes, zesty citrus acidity & warm finish from alc 14.3%; grapes ex-Fhoek & Piekenklf; ±70/30 blend, 9 mths Fr oak, 60% new.

Pinotage ★★★★ Opulent, succulent New World style with creamy texture. **05** ripe mulberry conserve with sweet vanilla spice & liquorice. Bold 15% alc, showing warmer vintage, needs food. Piekenklf vyds; 50% new wood, 20% Am, yr. Similar style to MIWA trophy awarded **04**. **Shiraz** ★★★ Warm, spicy & juicy **05** tempered by dry dusty tannin. Similar ±15 alc to pvs makes for rounded, powerful wine with long, glowing farewell. Half new oak, 20% Rssian, yr. WO Breede Rvr Vlly. **Cabernet Sauvignon-Merlot** ★★★★ 60/40 complex blend with wild mint & mocha choc aromas, richly fruited. **05** bright acidity & firm, cedary, dry tannins streamline balanced & juicy midpalate with long dry finish. 15% alc not evident. Yr Fr oak, 50% new. **L'Amour Toujours** ★★★★ Rich, New World style red with properly dry finish despite 15% alc; **05** again blends cab (40%), merlot, shiraz & grenache; abundance of ripe black fruit only just reined in by cedary dry tannin; gd with hearty fare. 60% new Fr oak. Swiss gold & VDG for **04**. **Rosé** ★★★ This yr pure shiraz, imparting savoury, juicy red berried flavours & well judged hint of tannin in **05**; 9 mths older wood add structure, help counter big alc (15%), making a great food partner. **Starlette Rouge** ★★★ Now pinotage led (with shiraz, grenache, cab & merlot) but **05** similar wood, alc & style to pvs; smooth approachable palate redolent of sweet spice & earth. 9 mths wood; 'cellar std' 15% alc. **Starlette Blanc** NEW ★★★ Gentle, understated, lighter style for lunchtime or aperitif quaffing. **06** just off-dry blend sauvignon, chenin & semillon (55/34/11), all in harmony; restrained lemongrass, waxy aromas & chenin's ripe-fruited flavours. **Sauvignon Blanc** NEW ★★★★ **06** off S/West, Paarl vyds; herbaceous hints overtaken by riot of tropical pineapple & passionfruit. Same abundant flavour profile balanced by zesty acidity. Refreshing, lighter style (12.9 alc), solo or with food, tangy sweet/sour farewell. All above WO W Cape unless noted. **Pinotage Natural Sweet** discontinued.— MW

Allesverloren Estate

Swartland ▪ *Est 1704* ▪ *Tasting & sales Mon-Fri 8.30-5 Sat 8.30-2 Phone ahead on pub hols* ▪ *Tours by appt* ▪ *Steakhouse style meals or BYO picnic* ▪ *Play area for children* ▪ *Owner/ winemaker/viticulturist Danie Malan (Nov 1987)* ▪ *187 ha (cab, shiraz & various port varieties)* ▪ *50 000 cs 100% red* ▪ *PO Box 23 Riebeek West 7306* ▪ *info@allesverloren.co.za* ▪ *www. allesverloren.co.za* ▪ **T** *022·461·2320* ▪ F *022·461·2444*

'All is Lost' the owners renamed this farm back in 1704 on returning from the Cape to find their house razed to the ground, their lands destroyed. The recovery from that disaster and rebirth of the property would have been much on the minds of the Malans last year, when they celebrated 200 years of winemaking at Allesverloren by opening a new tasting centre in one of the farm's oldest buildings. The old tasting venue is now an eatery (the steakhouse fare appropriate to their beefy wines!). Another innovation is new packaging, being phased in across the range.

★★★★ **Shiraz** These generously built, chunky & powerful — 14.4% alc for ripe, red-fruited **03**, the bottling last tasted. Skip to **05** (★★★★) a gentle, amiable, slightly lower keyed giant. Juicy, spicy, balanced, but has less concentrated fruit & more accessible structure than pvs. Combo new/older oak Fr & Am.

★★★★☆ **Port** Ingratiating & effortless LBV styling something of a Cape institution; **02** deliciously rich dark prune & mocha, long savoury-nutty flavours. Bit sweeter at 120 g/ℓ than last-tasted **99** but otherwise similar components (dash malvasia rey souping up customary souzão, pontac, touriga & trio of tintas – b, r & f) & character. Older oak aged.

Cabernet Sauvignon ★★★★ 04 restrained cedar & berry nose belies ripe cassis/choc palate with protracted finish. Tannins firm, ripe but dry, not gruff as pvs. Smooth, with well woven oak (18 mths Fr, 30% new); accessible now, shd develop further over few yrs. **Tinta Barocca★★★★ 05** generously fruited, riper & rounded rather than rustic as pvs. Broachable; lively acidity given vintage, so unblowsy; attractive mocha farewell. 8 mths equal parts barrel/tank fermentation, with micro-oxygenation. **Touriga Nacional ★★★ 05** explosion of ripe dark fruit on palate after shy perfumed aroma, silky texture thanks to warm-yr fruit ripeness & ±15% alc. Attractive spicy note from older wood. Drinks beautifully now. — *MW*

Alluvia

Stellenbosch ▪ Est 2002 ▪ 1stB 2005 ▪ Tasting by appt ▪ Sales office open daily ▪ Tours for pvt clients only ▪ Luxury guest suites (see Stay-over section) ▪ Facilities for children ▪ Gifts ▪ Conferences ▪ Walks ▪ Mountain bike trails ▪ Owners Delarey & Sandie Brugman ▪ Production team Kevin Watt, Neil Moorhouse & Delarey Brugman ▪ 8 ha (cab) ▪ 18 tons 1 100 cs 88% red 12% white ▪ PO Box 6365 Uniedal 7612 ▪ info@alluvia.co.za or ilka@alluvia.co.za ▪ www.alluvia. co.za ▪ T 0861·80·70·60/021·885·1661 F 021·885·2064

While Delarey Brugman is busy establishing Alluvia as a premium lifestyle getaway (offering a spa, fly-fishing, scenic winelands and breakfast flights in their Cessna, and a golf green among the vineyards, where young cab is coming on-stream this year), his Gauteng business savvy prompted him and a group of producers to form a 'value chain optimisation' consortium, 'Bring it Home', bypassing the traditional distribution chain and selling directly to upmarket customers.

Ilka range

★★★★ Sauvignon Blanc Dramatically styled **06** has sumptuous tropical aromas, yet fine crisp acidity; flamboyancy in this tank sample suggests early drinkability. Elegant successor to more floral, sweeter **05**.

Cabernet Sauvignon ★★★★ Restrained fruit but incipient complexity & gd depth, balance on **04** (tasted last ed), with tiny splashes petit v, merlot. 14 mths oak, third new. — *MF*

■ *Alphen Hill see* Cru Wines

Alter Ego Wines

Rustenburg ▪ Est 2001 ▪ 1stB 2002 ▪ visits by appt ▪ Attractions/amenities: see intro ▪ Owner Vin de Parr cc ▪ Winemaker/viticulturist John Parr (Sep 2001) ▪ 35 tons 2 000 cs 50% red 40% white 10% port ▪ Postnet Suite #75, Private Bag X7, Parkview, 2122 ▪ alterego@icon.co.za ▪ www.alteregowine.co.za ▪ T 014·577·4762/082·466·459

John Parr, having sold up in Tulbagh and trekked north — the new cellar in the Boons area between Magaliesburg and Rustenburg opens this year. Intention? Establish a traditional Cape winery next to the Gauteng market ('take the farm to the wine lovers'). Grapes still to be sourced in Tulbagh, wine to be made on Boonducks Farm (fresh free-range birds, stock and pâté can be purchased). Other attractions: mountain biking and amateur winemaking (for a fee, 10 'volunteers' get hands-on experience).

Boonducks Red ★★★★ (Pvsly 'Cabernet Sauvignon'.) **04** balanced, long & concentrated — but not overpoweringly so; wafts of cedar, then brimming blackberries, finishes savoury. Appropriate oaking (16 mths Fr, 2nd & 4th fill) provides frame to improve 3+ yrs. **Ethan Asher ★★** Cab/merlot (60/40) blend. **04** less claret-like, ageworthy than pvs; touch more rustic & vegetal, but same taut mineral core & tannins. 16 mths oak, some new. EW. Following duo not retasted: **Semillon ★★★** Fine acidity on **04**, unoaked but 3 mths on lees, last yr gave refreshment to the honey & lemon character. **Elroy's Pawt 00** unrated sweet fortified from cab & merlot, with plenty of personality, like the Labrador it's named for. 375ml. All WO Tulbagh, with 'very low' sulphur additions, says winemaker. — *CT*

Alto Estate

Stellenbosch • Est 1906 • 1stB 1918 • Tasting & sales Mon-Fri 9-5 Sat & pub hols 10-4 • Fee R10 (R20 incl glass) • Owner Lusan Premium Wines • Winemaker Schalk van der Westhuizen (Jul 2000) • Vineyard manager Danie van Zyl • Viticulturist Eben Archer • 93 ha • 25 000 cs 100% red • PO Box 104 Stellenbosch 7599 • altoestate@telkomsa.net • www.alto.co.za • **T 021·881·3884** • *F 021·881·3894*

Grown on a high altitude granite belt on the slopes of the Helderberg, Alto's vines enjoy ideal conditions for making fine reds. The blend which launched the estate's enduring reputation back in the 1920s is once again labelled Alto Rouge locally (though still 'Estate' abroad). For the first time in a decade, the estate will be producing a Port, though it won't be released for at least two years.

★★★★ **Cabernet Sauvignon** Stylistically one of SA's slow-maturing wines, its cellarability conferred by cab's typical austere tannins. **04** delivers faultless styling: cassis, cedar, meat-extract nuances on firm bed of fine-grained tannins. Worthy addition to any collection. Oaking regimen 18–24 mths 300ℓ Fr oak, 50% new, rest 2nd/3rd fill.

★★★★ **Shiraz** Off unirrigated vyds, 200-400m up the Hldrberg. Maiden **01** set tone: more elegant than powerful. *Decanter* 2006 trophy. **04** a worthy successor: luscious berries with oak-spicy dimension, smoky whiffs, liquorice. Poised, beautifully balanced & ageworthy. Sample tasted. Oak as for Rouge.

★★★★ **Alto Rouge** ('Estate' outside SA) One of Cape's oldest & best-loved labels, from older, low yielding vines. Has morphed from cab/cinsaut of yesteryear via bdx blend to current mix merlot, cabs s/f, shiraz (45/25/15/15). Intense cherry, dried herb approach in **04**, with trademark serious tannins adding stiffening, tobacco notes, promising rewarding future. Will show better in yr, develop for 5+ more. 18 mths oak, mainly Fr, 1st-3rd fill. — *CR*

Altydgedacht Estate

Durbanville • Est 1698 • 1stB 1981 • Tasting & sales Mon-Fri 9-5 Sat 9-3 • Closed Easter Fri, Dec 25 & Jan 1 • Tours by appt • Pampoenkraal boma-style function venue T 021·913·4962/3 • Conferencing • Conservation area • Owners Parker family • Cellarmaster Oliver Parker • Winemaker Etienne Louw (Jan 2006), advised by Mark Carmichael-Green • Viticulturists John Parker, with Adanté Roux (2002) • 170 ha (12 varieties, r/w) • 1 500 tons ±5 000 cs own label 55% red 45% white • Export label: Tygerberg • PO Box 213 Durbanville 7551 • altydgedacht@ mweb.co.za • www.altydgedacht.co.za • T 021·976·1295 • F 021·976·4318/8521

Withstanding Durbanville's urban sprawl continues to be Oliver Parker's biggest challenge — but he and his team are fighting back by planting more vineyards. An important development is the arrival of 'easy-going, guitar playing' winemaker Etienne Louw. No stranger to Altydgedacht, having worked the 2001 and 2002 harvests here after studying chemical engineering, Louw also boasts an oenology degree. 'We look forward to benefiting from his winemaking, tasting and people skills,' says Parker.

Chatelaine ☺ ★★★ Delightful, perfumed semi-sweet; **06** nimble & light-hearted blend gewürz & riesling, with low 12% alc.

Cabernet Sauvignon ★★★ Dry-finishing **02** has good tannins, but less fruit presence than pvs. Yr Fr/Am oak. Not retasted. **Barbera** ★★★ SA pioneer of this Italian grape. **03** hint forest fungus to dark, tangy varietal fruit; noticeably fresh, with fine tannins; very food-amenable. Mix Fr/Am oak, quarter new. **Merlot** ★★★★ Last yr's barrel sample **04** now bottled; retains its pleasant herbal character with woodland hint, trim but well tailored fruit, ripe tannin. Fr oak, 25% new. **Pinotage** ★★★★ **03** elegant & clean-cut, with good (if not overtly varietal) flavours, chalky tannins. Still somewhat tight – needs time. **Shiraz** ★★★★ **04** invites with lovely ripe red fruits display, smoky touch; well-judged wood (only Fr this time, 50% new); elegant meaty flavours. **Chardonnay** ★★★★ Mostly oak-fermented/aged 5 mths. Current **05** not retasted; last ed noted as pleasant, fresh, well balanced. **Chenin Blanc** ★★★ From 33 yr old bushvines; 33% barrel fermented. **06**

bit timid mid-2006 compared with rich & rounded pvs; might grow become expressive with time. **Sauvignon Blanc** ★★★★ Invariably ripely flavourful, freshly & fruitily succulent; **06** with usual touch sugar (3.5g/ℓ) adding to immediate appeal. NE. **Gewürztraminer** ★★★ Reliably charming example – ideal aperitif. **06** delicate honeysuckle & spice, smooth dryish finish. Small portion barrel fermented. – *IvH/TJ*

Alvi's Drift Private Cellar

*Worcester ▪ Est 1928 ▪ 1stB 2002 ▪ Tasting, sales & tours by appt ▪ Canoe trips, game drives, visits to dairy/cheesery, BYO picnics, walks, eco-friendly 4×4 excursions by arrangement ▪ Owners Bertie, Alvi & Johan van der Merwe ▪ Winemaker Alvi van der Merwe ▪ Viti consultant Pierre Snyman ▪ 350 ha (17 varieties w/r) ▪ 5 000 tons ▪ PO Box 827 Worcester 6850 ▪ alvi@intekom.co.za ▪ **T 023·340·4117** ▪ F 023·340·4557*

Former GP Alvi van der Merwe has expanded his Alvi's Drift range to include a Sauvignon, a 'Cape blend' and a red Muscat de Frontignan. In 2005, only three wines were bottled – a Chenin, Chardonnay and white Muscat de Frontignan – which, gratifyingly, earned recognition from the Muscadel Association, Veritas and Swiss Airlines. Not to be outdone, the farm cheesery's feta was voted the best in the SA National Dairy Championships!

★★★★☆ **Muscat de Frontignan 04** last ed noted as perfect example of SA muscadel; complex, perfumed nose; sweet entry, tangy & uncloying finish; superb balance. For winter or summer, even over ice. 14 mths Fr oak. Muscadel Awards 'platinum'.

★★★★ **Chardonnay** new Deep tropical fruit richness follows through to **05** palate, voluptuous mouthfeel held together by solid structure, tight vein of citrus acidity. Poised, seamless, oak (Fr, 50% new) already woven into the elegant fabric.

Cape Fusion new ★★★★ Name creates expectation of pinotage blend – correctly: **05** has 30% of the grape, equal portion cab, majority shiraz. Warm & aromatic rhubarb tone, excellent ripe but still firm tannins. Deserves yr/2 to develop. Mainly Fr oak, third new. Following pair not retasted: **Chenin Blanc** ★★★ Unoaked, appealing **05**; juicy tropical fruit salad, zingy acid. Happy mouthful, thanks to high extract & 14.3% alcl **Chenin Blanc** ★★★ Barrel fermented, complete, well structured **05** with broad flavours, acids & fruit tannins; oak adding interest/mouthfeel. **Sauvignon Blanc** new **06** unready for tasting. – *CR*

▪ ■ *Amalienstein* see Southern Cape Vineyards
▪ ■ *Amandalia* see Rooiberg

Amani Vineyards

*Stellenbosch ▪ Est/1stB 1997 ▪ Tasting & sales Mon-Sat 9-4 ▪ Closed pub hols ▪ Tours by appt ▪ Owner Jim Atkinson ▪ Winemaker Carmen Stevens-Kelly, with Dirk Tredoux (both 2005) ▪ Viti consultant Kevin Watt ▪ Vineyard manager JD Stassen ▪ 32 ha (cabs s/f, merlot, mourvèdre, shiraz, chard, sauvignon, viognier) ▪ 20 500 cs 53% red 47% white ▪ PO Box 12422 Die Boord 7613 ▪ wine@amani.co.za ▪ www.amani.co.za ▪ **T 021·905·1126** ▪ F 021·905·4404*

Winemaker Carmen Stevens-Kelly crafts the best boutique wines she possibly can. However, she believes quality boils down to 'maximum time input in the Amani vineyards', and to this end JD Stassen has been appointed vineyard manager. And when it comes to the end product, 'knowledgeable and friendly' new cellar door salesperson Cindy Swiegelaar will greet you in the tasting room.

Atkinson Ridge range

Sauvignon Blanc 06 (sample) has all the cool fruit attributes that impress: intense greenpepper grassiness throughout, giving the tastebuds a wake-up call; overall effect is spring in a glass, perfectly captured. Delicious. Provisional ★★★★. **Chardonnay** ★★★★ Oaked version showing a savoury, steely European character. Last tasted was sophisticated **04**, with all components in place for development over 2-5 yrs. Wine to watch.

Amani range

★★★★ **Merlot 05** sample already shows delights to come; perfectly ripe dark berries & cassis, smooth creamy texture, oak busy integrating, fine tannins, well judged. These

±30% new Fr barriques, 11-18 mths; usually with splash cab s or f (or, as here, shiraz) for complexity/stiffening.

★★★★ **Chardonnay Reserve** new No New World brashness here; **04** subtle citrus & white peach, noticeable mineral seam, expertly oaked – fruit & oak walk hand in hand. Shows breed, class; also likely to unfold further over next 2-3 yrs. 100% fermented/±11 mths Fr oak, 30% new.

Cabernet Franc-Merlot ★★★★ Shiraz addition (18%) makes its presence felt in previewed **05**, introducing savoury/smoky note to the proceedings; layers of complexity – plums, some herbaceous notes & spice; accessible already with gd few yrs ahead. ±30% new Fr oak, ±11 mths. **I Am 1** ★★★★ Mulberry-dominated berry melange introduces stylish **05** (sample), mainly merlot with cab, shiraz & petit v. Still austere mid-2006, early days for oak assimilation but no hardness, just needs time. Yr Fr wood, 30% new. **Forest Myers Shiraz** new ★★★★ A tribute to GM Rusty Myers's late son; incl touches viognier & cab; **06**, ex-barrel, brambleberries & hedgerow fruit find juicy expression on palate; balanced oaking (yr Fr, 30% new) not to interfere with drinkability, which this offers with panache. **Chardonnay 05** (★★★★) peach & shortbread entry, citrus peel nuances on palate; gd drinkability but not the same palate fullness, concentration of **04** (★★★★) or some pvs. Fermented/aged ±10 mths Fr barrels, some new. **Sauvignon Blanc** ★★★★ **05** signals style change to portion barrel fermented (Fr oak), also dash viognier, hence riper, less aggressive character without sacrificing any nettly/grapefruit punch. Invigorating layered freshness; lovely food wine. — CR

Amarava Wines

Stellenbosch ▪ *Est 1999* ▪ *1stB 2004* ▪ *Closed to public* ▪ *Owner Bernard Rodenberg* ▪ *GM Louis Smit* ▪ *Vini consultant Teddy Hall* ▪ *17 ha (cabs s/f, merlot, shiraz, sauvignon)* ▪ *20 tons* ▪ *PO Box 1083 Somerset West 7129* ▪ *info@amaravawines.com* ▪ *www.amaravawines.com* ▪ *T 084·587·7270*

Having launched his brand with a promising 05 Sauvignon, off own vineyards in the Helderberg foothills, Netherlands-based Bernard Rodenberg confirmed as the guide went to bed that a Merlot 05 would be next. 'In 2007 we will have a full crop again,' he emailed. 'including cab, merlot, shiraz and sauvignon.' To be vinified by Rudera's Teddy Hall.

■ *Ama Ulibo* see Goedverwacht

Ambeloui Wine Cellar

Hout Bay (see Constantia map) ▪ *Est 1995* ▪ *1stB 1998* ▪ *Visits by appt* ▪ *Owners Nick & Ann Christodoulou* ▪ *Winemaker/viticulturist Nick Christodoulou, with Alexis Christodoulou* ▪ *0.6 ha (pinot, chard)* ▪ *600 cs 100% MCC* ▪ *PO Box 26800 Hout Bay 7872* ▪ *wine@ambeloui.co.za* ▪ *www.ambeloui.co.za* ▪ *T 082·441·6039* ▪ *F 021·790·7386*

Nick, patriarch of the Christodoulou clan of Hout Bay, now has an assistant winemaker — youngest child Alexis, for whom the 2001 vintage in the tiny farm's sparkling series was named. Released in 2006 were the Nicholas (after the founding father); the Alex, for his first grandson, who refers to the sparklers as 'papou's juice'; and limited quantities of the Ann Reserve, blended in 2001 to celebrate co-owner, wife and mother Ann's 50th birthday. We wonder — will they ever run out of offspring or celebrations?

★★★★ **MCC** Delicious & well-made dry sparkling from pinot & chard, proportions vary with vintage. Degorged early 2006, **04** ('Alex') soothing pick-me-up with honey & baked apple, freshening mineral acidity from 60% chard. Best cellared few yrs but delicious now. Weightier **03** similar to **01** (★★★★★), showing pinot predominance. **02** ('Ann') mainly chard (66%) had appetising bakery notes. RS ±10g/ℓ for all.

★★★★ **Rosanne Rosé** Lively blush-coloured MCC, portion of base-wine barrel fermented; **04** (pvs were NV) fine, vibrant bubbles, berry & savoury aromas. Chard (80%, with pinot) asserts itself on crisp & appley palate, finishes candyfloss-sweet (RS ±10g/ℓ). Limited release: only 100 cs. Both WO Coastal. — CvZ

■ *Amira* see Avondale

Anatu Wines ◑♀

*Stellenbosch • Est/1stB 2002 • Visits by appt • Owners André & Freda Hamersma, Wickus & Anina Guelpa, Dries van Zyl • Winemaker Anina Guelpa • 670 cs 50% red 50% white • PO Box 5792 Cresta 2118 • sales@anatu.co.za • www.anatu.co.za • **T 0861·262·889***

As a hobby, winemaking is relegated to holidays and after hours. If anything needs to be done urgently, it's always a scramble. No more at Anatu. Inspired by the success of their Shiraz, new mother Anina Guelpa is now Anatu's full-time winemaker, allowing her not only to increase their red wine production but to produce a new baby in 2006: a maiden Sauvignon.

★★★★ **Shiraz** Robust, fruit lashed number from Dbnville grapes; **04** ripeness (15.5% alc), sweet raisiny lushness shored up by spicy tannins. Loads of personaliy, interest. 50% barrel fermented.

Sauvignon Blanc new ★★★ Lightish, aperitif friendly **06**, offers zip & zing without jarring acidity. Clean gooseberry/greenpepper tang. — *CT*

■ *Ancient Africa* see Baarsma
■ *Andreas* see Groenendal
■ *Andrew Bain* see Cape Vineyards

Andy Mitchell Wines ♀

Greyton • Est/1stB 2003 • Visits by appt • Owners/winemakers Andy & Vikki Mitchell, advised by Marais de Villiers (vini) & Terroir Wines (viti) • 250 cs 80% red 20% rosé • PO Box 543 Paarden Eiland 7420 • andy@za.northsails.com • www.andymitchellwines.com • T 028·254·9045/083·558·5085 F 021·510·1266

A continuing affair with rhône-style wines has kept Andy Mitchell buying grapes from the same vineyards in the Helderberg to go into his shiraz. Until this aspirant Cape Wine Master can find the time to make the long-promised white wine, he's compromised with a new Shiraz Rosé — light and fruity, he says, perfect for summer alfresco drinking.

Breakfast Rock Syrah ★★★★ **04** has integrated well since pre-bottling tasting, showing nutmeg, raspberry & coconut notes, & more spice than vinosity. 14.7% alc evident.15 mths oak, mixed 1st to 3rd fill. **Nerina Shiraz Rosé** new ★★★★ **06** deeply pink, free-run blanc de noir, partly barrel fermented. Just-dry, with voluptuous mid-palate spice; slight fizz lifts freshness, ensures quaffability — as does moderate 12.8% alc. These both off 'Helvetica' vyd on Hldrberg. — *MF*

■ *Angels Tears* see Grande Provence

Angora ♀

Robertson • Est/1stB 2002 • Tasting & sales by appt • Closed pub hols • Owner Gerrit Joubert • Winemakers Gerrit Joubert & sons, with Danie Slabber • Viticulturist Danie Slabber • 16 ha (cab, port varieties, ruby cab, shiraz, chenin, muscadel) • 300 tons 900 cs own label 100% red • PO Box 343 Bonnievale 6730 • chris.joubert@gilga.com • T 021·881·3475 • F 021·881·3248

Among their other wine commitments, the Jouberts have managed to find time to expand the Angora range from their Bonnievale family farm, trebling production. While there is no 05 Shiraz, reports Chris J, also winemaker at Overgaauw, the Rosé comes from the same vineyard block. The Chenin was made by brother Johan, Kleine Zalze's winemaker.

Shiraz ★★★★ Tasted mid-2005, **04** was improvement on pvs, with fleshier, earthy palate & individual cream-soda-like finish. Following both new: **Shiraz Rosé** ★★★ **06** pale pink in off-dry style, simple strawberry aromas, sweet raspberry flavours, some structure with sweet-sour finish. Bonnievale WO. **Chenin Blanc** ★★ Light bodied **06**, tasted newly bottled, popularly styled sweetish entry, tropical pineapple aromas & flavours. — *IM/DS*

Annandale Wines

Stellenbosch ▪ Est/1stB 1996 ▪ Tasting & sales Mon-Sat 9-5 ▪ Fee R15 refundable on purchase ▪ Closed Christian holidays ▪ Tours by appt ▪ Collection of antique wine objects ▪ Owner/winemaker/viticulturist Hempies du Toit ▪ 45 ha (cabs s/f, merlot, shiraz) ▪ 5 000 cs own label ▪ 100% red ▪ PO Box 12681 Die Boord 7613 ▪ annandale@telkomsa.net ▪ www.annandale.co.za ▪ T 021·881·3560 ▪ F 021·881·3562

With son Gerhard putting his European experience to effect handling marketing and finance at Annandale (when not drafted-in for 6th-generation Du Toit winemaking duties), ex-rugby Springbok 'Hempies' dT carries on doing what he knows best: making long-matured, Old World-style reds – and welcoming visitors to their old-Cape cellar and tasting area, among the most hospitable and atmospheric in the winelands.

★★★★ **Cabernet Sauvignon 01** 'masculine' cab, with classic cedar, blackcurrant aromas, solid, dry finish; 15.5% alc no drawback; neither is no-holds-barred 3 yrs new Nevers oak; Winemakers Choice; currently available, along with following duo: **98** touch organic, savoury; **99** silk-textured & seamless. No **00**.

★★★★ **Shiraz 01** only vintage available so far, beautifully packaged. Last time we noted as quintessential Cape shiraz: warm, spicily intense, properly dry, neither over-rich nor showy, 30 mths 2nd fill barrels, all Fr.

Cavalier ★★★★ Blend merlot, cab s & f, shiraz (40/25/25/10), 36 mths oak, all Fr; **01** noted as balanced & classy when tasted mid-2004. **CVP** ★★★★ 'Cape Vintage Port' always 100% shiraz, fortified with matured brandy, contributing to rich spiciness of **03**; sweet fruitcake flavours; youthful, ready to drink or keep a few yrs. 76g/ℓ, 20% alc. – *IM*

AntHill Wines

Somerset West ▪ Est/1stB 2000 ▪ Tasting by appt ▪ Owners Mark Howell & Hylton Schwenk ▪ Winemaker Mark Howell ▪ 1 000 cs ▪ 14 Somerset Str, Somerset West 7130 ▪ anthill@absamail.co.za ▪ T 021·852·6349/082·895·9008 ▪ F 021·851·5914

'It's a buyer's market,' say Mark Howell, barrel supplier to the trade, and Hylton Schwenk, construction project manager, but these partners-in-wine remain unperturbed. Their venture is 'simply a bit of fun' and neither of them have any intention of giving up their day jobs. 'We think we offer really good value,' they say, of their handcrafted wines, sold to friends, family and faithful followers.

★★★★ **Ietermagô Chardonnay** More elegant & classy animal than name ('armadillo') would suggest. **04** (★★★★) rich melon, clementine & shortbread aromas; lighter (12.5% alc), shade less opulent than maiden **03**, which had enough substance for good few yrs. Ex-miserly Koue Bokkeveld vyd, fermented/±yr new Fr oak; unfiltered.

The Persian Shiraz ★★★★ Mark H's goal of southern rhône-style red achieved with **04**, replete with whiffs wild scrub & asphalt. Elegant, juicy, well-managed oak. Layered, lots of interest, drinkability & prospects. Incl dash viognier. Sbosch/Pdberg fruit, 16 mths oak, mainly Fr, 50% new. Both W Cape WOs. – *CR*

Anthony de Jager Wines

Paarl ▪ Est/1stB 2001 ▪ Closed to public ▪ Owner/winemaker Anthony de Jager ▪ 175 cs 100% red ▪ PO Box 583 Suider-Paarl 7624 ▪ homtini@absamail.co.za ▪ T 021·863·2450 ▪ F 021·863·2591

'There's not much to say as not much has changed,' says Fairview winemaker Anthony de Jager about his own-venture, small-scale production of one of SA's finest shirazes. Quantities remain small, snapped up mainly by the local market and UK trade. He does divulge vinifying some grapes from 'cooler, higher elevations', but declines to be more specific, other than he hopes to achieve a little more refinement by blending the results into his Agter Paarl barrels. 'The results seem quite nice,' says the unassuming mountain-biking fanatic.

★★★★☆ **Homtini Shiraz** Since debut **00** (★★★★★) successfully merges shiraz & dash viognier – 4% in very ripe **05**, which lifts, brightens the aromas. Carefully handled to minimise burly

15% alc; maintains gentle, rounded mouthfeel, satisfyingly savoury, balanced drinking for medium term. Co-fermented/14 mths, 15% new oak. Old Paarl Mntn vines. — *AL*

Anthony Smook Wines

Voor Paardeberg (see Paarl map) ▪ Est/1stB 2000 ▪ Visits by appt; tasting/sales also at I Love Wine (see entry) ▪ Owner Anthony Smook ▪ Winemakers Anthony Smook & Francois Louw (2000) ▪ Viti consultant Johan Wiese (2001) ▪ 30 ha (cab, merlot, pinotage, shiraz, chard, chenin) ▪ 36 tons 2 500 cs 65% red 35% white ▪ PO Box 7038 Noorder-Paarl 7623 ▪ info@smookwines.co.za ▪ www.smookwines.co.za ▪ ***T 083·376·9924/082·294·4051*** *▪ F 021·872·2867*

A double-gold medal at Veritas for the Shiraz Reserve 03, which 'clearly improved with bottle maturation', was great news for Anthony Smook & co, now joined by marketing representative Zelda Furstenburg who also lectures part-time at the Cape Wine Academy on various subjects. Keen to show off their improved tasting facilities, they offer personalised bottle and barrel tastings, as well as food and wine matching, all by appointment.

★★★★ **Shiraz Reserve** All-new oak (90% Fr) for these; **03** more structure, complexity, ripeness than regular version; VDG; **04** (★★★★) similar bold-but-controlled quality, ripe & spicy/smoky profile, yet shade less convincing. Possibly just needs time.

Pinotage ★★★ **04** continues established, appealing burgundian style; dark, soft, rich yet elegant despite usual big alc (14.7%). Yr Am oak. **Shiraz** ★★★★ **04**, as pvs, cask aged (50% new, mainly Fr). Beefy (15%), but well fruited; firm, ripe & banalcned peppery tannin, clean dry conclusion. **Cabernet Sauvignon-Merlot** ★★★ Pvs was merlot-led (so 'Merlot-Cab' last ed), cab preponderant in current **03** (55%, with 10% shiraz), hence slightly steelier, more savoury character; still well- and elegantly fruited. 15 mth Fr oak. **Chardonnay Reserve** ★★★★ **04** last ed showed similar lime/mineral profile as regular version, but greater intensity, focus & freshness. **05** unready. **Chardonnay** ★★★ Rounded & comfortable **05**, tangy citrus fruit with hints butterscotch & clean vanilla from new-oak barrelling (50%, rest unwooded). — *MM*

Anura Vineyards

Paarl ▪ Est 1990 ▪ 1stB 2001 ▪ Tasting & sales daily 9.30-5 ▪ Closed Easter Fri/Mon, Dec 25/26 & Jan 1 ▪ Fee R15 (cheese & wine) ▪ Lilly Pad Restaurant ▪ Tours by appt ▪ Farm produce sold ▪ Owners Tymen & Jenny Bouma ▪ Winemakers Tymen Bouma & Carla van der Mescht (Jan 2002) ▪ Viticulturist Hannes Kloppers (Oct 1997) ▪ 118 ha (cab, malbec, merlot, mourvèdre, pinotage, sangiovese, shiraz, chard, sauvignon) ▪ 45 000 cs own label 80% red 20% white ▪ PO Box 244 Klapmuts 7625 ▪ info@anura.co.za sales@anura.co.za ▪ www.anura.co.za ▪ ***T 021·875·5360*** *▪ F 021·875·5657*

Amphibian-themed Anura, with its large new wine tasting centre and Lily Pad Restaurant, offers a relaxing winelands experience. But behind the scenes they're forever at work, having increased production to about 45 000 cases (from 20 000 in 2005!). They're now planning to build a new barrel cellar with 'extensive modifications to existing infrastructure' and a function/wedding venue. Oblivious to this activity, visitors continue to enjoy added attractions like the Forest Hill cheeses and a metalwork art exhibition.

Reserve range

★★★★ **Cabernet Sauvignon** Elegantly crafted, complex **04** has tight structure showing firm, fine tannins. Sumptuously rich & juicy palate with cassis & cedar nuances from serious oaking (23 mths 2nd & 3rd fill barrels). Long, dry, scented black fruit on finish. 15% alc in balance with fruit & wood. Built to last.

★★★★ **Merlot 04** similar nirvana-for-hedonists styling, oaking & flavour to pvs, plus thread mocha & spicy liquorice in richly textured palate, controlled by bright acidity. **03** luxuriously chocolaty with swanky wood 18 mths new Fr, creamy texture. This, above, Smnsberg-Paarl WO.

Syrah-Mourvèdre Reserve ★★★★ **04** similar to pvs, with some spicy floral notes; 15% alc subsumed in dark-berried appeal, ripe but discreet tannins. WO W Cape. Similarly benign & approachable **03** SAA Best Red trophy.

Limited Release range

new

Syrah ★★★★ Opulent dark fruit in showy, New World **04**. Concentrated & juicy – like biting into a dark ripe plum. Supple tannins with 20 mths oak maturation (40% new) providing support & a dry note to sustained finish. 15% alc. **Petit Verdot** ★★★★ Restrained, inky red-fruit nuances in lively **04**, balanced, with toned tannins, more elegant than other reds. Subtly oaked (18 mths older Fr), approachable with food friendly mineral farewell. Gd potential. Both Smnsberg-Paarl origin.

Anura range

★★★★ **Merlot** Bottled version of sullen sample **04** (★★★★) shows a leaner, edgier style with sour plum & herbaceous nuances. Taut tannins make it better suited as a food wine. 15 mths Fr oak. Pvsly tasted was fragrant **02**.

No new vintages tasted for following three reds: **Pinotage** ★★★★ **04** more serious; plummy, rich & dense with gd oak support. Shd last 4-6 yrs. **05**, sample last ed, lighter, still grippy. **Shiraz** ★★★ Classic style **02** well-bred, dry, with dense & compact fruit, firmish tannins. 20% barrel fermented; Fr oak, 50% new. **Syrah-Mourvèdre** Maiden **03** (sample last ed, provisional ★★★★) gd depth, dark berried juiciness, enough grip in classic styling. Part native yeast ferment; 18 mths Fr oak, 40% new. **Malbec** ★★★★ **05** (sample) restrained aromas develop into riper cedar-spiced mulberry, with juicy acidity. Lighter textured & less dense than pvs with food-consorting savoury tannins. **Sangiovese** ★★★★ **05** (sample) a trattoria in a glass! Savoury dried tomato, pesto & prosciutto hints carrying through to concentrated, textured palate with bright acidity. Highly appealing combo approachability & structure, partly through serious oaking (18 mths new Fr). WO Swtland. **'Bordeaux Blend'** **new** ★★★★ **05** merlot/cab (54/46) composition with lead pencil & ripe dark fruit. Rich, complex, though mid-2006 still incorporating supportive wood (yr 2nd & 3rd) into its powerful structure; needs yr/2; shd be delicious for several more. Smnsberg-Paarl WO. **Chardonnay** ★★★★ **05** more oak than pvs (11 mths, 10% new) but this well integrated with clean-cut fruit & limy acidity. Trimmer (±14% alc) & lively food styling. Classically formed **03** MIWA DG. This WO W Cape, following pair Smnsberg-Paarl. **Chenin Blanc** ★★★ **05** unashamedly ripe & showy, with 16% alc brazier. Gorgeous & different baklava/wild honey notes on palate, unchecked by soft acidity. Not for the faint-hearted. Similarly generous **04** Wine ★★★★★. **Sauvignon Blanc** ★★★ **05** bottled version of last yr's sample shows more of the figgy/tropical notes & breadth from 7 mths on lees. Less verve, concentration, but pleasing freshness.

Frog Hill range

Rana ★★★ Replaces 'Shiraz-'Merlot-Cab' with **05** red-blooded, extra-savoury four-way blend; wild & spicy; powerful chunky tannin makes for a real barbeque styled wine – with no need for the meat. **Rosé** **new** ★★★ Unwooded & lightish **05**, refreshingly tart cranberry flavours from cab (with dash merlot); gentle tannic twist & appealing vermillion hue make a gd alfresco option. 12.6% alc. Above pair WO W Cape. **Chenin Blanc** ★★★ **05** ripe & generously juicy explosion of tropical fruit balanced by lively acidity. Ends touch brash with bitter almond note that wld be tempered by food. — *MW*

Anwilka

Stellenbosch • Est 1997 • 1stB 2005 • Closed to public; sales from Klein Constantia • Owners Bruno Prats, Hubert de Boüard & Lowell Jooste • Winemaker Trizanne Pansegrouw (2005), with Hubert de Boüard & Bruno Prats • Viticulturist Piet Neethling, advised by Johan Wiese (May 1998/Dec 1997) • 40 ha (cab, merlot, shiraz) • 250 tons total ±100 tons own label 100% red • PO Box 5298 Helderberg 7135 • anwilka@mweb.co.za • www.anwilka.com • T 021·842·3225 • F 021·842·3983

Buyers received the 05 blend on debut last year with as much enthusiasm as all-powerful US critic, Robert Parker, who commented (after tasting more than 200 'rather astonishing' bordeaux of the same vintage): 'This is the finest red wine I have ever had from SA.' But alas! It's all but sold out: Lowell Jooste, the local partner (with Bruno Prats, former owner of Bordeaux second growth Château Cos-d'Estournel, and Hubert de Boüard de Laforest, co-proprietor of

Unlock a whole
new wine experiance.

Changing the way you look
at liquor stores.

Contender for the longest brand name in the guide, Hermanuspietersfontein Vineyards is a new partnership between Stanford vinegrowers Johan and Mariette Pretorius, and avuncular winemaker **Bartho Eksteen** (pictured). The name a tribute to Hermanus Pieters, 19th century founder of seaside town Hermanus. Pastoral cultural references blend with state-of-the-art technology and a sophisticated cellar-door experience to form one of the more interesting and different debuts in this year's guide.

WINE FREIGHT SPECIALISTS AND FINE WINE MERCHANTS

When it comes to the professional export and shipping of wines, our proud reputation spans more than 20 years. We will ship anything upwards of three bottles right to your door - anywhere in the world.

POLKADRAAI ROAD (M12) STELLENBOSCH 7600 SOUTH AFRICA
TEL: 27 (0) 860 10 30 34 FAX: 27 (0) 21 905 0293
EMAIL wine@capegrape.co.za OR freight@capegrape.co.za

CAPE GRAPE & WINE COMPANY

SPECIALIST WINE FREIGHT SERVICES	
FINE WINE MERCHANTS	
www.capegrape.co.za	TEL: +27 21 905 0290

Trust debonair *homme du vin* **Jean-Vincent Ridon** (left) to land himself and his Signal Hill team, **Laurence Buthelezi** and **Wade Metzer**, one of the most sought-after winemaking locations in SA: the glamorous new Mandela Rhodes Place in the tourist heart of Cape Town. Our early-harvest photo speaks eloquently of the artisanal methods but does little justice to the eventual setting, which will stylefully combine a production cellar, maturation facilities and tasting area, all visible from Church Street through a glass curtain.

So you'd like to acquire some wine?

Which estate?

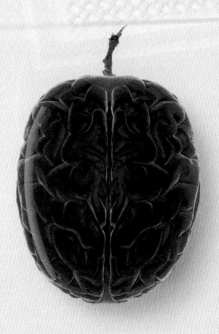

GRAPE MINDS NEVER THINK ALIKE (THANK GOODNESS)

Rand Merchant Bank's long and fruitful association with the South African wine industry is no coincidence. The wine-maker's skill for blending time-honoured techniques with cutting-edge thinking

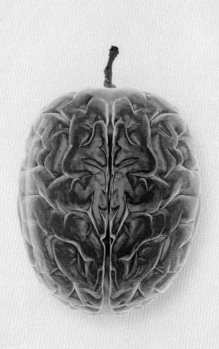

Traditional values. Innovative ideas.

reflects the way that we too develop financial solutions for our clients. This spirit is encapsulated in our 29-year-old pay-off line 'Traditional Values. Innovative Ideas'.

Within earshot of the Atlantic breakers at Strandfontein on the West Coast, winemaker **Wynand Hamman** (left), partner and brother-in-law **Jan van Zyl** (right), and father-in-law **'Ponk' van Zyl** grow some remarkably characterful and attractive wines, including a new Pinot, from infant vines. A hen's-teeth-rare 5-star rating from *Wine* for their Sauvignon sparked a frenzy of orders – and welcome recognition for a team ready to push the boundaries of SA winegrowing.

WEDDERWILL

RESIDENTIAL WINE ESTATE

• THE GATEWAY TO A COUNTRY LIFESTYLE •

This secluded residential mountain estate is set amongst beautiful vineyards, high above the sea. It overlooks Somerset West, False Bay and the Helderberg/Hottentots Holland mountains. Wedderwill offers low density living, an escape from a hectic city existence.
Enjoy natural beauty, space & wild life. Live on a romantic estate which boasts carefully chosen vines, fitting the unique terroir, producing a selected range of three high quality wines:
a Shiraz, a Bordeaux style and a Sauvignon Blanc.

Security • full title Plots from 4000sqm • Equestrian facilities • Fishing •
• 140ha private Nature Reserve • Walking trails • Private wine estate •

Property Sales:
Wolf Vosse 083 390 2250 • Willem Steyn 082 576 0048.
Discover our wines at www.wedderwill.co.za

The businesslike folder on the table beside **Vivian Kleynhans**, MD of Mia Cara Wines, suggests a no-nonsense attitude. But the bouquet of roses and lyrical background hint at the 'romantic secret' which this new entrant to the wine business wants to share with her customers. In partnership with Paarl-area winery Rose Garden Vineyards, Kleynhans aims to become one of SA's leading black female-owned wine companies.

top St-Emilion estate Château Angelus) says the maiden vintage was sold out sooner than you can say 'santé!', both locally and to the Bordeaux trade's leading international accounts. However, a small quantity may still be available from Klein Constantia tasting room. And there's more to good stuff come: the winemaking team is 'particularly pleased with the quality of the 2006 wines'.

★★★★☆ **Anwilka** new Maiden cab/shiraz blend as classy, chic, as the SA/Fr partnership behind it. **05** refreshingly unshowy, vinous; lovely broad, silky mouthfeel with sophisticated, gently resistant tannins; classically dry & long; stylish oaking (9 mths, 75% new Fr barriques), balance, harmony, all suggest min 5 yr potential. — AL

■ *Apiesklip* see Baarsma
■ *Aprilskloof* see Lammershoek

Arabella ♀ ♀ new

Robertson • Est 2005 • 1stB 2006 • Tasting & sales Mon-Fri 9-4 Sat 9-3 • Tours by arrangement • Owners Stephen & Jamie de Wet • Winemaker/viticulturist Stephen de Wet • 176 ha (cab, sauvignon) • 1 250 tons ±20 000 cs 50% red 50% white • HACCP certification in progress • PO Box 155 Ashton 6715 • info@arabellawines.com • www.arabellawines.com

This venture, formed after the division of Excelsior Estate between the two De Wet brothers, sees Stephen and son Jamie embark on their own brand, Arabella (a play on words referring to the property's beautiful Arabian horses). Daughter Nicky does the marketing, so it's a true family undertaking. The maiden wines were vinified off-site but a brand-new R30m cellar is ready for future vintages. Small quantities of 05 reds were bought in to complement Arabella's own 06 whites — making for some 'exciting' wines, says Nicky dW.

Cabernet Sauvignon 05 difficult to rate mid-2006, still being held captive by tannins; some herbal notes, red berries, but will show better in yr, unfold & reveal more over time. **Shiraz ★★★** Smooth, flavourful, made for drinking, **05** has variety-true smoky, plummy fruit, well balanced oak. **Merlot ★★★** Elegant **05** shows a cassis, toasty oak character, with 1-2 yrs ageing potential from the firm (but not harsh) tannins. **Chenin Blanc ★★★** Good varietal definition on **06**, aromatic, floral; a light textured, 'feminine' & charming drink. Screwcapped, as are next. **Sauvignon Blanc ★★** A blend of early & later picked fruit, quaffable **06** shows pear-drop, sherbet youthfulness & a crisp, food-friendly finish. **Viognier ★★ 06** pleasant clean nose, melon & fruit salad, with a fresh, undemanding drinkability. — CR

■ *Ardens Andreu* see Groenendal

Arendsig Hand-Crafted Wines ♀

Robertson • Est/1stB 2004 • Vineyard tour & tasting with winemaker by appt Mon-Fri 9-4 • Tasting by appt Sat 9.30-1 • Owner GF van der Westhuizen Trust • Winemaker Lourens van der Westhuizen • 15 ha (cab, shiraz, chard, sauvignon, viognier) • 15 tons 500 cs • PO Box 170 Robertson 6705 • info@arendsig.co.za • www.arendsig.co.za • T 023·616·2835/ 084·200·2163 • F 023·616·2090

Lourens van der Westhuizen knew his brand would find recognition, he reminisces, way back, when he scrambled over rocky, well-drained soil, watched vineyards planted on south-facing slopes, a south-easter cooling the vines… Three years of nurturing those vines and making wine on the family farm, as well as experience abroad, have taught him 'what makes chardonnay and shiraz so special'. Markets now include Swedish restaurants and upmarket local establishments, including top-rated golf resort, Leopard Creek.

Shiraz ★★★☆ Individual, attractive **05** more Rhône than New World: wild berries, meaty, tarry, with smooth texture, oak fully integrated. Drinking well but can still age. Yr Fr barriques. **Chardonnay ★★★★** Appealing peach & citrus peel in **05**, nice nutty oak element. Palate perked up by tangy acidity, stimulates the tastebuds, making it really delicious to drink. Fermented/matured 8 mths Fr oak. — CR

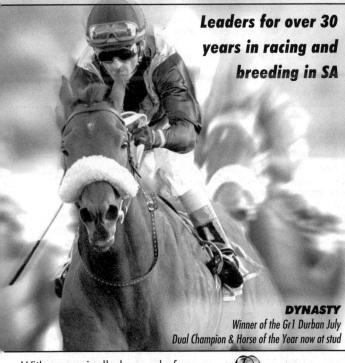

Arlington Beverage Group

Est 1996 • 1stB 1997 • Closed to public • Owner Richard Addison • ±200 000 cs 45% red 55% white • UK head office: 162-164 Arthur Rd, London SW19 8AQ • PO Box 1376 Stellenbosch 7599 • sarah@arlingtonbeverage.com • www.arlingtonbeverage.com

Arlington markets and sells SA wines to countries such as the UK, Ireland and Argentina. With local partners, it has built a number of successful on-trade brands including Broken Rock, Landsdowne, Millbrook and Rocheburg. Arlington also represents a number of leading Cape properties in the international markets, including Riebeek and Ridgeback.

Armajaro   ♂♀ [new]

Paarl • Est 2001 • 1stB 2005 • Visits by appt • Owner Armajaro Holdings UK • Winemaker Callie Louw (Jun 2004) • Viti adviser Andrew Teubes • 40 ha (cab, carignan, grenache, merlot, mourvèdre, shiraz, muscadel, chardonnay chenin, sauvignon, viognier) • 160 tons 10 000 cs 45% red 55% white • Export brand: Vondeling • PO Box 57 Wellington 7654 • armajaro@ iafrica.com • www.armajaro.com • T 021·869·8595 • F 021·869·8219

A high-potential property, given the investment, expertise and philosophy of the owners, Richard Gower and Anthony Ward of global financial services and commodities business Armajaro Holdings UK. Managed by former proprietor and fellow Englishman Julian Johnsen, 40ha of vineyard are vinified into mainly blends, one bearing the scientific name of a fynbos species native to the Perdeberg area. Winemaker Callie Louw, inspired by a stint at Rousillon's Domaine Gauby, which boasts Mediterranean conditions similar to this Voor Paardeberg farm's, seeks 'minimal intervention, old oak, purity, elegance and wines with the fingerprint of origin'.

Vondeling range

All WO Voor Pdberg unless noted. **Cabernet Sauvignon-Merlot** Cab-merlot blend (64:36) gives tobacco, dry herb aromas. Plenty of gd berry fruit to taste, but rather dryly tannic finish now (ex-barrel). Likely ★★★☆. **Shiraz** ★★★ Barrel sample **05**, so rating provisional. Shiraz with dollops mourvèdre, carignan, shows ultra-ripe aromas. Palate a bit fresher — plump, plum-sweet, with substantial soft tannins, good wooding (±16 mths, 20% new). **'Unwooded White Blend'** ★★★☆ Herbal, sunny hillside aromas on **06** blend chenin, sauvignon, viognier, chard — no varietal dominance. As with other whites, not about power but expressive restraint; here a gd texture, fresh poise, all in balance. Surely a label to watch. **Sauvignon Blanc** ★★★★ Pretty **06** flavourful & not too green, though welcome moderate 12.5% alc. Generally lightish, but some richness from 5 mths on lees. **Semillon** ★★★☆ Classic varietal character on **05**, notably lemon, lanolin; nicely succulent & fresh, good grip, supportive barrelling adding breadth (9 mths older oak), dry limy length. WO Swtlnd. **Babiana noctiflora** ★★★☆ Pleasing, chenin-based **05**, with 29% viognier adding perfume & peach component to delicate but full-fruited, quite weighty whole. A little enriching sugar not obvious, nor clever use of older oak. Part native fermentation. — TJ

■ **Arniston Bay** *see* The Company of Wine People
■ **Arumdale** *see* Thelema

Asara Estate   ♂♀⚇⌂♨&♿

Stellenbosch • Est 1691 • 1stB 1970 • Tasting & sales Mon-Fri 9-5 Sat 10-5 (Oct-Apr), 10-2 (May-Sep) • Fee R15 • Closed Easter Fri, Dec 25/26 & Jan 1 • Tours by appt • BYO picnic (see also intro) • Owner Markus & Christiane Rahmann • Winemaker Jan van Rooyen (Oct 1999) • Viticulturist Pieter Rossouw (1995) • 120 ha (cab, merlot, shiraz, chard, sauvignon) • ±500 tons avg • 25 000 cs 60% red 40% white • PO Box 882 Stellenbosch 7599 • info@AsaraWine. com • www.AsaraWine.com • T 021·888·8000 • F 021·888·8001

The African gods after whom Asara is named were smiling in 2006, when the estate escaped summer heatwaves and wind damage to crush a record 655 tons. 'The vintage can truly be described as the greatest in 10 years,' enthuses winemaker Jan van Rooyen. The philosophy here is 'allowing the wine its time and not rushing it into bottle'. Something else worth waiting for is a boutique hotel and fine-dining restaurant, under construction at press time.

★★★★ **Bell Tower Collection Estate Wine** Sets the tone of restrained classic-mindedness of this estate's reds. Splendid, serious **98** (★★★★☆) had fine fruit & balanced structure. 90% cab in pvsly reviewed **99**, with merlot, cab f, petit v, malbec, in same classy tradition, but a trifle lighter in feel despite bigger 14.5% alc. Integrated support from 2 yrs Fr oak, 50% new. IWSC 2006 gold. Shd easily see out their decades.

★★★★ **Avalon** ('Amaro' pvs ed) Fascinating amarone-inspired *vino di meditazione* ('meditation wine') from vine-dried pinotage. Hedonistic, high-toned (as per style), savoury & intense, with pleasing tannic grip; **05** carries hefty price tag, most wld say worth it. Sample tasted. Maiden **04** beguiled with richly firm, fleshy palate & smooth ripe tannins, ±16.5% alc, & dry finish despite ±7.5g/ℓ sugar.

★★★★☆ **Cabernet Sauvignon** Initially subdued, **00** evolves in glass to reveal black cherries & coffee jostling comfortably with powdery tannins, providing measured astringency; ripe alc (14%); mineral finish lingers. 24 mths Fr oak, half new.

★★★★ **Merlot** Elegance & grace are hallmarks of these. **01** pensive & brooding mid-2006, its opulent fruit still tightly wrapped around a mineral core, begging time. As usual, well managed oak (18 mths Fr, combo 1st/2nd/4th fill) provides foundation for growth over gd few yrs. Frequent Concours Mondial golds.

★★★★ **Cape Fusion** As name implies, a 'Cape blend' of pinotage, merlot & cab in equal proportions; to date the **01**, last ed showing whiffs of red fruit wildness, deliciously decadent richness kept in check by house's firm tannins. Unobtrusive 18 mths oak.

★★★★ **Shiraz** Vibrant & sexy **03** (★★★★★) allures with lily, black pepper & red berry scents, deliciously tangy fruity tannins. As engagingly forward & drinkable as **01** & **02**, with greater depth & concentration. Complex oaking: 25% in 50/50 split Am/Fr 1st fill, 28% 2nd, 47% 3rd — go figure!

★★★★ **Chardonnay Reserve** Restrained, judiciously oaked version. **04** wafts lemon & lime, hints vanilla & intriguing nutmeg; focused acidity & well knit tannins, long & dry. Silky, well balanced **03** flew SAA, brought home Concours Mondial gold. Fermented/±yr *sur lie*, combo new & older Fr oak.

★★★★☆ **Noble Late Harvest** Luscious dessert from barrel fermented chenin. **03** mid-2005 was lightly intense, with honeyed apricot & pineapple aromas & flavours governed by 11.5% alc, fine acidity. Concours Mondial gold, *Wine* ★★★★. **02** (★★★★) was unctuous & lingering.

Ebony ★★★ Estate's other take on the 'Cape blend'; this mainly cab & merlot (54/36) with dollop pinotage in easy, ready **00**, with moderate structure & flavour to enjoy with your favourite pasta. **Rosé** ★★★ Very dry rendition (1.5g/ℓ sugar), with just a nudge of tannin in **06**; full-flavoured shiraz & gamay, earthy with hint of boiled sweets. **Chardonnay Unwooded** ★★★ **06** sample exhibits estate's typical balance: rich citrus fruit on palate, with steely acid counterfoil. Ends quickly though. **Ivory** ★★★☆ Breezy dry white with sufficient versatility to make the transition from sunset toast to casual dinner companion. Early drinking **05** grass/hay notes, zippy acidity from 71% sauvignon; lemon-cream tones & palate weight from chard. **Sauvignon Blanc** ★★★ Shows lively acidity & gd depth of flavour; **06** previewed pre-bottling — might rate higher on release. **Spirit of Chenin** ★★★☆ White-port-style fortified from chenin, made intermittently. **04** complex nut & peach interplay with diesel whiff, nicely integrated spirit. At 108 g/ℓ, 20% alc, drier, warmer than pvs **98**. 14 mths Fr oak. — *CvZ*

Ashanti

Paarl • Est 1997 • 1stB 1998 • Temporarily closed to public • Winemaker Nelson Buthelezi (1999) • 66 ha • 250 0000ℓ • PO Box 934 Huguenot 7645 • info@ashantiwines.com • www. ashantiwines.com • T 021·862·0789 • F 021·862·2864

The property has been bought by a new group from abroad whose intentions had not been formulated at time of going to print. However, production has continued unabated, blocks have been uprooted and await replanting, and the visitor facilities are ready for re-opening if and when.

★★★★ **Chiwara** Attractively different blend pinotage, cab, shiraz; **02** more elegant than pvs, still full of taste, life; potential over next few yrs. ±15 mths Fr oak. No newer vintages of this, wines below, ready for review this ed.

★★★★ **Pinotage** Fruity & modern, lots of flesh to match the chewy tannins; sample **04** (★★★) sweet, ripe plummy fruit, tannins busy integrating, need time. Oaked yr Fr/Am. **03** appealing plum pudding & custard tone; quite firm on release, begging yr/2. 10–12 mths Fr oak.

Cabernet Sauvignon ★★★ **04** (sample) likeable red berry profile, though tannins fairly dominant in youth. Yr Fr/Am oak. Few yrs ageing potential. **Malbec** ★★★★ Last tasted was **02**, with veritable berry orchard of fruit. **Merlot** ★★★ **04** has variety's trademark elegance, mixed red fruit tones. Accessible, no hard edges; sinewy tannins provide support for 2/3 yrs. Oak as for Cab. **Shiraz** ★★★ **04** (sample) simpler than pvs. Midweight, ripe, red-fruited, with juicy, youthful appeal. Oak as above.

Concept wines

Joseph's Hat ★★★ A tasty early-drinker. **04** lovely raspberry, mulberry tones, 8 mths supportive oaking. 70/30 pinotage, merlot. **Sunset Hat** ★★☆ Charming & perfectly named dry rosé. **05** light hearted, redcurrant-toned sipper to mark the end of the day. 80/20 pinotage, cab. **Nicole's Hat** ★★☆ Working well together, **05**'s chardonnay/chenin equal partnership contributes pear-drop, melon flavour to this light textured, refreshingly dry quaffer. **French Kiss** ★★★ Natural Sweet chenin. **05** curvaceous, fruit-salad toned, uncomplicated & sweet. 60g/ℓ sugar. Friendly 11% alc. — *CR*

Ashbourne

Hemel-en-Aarde Valley ▪ Est 1996 ▪ 1stB 2001 ▪ Closed to public ▪ Owner Anthony Hamilton Russell ▪ Winemaker Hannes Storm ▪ Viticulturist Johan Montgomery ▪ ±13 ha (pinotage, sauvignon) ▪ 8 tons 600 cs 70% red 30 white ▪ PO Box 158 Hermanus 7200 ▪ hrv@hermanus.co.za ▪ T 028·312·3595 ▪ F 028·312·1797

The 113ha property on Hamilton Russell Vineyards' eastern boundary, previously devoted to HRV owner Anthony Hamilton Russell's Southern Right wine venture (see separate entry), has been renamed Ashbourne for development as a stand-alone wine farm. 'With four daughters, I'm committed to developing four separate projects before I retire. Wine farms with more than one child in ownership are much more likely to be sold!' The aim: two wines. Named for AHR's maternal great-great-grandfather, Ireland's late 19th-century Lord Chancellor, the pinotage-driven Ashbourne (future possible ingredients include cab, cab franc, malbec, petit verdot, shiraz) will attempt to become one of the world's benchmark reds. It now also has a white partner, Sandstone.

★★★★★ **Ashbourne** First of these elegant, bdx-styled pinotages since maiden **01** is excellent, raspberry-fruited **04**, with fresh charm, but mineral undertone & serious subtle structure of smooth ripe tannin; beautifully integrated & supportive Fr oak, restrained 14.1% alc. Shd develop over 5+ yrs.

★★★★ **Sandstone** new **06**'s aroma, flavour dominated by sauvignon (60%); mid-2006 needs decanting to bring out contribution of chard (30%), with barrel fermented semillon adding lemon twist to passionfruit, guava, peach: yr/2 shd augment present simplicity & hopefully justify rating. Nicely balanced, firm acidic core, bone-dry finish: gd food wine. These both WO W Bay. — *TJ*

Ashton Winery

Ashton ▪ Est 1962 ▪ 1stB ca 1970 ▪ Tasting & sales Mon-Fri 8-5 Sat 9-12.30 ▪ Closed pub hols ▪ Tours by appt ▪ BYO picnic ▪ Owners 68 members ▪ Winemakers Philip Louw (Aug 2000) & Jozua Joubert ▪ Viticulturist to be apptd ▪ 1 200 ha (cab, ruby cab, shiraz, chard) ▪ 18 000 tons (6 000 cs own label) 35% red 65% white ▪ PO Box 40 Ashton 6715 ▪ info@ashtoncellar.co.za or kcilliers@ashtoncellar.co.za ▪ T 023·615·1135/7 ▪ F 023·615·1284

Cellarmaster Philip Louw and his assistant, newcomer Jozua Joubert, were all smiles after last season, 'the next best thing to a perfect harvest'. New energy's evident here: the cellar's been renovated, the gardens have been prettied up and the staff complement's grown. A report-back on CEO Jakes de Wet's drive for new markets adds northern Europe and Mauritius to the list; added to the range are a red and a white sparkler and four limited edition Reserve wines.

Reserve range

Shiraz new ★★★ **04** ripe & rich with mouthwatering savoury notes, lithe tannins; delicious now but should improve over ±4 yrs. 14 mths, new Fr oak. **Chardonnay** ★★★ Last tasted was unsophisticated yet appealing **03**, 6 mths 1st/2nd fill Fr oak.

Ashton Winery range

Cabernet Sauvignon ★★★ **03** sample tasted mid-2005 grainy tannins matched by ripe red/black fruit, juicy acid. Reverted to older Fr barrels (**02** oak-staved); incl splash petit v. **Pinot Noir** ★★☆ **03** last ed was impressively dark, alcoholic (15%) yet agreeable, with soft red fruit. **Shiraz** ★★★ **03** chunky, savoury & spicy with lively dark fruit; last yr's gruff & mouthcoating tannins shd have softened by now. Yr Fr oak, none new. **Cabernet Sauvignon-Merlot** new ★★ Approachable 66/34 blend, **04** restrained red fruits on nose & palate, with soft tannins for early drinking. **Satyn Rooi** ★★★ Smooth equal blend 50/50 ruby cab & pinotage, unoaked; **04** sold out before we cld taste; **03** was supple & juicy, medium bodied, for early drinking. Also in 6x500ml packs. **Rosé** new ★★ 'Charming picnic partner' say the team, correctly; **06** sweetish (±14g/ℓ sugar) with strawberry note, jammy finish. **Chardonnay Unwooded** ★★ **06** not up to par: lacks varietal character, is warm (14% alc) & unconcentrated. **Chenin Blanc** new ★ **06** shy & restrained, muted fruit & bracing acidity. **Colombar** ★★ **06** vibrant & bright with hints guava & tropical fruits, moderate 12.5% alc. **Sauvignon Blanc** ★★ Always early-picked, kept under dry ice for lively crispness. **06** sherbety, bone-dry &, at 13.5% alc, not as light as pvs. **Colombar-Chardonnay** ★★★ **05**, tasted as a sample last yr, charming poolside sipper with light pear & citrus scents. No **06**. **Pétillant Blanc** ★★ Lightly perlant crowd-pleaser. **06** fresh, sweetish & faintly aromatic, with fairly modest 13% alc. **Late Harvest** ★ **05** manageably sweet & lightish (11.5% alc) but tiring, drink up. **Special Late Harvest** ★★ Ethereal **05** from white muscadel; last ed had talcum & green apple hints, very sweet & light (11%alc). Following fortifieds not retasted: **Red Muscadel** ★★ **05** strictly for the sweet toothed: one-dimensional spicy tea-leaf character. **White Muscadel** ★★★★ Luxurious **02** jasmine & honeysuckle aromas, silky peach & honey flavours. 16.8% alc. **Port** ★★ Honest, unpretentious winter warmer; **NV** (04) has flavours of raspberry & treacle, lifted by spirituous body & finish. **Blanc de Noir** discontinued. — *CT*

Assegai Selection   🍷 📂

*Stellenbosch (see Helderberg map) ▪ Est 1999 ▪ Tasting & sales by appt ▪ Assegai Guest Lodge ▪ Owner Woodlands Import Export ▪ 15 000 cs 80% red 20% white ▪ 10 Harewood Ave Somerset West 7130 ▪ rbuchner@worldonline.co.za ▪ **T** 021·855·2249 ▪ F 021·855·4924*

An export label featuring that ancient African weapon, the long throwing spear or assegai. No new wines in sight for this or owner Raimund Buchner's other brands, Patrys and Tarentaal.

■ *Astonvale* see Zandvliet

Ataraxia Mountain Vineyards   🍷 🌿

*Walker Bay ▪ Est 2004 ▪ 1stB 2005 ▪ Tasting by appt ▪ See intro for attractions ▪ Owner Kevin Grant Wines (Pty) Ltd ▪ Winemaker/viticulturist Kevin Grant ▪ 25 ha planned ▪ 5 000 cs 40% red 60% white ▪ PO Box 603 Hermanus 7200 ▪ ataraxia@kingsley.co.za ▪ **T** 028·212·2007/ 083·697·8292 ▪ F 028·212·1921*

Into his second vintage as a soloist, Kevin Grant and his wines have attracted enthusiastic local fans, and his sights are now moving abroad, aided by a new logo portraying the 'emotional tranquillity' alluded to in the winery's ancient Greek name. August 2006 saw the first vineyard plantings — Grant carefully matching rootstock to soil type, sourcing the best scion material available. His philosophy is to defer to the site to determine wine style, reflecting the variables and vagaries of each vintage. A new 'Overberg chapel' reception facility awaits visitors, offering wrap-around vistas down the Hemel-en-Aarde Valley.

★★★★ **Ataraxia** new **05** red blend from various vyds – but varieties not named (as 'merely vehicles of terroir expression' says KG). Black cherry/cassis aromas, primary fruit dominant mid-2006; unshowy elegance, supple tannins, persistent length. 18 mths Fr oak (65% new).

★★★★☆ **Chardonnay** new Classically styled **05** intense yet austere, with great linearity. Lime/grapefruit aromas, citrus concentration, mineral notes. Fermented/9 mths oak well integrated. From (a great rarity: ungrafted vines) remote Agter Witzenberg Vly.

Sauvignon Blanc 05 (★★★★) was attractively lean; **06** (★★★★) sample promises more, with capsicum/flint fragrance, racy yet reined-in acidity. Evident cool-climate fruit, ample palate length, moderate 13% alc enhancing freshness. Has ageing potential. – MF

- ■ **Atkinson Ridge** see Amani
- ■ **At The Limiet** see Nabygelegen
- ■ **Auberge du Paysan** see L'Auberge du Paysan

Audacia Wines

Stellenbosch ▪ Est 1930 ▪ Tasting & sales Mon-Fri 8-5 Sat 10-3 ▪ Fee R10 refundable on purchase ▪ Closed Christian holidays & Jan 1st ▪ Tours by appointment ▪ Owners Strydom & Harris families ▪ Winemaker Elsa Carstens (since Apr 1999), with Louis van Zyl ▪ Viticulturist Elsa Carstens, with Willem Booysen ▪ 20 ha (five bdx reds, rooibernet, shiraz) ▪ 154 tons 12 000 cs 100% red ▪ PO Box 12679 Die Boord 7613 ▪ info@audacia.co.za ▪ www.audacia.co.za ▪ T 021·881·3052 ▪ F 021·881·3137

Leaping onto centre stage last year was an own-label wine from Audacia co-owner and former ballerina, Diane Strydom. But the chief choreographer at this boutique red-wine specialist winery continues to be Elsa Carstens, now in her 7th year as winemaker and general manager. She reveals the new wine, named Dancing Vines Jeté, was 'specially selected and matured under perfect conditions to allow for an exquisite product', but modestly refuses to take a bow for it, simply saying: '2001 was a great year for Audacia'.

Rouge Noble 03 (★★☆) blend (half merlot, +cab, shiraz) dominated by gamey vegetal whiffs, with tannins flattening the finish. Yr Fr oak. Lacks aromatic sweetness of pvsly launched **04** (★★★★) from cab f. **Cabernet Sauvignon** ★★★ Brambly, nutty aromas on **02**; light but not insubstantial, with strikingly tannic finish. Just 9 mths oak 'because of light vintage' says Elsa C. **Dancing Vines Jeté Cabernet Sauvignon** new ★★★ **01** nicely matured in bottle. Gd concentration & dense tannins notwithstanding leafy notes. Yr Fr oak, 25% new. 14.4% alc. **Merlot** ★★★★ Food-friendly, modestly oaked **02** with succulent, soft-textured flavours, fine tannins. Like next 2, not retasted. **Shiraz** ★★★ Pleasantly savoury **02**, lightish in colour/body, slightly less fruit than pvs – all in line with vintage – but tasty. **Coeur de Rouge** ★★★ **01** oaked cab-merlot partnership showing gd mature touches to bright cassis fruit, prominent tobacco/cigarbox characters. – MF

Aufwaerts Co-operative

Rawsonville ▪ Visits by appointment ▪ PO Box 15 Rawsonville ▪ aufwaerts@breede.co.za ▪ T 023·349·1202/082·349·4001 ▪ F 023·349·1202

This well-established winery, owned by the De Villiers family, now markets a portion of its bulk production under an own-label, and invites visitors to pop in anytime for a tasting of the Dry Red and Dry White. ('Best to phone ahead though,' says Hennie de V, 'as we bottle very small batches at a time.') Also available is the Twee Eeue 5-year-old potstill brandy.

Autumn Harvest Crackling

Wallet-pleasing, lightly petillant blend chenin, colombard & crouchen, by Distell. **NV** ★★ Latest with zippy acidity, perky Granny Smith apple flavours to control the sweetness, ensure uncloying drinkability. Screwcapped. – CvZ

■ *Avoca* see Douglas Wine Cellar

Avondale ○♀♫☜&

Paarl • Est 1997 • 1stB 1999 • Tasting & sales Mon-Sat & pub hols 10-4 • Fee R12, refunded on purchase • Tours by appt • Conferencing • Owner John Grieve/Avondale Trust • Winemaker Bertus Albertyn, with Corné Marais • Viticulturist Johnathan Grieve (2000) • 100 ha (cab, grenache, malbec, merlot, mourvèdre, shiraz, chard, chenin, muscat d'A, roussanne, semillon, viognier) • 290 tons 15 000 cs 74% red 20% white 6% fortified • PO Box 602 Suider-Paarl 7624 • wine@avondalewine.co.za • T 021·863·1976 • F 021·863·1534

When it comes to working a farm 'as nature intended', the Grieve family – who propagated the line 'Nature's Way' for their health products – doesn't believe in half measures. Since 1999 all new plantings have been cultivated organically, while the rest of their Klein Drakenstein vineyards were slowly converted to what they call 'biological' farming practices (a combination of organic and biodiversity-conscious). It's all paid off: Avondale is now registered as biodiversity-compliant by Wines of SA and certified organic by Dutch-based authority Control Union (previously SKAL International).

Les Pleurs range

★★★★☆ **Syrah** The flagship from a single vyd, bearing Avondale signatures of rich savouriness, warming alc (±14.5%). **02** (not retasted) supple & svelte, released ahead of 01, with dense meaty/savoury flavours. VDG. Fermented/17 mths oak, 80% new.

★★★★☆ **Merlot 00** tasted mid-2004 understated & seamless. Notes of spiced dried fruits & 'rain forest'; sumptuous; long, fennel finish. Fermented new Fr oak.

Avondale range

★★★★ **Graham Reserve** Premium reserve cuvée named for the Grieves's Scottish clan. **03** blends selection of best barrels cab, merlot, shiraz (50/25/25). Classy cassis, cedar & choc, multi-layered & interwoven with fine oak (80%+ new, 17 mths), properly dry, lengthy warm finish (14.8% alc). Already approachable, will easily last 8-10 yrs. Pvs **01** had cab f also in equation; VDG.

★★★★ **Cabernet Sauvignon** Demanding warm-climate cab (±14.5% alc), usually unready on release but promising gd development. **02** (not retasted) lighter, softer than pvs – consonant with vintage. Fermented/matured ±14 mths Fr oak, 55-65% new. No **03** made.

★★★★ **Syrah 04** more New World than pvs (though 14.3% alc a little lower), with opulent black cherry & pepper bouquet; loads of black choc flavour combine with luxurious oak (14 mths, 60% new) for sleek, smart production. Shd keep 5-7 yrs. VDG for **03**.

★★★★ **Sauvignon Blanc** Less arresting than lip-smacking **05**, latest **06** (★★★★) more restrained, cool; less tropical in flavour despite riper harvesting – alc ups a little to 13. 3%. Herbal, green nettle flavours; tangy acidity adds elegant build with signature 'wet pebble' & slate textures. Gd for 2-3 yrs. WO Coastal.

★★★★ **Muscat Rouge** ✓ From fortified red muscat de F. Billowing muscat aromas on **04** conjure up spice souks – incense, exotic fruits, spices. Intensely sweet & raisiny (192g/ℓ sugar), slight tannic grip adding textural contrast, subtle grip to finish. Alc 18%. Small portion in old oak. 375ml, like white version.

★★★★ **Muscat Blanc** ✓ Nightcap from muscat de F. Muscadel Awards 'platinum' plaudit for **05**, gorgeous whiffs orange zest, apricot. Sweet, fleshy, but zesty acidity adds lovely fresh liveliness, ensures balance & non-cloying finish. Sugar 188g/ℓ, alc 16.1%.

Julia ★★★☆ Cab-dominated **04** (with merlot, cab f) tad more serious than pvsly tasted **02**, some gd cassis fruit, firmer tannic grip. Yr Fr oak, none new. WO Coastal. **Pinotage** ★★★ Previewed **06** with upfront crushed raspberry/red cherry flavours; mouthwatering & cheerful; light oaking. **Pinotage Reserve** new **06**, tasted ex-barrel, ripe & lush; plummy fruit (accentuated by partial carbonic maceration) putting on oak cloak, will be rich & sumptuous. Too early to rate realistically, but aiming higher than std. **Proprietor's Shiraz** ★★★ **04** warm leather & mocha notes follow through onto palate: meaty, beefy wine, great as a warming winter tipple & pretty alcoholic at 14.5%. 14 mths oak, some new. **Rosé** ★★ From muscat de F, pinotage (80/20). **06** dryish & crisp, firm taut fruit – but, sadly, no real evidence of muscat. **Chardonnay** ★★★ **05** (sample tasted last yr) emphasises fruit rather than oak (portion 9 mths in barrel); dried peach, bouncy fruit/acid balance, marginally more weight than unoaked cellarmate, lingering finish. **Chardonnay Sur Lie** ★★★ **06** gentle peach attractions & soft acid make for delightful charmer with some style. Gd juicy fruit, punchy finish; just dry. **Chenin Blanc** ★★★★ √ **06** in established style: delicate floral bouquet, main action on palate which bursts with tangy lime-tinged melon & quince, lengthy finish.

Amira range

Export wines. **Cabernet Sauvignon Rosé** new ★★ For gd summer quaffing, **06** has cherry aroma/flavour; dry, soft & fruity. For US, as is... **Cabernet Franc** ★★★ **04** deep, dark. Next-tasted **06** (sample; possible ★★★★) has big whiffs greenpepper, cedar — more like cab s, but less tannic: soft, more charm & gentle blackberry fruit in youth. Modest oaking. **Syrah** ★★★ **03** supple fruit, soft furry tannins from gentle oaking (mostly older Fr/Am), warming finish (14.5% alc). Not retasted, nor was... **Cape Red** ★★★★ **01** for German retail trade. Lively 5-way blend quite complex & integrated; drank well mid-2005. Mix new/old, Fr/Am barrels. — *IvH*

Avondvrede Private Wine Farm ö♀🍷🍴

Paarl • Est 1995 • 1stB 1999 • Tasting, sales, cellar tours & light lunches by appt • Tour groups • Function room • Owners John & Christine Enthoven • Winemaker John Enthoven • 4 ha (cabs s/f, merlot) • 20 tons ±5 000 cs 100% red • PO Box 152 Klapmuts 7625 • **T 083·658·0595** *• F 021·875·5609*

Back in 2006 after a brief break from winemaking, John and Christine Enthoven vinified and blended a pair of bordeaux-style reds, one a mirror of the other: the Koningshof Noble Red is 70/30 cab and merlot, while the Masters Noble Red is 70/30 merlot and cab. They also made a varietal merlot under their Cuvée Marie Christine label. All will become available later this year.

Avontuur Estate ö♀🍷🍴♿

Stellenbosch (see Helderberg map) • Est 1850 • 1stB 1990 • Tasting & sales Mon-Fri 8.30-5 Sat & Sun 8.30-4 • Fee R20 for 5 tastings, incl glass • Closed Easter Fri, Dec 25 & Jan 1 • Tours by appt • The Avontuur Restaurant • Owner Tony Taberer • Winemaker Adél van der Merwe (2006) • Viticulturist Pippa Mickleburgh (Sep 1999) • 50 ha (cab s/f, merlot, pinot, pinotage, shiraz, chard, sauvignon) • 20 000 cs own label 70% red 30% white • Export brand: Klein Avontuur • PO Box 1128 Somerset West 7129 • info@avontuurestate.co.za • www. avontuurestate.co.za • **T 021·855·3450** *• F 021·855·4600*

It's back to an all-women team at this Helderberg wine and equine stud farm. Winemaker Willie Malherbe left to focus full-time on his property development business (though he assures he'll still make a barrel or two for personal consumption). His successor, Adél van der Merwe, who cut her teeth at Hartenberg and Waterford, settled in mid-winter, assured of ongoing expert mentorship from respective (and respected) winemakers Carl Schultz and Kevin Arnold. Additional seating in the restaurant, and monthly tasting room specials make this farm even more visitor-friendly.

★★★★ **Baccarat** Brooding bdx blend cabs s/f & merlot; 16 mths new Fr oak. **01** last ed deep & dark for its age; some bottle-maturity revealed via forest-floor hint. Ready, shd improve another few yrs.

★★★★ **Pinotage** A fine Cape offering. **01** mid-2004 showed vivid raspberry, strawberry & vanilla-cream flavours, judicious wood (±18 mths Fr, some new). Probably best enjoyed soon.

★★★★★ **Luna de Miel** Barrel-fermented chard. **04** tasted last yr, exotic & pungent with asparagus suggestion, tangy grapefruit. Touch sugar (5.8g/ℓ) & viscous alc (14.5%) give sweet tail. 8 mths Fr oak. **01** Wine ★★★★.

★★★★ **Brut Cap Classique** Refined bone-dry sparkling from chard & pinot; latest (**NV**) equal blend, bottle matured 4 yrs. Luxurious aromas of toffee-apple & honey; rich but zesty lemon flavours.

Cabernet Sauvignon ★★★ Misreported 'discontinued' last ed; **02** nicely dry, with herby cassis tone. Big alc (14.5%), over-firm tannins need yr/2 to settle, meld. 18 mths 50% new Fr oak. **Shiraz** ★★★☆ **04** smoky red fruits well-knit with approachable tannins, white pepper hint adds interest. Combo new Am/old Fr oak. **Vintner's Red** ★★★ Fruity wallet-pleaser. Healthy dash merlot adds flesh, weight, to usual cabs f/s duet (50/25) in **04**. Dusty finish from oak (yr older Fr), freshened by acid. **Sauvignon Blanc** ★★★ Water-white **06** (sample) gd food partner: fair palate weight (though low 12% alc), cleansing acidity, subtle greenpepper, cut grass aromas. **Vintner's Blend** ★★★ Sunset-pink, medium bodied easy-drinker from chard/pinot (60/40), briefly barrelled. More pinot grip in **06** (sample), chard adds pleasing lime/lemon tone. Tasty picnic accoutrement. Following still-available wines not retasted: **Cabernet Franc** ★★★☆ **01** attractive 'fresh compost' fragrance. Nimble tannins spotlight gentle, perky flavours. Less than yr in older oak. **Merlot** ★★★☆ Confident **00** with choc/spice, maraschino cherry character. Lightly oaked (±yr older Fr barrels); drink or cellar another few yrs. **Minelli** ★★ Peach, strawberry & raspberry aromas abound on this rustic **04** pinot. Tough tannins dominated ripe-prune palate mid-2005. Will they soften? **Vintner's Pinotage** ★★★ Gluggable mulberry hued & raspberry toned **03**; fruit well-meshed with yr older wood. **Cabernet Sauvignon-Merlot** ★★★ Lighter in tone than single-variety bottlings. **01** melange black/red fruits, ripe tannins; shd be ready now. Yr used Fr oak. **Chardonnay, Chenin Blanc, Dolce Vita Red** discontinued. — *CvZ*

Ayama Wines [new]

Paarl ▪ Est 2004 ▪ 1stB 2005 ▪ Closed to public ▪ Owner Slent Farms (Pty) Ltd (6 partners) ▪ Winemakers Kobus de Kock & Pieter Carstens (Perdeberg Co-op) ▪ Viticulturist Morné Kruger (2004) ▪ 41 ha (cab, merlot, shiraz, chenin) ▪ 416 tons 20 000 cs 60% red 40% white ▪ PO Box 2180 Windmeul 7630 ▪ info@slentfarms.com ▪ www.slentfarms.com ▪ T/F 021-869-8313

An affair of the heart. Proudly Italian Michela and Attilio Dalpiaz, bowled over by SA's 'beautiful people, kind and smiling, great wines and a natural environment still intact', fell in love with Slent Farm in the Voor Paardeberg in 2003. At 172ha (41ha vines, 14.5ha plums, 2.5ha pears) with a loyal labourers' community, it was bigger than envisaged. But friends back home provided impetus and investment, and the delighted couple, supported by Perdeberg's Kobus de Kock and Pieter Carstens, and farm manager/viticulturist Morné Kruger, recall their maiden 2005 harvest with 'tears of happiness'.

> **Cabernet Sauvignon** ☺ ★★★ This **05**, like following reds, demonstrates satisfaction achievable without oak. Ripe ruby clarity; expansive dark berry fruits; well structured, with fresh tannin integration. Good drinking now & over yr/18 mths. **Merlot** ☺ ★★★ **05** comfortably plump with ripe plum compote filling. Substantial but not overpowering; lively, rounded & dry. **Shiraz** ☺ ★★★ Fruitily accented **05**. Straightforward yet pleasing choc/red berry persistence. Balanced,freshness & grip for current enjoyment.

Chenin Blanc ★★★ Full bodied, dry **05** with mellowing honeysuckle, floral tones. Richness cut by sharpish acid; alc kick in tail. — *AL*

Axe Hill ♀

Calitzdorp (see Little Karoo map) ▪ Est 1993 ▪ 1stB 1997 ▪ Open by appt; when closed, sales from Queens Bottle Store, Voortrekker Road (R62), Calitzdorp ▪ Owners Axe Hill Trust ▪ Winemaker Miles Mossop ▪ 1.3 ha (touriga, tinta, souzão) ▪ 6-9 tons 1 600 cs 100% port ▪ PO Box 43942 Scarborough 7975 ▪ lyn@axehill.co.za ▪ T 021-780-1051/044-213-3585/ 082-557-4477 ▪ F 021-780-1178

Shortly after the previous edition of this guide went to print, Tony Mossop (Cape Wine Master, self-taught winemaker, port champion, wine journalist, veteran taster and contributor to this guide) passed away. The many who mourned were soon saluting wife and partner Lyn for taking over the reins, assisted by younger son and Tokara winemaker, Miles. They vinified a 'bumper 9-ton crop'; bottled a barrel of Touriga Dry Red (a TM experiment); and released their long-gestated solera-aged white port.

★★★★★ **Cape Vintage Port** Multiple accolades for this stylish, consistently stellar port celebrate the legacy of Tony M. Marked by balance rather than opulence; 04 tighter, less
overt in youth than pvs, same intricate mould: alluring spice, smoke & nuts abound.
Traditionally vinified touriga/tinta blend (70/30) from low-yielding vyds (±5 t/ha); 14
mths seasoned casks. 20% alc, 95g/ℓ sugar.

★★★★ **Dry White Port** [new] Stunning fortified linctus coaxed 'solera-style' from chenin.
450ℓ made per yr & matured in two casks; first release blend of cask each of 03 & 04
(so **NV**) — remaining barrels will build reserve for future bottlings. Crisp liveliness
freshens oxidative girth, alc stiffens, doesn't detract. Best icy as an aperitif.

Touriga Nacional [new] ★★★★ ✓ 04 Tony M's only ever dry red: wild, musky cherry tang,
chewy breadth. Just 560 x 500ml btls. — *DS*

Baarsma Wine Group

Stellenbosch ▪ *Closed to public* ▪ *Owner Baarsma Wine Group B.V.* ▪ *MD Chris Rabie (since Jul
2001)* ▪ *Cellarmaster Hannes Louw (since Jan 2005)* ▪ *PO Box 7275 Stellenbosch 7599* ▪
phelia@baarsma.co.za ▪ *www.baarsma.com* ▪ **T 021·880·1221** ▪ *F 021·880·0851*

Baarsma SA, headquartered in Stellenbosch, is a major export marketer of SA wines, shipping more than 1m cases a year to the major international wine markets, notably Europe.
Ranges owned or exported include Ancient Africa, Apiesklip, Blydskap, Boschveld, Cape Reality, Drie Berge, Goede Moed, Goedgenoegen, Jacobus de Wet, Lazy Bay, Lyngrove (see entry), Meerland, Podium, Rotsvast, The Mask, Veelplesier, Volmaak, Voorspoed, Vreughvol and
Wild Tales. Baarsma also represents a number of top SA brands in Europe.

■ *Babbling Brook see Makro*

Babylon's Peak Private Cellar

Swartland ▪ *Est/1stB 2003* ▪ *Visits by appt* ▪ *Self-catering guest house* ▪ *Walks* ▪ *Conservation
area* ▪ *Owner/winemaker/viticulturist Stephan Basson* ▪ *200 ha (cab, carignan, merlot,
pinotage, ruby cab, shiraz, chard, chenin, sauvignon)* ▪ *80 tons 1 200 cs own label (70% red
30% white)* + *±40 000ℓ bulk wine* ▪ *PO Box 161 Malmesbury 7299* ▪ *info@babylonspeak.co.
za* ▪ **T/F 022·487·1614**

There's something quietly confident about putting your own name on a new product, and
that's what Stephan Basson did last year. His Basson range honours four generations of
winegrowers on the family farm, and is positioned as an entry-level offering complementary to the flagship Babylon's Peak range. The latter, named after the granite spire that shades the
vineyards of this Swartland farm, now features a Cab and a trio of whites.

Syrah ★★★★ Handsome 04 with mocha, black choc, nudges next rung up; taut, muscular
& dry, fine-grained tannins — but watch 15% alc. Still with lots in reserve. **Babylon** ★★★☆
04 blends pinotage, cab, merlot (40/30/30) from low-yielding Pdberg vyds. Offers mulberry, pencil shavings; still taut, very dry, some austerity. Following all [new], barrel samples. **Cabernet Sauvignon 05** sample has arresting mulberry leaf aroma, like opening
silkworm box! Ripe mulberry flavours to match; soft pulpy fruit, ultra-soft tannins, very
modern fresh-faced style: almost unbelievably full. 18 mths older oak. Heading for ★★★★,
as is... **Chardonnay 06** ripe pears & custard aromas/flavours — richly endowed, full-bodied & ripe. Fermented/6 mths older oak. **Viognier** Very correct 06 fragrance white peach
& evening flowers reined in by oak (as for Chard). Less rich than other white, but still substantial (both 14.5% alc). With dollops chard, chenin. Should rate min ★★★.

Basson Wines   [new]

Stephan's Blend ★★★ 04 irresistible spicy rustic blend led by 40% carignan, with cab,
merlot, pinotage. Huge concentration plums & dried currants, with earthy dry finish. Yr
oak, mainly Fr. **Chenin Blanc** Light & easy 06 sample (quaffable 12.5% alc), early harvested melon-tinged fruit arranged around steely core. Likely ★★. — *IvH*

■ *Babylons Toren see Backsberg*

■ *Babylon Wines* see La Vierge

Backsberg Estate Cellars

Paarl ▪ Est 1916 ▪ 1stB 1970 ▪ Tasting & sales Mon-Fri 8-5 Sat 9.30-4.30 Sun 10.30-4.30 ▪ Fee R10 refunded on purchase ▪ Closed Easter Fri, Dec 25 ▪ Self-guided tours during tasting hours ▪ Backsberg Restaurant Tue-Sun (see Eat-out section); cheese platters at tasting room ▪ Play area for children ▪ Maze ▪ Gifts ▪ Conferences & weddings by appt ▪ Owner Backsberg Estate Cellars ▪ Winemaker Alicia Rechner ▪ Viticulturist Clive Trent (Jul 1992) ▪ 130 ha (cab, merlot, shiraz, chard) ▪ 1 000 tons ±90 000 cs 65% red 30% white 5% rosé ▪ PO Box 537 Suider-Paarl 7624 ▪ info@backsberg.co.za ▪ www.backsberg.co.za ▪ T 021·875·5141 ▪ F 021·875·5144

The restaurant mooted last edition is now open six days a week and promises to braai a lamb on a spit every single one of them. To accompany it, Alicia Rechner has introduced a new Rosé named Bella Rosa, made from the juice of several red varieties (she playfully describes it as 'made of the rib of Elba,' an 'Eve' counterpart to their Mediterranean-style red). Backsberg's internal compass meanwhile is pointing towards offering a more holistic visitors' experience. Now a member of the Biodiversity & Wine Initiative, the farm has even engaged an environmentalist to audit energy effi-ciency and greenhouse gas emissions from the winery.

Babylons Toren range

★★★★ **Red 02** was 'Cabernet Sauvignon-Merlot' pvs ed; **03** gets 33% shiraz injection plus powerful shot new oak (3 yrs!). Ripe but embryonic mint-plum fruit holds its own, but needs yr/2 to grow into massive structure of tannin & alc (15%), which shd carry the wine decade or more.

★★★★ **Chardonnay** Bold & characterful **03**, pvsly a sample, has come together nicely in bot-tle: plentiful lime/greengage fruit, toasted hazelnut extra; appealing combo leesy breadth, racy-dry freshness; Fermented/yr oak, 100% new. Screwcapped, as is wine below.

★★★★ **Viognier** Last ed **05** (★★★★) a preview, now bottled, improved; peach/savoury tones & wet fynbos hint; warmly ripe palate with big alc meshed. Same insinuating sweet-ness (8g/ℓ RS) as generally more convincing **04**. ±6 mths barrelled. WO Coastal.

Cabernet Sauvignon discontinued.

Black Label range

★★★★ **Klein Babylonstoren** Balance the watchword, in both make-up (50:50 blend cab, merlot) & character. **03** last yr showed fine tannins, rich flavours, good length — all well integrated with serious structure. A stayer. 16 mths Fr oak, 25% new vs.

★★★★ **Elba** ✓ Individual, idiosyncratic medley of six red grapes & viognier, some ex-Dbnvlle, small oak aged 18 mths. Aromatic **05** well built, full, sturdy (rib)cage of tannin hung with enough dark-berried flesh to broach now & keep few yrs. Sample tasted.

Pumphouse Shiraz 04 (★★★) attractive soft, slightly earthy dark-fruit compote character; quickish flavours end in warming flow from usual robust alc (15%). 18 mths oak, 15% Am. Crackerjack **03** (★★★★) was multi-layered, with notes of mocha, vanilla & spice. **Elba Bella Rosa** ★★★ **06** juice bled from varieties headed for Elba red (mourvèdre mainly, sangiovese, petit v & zin). Dry, fruity & light but charming. **John Martin Reserve Sauvignon Blanc** ★★★★ **05** bottled (& screwcapped) version of last yr's sample offers fresh & light ruby grapefruit & apple flavours, bis-cuit overlay from 15% new-oak fermentation, racy acidity. Own, Dbnvlle fruit.

Premium range

Cabernet Sauvignon ★★★ **04** juicy, lively vintage, full bodied; dusting of spicy oak to classic blackcurrant fruit; nice now & for next few yrs. Barrelled 12 mths. **Merlot** ★★★ **05** easier, more fun than last; firm but yielding tannins, undaunting 15% alc, vanilla spicing to ripe dark fruit. Yr Fr oak, 10% new. Some Dbnvlle fruit. **Pinotage** ★★★ **05** again sets up contrast between mellifluous black pastille fruit & dry, niggling tannins. Might meld, soften with time. **Dry Red** ★★★ Sweet-fruited, unoaked everyday drink. Latest **NV** (05) appealing plummy ripeness, midweight, gently gripping tannins. Sizeable 18 000 cs off Coastal vyds. **Rosé** ★★★ **NV** (05) melange mourvèdre, chardonnay & chenin (54/40/6), last ed had ripe berry compote flavours with 20g/ℓ RS well cloaked. **Organic**

Chardonnay ★★★★ Last tasted was characterful **03**; medium bodied, balanced creamy/crisp contrast, roundly dry. Following trio WO Coastal: **Chardonnay ★★★ 05** showier, more flavoursome than pvs; textbook citrus peel & buttered toast character; attractive rounded mouthfeel from 50% Fr oak fermentation. **Chenin Blanc ★★★** Friendly, easy quaffing **06** gains length & fatness from few grams sugar, light but well ripened melon/guava fruit. **Sauvignon Blanc ★★★ 06** straightforwardly pleasant; fresh, clean & light, with hints gooseberry & nettle.

Niche range

Pinneau ★★★ Long-time tasting room favourite. Pineau des Charentes-style aperitif; unfermented semillon fortified with Backsberg potstill brandy. **04** fruity/toffee flavours with medicinal finish. **Port ★★★★** Attractive & different **04** from cab f, fortified with 3 yr old house brandy. Choc-sloshed burnt toffee character; pungent flavours & grip. Neither above retasted. **Camp Cabernet Sauvignon** & **Chardonnay** to be discontinued.

Kosher range

Made under supervision of Cape Town Beth Din. No newer vintages tasted . **Pinotage ★★** Highlights variety's sometimes tropical tone; **04** fruit salad melange with banana hint. **Chardonnay ★★ 04** whiffs of lawn cuttings & fresh compost; drier & less creamy than pvs. Oak-influenced. — *CR/MW*

Badsberg Wine Cellar

Breedekloof (see Worcester map) ▪ *Est 1951* ▪ *Tasting & sales Mon-Fri 8-5 Sat 10-1* ▪ *Closed Easter Fri-Mon & pub hols* ▪ *Tours by appt during Dec* ▪ *BYO picnic* ▪ *Tour groups* ▪ *Play area for children* ▪ *Walks* ▪ *Conservation area* ▪ *Owners 26 members* ▪ *Winemakers Willie Burger & Henri Swiegers, with Johann Fourie (Oct 1998/Dec 2002/Dec 2003)* ▪ *1 000 ha* ▪ *16 000 tons 20% red 74% white 2% rosé 4% fortified* ▪ *PO Box 72 Rawsonville 6845* ▪ *enquiries@ badsberg.co.za* ▪ *www.badsberg.co.za* ▪ **T 023·344·3021** ▪ *F 023·344·3023*

Willie Burger, Henri Swiegers & co bottle just 1% of their production but, they assure, only the best finds its way into glass. Competition judges appear to agree, as evidenced by recent good showings by the Chardonnay Sur Lie and Red Jerepigo in particular. When it comes to sharing the secrets of their success, the team play their cards close to their chest, ascribing it to the quality of the harvest. New blocks of petit verdot, viognier and nouvelle will bear fruit this year, enabling further experimentation with blends.

> **Merlot ☺ ★★★ 05** happy, berry-filled red, medium bodied; supportively oaked; dry but balanced tannins give a pleasant grip.

Pinotage & **Shiraz** sold out. **Rosé ★** From shiraz, **05** reverts to semi-sweet styling; light, still fruity but tiring a bit — drink up. **Chardonnay Sur Lie ★★★★ 05** SAYWS champ — & it shows: generous lemon/lime fruit, touch buttered toast, discreet oaking (5 mths, Fr/Hngrian oak). V pleasant indeed. **Chenin Blanc ★★** Delicate, soft & sappy **06**, floral aromas & soft acidity. **Sauvignon Blanc ★★★ 06** capsicum & greenpepper this yr; light, fresh, crisp, delightful early-drinker. **Special Late Harvest ★★★** Hanepoot & chenin team up again in **06**, light, attractively balanced, with a genteel sweetness. **Noble Late Harvest ★★★★** Usually chenin & hanepoot; **04** light bodied but unctuously sweet orange marmalade character, with hint of stalk; gentle, slightly fading charms, needs drinking. **Vin Doux Sparkling ★★★ 05** delightfully light & aromatic bubbles for the sweeter-inclined; from hanepoot & chenin; *Wine* value pick. **Red Muscadel 05 (★★★★ ✓)** gorgeous fortified dessert; masses of muscat flavour but not over-rich, touch savouriness & well judged alc (17%) lift & invigorate. Muscadel Awards gold. Notch above **03 (★★★★)**, with intense sweetness saved by lively alc & acidity. **Red Jerepigo ★★★★ 02** last ed had a lavender bouquet, & sweetness livened by alc (15.6%) for agreeably warming fruity finish. **01** also still available. **Hanepoot Jerepigo** Another outstanding **05 (★★★★ ✓)** fortified from this cellar; this one is abundantly sweet but fresh, almost dainty; excellent fruit concentration in an elegant frame. Youthful & delightful **03 (★★★)** oozed hanepoot. **Port ★★ 01** unclassic mix shiraz, cab f, ruby cab, Fr-oaked; plain but pleasant. Still selling. All WO Wrcstr. — *IvH*

▪ *Bain's Way* see Wamakersvallei
▪ *Bakenskop* see Jonkheer
▪ *Balance* see Overhex
▪ *Barefoot Wine Company* see BWC & Catherine Marshall
▪ *Barrydale Wine & Brandy Cellar* see Southern Cape Vineyards

Barry Gould Family Wines ☗ 🗫 `new`

Elgin ▪ Est 2003 ▪ 1stB 2004 ▪ Visits by appt ▪ B&B/self-catering accommodation ▪ Owner/ winemaker Barry Gould, with Niels Verburg & Gould family ▪ 100 cs 50% red 50% white ▪ PO Box 7 Elgin 7180 ▪ gould.arc@wildekrans.co.za ▪ T 028·284·9533/082·901·4896 ▪ F 028·284·9533

Some of architect Barry Gould's clients are puzzled by his hands, stained like those of a diesel mechanic; others know that since 2004 he's been playing truant in the Tinanda cellar near Elgin. The grapes are bought in, Luddite's Niels Verburg provides 'advice and inspiration' and the Gould family play assistant winemaker. The wines are on sale at Tinanda, with tastings by appointment at the Goulds' home, the historic Wildekrans Country House.

Simply Red ★★★ Characterful **04** equal cab/merlot ensemble showing restrained fruit styling, fairly evident oak & tannins, attractive 'wild' touch (from natural yeast ferment?); combo Fr barrels/staves 23 mths. **Chenin Blanc 06** sample too embryonic to rate; promising leesy fruit & overt but gd barrel character (fermented in Fr oak, none new). Both wines from Bot Rvr fruit. — *CT*

▪ *Bartho Eksteen Family Wines* see Hermanuspietersfontein —

Bartinney Cellars

Stellenbosch ▪ Est/1stB 1999 ▪ Sales Mon-Fri 9-5 ▪ Tours by appt ▪ Owner Thabana Li Meli (Pty) Ltd ▪ Winemaker/viticulturist Carl Potgieter (1999) ▪ 13 ha (cab, chard, sauvignon) ▪ 4 000 cs 33.3% red 66.6% white ▪ PO Box 2285 Dennesig 7601 ▪ thabana@mweb.co.za ▪ T 021·885·1013 ▪ F 021·885·2852

This farm high on Helshoogte Pass is owned by a company with a strong black economic empowerment component, and it adheres to eco-friendly Integrated Production of Wine principles. Winemaker Carl Potgieter focuses on varietal wines (his 03 Cab earning silver at the Swiss International Awards last year), but occasionally he makes a chardonnay-sauvignon blend named Select.

Thabana Li Meli range

Cabernet Sauvignon ★★★ **04** distinctly cab; blackcurrant on nose augmented by choc from oak (18 mths); soft & broad (15% alc), with pliant tannins which accessible now, gd for another 2/3 yrs. Samples tasted of following: **Chardonnay** ★☆ Unwooded & shorter lees-aged than pvs; **06** clean, uncomplicated, subtly tropical. **Sauvignon Blanc 06** too unformed to rate. — *JN*

Barton Farm ☗🗫

Walker Bay ▪ Est 2001 ▪ 1stB 2003 ▪ Tasting & sales Mon-Fri 9-5 Sat 9-1 ▪ Four self-catering villas ▪ Owners Peter Neill & Charles Lousada ▪ Winemakers Danie Truter & Niels Verburg (Onderkloof/Luddite) ▪ Viticulturist Noeil Vorster (Oct 2005) ▪ 28 ha (cab, malbec, merlot, mourvèdre, shiraz, chenin, sauvignon, semillon) ▪ 2 430 cs ▪ PO Box 100 Bot River 7815 ▪ peterjneill@aol.com ▪ www.bartonfarm.co.za ▪ T 028·284·9283 ▪ F 028·284·9776

Big progress at this farm in the Kogelberg Biosphere Reserve in the past year. The property is now open for tasting and sales, after having completed construction of a maturation cellar and tasting facility, as well as four guest villas. Winery authorisation is underway, and in the vineyards more sauvignon and cab were planted as well as the first mourvèdre.

★★★★ **Shiraz-Cabernet Sauvignon 05** from 60% Elgin shiraz & W Bay cab. Overtly fruity, ripe raspberry notes dominating mid-2006, food-friendly & finely textured tannins reflecting yr in oak (mainly Fr, 25% new). Lighter, less grippy than cab-driven **04**, labelled 'Cab-Shiraz'.

Chenin Blanc ★★★☆ Striking fruit selection for **06**; lovely pear-drop character in barrel sample, fine crisp acidity (6.8g/ℓ), some complexity from woodchip & lees vinification. — *MF*

- **Basson Wines** *see Babylon's Peak*
- **Bastiaans Klooff** *see Lateganskop*
- **Bat's Rock** *see Lutzville*
- **Bay View** *see Longridge*
- **BC Wines** *see Brandvlei*
- **Beacon Hill** *see Jonkheer*
- **Beacon Trail** *see Overhex*
- **Beaufort** *see Ultra Liquors*

Beau Joubert Vineyards & Winery

*Stellenbosch ▪ 1stB 2000 ▪ Visits by appt ▪ Self-catering guest houses ▪ Conference facility for max 100 ▪ Functions & weddings for max 150 ▪ Owners Joubert family & US investors led by Andrew Hilliard ▪ Winemaker Jannie Joubert, advised by Mark Carmichael-Green ▪ Viticulturist Lukas Joubert ▪ 80 ha (cab, merlot, chard, sauvignon) ▪ 600 tons 20 000 cs own label 50/50 red/white ▪ Other export brands: Oak Lane & Veelverjaaght ▪ PO Box 1114 Stellenbosch 7599 ▪ info@beaujoubert.com ▪ www.beaujoubert.com ▪ **T** 021·881·3103 ▪ F 021·881·3377*

A veritable beehive of activity, from continual fine-tuning of the vineyards and cellar, to landscaping enhancements, this farm improves each year. Exports to Europe and the US continue apace and local distribution makes the Beau Joubert and Oak Lane labels available nationally. Expansions to the guest cottages and function venues are underway to meet increasing demand for getaways in the waiting-to-be-explored Polkadraai Hills area of Stellenbosch.

Cabernet-Sauvignon ★★★ **02** balanced & rounded from almost 4 yrs in bottle; intense black fruit mingles with tertiary forest floor/fungi. Drinks well, don't keep much longer. **Merlot** ★★★★ Cleverly constructed **02**; appealingly ripe nose, generously fruited palate, smoky cocoa finish, supple tannins. Ready. This, cab above, seasoned in new/old Fr oak, yr. Following both samples: **Chardonnay** ★★★ **06** bit muted, some floral hints; well balanced though, with vibrant acidity & good vinosity. **Sauvignon Blanc** ★★★ Intensely flavoured **06** shows loads of tropical notes, zesty acidity, focus. A 'quaffer plus'. — *MM*

Beaumont Wines

*Walker Bay ▪ Est 1750 ▪ 1stB 1994 ▪ Tasting, sales & tours Mon-Fri 9.30–12.30; 1.30–4.30 Sat 9.30–1.30 ▪ Fee R20 for groups of 10+ ▪ Closed Easter Sat/Sun, Dec 25 & Jan 1 ▪ Meals for small groups by appt ▪ 2 self-catering guest houses ▪ Art/jewellery exhibits ▪ Conservation area ▪ Owners Raoul & Jayne Beaumont ▪ Winemaker Sebastian Beaumont (Aug 2003) ▪ Viticulturist Leon Engelke (May 2003) ▪ 34 ha (13 varieties, r/w) ▪ 200 tons 12 000 cs 55% red 45% white ▪ PO Box 3 Bot River 7185 ▪ info@beaumont.co.za ▪ www.beaumont.co.za ▪ **T** 028·284·9194 ▪ F 028·284·9733*

There have been changes aplenty since son Sebastian Beaumont took over the winemaking reins some three years ago. He has positively blossomed and so too the wines. The focus on chenin has seen the addition of another vineyard and a fresh new look for the barrel-matured version, named after late grandmother Hope Marguerite, as well as father Raoul's Old Basket Press Red, no longer 'Rustic'. Daughter Ariane now also gets help from Schalk Joubert in the marketing department — keep your eyes peeled for the Beaumont 'Bajaj' scooter around Cape Town.

★★★★ **Pinotage** 'Real Walker Bay pinotage, on the classic side,' says Sebastian B. **04** elegant, juicy & already moreish. Loads of red cherry fruit, tannins not overdone; dry, earthy finish. Traditional open *kuip* cold soak/ferment for these. 70% from 30 yr old vines. Yr oak Fr/Am, 80/20, 25% new.

★★★★ **Shiraz 04** retains classic style & feel despite ultra-ripeness (watch ±15% alc!), though some loss of fruit. Black cherry, smoked beef & warm oak spice move easily onto palate. Savoury, tangy flavours, the tannins unobtrusive. Includes touch mourvèdre. Oak as above.

★★★★ **Mourvèdre** SA's first varietal bottling. A brute, it takes some taming … **04** more groomed (quite a feat!) & stylish than some pvs. Dry earth, scrub & plum notes, savoury unyielding style reluctantly sleeked by oak. Needs time – say 3-5 yrs. Part natural ferment, 16 mths oak, whopping 15.4% alc.

★★★★ **Hope Marguerite Chenin Blanc Barrel Reserve** 'My baby,' says Sebastian B gleefully. Distinctive, single-vyd selection from older vines, curvaceous **05** does not disappoint: honeycomb, stewed quince, sprinkling spice; supportive oak, thrilling acidity. Give 3-5 yrs to show its best. Now natural ferment, 10 mths 400ℓ Fr oak. No malo.

★★★★ **Chenin Blanc** ✓ Fine example from 30+ yr old vines. Rounded, coolly elegant **06** has delicate almond blossom, bruised apple, subtle spice character, poised acidity. Will grow into its personality over 3-5 yrs. 15% oaked for 2-3 mths.

★★★★ **Chardonnay** Ageworthy **04** (not retasted) wears its big roundness well, thanks to lively acidity. Fermented/10 mths oak, 30% new. Final vintage; replaced by Jackals River version.

Raoul's Old Basket Press Red ☺ ★★★ In smart new livery, **05** has lost the 'Rustic' on the label (& in the glass). Tinta down to 40% of blend, with shiraz, merlot, all unoaked. Ripe & plummy, dusting of white pepper; dry, with subtle grip on tail.

Ariane ★★★☆ **04** adds dollops malbec, petit v to merlot, cabs s & f. Ultra-ripe harvesting shows on nose & palate as slight loss of fruit. Baked plum quality to merlot aromas/flavours; cab gives firm dry tannic grip. 14 mths oak, 30% new. Follows step-up **03** (★★★★). **Shiraz Rosé** 𝗻𝗲𝘄 ★★★ Fun fruit pastille, raspberry flavours on **06**, off-dry 9.8g/ℓ but lively acidity to balance. Should be a wow at a picnic. **Jackals River Unwooded Chardonnay** ★★★ For UK market. **06** terrific burst of greengage, apricot, lime perfume, follows through onto palate. Lively, mouthwatering, very much in house style. **Sauvignon Blanc** ★★★ **06** needs coaxing from glass, then features greengage, lime, gooseberry; tangy, juicy & individual. Suggest drink this summer. **Goutte d'Or** Botrytised blend: **04** (★★★★) had 80% semillon with the sauvignon; **05** (★★★★) lowers this to 64%. Gorgeous glacé pineapple & honey bouquet; sweetness (not excessive at 115g/ℓ RS) lifted by clean acidity, gd dry finish. Needs 5 yrs to reach peak. 10 mths oak. **Cape Vintage** ★★★ Cape/Portuguese compromise: 50/50 tinta/pinotage (all foot-trodden). 2+ yrs in old casks. **03** prune fruit, hints of coffee bean, rather like a liqueur but drier at 74g/ℓ RS, 19% alc.— *IvH*

Bein Wine ♀

Stellenbosch ▪ Est/1stB 2002 ▪ Open by appt only ▪ Owners/ winemakers/viticulturists Luca & Ingrid Bein ▪ 2.2 ha (merlot) 1 000 cs 100% red ▪ PO Box 3408 Matieland 7602 ▪ lib@ beinwine.com ▪ www.beinwine.com ▪ T 021·881·3025 F 021·881·3025

Small is beautiful for Swiss vets-turned-winemakers Ingrid and Luca Bein – just 80 rows of merlot – and even the egg whites used for fining come from their own contented free-range hens. The newly invented family crest sports their Bull Terrier and Ridgeback, among various other beasts. Helvetic thoroughness compelled both of them to study oenology at Stellenbosch which, combined with perfectionism and a loving personal touch, was sufficient to propel their second vintage into the ranks of the Diners Club Top 10 SA Merlots.

★★★★ **Merlot** Growing to be among best Cape merlots as vines mature. **04** (tasted last ed) well balanced & restrained, fresh & sweet cassis fruit emerging over ripe tannic core. Sensitively oaked – yr, ±40% new.

Following the 𝗻𝗲𝘄 **Little Merlot** ★★★ Vehicle for young-vine fruit, with 14% Breede Rvr petit v in **05**. Appropriate lighter structure than above for pleasant drinkability – yr older oak. Sweet fruit, dry finish. **Pink Merlot** ★★★ Blanc de noir **06**, juice bled from senior wine. Pretty colour, aromas & flavours, with fresh, easy-going, just-dry charm.— *TJ*

Belbon Hills

Worcester ▪ Est/1stB 1999 ▪ Closed to public ▪ Directors Mirella Corsetti Kruger & Pedro Estrada Belli ▪ 30 ha (cab, pinotage, ruby cab, shiraz, chenin, colombard, sauvignon) ▪ 260 tons 10 000 cs own label 60% red 40% white • *PO Box 457 Bloubergstrand 7436* • *winery@ belbonhills.com* • **T** *021·557·7143* • F *021·557·1351*

With their Italian wine roots, Breede River Valley duo Mirella Corsetti Kruger and Pedro Estrada Belli have put their import-export business background to good use, working closely with partners in Europe and North Africa to produce SA wines tailor-made for these markets. This consolidation in the export market is part of their plan to 'build up strength' to stake a claim in what they consider the competitive local market.

Cabernet Sauvignon ★★ 04 balanced, fruity easy-sipper offering plentiful red berries, dry wood tannins & a wide body from 14% alc. **Shiraz ★★** Unwooded **04** *vin ordinaire* with ultra-ripe fruit & warming flush from brawny alc. Oak staved. **Sauvignon Blanc ★★** Green pea & leafy vegetable notes on light bodied **05**, beginning to flag, drink soonest. **Passito** new **★★★** Named after traditional Italian dessert: hanepoot grapes dried on vines (30 yrs old), vinified jerepiko-style without fermentation. **NV**. Barley sugar & hint muscat, manageably sweet & easy to sip. 375ml. Above mainly W Cape WOs. **Red**, **Pinotage**, **Chenin Blanc** & **White** sold out.— *CT*

Belfield

Elgin • *Est 2000* • *1stB 2005* • *Closed to public* • *Owners Mike & Mel Kreft* • *Winemaker Mike Kreft, with Lawrence Lebenya & Kreft family, advised by Mark Carmichael-Green (2004)* • *Viti adviser Paul Wallace (2002)* • *2.5 ha (cabs s/f, merlot, shiraz)* • *±16 tons total 75 cs own label 100% red* • *PO Box 191 Elgin 7180* • *phkreft@mweb.co.za* • **T/F** *021·848·9840*

The second harvest on this tiny Elgin farm saw tonnage almost double, and owners Mike and Mel Kreft were looking to release their first wines — 750 bottles of Cab (untasted) — as the guide went to press. They've linked up with near-neighbour David Bridgman, and will use his new Valley Green cellar for vinification until the time is ripe for their own facility. New shiraz and cab franc see a significant rise in hectarage — to 2.5!

Bellevue Estate   ☝♀

Stellenbosch • *Est 1701* • *1stB 1999* • *Tasting Mon-Fri 10-4 Sat & non-religious pub hols 10-3* • *Owner Dirkie Morkel* • *Winemaker Wilhelm Kritzinger (Feb 2002)* • *Viticulturist Dirkie Morkel (1979)* • *193 ha (14 varieties, incl 5 bdx varieties, pinotage, shiraz, sauvignon)* • *13 000 cs own label 97% red 3% white* • *PO Box 33 Koelenhof 7605* • *info@bellevue.co.za* • *www.belle-vue.co.za* • **T** *021·865·2055* • F *021·865·2899*

This team clocked up air miles last year with three trips to the East and one to Brazil to develop markets. Social responsibility is close to Dirkie Morkel's heart, and his (and many others') were gladdened when the farm crèche was brightened up with the help of the Pebbles Project, which provides educational resources for children with special needs. Francina Swarts completed a National Agricultural Diploma at Elsenburg, their third staff member to do so, and PRO Randall Peceur embarked on the Certificate for Youth Trainer course to enable him to teach and inspire the next generation in this close-knit community.

Morkel range

★★★★★ **PK Morkel Pinotage** Site of SA's first released commercial pinotage, now a vyd selection. **04** accessible, with up-front fruit, soft velvety texture; ripe tannins mere ruffling of the surface. Richer, softer fruit than **03**, & oaking all-new Fr (pvs 50% new Am). Like next three reds, tasted last yr.

★★★★ **Pinotage** In bright modern guise, immediately accessible. Subtle **04**'s soft plush plummy fruit showcases variety's attractions. Slight sweetness to fruit balanced by dry oak tannins adding subtle texture, seriousness; all in gd balance. Yr Am oak, half new.

★★★★ **Tumara 03** all bdx's main red varieties: cabs s/f, merlot, malbec, petit v (69/6/10/5/ 10). Sleek subtle & stylish, more restrained, classically inclined than single variety cellarmates; dry & savoury, not over-rich, with submissive tannins. Yr Fr oak, half new. Cellar 5-7 yrs.

★★★★ **Limited Release Malbec** Stylish **03** (tasted ex-barrel) minted black plum fruit, fine tannins, savoury long finish. Yr new oak. **04** all to Woolworths.

★★★★ Sauvignon Blanc Pleasingly full & lively **05** (★★★★, not retasted) mixes tropical passionfruit, gooseberry with fig, grass, & some sweet/sour tension — but all in lower key than hugely concentrated **04**.

Malbec ★★★★ 'These always sell out quickly' is happy producer's warning. Bone-dry **04** shows maritime iodine notes, along with smoky whiffs & ample spice. Gd sappy texture on finish. Yr oak, 25% new, but all new barrels in... **Petit Verdot ★★★★** Near-black **04** has jammy notes, but quite mineral character, with velour-like tannins. **Pinot Noir ★★★** Last tasted was vinous, soft-berried **02**. **Atticus ★★★** Blend cab/pinotage/petit v — intended as 'Cape blend' sister to bdx-style Tumara. **03** sampled last ed, sweet plummy fruit, whiff gd oak, soft tannins. Fr/Am oak, 25% new. **Shiraz 03** (★★★★) showed controlled opulence; **04** barrel sample (likely ★★★), with light spicy notes, elegant but a little dilute & evanescent on finish. **Rozanne ★★☆** Oak dominates light fruited **05** with sappy, smoky whiffs. Mostly merlot (60%), with shiraz, pinotage. — *IvH*

Bellingham ⚱

*Wellington ▪ Est 1693 ▪ 1stB 1947 ▪ Closed to public ▪ Owner DGB ▪ Winemaker Niël Groenewald, with Mario Damon (Jul/Aug 2004, Jan 2002) ▪ Viti consultants Johan Wiese & Kevin Watt (1994/2002) ▪ 5 000 tons 350 000 cs 50% red 49% white 1% rosé ▪ HACCP & ISO 9002:2000 certified ▪ PO Box 246 Wellington 7654 ▪ bellingham@dgb.co.za ▪ www. bellingham.co.za ▪ **T 021·864·5300** ▪ F 021·864·1287*

Bellingham's celebrated founder Bernard Podlashuk broke with the winemaking traditions of his time, producing several SA firsts: a rosé, varietal shiraz, and bone-dry white blend. With their Maverick range, they have continued to live up to a reputation for innovation by giving their winemaking team (now minus Lizelle Gerber, who has relocated to sister brand Boschendal) licence to experiment and showcase their talents. The Chenin from this range is doing particularly well on the awards front. A wooded version from mature Perdeberg bushvines recently joined the range, and promptly sold out, with the next vintage yet to be bottled.

Spitz range

No new vintages tasted in this range: pvs were **Cabernet Franc**, **Merlot**, **Pinotage**, **Chardonnay**; all ★★★★.

The Maverick range

★★★★ Syrah Opaque core with vibrant purple rim showing youth of seriously bold **04**; splash co-fermented viognier adds perfumed floral notes to spicy aromas. Vigorous oak tannins (mostly new Fr 14 mths) pummel the dense fruit & dominate long, warm, dry finish.

★★★★ SMV new 03 serious, opaque, spicy 70/20/10 blend syrah, mourvèdre, viognier, all seamlessly integrated with oak & acidity; ripe mulberry fruit supported by tannins which provide structure to keep few yrs; strapping 15% alc not out of place; *Decanter* gold.

★★★★ Chenin Blanc Low-yield Sbosch vines & barrel ferment contribute to limpid gold colour & ripe, round style; **05** lanolin & white peach more evident on nose than palate, which avoids being overblown, despite 15% alc & 7g/ℓ sugar; fresh acidity ensures clean finish. **04** clanks with medals: *Wine* ★★★★★, VDG, Winemakers Choice, *Decanter* trophy, IWSC gold.

★★★★ Viognier Bright gold **05** proffers hedonistic peach, apricot & spice, mingling with oak from barrel fermentation; surprisingly demure palate, esp. given stats suggesting otherwise (15% alc, 10g/ℓ sugar!). Lively acidity through to dry-seeming finish. Perfect partner for spicy food.

★★★★ Sauvignon Blanc new Wooded, seriously styled, pale-gold coloured **05** from low-yield Darling fruit; oak nuttiness adds complexity & breadth to shy, ripe fig nose & palate. Genteel, not pungent, so versatile food partner; 14.5% alc leaves only slight impression.

Founders range

★★★★ Cabernet Sauvignon 04 grapes from Sbosch, Paarl, Darling; pronounced blackcurrant, choc-mint & cedar, succulent berries, suave tannins (yr Fr oak) & acid thread persist to savoury, herbal finish. Promise of improvement.

★★★★ Shiraz Spicy, peppery, smokiness & soft blackberry fruit of **04** (★★★☆) create approachable, balanced wine for immediate enjoyment; tannins from yr in barrel provide gentle grip.

Merlot ★★★★ Elegant, cedary **04** with mature colour, from Klpmuts fruit; plum & maraschino aromas & flavours balance tannins & yr oak; drink well now & preferably soon-ish. **Pinotage ★★★** Youthfully purple **05** from ripe Paarl fruit, dominated by smoked bacon aromas & ripe, tangy sour plum. Vinified/oaked for early drinking. **Chardonnay ★★★☆** Nutty vanilla & ripe stone-fruit flavours suggest **05** a popular winner. Neither high-ish alc nor sugar overly apparent on finish. **Sauvignon Blanc ★★★** **06** dry, herbaceous style from cool Darling/Dbnvlle; lean grassiness & asparagus in balance with refreshing acidity. All ranges above WO Coastal.

The Blends range

New vintages for the following not ready at press time: **Cabernet Sauvignon-Merlot (Classic) ★★★** **03** equal blend spotlights latter's choc coating for reticent cassis. Firmer grip than pvs. **Rosé ★★** The first Cape rosé. **05** coral-ruby hues from pinotage; candyfloss nose, sweet cherry send-off. **Sauvignon Blanc-Chardonnay (Sauvenay) ★★☆** Dependable easy-going style. Last tasted was **04**; polished & bright pear flavours, medium bodied, dry-enough tail. **Chardonnay-Semillon ★★★** Export only. Unwooded 50/50 mix in **04**, full & firm, waxy sheen to figgy flesh. **Premier Grand Cru ★★** Crisp & dry **NV** blend (including chenin, sauvignon, colombard), delivering the goods – & refreshingly light 12% alc – consistently since 1951. **Johannisberger ★★** Launched 1957; light-bodied **NV** (8% alc); aromatic, grapey sweetness in tangy tail. – IM

Benguela Cove `new`

Walker Bay ▪ Est 2004 ▪ 1stB 2007 ▪ Visits by appt ▪ Owners Chris Drummond & Mike Nixon ▪ Viticulturist Schalk du Toit (2004) ▪ 65 ha projected (cabs s/f, merlot, mourvèdre, petit v, pinot, shiraz, chard, sauvignon, semillon, viognier) ▪ Great Cellar, Alphen Estate Office Park, Alphen Drive, Constantia 7806 ▪ npv@icon.co.za ▪ www.benguelacove.co.za ▪ T 021·794·0751 ▪ F 021·794·0737

This new 'lifestyle estate' with its vineyards, lavender fields and olive groves on the banks of the Bot River lagoon will soon boast a 500-ton cellar, tasting facilities and restaurant, boutique hotel and spa. Experienced viticulturist Schalk du Toit (ex-VinPro) gauged the viability of growing vines where 'cooling sea breezes' are much more than just the copywriter's friend. The verdict? Plantings of some 12 red and white grape varieties will be completed by next year. Wines will be available as the vineyards come on stream.

Bergheim

Paarl ▪ Est/1stB 2000 ▪ Visits by appt; tasting/sales also at I Love Wine (see entry) ▪ Owners E & H Jordaan ▪ Winemaker Edwin Jordaan ▪ 500 cs 80% red 20% white ▪ PO Box 6020 Main Street Paarl 7622 ▪ T 082·770·8001 ▪ F 021·862·7852

Winemaker/owner 'Jorries' Jordaan, aka 'Dr Jordaan' to his patients in Paarl and 'chief cook and bottle washer' (self-designation), gives us fresh insight into his after-hours craft: 'I always thought you made wine with grapes. Now I know you make it with a bakkie (pick-up truck) – mine was stolen just before harvest.' Somehow he managed – so well, in fact, he found time to venture into white-wine-making with bought-in semillon from Franschhoek.

Pinotage ★★★ Dense & chewy **04** an appealing rustic; big brambly fruit spiced with vanilla from enthusastic oaking (combo Fr chips/barrels). Grapes ex-Knollefontein, largest pinotage block in SA. Incl soupçon 05. **Shiraz** `new` **★★** House's forthright styling on earthy **04**, spicy tannins evince extraction & lusty wooding (17 mths Fr/Am, some new). – CT

Bergkelder Wine Centre

Stellenbosch ▪ Tasting & sales Mon-Fri 8-5 Sat 9-2 ▪ Fee R20 ▪ Open non-religious pub hols ▪ Tours Mon-Fri 10 (Eng or Afr), 11 (Eng, Ger or Fr), 3 (Eng or Afr); Sat 10, 11 & 12 (Eng or Afr); incl AV presentation; bookings: tours@bergkelder.co.za ▪ Special group tours, private func-

tions by appt · Owner Distell · Cellarmaster Andrea Freeborough · Winemakers Kobus Gerber (white wines) & Justin Corrans (red wines), with Schalk van der Merwe & Jaco van der Walt · Viticulturist Bennie Liebenberg · 20 000 tons 60% red 40% white · PO Box 184 Stellenbosch 7599 · www.bergkelder.co.za · T 021·809·8492 · F 021·883·813

Literally 'Mountain Cellar', after the maturation halls cut into Stellenbosch's Papegaaiberg, the Bergkelder winery is responsible for production of the Fleur du Cap range, listed separately. Also on the premises are a visitor centre, where FdC and other ranges in the Distell portfolio are available for tasting/sale, and the Vinoteque Wine Bank (www.vinoteque.co.za), now in its 23rd year, which markets fine wines with the option of having purchases stored in perfect cellar conditions at surprisingly low cost.

Bergsig Estate

Breede River Valley (see Worcester map) · Est 1843 · 1stB 1977 · Tasting & sales Mon-Fri 8-5 Sat 9-5 · Tasting fee for groups · Closed Easter Fri & Dec 25 · Tours by appt · Bistro serving traditional food · Conference/function facilities · Owners Lategan family · Winemaker De Wet Lategan, with Chris du Toit (Jan 1989/Jul 2003) · 253 ha (cab, pinotage, shiraz, chard, chenin, sauvignon) · 3 200 tons 50 000 cs own label · 35% red 60% white 4% rosé 1% port · Exported as Lategan & White River · PO Box 15 Breede River 6858 · wine@bergsig.co.za · www.bergsig.co.za · T 023·355·1603 · F 023·355·1658

Thanks to handsome winnings for the Breedekloof Winemaker of the Year award, De Wet Lategan visited California last year, in part to see how family wineries like his handle business in a similar New World setting. Those who know the Lategans, however, might suspect a pair of binoculars tucked in the luggage — this conservation oriented family are bird-spotting mad and a chart in the winery documents the 120+ species they've sighted on the estate to date. Their elegant new Bistro makes the most of delightful vineyard and mountain views.

★★★★ **Pinotage** Elegant, minerally wine, from selected ±30 yr old shy-bearing vyds. Tasted last ed **03** (★★★) an unheralded blip, in contrast with stellar, ageworthy **02** (★★★★★) & **01**.

★★★★ **Chardonnay** Much awarded new-oak fermented version. Latest **05** full, fat, popular style with buttery vanilla aromas, rich tangerine flavours & high alc 14.5% contributing to sweet impression. **04** (★★★★) barrel character very obvious mid-2005, needed time to meld.

★★★★ **Cape Ruby** Current bottling of this multi-vintage **NV** blend, reviewed last ed, their finest to date. From tinta, as usual, fermented in open cement tanks, no oak maturation 'to allow fruit to be main focus'. 19.3% alc.

★★★★ **Cape Vintage** As above, from tinta, traditionally vinified, fortified with brandy spirit, 36 mths older oak; **00** was succulent & smooth last yr, harmonious, shd mature fruitfully.

Cabernet Sauvignon ★★★★ **04** attractive red-berry intro, stern & gripping tannins on finish mid-2005; might since have attained greater harmony. **Ruby Cabernet-Merlot** ★★☆ Usual ripe plum & cherry fruit on **04**, but tannins chewier, last ed noted as needing more time. **Shiraz Rosé** ★★★ Quaffable bone-dry blush with strawberry flavours; **05** gd refreshing summertime drink. **Chenin Blanc** ★★ **05**, a sample last yr, slight tropical tone, slender fruit, very firm in the mouth. **White River Chenin Blanc** ★★ The White Rvr label occasionally featured in the guide. Simple, sweet gumdrop aromas on **05**, otherwise a straightforwardly pleasant quaffer. **Sauvignon Blanc** ★★☆ Balanced everyday white with low 12% alc. **06** pear-drop aromas & simple quince flavours; WOM selection. **Gewürztraminer** ★★★ Balanced, fresh, delightful **06**; exotic Turkish Delight flavours, moderate 13.5% alc. **Weisser Riesling** ★★★ Last tasted as **03**, with potential for cellaring few yrs. **Bouquet Light** Await new release. **Sauvignon Blanc Brut** ★★★ Energetic carbonated dry sparkler; **05** last ed had lighter than usual tropical flavours, slightly less generous & well-padded finish than pvs. **Special Late Harvest** & **Noble Late Harvest** made in conducive yrs, currently sold out.

Lategan Family Reserve range

★★★★ **Touriga Nacional** Attractively porty, spicy **05**, rich fruitcake aromas, same sweet baked plum & allspice on palate; tannins keep fruit sweetness & alc high (15.5%) alc in check for pleasantly dry finish. Enjoy soon. 6 mths wooded. TriNations 2006 'Other reds' category winner.

Shiraz ★★★★ Softly structured for early drinking. **05** ripe mulberry & roasted spice whiffs, raspberry jam flavours. **Merlot-Petit Verdot** ★★★★ Toasty vanilla oak & sweet red berry fruit on **05**, 76/24 blend, with acidity zipping through ripeness to ensure dry finish; perceptible warmth from 14.7% alc. This established range, not pvsly featured in the guide, exclusively for export customer Direct Wines. — *IM*

Bergwater Vineyards

Prince Albert ▪ Est 1999 ▪ 1stB 2002 ▪ Tasting & sales Mon-Fri 9-4 ▪ Owners Heimie & Stephan Schoeman & DKPG (Dutch Investors Group) ▪ Winemaker Mariska Schreuder (Jan 2003) ▪ Viti advisers VinPro (1999) ▪ 70 ha (cab, merlot, shiraz, sauvignon) ▪ 90% red 10% white ▪ PO Box 40 Prince Albert 6930 ▪ wine@bergwater.co.za ▪ www.bergwater.com ▪ T 023·541·1703 ▪ F 023·541·1081

News from this winery in the Great Karoo is that the cellar is more or less completed, the wines have been released for sale to the public and there is a tasting locale in which to sample them. At some 900m above sea level — 'high enough', as one journalist cracked, 'to test the theory that alcohol is more intoxicating at altitude' — and comprising 3 000 hectares, this spread is worth visiting for its remarkable location alone.

These all NEW. **Royal Reserve** ★★★ Sturdy blend cab, merlot & shiraz (45/40/15). **04** heady cassis & plum aromas; very ripe, juicy palate cut by cab's lemon-like freshness; balanced, with firm tannin. ±14 mths 2nd fill oak, Am for shiraz. **Cabernet Sauvignon** ★★★ Oodles of black berries & plums on **05**; sweet fruit entry, then rather quick, gripping & chunky farewell. Fr oak chips, 3 mths. Similar fruit profile to.... **Cabernet Sauvignon Reserve** ★★★ As name implies, this seriously wooded (14 mths 2nd fill Fr); **04** juicy, fruit-sweet, palate pierced by green astringency. **Merlot** ★★★ Promising nose on **05**, black plums & dusty oak; dollops fruit on palate, broad midpalate tannins mask 14.5% alc but not the bitterness on the finish. **Shiraz** ★★ **05** with barnyard notes, unyielding, 'unsweetened' even by sojourn on Am oak. **Shiraz Reserve** ★★★ Contrast with above: **04** lively & fresh with cranberry fruit, touch pepper & friendly vanilla tannins from 14 mths 2nd fill Am wood; bitter hint won't be noticeable paired with a steak or hearty stew. **Rosé Reserve** ★★★ Unwooded, succulent pink sipper from pinotage & smidgen shiraz. **05** strawberries & cream whiffs complemented by gently sweet & balanced palate (14.7g/ℓ sugar). Active 14% alc. **Sauvignon Blanc Reserve** ★★ Lightish quaffer; **06** sweet-sour bouquet, zesty acidity, uncomplex flavours. All WO Prince Albert Vlly. — *CvZ*

Bernheim Wines

Paarl ▪ Est/1stB 2004 ▪ Tasting & sales Mon-Fri 8.30-5 Sat 9-12 ▪ Fee R5 refunded with purchase ▪ Closed Christian holidays ▪ Tours by appt ▪ Owners Pieter & Anneke Taljaard, Hermann Helmbold, Jacques Kruger/Pacas Winery (Pty) Ltd ▪ Winemaker Jacques Kruger (Feb 2004) ▪ Viti consultant Gawie Kriel (Mar 2004) ▪ 11 ha (cabs s/f, merlot, pinotage, shiraz) ▪ 6 000 cs 100% red ▪ PO Box 7274 Noorder-Paarl 7623 ▪ bernheim@iafrica.com ▪ www. bernheimwines.com ▪ T 021·872·8358 ▪ F 021·872·5618

The third harvest for this small Paarl producer has seen winemaker Jacques Kruger commit himself to reds, 'because the soil and climate are better suited'. Cellar upgrades are going ahead as planned, with the arrival of new stainless steel tanks. The premium range, JH Pacas & Co (initials of family and shareholders), now includes the Shiraz noted as slumbering in barrel last edition.

JH Pacas & Co range

Cabernet Sauvignon ★★★★ Harmonious & supple **03**, last yr was restrainedly flavourful, with well handled oak (17 mths Fr, 85% new). Sbosch fruit. **04 Shiraz** ★★★★ Unblushingly New World **04**; showy, chewy & ripe; lovely touches cardamom & sweet spice; lively despite 14.3% alc. 90% new oak, Fr/Am, 17 mths.

Bernheim range

Pinotage ★★★ Straightforwardly pleasant & drinkable; **05** fairly sturdy, wholesome tannins, so won't be overwhelmed by braaied meat or traditional *smoorsnoek* (spicy braised fish), Kruger's food recommendations. **Merlot-Cabernet Sauvignon** ★★ Eucalyptus-fragrant **04**, retasted, now tad too fresh, taut, for solo; try with a lazy-aged steak. 61/39 blend, fermented/ 4 mths Fr staves. No newer vintages of the following **04**s reviewed: **Rosé** ★★ Lightish equal mix colombard, chenin, dollop cab for colour; coming off the boil – drink up. **Chenin Blanc** ★★ Light, shy pear-drop aroma with leesy note, bone-dry palate. **Chenin Blanc Oak Fermented** ★★ Slightly floral nose, bit fuller than unwooded version, very dry finish. **Late Vintage** ★★ Medium bodied semi-sweet with hint of clove. – *CT*

■ **Berrio** see Flagstone

Beyerskloof

Stellenbosch • Est 1988 • 1stB 1989 • Tasting & sales Mon-Fri 8.30-4.30 Sat 10-2 • Closed Easter Fri/Sun/Mon, Dec 25/26 & Jan 1 • Farm produce • Owners Beyers Truter & Simon Halliday • Winemaker Beyers Truter, with Anri Truter (Jan 2004) • Viti consultant Johan Pienaar (2000) • 70 ha (cab, merlot, pinotage) • 490 tons 100 000 cs + 225 000ℓ for customers • 98% red 2% rosé • PO Box 107 Koelenhof 7605 • wine@beyerskloof.co.za • T 021·865·2135 • F 021·865·2683

Their Pinotage – still among the best-value wines in its class – is maintaining its popularity and business is ticking over nicely, freeing people-person Beyers Truter to spend more time on philanthropic projects like helping to launch the Faith Fund, a winelands initiative to tackle foetal alcohol syndrome. Improvements to the more immediate environment at Beyerskloof in the last year have focused on making visits ever more pleasant – a warm and welcoming tasting room and a brasserie being cases in point.

★★★★★ **Beyerskloof** Fine, modern blend cab, merlot, from 5ha planted 80/20, harvested enbloc, vinified traditionally, 2+ yrs new Fr oak. Last tasted was **02**, with 15% alc adding to forceful, macho presence; darkly savoury, yet sweet-fruited. Decant in youth – but 8-10 yrs in bottle even better.

★★★★ **Synergy Reserve** Cab in majority here (pinotage 37%, merlot 8%), so maiden **01** firmer than version below. Fresh, dynamic **02** (★★★★★, tasted last ed) forceful but focused, with delicious rich-fruited savouriness, pleasantly gripping tannin. VDG, *Wine* ★★★★. Enjoyable young, shd develop well over 5+ yrs.

★★★★★ **Pinotage Reserve** Serious & suavely refined. After sophisticated, light-hearted **03**, youthfully oak-dominated & touch sombre **04** (★★★★, perhaps tasted in dumb phase) has ripe but drying tannins with sweet, jammy core; unlingering finish. Traditional open fermenters; 14 mths oak (half new).

Synergy ★★★★ 'Cape blend', with cab & merlot, pinotage amount varying: **04** 38% pinotage, 57% cab; more succulently tannic than pvs, focused & fresh; bright fruitcake notes, lightly jammy. Yr Fr oak. **Pinotage** ★★★★ ✓ Extraordinary quality & value for 95 000 cs! Cherry/banana character, light ripe tannins beautifully managed, integrated oak influence; dry. **05** particularly delicious, refreshing. **Pinotage Rosé** ★★★ **05** (not retasted) attractive & tastily dry, well balanced with subtle tannin; notes of sweet red berries, gd earthy undertone. **Brut Pinotage Rosé** new ★★★ Truter's favourite grape finds another – foamily sparkling, v pleasant – outlet: **05** light earthy strawberry aromas, sweetly fruited but dry & fresh; interesting notes of sour cherry. Charmat process. **Lagare Cape Vintage** ★★★★ Traditional port style, **05** has equal tinta, touriga &, unsurprisingly, pinotage. Lightly gripping & fresh; sweet, ripe fruit; more easy charm than profundity. 19% alc; 85g/ℓ sugar. In handy 500ml. – *TJ*

Bianco Fine Wines

Tulbagh • Est/1stB 1997 • Tasting & sales Mon-Fri 8.30-5 Sat 9-2 • Fee R10 p/p for groups • Closed Easter Fri/Sun, Dec 25 & Jan 1 • Tours Mon-Fri 9-4.30 • Olive oil/olive products • Owner Gaëtan Bovit • Winemaker/viticulturist Marinus Potgieter (2005) • 16 ha (cab, nebbiolo, pinotage, shiraz) ▪ *70 tons 6 000 cs 70% red 30% white* ▪ *PO Box 103 Tulbagh 6820* ▪ *bianco@lando.co.za* ▪ *www.bianco.co.za* ▪ **T** *023·231·0350* ▪ F *023·231·0938*

Belgian Gaëtan Bovit fell in love with SA before he'd even set foot in the country; once here he was truly smitten. Then a property agent introduced him to the Bianco winery and farm, and he knew he'd never leave. She became his in July last year, and a very happy Bovit plans to do it the Billy Joel way — leaving things just the way they are. At least until he gets to know her a little better.

Cabernet Sauvignon ★★★ Sedate **04** in line with house's low-fruit, high-tannin style; faintly plummy, lingering & dry, commendably modest 12.5%. 16 mths Fr/Am oak (80/50), 50% new. **Nebbiolo Classico ★ 04** not retasted; pale, almost rosé style; delicate strawberry flavours masked by strong astringency. **Pinotage ★★★** Easy-drinking **04**, especially at 12.6% alc, pleasantly idiosyncratic with minty scents to fleshy red fruit. 16 mths Fr wood. **Shiraz ★★★** Rustic **04** needs yr/2 for obvious tannins to knit with dark berried fruit. Oak ± as for cab, slightly more powerful at 13.5% alc. **Boulder Red ★★★** Not retasted; everyday **NV** blend cab, shiraz, pinotage (48/20/32), salty dried fruit notes, manageably big dusty tannins. **Dry Muscat ★** Wolseley fruit, vinified traditional Italian way (fermented on skins 1st 2 days, as for next wine). **05** soft, for early enjoyment, not retasted. **Semi-Sweet Muscat ★★★ 05** pretty & gently sweet; honeysuckle & spice tones, lightish 11.5% alc; sip soon. This WO Coastal, others WO Tulbagh unless noted. — *IvH*

■ *Big Six see* Old Bridge Wines

Bilton Wines

Stellenbosch ▪ *1stB 1998* ▪ *Tasting & sales Mon-Fri 9.30-5 Sat 9.30-1* ▪ *Fee R20* ▪ *Refreshments & summer picnics; wine & choc tastings by appt (R30)* ▪ *Function venue* ▪ *Owner Mark Bilton* ▪ *Winemaker Rudi de Wet (Nov 2005), advised by Giorgio Dalla Cia* ▪ *Viticulturist Ruan du Plessis (Dec 2004)* ▪ *89 ha (cab, merlot, mourvèdre, petit v, pinotage, shiraz, chenin, sauvignon, semillon)* ▪ *100 tons own label 80% red 20% white* ▪ *PO Box 60 Lynedoch 7603* ▪ *info@biltonwines.com* ▪ *www.biltonwines.co.za* ▪ **T** *021·881·3714* ▪ F *021·881·3721*

While Bilton may have outgrown its previously *'garagiste*-like' approach to winemaking, as owner Mark Bilton puts it, bigger quantities have not come at the expense of quality. The property's first-ever Pinotage was champion at the 2006 National Young Wine Show — not bad for what Rudi de Wet and consultant Giorgio Dalla Cia describe as an 'experiment'. While the recently upgraded cellar will enable them to continue specialising in reds, they have also launched their very first white.

★★★★☆ **Matt Black** Named jointly after wine loving 17th-century pirate & combo Bilton family names. Shiraz, merlot, petit v blend (53/31/16) bearing fingerprint of vini guru Giorgio Dalla Cia. Impressive debut: **04** suitably inky hues; dark fruit, traces liquorice, game, campfire; misleadingly accessible palate — supple, juicy, vibrates with health, but 18 mths Fr/Am oaking confirms seriousness & ageing potential. Like next red, new.

★★★★ **Sir Percy** Statement bdx blend honours owner's grandfather, knighted for charitable work. Another Giorgio hand in **04** whose classic 60/30/10 proportions (cab, merlot, petit v) have New World concentration: cassis, mature beef, savoury oak. Tight structure, built to last gd few yrs. 18 mths combo new/used oak, mainly Fr.

★★★★ **Cabernet Sauvignon** Built on sleekly powerful lines, **04**'s rich cassis, plum fruit reined in by fine, beautifully judged tannins: a class act. 18 mths 300ℓ barrels, mainly Fr. **03**; with 10% petit v, *Wine* ★★★★. This, below, from registered single vyd.

★★★★ **Merlot** Succulent & sophisticated. **04** (★★★★☆) lesson in grape's local potential: deeply fruit-rich, raspberries, fresh prunes, layered with dried herbs & smoke; beguiling complexity. Deft oaking provides backbone for 4+ yrs ageing. Oak as for Cab. **03**, with 10% cab, similarly multi-layered, firm but harmonious tannins.

★★★★ **Shiraz** Modern, showy, voluptuous, lashings creamy vanilla-oak. Intensity continues into **04**'s fruit, raspberries, cherries, with prosciutto hovering in background. Svelte structure, harmonious tannins mean it's accessible already, but min. 4 yrs ahead. Oak as for Cab.

Following not ready for review, both new, both **06**: **Pinotage** SA champ for variety at 2006 SAYWS; **Sauvignon Blanc**. — *CR*

■ *Birdfield* see Klawer

Blaauwklippen Agricultural Estate

Stellenbosch • Est 1690 • 1stB 1974 • Tasting & sales Mon-Sat 9-5 Sun 9-4 • Fee: R25 formal tasting (incl tour); R25 informal (incl tasting glass); R35 informal (incl red wine glass) • Closed Jan 1 • Tours by appt 10-3 • Restaurant & many other amenities (see intro) • Owners Mr & Mrs Stephan Schörghuber • Winemaker Rolf Zeitvogel, with Piet Geldenhuys (Oct/Dec 2003) • Viticulturist Kowie Kotzé (1987) • 80 ha (cabs s/f, malbec, merlot, mourvèdre, petit v, pinot, shiraz, zin, viognier) • 440 tons 25 000 cs own label • 90% red 10% white • HACCP certification in progress • PO Box 54 Stellenbosch 7599 • mail@blaauwklippen.com • www.blaauwklippen. com • T 021·880·0133 • F 021·880·0136

Another attraction for visitors to this farm in the Arabella Stable — a centre dedicated to the whole wine experience, which includes a history of the SA industry, a soil display and a fragrant herb garden exemplifying herbal nuances in wine. In the vineyards, Kowie Kotzé (now in his 20th Blaauwklippen year) has instituted closer planting, his goal being more concentrated fruit flavours, and the sowing of permanent groundcover. The cellar's not standing still either — the use of natural yeasts was introduced last year.

Blaauwklippen Vineyard Selection (BVS)

★★★★ Cabernet Sauvignon Elegant, understated food wine from home vyds. **03** alluring black berry, plum & mint notes; tangy acidity; tannins taut & leafy but in harmony with fruit; shd improve over few yrs. Modest ±13% alc in keeping with Old World styling. 2 yrs new Fr oak.

Cabriolet Stylish cab-led bdx blend, ± 18 mths oak, 50% new. Concentrated **03** (★★★★) loses cab f of last tasted **01** (★★★☆), gains petit verdot — & extra star qualities: plush berry/spicy scents; poised, fleshy flavorous with long, pleasantly gripping tannins. **Merlot** ★★★☆ Fine fruit quality in SAYWS 2004 class-winning **04** prompts re-entry to flagship range. Ripe but still brooding, loads of black plum flavour, slightly savoury tannin, not unattractive bitter flick to tail. **Shiraz** ★★★☆ Another re-entry to top range; **05** packs a tannic punch, but has fruit density to absorb it; notes of toasted almond & hazelnut add complexity. This, Merlot above, 14 mths Fr oak. Satisfying drinking over next ±5 yrs. **Zinfandel** ★★★☆ Rare-in-Cape variety vinified for open-textured conviviality: **04** has bright, effusive cranberry & tomato flavours, savoury tannins, light feel despite beefy ±14.5% alc.

Blaauwklippen range

Barouche Cape Blend ★★★ Has origins in 2000 B'klippen Blending Competition. No **04** made; pinotage-led **03** with cab, shiraz, cinsaut tasted mid-2005 was ripe with juicy tannins, clean dry finish. 14 mths Fr oak. **Cabernet Sauvignon** ★★★ **04** not ready for tasting. **03** when last tasted neatly combined fruit-rich nose with dry mineral palate. 66% in Fr oak. **Merlot** ★★★★ **04**, previewed last ed, now appeals with aromas of vanilla ice-cream & plum sauce, spicy lead pencil whiffs from Fr oak, fine drying tannins. **Shiraz 03** (★★★★) well-fused but tight tannins, brisk red-plum fruit & farmyard notes, & gently astringent tealeaf finish. **04** mid-2005 showed ★★★★ potential. Neither revisited. **Red Landau** ★★★ A seven-variety 'A to Z' (incl zin) wine aged in large, older oak. **03** dusty & savoury food friend with grainy tannins. To drink early. **Rosé Landau** ★ Shiraz loses cab f partner in **06**, shows strawberries & cream flavours, sweet-sour mouthfeel & quite active 12.6% alc. WO Coastal. **Sauvignon Blanc** ★★★ Moves down from hero range above in **06**, but still a pleasing expression of the variety: tropical fruit, freshly cut grass, figgy flavours, mineral finish. **White Landau** ★★ Blend changes to 70% chenin (ex-Post House farm) & viognier in **05**. More vinous than variety-specific or 'fruity', satisfying weight if a tad short. **Semi-Sweet Landau** ★★ Pvsly from ottonel, gewürz; **05** is all muscat d'A. Rosewater & raisin whiffs, sweet musky flavours; not as vibrant or flavoursome as pvs. — *CvZ*

Black Oystercatcher

Elim (see Southern Cape map) ▪ *Est 1998* ▪ *1stB 2003* ▪ *Tasting by appt* ▪ *Owner/winemaker/viticulturist Dirk Human* ▪ *14.5 ha (cab, merlot, shiraz, sauvignon, semillon)* ▪ *±90 tons 48% red 52% white* ▪ *PO Box 199 Bredasdorp 7280* ▪ *dirk@blackoystercatcher.co.za* ▪ **T** *082·779·5439*

Dirk Human, who has set his sights on the eco-sensitive development of picturesque Elim, is paving the way for the local community and 15 surrounding farmers to join forces. The area has taken off, he says, and 'we're developing a reputation for producing sauvignons which have a distinct regional style'. Having sold off 2km of pristine coastline to plant his vineyards, this fifth-generation Moddervlei farmer still delights in the 1 000ha of woodlands stretching towards Struisbaai: 'It's pure magic and we need to protect it.'

★★★★★ **Semillon** Debut **05** expresses Elim provenance through taut, brisk minerality, grapefruit pith tanginess. Dusty, dry fynbos/lanolin flavours pierced by whiff capsicum (from 15% sauvignon). Barrel fermentation/ageing impart sense of completeness, hint vanilla/butter. 8 mths 4th fill Fr oak. Structure to age/improve good few yrs.

★★★★ **Sauvignon Blanc** Poised & delicate, but brimming with confidence, water-white **06** quintessential cool-climate aromas — cat's pee, hay, cut grass; equally complex flavours with appley fruit & acidity, persistent 'wet stone' aftertaste.

★★★★ **Blanc Fumé** new Food-friendly **05** from sauvignon, greater richness than Semillon above despite same oak regime. Wafts Cape gooseberry, lemonblossom, complementary buttery touch; midweight, with cleansing acidity & pleasant bitter lift at end. Will benefit from few yrs bottle-age.

Cabernet Sauvignon-Merlot new **05** preview of 62/38 blend; supple, vibrant cassis, plum, cardamom nose & gentle oak (Fr, 15 mths). Unknit mid-2006, needs short time to meld, as does of… **Shiraz** ★★★★ More smoke/white pepper than fruit on **05** barrel sample; tannins, overt oak (Fr, 15 mths, 25% new), add grip to palate. Red berry/plum ripeness on finish hints at quality waiting to be revealed. — *CvZ*

Black Pearl Wines

Paarl ▪ *Est 1998* ▪ *1stB 2001* ▪ *Tasting, sales & tours just about anytime but please phone ahead (note: no credit cards)* ▪ *Closed Dec 25* ▪ *Walks* ▪ *Conservation area* ▪ *Owner Lance Nash* ▪ *Winemaker/viticulturist Mary-Lou Nash* ▪ *8 ha (cab, shiraz)* ▪ *±1 800 cs 100% red* ▪ *PO Box 609 Suider-Paarl 7624* ▪ *info@blackpearlwines.com* ▪ *www.blackpearlwines.com* ▪ **T** *021·863·2900 / 083·395·6999 / 083·297·9796*

The self-taught Nash family has gone from micro-production to first class (SAA) and Wine of the Month Reserve Club within only a couple of years. The future? A marketing trip to the States in ski season ('They're lapping up our wine'), more photo shoots of the Nash toddlers for Pampers ('To support my winemaking habit,' quips winemaker, viticulturist, tractor driver and mother Mary-Lou N) and developing their new export markets, Ireland and Poland.

★★★★ **Shiraz** Restrained red-fruit aromas don't prepare you for an explosion of dark fruit & spicy black pepper on **04**. Big (14.5% alc) & powerful, its 60% new oak (15% Am) fused into dense core of liquorice tinged fruit. Long, juicy farewell with wafts of smoky veld fire. Quite an experience! Incl dash cab.

★★★★ **Shiraz-Cabernet Sauvignon** Listed as 'Cab-Shiraz' pvs ed when in fact shiraz (55%) dominates the blend. Last we enjoyed Aussie-styled **03**'s intensely ripe berry flavours, with spice/leather tones & ingratiating smoothness. 13 mths oak.

Cabernet Sauvignon ★★★★ Concentrated, robust **04**, ripe cassis & some leafier notes, sweet tobacco all repeat on bold, showy palate with liquorice hint. Firm tannins smoothed by 14% alc make for a compatible hearty food partner. 300ℓ barrels, yr; like… **Oro** ★★★★ New World styled, generously fruited shiraz/cab (60/40), **04** abounds with spicy, brambly fruit. Full (14.5% alc), smoothly textured with fine ripe tannins; delicious now with structure to improve in bottle. — *MW*

▪ **Black Rock** see The Winery of Good Hope

BlankBottle ♀ new

Somerset West ▪ Est 2005 ▪ Tasting by appt ▪ Owner/winemaker Pieter Walser ▪ 2 890 cs 90% red 10% white ▪ Postnet Suite 160, Pvt Bag X15, Somerset West 7129 ▪ thebestwines@ blankbottle.co.za ▪ www.blankbottle.co.za ▪ T 082·872·8658 ▪ F 0865·030·974

An interesting new concept from winemaker Pieter Walser: eschewing sampling and traditional distribution outlets, he sells only by phone and the Internet, and every sale comes with a 100% money-back guarantee. So, assuming you don't like the first bottle, simply replace the cork and he'll have the case collected. Walser, who says his focus is on producing small batches of affordable premium quality wine, promises delivery within five working days.

Merlot ★★★ Appealing **05** offers cool-grown berry fruit touched with white pepper; accessible & restrained; freshening acidity makes this an ideal summer red. W Bay WO. **Syrah** ★★★★ With more than a nod to the Rhône: **05** creamy, textured mouthfeel from perfectly ripe fruit, but major tone is savoury & dark, hints liquorice & tar; lovely juicy drinkability. W Bay fruit. **Isa 42** ★★★ Merlot under a different name, ex-Smnsberg. **03** minty style with berry grounding, some pepper; dry tannic finish which cld handle rich sauces. **Abrina** ★★★★ ✓ Attractive fruit expression of berries & cherries on **NV** blend merlot, cabs s & f, malbec; some complexity via violets & choc notes; a stylish early drinker with lots of freshness, vibrancy. W Bay/Sbosch vyds. Striking minimalist packaging a feature throughout. — *CR*

Bloemendal Estate 🍷🥂♟♿

Durbanville ▪ Est 1902 ▪ 1stB 1987 ▪ Tasting & sales Mon-Fri 9-5 Sat 9-4 Sun 11-3 ▪ Fee R15 pp for groups ▪ Closed Dec 25 ▪ Deli/oyster bar, weddings, evening functions & full conference facilities etc (see also intro) ▪ Owner Bloemendal Trust ▪ Winemaker Jackie Coetzee ▪ Viti consultant Johan Pienaar ▪ 140 ha (cab, merlot, shiraz, sauvignon) ▪ 5 000 cs own label 73% red 25% white 2% rosé ▪ PO Box 466 Durbanville 7551 ▪ bloemendal@isoft.co.za ▪ T/F 021·976·2682

The 05 Sauvignon took the inaugural Terroir Wine Award for the variety, a feather in winemaker Jackie Coetzee's cap and confirmation of the estate's reputation as prime terrain for the fashionable variety. Tweaking of attractions at the winery, deli and oyster bar continue — ceramic and art exhibitions, as well as weekend craft stalls have been added to the programme, and breakfasts, lunches and cheese platters to the eating options. As do efforts to drive off visiting kingfishers: 'They're destroying my koi,' laments Jackie C.

★★★★ **Cabernet Sauvignon** Showcases house's signature drinkabilty with stylish aplomb. **01** (★★★★) dark cassis, velvet texture & soft supple tannins. **00** rich cordial-like concentration, deep-pile texture. Traditional open *kuip* fermentation, as are all reds, Yr Fr oak. Note: no new wines tasted this ed.

★★★★ **Shiraz** Smoked beef, veldfire aromas/flavours on **03** (★★★★), savoury & very dry, verging on austere — less rich than burly **02**, whose tannins were approachable on release, dry tang on finish. Yr Am oak.

★★★★ **Sauvignon Blanc Suider Terras** Named for mature s-facing vyd, 30 yr old bushvines benefiting from bracing sea breezes. Riveting **05** distinctive dusty capsicum, green fig, nettles, translate easily onto assertive but elegantly built palate; rapier acidity, some softer ripeness on finish.

★★★★ **Semillon 05** (sample, potentially ★★★) very quiet, lacking flamboyance of Sauvignon above; modestly rounded profile, helped by brush oak — third Fr oak fermented. Friendly (but big: 14.6% alc) **04** also tasted as sample.

Merlot ★★★★ Properly dry & savoury **02** has charming cassis flavours, gd oak (yr Fr) helping gentle firmness on dry finish. Ready to drink. **Blosend Rooi** ★★ (Translates as 'Blushing Red'.) Barrel fermented dry rosé, **04** blending shiraz (70%), merlot; more a light red than rosé, barrel ferment giving more weight, less fresh fruitiness. **Brut** ★★ Light textured & focused cap classique; attractive citrus tones, busy bubbles, shd have settled, gained weight by now. **NV** from chard, 9 mths lees before disgorging. **Natural Sweet** In abeyance. — *IvH*

■ *Blouberg* see Graça

Blouvlei Wines

Wellington • Est/1stB 2003 • Visits Mon-Fri 8-5 Sat by appt • Fee R7/tasting • Closed pub hols • Meals by appt • Guesthouse • Owner BEE company • Winemaker Pieter-Niel Rossouw, with Jerome van Wyk • 8 000 cs 100% red • PO Box 817 Wellington 7654 • blouvlei@cknet.co.za • T 021·873·7745 • F 021·864·2737

Owned by a workers' trust established by Mont Du Toit Kelder, Blouvlei also produces wine to order — supply your label design and specs and, voila! The results may surpass your fondest expectations: last year, a Cape-based businessman requested 'a light, dry rosé'; the results were so good that the wine is now to join the Blouvlei line-up, says director Abelia Lawrence.

Klassique ★★★★ Senior bdx-style **03** blend (60/40 cab/merlot), gd ripe red fruit, serious-minded structural support in satisfying balance; savoury dry finish. ±17 mths barrelled. Mainly Wllngtn fruit. Like next, not retasted. **Red ★★★** Ripe, warmly inviting aromas on **03** announced a great value blend cabs s & f, merlot; firm palate with fresh acidity, dry tannic grip. Unobtrusive yr in oak. **White ★★ 05** from sauvignon, satisfyingly bone-dry, & moderate 13% alc, but seems to be tiring mid-2006 — less varietal punch than pvs. These WO Coastal. — *IvH*

Blueberry Hill

Franschhoek • Est/1stB 1998 • Visits by appt • 2 self-catering cottages • Owners Blueberry Hill Trust (Brian & Lindy Heyman) • Vini/viti advisers Nigel McNaught & Paul Wallace (1998/2000) • 0.6 ha • 350-400 cs 100% red • PO Box 580 Franschhoek 7690 • bhwine@iafrica.com • www.blueberryhillcottages.co.za • T 021·876·3362 • F 021·876·2114

This small wine farm beneath the Middagkrans peak in Franschhoek also offers four-star self-catering cottages overlooking the tiny vineyard, with fantastic mountain views (best enjoyed from the rim-flow pool in summer). Co-owner Brian Heyman pronounces himself happy with progress on the quality of his Merlot and confesses to having no new plans right now — a comfortable position indeed.

Merlot ★★★☆ Engaging aromas introduce muscular, solidly knit **04**, with big 14.5% alc, dry tannin & wood (70% new Fr oak) dominating ripe fruit in youth. Serious but tough. — *TJ*

Blue Cove Wines

Robertson • Est/1stB 2006 • Tasting by appt • Owner Blue Cove Brands Ltd (UK) • Winemaker/ viticulturist Stephen de Wet (Jan 2006) • 176 ha owned plus grower partnerships (cab, merlot, shiraz, chenin, nouvelle, sauvignon, viognier) • 1 250 tons 72 000 cs 42% red 6% rosé 52% white • HACCP accreditation in progress • PO Box 155 Ashton 6715 • info@ bluecovewines.co.uk • www.bluecovewines.com • T 082·492·3213 • F 021·671·9031

Shareholders Murray Giggins, Michael Bampfield-Duggan and winemaker/viticulturist Stephen de Wet are up and running with this large-volume premium label. Partnered with top UK marketers, they launched an impressive 72 000 cases in maiden vintage 2006. The brand boasts a spanking new R30m winery — with its own bottling and labelling lines — situated among vineyards on a farm known as Arabella, previously half of Excelsior Estate. While an enthused Giggins says the wines are largely destined offshore, they can also be found on SA shelves.

Trio of reds (**Cabernet Sauvignon**, **Merlot** & **Shiraz**) and a **Rosé** unready for tasting. **Chenin Blanc ★★★★ 06** satisfying mouthful; ripe & fleshy with Golden Delicious apple revved up by tangy acidity. **Sauvignon Blanc ★★★** For drinking rather than contemplating; **06** figs & fruit salad trademark of a riper style, refreshing lemony flick to tail. **Viognier ★★★** Highly aromatic & perfumed **06** has notes of jasmine & muscat, sufficient acidity to partner rich, spicy foods. — *CR*

Blue Crane Vineyards

Tulbagh • Est 2001 • 1stB 2004 • Visitors welcome but phone ahead • Owners Henk & Anita Jordaan • Winemaker/viticulturist Henk Jordaan, advised by viticulturist Andrew Teubes & suppliers • 6 ha (cab, merlot, shiraz, sauvignon) • 2 000 cs 75% red 25% white • PO Box 306

Tulbagh 6820 · *info@bluecrane.co.za* · *www.bluecrane.co.za* · **T 023·230·0823/ 083·266·0156** · *F 023·230·0825*

Having noted in last year's guide they were delaying the release of their flagship bottlings pending the wines' development, Henk and Anita Jordaan now have sufficient confidence to present their debut Blue Crane Cab and Full Flight (a blend of cab, merlot and shiraz) — neither, unfortunately, ready for review at press time. Vintage 2006, their third, was marked by further boosts: accolades for their Jagger's Peak wines, the name a nod to the outcrop towering over their tiny Tulbagh cellar, where hands-on Jordaan can do what larger operations may find 'impossible or unaffordable'.

Jagger's Peak range

Cabernet Sauvignon ★★★★ Too late for deadline last ed, choc-minty **04** full & ripe but well formed, partly thanks to 50% new oak (yr, Fr) which stiffens, gives structure for few yrs ageing. **05** unready. **Merlot** ★★★ For those who like their merlots big & generous. **05** ultra-ripe cassis & plums given tasty drinkability by refreshing acidity. Subtly wooded (yr, Fr, none new). 15% alc. **Shiraz** ★★★ A real extrovert, **05** has loads of fleshy berry/plum fruit gently supported by oak (yr, combo Fr/Am, 30% new). Soft, easy to drink. **Chenin Blanc** ★★★ Swiss gold winner **05** last ed was complex & distinctive, with hints resin & fynbos, food-friendly savoury flavours. No **06**. **Sauvignon Blanc** ★★★★ **06** fresh, lively & eminently drinkable; achieves attractive balance between gooseberry/pear ripeness & nervy acidity. — *CR*

Blue Creek Wines   ◊♀

Stellenbosch · *Est 1995* · *1stB 1996* · *Visits by appt* · *Owner/winemaker Piet Smal* · *Viti consultant Johan Smith (1996)* · *7.5 ha (cab, merlot, pinotage)* · *1 000 cs own label 100% red* · *26 Piet Retief Str Stellenbosch 7600* · *blue_creek@email.com* · **T 021·887·6938 / 021·880·0522 / 082·928·5157** · *F 021·886·5462*

Dentist by day, winemaker after hours, Piet Smal was particularly pleased with his cab's reception in the past year. Good write-ups perhaps came second to selection for the vinous Tri-Nations taste-off, pitting wines from SA, Australia and New Zealand against one another. Small quantities, well priced, beg to be snapped up after a visit to the new tasting room in the Blaauwklippen Valley.

★★★★ **Cabernet Sauvignon** From own vyds in Sbosch's reputed 'Golden Triangle'. **04** (★★★★★) last yr ed was sumptuously scented & flavoured; opulence checked by strong acid backbone & tannins. 14 mths Fr oak; 13.5% alc. Worth cellaring several yrs. **02** also classy; enticing & chewy yet pliable fruit. *Wine* ★★★★. — *CvZ*

■ *Blue Grove Hill* see Capaia
■ *Blue White* see Old Vines

Blyde Wines   ◊♀

Paarl · *Est/1stB 2000* · *Tasting & sales at I Love Wine (see entry)* · *Tours by appt* · *Owner/ winemaker Lieb Loots* · *400 cs 90% red 10% white* · *PO Box 3231 Paarl 7620* · *lajanc@ iafrica.com* · *www.blyde.com* · **T 083·270·5706** · *F 021·871·1619*

Lieb Loots was one of the first *garagistes* to start handcrafting wines in Paarl's Main Street Winery — according to this northern-Cape maize and wheat farmer, it's the only New Year's resolution he has ever kept. That said, Loots didn't make any wines in 2006, opting instead to focus his energy on training for the new Cape Epic cycle tour (he and his partner placed third in the Masters category). But with wine stocks now depleting, Loots assures us it's back to business in 2007.

Bona Dea ★★★★ Classy blend rings the changes in **03**: shiraz takes the lead (46%), relegates cab to support role with merlot; Fr oak (18 mths) now all-new, effortlessly absorbed by layered spicy fruit. Structure for the long haul. Not retasted, as for… **Jacobus Petrus Shiraz** ★★★ **03** heavy on the toast, smoke, thatch character, somewhat lighter on fruit. — *CT*

■ *Blydskap* see Baarsma

Bodraai Private Cellar

*Stellenbosch · Est 1999 · 1stB 2001 · Closed to public · Gabriël Kriel & Theo Beukes · Vini consultant PG Slabbert (2001) · Viticulturist Gabriël Kriel · 4 ha (cab, shiraz) · 1 000 cs 100% red · PO Box 321 Stellenbosch 7599 · minpro@adept.co.za · **T 083·601·9030** · F 021·881·3211*

Two Stellenbosch Hills neighbours, friends and winelovers — Gabriël Kriel and Theo Beukes — were rather pleased to have their two bottlings recognised at the Swiss Wine Awards (both exported to the UK, Canada and Benelux countries). But the aim remains drinking pleasure, just as the focus remains reds, the output small, the mantra 'wine and friends improve with age'.

Cabernet Sauvignon ★★★☆ Forthcoming varietal flavours, cedary hints on mature, ready **01**. Decent, appealing wine, well balanced with gentle but firm tannins. Yr Fr oak in unobtrusive support. Not revisited, nor next wine. **Cabernet Sauvignon-Shiraz** ★★★☆ **02** blend (85/15) has inviting herby/spicy character. A little longer oaking, more power, than above, but as unpretentious & rewarding. — *TJ*

Boekenhoutskloof

*Franschhoek · Tasting & sales Mon-Fri 9-5 · Sales Mon-Fri 9-5 · Owner Boekenhoutskloof Investments (Pty) Ltd · Winemakers Marc Kent & Rudiger Gretschel, with Heinrich Tait & Heinrich Hugo · Viticulturist Pieter Siebrits · PO Box 433 Franschhoek 7690 · boeken@mweb.co.za · www.boekenhoutskloof.co.za · **T 021·876·3320** · F 021·876·3793*

Good news for aficionados: after a revamp of the tasting area, the Franschhoek farm is now open to the public at set hours (previously only by appointment). Porcupine Ridge continues to grow locally, and The Chocolate Block 'has been awesome', says winemaker/marketer Marc Kent of his newer Mediterranean-style blend's sales. He and Rudiger Gretschel have been working on 'some other interesting blends' for the past three years, and are helping to develop a French system which Marc K dubs 'the latest in multi-stage berry selection' (see also Photo Gallery). It removes the fine stalks which may remain after the grapes have passed through the de-stemmer and the vibrating table. Among the first to introduce the triage table to SA, back in 1997, they see this as 'the next step in ensuring only perfect fruit comes into the cellar'.

★★★★☆ **Cabernet Sauvignon** Classic in style & ageworthiness. Superb **04** (★★★★★) echoes with claret-like minerality; fresh, intense fruit, fragrance & spice from complementary new Fr oak (27 mths). Sophisticated focus, tension; only in youth are brooding tannins curtailing sweet-fruited richness. Single hillside Fhoek vyd. Unfiltered. **03** *Wine* ★★★★; 90 pts *WS*.

★★★★★ **Syrah** Admired for remarkable consistency, traditional styling. Splendid **04** tighter knit, more focused than ever, both sensuous & sophisticated. Gorgeous spicy red-fruit intensity, delicious savoury concentration will reward 8-10 yrs cellaring. **03** (★★★★☆) full of measured oomph, finishes with ripe flourish. Single old Wllngtn vyd, producing ±600 sought-after cs. Native yeast ferment, 27 mths used Fr oak. Consistent 90+ pts *WS*.

★★★★☆ **CWG Auction Reserve Syrah** Only **03** tasted to date. Selection best 2 barrels of above wine, one new. Plush, polished, friendly & delicious.

★★★★☆ **Semillon** Refined, with charm & personality. **04** now settled, with some complexity, but still gd 3-4 yrs off peak. Subtle though richly vinous; fresh, savoury acid thread keeping full sumptuousness at bay; bone-dry, clean, very long. Fhoek vyds, some 100+ yrs old; fermented/aged new oak.

★★★★★ **Noble Late Harvest** Just **02** (from semillon) so far, but queue of botrytis desserts in cask.

★★★★★ **The Chocolate Block** Aptly named, given hedonistic (but serious) **05**'s spiced dark choc notes amongst much more. Intense, warm & sensuous, but fresh, with light touch to fully express its make up of syrah, grenache, cinsaut, cab & viognier (44/24/14/14/4). Already irresistible but better still in 5-6 yrs. 15 mths 600ℓ Fr oak, 40% new. WO W Cape.

> **The Wolftrap** ☺ ★★★ Unpretentious yet satisfying all-sorts red blend with rhônish leanings. **05** hearty, spicy chutney nose; juicy flavours; brisk, clean finish. Fr oaked to smooth any edges. Screwcapped. WO W Cape.

Wolftrap Rosé ★★★ Last tasted was shiraz-based **04**. No **05**.

Porcupine Ridge range

★★★★ **Syrah** ✓ Offers outstanding value & consistency; **05** at riper end of spectrum, but maintains balance despite big, chewy concentration. Spicy, rich & warmingly long. Best enjoyed soonish; some have few yrs in them. Mbury, Wllngtn vyds. Third unoaked.

Cabernet Sauvignon ★★★☆ **05** generous aromas of fresh black berries & currants; sweet & juicy with friendly but significant tannins, & clean, mineral finish. Incl important 8% petit v; 5% malbec. Fr oak; mainly Mbury fruit. **Merlot** ★★★☆ **05**, with dollop cab, perky, trim & fresh. Cool, mint-bordered red plum fragrance; juicy ripeness contained by neat dry tannins. 9 mths oak. **Sauvignon Blanc** ★★★ **06** clear varietal notes but not showy or aggressive; medium body, refreshing, juicy acids provide perfect lunchtime style. WO W Cape. — AL

■ *Boland Cellar* see Boland Kelder

Boland Kelder

Paarl · Est 1947 · 1stB 1948 · Tasting & sales Mon-Fri 8-5 Sat 9-2 · Closed Easter Fri/Sun, Dec 25/26 & Jan 1 · Tours by appt · Underground cellar for functions & gatherings (max 45 people) · Events programme during Dec/Jan; phone for details · Tour groups · Owners 96 producing shareholders · Cellarmaster Altus le Roux (Sep 1984) · Winemakers Naudé Bruwer & Bernard Smuts (Dec 1996/Nov 1999), with JG Auret & Chris Crawford (Dec 2002/July 2005) · Viticulturist Jurie Germishuys (Jul 1998) · 2 400 ha (cab, merlot, pinotage, shiraz, chard, chenin, sauvignon) · ±21 500 tons 56% red 44% white · Export brands: Boland Cellar, Lindenhof & Montestell · PO Box 7007 Northern Paarl 7623 · info@bolandkelder.co.za · www. bolandkelder.co.za · **T 021·862·6190** · F 021·862·5379

Boland has had much to boast about, garnering numerous accolades including being named best overseas producer at Germany's Mundus Vini, one of SA's top 20 export companies, and one of the world's top 100 wine producers by the World Association of Wine & Spirits Writers. On the ownership front, an empowerment deal through a subsidiary company saw a group of black women and a farmworkers' trust become stakeholders. Further BEE plans are underway.

No 1 Reserve range

★★★★ **Cabernet Sauvignon** Sleek & well groomed showstopper; latest **03** more overtly fruity than pvs, in line with vintage. Cinnamon whiff to opulent spicy berries; evident but classy wooding (60/40 Am/Fr, all new, 2 yrs). Modern, already harmonious, deserves keeping few yrs. Native yeast ferment. Strings of awards, incl VDG, Swiss gold, Wine ★★★★.

★★★★ **Shiraz** Powerful, flamboyant wine, new Am oak part of its personality; **03** carbon copy of **02**, which lauded by Concours Mondial, Paarl Shiraz Challenge, Swiss judges. Chockablock with beef, coconut milk & vanilla, savoury-sour red fruit flavours; protracted tannic finish. At 15+% alc, these not for the faint-hearted. Natural ferments, 20-22 mths wood.

Follow-ups to following unready: **Chardonnay** ★★★★ Delicate but serious **04**; lemon zest, mandarin & cream hints, concentrated citrus flavours gain weight, complexity, from partial barrel ferment, ±16 mths on lees, all new Fr oak. **Sauvignon Blanc** ★★★ **05** shows heavy hand with wood, though zingy acidity does provides freshness to floral/tropical flesh. Barrique fermented/aged, all new Fr, no malo.

Winemakers Selection   new

Native yeast ferments, serious oaking (malo/ageing in barrel), features of these; both need/deserve further bottle-maturation to show their best. **Merlot** ★★★ **04** mid-2006 shrouded in oak (2nd fill Fr, yr), very firm tannins, but shows an impressive ripe fruit core waiting to emerge. **Pinotage** ★★★ 100% new Am oak for **04**, showy, still overtly woody but ripe-fruited, characterful, promising; attractive savoury undertone to well expressed varietal fruit. Concours Mondial gold.

Boland range

★★★★ **White Muscadel** Elegant version always flies out of the cellar. **04** last ed noted as offering myriad nut, citrus aromas/flavours. Modest alc for style (15%), sweet but not sugary thanks to freshening acidity.

Cabernet Sauvignon ★★★ Ready-on-release **05** abounds with sweet, ripe cassis fruit, juicy tannins, attractive freshness. Legs for few yrs. 12 mths Am/Fr oak. **Merlot** ★★★ **05** somewhat darker toned than pvs; black choc/fruit flavours, leafy touch, fresh acidity, pleasant dusty/dry farewell. 8 mths Fr oak. **Pinotage** ★★ Strangely ungenerous **05**, starts sweetly but soon weighs in with big, dry tannins, quinine twist to tail. Third aged in small oak, 3rd fill, 10 mths. **Shiraz** ★★★ Early drinking **05** brimful with dark berried fruit; notes of leather & savoury meat; attractive dry, friendly tannins. Yr Am/Fr oak. **Cabernet Sauvignon-Shiraz** ★★★ Misses complexity of pvs, but **05** compensates with ripe, juicy drinkability, earthy/leathery aromatics, supple balanced tannins; unwooded. **Chardonnay** ★★ Amiable **06** a clone of pvs: light textured, peachy, smoothly accessible, though last yr's oak (fermentation, brief ageing) all but invisible; undaunting 13.5% alc. **Chenin Blanc** ★★ **06** firm-fleshed & tart, hint of tropical fruit, no rounding sugar this yr. Light 12.5% alc. **Nouvelle** ★★★ First varietal bottling of this semillon-crouchen (Cape riesling) cross. Easy, aromatic **06** similar exotic fruits & khaki bush tones to pvs, quite weighty, full, despite only 13.5% alc. **Sauvignon Blanc** ★★★ **06** tad more straightforward but appealingly bright, fresh; tropical tones laced with grapefruit. Comfortable 12.7% alc. Newer versions of following pair unready: **Red Muscadel** ★★★ **04** dessert wine for sweeter toothed. Crystallised fruit tone, dusty/earthy nuance & stalky finish. **Port** ★★★ **03** from shiraz; not overly sweet or alcoholic; prune fruit with dry tannic grip. 14 mths 2nd fill casks. **Riesling** discontinued.

Bon Vino range

In 500ml bottles; 2ℓ & 5ℓ packs. All **NV**, bargain priced. New versions unready, notes from pvs ed: **Dry Red** ★★★ Perfect for drinking round the braai. Unwooded fruit full of fun, cab tannins lend structure. 14% alc all but guarantees jollity. **Dry White** ★★ Designed for carefree drinking (incl moderate alc), enticing floral nose & crisp finish. Mainly chenin, with colombard. **Semi-Sweet** ★★ Will appeal widely. Mainly chenin; charming floral, grapey character & soft sweetness abets easy drinking. Low 11.5% alc. — *DH*

Bon Cap Organic Winery ◯⑧❀◻🍴⛏🚶

*Robertson ▪ Est 2001 ▪ 1stB 2002 ▪ Tasting & sales Mon-Fri 8-5 at winery; Sat, Sun & pub hols 10-4 at Bon Rouge Bistro ▪ Fee R15 for groups of 10+ ▪ Tours only by appt ▪ Bistro/function/ conference centre serving meals Mon-Sun 8-5; evenings by appt ▪ Guest house (self-catering & B&B by appt), weddings & conferences T 023·626·2073 ▪ Farm produce ▪ Facilities for children ▪ Tour groups ▪ Walks ▪ Owners Roelf & Michelle du Preez/SHZ Winecellar (Pty) Ltd ▪ Winemakers Roelf du Preez & Jacques Conradie (2002/2004) ▪ Viticulturist Roelf du Preez ▪ 45 ha (cab, pinotage, shiraz) ▪ 500 tons 21 000 cs + 1 200 cs for clients, incl Woolworths ▪ 80% red 10% white 10% grape juice ▪ PO Box 356 Robertson 6705 ▪ info@boncap.co.za ▪ www. boncaporganic.co.za ▪ **T 023·626·1628** ▪ F 023·626·1895*

Though opposed to selling wines solely on their organic credentials, Bon Cap's continuing commitment to organic wine production paid off with the best award — an empty cellar. No shortage of medals either, with golds from Michelangelo and German Biofach — their first-ever entry in an exclusively organic competition. The Du Preez family realise their wines must compare on their merits but when they can do well in both categories, the 'value added' for the consumer by sustainable holistic farming methods really comes through.

Organic range

Cabernet Sauvignon 05 previewed from barrel (60:40 Fr/Am); youthful purple hue with impressive blackcurrant purity; smoked meat notes & plush texture; more fruit concentration than rest of range. Potential ★★★★. Last tasted **03** (★★★★) continued neatly tailored style. **Pinotage** ★★★ Lighter-weight **04** a change from deeply fruity yet unshowy **03**. Smoked meat savouriness, but with appealingly fresh raspberry fruit. MIWA DG/trophy. **Syrah** ★★★☆ **04** previewed last ed, now beguiling fruit aromas, bright red cherry fruit flavours, some tannic grip and sweet-sour finish. Fermented with viognier skins. Yr oak, 60/40, Fr/Am. *Wine* ★★★★. **Viognier** ★★★★ Understood to be Cape's first organic version of this Rhône variety. Limpid **06** abundant varietal aromas: spice, apricot, dried peach; balanced, unshowy, with brisk acidity carrying finish. Fermented/3 mths 50:50 Fr/Hngrian oak. **Chardonnay** new Sample **06** too unsettled to rate. Above, below, WO Eilandia unless noted.

The Ruins range

> **Rosé** ☺ ★★★ Believed to be SA's first organic rosé, from pinotage. **06** fresh raspberry flavours with attractive bitter-almond finish. **Sauvignon Blanc** ☺ ★★★ **06** stylish packaging belies the quaffer within; fresh pineapple zinginess preserved with screwcap, as are all these. From Tradouw vyds.

Still whites non-organic. **Pinotage** ★★★ Fresh cherry aromas & flavours in **05**, tough tannins & a sour-plum bite to the finish. **Syrah-Cabernet Sauvignon** ★★★ **05** 70:30 blend; youthful purple rim, oaky notes with ripe red fruit & spiciness; acid & tannin in balance with plummy fruit. **Chardonnay-Viognier** ★★★ Apricot & white peach from 12% viognier on **06**; zippy acidity & fresh, clean finish. WO W Cape. **Sparkling Vin Sec** ★★★ Claimed SA's first organic sparkling, **06** made in simple, aromatic, fruity & not-too-fizzy style with attractively low alc (12%) & sweet finish; ideal for celebrations. — *IM*

Bon Courage Estate

Robertson • Est 1927 • 1stB 1983 • Tasting & sales Mon-Fri 8-5 Sat 9-3 • Restaurant Mon-Fri 9-4. 30 Sat 9-3 • Closed Easter Fri & Dec 25 • Play area for children • Owner/viticulturist André Bruwer • Winemaker Jacques Bruwer • 150 ha • Export brand: Three Rivers • PO Box 589 Robertson 6705 • wine@boncourage.co.za • www.boncourage.co.za • T 023·626·4178 • F 023·626·3581

A strong family business, this, presided over by André Bruwer, with much-applauded vinifying son Jacques making his mark and now second son, Pieter, coming in as accountant. Daughter Maude recently opened a restaurant, Café Maude, next to the tasting rooms on the historic estate: a bigger and better eatery (replacing what was a coffee shop), with plenty of seating inside and tables on the terrace. Enormous pepper trees offer yet another tranquil spot to relax in and enjoy the breathtaking view of the Langeberg in the distance.

★★★★ **Shiraz Inkará** Seductive choc-mocha & toasty oak on **04**, richly flavoured with languid black fruits & sleeked in expensive oak (12-18 mths all new): complex as a Persian carpet. But watch 15% alc. Shd mature 3-5 yrs.

★★★★ **Chardonnay Prestige Cuvée** Barrel matured version, 8 mths on lees in new to 3rd fill Fr oak. After showy **04**, less successful in **05** (★★★★): quieter, more reticent flavours, with lime-lemon zest character & subtle oak interplay.

★★★★★ **Cap Classique Jacques Bruère Brut Reserve Blanc de Blancs** Impressive debut with **00** chardonnay MCC. Latest **02** (★★★★) restrained brioche intro, then firm limy fruit tinged with spice & toast. Attractive bone-dry palate, with expansiveness from 10% oak fermented base wine. Shd age with interest, say 3-5 yrs.

★★★★ **Cap Classique Jacques Bruère Brut Reserve** Pvs was **NV** (00); now **02** — like above, aged for 36-60 mths following bottle fermentation, before disgorging (also 10% wooded). Supple, stylish, dry, with lively citrus set against yeasty undertones. Plenty of frothy mousse. From 60:40 pinot/chard.

★★★★ **Noble Late Harvest** Sumptuously sweet riesling dessert, with rapier fruit acid to balance. Following **02**, standout **04** (★★★★★) pvsly noted for its ethereal aromas/flavours, peaches & cream texture, some terpene oiliness & racy/steely finish. 9.5% alc.

★★★★ **White Muscadel** ✓ Long lineage of concentration, richness; **05** now bottled & settled: billowing barley sugar, sultanas, caramel. Heavy with sugar (215g/ℓ), voluptuous & slow-moving — alc perhaps a little low for ideal balance at 15.5% (was 18% in last tasted **03**).

Colombard ☺ ★★★ **06** a cracker, bursting with ripe guava flavour, just off-dry, but sweet touch balanced by bouncy acids; drink this summer while at its show-off best. **05** Winemakers Choice.

Cabernet Sauvignon Inkará Harmonious 03 (★★★★, VDG, *Wine* ★★★★★) followed by step-up 04 (★★★★), with complex whiffs mocha, cedar, cassis, pencil shavings all moving easily to toned, well muscled palate. In cab's tougher, firmer guise — but here well balanced, impressive. 8-24 mths new Fr oak. Accessible, but 4-6 more yrs potential. **Bruére Gold Reserve** [new] ★★★☆ **04** pinot made as 'tribute to estate's gold-awarded wines'. Lovely typicity with organic, forest floor aromas, dark berried flavours, velvety dry tannins, lingering finish. Half barrel fermented, all in oak 2 yrs (20% new). Notably modest 12% alc. **Cabernet Sauvignon** ★★★☆ **04**'s inviting black-currant/oak aromas follow through onto palate, joining softish tannins for delicious glassful: juicy but some seriousness. 12-15 mths oak. 03 ★★★ but VDG. **Pinotage** ★★★ A touch less opulent than when tasted ex-barrel last ed, but pleasing & modern-style **04** with rhubarb, pepper & red-fruit notes; silky texture & fully integrated oak. 18 mths Fr/Am mix new/used. **Shiraz** ★★★☆ Fruit-dominant **04** (tasted as sample last yr) big in flavour & structure: ripe black plum, some pepper; plenty of oak (yr, mixed ages), chewy but not harsh. 03 *Wine* ★★★★. **Cabernet Sauvignon-Shiraz** ★★★ **04**'s oak-matured 60:40 blend gives warm, baked fruit, pruney flavours; tannins approachable, but slight earthiness on dry finish. **Sauvignon Blanc** ★★★ Bone-dry **06** less arresting than pvs, seems lighter than 13% alc suggests & lacks varietal punch, though lively & balanced. **Chardonnay** ★★★ **06**'s peach bon-bon flavours & soft acidity make for casual summer drinking (this summer, NB, not next!) in easy unwooded style. **Riesling** ★★★ Food-friendly **06** from crouchen shows good typicity with fresh-mown hay aromas; firm acid softened by nearly 10g/ℓ sugar. **Colombard-Chardonnay** ★★★ **06** a 60:40 blend, an appealing bone-dry summer quaffer, with some limy touches & smooth acidity. **Gewürztraminer Special Late Harvest** ★★★☆ More spice than rosepetals in **06**, but usual lilting sweet-sour music for the palate; now up to 66g/ℓ sugar, mere 12% alc. **Weisser Riesling Natural Sweet** ★★★★ Last sampled was **03**: lush fruit, pineapple & lime notes; smoothly rounded body; racy acidity giving crisply clean finish. 11% alc. **Blush Vin Doux** ★★ Noted last ed, a frothy pink **NV** sweet bubbly from pinot & muscadel; light-hearted, uncomplicated. **Red Muscadel** ★★★☆ **04** (sample) combines elegance & pristine muscat flavours with warm, sweet raisin character. Sweetness is delicate rather than cloying; poised, well balanced. Heart-warming, too! **Vintage Port** ★★★ **04** from tinta/touriga, reprises drinkability & character of pvs: mocha, plums & molasses, with richly savoury flavour. 18% alc, 95g/ℓ sugar. — *IvH*

Bonfoi Estate

Stellenbosch ▪ Est 1699 ▪ 1stB 1974 ▪ Tasting & sales Mon-Fri 9-5 Sat 10-2.30 ▪ Fee R10, refunded with purchase ▪ Closed pub hols ▪ BYO picnic ▪ Walks ▪ Conservation area ▪ Owner/winemaker/viticulturist Johannes van der Westhuizen ▪ 101 ha (cabs s/f, merlot, pinot meunier, pinotage, shiraz, chard, chenin, sauvignon, semillon) ▪ 700 tons 3 000 cs own label 60% red 40% white ▪ PO Box 9 Vlottenburg 7604 ▪ bonfoi@wo.co.za & bonfoi@mweb.co.za ▪ www.bonfoiwines.co.za ▪ T 021·881·3774 ▪ F 021·881·3807

Johannes van der Westhuizen has installed a number of smaller tanks so all his reds can be vinified using the time-honoured 'punch-down' technique of submerging the cap of skins during vinification — pumping the must over the cap is no longer de rigueur here. The new vessels also have closures, allowing extended maceration after fermentation, which is 'most important for the cab and shiraz'. JvdW has also added a cooling facility to the press, particularly to keep the sauvignon on its skins overnight at a brisk 10°C.

★★★★ **Ouverture** Beautifully crafted & elegant blend, selected best barrels. **02** cab, merlot & shiraz (45/30/25) in warm, seamless weave; generous but still bdx-like. Last ed noted as unfolding stylishly, shd keep few more yrs. 18 mths oaked.

★★★★ **Cabernet Sauvignon** Established styling (dark mulberry, cool cedar, fine oak to black velvety fruit) somewhat impeded by difficult vintage in **02** (★★★☆); slightly green but, like **01**, lively & clean-cut, with fresh acidity & good depth. Yr Fr oak.

★★★★ **Shiraz 04** another terrific vintage, sensitively handled; usual smoked beef aroma, here with peppery tang, charry black cherry flavour, fine dry tannins. Delicious & not too full bodied. For now & over 3-5 yrs. Malo in barrel.

Merlot ★★★ Attractive dark cassis/mulberry flavours, some mulberry leaf tones adding freshness on **03**; acidity last ed bit unbalanced, diminishing usual generous feel. Yr oak. **Chardonnay** ★★★☆ **05** fuller & better balanced than pvs; some leesy richness to generous tangerine palate; integrated oaking (fermented/6 mths aged). **Sauvignon Blanc** ★★★☆ **06** (sample) offers usual balanced bounce, juicy curvaceousness; gooseberry & fig aromas, tangy grapefruit flavours, moderate alc. — *IvH*

■ *Bonne Esperance see* KWV Ltd

Bonnievale Wine Cellar   🍷♿

Robertson ▪ Tasting & sales Mon-Fri 8-5 Sat & pub hols 10-1 ▪ Closed Easter Fri-Mon, Dec 25/26 & Jan 1 ▪ Owners 135 members ▪ Production Sakkie Bosman ▪ Winemakers Gerhard Swart, Esmarie Smuts & Simon Basson ▪ Viti consultants Newald Marais & Willem Botha ▪ 1 771 ha (15 varieties r/ w) ▪ 23 500 tons 60 000 cs 25% red 75% white ▪ PO Box 206 Bonnievale 6730 ▪ info@ bonnievalecellar.co.za ▪ www.bonnievalecellar.co.za ▪ T·023·616·2795 ▪ F 023·616·2332

Stop press! Members of Merwespont, Nordale and Bonnievale wineries have voted to pool their resources under the Bonnievale Wine Cellar banner. 'The merger will position the business for future growth, as the Bonnievale area has proven its ability to produce wines suited to the consumer's palate,' says new CEO John Barnardt, formely specialist relationship manager for the fruit and wine industries at Nedbank. A stakeholding in Juno Wine Company (where consultant Newald Marais is also active) brings the 'buxom' Cape Maidens wines (listed under Juno in the guide) into the Bonnievale portfolio. Unveiled locally, in the UK and the Netherlands as the guide went to press was the Southern Lights range, from which a portion of sales will benefit each country's Sea Rescue Institution.

Vertex Reserve range

Cabernet Sauvignon ★★★★ **04** reflects a light, sympathetic touch; fruit & tannins ripe & in harmony, wild berry flavours well extracted, cedary hint from 50% new oak (70% Fr, 18 mths — same for all these). **Shiraz** ★★★ Style change from benign monster to man-about-town in **04**; trimmer oaking (pvsly 100% new), less flagrant alc (now 'only' 14.6%), still plenty fruit, structure & interest. **Chardonnay** ★★★★ **05** particularly well wooded, providing near-invisible scaffold for fine, creamy, lime zest fruit; light-tripping mineral texture balances ±14% alc.

Bonnievale range

> **Cabernet Sauvignon-Merlot** ☺ ★★★ Usual smooth drinkabilty delivered with delightful fruity exuberance in **04**; 70/30 blend, well oaked (as for Shiraz, plus unwooded portion); for early enjoyment.

Shiraz ★★★ More savoury & restrained this yr. **04** smoke & thatch notes, tangy tannins, any edges nicely rounded by combo Fr/Am staves & barrels. **Kelkierooi** ★★★ Lightish, quaffable, unwooded **NV** medley of pinotage & merlot, with former's banana whiffs & sweet fruit. Lightly chill in summer. 500ml. **Chardonnay** ★★ Well travelled **05** flew with SAA, BA, & is now tired: some dried pear flavours, charry notes from stave fermentation; drink soon. **Sauvignon Blanc** ★★★ Lightish **06** repeats pvs's (attractive) salad-leaf tone; soupçon sugar cushions the steely tartness. Following pair are equal chenin/colombard blends, **NV: Kelkiewit** ★★ Dry version, in 500ml; balanced, light, crisp, summertime tipple. **Pik 'n Wyntjie** ★★ With Late Harvest-style yielding sweetness. Light & simple, some delicate straw whiffs. **Sauvignon Blanc Brut** ★★ New packaging/label for this crisp, refreshing carbonated sparkling; **06** foamy, with fruit salad flavours. **NV. Cape Vintage** ★★ Port-style winter warmer last ed sampled pre-bottling; **03** no longer cloying, not unattractive charry character now fairly evident. **Cabernet Sauvignon Rosé, Chenin Blanc** & **Late Harvest** discontinued.

CCC range

Red ★★★ 'Cabernet Sauvignon-Cinsaut-Cabernet Franc' pvs ed, the varieties which make up partly oaked, braai-friendly **05**, with hearty tannins & green walnut flavours. **White** ★★★ 'Colombard-Chenin Blanc-Chardonnay' pvs ed; same varieties, slightly different proportions in lightly wooded **06**, same zinging freshness, 'drink soonest' caveat. — *CT*

Boplaas Family Vineyards　　　　　　　　　　　 🍷👤♨

Calitzdorp (see Little Karoo map) • *Est 1880* • *1stB 1982* • *Tasting & sales Mon-Fri 8-5 Sat 9-3* • *Fee R15 p/p for tour groups* • *Closed Easter Fri/Sun & Dec 25* • *Tours by appt* • *Gifts* • *Owner Carel Nel* • *Winemaker Carel Nel* • *Viti consultant Willem Botha* • *70 ha (cab, merlot, pinotage, shiraz, touriga, chard, sauvignon)* • *35 000 cs 50% red 45% white 5% blanc de noir* • *PO Box 156 Calitzdorp 6660* • *boplaas@mweb.co.za* • *www.boplaas.co.za* • **T 044·213·3326** • F 044 213·3750

Sweet victory for Boplaas owner/winemaker Carel Nel and SA Port Producers' Association colleagues after an EU ruling in favour of non-Portuguese port-makers using Ruby, Tawny, Vintage (but not Port) as label descriptors. As for the promised €4-million to market the alternative terms Cape Ruby, Cape Tawny Cape Vintage worldwide: *aluta continua*! Validation came from visiting Paul Symington of the eponymous Portuguese port house who pronounced Boplaas a top New World port-maker, making 'frightfully good' stuff. No resting on laurels for Nel, who continues to experiment with different spirits and fortification methods. Pioneering work in the southern Cape continues, with skin contact, various yeasts used on exciting new cool-climate Upper Langkloof and Outeniqua fruit, vinified at Boplaas.

Family Reserve range

★★★★ **Pinotage** Complexity, balance, suppleness in last-tasted **02** (★★★☆), generous with plums & black cherries, warming 14.9% alc. Creamy **01** had appealing banana-custard tones, ripe tannins for 3-4 yrs.

★★★★ **Kuip & Clay** Sample **03** tasted mid-2004 named 'Kuip & Klei'. Blend touriga, cab, merlot (30/35/35), with lavish black/red fruit & herby top-note; commanding but not overpowering.

★★★★ **Sauvignon Blanc** new **06**'s fruit from chilly Outeniqua mountain slope. Racy & slick; cool aromas of nettle, gooseberry, asparagus; similar palate tones of mineral & slate; poised, ultra-long chalky finish. 10% oak-influenced.

Cabernet Sauvignon ★★★ **05** classical cassis/cedar scents & gripping tannins, slightly bitter oak (9 mths Fr) & 15.3% alc showing on the finish. **Shiraz** Heady fruit, sweet Am oak vanilla its hallmark. Step up on last-tasted **02** (★★★☆), latest **05** (★★★★) has buxom berries, lofty lily aromas & flavours, some spicy choc. Smooth now, shd improve ±5 yrs. Forthrightly modern, with 9 mths Fr/Am oak — same goes for… **Shiraz-Cabernet Sauvignon** new ★★★★ Perfumed, red-toned, refreshing cab acidity/astringency mingling with sweet Am oak.

Boplaas range

★★★★★ **Cape Tawny Vintner's Reserve Port** new **1980** vintage — not a misprint here or on label: glorious mahogany colour from 15 yrs seasoning in old oak; bouquet of nuts & maraschino cherries seeped in spirit, satin texture, poised & sedate, endless nutty farewell. Pure tinta; 17.5% alc; 102g/ℓ sugar.

★★★★☆ **Red Muscadel Vintner's Reserve** Smooth & soft **75** an olive-rimmed beauty, tasted mid-2004. Complex, indulgent; dried-fruit finish.

★★★★★ **Vintage Reserve Port** Dignified fortified dessert, made only in exceptional yrs from mature touriga vines (15 yrs) & ungrafted ±30-yr-old tinta. **04** brooding & hedonistic; layered choc, charcuterie & oak flavours, vice-like tannins promise not to relinquish grip within 10 yrs. 'My monster', croons Nel. *Wine* ★★★★, TWS trophy. Hedonistic **03** (★★★★, VDG, *Wine* ★★★★) missed refinement & structure of pvs. Oak/fortification as below.

★★★★☆ **Vintage CWG Auction Reserve Port** Selection of best barrels, tiny quantities. Concentrated, structured **03** (not retasted), nutty/coffee whiffs, sweetness (92g/ℓ) corralled by tannins & knife-edge acidity/fortification. Made to Duoro specs, incl 500ℓ port 'pipes' (18-24 mths) to finish wine. Touriga, tinta b, souzão; fortified with brandy spirit.

★★★★ Cape Tawny Port ✓ SA flagship; 100% tinta, wood-matured 12 yrs. Following **02**, latest **NV** (★★★★★) classically flavoured & balanced; nutty, flor-like with caramel/tea leaf nuances & silky finish, 18.6% alc wave goodbye. Multi-awarded, inc VDG, TWS trophy, *Wine* ★★★★.

Tinta Barocca ☺ ★★☆ **05** very grippy but has raspberry nose & palate, to cope; fynbos/pepper hints add interest. 6 mths Fr oak. **Dry Red** ☺ ★★★ Generous blend of merlot, cab, shiraz pinotage & tinta b; pvsly unwooded, latest **NV** 3 mths Fr oak. Bright & joyful, soft tannins for easy drinking. **Late Harvest** ☺ ★★★ Equal blend hanepoot/colombard; **06** full of dried mango & muscat aromas/flavours. Cleansing acidity, light 11% alc suitable for lunchtime quaffing. **Red Dessert** ☺ ★★★ Tinta/muscadel mix (50/50) fortified to 16% alc. Latest **NV** uncloying despite 137g/ℓ sugar; ambrosial coffee/choc-raisin, berry sipper. **Muscadel** ☺ ★★★ Fortified white dessert. **06** very raisined, slightly oxidised, tealeaf lift to finish but we suggest cutting its richness with lime/ice for real summer fun.

Cabernet Sauvignon ★★ **04**'s jammy bouquet at odds with austere palate & slightly bitter finish. Some vanilla softness from 9 mths Fr oak. Tasted last ed, as was… **Merlot** ★★★ **04** fruit-driven & easy, pleasant plummy aromas, flavours plumped out by 8 mths Fr oak. Slipped down easily. **Pinotage** ★★★ Lightly oaked **05** cheery & sippable; strawberry/mulberry bouquet mimicked by palate, juicy, scrubby finish. Moderate 13% alc a bonus. **Shiraz** ★★★ **04**'s reticent red berries & plums mingle with whiffs smoke on the nose; palate more characterful: firm tannins plumped out by fleshy fruit. Drink soon. **Touriga Nacional** ★★★ One of few SA varietal bottlings; **05** lacks fruit weight of pvs, but still nicely different — marzipan & almond scents spice up black berries/violet tones, long peppery palate stoutly tannic. 9 mths oak. **Blanc de Noir** ★★ Semi-sweet with relatively low 12% alc. **06** fun & inviting with bubble gum, red fruit aromas & flavours. **Rosé** ★★ Muscadel, colombard & shiraz star in this sweetish (42g/ℓ sugar) **NV**. Spicy & earthy, with some red tones, fruity core, sweet farewell. **Chardonnay Unwooded** ★★ Subdued **06** shows slight citrus tone, floral hints; fresh & balanced. **Sauvignon Blanc** ★★ **05** slimmer's friend with only 1.2 g/ℓ sugar (though 13% alc); muted nose & palate, more steely than vinous. **Classic Dry White** ★★★ **06** bright & light (11.9% alc) patio companion; sauvignon, chard, colombard for fruit, viognier for palate. **Pinot Noir Sparkling** ★★ Lively mousse on **06** could start any party; raspberry aromas & flavours with hint of smoked ham. **Sweet Sparkling** ★★ Frothy, lightish (11% alc) but full-flavoured **NV** mood-lifter from hanepoot & colombard. **Hanepoot** ★★★ Silky fortified dessert. **05** tasted last ed, luscious raisins & dried fig aroma; persistent raisin finish. Slips down easily. **Muscadel Reserve** ★★★★ Back in the line up with **04**. Brassy hue belies creamy/nutty aromas & flavours. Scintillating orange peel/lemon zest entry, syrupy finish (200g/ℓ sugar). **Cape Vintage Port** Perennial award winner, ageing/fortification as per Rsv above; moderate sweetness: 90g/ℓ. Velvety **03** (★★★★) a tad short, but **04** (★★★★) blend successfully ups tinta to 60%, decreases touriga to 25%, maintains souzão at 15%; and boosts alc to 19.5%. Luscious & long, with choc & red raisins, creamy indulgence. Could sip now, best to wait ±5 yrs. *Wine* ★★★★. **Cape Ruby Port** Best-selling **NV** ruby, always in drier Douro style (±89 g/ℓ sugar, 18.5% alc). Souzão now solid partner in the blend with tinta (60%), touriga (25%). latest version's (★★★★) velvety fruit, integrated oak/alc make this super-sippable; Xmas-cake, marzipan notes joined by tealeaf hints. **Late Bottled Vintage Option Port** ★★★★ Last-tasted **93** spicily opulent, deliciously harmonious & balanced. Tinta, touriga, 4½ yrs Portuguese oak. 18.5% alc. **Ruby Light** NEW ★★☆ Billed as 'sweet after dinner drink', targeting those who like port's aromas & flavours, but not its alcs — this only 12.5%, exposing 74 g/ℓ sugar as decidedly sweet. Plummy, touches scrub & spice. **Cape White Port** ★★★ From colombard, yr old oak. Latest **NV** billows nuts, cream, sherry's oxidative notes; lively acidity for refreshing zip. 17.2% alc. — *CvZ*

Boschendal Wines   ☗♀♨♬♒⛝

Franschhoek ▪ Est 1685 ▪ 1stB 1976 ▪ Tasting & sales daily May-Oct 9-4.30 Nov-Apr 10-6.30 Fee R15 for 5 wines ▪ Closed Easter Fri, May 1, Jun 16 & Dec 25 ▪ Tours (vyd & cellar in minibus) 10.30, 11.30 & 3 by appt ▪ Restaurants & picnics ▪ Tour groups ▪ Gifts ▪ Conservation area ▪ Museum visits 9.30-5 ▪ Owner DGB ▪ Cellarmaster JC Bekker (1996) ▪ Winemakers Lizelle

Gerber (whites, 2006) & James Farquharson (reds, 2004), with Lionel Leibbrandt (1999) · Viticulturist Spekkies van Breda (1995) · 200 ha (cabs s/f, merlot, shiraz, chard, sauvignon) · 3 600 tons 250 000 cs 40% red 44% white 14% rosé 2% sparkling · ISO 9001 & 14001 certified · Pvt Bag X03 Groot Drakenstein 7680 · taphuis@dgb.co.za · www.boschendalwines.com · T 021·870·4200 · F 021·874·1531

With DGB's acquisition of the renowned brand, winery, cellar, production facilities and sales centre smoothly completed, CE Tim Hutchinson promises a boosted marketing drive. Jacques Roux, ex-Graham Beck, has come in as marketing director and will work closely with UK agent Paragon to make an impression on the £7 to £10 category of the British market. Five tiers of wine have emerged in a reshuffling exercise, including the premium 1685, the Reserve Collection and the new flagship Cecil John Reserve, each with a Sauvignon and a Shiraz in its ranks, the favourites respectively of cellarmaster JC Bekker (who celebrated 10 years on the historic spread last year) and red-wine maker James Farquharson. Also getting a boost are the farm's conservation areas, with R20m set aside for an alien eradication programme.

Cecil John range   `new`

★★★★ **Shiraz** These named after Cecil John Rhodes, famous founder of Rhodes Fruit Farms, which included Boschendal. **03** is cinemascope shiraz, exuberantly fruity yet complex: brambleberries, candied violets, white pepper, but don't be fooled: this is a serious wine, requiring yrs to reveal other layers. Bold in every way, including 15.5% alc, 27 mths oaking, 25% new.

★★★★ **Sauvignon Blanc** A worthy first release under this new label; previewed **06** captures all the green notes the variety develops under cool growing conditions. Abounds with capsicum, grapefruit, leafy minerality & steely acidity; with tastebuds alive, you'll be looking for food.

Reserve Collection

★★★★★ **Grand Reserve** Classically crafted & ageworthy blend, mainly cab f, from selected casks. **01** grandly serious, as pvs, but a little easier-going. IWSC gold in 2005. **02** not released. **03** (★★★★) needs time. Green walnuts, summer heath tones from 70% cab f (with equal cab, malbec, shiraz); serious oaking explains peppery nuances, firm structure. Still tightly buttoned mid-2006, shd show better in yr/2. 21 mths Fr, half new.

★★★★ **Cabernet Sauvignon** Elegantly styled red. Brooding, dark, with cassis peeping through, but **03** still evolving; tannins, though ripe, mask true potential. Give another yr, cellar 8+ more. Fr oak 18 mths, half new.

★★★★★ **Shiraz** Deeply coloured **02** offered mixed herb, red-fruited aromas, big structure, needing time to harmonise. *Wine* ★★★★. Philosophy of allowing fruit full expression, amply demonstrated in earlier maturing **03** (★★★★): opulent wild berries, smoothly rounded, fleshy palate, accommodating 15.5% alc. Expertly judged oak: 20 mths 300ℓ Fr, qtr new. Drink within 5 yrs.

Sauvignon Blanc ★★★★ Ripe-yet-green **05** has a figgy base, seamed with leafy, fynbos notes, racy acidity. Gd food partner. SAA. Discontinued: **Merlot**, **Chardonnay Reserve**, **Jean le Long Sauvignon Blanc**.

1685 range

★★★★ **Brut** Supple, yeasty, vintaged MCC from pinot (60% in **99**), chard. Last tasted disgorged Jan 2003 (date on label). Biscuit/brioche bouquet presaged almost decadently rich but well-balanced palate offering strawberry, ripe apple notes, sweet touch from 13g/ℓ sugar.

Range named after farm's founding date; packaged in distinctive bottle shape originally reserved for Grand Vin Blanc. **Shiraz** ★★★★ Good varietal typicity in **04**'s dark fruit & smoky, peppery tones. Given firm backbone, 2-3 yr ageing potential by 16 mths oak maturation, 20% new. **Shiraz-Cabernet Sauvignon** `new` ★★★★ **04** amiable 60/40 partnership, each showing off its wares. Bright, perky berries & no-nonsense firm foundation from cab, shiraz sprinkles fleshier notes, savoury, smoky spice finish. Oak as above. **Chardonnay-Pinot Noir** ★★★★ Replaces SA pioneer 'Pinot Noir-Chardonnay'. **06** retains touch pink, peach/strawberry fruit profile & appetite appeal of pvs. Now dry; oak % increased by fermenting/maturing chard in older barrels. **Chardonnay**

★★★★ Bold, fleshy **05** has toasty oak, a canned peaches character, livening acidity to offset richness, ripeness. 75% fermented/matured 9 mths Fr oak, third new. 50% native yeast. Watch 14.8% alc. **Sauvignon Blanc Grand Vin Blanc** ★★★☆ (Grand Cuvée internationally). Now made dry & upgraded to include small portion oak. **05** includes dab semillon, but wine has gooseberry/passionfruit vitality that shouts sauvignon. Discontinued: **Pinot Noir-Chardonnay, Cabernet Sauvignon, Jean le Long White**.

Boschendal Favourites

Lanoy ★★★☆ Big-volume blend named after 17th-century part-owner Nicolas de Lanoy. Chunky, satisfyingly robust **03** is cab-based with merlot (25%), shiraz (10%); prunes, smoky nuances speak of ripeness, good oak regime. Accessible, cld age 2+ yrs further. **Blanc de Noir** ★★★ Light, pretty, uncomplicated. Pale salmon-coloured **06** from red grape all-sorts, offers delicate red-berry perfume, just-off-dry styling to gain more fans. **Blanc de Blanc** ★★★★ Mainly chenin/chardonnay. **06** has 'drink me' written all over it: tangy lemon-drop character, quivering freshness. Incl semillon, sauvignon. **Chenin Blanc** ★★★☆ From 26 year old bushvines, giving gd fruit concentration, apple, melon in **06**, with trademark varietal enlivening acid balance. Touch palate-lengthening sugar adds to the appeal. **Le Bouquet** ★★★ Light textured off-dry blend. Delightfully aromatic **06** is designed to charm its audience, brighten any drinking occasion. Muscat d'A, riesling, gewürz 40/40/20.

The Pavillion range

Blanc ☺ ★★★ Unwooded chard & semillon. With peachy fruit salad flavours, **06** is bursting with vitality, appetite appeal. 80/20 proportions.

Shiraz-Cabernet Sauvignon ★★★ Lightly oaked & fruit-focused **05** has charming, juicy, fresh-faced drinkability. 55/45 blend. This, following, both new. **Rosé** ★★★ Light-hearted quaffer from mix of red varieties. **06** perky cranberry/fruitgum tones, rounded mouthfeel from touch sugar. **The Grand Pavillion** ★★★★ Reliable **NV** cap classique brut, available ex-farm only. Last had attractively yeasty, mature bouquet & spicy baked apple notes on light, fresh dryness. All ranges WO Coastal/W Cape. Discontinued: **Rouge**. —CR

■ *Boschetto* see Stellakaya

Boschheim   ♀

Stellenbosch ▪ 1stB 2003 ▪ Visits by appt ▪ Owner/winemaker Andy Roediger ▪ 750 cs 100% red ▪ PO Box 3202 Matieland 7602 ▪ ahar@sun.ac.za ▪ T 021·808·3175 F 021·886·4731

Aspirant Cape Wine Master Andy Roediger has found time to treble production in the past year. His small garage has been converted to a proper winery, with new cooling and other equipment making things easier. On the horizon is a cab-merlot blend, says he, and marketing is the next challenge, though with earlier vintages sold out, this should come easy for him.

Elemental ★★★★ ✓ Shiraz, fashionably laced with viognier (6%) — though the aromatic white grape less overt on **05** — less floral, more pervasively spicy, hints bramble & liquorice; new oak (30%, Fr, yr) better wielded than on pvs (& Cab below); confident, lifted finish. **Cabernet Sauvignon** ★★★ No follow-up yet to foursquare **03**, sweet-fruited juiciness trimmed by enthusiastic wooding.—CT

Boschkloof   ♂♀

Stellenbosch ▪ Est/1stB 1996 ▪ Tasting & sales by appt only Mon-Fri 8-6 (sales 8-5) Sat 8-1 ▪ Tours by appt ▪ Owners Reenen Furter & Jacques Borman ▪ Winemaker Jacques Borman ▪ Viticulturist Reenen Furter ▪ 19 ha (cab, merlot, shiraz) ▪ 120 tons ▪ 8 000 cs 89% red 11% white ▪ PO Box 1340 Stellenbosch 7599 ▪ boschkloof@adept.co.za or jborman@adept.co.za ▪ www. boschkloof.co.za ▪ T 021·881·3293 & F 021·881·3032 (office); T 021·881·3268 (cellar)

A vintage year for winemaker Jacques Borman, who was invited to join the prestigious ranks of the Cape Winemakers Guild, received excellent ratings from US *Wine Spectator*, and made Boschkloof's first viognier and mourvèdre, with 'exciting' results. So much so, he and wine-partner Reenen Furter think they should look at the possibilities afforded by other Rhône specialities such as marsanne and roussanne. Noteworthy too were vinifications of selected reds in new barrels, with long macerations on skins in certain instances. The verdict: 'Very exciting!'

**** **Conclusion** new Replaces 'Reserve' as flagship, portions shiraz & cab f add fillip to cab/merlot density. **04**'s deep colour & muted cassis harbingers of future pleasure, confirmed by ripe fruit stacked on sturdy tannic frame mid-2006. Shd unfurl post 2010. All new oak 2 yrs, 15% alc. **02** Winemakers Choice.

**** **Syrah** Considerable power within svelte frame. **04** from home vyds; generous scents laced with oriental spice; spiciness returns in rich, warming conclusion (14.7% alc). *WS* 91 pts; Winemakers Choice trophy. Fr & Am oak 14 mths, half new.

**** **Five Acres Shiraz-Viognier** new Rather more boisterous than above. **04** burly, ripe black fruit buffed by fragrant blending partner; imposing 15.7% alc tethers jostling tannins. Own shiraz, Darling viognier, natural ferment in oak. Mourvèdre may join party in future.

**** **Cabernet Sauvignon-Merlot** Stylish, accessible blend, easier — not lesser — than heavy-duties above. **04** replete with choc-vanilla sheen to plum fruits, coffee interest in tannin lattice. 19 mths Fr oak, 30% new.

Chardonnay ★★★☆ **05** bold, butterscotch fruit, tangy finish, 20% new Fr oak. Not reviewed for this ed: **Cabernet Sauvignon** ★★★ Measured house elegance woven into lighter **02**. **Merlot** ★★★ **02** sappy vinosity lends austerity to berry fruit, no loud choc-nut flavours of pvs. — *DS*

Boschrivier Cellar ⚲

Klein River • Est 1997 • 1stB 2002 • Tasting by appt (T 028·341·0630/072·208·6572 — Louise van der Merwe) • Owner Theo de Villiers • Winemaker Mike Dobrovic (Mulderbosch) • Viticulturist Johan van der Merwe • 14 ha (cab, shiraz) • 367 cs 100% red • PO Box 809 Caledon 7230 • njtdevill@mweb.co.za • www.boschrivier.co.za • **T 028·341·0630/023·347·3313** *• F 028·341·0630*

'We're now open for pre-booked tastings,' say viticulturist Johan and manager/marketer Louise van der Merwe, ensconced on this property near Stanford, once 18th-century wheat-and-onion land, inherited by paediatrician Theo de Villiers and selectively replanted with vines in 1997. Made by Mulderbosch's Mike Dobrovic, the Shiraz has won approval in *Wine* and Michelangelo judgings; the 04, maturing in bottle, will be released in due course. All evidence that Boschrivier is living up to the De Villiers' family motto: *'la main a l'oevre'* (hand at work).

Shiraz ★★★☆ First impression is of ultra-ripeness, but **03** flavours fresher than nose suggests. Warm & chunky; restrained tannins increase approachability, as does smidgen sugar to offset heartier features of 14.7% alc. 18 mths Fr oak, mainly new. WO Overberg. — *AL*

■ **Boschveld** *see Baarsma*

Bosman Family Vineyards ⚱♀ new

Wellington • Est 1699 • 1stB 2004 • Visits by appt • Owner Jan C Bosman Family Trust • Winemaker Petrus Bosman • Viticulturist Gerhard van Rensburg (Nov 1997) • 250 ha (cab, chenin) • 2 500 tons 300 cs own label 65% red 35% white • PO Box 9 Wellington 7654 • info@bosmanwines.com • www.bosmanwines.com • **T 021·873·3170** *• F 021·864·1705*

Young Petrus Bosman draws on much for a cab combining 'Old World elegance and bright New World fruit': eight generations of viticulture/winemaking on the farm Lelienfontein (circa 1798); all-new rootstocks; clones from the family's commercial nursery; pick of the crop from prime Groenberg sites; winemaking passion absorbed at his grandfather's knee; university qualifications and a stint under veteran vintner Charles Stassen, whose 01 Wamakersvallei La Cave Cab (source: Lelienfontein) was world's best at the 2003 London IWSC.

Cabernet Sauvignon ★★★ Ripe black berry aromas, spicy currant flavours on **04**, selected from 3 vyd blocks; opulent (15% alc) with ample tannin in support; yr Fr oak, half new. — *MF*

■ **Bosman's Hill** *see Saxenburg*

Botha Wine Cellar

Breedekloof (see Worcester/Breedekloof map) • Est 1949 • 1stB 1974 • Tasting & sales Mon-Fri 7. 30-5.30 Sat 9-1 • Closed Easter Fri/Sun, Dec 25 & Jan 1 • Tours by appt • BYO picnic • Facilities for children • Tour groups • Conservation area • Owners 71 members • Manager/cellarmaster JC 'Dassie' Smith (Nov 1996) • Winemakers Johan Linde & Michiel Visser (Nov 1996/1999), with Pierre Hugo & Cobus Brink • Viticulturist Hennie Visser • 1 880 ha • 30 000 tons 35% red 65% white • PO Box 30 Botha 6857 • admin@bothakelder.co.za • T 023·355·1740/789 • F 023·355·1615

A first wooded chardonnay is in the pipeline, and yet more variety is promised as this winery's viognier, malbec and petit verdot come into production. Johan Linde rates the 06 Sauvignon (not ready for tasting) as one of the best vintages yet produced at Botha. Certainly they are upping the stakes in the value-for-money race, with their Dassie's Rood in the running for our 'Superquaffer' of the Year.

Dassie's Reserve range

Cabernet Sauvignon ★★★ **02** whiffs currant jam & tobacco; dry powdery tannins & obvious wood. Matured in Fr barriques, as are all these reds. **Pinotage** ★★★★ **02** Oak/acid better handled here; **02** plum-jam fruit tones complemented by wood, spicy dry finish. Neither above retasted. **Merlot** ★★ Over-ripe style **03**, volatile whiffs & hints oak-char & raisin, not for keeping. **Shiraz** ★★★ **03** much riper-picked than pvs (26°B), yielding curranty/raisined aromas but little fruity substance on palate, v tight dry tannins. **Chardonnay** ★★ **05** retiring hints of pear on nose, some butteriness still on palate but acidity beginning to show — needs drinking soon; ditto for all these whites. **Chenin Blanc** ★★ A Young Wine Show favourite (both local & national); **05** light, just-dry, soft tropical fruit starting to fade **Colombard** ★★ Light bodied **05** showing some maturity, still enough fruit to enjoy; soft roundness via ±10g/ℓ sugar. **Sauvignon Blanc** ★★ **05** hints artichoke & celery, touch oxidative, losing its youthful freshness. **Special Late Harvest** ★★ **05** light, honeyed & very sweet chenin (80%) & hanepoot, with light barley sugar softness & hint of raisin.

Botha range

> **Dassie's Rood** ☺ ★★★ **05** medium bodied anytime red; half cinsaut, with cab & ruby cab. Appealing leathery/savoury sides to succulent ripe fruit, balanced, swiggably fresh.

All reds in range unwooded. **Cabernet Sauvignon** ★★★ **04** last yr was punchy but with well managed tannins, in harmony with fruit. **Merlot** ★★ **05** full bodied but soft, ripe & undemanding; farmyard whiffs, more pleasant with food. **Pinotage** ★★★ **05** gold on local Young Wine Show; lively fruit tannins, slightly 'wild' berry, banana & savoury notes, lots of personality, flavour. **Shiraz** ★★★ **04**, retasted, delivers fruity drinkability via wild berry jam aromatics, soft, medium bodied fruit-sweet flavours. **Blanc de Blanc** ★ **05** semi-dry equal mix colombard, chenin; retains some fruity flavour but must be drunk soonest. Following pair of sparklers carbonated: **Chardonnay Brut** ★★★ Refreshing, dryish **05**, fruity, with creamy bubbles & balanced freshness. **Chardonnay Demi-sec** ★★ Appealing **05**, ripe but not over-sweet sparkling, packed with prickly bubbles. **Hanepoot Jerepigo** ★★★ Lovely **04** anytime sweetie delicately billows pineapple & jasmine; luscious but balanced sweetness & well judged 16.5% alc. **Red Jerepigo** ★★ **04** from pinotage; redolent of treacle & fruit cordial; low acid, alc, & 230+g/ℓ sugar means there's no need for pudding. **Late Bottled Vintage Port** ★★★★ ✓ Bargain priced **02** from shiraz, unclassic but appealing; dry finish, gently gripping alc (19.5%), characterful wet slate/damp earth fruit flavours. Both ranges WO Wrcstr or Breede Rvr Vlly.— *CT*

Bottelary Hills Wines

Est/1stB 2003 • Tasting, sales & tours see Bellevue, Goede Hoop, Groenland, Kaapzicht & Mooiplaas • Owners Bottelary Hills Wines (Pty) Ltd • 70% red 30% white • PO Box 42 Koelenhof 7605 • goede@adept.co.za • www.bottelaryhills.co.za • T 021·903·6286 • F 021·906-1553

Inspired by long friendships and history, a group of neighbouring Bottelary Hills farms contribute selected wines for blending and sale under the flagship Bottelary Hills label and easy-drinking brand, M23 (the road runs through it). The following are available (but not tasted):

Bottelary Hills Cabernet Sauvignon-Pinotage 01 and Shiraz 03, and M23 Cabernet Sauvignon-Merlot 01, Rhapsody NV red blend, Limerick 06 (sauvignon/chenin), Sauvignon Blanc 06. Buoyed by success, the venture moves to new premises at Koelenhof this year.

Bottelary Winery International

Stellenbosch • Tasting & sales Mon-Fri 8-5.30 Sat 9-1 • Closed Easter Fri & Sat, Dec 25 & Jan 1 • Tours by appt • Light meals during office hours • Private functions after-hours/weekends by appt • Facilities for children • Winemakers Ewald Kellerman & Pieter Carstens (both 2004), with Carla Myburgh (Dec 2005) • Viticulturist Stephan Joubert (2004) • ±3 000 tons from contract vyds • 100 000 cs 48% red 48% white 4% rosé • Also exported as Rocco Bay • PO Box 214 Paarl 7620 • bottelary@mweb.co.za • T 021·865·2781 • F 021·865·2780

Now back in full force after a few years' hibernation, this winery's attractive tasting venue and restaurant in the Bottelary Hills are open for visitors. Children are treated to activities and games which have been approved by occupational therapists, leaving adults free to browse through ceramicist Johan Swart's studio before enjoying a tasting of their wines, followed by a family picnic on the lawn.

Reserve range

Cabernet Sauvignon ★★★☆ Modern yet elegant **03**, combines fruit-richness with restraint & seriousness; deserves another yr/2 to show its best. 14 mths Fr/Am small-oak (ditto all Rsv reds). **Merlot** ★★★★ Supple tannins underpin **02**, impart backbone to ripe red/black fruit & platform for growth; pity to open too soon. **Pinotage** ★★★★ **02** a polished performance; delicious black cherry fruit, elegant dry tannins, tangy sweet-sour touch. **Shiraz** ★★★☆ **02** ripe red fruit firmly supported by savoury tannins, twist liquorice in tail. Gd potential. **Chardonnay 04** untasted. **Sauvignon Blanc** ★★★ **04** still vibrant last yr, fruitily persistent, passionfruit & gooseberry combo, well-balanced acidity. New vintages for above, range below, not ready at press time:

Bottelary range

Reds in this range unoaked. **Cabernet Sauvignon** ★★★ Spicy, juicy **03**, well-made, unpretentious, light textured despite 14% alc. **Shiraz** ★★★ **03** forthright & attractive expression of the variety; smooth, friendly tannins, easy to drink. **Cabernet Sauvignon-Merlot** ★★★ **04** modern fruity style; satisfying juicy black fruit, easy tannins for solo or with food. **Cinsaut-Shiraz** ★★★ **03** lively, jovial 70/30 blend; smooth & seamless without being simple. **Chenin Blanc Dry** ★★☆ Ideal summer picnic wine: **06** light, easy, fruit-driven with ripe guava flavours. **Sauvignon Blanc** ★★★ **06** fresh, zingy, early-harvested style; 'Dbnvlle dust' on nose (source of 20% of fruit, rest Paarl), light & quaffable. **Hanepoot** ★★★ Jerepiko-style fortified from Breedeklf fruit; **05** pleasing grapey perfumes, flavours; soft & ripe, well balanced sweetness.

Rocco Bay range

Mainly for export, this established range is NEW to the guide. **Soft Smooth Red** ★★☆ Crowd-pleaser ex cab, shiraz & dollop cinsaut; sweet & undemanding, with wild-berry flavours. 17 g/ℓ sugar. **NV**, unwooded. **Pinotage 03** available but untasted. **Rosé** ★★ Attractively fresh, light & dry **05** from pinotage; interesting savoury rosepetal character. All ranges WO Coastal/W Cape. — CT

Bouchard Finlayson

Walker Bay • Est 1989 • 1stB 1991 • Tasting & sales Mon-Fri 9-5 Sat 9.30-12.30 • Fee R20 for groups of 8+ • Closed pub hols • Owner Bouchard Finlayson (Pty) Ltd • Winemaker/viticulturist Peter Finlayson • 17 ha (pinot, nebbiolo, sangiovese, chard, sauvignon) • 180 tons 12 000 cs 20% red 80% white • PO Box 303 Hermanus 7200 • info@bouchardfinlayson.co.za • www.bouchardfinlayson.co.za • T 028·312·3515 • F 028·312·2317

As Peter Finlayson says: 'The wine world is awash with choice; only quality will maintain the respect of customers.' Bearing that in mind, he has tightened up even further on final blend selection for his flagship Pinot. He has also upped his complement of new barrels, switched to using a cooper from Nuits St George whose production is small but excellent, and taken stock of the smoothness of the wines: 'Pinot can so easily offer too much tannin or bitterness. ' Last year saw the release of the Limited Edition (only 4000 bottles) Kaaimansgat Chardonnay, a special blend half matured in French oak and half unoaked. It also marked the 'release' (to well-deserved retirement!) of Michael Clark, after 15 successful years as BF director/ financial manager.

★★★★☆ **Galpin Peak Pinot Noir** Burgundy the touchstone for this leading Cape example. More recently riper, softer, without sacrifice of classic pinot tension. **04** waves of red fruits entice, but beauty's in the texture: fabulous grip, echoing length, sweet-fruit finish. Own vyds, concentrated yield 1kg/vine. Now less new oak (±third), yr.

★★★★★ **Tête de Cuvée Galpin Peak Pinot Noir** Cellarmaster's barrel selection in best yrs makes comeback after hiatus with terrific **03**. Waxy layers of subtle aromas lead to pervasive, enduring grip & substance, sensual tannic tail. Winemakers Choice. Pvs was tremendous **01**, redolent of truffles; velvet textured. Seriously oaked: 75% new Burgundian barrels, 14 mths, 14% alc.

★★★★ **Hannibal** Substantial power threaded with finesse in this sangiovese-pinot led blend, with 'Mediterranean partners' nebbiolo, mourvèdre, barbera — shiraz adding interest. **04** funky juniper berry flavours, savoury tannins add to tangy finish. Tank-fermented, matured 15 mths Fr oak, third new. **03** JCWCA 'first'/gold.

★★★★ **Missionvale Chardonnay** A fitting white flagship from home grapes — substantial, yet carries house's elegant stamp. **05** full, broad & smoky, complex mineral seam within super texture leads out stunning length of finish. Fr oak 7 mths.

★★★★ **Kaaimansgat Chardonnay** ('Crocodile's Lair') Elevated, cool Vllrsdorp vines massaged into most overt style of the regular trio: **05** vanilla butter nose cut by ripe citrus fruit, temperate 13% alc. 8 mths in cask, 30% new. **04** Santé Classic gold. WO Ovrberg.

★★★★ **Kaaimansgat Chardonnay Limited Edition** [new] Same source as above, but different handling for this 375 cs parcel of **04**. Half barrelled (8 mths), rest unoaked, which shows in clear peach/pear flesh, toned by nutty breadth from extra yr in bottle. 14% alc.

★★★★ **Sans Barrique Chardonnay** Unoaked, so shade less complicated than above, fresh lemon/lime fruit to the fore. **05** (★★★★) quieter, without flavour intensity of pvs. WO Ovrberg.

Sauvignon Blanc ★★★★ Sample **06** in recent louder style; broad passionfruit flesh, tingling dry finish. **Blanc de Mer** ★★★★ Viognier leads blend with sauvignon from **06**, now more flashy, tropical & peachy. WO W Cape. — *DS*

Bouwland   ♀

Stellenbosch ▪ Est 1996 ▪ 1stB 1997 ▪ Tasting & sales at Beyerskloof ▪ Owners Bouwland Deelnemings Trust & Beyerskloof ▪ Winemaker Beyers Truter, with Anri Truter (1997/2004) ▪ Viti consultant Johan Pienaar (2003) ▪ 40 ha (cab, merlot, pinotage) ▪ 350 tons 30 000 cs 100% red ▪ PO Box 62 Koelenhof 7605 ▪ bouwland@adept.co.za ▪ T 021·865·2135 ▪ F 021·865·2683

'In contrast to some empowerment projects, we are still growing,' says Andre Franzsen, the marketing manager of this Bottelary property owned by farmworkers at Bouwland, Beyerskloof and Kanonkop. Production, which has increased to cater for export growth and 'very exciting' developments in the local market, is still in the safe hands of Beyers Truter and son Anri at Beyerskloof, where the wines can be tasted.

Cabernet Sauvignon-Merlot ★★★★ ✓ Engaging, well made blend should win friends with its honest decency — & entertain them well alongside food. Gently firm tannins, light oaking support gd fruit on **04**. **Cabernet Sauvignon-Merlot Reserve** [new] ★★★★ Richer, fuller version of above **04**, with sweeter, more focused berry fruit; a little more structure & wood. Nudges higher rating (as other nudges lower one). These both drink well now but should keep gd few yrs. **Chenin Blanc** ★★★ In abeyance. Last was freshly flavoursome **03**. — *TJ*

Bovlei Winery   ♀ ℒ ♿

Wellington ▪ Est 1907 ▪ Tasting & sales Mon-Fri 8.30–5 Sat 8.30-12.30 Non-religious pub hols 9-4.30 ▪ Olive & grape seed products ▪ Owners 39 members ▪ Wine production manager Frank Meaker ▪ Viti consultant Dawie le Roux ▪ 560 ha (cab, merlot, shiraz, chard) ▪ 120 000 cs own

labels + 920k ℓ bulk ▪ 40% red 60% white ▪ PO Box 82 Wellington 7654 ▪ wines@bovlei.co.za
▪ www.bovlei.co.za ▪ **T** *021·873·1567/021·864·1283 ▪* F *021·864·1483*

Bovlei is celebrating its centennial this year and Frank Meaker, who has added winemaker to his production manager title, says that 'after 100 years of delivering quality wines, we still have great expectations for the future'. The occasion will see the release of a Centennial range of single-vineyard wines from small, tried-and-tested vineyards. Meanwhile, selected 2005 wines have benefited from the introduction of oxygenation and stave treatments, Meaker reports, while the 2006 vintage was a particularly good one for the cellar.

The Centennial range
new

★★★★ **Shiraz-Mourvèdre 05** stands head & shoulders above its stablemates in its full bodied complexity. Enchanting black fruit melange, white & black pepper, sweet spices;
high alc (15% vs 14.5% of many below) somehow also works bewitchingly! Will reward 5-8 yrs' patience.

This Rsv range specially made for release this yr, celebrating 100th anniversary of winemaking at Bovlei. All barrel aged 9 mths & oxygenated. **Cabernet Sauvignon** ★★★☆ Dark choc & lavender whiffs provide top notes, plus ripe berry succulence on boisterous **05**, needing ±3 yrs to settle down, round out pliable tannins. **Merlot** ★★★☆ **05** ambitious & complex. Well meshed thanks to generous plummy fruit, deft oaking. Long espresso-tinged finish. **Shiraz** ★★★☆ Touch mourvèdre adds spice to broad, peppery, red-fruited **05**. Ripe, supple tannins welcome early consumption. Moderate 13.4% alc. Note: pvs Rsv wines, **Merlot 03, Shiraz 03, Cabernet Sauvignon-Mer-lot 02, Chardonnay & Sauvignon Blanc 04**, not revisited this ed.

Bovlei range

Cabernet Sauvignon ☺ ★★★ **05** well crafted, appealing & accessible. Rich & full but
also delicately perfumed. Like all reds in this range, lightly wooded. **Merlot** ☺ ★★★ Gd everyday drinking **05**, rich choc & floral backdrop, ripe plum aromas & flavours perform centre-stage. **Grand Rouge** ☺ ★★★ Easy-going blend; was bdx pvsly, in **04** 10% shiraz joins
±equal partners merlot & cabs s/f. Tasty choc-mint, red-berried mouthful. **Chenin Blanc**
☺ ★★★ **06** steps up with lovely fruit depth & zesty acidity, best in bloom of youth —
friendly 12% alc makes that even easier.

Following quartet not retasted. **Pinotage** ★★ Classic mulberries & plums on **04**, noticeably firm dry tannins, better in yr/2 or with food. **Shiraz** ★★★ Most approachable of these reds; **04** sweet fruited, slightly smoky, toasty backing from well-executed oak staving. **Pinotage Rosé** ★★ Pale cerise **05**, youthfully fresh & appealing, light, its sweetness well balanced by keen acidity. **Char-donnay** ★★ **04** light tropical tones with honeyed notes; pleasing, but not for further keeping. **Sau-vignon Blanc** ★★ Picnic sipper **06**, light in body & flavour; fleeting lemon hints, clean & dry. **Beaukett** ★★ Medium-sweet **NV** blend muscat, colombard & chenin; tropical toned, light bod-ied, tad tired. **Port** ★★ Ruby-style **NV** offers fresh ripe-plum flavour, as expected from ruby cab (50%, with cab f, roobernet & grenache); traditional low fortification (15.3%). **Bukettraube** discontinued. — *DH*

■ *BoweJoubert see Beau Joubert*

Bracken Wines
♀♂ new

KwaZulu-Natal ▪ Est 2002 ▪ 1stB 2005 ▪ Tasting, sales & tours Mon-Fri 7.30-4 Sat 8-3 ▪ Closed Easter Fri-Mon, Dec 16/25/26, Jan 1 ▪ Owner Martin Hill ▪ Winemaker/viticulturist Silindile Msimango (Jul 2004) ▪ 15 ha (cab, merlot, pinotage, shiraz, sauvignon) ▪ 24 tons 3 000 cs 78% red 22% white ▪ PO Box 141 Greytown 3250 ▪ brackwine@gom.co.za ▪ **T** *033·413·2443 ▪* F *033·413·2474*

'If it works here it could work back home,' mused timberman Martin Hill when he visited Can-ada. With Stellenbosch graduate Silindile Msimango handling the vini/viti portfolio, he's pio-neering wine-farming in the Greytown area of KwaZulu Natal. 'Don't think Durban's humidity,' says Msimango, 'and we're cooled by breezes from the Drakensberg.' She's a long way from

UCT's MBA school, where she's studying wine management, but doubling production in the 2006 vintage, her second, is just one of the milestones she's planting.

White 06 from sauvignon — scarcely ripe: bone-dry, mere 10% alc. Bright verjuice character, lemony tang, green apple finish. — *MF*

■ *Bradgate* see Jordan
■ *Brahms* see Domaine Brahms

Bramon Wines

Plettenberg Bay ▪ Est 2000 ▪ 1stB 2004 ▪ Tasting, sales & tours Tue-Sun 11-sunset ▪ Fee R25 (full glass) ▪ Closed Dec 25 ▪ Light lunches ▪ Gifts ▪ Cheeses ▪ Owner: Private company ▪ Winemaker Pieter Ferreira, with Irene Waller (Graham Beck Wines) ▪ 5 ha (sauvignon) ▪ 100% white ▪ PO Box 1606 Plettenberg Bay 6600 ▪ peter@bramonwines.co.za ▪ www.bramonwines.co.za ▪ T/F 044·534·8007

Upmarket resort town Plettenberg Bay now has Wine of Origin status thanks to Bramon Wines, situated in the mountainous Crags area just 3km from the sea (and next to an elephant sanctuary!). 'The closest vineyards are in the Oudtshoorn vicinity 150km away,' says owner Peter Thorpe. His grapes make an even longer journey — by refrigerated truck to Graham Beck Wines in Robertson, where bubbly supremo Pieter Ferreira turns them into 'unusual but excellent' Cap Classique. 'Once production justifies it, a cellar will be established on the farm,' says Peter T.

Cap Classique ★★★ 05 brut-style MCC from sauvignon, so flinty, capsicum notes to be expected. Racy acidity lifts & refreshes palate; exuberant mousse needs time to integrate; persistent lime-tinged finish. — *MF*

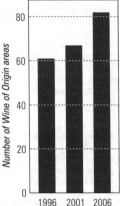

■ *Brampton* see Rustenberg

Brandvlei Cellar

Worcester ▪ Est 1955 ▪ 1stB 1956 ▪ Tasting & sales Mon-Thu 7.30-5.30 ▪ Closed pub hols ▪ Tours & group tastings by appt ▪ Owners 32 members ▪ Manager/winemaker Jean le Roux, with Jandré Human & Tertius Jonck ▪ Viticulturist Danie Conradie (2004) ▪ 1 400 ha (13 varieties r/w) ▪ 10 000 cs own label 20% red 75% white 10% jerepiko ▪ PO Box 595 Worcester 6849 ▪ brandvlei@breede.co.za ▪ www.brandvlei.co.za ▪ T/F 023·340·4215 ▪ F 023·340·4332

The 'terroir approach' in both vineyard (matching varieties to the most suitable sites) and cellar (special-selection tanks for separate vinification) is doing the trick, says manager/winemaker Jean le Roux, citing the Chenin and Sauvignon being snapped up soon after their release. 'People are crazy about these fresh young wines.' Good thing, then, that coinciding with the cellar's 50th anniversary, the crowd pleasing BC range has doubled in volume, to 4% of the 23 000-ton production — most of the balance still goes abroad.

BC range

Ruby Cabernet-Merlot ☺ **★★★** Always a happy wine; **05** fruity, fun to drink; fullish mulberry & choc flavours, amenable tannins. 60/40 blend.

Cabernet Sauvignon new **★★** Celebrates the cellar's 50th; restrained, light-textured **NV** shows variety's sturdy tannins, some berry fruit & touch earthiness. Oak matured 14 mths. **Chardonnay ★★ 06** straightforward dry white, crisp, with hay-like hint. **Chenin Blanc ★★** Racy, light (±12%

alc) **06**, slight stalky hint & bone-dry finish. **Sauvignon Blanc ★★ 06**, like pvs, picked early for 'grand cru' style racy freshness, low alc. **Bacchanté ★★ 06** semi-sweet but zesty white from chenin, fresh, light, tropical & easy to drink. **Hanepoot Jerepiko ★★★ ✓ 05** last ed delighted with tangy citrus/honeysuckle aroma, well-managed sweetness & alc. For delicious aperitif, pour over crushed ice. — *CT*

■ *Bredell's see* JP Bredell

Breeland Winery

*Rawsonville ▪ Closed to public ▪ PO Box 109 Rawsonville 6845 ▪ mlalee@xpoint.co.za ▪ **T/F 023·344·3137***
No update available on this winery; contact details from previous edition.

Brenthurst Winery

*Paarl ▪ Est 1993 ▪ 1stB 1994 ▪ Open to public only by special appt ▪ Owner/winemaker José Jordaan, with viti consultant Johan Wiese (1991) & other advisers ▪ 5 ha (cabs s/f, merlot, petit v) ▪ 50-70 tons ▪ PO Box 6091 Paarl 7622 ▪ **T 021·863·1154/1375** ▪ F 021·424·5666*
No update available on this winery; contact details from previous edition.

■ *Britz Vineyards see* Under Oaks
■ *Broken Rock see* Arlington, Riebeek Cellars
■ *Broken Stone see* Slaley
■ *Bryde see* ACJ Fine Wines

Buck's Ridge Wines & Olives

*Tulbagh ▪ Est 2005 ▪ Visits by appt ▪ Self-catering cottages & camping site ▪ Olives & olive products ▪ Walks, mountain biking & other attractions ▪ Owners Brendon & Sue McHugh ▪ Winemaker/viticulturist Brendon McHugh, with Craig Bianco ▪ 10 ha (cab, mourvèdre, petit v, shiraz, viognier) ▪ 2 555 cs (est.) 80% red 20% white ▪ PO Box 222 Tulbagh 6820 ▪ info@bucksridge.co.za ▪ www.bucksridge.co.za ▪ **T 023·230·1160** ▪ F 023·230·0444*

One shed converted, six hectares planted and voila! — the McHughs' working guest farm became a boutique winery. Two years on, Brendon McH has added a Chardonnay-Chenin (untasted) and a Cab to the original Shiraz and Chenin. Next up are rhône blends, as young vines come on stream. Last year, a third of production was sold to visiting corporate guests, who were so impressed after sampling the wines from barrel, they affixed their company labels and presented them as rather special and unique Christmas gifts. A win-win: 'We are credited on the back label.'

Chenin Blanc ☺ ★★★ Nutty, thatchy, stony notes on unpretentious & satisfying **05**. Well-used wood (25% on lees in older oak, 8 mths) adds richness, tannic touch. Dry, nicely balanced.

Cabernet Sauvignon new ★★★ 05 cedar, tobacco aromas, plus lurking black fruit. Modest oaking (14 mths older Fr), modest fruit on palate, finishing dryly tannic. **Shiraz ★★★★** Similarly wooded to Cab, but **05** richer, more forward fruit, nice ripe tannins. 15.3% alc obtrusive, but gratifying toasty, smoky, tasty persistence. WO Coastal. — *TJ*

Buitenverwachting

Constantia ▪ Est 1796 ▪ 1stB 1985 ▪ Tasting & sales Mon-Fri 9-5 Sat 9-1 ▪ Closed pub hols ▪ Tours by appt ▪ Buitenverwachting Restaurant Mon-Sat ▪ T 021·794·3522. Summer only: Café Petite for light lunches (tel as above) & picnic baskets by appt (T 083·257·6083) ▪ Teddy Bear Fair May 1; Valentine's Day Picnic ▪ Conferences ▪ Owners Richard & Sieglinde (Christine) Mueller, Lars Maack ▪ Winemakers Hermann Kirschbaum & Brad Paton (Dec 1992/Dec 2004) ▪ Vineyards Peter Reynolds (Jun 1997), advised by Johan Pienaar ▪ 120 ha (cabs s/f, merlot, pinot, chard, sauvignon, riesling) ▪ *1 300 tons 90 000 cs 18% red 80% white 1% rosé 1% sparkling* ▪ *PO Box 281 Constantia 7848* ▪ *info@buitenverwachting.com* ▪ *www.buiten= verwachting.com* ▪ *T 021·794·5190* ▪ *F 021·794·1351*

This Constantia grande dame is as famous for romance (at its annual Valentine's Day Picnic) and fun (at its Teddy Bear Fair in May) as for its award winning cuisine and wines. The main focus continues to be unquestionable quality, and to this end cellarmaster Hermann Kirschbaum has overseen the installation of additional tanks 'to ensure that all the new sauvignon coming on-line will be vinified separately'. This is in keeping with Buitenverwachting's pursuit of wines from grapes selected from the best blocks. 'We're not re-inventing the wheel but like to make life interesting by experimenting with some wild and wonderful yeasts, various blends...' says HK (assisted by Brad Paton, who studied at Geisenheim), from this cellar often overflowing with young winemakers who keep this mentor-of-many on his toes.

★★★★☆ **Christine** Cape fixture as one of finest classically minded bdx blends, released few yrs later than most, to winelover's benefit. All these **02** reds scarcely marred by poor vintage. Here, usual blend cabs s/f, merlot & dollop malbec offers enticing dusty cedar, spice, blackcurrant & a little fragrance; savoury, elegant palate – gd balance & length. Big but refined, with yrs to mature. Like other reds, 18–24 mths Fr oak – this 100% new.

★★★★ **Merlot** Tobacco-scented fruit to sniff on typically unshowy, elegant **02**, perhaps a touch more austere than usual – but structure, restraint & savoury freshness for fine food companion. 80% new barrels.

★★★★ **Cabernet Sauvignon** Following splendid **01** (★★★★★; a standout yr for Hermann K's reds), rather smart **02** has big tannic structure, but this succulently savoury rather than drying, with fruit concentration sufficiently satisfying.

★★★★ **Sauvignon Blanc** Sample **06** usual scents/flavours dried grass, passionfruit; bright, well balanced acidity; perhaps particularly concentrated, focused & succulent. Gd food wines: dry, moderate ±13% alcs.

★★★★ **Husseys Vlei Sauvignon Blanc 05** 'from some of the more interesting blocks on the farm'. Lightish (12.5% alc), with dried-grass aromas & pungent green core, though soft silky texture supported by crisp acidity & just a little noticeable sugar (3.8g/ℓ).

★★★★ **Chardonnay** Gd example of variety sympathetically vinified (two thirds fermented/11 mths 70% new oak; all through malo). **05** nutty, mealy bouquet; well balanced palate; fresh, sappy, succulent, with lime marmalade length. **04** SAA.

★★★★☆ **Husseys Vlei Chardonnay 05** vyd selection of above. More subtle, refined, less gregarious wine, adding citrus & gingery spice. Quietly forceful & will become more gorgeously so with few yrs. Gd balance. 90% new oak.

★★★★ **Semillon** Last savoured was flavourful, crisp **03**. ±15% wooded, ultra-ripe sauvignon augments richness, complexity. Typically for this cellar, to partner & not overwhelm food. TWS gold.

★★★★ **Rhine Riesling Noble Late Harvest 02** had aromas of honey, pineapple, peach when last tried. Lightly, seductively delicious. Fermented/6 mths oak.

Meifort ★★★★ ✓ Second-best (could be best for many wineries) but serious-minded blend, **02** with 68% cab, rest cab f. Plenty of dark, savoury fruit partnered by firm tannic grip. **Pinot Noir** ★★★ No follow-up yet to earthy, chunkily acidic **01**. **Blanc de Noir** ★★★ Dithering between white & red for lunch, slightly favouring red? This fresh, dry, substantial **06** the perfect solution. Juice 'bled' from top cab (mostly), cab f, merlot. **Buiten Blanc** ★★★★ 50 000 cs of this dependably good, flavourful sauvignon-based blend, with some chenin. **06** flows with floral, fruity, easy appeal, but not overdoing it. WO Coastal. **Gewürztraminer** ★★★ **05** abundant, straightforwardly varietal rosepetal character, pleasant fresh balance, almost dry. Lightly oaked. **Rhine Riesling** ★★★★ Freshly balanced **05** was attractively aromatic, redolent of peach & crisp apple, & lipsmacking; effectively dry, with light 10.8% alc. Ex-tank **06** offers more substance, thrilling acid counterpoint. **Brut MCC** ★★★★ NV bubbly from 66/44 pinot/chard, tasted last ed had attractive spiced apple & brioche character, dryly elegant but ending with sweet-sour hint. **Natural Sweet** ★★★ Last-tasted **02** from riesling offered pineapple, honey, nuts & terpene notes; lightly sweet, lovely to sip. 90g/ℓ sugar; 12% alc; unobtrusively wooded. – *TJ*

■ *BunduStar* see Vin-X-Port

■ *Bushbuck Ridge* see Long Mountain
■ *Bushman's Creek* see Cru Wines

Bushmanspad

Robertson · Est 2000 · 1stB 2006 · Visits (from Oct 2007) Mon-Fri 8-5 Sat/Sun 9-3 · Closed Easter Sun, Dec 25 & Jan 1 · Luxury B&B/self-catering cottages · BYO picnic · Gifts · Walks · 4×4 trail · Mountain biking · Facilities for children · Tour groups · Owner Menno Schaafsma · Winemaker Pieter Ferreira & Irene Waller (Graham Beck, Mar 2006) · Viticulturist Marco Ventrella (Graham Beck, Dec 2005) · 51.5 ha (cabs s/f, malbec, merlot, mourvèdre, shiraz, sauvignon) · 190 tons 1 500 cs own label · Export brand: Bushmanspad Red Gold · PO Box 227 Bonnievale 6730 · info@ bushmanspad.co.za · www.bushmanspad.co.za · T/F 023·616·2961

It's never too late to follow your dream, believes Menno Schaafsma who, at 49, completed a year of practical winemaking at Stellenbosch University. 'The results so far are very promising,' he says, referring to his 'New World wines with Old World finesse' (regrettably not ready for review). Grapes grown high up on the slopes of the Langeberg are vinified at Graham Beck's Robertson winery until a small own-cellar is ready. The first vintage, matured on the property in a refurbished 200-year-old barn, appears under the Red Gold label.

■ *Bush Vines* see Cloof

Buthelezi Wines

Cape Town · Est/1stB 2002 · Closed to public · Owner/winemaker Khulekani Laurence Buthelezi · 800 cs 100% red · PO Box 12481 Mill Street Cape Town 8010 · buthelezi@winery. co.za · T 021·422·5206 · F 021·422·5238

Laurence Buthelezi and mentor Jean-Vincent Ridon (of Signal Hill) have moved into new premises. 23 Church Street, part of the R1-billion Mandela Rhodes Place development, is now home to the Cape's first inner-city winery. Buthelezi's own-label Tutuka Syrah is making international waves (4½ stars in Revue du Vins de France), so the focus remains on export as he feels 'the local market does not believe in the quality of small black empowerment wineries'. Yet...

Tutuka Syrah ★★★ Still introverted mid-2006, but **05** already hinting at complexities to come: prosciutto, blackberries, freshly ground spices. Tannins ripe yet firm, holding flavours captive; shd show better in yr, keep 2-3 more. 2nd fill Fr oak, 18 mths. WO W Cape. — *CR*

BWC Wines

Paarl · Est/1stB 1997 · Tasting by appt · Owners Jeff Jolly, Cathy Marshall, Greg Mitchell & Peter Oxenham · Winemaker Cathy Marshall (1997) · 40 tons · 2 500 cs + 300 cs for Woolworths · 75% red 25% white · PO Box 13404 Mowbray 7705 · info@bwcwines.co.za · www. bwcwines.co.za · T/F 021·788·8390

Property hounds, note! Winemaker Catherine Marshall tips Elgin as 'the new hot and happening place' and wants to be part of developments there. Another reason for setting up in Elgin is the quality of the pinot she's bought in from the area ('fabulous', she enthuses). She's found four small blocks to manage, and eventually would like to own vineyards with a winery which is exclusively hers. In line with the move is a re-branding of BWC to 'Catherine Marshall' — see separate entry for the first Syrah under this new banner.

★★★★ **Pinot Noir** Cathy M deserves wider recognition for her characterful, assured pinots; **05** beguiling black cherry/forest floor perfume; quite dainty (12.5% alc), fresh but rich underlying fruit, balance, length — all hint at charming maturity in a few yrs. Fr barriques, 11 mths, skilfully judged. Elgin/Sbosch vyds.

★★★★ **Syrah** See under 'Catherine Marshall'.

Wholeberry Cabernet Sauvignon ★★★★ Supple-textured **03** with splash merlot (15%); subtly oaked, 2 yrs Fr. A one-off. **Sauvignon Blanc ★★★★** Vigour, ripeness, in friendly jostle on **06**. Bright grassy/figgy aromas; comfortable fruity-rich feel with steely edge; bone dry, clean & lingering. Screwcap closure. WO Sbosch. **Myriad ★★★** Latest **03** not tasted. Part-fermented, brandy-fortified pinot/merlot, hand/footmade. — *AL*

Cabrière Estate

*Franschhoek ▪ Est 1982 ▪ 1stB 1984 ▪ Tasting Mon-Fri 9-5 Sat & pub hols 10-4 ▪ Fee R15 for 3 wines ▪ Formal tasting/tour Mon-Fri 11 & 3 Fee R25 p/p ▪ Private tasting/tour (pre-booked) Fee R30 p/p ▪ Achim vA's tasting/tour Sat 11 Fee R25 p/p ▪ Closed Good Fri, Dec 25 & Jan 1 ▪ Haute Cabrière Cellar Restaurant (see Eat-out section) ▪ Tour groups ▪ Conferencing for groups of max 60 ▪ Owner Clos Cabrière Ltd ▪ Cellarmaster Achim von Arnim (1984), with Takuan von Arnim (2005) ▪ Viticulturist Sakkie Lourens (May 2002) ▪ 30 ha (pinot, chardonnay) ▪ 500 000ℓ 40% red 60% white ▪ PO Box 245 Franschhoek 7690 ▪ cabriere@iafrica.com or cabrierepr@iafrica.com ▪ www.cabriere.co.za ▪ **T** 021·876·8500 ▪ F 021·876·8501*

Achim von Arnim shows no signs of waning enthusiasm for crafting his popular bubblies, despite the acclaim garnered by his book of poems and paintings, *Naked*. The title verse – 'Naked/is/nothing more/nothing less/but a fearless/expression/of self' – applies equally well to his winegrowing philosophy, while his Ode to Pinot Noir reveals his passion for the grape. Haute Cabrière was named SA's best winery restaurant last year by the Great Wine Capitals Global Network. Von A's Saturday Tours, complete with flamboyant 'sabrage' demonstrations, are so popular they're reserved for 'customers only' in groups smaller than eight (book in advance).

Haute Cabrière range

★★★★ **Pinot Noir** Densely planted (10 000 vines/ha) Burgundian clones, gently handled in cellar. Vintage-boosted **04** (★★★★★) one of their finest: gorgeous bright cherry/strawberry fruits & flawless tannin/acid integration; ripe, so fewer herby/earthy qualities; satiny texture due, in part, to 14% alc. Gd prospects. Characterful **03** (★★★) had less fruit & substance; **02** was generous, with juicy flavours. ±10 mths Fr oak, 35% new.

Chardonnay-Pinot Noir ★★★☆ Versatile dining companion. **06** blushes delicately, shows 55% chard component in tropical fruits & citrus; pinot adds hint of smoked ham; barely sweet lift on finish (6g/ℓ). **Arnim Sauvignon Rouge** ★★★ Light, upbeat summer refresher from cab & sauvignon (blanc). Melange asparagus & cassis with supple tannins. Serve chilled, soon. **NV**. WO W Cape.

Pierre Jourdan range

★★★★☆ **Cuvée Reserve** Sumptuous cap classique from chard & pinot (60/40), estate fruit only; vinified from first fraction (500ℓ) of press juice, 5+ yrs on lees (disgorged on demand). Latest has enticing mousse tinged with pear, prosciutto & honey, & just a suggestion of fruit-sweetness (though still decidedly 'brut' at only 4.5g/ℓ RS). Will reward those with patience.

★★★★ **Cuvée Belle Rose** SA's first rose (not 'rosé', insists AvA) MCC, from pinot. Enchanting 'partridge eye' hue lit by tendrils of energetic bubbles, mood-enhancing sugared berry & boiled sweet tones. Drink soon to get the best expression of its lovely fruit, toned by 6g/ℓ sugar.

★★★★★ **Blanc de Blancs** From estate's top chard vyds; 40% of base wine wooded 6 mths in Fr (Argonne) barrels. Latest is sublime now but shd gain honeyed complexity with cellaring ±5 yrs. Pale, delicate & poised, with signature 'wet pebble' minerality, nuance of vanilla. Finishes Granny-Smith-apple crisp & dry (3.4g/ℓ sugar).

★★★★ **Brut Sauvage** The 'savageness' lies in the residual sugar – zero – which yields an absolutely & uncompromisingly dry MCC shot through with minerals & 'ocean spray'. Very unforgiving but very sexy. 60/40 chard/pinot, 36 mths on lees. Pause only to chill before drinking.

These named for estate's French Huguenot founder, mostly traditionally made cap classiques; bunch-pressed, unoaked, alc ±12%. **NV** unless stated. **Brut** ★★★★ ✓ Estate's best selling sparkling; same blend as 'Sauvage' but less time on lees. Antique satin hue, racy mousse, shy apple & lemon bouquet; satisfying breadth, length & dryness thanks to brut 4.5g/ℓ RS. Enjoyable now but shd improve ±3 yrs. 375ml, 750ml & 1.5ℓ. **Tranquille** ★★★ This, wine below, the non-sparklers in range. From the *première taille* juice (from near end of pressing time), blend pinot/chard 55/45. Lunchtime light 11.5% alc, delightful strawberry whiffs, sufficient grip from fruit tannins to complement food. **Ratafia** ★★★★ Jerepiko-style aperitif from chard, fortified with estate's (chard) potstill brandy. Latest has welcoming peaches & cream aroma, characteristic mead-like touches;

decidedly sweet & spirituous farewell in the tradition of the Champagne region of France (115g/ℓ RS, 20% alc). — *CvZ*

Calitzdorp Cellar

Calitzdorp (see Little Karoo map) ▪ *Est 1928* ▪ *1stB 1977* ▪ *Tasting & sales Mon-Fri 8-1; 2-5 Sat 8-12* ▪ *Closed Easter Fri & Dec 25* ▪ *Tours by appt* ▪ *Tour groups* ▪ *BYO picnic* ▪ *Farm produce* ▪ *Owners 60 members* ▪ *Winemaker Alwyn Burger (Nov 1990)* ▪ *Viti consultant Johannes Mallet* ▪ *160 ha (13 varieties, r/w)* ▪ *3 000 cs 60% red 30% white* ▪ *PO Box 193 Calitzdorp 6660* ▪ *calitzwynk@telkomsa.net* ▪ **T** *044·213·3301* ▪ **F** *044·213·3328*

Four Champions (plus one Reserve) and Best Little Karoo Cellar awards at the Young Wine Show is evidence that the promised shift from quantity to quality is bearing fruit. With more wine now maturing in oak, and team member Abraham Pretorius travelling to Burgundy to fine-tune his winemaking skills as part of an exchange programme, the cellar seems destined to produce even more standouts.

Cabernet Sauvignon ★★★ Returns to lineup after several yrs absence; **05** attractive, with variety's slightly firmer tannins well cushioned by ripe mulberry & black choc fruit. **Merlot** ★★ Softer styled **05** has honest flavours of cassis & dry food-friendly tannins. **Shiraz** ★★★ **05** sound everyday quaffer with smoky aromas, ripe fruity flavours & nice dry finish. These reds 10-14 mths Fr/Am oak. **Touriga Nacional** ★★★ Well made **05**, rounded soft red fruit, slight earthy note, drinkable & satisfying. **Blanc de Noir** ★ Orange-tinted **05** from shiraz; pleasant, sweet, with hint of balancing tannin. Needs drinking. **Chardonnay** ★★★ Local young wine show champ **05**, gentle & unassuming citrus flavours, slight butteriness & hint of oak. **Sauvignon Blanc** ★ Sweetish & soft **06**, pleasant without showing varietal character. **Late Harvest** new ★★ NV appeals with lovely sunripe grape flavour, balanced sweetness & crisp finish. **Golden Jerepigo** ★★ Syrupy, raisined **NV** from hanepoot & muscadel; not retasted. **White Muscadel** ★★★ **05** amiable, rich & sweet, with enough freshness to balance. Serve on crushed ice in summer. **Hanepoot** ★★★★ **04** still available; last ed offered fresh raisins & honeysuckle, lemony acidity ensuring freshness & uncloying pleasure. **Cape Vintage** ★★★★ √ Improved **05** port-style fortified from tinta offers typical Cdorp plum pudding richness, touch of raisin; lovely balance of flavour, grip & freshness. Shd improve/hold gd few yrs. **Cape Ruby** ★★★ Equal tinta & touriga in delicious new **NV** bottling; richer, fuller than classic Ruby style, well wooded/fortified (yr seasoned Fr) for spice, grip. — *JN*

Camberley Wines

Stellenbosch ▪ *Est 1990* ▪ *1stB 1996* ▪ *Tasting & sales Mon-Sat & pub hols 9-5 Sun preferably by appt* ▪ *Fee R10* ▪ *Closed Dec 25 & Jan 1* ▪ *Tours by appt* ▪ *B&B guest cottage* ▪ *Owners John & Gaël Nel* ▪ *Winemaker John Nel* ▪ *7 ha (cabs s/f, merlot, petit v, touriga, shiraz)* ▪ *±35 tons 2 500 cs 100% red* ▪ *PO Box 6120 Uniedal 7612* ▪ *john@camberley.co.za* ▪ *www.camberley. co.za* ▪ **T/F** *021·885·1176/082·808·0176*

Adding an olive oil to what owner/winemaker John Nel offers (the olives from a friend's farm, pressed at nearby Tokara) didn't do enough to satisfy visitors, so he's taken another step — a sparkling red made from shiraz. 'Not as good as (Aussie benchmark) Seppelt,' he deadpans, 'but I can live with that.' Port's always been on the Camberley agenda, but as John N's vines aren't yet in production, he had a dummy run with bought-in shiraz. It wasn't that easy: 'We wanted to make only 1 500ℓ but by the time I eventually got the maths right with the addition of spirits, we ended up with a small distillery of 4000ℓ!'

★★★★ **Cabernet Sauvignon-Merlot** Offers that elusive quality in fine wines, immediate access yet ageing ability, **04** has an array of attractions: plums & cassis seamed with mint, cedar; plenty of pep & juiciness. 14 mths Fr, half new. 72/28 blend; also 500ml.

★★★★★ **Shiraz** Succulent, full-ripe **04** has the peppery, mulberry, salty/savoury notes good shiraz brings, within a smoothly curvaceous body. Richness & oaking — 14 mths Fr/Am, 70/30, all new — tames the 15.5% alc. Framework for long, gentle development.

★★★★★ **Philosopher's Stone** Changing base metals into gold – or at least grapes into powerful, impressive wine! **04**, 3rd release of this bdx blend, is opulent, unabashedly New World: intense cassis, mint-laden choc, vanilla spicing; well crafted wooding fully absorbed (14 mths 2nd fill, mainly Fr). Cabs s & f, merlot (61/23/16); 15% alc.

★★★★ **Merlot** No **03**. Last tasted **02**, well built, soft & mellow, with supple grip from seasoned oak (14 mths).

★★★★ **Charisma** Unusual teaming of cab f with shiraz, merlot (65/20/15); bears cellar's trademark fruit intensity, ripe tannins. Terrific **03** last ed was smoke-infused, with creamy cassis/cherry flavouring. Robust oaking (14 mths Fr, 50% new) gave 5+ yrs cellar-worthiness.

★★★★☆ **Pinotage** House's ripeness, richness also in **05** (★★★★), but in hot vintage loses some mid-palate definition, concentration. Still drinks nicely: harmonious tannins, dark plum & dried herb tones. 13 mths Fr, half new. Soupçons merlot, shiraz. Invisible big alc a feature of the wine: 15.4% here, heady 16% for **04** VDG. Ready young, shd age well over 6-7 yrs. Also 500ml.

Cabernet Franc-Merlot ★★★☆ Last available was maiden **02**, cedar-dusted 80/20 blend, with lithe, supple tannins. Could age 4+ yrs. 14 mths mainly Fr oak, 25% new. 14.9% alc. – *CR*

Cameradi Wines

Wellington • Est 1998 • 1stB 2000 • Closed to public • Owners Stelvest cc (Pieter Laubscher, Niel Smith, Nic Swingler, Hendrik du Preez & Casper Lategan) • Winemaker Casper Lategan (Jan 1999) • 8 tons 600 cs 100% red • 48 Bain Str, Wellington 7655 • sonellel@telkomsa.net • **T 021·873·1225/082·323·4244** *• F 021·873·4910*

When after-hours winemaker Casper Lategan wasn't up to his knees in the latest construction project, he was trying his hand at the new cab-shiraz blend below, 'hopefully' available from the beginning of this year. The job for the remaining four comrades, spread across two continents, is to consume and distribute.

★★★★ **Cabernet Sauvignon-Shiraz** new Beefy **04** from Sbosch fruit ups the ante for this winery. Full-bodied with a confident tannic handshake; balanced, vibrant, clean finish. Intense wet earth, clove & mulberry characters marry well with spicy vanilla from 50% new oak, mainly Fr.

No successors to following provisionally rated vintages: **Cabernet Sauvignon** ★★★ **03** with strapping tannins dominating pungent greenpepper/mulberry fruit. **Shiraz** ★★★ **03** impenetrably dark & deep; hints black pepper, lily & vanilla, tarry oak finish. – *CvZ*

Capaia Wines

Philadelphia (see Durbanville/Philadelphia map) • Est 1997 • 1stB 2003 • Visits by appt • Owners Alexander & Ingrid von Essen • Winemakers Stephan von Neipperg & Mark van Buuren • Viticulturist Mattie Bothma (Jan 2004) • 59 ha (cabs s/f, merlot, petit v, shiraz, sauvignon) • 120 tons ±8 300 cs 83% red 17% white • PO Box 25 Philadelphia 7304 • info@capaia.co.za • www.capaia.co.za • **T 021·972·1081** *• F 021·972·1894*

This must-see winery, having impressed with its reds, is placing new bets on sauvignon: never shy to seek top-flight advice, (St-Emilion château owner Stephan von Neipperg still consults) the team has welcomed the expertise of Styrian oeno-star Manfred Tement. Slow ripening in 2006 demanded patience, but the rewards are showing and winemaker Mark van Buuren is keen to follow development. Further 'aforestation' of the cellar saw the number of wooden fermentation tanks grow to 54, creating the second biggest installation in the world. The future? A small crop of shiraz is due this year (expectations are already high); a sorting table to improve quality; and possible olive production.

★★★★☆ **Capaia** Deep-fruited, darkly handsome & suave. Third in a line that promises to be illustrious, **05** inky, with cool minerality; elegant berry fruits in weft of super-fine tannins. Deceptively – dangerously – delicious in youth. 55% merlot with cab & dollop petit v. 15 mths new Fr oak.

Blue Grove Hill range

Blue Grove Hill ★★★★ Now in more serious style, **05** offers meaty red fruits, lush accessible tannins. Two-thirds merlot, rest cabs s & f. 8 mths 2nd fill Fr oak. Fine, deep flavoured **04** (★★★★). **Sauvignon Blanc** ★★★★ **06** oak (portion, 2 mths) jostles with ripe tropical fruits, mineral send-off. — *DS*

■ *Cape 1652 see* Origin Wine

Cape Bay

Well established, nautical-themed range of easy-drinkers by Newton Johnson. Ready on release, and well priced.

Admiralty House range

Export only; neither retasted for this ed. **Cabernet Sauvignon-Shiraz** ★★★★ Elegant **04** spicy red fruit, lavender & pepper scents, choc-mocha flavours; integrated; added interest from ±yr Fr oak. **Sauvignon Blanc** ★★★ Restrained 'European' feel to mineral **05**, mainly Wrcstr fruit given extra zing by 35% ex-cooler Hemel-&-Aarde Vlly & Firgrove.

Cape Bay range

Cabernet Sauvignon-Merlot ☺ ★★★ **06** incl dashes petit v & shiraz. Rather nice: opens in glass to dark fruits & tealeaf; balanced, satisfying weight & length; slips down cheerfully. Sample tasted, as for… **Mellow Red** ☺ ★★★ Berried quick-quaffing quartet of pinotage, cab f, shiraz & cab. **06** dusty nose, refreshing acidity; ideal with steak or solo, even slightly chilled. **Pinotage** ☺ ★★★ Lovely carmine coat for **06**, mulberry, strawberry & hint banana; softly fruity middle & friendly tannic hug. **Chardonnay** ☺ ★★★ Tangerine & lemon bouquet on previewed **06**, attractive nutty/citrus flavours with slight alc glow. **Bouquet Blanc** ☺ ★★★ New blend in **06** for genteel off-dry white; colombard (65%), with muscadel & chard replacing gewürz. Dusty floral & guava scents, softly sweet flavours.

Chenin Blanc ★★ **06** quaffable slimmer's friend with low 1.5g/ℓ sugar & chenin's feel-good acidity. Appealing thatch & floral notes, tangy finish. **Sauvignon Blanc** ★★ Refreshing anytime dry white with moderate alc; **06** muted aromas & flavours, hints of grass & gentle acidity. All Cape Bays unwooded; both ranges WO W Cape. — *CvZ*

■ *Cape Boar see* Doolhof Estate

Cape Chamonix Wine Farm

Franschhoek ▪ Est 1991 ▪ 1stB 1992 ▪ Tasting & sales daily 9.30-4 ▪ Fee R15 ▪ The Chamonix Restaurant (see Eat-out section) ▪ Fully equipped self-catering cottages ▪ Facilities for children ▪ Tours by appt ▪ Gifts ▪ Tour groups by appt ▪ Farm-distilled schnapps & spring water ▪ Owners Chris & Sonja Hellinger ▪ Winemaker Gottfried Mocke (Sep 2001) ▪ Viticulturist Rodney Kitching, with Gottfried Mocke ▪ 50 ha (cabs s/f, merlot, pinot, pinotage, chard, chenin, sauvignon) ▪ 200 tons 17 000 cs 60% red 36% white 4% MCC ▪ PO Box 28 Franschhoek 7690 ▪ marketing@chamonix.co.za or office@chamonix.co.za ▪ www.chamonix.co.za ▪ T 021·876·2494 ▪ F 021·876·3237

Winemaker Gottfried Mocke seems to have been juggling a lot of changes over the past year, including a conversion to totally organic soil management and a complete revamp of labels aimed at better representing the classically European style of this Franschhoek farm. Mocke hopes that when the organic venture is completed, the wines will better reflect their terroir. But, he assures, they will still follow their quest to create wines that are 'traditional and individual in style'.

★★★★ **Troika** Serious-minded blend cabs s/f, merlot. Vinous, dryly tannic **03** (★★★★, but TWS trophy) followed by richer, smoother **04**, with elegant, even slightly austere tannic force structuring juicily sweet red fruit. Balanced, with 2 yrs new Fr oak; shd develop more harmony in bottle. Like Pinot, partly native ferment, in open-topped wood.

★★★★ Pinot Noir Fine **05** (★★★★★) confirms & continues pvs vintage's advance, with more intensity (& a trifle less elegance?) than **04**, also with forest floor, earth, red berries. Still reticent mid-2006, but redolent of lovely fruit, with muscular tannins & clean, bright acidity. 80% new oak. Deserves few yrs bottle slumber.

★★★★★ Chardonnay Reserve Elegantly forceful flagship, in classic mode, long internationally applauded. Youthful **04** more understated than pvs, should still blossom (benefits from decanting mid-2006). Silky, with pure & lingering varietal aromas/flavours, lightly limy plus mineral streak, gd natural acid; enriched by subtle oaking: fermented (half native yeast)/14 mths new Allier.

★★★★ Chardonnay An enviable 2nd label. **04** (★★★★) slightly lesser, lighter, shorter than focused **03**, but still refined, satisfying; only gently oaky from ferment/yr in new wood, with pleasant citrus tone. Native yeasts.

★★★★★ Sauvignon Blanc Reserve ✓ Subtle, steely sauvignon, fermented/11 mths in mostly older oak — for structure rather than flavour. **05** has earth, passionfruit, citrus notes along with non-pungent greenness. Vibrant & fresh, lovely mouthfeel, persistent flavours, for partnering rather than dominating food.

★★★★ MCC Blanc de Blancs Chardonnay bubbly, 11 mths big older oak, 3 yrs on fine lees. **03** follows establish pattern of undemonstrative elegance; subtle yeast, apple-pie character; fine mousse & texture, notably dry green-apple finish.

★★★★ MCC Reserve Occasional special release, degorged after 5 yrs lees-ageing. Last was expressive **00**, with brioche, baked apple notes, creamy refined richness & dry elegance.

Rouge ☺ **★★★** Last was **NV**, latest is vintaged **04** — another smartly structured though juicily red-berried blend cab, merlot, pinotage; lightly wooded. **Rosé** ☺ **★★★** **06** blends pinot, merlot, cab, chard chenin, for fresh, fruity, not-quite-dry easy-drinker, with a little earthiness adding interest; lightly tannic, small oak influence.

Cabernet Sauvignon ★★★★ Serious but flavourful, neatly compact **04**, with pleasing savoury fruit & clean dry finish; well structured; unobtrusively supportive oaking (22 mths). Has 10% merlot. **Pinotage ★★★** **04** usual good varietal character, fruitily scented, with light & bright flavours & firm tannic grip. Moderately, effectively oaked. **Sauvignon Blanc ★★★★** Last tasted was generously flavoured **05** sample promising ripe tropicality, good crisp lemony finish. **Blanc ★★★★** ✓ 53% lightly wooded chard adds depth to well-balanced, food-friendly & very drinkable **06**, but sauvignon's (31%) green grassiness dominates; plus semillon. — *TJ*

■ *Cape Circle* see Vin-X-Port & Rooiberg

Cape Classics

Somerset West ▪ Est 1991 ▪ 1stB 1995 ▪ Closed to public ▪ Owners Gary & André Shearer ▪ Winemaker Mzokhona Mvemve (Jan 2002) ▪ 83 000 cs own label 45% red 55% white ▪ PO Box 3273 Matieland Stellenbosch 7602 ▪ info@capeclassics.com ▪ www.capeclassics.com ▪ T 021·847·2400 ▪ F 021·847·2414

Following on the ongoing success of the Indaba range in the US, where the brand is supported by the likes of Disney World and Whole Foods, the Cape Classics team had yet another reason to raise their glasses: this time to a launch in the local market. Having led the way into the US, they are again focusing on hitherto untapped but potentially voluminous markets, like the trend-setting Soweto community, not only host to a burgeoning Wine Festival but also now boasting their first wine emporium.

Indaba range

Pinotage ★★★ Part barrel maturation imparts pleasant dry tannic grip to rein in abundant warm, dark mulberry fruit. Robust (14.5% alc), with hint of liquorice on farewell. Needs food. All below tasted as samples last yr, now bottled; all **05**, as is above. **Shiraz ★★★** ✓ Abundant roast beef, cracked pepper & some spicy red fruit. Smoky/charry notes from wooding (Fr/Am) persist, though less obtrusively, components now more in balance. Ripe vintage well managed (13.5 alc), with long finish. **Merlot** ★★★ Crowd pleasing, ripe & juicy, now more blueberries on taste with subtle vanilla overlay (3 mths Fr/Am oak), silky tannins in this friendly solo glassful. **Chardonnay** ★★★ Has developed into softer, rounded, earlier drinking style (only 6% barrel fermented); ripe melon & pear flavours lifted on finish by sweet/sour citrus suggestion. **Chenin Blanc** ★★★ ✓ Ripe Golden Delicious apple & tangy quince with thread of nutty almond throughout. Core of acidity elevates fruit & livens mid-palate. Balanced, midweight, bottled version improves on sample's 'journeyman' status. **Sauvignon Blanc** ★★★ Yr on, shows more fresh citrus, grapefruit & kumquat notes. Mid-palate vibrant with zesty acidity & clean-cut flavours that linger. Lighter-food-styled wine with some richness ex-lees ageing. 12% alc. All WO W Cape. — *MW*

Cape Coastal Vintners ♀

*Paarl ▪ Est/1stB 2004 ▪ Sales Mon-Sat 9-5 Sun 11-3 from Matuba Wine Shoppe at Pontac Manor, Paarl ▪ Owners: see intro ▪ Winemaker Koos Jordaan, with Johan Pietersen (Feb/Jun 2005) ▪ 65 000 tons 300 000 cs 45% red 55% white ▪ Export brands: Matuba, Kleinbosch & Jabulani ▪ ISO, HACCP, BRC certified ▪ PO Box 6141 Paarl 7620 ▪ office@ccvintners.com ▪ www.matuba.co.za ▪ **T 021·860·8840** ▪ F 021·872·9262*

Owned by management group Strategy Partners, a black empowerment company, and five wine producers — Boland, Bovlei, Wamakersvallei, Wellington and Riebeek Cellars — Cape Coastal Vintners has stepped up its campaign in the US market. It's bought a 50% stake in sales and marketing venture SA Premium Wines, and opened an office in Florida headed by Norman Cilliers. At home in Paarl, it's unveiled the Matuba Wine Shoppe on the premises of Pontac Manor Hotel & Restaurant where selected wines can now be tasted.

Matuba Vineyard Specific range
Shiraz-Viognier ★★★ Distinct varietal characters light up **05**: white pepper, lilies & red fruits from shiraz; peach & floral nuances from 6% viognier. Needs bit of time to knit fully & settle slight astringency on finish. Fr oak, 16 mths. Sample tasted, as for next wine. **Chardonnay-Viognier** new ★★★★ Appealing notes of citrus, white stonefruit & florals on **05**, separately fermented/7 mths matured then blended. Oak seamlessly integrated with ripe fruit, though alc (14.6%) just a little hard work. Both in unusual square-sided 'Johnny Walker' bottle; WO Coastal. **Sauvignon Blanc 06** tasting sample not ready at press time. Discontinued: **Chardonnay**.

Matuba Premium Select range
Cabernet Sauvignon ★★ **03** savoury styling; last ed whispered dried leaf & damp earth, dry leathery tannins. Briefly oaked. **04** unready. **Shiraz** ★★★ **04** showed restrained fruit (despite big 14% alc) when last tasted, roast beef whiffs, enough tannin to go 2+ yrs. 25% unwooded. **Chardonnay** ★★ Soft, slightly sweet, accommodating **04** last had moderate melon flavours. **Chenin Blanc** ★★★ Raises the bar with ripe-style **05**, without pvs's dollop chard; thatch & spice aromas, well meshed vinous palate with tangy finish. 50% wood fermented/5 mths; screwcapped. **Sauvignon Blanc** ★★★ Ante-upping **06** (sample) similar soft wet hay/fynbos bouquet & food-styled crispness as pvs, but better balance, with persistent mineral finish. Coastal/W Cape WOs.

Kleinbosch range
Merlot ★★ Plummy fruit on quick-quaffer **04** is in sufficient concentration to stand up to unsubtle oaking, suggestion of greenness on finish. 20% staved. **Pinotage** ★★ **04**, tasted last ed, green banana & wild berry hints, quite lean & short, very dry. **Shiraz** ★★ **04** has intense herby red-fruit bouquet, modest fruiting, similar woody 'green stick' character as the Merlot. **Pretty Pink** new ★★ Low-alc Natural Sweet rosé from pinotage & colombard serves up flavours of crushed strawberry dusted with castor sugar, manageably sweet, not syrupy. **NV**. **Chardonnay** ★★ Sample unoaked **05** short on aroma, flavour & finesse; slight whiffs of orange zest & nuts. **Chenin Blanc** new ★★ **06** light (11.8% alc), semi-dry aperitif with papaya flavours & gentle musky farewell. **Sauvignon Blanc** ★★★ Preview **06** a quaffer with some substance, panache. Tropical flavours & perky acidity, all nicely toned & balanced. All WO W Cape. Discontinued: **Cabernet Sauvignon, Cabernet Sauvignon-Shiraz**.

Jabulani range

Range moves here from pvs listing under SA Premium Wines. **Shiraz ★★ 04** fruity, light textured & versatile enough for fireside sipping or lightly chilling in summer. 20% oak staved, same for…
Merlot-Cabernet Sauvignon ★★ Berry aromas & charry oak flavours on **05**, insubstantial despite 14% alc. **Chardonnay ★★** Unoaked **05** modest & unforthcoming, some floral/citrus hints & warmth from 14% alc. All screwcapped, WO Coastal. — *CvZ*

■ *Cape Concert* see Daschbosch

Cape First Wines
Ⓨ

Stellenbosch ▪ Est 2003 ▪ 1stB 2004 ▪ Visits by appt at Blue Creek (see entry) ▪ Owners Cape Five Fruit Export & Christo Versfeld ▪ Winemaker Christo Versfeld (2004) ▪ 70 000 cs own label ▪ 40% red 60% white ▪ PO Box 3294 Somerset West 7129 ▪ marcschonland@capefive.com ▪ www.capefirstwines.co.za ▪ T 021·880·2541 ▪ F 021·880·2547

Now heading up this specialist wine company is MD Marc Schonland, a South African who's been abroad for a decade, managing purchasing and procurement for Starbucks. A new challenge, this, for an experienced palate! The company's product portfolio and export markets have grown: Makana is now a four-tier range, selling into Russia as well as the UK; co-owner/winemaker Christo Versfeld has launched his eponymous bordeaux-style blend; and Hill Station and new Hill Station Reserve have been well accepted in Germany, among other countries.

Christo Versveld Bordeaux Blend `new` **★★★★** Attractive berry spread with sweet cedar notes in **04**; palate has similar character, but tannins still strong presence, with firm dry finish, not yet pliable. Shd integrate with time, the fruit foundation is there. Sbosch fruit; 19 mths Fr barrels, half new. Calyon Top Ten 2006.

Makana Reserve range

new

Cabernet Sauvignon ★★★ 05 Meaty notes, deep dark fruit, smoky spice & cellar's trademark firm tannin, not fully integrated. Cld do with another yr, will go 3+ more. ± 10 mths on staves, as all red Rsvs. **Pinotage ★★★** Herb garden & rhubarb, some white pepper in **05**; structure still tightly held, needing another yr to relax, meld. Varietal juiciness is already in place. **Shiraz ★★★** Full-ripe plummy fruit, some spiced biltong notes, but **05** becomes fresher, lighter textured on the palate, with verve, juiciness. A quaffer for cool days or around the campfire. **Merlot ★★★** A forceful personality, **05** is a vanilla, toast & red berry melange, for those who like to meet the oak. Accessible now, but another yr will soften more edges. **Chardonnay ★★** Fresh citric styling in **06**, with gentle fruit on palate. Uncomplicated, for earlier drinking. **Sauvignon Blanc ★★★** Pear-rich summer fruit salad, nice rounded mouthfeel in **06**, but a quiet fellow, a bit introverted mid-2006, might show more with time. **Chenin Blanc ★★★** A quaffer with gd food styling, **06** has apple, pear-drop freshness throughout, some minerality on the finish. Modest alc (12.6%) will please diners. All in range W Cape WOs.

Makana Boutique range

Pinot Noir ★★★ Tasted pvs ed, **04** had cherry, sherbet & subtle spice; earthy notes & mineral finish. Fruit concentration easily soaks up 14.5% alc. 11 mths Fr oak, 25% new. WO W Cape, rest of range Coastal. **Cabernet Sauvignon-Merlot-Cabernet Franc ★★★** Last tasted as sample **04**, ripe berry compôte & spice on 50/30/20 blend; mouth-puckering tannins & acidity needed some time to settle; big finish (15% alc). Went on to receive cellar's 2nd 2006 Calyon award. **Chardonnay** Big quality jump from **04** (★★★ but MIWA DG, *Wine* ★★★★) to bold & delicious **05** (★★★★), with powerful peach & lime perfume, 'shortbread biscuit' oak influence, long tangy finish. Fermented/11 mths mainly Fr oak, 60% new. **Sauvignon Blanc ★★★ 06** (sample) nice gooseberry, Bosch pear entry, really invigorating acidity, with nettly whiffs to accompany that freshness.

Hill Station Reserve range

new

Cabernet Sauvignon ★★★ 05 molten dark fruit still held captive by tannins; would be better integrated in yr, hold for 3 more. 10 mths on staves. **Sauvignon Blanc ★★★ 06** has a pear-drop, gooseberry fruit profile, crisp finish. An easy, just-dry uncomplicated summer quaffer. Both W Cape, ditto next range.

Hill Station range
Cabernet Sauvignon-Merlot new ★★★ A lot of richness, ripeness in **05**, plums, mulberries & plenty of vanilla spicing. Harmonious oaking; a restrained elegance despite fruit power. **Chenin Blanc-Chardonnay** ★★★ **06** has softly rounded drinkability, melon, gentle peach; quite light, goes down easily. 85/15 blend. Discontinued: **Shiraz-Pinotage** & **Three Anchor Bay** range. — *CR*

Cape Grace Wines

Stellenbosch • Est/1stB 2004 • Closed to public • Owners Thierry's Wine Services & Afrifresh • Winemaker Carno du Toit • 200 000 cs for export only, incl Waitrose, Asda, Sainsbury's, Tesco, Somerfield & Thresher • 40% red 40% white 20% rosé • PO Box 1376 Stellenbosch 7599 • info@capegracewine.co.za • www.capegracewine.co.za • T/F 021·855·5639

A joint venture between UK importer Thierry's Wine Services and Vineyard 41 (a division of Afrifresh, the fruit exporter), the Cape Grace range has swiftly spirited itself into a slew of UK grocery chains, the Pinotage Rosé attracting particular attention. Their recently launched Diversity label is also gaining momentum there (it's currently sold through the Thresher chain). On the ground here, portfolio manager Lucy Warner has established a Grower's Club. The stakeholders are staunch supporters of The Pebbles Project, for children affected by foetal alcohol syndrome.

Cabernet Franc ★★★★ **02** notes of black plum & dried leaves; firmish, concentrated; lead pencil whiffs from 16 mths in 2nd/3rd fill barrels. Sbosch grapes. **Pinotage-Shiraz** ★★★ Preview **05** consistent with style of pvs: ripe rasp/blackberry notes, sweet fruit, comfortable furry tannins. Oak influenced. Neither above retasted. **Pinotage Rosé** ★★★ Ideal sundowner, with delicate potpourri aroma & strawberry flavour; **06** tad soft, sweet, but comfortable, won't offend. **Merlot** ★★★ Pleasant enough but less complete than pvs; **05** tidy mulberry fruit, whiff mint; acid wellpitched but touch too much of 14.5% alc showing. Portion seasoned Fr oak. **Chardonnay-Semillon** ★★★ Again equal blend in **05**, lightish but vibrant flavour/feel, with hint of guava. Following not retasted. **Chardonnay** ★★★ Easy drinker, should appeal widely. 10% new-oak-fermented shows subtly as hazelnut/butterscotch tint to **04**'s pear flavours. **Sauvignon Blanc-Chenin Blanc** ★★★ 50/50 light-bodied blend, **05** forthcoming, firmly dry & refreshing. **Cabernet Sauvignon-Merlot** discontinued.

Diversity range new
Red ★★★ **05** bdx-rhône partnership of mainly cab, petit v, merlot, shiraz, dash viognier, bit fractious mid-2006, needs time to settle, cooperate; but shows potential. **White** ★★★★ Delicious, well-composed medley of varieties, textures & flavours; **05** zesty sauvignon, creamy chard (portion barrel vinified, tropical chenin & delightful peachy touch from viognier). Both ranges W Cape & Coastal WOs. — *CT*

■ *Cape Haven* see Pulpit Rock
■ *Cape Heights* see False Bay Vineyards

Cape Hutton

Stellenbosch • Est 2003 • 1stB 2004 • Visits by appt • Owners/viticulturists Gerrit & Lesley Wyma • Winemaker Piet Smal (Blue Creek), with owners • 4 ha (cab, merlot) • 19 tons 1 000 cs 93% red 7% rosé • PO Box 2200 Somerset West 7130 • info@capehutton.com or lesley@capehutton.com • www.capehutton.com • T 021·880·0527/082·322·8489 • F 021·880·0666

Last year the Wymas harvested their first merlot and, after maturation, expect to bottle around 2 000 litres. They also made a Merlot Rosé, packaged in consumer-friendly 500ml bottles. Piet Smal, dentist and after-hours winemaker from neighbouring Blue Creek, consulted in the cellar again.

Cabernet Sauvignon ★★★ **04** elegant blackcurrant, lead pencil aromas last ed suggested classically styled if slightly austere red. More spice, tea-leaf & cedar character than fruit, restrained finish. 14 mths Fr oak. — *MF*

■ *Capell's Court* see Linton Park

Cape Legends

Stellenbosch ▪ Closed to public ▪ Owner Distell ▪ PO Box 184 Stellenbosch 7599 ▪ ekrige@ capelegends.co.za ▪ www.capelegends.co.za ▪ T 021·809·8330 ▪ F 021·882·9575

Stand-alone marketing and sales organisation within the Distell group representing a portfolio of well-regarded brands including Alto, Allesverloren, Flat Roof Manor, Hill & Dale, Ixia, Jacobsdal, Le Bonheur, Lomond, Neethlingshof, Plaisir de Merle, Stellenzicht, Theuniskraal, Tukulu and Uitkyk, all listed separately.

■ *Cape Maclear see* African Pride
■ *Cape Maidens see* Bonnievale Wine Cellar, Juno
■ *Cape Mist see* Thorntree & Overhex
■ *Cape Nature Organic see* Origin Wine

Capenheimer

SA's original perlé wine, launched 1962. By Distell. Always gently petillant, delicate. **NV** ★★ Latest 50/50 chenin/colombard mix, with fresh-cut pear & pink musk sweet aromas. – *CvZ*

■ *Cape Original see* Origin Wine

Cape Point Vineyards   ♂♀

Cape Point ▪ Est 1996 ▪ 1stB 2000 ▪ Visits by appt ▪ Owner Sybrand van der Spuy ▪ Winemaker Duncan Savage (Dec 2002), with viticultural adviser Kevin Watt ▪ 31 ha (cab, shiraz, chard, sauvignon, semillon) ▪ 140 tons 7 000 cs own label 1 500 cs for Woolworths ▪ 20% red 80% white ▪ PO Box 100 Noordhoek 7985 ▪ info@cape-point.com ▪ www.capepointvineyards.co. za ▪ T 021·785·7660 ▪ F 021·785·7662

Duncan Savage rates 2006 a great season, in spite of greedy winds which reduced his sauvignon crop by half. What lacked in tonnage showed in concentration and a promise of longevity, he reckons, also discerning in his wines the positive effects of the advancing maturity of the vineyards. Convinced of the ultimate match for whites of the cool, south-facing Noordhoek site, he has grubbed up the remaining pinot in order to go 100% sauvignon, semillon and chardonnay. Cab and shiraz are meanwhile responding well to the relative warmth of the north facing Scarborough site.

★★★★ **Isliedh** (Pronounced '*Eye*-lay') Maiden **04**, barrel-fermented sauvignon, turned from sombre duckling to beautiful swan, taking 2006 TWS Sauvignon trophy; also *Wine* ★★★★★. **05** (★★★★★) sauvignon/semillon (85/15) fusion, has glorious plumage from start (White Blend trophy on same show). Exemplifies power with cool-climate subtlety; deeply flavoursome, steely nucleus holds full richness. Excellent potential. Fermented/10 mths Fr oak, 70% new.

★★★★★ **Sauvignon Blanc** Sophisticated Loire-inspired dry white, its racy coolness, intricate complexity, fully realised only after 3-4 yrs. **05** incl usual ±7% splash semillon but no small oaked portion as pvsly; sleek, richly flavoured, hints tangerine, steely minerals, delivered with vigour, intensity. **04** *Wine* ★★★★★.

★★★★ **Stonehaven Sauvignon Blanc** Their 'second tier' sauvignon, but **06** better than many premium labels. Vivid lemon-zest/dried herbs scents, simultaneously expressive & elegant; fresh-as-a-daisy flavours, emphatic mineral tang on finish. Delicious in youth, can age yr/2.

★★★★ **Semillon** After break in 2004, **05** (★★★★★) returns in splendid form: distinctive coolclimate minerals, tantalising whiffs tangerine, lemon peel, dried grass all poised for grand evolution. Wood-matured portion adds polish, texture, though mid-2006 still youthfully tight. Uncompromisingly dry (as is entire range). 48% fermented/10 mths used Fr oak; incl 6% sauvignon. **03** (★★★★★) only war at best.

★★★★ **Semillon Noble Late Harvest**. None since **01**, due to insufficient botrytis.

Scarborough Red new ★★★★ Cellar's first red, **04** cab-led blend with shiraz/merlot (68/27/5) from Redhill vyd, Scarborough. Open fruited, supple; friendly yet firm tannins. Easy, satisfying drinking now & for few yrs. 16 mths Fr oak, 30% new. **Chardonnay** ★★★★ No Cinderella in this quality range; **04** previewed last ed, has filled out, gained weight, richness to complement citrus freshness & spicy oak (Fr, fermented/11 mths, 35% new). *Wine* ★★★★. — *AL*

Cape Promise

Est 2002 • Owners UK-based WaverleyTBS • UK office: WaverleyTBS, Unit 2, G Park, Maxted Road, Hemel Hempstead, Herts, HP2-7DX • T 09·44·1442·206800 • F 09·44·1442·206888 www.waverleytbs.co.uk • SA partners: LGB Wines (Daschbosch, Badsberg & Groot Eiland) • T 023·349·1017 • F 023·349·1012

Cape Promise was developed in 2002 by WaverleyTBS, the UK's largest wine and spirits distributor, with SA winery partners Daschbosch, Badsberg and Groot Eiland. The brand continues to grow steadily in the UK, Northern Ireland and mainland Europe, where it's met with strong consumer approval. Marketed under the strapline 'Have you been there yet?', the range features eye-catching labels depicting African animals against a sunset backdrop.

Pinotage ★★ **06** bright & fruity, like beaujolais nouveau. Chillable, easy-sipping, but heed 14.6% alc. **Cabernet Sauvignon-Merlot** new ★★ Not for keeping **05**, 60/40 blend with chemical whiffs to red candy flavour, tight tannic grip. **Ruby Cabernet-Pinotage** ★★ Rustic but tasty **05**, dry & firm braai companion; 60/40 mix. **Chardonnay** ★★☆ **06** fruity rather than oaky flavours this yr, hints lemongrass & citrus, glows with 14.3% alc. **Oak Chenin Blanc** ★★★ Attractively wooded **06** has a creamy texture yet is lively & light, sun-ripe tropical notes mingle with brisk acidity. **Chenin Blanc** ★★ Lively & crisp quaffing wine. **06** grass-scented with firm, dry flavours. **Sauvignon Blanc** ★★★★ Forthcoming **06** varietally pure & flavourful with gooseberry & tropical tones, racy acidity; well-made & -balanced. **Chardonnay-Colombard** ★★☆ **06** enters gently sweet with dried pear flavours, finishes dry & brisk. **Dry Muscat** ★ **06** leaner with less concentration & flavour than pvs, whispered notes of rosepetal & honeysuckle. **Noble Late Harvest** new ★★★ From chenin; **03** billows honey, raisin & treacle; long, syrupy flavours shd appeal to the sweeter-toothed. Following duo sold out before we cld taste new vintage: **Merlot** ★★☆ Uncomplicated **03**, shy; soft jammy sweetness firmed by powdery tannins. **Shiraz** ★★★ **03** meaty/peppery whiffs, charred mocha wood spices up red fruit. 6 mths oak. Range sourced widely, so various WOs. **Cape Promise Reserve** range discontinued. — *CR/CT*

■ *Cape Reality* see Baarsma
■ *Cape Roan* see Doolhof Estate

Cape Rock Wines ♀♨☕🎵 new

Olifants River • Est 2001 • 1stB 2002 • Visits by appt • BYO picnic • Permanent art exhibit • Owner Willie Brand • Winemakers WP Brand & Gavin Brand (Jan 2002/Feb 2005) • Viticulturists Jeff Joubert & WP Brand • 30 ha (cab, merlot, pinotage, roobernet, ruby cab, shiraz, chard, chenin, sauvignon) • 605 tons 140 cs own label 100% red • PO Box 261 Vredendal 8160 • oerwoud@ telkomsa.net • www.caperockwines.co.za • T 027·213·2567 • F 027·213·5567

Visitors to this boutique cellar on the Olifants riverbanks will get more than the usual cheese and biscuits: a pristine natural environment with abundant wildlife and rare bird species, leisurely picnics under shady trees, and a shiraz-viognier blend inspired by owner Willie Brand's visit to Australia's Adelaide Hills. 'It motivated me to try something similar for the local market,' says this qualified Wine & Spirit Board taster. He's determined to make world-class wine, as well as to boost wine appreciation in SA — particularly when paired with food.

Shiraz-Viognier ★★★ Plum-pudding, coconut aromas on sumptuous, soft-tannined **05**, with big 15.3% alc well tucked away in the opulent fruit — 7% of the aromatic white grape adds floral notes & a bit of polish. WO W Cape. — *MF*

■ *Cape Table* see Riebeek Cellars
■ *Cape View* see Kaapzicht

Cape Vineyards

*Rawsonville · Est 1994 · 1stB 1996 · Closed to public · Owners 4 shareholders · 47 300 cs + 2m litres bulk · 70% red 30% white · Ranges for customers: Pearl Springs (UK/Japan); Andrew Bain Reserve, Jantara, Wildfire (all UK) · PO Box 106 Rawsonville 6845 · marleze@ cape-vineyards.com or monique@cape-vineyards.com · www.cape-vineyards.com · **T** 023·349·1585/1466 · F 023·349·1592*

Four wineries, Opstal, Bergsig, Merwida and Slanghoek, form the core of this export venture for bulk and bottled wines. The portfolio includes the Rawsons and Andrew Bain ranges. UK importer Bottle Green's flying winemaker, Mark Nairn, oversees the making of joint-venture brand Jantara. Cape Vineyards also sources wine for Bottle G's Wildfire and Andrew Bain Reserve ranges.

Andrew Bain Reserve range
Pinotage ★★★ **05** a sleeping giant; incl 15% shiraz, packed with dense savoury/spicy fruit & powerful tannins. Shd hold gd few yrs. 30% 1st fill oak. **Chardonnay** ★★ **05**, with 15% chenin; muted varietal character, understated oak (though 40% is new), unheavy styling makes for food compatibility. Slnghoek fruit for these.

Andrew Bain range
No new vintages ready for review. Added tannins for merlot component & chard. **Cabernet Sauvignon-Merlot** ★★★ **05** generous & warming (14.5% alc); 60% cab & equal dollops merlot/malbec provide flavoursome mouthful coffee, choc & red fruit. **Chardonnay** ★★★ Tropical **05** weighty, with zesty lift; appealing.

Jantara range
No new vintages reviewed for this or range below. **Pinotage** ★★★ Splash malbec adds extra colour & fruit-richness to **05**, dry tannins & bitter lift make it a food wine. Fr/Am oak, 2 mths, as for… **Shiraz** ★★★ Juicy **05** gets density & flavour boost from 15% malbec; last yr dry raspy tannins needed rustic food. **Chardonnay** ★★ **05** restrained & shy; fruit aromas & flavours gently buoyed by 6 wks combo Fr/Am oak. **Chenin Blanc** ★★★ **05** attractive nectarine & lime tones balanced by light vanilla whiff (oak as for Chard). Sensible 13% alc. **Sauvignon Blanc** ★★★ **03** had unusual peach whiff; bright, zesty finish. None in range for keeping.

Rawson's range
Ruby Cabernet-Merlot ★★★ Unoaked blend. **05** ready to drink, merlot/malbec (20/10) add structure to ruby cab's sweet fruit & accessibility.

Wildfire range
Slnghoek fruit for these. **Malbec** ★★ Vibrant fruit runs riot on **05**, spicy aromas & tannic bite add interest. Drink in vibrant youth. **Chardonnay** ★★ **06** friendly poolside quaffer; lightish pine & peach notes, not-so-light 14% alc. W Cape/Breede Rvr Vlly WOs for all above. — *CT*

■ *Cape Wine Cellars* see Cape Coastal Vintners

Cape Winemakers Guild (CWG)

*Chair: Gary Jordan · General Manager: Kate Jonker · **T** 021·852·0408 · F 021·852·0409 · info@capewinemakersguild.com · www.capewinemakersguild.com*

Independent, invitation-only association, founded in 1982 to promote winemaking excellence among its members. Since 1985, the CWG has held a highly regarded annual public auction. A Development Trust, formed in 1999 with auction sponsor Nedbank, benefits disadvantaged communities living and working in the winegrowing regions. The current guild members are (new inductees in bold): Kevin Arnold, Waterford; **Jacques Borman**, Boschkloof; Anton Bredell, JP Bredell Wines; Jan Coetzee, Vriesenhof Vineyards; Philip Costandius, Lourensford; Jean Daneel, Jean Daneel Wines; Neil Ellis, Neil Ellis Wines; Pieter Ferreira, Graham Beck Robertson; Peter Finlayson, Bouchard Finlayson; David Finlayson, Glen Carlou; Ross Gower, Ross Gower Wines; Kevin Grant, Ataraxia; Jeff Grier,

Villiera; Teddy Hall, Rudera; Charles Hopkins, De Grendel; Bruce Jack, Flagstone Winery; Gary Jordan, Jordan Winery; Christopher Keet, Cordoba; Marc Kent, Boekenhoutskloof; Etienne le Riche, Etienne le Riche Wines; John Loubser, Steenberg; Johan Malan, Simonsig; Carel Nel, Boplaas; **Louis Nel**, Warwick; **David Nieuwoudt**, Cederberg Private Cellars; Carl Schultz, Hartenberg; Danie Steytler, Kaapzicht; Louis Strydom, Ernie Els; David Trafford, De Trafford; Beyers Truter, Beyerskloof; André van Rensburg, Vergelegen; Braam van Velden, Overgaauw; Bernhard Veller, Nitida; Niels Verburg, Luddite; Nicky Versfeld, The Company of Wine People; Jeremy Walker, Grangehurst; Gyles Webb, Thelema. Most members have bottlings on the latest (2006) Auction; wines tasted are listed separately under the winery name. Honorary 'Keepers of the Key': Francois Naudé and Norma Ratcliffe.

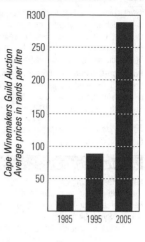

- ▪ **Cap Vino** see Winkelshoek
- ▪ **Cardouw** see Citrusdal Cellars
- ▪ **Caresse Marine** see Wildekrans

Carisbrooke Wines

*Stellenbosch ▪ Est 1989 ▪ 1stB 1996 ▪ Tasting & sales Mon-Fri 9.30-2 (all day & Sat 9-12 during Dec/Jan) ▪ Closed Easter Fri-Mon, Dec 24/25 & Jan 1 ▪ Owner/winemaker Willem Pretorius ▪ Viti/vini consultant Kowie du Toit (Jan 1997) ▪ 6 ha (cab, shiraz) ▪ 40 tons 1 500 cs own label 100% red ▪ PO Box 25 Vlottenburg 7604 ▪ wjpret@mweb.co.za ▪ **T/F 881·3798***

No new vintages reviewed for the Cabernet Sauvignon and cab-shiraz blend made by Stellenbosch senior counsel Willem Pretorius in conjunction with Kowie du Toit. The brand takes its name for the little train station of Carisbrooke, made famous by Alan Paton's masterpiece *Cry, the Beloved Country*.

▪ **Carl Everson** see Opstal

Carnival

Private-label range of the Spar chain of convenience stores; available in 1, 3 & 5ℓ casks. See also Country Cellars and Spar SA.

All **NV**; alcs ±12% unless noted. **Classic Red** ★★ Fresh & plummy early drinker with supple tannins. Ruby cab/pinotage mix, latter oak-staved for extra grip & flavour. 13.5% alc. **Rosé** ★★★ Semi-sweet blush from colombard, tinted by pinotage. **06** zesty & berry toned. **Grand Cru** ★★ Chirpy equal partnership between chenin & colombard. Bright tropical fruit & crisp acidity. **Stein** ★★ Attractive tropical notes of guava & ripe pineapple, balanced sweetness; from colombard & chenin. **Late Harvest** ★★ Tropical fruit & honey notes, rich rather than sweet thanks to gd acidity. All are best consumed as young as possible. — *DH*

Carolinahoeve Boutique Wine Cellar

*Wellington ▪ Est 2004 ▪ 1stB 2005 ▪ Sales daily 11 till late (incl pub hols) ▪ Italian restaurant (see Eat-out section) ▪ Exhibition of railway artefacts & watercolour paintings ▪ Owners Lee-Ann Millin & Carolina Dagevos-Millin ▪ Winemaker Lee-Ann Millin, advised by Pierre Marais (Jan 2005) ▪ 4 ha (cinsaut, chenin) ▪ 10 tons ±1 100 cs 75% red 25% white ▪ PO Box 974 Wellington 7654 ▪ info@ carolinahoeve.com ▪ www.carolinahoeve.com ▪ **T 021·873·0741** ▪ F 021·873·0742*

If exclusivity is your thing, the wines of Lee-Ann Millin and Carolina Dagevos-Millin will have a special appeal: they're available only from the Italian restaurant which the partners have opened in the old stationmaster's residence in Wellington; from a sister establishment in the Netherlands, De Carolinahoeve; and a handful of local wine shops. With two vintages under their belt, the Millins continue making wine with advice from seasoned consultant Pierre Marais.

Pinotage-Cinsaut ★★★ **05** still selling; pleasantly dry *vin ordinaire* with bright spicy red fruits; 55/45 blend. Available in wooded & unwooded versions. **Chenin Blanc** ★★★ **06** crisp Granny Smith apple & lanolin notes, racy acidity throughout, masking fruit for now; Sbosch & own grapes; 750/187ml. Both WO Coastal. — *IM*

■ *Carpe Diem* see Diemersfontein
Cathedral Cellar *see* KWV Ltd

Catherine Marshall [new]

Phased re-branding will see the wines of BWC (Barefoot Wine Company) marketed under the name of their winemaker and co-director, Cathy Marshall, beginning with the Syrah below. See separate BWC entry for further details.

★★★★ **Syrah 04** attractions of pure varietal red fruits & lilies, embroidered with whiff toasty oak. Elegant 13% alc yet agreeably rich flavours, texture enlivened by fresh mineral core; supportive oaking. Malo/matured yr in Burgundy barrels, mainly used. WO Paarl. — *AL*

■ *Cattle Baron* see ACJ Fine Wines
■ *CCC* see Bonnievale

Cederberg Private Cellars

Cederberg (see Olifants River map) ▪ Est/1stB 1977 ▪ Tasting, sales & tours Mon-Sat 8-12.30; 2-5 Pub hols 9-12;4-6 ▪ Fee R10 ▪ Closed Easter Fri/Sun/Mon & Dec 16/25 ▪ BYO picnic ▪ Fully equipped self-catering cottages (see Stay-over section) ▪ Walks/hikes ▪ Mountain biking ▪ Owners Nieuwoudt family ▪ Winemaker David Nieuwoudt, with Jan Taylor (1997/1998) ▪ Viticulturist Ernst Nieuwoudt ▪ 56 ha (cab, shiraz, chenin, sauvignon) ▪ 14 000 cs 60% red 40% white ▪ PO Box 84 Clanwilliam 8135 ▪ info@cederbergwine.com ▪ www.cederbergwine.com ▪ T 027·482·2827 ▪ F 027·482·1188

It almost seems like business as usual at SA's highest vineyards, located in the rugged Cederberg mountains. 'We have replanted the sauvignon and chenin on more suitable slopes and soils,' recounts winemaker David Nieuwoudt. 'We have also planted our first viognier and 4 ha of sauvignon on beautiful south-east facing slopes — a prime spot.' But in between all this, Nieuwoudt has been elected to the prestigious Cape Winemakers Guild — to his great delight. 'As a young winemaker, it's fantastic to be part of this group of heavyweights, at the forefront of SA wine.' His first CWG wine is a Shiraz, appropriately named Teen Die Hoog, a poetic reference to the high climbing vines.

★★★★★ **V Generations Cabernet Sauvignon** In homage to the family's guardianship of this snowline wilderness area; fruit ex 28 yr old vyd enjoys hand crafting, indulged with new Fr oak (18 mths). **04** (★★★★) softer, more open structure suggests earlier accessibility than cellar-worthy **03**: overt mocha, some liquorice; layered cassis/mulberry balance in trademark clean lines. 120 cs.

★★★★ **Cabernet Sauvignon** Well established quality level & style; cool, pure, focused fruit, ample & sweet, ripe dry tannins. Pent-up cassis shoe-horned into spicy **05**, more leafy than warmer mulberry/blackberry profile of **04**. Needs few yrs to unwind. 13 mths Fr oak, 60% new. **03** *Decanter* ★★★★.

★★★★ **Shiraz** Authoritative & characterful yet refreshingly unflamboyant; much garlanded since maiden **02**, incl *Wine* ★★★★ for **04**. Latest shimmers with cool elegance; **05** spices on nose, glossy mulberry fruit, fantastic carry-through into lasting finish. 15 mths, 70/30 Fr/Am oak, 70% new. Probably for earlier enjoyment, unlike following wine.

★★★★★ **CWG Auction Reserve Teen die Hoog Shiraz** [new] Small-berried fruit from upper portion of best vyd, pampered 18 mths in new Allier oak; then only four best barrels selected for 100cs production. Critics may suggest it's the old style: 'Multi-dimensional!' is David N's retort. **04** a showstopper either way: musky asphalt aromas, scented black berry fruits in muscular structure; powder-fine tannins escort lovely elegance on exit. Will reward many yrs in the cellar.

★★★★ **V Generations Chenin Blanc** Ageworthy version from small (1.2ha), older vyd. **05** melange of white-pear fruit, broad oak & nutty bottle-age; oodles of character, ends brisk & dry. Long fermented (44 days) in 60% new Fr oak, 11 mths matured.

★★★★ **Sauvignon Blanc** Wow! Racy, explosive **06** bristles with cut grass, flashes of pea soup character & tingling, rapier-like flintiness: in short, arresting. Pleasing 13% alc. **05** Wine ★★★★.

Cederberger ★★★★ Frequent WOM selection; mainly merlot & pinotage, with shiraz (50/30/20); **05** sweet ripe plum & blackberry flavours lifted by spicy finish. Used casks 14 mths. **Chenin Blanc** ★★★★ Interesting, flavourful without being tropical, over-ripe or blowsy. **06** brisk citrus seam in balanced weight, invigorating finish. **Bukettraube** ★★★ **06** enticing floral, honey & cumin complexity to sweet grapiness (±27g/ℓ sugar). —DS

Cellar Cask

Well-established budget range; first in SA, in 1979, with a bag-in-a-box. All NV, all ±11.5% alc, all semi-sweet. By Distell.

Johannisberger Red ★★ Berry-rich bouquet, fresh tea-leaf grip, gently sweet goodbye. A red for curries? **Johannisberger Rosé** ★★ Candyfloss-hued & -scented, fair zip on the palate. **Select Johannisberger White** ★★ Chenin/colombard/riesling medley, shy & floral with some bruised apple/melon aromas. All WO Coastal. **Premier Claret**, **Grand Cru**, **Semi Sweet** & **Late Harvest** discontinued. — CvZ

■ *Cellar Door* see Villiera
■ *Cellar Hand* see Flagstone
■ *Cellar Selection* see Kleine Zalze

Cellar-Vie Wines

Est/1stB 2004 • Closed to public • Owners Hendri Nagel & Adam Simcock • Vini consultants Teddy Hall & Bob Cartwright (Rudera/Leeuwin Estate) • 320 cs 50% red 50% white • PO Box 10136 Edleen 1625 • hermitage@absamail.co.za • T 083·713·9256 • F 011·975·4482

Wine partners Hendri Nagel and Adam Simcock buy in grapes and juice from various regions for vinification by selected high-profile winemakers such as Rudera's Teddy Hall, who created the red blend below. In an Antipodean venture, Bob Cartwright of Western Australia's Leeuwin Estate flew in to help produce an as-yet-unreleased 06 Chardonnay with Weltevrede's Philip Jonker.

Commitment Reserve new ★★★★ Modern but serious bdx blend cab/merlot (53/47); **04** has generous padding of cranberry fruit to absorb rich vanilla flavours ex-new Fr oak, 23 mths, lovely fresh acidity, moderate 13.5% alc. Shows promise, shortish finish only detraction. Sbosch fruit. —CvZ

■ *Chacma's Bark* see African Pride
■ *Chamonix* see Cape Chamonix
■ *Chapman's Peak* see Cape Classics

Chateau Libertas

SA's 'iconic' affordable red blend, made every year since 1932. By Distell. **04** ★★ Cab-dominated (45%), given depth by dollops merlot, shiraz, malbec (30/20/5). Firm & food-friendly, chunky tannin from staves. WO Coastal. — CvZ

■ *Cherry Hill* see Liquor World

Christo Wiese Portfolio

Owner Christo Wiese • *Contact Anton du Toit* • *PO Box 16 Somerset West 7129* • *cwp@ loursenford.co.za* • *T 021·847·2200* • *F 021·847·0910/1669*

This is the umbrella for big-businessman Christo Wiese's extensive wine interests, which include Stellenbosch farms Lanzerac and Loursenford, and branded ranges Five Heirs and Eden Crest (the latter pair now listed under Loursenford).

Cilandia

Robertson • *Est 2002* • *1stB 2003* • *Visits by appt* • *Owners AA Cilliers Jnr & AA Cilliers* • *Winemaker Albie Cilliers* • *Viticulturist Abraham Cilliers* • *60 ha (cab, cinsaut, pinotage, roobernet, shiraz, chard, chenin)* • *700 tons 1 200 cs own label 100% red* • *PO Box 504 Robertson 6705* • *Cilandia@telkomsa.net* • *T/F 023·626·5209*

Fruit for the Cilandia brand (a blend of family name, Cilliers, and Robertson winegrowing ward Eilandia) is from selected fruit off 60 hectares on the home farm, vinified by third-generation AA 'Albie' Cilliers, who is intent on restoring winemaking pride to the family spread. No new vintages tasted of the **Cabernet Sauvignon**, **Pinotage** or **Shiraz**.

■ ***Cilliers Cellars*** see Stellendrift
■ ***Cilmor*** see African Terroir
■ ***Cinzano*** see African Wines & Spirits
■ ***Circumstance*** see Waterkloof
■ ***Cirrus*** see Ernie Els Wines

Citrusdal Cellars

Citrusdal (see Swartland map) • *Est 1957* • *1stB 1958* • *Tasting & sales Mon-Fri 8-5 Sat 9-12. 30 (sales also at retail outlet in Citrusdal village Mon-Fri 9-7 Sat 8-5)* • *Closed all pub hols except Easter Sat* • *Tours by appt* • *BYO picnic* • *Citrusdal Cellars Guest House* • *Tour groups* • *Owners 78 members* • *Winemaker Ian Nieuwoudt, with Jaco Brand & Andries de Klerk (2005)* • *Viti advisers: VinPro* • *1 200 ha (grenache, pinotage, chenin)* • *6 000 tons 90 000 cs own label + 20 000 cs for clients* • *30% red 60% white 5% rosé 5% dessert* • *Export brands: Cardouw, Ivory Creek & Danckaert* • *HACCP certified* • *PO Box 41 Citrusdal 7340* • *info@gouevallei.co.za* • *www.gouevallei.co.za* • *T 022·921·2233* • *F 022·921·3937*

GM De Witt la Grange is fending off attempts by overseas marketers to discard the Goue Vallei moniker – it may not roll off the foreign tongue but its 45-year history argues strongly for its retention. In fact the label, if the GM has his way, will identify a premier red and a premier white blend, with Goue Vallei Classic used for entry-level wines. He and cellar stakeholders are dedicated to management of the environment, with involvement in the Cape Leopard Trust and conservation of the Cederberg, Witzenberg and Sneeukop wilderness areas.

Goue Vallei range

Shiraz ★★★ Fleshy & approachable **05**; warm black plum flavours & lively but soft tannins. Wooding as for Cab.

Cabernet Sauvignon ★★ 05 in customary style of big, tight, tannins, food-imploring drynesss via rigorous oaking (Am chip fermentation, 6 mths Fr staving). Whereas...
Cabernet Sauvignon-Merlot ★★★ Again 60/40 blend, but **05** miles better than pvs; has interest, some structure; agreeably gruff tannins to plummy fruit; Am chips & Fr staves.
Pinotage ★★ 05 full-bore Am oak bouquet (from chip/stave combo, 6 mths), palate rather pleasant, nice dry pinotage thwack on finish. Following pair tasted as samples:
Classique Rouge ★★★ Crowd pleasing red, quaffably light (13.5% alc), comfortably dry; gd with pastas/pizzas; latest **NV** multi-vintage/variety blend with savoury/earthy touches. Also in 3ℓ cask. **Chianti ★★★** Appealing everyday red; tangy red fruit flavours in **06**, unwooded grenache/cinsaut; juicy-dry tannins equally suited to table, patio or picnic.
Chardonnay ★★ 05 unwooded; brief lees-ageing yields placid dry white with mild

Golden Delicious apple flavour. **Chenin Blanc** ★★ Notch-up **06** riper, friendlier than pvs; fresh, pear-toned quaffer, gently dry. **Sauvignon Blanc** ★★ Ethereal **05** 'crisply dry' rather than pvs 'perky', with suggestion of grassiness. Not re-tasted. 11.5% alc. **Classique Blanc** ★★ Latest again **NV** (06, uncertified); lightish-textured just-off-dry summer quaffer with hints of flowers & boiled sweets. Mainly chenin. **Bukettraube** ★ **05** off-dry white, feather-light in every respect.**Classique Natural Sweet Rosé** new ★★ **06** ultra-soft sweetie with fleeting rosepetal & cherry cordial hints, low 7.5% alc. **Late Vintage** ★★ Semi-sweet in 3ℓ cask; candied fruit flavours, hints spice/mint — good with glazed chicken or Thai curry. **NV**/uncertified, not retasted, ditto following **NV** pair... **Brut** ★★★ Chardonnay & clairette; stylish dry fizz with appetising fresh baked bread tone. **Vin Doux** ★★★ Lovely bouncy bubbles with honeysuckle fragrance, uncloyingly sweet. Following fortifieds all **NV**/uncertified: **White Jerepiko** new ★★★★ ✓ Low-for-style but efficacious 15.5% alc imparts tangy tingle to lemongrass/barley flavours; minty note makes this a natural for pouring over crushed ice in summer. **Red Jerepiko** ★★★ Nippynight campfire warmer from pinotage. Preview offers delightful flavours of liquid raisin & plum; comforting sweetness nipped by touch tangy acidity. Following four not retasted: **White Muscadel** ★★★★ Almost a dessert in itself, complete with ripe mango, pineapple & apricot flavours; silky smooth (partly due to low 15% fortification). **Sacramental Wine** ★★ For the Roman Catholic Church; aromatic blend pale dry sherry, muscadel & colombard. 14.8% alc. **Hanepoot Jerepiko** ★★★ Last bottling was wickedly smooth & sweet; grapey nose & herbal palate with hints mint & buchu. **Ruby** ★★ From shiraz, straightforwardly sweet, dry for style (86g/ℓ sugar). WO W Cape unless noted. – *IvH*

Clairvaux Private Cellar

Robertson ▪ Est 2000 ▪ 1stB 2001 ▪ Tasting & sales Mon-Fri 8-5 Sat & pub hols 9-12.30 ▪ Closed Easter Fri-Mon, Dec 25/26 & Jan 1 ▪ Tours by appt ▪ BYO picnic ▪ Owners Wouter de Wet Snr & Jnr ▪ Winemaker Pieter van Aarde (Jan 2004) ▪ Viti consultant Briaan Stipp ▪ 100 ha (cab, malbec, merlot, pinotage, petit v, shiraz, chard, colombard, muscadel, sauvignon) ▪ 3 100 tons ▪ PO Box 179 Robertson 6705 ▪ clairvaux@lando.co.za ▪ www.wine.co.za ▪ T 023·626·3842 ▪ F 023·626·1925

A new vintage, a new baby at Clairvaux. Winemaker Pieter van Aarde and wife Ria welcomed first-born son Pieter Jnr pre-harvest. The previous year, it was third-generation owner Wouter de Wet's turn when his son – yes, Wouter Jnr, was also born pre-harvest. For the rest, focus continues on upping quality, bottling more serious wines and increasing sales.

Cabernet Sauvignon ★★★ **04** opposite of nervy & lean pvs: ripe & succulent berry fruit, silky tannins, good persistence. **Shiraz** ★★★ Riper & fuller this yr; also more dry wood tannins evident. **05** pleasant enough but better with food. **Sandberg Purple** ★★★ **04** delightful medium bodied quaffer; roughly equal mix pinotage, ruby cab, merlot, showing spicy red fruit, slippery tannins. **Rosé** ★ Overtly sweet, somewhat simple **05**, with talcum powder whiff from white muscadel. **Chardonnay** ★★ **05** amiable & plump, well flavoured & supportively oaked. **Sauvignon Blanc** ★★★ Uncomplicated picnic wine. **05** light bodied, lemon toned, briskly dry with long finish. **Chardonnay-Colombar** ★★ Friendly, light dry white; **05** orange zest aroma, gentle dryness; suggest drink soon. **Soleil** ★★ Sweet but refreshing **05**, mainly white muscadel & colombard, straightforwardly pleasant. **Madonna's Kisses Golden Muscadel** ★★★ Luscious full-sweet jerepiko; **05** billows marmalade & muscat; combo lively acidity, uplifting alc (17.7%), give an airy, silk-like tone. Note: newer versions of only this wine, Shiraz above, tasted for current ed; all others still selling. **Port** ★ Old-style fireside fortifier from ruby cab; **03** showing treacle-like sweetness. – *MM*

Cloof

Darling (see Durbanville/Darling map) ▪ Est 1997 ▪ 1stB 1998 ▪ Tasting & sales Mon-Fri 10-5 Sat 10-2 ▪ Closed Easter Fri/Sun, Dec 25/26, Jan 1 ▪ Tasting room lunches Mon-Sat; occasional Sun gourmet BBQ events – pre-bookings only ▪ Owner Cloof Wine Estate (Pty) Ltd ▪

Winemaker Christopher van Dieren (Jan 2002) • Viticulturist Peter Duckitt (2005) • 166 ha (cabs s/f, cinsaut, merlot, pinotage, shiraz, chard, chenin) • 600 tons 90 000 cs 88% red 5% white 7% rosé • PO Box 269 Darling 7345 • info@cloof.co.za • www.cloof.co.za • T 022·492·2839 • F 022·492·3261

As if the emerging track record of Cloof's Crucible Shiraz isn't enough (trophies, medals and listings galore), marketing manager Oscar Foulkes says they're working towards attracting more customers by developing their cellar-door experience. 'The catch-22 is that one needs foot traffic to justify the investment but if one hasn't made the investment there is less of a drawcard to bring in the foot traffic!' Sundays are already sorted, at least, thanks to the popular Gourmet BBQs (by appointment) where self-declared 'closet chef' Foulkes himself wields the tongs.

★★★★☆ **Cloof Crucible Shiraz 04** similar concentration, flavour & oaking to showstopper **03**. Spicy red fruit even more focused by bright acidity & lower sugar (2.2 vs 5.6g/ℓ) & alc (14. 8 vs 15.5%). Still powerful & well crafted with sustained sappy finish; loads of potential. Remarkably concentrated **03** vigorously but harmoniously oaked (15 mths new Fr). These widely gonged: *Decanter* gold, MIWA trophy, VDG among latest felicitations.

★★★★ **Cloof Merlot-Cabernet Franc** New name for new take on their bdx blend (pvsly 'Cabernet Sauvignon-Cabernet Franc-Merlot'); 67/33 assemblage in **04** (★★★), choc & sweet tobacco jostle with racy acidity & firm, almost austere dry tannin. Nervy mid-2006, needs food & time to tame. Concours Mondial 2006 judges felt differently & awarded gold. **03**, wearing pvs tag, flew with SAA, impressed *Wine* judges (★★★★).

★★★★ **The Cloof Cellar Blend** Cab exits the mix in **05** (★★★), leaving tinta, pinotage & shiraz to star in what Oscar F dubs a Quentin Tarantino remake of 'Sideways'. Unsurprisingly, subtlety & finesse outgunned by vintage's extreme ripeness (6g/ℓ RS, 14.5% alc); warm, hollow palate with notes of dark spice & liquorice. Shade less alluring than sweetly rustic **04**, with wild red fruit & richness from ±5g/ℓ sugar. Yr Fr oak, 20-30% new.

Cloof Pinotage ★★★ **04** wild red berries & some spice masked by brusque tannins. Yr new Fr oak dominates mid-2006 leaving ungenerous austere impression. Food pairing & time may reward. Ex-single bushvine vyd established 1976. **The Very Sexy Shiraz** ★★★★ Less allure & panache than new name suggests; **04** some perfumed red fruit with spicy nuances, smoothly textured palate with savoury overlay, tangy farewell. Yr Fr oak, 75% new. **'Cloof Ubuntu'** new ★★★ Name to be confirmed; alludes to 'the African principle of humanity' implicit in initiative to channel proceeds from sales to worthy education initiatives; **05** (sample) cab-led blend with shiraz & merlot (roughly 50/38/12), bold & powerful (15.5 alc) but gd with robust fare. **Cloof Bush Vines CPS** new ★★★ Blend cab, pinotage, shiraz (44/29/27); **04** earthy, with spicy wild berry flavours, dry chalky tannins. Portion barrel matured, 20% new. Currently gruff & brooding but has character, deserves time to show its latent charms. **Cloof Dusty Road Cabernet Sauvignon** ★★☆ **05** ripe cassis with whiff spice (from dash shiraz) imparts sweet impression to chunky wine, with dry dusty finish. Touch hot & hollow, unsurprising for vintage. **Cloof Dusty Road Pinotage** ★★☆ **05** (sample) unwooded & softer than pvs with ripe squishy fruit & friendlier 12.4% alc. **Cloof Dusty Road Cabernet Sauvignon-Shiraz** Made intermittently for particular customers. Last was smoky & austere **03** (★★★). **Cloof Dusty Road Rosé** ★★ **06** equal parts cinsaut & shiraz infuse dry crisp quaffer with some spicy, savoury nuances. Short & brisk. **Cloof Dusty Road Chardonnay Unwooded** ★★ Soft, understated, light & brisk **06**, with limy acidity & short sherbetty finish. **Cloof Dusty Road Chenin Blanc** ★★ **06** lighter styled with shy winter melon aromas & very brisk palate. Note: range refinement leaves the above line-up on the available list for 2007; all other ranges & labels discontinued or in abeyance. — MW

■ ***Clos Cabrière*** see Cabrière Estate

Clos Malverne

Stellenbosch • Est/1stB 1988 • Tasting & sales Mon-Fri 10-4.30 Sat 10-1 • Fee R15 • Closed Christian hols & Jan 1 • Tours by appt • Free picnic facilities • Owners Seymour & Sophia Pritchard • Winemaker/viticulturist Isak 'Ippie' Smit (Nov 1997) • 25 ha (cab, merlot, pinotage, *shiraz, sauvignon) • 350 tons 24 000 cs 80% red 20% white • Main export brands: Clos Malverne, Heron's Nest & Kleinrivier • PO Box 187 Stellenbosch 7599 • closma@mweb.co.za • www.closmalverne.co.za www.capeblend.co.za • **T** 021·865·2022 • F 021·865·2518*

Mindful of the perceived increased resistance towards blockbuster styles, the Pritchards are turning the clock back from what Seymour P calls the 'gorilla style' of their recent vintages (2000 to 2003) to 'the more elegant, finessed sweet spot' achieved in the late 90s. The goal is to slightly shorten hang-times for their reds (some previous harvests languished on the vines till April), thereby reducing potential alcohol levels without compromising ripeness. Their Sauvignon is doing particularly well for them, and they're looking to expand production. Marketing wise, they say they're 'going flat out' so they can reap the benefits when the current slower market turns.

★★★★ **Auret Cape Blend** Cellar's flagship — cab/pinotage/merlot blend (60/25/15); standout **03** (★★★★☆) youthful yet harmonious, compact, with rich, ripe blackberry fruit; oozing luxurious sleekness; perfectly integrated tannins provide structure for 6-8 yrs, though happily drink sooner. ±Yr Fr oak. Swiss gold. **02** (★★★★) stylish, but less presence. Magisterial **01** was firm & unyielding in youth. All reds basket-pressed, fermented in traditional open-topped *kuipe*.

★★★★★ **Auret Cape Blend Limited Release 01** still offered; features SAYWS winning cab (60%) & merlot, plus cellar's best pinotage (25%). Mid-2004 showed dense, compact flavours, impressive understated power. Yr Fr oak adds opulence.

★★★★ **Pinotage Reserve 03** elegant rather than showy; intriguing lavender & cherry tobacco aromas, bright, juicy fruit flavours, fresh acidity, decent structure, long savoury, mint tinged finish. Drink now or cellar few yrs. Concours Mondial gold. Yr Fr/Am oak.

★★★★ **Cabernet Sauvignon-Merlot Limited Release 01** once-off showcase for 60/40 blend which won Jan Smuts Trophy at SAYWS 2001; held back for further bottle maturation. Much medalled since, incl *Decanter* gold, Winemakers Choice & Calyon top ten; released early 2006. Mid-2005 noted as being beautifully proportioned, with deep-pile velvety richness.

★★★★ **Cabernet Sauvignon-Shiraz** Appealing balancing act between shiraz juiciness & cab austerity; **04** (★★★★) revisits **03**'s blend proportions (75/25) without repeating its style, complexity; roasted herb & spice touches to blackberry fruit. Well balanced; drink over next 2 yrs. Briefer oaking than pvs (4 mths Fr/Am).

★★★★ **Cabernet Sauvignon-Pinotage Cape Blend ✓ 03** seriously styled, complex 75/25 blend offering sour plum, maraschino aromas & flavours; firm tannins provide structure; well-knitted, good acid thread gives freshness; savoury finish. Fr oak yr.

Cabernet Sauvignon ★★★★ Classically styled **03** sweet blackcurrant fruit framed by foursquare structure from yr Fr oak; dry savoury finish; will hold few yrs. **Shiraz** ★★★★ **03** last noted as fragrant dark cherry, soft ripe tannins sculpting fruit to pleasing roundness. Yr Fr/Am oak. **Pinotage** ★★★ **04** smoky oak & sweet red berry aromas; savoury spiciness combines well with ripe fruit; dry tannins accentuate slightly bitter finish. 4 mths Fr/Am oak. **Cabernet Sauvignon-Merlot** ★★★ **04** pronounced barnyard & blackberry aromas, dry tannins masking fruit of 80/20 blend; smokiness from just 4 mths Fr/Am oak. **Devonet Merlot-Pinotage** ★★★ **05** youthfully appealing 51/49 blend; sweet cherry, some vanilla; immediate oaky, juicy plum fruit; mild grip from 4 mths Fr/Am oak. **Sauvignon Blanc** ★★★☆ All home-grown grapes, **06** abundant fresh, upfront pineapple/tropical fruit aromas; intense, sweet passionfruit flavours carry through to zingy finish. Discontinued: **Shepherds Creek Classic Red** & **Chardonnay**. — *IM*

Clouds Vineyards

*Stellenbosch • Est 2002 • 1stB 2003 • Visits by appt • Lunches/dinners for small groups by appt • Luxury self-catering & B&B suites (see Stay-over section) • Weddings & functions • Owners Bernard & Petro Immelman • Winemakers Gyles Webb & Rudi Schultz (Thelema) • Viticulturist Matthew Castle • 2.5 ha (sauvignon) • 750 cs 100% white • PO Box 540 Stellenbosch 7599 • info@cloudsvineyards.co.za • www.cloudsguesthouse.com • **T** 021·885·1819 • F 021·885·2829*

This winery continues to make the most of its great location on the Helshoogte Pass with the recent completion of a chapel and entertainment *piazza* — if you're planning a wedding (guest list

100; luxury accommodation 10), this is one well worth booking. And the white wine served will, of course, be their single vineyard Sauvignon, made to spec by neighbouring Thelema.

Sauvignon Blanc ★★★★ Rich, bone dry **06**; full-throttle ripe gooseberry concentration paced by bright acidity; invigorating but not harsh. — *AL*

Clovelly Wines

Stellenbosch • Est/1stB 2000 • Visits by appt • Owners Mineke Toerien-Fourie, Jacques Fourie & Deon Toerien • Winemaker Jacques Fourie • 3 ha (cab) • 6 tons 2 600 cs 70% red 30% white • Postnet Suite 215 Private Bag X5061 Stellenbosch 7599 • info@clovellywines.com • www. clovellywines.com • T/F 021·865·2511/082·853·7190

This tiny family-owned vineyard — 3ha cab, the rest bought in — garnered two UK wine awards for its home-grown 03 Cab. The partnership of Deon Toerien, daughter Mineke and winemaker husband Jacques Fourie (Delaire, Wildekrans, Mount Rozier) hopes to further impress its growing local and overseas markets with six barrels of premium shiraz (see below).

Patina Shiraz new ★★★★ 100% new Fr oak matured — 'needs time to develop its own patina', explains JF. **05** classically styled & well groomed, quickish mid-palate mid-2006 but does show potential to improve with bottle-ageing. **Cabernet Sauvignon** ★★★ **03** last ed was few yrs off peak; very ripe dark-choc/cherry aromas & flavours balanced by tangy acids & savoury tannins. 14 mths oak, some new. **Triangle** ★★★ Allusion to trio of partners in this venture. Some yrs a 3-way blend, others a single variety; latter in **03**, from merlot, seasoned in older Fr oak; meaty, firm, medium-bodied, food-friendly dry tannins. **Chardonnay** ★★★ **04** not re-tasted. Pvsly we noted lovely peachy fruit somewhat blemished by alc/acid bite & obvious oak. Portion barrel fermented/aged 9-10 mths. — *IvH*

Cloverfield Private Cellar

Robertson • Est ca 1920 • 1stB 2002 • Tasting & sales Mon-Fri 9-5 Sat 10-2 • Closed Easter Fri-Sun, Dec 25 & Jan 1 • Owner Pieter Marais • Winemaker Cobus Marais (Jan 2002) • Viticulturist Pieter Marais • 120 ha (10 varieties r/w) • ±1 700 tons ±2 000 cs own label 40% red 60% white • PO Box 429 Robertson 6705 • info@cloverfield.co.za • T 023·626·4118/3 • F 023·626·3203

One could be forgiven for thinking that things happen rather slowly in this corner of the Robertson Valley, with the farm established around 1920 and the first bottling of own-wines taking place in 2002. Actually Pieter and Liz Marais' large property produces mostly for the bulk-wine market but a small percentage makes it into the own-label wines which are receiving acclaim. Their Winemaker's Selection Chardonnay claimed Michelangelo gold for the third successive year. Upgrading and expansion of the red wine cellar continues.

Winemaker's Selection

★★★★ **Chardonnay Wooded** ✓ New-oak fermented attention-grabber, shows house's penchant for crafting elegantly voluptuous chards. Fr wood, 6 mths, gives lovely rounded richness to lime fruit, pert acidity easily sees off cloy, reins in 15% alc. MIWA-applauded **05**, as pvs, has got few yrs to go.

Shiraz ★★★ Medium bodied **04** satisfying winter table companion; warm, creamy fruit-compote flavours, touch of spice, clean sweet-sour twist. Yr Fr casks, 2nd fill.

Four Clover range

Chardonnay Unwooded ★★★★ ✓ Characterful **05** similar to pvs's boldly ripe styling; fluid, almost opulent lime/dried grass flavours, citrusy acid to tame the usual brawny alc (15%). **Chenin Blanc** ★★★★ None since richly fruited, charcterful (& v ready) **04**. **Sauvignon Blanc** ★★★ Early harvesting (19°B) gives **06** a fairly raw acidity, green-spectrum flavours of grass & pea, & light body (11% alc). — *CT*

■ **Cogmans Kloof/River** see Zandvliet

Cold Duck (5th Avenue)

Carbonated sparkler by Distell. Signatures are its gentle sweetness, low alc (8%) & pineapple scents from Ferdinand de Lesseps grapes (50%, with pinotage, chenin). Latest **NV** ☺ ★★ exuberant bubbles, candyfloss highlights to tickle your fancy. Try with prosciutto! — *CvZ*

Coleraine Wines

Paarl • Est 1998 • 1stB 1999 • Tasting & sales Mon-Fri 10-3 Sat 10-1 • Fee R10 • Closed Easter Fri-Mon, Dec 25/26 & Jan 1; phone ahead on other pub hols • Tours by appt • Walks • Owners C & HK Kerr • Winemaker/viticulturist Clive Kerr • 30 ha (cab, cinsaut, merlot, mourvèdre, petit v, ruby cab, shiraz, chard, sauvignon, viognier) • 4-5 000 cs own label 100% red • PO Box 579 Suider-Paarl 7624 • info@coleraine.co.za • www.coleraine.co.za • T 021·863·3443 • F 086·617·8723

'Another stunning harvest,' enthuses owner/winemaker Clive Kerr of the 2006 intake. Now that he's got Merlot down pat, and is happy with the Cab and Shiraz, he'll be glad to welcome visitors to taste them on the Paarl farm. An old barn, circa 1800s, has been revamped as the new tasting room. Honours at the Paarl Shiraz Challenge and Trophy Wine Show, among others, will take pride of place on the walls.

★★★★ **Culraithin Syrah** Deeply scented & amply fruited, but with lingering elegance. Sample **04** retains refined, minty, spiced berry character but in broader mould that manages (just!) — whopping 15.5% alc. No **03**. Exceptional **02** (★★★★☆) won Paarl Vintners Challenge. Yr Fr barrels, 25% new.

★★★★ **Culraithin Merlot 04** unready for tasting at press time. 2005 TWS trophy for **03**, last ed noted as showing plump magenta-toned fruits, butcher-shop richness & finely tuned tannins. 2 yrs in cask, 10% new Fr.

Culraithin Cabernet Sauvignon Sample **04** heady, touch volatile; choc-plum flesh shot with cellar-standard 15% alc. Yr Fr barriques, 25% new. **Culraithin Cabernet Sauvignon-Merlot** ★★★ Once-off **99** still available, not retasted. 60/40 blend, 40% new Fr oak. **Fire Engine Red** ★★★ **05** easy drinking equal merlot/shiraz blend proffers generous fruit, ends touch sweet. Seasoned oak matured. **Culraithin Viognier** new ★★★ **06** opulent & unambiguous; almond/peach pip & tropical flesh to girth, astringent finish on sample tasted mid-2006. — *DS*

Colmant Cap Classique & Champagne   new

Franschhoek • Est/1stB 2005 • Visits Fri 10-6 & Sat 10-1 or by appt (T 072·368·4942) • Fee R15 for glass of champagne • Owners Jean-Philippe & Isabelle Colmant • Winemaker Jean-Philippe Colmant, with Nicolas Follet (2006) • Viti adviser Paul Wallace • 2.8 ha (chardonnay) • 18 tons 3 000 cs 100% MCC • PO Box 602 Franschhoek 7690 • info@colmant.co.za • www.colmant.co.za • T 021·876·4348/072·368·4942 • F 021·876·3732

The Colmants relocated from Belgium to this subdivision of the original 1694 La Motte farm with the sole purpose of making sparkling wine: a chardonnay/pinot blend, sourced from Somerset West and Robertson vineyards. Bubbly being a blender's art, they are delighted to have experts Pieter Ferreira (Graham Beck Wines) and champenois Nicolas Follet advising, and while their first own cap classique gently matures, they are building their local clientele by plying them with imported French examples, which can also be ordered from their website.

■ **Compagnies Wijne** see Oude Compagnies Post
■ **Condé** see Stark-Condé
■ **Confluence** see Douglas Wine Cellar, Landzicht

Conradie Family Vineyards

Worcester • Est/1stB 2004 • Tasting, sales & tours daily 9-5; sales also after-hours by appt • Closed Good Fri, Ascension Day, Dec 25 & Jan 1 • Fully licensed restaurant, guest house & other amenities • Owners Conradie family • Winemaker CP Conradie, with Colin Ciliers (both Jan 2004) • Viticultur-

ist CP Conradie • 91 ha (cabs s/f, merlot, pinotage, red muscadel, chard, chenin, colombard, crouchen, sauvignon) • *1 500 tons 5 300 cs own label* • *Other export brand: Saw Edge Peak* • *45% red 45% white 10% rosé* • *PO Box 5298 Worcester 6851* • *wine@conradievineyards.co.za* • *www.conradie-vineyards.co.za* • **T 023·342·1258/7025** • F 023·347·1356

Tentative steps have become bolder: heartened by a Michelangelo gold for his maiden Chenin and a quick sell-out (and no marketing!) of all he had to offer in 2005, winemaker CP Conradie expanded his cellar to cope with doubled production in 2006. An extended range will include an MCC, 'an experiment, but the base wine turned out to be very good'. Sister Elsabe will join the family business this year after completing her oenology course, making it a trio – Pieter C is the financial man.

Cabernet Sauvignon ★★★ **05** restrained expression of this sometimes exuberant variety; muted cassis aromas, flavours, coconut nuance from new Am oak (25%, rest new Fr, 13 mths), obvious tannins need yr/2 to mesh. **Chardonnay** ★★★★ Last tasted was MIWA-lauded **05**, with bright citrus notes, subtle oak (only third barrel fermented), food-friendly mien. Following all **new**: **Pinotage** ★★☆ Savoury glassful with smoked ham, bacon & sweet vanilla-oak notes. **05** lightish textured, firm tannic tail. Similar oak as Cab. **Sweet Rosaline Perlé Rosé** ★★ Feather-light, sweet, gently frothy quaffer in flirtatious frosted bottle; just 9.5% alc. **NV** blend muscat de F, sauv bl & cab, screwcapped. **Chenin Blanc** ★★★ Floral/thatch toned **06** quick-quaff with zippy acidity; texture firmed & slightly broadened by lees ageing. **Sauvignon Blanc** ★★ **06** demure summer white with leanish fruit, plumped out by touch sugar (4.5g/ℓ). **Werdoux Semi Sweet** ★★ Pretty, floral, gently sweet tipple from colombard. **06** enlivened by tangy acidity. 12% alc. Above mostly WO Nuy. – *CvZ/MF*

Conspirare

Stellenbosch (see Helderberg map) • *Est/1stB 2002* • *Tasting by appt* • *Owners HB Dowling/ LRD Trust* • *Winemaker Henry Dowling* • *Viticulturist Francois de Villiers* • *24 ha (cab s/f, merlot, shiraz, chenin)* • *250 tons 425 cs own label 100% red* • *PO Box 1210 Stellenbosch 7599* • *dowls@mweb.co.za* • **T 021·855·0722** • F 021·855·0706

Henry Dowling and singer wife Lesley-Rae have taken a three-year sabbatical from winemaking for their boutique label, Conspirare ('Breathing Together'), but they intend to vinify the current harvest. Their improbably beautiful eyrie on the Helderberg is open to visitors by appointment.

★★★★   **Conspirare** Last was quietly powerful & intense **03**, which added 14% shiraz to pvs cabs s/f, merlot blend, with no reduction of appeal. Last ed noted as good for few yrs maturation yet. 27 mths oak, 30% new. – *TJ*

Constantia de Tulbagh/Montpellier du Sud

Tulbagh • *Est 1965* • *1stB 2000* • *Visits by appt* • *Owner Lucas J van Tonder* • *35 ha (cab, merlot, pinot, chenin, riesling, sauvignon)* • *3-5 000 cs own label 15% red 80% white 5% blanc de noir* • *PO Box 79 Tulbagh 6820* • *montpellierwine@tiscali.co.za* • *www.montpellier.co.za* • **T 023·230·0656 / 083·300·6777** • F 023-230-1574

At this 330ha property, a Constantia de Tulbagh range of hand-crafted wines will reflect Johannesburg advocate Lucas van Tonder's mission to make only top quality in the upgraded 600-ton cellar. The hillside sites are ready for extensive additional planting – varieties such as cab, pinot, chardonnay, chenin, riesling and sauvignon are contemplated.

Merlot ★★★ **06** unwooded; simple & undemanding red, with volatile whiffs. Sample tasted, as for... **Pinot Noir** ★ **06** very light coloured/styled, fruity, with a hint of the variety's fragrance. **Chenin Blanc** & **Weisser Riesling**, both **04**, unrated/tasted last ed. **Méthode Cap Classique** ★★★ Last was lightish, fruity & refreshingly frothy **02**, from mostly semillon. Latest is **NV**, untasted. – *CT*

Constantia Glen

Constantia • *Est 2000* • *1stB 2005* • *Closed to public* • *Owners Tumado Investments* • *Winemaker John Loubser (Steenberg), 2005 harvest* • *Viticulturist Andrew Teubes (1999)* • *29 ha (cabs s/f,*

malbec, merlot, petit v, sauvignon) ▪ *102 tons 600 cs 100% white* ▪ *PO Box 780 Constantia 7848* ▪
wine@constantiaglen.com ▪ *www.constantiaglen.com* ▪ *T 021·794·7865* ▪ *F 021·794·9705*

This year, the fruit from Glen Alpine — a 60ha forested spread that became an Angus cattle stud
and then, at the start of this century, a wine farm — will be vinified in the new 100-ton, state-of-
the-art gravity fed cellar. The maiden vintage, a well-awarded Sauvignon, has made its way into
local restaurants and retail stores — and into top-end London eateries, most notably Mayfair's
Greenhouse, whose wine list was last year named the best in the world by *Wine Spectator*.

★★★★☆ **Sauvignon Blanc** After maiden **05** *Wine* ★★★★, another cool-climate classic in **06**,
but green flavours not exaggerated or pungent: some greenpepper, citrus, flint. Asparagus, tinned pea notes will develop with the added interest bestowed by deserved yr/
2 bottle age — certainly the beautifully balanced, taut-silk structure can cope with that,
& more. — *TJ*

Constantia Uitsig

Constantia ▪ *Est 1988* ▪ *1stB 1993* ▪ *Tasting & sales Mon-Fri 9-5 Sat & Sun 10-5* ▪ *Closed Easter
Fri, Dec 25/26, Jan 1* ▪ *Constantia Uitsig & La Colombe restaurants (see Eat-Out section);
Spaanschemat River Café for light meals 8-5* ▪ *Constantia Uitsig Hotel (see Stay-over section)*
▪ *Owners David & Marlene McCay* ▪ *Vini/viti consultants André Rousseau & John Loubser (Mar
1998/2001)* ▪ *32 ha (cab, merlot, chard, sauvignon, semillon)* ▪ *±200 tons ±12 000 cs 30% red
70% white* ▪ *PO Box 402 Constantia 7848* ▪ *wine@uitsig.co.za* ▪ *www.uitsig.co.za* ▪ *T
021·794·1810* ▪ *F 021·794·1812*

Despite a three-week late start due to the cool temperatures, harvest 2006 was a fairly easy
one for André Rousseau, producing lower yields and good quality fruit. He planted a hectare
of sauvignon, choosing clone 108 for its greener, more mineral and flinty character. André R
and the viti men of the Constantia Valley have taken up the Biodiversity & Wine Initiative
cause wholeheartedly, and are advancing a valley-wide initiative to control mealy bug by releasing natural parasites in the vineyards. A revamp of the cellar door facilities will include
new disabled-friendly features. In a well-deserved international culinary flourish, their celebrated La Colombe restaurant was named Best in the Middle East & Africa by the World's 50
Best Restaurants Academy.

★★★★ **Constantia Red** Half merlot, with cab s & 9% cab f ex-Steenberg; **03** last ed was
more showy, lushly ripe, woodier than pvs. Rich fruit, fresh acidity, soft reclusive tannins. 19 mths oak, mostly Fr 70% new, a little Am. Shd develop well few yrs or more.

★★★★☆ **Chardonnay Reserve** Lovely aromas of oatmeal, citrus on **04** (★★★★, tasted last
ed), full flavours & silky texture on palate, complemented by admirable oaking (11
mths, 70% new) — but a rather hard, hot alc glow tending to dominate finish (alc 14.
5%). **03** was full, rich & deep.

★★★★☆ **Semillon Reserve** Always serious & rather grand, but needing yr/2 to open up & to
harmonise various elements: pungent **05** typically quiet mid-2006, with emergent
nutty, toasty, lemon & lanolin hints. Elegant despite being not quite bone-dry, subtly
wooded (fermented/8 mths in 2nd/3rd fill Fr oak).

★★★★ **Constantia White** Varying blend semillon/sauvignon. After more equal partnership in
fine, serious 13% alc **04** (★★★★★), **05** returns to earlier style with 70:30 proportions,
14% alc, & not quite dry 5g/ℓ RS. Intense, powerful, with toasty citrus semillon mesh-
ing well with passionfruit of sauvignon. Big, integral acidity will assist beneficial bottle
age for few yrs — unthreatened by cork taint, like all these screwcapped whites. **03**
Wine ★★★★.

★★★★ **Sauvignon Blanc** Intense, full flavoured **06** splendidly combines green fruit &
tropicality. Some skin & lees contact abets richness which fresh acid makes all the
more appealing, while moderate 13% alc aids drinkability. These, like all the Uitsig
whites, benefit greatly from bottle.

★★★★ **Chardonnay Unwooded** Always convincing & really attractive example in increasingly popular genre; **06**, pure, untrammelled varietal aromas & flavours, broad
mouthfilling power focused by cool acidity, gd long finish — though alc (14.5%)
becoming apparent. — *TJ*

Cordoba Winery ♂♀

Stellenbosch (see Helderberg map) · Est 1982 · 1stB 1994 · Tasting only by appt Mon-Fri 8. 30-5 · Sales Mon-Fri 8.30-5 · Closed pub hols · Tours by appt · Owner Jannie Jooste · Winemaker/viticulturist Christopher Keet (Oct 1993) · 31 ha (cabs s/f, merlot, shiraz, chard) · 100 tons 7 000 cs 90% red 10% white · PO Box 5609 Helderberg 7135 · mail@ cordobawines.co.za · www.cordobawines.co.za · T 021·855·3744 · F 021·855·1690

Having been 'inwardly focused' on vineyard renewal since 2000, replacing 50% of this mountain eyrie's well-tended vines, grower-vintner Christopher Keet faces 'a great challenge': marketing Cordoba's select range of classics amid the plethora of new wines and brands, the flood of export labels, the plenitude of quality reds. But he's thrilled with the results of his team's hard work in the vineyard: 'stunning' cab franc (his métier), cab and merlot. Another challenge — disproving the myth that young vines cannot produce quality wine — is being well met...

★★★★☆ **Crescendo** Classically oriented fine blend based on cab f — proportions may vary. Quietly assertive **03** 15% each cab s & merlot. Unusually early emergence of charm for this long developer: lovely berry fruits, cherries, minerality supported in harmonious whole by fine tannins, savoury acid, good oak (18 mths new Fr), 13.9% alc. Last yr noted as delicate, fresh, exciting, with a fine future. Note: no new Cordoba vintages tasted this ed.

★★★★ **Merlot** This always one of Cape's more serious. After refined, refreshing & persistent **01** (★★★★☆) with characteristic roast coffee/dark choc notes over cherries & minty-leafy element, **02** was more severe, though fragrant, savoury & well structured, deserving attention, time, decanting, & food. 17 mths Fr oak, 20% new.

Merlot-Cabernet Sauvignon ★★★ Typically dry, firm **02** plummy & slightly dour flavours; lightish fruit flesh over strong bones. 17 mths Fr oak, 20% new. **Chardonnay** ★★★★ Oak fermented/matured (9 mths, 33% new) **04** as usual rounded but elegant, with lime-marmalade & toast-vanilla notes of oak; drinkability helped by easy 13% alc. Discontinued: **Mount Claire Mountain Red**. — *TJ*

Country Cellars

Private-label range of he Spar chain of convenience stores; mainly cork-closed, though some in vintage-dated 3ℓ 'flat pack' casks. See also under Carnival and Spar SA.

Vintage-dated range

Claret ★★ **05** unready; **04**, tasted pvs ed, pleasing blend shiraz & ruby cab, with red fruit & choc flavours; slips down easily. **Shiraz-Cabernet Sauvignon** ★★☆ **05** savoury sipper with gentle tannins & softly ripe red berry fruit. Also in 3ℓ, as for... **Rosé** ★★☆ Colombard-fruited, pinotage-tinted **05**, aromas of ripe banana & blackcurrant, dry & savoury flavours. **Chardonnay** ★★ Brief oaking rounds, adds buttery touch to **06**, very soft & easy, sure not to offend. **Sauvignon Blanc** ★ Early picked **06** plain & simple, with waist-friendly low sugar & alc. **Blanc de Blanc** new ★★ From colombard; light textured **05** fruity, forthcoming & tropical; drink soon. **Chenin Blanc-Chardonnay** ★★ **05** light bodied 80/20 blend with shy fruit & brisk acidity. Also in 3ℓ cask. N/W Cape WO.

Non-vintage range

All **NV**, now in more serious looking packaging; alcs ±12% unless noted. **Classic Red** ★★ Perennial consumer favourite; latest bottling from ruby cab & pinotage, with healthy tannins, savoury goodbye. **Rosé** ★★★ Colombard replaces chenin in latest incarnation, but still tinted by pinotage, so aromas of ripe banana & blackcurrant, dry & savoury flavours. **Caresse** ★★ Blanc de noir-style semi-sweet from chenin, with dash pinotage. Aromas as light as the alc (8.5%), but a few soft berries to taste. **Dry White** ★★ Tropical-toned quaffer with some honeyed notes but ending dry. From chenin, as is... **Light** ★ As in name & alc (9.5%), so in character: light & lean as dieting drinkers would like to see themselves. **Stein** ★★ 30g/ℓ sugar does the trick, helping guava/pineapple notes to come forth; from colombard, chenin. **Late Harvest** ★★ Balanced sweetie from chenin; quite rich but not cloying, sprightly tropical nuances. All these for drinking soon. — *DH*

Cowlin Wines

Paarl • Est 2001 • Tasting & sales Mon-Fri 8-5 Sat 10-1 • Picnics: please phone for details • Closed Easter Fri, Dec 25 & Jan 1 • Tours by appt • Farm produce • Facilities for children • Walks • Small tour groups • Owners Cowlin & Malherbe families • Vini consultant Hardy Laubser (2002) • Viti consultant Gideon Malherbe • 17 ha (cab, merlot, shiraz, mourvèdre, chard, viognier) • 150 tons 5 000 cs own label 90% red 10% white • PO Box 174 Simondium 7670 • cowlinwines@iafrica.com • www.cowlinwines.co.za • T 021·874·3844 • F 021·874·2948

Although Mother Nature was really good to them last year, not all credit should go to her, say the Cowlin team. Rodney Zimba, a dab hand in the cellar, also has green fingers and under his care trees have flourished, providing welcome shade for picnickers in summer. New viognier and mourvèdre plantings are also thriving. The bird population has grown too, with many different species flocking to this twitcher's paradise.

★★★★ **Shiraz 05** alluded to pvs ed unready; when last tasted **02** showed good varietal character, generous, accommodating tannins; all in elegant, not overblown package (13.5% alc). 6 mths oak, casks/staves.

Cabernet Sauvignon ★★★ Much more open weave this yr; **03** warm, plummy fruit (just a touch raisined), pleasantly dry ripe tannic farewell. Yr Fr oak, 30% new. **Merlot ★★★★** Soft, fleshy **04** opens with classic pencil shavings & dark berried fruit, concludes with serious-minded dryness. Oak as per Cab. **Noble Hill ★★★★** Stylish (wine & packaging) cab-driven blend with merlot (39%) & introducing petit v (11%) in **04**; less beefy, more silky than last, rounded with elegant dry finish. 14 mths oak, otherwise as for Cab. **Jack's Jug ★★★** Now vintage-dated (**05**) near equal mix shiraz, cab, showing full, concentrated red plum fruit, shiraz's leathery smoke, sturdy steakhouse-friendly tannins. 6 mths Fr staves. **Poodle's Passion Sauvignon Blanc ★★★** Light textured **06** features fruit ex-Sbosch/Dbnvlle; echoes of fig leaf & gooseberry; dry, slightly gravelly acidity in tail. **Chardonnay-Semillon ★★★** Pvs **NV** was 70/30 chard-semillon; blend now reversed but quality's still same, flavours as appealing (fleshy peaches) & oak equally well integrated (3 mths with staves). — *IvH*

Craighall

Popular range of early/easy-drinkers, budget priced, by African Wines & Spirits.

> **Cabernet Sauvignon-Merlot ☺ ★★★** Excellent this yr! Distinct claret feel to **05** unpretentious red: a pleasant leafiness to well tended, fullish fruit, gentle minty/earthy notes. 60/40 mix achieves both elegance & carefree quaffability.

Rosé ★★ Ripe & slightly jammy pink from shiraz; soft, gentle, uncomplicated dry flavours. Latest bottling (**NV**) unready. **Chardonnay-Sauvignon Blanc ★★★** Introduces dash colombard to the mix (60/30) in **06**; sample shows delightful clean tropical tone, balanced fleshiness/zing for easy tippling this summer. **Sauvignon Blanc 06** sample too unformed to rate; seems bit lighter, edgier than pvs, dry & racy. All above WO W Cape. — *CT/MM*

■ **Credo** see The Company of Wine People

Crossroads Wines   <u>new</u>

Cape Town • Est/1stB 2005 • Closed to public • 5 000 cs • simphiwe@crossroadsmail.co.za • T/F 021·461·0360

The name speaks of inclusivity, and that's what this urban focused, black empowered company's all about. Its founders, and owners with shareholders on the Cape Flats and in Gauteng, include designer Simphiwe Mavuya, creative force behind the colourful labels; and brand strategist and custodian Frans Roelofse. Made by Cru Wines, the current line-up includes a premium red, Frans Antonie, an Imbongi Chenin and Shiraz, and Soweto White. Their raison d'être: 'We have a passion for wine.'

Crows Nest

Paarl ▪ Est/1stB 2003 ▪ Tasting & sales daily 8-5 ▪ Tours Mon-Sat 9-5 ▪ Farm/country-style lunches 12-3; also picnics in summer by appt ▪ Farm produce ▪ Facilities for children ▪ Tour groups ▪ Owners Marcel & Deidre de Reuck ▪ Winemaker Marcel de Reuck ▪ Viti consultant Paul Wallace (Aug 2003) ▪ 11 ha (cab, mourvèdre, shiraz, chard, viognier) ▪ 48 tons 4 000 cs 85% red 15% white ▪ PO Box 2571 Paarl 7620 ▪ info@dereuckwines.co.za ▪ T 021·869·8712 ▪ F 021·869·8714

A few notable changes, the best of which is that you no longer need to make an appointment to visit: the tasting room is now open all day, every day. You can also enjoy a farm-style lunch here, or – if you call ahead the day before – order a picnic (ie it's no longer *de rigeur* to BYO). With all catering, as Marcel de Reuck so sweetly puts it, 'by my loving wife', the Nest has never been more nurturing.

Marcel de Reuck range

★★★★ **Cabernet Sauvignon** ('Marcel de Reuck' pvs ed.) Combines power, extraction & elegance; **04** virtual clone of pvs: same dense tannins, opulent blackcurrant flavours. Very youthful still, deserves few yrs to show its true potential. Yr Fr oak, 20% new. Paarl, Dbnvlle fruit, ditto for following red.

Syrah 03 (★★★★, MIWA DG) showed excellent fruit extraction, flavour, persistence; latest **04** (★★★✩) juicy, rich, similar attractive spicy barrel character (20% new oak) but mid-2006 yard short of seriousness, complexity, needed for higher rating. 20% new oak. **Cabernet Sauvignon-Merlot** ★★★ A more sinewy, even austere styling here, aeration needed if opening in youth; **04** powerful tannins & herbaceous green walnut fruit, hot finish from 14.5% alc. Oak as for Syrah. WO Coastal. **Chardonnay** ★★★✩ Last was well crafted & harmonious **04**. Fhoek grapes; yr new oak. **Sauvignon Blanc** ★★★ From Rbtson fruit, lees-aged 10 mths, further 4 mths at cellar before release, hence attractive bottle-age nuance on **05**; medium bodied with fig & nettle flavours, clean acid bite.

Crows Nest range

No newer releases of **03** red blends **La Karnel** & **Torres Claude**. – *CT*

Croydon Vineyard Residential Estate

Stellenbosch (see Helderberg map) ▪ Est 2005 ▪ Visits by appt (see intro) ▪ Owners Croydon Vineyard Estate Homeowners Association ▪ Winemaker Corius Visser (2005), advised by Beyers Truter ▪ Viticulturist Corius Visser ▪ 7 ha (cabs s/f, malbec, merlot, pinotage, shiraz) ▪ 56 tons ±5 000 cs ▪ 100% red ▪ Croydon Wine Company, Unit 1, Croydon Vineyard Estate, Croydon, Somerset West 7130 ▪ winemaker@croydon-estate.co.za ▪ www.croydon-estate.co.za ▪ T 021·843·3610 ▪ F 021·843·3609

This residential-cum-wine estate (a Beyers Truter 'signature' development), is in full swing: 17 000 bottles were made last year, the winery is now open for tastings and a function venue available for hire. Residents are allocated a fifth of production. Last year, Corius Visser planted malbec to extend play when blending but he remains committed to being a 'Cape blend' producer – wines will always show a ±30% pinotage content.

Both ★★★✩ **04**. **Title Deed** ✓ Red berry notes reflect 58% cab, 12% merlot, with plum/mulberry whiffs & ample tannin from pinotage. Mouthfilling flavours & gd length – altogether food-friendly. **Covenant** Another 'Cape blend' – cab/pinotage/merlot/petit v in 42/30/18/10 proportions. Blackcurrant, raspberry aroma & persistent, spicy finish. Robust & sumptuous, yet not unrefined. Both yr in oak, none new. Some magnums. – *MF*

Cru Wines

Paarl ▪ Tasting & sales Mon-Sat 9-5 ▪ Deli/bistro & other attractions (see intro) ▪ Owner DS Sarnia (Pty) Ltd ▪ Cellarmaster Wrensch Roux ▪ Assistant winemaker Samantha Hughes ▪ Viticulturist Wilhelm van Rooyen ▪ Export brands: Due South, Rising River, Withof, Marimba & ranges below ▪ PO Box 1317 Paarl 7620 ▪ info@cruwines.co.za ▪ T 021·863·1471 ▪ F 021·863·1473

Though relatively young, this production and marketing company reports that it's going from strength to strength. Its focus is to continue expanding both the local and international markets. Wines can be tasted on the Zonnebloem Vineyards property, where visitors can also enjoy a picnic with a view of the Berg River or choose from the alfresco menu at the deli.

Alphen Hill range

Cabernet Sauvignon ★★★ 03 sold out, **04** not ready for tasting. **Merlot ★★★ 04** step up in quality; delicate & understated, gentle black fruits, signature soft tannins for early drinking. **Pinotage ★★★ 04** unmistakable high-toned red fruit, sweet raspberry entry, supple tannins; eminently drinkable. **Shiraz ★★ 04** ultra soft acidity & tannins for early enjoyment; sweet fruit dusted with light spices. **06**s of following duo unready: **Chenin Blanc ★★★ 05** (sample) was fairly neutral, tastes off-dry despite low 2.9g/ℓ RS. **Sauvignon Blanc ★★★ 05** last ed noted as plump & jolly, tropical fruit delivered with charm & some flair.

Bushman's Creek range

Cabernet Sauvignon new **★★★** Light textured **04** restrained & soft; sweet cassis fruit wraps around integrated oak, alc & fruit. For early enjoyment. **Shiraz ★★★** Slightly built **04**'s medicinal aromas lifted by sour cherries & spice; soft tannins encourage early drinking. **Cabernet Sauvignon-Merlot ★★★ 04**'s berried tone touched with slight earthy note; lightweight mid-palate, low tannins aid approachability. **Chardonnay ★★★ 06** in pipeline, no **05**; **04** more heavily wood influenced than pvs, but well knit; caramel patina to peach fruit; fleshy yet finishes dry. **Sauvignon Blanc ★★★ 06** unready. **05** last ed was appealing, with lots of vitality & youth.

Dolphin Bay range:

Pinotage-Ruby Cabernet ★★★ 04 lively 70/30 blend with wild berry & strawberry on nose, soft & smooth on palate. Not retasted. **Pinotage Rosé ★★** Semi-dry sunset sipper with active 13% alc; **06** melange of berry fruit, light tannins go well with food. **Chenin Blanc ★★ 06** a sleek runway model compared to generously proportioned **05**; latest is crisp & dry with delicate floral scents. **Sparkling Brut ★★** Carbonated fizz from chenin; **NV** (06); frothy, fresh & fun with charming lemony notes. All ranges WO W Cape. — IvH

Culemborg

This big-volume range of easy-drinkers is made by DGB.

No new vintages tasted for these. Note: some reds lightly seasoned with Fr oak. **Cabernet Sauvignon ★★★★** Classic cab aromas/flavours on **03**, dry but soft dusty tannins, easy drinking. **Pinotage ★★★** Muted but quintessential mulberry aromas/flavours; **03** soft, sweet jammy finish. **Merlot ★★★** Balanced, well made everyday red; **03** smooth choc/plum flavours, mere suggestion of tannin. **Cinsault ★★** Undemanding **05**, plum & fruitcake flavours, soft dry tannins. **Cape Red ★★** Mainly cinsaut & ruby cab, **04** with those varieties' ripe-berried friendliness & generosity. **Rosé ★★** Off-dry & gluggable **05**, hints strawberry & dried fruit, tangy fruit-cordial flavours from pinotage. **Blanc de Noir ★★ 05** similar to Rosé. **Chardonnay ★★** Quaffable commercial style. **04** subtle but fresh melon/peach tone. Fermented with Fr oak. **Chenin Blanc ★★** Not overtly chenin, but **05** a pleasant, fresh, juicy dry white. **Sauvignon Blanc ★★ 05**, light (12.4% alc) zesty dry white, for casual quaffing within yr of harvest. **Cape White ★★★** Pleasantly rounded from bottle-age, **04** equal chenin/colombard mix; light, with sweet grape/floral aroma. All WO W Cape. — DH

■ **Culraithin** see Coleraine

Dalla Cia Wine & Spirit Company 🍷👨‍🍳

Stellenbosch ▪ Est 2004 ▪ Tasting venue & bistro opening Jan 2007 (see intro) ▪ Owner Giorgio Dalla Cia ▪ 9 000 cs ▪ 11 Papegaai St Stellenbosch 7600 ▪ info@dallacia.com ▪ www.dallacia. com ▪ T/F 021·887·2480

'We always have a great vintage in the Cape,' says an upbeat Giorgio Dalla Cia, the winemaker who helped introduce bordeaux-style reds to SA while at Meerlust and now makes a cracking 'claret' for the his family's Dalla Cia label. Wife Simonetta and daughter-in-law Elana are an accomplished catering team, and with GDC and son George, who's MD of the company, opened an Italian-style wine and espresso bar-cum-bistro in Stellenbosch last year. Now GDC is keen to track down some quality petit verdot. Because the variety can add structure, finesse and longevity to a blend, Dalla Cia believes 'it could become the greatest winning card for the Cape'. Growers take note.

★★★★ **Giorgio** Gets even better, **03** (★★★★☆) is deep & intensely perfumed, a wine of finesse, craftsmanship. Complex layers of cool-grown berry fruit, herbal nuances, dark choc, a pinch of spice. Svelte tannins offer immediate drinking pleasure but 18 mths mainly new Fr oak ensure longevity. Cabs s/f, merlot 46/29/24. Deliciously drinkable **02** cab/merlot (70/30) similarly well structured for ageing. Also in magnums.

Chardonnay ★★★ **06** this & next first SA wines closed with synthetic Guala Seal. Just bottled, still muted mid-2006 but quite individual: fresh peach, biscuit tones plus intriguing floral & fennel layers. Drinkability is assured by the zesty acidity. 9 mths on lees. **Sauvignon Blanc** ★★★★ Reflecting the vintage, lovely fruit purity in **06**, gooseberry & lime, with trademark food-friendly palate minerality, racy finish. — *CR*

■ *Danckaert* see Citrusdal Cellars
■ *Danie de Wet* see De Wetshof

Darling Cellars

Groenekloof/Darling (see Durbanville/Darling map) • *Est/1stB 1996* • *Tasting & sales Mon-Thu 8-5 Fri 8-4 Sat 10-2* • *Closed Easter Fri/Sun, Dec 25 & Jan 1* • *BYO picnic* • *Tours by appt* • *Owners ±20 shareholders* • *Cellarmaster Abé Beukes (Dec 1997)* • *Winemakers Johan Nesenberend (reds, Dec 1996) & Albé Truter (whites, Dec 2003)* • *Viti consultant Gawie Kriel (Sep 2001)* • *1 300 ha (cab, merlot, pinotage, shiraz, cinsaut, chard, chenin, sauvignon)* • *6-7 000 tons 300 000 cs* • *65% red 33% white 2% rosé* • *BRC, IFS & ISO 9001:2000 certified* • *PO Box 114 Darling 7345* • *info@darlingcellars.co.za or jsheppard@darlingcellars.co.za or mnel@darlingcellars.co.za* • *www.darlingcellars.co.za* • *T 022·492·2276* • *F 022·492·2647*

This can-do cellar has added HACCP certification to their growing list of international quality management testimonials. Another credit: the Flamingo Bay and DC ranges are to be screwcapped to avoid any (corky) disappointments. On a celebratory note, red-wine maker Johan Nesenberend has plenty to smile about: 2006 brought his first-born (Sophia) into the world; and he now has ten vintages under his belt. And 2007 sees Darling Cellars reach its first decade. Any plans to celebrate these milestones? Limited releases plus a HUGE party!

Onyx range

★★★★☆ **Kroon** Cellar's flagship, unusual & stylish blend shiraz, pinotage, grenache & cinsaut, co-fermented; **03** slightly more shiraz, less pinotage (55/35/5/5); layered dark fruits with savoury & spicy notes working in complex, richly textured harmony. New Fr 300ℓ barrels (13 mths) add support & spice. Powerful (14.6 alc) yet sleek, long juicy finish with gd ageing potential.

★★★★ **Cabernet Sauvignon 03** abundance of ripe cassis woven with liquorice, spice & scented violets. Sleekly textured with supportive dry tannins keeping all in tailored line. Layers of flavour — coffee, sweet tobacco & choc — continue on sustained finish. Gd food wine with some yrs potential. 60-70% new Fr oak , ±14.5% alc. Off ±10 yr old dryland bushvines, low cropped.

★★★★ **Pinotage** Extrovert, fruitier style. Whiffs cardamom, vanilla, violets & strawberry added impressive complexity to **03** when tasted mid-2005; made an elegant statement despite 14.8% alc. 100% new Fr oak.

★★★★ **Shiraz 03** last ed was bold & impressive, with fresh acidity, finely focused tannins. Gamey, less alcoholic but with similar peppery black fruit profile as **02**. Fr oak, 60% new, ±yr.

★★★★☆ **Noble Late Harvest 03** sold out unreviewed. **02** (from chenin) mid-2005 showed daunting sweetness enlivened by tangy fruit-acid that raced across palate. 240g/ℓ RS, 9.5g/ℓ, 11.5% alc; 5-9 mths Fr barrels. **Barrel Selection** The 2 best **02** casks, 14 mths older wood; drier (120g/ℓ), firmer; botrytis more evident among candied fruit flavours.

Sauvignon Blanc ★★★★ **06** similar green & racy character to pvs, hints herb, nettle & 'wet slate', vibrant acidity balanced by fruit. 12.5% alc. This WO Darling, all above Groenekloof WO.

DC range

★★★★ **Black Granite Shiraz** Flagship of this fruit driven varietal range back on form in **05** with dense profusion of spicy red fruit & black pepper. Firm tannins keep abundance in check, bright acidity gives juicy concentrated impression. Shd develop well over 3-5 yrs. Attractive **04** (★★★★) left wanting for fruit-shy palate. Now barrels only for all these reds — no staves of pvs — none new.

Terra Hutton Cabernet Sauvignon ★★★★ **04** differs from pvs ripe & porty style: leafier & more restrained with notes of cassis. Balanced fruit-pastille palate with dry tannins & integrated oaking. Some potential to develop. **Six Tonner Merlot** ★★★ **05** brasher than plummy/minerally pvs, though similar bold alc (14.7%). Very ripe, with tarry tannins, macho & chunky, needs suitably robust fare. **Old Block Pinotage** ★★★★ Ex-35 yr old vyd, **05** soft smoky notes, leather & red plum fruit; as pvs, well structured with firm tannins, bright acidity. **Quercus Gold Chardonnay** ★★★ In fact, these are 'quercus-free' — unwooded, early picked & undemanding; **06** lighter (11.9% alc) than pvs with similar floral acacia, lemon/lime character; promising palate, citrus grip & chalky finish. **'Chenin Blanc'** new ★★★ Name undecided at press time; soft, rounded style (14% alc) with ripe Golden Delicious apple & some toasty notes from light oaking; acidity tad spiky & unknit on **06** sample. **Bush Vine Sauvignon Blanc** ★★★★ ✓ **06** similar style to pvs. Grassy, dusty & flinty flavours & textures, racy acidity. Early picked (±11.5 % alc) dryland bushvines. Above WO Darling, ranges below, Coastal.

Flamingo Bay range

'Buy by the caseload!' winemakers suggest these well priced quaffers. **Cinsaut-Cabernet Sauvignon** ☺ ★★★ **05** 70/30 blend with ripe dark fruit & toasty nuances ex-staves. Balanced, friendly medium bodied drinkability. **Lagoon Rosé** ☺ ★★★ Flamingo-pink (ex-pinotage) **06** light & dry with refreshing sweet/sour twist on the finish. Flavoursome summer sipper. **Chenin Blanc-Sauvignon Blanc** ☺ ★★★ **06** brighter, fresher version of pvs, same 80/20 blend, same light (11.6% alc) dry & fruity drinkability. Enjoy young.

Zantsi Natural Sweet range

Both **NV** & just over 10% alc. **Rosé** ★ Coral hued sweetie from buket & pinotage; sherbetty acidity freshens light-styled palate. **White** ★★ 100% buket; sweet-sour nose & palate, with some passionfruit; short, light & bright. Finds favour in France as aperitif. — *MW*

Daschbosch Wine Cellar

*Breedekloof (see Worcester map) ▪ Est 1956 ▪ 1stB 1965 ▪ Tasting & sales Mon-Fri 8-5 Sat & pub hols 10-2 ▪ Closed Christian holidays ▪ BYO picnic ▪ Children welcome ▪ 'Fear Factor' wine tasting, cheese platters & accommodation by prior arrangement ▪ Conference facilities for max 50 ▪ Tour groups ▪ Walks ▪ Owners 30 shareholders ▪ Winemakers Gerrit van Zyl & Johan Lotz (Jun 2000/Jun 2004), with Wilhelm le Roux (Sep 2002) ▪ Viticulturist Gerrit van Zyl (Jun 2000) ▪ 890 ha (15 varieties, r/w) ▪ 14 700 tons 3 500 cs own label 50% red 40% white 10% fortified ▪ Ranges for customers: Welgevonde (Nthrlnds/Belgium); Sebeko & Cape Concert (Shoprite Checkers), Cape Promise (UK) & Waverley (TBS) ▪ BRC & HACCP accredited ▪ PO Box 174 Rawsonville 6845 ▪ cellar@daschbosch.co.za ▪ www.daschbosch.co.za ▪ **T** 023·349·1110 ▪ **F** 023·349·1980*

For an unusual food and wine pairing, book here — in four easy steps you'll teach your palate what wine's all about. The first event, held on a mountain-top reached in a tractor-drawn vehicle, was immediately dubbed Fear Factor, after one guest was almost shaken off en route and all were met by a hostile puff adder! On a more delicate note, there are several additions to the range — a Red Nectar, a Shiraz and a demi-sec sparkler — launched to mark the cellar's 50th anniversary.

Sauvignon Blanc ☺ ★★★ **06** brims with cool fruit, buoyed by zesty lemon acidity & finishes with a gooseberry/greengage flourish.

Pinotage Reserve ★★ Oak-derived vanilla & coconut aromas/flavours (18 mths new wood) sadly overwhelm varietal characteristics on **03**. Flavours seem dilute, lacking concentration, as with… **Shiraz** new ★★ **04** eucalyptus, resin & smoke notes dominate the fruit, leading to firm, dryly tannic finish. 60% oak, 18 mths. **Cabernet Sauvignon-Cabernet Franc** ★★★ Well rounded 60/40 mix tasted pvs ed; **02** muted but ripe mint & plum tones. **Rosé** new ★★ **05** a happy off-dry strawberry/plum tipple from pinotage, spruced up by tangy acidity. **Chenin Blanc** new ★★ Pleasant summer quaffer **06**, with tropical tones, brightly fresh. **Sparkling Demi-Sec** new Carbonated bubbly from hanepoot. **06** not ready for tasting. **Nectar de Provision Red** new ★★ **NV** red version of white below; from unfermented merlot juice fortified to 16.5% alc with oak matured brandy, then portion yr in wood. Sample shows subdued berry & plum character, spirituous & vibrant entry & unctuous finish. Though 245g/ℓ sugar a smidgen lower, it seems sweeter than… **Nectar de Provision White** ★★★★ ✓ First local version of Cognac's classic aperitif, Pineau des Charentes; made like red, but from colombard, 12-18 mths wooded. Latest **NV** bursts with orange, choc-mint & vanilla notes; silky, decadent but not cloying. These seem to be ageless. **Ruby Cabernet**, **Chardonnay** & **Louwshoek-Voorsorg Hanepoot** discontinued. — *DH*

■ *Dassie's Reserve* see Botha Wine Cellar

David Frost Estate ♙♟♞

Paarl ▪ Est 1994 ▪ 1stB 1997 ▪ Tasting & sales Mon-Fri 10-5 ▪ Owner David Frost ▪ ±24 ha (five bdx reds, shiraz) ▪ 100% red ▪ PO Box 7358 Noorder-Paarl 7623 ▪ davidfrost@global.co.za ▪ www.frostwine.com ▪ T 021·869·8339 / 072·417·4527 ▪ F 021·869·8732

A name change (from last edition's Daview Vineyards) for pro-golfer David Frost's wine farm. Awaiting admission onto the masters golf circuit, Frost completed the tasting room (a showcase for his golfing memorabilia), re-jigged his labels and re-negotiated working relationships (wines and vineyards will now be tended by Wynand Pienaar, assisted by farm stalwart Freddie Theunissen).

★★★★ **Cabernet Sauvignon Reserve** With dash merlot, **00** intensely plummy, fine-grained tannins but mid-2004 needed 2-3 yrs more to harmonise. 22 mths Fr oak.

★★★★ **Cabernet Sauvignon 02** (★★★) powdery tannins & big alc (15%) last yr fought for dominance over ripe blackcurrant flavours. Cellaring shd give fruit the upper hand. 18 mths 42% new Fr oak. **01** had velvet tannins, tapered slowly to persistent finish.

★★★★ **Par Excellence 02** cab-dominated bdx-style blend, aptly named, given David F's golfing links. Last ed showed excellence in flavour department too. Deep, slightly decadent choc-truffle tones; structure & intensity to improve 6-7yrs. 18 mths new Fr oak.

Merlot Reserve ★★★★ Massive **00** ripe plum, prune flavours & 'hot' 15.5% alc. Generous tannins from 20 mths Fr oak (30% new) & sweet jammy finish. No new vintage in sight; ditto for… **Merlot** ★★★ **02** savoury & high-toned, packs tremendous fruit & alc (15.4%) on the finish. Shd mellow with time in bottle. **Shiraz 04** barrel sample showed ★★★★ potential mid-2005. Powerful, with very ripe, concentrated fruit; bold tannins. Needs 2-3 yrs to integrate, grow into its frame. **Cabernet Sauvignon-Merlot** Elegant structure & opulent fruit last ed augured well for fine integration; already creamy, velvety, nodding at ★★★★. — *CR*

■ *Daview Vineyards* see David Frost Estate
■ *DC Wines* see Darling Cellars
■ *Decent Red* see Southern Cape Vineyards

De Compagnie

*Wellington ▪ Est/1stB 2002 ▪ Tasting & tours by appt ▪ Fee R10 ▪ Sales Mon-Fri 8-4.30 or by appt ▪ Meals for groups of 2-30 by appt ▪ Owners 2 shareholders ▪ PO Box 395 Wellington 7654 ▪ mail@ decompagnie.co.za ▪ www.decompagnie.co.za ▪ **T** 021·864·1241 ▪ F 021·864·3620*

Johann Loubser and wife Riana Scheepers, co-owners of this 300-year-old Wellington property, are winding down production of their Cabernet Sauvignon and bordeaux-styled red, Privaatkeur, and focusing on a Natural Estate Potstill Brandy in 5- and 10-year-old variants.

De Doorns Winery

*Worcester ▪ Est 1968 ▪ Tasting & sales Mon-Fri 8-5 Sat 8-12 ▪ Winemaker/manager Danie Koen, with Ferdie Coetzee ▪ PO Box 129 De Doorns 6875 ▪ ddwk@hexvallei.co.za ▪ **T/F** 023·356·2835 ▪ F 023·356·2101*

This co-op in the scenic Hex River Valley has a friendly, welcoming face in the form of a Cape Dutch 'wine house' near the N1 highway, open on weekdays and Saturday mornings. Regulars on the wine list are a Cab, Roodehof Dry Red, Chardonnay, Chenin, Colombar, Late Harvest, Red Muscadel, Hanepoot and Demi-sec Sparkling, none tasted.

Deetlefs Estate

*Breedekloof (see Worcester/Breedekloof map) ▪ Est 1822 ▪ Tasting, sales & tours Mon-Fri 8-5 Sat 10-4 ▪ Closed Easter Fri, Dec 25 & Jan 1 ▪ Picnic baskets by appt or BYO ▪ Owner Kobus Deetlefs ▪ Cellarmaster Willie Stofberg (Aug 2004) ▪ Viticulturist Coenie van Dyk (Sep 2003) ▪ 100 ha (cab, malbec, merlot, pinotage, shiraz, chard, chenin, sauvignon, semillon) ▪ ±1 000 tons 40% red 50% white 5% rosé 5% fortified ▪ BRC certified ▪ PO Box 36 Rawsonville 6845 ▪ sales@deetlefs.com ▪ www.deetlefs.com ▪ **T** 023·349·1260 ▪ F 023·349·1951*

The Deetlefs family have farmed in the cool shadow of the Du Toitskloof mountains since 1822. Sixth-generation incumbent Kobus Deetlefs heads a wide ranging wine enterprise whose focus on quality has seen plaudits for the independent wine laboratory, while eco-credentials include a fully fledged biological waste-water treatment plant on the estate. Enjoying a boost from the release of his Deetlefs Familie range and the granting of Breedekloof Wine of Origin status, Kobus D is especially upbeat about the future.

★★★★ **Philippus Petrus Muscat d'Alexandrie** Superb old muscat, a rarity; individual & exotic, to drink by the thimbleful at end of a fine dinner. To date the **74**, next release in 2025!

Deetlefs Familie range

★★★★ **Semillon** Limpid, golden **05** has best barrel of sauvignon making 12% of blend; 5% botrytised semillon & oak fermentation adds dimension & complexity to fresh herbaceousness. Still in restrained, minerally youth, needs time to develop. 9 mths 20% new Fr. Swiss gold.

★★★★ **Semillon Noble Late Harvest** Pale yellow-gold **06** complex orange peel & apricot aromas, flavours; unctuously textured sweetness (140g/ℓ RS) avoids cloying, with fresh, fine acidity giving delightfully zesty finish, underpinned by 9 mths 2nd fill Fr oak. Unfiltered.

Weisser Riesling ★★★☆ **06** sample more spicy than floral rendition of this fine variety; peppery, aromatic intensity & attractively low 11.7% alc; mineral finish. **Méthode Cap Classique** Moves here from range below; sold-out **00** was last vintage tasted.

Deetlefs Estate range

★★★★ **Oak Matured Pinotage** new Dense, brambly fruit charms in **05**, compact sweet-fruit flavours, tannins & alc maintain balance & lead flavour-packed finish. Judicious 9 mths Fr stave maturation.

Merlot ★★★ Ripe, sweet plum & mocha aromas abound in **04**; surprisingly savoury palate & firm tannins through to finish; moderate 13.5% alc welcome. Older Fr barrels. **Pinotage** ★★★☆ Succulent berry flavours are restrained by firm, ripe grape tannins in lightly staved **05**. **Shiraz** ★★★ **02** was last tasted; showed elegant red fruit & pepper tones.

. **Chardonnay** ★★★ Aromas of pear-drops in lightly wooded **05** with some white peach & spice; oak evident on finish. **Sauvignon Blanc** ★★★ Preview **06** has 10% semillon; melange tropical fruits; vibrant passionfruit flavours & lively acidity; substantial weight despite low 11.8% alc. **Semillon** ★★★ Fresh, lean & balanced **06**, unwooded, lightweight & minerally with soft lemon finish. **Weisser Riesling** ★★★★ Charming & youthful **05** offers delightfully floral aromas typical of variety, apple & citrus flavours & zingy acidity; 21g/ℓ sugar and 11.8% alc impart soft charm before dryish, minerally farewell. **Hanepoot** new ★★★★ Fortified **06** in tall 375ml bottle; lovely yellow-gold glints; perfumed grapey muscat aromas, intense dried peach & spicy raisin sweetness, with clean finish. **Chenin Blanc** Latest **05** not reviewed, to be discontinued.

Stonecross range

Shiraz new ★★★ **04** vanilla & smoked bacon precede spicy blackberry fruit & firm chewy tannins, providing grip. **Pinotage** ★★★★ Pronounced sweet dark fruit & serious, meaty aromas, concentrated flavours in ripe **05**, balanced by soft tannins & dry finish; 14.5% alc well concealed. **Merlot-Pinotage** ★★★ Agreeably drinkable juicy, plummy **05**, 60:40 blend offers sweet fruit & soft, well meshed tannins. **Rosé** ★★ **06** attractive onion skin colour from pinotage, subtle strawberry aromas & flavours, finishes dry. W Cape vyds, so NE. **Chardonnay** new ★★★ **06** appealing peachy aromas with citrus flavours offering some concentration & weight. Balanced, crisp acidity. **Sauvignon Blanc** new ★★ Lightly herbaceous **06** with pineapple fruit & low 12.5% alc for uncomplicated drinking. **Chenin Blanc-Chardonnay** ★★ **05** medium bodied, balanced 80/20 blend with some discernible melon & peach tones. **Sauvignon Blanc-Semillon** ★★ **05** 60:40 mix with low 12.5% alc & light lime cordial finish. All ranges WO Brdekloof unless noted. — *IM*

De Grendel Wines

Durbanville • Est 1720 • 1stB 2004 • Visits Mon-Fri 9-5 Sat 9-4 • Closed Good Fri, Dec 25 & Jan 1 • Farm produce • Walks • Conservation area • Owner David Graaff • Winemaker Charles Hopkins (Oct 2005), with Elzette du Preez • Viticulturists Johnnie de Flamingh & Granville Klerk • 104 ha (cabs s/f, malbec, merlot, mourvèdre, petit v, pinot, shiraz, chard, semillon, viognier) • 15 000 cs 40% red 60% white • PO Box 15282, Panorama, Cape Town 7506 • info@ degrendel.co.za • www.degrendel.co.za • T 021·558·6280 • F 021·558·7083

Harvest 2006 was the first handled in the new 600-ton cellar — cellarmaster Charles Hopkins consulted on design aspects and is delighted with its functionality and practicality. Hopkins and assistant Elzette du Preez are equally pleased with their location, invoking the movie title *A Room with a View* to describe this Tygerberg Hills property overlooking Table Mountain. 'The support of the Graaff family, vineyards 120-350m above sea level and just 7km from the Atlantic, a motivated winemaking team... it must all add up to something special in the bottle.'

★★★★ **Sauvignon Blanc** Nine vyd blocks blended to create the layered house style captured in **06**, showing pungent & classic whiffs of 'Dbnvlle dust', with tangy grapefruit & granadilla broadened by 4 mths *sur lie* ageing; lovely cleansing acidity begs another glass.

★★★★ **Winifred** new Elegant & restrainedly flavourful white named for wife of owner David G. **06** 40% each semillon & chard, 20% viognier. Captivating bouquet of vanilla & thatch with spicy lemon accents, zesty acidity & long, measured finish. Chard & viognier fermented/4 mths in Fr oak; natural acidity reined in by partial malo. Hugely appealing now, has structure & intensity to improve few yrs.

Merlot ★★★★ Sensuous **05** ups the wattage with elegant bouquet of candied plum & dusty spice, plummy mid-palate controlled by firm but svelte tannins, warm, lingering farewell (14.5%). **Shiraz** ★★★★ High quality fruit evident in **05**'s pure red berry character, notes of sour cherry & black pepper, all easily hiding muscular 15% alc. Well judged grip & spice from complex oaking (13 mths 30% new Am, 30% new Fr, 30% 2nd/3rd fill Fr!). — *CvZ*

■ **De Groene Heuwel** *see* Linton Park
■ **De Heuvel Estate** *see* Bianco
■ **Dekker's Valley** *see* Mellasat

De Krans ♀♨🐌♌👤

*Calitzdorp (see Little Karoo map) • Est 1964 • 1stB 1977 • Tasting & sales Mon-Fri 8-5 Sat 9-3 • Tasting fee for groups R10 pp • Closed Easter Fri/Sun, Dec 25 • Tours by appt • Vintners platters 12-2 Wed & Sat during Feb (also pick your own hanepoot grapes) • BYO picnic • Olive oil for sale • Tour groups • Self-guided vineyard walks year round • Owners/winemakers Boets & Stroebel Nel (1982, 1988) • Viti consultant Willem Botha (2001) • 45 ha (cab, pinotage, tempranillo & port varieties, chard, chenin & muscats) • 500 tons • 20-25 000 cs 50% red 10% white 3% rosé 37% fortifieds • PO Box 28 Calitzdorp 6660 • diekrans@mweb.co.za • www. dekrans.co.za • **T 044·213·3314/64** • F 044·213·3562*

After a difficult 2005 — the brothers Nel decided to bottle no Cab or Pinotage — the 2006 vintage was 'the smallest harvest ever but probably the best quality in more than five years,' says Boets N. Port's his forte — the Vintage Reserve went for the second highest price at last year's Nederburg Auction — and producing wines that speak of Calitzdorp is his goal: 'There are too many boring wines, produced in different regions, that ultimately have the same characteristics.'

★★★★ Red Stone Reserve Front-runner of the reds, named for ruddy cliffs visible from the cellar. **05**, touriga + 30% cab as usual, flaunts showy plum/fynbos scents, then savoury/salty flavours. Continues on path set by focused, fruit-rich **04**, & shares its considerable tannic profile, needing 4-7 yrs to soften. These 10 mths Fr oak, half new.

★★★★ White Muscadel Jerepigo ✓ Varietal character preserved by picking before too many grapes raisin. Tasted last ed, **05** intense muscat aromas with curry leaf, nut, khaki-bush. Refreshing smack of tealeaf on long finish. At 205g/ℓ RS, touch sweeter than **03**. **04** untasted.

★★★★ White Muscadel Reserve ✓ Muscat de F vyd close to 20 yrs old, fortified to just 15. 5% alc. **05**, tasted ex-tank, silky, gentle & uncloying; ample lychee/marmalade flavours & fresh, citrus persistence. Now 160g/ℓ RS, for 'drinkability & balance'. **04** (★★★★) more delicate flavours, shortish finish. Almost 70% goes to warm admirers in cooler European climes.

★★★★★ Vintage Reserve Port A Cape flagship, declared only in best yrs. Time-honoured tinta, touriga, souzão (50/38/10) & smidgen tinta r, fortified with unmatured spirit to 20%, balancing 90g/ℓ RS. Violet/tobacco notes; fruit sweetness integrates seamlessly with alc, tannin for quintessential elegance — but shd still develop ±15 yrs. These typically16 mths in 4 000ℓ vats, **04** given firmer grip/structure from 22 mths in cask. Flawless structure, brooding fruit also marked **03** (Wine ★★★★★).

★★★★ Cape Vintage Port ✓ Consistent charmer, made every year; from tinta b, touriga, souzão (50/40/10 in **04**); ±18 mths in 500ℓ oak, 19% alc. **04**, tasted ex-barrel, won't disappoint, with choc/Xmas-cake nose & gd spirit/tannic grip & length. Similar character & wonderful smoothness on **03**. These drinkable earlier than VR, but better after 2-3 yrs min.

★★★★★ Cape Tawny Port ✓ **NV**, mainly tinta b with touriga, tinta r from ±8 yr old vines, lifted by drop younger touriga port. Usually 104g/ℓ RS, 19% alc. Current version, flamboyantly deploys toffee/fudge/coffee aromas & flavours, revved up with cinnamon & cardamom scents. Lively acid/spirit grip, silky. SAA, Santé gold, JCWCA 'first'/gold. Pvs was tangy, weighty, also well-awarded. In 375ml too.

★★★★ Cape Ruby Port ✓ Perky, dependable **NV** blend tinta, touriga, souzão (50/45/5). Latest has dried herbs/tealeaf scents mingling with generous fruitcake/marzipan aromas/flavours; 'iron fist in velvet glove' tannins & alc (18.5%), with 95g/ℓ sugar. 50% in 500ℓ casks, rest in 4 500ℓ. Also in screwcapped 250ml.

Touriga Nacional Among pioneers of unfortified reds from stalwart port variety. Big acidity, hefty tannins at odds (mid-2006) with **05**'s (★★★★) abundant berries; leave 3-4 yrs to mesh. **04** (★★★★) well groomed & knit. 5 mths wood. **Pinotage** ★★★ Unpretentious easy-drinker. **04**, not retasted, had temperate plum & licorice nuances, forgiving tannins (4 mths, older oak), & bitter hint. No **05**. **Tempranillo** SA's only stand-alone bottling. We last tasted sour-cherry-toned **04** (★★★★ ✓), but Nel believes **06** 'best so far' — & unrated sample suggests he may be right: has wonderfully vibrant palate. **Tinta Barocca** ★★★★ ✓ A favourite in Europe, gaining popularity back home. Salt & pepper abound on unwooded, slippery, balanced **05**, as does refreshing raspberry/spicy fruit. **Merlot-Pinotage** ★★★ Unwooded 60/40 blend; no **05**; last ed, **04** showed plums & strawberries with comfortably dry tannins, pinotage giving a tad bitter lift. **Rosé** Following gd value **04** (★★★), with strawberry/earth tones & sweet lift to finish, **06** cab/merlot blend looks to be just as gulpable (unrated, as unfinished sample tasted). **Chardonnay** ★★★ Unwooded, but 4 mths on lees for weight. **06** (tasted ex-tank) picked slightly riper than pvs for fruit intensity; restrained nose with creamy, floral & lemon notes; also cool 'wet stone' nuances. Rounded finish. **White Port** ★★★ **NV** from chenin; drier (65g/ℓ) than red stablemates; 19.5% alc. Tealeaf, nuts & cream mingle in latest, with evocative oxidative tail adding complexity. **Heritage Collection White Jerepigo** discontinued.

Cabernet Sauvignon ☺ ★★★ **04** creamy vanilla/cassis nose & palate, friendly tannins from judicious 4 mths oaking. **Relishing Red** ☺ ★★★ Juicy easy-drinker from pinotage (50%), ruby cab & merlot, partly wooded 3 mths for grip/interest. Newest **NV** gets the nod for modeate 13.5% alc – 'brought down for better drinkability', says Boets N. **Chenin Blanc** ☺ ★★★ **06** crisp, dry & lightish (12.5% alc); floral/honey aromas & flavours, toffee-apple goodbye; pithy grip from 2 mths lees-ageing. **Golden Harvest** ☺ ★★★ Delightful natural sweet **NV** from 50/50 hanepoot & gewürz. Latest with rosepetal/lime hints & a nice tickle from 40g/ℓ sugar. Drink soon. — CvZ

Delaire Winery   ◊ 🍷 🍇 ♿

Stellenbosch ▪ Est 1982 ▪ 1stB 1986 ▪ Tasting & sales Mon-Fri 9-5 Sat/ Sun 10-5 ▪ Fee R40 ▪ Closed Easter Fri, Dec 25/26 & Jan 1 ▪ Tours by appt ▪ Gifts ▪ Owner Laurence Graff ▪ Winemaker Gunter Schultz (Jan 2004) ▪ Viticulturist Bennie Booysen (Oct 2002) ▪ ±20 ha (cabs s/f, merlot, petit v, shiraz, chard, sauvignon) ▪ 170 tons 12 500 cs 60% red 40% white ▪ PO Box 3058 Stellenbosch 7602 ▪ info@delaire.co.za ▪ www.delairewinery.co.za ▪ T 021·885·1756 ▪ F 021·885·1270

Owner Laurence Graff, whose Graff Diamonds in the UK won the Queen's Award for Export Excellence for the fourth time, believes these 'Vineyards in the Sky' are among the most beautiful places on earth. They're set to become glossier still with considerable capital channelled into further polishing of the property. The wines, too, are taking on renewed focus under Gunter Schultz, assisted by old hands Mzimasi Ncoko and Mjaceni Goza. Praiseworthy is the undertaking by the Rolf Frischknecht Foundation to repatriate part of Swiss export revenues to benefit local children with hearing issues.

★★★★☆ **Botmaskop** Small quantities of cab from best vintages; named for peak above farm; style 'One third Old World & two thirds New'. **04** (★★★★) robust & concentrated; brooding bouquet of smoky meat & black plums, ripe fruit tannins. Needs ±5 yrs to show its mettle. 14 mths Fr oak, 40% first fill. Departure from pvs **02**, which was elegant, soft & silky on release.

★★★★ **Delaire** Like maiden **03**, **04** blends cab, merlot, cab f (43/41/16). So seductive & complex when tasted last ed, seemed a pity tannins still too tight, needed ±yr to soften. 14 mths barriques Fr/Am/Hungarian (50/38/12), 45% new.

★★★★ **Chardonnay Barrel Fermented 05** (★★★★) bottled version shows distinct toasty charriness that dominates grapefruit, citrus flavours. Somewhat austere – pairing with food would restore some amicability. 90% in oak 8 mths, 30% first fill. **04** was entirely barrel fermented in Fr oak; soft & sweetish, courtesy 6g/ℓ sugar.

★★★★ **Sauvignon Blanc** From four mountain vyds picked at varying degrees of ripeness. **06** (★★★★) complex green aromas & flavours (greengage, guava & fynbos), quivering freshness, elegant nervosity but not quite as much authority as **05**, with mouth-tingling, ultra-fresh body, gorgeous long finish.

Blush new ★★★ Dainty dry rosé from four-way mix led by cab f, with almost equal portions merlot, chardonnay, sauvignon. **06** strawberry hues & flavours, light textured but juicy, ideal when dining alfresco. 14% alc. **Chardonnay Unwooded** ★★★ More delicate & restrained version this vintage; **06** still attractive, lightish & crisply refreshing. — CR

■ *De Leuwen Jagt* see Seidelberg

Delheim

👁💈🍷♿

*Stellenbosch • 1stB 1961 • Tasting & sales Mon-Fri 9-5 Sat 10-4 Sun (Sep-May) 10-4 • Fee R15 (tasting) R20 (tour & tasting) • Tours Mon-Fri 10.30 & 2.30 Sat (Sep-May) 10.30 • Closed Easter Fri/Sun, Dec 25 & Jan 1 • Delheim Garden Restaurant for country/traditional meals Mon-Sat 12-3 Sun (Sep-May) 12-3 • Tour groups • Gifts • Farm produce • Winemaker Brenda van Niekerk, with Karen Bruwer (Oct 2002/Sep 2004) • Viticulturist/cellarmaster Victor Sperling (Aug 1993) • 148 ha (15 varieties, r/w) • 850 tons 60 000 cs 70% red 28% white 2% rosé • Wines for client: Woolworths • PO Box 210 Stellenbosch 7599 • delheim@delheim. com • www.delheim.com • **T021·888·4600** • F 021·888·4601*

The Sperlings have registered three of their wines as originating from single vineyards: Vera Cruz Shiraz (from the eponymous parcel), Gewürtraminer (ex-'Reservoir' block) and Edelspatz (off somewhat cryptically named 'Office' — it does the business?). Limited vineyard extent, careful harvesting and production (including selective handpicking and bunch-pressing) ensure special, site-specific wines. Their Pinotage Rosé celebrated its 30th anniversary with a new screwcap closure (Sauvignon & Heerenwijn to follow suit), with marketer Nora Thiel (daughter of patriarch and Cape pioneer vintner 'Spatz') reporting a new 'pink' wine trend. Viticulturist/cellarmaster son Victor followed last season's malbec, cab franc and petit verdot plantings with some semillon.

Vera Cruz Estate range

★★★★☆ **Shiraz 04** darkly handsome, muscular too — but so well groomed… Firm dark fruit, meaty & rich with hints of smoked beef; big 14.5% alc but still manages elegance. Formidable tannin suggests wait until 2008 at earliest, will easily last 8-10 yrs. 16 mths Fr/Am oak.

Delheim range

★★★★ **Grand Reserve** Well over 2 decades on, still successful. **03** (tasted last ed, some info updated) includes 6% merlot (some pvs only cab). Whiffs mulberry, gentle mint, makes interesting comparison with Cab below: similarly dark berried but GR hiding much while cab more accessible. Tannins firm. Will keep 10 yrs — drink Cab while waiting. 18 mths Fr oak, 79% new.

★★★★ **Cabernet Sauvignon 04** confirms recent new seriousness. Intense blackcurrant fruit, attractive sweetness from ripe grapes, ripe tannins to match. Well judged oaking (16 mths, 20% new). Already approachable, shd peak around 2007.

★★★★ **Shiraz** Sleek, polished **04** quieter than pvs but still poised & stylish, a dark-berried charmer, keeping something in reserve: shd unfold in yr/2. Black cherry notes interwoven with subtle oak (yr European/Am, 25% new), but fruit centre-stage.

★★★★ **Edelspatz Noble Late Harvest** Now from registered single vyd of riesling. Youthfully seductive, **06** spills a cornucopia of scented fruits dusted with botrytis. 154g/ℓ sugar (**05** had 117), but elegant & refined, with lusciousness not overdone, finishes very clean. 11.5% alc. Unoaked.

Pinotage Rosé ☺ ★★★ Almost-dry **06**, candyfloss pink, whiff of 'Star' sweets & raspberry, flavoured to match. 10% muscat adds lilting florality. Tuck into picnic basket this summer; screwcapped. **Sauvignon Blanc-Chenin Blanc Heerenwijn** ☺ ★★★ In smart new livery for pleasingly plump **06**, blend tweaked, too: still 55% sauvignon, with more chenin, 8% colombard. Crisp & properly dry.

Merlot ★★★☆ Attractive mulberry leaf, cedary aroma on **04**. Neat build, with pleasing flavours, fresh acidity, easy soft tannins, green hint on finish. Oak subtle & supportive: 11 mths Fr, 11% new. **Pinotage** ★★★ Curiously sullen **04**, after stylish **03**, but gd sweet-sour red cherry flavours, suitably plump & juicy; soft tannins. Yr 70/30 Fr/Am oak. **Cabernet Sauvignon-Shiraz Dry Red** ★★★ (Pvsly 'Cab-Pinotage DR'.) Smarter image & smarter wine in **04**. A few other varieties involved in small way in **04**, but cab cedar leads the way; meaty/savoury flavours, firm tannins — & dry it is, as said. Yr Fr oak. **Chardonnay Sur Lie** Oaked version from cool-grown grapes up on Smnsberg, more weighty than cellarmate below. Gd follow-up to rich **04** (★★★★), well flavoured

05 (★★★★) suggests toast, grilled nuts, stone fruits, with interplay of fine oak (10 mths, 37% new). Will last 2-3 yrs. **Chardonnay ★★★ 06** aromas melon, peach lead to ripe & juicy palate, bursting with pristine fruit, nicely rounded. Only 16% oaked. **05** sold out before we cld taste. **Sauvignon Blanc ★★★** Revved up in **06**, nudges next notch up, with tropical aromas/flavours – passionfruit, green fig; juicy with gd crisp acidity, races to lengthy finish. A real show-off! **Gewürztraminer ★★★★** Bang on form in pretty **06**, fresh rosebud/ talcum powder to sniff; delicate sweetness (less sugar each yr, now 17g/ℓ), softish acidity, lingering finish. **Spatzendreck Late Harvest ★★★ 05** (not retasted) saw pinot blanc (29%) blended with chenin. Wafting pineapple/honey, attractive fresh sweetness; slightly less charm than pvs. **Rhine Riesling** (a special: winemaker's choice), **Brut** not tasted; both available ex-farm. Smnsberg-Sbosch WOs. – IvH

Dellrust Wines

Stellenbosch (see Helderberg map) ▪ *Est/1stB 1998* ▪ *Tasting & sales Mon-Fri 8-5 Sat 10-2* ▪ *Closed pub hols* ▪ *Tours on request* ▪ *Restaurant Tue-Sat 9.30-3.30 Sun 12-4* ▪ *Play area for children* ▪ *Owner/winemaker Albert Bredell* ▪ *Viticulturist Francois Hanekom (Jul 2003)* ▪ *97 ha (11 varieties, r/w)* ▪ *600 tons 6 000 cs own label 75% red 25% white* ▪ *PO Box 5666 Helderberg 7135* ▪ *dellrust@mweb.co.za* ▪ *www.dellrust.co.za* ▪ **T** *021·842·2752/842·2457* ▪ F *021·842·2456*

Fancy touring the Dellrust vineyards on a quad-bike, the wind in your hair? Harvesting your own grapes, then barefoot pressing them in vats? Manager Francois Hanekom came up with this interactive wine tour last year and it's been a roaring success. And for more sedentary types, there's Three Vines, the new Dellrust restaurant, where you can dine alfresco on young chef Robyn Hagen's fresh Mediterranean flavours.

★★★★ Three Vines Cellar's flagship, harmonious blend merlot, pinotage, shiraz; selected blocks vinified & blended pre-maturation in small Fr oak, ±14 mths. Still-current **03**, 40/30/30 ratio; darker, chunkier than pvs; last ed noted as plummy with lead pencil hint. **Merlot ★★★ 03** elegant, unforced & appealing, everything present & in position for satisfying shorter term drinking, solo or with food; 16 mths Fr oak. **Pinotage ★★★ 02** misreported '03' last yr; noted as pleasingly rustic & earthy, with barnyard sniff, well behaved tannins & acidity. Pvs were 14 mths Fr oak. **Tinta Barocca-Cinsaut ★★★** 50/50 blend; 16 mths older oak. **03**, retasted, light textured & -structured; shows rather less fruity charm than expected of the varieties. **Rosé ★★★** Fun & friendly red-berried **05**, off-dry pink from merlot & shiraz; still listed, not retasted. **Sauvignon Blanc ★★★★** ✓ Consistent styling, value pricing, make this a standout in range. Usual gutsy mineral attack on **06**, fresh, zinging grapefruit tone, rousing full flavoured finish. **Steen & Groen ★★★** After the old-Cape monikers for chenin and semillon; **06** 60/40 combo, tasted very young, still embryonic; but complementary varietal expression, freshness, all augur well. **Jerepigo ★★** Swings from rich & lovely botrytised chenin of pvs to sweet & light textured tinta in **06**, fairly shy on fruit, freshness & zing. **Cape Late Bottled Vintage ★★ 02** sweet & oaky entry, finish beginning to dry slightly, so not for further ageing. Tinta (88%), touriga, 36 mths Fr oaked. – MM

De Meye Wines

Stellenbosch ▪ *Est/1stB 1998* ▪ *Tasting & sales Mon-Fri 9.30-5 Sat 9.30-2* ▪ *Closed Easter Fri, Dec 25/26 & Jan 1* ▪ *Home-grown lavender & lavender essential oil* ▪ *Owner Jan Myburgh Family Trust* ▪ *Winemaker Marcus Milner, with Aby Bodlani (Sep 1999/Sep 2000)* ▪ *Viticulturist Philip Myburgh* ▪ *60 ha (cab, shiraz, pinotage, chard)* ▪ *13 000 cs 90% red 10% white* ▪ *PO Box 20 Muldersvlei 7607* ▪ *info@demeye.co.za* ▪ *www.demeye.co.za* ▪ **T** *021·884·4131* ▪ F *021·884·4154*

Even boutique wineries need to stretch their girth occasionally, and the De Meye team is expanding cellaring space so there's more room to move between barrels – also allowing for a 15% increase in production. Virgin merlot and cab franc blocks deliver their first grapes this year, giving more blending options to winemaker Marcus Milner. Conservation-minded viticulturist Philip Myburgh is overseeing renosterveld rehabilitation on the farm and replacing invasive trees with water-wise indigenous plants – not for the marketing draw but because it's the responsible thing to do.

★★★★ Trutina As balanced as translation of Latin name implies. **03** favourable vintage reflected in warm, expressive aromas of 80/20 cab/shiraz partnership. Rich, mouthfilling, without heaviness; savoury acid, fine vibrant tannins add to convincing potential. Classily buffed with 2 yrs Fr oak, 35% new. Unfiltered.

★★★★ **Shiraz** ✓ Delicate, fragrant **03** still selling. Convincing sweet fruit, decent structure; deliciously approachable but understated. 18 mths Fr oak (25% new) well integrated.

★★★★ **Chardonnay** ✓ Reliably attractive, well wooded (50% new). **05** last ed showed honeyed element with customary spice, nuts, orange-peel.

Shiraz Rosé ☺ ★★★ ('Blanc de Noir' pvs ed.) **06** fashionably dry with pleasing spicy red fruits; savoury extras from fermentation/maturation in used oak.

Cabernet Sauvignon ★★★★ Clear, forward-fruited face of modern cab; more classic resolute grip, savoury dryness. **03** enhanced by carefully applied oak (18 mths, 20% new Fr).
Chardonnay Unwooded ★★★ Well-defined pithy lime/lemon varietal notes; **06** light (12.5% alc), comfortably textured for aperitif or as food partner.

Little River range

Cabernet Sauvignon ☺ ★★★ Accessible **04**, with quiet presence; fresh, dark-fruited profile held by moderate grip. **Shiraz** ☺ ★★★ **04** mirrors pvs with purity of sweet fruit, rounded drinkability. Smoothed (as are other reds) by ±yr older wood. **Blend** ☺ ★★★ Characterful, easy-drinking cab/shiraz blend; **04** appeal enhanced by fresh, juicily sweet fruit, gentle tannins. Moderate alc (13.5% or lower), feature of this range. **Chenin Blanc** new ☺ ★★★ Unpretentious yet charming **06**, pleasing bounce, vivacity; outgoing but not showy fruit; rounded, dry persistence. — *AL/TJ*

■ *De Mooie Opstal* see Bon Cap

De Morgenzon

*Stellenbosch ▪ Closed to public ▪ Owners Wendy & Hylton Appelbaum ▪ Manager Anton Ferreira ▪ Vini consultant Teddy Hall (2005) ▪ Viti consultant Kevin Watt (Sep 2003) ▪ PO Box 1388 Stellenbosch 7599 ▪ info@demorgenzon.co.za or anton@demorgenzon.co.za ▪ **T 021·881·3030** ▪ F 021·881·3773*

A plan is coming together — winemaker Teddy Hall's maiden Chenin attracted notice (including an invitation to enter the Tri-Nations competition); replanting of the Stellenboschkloof farm is more than half done; nursery staff are building up the stock ('hundreds of thousands of plants', estimates owner Hylton Appelbaum) to restore De M's fynbos and renosterveld; roads have been built and a new winery is more than a dream. 'GPS, extensive climatic data and a detailed soil analysis proved invaluable in helping us understand our terroir,' comments Hylton A.

★★★★★ **Chenin Blanc** new Debut **05**, 'best Chenin I ever made', opines Teddy H. Opulent lemon blossom, honey & spice bouquet; equally alluring satin palate, touch tannin, interminable finish. TH's trademark sugar (6.8g/ℓ) matched almost gram for gram by bracing natural acidity. An individual, strikingly packaged head-turner. Fermented/8 mths 100% new Fr oak. Great prospects. Wine ★★★★. — *CvZ*

■ *Den Dulk & Siddle* see De Toren
■ *Denneboom* see Oude Denneboom
■ *De Sonnenberg* see Premium Cape Wines
■ *Destiny* see Mont Destin

Détendu Wines   ☺ ♈

Paarl ▪ Est 1995 ▪ 1stB 2001 ▪ Visits by appt ▪ Owner Western Investments Company ▪ Winemaker Anthony Smook, with Francois Louw (Jan 2001/2003) ▪ Viti consultant Johan Wiese (2002) ▪ 33 ha (cab, merlot, pinotage, shiraz, chard, chenin, colombard) ▪ 300 tons 1

*500 cs own label 90% red 10% white • PO Box 2917 Paarl 7620 • info@detendu.co.za • **T 021·863·3282** • F 021·863·2480*

The 2006 harvest, the fourth in their own cellar, 'flowed and worked like a charm'. The quality of the 2006 grapes was much improved, benefiting from a continued focus on vineyard management and a better understanding of the site, and it showed in the cellar, says Garry Roberts. The entire winemaking process is still very hands-on, with an emphasis on the pre-selection of grapes and a continuation of the practice of cooling the berries prior to crushing.

Cabernet Sauvignon-Merlot ★★★ Cab-led (60%) in **03**; last ed interesting oliveaceous character, pliable tannins, deep black-fruit concentration. Shd develop over 2-3 yrs. **02** also still selling. **Pinotage** ★★★ Ripe-style **04**, red fruit & toasty vanilla from 18 mths Fr oak, 2nd/3rd fill; sweeter tannins than pvs; fleeting finish. **Shiraz** ★★★ 30% new Fr oak (18 mths) for this version, which pleasant on nose but rather less so on dry, tannic taste; big 15% alc gives **04** a ripe glow. **Shiraz Reserve** ★★★ All-new oak (mainly Fr) distinguishes this rendering; **04** sweet berry flavours, smoother tannins, better-tuned wood, similar intrusive alc as std version only quibble. **Chardonnay** ★★★ **05** again enriched by well balanced wooding (only 50% oaked, 6 mths new Fr), enlivened by citric thread; restrained alc; clean finish. — *MM*

De Toren Private Cellar　　ô\♀

*Stellenbosch • Est 1996 • 1stB 1999 • Visits by appt • Fee R180, waived on purchase • Owner Edenhall Trust • Winemaker Albie Koch (Aug 1998) • Viticulturist Ernest Manuel (Mar 2003), advised by Johan Pienaar • 20 ha (cabs s/f, malbec, merlot, petit v) • 7 000 cs 100% red • PO Box 48 Vlottenburg 7604 • info@de-toren.com • www.de-toren.com • **T 021·881·3119** • F 021·881·3335*

If Fusion V — a regular Best Red on Show at WineX — is De Toren's answer to Bordeaux's Left Bank, then 'Z' (pronounced 'zee') is its new merlot-dominated Right Bank counterpart. 'We decided to keep it simple and name it after the vineyard block,' says director Emil den Dulk. Not just any block, mind, but the one in front of the manor house, where you might spot 50 resident ducks 'having a ball and solving our snail problem with a quack and a waddle'.

★★★★★ **Fusion V** Acclaimed locally & abroad ('Global A-list' US *Food & Wine*, *Decanter* ★★★★, IWSC gold, 91 pts *WS*), this a glossy, modern top-ranker. Aerial imaging at ul used to monitor ripening of quintet bdx black grapes. Invariably cab-led (55%), **04** also features 20% cab f (plus merlot, malbec, petit v); dense concentration of bright fruit in rippling structure, brooding, unyielding; needs good ten yrs. 90:10 Fr/Am oak, 50% new. 14.5% alc.

★★★★ **Z** new 'Not a 2nd wine, but *another* wine.' Merlot leads pack in maiden **04**, cabs s/f, malbec & splash petit v (ex-Wllngton) complete the palette. Deep mocha, violets & bacon intro to plump mulberries, textured tannins. More accessible than partner, could go as long though. After new sea-facing vyd. Yr oak, 30% new.

★★★★ **DDS Shiraz** new Den Dulk & Siddle (Domaine Bertanga), with respective winemakers (who 'democratically decide on harvest date'), in a Franco/African take on the northern Rhône. Contents of **04** far more classy than lurid label: spicy toasted oak, pulpy blackberry fruit whisked into elegance, delectable lightness in finish. Hand-sorted, no berry crush, yr new Burgundian wood.

Diversity discontinued. — *DS*

De Trafford Wines　　ô\♀

*Stellenbosch • Est/1stB 1992 • Tasting, sales & tours Fri & Sat 10-1 • Owners David & Rita Trafford • Winemaker David Trafford • 5 ha (cabs s/f, merlot, pinot, shiraz) • 80 tons 3 500 cs 75% red 25% white • PO Box 495 Stellenbosch 7599 • info@detrafford.co.za • www. detrafford.co.za • **T/F 021·880·1611***

The Traffords' boutique winery holds the highest *Wine Spectator* rating for any SA wine — 94 points, for both the Shiraz 01 and 03. 'It feels dishonest talking up another vintage,' says architect/winemaker David T of 2006, 'but the truth is we've had a string of wonderful vintages since 1997.' He's wary of taking conditions for granted, bearing in mind that Bordeaux's amazing run 1982-1990 was followed by some of the poorest vintages of the last century. The family involve themselves with their community: in the past they've sponsored a local primary school outing to De Hoop Nature Reserve, and recently hosted a visit to the winery by their son's eight- and nine-year-old classmates. ('I learnt that you must keep a lid on the barrel to keep the flies out' was one of the pearls of wisdom gleaned!)

★★★★☆ **Elevation 393** Allusion to height above sea level of Mt Fleur home vyd; Selection best cab, merlot & shiraz lavished with 100% new Fr oak nearly 2 yrs. **04** darkly handsome forest floor fruits ordered by tight-knit structure; fabulous integration, balance, effortlessly manages elevated alc (±15%, which part of wine's persona). **03**, with soupçon cab f, took this label to next level; WS 90 pts; no **02**; **01** 90 pts WS.

★★★★☆ **Cabernet Sauvignon** Aristocratic Cape cab with deluxe lineage. **04** concentrated, complex; finely etched cassis tints to ripe-fruit elegance; pure, clean & classy. Carries 14.5% alc with ease. **03** WS 91 pts; **02** to us more austere, but Wine ★★★★☆, WS 90 pts. Low-yielding Sbosch cab supported by 12% merlot, dash petit v. 21 mths oak, mainly Fr, 40% new.

★★★★ **Merlot** Hallmark elegance derived from polished plum & mulberry fruits, shaped by careful wooding (35% new Fr, 19 mths) & splashes cab f & petit v. Last ed a preview (as was next wine), **04** has blossomed into stunning beauty: minty, deep violet scents mingle with nutty black fruits, beguiling lithe tannins.

★★★★☆ **Shiraz** An exposition of hand-made craft, lauded with regular WS 90+ ratings, heads cellar's three interpretations of the grape. **04** magical after yr in btl; plumes of roast spice & succulent mulberry fruits in embroidered framework, stamped with singular elegance. 20 mths wood, half new, 10% Am. 258 cs.

★★★★ **Blueprint Shiraz** Fruit of younger Keermont vyds accorded cellar's standards: gentle hand-picking/crush, native yeast ferment, full malo in barrel, limited racking/handling. More aromatic, fruitier, somewhat lighter than above, **04** offers liquorice berry fruit accessibility in youth; best around 2010. Maiden **03** WS 91 pts, Wine ★★★★. Barrelled 19 mths 25% new casks, mix Fr/Am.

★★★★ **Heap of Stones Shiraz** new One-off made by assist. wnmkr Hendry Hess & Keermont grower Alex Starey from Pru Crawley's 'HoS' vyd. **04** more scrub-like, herbaceous than above siblings, tightly structured — best with food. Fr oak, 25% new. Mere 42 cs.

★★★★ **Pinot Noir** Only 2 barrels given individual attention — & fly out of cellar door. Sample **04** last ed showed black cherry gloss to earthy/tar aromas, breathtaking concentration. 18 mths used Fr wood, 15% alc. Mix Burgundian (±80%) & older BK5 clones.

★★★★ **Chenin Blanc** New-wave chenin, exclusively from venerable Hldrberg vyds, full & complex but laced with elegance: sample **06** in usual rich vein; luscious yet brisk, fruit with flair. Equally delicious **04** & **03** both 90 pts WS. Naturally fermented/8 mths half each Fr/Am oak, 15% new; unfiltered.

★★★★☆ **Straw Wine** Passion & commitment taken to the edge with this elixir from 'air-dried' chenin; languid ferment takes yr to complete. Sample **05** suggests return to earlier lighter, sweeter style (±13% alc, 153g/ℓ sugar); shimmering tangerine hues; heady marmalade characters in luxurious, viscous mouthful. Mostly new oak, 50% Fr/Am, 17 mths. **03** WS 92 pts, Wine ★★★★. 375ml. — DS

De Villiers Wines

Paarl ▪ *Tasting & sales by appt* ▪ *Owner De Villiers Family Trust* ▪ *50 000 cs 60% red 40% white* ▪ *PO Box 659 Southern Paarl 7624* ▪ *devwines@mweb.co.za or vadev@mweb.co.za* ▪ *www.devwines.co.za* ▪ **T 021·863·4441** ▪ *F 086·6538·988*

CEO Villiers de Villiers and marketer Wayne Fredericks have achieved their goal nationally: penetration of the retail sector, with listings by all major supermarket groups, and, reports VdV, top-seller status for his Cab and Pinotage in a leading chain. Next step is to take De Villiers Heritage wines and their new slogan, 'The Cape's leading brand of quality wines', into overseas markets.

De Villiers Heritage Wines

> **Cabernet Sauvignon** ☺ ★★★ **05** fruitily quaffable as pvs. Rounded, well-fattened with wild berries, punchy ripe tannins add friendly firmness.

Pinotage ★★★ Food & wallet-friendly **04** last ed noted as showing classic pinotage notes of strawberry, smoke & ripe banana. Modest 11.9% alc. **Shiraz** ★★★ **04** last ed had promising nose of dark choc, red fruit, dust & coffee; slightly less convincing palate, warming finish (14.7% alc). **Rosé** new ★★ Dry **04** from pinotage shows no signs of weariness; quite punchy (14% alc), red berried fruit shot through with rhubarb. **Chardonnay** ★★★ Lightish **06** perky fruit acids, as pvsly, good flavour layering, pretty musk sweet perfumes; no sign of wood. **Chenin Blanc** ★★★ Step up on pvs; **06** light but flavourful, easy pineapple & guava flavours, softly dry. **Sauvignon Blanc** ★★★ Lightish **05** uncomplicated but tasty; herbaceous flavours end with refreshing crunch. **Blanc de Blanc** ★★ **05** starting to flag slightly, needs drinking soon to enjoy subtle green apple flavours. **Riesling** ★★ Pleasant grassy easy-drinker from Cape riesling; **05** smoothed & balanced by iota sugar. All W Cape WOs. — *CT/MM*

■ *Devon Air see* Terroir Wines

Devon Hill Winery

Stellenbosch ▪ Est 1996 ▪ 1stB 1997 ▪ Tasting & sales Mon-Fri 10-4 Sat by appt ▪ Fee R10 ▪ Closed pub hols ▪ Tours by appt ▪ Walks ▪ Winemaker Erhard Roux (May 2004) ▪ 46 ha (cabs s/f, merlot, pinotage, shiraz, sauvignon) ▪ ±300 tons 80% red 20% white ▪ PO Box 541 Stellenbosch 7599 ▪ info@devonhill.co.za ▪ www.devonhill.co.za ▪ T 021·865·2453 ▪ F 021·865·2444

The performance of the 02 Pinotage in the ABSA Top Ten gave winemaker Erhard Roux and the farm's Swiss owners pause for thought – the variety obviously has potential at Devon Hill and should be nurtured. Roux's first harvest on this Stellenbosch farm was, coincidentally, 2002, as assistant to Theo Brink, since retired to the seaside. Roux describes his astonishment when, working for the owners at Grandvaux near Geneva, he watched helicopters deliver the grapes to the cellar!

★★★★ **Blue Bird** Elegant, full flavoured 'Cape blend', varieties/proportions vary with the vintage. Merlot (50%), pinotage & cab in beautifully balanced **02**, with floral hint to luxurious, well modulated berry character. Pinotage & cab portions double that of pvs, now only Fr oak (yr, 80% new) – tighter tannin structure reflects this.

Cabernet Sauvignon ★★★ **05** preview continues along more elegant & restrained path set by last tasted **03** (no 04 made). Layered, full-fruited yet bone dry, supple & long. Oak less dominant thanks to greater use of seasoned barrels. **03** *Wine* ★★★★. **Sauvignon Blanc** ★★★★ Cellar style leans towards green flavours & racy acidity. Sample **06** true to form: greenpepper & nettle in foreground, but riper gooseberry too, giving fleshier feel; zesty & dry. New vintages of following not ready for review: **Shiraz Reserve** ★★★ Cellar's flagship. Lean & spartan **03** last yr noted as deserving fuller maturation. Distinct varietal aromas/flavours of pepper, leather, spice very prevalent, as they are on std version. **Shiraz** ★★★ **03** fleshier than Rsv, fuller flavoured, enough red fruit to match fairly strong tannins. Yr oak, third new. **Four Stars** ★★★★ Easy-drinking pleasure with touch of seriousness; **02** light textured blend pinotage, merlot, shiraz, cab (40/30/15/15). Yr oak, none new. **Pinotage** ★★ Pinotage Top Ten selection, though when last we tasted **02**, we noted an old-style 'nail varnish' tone. Yr Fr oak. **Merlot 03** sample was shrouded in dusty dry oak mid-2005, impossible to rate conclusively. — *DH/CR*

Devon Rocks   new

Stellenbosch ▪ Est 1998 ▪ 1stB 2003 ▪ Visits by appt ▪ B&B ▪ Owners Jürgen & Brita Heinrich ▪ Vini consultant Simon Smith (Louisvale) ▪ Viti advisers Gawie du Bois & Paul Wallace ▪ 3.5 ha (pinotage, shiraz) ▪ 775 cs 100% red ▪ PO Box 12483 Die Boord 7613 ▪ info@devonrocks.co. za ▪ www.devonrocks.co.za ▪ T 021·865·2536 ▪ F 021·865·2621

Started by Jürgen Heinrich and his Swedish wife Brita as a retirement project, the winery has grown to include Simon Smith of Louisvale as consultant. Despite the *garagiste* quantities, Jürgen H has made inroads on his biggest challenge, sales and distribution, with the first exports to his native Germany and the Netherlands leading what are sure to be many more.

Pinotage ★★★ Varnishy whiffs on tannin-dominated, robust & rustic **05**, but plenty of sweet fruit on palate. 14.5% alc; in new Fr barrels for yr. Chunkier than softer, more jammy & berry-charactered **04**. From dryland bushvines. — *MF*

Devonvale Golf & Wine Estate

Stellenbosch ▪ Est/1stB 2004 ▪ Tasting by appt ▪ Sales daily 10-6 ▪ Fee R25 (incl glass) ▪ Closed Easter Fri-Mon, Dec 25 & Jan 1 ▪ Breakfasts & lunches ▪ Gifts ▪ Conferences ▪ Tour groups ▪ Owner Devonmus (Pty) Ltd ▪ Winemaker Wilhelm Kritzinger (Bellevue, Feb 2004) ▪ Viticulturists Ruben Nienaber & Dirkie Morkel (Bellevue) ▪ 5.5 ha (cab, shiraz) ▪ 40 tons 3 362 cs 100% red ▪ PO Box 187, Bottelary Road, Koelenhof 7605 ▪ proshop@devonvale.co.za ▪ www. devonvale.co.za ▪ T 021·865·2080 ▪ F 021·865·2601

When vines became part of the landscaping, it was inevitable that wine would one day feature at this golf and housing estate in the heart of the winelands. MD JJ Provoyeur, for whom wine remains a passion, brought in the winemaking team from Bellevue from the start of the 2004 vintage. Their mandate is to make 'pleasant wines at affordable prices'.

Broad Reach range

Cabernet Sauvignon ★★ Maiden **04** more Old World than New with restrained fruit, leafy/fungi notes & taut tannins. Needs a few yrs to integrate, soften. Innovative 'wooding' technique: combo 235ℓ polyethylene barrels & Fr staves. Same treatment for… **Cabernet Sauvignon-Shiraz** Sample **05** too unknit to rate. — *DH*

■ *Devon View* see Devon Hill

DeWaal Wines

Stellenbosch ▪ Est 1682 ▪ 1stB 1972 ▪ Tasting & sales Mon-Fri 9-4.30 (Oct-Apr) Mon-Fri 10-12. 30; 2-4.30 (May-Sep) Sat 9-4.30 (Aug-May only) ▪ Fee R10 ▪ Closed Easter Fri/Sun, Dec 25/ 26 & Jan 1 ▪ Owners De Waal brothers ▪ Winemakers/viticulturists Chris de Waal & Daniël de Waal (whites/reds, Jan 1976/1989) ▪ MD Pieter de Waal ▪ 120 ha (pinotage, shiraz, sauvignon) ▪ 800 tons 20 000 cs 50% red 50% white ▪ PO Box 15 Vlottenburg 7604 ▪ dewaal@ uiterwyk.co.za ▪ www.dewaal.co.za ▪ T 021·881·3711 ▪ F 021·881·3776

The ninth-generation De Waal brothers of Uiterwyk Estate are going stronger than ever. Daniël makes the red wines while Chris takes care of white, and it's MD Pieter's job to make sure the world hears about it (to this end, Ryan Sowray has been appointed as sales and marketing manager). The Top of the Hill Pinotage — from one of SA's oldest pinotage vineyards — has attained ABSA Top 10 status five times (and scooped DdW the Diners Club Winemaker of the Year title in 2002). Meanwhile, more people can now enjoy his interpretation of SA's home-grown grape — volumes of DeWaal Pinotage have increased substantially.

★★★★☆ **Top of the Hill Pinotage** One of the more elegant & serious expressions of this grape, from small bushvine vyd 50+ yrs old. **04** a lesson in sheathed power; remarkably supple tannins (given 2 yrs all new oak), shimmering dark fruit, tantalising dried herb & banana nuances. Sophisticated & brilliantly executed. Like pvs, deserves gd few yrs in bottle.

★★★★ **CT de Waal Pinotage** From low-cropping ±40 yr old vines, a label to rival illustrious partner — some will prefer its somewhat lesser oakiness. **04** showcases variety's layered complexity: brambleberries, liquorice, violets plus a lifting herbaceousness but, like **03**, still tight, needs few yrs to soften; potential over 6+. 65% new Fr, 18 mths.

★★★★☆ **Cape Blend** Maiden **93** was first of the 90s wave of blends with pinotage — this one a serious-minded, soberly elegant version. Last reviewed **03** had merlot dominant at 50% (pinotage/shiraz 30/20), though pinotage also assertive. Plenty of oak character (50% new Fr); shd develop well at least 5 yrs, keep longer.

★★★★☆ **Shiraz** Beautifully crafted **04** draws you into its smoky depths, scrub & blackberry-veined opulence; fine-grained tannins hold everything in place, promise 5+ yr future. Fr oak 35% new, rest 2nd fill. No **03** made.

★★★★ **Merlot** Given estate's credentials, **04** (★★★★) shd show better with time, but mid-2006 dominated by oak (45% new Fr), masking fruit. Give another yr or so. Early-harmonious **03** had bags of plummy flavour to match big structure.

Pinotage ★★★☆ From 35+ yr old vyds. Lightest of the pinotage trio, well made **04** shows varietal-true rhubarb & dried banana, juicy palate appeal. Already accessible thanks to balanced oaking, but also a few more yrs ahead. 18 mths Fr wood, third new. NE. **Sauvignon Blanc** ★★★☆ Always a serious-minded example: vivacious asparagus/greenpepper-toned **06** ex-tank captures the essence of sauvignon, steely freshness personified. **Viognier** ★★★ First Sbosch version of this white Rhône variety, from 12 yr old vyds. Previewed **06** peach kernel, floral typicity, but still quiet, reserved mid-2006; might perk up with time. Fr oak, 20% new. **Young Vines Red** ★★★ This, next, pvsly branded 'Uiterwyk'. Perky plummy fruit in **04**; allowed limelight by oak's gentle support role, shows youthful charm. Merlot 60%, balance equal shiraz, pinotage. **Young Vines White** ★★ Uncomplicated quaffer; crisply dry, pear-drop character in **06**. Sauvignon, chenin, colombard; modest 12.5% alc.

Uiterwyk range

★★★★ **Shiraz** Last tasted was well-structured, velvety **00**, viognier perfume adding to spice, plum & toasty oakiness. 40% new Fr oak.

Merlot ★★★ Fr-oaked **00** had spicy, dusty plum notes, pleasing balance. — *CR*

De Wet Co-op Winery

Worcester ▪ *Est 1946* ▪ *Tasting & sales Mon-Fri 8-5 Sat 9-12* ▪ *Fee R1/wine* ▪ *Closed pub hols* ▪ *BYO picnics* ▪ *Conferencing* ▪ *Owners 60 members* ▪ *Winemaker/manager Piet le Roux (1995) & Hugo Conradie (2003)* ▪ *Viti consultant Newald Marais (Jan 2003)* ▪ *±1 000 ha (chard, chenin)* ▪ *19 000 tons 20% red 80% white* ▪ *PO Box 16 De Wet 6853* ▪ *admin@dewetcellar.co.za* ▪ *www.worcesterwinelands.co.za* ▪ *T 023·341·2710* ▪ *F 023·341·2762*

Manager/winemaker Piet le Roux has been busy of late, what with new labels and an expansion programme. The latter was a matter of urgency, given harvests of the size experienced in 2006 and their concomitant challenges. As a founder shareholder in FirstCape, among the UK's Top 10 brands by value, the winery is set to benefit from a big promotion launched in Thresher and Wine Rack stores across Britain by Brand Phoenix, a FirstCape partner.

Pinotage ☺ ★★★ Gluggable & wallet-friendly. **05** lightly scented, flavoured (& oaked) but still bright & breezy; charming front label features artwork by student at local special-needs school. **Sauvignon Blanc** ☺ ★★★ **06** oodles of varietal zing; grass & hay whiffs followed by passionfruit flavours, lively acidity. Lightish ±11.5% alc just enough to provide silky mouthfeel. **Bouquet Blanc** ☺ ★★★ Unpretentious off-dry white, now mainly colombard with dollop muscat de F/dash chardonnay. **06** fairly intricate white-fruit bouquet, pithy acidity balances 9.8g/ℓ sugar. **Petillant Fronté** ☺ ★★★ Cellar door stalwart; extra-low-alc white (±8%) from muscat de F, Heart Foundation endorsed. Rousing muscat nose, fair froth, gentle sweetness. **NV**.

Shiraz ⃞new⃞ ★★★ Undemanding **05** leanish fruit, almost raisin-like character on nose, gentle tannins. 6 mths older oak. **Dry Red** ★★★ Blend varies from yr to yr, **06** equal shiraz/cab/merlot, lightly oaked. Hint strawberry bubblegum to unlingering fruit, gently squeezing tannins. 5ℓ party-ready packs. **Chardonnay** ★ New wine not ready for tasting. Last **02** v oaky; better in youth. **Chenin Blanc** ⃞new⃞ ★★ Light bodied **06**'s delicate floral, thatch, aromas/flavours well served by balanced alc (13%) & oak (part barrel-fermented). **Special Late Harvest** ★★ Another change from 100% gewürz to only 33%, majority muscat de F. **06** pretty bouquet of rose & muscat; light, balanced off-dry potpourri tastes. **Muscadel** ★★★★✓ Critically acclaimed but unselfconscious fortified dessert, chillable in summer; **03** grapey with some tropical notes; nutty flavours & cleansing spirituous grip. VDG, gold at 2006 Muscadel Awards. **Port** ★★★★ ✓ Uncomplex but attractive ruby-style **03** has savoury tone rather than more usual fruitcake; dry (85g/ℓ), well-woven spirit (17.3% alc). **Cape Riesling, Hanepoot** discontinued. — *CvZ*

De Wetshof Estate

*Robertson • Est 1949 • 1stB 1972 • Tasting & sales Mon-Fri 8.30-4.30 Sat 9.30-12.30 • Closed Easter Fri/Mon, Dec 25/26 & Jan 1 • Tours by appt • Owner Danie de Wet • Winemaker Danie de Wet (1973), with Mervyn Williams (2001) • Viticulturist George Thom (1996), advised by Phil Freese & Francois Viljoen (both 1997) • 180 ha (cab, merlot, pinot, chard, sauvignon, semillon, riesling) • 10% red 90% white • ISO 9001, BRC & HACCP certified • PO Box 31 Robertson 6705 • info@ dewetshof.com • www.dewetshof.com • **T 023·615·1853** • F 023·615·1915*

Though still championing chardonnay (latest innovation: the Chardonnay Club @ De Wetshof, for aficionados), Danie de Wet's more recent emphasis has been on reds. The pinot was subjected to a 'hailstorm pruning' early in last season, but quality was undamaged. Highlights included a new bordeaux-style blend for Woolworths and top prices for his Merlot at the Nederburg Auction. Grooming of former gardener, Mervyn Williams, as cellar assistant has re-enthused the seasoned winemaker. Adjusted strategies have seen the appointment of additional export agents and the list of foreign markets swell to 22, including the US.

★★★★ **Bateleur Chardonnay** Serious example, showing style & finesse. Epitomised by **05**, with toasty oak, grilled hazelnut, ripe stonefruit — but restrained, nothing overdone, fruit tautened by racy acidity. New Fr oak, fermented/yr. These age well. No **04**.

★★★★ **Rhine Riesling** Well regarded example; in good vintages allows maturation over 5-7 yrs. Usually delicate & refined but **04** (★★★★, tasted last ed) more austere than pvs. Bone-dry & moderate 12.7% alc — might unfold over time. No **03**. **02**'s 8g/ℓ sugar was balanced by acidity, finishing dry.

★★★★★ **Edeloes** Gorgeous botrytis dessert from riesling. Last tasted was **00**, honeyed, with lovely balance between opulent sweetness & firm, clean acid. **01** is next.

Chardonnay D'Honneur ★★★★ Bigger in style than some others in range, with generous ripe fruit, though less oaky lately. Ripe & plump **04** hints at peaches & vanilla custard, but with estate's signature clean acidity. Previewed **05** right on form. Fermented/±yr new Fr oak. **Finesse Chardonnay** ★★★★ Lightest-oaked of the trio of barrel fermented chards; named **Lesca** for export. **06** quieter than pvsly tasted **04**, but rounded, stylish, showing citrus & stonefruit character with subtle oak overlay. **Bon Vallon Chardonnay** ★★★★ SA's first unwooded version, still dependable. **06** quietly soft, approachable, fresh & limy with touch of chalkiness in lengthy mouthwatering finish. Fine lunch companion. **Blanc Fumé** ★★★ Lightly wooded sauvignon. **06** shows gentle lime & lemon, with oak barely perceptible. Citrus finish, with gravelly touch. **Sauvignon Blanc 06** & **05** (both tasted mid-2006) signal move to riper, more relaxed tropical style. Bone-dry **06** (★★★★), with vibrant passionfruit, papaya, gooseberry, is plump & tangy. Quieter, softer **05** (★★★) a bit dull in comparison, but also a gd food partner.

Danie de Wet range

★★★★ **Cape Muscadel** Refined new-wave Cape fortified. Last was **00**, with lovely sweet/ sour tussle, uncloying. 15.3% alc. 500ml. Next is **06**.

★★★★ **Limestone Hill Chardonnay** Fragrant unwooded version harvested ultra-ripe — a local spin on chablis, perhaps. **06**'s exotic blossom, passionfruit, lime do not obscure mineral undertones. Plump & juicy, just-dry, with a terrific concentration of gd fruit seen in lengthy finish. Watch that 14.8% alc.

Dukesfield Cape Blend new ★★★★ ✓ Territory-reclaiming name? Contains no pinotage, as implied in moniker — just cab, with 10% merlot. **03** forward bouquet mocha, toast, ripe prune; warm soft palate, fleshy (4.5g/ℓ sugar) but with dry tannic grip. 10 mths wood contact. **Cabernet Sauvignon Naissance** ★★★★ **04** even nicer than **03**, & unusually approachable for variety — attractive cedary whiff to soft juicy blackberry & warm spice of oak (15 mths Fr); big 14.6% alc. **Merlot** new ★★★ Attractive ripe blackcurrant pastille, dried prune touches on **04**; softly structured, with ripe unintimidating tannins. Shd be a hit. Oak 13 mths. **Nature in Concert Pinot Noir** ★★★ **04**, intriguing toast & warm hay/

organic notes to soft strawberry-tinged palate; dry tannins. Fermented/yr small Fr oak. JCWCA 'first'/gold. **Chardonnay Sur Lie** ★★★ **06** soft & easy unwooded version, a sipper with style. Light lemon-tinged flavours, honest varietal fruit, bone-dry. **Sauvignon Blanc 06** unready. **Call of the African Eagle** for foreign supermarkets; **Blanc De Wet** discontinued. *— IvH*

■ *Deza* see Oaklands Wine Exporters

De Zoete Inval Estate

Paarl • Est 1878 • 1stB 1976 • Tasting & sales at I Love Wine (see entry); farm tastings & tours by appt • Owner AR Frater Trust • Winemaker/viticulturist John Robert Frater (1999/2004) • 20 ha (cab, petit v, port varieties, shiraz, chard, sauvignon) • 100 tons 5 000 cs own label 50% red 50% white • PO Box 591 Suider-Paarl 7624 • dezoeteinval@wine.co.za • www.dezoeteinval. co.za • T 021·863·1535 • F 021·863·2158

The last was a rather quiet year for the Fraters, but at time of going to press preparations were being made for the planting of Rhône varieties which seem to suit the climate of Paarl. Further work in progress is the clearing of alien vegetation and replacement with indigenous trees. Those seeking older vintages (particularly cab) should call here.

Cabernet Sauvignon ★★ **03** light coloured/textured red with tart cranberry flavour, dusty dry conclusion. 20 mths oaked. **Yvette Dry Red** ★★ Light, slightly dusty **NV** from cab, yr Fr oaked. 1 000ml bottle. **Shiraz Rosé** ★ **05** light in tone & taste, with slight salty tang. **Blanc de Blanc** new ★ **05** light bodied dry white from sauvignon, with some chenin. **Vin Sec Sparkling** new ★★ From chenin; delicate, effervescent **06**, with decidedly sweet crème caramel note. Following not re-tasted: **Cabernet Sauvignon-Shiraz** ★★★ Rustic yet not unappealing **NV**. Almost porty nose of prunes & plums, savoury touch; chunky 15+% alc. **Chardonnay** ★★★ Last was **03**, which revealed some complexity; dry, attractively austere on finish. **Late Harvest** ★★★ From sauvignon. Last was **03**, with supple, light fruit salad tastes. **Vintage Brut** ★★★ **03** maiden MCC from chard. Fine bubbles, arresting acidity, bone-dry (just 3g/ℓ sugar) yet balanced. **Cape Vintage** ★★ Port-style fortified; **01** with mature tawny tint; dusty dried-fruit nose, soft, silky & attractively dry. Next is **03**. **Grand Rouge** discontinued.

Eskdale range

Last tasted were **03** vintages of **Merlot**, **Pinotage** and **Shiraz**, all ★★★. New releases not ready. *— MM*

DGB

Wellington • Est 1942 • Closed to public • Owners DGB management, Brait Capital Partners & Kangra • Winemakers/viticulturists: see Bellingham & Boschendal • PO Box 246 Wellington 7654 • exports@dgb.co.za • www.dgb.co.za • T 021·864·5300 • F 021·864·1287

Well established merchant house with a strong portfolio of premium and own-brand table wines, ports and sherries. See separate listings for Bellingham, Boschendal, Culemborg, Douglas Green, Millstream, Oude Kaap, Tall Horse, Text and The Saints.

Die Huis van Anjé   new

Villiersdorp (see Worcester map) • Est/1stB 2006 • Visits by appt • Fee R10 p/p • BYO picnic • Owner Petrus Roux Trust • Winemaker Petrus Roux • 6 tons 100% white • 1 Upington Str, Villiersdorp 6848 • huisvananje@lando.co.za • T/F 028·840·2115 / 083·748·6260

For a 'meaningful' occupation after retirement, former apple farmer Petrus Roux turned to winemaking at his home in the hamlet of Villiersdorp. Believing his facilities too modest for a 'Winery' or 'Cellar' moniker, he opted for 'The House of Anjé' (a tribute to wife Annetjie). A few tanks, a DIY vinification system (courtesy of Main Street Winery's Marais de Villiers) and endless calls to a KWV family friend later, he's produced a chenin for friends, chardonnay for his brother, sauvignon for himself. The latter two are from a rather famous vineyard: Kaaimansgat, conveniently part of the family vineholding.

All **06**. **Kroonland Chardonnay** ★★★ Light lime fruit, bone-dry mouth-puckering flintiness, moderate 12.9% alc, very lightly oaked. **Pastorie Chenin** ★★ Guava, papaya aromas, then some soft, slightly spicy sweetness on the unconcentrated, light bodied (12% alc) but harmonious palate. **Sauvignon Blanc** ★★★★ Pale straw-coloured example from slow-ripening Vllrsdorp vyds; crisp capsicum aromas, fresh gooseberry notes, light citrusy finish. 14.5% alc well tucked away among the flavour. — *MF*

■ *Die Krans* see De Krans

Diemersdal Estate

Durbanville ▪ *Est 1698* ▪ *1stB 1990* ▪ *Tasting & sales Mon-Fri 9-5 Sat 9-3* ▪ *Closed Easter Fri/ Sun, Dec 25 & Jan 1* ▪ *Tours by appt* ▪ *Restaurant or BYO picnics* ▪ *Walks* ▪ *Owner Tienie Louw* ▪ *Winemakers Tienie & Thys Louw* ▪ *Viticulturist Div van Niekerk (1980)* ▪ *172 ha (cab, merlot, pinotage, shiraz, chard, sauvignon)* ▪ *1 730 tons 15 000 cs own label 79% red 21% white* ▪ *PO Box 27 Durbanville 7551* ▪ *wines@diemersdal.co.za* ▪ **T 021·976·3361** ▪ *F 021·976·1810*

Representing the sixth generation of his family, Thys Louw has taken over from Johan Kruger (see Sterhuis) as winemaker after completing his 'tutorship' with Hermann Kirschbaum at Buitenverwachting. 'With the arrival of the new generation, many things are happening,' says father Tienie. 'The labels are changing, a new tasting room is being established and new wines are seeing the light of day.' It was also Louw Jnr's idea to host a harvest picnic at full moon, which proved such a success it will now become an annual event.

★★★★ **Shiraz** Modern, accessible style with a hint of the classics. **04** (★★★★) more open, affable, than pvs; sweet fleshy fruit with smoky vanilla nuance, but no great dimension, complexity. Unlike **03**, which has many varietal & oak-derived layers. These 14% alc, 12-15 mths Fr oak.

★★★★ **Chardonnay Reserve** Opulent aromatics the keynote here, partly through new oak fermentation, for luxurious toasted nut effect, partly through bold (not extravagant) fruit styling (hints clementine & peach), further abetted by dollop sugar — 6g/ℓ in second-vintage **05**. Delicious now, structure & stuffing for yr/3. Fr oak, 9 mths.

★★★★ **Sauvignon Blanc Single Vineyard** new 'Small block nursed to bring flavour & acidity into balance,' says Thys L. Mission well & truly accomplished: **06** concentrated full-spectrum sauvignon aromas/flavours (gooseberry, catbox et al); impressively harmonious despite huge acid & slender build (7.2g/ℓ, 13% alc). Unfiltered.

★★★★ **Sauvignon Blanc 8 Rows** new Selected bunches from 320-row block (also officially a single-vyd). **06** will delight fans of an edgier, 'sauvage' style; greener toned than SV above, not unripe; sleek, concentrated, concludes with surge of mouthwatering acidity.

Matys ☺ ★★★ Pronounced Mah-*tace*, gently wooded equal blend cab, merlot, shiraz, with 10% pinotage; now screwcapped. **05** honest, well-made quaffer, lively & plummy. **Blanc de Blanc** ☺ ★★★ Pvs 4-way blend halved to just sauvignon, chard in **06**, but pleasure's doubled: delicious fresh-sliced pear tone; racy, lightish (13% alc); screwcapped for convenience.

Cabernet Sauvignon ★★★★ **04** rated by Tienie L as his best ever. Certainly shows potential — tightly packed ripe fruit, serious oaking (15 mths Fr), structure for keeping — but needs time to develop. **Merlot** new ★★★★ A little gem. Truly ripe fruit, supportive oaking (16 mths Fr), fine savoury spiciness to **04**'s raspberry/cherry flavours. **Pinotage** ★★★★ Hallmark charm & grace (rather than the variety's more usual power) on **04**, dark fruit & dried banana whiffs, pleasantly understated oak (14 mths Fr); usual not overpowering 14. 5 % alc. **Private Collection** ★★★★ 'Vintage' red, blend make-up varies from yr to yr. Bdx line-up of cab, merlot, cab f (60/30/10) in **04**; fairly juicy, with undaunting tannins but seems embryonic mid-2006, has more to give — cellar yr/3. Fr oak, 2 yrs. **Blanc de Noir** new ★★☆ Dry, light, toothsome **06** from cab, merlot; ripe red berries with lighter grassy herbaceous nuance. Screwcapped. **Chardonnay Single Vineyard** ★★★★ Simply 'Chardonnay' last ed; block since registered. **06** quietly charming sister to brazen Rsv; subtly oaked (only 50%, rest tank-vinified), 3 mths lees gives breadth, silkiness to excellent but still tight fruit. Vg potential. **Sauvignon Blanc** ★★★ Unmistakably 'Dbnvlle' — nettles & sundry green fruit, again sensible 13% alc, zinging freshness, but **06** perhaps too austere for solo enjoyment. **Noble Late Harvest** ★★★ ('Elixir' last ed.) Bunch pressed, barrel fermented/matured dessert from sauvignon. To date only **03**, mid-2005 billowed ripe peach fruit & fresh baked bread; racy acidity, nutty flavours & long, elegant finish. Unobtrusive 14%. — CR

Diemersfontein Wines

Wellington · Est/1stB 2001 · Tasting & sales daily 10-5 · Fee R15 · Closed Dec 25 · Tours by appt · Restaurant & guest house (see Eat-out & Stay-over sections) · Conferencing · Walks · Mountain biking · Owners David & Susan Sonnenberg · Winemakers Francois Roode & Brett Rightford (Sep 2003/Nov 2005) · 55 ha (cab, merlot, mourvèdre, petit v, pinotage, shiraz, viognier) · 400 tons 25 000 cs · 95% red 4% white 1% rosé · HACCP & ISO 9001 accredited · PO Box 41 Wellington 7654 · wine@diemersfontein.co.za · www.diemersfontein.co.za · T 021·864·5050 · F 021·864·2095

Diemersfontein is a far busier place than it was in 2000, when David and Sue Sonnenberg returned from the UK to develop the family farm. 'It's largely, but not exclusively, pinotage that's done it,' acknowledges David S, referring to their much-applauded Carpe Diem Pinotage and popular 'coffee-and-chocolate-toned' Diemersfontein Pinotage, now launched annually at a gala Pinotage-on-Tap party. Elaborating, Sonnenberg says: 'I feel like the parent of two teenage daughters — one is a classically trained violinist who dresses modestly and pulls the crowds in the exclusive concert halls; the other, a mini-skirted and occasionally provocative pop star who wows the younger generation but has fans of all ages. Who'd choose between them?'

Carpe Diem range

★★★★ **Cabernet Sauvignon 05** work in progress but already has exuberant cassis, livening touch mint, oak as 'wood shaving' presence. Busy integrating, firm but fine-grained tannins, dry finish. 15 mths new Fr. **04**, also a sample, had pencil shavings & minerals, taut austerity; weightier (14.5% alc) than pleasantly sweet **03**, *Wine* ★★★★.

★★★★★ **Pinotage** Last tasted sample **04**, destined for greatness. Toasty nose led to fruity sweetness, well structured tannins with lingering aftertaste. Serious oaking: new Fr/Am, 15 mths, 70/30. Poised to continue assertive wine show presence of **03**, whose newer laurels incl IWSC gold & Pinotage Top Ten.

★★★★ **Shiraz 05** ex-barrel shows dark choc, anise & sweet red-fruit perfume but palate till evolving. Elegant structure not yet fully accommodating sinewy tannins. Difficult to rate mid-2006, might equal sample **04**, which returned to form after vegetal & milky **03** (★★★ but *Wine* ★★★★).

Merlot ★★★★ Last ed **03** showed house style, delivered herbal warmth to tightly arrayed palate. ±18 mths oak. **Malbec** new Dark hued **05** ex-barrel shows trademark vegetal leanings, wet heath, hedgerow fruit; chunky construction, still assimilating oak mid-2006, difficult to rate, possible ★★★★. Incl 10% cab f. **Viognier** ★★★★ Trim but well formed **05** transports you to southern France with its violets & lavender perfume. Intriguing, stylish.

Diemersfontein range

★★★★ **Pinotage** Work in progress **06** already showy with luscious wild berries, rhubarb nuances, creamy mocha spicing. When bottled, shd match quality of MIWA gonged **03**. **05** sold out before we cld taste. **04** (★★★) was super-ripe & not as arresting.

★★★★ **Heaven's Eye** Trademark dark-fruit core lifted by cranberry piquancy from blend change in **04** to mainly cab, with petit v, shiraz, roobernet. Oodles of sweet spice accompany stern tannins from 10 mths mainly Fr oak; wine built for longer haul, 10+ yrs, as rest.

★★★★ **Summer's Lease 04** blend now 65/35 shiraz, mourvèdre, dab viognier, bringing out rhône quality of wine: dark fruit, salty liquorice, nuances of scrub, white pepper. Already delicious, palate's lithe juiciness balances the firm, ripe tannins. Give more time to show true potential, keep 5+ yrs, as all these. Mix Fr/Am oak, 10 mths.

★★★★ **Shiraz 04** forceful black cherry, brambleberry frame on which hangs all variety's expected perfumes, flavours: campfire smoke, savoury spice, touch of tar. Supple body shows juiciness of good fruit, harmonious oaking. Yr Fr/Am.

Cabernet Sauvignon ★★★ **05**'s plummy fruit holds centre stage, with oak in support role, adding stiffening to elegant, juicy palate. Yr 2nd fill, mostly Fr. **Merlot** ★★★ Bright red-berry & prominent cedar aromas prepare you for **04**'s medium weight but firmly held tannins, needing another yr to meld, gd for ±2 more. **Maiden's Prayer** ★★ Unoaked merlot, cab, shiraz, pinotage blend, fruit driven & designed for early drinking — though last ed **04** was neither: unripe vegetal tone & bitter finish. — *CR*

■ *Die Rivierkloof see* Viljoensdrift
■ *Die Tweede Droom see* Groot Parys

Dieu Donné Vineyards   ◊♀🖑

Franschhoek ▪ Est 1984 ▪ 1stB 1986 ▪ Tasting & sales Mon-Fri 9-4 Sat/Sun 10.30-4 ▪ Fee R10 ▪ Closed Dec 25/26 & Jan 1 ▪ Cheese platters ▪ Picnic lunches in summer (booking essential) ▪ Tours by appt ▪ Tour groups ▪ Owner Robert Maingard ▪ Winemaker Stephan du Toit (May 1996) ▪ Viticulturist Hennie du Toit (Apr 1988) ▪ 40 ha (cab, merlot, pinotage, shiraz, chard, sauvignon) ▪ ±280 tons 16 500 cs 60% red 35% white 3% rosé 2% MCC ▪ PO Box 94 Franschhoek 7690 ▪ info@dieudonnevineyards.com ▪ www.dieudonnevineyards.com ▪ T 021·876·2493 ▪ F 021·876·2102

The best seats in this natural theatre will be those in the new restaurant being built next to the tasting room — the view from the farm, high up on the slopes of the Franschhoek Mountains, is breathtaking. Winemaker and Cape Wine Master Stephan du Toit has his range sorted: 60% red and 30% white, with his production of MCC increased dramatically in 2006, thanks to its popularity. 'Our terroir suits the style perfectly,' he elaborates.

Cabernet Sauvignon ★★★★ House's low-fruit, tight-tannin style will be appreciated by classicists. **02** offers black berry, herby complexity & typical firm, long-lived cab tannin/acid structure. 16 mths Fr oak, third new. **Chardonnay Wooded** ★★★★ Change from delicate citrus-dominated pvs to a more pronounced barrel character in **04**, still attractive; spice, biscuit & cream aromas; on palate, wood more supportive, underpinning luscious long lime flavours. Yr Fr oak, 50% new. **Sauvignon Blanc** ★★★ Grassy **06** pleasant enough but somewhat lacking verve, persistence; for early drinking. **Noble Late Harvest** ★★★★ Wafts of botrytis entwine with pineapple, marzipan & vanilla in this delicate dessert. **05** subtly oaked, vibrant, touch sweeter than pvs (126g/ℓ sugar) but uncloying & persistent. 6 mths Fr oak. JCWCA 'first'/gold. No new vintages tasted for the following: **Merlot** ★★ Generous plum fruit on nose/palate of **02**, finishes with bitter almond suggestion. 18 mths Fr oak. **Pinotage** ★★★ **03** lightish version (13.6% alc) with charming raspberry aroma; dry, elegant finish showing hint of Am oak. Concours Mondial gold. **Shiraz** ★★★ Earthy & spicy **03** lighter than pvs (14% alc vs 15.5%), very dry & food-friendly. Yr mainly Fr oak. **Cabernet Sauvignon-Shiraz** ★★★ **03** smooth & accessible debut; balanced New World fruitiness, light oak touch will please widely. **Rosé** ★★★ Usually from two sauvignons, one red (cab-), other white (-blanc); **05** cherry nose, raspberry-toned sweet/sour palate; for early consumption. **Chardonnay Unwooded** ★★★ **05** gains weight & texture from 4 mths *sur lie* ageing, nicely balanced by refreshing Granny Smith apple acidity. **Maingard Brut MCC** ★★★★ **02** light & delicate styling with fine toasty mousse, brioche whiff. Some honey, cream on finish. 30 mths matured on lees. *Wine* ★★★★. Discontinued: **Cabernet Sauvignon Reserve**, **Cabernet Sauvignon-Merlot**. — *CvZ*

■ *Die Vlakte see* Cloverfield
■ *Disa see* Tulbagh Wineries Co-op
■ *Discover see* Spier

Dispore Kamma Boutique Winery   ◊

Caledon ▪ Est/1stB 2002 ▪ Visits by appt ▪ Owners Philip Mostert & Hannes Coetzee ▪ Winemaker Philip Mostert, with Hannes Coetzee (Jan/Jun 2002) ▪ Viti consultant Willie de

Waal ▪ ±150-200 cs 100% red ▪ PO Box 272 Caledon 7230 ▪ *disporekamma@overnet.co.za* ▪ **T 083·448·1670** ▪ *F* 028·214·1077

Shiraz was country GP Philip Mostert's first love even before it became fashionable: 'It adapts itself to your own style'. The demands of being a GP shelved Cape Wine Master plans but didn't stop Mostert from working a harvest in Burgundy with Topaz's Clive Torr, nor from opening a boutique cellar in rented premises in his home town, Caledon. Syrah will always be the lead act but a Cab and Merlot play strong supporting roles.

Cabernet Sauvignon ★★★ Lasted tasted was well balanced, eminently approachable **04**, packed with ripe fruit & spice. **Merlot** new ★★ One-off from organically grown Ovrberg vines; **05** ripe-style country red with obvious oak & alc, bountiful dry tannins. 14 mths 3rd fill Fr oak. **Syrah** ★★★ Blend of Paarl, Sbosch & Rbtson fruit for **05**; vintage's big bones evident in ultra-ripe dark berry fruit, brawny alc (15.2%), generous oak spicing (14 mths Fr/Am, none new). Now lightly filtered.— *MM*

Distell

Stellenbosch ▪ PO Box 184 Stellenbosch 7599 ▪ *www.distell.co.za* ▪ **T 021·809·7000**

Operating from two corporate-owned wineries in Stellenbosch (Bergkelder and Adam Tas), Distell vinifies some of SA's most successful and enduring wine brands. They are: 5th Avenue Cold Duck, Autumn Harvest Crackling, Capenheimer, Cellar Cask, Chateau Libertas, Drostdy-Hof, Flat Roof Manor, Fleur du Cap, Graça, Grand Mousseux, Grünberger, Hill & Dale, Ixia, Kellerprinz, Kupferberger Auslese, Libertas, Lomond, Monis, Obikwa, Oom Tas, Oracle, Overmeer, Pongrácz, Sedgwick's, Ship Sherry, Table Mountain, Tassenberg, Taverna, Two Oceans, Virginia and Zonnebloem. Distell also owns the House of JC le Roux, a dedicated sparkling-wine cellar in Devon Valley. Then there are the stand-alone 'estate' labels: Nederburg, Plaisir de Merle and Lomond. Distell is also the co-owner, together with Lusan Holdings, of a handful of top Stellenbosch properties (Alto, Le Bonheur, Neethlingshof, Stellenzicht, Uitkyk), and, with seven local growers, of Durbanville Hills. Distell also has agreements with a few independently owned cellars (Allesverloren, Jacobsdal, Theuniskraal) for which it provides a range of services. Finally, there's the black empowerment venture on Papkuilsfontein farm near Darling, source of Tukulu wines. See Bergkelder for details about the Vinoteque Wine Bank, and separate entries for the above brands and properties.

■ *Dixon's Peak* see Waverley Hills
■ *Dolphin Bay* see Cru Wines

Domaine Brahms Wineries   ◔♀

Paarl ▪ Est 1998 ▪ 1stB 1999 ▪ Tasting & sales Mon-Fri 9.30-5 Sat & pub hols by appt (closed Easter Fri-Mon, Jun 16, Sep 24, Dec 25/26 & Jan 1) ▪ Fee R5/wine ▪ Tours anytime by appt ▪ Owners Johan & Gesie van Deventer ▪ Winemaker/viticulturist Gesie van Deventer (Lategan) (1998) ▪ 15 ha (cab, merlot, pinotage, shiraz) ▪ 100% red ▪ PO Box 2136 Windmeul 7630 ▪ *brahms@iafrica.com* ▪ **T 021·869·8555** ▪ *F* 021·869·8590

Former advocate Gesie van Deventer's remarriage doesn't signal any changes to the Domaine Brahms brand but new husband and MD of Freshmark Johan vD's marketing savvy will doubtless provide an extra fillip. Gesie vD in the meantime is becoming more involved in women's issues, helping to uplift female farmers locally with legal advice and mentoring, and judging female entrepreneurs in a national competition sponsored by Old Mutual. Winemaking too is on the right track, the farm savouring many awards including an IWSC 'Best in Class' award for their 04 Pinotage.

★★★★ **Shiraz 02** (★★★) difficult vintage with high acidity & greenish tannins. Pvsly noted as developing similarly to **01**, with herbal notes & greener tannins. From low yielding vyds (±6 t/ha); Fr oak, 15-20% new.

★★★★ **Pinotage** Sample **04** tasted mid-2005 was suave, well behaved but still varietally true pinotage. 9 mths Fr oak.

Quartet ★★★★ **03** last ed was stylish blend merlot, pinotage, cab, shiraz (50/30/10/10). Attractive cassis, spice, smoke, hint biltong migrate easily onto palate, nicely proportioned, unobtrusive oak (only 40% wooded). **Judex Provisional Judgement** ★★★ Earthy blend pinotage, merlot, ruby cab, shiraz (39/30/28/3); **02** attractive berry, herb & oaky tones. No new releases ready for wines above. **Cabernet Sauvignon** ★★★★ Ripe **03** expressive dark plum aromas; surprisingly delicate entry, then rich fruit, supple tannins & textured finish. Yr Fr oak, 20% new. **Chenin Blanc** ★★★★ Bright, golden **05** with oak, tangerine & sweet almond aromas; harmonious & integrated, fruit adequately supporting 60% new Fr oak (yr). Ex-35 yr old bushvines. — *IM*

Domaine Finlayson-Edgebaston [new]

Stellenbosch • Est/1stB 2004 • Closed to public • Owners Woodlands & Finlayson Family trusts • Winemaker Walter Finlayson, with Riaan Coetzee (Jan 2004/Jan 2006) • Viticulturist David Finlayson, with Riaan Coetzee (Jan 2004/Jan 2006) • 24 ha (cab, merlot, mourvèdre, shiraz, sauvignon) • 35 tons ±1 000 cs 80% red 20% white • Export brands: The Edge/Edgebaston • PO Box 2033 Dennesig 7601 • lizelf@lantic.net • T/F 021·880·1633

It's back to the roots for the Finlayson family as these doyens of Cape wine come together once again to map out new territory in the Simonsberg foothills. (Edgebaston the original name of the farm). David F's at the helm of vineyard development; father Walter (who put Hartenberg and Blaauwklippen on the chart, then set Glen Carlou on its upward course) is overseeing winemaking and marketing, while David F's wife Lizel has taken on sales. Says DF: 'Times are tough in the industry but family credentials should prove true.' They're already making their mark internationally with exports to the UK, Holland and Scandinavia.

★★★★ **First Release Shiraz** Name commemorates the property's first wine. Polished **04**'s ripe raspberry fruit beautifully integrated with effects of 16 mths new Fr oak, which adds creamy mocha notes, attractive soft tannins, persistent flavours. Just 150 cs (x 12).

Shiraz ★★★★ Light peppery fruit on **04**, & ample spice; well oaked (14 mths, 65% half new Fr, rest Am). 10% cab adds to the structure & grip, but the 14.2% alc rather evident. — *MF*

■ **Domaines Paradyskloof** *see Vriesenhof*
■ **Dombeya Vineyards** *see Haskell Vineyards*

Domein Doornkraal

Little Karoo • Est 1890 • 1stB 1973 • Tasting & sales Mon-Fri 9-5 Sat 8-1 (Sep-May) & Sat 9-1 (Jun-Aug) • Pub & school hols 8-5; school hols (summer) 8-6 • Closed Easter Fri/Sun, Dec 25/ 26 & Jan 1 • Tours by appt • Seasonal farm produce • Tour groups • Gifts • Owners/winemakers Swepie & Piet le Roux • 22 ha • 2 000 cs own label 50% white 50% red • PO Box 14 De Rust 6650 • doornkraal@xsinet.co.za • www.doornkraal.co.za • T/F 044·251·6715

The worst drought in memory ended with a gentle rain which started in July and continued for over a month. For the first time, the Stompdrift dam was full, waterfalls cascaded from unlikely places and plants which had not flowered for many years transformed the landscape into a colourful carpet. It was 'a sight for sore eyes' say the Le Rouxs, after a challenging 2006 harvest which was 'not for sissies', according to Piet le R.

★★★★ **Pinta** ✓ Luscious jerepiko-style dessert from pinotage, tinta; lately dash touriga too (necessitating name change?); new bottling not tasted (ditto for all following); pvs was harmonious with fresh dry finish. 30/50/20 mix; alc now set at 17%. **NV**.

★★★★ **Ten Year Old Tawny Port** Among handful of SA vintaged tawnies; old-fashioned but delicious. last tasted **92** VDG was beautifully balanced; from pinotage, tinta. Premium priced: R150 ex-tasting room.

Cabernet Sauvignon ★★★ **02** ripe cassis aromas; focused & quite rich; quick finish but pleasant enough. **Merlot** ★★ Quirky, sweet & simple **03**, fermented with native yeasts. **Kannaland (Red)** ★★★ **05** cab, merlot mix (60/40), unwooded; undemanding, lightish red berry flavours finishing slightly sweet. **Kannaland (White)** ★★ **05** chardonnay/semillon liaison under screwcap; semi-dry boiled-sweet flavours, lively, for early enjoyment. **Tickled Pink** ★★ Light (12% alc), friskily foamy blanc de noir sparkler, intense grapey aromas, sweet but very fresh finish; sold with shocking pink home-grown ostrich feather.

Muscadel Jerepigo ★★★ Comfortable & warming fortified dessert; rich raisiny flavours with hint of pipe-tobacco. 18% alc. **NV**. Also available but not tasted: **Kuierwyn** (dry & Natural Sweet), **Ruby/White Port**.

'Military' range

NV fortified desserts. **Majoor** ★★★ Idiosyncratic white jerepiko from chenin; 'Great Martini mixer,' avers Piet le R, 'or pour over crushed ice.' **Kaptein** & **Luitenant** not assessed (both still AWOL). — DH

Dominion Wine Company

*Stellenbosch ▪ Est/1stB 2002 ▪ Closed to public ▪ Winemaker Lelanie Germishuys (2004) ▪ 12 000 cs own label 40% red 60% white ▪ Export brands: Longwood, Harvest Moon & Dominion ▪ Postnet Suite 280, Private Bag X29, Somerset West 7135 ▪ info@dominionwineco.co.za ▪ www.dominionwineco.co.za ▪ **T 021·883·8879** ▪ F 021·883·8782*

This Stellenbosch-based company — 50% of its equity recently sold to G3 Capital, a black owned investor consortium with interests in media and hospitality — has opened an office in West Yorkshire, manned by John Murch, a seasoned wine marketer with 20 of his 30 years experience focused on SA wines. Dominion is confident of making their mark in the competitive UK market, says new MD Anzill Adams, who played a significant role in bringing G3 and Dominion together.

Kingsview Pinotage ★★ Still-listed **03** lusty version with high-toned red-berry pungency, big tannins, warming 14.3% alc. Fr barrels, 9 mths. **Big Red** ★★ Cab/merlot blend sold in magnum (1.5ℓ) only; latest is **NV**; surprisingly robust compared with pvs; strong tannins & tight, leathery, slightly stewed fruit. Following **03** chards still selling, not revisited: **Rolling Hills Chardonnay** ★★★★ Flavoursome & big **03**, will be liked by lovers of woodier styles. **Milestone Chardonnay Limited Release** ★★★★ **03** less oak-powered than above; fruit salad & peach tones; lightly toasty caramel finish. Yr 1st/2nd fill barrels. **Sauvignon Blanc** ★★ Similar character to versions below; **06** (sample) vinified for light bodied freshness & verve. **Sauvignon Blanc Brut** ★★ Gently dry sparkling; **NV**; showing soft honeyed tone, inviting early drinking. **Merlot**, **Milestone Syrah**, **Shiraz**, **Cabernet Sauvignon-Merlot** & **Rosé de Syrah** discontinued.

Longwood range   new

Pinotage-Shiraz ★★ **05** light textured blend with banana whiff, sprinkle of spice & slight astringency on finish. **Chenin Blanc-Colombard 06** (preview) a sound commercial proposition: ripe tropical fruit, slightly sweet yet crisp, quaffable. Potential ★★ stars. **Sauvignon Blanc** ★★ **06** similar to versions below; zingingly fresh & light.

Sugar Bush Ridge range

> **Cabernet Sauvignon-Merlot** ☺ ★★★ Delicious & approachable **05**, harmonious, flavourful combo dried leaves & damp earth from cab, ripe mulberry & plum from merlot.

Sauvignon Blanc ★★ **06** crisp, light & dry with green flavours in a slight frame.

Harvest Moon range

Charming & whimsical labels for these quick-quaffs. **Shiraz** ★★ Aussie-style pulpy fruit on **04**, slightly sweet & effortless. **Chardonnay** new ★★ Soft, easy **05**, ripe pineapple flavours & hint of botrytis adding interest. **Sauvignon Blanc** ★★ Green-spectrum nettle & grass on **06** sample, slender & light with racy acid. All wines sourced widely, so various WOs. — CT

Doolhof Estate

*Wellington ▪ Est 1995 ▪ 1stB 2001 ▪ Visits Mon-Fri 8.30-4 or by appt ▪ Fee R20 ▪ Guest cottage (see Stay-over section) ▪ Walks ▪ Mountain biking ▪ MD Dennis Kerrison ▪ Winemaker Therese Swart (Aug 2004) ▪ Viticulturist Hendrik Laubscher (Aug 1996) ▪ ±36 ha (cabs s/f, malbec, merlot, petit v, pinotage, shiraz, chard, sauvignon) ▪ 220 tons 25 000 cs ▪ PO Box 157 Wellington 7654 ▪ wine@ doolhof.com ▪ www.doolhof.com ▪ **T 021·873·6911** ▪ F 021·864·2321*

Last year's highlights for Doolhof were gaining official sanction to produce 'estate' wines — and escaping the worst of Wellington's rampaging fires: only one row of sauvignon was singed. The 2006 harvest saw both quality and yield improved, while the first 2005 reds made in the new cellar were released. The Doolhof brand is proving popular overseas and at home, evidenced by the addition of four wines to the Signatures range.

Cape Boar ★★★☆ Partly oaked blend led by cab (60%) in **04**, equal portions shiraz/merlot. Explosive plum pudding fruit, gutsy tannins make for robust quaffing wine. 15% alc not unbalanced. **Cape Roan** ★★★★ No **04**. Shiraz led the charge in **03** (70%) with cab/merlot (20/10); similar character to above, slightly more pepper; massive alc (15%) but more control, less overt sweetness. Both 'Capes' WO Coastal. **Renaissance Cabernet Sauvignon-Merlot** new ★★★ Similar styling to version below with addition of dried herbs; **04** warm ripe fruit throughout; harmonious tannins but brawny alc (15%) out of kilter. Wine ex-Wllngtn & Darling, matured at estate (Fr oak, 20% new, 11 mths). **Maiden's Prayer** ★★★★ Joint venture with Diemersfontein (see entry). **The Dukes Blend 03** available but not tasted. **Renaissance Cabernet Sauvignon** & **Renaissance Pinotage** discontinued.

Signatures of Doolhof range

★★★★ **Chardonnay Wooded** Characterful **05** achieves buttered toast richness from fermentation/11 mths in 25% new Fr oak without sacrificing citrus-freshened drinkability; assured winemaking! Luxurious silky texture; lively acidity gives length, definition. new, as are next 3 wines.

Cabernet Sauvignon ★★★ **05** distinctive & appealing profile of roasted corn & pruney fruit; balanced oaking, though a tad 'hot' from high alc (15%). New Fr oak, yr. All reds tasted ex-barrel. **Merlot** ★★★ Full-frontal merlot, **05** oozes ripe cassis, 90% new Fr oak fully absorbed into smooth body, so fruit is the star. **Pinotage** ★★★★ A smooth textured charmer showing gd typicity in mulberry/rhubarb tone; **05** shows what drinking pleasure variety can give. Yr Fr oak, 50% new. **Chardonnay Unoaked** ★★★ **05** last ed noted as a step up. More passionfruit & citrus notes, tasty & satisfying, zestier, drier. Blend Wllngtn/Stbosch fruit. **Sauvignon Blanc** ★★★★ Bursting with vitality, **06** has a delicious tangy zestiness & just-picked fruit character, making it an ideal food companion. — CR

Dormershire   👓🍷

*Stellenbosch • Est 1996 • 1stB 2001 • Visits Mon-Fri 10-5 Sat 10-4 • Owner SPF Family Trust • Winemaker Sunette Frost, advised by Kowie du Toit • Viti consultant Johan Pienaar • 7 ha (cab, shiraz, sauvignon) • 60 tons 4 000 cs 75% red 15% white 10% rosé • PO Box 491 Bellville 7535 • frostyr@iafrica.com wine@dormershire.co.za • **T/F** 021·903·1784 • F 021·945·1174*

The closest to Cape Town of the Stellenbosch wineries, the Frosts' estate now has a small function and conference venue (so that even more visitors can enjoy that Table Mountain view). Paul F has his hands full with lawyering, farming and marketing, while Sunette makes wine (with input from Kowie du Toit) and manages their spread. 'All the wines are now made here,' she notes, 'and I believe that's evident from the improvement in their quality.'

Cabernet Sauvignon ★★★★ Classically constructed, stylish **04**; finished wine shows some of the promise of last yr's preview in liberal cassis fruit, fragrant pencil-shaving oak; but present inwardness suggests more time's needed to show true worth. 15 mths Fr oak, 20% new. **Shiraz** ★★★ **04** similar uninhibited ripe-fruit expressivity as pvs, plus aromatic enticements incl smoked bacon, though tannins drier, bit more herbaceous than pvs. 15 mths mainly Fr oak, 20% new. **Stoep Shiraz** ★★★★ Higher rating for this new version courtesy riper tannins/fruit, more generosity & concentration. **04** similar attractive flavours. Wood as above, exclusively Fr. **Rosé** ★★★ Barrel-aged **05** from shiraz/cab, revisited, remains interesting & unusual: emphatic dry finish, coffee/caramel aromas, red-wine fleshiness (yet only 12.5% alc); needs bit more freshness for higher rating. **Sauvignon Blanc** ★★★ Restrainedly flavourful & appealing **06** (sample), subtle capsicum/herb tones with fresh acidity; again commendably low 13% alc. All above EW. — IvH

Dornier Wines

Stellenbosch · 1stB 2002 · *Tasting & sales Mon-Fri 9.30-4.30 Sat 11-4 Sun 11-4 (Nov-Apr only)* · *Fee R20* · *Closed Easter Fri-Mon, Dec 25/26, Jan 1* · *Tours by appt* · *Tour groups* · *Owner Christoph Dornier* · *Winemaker JC Steyn (2005)* · *Viticulturist Bob Hobson (2005)* · 67 ha (cabs s/f, malbec, merlot, petit v, pinotage, shiraz, chenin, sauvignon, semillon) · 300 tons 85% red 15% white · PO Box 7518 Stellenbosch 7599 · info@dornierwines.co.za · www. dornierwines.co.za · **T** 021·880·0557 · F 021·880·1499*

It's all about precision fine-tuning at this architectural showpiece, focusing on the hillside vineyards: striving for homogeneity regarding levels of ripeness via infrared aerial photography to manage irrigation and vine stress levels; and identifying micro-blocks within vineyards (which are separately vinified, with Bordeaux oenologist Florent Dumeau's input). The range has been neatly tiered: the flagship Dornier Donatus for premium classic blends; good value Dornier single varieties intended to offer elegance and finesse ('Check out our Pinotage!' exhorts winemaker JC Steyn); and the new Cocoa Hill wines for easy accessibility. A new restaurant opens in the historic barn in April.

Donatus range

★★★★ **Donatus** Bdx-inspired red with regal bearing; selection of best blocks, vinified & matured apart before blending. Classic melding of cab f, merlot & cab in **03** gives way to duo cab f/merlot (71/29) in **04** (★★★★★). Alluring herb/spice aromas (green tea, cardamom, anise); taut palate with focused tannin, brisk acidity, typical claret tealeaf note on finish. New Fr oak, 18 mths. Holding back: deserves 5+ yrs cellaring to show best.

★★★★ **White** Blend chenin, semillon, sauvignon (cleverly, only chenin oaked, 5 mths) impressed wine critics on **03** debut (considered one of world's best wines by UK's Matthew Jukes). Current **05** (★★★★★) has no sauvignon but is even more delicious; wax, spice & thatch prelude to the main act: arresting acidity & slate-like core, fine structure for fruitful bottle maturation. Slightly longer oaked (8 mths new Fr barrels).

Dornier range

Merlot Fine tannins & minerals underpin poised, well fruited **04** (★★★★); sugared plum character tempts on first sip, encourages return visits. 18 Fr oak, combo new/2nd fill. **03** (★★★) similar plum compôte richness but slightly astringent tannin. **Pinotage** new ★★★★ 'V well received' by customers, critics (*Wine* ★★★★), advises JCS; **04** outspoken oak (18 mths 2nd fill Fr oak) subdues mulberry fruit mid-2006; gd vinosity but astringent finish, give more time.

Cocoa Hill range   new

Cocoa Hill ★★★ Wallet-friendly cab, shiraz, merlot assembly (41/36/23), smidgen fruit ex-Dbnvlle; **04** plump plum flavours, touch woody still (12-16 mths combo new/old Fr oak). **Chenin Blanc** ★★★★ ✓ Engaging version with presence, personality; previewed **06** bouquet of hay & apricot; zesty cinnamon-dusted green apple flavours, tight mineral core. Weighty & round, slightly spicy thanks to judicious oaking (only 30% barrelled 5 mths) & regular lees stirring. — *CvZ*

Douglas Green

Wellington · Est/1stB 1938 · *Closed to public* · *Owner DGB* · *Cellarmaster (blending cellar) Gerhard Carstens, with Liesl Carstens-Herbst (2003)* · *Oenologist Jaco Potgieter (2000)* · *Vini advisor John Worontschak* · *Viti advisers VinPro (May 2000)* · 6 000 tons 580 000 cs 50% red 50% white · ISO 9002 & HACCP certified · PO Box 246 Wellington 7654 · douglasgreen@ dgb.co.za · www.douglasgreen.co.za · **T** 021·864·5300 · F 021·864·1287*

As early as 1938, Douglas Green, the Cape's first true negociant, was bucking the regionalist trend in favour of quality and price, blending products from scattered but select vineyards and cellars. Parent company DGB has overseen a reinvigoration, oenologist Jaco Potgieter teaming up with flying viticulturist/winemaker John Worontschak to oversee primary production and relations with growers, while Wellington cellarmaster Gerhard Carstens adds his touch to the vinification and blending process. A new brand, The Beach House, was recently released in Europe and the US; the local launch is set for September this year.

Cabernet Sauvignon ★★★ **04** repeats somewhat restrained style of pvs; savoury/meaty fruit spectrum, enough cab backbone to go few yrs. **Merlot** ★★★★ ✓ **03** again well fruited, aromatic red berry nose, well constructed & balanced, with integrated oak (Fr staves, 3 mths). **Pinotage** ★★★★ ✓ **03** banana custard aroma imparts impression of richness, belied by leaner, fairly firm palate; accessible but best in few yrs. 3 mths Fr staves. **Shiraz** ★★★ **03** tasty commercial style with typical smoky/meaty whiffs, soft, accessible flavours, lots of vanilla from 3 mths on Am/Fr staves. **St Augustine** ★★★★ Favourite SA red since the 1940s; now equal cab & merlot, with 20% shiraz in unwooded **03**, warm & generous red (14% alc), approachable, with few yrs in hand. **Chardonnay** ★★★ **04** melon & lightly buttered-toast whiffs; soft & easy but quite quick. Stave fermented. **Sauvignon Blanc** ★★★ **04** with crunchy acidity, appley fruit salad tones, low 12.4% alc. **Cape Ruby Port** ★★★★ **NV** winter snuggler; last we noted an LBV (rather than Ruby) style, fragrant & warming. Both ranges WO W Cape. No new wines ready for review for either.

Faces of Africa range

Cinsault-Pinotage ★★ 50/50 blend in **04**, wood (Fr/Am staves) a more commanding presence than pvs, firmish fruit-pastille palate ends furrily. **Colombar-Chardonnay** ★★★ Light-textured **04**, up-tempo lemon-drop flavours, refreshing crisp acidity. — *CR*

Douglas Wine Cellar   🍷🕮♿

Northern Cape • Est 1968 • 1stB 1977 • Tasting & sales Mon-Fri 8-5 • Fee R5 • Closed pub hols • Tours by appt • BYO picnic • Gifts • Owners 45 shareholders • Winemaker Chrisna Botha • Viticulturist Stefan Gerber (May 2005) • 360 ha (cab, merlot, ruby cab, shiraz, chard, chenin, colombard, gewürz) • 6 000 cs own label 19% red 43% white 8% rosé 30% dessert • PO Box 47 Douglas 8730 • wynkelder@gwk.co.za • www.confluencewines.co.za • T 053·298·8314 • F 053·298·1845

The focus over the past year at this Northern Cape winery has continued to be on upgrading the cellar. The big spend has been on winery equipment with one goal in mind, says Douglas marketing advisor Pieter Louw: the drive for premium quality.

Confluence range

Shiraz-Cabernet Sauvignon ★★ 60/40 mix with briary red-fruit aromas; **03** soft, juicy, medium bodied; lightly oaked. **Chenin Blanc-Colombard** ★★ Clean but quiet & four-square 65/35 blend; **03** light bodied. **Classic Red** ★★ **03** braai quaffer with wild berries, spicy, dry finish. **Classic White** ★★ **05** attractive summer sipper from chenin, colombar & chard (50/30/20). Tropical bouquet, guava & melon palate. Three Natural Sweets in the range vary in sweetness, alcohol levels: **Johannisberger Red** ★ **05** Tutti-frutti medium bodied (12.5% alc; 45g/ℓ sugar), soft tannins. Cloying, strawberry **Classic Rose** ☆ **05**, barely vinous; 80g/ℓ sugar, 8% alc. **Johannisberger White** ★★ **05** Crowd pleasing sun-kissed peaches & melons with good sugar/acid balance; 30g/ℓ sugar, 11% alc. **Red Muscadel** ★★ Well-crafted winter warmer. **04** full of raisins & treacle, well integrated alc, not cloying despite 200g/ℓ sugar. **Red Jerepigo** ★★ Fortified dessert sipper. **04** Xmas cake aromas, full-sweet molasses palate. 230g/ℓ sugar. No new vintages tasted for above, below.

Provin range

These in 2/5ℓ casks: **Dry Red**, **Grand Cru**, **Stein**, **Special Harvest** & Late Harvest. Also **Vin Doux Sparkling**. — *CT*

Drakensig Wines   🍷🕮♿

Paarl • Est 1999 • 1stB 2000 • Tasting & sales Mon-Fri 9-5 Sat 9-1; low season by appt • Closed Easter Sun, Dec 25/26 & Jan 1 • Farm-grown olive oil for sale • Conference facilities for groups of 5-10 • Owner/winemaker/viticulturist Marais Viljoen • 13 ha (cab, pinotage, shiraz) • 4 000 cs 80% red 20% white • HACCP implementation in progress • PO Box 22 Simondium 7670 • drakensig@mweb.co.za • T 021·874·3881 • F 021·874·3882

Marais Viljoen would rather be making his wines and olive oil than talking about them, but admits to being rather pleased with his recent awards, and enthused about the 2006 grapes — the first big harvest from Drakensig vines (previously grapes were bought in); this may signal an increase in volumes of the Reserve range. He's also increasing his olive oil production — it's become incredibly popular and besides 'olives and wine just go so well together'.

Marais Viljoen range

★★★★ **Shiraz** Spicy wild-berry fruit intro to **04**, off Darling vyds (as are all in range); full-bodied, robustly (but not overly) extracted, with strong, tight tannins promising gd few yrs development. 14 mths 50/50 Am/Fr oak.

Cabernet Sauvignon Returns to guide with **04** (★★), showing rather less of the vibrant fruit character of sibling above (or last-featured **01** ★★★★), & more chalky-dry tannins tending towards austerity. Oak as for Cab, ditto next wine. **Merlot** ★★★ new to this guide. **05** lashings sweet-ripe plummy fruit, low acid, ±15% alc, all make a big, rich, winter warmer. No need for a heater: once sipped, the fire's inside. **Pinotage** ★★ **01** statement wine, big & unsubtle; last ed showed a porty character, gamey palate-coating flavours.

Drakensig range

Shiraz ★★★ **03** unready. Still-selling **02** last ed was easy drinking despite high 14.5% alc, with smoky mocha whiffs & soft brambly fruit. Following reviewed as samples last yr, so revisited here: **Cabernet Sauvignon** ★★★ **03**'s healthy but embryonic fruit core still masked by wood tannins; needs another yr/2 to come round. Yr Fr oak, 1st/2nd fill. **Merlot** ★★★ Last yr's chunky tannins have melded with plummy choc fruit, turning **03** into a pleasant, lightly savoury drink. Oak as for Cab, ditto... **Pinotage** ★★★ **03** has evolved into a ripe-fruited crowd-pleaser. Big (14.5% alc), touch jammy, though initial sweetness no longer bothersome. **Sauvignon Blanc** ★★★ Better, more expressive than pvs; **06** appealing green/flinty tone, still racily fresh — needs a rich food counterfoil. — *CT*

Dreamview Hill

Stellenbosch (see Helderberg map) ▪ *Est 2004* ▪ *Winery closed to public; sales Wed-Mon 12-late from restaurant (T 021·858·1453)* ▪ *Functions* ▪ *Owners Capelands Estate (Johann Innerhofer & Laura Mauri)* ▪ *4 ha (cab, malbec)* ▪ *18 tons 200 cs 100% red* ▪ *PO Box 3835 Somerset West 7129* ▪ *office@capelands.com* ▪ *www.capelands.com* ▪ ***T 021·858·1477***

Italians Johann Innerhofer and Laura Mauri indulge their passions in this small-scale wine and food venture in the Helderberg. Grapes from the property high on Schapenberg Hill find their way to nearby Ingwe for vinification, and thence to the dining tables of the couple's restaurant, recently renamed to 'O de V'.

Redstone ★★★ Ready-to-drink **03** barrel sample was last tasted; succulent if straightforward bdx-style blend lifted by 10% shiraz, with ripe red berry & plum flavours. — *MF*

■ *Drie Berge* see Baarsma

Drostdy-Hof Wines

Tulbagh ▪ *Est 1804* ▪ *Tasting & wine sales at De Oude Drostdy Mon-Fri 10-5 Sat 10-2* ▪ *Owner Distell* ▪ *PO Box 213 Tulbagh 6820* ▪ *www.drostdywines.co.za* ▪ ***T 023·230·0203*** ▪ *F 023·230·0211*

De Oude Drostdy, Tulbagh's old magistracy, built in 1804 and now a national monument, is the spiritual home of Drostdy-Hof wines. The range, intended to be fruity and accessible early, is now distributed globally.

Merlot ☺ ★★★ Most pleasing red in range; cardamom & vanilla scents on plummy **05**; supple, with warming 14.5% alc; integrated oak (yr Fr, mix old/new). **Chardonnay-Viognier** ☺ ★★★ **05** smidgen of the aromatic Rhône grape adds dimension to the Burgundian leader. Wide-awake citrus/melon nose & palate; butterscotch tones from well-knit wood (9 mths Fr, combo staves/barrels, some new).

Cabernet Sauvignon ★★ Quintessential cassis/mint aromas & flavours on **04**; four-square with some astringency on finish. Fr barrels/staves, 9 mths. Better with food, as is... **Pinotage** ★★ **05**, unlike polite & soft-spoken pvs, rather churlish, with puckering tannins & tart berry tail. Fr oak staves, 9 mths. **Shiraz** ★★★ Burly but satisfying **05**, smoked meat/game notes in keeping with the gruffish tannins. Combo Fr/Am staves, 9 mths. **Cape Red** ★★★ Fireside sipper with touch oak (small portion Fr staved). Dollop shiraz in **05** joins usual cab, pinotage, ruby cab medley. Oozes red berries, ends on refreshing note. **Claret Select** ★★ Vat-matured, lightish blend tinta/pinotage/cab. Latest **NV** spicy, vinous, pleasantly dry with fruit-tannin tug. 12% alc. **Rosé** ★★ Switch from four-way blend to 100% cab in **06**; still cheery, light, but relies on acidity for its character. **Chardonnay** ★★ **05** furtive tangerine & oak (chip) aromas, hint grapefruit-pith on palate, usual bracing acidity. **Sauvignon Blanc** ★★ **06** lightish bodied (11.6% alc) & light on aroma/favour. Some granadilla, sweaty whiffs, brisk acidity. **Chardonnay-Semillon** ★★★ 60/40 blend in **05**, layered lemon/wax bouquet, whiff vanilla; well weighted, courtesy 6 mths on oak chips/lees; vibrant orange-toned flavours. **Extra Light** ★ Big-selling, low-alc (9.5%) white. Latest **NV** swingeingly dry, from barely ripe chenin. **Steen/Chenin Blanc** ★★ **06** apparently made to partner oysters: suitably subtle flavours, a touch of fresh hay, bright flinty acidity. **Premier Grand Cru** ★★ **NV** blend of blancs (chenin, sauvignon), colombard, riesling; vinous, slightly salty, appropriately (for this style) bone-dry finish. **Stein Select** ★★ Shy but amenable five-way blend; semi-sweet, vaguely tropical; balanced, with honeyed tail. **NV. Late Harvest** ★★★ Perky **NV** from chenin with honeyed fruit on nose, sweet but uncloying texture. Enjoy well chilled. **Adelpracht** ★★ SLH from chenin. Dried mango notes on **05**; rich, but freshened by sweet-sour finish. All above for early drinking. Some also available in 340ml, 2ℓ and 5ℓ packs. WO W Cape.

African Sky range

Untasted export wines: **Cabernet Sauvignon**, **Merlot**, **Shiraz**, **Cirrus** (mainly pinotage, with cab, merlot, cab & shiraz), **Crux** (chiefly cab, splash ruby cab), **Cape Red**, **Cumulus** (chenin), **Chenin Blanc**, **Cape White** (chenin), **Sauvignon**, **Celeste** (sauvignon, semillon). — *CvZ*

■ **Dry Creek** see Du Preez Estate
■ **Due South** see Cru Wines
■ **Dumisani** see Winecorp
■ **Duncan's Creek** see Rickety Bridge
■ **Du Plessis** see Havana Hills

Du Preez Estate

Goudini (see Worcester map) ▪ *Est 1995* ▪ *1stB 1998* ▪ *Tasting & sales Mon-Fri 8-12.30; 1.30-5 Sat 10-1* ▪ *Closed public holidays* ▪ *Tours by appt* ▪ *BYO picnic* ▪ *Facilities for children* ▪ *Tour groups* ▪ *Owners Du Preez family* ▪ *Winemaker Hennie du Preez Jnr (1995)* ▪ *Viticulturist Jean du Preez (Dec 1996)* ▪ *300 ha (cab, merlot, petit v, chard, chenin, sauvignon) 56% red 40% white 2% rosé 2% sparkling* ▪ *Export brands: Du Preez Estate, Rockfield Wines, Dry Creek, Route 101* ▪ *PO Box 12 Rawsonville 6845* ▪ *info@dupreezestate.co.za* ▪ **T 023·349·1995** ▪ *F 023·349·1923*

'Look out for our new bubbly,' advise the brothers Du Preez, winemaker Hennie based on the family's Goudini estate and viticulturist Jean at Rockfield Vineyards, their farm in Rawsonville. Bearing a five-generation-old family name, (untasted) newcomer to the range is the Hendrik Lodewyk Cap Classique, wearing the modern livery now being extended to all Du Preez products. Newer than the label is a 'factory roof' vine training system, part of a drive for better quality sauvignon. And most recent of all is the arrival of a daughter for Hennie dP.

★★★★ **Hendrik Lodewyk Petit Verdot** One of still few solo SA bottlings of grape. **01** was youthful but promising when last tasted, deserved time. Seriously wooded (30 mths small oak), giving clean, attractive spiciness. NE. No newer vintages yet for this, next two wines.

★★★★ **Merlot Reserve** Easily recognisable by its attractive spiciness; **01** edgy style, zingy but ripe. Fermented with oak chips, then barrelled 18 mths, some Am.

★★★★ **Hanepoot** Invariably smooth jerepiko-style dessert. Last we tasted the **03**.

Polla's Red ★★★★ Character/flavourful vintage blend. Bouquet of **02** four-way mix pinotage, cab, petit v & shiraz (45/25/20/10) has spicy welcome of roasted cardamom & cinnamon, ripe plummy flavours; richly textured, juicy with supple tannin, well fused oak (6-12 mths). NE. **Merlot** ★★★★ Ripe, dark fruited **04** with mocha choc & hint of eucalyptus; creamy, persistent, balanced flavours with smoke & spice from integrated wooding (9-18 mths). **03** (★★★) misreported as 'Rsv' last ed. **Shiraz** ★★ **05** not ready for review. Unfruity **04** had hints of smoke, mocha & vanilla. **Chardonnay** ★★★ **06** (sample) has lemoncurd & pear nuances which increase on ripe, leesy palate; lime/lemon-cream twist on finish. This, following, WO Breedeklf. **Sauvignon Blanc** ★★★★ Lower alc (±12%) but bigger fruit concentration on zesty, fresh, herbaceous **06**; buchu, nettle & food-friendly mineral notes.

Rockfield range

Cabernet Sauvignon new ★★★ Ripe cassis & fruit pastille combine with bright acidity on clean, juicy **04**. Medium bodied & unoaked, for early drinking. **Merlot** new ★★ Leaner, fresh style (±13 alc), **04** unwooded with sweet/sour cranberry & rhubarb finish. **Shiraz** new ★★ Spicy wild-berry & fynbos scrub introduce a lighter but sappy **04**; mildly gripping tannins & a tangy touch make this a good barbeque red. **Red Stone** ★★★★ Spicy, red berried **02** was last tasted. **Dry Creek Red** ★★★ **04** still selling, not retasted. *Wine* 'Best Value' selection. **Chenin Blanc** ★★☆ **06** refreshing summer quaffer with Granny Smith apple nuances. **Sauvignon Blanc** ★★ **06** light bodied/styled; hint white peach with fresh sherbetty acidity; short, tart, lemongrass farewell. WO Breedeklf. **Dry Creek White** ★★ **05** from chenin, colombard & sauvignon, currently selling; follow-up not ready for review. **Dry Creek Bouquet Blanc** ★★★ new to the guide; equal blend chenin & colombard; aromatic, light & off-dry summer quaffer. **04** delicate & still fresh. **06** unready. This range NE.— *MW*

Durbanville Hills

Durbanville • Est 1998 • 1stB 1999 • Tasting & sales Mon-Fri 9-4.30 Sat & pub hols 9.30-2.30 Sun 11-3; fee R10 • Tours Mon-Fri 11 & 3; Sat/Sun by appt; fee R20 • Closed Easter Fri/Sun, Dec 25/26 & Jan 1 • @ The Hills Restaurant (see Eat-out section) • Facilities for children • Tour groups • Owners Distell, 8 farmers & workers' trust • Cellarmaster Martin Moore with winemakers Louw Engelbrecht & Günther Kellerman (Nov 1998/Jun 2005/Nov 2003) • Viti consultant Johan Pienaar • 770 ha (cab, merlot, pinotage, shiraz, chard, sauvignon) • 6 000 tons 140 000 cs own label 50% red 50% white • ISO 9000,14000 & BRC certified • PO Box 3276 Durbanville 7551 • info@durbanvillehills.co.za • www.durbanvillehills.co.za • T 021·558·1300 • F 021·559·8169

These cool hills produce fine sauvignon, among SA's best. Going all out, Martin Moore has decided to inaugurate a 'mini-Olympics', pitting his own vineyard blocks against each other: at the starting line, we have the current contenders — single-vineyard Biesjes Craal; Rhinofields, from a carefully selected combination; and the value priced Hills Range — as well as two newcomers, released end-2006: Inner Valley, showcasing the character of Clone 108, which is new to the area; and Outer Valley, which bottles bushvines on an early-ripening slope. Regardless of who takes home gold, the real victor is the sauvignon lover.

★★★★★ **Caapmans Cabernet Sauvignon-Merlot** Back on track, well crafted **01** enthrals with complex interplay of blackberries, cigar box, Dutch liquorice, supple athleticism. 2 yr Fr, all new. Ready, also has glorious future. Fruit from 3 vyds. 64/36 blend. Calyon Top Ten. **00** (★★★★) had expected fruit intensity, but too obvious tannins, needing time to unfold.

★★★★ **Luipaardsberg Merlot Reserve** Designed to impress — & does; **01** remarkable combination of structural elegance & fleshiness to immediately please, but as with pvs vintages, has a long life. Prune, cassis richness easily assimilates the serious oaking (2 yrs new Fr). Ex-single vyd on Klein Roosboom property.

★★★★★ **Biesjes Craal Sauvignon Blanc** In cool vintages only, & steep, mature south-facing vyd. Reflecting conducive vintage, **06** preview has riveting concentration & length: expected asparagus, nettles, but also deep seated passionfruit ripeness. Uncompromising sauvignon, the perfect food match, especially at only 11.8% alc.

Rhinofields Reserve range

★★★★☆ **Chardonnay** Ex-barrel 05, already powerhouse of toast, yellow cling peach & citrus peel, with an irresistible tangy, lively drinkability. Robust oaking (5 mths lees, further yr new Fr) fully integrated.

★★★★ **Sauvignon Blanc** Grapes from 4 producers add layered complexity, riper elements, to 06 (sample): gooseberry, lime, summer fruits. Delicious, characterful, with added bonus of only 12.2% alc.

★★★★☆ **Inner Valley Sauvignon Blanc** This & next `new`, designed to show diversity of terroir. Previewed 06 has fantastic potential; reductively made to capture essence of the grape: passionfruit, piercing lime, a leafy nuance. Mouth-awakening racy acidity secures flavours, giving ultra-long finish.

★★★★ **Outer Valley Sauvignon Blanc** Fuller, riper than sibling, 06 sample is still quintessential sauvignon: apple, melon-rich fruit salad, with greengage making an appearance on the palate. Delicious solo or with food.

Merlot Raising the bar, 01 (★★★★) from 2 vyd selections, which may explain vivid raspberry/mulberry fruit yet grassy, herbaceous notes. Svelte, well crafted & drinking perfectly, with few yrs ageing potential. Yr Fr oak, third new. 00 (★★★☆) had appealing elegance, accessibility.

The Hill Range

★★★★ **Bastion** `new` ✓ Confident & classy 60/40 blend cab/shiraz named for cellar's viewing platform, recalling the bastions of the Castle of Good Hope. Dark-fruited, aromatic, black pepper & cardamom notes; refreshing cab acidity & lithe shiraz tannins; finishes dry. Already smooth, has structure to reward 3-5 yrs patience. 12-18 mths Fr oak.

Cabernet Sauvignon ★★★★ Like reds below, for earlier drinking. Classically profiled 03's cassis tone slight herbaceous edge, attractive spicing. Elegant structure delivers stylish drinkability & enough stiffening for couple yrs ageing. Yr Fr oak, 40% new; rest reds similar. **Merlot** ★★★ 04's appeal lies in its dark berries, mocha choc textures on sleek frame. Oaking supports, doesn't intrude. **Pinotage** ★★★ Riper than pvs (14.6% alc), 04 dominated by opulent fruit, brambleberries, black cherries. Oaking evident in dry finish. **Shiraz** ★★★★ 04 satisfyingly text-book: meat extract, savoury spice, with wild berry core. Tasty, appealing fleshy ripeness gets centre stage on palate. Some Am oak with Fr. **Chardonnay** ★★★ 05 earlier drinking; dried peach character from riper harvesting; extended lees-ageing for creamy roundness. Partially oaked. **Sauvignon Blanc** ★★★ Entry-level, high-volume (±26 000 cs) version. 06 pleasing varietal green fig notes on a gooseberry bed; light textured, for easy consumption. — CR/CvZ

■ *Dusty Road* see Cloof

Du Toitskloof Winery 🍷🐘♿

*Rawsonville (see Worcester map) ▪ Est 1962 ▪ 1stB 1970 ▪ Tasting & sales — Winery: Mon-Fri 8-5 Sat 9-12.30; wine shop: Mon-Fri 9-5 Sat 10-5 Sun 11-6 ▪ Closed Easter Fri/Mon, Apr 27, Sep 24, Dec 16/25/26, Jan 1 ▪ BYO picnic ▪ Tours by appt ▪ Formal tasting for groups max 20 ▪ Owners 17 members ▪ Winemakers Philip Jordaan & Shawn Thomson (May 1983/Oct 1999), with Derrick Cupido & Christo Basson (1993/Jan 2002) ▪ Viti consultant Leon Dippenaar (2005) ▪ 750 ha ▪ 13 500 tons 30% red 70% white ▪ PO Box 55 Rawsonville 6845 ▪ dutoitcellar@intekom.co.za; info@ dutoitskloof.co.za ▪ www.dutoitskloof.co.za ▪ **T 023·349·1601** ▪ F 023·349·1581*

Value for money is the name of the game here, with Du Toitskloof last year again rated as the Best Value Cellar by *Wine* (the third time in five years). Expansion has also been a focus, and the winery has purchased the brands of the Lost Horizons stable (for which they supplied some wines) from the Philadelphia-based owner, Charles Jacquins Inc. Says DuT chair Johan de Wet: 'Taking the Lost Horizons brands in-house makes sense. To survive and grow, the marketing chain must be as short and efficient as possible.'

★★★★ **Red Muscadel** ✓ No simpering sweetie: this fortified dessert has real complexity, substance & structure; epitomised by current 05, gorgeous aromatic intensity, fine texture thanks to lively acidity, even an impression of dryness amid the massive 222g/ℓ sugar, courtesy of a kiss of tannin.

★★★★ **Hanepoot Jerepigo 03** interesting & ingratiating fortified dessert with muscat & Cointreau-like citrus notes, lingering fruitiness. Massively sweet but not cloying or heavy. Not retasted.

Sauvignon Blanc ☺ ★★☆ Appealing, light bodied but flavourful **06**, whiffs passionfruit & pineapple, ingratiating smoothness assisted by few grams sugar. Screwcapped. **05** SAA. **Bukettraube** ☺ ★★☆ **06** again surprisingly full-flavoured for variety; gorgeous rose & incense bouquet, usual well balanced sweetness.

Following pair still selling, not retasted: **Cabernet Sauvignon** ★★★☆ **03** pleasing dusty blackcurrant aromas; savoury & succulent with firm, dry tannin. All reds ±8 mths Fr oak unless noted. **Merlot** ★★★ Gains extra juiciness from partial carbonic maceration. **03** interesting & charming aromas; succulent flavours, decent balance. **Pinotage** ★★★ **04** cool cedar & mulberry intro to honest, well made, big-on-flavour red; properly dry, decidedly moreish. *Wine* 'Best Value' selection. 7 mths Fr staves. **Shiraz** ★★★★ **03**'s shy smoky nose last ed led to harmonious savoury flavours; lightish, elegant tone despite 14% alc. **Cabernet Sauvignon-Shiraz** new NV equal blend not tasted. **Pinotage-Merlot-Ruby Cabernet** ★★ Soft, fruity, semi-dry braai buddy. Blend pinotage, merlot, ruby cab, none dominating, oaked 4 mths. **NV** in 500ml screwcapped bottle, as is next wine. **Rosé** new ★★ Fresh, sweetish, with soft acidity & tinge of tannin on the exit. **Blanc de Noir** ★ **05** switches from cinsaut to pinotage: pretty colour, dryish, but fading, drink up. **Chardonnay** ★★ **06** earthy & foursquare; near-invisibly oaked (3 mths new Fr staves); 14% alc high for this cellar. **Chenin Blanc** ★★★ **06** another tropical-toned glassful of softly dry, easygoing pleasure, with the now std low 12% alc. **Riesling** ★★ Unusually characterful for crouchen; **06** soft salad leaf aromas, light & easy just-dry flavours. **Blanc de Blanc** ★★ **06** effortless chenin, sauvignon blend, softly dry & uncomplex. Also as **NV** in 500ml twist-open bottle. **Special Late Harvest** ★★★ Light bodied semi-sweet muscat d'A. **06** luscious ripe pineapple tone from nose to tail, attractively poised sweetness. **Noble Late Harvest** ★★★★ Botrytised dessert from muscat & chenin; to date the debut **99**, SAYWS champ. **Sparkling Brut** ★★★ Light & fresh **06**, brisk, clean mousse, perceptibly dry; white muscadel (here with sauvignon, chenin) a fleeting fragrance. **Cape Ruby** ★★★☆ **03** still selling; more modern styling with tinta, souzão, touriga; inviting, rich & supple, dryish & smooth. 18% alc; yr small oak. Mostly W Cape WOs for this, ranges below. **Late Vintage** discontinued.

Lost Horizons range

Cabernet Sauvignon ★★☆ Unwooded **03** easy everyday red, smoothness boosted by ±6g/ℓ sugar, ditto for Cab-Merlot (neither retasted this ed). **Merlot** ★ Not-so-pretty sister to fruity charmer below: **04** unripe & watery, with 'green stick' tone. **Pinotage** new ★★ Lightly wooded **05**, attractive breakfast aromas of bacon & banana, savoury flavours, tangy tannins, gd dry finish. **Cabernet Sauvignon-Merlot** ★★ 60/40 blend in **03**, trattoria-friendly as always; very soft, juicy, sweetish fruit flavours. Not retasted. **Classic Red** ★★ Unpretentious **05** repeats pvs mix pinotage, ruby cab, merlot; spicy bananas to taste, cheerful & undemanding. **Chardonnay** ★★ **05** uncomplicated but nice (& still available); sweet-ripe fruit, peach/mango flavours, crisp, well juiced finish. **Sauvignon Blanc** Currently unavailable. **Classic White** ★★ **NV** from chenin; guava/pear/apple melange, dry; last ed still fresh & fruity.

Quantum range

Classic Ruby Red ☺ ★★ Usual suspects pinotage, ruby cab & merlot in gulpable, juicy cahoots; lightly wooded **05** delightfully smooth & unpretentious.

Pettilant Rosé ★ Delicately spritzy **05**, now technically semi-sweet at ±23g/ℓ sugar, lively & fruity albeit markedly sweet. **Pettilant Blanc** ★★ **06** again from chenin; usual slight prickle on palate; pretty fresh-guava aroma; light, lifted tropical flavours. **Chenin Blanc** discontinued.

Hemisphere range

Cabernet Sauvignon ★★ Very ripe **03**, soft, squishy near-raisined fruit, needing drinking before it devolves into decadence. **Merlot** ★★★ **04** a basket of juicy plums & mulberries, lightly oaked; full, ripe, soft & easy to drink. **Shiraz** new ★★ **04** pleasantly spicy on nose but debut marred by unpolished, drying oak. **Classic Ruby Red** ★★ Good anytime red, unwooded; mix pinotage, ruby cab, merlot in still-available **04**. **Rosé** new ★★ Appealingly fruity & light quaffer from chenin, muscadel & ruby cab. **06** interesting hints wet wool & dried peach, 9g/ℓ sugar carefully hidden by crisp acidity. **Chardonnay** ★★ Light wooding adds some dimension to ripe but otherwise foursquare **06**. **Chenin Blanc** new ★★ **06** light, tropical toned quaffer, with hint of sugar cushioning brisk acidity. **Sauvignon Blanc** ★★ Light & ultra-green **06**, whiffs leaf & grass, racy freshness unbuffered by 6g/ℓ sugar. **Cabernet Sauvignon-Merlot** & **Select Rosé** discontinued. — *CT/IvH*

■ *D'Vine* see Swartland Winery
■ *Dwyka Hills* see New Cape Wines
■ *Eagle's Cliff* see New Cape Wines

Eagles Nest Farm ♀ new

Constantia • Est 2001 • 1stB 2005 • Visits by appt • Winemaker Martin Meinert (July 2004), with Steve Roche • Viticulturist Steve Roche (Oct 2001) • 12 ha (merlot, shiraz, viognier) • 36 tons 95% red 5% white • info@eaglesnestwines.com • www.eaglesnestwines.com • T 021·794·4095 • F 021·794·7113

A phoenix rising from the ashes… The Mylrea's Constantiaberg farm lost a pine plantation, export protea and kiwifruit crops plus all farming infrastructure in a raging 2000 bush fire. Careful research, perseverance and businesslike planning took them the viticultural route: 12ha of densely-planted (5 000 vines/ha) varieties on steep, terraced slopes 400m up, overseen by viticulturist/assistant winemaker Steve Roche, vinified by Martin Meinert in his Devon Valley cellar. An own-production facility follows this year.

Viognier ★★★★ Refined **05** newcomer. Attractive straw-gold lights; understated though pure aromatic, flavour distinction with controlled whisper oak. Weight, freshness balanced by 5.3g/ℓ fruit-lengthening sugar. Used Fr oak fermented. — *AL*

Eaglevlei

Stellenbosch • Est/1stB 1997 • Visits daily 10-6 • Restaurant & other attractions (see intro) • Owner Tony Hindhaugh • Vini consultant Jacques Borman, with Tony Hindhaugh • Viti consultant Johan Pienaar • PO Box 969 Stellenbosch 7599 • tony@eaglevlei.com • www.eaglevlei. com • T 021·884·4713 • F 021·884·4716

Previously low-key Eaglevlei has been turned into a hive of activity by new owner Tony Hindhaugh from the UK, whose vineyard experiences down south have been documented on the Discovery channel. Significant investment has manifested in a floor-to-ceiling glass-walled tasting room, a restaurant, art gallery and an arts foundation, opening up the creative world to neighbouring children. A first for Eaglevlei is a premium range of white wines and a Pinotage Rosé named Beccy's Blush after Hindhaugh's daughter.

★★★★ **Cabernet Sauvignon** Our last example was subtly savoury **03**. Now **05** (★★★★) offers classic blackcurrant/cedar aromas; full sweet fruit to taste; solid & extracted, with big tannins asking for decanting now, or (better) a few more yrs. Yr Fr oak.
Cabernet Sauvignon Reserve ★★★ Last yr, **02**'s oak overwhelmed attractive aromas & sweetly ripe fruit, giving drying hard tannic finish. **Pinotage** ★★★ **05** lovely ripe raspberry/banana aromas/flavours & first sweet softness don't prepare for powerful dry tannins on lingering sweet finish (4.6g/ℓ RS). Fr/Am oak. **Merlot** ★★★ Bold, appealing aromas of choc & vanilla on very ripe **05**. Chunky flavours too, with gd ripe fruit squeezing past oak & tannins. Not quite dry. Following all new: **Shiraz** ★★★ Another attractive set of

varietally typical aromas. Pleasant, easy **05** is lightly, softly lush, though firm & fresh finish. Wood (Fr/Am) more subdued here. **Beccy's Blush Pinotage Rosé ★** The palest of pinks for this crisp **06** (less than 2 hrs skin contact) & equally pale raspberry flavour. **Sauvignon Blanc ★★★ 06**, like all these whites. Enjoyable combo greenpepper & passionfruit aroma/flavour, with greenly fresh grip. **Chardonnay, Chenin Blanc, Sauvignon Blanc Reserve** too unready to satisfactorily taste & rate. — *TJ*

■ *Eden Crest* see Lourensford
■ *Edenhof* see Schalkenbosch

Eikehof Wines

*Franschhoek • Visits by appt • Owner/winemaker/viticulturist Francois Malherbe • 43 ha (cab, merlot, shiraz, chardonnay) • 70 tons 4 000 cs 60% red 40% white • PO Box 222 Franschhoek 7690 • eikehof@mweb.co.za • www.eikehof.com • **T/F 021·876·2469***

Francois Malherbe has scaled back wine production in recent years, citing the sobering draught from the downturn in the market. No matter: at best he vinifies no more than a fifth of his grapes for his Eikehof label. Best of all, with a little more time on hand, the family gets to head north and spend more of it at his father's game farm in Namibia.

★★★★ **Cabernet Sauvignon** Pvs were dense, showy, chunky, but current **03** (★★★★, not retasted) is none of these: soft, touch savoury, dry but sweet-tannined. **02** layered with ripe berry flavours, fairly evident oak. ±5 mths oak (ditto all the reds).

Merlot ★★★ Cool, herbaceous feel to **04**; restrained & elegant fruit; maybe too nervy for solo but good foil for richer foods. **Shiraz ★★★** In contrast with Merlot, **04** fruity & well-spiced; soft, rounded, slips down easily. Enjoy soon. **Chardonnay** Bunch-pressed, briefly oaked **06** more rounded, silky, satisfying than pvs; pre-bottling sample quite mouthfilling (14% alc), liberal citrus/hazelnut flavours. Potential ★★★★. **Bush Vine Semillon ★★★** Off ancient low-cropped bushvines; last tasted was light-toned **03**, with lime/lemon bouquet. — *CR/IvH*

Eikendal Vineyards

*Stellenbosch (see Helderberg map) • Est 1981 • 1stB 1984 • Tasting & sales — Sep-May: Mon-Sat 9.30-4.30 Sun & pub hols 10-4; Jun-Aug: Mon-Sun & pub hols 10-4 • Fee R10 (5 wines) • Tours Mon-Fri 10 & 2.30 • Closed Easter Fri/Sun, Mothers Day, Jun 16, Dec 25/26 & Jan 1 • Harald's@ Eikendal for lunch/dinner (cheese fondue in winter) T 021·855·5033 for opening times • Eikendal Lodge Guest House/B&B; lodge@eikendal.co.za; T 021·855·3617; F 021·855·3862 • Facilities for children • Tour groups • Small conferences • Walks • Winemaker Henry Kotzé (Sep 2004) • Viti consultant Johan Pienaar (Sep 2001) • ±65 ha (cabs s/f, merlot, shiraz, chard, chenin, sauvignon, semillon) • ±350 tons ±20 000 cs 65% red 35% white • PO Box 2261 Stellenbosch 7601 • info@ eikendal.co.za • www.eikendal.com • **T 021·855·1422** • F 021·855·1027*

Eikendal marked its 25th anniversary by labelling its 2006 wines with a special logo — an acorn. 'It's a symbol of our success,' explains marketing manager Grant Newton. 'As an acorn eventually becomes a towering oak tree, so we have come from small beginnings to where we are today.' One new development is winemaker Henry Kotzé's decision to channel blocks unsuitable for vinifying into red wine into slaking the ever-growing thirst for rosé. 'This also allows us to give the good red blocks some extra-special treatment,' he says. Resident chef Harald Siedler is particularly pleased about last year's 'green harvest', which yielded Eikendal's own verjuice.

★★★★ **Merlot** Pleasing **04** approachable & friendly but sufficiently serious, rich & round, dryly refined; sweet red fruit & choc-mint character well supported by oak (21 mths, partly new).

★★★★ **Cabernet Franc** Touch of spicy fragrance just one attraction on **04** barrel sample, still quiet but promising satisfaction, though more dry tannin under ripe softness than there was in elegant, delicious **03** (*Wine ★★★★*). Latest has 16 mths Fr oak, 30% new.

★★★★ **Classique 02** not tasted (reduced quantity disappeared soon!), but **03** more elegant than bold **01**; blends cab, merlot, cab f (60/30/10), vinified separately. Still tight — & oaky, with strong spicy tobacco notes obscuring rich fruit, & tannic dryness. Needs few yrs to give its best.

★★★★ Chardonnay Reliably pleasing, not too showy. **05** smoothly rich & forceful, good limy length with background toastiness; balanced structure. Part native yeast barrel ferment; 9 mths half new Fr oak. Track record for developing over 3-5 yrs. **04** Classic Trophy gold.

Rouge ☺ ★★★ Friendly, fruity, nice & easy but not trivial **NV** blend merlot, cab, shiraz. Lightly oaked, dry & firm, though a little 'hot' from big 14.5% alc. **Rosé** new ☺ ★★☆ **06** forward, fruity & fresh, just off-dry. Really pleasant flavours given by young-vine merlot & a few other reds. **Blanc** ☺ ★★☆ Sauvignon & chard co-operate happily to offer generous flavours; sweet undercurrent controlled by freshness. **NV**. W Cape WO.

Cabernet Sauvignon ★★★★ Oak dominates aromas of **03**, noticeable also on palate, abetting big dry tannins; but also gd red berry fruit, making for gratifying but slightly severe effect. 20 mths oak, half new. **Shiraz** After spicy, soft **03** (★★★★), ultra-ripe, slightly porty nose on previewed **04** (rating uncertain), faded but lush sweet fruit, dry oak (22 mths, ±50% new) 14.5% alc. **Janina Chardonnay** ★★★ Scarcely oaked **04** was packed with flavour; richness cut by vivid acidity. No **05** made. **Chenin Blanc** ★★★★ New ambitious look with **06**: trendy, showy styling with very ripe honeyed fruit, spicy oak (50% new, barrel fermented) & subtly off-dry. Finishes warmly from 14.5% alc, but impressive. **Sauvignon Blanc** ★★★ Gushing tropicality & grassiness on **06**, full-flavoured, with greengage edge disguising 4.5g/ℓ RS; fresh, lusciously tart. **Semillon** ★★★★ **04** showed citrus, honey, nuts; step-up **05** (★★★★) good varietal lemon-lanolin character; satin texture, concentrated, interesting, dry. Well integrated oak (fermented in new Fr/Am), balanced acidity. Shd develop over yrs. **Noble Late Harvest** ★★★★ Lightly oaked **05** from chenin with gentle, rather fugitive marmalade flavours, uncloying sweetness complemented by fresh, almost sharp acidity. **Sparkling Brut** ★★★ Latest **NV** bubbly from sauvignon & chard pleasant as ever, with tropical & peach aromas/flavours, nice sour twist in tail. **Cabernet Sauvignon Reserve** discontinued — to be replaced by new prestige label. — *TJ*

■ *Elandsberg see* Viljoensdrift

Elberti Wines   ♀ new

Stellenbosch (see Helderberg map) • Est 2005 • Tasting & sales by appt • Owners Steyn family • Winemaker Pieter Steyn • 8 000 cs own label 75% red 25% white • PO Box 2401 Somerset West 7129 • info@elbertiwines.com • www.elbertiwines.com • T 021·851·4760 • F 021·851·4761

The concept behind Elberti Wines is that of a journey, with 'the beginning' signified by their entry-level wines, Dawning. Then follows the passage to the midpoint, Sojourn, 'a place to pause or rest', before tackling the last stretch to 'the destination', Cape Cana. Not all wines will have the legs to attain flagship status, advises MD Eppie Steyn, the man behind the lyrical marketing (son Pieter is the winemaker). But those that do will be 'superior premium icons, with packaging and price tickets to suit'.

Dawning range

Merlot ★★★ **03** has lots of ripe fruit aromas (plum, mulberry), promising greater richness than the lean, slightly austere palate delivers. 14 mths new Hngrian oak, like ... **Cabernet Sauvignon** ★★☆ **03** shows similar contradiction, with nutty, black fruit notes, but slightly green & grippy finish. **Syrah-Malbec** ★★ Wooded 15% malbec joins majority unoaked shiraz on **05**, marked by smoky tones & persistent sappy tannins. **Sauvignon Blanc** ★★ Limy citrus/lime notes dominate bone-dry, crisp-finishing **05**. Moderate 13% alc adds to food-friendliness. — *MF*

Eldorado Wines   ♂

Paarl • Est 1999 • 1stB 2001 • Closed to public • Owner Proteus Trust • Winemaker/viticulturist Shannon Booth (1999) • 1 ha • 4 tons 300 cs 100% red • PO Box 2042 Windmeul 7630 • tmurray@iafrica.com • www.eldorado.co.za • T/F 021·869·8830

Each vintage of this boutique winery's blend carries the name of a Booth offspring, says Shannon B (mistakenly identified by our resident gremlin last edition as female – our apologies). Aquila, the first, is named after his second-born. It wasn't 'feminine' enough to be 'Farris Annabella' – she gets the 03. When asked about the next version, the father of two laughingly responds: 'We'll just have to adopt!' Due later this year are the 05 (no 04 bottled) and a maiden Shiraz.

Farris Annabella ★★★ **03** again 80/20 cab-merlot blend; chunky, chewy, high toned; lots of fruit ripeness & muscular cab tannins, needing plenty of time. Ex-single vyd; 18 mths Fr oak. – *MM*

■ *Elements* see Hartswater

Elgin Vintners

*Elgin ▪ Est 2003 ▪ 1stB 2004 ▪ Tasting & sales Mon-Fri 9-5 by appt ▪ Closed pub hols ▪ Owners Derek Corder, Max Hahn, Alastair Moodie, James Rawbone-Viljoen, Rob Semple & Paul Wallace ▪ Winemakers see intro ▪ Viticulturist Paul Wallace ▪ 75.5 ha (cab, malbec, merlot, shiraz, pinot, chard, sauvignon, viognier) ▪ 3 950 cs ▪ PO Box 121 Elgin 7180 ▪ elginvintner@ mweb.co.za ▪ **T/F 021·848·9587**

Cometh the season cometh the men! The 'Elgin Six' have decided to replace original winemaker Ross Gower (who went solo) with not one but four winemakers – Jeff Grier, Justin Hoy, Niels Verburg and Clive Torr, each chosen with specific wines and styles in mind. Plantings up to 76ha, and the group now selects for its needs (which include an expanding local consumer base and a UK market) and sells off the rest. Its tasting room is now open on Beaulieu Farm.

Shiraz new ★★★★ **05** 50/50 blend wines independently crafted by Niels Verburg & Clive Torr from young vyds. Lightly weighted, more spice than pepper, elegant exit. **Easy Red** ★★★ ('Pinot Noir pvs ed.) **05** attractive clean cherry fruit, unobtrusive oak, demure 12% alc. **Sauvignon Blanc** ★★★★ **06** 2nd edition from these 'Publishers of Fine Wines'; cut grass interplay with capsicum, complexity woven into quite impressive length. Fresh cool-area acidity. Following **05**s untasted pending release: **Cabernet Sauvignon-Merlot** & **Merlot**, both new, **Cabernet Sauvignon**. – *DS*

■ *Elixir* see African Terroir
■ *Engelbrecht-Els* see Ernie Els
■ *Enon* see Zandvliet

Ernie Els Wines

*Stellenbosch ▪ Est 1999 ▪ 1stB 2000 ▪ Tasting & sales Mon-Fri 9-5 Sat: May-Sep 9-3 Oct-Apr 9-4 ▪ Closed Easter Fri, Dec 16/25 & Jan 1 ▪ Gifts & amenities: see intro ▪ Owners Ernie Els & Jean Engelbrecht ▪ Winemakers Louis Strydom & Coenie Snyman (2000/2005) ▪ Viti consultant Paul Wallace (2004) ▪ 72 ha (cab, merlot) ▪ 45 000 cs 100% red ▪ PO Box 7595 Stellenbosch 7599 ▪ info@ernieelswines.com ▪ www.ernieelswines.com ▪ **T 021·881·3588** ▪ F 021·881·3688*

A rising star shines again in this year's guide (see five-star rating for the flagship), matching the achievements of co-owner, champion golf pro Ernie Els, back on the circuit after knee surgery. This prime red-wine property with stylish cellar hewn from Helderberg rock is set to assume an even higher international profile courtesy of its Cirrus Wine Company joint venture with Napa Valley's Silver Oak. Meanwhile, the Guardian Peak range now boasts its own 500-ton cellar and tasting room (formerly Helderkruin's). All these classy wines are matched to gourmet dishes at the adjoining new Guardian Peak restaurant.

★★★★★ **Ernie Els** From **04** (★★★★★) this cab-headed, bdx-style red presents purer, fresher face without loss of distinctive intricacy. Class revealed in striking spice & cassis aromas; palate attractions still uncompromisingly wrapped in fine, grainy tannin. Lavishly oaked (100% new Fr) but balanced within overall youthful frame; deserves yr/2. **03** Concours Mondial gold; 92 pts *WS*. Blend cab, merlot, petit v, malbec, cab f (62/24/6/4/4/); combo Smnsberg & Hldrberg fruit.

★★★★★ **Engelbrecht-Els Proprietor's Blend** Homogenous cab/shiraz (50/23) ensemble embroidered with merlot, equal splashes petit v, malbec, cab f. **04** ex-cask last yr, bigger yet worthy follow up to sophisticated **03**. Dark, dense, ripe, with rustle of resilient tannins, still-plush new wood evidence of youth. Fr/Am oak, 80% new, 18 mths. **03** IWC gold. Dbnvlle, Elgin, Sbosch vyds. WO W Cape, as is following wine.

★★★★ **Cirrus Syrah** new Joint venture with US winery, Silver Oak, launched with **03**, sold out before we tasted (but *Wine* ★★★★½). **04** incl aroma-lifting viognier. For Am market, so suitably sumptuous & ripe yet pleasantly fresh, not evidently sweet (despite 6g/ℓ sugar) or over the top. New oak, 15 mths. TWS gold. Sbosch & Wllngton vyds.

Guardian Peak range

★★★★ **Cabernet Sauvignon** new Most serious & classic of varietal GPs; **04** shows fruit restraint, nutty vinosity, determined grip, though nothing mean, unripe about luxurious concentration. Carefully oaked, all Fr, 70% new, enhances elegant demeanour. Will benefit from few yrs ageing.

★★★★ **SMG** Aka 'Syrah-Mourvèdre-Grenache', since maiden **01** regular local & int. award winner. Behind initially quiet **04** (★★★★) lurk soft choc, mushroom smells. Restraint also watchword for placid, lush mouthfeel; pleasant current drinking, if lacking distinction, punch, length of pvs. **03** IWSC gold. Fr/Am oak, 50% new.

★★★★ **Frontier** ✓ Hedonistic cab blend, with shiraz/merlot (41/11) from Sbosch & Elgin in **05**; sample bears striking resemblance to pvs: creamy opulence, silky tannins & bright raspberry/cherry freshness. Delicious, savoury; overt modernity not at expense of interesting layers, ageworthy structure. Yr oak, none new. **04** TWS trophy.

Merlot ★★★★ ✓ Satisfying, pure-fruited **05**; fresh, lively with gentle mouthcoating richness, delicious, clean bitter choc tail. 6/12 mths, staves/barrels. Sbosch grapes. **04** Concours Mondial gold. **Shiraz** ★★★★ ✓ Sbosch, Tygerberg, Paarl vyds new sources for finely scented **05** (sample). Flavour definition, fresh lift, lend agreeable delicacy to 14% alc; suppleness, rounded tannins add to drinkability. Stave/barrel matured. These all WO W Cape.—*AL*

Ernst & Co Wines ♂♀

Stellenbosch • Est/1stB 2004 • Tasting by appt • Owners Ernst & Gwenda Gouws • Winemaker Ernst Gouws • 12 ha (chenin, sauvignon) • 10 000 cs 50% red 50% white + 10 000 cs under export brand Imbizo; also for export: Four Gates & Timbili • PO Box 7450 Stellenbosch 7599 • info@ggwines.co.za • www.ernstco.co.za • T 021·865·2895 • F 021·865·2894

Adventurous Ezanne Gouws, who joined long-distance-running dad Ernst for the 2006 harvest, shares his other great passions: chardonnay and pinot. Her enthusiasm took her postharvest to Wither Hills in Blenheim, New Zealand, to tweak her talent with pinot (and gain sauvignon experience). New offices, a wood maturation cellar, tasting facilities and vineyard development are all taking shape while Ezanne is away, so Ernst G has hung up his marathon shoes for now — no time for Comrades training, he sighs.

No new vintages ready for following four wines: **Cabernet Sauvignon** ★★★ **03** promising debut; fruity, layered with cedar/herbaceous notes, fresh balanced palate. ±4 yrs potential. Yr new Fr oak, as for all reds in range. **Merlot** ★★★ **03** meaty & savoury with anise nuances; stronger tannins than pvs, long blackberry tail with warm wag from 14.5% alc. Cld keep ± 3-5 yrs. **Shiraz** ★★★★ Accessible, New Worldish **04**, with dash viognier adding floral highlights; dry tannins softened by hint sugar. Shd hold another few yrs. **Chardonnay** ★★★★ **05** richer than pvs, also more alcoholic (14.5% alc vs 12%). New oak (5 mths Fr) gives fleshier/flashier style. Fruit ex-Mbury. **Chenin Blanc** new ★★ Crisp, melon-toned **06**, fresh, lightish, rounded flavours for uncomplicated summer sipping. **Sauvignon Blanc** ★★★★ **06** (sample) greener flavours than pvs tropical; light, almost delicate, won't overwhelm food. Sensible 12% alc. WO Coastal.

Imbizo range

Aimed at supermarket trade. **Merlot** ★★★ **03** generous cassis/blueberry fruit on offer last ed, soft tannins & smooth finish. Yr Fr oak. **Chenin Blanc-Sauvignon Blanc** ★★★ Charming lunchtime refresher; chenin's trademark acidity buoys sauvignon's gooseberry

& melon; **06** (sample) served with modest 12% alc. Above ranges WO Sbosch unless noted. **Timbili** range export only, not tasted. — *CR*

Eshkol Kosher Winery

Wellington · Est/1stB 2003 · Tasting & sales only by appt Mon-Thu 10-5 Fri 10-12 Sun by appt · Fee R15 · Closed Jewish holidays · Tours by appt · Cheese platters by appt; also (non-kosher) meals at Onverwacht Restaurant · Small tour groups · Owner ERIE Trading · Winemakers Shalom Epstein & Hein Hesebeck (2003/2004) · Viticulturist Hein Hesebeck (2004) · 15 ha (merlot, pinotage, ruby cab, shiraz, chenin) · 10 000 cs 90% red 10% white · PO Box 151 Wellington 7654 · eshkol@ezinet.co.za · www.eshkol.co.za · T 021·864·3356 · F 021·873·0871

From the outset, Eshkol Winery has made inroads into the international kosher market but their big break came last year with the announcement that Royal Wines, the largest kosher wine distributor in the world, had chosen Eshkol as its sole SA supplier. Evidence that Shalom Epstein and Ori Ilan, the owners who work under the strict supervision of Rabbi Desmond Maizles and the OU (Orthodox Union of North America) are realising their dream: to make premium boutique wines… which just happen to be kosher.

King Solomon range

Premier Chenin Blanc ★★★ Ex 30 yr old vyd on Rose Garden farm, Paarl; **06** pleasing citrus flavours & dry straw hint; light, clean & balanced. No newer releases of following ready for tasting; notes from pvs ed: **Cellar Masters Choice Red** ★★ **04** roughly equal four-way blend with dusty dried-currant fruit, sweet-stalky finish. **Shiraz Rosé** ★★ Crushed raspberry whiffs on semi-sweet **05**, juicy, balanced by touch dry tannin. **Chardonnay** ★★ **05** tasty dry white, 100% Am oak a surprisingly subtle backdrop; grapefruit hints, citrus-salad flavours. **Cellar Masters Choice White** ★★ Chardonnay, chenin blend (53/47), **04** high-toned, with pleasing fresh acidity. **Kiddush** ★★ Very soft & sweet sacramental wine from cinsaut, shiraz, ruby cab.

Eshkol range

Cabernet Sauvignon Reserve ★★★ new 04 ripe-fruit style with raisined nuance; touches cinnamon & damp earth to cassis fruit; comfortable — not too full-bodied. Wellngtn vyds. Yr new Romanian oak; ditto for… **Merlot Reserve** new ★★ **04** off own vyds; jammy plum whiffs with volatile touch, tart flavours, unsustained dry finish. **Shiraz** ★★★ Medium-bodied **04** expressive leather & spice aromas, bluegum whiff; tangy tannins & sweet-sour farewell. Wellngtn fruit, fermented with new Am oak. Newer releases of the following unready; notes from pvs ed: **Cabernet Sauvignon** ★★ Hot-country 'baked' quality on **04**, flavours of plum jam with slight stalky edge, concluding sweet nuance. **Merlot** ★★★ Restrained but appealing **03**, leafy cassis hint; light (12%), harmonious, accessible dry flavours. Am oaked. **Pinotage** ★★ **04** lightish country-style red with choc-prune fruit, tangy dry savoury flavour. Paarl fruit, unwooded, whereas … **Walker Bay Pinotage** ★★★ 100% Am oak — yet amazingly unwoody; pinot-like delicacy on **04**; red berry flavour, juicy & dry. **Classic Dry Red** ★★★ Light but succulent cab, merlot, shiraz convivium; **03** classy cedar whiff & berry ripeness from cab, balanced by leafy tannins. — *CT*

■ *Eskdale* see De Zoete Inval
■ *Eventide* see Mischa
■ *Evolution* see Origin Wine

Excelsior Estate

Robertson · Est 1859 · 1stB 1997 · Closed to public · Owners Freddie & Peter de Wet · Winemaker Johan Stemmet (Nov 2003) · 190 ha · 150 000 cs own label 67% red 33% white · HACCP certified · PO Box 17 Ashton 6715 · info@excelsior.co.za · www.excelsior.co.za · T 023 615·1980 · F 023·615·2019

'Business as usual' is winemaker Johan Stemmet's bird's eye view of 2006: sales are going well, especially in the States, where Excelsior is one of the top-selling SA wine brands, and the first harvest of newly planted mourvèdre and petit verdot is 'very promising'. The trick now, says Stemmet, is to improve quality and consistency while maintaining pocket-friendly prices.

Merlot Rosé ☺ ★★★ Ideal picnic wine: **06** smoothly dry, juicy, fresh, with appealing Cherry Lifesavers tone & rounded mouthfeel.

Cabernet Sauvignon Reserve ★★★ Black fruit & tarry whiff on massively ripe **04** (14.8% alc), 22 mths oaked, some new. Baked fruit, dry tannins suggest this not, as Rsv moniker implies, for long haul. **Cabernet Sauvignon** ★★★ Always pleasing; **05** (sample) usual pulpy fruit, supple tannins, touch sugar; cedar whiff gives luxurious feel to honest, well-made red. Screwcap. **Merlot** ★★★ **05** a notch up; earthy whiffs, good food-friendly tannins, 14.5% alc not obvious. Already shows some age – drink soon. **Paddock Shiraz** ★★★ Different styling for **05** (sample): mega-ripe 'hot-climate' character with earth/dried-fruit sniffs, porty note invites (screwcap) to be opened soonest. **Pure-bred Red** ★★★ Raisiny, somewhat rustic & dry **05**; blue blood in name but bit of a bronco in tannin department – tame with richer foods. **Chardonnay** ★★ Lightly wooded **06**, confected peach cordial tone, marked sweetness (5.6g/ℓ sugar) without the customary uplift on finish. **Sauvignon Blanc** ★★★ Plumper **06**, shade less razzmatazz than pvs but still satisfying, affordable everyday white. Usual moderate 13% alc. **Paddock Viognier** ★★★ Last tasted was fresh, zesty **05**, super varietal expression & lots of characterful fun. Screwcap for easy access. – IvH

Excelsior Vlakteplaas

Little Karoo • Est 1934 • 1stB 1998 • Tasting & sales Mon-Fri 9-5 • Closed Easter Fri-Mon, Ascension Day, Dec 16/25/26 & Jan 1 • Owners Jurie & Danie Schoeman • Winemaker Danie Schoeman (1981) • 41 ha (merlot, pinotage, ruby cab, chenin, muscadel r/w) • 490 tons 1 000 cs own label 50% red 50% white • Export brand: His Master's Choice • PO Box 112 De Rust 6650 • jjschoeman@telkomsa.net • T 082·821·3556 • F 044·241·2240

Danie Schoeman completed a university degree but says his real training started when he returned to the farm to learn from the 'Muscadel Master', aka Schoeman Snr. Danie S's stated aim is to bottle only the very best Muscadel for 'His Master's Choice'. And he has Mother Nature on his side – the farm is situated on the flanks of the Swartberg mountains, in the heart of the Little Karoo, birthplace of some of SA's best fortified wines.

Red Muscadel ★★ **04** has lost its youthful muscat perfume, shows mature caramel/thatch aromas & soft raisiny sweetness. 17.5% alc. **06** version unready; ditto… **White Muscadel** ★★ 2004 Young Wine Show & Veritas gold medalist **04** also revealing some middle-age spread (which attractive to some); ultra-smooth, syrupy. Both wines best enjoyed soon. – IvH

■ **Excelsious Wines** see Stoumann's Wines
■ **Faces of Africa** see Douglas Green
■ **Fairbridge** see Paarl Wine Company
■ **Fairhills** see Origin Wine

Fairseat Cellars

Cape Town • Closed to public • Owner Dick Davidson • PO Box 53058 Kenilworth 7745 • fairseat@mweb.co.za • T 021·797·1951

Negociant and Cape Wine Master Dick Davidson sources wines locally for export to Europe, chiefly buyers' own brands (BOBs) for the German market. Current production (untasted) includes the Fairseat Cellars Ruby Cab; and Mountainside Shiraz 04, Pinotage 05 and Sauvignon 05. An NV sparkling Mountainside Blanc de Blanc Cuvée Afrique was added during the year. Some previous releases have flown with Lufthansa.

Fairvalley Farmworkers Association

Paarl • Est 1997 • 1stB 1998 • Tasting & sales at Fairview (see entry) • Owners Fairvalley Community • Winemaker Awie Adolph (Feb 1997) • 18 ha • ±50 000ℓ for own label 50/50 red/white • PO Box 6219 Paarl 7620 • marlene@fairview.co.za • T 021·863·2450 • F 021·863·2591

This venture has grown from strength to strength, with an increased footprint in the US (their primary market), strides into the UK and Japan, and new interest from Scandinavia. Proof that empowerment projects can – if there is genuine investment and upliftment – count on considerable support abroad. To this end Fairview, who started this farmworkers initiative, are looking at Fairtrade accreditation on their behalf.

Pinotage ★★ **04** when tasted was tannic with lower fruit & approachability than pvs, though might have softened since. Combo tank/oak ageing (older Am/Fr). **Chenin Blanc** ★★ **05** pleasant easy-drinker with lemon/herbaceous fragrance & mineral core. **Sauvignon Blanc** ★★ **05** fairly neutral, whiffs tropical fruit & grass. All WO Coastal, none retasted this ed. — *JP*

Fairview

Paarl · Est 1693 · 1stB 1974 · Tasting & sales Mon-Fri 8.30-5 Sat 9-4 Sun 9.30-4 · Fee R15 · Closed Easter Fri, Dec 25, Jan 1 · Goatshed Eatery for meals/refreshments daily 9-5 (see Eat-out section) · Groups by appt · Also tasting & sales of Fairview cheese · Owner Charles Back · Winemakers Charles Back & Anthony de Jager (Dec 1996), with Erlank Erasmus (Jan 2001) · Viticulturist Johan Botha, advised by Andrew Teubes · 300 ha (cab, barbera, malbec, merlot, mourvèdre, nebbiolo, pinotage, shiraz, sauvignon, viognier) · 1 700 tons 80% red 15% white 5% rosé · ISO 9001:2001 & HACCP certified · PO Box 583 Suider-Paarl 7624 · info@fairview. co.za · www.fairview.co.za · T 021·863·2450 · F 021·863·2591

There is simply no end to Charles Back's exuberant winery's growth and innovation. Extensive indoor revamps and outdoor landscaping in recent years continued with yet another cellar expansion and upgraded bottling and labelling lines. All to handle increased demand, particularly in Scandinavia, Canada and the US. As if not suitably stimulated by Fairview's eclectic range of wines, winkled out on Back's forays into new viticultural territory, cellarman Anthony de Jager (celebrating a decade here) still found time to 'have a bit of a go' at a dessert-wine-style viognier. This busy, buzzing operation, as renowned for its hand-crafted cheeses as its wines, is also enlarging its cheese shop. Add spacious winetasting and casual dining facilities to the mix and you have one of the Cape's most convivial destinations.

Red Seal range

★★★★ **Caldera** From selected Swtland vyds of grenache, mourvèdre, shiraz; 2nd release **04** last ed recalled Châteauneuf-du-Pape: elegant sweet, ripe nose; choc & intriguing orange notes; potential to evolve.

★★★★ **Pegleg Carignan** Features some of the oldest carignan in SA. Last reviewed **04** showed high toned sweet nose of ripe fruit & oak, typical firm acid of the variety.

★★★★★ **Primo Pinotage** Massively flavourful & aromatic; off bushvines on eponymous Agter-Paarl farm. **04** still available; deep, concentrated, with gd varietal definition. Serious wine with positive savoury elements, firm tannins needing to settle.

★★★★☆ **Solitude Shiraz** Ex-dryland Pdberg vyd, standout **04** (★★★★★) reveals an intriguing sweet/savoury character, loads of spice, hedgerow fruit, even scrub, all the while showing restraint, promising more layers to come over further 5+ yr development. Oak fermented, further 16 mths Fr barrels. Earlier accessible **03** widely hailed: 91 pts *WS*, Concours Mondial & Santé Classic golds.

★★★★☆ **The Beacon Shiraz** From low-vigour Koelenhof vyd. Ultra-ripe **04** (★★★★) lost some mid-palate definition, class, in going bolder (15.1% alc); sweet spice, liquorice, opulent dark fruit & broad-textures, able to handle the serious oaking. Dry finish, can be aged. Fermented/matured Fr oak, 40% new. Gold IWSC. **03** elegantly styled with pure fruit expression.

★★★★ **Jakkalsfontein Shiraz** Mature bushvine vyd on western Pdberg slopes. Reviewed pvs ed, **03** serious, sturdy but showing integrity of its origin. Juicy fruit, great structure & vibrant acidity, so holds its 15% alc well; will benefit with keeping. 91 pts *WS*.

★★★★ **Oom Pagal Semillon** One of the more serious Cape examples. **06** (sample) no longer single vyd, combo own & Darling fruit giving fresher styling. Layers of interest unfolding, showing tropical/peachy, waxy notes, with palate weight speaking of fruit concentration. Portion tank fermented, rest Fr oak.

Fairview range

★★★★ **Shiraz** This winery's signature since **74**. Last reviewed **04**, high toned, light & elegant, with lily perfume. Obvious shiraz fruit, juicy acidity & soft tannins.

★★★★ **Stellenbosch Cabernet Sauvignon** From 2 Firgrove vyds giving authentic maritime influenced fruit. **04** likeable extrovert; perfectly ripe plums, blackcurrants, well partnered by 14 mths Fr oaking, partial barrel ferment. Already drinking well, but there's a gd future.

★★★★ **Sauvignon Blanc** Ex-unirrigated Swtland bushvines, some Dbnvlle fruit. Perfect for food & long summer days but not simple. Elegant **06** has gentle gooseberry, grapefruit & minerals on the palate, enough racy acidity to kick-start any meal. 12.5% alc.

★★★★ **Viognier** Lauded example of the fashionable Rhône variety. Nothing overt in **06**, shows the class variety can deliver in good hands: wafting jasmine, peach pip perfume partnering savoury oak nuances. Majority fermented/4 mths seasoned barrels. Despite 14.9% alc, elegant, poised. Grande Médaille d'Or at Concours Mondial 2006 for **05**, which sold out before we cld taste.

★★★★ **La Beryl Rouge** Returned after some yrs hiatus with **04**, tasted pvs ed, a single barrel of straw-dried shiraz. Concentrated, smoky, well focused & juicy. A worthy curiosity.

★★★★☆ **La Beryl Blanc** Chenin grapes air-dried on straw mats. **05** sold out untasted, but secured winery's 2nd 'great gold' at 2006 Concours Mondial. **04** had 50% semillon; sweet (206g/ℓ RS), but with fantastic balancing acid & concentrated fruit; amenable 12% alc. *Wine* ★★★★.

Rosé ★★★ Cerise hue already enough reason to display **06** on alfresco tables, but 6-variety fruit mix tastily lifts the dry structure with lovely berry tones. **Formosa Peak Cabernet-Shiraz** ★★ Last reviewed **03** from high, Garden Route vyds — 600km away. Smoky, cool-climate nose with charry wood (14 mths Fr); minty & leafy character; soft tannins. *Wine* ★★★★. WO Upper Langkloof. **Mourvèdre** ★★★ Sturdy & tarry **04**, still available, expresses variety's typical monolithic girth, flattered in youth by oak (9 mths older Am). From dryland Swtland grapes. **Stellenbosch Merlot** ★★★ **04** tasted pvs ed; from Firgrove, as with Cab above. Good, bright varietal fruit; taut palate that would benefit with some ageing. **Pinotage** ★★★★ Starting with a colour you could use in pens, **05** is textbook pinotage: rhubarb, mulberry & some wild herbs, all in a juicy, vibrant package. Very inviting, yet enough oak backbone for some ageing. WO Paarl. **04** Concours Mondial gold. **Pinotage-Viognier** ★★★★ 2nd commercial release **04** shows varieties' compatibility: ripe red fruit allowed full sway, ultra-smooth, juicy mouthfeel given aromatic lift by 4% viognier. 25 yr old bushvine pinotage; varieties co-vinified in open fermenters; yr Fr/Am seasoned oak. **Viognier Special Late Harvest** NEW ★★★★ Unusual & delicious **06**'s heady perfume jumps out of the glass, jasmine, rosepetal & an interesting fresh pineapple note. Beautifully balanced, 8g/ℓ acidity reining in the sugar for an almost-dry effect, easy to match with food. **Chardonnay** ★★★ **03**, as per earlier ed, clean citrus & slightly mineral tone. Bunch-pressed, fermented/6 mths Fr/Am oak, some new. No **04** or **05**. **Sweet Red** ★★★ Fairview's fortified winter warmers tend to change variety every yr; last from merlot. Touch rustic & very sweet with firm acid. Just about held its 17% alc. Mainly screwcap closures. This, range below, WO Coastal unless noted. **Akkerbos Chardonnay** discontinued.

Agostinelli range

Bright Italianate packaging, cork closures, for these. **Agostinelli** ★★★★ Blend of barbera, sangiovese, nebbiolo, primitivo (aka zinfandel) 43/25/18/14 in **04**. Tasted pvs ed, juicy & fresh, with sweet/sour notes, grainy tannins demanding food. Ex-young vyds; fermented in 'neutral' oak for fruitier profile. **Barbera** ★★★★ Herbal whiffs in piquant sour cherry compote, **05** sparks with youthful vibrancy, sinuous appeal. 10 mths used Fr wood. WO Swtland, as is next wine. **Sangiovese** ★★★★ Ripe cherries, plum core in **05**, with savoury, dried herb elements adding intrigue. Streamlined, drinkable; has attractive lifting freshness. 14 mths Fr oak, third new. — *CR*

False Bay Vineyards

Est/1stB 2000 ▪ Closed to public ▪ Owner Boutinot UK ▪ Winemakers Werner Engelbrecht & Paul Boutinot (2004/2000) ▪ Viti consultant Johan Pienaar, with Werner Engelbrecht ▪ 380 000 cs 45% red 40% white 15% rosé ▪ Export brands: Cape Heights, Hoop Huis, Paarl Heights, Vals Baai/False Bay ▪ PO Box 1286 Wellington 7654 ▪ ceo@boutinotsa.co.za admin@ boutinotsa.co.za ▪ T 021·873·2418 ▪ F 021·873·7580

Part of the UK Boutinot group, whose reach has extended from humble beginnings in France 25 years go to encompass an impressive international wine production and distribution business, False Bay Vineyards was established in 2000. A traditionalist at heart, founder Paul Boutinot believes in making wine in a far less interventionist way than might be thought appropriate for the high volumes concerned, willing, for example, to risk a few stuck fermentations from relying on wild yeasts in pursuit of softer, more individual styles. See separate entry for Waterkloof, their Somerset West farm.

All below `new`; whites all **06**, tasted as samples. **Shiraz** Naturally fermented **05** untasted. **Chardonnay** ★★★ Fairly reticent on nose; more expressive, well balanced lemon-butter flavours, tangerine acidity & rounded vinosity. For early consumption, as all here. **Chenin Blanc** ★★★ Promising debut with restrained fynbos, wet wool & nutty notes, fine weight & persistence. Pdberg fruit, wild yeast fermented, small portion in 600ℓ barrels. Shd gain complexity over next 2-3 yrs. **Sauvignon Blanc** ★★★ Smart & interesting wine with unusual white pepper note, slight fruit-tannin grip, tropical flavours with crisp appley acid. Shd please widely. Mainly W Cape WOs.—*CvZ*

■ *Family Reserve* see Jonkheer, Kleine Zalze, Riverstone, Waterford
■ *Fantail* see Morgenhof

Fat Bastard

Tongue-in-jowl international label created by European wine-partners Thierry Boudinaud and Guy Anderson. Now made in serious quantities (500 000+ cartons) and distributed in Europe, America and the Far East. The SA versions, featuring a cartoon hippo on the front-label, are from Robertson Winery.

Shiraz While **03** (★★★★) was big (14% alc) & lumbering, **04** (★★★★) is elegant & classy — though still of the same ripe, brambly, aromatic family; supple tannins, much improved wooding (new small-oak 10 mths) & sweet-fruited finish make a delicious, widely pleasing package. **Chardonnay** ★★★★ Much nicer than name suggests, & not podgy either. Partial oak fermentation adds buttery layer to **06**'s ripe tropical tones; soft, fullish, rewarding easy drinking. **Sauvignon Blanc** ★★★★ **06** well textured & flavoured as pvs; passionfruit & pineapple ripeness, up-tempo Granny Smith apple finish; low 13% alc. Enjoy in fruity youth. All WO Rbtson.—*DH*

■ *Fat Ladies* see Winecorp

Feiteiras Vineyards   ◊?

*Walker Bay ▪ Est 2003 ▪ 1stB 2004 ▪ Visits by appt Mon-Fri 9-5 Sat/Sun 9-12 ▪ Closed Easter Fri/Sun, Dec 25 & Jan 1 ▪ Owners De Andrade family ▪ Winemaker Jose de Andrade (Mar 2003) ▪ Viticulturist Manuel de Andrade (Mar 2003) ▪ 4.5 ha (cab, merlot, mourvèdre, petit v, shiraz, verdelho) ▪ 1 200 cs ▪ 80% red 20% fortified ▪ PO Box 234 Bot River 7185 ▪ feiteiraswine@icon.co.za ▪ www.feiteiraswine.co.za ▪ **T 082·453·1597** ▪ F 028·284·9525*

The De Andrade brothers have the only working 'foot press' (also known as a *lagar*) in the Cape. Built from scratch and housed in an open fermentation tank, its wooden screw was hand-turned in Madeira, where the De Andrades hail from, and it needs two men to turn the 7m gum pole to work it. A sentimental but functional déjà vu for José and Manuel de A, whose winemaking is deeply informed by their heritage. 'This truly is handmade wine,' says JdA, who learned winemaking as a young man during his annual visits to Madeira.

Following all `new`, WO Ovrbrg: **Troca Tintas** ★★ Concentrated mulberry character on chunky & robust **05**, mostly merlot, plus 15% tinta with dense dry tannins. **Vinho Fino Tinto** ★★★★ **05**, like next, a traditionally foot-crushed, port-style wine; this from tinta, with 10% merlot. Jammy black fruit aromas, rich texture, & tealeaf/forest floor notes. Gd long flavours. Classic build of 19% alc, 124g/ℓ sugar. **Vinho Fino Branco** ★★★★ **05** from chenin: this white version has nutty aromas, with concentrated melon/marzipan whiffs & raisiny finish. Same alc as above, but sweeter, with 154g/ℓ RS.—*MF*

■ *Fernkloof* see Cape Wine Exports
■ *Firefly* see Stellar Winery

FirstCape Vineyards

Paarl • Closed to public • Est 2002 • Owners De Wet, Aan de Doorns, Stettyn & Badsberg co-op wineries, Goudini Wines, Newton Johnson family & BrandPhoenix • Winemakers Gordon Newton Johnson & Newald Marais • 60% red 40% white • UK office +44 (0) 1306·875·219 • PO Box 6213 Paarl 7622 • info@firstcape.com • www.firstcape.com • T 021·872·0837 • F 021·872·2534

Mind-boggling growth for this young giant, the fastest-growing SA brand in the UK for two years running and now sporting entry level, Limited Release and First Selection ranges. Export manager Charmaine Alger reckons that by early this year the brand's sales in Britain will reach one million 9ℓ cases, making it the second biggest SA bottled brand there. The sales avalanche has put pressure on production and in response, Aan de Doorns, Stettyn and Badsberg joined the originals, Goudini and De Wet Co-op, as FC suppliers. Imminent is the building of a visitor-friendly home base, a Worcester winery with 'massive capacity' — a must, given Alger's disclosure that plans for distribution into Europe are also on the cards.

First Selection range   `new`

Shiraz ★★★ Appealing **05** fireside red with lively savoury red fruit, tealeaf tannins, pleasing roundness from suggestions Am oak & sugar. **Shiraz-Cabernet Sauvignon** ★★★ **05** gentle tannic tug at end of juicy red/black berry palate, balanced, with decent length. **Shiraz Rosé** ★★ **06** light, unpretentious sundowner with earthy red plum aromas, flavours sweetened by few grams sugar. **Chardonnay** ★★★ **06** shy, delicate citrus flavours, touch of spice from small portion Fr staves/barrels, gains bit of fatness from 13.7% alc. **Chardonnay-Viognier** ★★★ Charming **06** blend with dollop sauvignon; tropical whiffs & viognier's floral/apricot flavours on palate. Deft oaking (combo Fr staves/Am barrels) adds spice & some breadth; slightly warm farewell (13.6% alc).

Limited Release range

Cabernet Sauvignon ★★★ Lush blackcurrant teams with cab's typical astringency to deliver fruity, uncomplicated **04**, tasted last ed. **Merlot** ★★★ Moreish **05** with sugar-plum fruit, supple tannins & soft acidity, begs to be shared. **Shiraz** ★★★ **05** sweet-sour character, fairly firm tannins though still easy to drink; acidity refreshes just-too-ripe fruit. **Pinotage Rosé** `new` ★★ Earthy strawberry tones on **06**; sweetish entry checked by pleasantly drying fruit tannins. **Chenin Blanc** ★★ As pvs, **06** a weight-watchers friend with low 1.8g/ℓ sugar. Subdued fynbos bouquet, short, vinous palate. **Sauvignon Blanc** ★★★ **06** untasted; **05** had intense greenpepper aroma & bracing acidity, tangy grapefruit tail. **Sauvignon Blanc-Semillon** `new` ★★★ Shy, fresh **06**, some tropical & elderflower nuances, grassy acidity, satisfying weight. All above for current consumption.

FirstCape range

Pinotage ★★★ **04** last ed was juicy & elegant with strawberry tones, firm fruit tannins for structure; long earthy exit. **Shiraz-Pinotage** ★★★ Cheery **05** has vibrant raspberry/cranberry aromas & flavours; supple fruit tannins give structure & grip. **Cabernet Sauvignon-Merlot** ★★★ Ripe prunes mingle with cassis & black plums in sappy **05**, relaxed tannins & freshness make a gd summertime option. **Chardonnay-Semillon** ★★★ **06** flavoursome 50/50 blend; delightful herby lemon scents, lightish but flavoursome, finishes fresh. **Colombard-Chardonnay** ★★★ Quiet **06** shows subtle floral & fruit pastille notes, lemony acidity, pleasing vinosity. All ranges WO W Cape. — *CvZ*

■ *First Sighting* see Agulhas Wines
■ *Fish Hoek* see Flagstone
■ *Five Heirs* see Lourensford
■ *Five Senses* see Overhex
■ *Five's Reserve* see Van Loveren

Flagstone Winery

Somerset West (see Helderberg map) ▪ *Est 1998* ▪ *1stB 1999* ▪ *Tasting & sales Mon-Fri 10-5 Sat 10-3 Sun by appt ('phone to avoid disappointment')* ▪ *Fee R20 redeemable with any purchase* ▪ *Tours by appt* ▪ *Owners Jack family* ▪ *Winemakers Bruce Jack, Wilhelm Coetzee & Gerald Cakijana* ▪ *Viticulturist Bruce Jack* ▪ *90 ha under management* ▪ *400-600 tons 40-70 000 cs (varying % reds/ whites)* ▪ *PO Box 3636 Somerset West 7129* ▪ *admin@flagstonewinery.co.za* or *sales@ flagstonewinery.co.za* ▪ *www.flagstonewines.com* ▪ *T 021·852·5052* ▪ *F 021·852·5085*

Vintner-on-the-edge Bruce Jack, who manages vineyards across the Cape (including his own Napier rows), relished the challenges of vintage 2006. He fought raging fynbos fires pre-harvest and runaway fermentations during power outages mid-crush, but emerged inspired by 'the best-quality vintage since 1974'. Accolades continue to roll in for his out-of-box brand of winemaking/mongering. Jancis Robinson MW dubbed him SA's Randall Grahm (of California's Bonny Doon renown) and, in the UK, Flagstone has more wines retailing at over £8 than any other SA producer. He's cooperating with The Winery of Good Hope, Sagila, Sequillo and several other like-thinking wineries in Grape Minds, 'a coalition of confidence'. Energy unflagging, Ses'Fikile (see separate entry) is set 'to change the face of black empowerment winemaking'. And then there's La Bascula, a new venture in Spain...

★★★★☆ **CWG Auction Reserve Love Handles** new With a name derived from Bruce's physique (!!), this shiraz is also deserving of attention: **04** prosciutto, coffee beans, intense dark berries; quite New World on palate, plush fruit underpinned by spice. Impossibly smooth, accessible tannins, but cellaring will reveal more layers over time. 2 yrs new Am oak. Mainly Swtberg fruit, some Tbgh. For 2006 Auction.

★★★★☆ **Mary Le Bow** Cooperation with the Fraters of Rbtsn. A fruitcake richness & appetite appeal at first glance in **04** blend, then the intriguing nuances appear: mint choc, smoky cigarbox, roasted veggies, showing how clever it is to add shiraz to a bdx blend. A big wine (incl 14.9% alc,) & very impressive. 16 mths Fr/Am, some new.

★★★★ **Bowwood** A cab/merlot blend in technicolour, **04**'s cassis & black plums are given vanilla-rich 14 mths Am oak treatment; a lush-fruited velvety mouthful. Has 3-4 yr ageing ability but doubt there'll be any left: only 126 cs made. Partnership with the Johnsens in Pdberg.

★★★★★ **CWG Auction Reserve Month of Sundays** For 2005 Auction, not featured last time, so new to guide, **05** takes winemaking confidence or bold imagination or both (it's Bruce J, after all), but, amazingly, dry-but-fruity blend chard, riesling, morio muscat, sauvignon works. Tantalising layers of flowers, fruit & shortbread biscuit arise from 4 mths *sur lie* textures, Am oak & superb grapes ex-Elim, Swtberg. A must-have, also for back-label explaining its name.

The Berrio range

★★★★ **Cabernet Sauvignon** This, below, joint venture with Elim grower Francis Pratt. Previewed last ed, **04** in finished form has intriguing blueberry/wild fruit character, hints wintergreen, mocha choc; a refined elegance that speaks of careful handling, expert oaking (14 mths Am, 60% new). Individual. Dabs cab f, petit v, merlot. Gd 4-6 yr future. Incl dashes Wllngtn, Tbgh fruit.

★★★★ **Sauvignon Blanc** Refined & sophisticated, **06** shows nettles, grapefruit & a deep seam of minerality. Cool grown (Elim) & ideally suited to food, but good enough for solo enjoyment too.

Foundation range

★★★★ **Dragon Tree** Not for classicists perhaps, but Cape individuality in complex flagship blend mainly cab, pinotage, shiraz with 4 others. With succulent dark fruit **04**, sacrifices none of pinotage's juicy appeal, but enriches it with blending partners, yr Am oak, some new. For drinking rather than keeping, no hardship here.

★★★★ **Dark Horse Shiraz** As wild as cellar mantra: 'a moving target, our dreams reflected'. Aptly named, **04** has sheathed power, touch of the untamed in hedgerow fruit, scrub, moorland. Glossy texture, sleek & approachable tannins, but with yrs of pleasure ahead. Barrel selection: 14 mths two-thirds new Am, rest Fr/Am. Deep & brooding **03** houseful of awards incl VDG, SAA, *Wine* ★★★★.

★★★★ **The Music Room Cabernet Sauvignon** Jack's 'best attempt yet' **02**, topped, in our view, by vintage-finessed **03**, pvs ed packed with explosive cassis, succulent red berries in decadently smooth structure; Am oak-paved lingering finish. *Decanter* ★★★★.

★★★★ **Writer's Block Pinotage** Ever popular with pundits. **04** last ed confirmed upward quality trajectory: spicy plum richness mingled with sweet ripe fruit in medium-tannined tail. Third whole-berry crush, 14 mths barrelled, 30% new Am.

★★★★ **Two Roads** Cellar's 'icon white' a blend of changing varieties & origin. **05** near equal sauvignon, chard, with 4 others incl riesling, pinot bl, mostly Am barrel fermented/matured. Result an assault on the senses: preserved peach & pineapple, citrus peel, yet underlying green fig, herb garden, all coming together in a tangy sweet-sour way. Admirably creative, complex.

Longitude ★★★★ ✓ Consistent value, deftly orchestrated 7-fruit ensemble. Exuberant **05** has plums, dark berries, with oaking in support role, adding more flavour than structure. Lively, juicy &, as the label says, 'everyday'. Mainly cab, shiraz. Combo unoaked, staves, barrels. **BK5 Pinot Noir** ★★★ No follow up yet for **03**, where BK5 clone's propensity for organic notes held sway. **Semaphore** ★★★ Rosé from mainly pinotage, just-dry **06** (sample) has astonishing fresh banana tones (no kidding!) to go with its curvaceous approachability. **Free Run Sauvignon Blanc** ★★★★ Now just Elim fruit (pvsly some Rbtson), beefing up the leafy/fynbos tones in **06**; racy acidity balanced by soupçon body-plumping sugar. All designed for drinking pleasure. With 15% semillon. **Heywood House Barrel Fermented Sauvignon Blanc** ★★★★ Sophisticated handling of often fractious sauvignon/wood marriage. Last tasted **04**'s warm custard breadth of spiced oak softened sauvignon spikes. **Noon Gun** ★★★ Riesling/chenin-based dry miscellany of 6 white grapes, some just a pinch. **06** has less aromatics, more freshness & minerality than you'd expect, just perfect for lunch, any occasion. **The Field Day** See under Makro. **The Last Word Port** ★★★★ Exotica such as tannat jostle with mourvèdre, sangiovese & friends in eclectic take on higher alc/lower sugar genre. None since **02**.

Fiona range

★★★★ **Pinot Noir** Range not featured pvsly, so both new to guide. Textbook styling, has all the structural grace the variety can deliver under good, cool growing conditions (Faure, Elgin, Darling) **03** pure fruit expression, raspberries, red currants, then goes further: violets, cedar, even palate minerality. 10 mths Fr/Am oak. Bruce, you've got competition! (This & next is his sister's wine).

★★★★ **Sauvignon Blanc Reserve** From Elim fruit. **05** has grapefruit, green figs, an attractive minerality; quite classic & fine but unshowy; for food or long afternoons in conversation with friends.

Cellar Hand range

The Backchat Blend ☺ ★★★ Mix 7 varieties, mostly cab, shiraz. Gets surprising care for a quaffer: combo tank & oaked wine, Fr/Am. **05** attractively fruity, plums, berries, with a savoury note in its fleshy flavours.

These are joint ventures with employees committed 'beyond the monotonous security of a monthly salary'. **Chenin Blanc** ★★★ **06** crunchy apple & pear fruit salad, with the smooth textured drinkability its many fans expect. Both above in screwcap.

Strata Series

'Experimental, once-off & seriously adventurous' wines. **Cape Blend** See under Makro. **The Wallflower** ★★★★ Not to be found in the winemaker's primer; 65/35 morio muscat & sauvignon blend of Oudtshoorn, Elim fruit — muscat Am oaked 8 mths to boot. Sample **05** last ed had pastiche grapey fruit & charry wood whipped into form by sauvignon tartness in dry tail.

Fish Hoek range

Entry level wines – in fun 'fishmonger' packaging – mainly for export; all W Cape. **Merlot** ★★★ **04** pvs ed was chunky everyday red with fruity flesh beyond its price point; cabs s & f added some authority, Am oak gave vanilla warmth. 14.5% alc. **Shiraz** [new] ★★★☆ **05** sample to be enjoyed in its delicious youth; lightly oaked, a silky structure, with wild berries & scrub, some liquorice shading. **Shiraz Rosé** ★★★ Last tasted **05** offered sun, fruit & fun; grippy tail (partial Am cask ferment) encasing just-dry finish. **Sauvignon Blanc** ★★★ Swtlnd & Elim fruit give rounded tropical appeal in **06**, sample, with enough leafy tones to go well with food. All WO W Cape unless noted. – *CR*

■ *Flamingo Bay* see Darling Cellars

Flat Roof Manor

'Laid-back, unpretentious and quirky' screwcapped range made by Estelle Lourens of Uitkyk (where the wines may be tasted). The name an allusion to the flat-roofed, neoclassical manor house on the property.

Cabernet Sauvignon-Sangiovese [new] ★★★☆ 70/30 blend brings to mind 2006 football World Cup final: **05** exciting, with upbeat finish – & more Italian than French, with sangiovese's sour-cherry tone dominating. Oak (combo new/old, mainly Fr, 14 mths) well integrated. **Merlot 05** ★★★ Appealing plummy vanilla nose & palate, raspy oak exit less endearing. **Shiraz-Mourvèdre** [new] ★★★☆ 60/40 medley; **05** spicy, refreshing; vibrant fruit & judicious oak (as for blend above) mask 14.45% alc. **Semillon** ★★★★ ✓ Classy, medium-bodied **05**, delightful peach/lemon aromas & flavours with exotic curry leaf hint; enhanced by zesty acidity (no malo); 5 mths on lees give grip. **Pinot Grigio** ★★★ **06** more vinous than fruity. Pvs 6 mths fattening on lees down to 2, imparting more linear mineral quality; alc moderate 12%. All from Sbosch vyds; for early drinking. – *CvZ*

Fleur du Cap

Stellenbosch • 1stB 1968 • Tasting & sales at Bergkelder Wine Centre (see entry) • Owner Distell • Cellarmaster Andrea Freeborough • Winemakers Kobus Gerber (white wines) & Justin Corrans (red wines), with Schalk van der Merwe & Jaco van der Walt • Viticulturist Bennie Liebenberg • 2 100 tons 180 000 cs 55% red 45% white • fleurducap@distell.co.za • www.fleurducap.co.za • T 021·809·7000 • F 021·883·9651

At its home, the Bergkelder ('Mountain Cellar', recessed into the Papegaaiberg outside Stellenbosch), this long-lived Cape brand has reinvented itself with its top-end Unfiltered range. Traditionally vinified (hence the name), the wines have bowled over critics worldwide. Most are single-vineyard wines; some are blends from two sites. Joining the two dedicated teams under Bergkelder cellarmaster (and new mom) Andrea Freeborough is Schalk van der Merwe (ex-Boschendal, with experience at California's Kendall Jackson). He replaces Tariro Masayiti, now at Nederburg, as Kobus Gerber's fellow white-wine specialist.

Unfiltered Collection

★★★★ **Cabernet Sauvignon** Restrained **04** offers cassis, touches cedar, tobacco. Tannins still fairly taut mid-2006, should unravel over next 2-3 yrs – cellar up to 8. Moderate 13.2% alc, like pvs. Ex-single Bottlry vyd, as is Merlot below. 16 mths Fr oak, all new.

★★★★ **Chardonnay 05** shows ripe yellow peach, exotic nuance tropical lime. Authoritative oaking (fermented/9 mths, 80% new). Firm-fleshed & classy, needing till mid-2007 to hit its stride, but will keep few more. Classically styled **04** *Wine* ★★★★.

★★★★ **Sauvignon Blanc** Tropical nuances to headline flavours of gooseberry, grass in quiet, subtle & refined **06** (★★★★), which lacks oomph of pvs vintages. WO W Cape. **05** pulled in awards: MIWA DG, Winemakers Choice, *Wine* ★★★★.

★★★★☆ **Sauvignon Blanc Limited Release** Arresting **06** (★★★★) a shade less exciting than **05**, but the multi-faceted capsicum, gooseberry & cat-pee combo is in place. Taut & tangy, dressed in many shades of green but never unripe, with exciting fruit acid balance, bone-dry finish. **05** VDG.

★★★★ **Semillon** Slimmed down **04** (★★★★ but IWC gold 2006), now **05** shapely, even statu-esque — but stature carried with aplomb. Limes, other citrus set against subtle oak, though none of variety's usual lanolin. Firm acidity for mouthwatering freshness, un-compromisingly dry. Fermented/6 mths oak (50% new Fr/Am).

★★★★ **Viognier Limited Release 05** (★★★★), less outspoken than maiden **04** SAA. Gone the white peach, evening flowers: here some dried peach & lots of oak (though only seasoned oak for ferment/9 mths). Firm flesh, hiding massive 14.9% alc well, until 'warm' finish.

★★★★ **Viognier-Chardonnay-Sauvignon Blanc-Semillon 05** shows toasty oak, ripe peach, toasted almonds, marzipan threaded with lively citrus tang, long dry finish. Bold but elegant — with, says Kobus G, the creamy, nutty quality coming from the chard. Va-rieties equally blended, fermented/matured separately, 9 mths oak, some new. **05** Winemakers Choice.

Merlot Dense, thick & beefy **03** (★★★★) followed by **04** (★★★★) more neat & tidy than lush; restrained berry quality to mineral palate, well integrated oak (18 mths new). V dry; firm tannic backbone.

Fleur du Cap range

★★★★ **Cabernet Sauvignon** Reliable & quite stylish. Subtle mulberry, touch mint on **04** (★★★★). Classically constructed but less concentrated, intense than **03**, yet same fine-grained dry tannins, lingering dry finish with brush of oak (14 mths, mostly Fr, 30% new). Gd over next 5 yrs.

★★★★ **Chenin Blanc ✓ 06** in now-established style — intense fruit from older vines, subtle oak allows fruit to shine. Complex greengage, chamomile, mineral, with touches of spice in youth; firm flesh, mouthwatering acidity, 14.6% alc. These mature superbly.

★★★★ **Noble Late Harvest 05** (not retasted) has 25% chard, 18% gewürz added to riesling, to give fruit aromas & wafting botrytis. Lengthy finish tinged with orange zest. In mod-ern, less sweet style, with thrilling acidity (107g/ℓ sugar, 10g/ℓ acid).

Merlot ★★★ **04** interesting sprinkling black pepper to mulberry fruit, but fresh acidity forecloses on richness. Subtle oak, mainly Fr, some new. Ready to drink. **Pinotage** ★★★ **04** 'masculine' — & sin-ewy in its austerity rather than muscular. Very dry, with firmish tannic grip. 15 mths used Fr oak. **Shi-raz** ★★★ Very approachable **04** has black-berried fruit, soft tannins but dry grip on finish. Should keep few yrs. Fr/Am oak 14 mths, 30% new. **Chardonnay** ★★★ Very correct, lime & toast in **05**; nice minerally touch with firm acidity for freshness & tang. Unobtrusive oak (6 mths, mainly Fr); soft finish, will please many palates. **Sauvignon Blanc** ★★★ **06** back on form, tropical aromas, attrac-tively plump with sweet/sour tussle, freshness ensured by crisp acidity & faint spritz. **05** flew SAA 2005. **Natural Light** ★★ 'Light' refers to low ±9% alc, not 9.8g/ℓ sugar; so ideal for lunchtime tip-pling, not dieting! **05** (not retasted) crunchy acidity, appley tail, dryish-tasting. — *IvH*

■ **Foot of Africa** *see* Kleine Zalze
■ **Footprint** *see* African Pride
■ **Forellen** *see* Lanzerac
■ **Forge Mill** *see* Franschhoek Vineyards

For My Friends   ♂♀

Darling ▪ *Est/1stB 2002* ▪ *Tasting by appt* ▪ *Owners/winemakers Abé Beukes & Johan Nesenberend* ▪ *200 cs 100% red* ▪ *PO Box 114 Darling 7345* ▪ *winemaker@darlingcellars.co. za* ▪ *T 083·658·8691 (AB) / 083·379·3941 (JN)*

This is the private-label collaboration between Darling Cellars' cellarmaster Abé Beukes and red-wine maker Johan Nesenberend, who was delighted to win the Young Winemaker of the Year title for the maiden vintage. Beukes was just as chuffed that someone was willing to pay R7 500 for six bottles at a local school auction. 'It suggests that there are consumers who share our passion,' he says, adding: 'We believe our wine will win more friends than prizes.'

Shiraz ★★★★ Maiden **02** mid-2005 was modern, bright, generous, with good support from piquant acid, tannin & good oak; **03**, work in progress last ed, noted as more elegant, lingering, harmonious — though also on large scale. Possible ★★★★ rating. These 18 mths Fr oak, 60% new. — *CvZ*

■ *Forresters* see Ken Forrester
■ *Fortress Hill* see Fort Simon

Fort Simon Estate

Stellenbosch ▪ Est/1stB 1998 ▪ Tasting & sales Mon-Fri 9.30–5 Sat 10-2 ▪ Fee R1/wine ▪ Closed pub hols ▪ Tours by appt ▪ Meals & venue for after-hours receptions/conferences (max 40 guests) by appt ▪ Walks ▪ Owners Renier & Petrus Uys ▪ Winemaker Marinus Bredell (Jun 1997) ▪ Viticulturist Renier Uys ▪ 126 ha (cabs s/f, malbec, merlot, pinotage, shiraz, chard, chenin, sauvignon, viognier) ▪ 800 tons 30 000 cs own label 50% red 50% white ▪ PO Box 43 Sanlamhof 7532 ▪ fortsimon@telkomsa.net ▪ www.fortsimon.co.za ▪ T 021·906·0304 ▪ F 021·903·8034/021·906·2549

Colder than normal nights swept mists in over the lower-lying vineyards, causing noble rot in the viognier and affording Marinus Bredell the opportunity to make a 'delicious and unusual' Noble Late Harvest (untasted). At the time of writing a new limited-release Reserve label was being readied (to include a Chardonnay and possibly some reds). Meanwhile the 'regular' Chardonnay flew high after awards from SAA, KLM and Swiss Air. Also interesting and delicious are the new gourmet cheese platters (groups of 20+ book ahead), served in the updated tasting area.

★★★★ **Chardonnay** After relatively flamboyant, SAA selected **04**, **05** leans more towards house elegance, understatement without loss of concentration, verve. Balanced oaking spotlights tight textured fruit, provides stage for few yrs gd development. Fermented/aged 9 mths new Fr barriques.

★★★★ **Chenin Blanc Barrel Fermented** Last was **03**, poised, vigorous fruit with lively acidity, resonating finish. Shd easily last 5–7 yrs. Fermented/aged 4 mths, new Am oak.

★★★★ **Sauvignon Blanc 04** was showy & intense, vibrant, tangy, with mouth-watering green fig flavours, long limy finish. **05** (★★★★★) is all that – & even more concentration, complexity, scrumptiousness. Perfect ripeness at only 12.3% alc a major plus.

Cabernet Sauvignon ★★★★ Last tasted was maiden **01**, understated, compact, with ripe cassis & silky tannins. **Merlot** ★★★ Deft oak handling for **03** allows black cherry & cocoa flavours to shine, vibrant palate is confident & long. Pleasing now, shd improve over 3-4 yrs. 18 mths seasoned barrels. **Pinotage** ★★★ **03** lighter toned/bodied but ripe, lively, easy to drink; Ribena & sour cherry flavours, smoothly dry finish. Yr 2nd/3rd fill oak, third Am. **Shiraz** ★★★ Step-up **03**, warmer, riper tone (plumper body too: 14% alc); silky feel, savoury tinge & hints fynbos, leather. 18 mths Fr/Am oak. **Rosé** ★★★ Pretty musk sweet scented **06**, mainly pinotage with merlot; juicy berry flavours, easy dry finish. **Anna Simon Merlot-Pinotage** ★★★ None since **01**, interesting savoury, ground coffee aromas/flavours, tell-tale touch pinotage sweetness in finish. **Chenin Blanc** ★★★★ One-third barrel fermented (cf two-thirds for FH version), **05** light textured apple/citrus flavours with savoury extra, subtle oak overlay, exuberant juicy acidity. JCWCA 'first'/gold award. **Restelle** ★★★★ Export blend; last tasted was **04**, sauvignon, chard, chenin (65/25/10); sauvignon dominates, adds limy edge throughout; chard/chenin contribute palate weight & tropical flavours. **Sauvignon Blanc Barrel Fermented** ★★★ **03** wood prominent on release, had tamed wilder edges of sauvignon, plumped up profile of otherwise slender style. This, Chenin Barrel Fermented, are alternating releases.

Fortress Hill Reserve range

Merlot ★★★ **03** continues to lift the bar; dark fruit & spice integrated on nose & palate, smart oaking. Drink or keep ±3 yrs. 18 mths seasoned barrels. **Pinotage** ★★ Lightly oaked **02** still selling, not retasted, ripe & plummy, approachable tannins, savoury twist to tail. 30 yr old vines, since uprooted. **Merlot-Pinotage** ★★★ Lightly oaked **01**, last yr was amiable easy red, smooth tannins for early accessibility. **Chardonnay** new ★★★★ **05** smoky note from oak (combo staves/casks, 8 mths) marries well with medium bodied fruit, gives extra plumpness to ripe tropical tone. **Chenin Blanc** ★★★★ Step-up **05** gorgeous ripe melon & citrus bouquet; full, rich but racy, vibrantly fruity. Terrific – & more serious than last ed's 'tipple'. Two-thirds barrel fermented/aged. *Wine* ★★★★. **Sauvignon Blanc** ★★★ Last tasted was **03**, easy drinking version plumped with touch sugar. – *CR/IvH*

■ *Foundation Series* see Flagstone

- ■ *Fountain Head* see Jason's Hill
- ■ *Four Clover* see Cloverfield
- ■ *Four Cousins* see Van Loveren
- ■ *Four Gates* see Ernst & Co

Fraai Uitzicht 1798

*Klaas Voogds (see Robertson map) • Sales at reception/restaurant during opening hours (see Eat-out section) • Closed Jun-Aug & Jan 1 • Tours strictly by appt • For amenities & activities, see Stay-over section • Owner Karl Papesch • Winemaker/viticulturist Karl Papesch, advised by local experts • 10 ha (cab, merlot, shiraz) • 500 cs 100% red • PO Box 97 Robertson 6705 • info@fraaiuitzicht.com • www.fraaiuitzicht.com • **T/F 023·626·6156**

'Never change a winning idea,' wrote Karl Papesch from Europe as he wound up his life there before moving family and all to Fraai Uitzicht in October last year. Regular visitors here, they fell in love with the farm during the 2001 crush and leapt at the chance when the outgoing owners put it up for sale. Karl P says they'll keep the guesthouse and restaurant ('Janet Wells is an excellent chef') and get local consultants in to help with the wine.

Merlot ★★★★ Blueberry-toned 04, ripe & fragrant, well-made; similar inky notes & approachable tannins to pvs, but touch more intensity to fruit. Ready to enjoy. Yr Fr/Am oak, some new. — *MM*

Franschhoek Vineyards

*Franschhoek • Est 1945 • 1stB ca 1975 • Tasting & sales Mon-Fri 9.30-5 Sat 10-4 Sun 11-3 • Fee R15 • Closed Easter Fri & Dec 25 • La Cotte Restaurant (booking advised) • Owners 95 shareholders • Winemaker Jolene Calitz, with Richard Duckitt (Nov 2002/Dec 2005) • 2 300 tons 44 000 cs own label 45% red 55% white • Ranges for customers: Forge Mill, Keates Drift & Millberg • PO Box 52 Franschhoek 7690 • sales@franschhoek-vineyards.com • www.franschhoek-vineyards.co.za • **T 021·876·2086** • F 021·876·3440*

In 2003, new GM Daan Coetzee said of this winery: 'To survive, we have to make higher priced, market driven wines.' So, growers' vineyards were revitalised and the vintage cellar modernised; then a barrelling programme implemented, resulting in a Reserve range with re-vamped packaging. Now it's the turn of single-vineyard bottlings, managed and made by seasoned Jolene Calitz and newcomer Richard Duckitt, with help from characterful growers like Graham Severn, who tends his Klein Goederust vineyard with a vine leaf draped over his nose as protection against the African sun! Success has superseded survival: UK exports claim 45% of production; quality driven Woolworths takes 20%.

Stonewalker new ★★★★ Serious & classical-minded red from equal shiraz & cab, with 25% unwooded mourvèdre; 05 off Paarl vines in stony soils. Supportive oak for cedary mulberry fruit, ripeness well controlled & harmonised with firm structuring tannins. A pleasure to drink now & for few yrs. 8 mths Fr oak; fruit.

Franschhoek Cellar Reserve range

Cabernet Sauvignon new ★★★★ Sets the tone for range with ripe-fruited lushness on 04; pulpy mulberries controlled by rich but chewy tannins; concludes with winter warming glow from 14% alc. **Merlot** ★★★★ Very ripe & sweet blueberry fruit with touch of wildness about the nose; 04 ripe, balanced tannins; quite a chunky profile, with similar glowing farewell to above. **Petit Verdot** ★★★ 04 reticent on nose but opens up on palate to ripe black plum fruit still tightly gripped by stern tannins needing time or food. 18 mths Fr oak. **Shiraz** new ★★★ Ultra-ripe 04 has 'hot', slightly porty overtones to its sweet black-plum fruit, ripe earthy tannins. Unbridled style will have its adherents. Incl dash 06. **Chardonnay** ★★★★ 04 last ed was tinged with lime, lemon & vanilla; lively, tangy, with well-meshed wood. 6 mths Fr oak, 50% new. 05 untasted. **Semillon** ★★★ Eschews pvs sauvignon injection in 05, but styling is similar, with 100% new oak (35% Am) dominating well expressed limy fruit mid-2006 — needs more time to harmonise & rate higher.

Franschhoek Cellar Gold range

Cabernet Sauvignon ★★ **05** continues pvs's styling in bright mulberry intro, charry oak, healthy fruit waiting for lively tannins to settle. Incl smidgen 04. **Merlot** ★★ **05** similar to, but fruitier than pvs, with sweet cassis & touch of honey, same big wood tannins (8 mths on oak), inviting food. Incl dollop unwooded 06, ditto for… **Shiraz** ★★★ Again marked by a generous, open weave, **05** sweet, warm fruit with tobacco hints, soft ripe tannins & 15% alc, latter obvious this yr. Am oak. Paarl fruit, as for … **Pinotage** ★★ **05** leads with warm pruney notes, follows with chewy tannins which are sufficiently hearty for robust foods. Now 100% oaked, 8 mths. **Chardonnay** ★★ Barrel character fairly obvious on last-tasted **05**, needed time for delicate pear & citrus fruit to come to fore. **Sauvignon Blanc** ★★★ Attractive mineral feel to **06**, hints citrus, cut grass & capsicum; light & fresh, gently dry.

Franschhoek Cellar Silver range

Chenin Blanc ★★ Underplayed melon & spice on **06**, softish acidity & modest fruit, unlingering almost-dry finish. WO Paarl. Following not retasted: **Grande Rouge** ★★ Varietal quintet led by merlot, 8-9 mths oaked. Friendly red fruit given some backbone by light wood tannins. **NV. Blanc de Blanc** ★★ Light bodied **05** mainly semillon, with trio of white partners; waxy semillon whiffs, pleasing mineral-tinged fruity finish. **Semi-Soet** ★★ Chiefly hanepoot, with chenin & crouchen; **05** grapey muscat perfumes, spring blossom whiff, short but polite farewell. — *IvH*

▪ *Fredericksburg* see Rupert & Rothschild Vignerons

Fredine le Roux Wines

*Walker Bay/Caledon ▪ Est/1stB 2004 ▪ Tastings/sales at Goedvertrouw ▪ Owners Josias & Fredine le Roux ▪ Winemaker Fredine le Roux ▪ 240 cs 60% red 40% white ▪ PO Box 338 Caledon 7230 ▪ Josiasfredin@mweb.co.za ▪ **T 028·284·9765 / 082·944·4573** ▪ F 028·284·9765*

Fredine le Roux barely had time to confirm the above details before returning to her busy life in the Caledon area. Notes for the wines below are from the previous edition.

Cabernet Sauvignon ★★★★ Big-boned **04** oozes ultra-ripe but gorgeous cassis & plum fruit, toasty oak & pipesmoke notes add complexity. Prominent tannins might well have harmonised by now. 18 mths Fr oak. **Grenache-Cabernet Sauvignon** Sells out before we can taste. **Chenin Blanc** ★★★ **04** marked by sinewy elegance when tasted in youth; kiwi & passionfruit on nose, fairly prominent oak but enough vivacious lemon fruit to carry it. — *MM*

Freedom Hill Wines

*Paarl ▪ Est 1997 ▪ 1stB 2000 ▪ Tasting & sales Mon-Thu 9-5 Fri 9-4 Sat 10-3 ▪ Closed pub hols ▪ BYO picnic ▪ Owner Francois Klomp ▪ Winemaker/viticulturist Ryan Wyness (Aug 2005) ▪ ±19 ha (cab, merlot, pinotage, shiraz) ▪ 140 tons 6 000 cs 80% red 10% white 10% blanc de noir ▪ PO Box 6353 Uniedal 7612 ▪ info@freedomhill.co.za ▪ www.freedomhill.co.za ▪ **T 021·867·0085** ▪ F 021·867·0576*

Engineer Francois Klomp's winery was established with a love of good wines as its foundation. Market demand tells the success story here, with most previous vintages sold out. Named Freedom Hill, the property overlooks Victor Verster (now Drakenstein) prison, from where Nelson Mandela took his first steps to freedom in 1990. Many wines are available in 375ml bottles. Explains Francois K: 'Choice of wine is far more important for a wine lover than quantity, and also a motivating factor when ordering for a light lunch or dinner.'

Freedom Hill range

★★★★ **Shiraz-Cabernet Sauvignon** None since **01**; 50/40 blend (& splash merlot), generous New World ripeness, fairly extracted but harmonious.

★★★★ **Shiraz 03** last ed had acquired a maturer savoury/game dimension beyond its full, creamy plum pudding fruit; no urgent need to uncork, however: brisk acidity, ripe tannins augur well for further cellaring. 27 mths Fr oak, 30% new.

This range EW unless mentioned. No newer vintages tasted for following: **Cabernet Sauvignon** ★★★ **05** early drinking style; comfortable tannins, fruitcake & cream nose, slender mouthfeel despite 14.5% alc. **Pinotage** ★★★★ Introverted **05**; muted cappuccino/earth tones, well structured with fleshy fruit, lively acidity, generous tannins. Following pair ex-Sbosch, both NE: **Merlot** ★★ **03** 'dry red' rather than varietal standout; soft & fat as pvs, with earthy touch; wood (30% new Fr, 2 yrs) a pleasant background note. **Shibula Merlot** ★★★★ Last tasted was meaty **01**; big, juicy, supple wine, showing some complexity. **Merlot-Cabernet Sauvignon** ★★★ **02** is new to guide but clearly no callow youth: flavours, oak & tannins already harmonious, approachably soft; clean-cut cassis & berry polished with quality wood (regime as for Merlot). **Cape Blend** ★★★★ ('Liberty' pvs ed). Light bodied **05** aromatic rhubarb & wild berry fruit; toasty note; moderate tannin adds some structure. Blend pinotage, shiraz & cab (50/47/3), for earlier enjoyment. **Blanc de Noir** new ★ From shy-bearing cab; **06** slightly sweet red cherry flavours, soft, easy; dusty note on finish. **Sauvignon Blanc** new ★★★ Off Elgin vyds (therefore NE); **05** very delicate & demure, with light floral tone; dry & undemanding. — *IvH*

■ *Friends* see Lutzville
■ *Frog Hill* see Anura
■ *Frost Vineyards* see David Frost Estate

Fryer's Cove Vineyards

Bamboes Bay (see Olifants River map) ▪ *Est 1999* ▪ *1stB 2002* ▪ *Tasting/sales at Knorhoek (see entry)* ▪ *Owners Jan Ponk Trust, JH Laubscher Family Trust & Wynand Hamman* ▪ *Winemaker Wynand Hamman (Apr 1999)* ▪ *Viticulturist Jan van Zyl (Apr 1999)* ▪ *6 ha (cab, merlot, pinot, sauvignon)* ▪ *35 tons 2 500 cs 66% red 34% white* ▪ *PO Box 93 Vredendal 8160* ▪ *janponk@ kingsley.co.za* ▪ *T 082·550·8749/027·213·2312* ▪ *F 027·213·2212*

The partnership between winemaker Wynand Hamman, formerly of Lanzerac repute, and brother-in-law Jan van Zyl, is earning recognition for this enterprising boutique winery. In a career spanning 20 years, Hamman revels in being independent, especially now that their young sauvignon vineyards-by-the-sea are in full production and so better able to keep pace with demand boosted by an infrequent *Wine* 5-star rating. For a special experience, visit them at Strandfontein between Christmas and New Year or over the Easter weekend by appointment, or at their home-from-home, Knorhoek Winery outside Stellenbosch (see separate entry and Photo Gallery).

★★★★★ **Sauvignon Blanc** Vintage driven ripeness in **06** preview, but still 'cool' feel: leafy green melon aromas, with arrestingly fresh palate, capsicum, vibrant lemon/lime. Irresistible. Riveting, nettly **05** *Wine* ★★★★★.

Richard Fryer 04 (★★★★) near-equal blend cab, merlot, previewed last ed, now impressive finished wine. Molten dark fruit, veined with beef extract, tar. Tannins more integrated, less fierce, but this much sheathed power needs gd few yrs to show full potential. Yr Fr barriques, portion new. **03** (★★★★) sample had similar flavours, dominant tannins in youth. **Pinot Noir** new First crop; barrel sample **05** too young to rate, still in development: plenty mocha choc but no shortage fruit, busy assimilating oak. — *CR*

Furstenburg Wines

Stellenbosch ▪ *Est 2004* ▪ *1stB 2005* ▪ *Closed to public* ▪ *Owners Victor van Aswegen & Anton van Aswegen family trusts* ▪ *Vini consultant Jeff Wedgwood (Oct 2004)* ▪ *1 600 cs 67% red 33% white* ▪ *PO Box 212 Stellenbosch 7599* ▪ *victor@furstenburg.com* ▪ *www.furstenburg. com* ▪ *T 082·552·7063* ▪ *F 021·465·2428*

Victor van Aswegen, co-owner with brother Anton, is enthused about the prospect of bringing a partner into their virtual winery business, all the more so because his professional life revolves around black economic empowerment — 'matching skills outside the industry with opportunities within', as he puts it. Meanwhile, the Van Aswegens and consultant winemaker Jeff Wedgwood have been formulating ideas on a blend for release next year.

Cabernet Sauvignon ★★★ From old Sbosch vines, **03** herbaceous tea leaf & tobacco aromas & whiffs black cherry, dense tannined finish. 18 mths new Fr barrels. **Chardonnay** ★★ Aromas of stonefruit on **05**, golden straw colour with matching developed notes, some intensity. 15 year old Sbosch vines, barrel aged. Neither retasted. — *MF*

Galleon Wines   ♀♀🍇 new

Betty's Bay • Est 2003 • 1stB 2004 • Visits by appt • Owner BK Investments/Andries Brink • Winemaker Andries Brink, advised by Bertus Fourie (2004) • 600 cs 100% red • PO Box 62 Durbanville 7551 • andries.medcon@absamail.co.za • T 028·272·9511/021·976·1786 • F 021·976·8129

Inspired by fellow *garagistes*, retired cardiologist Andries Brink set up a small cellar in his… well, garage. Assisted by Bertus Fourie (KWV), he aims to make 'wines with heart' and claims this is the most fun he's had in years. To date, this Betty's Bay venture focused on small quantities of red. With one tank already in his garden, a second has been added to the 'cooled barrel room' (read: garage) for his first chardonnay.

Cabernet Sauvignon ★★★☆ Cassically styled **05** marked by gd but reined-in varietal aromas of lead pencil, blackcurrant. Tight tannins, slightly herbal finish. 13.5% alc; 10 mths oak, mostly Fr/Am. Dbnvlle fruit vinified at Betty's Bay — then back home for bottling! — *MF*

Gallop Hill   ♀🐎📇♟

Paarl • Est 2001 • 1stB 2002 • Visits by appt; contact Jax Parsons T 082·895·4110 • Attractions/amenities: see intro • Owners Dijonne du Preez & Jim Deane • Vini/viti consultant Stephan Gerber • 20 ha (cab, shiraz) • ±50 tons 2 500 cs 100% red • PO Box 7539 Stellenbosch 7599 • info@gallophill.co.za • www.gallophill.co.za • T 021·869·8956 • F 021·869·8133

If you're part of the Cape's polo playing fraternity, you'll know that First Chukka is the pukka wine to serve post-match, or younger sibling Sauvignon if you prefer. Novices can now learn to play at this stylish stud farm's new indoor polo arena, then sit down with Stephan Gerber to a luncheon and tasting (by special arrangement only, as quantities are limited with only 20ha under vine).

The First Chukka ★★★ 03 seamless blend shiraz, pinotage, cab (70/15/15). Ripe & fleshy, tannins pliable, oak supportive (14 mths used Fr/Am barrels). Ready, shd keep few yrs yet. **Sauvignon Blanc ★★★ 04** delicate, polite example, with gentle tropical nuances to smooth rounded profile; silky mouthfeel despite firm acidity. Neither wine retasted this ed. — *IvH*

■ *Gecko Ridge see* Long Mountain

Gehot Bosch Winery   ♀♀

Bot River (see Elgin/Walker Bay map) • Est 2005 • Visits Tue-Sat 9.30-5 Sun 10-3 • Closed Easter Fri & Dec 25 • Owners Pierre & Paulette van den Bosch • Winemaker Pierre van den Bosch • 185 cs 100% red • PO Box 1895 Hermanus 7200 • vdbosch@lando.co.za • T 082·349·8265 •T/F 028·284·9409

Former Robertson fruit farmers (via Zaire) Pierre and Paulette (née Gehot) van den Bosch have 2 000ℓ of cab in barrel from grapes bought in 2006 for vinification on their farm between Bot River and Hermanus. He makes the wine by hand (basket press, open fermenters); she sells property and a small selection of local and Robertson bottlings at their charming roadside wine outlet.

Cabernet Sauvignon ★★★★ Cheerful but not frivolous **03** last yr deftly packed lots of ripe red fruit around a firm armature. Spice/tobacco hints from 18 mths Fr oak. Rbtson fruit, open tank-fermented. — *TJ*

■ *GG Wines see* Ernst & Co

Gilga Wines ♂♀

Stellenbosch • Est/1stB 1998 • Visits by appt • Winemaker/viticulturist Chris Joubert • 2.5 ha (shiraz) • 700 cs 100% red • PO Box 3 Vlottenburg 7604 • chris.joubert@gilga.com • www. gilga.com • T 021·881·3475 • F 021·881·3248

'Gilga needed an address,' says Chris Joubert, and where better than next door to Overgaauw, where he's long served as winemaker, and currently crushes and vinifies for his own venture. A new silent partner helped facilitate the purchase of this prime site from the estate. Of the 4ha now belonging to Gilga, 2.5 are devoted to shiraz, his specialty grape, and the balance will be planted with cab, he says, signalling bigger things to come.

★★★★☆ **Syrah** Youthful magenta rim, opaque core of hand-crafted **04** in keeping with densely fruited, compact style; pronounced, complex roasted spice & blackberry fruit; tight but supple tannins embrace juicy black plums; weighty, persistent finish. Broach in ±3 yrs: has balance, concentration & ample oaking (18 mths Fr) for grand evolution in bottle. Pleasures of slightly earlier approachable **03** still yrs off.

★★★★ **Amurabi** new First of an envisaged blended range carrying name of fabled Persian king introduced to the pleasures of wine by shy young maiden Gilga. Preview of seriously styled **04**, complex violet, blackberry & liquorice aromas; sinewy grape & oak (18 mths Fr) tannins mask youthful fruit; shiraz/cab (80/20), cab contributes elegance, minerality; piquant savoury finish; vg potential for improvement. — *IM*

Glen Carlou ♂♀ 🎨♿

Paarl • Est 1984 • 1stB 1988 • Tasting & sales Nov-Mar: Mon-Fri 8.30-4.45 Sat & Sun 10-3; Apr-Oct: Mon-Fri 8.30-4.45 Sat 9-12.45 • Fee R15 p/p, refundable on any purchase of R100 or more per group • Closed Easter Fri/Sat/Sun, Dec 25/26 & Jan 1; phone ahead on other pub hols • Cellar tours by appt • Gifts • Conferences • Fine art gallery (book ahead for guided tour) • Owners The Hess Group (Switzerland) • Winemaker David Finlayson, with Arco Laarman & Gillie Beukes (1994/2000/2006) • Viticulturist Marius Cloete (2000), advised by Richard Camera • 75 ha (cab, pinot, shiraz, chard) • 8-900 tons 65 000 cs 60% red 40% white • PO Box 23 Klapmuts 7625 • welcome@glencarlou.co.za • www.glencarlou.co.za • T 021·875·5528/96 • F 021·875·5314

Its new-look public areas, post-extreme makeover, give visibility to the Paarl winery's Swiss ownership. An international tasting room offers wines from the Hess Group's other properties in Argentina (the Colomé brand), California (Hess Collection) and Australia (Peter Lehmann), and doubles as a function room, with a small conference venue next door. Beyond the general tasting area, now with a view into the new cellar below, is a gallery showcasing pieces from Donald Hess's contemporary art collection. A Zen garden and indigenous plantings complete a handsome picture.

★★★★☆ **Syrah** Complex, individual wine (extra intrigue from soupçons mourvèdre, viognier), lauded around the globe. **05** follows **04**'s winning styling, but deeper, darker, more brooding; bitter choc this time coupled with brambleberries. Classy, beautifully judged fine-grained tannins, lifted by juiciness; all building blocks in place, but a slower developer: has 8+ yr future. 50% new oak, 50% Am, yr. Stunning **04** (★★★★★) our 2006 Wine of Year; *WS* 90 pts, MIWA DG, *Decanter* gold. **03** Paarl Challenge winner, SAA trophy, *Wine* ★★★★.

★★★★★ **Gravel Quarry Cabernet Sauvignon** new Named for old quarry found by pvs founder Walter Finlayson when he bought farm. Hugely impressive concentration in **04**: molten black plums which soak up serious oaking with ease, becoming smoky-savoury on palate. So well crafted it's already delicious, but there are further delights to come over time. Incl 7% petit v. 16 mths new Nevers barriques.

★★★★ **Grand Classique** Historically, flagship red of range: classic 5 bdx varieties. Blend switch in **03**, cab takes lead, adds more cassis concentration, beefy layers. Lip-smacking juiciness perfect foil for serious but supple tannins: also a keeper. Step-up **02** (★★★★★) *Wine* ★★★★, TWS gold. Expert oaking (2 yrs Fr, half new); 10+ yr ageing potential. 14.8% alc.

★★★★ Pinot Noir 05 back on track with more amenable tannins, respecting pinot's fragility & elegance. Mixed berries cohabiting with herb-rich scrub; juicy palate, accessible now, but will reveal true class over next 3-4 yrs. 11 mths Fr oak, 25% 1st fill. **04** Santé Classic trophy.

★★★★ Chardonnay Impressive yet friendly **05** seduces with bold peach & citrus peel perfume, flavours, infused with English toffee. Lifting acidity ensures the pleasure extends to food compatibility. Swiss gold. Fermented/10 mths oak, mainly Fr, 30% new.

★★★★☆ Chardonnay Reserve Intense, rich & serious, under CWG Auction label for most of past 10 yrs. **02**, untasted, selected for 2006 Auction.

★★★★☆ Quartz Stone Chardonnay Replaces high-flying 'Reserve Black Label' &, as expected, **05** a glorious chard: canned peaches, quince marmalade, roasted nut oak influence & that trademark tangy freshness, length. Native yeast, fermented/yr new Fr oak. TWS gold. Ltd quantities available locally.

Tortoise Hill Red ★★★ Blend mainly cab, some zin, shiraz, touriga, merlot. **04** last ed charmed with fleshy youth, creamy spice ex-oak, textured finish. For easy-drinker, got surprising care: 14 mths Fr/Am oak. **Tortoise Hill White ★★★** Unpretentious varying blend. Higher proportion (77%) sauvignon in **06** partnering chard, touch viognier, beefs up freshness, lemon/gooseberry styling. Tasty quaffer. **Zinfandel** Last tasted was **01** for CWG auction. **Devereux** discontinued. — *CR*

■ *Glenhurst* see Quoin Rock

Glenview Wines

*Cape Town ▪ Est/1stB 1998 ▪ Closed to public ▪ Owner Robin Marks ▪ Vini consultant Reino Kruger ▪ 7 000 cs 50% red 50% white ▪ PO Box 32234 Camps Bay 8040 ▪ bayexport@ kingsley.co.za ▪ www.glenview.co.za ▪ **T** 021·438·1080 ▪ F 021·438·3167*

Negociant Robin Marks is aiming to improve quality — particularly his barrel-matured Merlot, sourced from Stellenbosch — but keeps his competitive edge honed with a pragmatic approach to pricing. He has added a Shiraz to the range and is toying with the idea of a Sauvignon — if he can get 'the right quality/price ratio'.

Merlot ★★ 03 for early drinking; super-ripe plummy aromas contrast with lean palate, firm acid & alc (14%). 18 mths Fr oak. WO Bosch; below WO Paarl. **Shiraz** new **★★** Intriguing vegetable notes of tomato & white asparagus on **05**, leading to fleshy palate lifted by bright acidity, friendly tannins. Enjoy soon with food. Yr Fr/Am oak. **Chenin Blanc ★★★** Cheery **06** has bright melon & tropical fruit, brisk acidity almost masks 10g/ℓ sugar, provides sweet-sour lift to tail. Lightish 12.5% alc. — *CvZ*

GlenWood   ⌀♀

*Franschhoek ▪ Est/1stB 2000 ▪ Tasting & sales Mon-Fri 11-4.30; weekends (Sep-Apr only) 11-3; pub hols (except Christian holy days) 11-3; Fee R20 ▪ Tours daily 11; Fee R30 ▪ Owner Alastair G Wood ▪ Winemaker/viticulturist DP Burger (May 1992) ▪ 23 ha (merlot, shiraz, chard, sauvignon, semillon) ▪ ±150 tons 5 800 cs own label 30% red 70% white ▪ PO Box 204 Franschhoek 7690 ▪ info@glenwoodvineyards.co.za ▪ www.glenwoodvineyards.co.za ▪ **T** 021·876·2044 ▪ F 021·876·3338*

Situated in the Robertsvlei Valley, natural home of the rare Blushing Bride protea, this small winery has given fresh impetus to the re-establishment of local indigenous flora and fauna by joining the Biodiversity & Wine Initiative. Caring for people and their development opportunities, too, Alastair Wood and his team received the Rudnet Farm Health Award for the past two years. The focus remains on the wines, production of which increased by 100% last year; they also made their first unwooded chardonnay.

★★★★ Chardonnay Vigneron's Selection Opulent, seductive **05** (★★★★★) is very showy: preserved citrus & butterscotch, bold use of oak but has the fruit to handle it; a limy tail lifts the whole experience. New Fr oak, 11 mths, as all these. TWS trophy. **03** also seriously & well wooded, balancing citrus freshness with structure. Both different league to quirky **04** (★★★★) with spirituous notes.

Merlot ★★★★ Star in the making. Achieved full ripeness in **05**, without losing tight, disciplined core; peppery red fruit, hints of mint & a lovely juicy accessibility. 9 mths seasoned Fr oak. **Shiraz** ★★★★ Fleshy **05** offers nice drinkability with its dark fruited, smoky, roasted spice styling, fully integrated oak (11 mths combo new/used Fr). WO Coastal. **04** Santé Classic gold. **Sauvignon Blanc** ★★★★ Coolly fresh **06** is perfect restaurant fare: leafy-lime styling, with gooseberry nuances. Now in screwcap, as is… **Unwooded Chardonnay** new ★★★ Light textured, characterful **06** has tropical, peachy tones throughout, enough crisp freshness for food or solo drinking. **Semillon-Sauvignon Blanc** discontinued. — *CR*

■ *Goat Roti* see The Goats do Roam Wine Company
■ *Goats do Roam* see The Goats do Roam Wine Company

Goede Hoop Estate

Stellenbosch ▪ Est 1928 ▪ 1stB 1974 ▪ Tasting & sales Mon-Thu 10-4 Fri 10-3 ▪ Open pub hols ▪ Tours, meals & refreshments by appt ▪ BYO picnic ▪ Conferencing for max 20 ▪ Owner Pieter Bestbier ▪ Winemaker Carel Hugo (Dec 2002) ▪ Viticulturist Johan de Beer (Apr 2000) ▪ 80 ha (cab, carignan, malbec, merlot, pinotage, shiraz, chard, chenin, sauvignon) ▪ 11 000 cs + 90-100 000ℓ bulk 91% red 9% white ▪ PO Box 25 Kuils River 7579 ▪ goede@adept.co.za ▪ www. goedehoop.co.za ▪ T 021·903·6286 ▪ F 021·906·1553

Replanting continue here, with a fair amount of chenin and sauvignon going into the ground as well as some chardonnay. Winemaker Carel Hugo now talks of a focus on marketing: 'That's me, going out one day a week!' he adds wryly. An innovation in another area is the bottling last year of the 02 Cab in half-litre, 3ℓ and 5ℓ volumes, in response to a request. Someone out there obviously likes lots of GH Cab.

★★★★ **Cabernet Sauvignon 00** nose more open than pvs; balanced tannin, fine structure for ageing. **99** Xmas cake aromas over leafy cassis notes, classic cigarbox whiffs, dry finish. 2nd/3rd fill Fr, 18 mths. This, following reds, not re-tasted.

★★★★ **Merlot-Cabernet Sauvignon** ✓ (Aka 'Vintage Rouge'.) Charming & delicious **01**, juicy, ripe, accessible with plenty to give. **00**'s 60/40 blend shows spice & complexity; restrained wooding makes for plush style. 19 mths 2nd/3rd fill barrels.

Shiraz ★★★★ Classy **02**, interesting combo black fruit & white pepper, some savoury spicing; quite chewy/youthful, needs time. **Pinotage** ★★★★ **02** somewhat leaner than pvs, slight vegetal hint with savoury undertone. 8 mths oak, 2nd/3rd fill. **Domaine** ★★★ **02** lightish unwooded cab/carignan blend (53/47). Redcurrants & cherries, accessible weave, savoury & peppery fruit, firm dry finish. **Chardonnay** ★★★★ Down-toned wood presence in **05** for appealing nutty citrus effect; rounded bonhomie thanks to grain sugar. 8 mths Fr wood, 20% unoaked. **Sauvignon Blanc** ★★★★ ✓ Expressive 'Loire on steroids' styling continues with **06**, pungent capsicum/green fig whiffs, zesty nettle palate. V good combo of minerality & juiciness. — *IvH*

■ *Goede Moed* see Baarsma
■ *Goedgenoegen* see Baarsma

Goedvertrouw Estate

Walker Bay ▪ Est 1990 ▪ 1stB 1991 ▪ Visits by appt ▪ Home-cooked meals & accommodation by appt ▪ Play area for children ▪ Farm produce ▪ Small conferences ▪ Conservation area ▪ Small art gallery ▪ Owner/winemaker/viticulturist Elreda Pillmann ▪ 8 ha (cab, pinot, chard, sauvignon) ▪ 70% red 30% white ▪ PO Box 37 Bot River 7185 ▪ Josiasfredin@mweb.co.za ▪ T/F (028) 284·9769

No update from this organically run estate near Bot River. The notes below are from last edition.

★★★★ **Cabernet Sauvignon** Native yeast-fermented (as are stable mates), matured ±yr seasoned Fr oak. **03** (sample) dense, ripe cassis fruit swathed in grainy tannins. **04** (★★★) leaner & more restrained; firm acid & dusty finish; unknit, needs yr/2 to marry.

Pinot Noir ★★★ Barrel sample **04** more 'correct' than pvs; fragrant mineral bouquet, hints game & damp earth; elegant, firm finish. Yr in old vats. **Chardonnay** Last sampled was **01** (★★★); next probably the **06**. **Sauvignon Blanc** Individual style, more 'white wine' than 'sauvignon'; **03** (★★★) was last tasted. **Pardoemps** ★★★ Once-off individual **03** blend pinot, pinotage, cab (50/25/25); onomatopoeic name a favourite of the late Arthur Pillmann's. —*MM*

Goedverwacht Estate ◊ 🍷 🦐

Robertson ▪ 1stB 1994 ▪ Tasting & sales Mon-Fri 8.30-4.30 Sat 10-2 ▪ Closed Easter Fri/Sun, Dec 25 & Jan 1 ▪ Tours by appt ▪ Snacks served with wine tasting; also BYO picnic ▪ Owner Jan du Toit & Sons (Pty) Ltd ▪ Winemaker Henry Conradie ▪ Viticulturist Jan du Toit, advised by Francois Viljoen ▪ 110 ha (cab, merlot, shiraz, chard, colombard, sauvignon) ▪ 1 500 tons 40 000 cs own label 43% red 50% white 7% rosé ▪ Exported as Soek die Geluk & Ama Ulibo ▪ PO Box 128 Bonnievale 6730 ▪ goedverwachtestate@lando.co.za ▪ www.goedverwacht.co. za ▪ T 023·616·3430 ▪ F 023·616·2073

New winemaker Henry Conradie (ex-Langverwacht, where he was assistant) waxes lyrical about his first harvest on the farm of Jan du Toit *et famille*: 'In terms of quality of fruit, it was just in another league, one of the best in a decade.' The estate's first barrel fermented Chardonnay was released late last year, to twin with the Maxim Cab as a flagship wine. Jan dT is now wearing the viti hat; last year he planted limited amounts of chenin and sauvignon.

★★★★ **Triangle** ✓ Refined cab s/f & merlot blend, each judiciously oaked prior to blending: 41/10/49 mix in latest **04**, after **03** (★★★★) first to feature cab f. Berry-filled **04** back on track with velvet texture & flavour packed body; delicious now, shd improve over 4-6yrs.

Shiraz Rosé ☺ ★★★ Brightly coloured & flavoured as ever. **06** well balanced, nicely dry with tangy lift to tail. **Crane White Colombar** ☺ ★★★ Easy & early summer-sipping pleasure. **06** brisk & vibrant; tempts with guava, pineapple & passionfruit.

Maxim Cabernet Sauvignon Following on maiden **03** (★★★★ VDG), raises bar with **04** (★★★★): suave mulberry & cherry mingle with smoky, cedary notes; stylish tannins suggest 4-6 yr ageing potential. From south-facing single vyd. 24 mths new Fr oak. 14.5% alc. **Crane Red Merlot** ★★★ Preview **05**, tasted mid-2005, was plump, with soft tannins. **Acre of Stone Shiraz** ★★★★ **05** ever improving as vyd matures. Darkly attractive, almost brooding; black choc, bramble & liquorice bouquet intrigues, then well judged oak (9 mths, none new) & silky farewell please the palate. **Great Expectations Chardonnay** ★★★ A consistent performer; **06** delicate lemon/lime freshness brushed by light wooding (subtly used oak staves); hides 14.5% alc well. **The Good Earth Sauvignon Blanc** ★★★ Underplayed flavours & nervy acidity of **06** lifted & smoothed by hint sugar. **Suiderkruis Vonkel** new ★★★ Attractive carbonated sparkler from 50/50 sauvignon/colombard. **05** 'puts a smile on your dial' with its creamy mousse, lively acidity & tropical tones. —*DH*

■ **Goeie Tye** see Rooiberg
■ **Golden Kaan** see KWV Ltd
■ **Golden Triangle** see Stellenzicht
■ **Gordon's Bay** see Zidela

Goudini Wines 🍷 🥃 🦐

Rawsonville (see Worcester map) ▪ Est 1948 ▪ Tasting & sales Mon-Fri 8-5 Sat 9.30-12.30 ▪ Closed Easter Fri-Mon, Dec 25/26, Jan 1 ▪ Coffee shop ▪ Conferences ▪ Gifts ▪ Owners 40 members ▪ Cellarmaster Hennie Hugo (Dec 1984) ▪ Senior winemaker Dominique Waso (Oct 2001), with Ruaan Terblanche & Samuel Viljoen (Nov 2001/Sep 2004) ▪ Viti advisor Hendrik Myburgh (Nov 2001) ▪ 1 040 ha (merlot, ruby cab, shiraz, chard, chenin, semillon) ▪ 20 000 tons 33 000 cs own label 45% red 45% white 10% rosé ▪ PO Box 132 Rawsonville 6845 ▪ winesales@goudiniwine.co. za ▪ www.goudiniwine.co.za ▪ T 023·349·1090 ▪ F 023·349·1988

The purchase of a new electro-dialysis machine affords a much gentler approach to cold stabilisation (no need to 'shock' the wines at -4°C) and cellarmaster Hennie Hugo is pleased

www.peugeot.co.za

Let it breathe

407 Coupé

PEUGEOT

While the 2006 harvest ripened on the vine, Crossroads Wines' creative director **Simphiwe Mavuya** (right) and sales manager **Patrick Danster** showed their company's 'proudly African' wines to customers and potential outlets around the Cape Peninsula. Judging from the reaction of winelover **Oscar Marshall** (left), the Robben Island Red and Soweto White poured on this happy occasion were an instant hit.

A backdrop of semi-arid scrubland tells you this is low-rainfall country – ideal for growing wine without pesticides or other chemical interventions. Which is what the Rossouw family and their international network of partners do here at Stellar Winery, SA's largest organic producer, on the Olifants riverbanks. Overseeing 100ha of vines is diminutive **Maria Malan**, who started here as a domestic worker 30 years ago, seen with winemaker **Dudley Wilson** and, in the foreground, one of the resident 'organic' pest control units.

Stockist of a wide variety of Quality
South African & Imported Wines
including Nederburg Auction Wines

For the **BEST** Prices in Town

cybercellar.co.uk

cybercellar.co.za

cybercellar.com/eu

cybercellar.us

cybercellar.ie

cybercellar●com

wineonline.co.za

johnplatter.co.za
platteronline.com
platters.co.za
platterwineguide.com

umkhulu.com

sa-wine.com

tastesouthafrica.com

Family farms such as Bordeaux, represented by owner **Deon Bruwer** (left), are birthplace to the succulently sweet Muscat de Frontignan, flagship wine of Montagu-based cellar Uitvlucht. Rejuvenation has seen a new, younger team take charge of the winery, under the baton of manager **Jacques Jordaan**, their goal to encourage consumers to venture beyond the conventional 'winter warmer' paradigm for muscadel and try it, among others, over ice as a trendy summer refresher.

Want help selecting the best Bordeaux blend? Just ask **John** or Jack or Graham or Nick or Michelle or Cherryl or Craig or Werner or Pietie or Allan or Andre or Emily or Tess or Leon or Deanne or Nuha or Warren or Lindsay or Judy or Rory or Kevin or Anne or Clinton or Lynne or Jeanette or Lindelwa or Tracy or Colin or Sandi or Murielle or Gigi or Farieda or Philadi or Andrew or Gillian or Lyall or Kerry or Francois or Patrick or Anthony or Grant or Brad or Carey or Selwyn or Rodney or Adrian or Richard or Gareth or Ryan or Anton or Neil or Jenny or Kim or Thomas or Lucy or Alex or Bianca or Steven or Sharon or Blanche or Allison or Brandon or Chris or Anna or Elton or Cindy or Frank or Jason or Keith or Zoe or Megan or Scott or Miles or Warren or Sarah or Robynne or Chad or Christiaan or Vincent. Now you can find out what your fellow wine lovers think of the world's leading vintages. Log on to winesense.co.za to access their personal tasting notes on everything from the pride of Paarl to the best of Bordeaux. Or visit our tasting rooms, sample our fine selection and then submit your very own tasting notes.

winesense™
www.winesense.co.za

Observant readers will note that the implements in the hands of Solms-Delta farm manager **Nico Jansen** (left front) and viticultural adviser **Paul Wallace** aren't the usual secateurs – they're pliers, here used for the unusual purpose of pinching the stems a portion of the grape bunches, causing the berries to dry on the vine and so intensify their luscious flavours. It's an ancient winegrowing technique harnessed with exciting results by co-owner and world renowned neuroscientist **Mark Solms**, pictured in the shiraz vineyard near the old manor house with navy-shirted winemaker **Hilko Hegewisch**.

0860 360 360 ☎

THE VINEYARD
CONNECTION

VISIT US
TASTE
BUY
FREIGHT

EXPORTERS OF WINES FROM THE CAPE

TO CAPE TOWN
R44 TO PAA
exit 47
N1
R101 KLAPMI
KLAPMUTSKOP
LIEVLAN
MULDERSVLEI ROAD
THE VINEYAR
CONNECTIO
AT DELVER
R44 KANONKOP
BOTTELARY ROAD
SIMONSIG TO STELLENBOSCH
KROMME RHEE ROAD

OPEN 7 DAYS A WEEK

wine shop .co.za

with the resultant quality improvement in his 2006 harvest. The focus here is on the local market (which grew around 30% last year) and on building a reputation for value for money wines within the reach of many consumers, rather than a small, affluent niche.

Reserve range

Ruby Cabernet ★★★☆ **04** yet to be bottled; last ed's sample was a generous varietal expression of sweet ripe plum, touches stalk & thatch, well massaged tannins/oak (some new, some Am). No **03**. **Chardonnay Barrel Fermented** discontinued.

Goudini range

> **Ruby Cabernet-Merlot** ☺ ★★★ Unoaked **05** ups ante; 55/45 mix, with thatch & lavender scents, choc-toffee flavours given grip by healthy tannins. Portion thermo-vinified. **Ruby Cabernet-Merlot Semi-Sweet** new ☺ ★★★ Same plummy character as dry version; **05**'s sweet fillip (18g/ℓ sugar) adds roundness, downplays any possible 'stalkiness'. **Brut Sparkling** ☺ ★★★ Carbonated **NV** bubbly from sauvignon; creamy mousse harbours intense gooseberry & capsicum character. Wrapped in 'shrink-sleeve', still only one in SA. **Natural Sweet** ☺ ★★★ Honey-toned **06** brightly fruited & engaging, zippy. From chenin.

Pinotage ★★★☆ ✓ Concours Mondial gold winner **05** leap-up in quality; abundant plums & choc-banana whiffs, very satisfying, with agile tannins. Yr oak, some new, 10% Am. **Shiraz** ★★★ **04** pvs ed a sample, now has supple tannins, loaded with peppery varietal fruit. Mix seasoned Am/Fr (60/40) oak. **Blanc de Noir** ★★ **05** light salmon-hued, gentle strawberry toned tipple. From cinsaut; off-dry. **Unwooded Chardonnay** ★★☆ **06** brims with tropical fruit; lively & flavoursome for this-year pleasure; bold 14.4% alc well tucked in. **Chenin Blanc** ★★ **06** slips down easily with fresh guava & passionfruit aromas; nearly dry at 6.5g/ℓ sugar. **Sauvignon Blanc** ★★ Vibrant **06** has lots of freshness, greenpepper/cut grass bounce. **Hanepoot** ★★★★ ✓ **05** luxuriously scented, with muscat & honeysuckle flavours. Alc down to 16% alc from pvs 17%. **Port** ★★★☆ Preview **02** reveals characterful choc-prune & smoke aromas, generous fruity palate, lengthy dry finish. Low for style 18% alc.

Umfiki range

> **Cabernet Sauvignon** new ☺ ★★★ Smooth, berry toned easy-drinker: what more to ask at this price? W Cape WO. **Merlot** ☺ ★★★ Latest lifts the bar; still unwooded, overflows with plums, violets & choc. Well-rounded, with agile tannins. **Pinotage-Cinsaut** ☺ ★★★ Attractive quaffer waving flag for pinotage: strawberries, tobacco; lively acid lift in its tail. **Sauvignon Blanc** new ☺ ★★★ Crisp & animated flavours for summer sipping; light-hearted — & lightish 12% alc too.

Clairette Blanche-Colombar ★★ Honest, zippy tropical blend, 50/50. **Dry White** ★★ Pretty & floral sipping for summer (might not keep its charm till autumn). All **NV**. – —*DH*

Goudveld Winery

*Free State (see Northern Cape/Free State map) ▪ Tasting & sales Mon-Fri 8-6 Sat by appt ▪ Tours on request ▪ Owner: see intro ▪ Winemaker/viticulturist Merkil Alers (1985), advised by Ian Sieg ▪ 15 ha ▪ 120 tons 1 000 cs own label ▪ PO Box 1091 Welkom 9460 ▪ **T 082·783·8272***

Pending change of ownership, business plans for Goudveld are in place and include a cellar upgrade and modernisation of the entire operation. New consultant winemaker Ian Sieg, who also lectures in vini/viticulture at the Free State's University of Technology, is looking forward to this challenge. 'I have a bit of experience of winemaking in summer rainfall areas…' he comments with understatement, as his 22 years as winemaker at Landzicht on the Northern Cape/Free State border and six seasons in Zimbabwe testify.

■ **Goue Vallei** *see Citrusdal Cellars*
■ **Goiya** *see WestCorp*

Graça

Vinho verde-inspired, lightly spritzy swiggers, the original white version still among SA's top-selling cork-closed wines. By Distell; exported as Blouberg.

Graça ★★ Crowd pleasing, light-bodied (11.8% alc), seafood-amenable tipple with thatch & hay nose, grassy flavours/zippy finish from sauvignon (60%, with semillon, crouchen). **Rosé** ★★ Now drier, still low alc (±11%). Mainly sauvignon; dollop pinotage giving healthy salmon colour & raspberry notes. Also in 375ml. Both **NV**; WO W Cape. — *CvZ*

Graceland Vineyards

Stellenbosch • Est 1997 • 1stB 1998 • Tasting & sales Mon-Fri 9-5 • Fee R30 • Closed pub hols • Two-bedroom B&B + self-catering vyd cottage • Owners Paul & Susan McNaughton • Winemaker/ viticulturist Susan McNaughton (2001) • 10 ha (cab, merlot, shiraz) • 60 tons 4 300 cs 100% red • PO Box 7066 Stellenbosch 7599 • graceland@iafrica.com • www.gracelandvineyards.com • T 021·881·3121 (admin) 021·881·3394 (cellar) • F 021·881·3341

Paul and Susan McNaughton admit that the strong rand has meant some biting of the proverbial bullet. But in no way is this going to affect quality. On the contrary, the 04 Three Graces was not up to scratch and not released. Better news: two new cab blocks are showing great promise, and Pasha, an Anatolian sheepdog, has been added to the valued canine squad. 'One of the most important winemaking principles remains that the grapes are ready to pick when the dogs start eating them,' chortle the McNaughtons.

- ★★★★ **Three Graces** Flagship blend, the varietal trio being cab (59%), shiraz (22%), merlot in **03** (tasted last ed). Restrained but ample fruit; oak evident but integrates components into food-friendly whole; persistent spiciness, succulence.

- ★★★★ **Cabernet Sauvignon** Fermented in traditional open *kuipe*. **04**'s ripe black fruit aromas integrating well in unshowy, elegant whole, with ample tannins, gd 18 mths oaking (mostly Fr, 30% new).

Merlot Showily opulent **03** (★★★★) followed by step-up **04** (★★★★), elegantly fruited with bright plum notes. Shows sweet mid-palate fruit, silky tannins, plus refined vanilla notes ex-14 mths oak, 27% new. **Shiraz** ★★★★ **04** raspberry whiffs, almond vanilla notes (announcing 18 mths in Fr wood, 30% new) adding spice, textured tannins carrying evident 14.5% alc well. — *MF*

Graham Beck Wines

Franschhoek/Robertson • Est 1983 • 1stB 1991 • Owner Graham Beck • Cellarmaster Pieter Ferreira (Aug 1990) • Viticulturist Marco Ventrella (Sep 2004) • ISO 14001 certified • market@grahambeckwines.co.za • www.grahambeckwines.com • Robertson Estate: Tasting & sales Mon-Fri 9-5 Sat & 1st Sun of mth 10-3 • Closed Easter Fri/Sun, Dec 25/26 & Jan 1 • Tours by appt • Winemaker Irene Waller (Dec 2004) • 168 ha (cab, merlot, pinot, sangiovese, shiraz, chard, viognier) • 1 500 tons • 45% red 20% white 35% MCC • PO Box 724 Robertson 6705 • T 023·626·1214 • F 023·626·5164 • Franschhoek Estate: Tasting & sales Mon-Fri 9-5 Sat 10-4 • Closed Easter Fri/Sun, Dec 25/26 & Jan 1 • Tours by appt • Winemaker Erika Obermeyer (Jan 2005) • 158 ha (cabs s/f, merlot, petit v, pinotage, shiraz, sauvignon, viognier) • 1 200 tons • PO Box 134 Franschhoek 7690 • T 012·874·1258 • F 021·874·1712

'Pieter Ferreira is the finest maker of fizz in SA,' avers *The Daily Mail*'s Matthew Jukes. 'The stunning Blanc de Blancs puts Champagne to shame.' Deserved praise for the long-resident winemaker whose skill, in tandem with Irene Waller and Erika Obermeyer, extends across the range. SA's second Biodiversity & Wine Initiative (BWI) 'Champion' — nearly half its Robertson farm was set aside for protection of renosterveld, succulent Karoo and critically endangered fynbos vegetation — boasts a gamekeeper-in-residence, conservationist Mossie Basson. The winery also wants to set a 'prime example of educating the local community' by building a skills centre for Robertson Valley's folk. The Franschhoek cellar complex gets a new tasting facility and, since its visitors' centre 'lies at the gateway of the Cape's gastronomic capital', this too is being spruced up.

Single Vineyard range

★★★★☆ **The Ridge Syrah** Icon wine named after its Rbtsn vyd. With finesse & style, **03** (not retasted) doesn't put a foot wrong; prosciutto, black plums, mocha choc held in place by elegant, harmonious structure. 14 mths 60/40 new Am/Fr oak assists 6-8 yr ageing potential. **02** Winemakers Choice.

★★★★ **Coffeestone Cabernet Sauvignon** From Sbosch decomposed granite 'coffee stone'. **03** last yr showed admirable concentration, cassis/blackberries, liquorice spice, smoky depths. Serious oaking (15 mths, mainly new) evident as steely backbone, cloaked by lush fruit. 10 yr development ahead. *Wine* ★★★★.

★★★★ **The Old Road Pinotage** From 1963-planted, low-yielding Fhoek vines. **02** (not retasted) sinuous structure, complex interweaving of sweet & savoury spices; concentrated red berry fruit, easily assimilated yr Fr/Am barriques. Pinotage Top Ten.

★★★★ **Lonehill Chardonnay 05**, from a Rbtsn mountainside single vyd, has hazelnuts & lime peel to sniff, lightly toasty oak on creamy, succulent, full flavoured palate. As usual, bunch pressed, fermented/10 mths Fr barrels, 80% new.

★★★★ **Pheasants' Run Sauvignon Blanc** (Gremlins had 'Peasant's Run' pvs ed!) Sample of tingling, satisfying **06**: nettles, gooseberries, greenpepper aplenty in concentration; hits the spot firmly & directly. Dbnvlle grapes. Sense-awakening **05**, also tasted as sample; VDG, MIWA DG, Winemakers Choice.

★★★★ **Rhona Muscadel** Unusually elegant version, though still richly sweet; generously released late, when fruit & spirit integrated. **02**'s perfumed muscatty, grapey, floral notes deepened by marmalade – also a mature terpene hint. 16.5% well calculated for lift, but greater acidity would have added zip. 500ml.

Barrel Select range

★★★★☆ **The William** Named for a Beck grandson. Barrel selected 60/40 blend cab, pinotage, vinified separately at Rbtsn & Fhoek cellars before blending. **03** rich dark fruit, meat extract, lashings oak spice. Sleekly muscular; drink now if you must, but shd develop beautifully 8+ yrs. WO Coastal. **02** (★★★★ but Winemakers Choice) needed time to meld, soften. Yr oak: Fr (cab)/Am (pinotage). All this range not retasted.

★★★★ **The Joshua** Adopts Beck's second name. Cellar flagship, with price to match. 9% viognier in **03** – varieties crushed, fermented together – not to soften but to bring perfume, more complexity. Tasted few yrs back, very ripe (enormous 15.5% alc) sour cherry, roasted spice flavours. Yr Fr/Am barrels, 60/40, promising 6+ yrs development. VDG. Fhoek.

★★★★ **The Andrew** Cellar's first bdx-style blend (cab, merlot, cab f: 41/35/24), another Beck grandson behind name. Serious, classy **03** (not retasted) with cassis, savoury spice & meat extract complexity, polished, sleekly appealing texture from supple tannins, & gd length. Yr Fr oak, 60% new. WO Coastal.

Graham Beck range

★★★★ **Cabernet Sauvignon** Serious & classic **01** tasted few yrs back. Latest **02** (★★★★☆) also elegantly built, reveals difficult yr with an edge of vegetal dankness to attractive aromas/flavours of valiantly succulent dark berry fruit. 14 mths Fr oak. WO Coastal (as Shiraz below); all others in range WO W Cape except where noted.

★★★★ **Shiraz 03** had dollops other varieties; mildly spicy **04** (★★★★☆) all ultra-ripe shiraz; fruity & chunky, with big stand-apart acidity rather than real freshness. 13 mths mostly Am oak; 14.8% alc.

★★★★☆ **Brut Blanc de Blancs** MCC from chard, amongst Cape's most celebrated & most used for classy celebrating. **01** maturing splendidly – shd reward further keeping with more complexity. As shd **02** – also rich but dry, verve-ful, but more rapier-like in its acidic thrust, apple-freshness. 50% of bunch-pressed grapes fermented in oak; ±4 yrs on lees adds to breadth/depth. WO Rbtsn. **99** *Wine* ★★★★, **00** Santé Classic gold.

★★★★ **Brut** Dependably delicious & stylish NV MCC. Lively, lightly rich & dry, generous, with classic yeast-hinting apple pie character. Dry but not tart. 10% 'reserve' wine, blended in with younger pinot, chard for consistency. **94** *Wine* ★★★★ in 2006.

★★★★ **Brut Rosé** Unique, says Peter F, through mixing bunches pinot/chard before crushing, rather than blending base wines. 20 mths on lees before disgorgement. Pinot (70%) gives **04**'s lovely partridge eye colour & earthy, raspberry, floral grace-notes. Interesting, nervy, high-strung wine, more piercing than versions above.

Merlot ★★★ Blend of wines vinified at both cellars. **04** in restrained, cool fruit style: violets, red berries, herbaceous thread & juicy palate in light tannin framework. Tasted last ed, as was ... **Shiraz-Cabernet Sauvignon** ★★★ UK only. Pepper & soft plummy fruit in accessible **04**; supportive tannins; 9 mths Fr/Am oak. **Pinotage** ★★★☆ Subtly wooded (13 mths mostly Am) **05**, tasted from barrel, has 5% each cab, tannat; gd red fruit but savoury too, nicely balanced with firm, slightly dry tannins. WO Coastal. **Railroad Red** ★★★☆ Smoky, spicy **05** again blends happily 60/40 shiraz, cab. An agreeable, elegantly styled food partner, with juicy fruit well supported by gd tannin, lightly oaked. **Pinno Pinotage** Sample **05** promises to be particularly charming example of unwooded & fruit-focused pinotage, with gentle tannic grip — likely ★★★. **Cabernet Sauvignon-Merlot** new ★★★ Slightly lean, lightly wooded 60/40 **03** blend, with subdued fruitcake notes accompanied by drying tannins. Respectable, if unexciting. **Pinno Rosé** ★★★ Copper-glinting light red **06** is berry-fragrant, flavourful, just off-dry, with a bit of substance to it. WO Rbtsn. **Chardonnay** ★★★☆ With tropical, peach notes, **05** nicely rounded, but good citrus bite aiding food-friendliness, as does usual judicious oaking (6 mths, 40% new). WO Rbtsn. **Chardonnay-Viognier** ★★★☆ Beautifully managed & vibrantly fresh blend for export, **06** with 16% viognier adding peach, floral fragrance, chardonnay in charge of balanced structure. **Sauvignon Blanc** ★★★☆ Forthcoming **06**, (ex-tank) grassy character, figs & tropical fruit on the side. Satisfyingly bone-dry. WO Coastal, as is... **Viognier 04** sample (★★★★) showed early promise; bottled **05** (★★★★) impresses even more with deliciously tasty, silky charm, more tactful in apricot/petal fragrance than many examples, well matched with oak's slight toastiness (50/50 barrel/tank). **Waterside Chardonnay** ★★★ **06**'s white peach character untrammelled by wood; altogether softly, smoothly fresh & easy-going. Has dollop colombard. **Pinno Chardonnay** ★★★ Unoaked, for USA only; **05**'s peachy flavours last ed given lift by crisp acidity. — *TJ*

Grande Provence

Franschhoek ▪ Est 1694 ▪ Tasting & sales daily 10-6 ▪ Fee R20 ▪ Tours Mon-Fri 11 & 3 ▪ 'The Restaurant' & 'The Owners Cottage' (see Stay-over & Eat-out sections) ▪ Fine art exhibit in 'The Gallery' ▪ Winemaker/viticulturist Jaco Marais (Oct 2003), advised by Kevin Watt (2001) ▪ 22 ha (cab, merlot, petit v, shiraz, chard, sauvignon) ▪ 250 tons 25 000 cs own labels 35% red 55% white 10% rosé ▪ PO Box 102 Franschhoek 7690 ▪ winesales@grandeprovence.co. za ▪ www.grandeprovence.co.za ▪ T 021-876-8600 ▪ F 021-876-8601

The extensive physical changes at this property in 2004 have moved to the wines, with Jaco Marais, recipient of the General Smuts Trophy at the 2005 Young Wine Show, developing a new Premier range of four single-variety wines from grapes sourced from Franschhoek and Elim, all sporting screwcaps. He also added a Sauvignon to the popular Angels Tears range, which got new-look 'sassy yet classical' labels. Meanwhile, the hospitality side of this upmarket spread made Condé Nast Traveller's 2006 Hot List of the top 60 new hotels worldwide.

Premier range

★★★★ **Cabernet Sauvignon** Well & seamlessly constructed **04**; dark-fruited, elegantly fleshed, with pronounced cool minty tone. Ready, shd continue improving over several yrs. 15 mths new Fr barrels.

★★★★ **Shiraz 04**, retasted (ditto above Cab), has over-delivered on initial promise. Savoury/aromatic styling, swirls smoke & dried herbs, copious vanilla spice from new oak (15 mths, 85/15 Fr/Am), sweet-fruited finish. Bit calculated, but the crowds won't mind. SAYWS gold.

Chardonnay ★★★ **04** sample last ed, shows maturing butterscotch tone, toasty flavours with some citrus fruit; turning savoury — drink soon. 11 mths Fr oak, 60% 1st fill. **Sauvignon Blanc** ★★★☆ **05** (sample) showed classic sauvignon character, minerality & freshness. Powerhouse **06** (also sample) raises the bar with blast of pungent varietal aromas, flavours (incl tinned peas, nettles). Rousing, athletic white from cool Elim vyds. Likely ★★★★.

Angels Tears range

Red ★★★ Pvs bottling (**NV**) was this guide's first 'Superquaffer of Year'; the new version still merlot/cab blend, still all previous easy drinking attributes in tad more subdued, streamlined form; 8 mths oak, 60/40 Fr, Am. **Pink** ★★★ Easy drinker from chenin with dollop pinotage, off-dry. Current bottling (**NV**) forthcoming sweet strawberry aromas; soft, rounded fruit-gum flavours. Light 12.5% alc. **Sauvignon Blanc** ★★★ [new] 06 supple, quaffable, with leafy freshness & riper hint gooseberry, smooth lemony finish. **White** ★★★ Uncomplicated off-dry, fruity white. Latest **NV** works its chenin/hanepoot charms with grapey, musk-sweet aromatics, softly rounded drinkability. Low alc as for Pink. All in this range WO W Cape. — *CR*

Grand Mousseux

Anytime, anywhere non-vintage carbonated bubbly by Distell. **Vin Doux** ★★ Rather shy for a sparkler — fleeting honeycomb & pear whiffs — titillating mousse, soft sweetness (32g/ℓ). — *CvZ*

Grangehurst Winery

Stellenbosch (see Helderberg map) ▪ *1stB 1992* ▪ *Tasting & sales Mon-Fri 9-4 Sat, Sun & pub hols 'take a chance' 10-4* ▪ *Self-catering Grange Cottage* ▪ *Owner Grangehurst Winery (Pty) Ltd* ▪ *Winemaker Jeremy Walker, with Gladys Brown (1992/2002)* ▪ *Viti consultant Thys Greeff* ▪ *±14 ha (cab, merlot, mourvèdre, petit v, pinotage, shiraz)* ▪ *70 tons 3 200-4 000 cs 100% red* ▪ *PO Box 206 Stellenbosch 7599* ▪ *winery@grangehurst.co.za* ▪ *www.grangehurst.co.za* ▪ **T 021·855·3625** ▪ *F 021·855·2143*

'Exporting wine to France is like selling ice to Eskimos,' says Jeremy Walker. But he was persuaded to do just that by three influential Frenchmen who visited last year: wine journal editor Denis Saverot, chef-sommelier Christian Martray and Oliver Poussier (World's Best Sommelier 2000). No doubt they appreciated the 'French style with fruit', as one UK buyer describes the wines. 'My intention is that Grangehurst always remains red,' says Walker, though this hasn't stopped him 'tinkering around' with a Rosé, bottled under the Woodhill label (see separate entry), which could eventually include an inexpensive red and white, all under screwcap. Other plans include relocating the tasting room to a prime spot with superb views, and converting the existing tasting room and offices into self-catering cottages.

★★★★☆ **Nikela** Richly austere in youth, ageworthy **01** has intense, winning aromas/flavours, bdx-like & meaty on nose, some sweet jam added on palate. Always ±50% cab, with merlot, pinotage — latter 31% (38% in engaging **00**). Luxury velvet of ripe, well extracted fruit, firm structure abetted by 22 mths oak, mostly Fr. Some will discern bitter note on finish.

★★★★☆ **Cabernet Sauvignon-Merlot** Authoritative & satisfying, sombrely rich fruit balanced with grippy tannins, savoury acid. Big, still-young **01** (72% cab), offering dusty, spicy blackcurrant, fits fine pattern. 14.2% alc. 2 yrs oak (mostly Fr) well integrated. Shd grow over a decade.

★★★★☆ **Cabernet Sauvignon Reserve** Pvs mostly under CWG Auction label; **02** (★★★★) interesting, gd & rich for lesser vintage, well structured with big dry tannins. **03** less austere, but forceful, even richer: big 14.8% alc balanced by dark-toned succulence of mouthfilling, generous fruit. From 3 prime Sbosch vyds. 25 mths Fr oak. Designed to mature decade; then, as Jeremy W says, 'to enjoy with fine cuisine'.

★★★★☆ **Shiraz-Cabernet Sauvignon Reserve** [new] **03** brighter, sweeter, lighter-seeming, though more forthright tannins than pure Cab — 55% shiraz generous with sweet, spicy red fruit, cab commanding the serious structure. Again, more than simply a stayer: shd develop. 28 mths mainly Fr oak.

★★★★ **Pinotage** Serious-minded version, with some cab — 11% in **01**. Gd varietal aromas lead to powerful, sweetly fruity flavours awaiting integration with big dry tannins. Impressive & rather tough mid-2006; few yrs shd do some softening. Like others, fermented in open tanks, then to basket press.

★★★★ **CWG Auction Reserve Cape Blend** Characterful, serious & long lived melding pinotage, cab & shiraz; **03** (★★★★★) gavelled at latest Auction, near-equal mix, pinotage just ahead. Delicious & sweet fruited, supported by ripe tannins, untroubling 14.8% alc. Similarly flavourful **01**, elegant structure rhymes with slightly bigger cab portion (49%). Like all Walker's wines, genuinely dry.

Cabernet Sauvignon ★★★★ Label re-emerges after many yrs with tobacco-spicy **01**. Restrained, austerely balanced, dryly tannic — fruit lurks, perhaps to fully emerge in few yrs. 2 yrs oak, mostly Fr. — *TJ*

■ *Griekwaland West Co-op* see Douglas
■ *Groblershoop* see Oranjerivier Wine Cellars
■ *Groenekloof* see Darling Cellars, Neil Ellis, The Company of Wine People, Woolworths

Groenendal Farm

Wellington ▪ Est/1stB 2003 ▪ Tasting & sales by appt Mon-Fri 9-5 ▪ Fee R10 ▪ Closed pub hols ▪ Tours by appt ▪ Owners Jan & Anita Bokdal ▪ Winemakers Tiaan Ellis & consultant (Oct 2005) ▪ Viticulturist Tiaan Ellis (Oct 2005) ▪ 4.6 ha (mourvèdre, shiraz) ▪ 30 tons 1 900 cs 100% red ▪ Export brands: Andreas & Ardens Andreu ▪ PO Box 892 Wellington 7654 ▪ andreas@ezinet. co.za ▪ **T** *021·873·2286 ▪* F *021·873·2268*

These shiraz specialists pay tribute to former owner, Hennie Andrews, who converted the old guava orchard and juice factory into a wine farm, with its farmhouse dating back to 1799. 'His passion and drive created Groenendal and put its wine on the map,' they say, adding that they'll be sticking to a winning recipe, working with nature and intervening as little as possible to make 'beautiful' shiraz, thereby realising their lifelong ambition to produce something that could be shared with others for years to come.

Andreas Shiraz ★★★★ Showy, outgoing **04** from Wllngtn grapes, has lots of ripe plum, raspberry fruit, effectively presaging the richly textured palate (with evident 14.2% alc). Yr Fr/Am oak; unfiltered. MIWA DG. **Andreu Shiraz** ★★★ **03** robust & rustic, with black berry fruit, some rhubarb notes; dense, silky tannins, finishing with cardamom spice. WO Coastal. — *MF*

Groenland

Stellenbosch ▪ Est 1932 ▪ 1stB 1997 ▪ Tasting & sales Mon-Fri 10-4 Sat & pub hols 10-1 ▪ Fee for large groups ▪ Closed Easter Fri/Sun, Dec 25, Jan 1 ▪ Meals for 20-60 by appt ▪ Tours by appt ▪ Conference & reception facilities ▪ Owner Kosie Steenkamp ▪ Winemaker Kosie Steenkamp, with Piet Steenkamp (1975/2001) ▪ Viticulturists Kosie & Piet Steenkamp ▪ 152 ha (cab, merlot, pinotage, shiraz, chard, chenin, sauvignon) ▪ 1 200 tons 6 250 cs own label + 75 000 blts ▪ 100% red ▪ PO Box 4 Kuils River 7579 ▪ steenkamp@groenland.co.za ▪ www.groenland.co.za ▪ **T** *021·903·8203 ▪* F *021·903·0250*

Small quantities from the 2004 crush, specially selected by father-and-son team Kosie and Piet Steenkamp, were treated to maturation in 100% new barrels, then bottled and released under their inaugural Reserve label. Two new 5 000-litre stainless steel tanks provide additional facilities for individual handling of smaller volumes, aimed at a more exclusive clientele.

Reserve range

new

Antoinette Marié ★★★★ Softly elegant **04** equal portions shiraz, cab, merlot, same oaking as below but all new barrels, which show in creamy vanilla overlay to generous ripe fruit; savoury finish. **Cabernet Sauvignon** ★★★★ Dark & brooding **04** less herbal, more berry-fruited than version below. Well meshed wood (Fr barrels), protracted cassis farewell. **Shiraz** ★★★★ Appropriately, has more of everything than version below — incl structure & keepability. **04** peppery note to rounded mouthfeel, attractive oaky/savoury finish. Am barrels, yr. All new oak for these.

Groenland range

Antoinette Marié ★★★ Usually a blend of varieties below, **04** has less cab than pvs, more shiraz plus dollop merlot (34/50/16). Tad lighter than pvs but well integrated, smooth, satisfying. Yr oak, Fr/Am 60/40. **Cabernet Sauvignon ★★★ 04** has hallmark herbaceous scent & firm yet ripe tannins, long savoury-tobacco finish. Better meshed & more approachable than pvs. Yr Fr oak. **Shiraz ★★★ 04** in usual New World style: lots of fruit richness & sweet vanilla oak (Yr 80% Am/20% Fr); very pleasant now (& soon). Moderate alc a feature of both ranges. Untasted **Cape Port 01** (500ml) also available from the cellar door. — *MM*

Groot Constantia Estate

Constantia • Est 1685 • 1stB 1688 • Tasting & sales daily 9-6 (Oct-Apr) 9-5 (May-Sep) • Fee R22, R25 (tasting & tour) • Closed Easter Fri, Dec 25 & Jan 1 • Tours on hour (large groups plse book ahead), every hour 10-4; also 'theme' tours/tastings • Simon's at Groot Constantia Restaurant (T 021·794·1143); Jonkershuis Restaurant (see Eat-out section) • Tour groups • Gift shop • Conferencing • Walks • Museum • Managed by Groot Constantia ('Section 21' company) • Winemaker Boela Gerber (Jan 2001), with Michelle Rhodes • Viticulturist Callie Bröcker, advised by Johan Pienaar (1996) • ±90 ha (12 varieties, r/w) • 448 tons 40 000 cs 75% red 25% white • Private Bag X1 Constantia 7848 • enquiries@grootconstantia.co.za • www.grootconstantia.co.za • T 021·794·5128 • F 021·794·1999

With its many attractions, historic Groot Constantia continues to shine among Cape Town's top tourist destinations. But what's really exciting winemaker Boela Gerber at the moment (in a valley generally considered white-wine territory) is the estate's reds. 'They make themselves,' he says 'with a classically restrained complexity you can still enjoy into the second bottle.' With a 75:25 ratio, GC is redder than its neighbours, and investment in fermentation and barrel maturation capacity attest to its continuing commitment.

Gouverneurs range

★★★★   **Reserve** Flagship blend, **04** mainly cab (54%) & 3 other bdx reds. Sensuous mocha, dark fruit & spice; rich cassis flavours supported by fine, firm tannins; vigorous oaking. Harmonious & elegant, accessible now, shd improve over next 5+ yrs. Merlot 23%, rest cab f & malbec. Swiss gold winner **03** showed same classic elegance.

★★★★   **Merlot** Unfiltered (as above) dense core of **03** heralds rich, bold, spicy plum pudding fruit. Plushly textured with integrated tannins providing structure. Serious oaking for these reds: 18 mths 100% new Fr.

★★★★   **Chardonnay** Similarly huge whack of oak on **05** as **04**, needing time to integrate (10 mths 60% new small Fr). Limpid gold, weighty in glass, shows ripe citrus peel & marmalade flavours beneath showy oak. Resolute, textured, lemony finish. Santé Classic, JCWCA gold/'first'.

Groot Constantia range

★★★★   **Sauvignon Blanc 06** exuberantly herbaceous, with trademark green fig, fresh vibrancy on palate with some fruit depth & breadth; pleasing minerality merging with crisp acidity on finish.

★★★★   **Grand Constance** Maiden **03** still available, flies flag for famous GC sweet muscat desserts of yesteryear. Sweet & seductive; satin textured with beguiling wafts fresh grape, litchi, tangerine peel & spice; ultra-long finish. Red & white muscat de F, oak fermented (none new), aged 18 mths.

Blanc de Noir ☺ **★★★ 06** pale onion-skin pink, freshly flavoured berry fruit from merlot/cab (60/40). Ideal for summer picnics, esp. low ±12%.

Cabernet Sauvignon Generously oaked **04** (**★★★★**) more leanly structured than luxurious **03** (**★★★★**), delicate raspberry fruit requires earlier drinking, though hearty tannins will preserve. 14 mths 40% new small Fr oak. **Merlot ★★★ 04** smoky oak aromas (from 15 mths Fr) mingle with plummy spiciness; structured ripe tannins embrace juicy plum fruit, with fine acidity adding elegance & freshness. **Pinotage ★★★ 04** more serious than fun, though attractively styled, with oak & redcurrant aromas, succulent flavours, solid & dry finish. Yr 40% new Fr; same for... **Shiraz** Sweet blackberry & caramelised sugar aromas, ripe fruit flavours lacking dimension on **04** (★★★). Classically constructed unshowy **03** (★★★★) exudes style. **Constantia Rood** ★★★ Multitude varieties in **04**, headed by shiraz/merlot for early, easy drinking, even though tannins, oak (15 mths older Fr), are evident. **Chardonnay** ★★★ Last tasted was distinctive **04**, ripe & fragrant mandarin & orange zest, modest oak (20%), fleshy yet lively. **Semillon-Sauvignon Blanc** ★★★☆ ✓ Bracing, grassy herbaceous **06**, with 60% dusty semillon, makes statement on entry but fades on finish; fine mineral acid backbone throughout. **Cap Classique** ★★★★ Last tasted was an **NV** (00); rich & not quite bone-dry. **Muscat** new ★★★ Barrel fermented/aged muscat in simple, sweet (101g/ℓ RS) grapey style; dried peach flavours, rich, not cloying. **NV. Cape Ruby Port** ★★★★ **03** almost equal blend pinotage, touriga, shiraz nearer a decently structured LBV style than ruby: sweet plum pudding, invitingly smooth & friendly. — *IM*

■ *Grootdrink* see Oranjerivier Wine Cellars

Groot Eiland Winery

*Breedekloof (see Worcester/Breedekloof map) ▪ Est 1962 ▪ 1stB 1980 ▪ Tasting & sales Mon-Fri 8-5 ▪ Tours by appt ▪ La Bri guest house (T 023·349·1547) ▪ Gifts ▪ Owners 30 members ▪ Winemakers Erik Schlünz & Albertus Louw (2000/2003), with Lindi Kotzé & Jacques Theron (both 2003) ▪ Viti consultant Johan Möller (2003) ▪ 1 000 ha (cab, merlot, pinotage, shiraz, chard, chenin, colombard, sauvignon) ▪ 50 000 cs own label 30% red 50% white 20% rosé ▪ PO Box 93 Rawsonville 6845 ▪ grooteiland@lando.co.za ▪ www.grooteiland.co.za ▪ **T 023 349·1140** ▪ F 023·349·1801*

Winemaker Erik Schlünz says its time to give more attention to local consumers, after bustling growth abroad. To this end, new marketers have been appointed. 'We're only bottling 2% under our own label,' ES explains, 'but it's growing nicely'. Exports are not getting the cold shoulder, however: Nuwehoop is the new range for European supermarkets. The tasting area has had a make-over and the La Bri guesthouse, owned by a member-grower, has opened on the next-door farm. At press time, news of their Merlot-Ruby Cab clinching the coveted General Smuts Trophy and SA Champion Red Blend titles at the National Young Wine Show had celebratory corks popping.

Cabernet Sauvignon ★★★ Brawny **04** with powerful tannic finish preceded by earthy scents, spicy blueberry tones. Tasted last ed, as was **Shiraz** ★★★ Sweet fruit & spicy oak on **04**, attractive savoury farewell, needing time for tannin to settle. **Merlot** ★★ Leafy bouquet & palate, tight & tarry tannins on **05**; more austere, fruit-shy, less supple than pvs. **Pinotage** ★★ Savoury & tight **05** has banana hints & just a little berry-fruitedness; alc ±14.5%, as for all these reds. **Rosé** ★★ Picnic-friendly semi-sweet summer quaffer. **06** with faint strawberry tones & hint of dried apricot. **Chardonnay** ★★ Early-drinking **05** pleasantly balanced, with citrus fruit, the sweetish note perhaps from big 14.6% alc. **Chenin Blanc** ★★ **06** refreshing & zesty pineapple scents & flavours; ideal as chilled partner to light summer salads; so too is… **Sauvignon Blanc** ★★ Early-drinking, rather shy **06** shot through with lemon/lime acidity, sherbety finish. **Honigtraube** ★★ Supple **04** from colombard with 15% chenin; last ed had forthcoming floral/honey aromas, easy uncloying sweetness. **Hanepoot Jerepigo** ★★★ Fortified raisin-scented dessert; **05**'s spirit, acidity & 16.6% alc twisted satisfactorily with fruit, giving tangy farewell.

Meander range

Fruity Red ★★ Undemanding early-drinker; **05** nicely fruity, touch sugar adds bounce & roundness. **Crisp Dry** ★★★ **04** from chenin — was living up to its name & tropical-fruity styling a few yrs back. **Fruity White** ★★ **05** floral & gently, unproblematically sweetish (16.9 g/ℓ RS) with honeysuckle nuances. Both ranges WO Goudini. — *CT*

Groote Post Vineyards

Darling (see Durbanville/Darling map) ▪ 1stB 1999 ▪ Tasting & sales Mon-Fri 9-5 Sat 9-2.30 Pub hols 9-5 ▪ Closed Easter Mon, Dec 25 & Jan 1 ▪ Fee R10 for groups of 10+ ▪ Hildas Kitchen Restaurant (see Eat-out section) or BYO picnic ▪ Tour groups (40 people) ▪ Conferencing ▪ Walks ▪ Game drives (T 022·492·2825) ▪ Conservation area & bird hide ▪ Owners Peter & Nich-

*olas Pentz ▪ Winemaker Lukas Wentzel (Nov 2000) ▪ Viticulturist Jannie de Clerk, advised by Johan Pienaar (1999) ▪ 117 ha (cabs s/f, merlot, pinot, shiraz, chard, chenin, sauvignon) ▪ 470 tons 28 000 cs 35% red 65% white ▪ PO Box 103 Darling 7345 ▪ wine@grootepost.co.za ▪ www.grootepost.com ▪ **T 022·492·2825** ▪ F 022·492·2693*

Quality wine production goes hand-in-hand with environmental conservation on historic Groote Post, whose massive 4 000ha spread includes 117ha of vines alongside 2 000ha dedicated to the UNESCO-proclaimed Cape West Coast Biosphere Reserve. Father-and-son team Peter and Nick Pentz are in hot pursuit of championship Biodiversity status — indigenous Swartland renosterveld and Atlantis fynbos is rich in buck and birds (accessible to visitors from a game vehicle/bird hide). Maturing vineyards (especially shiraz and sauvignon), and Pentz Snr's characterful anytime wine, The Old Man's Blend Red, particularly, are wooing winelovers. Adding allure is the eponymous restaurant, offering modern country cooking and a pastoral venue for weddings, small conferences and birthday parties.

★★★★ **Wooded Chardonnay 06** (sample) 80% new barrel fermentation/ageing imparts rich butterscotch, vanilla-infused caramel & lees character. Ripe pear fruit & hint sugar create sweet impression balanced by lipsmacking lime acidity. **05** sold out before we cld taste. Showy, sumptuous **04** *Wine* ★★★★.

★★★★ **Sauvignon Blanc Reserve** new The bottled quintessence of Darling! An array of cool scents excite & allure, incl fynbos, asparagus, lime & hints of minerals; focused deliciously crunchy flavours padded by lees-age richness & ±5g/ℓ sugar. **05** powerful Kiwi/SA crossover style, almost too intense for solo but great with gutsy food; great potential too.

Shiraz Ripe, rich style this yr (influence of portion Swtland fruit?), with arresting spicy, savoury & herbal scrub aromas. **04** vanilla nuances from oak (20% Am, 13 mths), peppery dark fruit still reined in by dry tannins. Sample shd rate at least ★★★★ when bottled. Youthfully taut **03** (★★★★) greatly impressed *Wine's* panel: ★★★★★. **Merlot** Previewed **04** (★★★★) needs 3/4 yrs to develop potential lurking in its minty dark fruit; lots of ripeness in evidence, but nicely controlled by cedary, dry tannins. Alc (14.5%) absorbed by concentration of fruit & oaking (20% new Fr, 14 mths) **Pinot Noir** Early barrel sample **06** seems bolder, riper, more New World. Enticing plummy red fruit & earthy forest-floor nuance. Hint of liquorice & unyielding tannic edge. Still integrating, hard to rate: minimum ★★★. 30% new oak, rest 2nd fill. **The Old Man's Blend (Red)** ★★★ A great fireside friend (optional 1.5ℓ format extends the conviviality). **05** (sample) accessible juicy melange mainly merlot, with cab, shiraz & pinot. Smooth, spicy & balanced, brushed with oak. WO Coastal. **Unwooded Chardonnay** ★★★★ **06** (sample) abounds with ripe pear & honey, additional creamy richness comes from 3 mths lees-ageing. Generous, rounded, suggestion sweetness from ripe fruit, alc (14%) & touch RS all balanced by limy flick. **Chenin Blanc** ★★★ **06** light styled (12.5% alc) gentle, fresh & fruitful, with ripe apple, pear & melon flavours best enjoyed this summer. Coastal bushvines. **Sauvignon Blanc** ★★★★ Delicious **06** offers widescreen capsicum, dusty fig leaf & nettle characters mingled with tangy lime zestiness on palate; refreshing & balanced, no edges. Nudges next rung up. Sleekly powerful & fresh **05** MIWA DG. **The Old Man's Blend (White)** ★★★ Summery aperitif-style **06**, sauvignon & chenin (70/30) with former's grassy aromas & latter's crisp ripe fruit, finishing with a fresh grapefruity twist. WO Coastal.— *MW*

Groot Parys

*Paarl ▪ Est 1699 ▪ 1stB 2003 ▪ Visits by appt ▪ Owners Eric Verhaak & Peter & Mariëtte Ras ▪ Vini consultant Naudé Bruwer ▪ Viti consultant Gawie Kriel ▪ 45 ha (ruby cab, chard, chenin, colombard) ▪ 550 tons ±1 500 cs ▪ PO Box 82 Huguenot 7645 ▪ grootparys@wam.co.za ▪ www.grootparys.co.za ▪ **T/F 021·872·7140***

A grand design here, beginning in 2002 with a gradual restoration of the balance of both soil and vines. The goal: 'Becoming in the near future one of the few specialists in the "truly SA" varieties of chenin and pinotage,' as co-owner Mariëtte Ras puts it. En route will be the certification, this year, of selected portions of the vineyards as organic. It's a cooperative effort — the cows contribute their manure and the ducks have been trained as a snail demolition squad.

Die Tweede Droom range

★★★★ **Chardonnay Wooded** new Impressive & well crafted **05**, tasted newly bottled, antithesis of Chenins below: opulent, weighty (15.2% alc), oak toast layered with creamy citrus fruit. Just two barrels, ex-'Miep's Blokkie' vyd, fermented/16 mths Fr oak, 50% 1st fill.

Chardonnay Unwooded ★★★☆ Last tasted was **04**, with more intensity, character than most. **Chenin Blanc Wooded** new ★★★☆ 10 mths oak (2nd fill Fr) imparts appealing fragrance, rotundity, to **05**; lovely sweet-straw/tropical fruit tone; more substance, mouthfeel, than 12.5% alc would suggest. Fruit off registered single vyd, as is... **Chenin Blanc Unwooded** ★★★ **05**, a sample last ed, still crisp, refreshing, cling peach hint; easy, but same low alc as above shows tad lean here. **06** to be bottled unfiltered; preview looks promising but too young to rate. — *CT*

Grünberger

Frankish 'bocksbeutel' bottles a nod to German oenologist Alfred Baumgartner, who originally developed this brand for the Bergkelder, now part of Distell. All are off-dry or semi-sweet, and quaffably light.

Rosenlese ★★ Natural Sweet gets its zest from sauvignon (80%); coral hue & raspberry flavours from ruby cab. **06** funfair nose, slippery palate. **Freudenlese** ★★ **06** also a Natural Sweet, also mainly sauvignon (70%). Gewürz/muscadel give raisin, honey notes. Blowsy palate lacks lead grape's zip. Following not retasted: **Stein** ★★ Semi-dry libation from chenin & sauvignon. **05** cheery, grassy, fresh. **Spritziger** ★★ Frothy poolside easy drinker, **05** with chenin's vivacious acidity. Screwcap. All WO W Cape. — *CvZ*

Grundheim Wines ◊ 🍸

*Little Karoo ▪ Est/1stB 1995 ▪ Tasting & sales Mon-Fri 8-5 Sat 9-1 ▪ Fee R10 for groups of 10+ ▪ Closed Easter Sun, Dec 25 & Jan 1 ▪ Owner Danie Grundling ▪ Winemaker Dys Grundling (1997) ▪ 25 ha (cinsaut, tinta, touriga, ruby cab, r/w muscadel, colombard, hanepoot, palomino) ▪ 360 tons 10 000ℓ for own labels 100% fortified ▪ PO Box 400 Oudtshoorn 6620 ▪ grundheim@absamail.co.za ▪ **T/F 044·272·6927***

Not content with producing a respectable range of fortified wines and liqueurs (winning two trophies in 2005 for 'best aged product' and 'best liqueur'), father-and-son team Danie and Dys Grundling recently decided to focus on making a good traditional potstill brandy. And what the Grundlings set their minds to, they're do well: Grundheim Potstill Brandy walked away with a gold medal at the Little Karoo Wine Show.

Red Muscat ★★★ Subtitled 'Muscat de Frontignan'. Well aged **95** lovely tawny hues; aromas of Karoo bush & raisins, soft caramel texture. ±17% alc. Not retasted. **Red Jerepigo** ★★★★ Delicious winter-warming **NV** from ruby cab, touriga & tinta, permeated with ripe, luscious blackcurrants & raisins. ±18% alc. 12 mths in barrel. **White Muscadel** ★★ Plump **06** has flavours & textures of liquid raisins, very soft acidity imparts little structure or refreshment. Ditto for... **Golden Jerepigo** ★★★ **04** a tad tired, syrupy. ±17% alc. **Cape Ruby Port** ★★★ Eccentric style: darker & richer than true Ruby, with notes of ground coffee & raisins; chunky & sweet, distinctly warming. **NV**. Also available: **Classic Red**, **Chenin Blanc**, **Late Harvest** & **Cape Vintage**. — *IvH*

■ *Guardian see* Du Toitskloof
■ *Guardian Peak see* Ernie Els Wines

Gusto Wines 🍸

*Stellenbosch ▪ Est 2001 ▪ 1stB 2002 ▪ Tasting by appt ▪ Owners PG Slabbert & Nicolette Waterford ▪ Winemaker Nicolette Waterford ▪ Viticulturist PG Slabbert ▪ 500 cs 30% red 70% white ▪ PO Box 6045 Uniedal 7612 ▪ wine@base4.co.za ▪ **T 082·807·4447** ▪ F 021·790·8000*

There are now two babies in Nicolette Waterford's life — her 50 sauvignon vines on the Waterfords' Llandudno property, and son Walter, born last year, three weeks after she'd put the finishing touches to the vintage. Looking after an infant, she admits with a smile, calls for much more effort than producing wine. But we think the lady doth protest too much: she finds time to act as consultant to several farms, as well as writing about wine and doing vino PR.

Sauvignon Blanc ★★★ **06** 's ripe sweet-fruited notes yield attractive quaffing wine, though not cultivar-typical. **Destino** ★★★★ Last tasted was unshowy **01**, firm merlot/cab blend. Both ex-Sbosch vyds. — *MF*

■ *Hagelsberg see* Middelvlei
■ *Hakuna Matata see* Remhoogte

Hamilton Russell Vineyards

Hemel-en-Aarde Valley (see Walker Bay map) ▪ *Est 1975* ▪ *1stB 1981* ▪ *Tasting & sales Mon-Fri 9-5 Sat 9-1* ▪ *Also tasting/sales of estate olive oil* ▪ *Closed Easter Fri/Sun, Dec 25/26 & Jan 1* ▪ *Tours by appt* ▪ *BYO picnic by appt* ▪ *Conservation area* ▪ *Owner Anthony Hamilton Russell* ▪ *Winemaker Hannes Storm (2004)* ▪ *Viticulturist Johan Montgomery (2005)* ▪ *52 ha (pinot, chard)* ▪ *150 tons 13 500 cs 40% red 60% white* ▪ *PO Box 158 Hermanus 7200* ▪ *hrv@ hermanus.co.za* ▪ **T 028·312·3595** ▪ *F 028·312·1797*

Anthony Hamilton Russell is unbundling. After 15 years of guiding one of the Cape's leading wineries, the eponymous Walker Bay estate founded by father Tim, HRV's second-generation custodian intends creating a vinous legacy for each of his four daughters. Accordingly HRV, home of internationally acclaimed Pinot and Chardonnay, has become the springboard for (to date) two standalone wine ventures, Ashbourne and Southern Right (see separate entries). Meanwhile, burnishing continues at the home farm. Two subtle but noteworthy steps forward in 2006 were no sterile filtration and significant use (in 30% of both wines) of indigenous vineyard yeasts. AHR's thrilled with the recently released 25th-anniversary Pinot 05 ('Best ever, some say!'), listings in two of the world's top restaurants (Spain's El Bulli and UK's The Fat Duck) and Biodiversity & Wine Initiative membership.

★★★★☆ **Pinot Noir** Experiments with native yeast fermentation & lighter filtration (as with Chard below) pay off with refined, intense mineral/fruit purity & focus of **05**, perfumed & elegant as ever; superbly managed oaking in early harmony. Silky length, deeply satisfying. International acclaim for pvs vintages unsurprising.

★★★★☆ **Chardonnay** Unlike restrained, powerful **04**, **05** (★★★★★) underwent malo, but with no loss of elegance, even perhaps gain in silky richness. Elegantly forceful structure, with obvious toasty, ginger-spice oak in youth destined for harmony with lemon/peach/nutty fruit & cool pebbly minerality; well-balanced acid. Persistent & already delicious. 8 mths oak, third new. Both EW. — *TJ*

Handcrafted Wines

Est 2006 ▪ *1stB 2006* ▪ *Tasting & sales Mon-Fri 9-5 Sat & Sun 9-5* ▪ *Closed religious holidays* ▪ *Tours by appointment* ▪ *Owner Handcrafted Wines* ▪ *Winemaker Oliver Meckler* ▪ *20 000 cs own label 100 % red* ▪ *Export brand: Ikapa* ▪ *PO Box* ▪ *781960 Sandton 2146 info@ handcraftedwines.co.za* ▪ *www.handcraftedwines.co.za* ▪ *T 0861·235·527* ▪ *F 086·688·9482*

This joint venture between Gauteng wine and food destination Cellar d'Or (with maturation facilities and corporate suites for lease) and winemaker Oliver Meckler of Adler Wines brings the winelands of the Cape to SA's most populous province. Groups of winelovers get to make and blend wines themselves, under Meckler's experienced tutelage, using grapes sourced from the same Cape vineyards as for the Adler label, at Cellar d'Or's premises in Sunninghill. In a complementary role, Meckler and the Handcrafted Wines team blend their own wines under the Ikapa label, mainly for export but also available locally.

Hartenberg Estate

Stellenbosch ▪ *1stB 1978* ▪ *Tasting & sales Mon-Fri 9-5 (Nov 1 till Easter 9-5.30) Sat 9-3 Sun Dec 1 till Jan 31 (tasting & lunches) 10-4 Closed all other Sundays & Easter Fri, Dec 25 & Jan 1* ▪ *Nominal tasting fee for groups, refunded with purchase* ▪ *Vintners lunches (alfresco, weather permitting) Mon-Sat 12-2 (picnic platters in summer; soup & vetkoek in winter);*

booking advisable ▪ *Seasonal cellar tours by appt* ▪ *Excellent birding (obtain permission via tasting room)* ▪ Owner Hartenberg Holdings ▪ Winemaker Carl Schultz, with Jaco van der Merwe (Jun 1993/Jan 2001) ▪ Viticulturist Wilhelm Joubert (2006) ▪ 95 ha (cab, merlot, pinotage, shiraz, chard, riesling, sauvignon) ▪ 500 tons 42 000 cs 80% red 20% white ▪ PO Box 69 Koelenhof 7605 ▪ paddy@hartenbergestate.com ▪ www.hartenbergestate.com ▪ **T** **865·2541** ▪ F 865·2153

The 2006 highlight for the close-knit Hartenberg 'family' was Carl Schultz's Diners Club Winemaker of the Year award (for the Merlot 04). Second was the release of three 'super-premium' wines. Long the preserve of a well-made, varietally sound range, Hartenberg (and unassuming yet assured Schultz) flexes toned muscles, showcasing its versatile capabilities. The Eleanor is a study in delicacy. The Mackenzie shows hallmark Hartenberg elegance. The Stork is an unabashed showstopper (with a five-star rating in this year's guide). But for all its fame, Hartenberg remains all heart; tasking new viticulturist Wilhelm Joubert with replanting of unfashionable riesling, to which Hartenberg has long been loyal; committed to the Biodiverstiy & Wine Initiative; delighting in its increased birdlife and lynx visits.

★★★★ **Cabernet Sauvignon 04** cloaks the fine grained tannin structure with shimmering berry fruit, crystallised violets, cedar spicing. Accessible, no hard edges, but the tannins are deeply veined, built for a 10+ yr life. 17 mths Fr oak, half new, half 2nd fill (±this for all the top reds).

★★★★ **Merlot** In sleek style that has become estate's trademark. **04** (★★★★★) classy step-up, riper, more complex; roasted spice, whiffs prosciutto, violets, on a dark plum base; elegant, silky texture & ultra-long finish. *Wine* ★★★★. Cool-grown **03** harmoniously oaked for ready accessibility, but shd develop beautifully over 4-6 yrs.

★★★★ **The Mackenzie** Cab/merlot blend named for family responsible for estate's regeneration. **04** (★★★★☆) confirms team's vyd selection, oaking expertise: textbook cassis, violets, cigarbox from cab (85%), given 100% new wood treatment. Fleshy palate offers immediate access but wine built for longer haul, as is classically styled **03** IWSC gold.

★★★★ **The Stork** Memorialises late Ken Mackenzie (nicknamed 'Stork' for his height & thin legs!), who loved the estate's shiraz. This version is from vyds with clay soils, to give a contrasting style to Gravel Hill. Awesome depth & concentration in **04** (★★★★★); nothing skinny here: opulent liquorice toned plums, black cherries; velvety texture, irresistibly delicious, but don't underestimate underlying structure, ageability. All new Fr oak, 18 mths. Only 550 cs. Generous **03** deeply rich, easily accommodates hefty 15.5% alc. All keepers, 7+ yrs.

★★★★★ **Shiraz** Always serious & complex. **04** doesn't put a foot wrong, delivers the expected deep rich fruit, smoky, savoury notes, fleshy accessibility. Already impressive, its supple tannins will reward 4+ yrs cellaring. Gorgeous **03** *Wine* ★★★★★.

★★★★★ **CWG Auction Reserve Gravel Hill Shiraz** From single vyd with gravelly red soil – 'poorest on the property', says Schultz. Awesome **03** (for 2006 Auction), tasted last ed, had colour you could write with; intense berry fruit; velvety tannins which misled about the sheathed power, longevity. 17 mths new Fr barrels. Only 47 cs.

★★★★ **The Eleanor Chardonnay** Named after Eleanor Finlayson, property's former doyenne; from premium vyd blocks. **05** refined, poised; perfectly judged oaking frames the citrus & peach fruit, adding palate definition, 2-3 yrs ageing potential. Fermented/ 10 mths new Fr barriques. Only 425 cs. Replaces Chard Rsv, whose last vintage **03**, awarded *Decanter* trophy.

★★★★ **Chardonnay** Selection from 5 vyds, 5 clones – all Burgundian or California Davis. Bold, concentrated. **05** same confident showiness as **04**: powerful house-style citrus peel & peach; nutty oak an integral part of profile, punctuated by tangy mouthfeel. Fermented/matured 11 mths, Fr oak, 60% new, rest 2nd fill.

Pinotage ★★★★ **04** easily manages to combine the dual personalities of voluptuous ripe fruit & lively drinkability, using all the variety's assets. Oak fully integrated (15 mths Fr, half new). **Cabernet Sauvignon-Shiraz** ★★★★ 'Ecurie' in US. **04** designed to please, & does, with smoky, plummy styling, smoothly rounded body. 14 mths seasoned barriques. 47/34 blend, rest merlo**03** Santé

Classic gold. **Bin 9** ★★★ **NV** juicy, flavourful quaffer. Only ex-estate & Gauteng restaurant, Luca's. Varying blend, tasted last ed was merlot, cab, shiraz; NE. **Sauvignon Blanc** ★★★★ **06** sample already showing well; green fig & gooseberry perfumes, flavours, a zesty freshness. Delicious solo or with food. **Weisser Riesling** Impressive **06** (★★★★), previewed mid-2006, abounds with aromatic charm, pineapple, honeysuckle, tantalising spicy notes. Off-dry, but signature balancing acidity, elegance, length make it irresistibly delicious. 30% botrytis. Jasmine scented **05** (★★★★ but flew SAA). NE. **Chatillon** ★★★ Easy-drinking characterful white. **06**, tasted ex-tank, from chenin; apple/pear styling with appealing rounded texture. **Bin 3**, **L'Estreux** made occasionally. — *CR*

Hartswater Wine Cellar

Northern Cape ▪ Tasting & sales Mon-Fri 8.30-5 Sat tasting by appt ▪ Sales also from outlet in Hartswater town; orders delivered to liquor stores in Northern Cape (350km radius), Free State & Pretoria ▪ Tours by appt ▪ Fully licensed restaurant with braai ▪ Conference facilities ▪ Owner Senwes ▪ Winemaker Roelof Maree (1978) ▪ 5 000 tons ▪ PO Box 2335 Hartswater 8570 ▪ wynkelder@senwes.co.za ▪ T (053) 474·0700 ▪ F (053) 474·0975

No update received from this Northern Cape winery; contact details and notes below from the previous edition.

Elements range

Thunder ★★ Rich & earthy glassful of bold, juicy fruit; weightier than 11% alc would suggest, sweetish finish. **Earth** ★★★ Dry red with herby hint to its red fruits, soft bite of tannin. Pinotage, shiraz, cab. **Fire** ★★★ Natural Sweet rosé from chenin, pinotage; strawberries & cream aromas, crisp finish. **Wind** ★★ Off-dry chenin-based white with peach blossom aroma; light, juicy, refreshing lemon acidity. **Rain** ★ Natural Sweet white from chenin, colombard, with soft, somewhat dilute fruit-salad flavours. All above light-bodied, low-alc wines (9.5-12.5%). All **NV**, for early drinking. Serve whites well chilled.

Hinterland range

Available but never tasted: Ruby Cabernet, Cabernet Sauvignon, Chardonnay, Chenin Blanc, Overvaal Grand Cru, Late Harvest, Special Late Harvest (in 3ℓ bag-in-boxes), Doux Sparkling, Red Jeropigo & Port. — *DH*

■ Harvest Moon *see* Dominion Wine Company

Haskell Vineyards

Stellenbosch ▪ Est 2002 ▪ 1stB 2003 ▪ Tasting, sales & tours Mon-Fri 9-5 Sat (Sep-Apr only) 10-3 ▪ Closed pub hols ▪ Vineyard Kitchen for breakfasts & light lunches Mon-Sat 9-4.30 ▪ Walks ▪ Owner Preston Haskell ▪ Winemaker Rianie Strydom (Jan 2005) ▪ Viticulturist Wikus Pretorius (Dec 2005) ▪ 15 ha (cab, merlot, shiraz, chard) ▪ ±65 tons ±6 000 cs 80% red 20% white ▪ Export brand: Dombeya ▪ PO Box 12766 Die Boord 7613 ▪ www.haskellvineyards.com ▪ info@haskellvineyards.com ▪ T 021·881·3895; F 021·881·3986 ▪ T 021·881·3491

Haskell Vineyards (previously listed as 'Dombeya') is owned by Preston Haskell, one of Russia's leading property developers and a frequent visitor to SA since 1986. He bought the farm in 2002 and built the cellar in time for former Morgenhof winemaker Rianie Strydom to conduct the 2005 maiden vintage. 'We are a small, passionate team of four waiting to serve you,' says Strydom, who promises a very 'personal' tasting experience. 'We also invite people to visit us in harvest-time to experience the crushing of grapes first-hand.'

Amalgam new **03** (★★★) cab-merlot combo dominated by gamey notes & grainy tannins. **04** (★★★★) very different: silky & sweet-fruited equal blend cab/merlot/shiraz, with cherry, blackcurrant notes, though palate dominated mid-2006 by oak (though only 2nd/3rd fill used, 14 mths) — may blend in soon. WO Coastal, as is... **Shiraz** new ★★★ **03** with a touch of cab. White pepper fruit marred by vegetal gamey notes; oak (20 mths, third new) evident but integrated. **Chardonnay** Contrasting with leaner **04** (★★★★) comes sumptuously tropical wood fermented **05** (★★★★) — bigger (14.5% alc), showier, with fruit/oak well integrated on creamy, leesy palate; mouthfilling, with long flavours. **Sauvignon Blanc** ★★★ Easy, delicious & softly rounded **05** was last tasted; no **06** made. — *MF*

Haut Espoir ♀♂

Franschhoek ▪ Est 1999 ▪ 1stB 2004 ▪ Tastings & tours by appt; sales Mon-Fri 9-4 (phone ahead) ▪ Owners Armstrong family ▪ Winemaker/viticulturist Nikey van Zyl (Oct 2003) ▪ 12 ha (cab, merlot, petit v, shiraz) ▪ 80 tons 4 000 cs 70% red 30% white ▪ PO Box 681 Franschhoek 7690 ▪ wine@hautespoir.co.za ▪ www.hautespoir.co.za ▪ T 021·876·4000 ▪ F 021·876·4038

'After a few award functions, the wines have literally flown out of the cellar,' beams Rob Armstrong. 'Availability is a constant problem – a nice one to have, though, so no complaints from this neck of the valley.' Winemaker Nikey van Zyl reckons 2006 is his best vintage yet. 'Especially fun' was making Sauvignon 'to send to the thirsty Kiwis...' (Dad Ian A has a home in New Zealand and connections remain strong, hence the 'coals to Newcastle' export channel).

Syrah ★★ 04 sold out; no **05** released. **Shiraz Rosé ★★★** Fermented in seasoned Fr oak; friendly & pleasant **05**; fresh strawberry intro; full, fattish, characterful dry fruit flavours. **Chardonnay Reserve** Delicious **05 (★★★★)** notch above pvs; oak subtler & more integrated, showcasing citrus peel fruit on nose & lively palate; lovely tangy finish. Potential to improve. Barrique fermented in native yeasts; 13 mths on lees. Woodier **04 (★★★** but DGs at Veritas, MIWA). **Sauvignon Blanc ★★** Last tasted was lightish **04** ('05' of pvs ed in fact not made); **06** unready. **Semillon ★★★ 05** gentle leafy aromas; pure & clean waxy fruit; little evidence of fattening dash chard in slender, almost delicate body (12% alc). Small portion oaked. *— CR*

Havana Hills ♀♂

Philadelphia (see Durbanville/Philadelphia map) ▪ Est 1999 ▪ 1stB 2000 ▪ Visits by appt ▪ Owner Kobus du Plessis ▪ Winemakers Nico Vermeulen & Paul Engelbrecht (Jun 1999/Jan 2006) with Joseph Gertse (Jan 2000) ▪ Viticulturist Rudi Benn (2001) ▪ 58 ha (cabs s/f, merlot, mourvèdre, shiraz, pinot, chard, sauvignon) ▪ 120 tons 20 000 cs 85% red 15% white ▪ Export brands: Lime Road 1481 & Virgin Earth (see entry) ▪ Postnet Suite 57, Pvt Bag X18, Milnerton 7435 ▪ sales@havanahills.co.za ▪ T 021·972·1110 ▪ F 021·972·1105

Owner Kobus du Plessis has introduced a third winemaker, Paul Engelbrecht (ex-Whalehaven), to his successful team, who are able to boast five consecutive Veritas double-gold medals for the Du Plessis Shiraz Reserve (vintages 99-03), making it the most consistent high performer in this competition to date. Recent plantings of viognier and mourvèdre, on south facing virgin soils overlooking Table Bay, are starting to bear fruit and will enhance the complexity of their various blends.

★★★★★ **Kobus** Flagship finally gets a name, albeit not the preliminary, edgy 'Kobus One' (doffing wry cap to Mondavi-Rothschild icon). Foxy front-label heightens intrigue – of both 'Name' & contents. Back-label of **03** far from modest, contents similarly unabashed: inky hues with glistening bitter-choc sheen; individual meaty/cassis palate wound like a golf ball... awaiting release! (Try ±2010.) 60/40 cab/merlot. 18 mths Fr oak, 30% new. Only 300 cs.

Du Plessis Reserve range

★★★★☆ **Du Plessis** Médoc-style blend carrying own West Coast watermark & making waves since maiden **00 (★★★★★,** VDG in 2006). **04** cements credentials, ageworthiness: neither gauche nor overt; munificent fruit jostles with integrated structure to suggest longevity. 65/20/10 cab, merlot, cab f, drop petit v. 18 mths Fr oak, 30% new. Coastal WO, as are above & next.

★★★★ **Shiraz** Only wine to secure VDGs 5 consecutive vintages. **04** nuanced & refined: truly beautiful clean pepper & spice aromas, lovely integration – fruit seamlessly etched into velvet structure, marvellous length of finish. Established oaking regimen: 85/15 Fr/Am, 30% Fr new, 18 mths. 14.5% alc.

Havana Hills range

Lime Road ★★★☆ Reliable member of this 'fruity & elegant' range. Now shiraz/cab with 22% merlot. **04** wisps of ethereal smoke & spice, cassis fruit & mocha add the filling. **Shiraz ★★★☆ 04** sweet vanilla notes to well spiced, fruit driven mouthful; trademark viscous 'glaze' on smooth finish. Yr 85/15 Fr/Am barrels, 30% new. **Italian Job** new ★★★ Melting pot of sangiovese, nebbiolo, barbera, shiraz, pinotage – even touriga! Trifle rustic **04**

more interesting on paper than in glass. WO W Cape. **Chardonnay ★★★★ 05** toasty, mature aromas counterpoised with fruity freshness, ends tad sweet. 40% barrel fermented/8 mths, 30% new. **Sauvignon Blanc ★★★★ 06** neatly packaged grass & flint, refreshing 12.5% alc, step-up on straightforward tropical **05**. Discontinued: **Du Plessis Cabernet Sauvignon, Du Plessis Merlot, Havana Hills Cabernet Sauvignon, Havana Hills Merlot.** — *DS*

Hazendal

*Stellenbosch • Est 1699 • 1stB ca 1950 • Tasting & sales Mon-Fri 8.30-4.30 Sat/Sun 9-3 • Fee R5; R10 incl tour • Tours Mon-Fri 11 & 3 • Closed Easter Fri, Dec 25 & Jan 1 • Hermitage Restaurant • Museum of Russian art & culture • Gifts • Conferencing • Owners Mark Voloshin & partners • Vini/ viti consultants Ronell Wiid & Schalk du Toit (Jan 1998/2000) • 60 ha (cab, merlot, shiraz, chenin, sauvignon) • 400 tons 25 000 cs own label 40% red 60% white • PO Box 336 Stellenbosch 7599 • info@hazendal.co.za • www.hazendal.co.za • **T 021·903·5112** • F 021·903·0057*

Putting paid to persistent rumours of Hazendal's imminent sale, Russian owner Mark Voloshin and business partner Leo Schumacher have handed over the reins to the next generation. Leonid Schumacher shepherds family interests abroad. Sister Rebecca and husband Roger Horn focus on Hazendal's hospitality side (including restaurant expansions and the historic slave quarters' conversion into luxury accommodation). Simone Voloshin handles wine marketing and sales. Which leaves winemaker Ronell Wiid busily, happily involved in a 'massive' clearing of old vineyards for new plantings, and enjoying her 'tricky 2004 reds blossoming into richness and depth of fruit'.

★★★★ **Shiraz-Cabernet Sauvignon** ✓ Retaste of last yrs' sample confirms everything in place for a gd drinking experience: **03** creamy, fully ripened berries, deepening savoury woodsmoke notes; balanced structure. But: drink only if you must the real pleasure is 4-5 yrs off. 54/46 blend, yr Fr barrels, 40% new.

★★★★ **Shiraz** ✓ 'High hopes for only supple, firm tannin' says Ronell W of stringent fruit sorting process for **04**; dark fruited, with hints liquorice & smoked salami; tannins well judged & … yes, supple, giving firm but accessible skeleton for 4-6+ yrs ageing. 18 mths Fr oak.

★★★★ **The Last Straw** Aptly & amusingly named meal-ending straw wine. **05** (★★★★☆) another notch up the scale: mouthcoating, resonating apricot & quince flavours as per **04**, but with richer, yet more delicious shortbread & toffee nuances. Sweeter than pvs (±200g/ℓ sugar) but active acidity cuts & refreshes. Simply irresistible. Fermented/9-10 mths Fr oak. **03** *Wine* ★★★★★.

> **Bushvine Chenin Blanc** ☺ ★★★ Off old vines, **05** (retasted) repeats the winning formula: old-vine concentration, succulent tropical flavours, loads of juicy liveliness for with food or solo, plus 2-3 yr ageability.

Merlot ★★★★ 04 recalls firmer (but well berried) structure of pvs, slightly more rigorous oaking contributes to higher-tannin, food-indicating profile. 15 mths Fr oak, 60% new. **Marvol Pinotage ★★★★** Made for Mark V's 60th birthday celebration in Russia. Last tasted was serious & elegant **02**, with perfectly ripe plummy fruit, attractive smoky spice. **Pinotage ★★★★** Limited quantities for UK market. **04** last ed captured the variety perfectly: rhubarb pie richness, with a touch of green fynbos to lift, enliven. **Blanc de Noir ★★★ 06** (sample) from pinot, a more restrained & savoury version, food-convivial, friendly (12.5% alc), for early drinking. **Chenin Blanc Wooded** From miserly 30 yr old bushvines. **04** (★★★★) generous oaking (yr Fr) gave structure for enjoying early or over 3-4 yrs. Same for **05** (★★★★), fuller & richer, with delightful peachy concentration set to unfold beautifully. **Sauvignon Blanc ★★★** Ex-30 yr old bushvines. **06** (sample) textbook styling for vibrant refreshment: gooseberries & passionfruit, some greener leafiness a great foil for food. Bonus 13% alc. **White Nights Brut Cap Classique ★★★** Recalls 'Beliye Nochi' - bright midsummer nights of St Petersburg. Pvs was fresh, very dry & lively **00** from chard/ pinot (60/40), **01** only pinot, 4 yrs on lees; touch richer, creamier; enjoy soon to catch at peak. **Chardonnay** ★★★ Pvs sample **04** still lively, tasty, nicely put together. Gd summer white with modest alc & ripe tropical fruit core. Fermented/aged Fr barrels, 20% new.

Kleine Hazen range

> **Konynwijn** ☺ ★★★ **05** (revisited) semi-sweet chenin quaffer with appealing glacé pineapple flavours & bags of character. Mostly for own restaurant.

Reserve Red ★★★ Latest rings the changes: now oaked & **NV**, & a bdx blend (cab, merlot); wood still shows a bit & tannins tad gruff, but nothing heartier foods wouldn't tame. — CR

Headbutt Wines ⚲ new

Wellington • Est/1stB 2003 • Tasting & sales at Bovlei Winery (see entry) • Owners Jan du Preez & Marius Erasmus • Winemaker Frank Meaker (Bovlei), with Jan du Preez • Viti adviser Dawie le Roux • 120 tons 10 000 cs 60% red 30% white 10% sparkling • BRC accreditation in progress • PO Box 7210 Stellenbosch 7599 • headbutt@leidersburgwines.co.za • www. leidersburgwines.co.za • T 021·873·1567 • F 021·864·1483

A fruitful collaboration between Leidersburg's Jan du Preez and wine industry administrator/ financial strategist Marius Erasmus has resulted in this colourful new range of affordable wines. Mostly exported to the US and Netherlands, Headbutt wines are also available locally. Tasting and sales are at Wellington's Bovlei winery, whose team produces the wines with Du Preez' input when it comes to selection and blending.

Vinters Reserve Pinotage ★★ **04** 'sweet' choc-nut nose belies lightly fruited, firm & taut palate. 40% oaked, as is... **Vinters Reserve Merlot-Pinotage-Cinsaut** ★ Burly **05** light on flavour, rich on tannins; quite leanly structured. **Chardonnay** ★ Unoaked **06** crisp & fresh; pleasantly gulpable if somewhat lacking varietal distinction. **Sauvignon Blanc-Steen** ★★ **06** equal partner sauvignon & chenin; green scented/flavoured, with sharp Granny Smith apple finish. All above WO Coastal. **Sparkling Brut** ★★★ Carbonated **NV** bubbly from chenin & chard (70/30). Frothy & fun; vibrant mousse, peaches & cream scents/tastes. —CT

- ■ *Hegewisch Wines* see Solms-Delta
- ■ *Helderberg Winery* see The Company of Wine People
- ■ *Helderkruin Wine Cellar* see Ernie Els
- ■ *Helgerson* see La Bri
- ■ *Helshoogte Vineyards* see Vuurberg

Hemelzicht ⚲

Upper Hemel-en-Aarde • Est 1998 • 1stB 2003 • Tasting & sales Mon-Fri 8.30-5 Sat 8.30-1 at 19 Long Street Hermanus • Closed pub hols • Owner Louis Saaiman • Winemaker Hannes Storm (2003) • 16 ha (cab, malbec, shiraz, chard, sauvignon) • 800 cs 100% white • PO Box 469 Onrusrivier 7201 • T/F 028·313·2215 (cellar) • T 028·312·3512 (a/h)

Changes to the Wine of Origin system see boutique vintner Louis Saaiman bottling his wines under a new appellation, Upper Hemel-en-Aarde. A Cabernet Sauvignon 05 and Sauvignon Blanc 06, untasted at press time, will be available during 2007.

■ *Hemisphere* see Du Toitskloof Hercules Paragon see Simonsvlei International

Hermanuspietersfontein Vineyards ♀⚲ 🎵 new

Walker Bay • Est/1stB 2005 • Tasting & sales Tue-Fri 10-6 Sat 9-5 Sun 10.30-3 (in season) • Closed Easter Sun/Mon, Dec 25/26 & Jan 1 • Farmers' market Sat 9-1 • Wine accessories, gifts & other attractions (see intro) • Owners Johan & Mariette Pretorius, Bartho Eksteen • Winemaker Bartho Eksteen, with Kim McFarlane • 250 tons 12 000 cs 68% red 32% white • Suite 47, Private Bag X15, Hermanus 7200 • kelder@hpf1855.co.za • www.hpf1855.co.za • T 028·316·1875 • F 028·316·1293

Maverick Walker Bay winemaker Bartho Eksteen's allusion in last year's edition to a collaborative project has materialised. Eksteen's partnered Stanford farmers Johan and Mariette Pretorius in a 250-ton high-tech cellar at the entrance to the Hemel-en-Aarde Valley. 'At last, a consistent supply of quality grapes!' he rejoices, intending indulging his passion for Sauvignon and Shiraz. The branding is vintage Eksteen individualism: only Afrikaans on labels; the mouthful-of-a-moniker commemorates Hermanus Pieters, the early 19th-century Dutch teacher after whom whale-watcher's paradise Hermanus is named.

★★★★☆ **Die Bartho 06** intense cool-provenance character sauvignon (mostly Elim grapes): grass (both fresh & dried), flint, greenpepper, but also a twist of ripe passionfruit. Concentrated, harmonious & complete; lightly gripping, with silky texture, fine integrated acidity, bone-dry finish. Includes some semillon (like all these whites) & nouvelle.

★★★★ **Sauvignon Blanc No 3** Nicely blended tropicality – figs, passionfruit – with cooler flourishes of greenpepper, grass. Broad mouthfeel; substantial acidity adds tingle to fairly straightforward but satisfying equation. **06**, like other versions, low-mid 13% alc.

★★★★ **Sauvignon Blanc No 7** More interesting version than above, perhaps, **06** a touch more austere: steely, flinty rather than fruity; compact, concentrated. WO W Cape.

Swartskaap ★★★★ A variable beast, this (red) black sheep, which might change variety/style annually: heavily wooded **05** from cab f, with a little leafy fragrance breaking though oaky spice, toast. Soft, sweet fruit goes down easily, pursued by a little tannin.

1855 range

All labelled simply 'Tafelwyn'. From cellar & Hermanus restaurants only. **'Red' ★★★** Clean, fresh firm lightly wooded **05** red from 5 varieties led by malbec (41%). Not a dumbed down fruity number, just simple, straightforward. **'Rosé' ★★** Fruit pastille, earthy notes to pleasant enough **06** blend of 7 red varieties; mild, fresh, dry. 'No problem!', the waitron might say of all these. **'White' ★★★** Dry (but only just) **06** white from sauvignon, some semillon & dash nouvelle. Lots of greenpepper & grass, but not too pungent; soft texture, fresh light feel. These WO W Cape. — *TJ*

Herold Wines ◊♟️🏠🎣

Outeniqua (see Little Karoo map) ▪ Est 1999 ▪ 1stB 2003 ▪ Tasting & sales weekdays; other times by appt ▪ Fee R15 refundable on purchase ▪ BYO picnic ▪ Walks ▪ Conservation area ▪ Owner Mark Chandler ▪ Winemakers Mark Chandler & Vivien Harpur ▪ Viticulturist Vivien Harpur (1999) ▪ 6 ha (pinot, sauvignon) ▪ 30 tons 1 200 cs 80% red 20% white ▪ PO Box 10 Herold 6615 ▪ heroldwines@mweb.co.za (Mark) or harpie@xsinet.co.za (Vivien) ▪ T 072·833·8223 ▪ F 0866·204·248

A bigger harvest than their Montague Pass cellar could handle saw grapes sold off and some pinot left on the vine; and unavailability of their winemaking consultant spurred siblings Mark Chandler and Vivien Harpur into going it alone last year. Vivien H laughs: 'Only time will tell if the wines develop some unusual qualities – the smell of fear on the nose and a hint of hysteria on the palate.' Adversity overcome, it's still a magical spot, with wines to match.

Pinot Noir Silky, sensual **03** (★★★★☆) trumped by burgundy-styled **04** (★★★★; retasted: pre-bottling last ed): forthcoming forest floor, organic aromas, touch wild strawberry; fresh cool-climate redcurrant fruit & subtle oak (11 mths, 30% new); lingering dry finish. Shd keep well 3-4 yrs. **Shiraz ★★★ 05** (tasted new-bottled) has distinctive dark choc, hint black cherry. Less ripe than pvs, but still richly fruited, fresh. 14 mths oaked. Volatile acidity on lingering finish precludes higher rating. Incl Bo-Langkloof fruit. **Cabernet Sauvignon-Shiraz** new ★★★ Ripe, rich **05** shows the fruit quality from these high vyds. Loads of fleshy black-berried fruit, almost cordial-like but saved by cool acidity, ripe tannins, dry finish. **Rosé ★★★** new to this guide. **06** aka 'Gertrude II' (we missed Gertrude I): 'to honour the grandmothers of the farm who gave us strength & sweetness!' says Vivien H. From pinot, with delicate strawberry, forest floor notes & lovely full flavour. Just off-dry, but long dryish finish. Massive 15.8% alc. **Sauvignon Blanc** Pungent **05** (★★★); now jump-up **06** (★★★★ ✓) with great varietal purity: fig-leaf, nettles, cut grass aromas, but more tropical & lush to taste; plump & rounded, with thrilling fruity acids mopped up by huge fruit concentration. 14.7% alc. — *IvH*

Heron Ridge

Stellenbosch (see Helderberg map) ▪ Est 1997 ▪ 1stB 2001 ▪ Visits by appt ▪ Fee R10 p/p for groups ▪ Closed pub hols ▪ Owners Pete & Jane Orpen ▪ Winemaker Pete Orpen ▪ Viti consultant Paul Wallace (Mar 1999) ▪ 4 ha (cab, shiraz) ▪ 30 tons 1 800-2 000 cs 100% red ▪ PO Box 5181 Helderberg 7135 ▪ orps@xsinet.co.za ▪ www.heronridge.co.za ▪ T/F 021·842·2501

This small-scale family winery has added several new strings to its bow: a Reserve Shiraz, a Cab-Shiraz blend and an assistant winemaker (daughter Pippa). Harvest 2006 saw stringent measures to guarantee quality: severe crop thinning (halving production), and hastily summoned friends to help in the cellar when power failures hit mid-harvest. Mother (Jane) and daughter collaborated on their first three open-top barrels of Ladies' Reserve, under the 'watchful but amused eye' of winemaker/husband/dad Pete.

★★★★ **Cabernet Sauvignon-Shiraz** new **05** blend (77/23) not yet quite knit — shiraz choc abuts cab cassis. Better balance than straight Shiraz: cab leavens richness, adds berries, improves texture. Ripe flavours, ripe tannins; gd concentration, long dry finish with brush of tannin. Yr oak 10% new.

★★★★ **Shiraz 04** when last tasted as sample offered sumptuous ripeness, fine texture & lovely concentration. 05 previewed last ed appears as Rsv below. ±Yr oak, 30% new; 70% Fr. Unfiltered.

Shiraz Reserve ★★★★ **05**, now bottled, less exciting. Layers of ripe choc flavour, thick & chunky, shows incipient portiness. Lacks elegance, but some will prefer. Mostly Fr oak, ±yr, 45% new. — *IvH*

■ **Heron's Nest** see Clos Malverne

Hex River Crossing Private Cellar   new

Worcester ▪ Est/1stB 2004 ▪ Visits Sat 10-2 ▪ Fee 10 ▪ Closed most pub hols ▪ Meals by appt ▪ Owners De Villiers Graaff, AJ Reyneke & Leon Dippenaar ▪ Winemaker/viticulturist Leon Dippenaar (2004) ▪ 2 ha (mourvèdre, shiraz, viognier) ▪ 15 tons 500 cs 90% red 10% white ▪ Export brand: The Auction Crossing ▪ PO Box 5 Hex River 6855 ▪ leon@vinpro.co.za ▪ T 083·455·5194 ▪ F 023·347·4734

When they acquired their Breede River valley farm four years ago, De Villiers Graaff and AJ Reyneke were delighted to find a well-preserved cellar, built in 1936 and then used as a store, next to the old Cape Dutch homestead. 'It was working well enough to make the traditional purist really jealous!' quips winemaker (and co-shareholder) Leon Dippenaar, now producing Côte Rôtie-style wine in the upgraded facility from bought-in shiraz and viognier. Initial plantings are of those two varieties, as well as mourvèdre.

The Auction Crossing range

★★★★ **Viognier** From low-yielding Dbnvlle vyd, **05**'s classic aromas of peach & flowers foreshadow lovely mid-palate viscosity & persistent spicy finish. Only just off-dry; balanced acidity & alc (14%). Well integrated new wood influence (fermented/5 mths).

Syrah-Viognier ★★★ **04** has raspberry, raisiny notes, with floral whiff from co-fermented white grape element (7%) — which also softens the shiraz tannins, helping make for easy-drinking wine. But serious oaking: 17 mths, 35% new. From widely sourced fruit, so WO W Cape (like abv). — *MF*

Hidden Valley Wines

Stellenbosch ▪ Est/1stB 1995 ▪ Tasting, sales & tours Mon-Fri 9-4.30 Sat, Sun & pub hols 9.30-3.30 ▪ Closed Good Fri, Dec 25 & Jan 1 ▪ Owners Dave & Marguerite Hidden ▪ Winemaker/GM Chris Kelly (2005), with Corina du Toit (Oct 2005) ▪ Viticulturist Johan 'Grobbie' Grobbelaar (Feb 1999) ▪ 44 ha (barbera, cabs s/f, malbec, merlot, mourvèdre, petit v, pinotage, shiraz, tannat, sauvignon, semillon) ▪ *220 tons 15 000 cs 75% red 25% white* ▪ *PO Box 12577 Die Board 7613* ▪ *info@ hiddenvalleywines.com* ▪ *www.hiddenvalleywines.com* ▪ **T** *021·880·2646* ▪ *F 021·880·2645*

Activity galore at this expanding operation: the recently completed 200-ton gravity-flow cellar is handling not only top-notch Helderberg fruit but also the reds (shiraz, cab, cab franc and petit verdot) from Dave Hidden's newly acquired property, Land's End, in Elim. The white grapes (sauvignon and semillon) from that farm are being vinified locally in rented cellar space. Visitors can taste selected Land's End bottlings at the Helderberg winery, pending a decision on whether or not to open the Elim spread, with its 24ha of preserved wetland, to the public.

★★★★ **Pinotage 04**, previewed last yr, distinctive, intriguing (from tiny shiraz/viognier additions?); fennel/rhubarb nuances & whiff mint, blueberry. Ripe, juicy; well managed tannins introduce delicious savoury dimension. Ideal partner for hearty game dishes. Pinotage from 30+ yr old Devon Valley vyd; balance other Sbosch grapes. Yr oak, 80/20 Fr/Am, 30% new.

★★★★ **Cabernet Sauvignon** Serious & approachable **01**, traditionally vinified, still available, not re-assessed. Svelte; beautifully judged silky tannins, deep-veined strength for ageing. 18 mths mainly Fr, touch Am, mix new/used oak. 10% shiraz. Also in magnums. Firgrove/Hldrberg vyds.

★★★★ **Shiraz** ★★★★ A sample last yr, **04** now shows mint/vanilla overlay to characteristic white spice. Light textured, fresh; suggestion of oak/fruit sweetness cushions tannin & hefty 14.5% alc. 13 mths new/2nd fill barrels, 20% Am. Made in Elgin by Niels Verburg. **Sauvignon Blanc** new Faure vyds source of pungent **06**. Sample flaunts passionfruit/ sweat aromas, balanced juicy zest; clean dry finish. Min ★★★★ when released. **Land's End Sauvignon Blanc** Returns to guide with sample **06**; eloquent contrast to above wine; delicate mineral/gooseberry fragrance; richer, weightier mouthfeel with cool, steely core, great length. Likely ★★★★. Incl 10% semillon. WO Elim.

Hidden Agenda range

Shiraz new ★★★ Replaces 'Red' in last ed. Ripe, warming **05** blended with splashes cab & pinotage. Plentiful spice, blackberry fruit, easy tannins; partially oaked for extra dimension. **Chenin Blanc** new Sample **06** shows traditional chenin floral/honey composition, accessorised by splash viognier; lots of fruity freshness, persistence; 20% barrel fermented portion for structure. Promising ★★★. **White** ★★★ Screwcapped **05**, previewed last yr, now pretty honeyed/floral bouquet; rounded, easy drinking with obvious 6.9g/ℓ sugar. Chenin with 10% viognier, dollop sauvignon, partly oaked. —AL/CR

High Constantia ⌀♀

Constantia ▪ *Est 1693* ▪ *1stB 2000* ▪ *Tasting, sales & tours 8-5* ▪ *Fee R25* ▪ *Closed Dec 25 & Jan 1* ▪ *Owner David van Niekerk* ▪ *Winemakers David van Niekerk & Roger Arendse* ▪ *14.5 ha (cabs s/f, malbec, merlot, pinot, chard, sauvignon)* ▪ *40 tons 5 500 cs own label* ▪ *64% red 1% white 5% rosé 30% MCC* ▪ *Range for customer: High Constantia (UK)* ▪ *Puck's Glen, Groot Constantia Rd, Constantia 7800* ▪ *david@highconstantia.co.za* ▪ *www.highconstantia.co.za* ▪ **T** *021·794·7171* ▪ *F 021·794·7999*

His 'Sebastiaan' affirmed by *Decanter* as part of a new wave of high-end bordeaux blends able to compete with the real thing, David van Niekerk is in a celebratory mood. But the best, he believes, is yet to come. This year he harvests sauvignon, cab and merlot he planted on nearby Nova Zonnestraal (previously a table grape farm), where 'the deep, rich, loamy soil will produce grapes befitting the quality the Constantia Valley is now producing'.

★★★★☆ **Sebastiaan** Splendid blend of cabs s/f (63:32), with a dab of malbec; understatedly handsome **03**'s dark-fruited, lightly fragrant depths show incipient complexity which shd happily absorb spicy oak (mix new/2nd fill Fr; 2+ yrs). Rich & well balanced, with forceful, muscular elegance & authoritative composure. 13.8% alc. Shd develop rewardingly 5+ yrs.

★★★★ **Cabernet Franc** Leafy fragrance, allied with dusty spice & earthy notes, making for an unusual, characterful **03**. Sweet fruit on smoothly tannic palate, with dusty finish, though elegantly dry, with moderate 13% alc. 32 mths new oak integrating well.

★★★★ **Malbec** [new] **04**'s spicy cedar, plummy fruitcake bouquet carries through to dark-fruited & vibrantly juicy palate, with quietly firm tannic grip. 2nd/3rd fill oak, 22 mths. Interesting & charming.

★★★★ **Sauvignon Blanc** [new] **05** cool-country aromas/flavours: gooseberry, grapefruit, but not too green, & edged with passionfruit. Lovely richness tempered by steely acidity, well balanced by very adequate 12.5% alc, all making for serious pleasure. **06** tank sample promises perhaps more richness, concentration.

★★★★ **Clos André MCC** One of the Cape's most refined — & about as dry as you can go. Various proportions chard/pinot. **04**, with 76% of the white grape, has subtle biscuit/apple/mineral character, just hinting at yeast; lightly rich, austerely elegant — that's the appeal. **05**, nearer a 50:50 blend, has more brioche, is a little fuller in flavour, but similarly delicate — like brittle, fine porcelain. Packaging beautiful, as it is for all these wines.

Cabernet Sauvignon ★★★ Herbal, herbaceous notes to **03** & **04** tell of a cool origin; with some varietal character (cassis, cedar) added to idiosyncrasies. Big dry tannins tend to overwhelm fruit on shortish finish. Lot of wood apparent; ±19 mths new. **Rosé** ★★★★ **05** a 'fun wine' says David vN, but actually a bit more: big (14.5% alc), quite rich, pure-fruited — though as vinous as it is fruity, with gd dry finishing grip. Mostly cab f, some MCC press-wine, & tiny dollops of this & that. — *TJ*

■ *High Gables* see Klein Constantia

Hildenbrand Wine & Olive Estate

Wellington ▪ Est 1998 ▪ 1stB 1999 ▪ Tasting & sales daily 10-4 ▪ Closed Easter Fri-Sun, Dec 25, Dec 31 & Jan 1 ▪ Tasting fee R15 ▪ Tours by appt ▪ Hildenbrand Restaurant (closed Tue in season & May 1-Aug 31) ▪ Klein Rhebokskloof Country & Guest House ▪ Farm-grown olives & olive oil ▪ Owner/viticulturist Reni Hildenbrand ▪ Winemaker Reni Hildenbrand, with Ruani Visser ▪ 18 ha (cab, malbec, shiraz, chard, chenin, semillon) ▪ 4 800 cs own label 50% red 50% white ▪ PO Box 270 Wellington 7655 ▪ info@wine-estate-hildenbrand.co.za ▪ www.wine-estate-hildenbrand.co.za ▪ T 021·873·4115 ▪ F 0866·700·147

Assisting owner Reni Hildenbrand last year, Ruani Visser had an exciting maiden vintage, from having a hand in the estate's first export to Sweden to helping produce the first Semillon NLH and putting 'a lovely port' on the path to maturity. Also participating, but for the third time, was consultant and friend Olivier Geffroy from ITV-France, the vini/viti research institute. 'A special vintage for him,' comments Reni H, drily, 'with no rain and no electricity.'

★★★★ **Shiraz** Dark, brooding **04**, reflection of Wllngtn's warmer climes; spicy/meaty depths lifted, freshened by gentle red fruits. Well mannered tannins & carefully judged oak lend smoothness/homogeneity yet no lack of potential (±6-8 yrs). Big 15% alc relieved by solid dry finish. 80/20 Hngrian/Fr oak, portion new. No **03**.

★★★★ **Chenin Blanc** Individual version from mature bushvines. Latest **05** (★★★★) sensitively handled in difficult yr. Portion tank fermented to enhance ripe floral character, subtle native yeast embroidery. Rounded, for current enjoyment. Third used-oak fermented, vs 100% in **04**.

★★★★ **Semillon 05** (★★★★) riper, less exuberant than TWS trophy winning **04**. Quite big, soft with gentle lanolin/lees creaminess, further enrichment from oak; finishing glow. Barrel fermented/matured with native yeast.

Rosé ★★★ ☺ Tasty **06** from shiraz. Gleaming ruby lights; generous spicy wild strawberry fruit, tweak of tannin offsets 4 g/ℓ sugar.

Cabernet Sauvignon Barrique ★★★★ **04** teams classic cassis notes with fragrant oak spice. Quite big, sumptuous, eased by firm tannins, dry finish. Fr/Hngrian oak aged, some new. **Cabernet Sauvignon Unwooded** ★★★★ Unoaked cabs a rarity but latest **05** illustrates style's enjoyment possibilities. Forthcoming fresh wild berries, well integrated tannin support; rounded & dry. Probably best within next yr/2. **Malbec** Popular flagship, sold ex-estate only; production miniscule 1-2 t/ha, 40 cs; sells out before we get to taste; last was lightly oaked **05**. **Chardonnay Barrique**

★★★☆ 04 follows pvs with butterscotch/toast appeal cut by taut lime/mineral freshness. Fr barrel fermented/matured, well judged to not dominate. Interesting future. **Chardonnay Unwooded** ★★★ Bright citrus peel, pineapple on **05**; quite sturdy, dry, shortish finish. **Sleepless Nights Semillon Noble Late Harvest** new Maiden **06** (sample) delicate botrytis veil over lanolin/lemon aromas; not too unctuous or sweet. Name records how winemaking team fared during production period. NE. Possible ★★★★. — *AL*

■ *Hilko Hegewisch* see Hegewisch Wines

Hill & Dale

Vinified from fruit off selected Stellenbosch vineyards by Guy Webber at Stellenzicht (see entry for tasting/sales information), this range aims to be 'classic but accessible'.

Cabernet Sauvignon-Shiraz ★★★ **04** 80/20 blend for fans of 'big & bold'. Gutsy flavours of sweet cassis, smoke & vanilla oak (Fr/Am). Tannins, alc, more in tune than pvs. Best enjoyed soon. **Merlot** new ★★★ Light (12% alc), unoaked pasta partner. **05** combo savoury/leafy/plummy aromas, flavours; soft tannins & modest fruit. **Pinotage** ★★☆ **04** rather foursquare; restrained raspberry fruitiness, austere finish despite sweet suggestion from Fr/Am oak. **Merlot Rosé** ★★ Bone-dry, diet-friendly **06**, sample shows muted hints raspberry & rose-hip, matching soft onionskin hue; ±12% alc better balanced than pvs. **Chardonnay** ★★★ Shy stewed peach & lime bouquet on **05**, also shy on flavour, intensity, ends touch bitter. Fr/Am oak fermented. **Sauvignon Blanc** ★★★ **06** vibrant, with lots of 'green' interest, incl greenpepper & peppercorn. Zesty, balanced, though flavours are quite short-lived. **Stellenbosch Red** discontinued. — *CvZ*

Hillcrest Estate

◯♀⚖

Durbanville • Est/1stB 2002 • Tasting & sales daily 9-5 • Closed Easter Fri, Dec 25 & Jan 1 • Restaurant for breakfast & lunches during tasting hours • Tours by appt • Owners PD Inglis, R Haw & G du Toit • Winemaker Graeme Read (Jan 2003) • Viticulturist G du Toit • 25 ha (cab, merlot, shiraz, chard, sauvignon) • 60 tons • ±3 000 cs 45% red 55% white • Private Bag X3 Durbanville 7551 • restaurant@hillcrestfarm.co.za • T 021·976·1110/975·2346 • F 021·975·2195

Ex-marine biologist Graeme Read is very enthusiastic about his winemaking, and will pull out all the stops to marry sauvignon fruit flavour with Hillcrest's signature 'crisp, zippy acidity'. Fortunately he suffered none of the power outages that threatened to impede many a cool ferment in the 2006 vintage — 'so there can be no excuses!'. Strategy for the year ahead includes focus on the vineyards to further raise fruit quality, with recently installed irrigation set to minimise vine stress.

★★★★ **Cabernet Sauvignon-Merlot** Name change from 'Merlot-Cab' pvs ed reflects rejigged proportions — 55/45 in **05**. Skilful handling allows cassis/plum richness to remain hero, gives sufficient oaking platform for future development. Already delicious, but a 6+ yr keeper if you can resist.

★★★★ **Sauvignon Blanc** Gets it right every time: **05** almost vibrates with gooseberry/lime intensity, freshness (7.9g/ℓ TA), expected taut minerality, awesome length. Good 3+ yrs ageing potential.

★★★★★ **Chardonnay Noble Late Harvest** new Astonishing perfume on **05**, dried peaches, preserved melon, liberally dosed with honey; but palate is the real surprise: tangy, zesty citrus. Irresistible. Third used barrels. 105g/ℓ sugar, 11.5% alc.

Merlot 05 (★★★★) has even greater concentration, complexity than **04** (★★★★). Trademark red berry fruit, candied violets, oak spice & backbone from 11 mths Fr barrels, 80% new. Ageing potential 5+ yrs. Incl touch cab s. **Chardonnay Wooded** ★★★☆ **05** final product (sample last ed) unfolds melon, citrus charms, balancing oak, enough zest for good food matching. Portion oaked, mix new/older Fr. **Chardonnay Unwooded** ★★★ Last was **05**, tropical tones, rounded fresh flavours. Tasted as sample, as was… **Sauvignon Blanc Reserve** ★★★★ Coolly austere whiffs nettle & grapefruit on **05**; tad lean, might settle once bottled. — *CR*

■ *Hill Station* see Cape First
■ *Hinterland* see Hartswater

Hippo Creek

By Vintage International Brands. Originally exclusive to the PicardiRebel chain, now more widely available following its success in the export arena. VIB's Colin Frith, viti consultant Paul Wallace and Hazendal winemaker Ronell Wiid join forces to provide 'good value wines without cutting corners'.

Cabernet Sauvignon ★★★ **02** vanilla & red berries lead aromas/flavours; ripe, rounded tannins (only 2nd fill oak) make for easy, early drinking. **Merlot** ★★ **03** less stellar than pvs, still juicy but uncomplex; smoky/savoury nuances. ±Yr Fr oak oak, 20% new. Drink soon. **Pinotage** ★★ Unwooded, swiggable **04** earthy & plummy with brusque tannins — good with hearty braai food. **Shiraz** ★★ Medium bodied **03**, fruity, dusty, from combo new/old Fr oak. Showing signs of maturity, time to pull the last corks. **Simply Red** ★★ Chunky & friendly (14% alc) blend pinotage/merlot/ruby cab, spilling over with plums & prunes; bright finish. **NV**. **Chardonnay** ★★★ **02** pvsly noted as low-keyed but attractive. **Sauvignon Blanc** ★ Light **05** (sample) lacks varietal character, somewhat dilute. **Simply White** ★★ Pleasant dry tropical quaffer from colombard & chardonnay. **NV**. All WO W Cape, none retasted this ed.— *DH*

■ *His Master's Choice* see Excelsior Vlakteplaas

Hofstraat Winery   🍷🍽

Swartland ▪ Est/1stB 2002 ▪ Visits by appt ▪ Owners/winemakers Wim Smit, Loch Nel & Jack de Clercq ▪ 3.5 tons 310 cs 100% red ▪ 30 Rainier Str, Malmesbury 7300 ▪ wimsmit@ wcaccess.co.za ▪ T 022·487·3202 F 022·487·3015

This young trio insist they're committed to keeping their winery a hobby, not making it a job. Still, quality is a priority, and on that note they're proud to have come out tops in an informal Shiraz Challenge against three other *garagiste* cellars, all using grapes harvested simultaneously from the same block. Now they're optimistic about their chances for the follow-up clash of the cabs.

Renosterbos range

Shiraz ★★★ Higher rating for improved oak management on **05**; now older Fr wood (pvsly new Am), so sweet-ripe fruit more in balance. A pleasant, smoky, fireside drink — 15.5% alc guaranteed to banish any winter chill. Rbtson fruit; an untasted **05** from Swtlnd grapes also made/released. **Barbera** ★★★ Italian grape showing Swtlnd heartiness in **05**; big smoky bouquet, sweet fruit, strong dry tannins, heady 15.3% alc. Liberal oak spice from yr Am barrels. Following still selling, not retasted: **Cabernet Sauvignon 04** (sample last ed) juicy, supple style; flavoursome fresh cassis teamed up with noticeable but good oak. Possible ★★★★. **Merlot** ★★★ **04** focused red plum, choc freshness; light textured but with some fruity succulence. WO Voor Pdberg. — *DH*

■ *Homtini* see Anthony de Jager Wines

Hoopenburg Wines   🍷🍴🏛🍷

Stellenbosch ▪ Est 1992 ▪ 1stB 1994 ▪ Tasting & sales Oct-Apr only Mon-Fri 9.30-4.30 Sat & pub hols 9.30-2 ▪ Fee R10 refunded with purchase of 6+ btls ▪ Closed Easter Fri-Mon & Dec 25/26 ▪ BYO picnic ▪ Tours by appt ▪ Art gallery ▪ Owner Gregor Schmitz ▪ Winemaker/viticulturist Neil Hawkins (Jan 2005) ▪ Farm manager Gert Snyders ▪ 34 ha (cab, merlot, pinot, shiraz, chard) ▪ 150 tons 10 000 cs 75% red 25% white ▪ PO Box 1233 Stellenbosch 7599 ▪ info@ hoopenburg.com ▪ www.hoopenburg.com ▪ T 021·884·4221/2/3 ▪ F 021·884·4904

The Schmitz family is celebrating 15 years at Hoopenburg, where renewal has been the recent byword. Neil Hawkins continues the cellar's rejuvenation with quality-enhancing techniques including reduced yields, hand-picking and suckering, and plans to tantalise consumers with their top-end South Barrel Chamber range. International marketer Higgo Jacobs, who also assisted in the cellar, went off to Europe to oversee a hands-on expansion of Hoopenburg's market which is generating new consumer interest, especially in Spain and Holland.

★★★★ **Cabernet Sauvignon 02 (★★★★)** pvs ed was big & bold in every respect, incl black/sour cherry flavours with warming 14.5% alc, strapping tannins. Needed few yrs to mesh. **01** was full flavoured yet more restrained. Yr 2nd & 3rd fill Fr oak.

Merlot ★★★★ 03 a satisfying marriage of meaty/savoury aromas with herby sweet plum flavours, firm tannins & refreshing lemon-like acidity. 18 mths Fr oak, 30% new; same duration but no new wood for... **Pinot Noir ★★★ 04** in vein of pvs though lighter textured; hints cherry, raspberry & charry oak; fairly firm tannins & acidity. **Shiraz ★★★ 03** last ed noted as somewhat rustic with noticeably drying tannins (though these might since have settled & melded with fruit). 18 mths Fr oak, 20% new. **Chardonnay ★★★** 'Feminine' **05** elegant & restrained, shows subtle varietal character; well textured, though, with fine acidity & judicious oaking (yr Fr oak, 20% new). **South Barrel Chamber Chardonnay 05** work-in-progress tasted last yr & provisionally rated ★★★★, destined for release in 2007. Acacia flower & lemon blossom on nose, lively lime acidity; buttery, creamy oak. **Sauvignon Blanc ★★★★** New Zealand-like **05** has whiff of sweaty armpit, abundant green grass & nettle, fine vinosity with controlled acidity, dry mineral finish. All above WO Sbosch. **Pinotage** discontinued; **Pinot Noir-Chardonnay** tasted as sample last ed never bottled. — *CvZ*

■ *Hoop Huis see* False Bay Vineyards

Horse Mountain Wines

Paarl ▪ Est 1997 ▪ 1stB 2001 ▪ Visits by appt Mon-Fri 9-5 Sat 9-1 ▪ BYO picnic ▪ Owner Far Horizons Wine Estate (Pty) Ltd ▪ Winemaker Charles Stassen (Jan 2002) ▪ Viti consultant Paul Wallace (Jan 2000) ▪ 45 ha (cabs s/f, merlot, pinotage, shiraz) ▪ 400 tons 20 000 cs own labels + 80 000ℓ for clients ▪ 70% red 20% white 10% rosé ▪ PO Box 2143 Windmeul 7630 ▪ wine@horsemountainwines.com ▪ www.horsemountainwines.com ▪ T 021·869·8328 ▪ F 021·869·8329

Supermodel-turned-actress Jerry Hall reportedly enjoyed a few glasses of Quagga Ridge while performing at London's Shaftesbury Theatre, where this 'lifestyle' range was selected as the only wine served for the second year running. Back at Horse Mountain Wines, MD Craig Lardner has been elected head coordinator of The Quagga Project, which aims to bring these 'wild horses' back from the brink of extinction and reintroduce them to their former habitat. You might even spot some of them in a newly formed conservation area on the farm.

★★★★ **Pinotage 04** worthy successor to perfumed **03**. Fresh, ripe red flavours, hint of acetone more heritage than hindrance; excellent balance. 20% Am oak for coconut lift.

★★★★★ **Michele 04** classic bdx recipe of cab, merlot, cab f provides a wealth of interesting flavours, richness & palate weight. New Fr oak applied with class & restraint.

★★★★★ **Shiraz 04** Italian coffee shop in liquid form: all mocha & spice, booming 14.5% alc. Fr & 20% Am oak. No new releases tasted for this or next range.

Quagga Ridge range

Red ★ 04 rustic, earthy melange of cab & merlot; quality-wise, not from same stable as pvs. **Rosé ★★★** Easy drinking **05**, boiled sweets nose & light, fragrant body (12.5% alc.); 80% pinotage, dash merlot. **White ★★** 60:40 blend of sauvignon/semillon in **05**, vegetal flavours & big acidity. Less convincing than unpretentious **04** quaffer. — *NP*

■ *Houmoed see* Teubes Family

Huguenot Wine Farmers

Wellington ▪ Closed to public ▪ Owner Kosie Botha ▪ Cellarmaster Bill Matthee (1984) ▪ Trade enquiries Gert Brynard ▪ PO Box 275 Wellington 7654 ▪ jcb@mynet.co.za ▪ T 021·864·1293 ▪ F 021·873·2075

Privately owned wholesaling company which blends, markets and distributes a wide range of wines, liqueurs and spirits. The range, not assessed, includes: Cabernet, Pinotage, Smooth

Red (cinsaut/pinotage), Premier Grand Cru (chenin/crouchen), Stein (chenin), Late Harvest (chenin), Hanepoot, Red/White Jeripico (red/white muscadel), Invalid Port, Tawny Port, Nagmaalwyn and Old Brown Sherry. And the Zellerhof 5ℓ vats: Stein, Late Harvest and Premier Grand Cru.

■ **Husseys Vlei** *see Buitenverwachting*
■ **Isis** *see Schalkenbosch*

Idiom

Sir Lowry's Pass ▪ Est/1stB 2003 ▪ Tasting & sales: see Whalehaven ▪ Tours by appt ▪ Owners Alberto & Valerie Bottega ▪ Winemaker Sydney Burke, with Reino Thiart (Oct/Jan 2005) ▪ Viticulturist Tim Clark ▪ 32 ha (cabs s/f, merlot, shiraz, mourvèdre, nebbiolo, pinotage, sangiovese, zinfandel, viognier) ▪ 90% red 10% white ▪ Private Bag X14 Hermanus 7200 ▪ wine@idiom.co.za ▪ www.idiom.co.za ▪ T 028·316·1633 ▪ F 028·316·1640

Having had its first vintage showered with medals, small wonder that Idiom reports an amazing response from the industry and customers alike. The three single varieties sold out within months but some Idiom wines can still be found at a handful of SA's top restaurants. Vini-consultant Giorgio Dalla Cia is becoming increasingly excited by the quality as the vines mature and the wines become more complex. He suspects the secret to Idiom's success may be the constant wind blowing down from the Hottentots Holland mountains onto the vineyards.

★★★★ **Cabernet Sauvignon-Merlot-Cabernet Franc** ('Bordeaux Blend' pvs ed.) Elegant 57/28/15 configuration, yr Fr oaked, 60% new; **04** maraschino cherry flavours & firm, classy tannins. Poised, shrugs off substantial alc, sweetness (14.8%, 3g/ℓ sugar). Good prospects.

Sangiovese ★★★★ 04 realises potential implied in maiden **03**; well crafted, so 15% alc barely noticeable; juicy berry fruit, lithe tannin, tangy tail. Yr Fr/Am, some new. **Zinfandel ★★★★** Muscled **04**, packed with dark berry & piquant redcurrant fruit, rich, spicy oak. Vibrant acidity, firm tannins suggest gd evolution over next few yrs. 60% new Am oak. 15% alc. **Shiraz-Mourvèdre ★★★★** **04** stylish rhône-style blend led by shiraz (71%), dollop mourvèdre (25%), tickle viognier. Peppery spice in bouquet; full, round, confident flavours shd grow more expressive with few yrs cellaring. Combo new/old Fr/Am barrels. **Wooded Viognier ★★★★ 04** stone fruits aromas, 'sweet' butterscotch & barley sugar flavours. Oak overwhelming on release but sufficient fruit to carry 2-3 yrs. Note: no wines retasted this ed; all WO Sbosch.—*DH*

■ **Ikapa** *see Handcrafted Wines*
■ **Ilka** *see Alluvia*

I Love Wine

Paarl ▪ Open Mon-Sat 9-5; pub hols 10-3 ▪ Closed Good Fri, Dec 25 & Jan 1 ▪ 40A Main Rd Paarl 7646 ▪ info@ilovewine.co.za ▪ www.ilovewine.co.za ▪ T 021·863·2375 ▪ F 021·863·3120

Paarl boutique-wine and fully licensed coffee shop, doubling as tasting venue for Anthony Smook Wines, Bergheim, Blyde Wines, De Zoete Inval, Southern Sky and The Mason's Winery, all listed separately.

■ **Imagine** *see Southern Sky*
■ **Imbizo** *see Ernst & Co*
■ **Imbongi** *see Crossroads Wines*
■ **Imvelo** *see Premium Cape Wines*
■ **Indaba** *see African Terroir, Cape Classics, Excelsior*
■ **Indalo** *see Swartland Winery*
■ **Infiniti** *see The Company of Wine People*
■ **Inglewood** *see Neil Ellis Wines*

Ingwe

Stellenbosch (see Helderberg map) • *Est 1998* • *1stB 1999* • *Visits Mon-Fri 10-4* • *Owner Alain Mouiex* • *Winemaker PJ Geyer (Sep 2001)* • *Viticulturist Francois Baard (Sep 1999)* • *28 ha (own/leased; cabs s/f, malbec, merlot, shiraz, tempranillo, chard, sauvignon)* • *110 tons 18 000 cs 95% red 5% white* • *PO Box 583 Somerset West 7129* • *ingwewine@eject.co.za; ingwewinepg@eject.co.za; riana.wine@mweb.co.za* • **T 083·280·0137 (FB) / 083·327·3887 (PJG)** • *F 021·858·1063/021·852·7346*

The welcome carpet is out at Bordeaux vintner Alain Mouiex's Cape 'micro-château' in the burgeoning wine enclave of Sir Lowry's Pass in the Helderberg. With the focus now on blends only — two serious reds, one white, using typical bordeaux varieties and combinations — the appointment of marketer Riana Olivier (ex-neighbouring Mount Rozier) speaks of spreading the word — and the wines — more widely. The farm is now open for tastings weekdays.

★★★★ **Ingwe** Refined & classic merlot-led red, it's name means 'Leopard' in Xhosa. Has 48% cab partnering standout **03** (★★★★★), where mineral, savoury & black cherry tones abound; exceptional oak integration assisted by micro-oxygenation. Sample tasted mid-2005. Classy **02** also displayed refined minerality & mid-palate fruit density; 60% new Fr oak compared to **03**'s 40%.

★★★★ **Amehlo White** Sophisticated & harmonious bdx-style blend sauvignon & semillon, former fermented in two tanks — one 'cold' (±15°C), the other 'warm' (±26°C) by PJ Geyer; semillon vinified in Fr barrels with natural yeasts. Textured, aromatic **06** (★★★★★) continues upward trend; polished, bone-dry, flavoursome & stonily persistent. Gd for another 3 yrs at least. Impressively taut, minerally **05** raised the bar.

Amehlo 'Leopard's Eye' is another take on the bdx style; this is cab dominated (46%) with merlot, malbec, shiraz (25/15/10) & touch petit v in exceptional **03** (★★★★★). Pvs ed showed enticing spicy perfumes & focused velvet texture. Leap up from austere & leafy **02** (★★★★). 14-18 mths Fr oak. — CvZ

■ *Initial Series see* Jean Daneel

Iona Vineyards

Elgin • *Est 1997* • *1stB 2001* • *Tasting, sales & tours Mon-Fri 8-5.30* • *Closed Easter Fri/Sat/Sun, Dec 25 & Jan 1* • *BYO picnic* • *Self-catering guest house* • *Walks* • *Mountain biking* • *Owner Andrew & Rozanne Gunn, Workers Trust* • *Vini consultant Niels Verburg, with Thapelo Hlasa (both Feb 2004)* • *Viticulturist Joseph Sebulawa, advised by Kevin Watt (Nov 2001)* • *35 ha (cab, merlot, petit v, shiraz, mourvèdre, chard, sauvignon, semillon, viognier)* • *10 000 cs 25% red 75% white* • *PO Box 527 Grabouw 7160* • *gunn@iona.co.za* • *www.iona.co.za* • **T 028·284·9678** • *F 028·284·9078*

Intent on producing wines 'more minerally than the overtly fruity New World styles', owner Andrew Gunn is more than satisfied with last season's vintage. He attributes the 'concentrated elegance' of his Sauvignon to the use of French yeast (influenced by a visit to Sancerre) and last year's long, cool, dry growing season. The Sauvignon doesn't shine alone: vini consultant Niels Verburg sings the praises of the maiden Chardonnay, to be released at the start of this year.

★★★★★ **Sauvignon Blanc** Classically styled cool-climate example, where fine herbaceous rather than tropical notes dominate, in lighter, less punchy style — only 13.1% alc in **06**. Pungent nettley aromas, green fig whiffs, lovely pulpy fruit texture on the palate, finishing dry rather than tart.

Merlot-Cabernet Sauvignon ★★★★ **04** bright fruit flavours, featuring mulberry notes. Savoury, herbal hints on palate, with tannins lending grip, adding to length. Yr Fr oak, 25% new; 13.2% alc. **Shiraz** ★★★★ We noted last yr intriguing bouquet on smooth & dry **04**, & refreshing mineral aftertaste. Accessible, with 3-4 yr potential. — MF

■ *Isabelo see* 32 Degrees South
■ *Ivory Creek see* Citrusdal Cellars

■ *Ivy du Toit* see Jason's Hill
■ *Ixia* see Theuniskraal, Cape Legends
■ *Jabulani* see Cape Coastal Vintners

Jacaranda Estate

*Wellington ▪ Est 1993 ▪ 1stB 1994 ▪ Tasting, sales & tours Mon-Sat 10-5 ▪ Closed Easter Fri & Dec 25 ▪ Self-catering/B&B cottage ▪ BYO picnic ▪ Farm-grown/made cheeses, jams & olives ▪ Owners Jan & Trish Tromp ▪ Winemaker/viticulturist Jan Tromp ▪ 2.8 ha (cab, merlot, chenin) ▪ 25 tons 300 cs own label ▪ 75% red 25% white ▪ PO Box 121 Wellington 7654 ▪ jacaranda@ iafrica.com ▪ www.jacarandawineestate.co.za ▪ **T 021·864·1235/082·579·2992***

Jan and Trish Tromp's holistic view of their farm takes us beyond the vineyards: 'Our bird count is now up to 170,' he reports with glee, 'and Daisy the dairy cow's lactation has stretched to 1 213 days!' Then, cryptically: 'Watch this space for further developments.' His 05 Jerepigo has been bottled, the 06 Debutante red blended, leaving a little 06 Merlot. All show promise, says he: again, watch this space…

Jerepigo ★★★ Individual & attractive **05** brimful of baked apples & sultana, very sweet (199g/ℓ sugar) & just a shade cloying. From chenin, 18% alc. New vintages of following unready: **Cabernet Sauvignon** ★★ **01** individual & rustically charming. **Merlot** ★★★ **03** soft & light textured with pleasing tannin structure & smart wooding (Fr staves). **Debutante** ★★★ Idiosyncratic **03** cab/merlot blend with scents of farmyard & wild scrub, stewed fruit flavours, firm dry finish. Lightly Fr oaked. **Chenin Blanc** ★★ Pear toned **03** soft, fruity-dry; unwooded. — *IvH*

■ *Jackals River* see Beaumont

Jack & Knox Winecraft

Est/1stB 2001 ▪ Tasting & sales at Flagstone (see entry) ▪ Owners Graham Knox & Bruce Jack ▪ See under Flagstone

Vinous chameleon Graham Knox (Siyabonga, Stormhoek, At The Limiet) here collaborates with Bruce Jack of Flagstone Winery, uncovering exciting and unusual vineyards, capturing the essence of variety, nurturing the young and nursing the old back to life. And bottling under the most descriptive names: Frostline – from high, not-quite-snowline Swartberg mountain vineyard; Outsider – shiraz, now a tri-regional blend; Green on Green – vineyard situated on lower foothills of Wellington's Groenberg ('Green Mountain'). Huge critical acclaim, great fun.

★★★★ **Green on Green Semillon** Textured rather than bright varietal tones garnered from Wllngtn vyd. Last tasted **04** beautifully elegant from candlewax notes through ripe quince flesh, tethered by limy seam. Native yeasts; Am/Fr oak, 30% new; now lighter 13% alc.

The Outsider Shiraz A step-up; lovely fleshy texture, fruit purity in **04** (★★★★). Complex layers violets, café au lait, dark plums, even hint of mint, coupled with svelte body, reward the drinker. 14-16 mths mainly Am, 20% new. WO W Cape. Pvs was brooding blockbuster **02** (★★★☆), with ultra-ripe waves liquorice & crushed dark spice. **Frostline Chardonnay** ★★★★ **04** reviewed last ed, proffered crème brûlée aromas, roast hazelnut girth cut by litchi & white pear; smooth, less robust (13% alc) than pvs. Barrel fermented 4 mths Am/Fr oak, 60% new. **Frostline Riesling** ★★★★ Variety's aromatic pepper/lime delicacy given steely glint in last tasted **05**: broad fruit richness to tingling bone-dry finish. — *CR*

■ *Jackson's of Stanford* see Stanford Hills Winery

Jacobsdal Estate

*Stellenbosch ▪ Est 1916 ▪ 1stB 1974 ▪ Tasting & sales at Bergkelder (see entry) or by appt ▪ Owner Dumas Ondernemings (Pty) Ltd ▪ Winemaker/viticulturist Cornelis Dumas, with Hannes Dumas ▪ 100 ha (cab, pinotage, chenin, sauvignon) ▪ 600 tons 9-13 000 cs own label 100% red ▪ PO Box 11 Kuils River 7579 ▪ dumas@iafrica.com ▪ www.jacobsdal.co.za ▪ **T/F 021·905·1360***

Cornelis Dumas is the third generation of this family of French origin to work this land, on the south-western edge of Stellenbosch. Nearly a quarter of the farm is planted with their speciality pinotage, vinified here for 40 years. Son Hannes assists with the winemaking, which is staunchly traditional, involving natural yeast fermentation, with manual punch-down of the grape skins in open cement tanks.

★★★★　**Pinotage** A sentimental favourite; the first was **66** & today's versions are still charmingly artisanal. **03** flush with jammy mulberry/raspberry fruit & hints varietal smoke & rubber; balanced, no rough edges despite hefty 14.5% alc. Long, with lovely fruit depth. Off 25-35 yr old dryland bushvines, free-run juice only, 12-18 mths small Fr oak.

Cabernet Sauvignon ★★★★ Made exactly as above, off dryland bushvines 10-15 yrs old. **03** a departure from pvs, which didn't pander to fleshy fruit pundits: more genteel, with creamy cassis & violet notes & supple but suitably astringent cab tannins; refreshing acidity still makes this an ideal partner for rich mutton *bredies*. — *CvZ*

▪ *Jacobus de Wet* see Baarsma
▪ *Jacoline Haasbroek Wines* see My Wyn

Jacques Smit Wines　　　　　♂♀ ☕ [new]

*Wellington ▪ Est/1stB 2003 ▪ Tasting, sales & tours Mon-Fri 9-5 Sat 8-1 ▪ Closed Easter Fri/Sun/ Mon, Ascension Day, Dec 25/26 & Jan 1 ▪ Facilities for children ▪ Owners Jacques & Marina Smit ▪ Winemaker Jacques Smit, with Jan Paul Louw (2003) ▪ Viticulturist Jacques Smit ▪ 32 ha (cab, shiraz, chenin, crouchen) ▪ 300 tons total 6 tons/±5 000 btls own label 100% red ▪ PO Box 137 Wellington 7654 ▪ wine_vines@mweb.co.za ▪ **T** 021·873·1265 ▪ F 021·873·2143*

Jacques Smit has always worked with vines: his nursery stocks them all — from the special varieties for the trade to the patio 'autumn vine' for the weekend gardener. Along came a particularly fine cab harvest and the winemaking bug bit deep. 'It was my 45-year itch. And it became a family passion — even my five-year-old son helped crush the first harvest.' That was four years ago and for the Smits there's no looking back.

These wines open-tank fermented, bottled unfiltered; names yet to be finalised at press time ('Please don't sue us!'). **Cabernet Sauvignon** ★★ Gamey aromas, black fruit hints on **04**, but 14. 6% alc pretty evident. 22 mths oak, some new. Unfiltered. First was **03**, but we missed it. **'The Full Circle'** ★★★ Aka 'Cabernet Sauvignon'; **NV** version pleasant, amply fruited, also from fully ripened grapes (14.9% alc). 18 mths small oak lends persistence to finish. **Shiraz** ★★★★ Massive **05** (tasted ex-barrel) delivers dollops of black fruit, pepper, savoury tannins, but unbalanced by huge 16.4% alc. 11 mths oak, 20% new. Maiden **04** (oaked 22 mths) untasted by us. **'Vine Valley'** ★★★ Aka 'Red Blend'; **04** sees cab/shiraz in 50/50 partnership, with dominant red & black fruit aromas & a lingering pepper/nutmeg finish — not to mention house-style sumptuous texture. **Roobernet Port** Robustly fashioned, foot-crushed **06** — the first in SA from this grape (a pontac-cab cross)? Fine leafy hints lift curranty palate, but alc (18.6%) & sugar (103g/l) still unintegrated in this tank sample; probably ★★★. — *MF*

▪ *Jagger's Peak* see Blue Crane

Janéza Private Cellar　　　　　♀ ☕

*Robertson ▪ Est 2000 ▪ 1stB 2001 ▪ Visits by appt ▪ Fee for tour groups R5 ▪ Open pub hols by appt ▪ Platters by appt Mon-Fri ▪ Owners Jan & Eza Wentzel ▪ Winemaker Jan Wentzel ▪ Viti consultant Willem Botha ▪ 18 ha (cab, merlot, petit v, shiraz, chard, sauvignon) ▪ 3 000 cs own label 60% red 40% white ▪ PO Box 306 Bonnievale 6730 ▪ jan.eza@lando.co.za ▪ www. janeza.co.za ▪ **T/F** 023·616·3547*

'In spite of hail damage, we had good quality grapes which produced lovely wines,' say the Wentzels from their Robertson farm, where the tasting room was recently enlarged and a fireplace installed. The range is now broadened by two new food- and pocket-friendly reds.

Cabernet Sauvignon [new] ★★★ **05** toasted hazelnut tone to broad shouldered newcomer; big, firm structure presently overshadows modest fruit — needs yr/2 to develop.

Merlot new ★★★ Off to gd start; **05** approachably ripe & comfortable; juicy wild berry fruit; decidedly ingratiating ±5g/ℓ sugar & 15% alc. **Tresuva** ★★★ Trio of grapes in wine's Spanish name now a quartet: cab (44%), shiraz, merlot & smattering petit v, vinified traditionally, 13 mths oaked. **03** riper than pvs though still medium bodied; quite rich, slightly raisined fruit. **Chardonnay** ★★★ Amiable & appealing **06**, pure, clean & bright pear flavours untrammelled by wood; touch sweetness in tail. **Sauvignon Blanc** ★★ Early picked, piercingly fresh & dry **05**, delicate green herb bouquet; at 11.5% alc, even lighter than pvs.—*CT*

▪ *Jantara see* Cape Vineyards
▪ *Jardin see* Jordan

Jason's Hill Private Cellar

Slanghoek (see Worcester map) ▪ Est/1stB 2001 ▪ Tasting & sales Mon-Fri 9-5 Sat 10-3 Sun by appt ▪ Fee R10 ▪ Closed Easter Fri, Dec 25 & Jan 1 ▪ Bistro @ Jason's Tue-Sat 9-5 (also available for functions) ▪ Facilities for children ▪ Farm produce ▪ Conferencing for max 50 ▪ Owner Sakkie du Toit ▪ Winemaker Ivy du Toit-Oates (Jan 2001) ▪ Viticulturist Alister Oates (2004) ▪ 100 ha (13 varieties r/w) ▪ 600 tons 50% red 45% white 5% rosé ▪ Brand for customer: Wolvenbosch Family Vineyards (UK) & Fountain Head (Denmark) ▪ PO Box 14 Rawsonville 6845 ▪ jasonshill@lando.co.za ▪ www.jasonshill.com ▪ T 023·344·3256 ▪ F 023·344·3146

Ivy du Toit-Oates began her vinous journey at the tender age of 21 when she telephoned through her resolve from the US: 'Dad, I want to make my own wine.' Her *garagiste* days now over (a cellar materialised in 2002), she and her wines are maturing nicely. A new addition to the farm: Bistro @ Jason's, which provides tasties and lovely views over the vineyards.

> **Jason's Creek Classic Red** ☺ new ★★★ **04** unusual combo petit verdot & malbec delivers explosion of earthy/smoky fruit; juicy, sleek, perfectly smooth, with lovely lithe tannins. A treat!

No new vintages ready for following trio: **Cabernet Sauvignon** ★★★ **01** mocha/mushroom features to dark-berried bouquet; solid mouthful, well integrated for early drinking. 15% alc. **Pinotage** ★★★ Vanilla toned **01** smooth, light textured & less weighty than 14.5% alc would suggest. 10 mths used Fr oak. **Shiraz** ★★★ **01** sweet-oak flavours dominate; 15% alc warmth in tail. 20% new Am oak, rest older Fr. **Merlot** ★★★ **05** ripe, soft, minty mulberry fruit, stronger tannin backup than pvs, so better cellared or served with food. Fr casks, 10 mths, none new. **Rosé** Off-dry **06** unready. **Chardonnay** ★★ **05** similar styling to pvs: sweetish tone, with butterscotch & vanilla, pleasant bottle-age honey creeping in, so drink soonish. Fermented in Fr oak, 1st/2nd fill. **Sauvignon Blanc** ★★★ **03** won Diners Club Young Winemaker of Year for Ivy dT. Current **05** light, easy-drinking style, crisply dry, with gooseberry & asparagus notes. **Chenin** ★★★ Last tasted in **04**, invitingly fresh in youth, lively medium bodied sipping. **Ivy du Toit Limited Edition Sauvignon Blanc-Semillon-Chardonnay** ★★★ ('White Blend' pvs eds.) SA Woman Winemaker of Yr award for last tasted **03**, equal blend with prominent sweet-oak vanilla, good thread balancing acid. Fermented/8 mths new Fr oak. An **Ivy du Toit Limited Release Pinotage 02** also made but not tasted. **Jason's Creek Classic White** new ★★★ **06** chenin & sauvignon in delightful summer-styled refresher, medium bodied, with a pleasing contrast of tropical fruit & greenpeppers. **Jasonté Sparkling** new Rosé from pinotage, **06** just missed our deadline. **Noble Late Harvest** ★★★★ Golden **03** dessert was last-tasted; 50/50 chenin/muscat d'A; luscious but not over-heavy.—*CT*

▪ *Jay Gatsby see* Third World Wines

JC le Roux

Stellenbosch ▪ 1stB 1983 ▪ Tasting & sales Mon-Fri 8.30-4.30 Sat 10-4 (Nov-Apr) 10-3 (May-Oct) Sun 10-3 (Nov-Apr only) ▪ Fee R20 ▪ Tour & AV show Mon-Fri 10, 11.30, 3 Sat 10, 12 Sun (Nov-Apr only) 11, 12 ▪ Closed Easter Fri/Sun, Dec 25 & Jan 1 ▪ Tour groups ▪ Gifts ▪ Owner

*Distell • Winemaker Wilhelm Pienaar (2006) with Hentie Germishuys (Oct 2002) • Farm manager Willem Laubscher; viticulturist Bennie Liebenberg (both Jan 2000) • 27 ha own vyds • 20% red 80% white • ISO 9200 certified • Devon Valley Rd, Stellenbosch 7599 • info@jcleroux.co.za • **T 021·865·2590** • F 021·865·2586*

Melanie vd Merwe having retired to hearth and home after more than a decade here, assistant winemaker Wilhelm Pienaar took over last year as cellarmaster. 'Rough, but it's good,' he opines of his new responsibilities, adding that there's been little change, production-wise, for the biggest bubbly-maker in the country: for now, the new broom is leaning against the cellar wall. Another thing that hasn't changed is the constant growth the sparkling sector continues to record. And still pleasing Stellenbosch wine-route visitors is the deli-style restaurant on the estate, Tables @ JC le Roux.

Méthode Cap Classique range

★★★★ **Scintilla** Chard-dominated sparkling (75%, with pinot), its class alluded to by weighty embossed bottle. Rich but refreshing **01** has a creamy mousse as delightful as its brioche & honey aromas, lengthy apple flavours. Ideal for solo or with food; fruit-weight also bodes well for cellaring. Bottle-matured 3 yrs (pvs 4½); at 9.7g/ℓ RS, slightly sweeter than predecessors. SAA trophy winner.

★★★★★ **Pinot Noir** Beautiful antique lace colour of **98** (★★★★☆) a reflection of the elegant, creamy wine, inviting with aromas of candy apple & patisserie. Quite delicious &, like **97**, step-up in quality. Sbosch grapes; ±7 yrs *sur lie*; undemandingly brut at 7.1g/ℓ RS.

★★★★ **Pinot Noir Rosé** Pink bubbly with something to say, partly from 6+ yrs on lees. **97**'s gorgeous salmon hue would complement any sunset, its candied raspberry fruit many romantic meals. Weighty & pleasantly dry (9g/ℓ RS); best enjoyed soonish to appreciate its delightful freshness.

★★★★ **La Vallée** Unconventional – it's from pinot gris – & popular semi-dry bubbly (33g/ℓ RS). **00** (★★★★) offers an orange & nutmeg bouquet, fresh yeasty aromas; gently sweet, uncloying, finishes with a honeyed tang from ±5 yrs bottle-age. Appealing, if just a shade lighter than **99**, with notes of toasted nut & chamomile.

Chardonnay ★★★☆ Brut sparkler from home vyds in Devon Vlly, classically long-matured (5+ yrs on lees). **01**, recently degorged, will reward patience by growing in complexity. Lemon, apple & coconut tones dominate; brisker & leaner (only 7.9g/ℓ RS) than apple toned **00**.

Sparkling range

These all carbonated; **NV** unless noted. **Le Domaine** ★★★ Frothy, sweet, party-friendly bubbles from white muscadel & sauvignon; floral & thatchy muscat aromas, lively, with low 7.5% alc, as for…. **La Chanson** ★★★ Big-volume sweet sparkler with a lovely ruby hue to lift jaded spirits. Abundant berry fruit from mix red varieties, predominantly pinotage. Tannins provide contrast, absorb some of the sweetness. **Sauvignon Blanc** ★★★ Perky, easy-drinking **06** offers gooseberry, hay & Granny Smith apple, suggestion of sweetness from 12g/ℓ sugar. **JC Blue** ★★ In 187ml screwcapped sapphire bottle complete with straw for easy sipping. Papaya & lime notes; soft semi-sweet flavours. Both ranges Coastal or W Cape origin. — *CvZ*

Jean Daneel Wines ☺

*Napier • Est/1stB 1997 • Visits by appt • Owners/winemakers Jean, Jean-Pierre & René Daneel • 3.25 ha • 57 tons 4 000 cs 30% red 70% white • PO Box 200 Napier 7270 • jdwines@worldonline.co.za • **T 028 423·3724** • F 028·423·3789*

Jean Daneel, wife René and two sons brought in the maiden harvest from their own vineyard just outside Napier last year. And when understated Daneel reports that it was a 'huge success', winelovers should stand up and start clearing cellar space. The family has added more rows, including shiraz, to their vine holdings. Hopefully this, as well as the planned new tasting room and deli in Napier, will go some way toward appeasing fans looking for more of his wines, which are invariably sold out.

Signature Series

★★★★ **Cabernet Sauvignon-Merlot** Standout **01** (★★★★☆) showed elegance & restraint. As does **02** (apart from 14.5% alc), appealingly generous & ripe, with sweet fruit, well structured — gd for difficult yr, but focus diffused, finish rather congested, tannins chewy. Most drinkable nonetheless. 65/35% blend. 22 mths oak, half new. WO Fhoek.

★★★★☆ **Chenin Blanc** Gorgeous, complex aromas on **05** (pineapple, wax, honey, fennel to say the least); dried apricot asserted on rich palate. Ripe but elegant, braced by fine acidity; 10 mths oak (20% new) noticeable, but rapidly integrating. Dryness, refinement (though big 14.5% alc) gives more drinkability than many trophy-seeking Cape chenins have. Sbosch grapes. Less striking **04** (★★★★) followed magnificent **03** (★★★★★), this guide's first Wine of the Year.

★★★★ **Chardonnay Brut** Elegant MCC from Fhoek chard. Last tasted **01** with biscuit notes, delicious suppleness on palate, great lift & focus.

Initial Series

Red ★★★☆ (Pvsly 'Cabernet Sauvignon-Merlot', now no varietal mix in name, as with next wine.) Forward blackcurrant aromas on **03**; smooth but classic-minded rather than showy, with firm acid/tannin structure & restained, integrated oak (22 mths, 20% new). 75/25 cab/merlot. WO Fhoek, like… **White** ★★★ Chenin attractively dominates aromas (though just under half of blend with sauvignon), with honeyed, grassy notes. Nice flavours too, but on lean side of elegance. Dry finish. **Port** ★★★ **00** from cab ex-Barrydale, 3 yrs wooded & showing rich barrel character last yr; raisiny oxidative berry aromas; dense, soft textures. — *TJ*

■ *Jewel of the Breede River* see Kingsriver Estate
■ *Kiss & Tell* see Leopard Frog Vineyards
■ *JH Pacas & Co* see Bernheim
■ *JJ Handmade Wines* see Stellenrust

Johan van Zyl Wines

Piekenierskloof (see Olifants River map) • Est/1stB 2002 • Visits by appt 10-5 • Owner Johan van Zyl • Winemaker Gerda Willers • Viticulturist Johan Viljoen • 50 ha (cab, cinsaut, grenache (r/w), pinotage, tempranillo, chard, viognier) • 250 tons 500 cs own label • PO Box 251 Citrusdal 7340 • hannalise@heidedal.co.za • T 022-921-3328/2740 • F 022-921-2740

A very dry winter in the Piekenierskloof deterred the vines and the Van Zyls not a jot: owner/winemaker Johan vZ declares the 2006 vintage 'very good, with intense flavours'. He's also buoyed up by his Grenache 05, released late last year. Improvements to the property include a tasting facility and a maturation cellar; newly introduced to the range is an unoaked Chardonnay, with a red blend in the pipeline.

Grenache ★★★ **05** more generous, approachable vintage; offers bright ripe red fruit, hint of spice, pleasing harmony among fruit, alc & acid. Mainly older oak, 9 mths. **Pinotage** ★★ **04** similar qualities to pvs: high-toned, 'sauvage' aromas, Am oak 'sweetening' (20%, yr, 50% new), spirituous rush from 15% alc. Might settle, mesh, with time. **Chardonnay** ★★★ Lovely & lively full-ripe entry to **05**; touch of pear; integrated & unobtrusive oak/alc (though 15%!); lowish acidity only cavil. 9 mths Fr wood, 20% new. **Chardonnay Unwooded** new ★★★ 'Not dry white!' asserts JvZ about deliberate sweetness (8g/ℓ sugar) on **06**, which gives extra plumpness to sunny-ripe tropical fruit (14% alc); some balance restored by fresh acidity. — *JN*

■ *John B* see Rietvallei
■ *John Faure* see Ruitersvlei

Jonkheer

Robertson • Est 1912 • 1stB 1956 • Visits by appt • Closed pub hols • Proclaimed conservation area • 4×4 trail • Owners Nicholas Jonker & sons • Winemakers Erhard Roothman & Dirk Jonker (1970/1992) • Viticulturists Andries Jonker & Gideon van Niekerk (1985/1981) • 185 ha (cab, chard, muscat de F) • 2 500 tons 15 000 cs own label + 130 000 cs for customers, incl

Semaya (US & Scandinavia) ▪ 30% red 70% white ▪ PO Box 13 Bonnievale 6730 ▪ info@
jonkheer.co.za ▪ www.jonkheer.co.za ▪ **T** 023·616·2137/8/9 ▪ F 023·616·3146

Dirk Jonker's enjoying the thought of a busy 2007, with plans to launch a Reserve Sauvignon
and two export ranges. Not that 2006 was a stroll on the Breede riverbank. The Jonkheer
range tripled its listings in premier hotels around the world and, back home, there was a flurry
of innovation: a Dead Frogge Merlot joined the thereby-hangs-a-tale amphibian range, the
first petit verdot was harvested, the first nouvelle vines went into the soil and a new tasting
room came into being.

Jonkheer range

★★★★ **Chardonnay Family Reserve** Serious & classically styled; from a single vyd, new Fr
oak fermented, *sur lie* ±18 mths, native yeasts. Pvs **04** (sample) held nothing back,
with crème brûlée intensity, palate-lengthening 6g/ℓ RS. **05** (★★☆) has similar opulence without a containing structure, giving an ultra-soft boneless character — which
will have its adherents. WO Rbtson.

★★★★ **Dead Frogge Chardonnay** Vastly less frivolous than name — block selection, 75%
fermented in new & 2nd fill oak, natural yeasts; **05** (★★★☆) bold & vibrant as pvs, a
ringing freshness to the yellow peach fruit, wood well integrated; only quibble is the
sweetish finish, which **04** (sample) avoided though it had more sugar (5.5g/ℓ).

★★★★ **Muscatheer Family Reserve Muscat de Frontignan** Last was massively sweet
04, which billowed fragrance/flavours of caramelised peel, dried fruit, toasted nuts.
IWSC Gold, Muscadel Assoc Platinum. 500ml.

Dead Frogge Merlot [new] ★★☆ Warm-hearted country red with soft squishy-sweet fruit &
savoury hints of roast beef. **03** partly Fr oaked, unfiltered. **Pinotage** ★★★ Characterful **05** ex-single vyd block; thick & chunky with high-toned edginess; rich, full, sweet flavours yet a firm tannic
grip, partly from portion barrel fermented/aged new Fr oak. Cld develop interestingly. New vintages of following quartet unready: **Cabernet Sauvignon Family Reserve** ★★★☆ **03** meat-
extract savouriness; juicy accessibility yet enough tannin foundation (18 mths in barrel) for few
more yrs in cellar. **Cabernet Sauvignon-Merlot** ★★★★ Yr oaked **03** evolved beautifully; curves
in the right places to please most palates. **Chardonnay** ★★★ Unoaked **04** showed delicate floral/
honeysuckle nose; full-flavoured with refreshing limy acidity. **Buccanheer Touriga Nacional**
★★★★ Ruby style port, 18 mths in 2nd fill oak; **02** Xmas cake, tea leaves & marzipan; lighter than
expected body doesn't detract from enjoyment. 500ml.

Bakenskop range

★★★★ **Red Muscadel** Traditional-style fortified muscatty dessert with intriguing complexity.
Impressive **04** tea leaf notes & Glühwein spice. Marvellous silky texture, delicious.

★★★★ **White Muscadel** Raisiny fortified dessert, beloved of competition judges. Gorgeous
04 clementine marmalade aromas, flavours; luscious, with enough alc zip to break the
richness. WO Rbtson, as is above.

Only the Rosé in range tasted this ed; new vintages unready. **Cabernet Sauvignon** ★★☆ **04**'s
plum & vanilla biscuit aromas, flavours punctuated by firm edginess, making it food-compatible. 7
mths barrel maturation, as are rest of reds. **Merlot** ★★★ **04** a real charmer: sappy red berry fruit,
silky mouthfeel helped by 4.7g/ℓ sugar. **Roothman Cape Red** ★★★ Fruit the hero of this **NV**
blend: bright, fresh-picked mulberries, blackcurrants, backed up by creamy, smoothly tasty palate.
Pinotage ★★☆ Textbook ripe-style pinotage, **04** forceful tannins in youth. **Natural Sweet Rosé**
[new] ★★ From red muscadel, with delicate spiciness & hint of muscat; easy, not too sweet, will
make many friends. **NV. Blanc de Noir** ★★ Simple & honest **05** redcurrant/cherry character from
its red muscadel source, light 11.7% alc & off-dry. **Chardonnay** ★★★ Unwooded **04** had pear/
marzipan aromas, nice melon mouthful. **Chenin Blanc** ★★ **05** refreshing easy-drinker with pear/
guava fruit salad character, approachable 12.3% alc. **Sauvignon Blanc** ★★ **05** shyer than pvs;
nettly minerality, light textured, bone-dry. **Muscat Perlé** ★★ Gentle bubbles emphasise the floral
tones, grapey flavours of **04**. Semi-sweet, friendly quaffer, with low 8.9% alc. All WO W-Cape
unless noted. — *IvH*

Joostenberg Wines

*Paarl • Est 1999 • Tasting & sales daily 10-5 at Klein Joostenberg Deli & Bistro • Tours by appt •
Bistro hours Tue-Sun 8-5 (see Eat-out section) • Owner Myburgh Winery (Pty) Ltd • Cellar-
master/viticulturist Tyrrel Myburgh • Winemaker Gareth Hardres-Williams • 31 ha (cab, merlot, mourvèdre, shiraz, touriga, chenin, viognier) • 200 tons 8 000 cs own label 35% red 50%
white 15% dessert • PO Box 82 Elsenburg 7607 • joostenberg@mweb.co.za • www.
joostenberg.co.za • **T 021·884·4932** • F 021·884·4135*

Gareth Hardres-Williams caught the wine bug while working as a game ranger at Londolozi.
Elsenburg, France, California and Rustenberg winery lionised his enthusiasm, which now boards
with the Myburghs at Joostenberg. This allows Tyrrel M to spend more time in the vineyards, his
first love. Last year saw the 250th anniversary of the manor house on this farm but the business
end of Joostenberg is across the N1 at Klein Joostenberg, where you can taste the wines and enjoy the cuisine of French brother-in-law Christophe Dehosse at the increasingly popular deli.

★★★★ **Bakermat** 'Birthplace' — farm's flagship, off their best performing vyds; **04** more robust & showy than pvs, but still seriously styled. Blend cab, merlot, shiraz (50/41/9) with
well judged 2 yrs Fr oak, 25% new. Compact blackberry fruit balanced by firm
tannins.

★★★★ **Shiraz-Viognier** From uncertified organic vineyards; **05** fresh & elegant (moderate
13.5% alc); viognier (7%) co-fermented with earlier-picked shiraz; beguiling fruit purity, vibrancy & balance make for delightful enjoyment. Native yeasts, 10 mths 500ℓ Fr
barrels. Swiss gold.

★★★★ **Walker Bay** new Tyrrel M 'fascinated by potential of s-Cape', hence experimental **04**
from young (5 yr) low-yield Stanford vines; mainly cab (86%), equal dollops cab f, merlot. Classic, elegant bdx style; sweet, pure blackcurrant fruit; rewarding now & probably over shorter term. Open *kuip* fermented; 18 mths older Fr barrels. Just 50 cs.

★★★★ **Chenin Blanc Noble Late Harvest** ✓ **05** (★★★★☆) not as flamboyant as some pvs
but notably sophisticated, sufficiently rich to ensure longevity; fine grapefruit acidity
balances unctuously sweet depth of peach/pineapple flavours (135g/ℓ sugar) for
thrillingly fresh, flavoursome, long finish. 6 pickings, last mid-May. **04** *Wine* ★★★★.

Merlot-Shiraz ★★★☆ ✓ Previewed **05** abundant spice & pepper; firm ripe tannins frame
rich, juicy blackberry fruit, delivering balance & drinkability in 50/50 blend. **Fairhead 05**
(★★★★) blend chenin/viognier/chard (55/38/7), latter from barreled 03 vintage, early
picked for freshness — successful strategy to counteract usual opulence & low acid of
viognier. Richly spicy; seamless, with remarkable texture & moderate 13.5% alc. Maiden
04 (★★★☆) noted last ed as one to watch. Wild yeasts, older barrels. **Chenin Blanc-
Viognier** Abundant honeysuckle & peach on exotically spiced **06** (★★★★ ✓); preview
shows much more fruit & texture than pvs minerally **05** (★★★☆); also more concentration
from harvesting 25 yr old bushvines. 5% viognier. — *IM*

Jordan Winery

*Stellenbosch • Est 1982 • 1stB 1993 • Tasting & sales Mon-Fri 10-4.30 Sat 9.30-2.30 Sun 10-
2.30 • Fee R15 refundable with purchase • Group tastings for up to 15 by appt • Closed Easter
Fri-Mon, Dec 25 & Jan 1 • Tours by appt only (no pub hols) • BYO picnic • Owners Jordan family • Winemakers Gary & Kathy Jordan • Production Sjaak Nelson (2002) • Viticulturists Ted &
Gary Jordan (1982) • 105 ha (cabs s/f, merlot, shiraz, chard, chenin, sauvignon, riesling) • 900
tons 65 000 cs 55/45 red/white • PO Box 12592 Die Boord 7613 • info@jordanwines.com or
sales@jordanwines.com • www.jordanwines.com • **T 021·881·3441** • F 021·881·3426*

Last year was one of comings and goings on the Stellenbosch farm: two Austrians and a
Namibian helped Gary and Kathy Jordan in the cellar, with Francis Carle from Bordeaux lending a hand for a few days, while a Californian expat vineyard manager (aka 'Druiwe') assisted
in the vineyards. Once the harvest was done — Gary J reports more balanced acidities and
better pHs than in previous years — the husband-and-wife team, accompanied by production
manager Sjaak Nelson, took a trip to Bordeaux; a little later in the year, Leon Nero, who has
worked at the winery for three years, went to Burgundy on a two-month SAWIT exchange

programme. A partnership with an English winery, Stanlake Park Estate, sees Jordan's wines offered in its 15th-century tasting room.

★★★★ **Cobblers Hill** Flagship bdx blend celebrating Jordan cobbler heritage. Mainly cab with merlot, cab f, from specific vyds. **04** held back for later release, not tasted. Majestic cab austerity on **03** (★★★★★, not retasted), more dimension than pvs, even better prospects. Blend cab, merlot, cab f (55/30/15). Swiss gold. **02** IWSC gold, *Wine* ★★★★.

★★★★★ **Sophia CWG Auction Reserve** Named for mother of Faith, Hope & Charity, representing the trio of best barrels selected from above wine for this impressive showcase bottling. Additional cab on **04** gives more austere, tannic feel; will need yrs to develop fully; underlying sweet fruited richness & freshening acid augur well for long haul. 46/33/21 cab, merlot, cab f, 26 mths new Fr barriques.

★★★★ **Cabernet Sauvignon** One of Cape's leading modern style cabs; maturing vyds now evident in greater core concentration, complexity. Macho **04** from dry, hot vintage, still relatively tight; unyielding yet ripe tannins will benefit from yr/2 to release array classic, deep flavours. Beautifully proportioned for 6–8 yr evolution. ±20 mths new/used Fr oak. **03** Winemakers' Choice.

★★★★ **Merlot 04** stylish & understated, as usual. Lithe yet confident; satisfying contrast of perfectly ripe fruit & freshness. Moderately oaked for harmony, ready drinkability – but don't underestimate potential: decade-old **96** recently rated ★★★★ by *Wine*. Fr oak, new/used, 16 mths.

★★★★★ **Nine Yards Chardonnay Reserve** A New World classic: bold, outspoken but also sophisticated, complex, ageworthy. **05** balances keen freshness with rich flavours & textures. Already polished, integrated; little suggestion of bold 14.5% alc. Barrel selection from their best vyd (17 yrs old); fermented/yr new Fr oak, portion native ferment for complexity. Glory-soaked **03** ★★★★★; *Wine* ★★★★; VDG; JCWCA 'first'/gold.

★★★★★ **CWG Auction Reserve Chardonnay** Stringent all-new-barrel selection from Nine Yards vyd, with yet more of everything than above, incl gorgeous buttery gold shine on **05**. Distinguished & refined, though shade more assertive, will need longer to round out, esp. spicy oak edges. 100% native yeast ferment, 14 mths new Fr oak.

★★★★ **Chardonnay** Consistent hit with show judges & consumers; ages beneficially, too, over 4–5 yrs. Youthful citrus, hazelnut & lees aromas, subtle oak on **05**, plus greater steely tautness than usual to balance creamy mouthfeel. Established oaking regime, incl 40–50% new Fr, *sur lie* 9 mths. Incl ±12% tank fermented portion. **04** Winemakers' Choice, VDG.

★★★★ **Sauvignon Blanc** ✓ **06** (★★★★★) best yet from excellent sauvignon vintage. Touch more dramatic than usual but nothing too aggressive, harsh. Fantastic cool purity of fruit; ripe, concentrated but agile; seemingly endless conclusion. **05** also stimulating, steely & brisk.

★★★★ **Blanc Fumé** ✓ Well defined contrast between this riper, more complex wooded sauvignon & above wine. **05** back on reliable form, with elegantly vanilla enhanced fig/citrus features. Balanced freshness, intensity derived from fruit concentration rather than alc, (a moderate 13%). Incl 40% tank fermented portion. Few yrs potential.

★★★★ **Mellifera Noble Late Harvest** Riesling's propensity for this botrytised dessert style again paraded in scintillating **06**. Spicy/limy aromas; lush concentrated fruit; sweetness pepped up by urgent, racy acid. Touch bigger than best-to-date **05** (★★★★★).

Syrah ★★★★ **04** from warm, west-facing vyds, richly textured, flavoursome with lifted spice for balanced freshness. Fullish but not too heavy. Harmoniously Am/Fr oaked, 16 mths. **Chameleon Cabernet Sauvignon-Merlot** ★★★★ Combines approachability, flavoursome layers & ageing potential. **04** with 17% shiraz not strictly bdx style as pvs, though similar character in bright cassis/plum fruit, firmly rounded structure. Fr oak, 14 mths. **Chardonnay Unoaked** ★★★★ Unlike many in genre, **05** has personality squared, from soft gold glints to concentrated limy farewell. Well harmonised firm structure, substantial nutty/citrus concentration with focusing freshness. On lees 4 mths. **Chenin Blanc** ★★★★ **05** full bodied, rich, with varied floral/honey notes; dense, supple texture harmonised by balanced acid, fruity 4.7g/ℓ sugar. 55% used Fr oak fermented/8 mths. **04** TWS trophy. **Chameleon Sauvignon Blanc-Chardonnay ★★★★** Standout sauvignon vintage reflected in **06**'s vivid varietal aromas; weight, silky richness & flavour contributed by chard. Equally tasty solo or with food. **Rhine Riesling ★★★ 05** mirrors **04**s pepper/kerosene personality; lightish, lively with spicy kick in tail. Whisper sugar to balance, complement Asian/poultry/fish dishes.

Bradgate range

These easy drinkers developed for world markets but also available locally. **Syrah ★★★ 04** exploits variety's palate-friendly qualities, offers freshness, structure & ample spice, savoury satisfaction. Fr/Am oak finish. **Cabernet Sauvignon-Merlot ★★★★** Bdx blend rounded with soupçon shiraz. Modern, bright-fruited, approachable. **05** not ready for tasting. **Chenin Blanc-Sauvignon Blanc ★★★ 05** with whiff attractive bottle-aged/honeyed flavours. Perky acid maintains character, drinkability. 65/35 mix. — *AL*

Joubert-Tradauw Private Cellar

Tradouw (see Little Karoo map) ▪ Est/1stB 1999 ▪ Tasting & sales Mon-Fri 9-5 Sat 10-2 ▪ Breakfasts, teas & tapas/alfresco lunches Mon-Sat ▪ Tours by appt ▪ Lentelus B&B (T 028·572·1636), facilities for children & many other attractions ▪ Owner Joubert Family Trust ▪ Winemaker/viticulturist Meyer Joubert (1995) ▪ 30 ha (cab, merlot, shiraz, chard) ▪ 2 500 cs own label 70% red 30% white ▪ PO Box 15 Barrydale 6750 ▪ joubert.r62@lando.co.za ▪ www. joubert-tradauw.co.za ▪ T 028·572·1619 ▪ F 028·572·1315

With decidedly cool nights promoting slow ripening, the Tradouw Valley is proving to be a place of vinous discovery. From Meyer Joubert's artisanal cellar, which wouldn't look out of place in France, an elegant Chardonnay has already emerged and a Pinot is in the pipeline. Next door, wife Beate's deli-cum-restaurant serves highly rated local fare with a Mediterranean flavour, accompanied by their wines, a warm ambience and sweeping views.

R62 ★★★ 'Cab-Merlot' pvs ed, indicating cab predominance; bdx-style blend switches to merlot-cab (70/30) in **04**, where wood (40% new, 19 mths) rather than the lead variety has ascendancy mid-2006. Needs time to settle, knit with ripe, soft black fruit. More classically styled **03** Caylon Top 10 in 2006. **Syrah ★★★★** Wild, spicy berries & smoke mingle on smoothly textured **05** palate. Well crafted given warm vintage: supple ripe tannins, bright acidity & sustained red fruit, lovely fragrant black pepper farewell — great with food. Now only Fr oak, 14 mths. **Chardonnay ★★★★** 'Classic, elegant, lekker!' says Meyer J, correctly as regards the latter, though classicists might find the toasty wood, opulent styling of **05** more ebulliently New World than restrainedly Old. Bright, tangy threads of lime marmalade tease the palate, awaiting melding with effects of 14 mths barrel fermentation/ageing. — *MW*

■ *Journey's End see* Western Wines

JP Bredell Wines

Stellenbosch (see Helderberg map) ▪ 1stB 1991 ▪ Tasting & sales Mon-Fri 9-5 Sat 10-2 ▪ Tours by appt ▪ Owner Helderzicht Trust ▪ Winemaker Anton Bredell ▪ 95 ha (cab, merlot, pinotage, shiraz, souzão, tinta, tourigas f/n) ▪ 15 000 cs own label 80% red 20% port ▪ PO Box 5266 Helderberg 7135 ▪ info@bredellwines.co.za ▪ www.bredellwines.co.za ▪ T 021·842·2478 ▪ F 021·842·3124

The focus at this cellar has increasingly been on making 'cleaner' wines, with hygiene a priority to 'eliminate any attacks from "Mr Brett" and compatriots', is the forthright message from MD Donald Keyes. 'Consumers have become more knowledgeable and producers should up their game to satisfy modern winelovers' more sophisticated palates.' In a further reflection of the times, Bredell's CWG wines have adopted a conservation theme — the name Terra Bewaria for the (untasted) 04 alludes to the growing importance of both biodiversity generally and in particular the 8 000ha Bredell Karoo game farm, a burgeoning ecotourism destination.

★★★★ De Rigueur Back in the saddle with uncompromising **03** (pvs was **00**). Sbosch bushvine cab/merlot (60/40); careful handling leaves all brambly/woodsmoke flavour unscathed; succulent, juicy frame; ripe tannins harness plump fruit – only just! Yr Fr oak prior to blending. Calyon Top 5.

★★★★ **Cabernet Sauvignon** In distinctly unbridled mould started by **00** ('held back to lose a bit of power' & released after relatively soft, easy **02**). **03** densely coloured; teems with cassis fruit in a huge – yet refined – structure, lingering finish with 15.5% alc fillip.

★★★★ **Bredell's CWG Auction Shiraz** Emphatic & individual **01**, with extra-fine tannins & tantalisingly 'different' finish. Yr mix Fr/Am wood, 25% new. Not retasted; 2nd lot offered at 2006 Auction.

★★★★★ **Cape Vintage Reserve** Benchmark Cape port for over 15 yrs. **01** splendid, eminently drinkable now but worthy of deferred (& amplified) gratification. Tantalisingly scented, beautifully built: fruit-mix, nuts, leather & spice all present & correct within powerfully elegant framework. **00** (★★★★☆, without 'Reserve' moniker pvs ed) an inch off fabulous **97**, TWS trophy in 2006. Melange tinta, tourigas & souzão. 20% alc, ±90g/ℓ sugar.

★★★★☆ **CWG Auction Reserve Port** When reviewed mid-2005, **03** needed to slumber for ±decade, in vintage style. Traditional Portuguese varieties, 2 yrs vintage old Fr oak; 87g/ℓ sugar.

★★★★ **Late Bottled Vintage** Not-so-serious but still weighty, rich & silky 'fireside port'. **02**, from barrel pvs ed, seduced with plush fruitcake features, promising velvety finish. Tinta, souzão, tourigas; 3 yrs old oak; 19% alc; ±90g/ℓ sugar.

Shiraz Back on shelves with revved-up **03** (★★★★); whiffs of oak cosset berry pith, laced with attractive spice in finish. Pvs was **01** (★★★★) full of juicy blackberry fruit & sweet vanilla Am oak. **Merlot** ★★★☆ None since big, plummy **01**.

Vineyard Collection range

Red ★★★ Merlot-led cheer which won't break the bank. Honest fruit, lightly wooded, easy without being a cordial. **NV** not revisited this ed. **Chenin Blanc** [new] ★★☆ **05** fleshy peach/pear aromas, straightforward chenin fruit, ends off-dry. 12.5% alc. – *DS*

■ *Juhantha* see Stellar Winery

Julien Schaal [new]

Walker Bay ▪ Est 2004 ▪ Closed to public ▪ Owner/Winemaker Julien Schaal ▪ 14 tons 1 000 cs 85% red 15% white ▪ 6 Royal Str, Hermanus 7200 ▪ julien@vins-schaal.com ▪ T +33-8-73-09-37-75 ▪ F +33-3-90-29-81-27

Young Alsace estate owner Julien Schaal fell in love with SA during the 2003 harvest at Bouchard Finlayson. Returning the next year, he befriended Walker Bay winemaker Gordon Newton Johnson and embarked on his own venture here: 'Making SA reds in February, Alsace whites in October!' Using the new Newton Johnson cellar, cool-climate fruit and traditional vinification methods, Schaal offers minute quantities of three exciting new wines.

★★★★ **Chardonnay** Opulent **05** debut with intense lime notes punctuating the lavish nut, biscuit & vanilla bouquet; wood initially dominates palate, too, then ripe tangerines stake a claim & persist into creamy finish, where 4.7g/ℓ RS adds hint sweetness. Already lovely, needs more time to show its best. Ovrberg fruit, fermented/9 mths new Fr barrels.

Syrah ★★★★ Promising **05** redolent of red berries, flowers & spice, all shining through well managed oak. Refreshing acidity & light tannic bite on long, slightly warm farewell. ±60% new Fr wood, combo small/large barrels. **Merlot-Petit Verdot** ★★★☆ **05**'s jewel-like appearance mirrored in pure plum & blackberry tones, with hint of scrub. Intense yet restrained. Lemony acidity & tailored tannins augur well for future. 14.5% alc afterglow. Oak ± as for Syrah. All WO W Cape. – *CvZ*

Juno Wine Company

Paarl ▪ Est/1stB 2004 ▪ Tasting at 191c Main Str, Paarl, Mon-Fri 10-4 Sat 10-3 ▪ Sales Mon-Fri 8-5 Sat 10-3 ▪ Closed Dec 16-Jan 3 & most pub hols ▪ Vini/viti consultant Newald Marais (Nov

2004) ▪ ±50 000 cs 50% red 50% white ▪ PO Box 68 Main Road Paarl 7622 ▪ info@junowines. com ▪ www.junowines.com ▪ T 021·872·0697 ▪ F 021·872·1863

Having done his time with the 'big guys' (notably Nederburg), Juno's winemaker Newald Marais is enjoying the individuality and creative spirit behind this Paarl-Bonnievale brand. A sauvignon and a cab-merlot have been added to the range and they, too, sport Juno's attractive packaging. The voluptuous beauties on the labels are the work of partner Johan du Toit's wife Tertia, and are meant to reflect the playful elegance of the wines. At press time, Juno was opening its doors to the public.

Cape Maidens range

Shiraz ★★★ Again approachable & unchallenging; **05** black pepper & dark fruit, balanced spicy tannins. **Cabernet Sauvignon-Merlot** new ★★ **05** similar fruit-filled quaffability to above but lighter (12.7% alc) & more straightforward. **Chardonnay** ★★★ **05** unoaked; last ed had a fruity nose packed with pear, apple & lime, plump middle, easy finish. **Sauvignon Blanc** new ★★ Early harvested 'slimmer's friend' type lightness, dryness & acidity on **06**, with suggestion of tropical fruit. All WO Rbtsn. — *MM*

■ *Kaapdal see Robertson Wide River, Vinimark*
■ *Kaap Hollands see Origin Wine*

Kaapzicht Estate

Stellenbosch ▪ Est 1946 ▪ 1stB 1984 ▪ Tasting & sales Mon-Fri 9-4.30 Sat & pub hols 9-12 ▪ Fee R10 ▪ Closed Easter Fri-Sun, Dec 25 & Jan 1 ▪ Tours by appt ▪ BYO picnic ▪ Self-catering chalet & separate 'Wingerd Kraal' braai area for ±70 people; conference/entertainment venue (T 082·737·8329 — Mandy Steytler) ▪ Conservation area ▪ Owner Steytdal Farm (Pty) Ltd ▪ Winemaker Danie Steytler, with Charl Coetzee (Jan 1979/2003) ▪ Viticulturists George Steytler, Charl Coetzee & Schalk du Toit (Jan 1984; Mar/Jun 2003) ▪ 146 ha (cab, merlot, pinotage, shiraz, chenin, sauvignon) ▪ 1 100 tons 40 000 cs own label 65% red 35% white ▪ PO Box 35 Koelenhof 7605 ▪ kaapzicht@mweb.co.za or sales@kaapzicht-wines.com or exports@kaapzicht-wines.com ▪ www.kaapzicht-wines.com ▪ T 021·906·1620 ▪ F 021·906·1622

This well established family winery continues to improve on all fronts: in the vineyards, where George Steytler has been soil-mapping; the cellar, where his brother Danie installed a new cooling system, upping the quality of the whites; and sales — intent on growing international markets, Yngvild S flew east for the first time, establishing new ties in Singapore, west on Wines of SA's marketing sortie to the US, and north to service existing European markets. All fuelled by accolades like the Best Red Trophy in the over-£10 category at the *Decanter* World Wine Awards for their Steytler Vision pinotage blend. Back home, Danie S remains intent on changing perceptions of cask wines with his quality offerings under the Cape View label.

Steytler range

★★★★★ **Vision** The Steytlers might as well put out the JCWCA's press release as their own, such is the showing of their wares at the event. This standout Cape blend (50% cab, 10% merlot &, of course, pinotage) swept aside its peers in 2006 with **03**: gently perfumed, tremendous intensity tightly woven into truckloads of powdery tannins; the triumph's in the structure. **02** *Wine* ★★★★. 2 yrs 100% new Fr oak. 14.8% alc.

★★★★★ **Pinotage** Topping the above's JCWCA 2006 show performance, **03** won both its class & overall best on show. Slightly volatile on entry, the sumptuous mouthful of fruit entangled with ripe tannins finishes with assertive 15% alc. Also Swiss, Concours Mondial golds. Single venerable vyd, 2 yrs new Fr (Taransaud) oak.

Kaapzicht range

★★★★☆ **CWG Auction Reserve Blend** Barrel selection of Vision above, but generally less yielding. **03** (★★★★) similarly burly build to magisterial, dark-berried **01** (no **02**). This, following two wines, not retasted.

★★★★☆ **CWG Cabernet Sauvignon 02** (★★★★) very dry, despite ripe mulberry fruit. Not as good as **01**, which promised to open out & be splendid. 19 mths new Fr oak.

★★★★ **Cabernet Sauvignon** Still available **02** has Steytler signature: ripe blackcurrant, dark choc fruit, authoritative oaking. For earlier drinking than outstanding **01** (★★★★☆), which showed classicism though still New World in breadth, generosity. 18 mths Fr oak, 50% new.

★★★★ **Pinotage** Pretty much the 'visiting card' in the cellar's portfolio, it should be super, & is. Heady aromas of **03** eschew acetone; obvious sweet plum features toned by soft, restraining tannins. 2 yrs Fr oak, 30% new. Lower 14% alc.

★★★★ **Shiraz** Strikingly perfumed, well spiced, more elegant than most: **04** a veritable censer; floral fruit tethered by super grip, near-15% alc. 20 mths small Fr oak, 40% new.

★★★★ **Bin-3** ✓ Approachable merlot/cab blend, with touch with near-inevitable pinotage (9%) adding some sweetness. After sleek, fat **03** DG, *Decanter* ★★★★, **04** (★★★☆) reviewed for this ed more demure, looser textured. Still, finesse beyond its price. Fr oak 9 mths.

Sauvignon Blanc ☺ ★★★ More flinty, grassy **06** follow up to big & juicy pvs; ripe fruit, sweet/sour finish — mouthwatering.

Merlot ★★★ **02** warm spiced-plum aromas, solid meaty texture with trademark grip. Firm oaking (19 mths Fr, 30% new) supports longevity. Medalled **03** (not tasted for this ed) waiting in the wings. **Estate Red** ★★★ Cab/shiraz blend (65/35), travels in 'dinkies' on German Bundesbahn. **04** full, chunky fruit rests on burly tannins; good lightly chilled. **Classic Red** ★★★ Allsorts red with cinsaut; **04** classy for its station; gamey, vinous grip. **Chardonnay** new ★★ 'More for the fun of it; my husband enjoys experimenting' says YS. **05** citrus/lime interplay, astringent tail. **Combination** ★★ 60/40 sauvignon combo with chenin, **06** bright, crisp & dry, refreshing 12.3% alc. **Chenin Blanc** ★★ **06** fleshy guava features with a nip & tuck, just 12.7% alc. Following not tasted for this ed: **Natural Sweet** ★★★ **05** pineapple/mint intro, delightful tropical flavours, fresh acidity. Catchy alternative to end summer dinners. JCWCA 2006. **Hanepoot Jerepigo** ★★★★ ✓ Incense & barley sugar invitation in **05**: like liquid raisins, sweet & intense, with thread of refreshing mint. High 19% alc.

Cape View range

Not rated; brand is now a vehicle for 3ℓ bag-in-box wines. **Classic Red** & **Classic White** contents similar to bottled Classic Red & Combination above. — *DS*

■ *Kakamas* see Oranjerivier Wine Cellars
■ *Kalkveld* see Zandvliet

Kango Winery ☺♟♨🍷🎺

Little Karoo ▪ Est 1976 ▪ 1stB 1977 ▪ Tasting & sales Mon-Thu 8-5 Fri 9-4.30 Sat 9-1 ▪ Tours by appt ▪ Cheese platters, picnic baskets by appt (or BYO) ▪ Conferences ▪ Owners 58 members ▪ Winemaker Flip Smith ▪ Viti consultant Johannes Mellet ▪ 295 ha (cab, merlot, pinotage, shiraz, chard, chenin, colombard, hanepoot, muscadel r/w, sauvignon) ▪ 3 000 tons 18% red 82% white ▪ PO Box 46 Oudtshoorn 6620 ▪ wynhuis@kangowines.com ▪ www.kangowines. com ▪ T 044·272·6065 ▪ F 044·279·1038/1339

Winemaker Flip Smith (aka 'Klein Dassie', after his father JC 'Dassie' Smith, cellarmaster at Botha Wine Cellar, who's his unofficial taster-in-chief and most trusted selection panel) is delighted with their new, hard-to-miss sales venue, Kango Wijnhuis, on Oudtshoorn's Van der Riet Street. It has a spacious tasting-room and covered veranda for visitors, as well as conference facilities for larger parties. And it's run by someone with the brand at heart — Caren, Flip's wife.

Kango Reserve range

Cabernet Sauvignon new ★★★ **04** reticent but distinct aromas of minty black fruit, herbal tea flavours; tense, uncompromising personality perhaps needs time to relax. No newer releases tasted for: **Pinotage** ★★ Hints mulberry & rhubarb on **04**, firm but juicy;

modestly fruited for lofty 'Reserve' labelling. **Chardonnay** ★★ Lightly wooded **04**, with baked character underlying subtle peachy fruit.

Swartberg Reserve range
new

Grapes from elevated vyds in Meiringspoort area, among highest in S Hemisphere. **Shiraz** ★★★ Pleasing varietal smoke & thatch on **05**, hint of salted meat, full-ripe fruit flavours & firm, full, hearty finish. **Pinotage** ★ **05** opulent bouquet of raisin-ripe fruit, yet palate shows little substance or weight (13.8% alc), concludes with slatey, tannic dryness. **Chardonnay** ★ Demure straw aromas on **05**, light, dry & briefly lingering flavours.

Kango range

All reds unwooded. **Cabernet Sauvignon** ★★★ Rounded, black berried **05**, meat extract & nutmeg whiffs; sustained amicable dry farewell. **Merlot** ★★ last tasted was **04**, lightish, easy dry red with ripe plummy fruit. **Pinotage** new ★★ Compact, medium bodied, **05** dusty-dry tail, savoury green banana whiffs, unceremonious braai slosher. **Ruby Cabernet** new ★★ Little Karoo show champ — yet unpretentious, quaffable; **05** juicy & balanced wild berry fruit, any edges smoothed. **Shiraz** ★★ **05** restrained, almost ethereal savoury intro, palate more presence, substance; fairly robust tannins for heartier foods. **Cabernet Sauvignon-Merlot-Shiraz** ★★★ **05** a step up; harmonious blend, earthy centre to the wild berry core; full, fairly gripping but sufficiently rounded to enjoy now. **Chenin Blanc** new ★ **05** soft, lightish, foursquare dry white with sweet-sour texture. **Sauvignon Blanc** ★★ **05** last ed noted as uncomplicated dry white with pear-drop & tropical fruit tone. **Morio Muscat Sparkling** ★★★ **04** charracterful bubbly with hints aniseed & muscat, lots of minty freshness, energetic bubbles. Not retasted. **Semi Sweet** new ★ **05** from Little Karoo sauvignon, muscat; light & sweet, with just a touch of muscat's perfume.

Rijkshof range

All fortified desserts in range **NV**, mainly W Cape origin. **Red Muscadel** ★★★★ Trophy for best RM at Trophy Show 2006 for this perfumed wine, more flatteringly fortified this time (alc upped to 17.5%) to balance the powerful sweetness of succulently ripe fruit. **White Muscadel** ★★★ Regular show medallist incl Muscadel Awards. Latest bottling is feather-soft & supple, with barley sugar flavours & rich, unctuous sweetness. **Red Jerepigo** ★★ Mahogany glints to these massively sweet (275g/ℓ sugar) comforting drops, latest version with malty maple syrup flavours. **Gold Jerepigo** ★★★ Appropriately golden hued sweetie; latest version enlivened with combo acid & spirit, for clean, uncloying feel. **Hanepoot** ★★ Subdued grapey character, not too sweet, appealing caramel & golden syrup overlay. **Ruby Port** ★★★ Pleasant fireside fortified ('port' something of a misnomer); the new version sweeter, more spirituous, with 'flintiness' on nose from 17.8% alc. **Vintage Port** In abeyance. All ranges WO W Cape unless noted. — *CT*

Kanonkop Estate
🍷🍵🛢🦽♿

Stellenbosch ▪ Est 1910 ▪ 1stB 1973 ▪ Tasting & sales Mon-Fri 8.30-5 Sat 9-12.30 (9-2 Sep-Mar) ▪ Fee R10 ▪ Closed Easter Fri , Dec 25 & Jan 1 ▪ Traditional snoek barbecue only by appt (min 15 people) or BYO picnic ▪ Owners Johann & Paul Krige ▪ Winemaker Abrie Beeslaar (2002), advised by Beyers Truter ▪ Viticulturist Koos du Toit ▪ 100 ha (cabs s/f, merlot, pinotage) ▪ 500 tons ±40 000 cs 100% red ▪ PO Box 19 Elsenburg 7607 ▪ wine@kanonkop.co. za ▪ www.kanonkop.co.za ▪ T 021·884·4656 ▪ F 021·884·4719

Illustrating what he means by 'Be innovative but don't reinvent the wheel', co-owner of this iconic brand, Johann Krige, refers to techniques like the refined hand-sorting the estate uses: 'It's infinitely more labour-intensive and a big cost, but essential if you want to reach the top end of the market. A lot of people do the same but only for their premium range. We do it for all our wines, and there's been a marked change as a result since the 2004 vintage.' Another JK guideline is 'Don't be static' if you want to stay ahead of the pack. So expect, for example, a slight change to the bdx-style Paul Sauer blend. And a third word of wisdom: 'Don't go over-the-top with the latest in technology. After all, it's about terroir.'

★★★★☆ **Paul Sauer** A classic since 1981: has Cape character plus international sophistication. Vinified traditionally, like all these, in open fermenters. **03**'s 64% cab in line with pvs, but just 6% merlot, rest cab f. Dominated in youth by oak's spicy tobacco, but rich fruit lurking: deserves at least half-decade maturation for violets, tea-leaf, black berries to play full role within firm, ripe structure. **02** was less sumptuous, more severe, but convincing: *WS* Top 100, *Decanter* ★★★★★. These 2 yrs new Fr oak. WO Smnsberg-Sbosch (as all are, bar Kadette which WO Stbosch/NE).

★★★★ **Cabernet Sauvignon 02** (★★★☆ at most) shows vintage in slight dankness, lighter fruit — appropriately managed, so gd balance & grip, but rather short. Unlike typically fine, sternly elegant **01**, not for long keeping. 2 yrs Fr oak, half new.

★★★★★ **Pinotage** Lovely, pure-fruited aromas/flavours on **04**, complicated but unspoilt by wood (16 mths mostly new Fr). Big 14.9% alc, but in balance with ripe, sweet fruit. Gd acid, well restrained tannic structure. Charm & power for long haul. **03** ABSA Top Ten, SAA.

★★★★ **Kadette** Just 26% pinotage on sophisticatedly rustic **03**, back to 51% (& apparent) on **04** (★★★☆) with cabs s & f, merlot. Pleasing, easy-going with ripe tannin, bright sweet fruit, obvious 14.3% alc. Well oaked, but ready now. — *TJ*

Kanu Wines 👁🍷🎵

Stellenbosch • Est/1stB 1998 • Tasting & sales Oct-Mar: Mon-Fri 10-5 Sat 9-1; Apr-Sep Mon-Fri 10-4.30 Sat closed • Fee R3/wine • Closed pub hols • Gifts • Cheese Bar for farm-style products • Functions venue • Permanent art exhibition • Owner Hydro Holdings • Winemaker Richard Kershaw, with Johan Grimbeek & Nadine Hector (Jan 2002/Oct 2005) • Viticulturists Werner de Villiers (Nov 2004) • 55 ha (cabs s/f, merlot, petit v, roobernet, shiraz, sauvignon, viognier) • 1 000 tons 50 000 cs own label 35% red 65% white • PO Box 548 Stellenbosch 7599 • info@kanu.co.za • www.kanu.co.za • T 021·881·8104 • F 021·881·3514

Legend has it that those who fall under the shadow of Kanu — a mythical bird of promise — will be blessed with a bountiful harvest and this certainly seems to have been the case here in 2006. 'The best winter rainfall for some years... virtually no rot... 80% picked under ideal conditions,' summarises winemaker Richard Kershaw. In the cellar, meanwhile, he continues his occasionally 'hair-raising' experiments with natural or 'wild' fermentation — with rewarding results. 'I may need to tread carefully with the yeast companies!'

Limited Release range

★★★★ **Merlot** Elegantly structured, Fr oaked **02** originally tasted as barrel sample, still available. Label to be discontinued.

★★★★ **Chenin Blanc Wooded** Very ripe **05** (★★★☆) not quite in league of pvs richly fruited, seriously oaked versions. Attractive tropical/floral scents with buttery background; forceful structure, glow from 14% alc dims fruit on palate. Sweeter than 7g/ℓ sugar suggests. Native ferment in mix Fr/Am/Hngrian oak/11 mths, 50% Fr new. **04** *Wine* ★★★★. Khof/Bottlry vyds.

★★★★★ **Kia-Ora Noble Late Harvest** Occasional botrytised dessert. **04**, from chenin, still available. Last yr's review mentioned luscious texture, riveting sweet/sour balance & enchanting array of flavours. 14 mths Fr oak, 60% new. **03** *Wine* ★★★★, 90 pts *WS*. 375ml.

Shiraz ★★★☆ Enjoyable, modern style; rich & plummy, vanilla spiced with amenable tannins noted in last yr's review of still-selling **03**. 18 mths older Fr oak.

Kanonkop Paul Sauer ex-farm selling price

| R3,50 | R195,00 |
| 1981 | 2006 |

Kanu range

★★★★ **Keystone** Cab-dominated bdx-style blend, 91% in **03**, with merlot. Blackberry/brambleberry fruit, toasty oak. Firm tannin, needs time, has good 6+ yr future. 18 mths Fr oak, half new. Not retasted.

★★★★ **Chardonnay 04** (★★★☆) still available, when last tasted perhaps at awkward stage; smoky oak (10 mths, mainly Fr, dab Am, equal new/2nd fill) gives extra dimension but unintegrated with zesty acid, tropical fruit. Khof grapes. Less impressive than deep, sophisticated **03**.

Rockwood ☺ ★★★ Freshly bottled **05** with clean, cool feel; plentiful spicy, mint edged interest, delivered in rounded, ready mode. Shiraz with cab, merlot & introducing roobernet. Light oak influence.

Sauvignon Blanc ★★★ **05** mirrors preview comments last yr; quiet grapefruit, figs; lightish, perky acid tamed by 6.6g/ℓ sugar. Incl 5% chenin. **Chenin Blanc** ★★★★ One of early leaders in chenin renaissance. **05** unfinished sample last yr, now still full of vitality, crunchy green apple stimulation; clean & with fruity length. Perked up by 13% sauvignon. Low yielding 26 yr old bushvines. Versatile food partner.

Reserve range

★★★★ **Sauvignon Blanc** ★★★★ Lively, food-friendly **05** with well assembled green fig & summer meadow character. Deep, full structure (aided by 7g/ℓ acid), long minerally finish. Not retasted, still on menu.

Escape range

Red ☺ ★★★ Deep coloured blend shiraz, cab, merlot, roobernet. Earthy/pruney nose, ripe, hearty flavours, matching gutsy tannins in happy **05** partnership for warming, winter dishes. **Rosé** ☺ ★★★ Pearly pink **06** from merlot, splash shiraz. Lightish, refreshing; tangy red fruits set off by 6g/ℓ sugar. **Chardonnay** new ☺ ★★★ Ripe tropical limy aromas/flavours, some toasty oak extras on **05**. Plump, juicy, with zesty freshness. Portion Fr oak fermented, third new.

No **06 Chenin Blanc** or **Sauvignon Blanc**, will feature again when sufficient quantity available. — *AL/CR*

■ *Karmosyn see* Terroir Wines

Karusa Vineyards

Robertson ▪ Est/1stB 2004 ▪ Tasting by appt ▪ Partner/oenologist Jacques Conradie ▪ 100 cs ▪ jacques@karusavineyards.co.za ▪ www.karusavineyards.co.za ▪ PO Box 529 Robertson 6705 ▪ T 023·626·1628 ▪ F 023·626·1895

'Wines have become boring,' is Jacques Conradie's take on big brands and marketing budget dictates, which is why he's determined that vineyard pockets tucked away in rugged terrain from Montagu to Oudtshoorn get their deserved recognition. Slowly working towards his own specialist cellar in his favoured Little Karoo, he currently makes his own-label wine at Bon Cap, where he's cellar chief.

★★★★ **The Fifth Element** Debuted impressively with refined **04** shiraz/viognier (88/12) blend. **05** (★★★★) equally characterful albeit shade lighter; lovely floral intro (5% viognier influence), spicy oak background, choc flavours. Maybe earlier peaking than pvs. Yr new Am, 2nd fill Hngrian oak. Unfiltered/fined. Montagu fruit. — *MM*

Katbakkies Wine

Est/1stB 1999 ▪ Tasting & sales by appt ▪ Owner Andries van der Walt ▪ Vini consultant Teddy Hall (2002) ▪ 700 cs 45% red 55% white ▪ PO Box 21675 Kloof Street 8008 ▪ Avdwalt@inds-ct.co.za ▪ T 021·424·6883 ▪ F 021·426·1967

Petit verdot from one of SA's highest vineyards in the Cederberg foothills continues to elude architect-turned-part-time-producer Andries van der Walt. 'Last year the grapes were decimated by drought and once again raided by baboons. But we did make some wonderful verjuice, a small conSolation. As for the Stellenbosch grapes, it was a great harvest.' An upcoming Syrah Reserve promises to be 'the cat's whiskers'.

★★★★☆ **Cabernet Sauvignon 03** made an impressive debut with balanced sweet-fruit opulence & classic herbal whiffs, fine dense tannins. Last ed noted as worthy of gd few yrs maturation. 22 mths new Fr oak. **04** unready.

★★★★ **Syrah** Prominent savoury & garrigue scrub aromas lead to lighter styled, more restrained **04** (★★★★☆), showing less concentration than pvs. Earthy red fruits, smoky charcuterie nuances lifted by bright acidity. 12.5% alc. **03**, also lighter toned, its red-fruits character punctuated by soft, spicy whiffs. These 11 mths matured, 1st/2nd fill oak.

★★★★ **Chenin Blanc** Like some thoroughbred tensed to sprint, **05** fuses lime, white peach & almond with taut acidity in a restrained, tightly contained structure. Barrel fermentation/8 mths in seasoned wood adds toned muscle & fine potential. Just a shade off sumptuous standout **04** (★★★★★).

Viognier ★★★★ Intricately perfumed **05** redolent with white peach & apricot; the aromatic loveliness continues on drier-than-pvs palate with concentrated lime fruit & brisk acidity. 11 mths oaking add opulence within a sleek, well tailored form. All above WO Sbosch. — *MW*

Kautzenburg

Stellenbosch ▪ Est 2000 ▪ 1stB 2002 ▪ Closed to public ▪ Owners Peter & Nina Ruch ▪ Winemaker Jeremy Walker (2002) ▪ Viticulturist Peter Ruch, advised by De Waal Koch ▪ 5 ha (pinotage) ▪ ±25 tons ±300 cs 100% red ▪ PO Box 91 Somerset West 7129 ▪ T/F 021·842·3903

It's apt this small cellar chose to specialise in pinotage: their small vineyard, sea breezed by nearby False Bay, is considered by Grangehurst's Jeremy Walker (who makes their wine) to be in a prime position for growing this variety. Contrary to previous reports, Peter and Nina Ruch are not 'summer swallows' but live here permanently, he dividing his time between the vines and his profession as a doctor of Chinese medicine, she dedicated to artistic pursuits.

Pinotage ★★★★ **04** (provisionally rated sample last ed) from low-yielding Hldrberg bushvines. Scrubby nose enlivened by dark fruit & tar, layered fruit complexity & fine tannins from deft oak touch (16 mths Fr). For the long haul: 6 yrs at least. — *CR*

■ *Kaya* see Overhex
■ *Keates Drift* see Franschhoek Vineyards
■ *Keimoes* see Oranjerivier Wine Cellars

Keisseskraal Vineyards

Bot River (see Walker Bay map) ▪ Est 2004 ▪ 1stB 2005 ▪ Tasting & sales Mon-Fri 10-4 Sat/Sun by appt ▪ Closed Christian holidays ▪ BYO picnic (if tasting) ▪ Farm produce ▪ Walks ▪ Owners Johann & Ulrike Mendelsöhn ▪ Winemaker Johann Mendelsöhn, advised by Bartho Eksteen (Jan 2005) ▪ Viticulturist Johann Mendelsöhn ▪ 4 ha (cab, malbec, merlot, mourvèdre, petit v, shiraz, viognier) ▪ 1.3 tons 250 cs 100% red ▪ PO Box 85 Bot River 7185 ▪ mendelsohn@ telkomsa.net ▪ T/F 028·284·9219

This year will see extensions and upgrades of the cellar and tasting facilities, and the birth of a pinotage, cab and cab-shiraz blend, all from his own and neighbouring grapes. Architect-winegrower Johann Mendelsöhn says the 2006 vintage shows excellent promise for the newcomers and his original Syrah. He plans to establish chenin and mourvèdre next year, and will continue to buy in some fruit until his own vines mature in 2009.

Galantskloof Syrah new ★★★★ Attractive, forward ripe fruit on **05**, appealing rustic richness with nice tannins, but oak (yr new Romanian) & alc (14.9%) a little prominent. Sweetly delicious. Native yeast, unfiltered. WO W Cape. — *TJ*

■ *Keizer's Creek see* Roodezandt

Kellerprinz

High-volume semi-sweet white glugger in 2ℓ jug; by Distell. **Late Harvest** ✱ From chenin/colombard, latest **NV** shows honey/biscuit nose, light body (11% alc). — *CvZ*

Ken Forrester Wines

Stellenbosch (see Helderberg map) ▪ *Est/1stB 1994* ▪ *Tasting & sales daily at 96 Winery Road Restaurant (see Eat-out section); also at new venue on home farm, cnr R44 & Winery Rd Mon-Fri 9-5 Sat 10.30-1.30* ▪ *Owners Ken & Teresa Forrester* ▪ *Vini consultant Martin Meinert (1995), with Allison Adams* ▪ *Viticulturist Jannie Fourie (Jan 2005)* ▪ *33 ha (cab f, grenache, merlot, mourvèdre, shiraz, chenin, sauvignon)* ▪ *200 tons/60 000 cs own label + 350 000ℓ for clients* ▪ *35% red 65% white* ▪ *HACCP, SEDEX certified; WIETA pending* ▪ *PO Box 1253 Stellenbosch 7599* ▪ info@ kenforresterwines.com ▪ *www.kenforresterwines.com* ▪ **T** *021·855·2374* ▪ *F 021·855·2373*

An ancient *veewagtershuisie* (stockman's hut) at the entrance to the Ken Forrester cellar, now restored, is more than a monument to the Boland's border-country past — inside, it's Ken & Teresa F's gift to the future: an ultra-modern classroom, complete with internet, where more than a dozen vineyard labourers are mastering courses from basic literacy to matric. 'All in all, it's been a hectic year,' says Ken F, 'with three visits to the US, our Chenin listed as a housewine at Spago Beverly Hills and Gordon Ramsay London, a 90 point rating by *Wine Spectator* for the flagship FMC and 'Best Value' selection by the same magazine for the Petit Chenin. Come to think of it, it's been a *chenin* year!'

Icon range

★★★★ **Gypsy** Impressive, individual New World fusion of grenache, shiraz, occasional smattering other varieties. Living up to name, flamboyant, unconventional **03** (★★★★✰) raises bar & surprises at every turn: piquant berries, brooding smoky depths, prosciutto & dried herbs. Accessible but 8+ yrs off peak. 77/23 shiraz, grenache, new oak pre- & post blending, yr. **02** (sample last ed, possible ★★★★★) sleekly muscular & generously oaked (18 mths). **01**'s instant appeal belied complexity. Grenache ex-50 yr old vyds delivering only ±2 t/ha.

★★★★★✰ **The FMC Chenin Blanc** Designed to 'put Cape chenin indelibly on the map'. Powerful & gorgeous **04** among their best: lush tropical fruit, citrus peel & roasted nuts; voluptuous body with ultra-long, satiny finish. 9.7g/ℓ sugar tastes dry. Perfect oaking: fermented/9 mths Fr, half new. Native yeasts. *Wine* ★★★★✰, IWC gold. Deeply rich **03** heaped with praise; latest incl *WS* 90 pts, IWSC gold, Winemakers Choice.

★★★★★ **'T' Noble Late Harvest Chenin Blanc** Mesmerising botrytised dessert, both solo-perfect & food-cordial. Sumptuously perfumed: preserved quince, liquidised apricots, barley sugar all vie for attention in **05**. Racy acidity balances the sweetness, giving an ultra-long, silky finish. No effort spared in these: native yeast fermented, up to 5 pickings off old bushvines. 18 mths new Fr oak. No **04**, **02**. Tantalising **03** (★★★★✰) *Wine* ★★★★; lush silky **01** IWC gold in 2005.

Ken Forrester range

★★★★ **Chenin Blanc** ✓ From 30+ yr old Hldrberg bushvines, pruned for low yields. **05** doesn't put a foot wrong, showing trademark concentration, breed. Melon & peach flavours, masterly oaking adds complexity, lively crisp finish. Worthy of cellaring ±4 yrs, as are all these. Fermented/9 mths Fr, 20% new. *Wine* ★★★★✰. Lush, intense **03** (★★★★✰) *Decanter* gold in 2006.

Merlot ★★★ Hedgerow fruit, herbaceous touch mark a style change in **04**, but elegant structure, discernable oak backbone remain. Will reward cellaring 3-4 yrs. 10 mths used barrels. **Shiraz-Grenache** (Last ed 'Grenache-Syrah'.) ★★★★ With more than a nod to southern France, near-equal blend **03** displays quirky wildness: tar, campfire smoke, cherry pip. Firm dry tannins hint at pleasures to come. 9 mths Fr oak, some new, touch Am. **Sauvignon Blanc** ★★★ Previewed **06** promises quality delivery of gooseberry & tangy lime, light textured drinkability, clean refreshing finish.

Petit range

Petit Pinotage ★★★ Juicy unwooded style. Vivid rhubarb, brambleberry character of **05** has enough grape tannin for structural definition, food-friendly dry finish. **Petit Chenin** ★★★★ ✓ Bursts out of its skin with freshness, appetite appeal, **06** offers a lime, apple, green melon melange, with 'another bottle please' palate vibrancy. — *CR*

Keukenhof Wines

Olifants River ▪ *1stB 2003* ▪ *Visits by appt Mon-Sat 8-5* ▪ *Fee R10 p/p* ▪ *Closed Good Fri-Mon, Ascension Day & Dec 25* ▪ *Play area for children* ▪ *Owners Smuts family* ▪ *Winemaker Riaan Smuts, with Nadine Smuts (both Jan 2003)* ▪ *Viticulturist Riaan Smuts (Jan 2003)* ▪ *65 ha (cab, merlot, chard, chenin, colombard, sauvignon)* ▪ *1 200 tons 250 cs own label* ▪ *PO Box 49 Lutzville 8165* ▪ *tazu@kingsley.co.za* ▪ ***T/F 027·217·2623***

No update from *garagistes* John and Lulaine Smuts; contact information and wine notes from previous edition.

Both **04s** Fr oak matured, unfiltered. **Cabernet Sauvignon** ★★ Sweet blackcurrant & fine herbal hints, some greenish tannin/alc evident. **Merlot** ★★ Chalky mulberry whiffs, succulent & soft tannins though fruit somewhat overpowered by nearly 15% alc. — *MF*

■ ***Keurfontein*** see Viljoensdrift
■ ***Kevin Arnold*** see Waterford
■ ***King Solomon*** see Eshkol

Kingsriver Estate

Robertson ▪ *Est 2004* ▪ *1stB 2005* ▪ *Visits Sun 10-4, otherwise by appt* ▪ *Walks* ▪ *Owners De Clercq family* ▪ *Winemaker Ruud de Clercq (2005), advised by Kobus van der Merwe* ▪ *Viti adviser Anton Laas (2004)* ▪ *26 ha (ruby cab, shiraz, chard, chenin, colombard)* ▪ *250 tons total 900 cs own label 100% red* ▪ *PO Box 203 McGregor 6708* ▪ *kingsriver@breede.co.za* ▪ *www-kingsriver-estate.com* ▪ ***T 023·625·1108***

Listed in last year's guide as Jewel of the Breede River, this historic property celebrated a return to its winemaking roots (and official 'wine estate' status) with the release of a red blend (unready for tasting). The farm's grapes were traditionally sold to the McGregor co-operative, before new co-owner Ruud de Clercq, a trained engineer and former theme park entrepreneur in Europe, decided to resurrect the property's oeno-tradition after unearthing four underground wine storage tanks in an old farm shed.

Klawervlei Estate

Stellenbosch ▪ *Est 1994* ▪ *1stB 1995* ▪ *Tours by appt* ▪ *Owner Quickstep 594 (Pty) Ltd* ▪ *PO Box 144 Koelenhof 7605* ▪ *chrisdejager@telkomsa.net* ▪ *www.klawervlei.com* ▪ ***T/F 021·865·2415***

Change of ownership in progress for this Cape pioneer of organic winegrowing. Visits by appointment for the time being.

Klawer Co-operative Cellars

Olifants River ▪ *Est 1956* ▪ *Tasting & sales Mon-Fri 8-5 Sat 9-1* ▪ *Fee R5* ▪ *Closed pub hols except during wildflower season* ▪ *BYO picnic* ▪ *Conferences* ▪ *Owners 120 members* ▪ *Winemakers Bob de Villiers (also General Manager, Dec 1999), Hermias Hugo (Dec 2002) & De Wet Hugo (Aug 2003), with Roelof van Schalkwyk (Jan 1999) & Dewald Huisamen (Nov 2003)* ▪ *Viticulturist De Wet Hugo* ▪ *2 095 ha ±40 000 tons 14% red 85% white 1% rosé* ▪ *PO Box 8 Klawer 8145* ▪ *klawerwyn@kingsley.co.za* ▪ *www.birdfieldwines.co.za* ▪ ***T 027·216·1530*** ▪ *F 027·216·1561*

Fiftieth birthday celebrations over and the tasting room spruced up by an interior designer, it was back to business for the two Hugos, Hermias and De Wet (no, they're not related), running the show post-harvest in absence of Bob de Villiers — his sense of smell still mysteriously absent despite several specialist consultations, he took long leave to motorbike across Africa. The focus is now firmly on quality, with a new Cape marketing manager flighting the Birdfield range locally.

Birdfield range

Merlot ★★ Now seriously styled (60% new Fr oak, 9 mths), but retains its easy-going, quaffable persona; **05** soft, slightly earthy mulberries to taste. **Pinotage** ★★ Six mths barrelled **05**, shows house's earthy nuance, bramble fruit & suggestion of over-ripeness, contrasting with bone-dry finish. **Shiraz** ★★★ Full bodied **05** has appealing & casserole-cordial savoury, caramelised character; hint old leather; v soft finish. New Am-Fr oak, 9-12 mths. Following pair still selling, not retasted: **Blanc de Noir** ★★ Coral pink summer sipper from pinotage; **05** strawberry fruited with off-dry, slightly savoury flavours. **Chardonnay** ★★★ **05** gentle tropical fruit lead-in, citrus-zest flavours, freshening acidity which initially stood slightly apart. **Chenin Blanc** ★★ Uncomplicated, mildly fruity everyday quaffer. **06** again light in all respects (11.5% alc). **Sauvignon Blanc** ★★ Early harvested **06** v light bodied/flavoured; grassy nuance, dry, with bracing acidity. **Special Late Harvest 05** untasted & sold out; no newer vintage. **Michelle Sparkling** ★★ Light (10% alc), frivolous froth for sweeter palates. **NV (06)** has Barbie-pink label which mirrors wine's colour & reads: 'For ladies only'. From red muscadel. **White Muscadel** ★★★ Soft, rounded, fortified dessert; **05** has generous sunripe melon flavours which not averse to being poured over crushed ice. Fairly hefty but unobtrusive 17% alc. **Red Muscadel** ★★★ Returns to guide with rosé-hued **06**, treacle-sweet fruitcake flavours nicely lifted by lively spirit (16.5%). Following available cellar door, untasted: **Shiraz-Merlot**, **Late Harvest**, **Hanepoot**, **Matador** (port). — *CT*

■ **Klein Avontuur** see Avontuur
■ **Klein Begin** see New Beginnings
■ **Kleinbosch** see Cape Coastal Vintners

Klein Constantia Estate ⚲♙&

Constantia ▪ Est 1823 ▪ 1stB 1986 ▪ Tasting & sales Mon-Fri 9-5 Sat 9-1 ▪ Fee R20 for groups ▪ Closed pub hols ▪ Owners Duggie & Lowell Jooste ▪ Winemaker Adam Mason, with Sebastiaan Cloete (Jul 2003/Jul 2006) ▪ Viticulturist Floricius Beukes (Jan 2006) ▪ 82 ha (cabs s/f, merlot, pinot, shiraz, chard, muscat de F, riesling, sauvignon) ▪ 500 tons 40 000 cs 25% red 75% white ▪ Export brand: High Gables ▪ PO Box 375 Constantia 7848 ▪ info@ kleinconstantia.com ▪ www.kleinconstantia.com ▪ T 021·794·5188 ▪ F 021·794·2464

Just as the Jooste family nursed this neglected historic property back to health, and world wine renown, over the past quarter-century, they take care of their people — and their customers. Farmworkers now own their own homes in a nearby housing development. Cellar worker Stemmer Isaacs did an educational stint in Burgundy. And Floricius Beukes, erstwhile assistant to winemaker Adam Mason, is now in charge of overseeing the vineyard regeneration programme slated for completion in 2010 (Beukes's successor is Sebastiaan Cloete). Warmly welcomed visitors can add home-grown honey (*The Bees' Knees*) and a mouthwatering coffee-table recipe book (*Vin de Constance with Michel Roux Jr* - he of London's famous Le Gavroche) to their shopping bag.

★★★★ **Marlbrook** Virtual relaunch with **05** — last was **01** (★★★★). From 'carefully selected vyd sections', says Adam M. Youthful, needing time to develop; now oaky, tarry surround to dark fruits, some austere richness with firm savoury tannins — making for promising whole. 15 mths oak, third new.

★★★★ **Mme Marlbrook** Consort for flagship red settling down stylistically: **05** (★★★★★) more serious 60% semillon with sauvignon & mere hint florally fragrant muscat de F to lemon, tropical fruit. Enriching sugar touch not apparent on fresh palate, nor beautifully controlled oak (fermented/11 mths in 50% new 500ℓ butts). Moderate, harmonious 12.8% alc. Lovely now, shd mature few yrs.

★★★★★ **Perdeblokke Sauvignon Blanc** Selection from one higher-altitude vyd — name recalls ploughing Percherons of old. Expressive aromas passionfruit, hints asparagus on **05** (not retasted) vibrant green grass-edged richness, lingering flavours. *Wine* ★★★★★. No **06** made.

★★★★ Sauvignon Blanc Enduring favourite, noted for rewarding ageability in some vintages, with ±10% semillon adding complexity. **06** subtly forceful, though still restrained mid-2006 — these need some time to open up. But emerging cool-origin aromas greenpepper, gooseberry, rounded by passionfruit. Succulent, fresh balance.

★★★★ Rhine Riesling Dry, since **05**; elegant **06** offers pineapple, peach & pepper notes, deliciously delicate yet concentrated, dry & lipsmacking. Should develop complexity over 5 or even more yrs.

★★★★ Sauvignon Blanc Noble Late Harvest After disappointingly heavy, woody **02** (**★★★**), welcome back to rich, focused botrytised pleasure with amber coloured **05**. Honey-lemon freshness, clean, tangy & lively balance. Modest 86g/ℓ sugar; 14% alc. Fermented/matured in older oak.

★★★★☆ Vin de Constance Reaching (in patented 500ml old-style bottles) for the international renown its ancestor enjoyed 2 centuries back; from usually unbotrytised but ripe muscat de F, generally giving a long-lived, silky wine with fine mineral acidity. **01** more obviously muscat, with floral/grapey/raisiny character; full-flavoured & sumptuous — gentler acid means effectively sweeter balance than many pvs, involving 135g/ℓ sugar, big 14.8% alc. Shd acquire more complexity with time. These up to 4 yrs in used 500ℓ Fr oak barrels.

Cabernet Sauvignon ★★★☆ Last was quietly austere **01**. **Pinot Noir ★★★** Pleasant **05** offers light earthy, strawberry/raspberry notes, well integrated oak, some drying tannin & chunky 14.7% alc. **Shiraz ★★★☆** Notably ripe **04**, soft, almost lush but restrained fruit in good firm structure, unobtrusively oaked. **Chardonnay** Attractive **04** (**★★★★**) a harbinger of an **05** (**★★★★**) with unusual but successful 14% semillon component. Unshowy style, but firm fruit & well integrated wood (70% fermented/11 mths in oak), invigorating freshness, lingering flavour. **Semillon ★★★★** Lemongrass, fennel, lanolin on immensely drinkable **05** (with 14% sauvignon); beautifully dry & tangy, sufficient but modest 12.3% alc. Fermented/yr on lees in older 500ℓ butts.

KC range

Includes grapes from Anwilka farm in Hldrberg, so NE. **Cabernet Sauvignon-Merlot ★★★★** **03** (not retasted) generous, ripe blend (53/39, balance cab f), more vinous than fruity, with firm tannins; moderately wooded. **Shiraz** new **★★★★** **04** darker, more forcefully structured than estate version, with focused, savoury tannins & bright, confident fruit. 18 mths oak. — *TJ*

■ *Kleindal* see Robertson Wide River, Vinimark

Klein DasBosch 🍷

*Stellenbosch • Open by appt • Owner James Wellwood Basson • Viti/vini consultant Jan Coetzee (1997) • Marketing director Nikki Herbst • 5.5 ha • 35 tons 16 000 cs own label 89% red 11% white • PO Box 826 Brackenfell 7561 • wine@kleindasbosch.co.za • www. kleindasbosch.co.za • **T** 021·880·0128/083·272·4575 • **F** 021·880·0999*

Range made at Vriesenhof Vineyards by rugby-and-wine legend Jan Coetzee for his neighbour James 'Whitey' Basson, CEO of retailing empire Shoprite/Checkers. Current releases include an 03 Merlot and 05 Chardonnay. Mostly exported, though some do appear on selected local restaurant lists. The wines can now be tasted by appointment.

Kleine Draken 🍷🍴&

*Paarl • Est 1983 • 1stB 1988 • Tasting & sales Mon-Fri 8-12.30; 1.30-5 • Closed pub hols & Jewish holy days • Tours strictly by appt • BYO picnic • Owner Cape Gate (Pty) Ltd • Winemaker Neil Schnoor, with Mabusa Nyaniso (Sep/Jul 1999) • Viticulturist Frank Pietersen (1984) • 9 ha (cabs s/ f, malbec, merlot, chard, riesling, sauvignon) • 90 tons 10 000 cs own label 50% red 50% white • Brand for customer: Tempel Wines • ISO 9000 certification in progress • PO Box 2674 Paarl 7620 • zandwijk@capegate.co.za • www.kosherwines.co.za • **T** 021·863·2368 • **F** 021·863·1884*

The trick, says GM/winemaker Neil Schnoor, is to produce wine that's of a good quality 'in spite of its being kosher'. Last season, the trick was to work around power outages, hence a new generator in the cellar! A Shiraz has joined the range, and Panama is one of several unusual names on a growing list of export destinations. 'We make sure that our local base is supplied,' says Neil S, 'and then we find ex-pat demand all over the world.'

> **Dry Red** ☺ ★★★ Bdx-style blend equal portions cab f, merlot, malbec. Lightish (11.9% alc), rather elegant red-berry character, **04** friendly tannins, touch oak thanks to brief sojourn in older Fr wood.

Cabernet Sauvignon ★★☆ **02** not retasted. Cassis & black berry scents; smartly oaked (6 mths old/new Fr) for good dry tannins. **Pinotage** ★★ Tannic **04** has distinct varietal plum & mulberry, slight bitter lift to tail. 6-12 mths seasoned Fr oak. **Shiraz** new ★ **05** attractive varietal bouquet of red berry & smoked beef let down by hard, astringent palate; 14.9% alc. Yr wooded. **Kiddush** ★★ Natural Sweet sacramental wine from cinsaut **01**, not revisited. **Chardonnay** ★★ Appealingly restrained **05**'s white peach gently brushed with vanilla oak notes from barrel-fermentation/maturation. **Sauvignon Blanc** ★★ **05** subdued, barely vinous, but (looking on the brighter side!) nicely fresh. **Bouquet Blanc** ★★★ **04** tasted mid-2005, upfront fruit, very pleasant; semi-dry from sauvignon. — DH

■ *Kleine Hazen* see Hazendal
■ *Kleine Parys* see Klein Parys

Kleine Zalze Wines

Stellenbosch • Est 1695 • 1stB 1997 • Tasting & sales Mon-Sat 9-6 Sun 11-6 • Closed Easter Fri, Dec 25 & Jan 1 • Fee R15 • Tours by appt • 'Terroir' Restaurant (see Eat-out section) • Guest cottages & golf lodges (see Stay-over section) • Play area for children • Tour groups • Conferences & functions • Owners Kobus Basson & Rolf Schulz • Winemaker Johan Joubert, with Bertho van der Westhuizen (Nov 2002/Dec 2004) • Viticulturist Henning Retief, advised by Schalk du Toit (May 2006/2000) • 60 ha (cab, merlot, shiraz) • ±2 000 tons 80 000 cs 50% red 50% white • PO Box 12837 Die Boord Stellenbosch 7613 • quality@kleinezalze.co.za • www. kleinezalze.com • T 021·880·0717 • F 021·880·0716

Another year, another clutch of awards. Best of all, sales to match — within 20 months of its launch in Sweden, Foot of Africa Chenin Blanc was the best-selling white wine in that country. Even the restaurant, Terroir, emerged with laurels, featuring in two national Top 10 listings. Appropriately, it is the Kleine Zalze terroir to which the winemakers — who monitor each vineyard block separately according to soil type — attribute much of their success. Vineyard management being a key element, the team is delighted to welcome Elsenburg graduate Henning Retief (ex-Bon Cap) on board as their new viticulturist.

Family Reserve range

★★★★★ **Shiraz** Much gilded **04** (incl Swiss, *Wine*, Winemakers Choice), sleek & confident but not brash, ripe smooth tannins supporting rich fruit which copes well with 18 mths new oak (85/15 Fr/Am) & 14.2% alc. Shd develop well over few yrs, last longer. All in this range tasted last ed. **03** *Wine* ★★★★★.

★★★★ **Cabernet Sauvignon** Serious, impressive wine, **04**'s potential seems to lurk in tightly packed, satisfyingly savoury balance. 18 mths new Fr oak well absorbed. 14.5% alc a little too assertive on finish. **03** Winemakers Choice.

★★★★ **Sauvignon Blanc** Reserved, rather stately **05** in riper grassy/green pea style. Big fresh acid lifts fruit on well balanced, textured palate, with a little sugar smoothing any edges. Shd benefit from ageing through 2006. Winemakers Choice, *Wine* ★★★★. WO W Cape.

Vineyard Selection

★★★★ **Cabernet Sauvignon Barrel Matured** After elegant **01**, next-up **03** (★★★☆) big & bold, now showing nice cedarwood touch to good, ripe fruit. Well managed oak in good balance with sweet fruit & soft, dry tannins.

★★★★ **Merlot Barrel Matured 03** (tasted last ed as sample) mint-choc aroma, slight leafy note & lead pencil; dark plummy palate, cedarwood tinge; dry tannins. Yr-18 mths Fr/ Am oak, some new.

★★★★ **Chardonnay Barrel Fermented** Quietly classy **05** ripe but understated, with orange zest notes, well integrated oak (20% new); creamy richness cut by fresh acidity.

Pinotage Barrel Matured ★★★★ More power than charm on **03**, last ed marked by severe tannins, dusty cedar notes from 18 mths new Fr oak — but dark fruit lay in wait. **Shiraz Barrel Matured** ★★★★ Bold, forthright **03**, spicy red fruit accompanying obvious oak (mix new/older Fr), supported by big tannic structure; savoury & vinous. **Chenin Blanc Barrel Fermented** While sugar on rich, serious **04** (★★★★; *Decanter* gold) not too obvious, ripe-flavoured **05** (★★★★) perhaps too sweet (9.2g/ℓ) & powerful (15% alc) for many. But uncloying, pleasant, with well-handled wood (7 mths, 30% new). *Wine* ★★★★.

Cellar Selection

Chenin Blanc Bush Vines ★★★★ Unwooded version, **06** just off-dry & a touch rich, though tempered by marked acidity. Attractive pineapple-peach notes. Tank samples tasted of these 06 whites. **05** flew SAA, *Wine* ★★★★; **04** *Decanter* trophy. **Sauvignon Blanc** ★★★★ Reliably fresh & appealing; **06** lively, forthcoming grassy tropicality on nose. Green, lipsmacking flavours, round & dry. **Chardonnay** ★★★ Unwooded, pleasingly zippy version as usual in **06**, only hinting at sweetness. Ripe, bruised apple & citrus tones, forward, engaging. WO Coastal, as is... **Gamay Noir** ★★★ Very ripe, rich **05** easy-drinker now showing softly sweet with tartly fresh edge & dense texture. Drink chilled, suggests winemaker. **Merlot** ★★★★ Light but ripely fruity **04** has friendly, savoury elegance; gently firm structure for plum, fruitcake flavours & nice earthy element. Yr in oak. **Cabernet Sauvignon** ★★★ **03** (like next, tasted last ed) has tobacco, red/blackcurrant aromas, leading through firmly tannic but balanced mouthful to slightly sweet-sour conclusion. Lightly wooded, like... **Pinotage** ★★★ Cheerful, fresh, spicy **04**; ripely sweet fruitiness matched with big dry tannins.

Foot of Africa range

Currently for Sweden only. **Chenin Blanc** ★★★ Yet another pleasant KZ chenin — this just-dry **06** delightful, crisp, ripely flavoured. WO W Cape, as is... **Chenin Blanc-Chardonnay** ★★★ **06** (sample) 70:30 blend has sweet hint to vibrant freshness. Big bones, big tropical/citrus flavours. Not elegant, but very tasty. **Cabernet Sauvignon** ★★★ Good varietal character on **03**, with black fruit & cigarbox wood (18 mths Fr oak); robust but not excessive tannins; nice fruit disappears as alc glow takes over (14.5%). Like next, not retasted. **Pinotage-Shiraz** ★★★ Lightly wooded 60:40 blend **04** ripe jammy aromas, soft fruit, mild tannins, short sweet adieu. Big 14.5% alc. **Shiraz-Viognier** 𝗻𝗲𝘄 ★★★ Fashionable blend gives floral note to burly, plump **05**; just about dry, with softly chewy, lush red-fruited ripeness. Rather hot finish from big 14.5% alc. WO W Cape. — *TJ*

Kleinfontein Private Cellar

◐ 💿 **new**

Wellington ▪ Est/1stB 2003 ▪ No winetasting ▪ Luxury guest house ▪ Owners Tim & Caroline Holdcroft ▪ Vini consultants Charles Stassen & Corlea Fourie (May 2004/Jan 2006) ▪ Viticulturist Tim Holdcroft ▪ 1 ha (cab, merlot) ▪ 5-6½ tons 375 cs 100% red ▪ PO Box 578 Wellington 7654 ▪ kleinfon@iafrica.com ▪ www.kleinfontein.com ▪ T/F 021·864·1202

'Small is beautiful', maintains British-born civil engineer Tim Holdcroft of this new Wellington *garagiste* operation. Their maiden vintage 03 Cab was a milestone after he and wife Caroline settled into semi-retirement here from Kenya in 1995. Work started with restoration of the 1830s Cape Dutch farmhouse, followed by planting a single hectare of cab and merlot three years later. Meanwhile Caroline H's bird-friendly indigenous garden is a picture for visitors staying in the luxurious two-room guesthouse.

Cabernet Sauvignon-Merlot ★★★★ **04** has cab dominant at 85%, evident in ripe blackcurrant notes; sweet berry-fruited mid-palate, ample weight (with 13.8% alc) & voluptuous tannins; persistent finish. Yr Fr oak, 18% new. **Merlot** ★★ **04** gamey, thatchy notes, with characteristic plum too, & vanilla from yr in oak (a third new); jammily ripe finish showing tannin. — *MF*

Klein Gustrouw Estate

Stellenbosch • Est 1817 • 1stB 1993 • Tasting, sales & tours by appt '24x7' but phone ahead (closed Dec 25/26) • Conservation area • Owners Chris & Athalie McDonald • Winemaker/viticulturist Chris McDonald • 16 ha (cab, merlot) • 21 tons 1 600 cs 100% red • PO Box 6064 Stellenbosch 7612 • T/F 021·887·4556

Chris McDonald on 2006. Vintage report: most difficult in 18 years. Grapes wouldn't ripen (probably stress: no rain, don't irrigate). But ripening eventually occurred, in a rush. Biggest crop ever, no doubt the usual excellent quality. Market report: Hitting new restaurant highs of £40 a bottle in London and Edinburgh. Vintner's report: Usual hands-on fruit selection, no mucking about in vineyards or cellar. Scottish deerhound breeder's report: Ghillie took himself a bride… very sweet but a bit young still… no consummation as yet. Will try again later.

★★★★☆ **Cabernet Sauvignon-Merlot** Finely tailored **03** promised seamless elegance by 2008. Equally impressive **04**, from lovely, intense, perfumed aromas to lingering finish, has restrained elegance as well as early charm — but don't doubt the subtle strength working along with harmoniousness for ageability. Subtle oaking too: 12-17 mths, third new (mostly for cab). — *TJ*

Kleinood

Stellenbosch • Est 2000 • 1stB 2002 • Visits by appt • Owner Gerard de Villiers • Winemaker Willem Grobbelaar (Sep 2004) • Viti consultant Aidan Morton (Dec 2000) • 9.6 ha (mourvèdre, shiraz, viognier) • 1 200 cs own label 100% red • PO Box 12584 Die Boord 7613 • winemaker@kleinood.co.za • www.kleinood.com • T 021·880·2527 • F 021·880·2884

Quiet gratification at this small, cherished ('kleinood' in Afrikaans) property beneath Stellenbosch Mountain. Harvest 2006 saw the first intake from young viognier and mourvèdre, to be blended with Willem Grobbelaar's shiraz. Owners Gerard and Libby de Villiers (he an engineer involved in big-name cellars for Graham Beck, the Ruperts and Distell; she a former actress), resident in Tamboerskloof in Cape Town (hence the label name), see this as their dream country retreat. Tasteful landscaping and interiors welcome visitors.

Tamboerskloof Syrah ★★★★ ('Shiraz pvs ed'.) **04** notch up on **03** debut. Cranberry aromas & flavours, floral notes ex-5% viognier. Tannins (from Fr, Am & Russian oak, 14 mths, 35% new) give friendly grip, warming glow from 14.5% alc. Mix Sbosch, Klapmuts fruit. — *MF*

Klein Optenhorst

Wellington • Est/1stB 2001 • Closed to public • ±150 cs 100% red • See Siyabonga for details.

Marketer-about-the-globe Graham Knox (latterly, Stormhoek) and Wellington winefarmer Naas Ferreira have introduced a new partner to their gem of a Pinot venture: Poppie the percheron. She draws a humble iron plough to help remove the weeds from rows planted — unusually — a mere metre apart; farmworkers with straw, hoe and backpack finish off the weeding, and control disease as well. The fruit of their labours was once again, in 2006, selected for the luxury Blue Train.

★★★★ **Pinot Noir** Individual SA take on classic grape. **05** (★★★★) hits market ahead of heldback **04**, as former 'more developed, open'; softly textured, ends touch sweet. 11 mths Fr casks — just six of them. 13% alc. — *DS*

Klein Parys Vineyards

Paarl • Est 1692 • 1stB 2003 • Tasting & sales Mon-Fri 10-6 Sat 10-4 • Closed Easter Fri/Sun, Dec 16/25/26 & Jan 1 • Tours by appt • Restaurant, cheese platters, olives, olive oil & other farm-style produce • Self-catering accommodation • Tour groups • Gifts • Art, clothing & other exhibitions • Owner Kosie Möller • Winemaker/viticulturist Kosie Möller • 56 ha (cab, chard, chenin, nouvelle, semillon, viognier) • 700 tons 80 000 cs 50% red 50% white • Export brands: Kleine Parys & Miller's Mile • PO Box 1362 Suider-Paarl 7624 • kmoller@kparys.co.za. • T 021·872·9848 • F 021·872·8527

In just three years, Kosie Möller has virtually transformed one of Paarl's oldest wine farms, replanting and upgrading vineyards (nouvelle and viognier feature in the new portfolio), and pulling in new visitors with redeveloped facilities – last year Klein Parys opened the doors to their new restaurant; this year the first self-catering units will be built. Things are moving on the cellar front too: exports have grown appreciably, and Möller plans to extend his line-up with new 'icon' and entry-level ranges.

Kleine Parys range

Sangiovese new ★★★☆ Screwcapped **05** a hit in Sweden, says Kosie M. Intrigues with spicy melange of aromas, tastes (incl anise, salt), all still tightly bound; needs yr/2 or decanting if opened now. Yr 2nd fill barrels. WO W Cape. Follow-up vintages for following 8 wines unready: **Cabernet Sauvignon** ★★★ Different & characterful **04**, touches tar & eucalyptus; extracted 'hot' character well balanced by freshening acidity. Yr oak, 20% Am, whereas… **Shiraz** ★★★ 80% Am oak for **04**, stylish, welcoming, warm; succulent fruit subtly tensioned by well extracted tannins. **Pinotage** ★★ **04** different bowl of fruit to pvs: old-style with whiff acetone, big (14.5% alc) & boisterous. 40% Am oak, yr. **Beatrix Selection** ★★★☆ Meaty/spicy blend shiraz (60%), cab, pinotage; **02** fruitcake flavours, rich & ripe. Contrived & obvious in the nicest way. New oak 18 mths, 40% Am. **Classic Red** ★★★ Baked fruit character with soft, easy, sweet-sour twist; **04** varieties as per Beatrix. WO W Cape. **Pinotage Blanc de Noir** ★★★ Palest shell-pink **06**, softly dry, delicate honeysuckle scents & flavours, unobtrusive 14% alc. **Chardonnay** ★★ **05** barrel fermentation not obvious; sniffs warm hay & peach; soft, fruit-sweet, eager to please. **Chenin Blanc** ★★★ **05** spring flowers & confected peach ice-cream on nose; light-bodied, lingering flavours, good acidity. **Sauvignon Blanc** ★★★ Fruit-driven quaffer, clean & fresh, **06** light bodied but well layered with capsicum & green-pea. **Cuvée Brut** ★★★ Foamy summer bubbles, crisply dry with fruit salad flavours; **NV** from chenin, colombard, chard.

Miller's Mile range

Cabernet Sauvignon ★★★ Last was honest & typical **04**, lingering cedar/mulberry aromas, medium body, dry; youthful slightly savoury tannins. 8 mths oak, 20% Am. **Pinotage** ★★★ Change from dusty-dry pvs to soft, fruity-smooth **05**, with typical pinotage banana; most quaffable. 6 mths oak. **Shiraz** ★★★ **05**, like pvs, unshowy but satisfying; appealing hints of old leather, dried fruit & roasted veg. Only Am oak this time, 6 mths. **Pinotage-Shiraz** ★★ We last tasted light textured **04**, 60/40 blend, oak as for Cab, shy & dry, some red fruit lying in wait – possibly needs time. **Chardonnay** ★★☆ **06** well-made easy-drinker; fresh, clean-cut pear flavours, only 13% alc. 5 mths Fr oak. **Chenin Blanc** ★★ Demure, light textured quick-quaff. **06** leanish winter melon flavours, gently dry. WO W Cape for all. — *CT*

■ **Kleinrivier** see Clos Malverne
■ **Klein Simonsvlei** see Niel Joubert
■ **Klein Tulbagh** see Tulbagh Wineries Co-op

Kleinvallei Winery ♂♀

Paarl • Est/1stB 2000 • Tasting by appt • Owners Piet & Sandra van Schaik • Vini consultant Helene van der Westhuizen • 10 ha (cab, malbec, merlot, petit v, pinotage, shiraz, chard) • 17 tons 940 cs 90% red 10% white • PO Box 9060 Klein Drakenstein 7628 • kleinvallei@mweb. co.za • www.kleinvallei.co.za • T 021-868-3662 / 082-399-5075 • F 021-868-3130

Helene van der Westhuizen, seasoned at (among others) Distell and African Terroir before turning boutique winery consultant, takes over here as adviser to Piet van Schaik, economist, retired stock-broker and hands-on owner, who oversees the vineyards and makes the limited-release wines.

Cabernet Sauvignon ★★★ **01** blackcurrant, cream & toast aromas; slightly leafy & austere; best enjoyed early. 20 mths Fr, some new. ±14% alc. **Bel Canto** ★★★ **03** raises the bar on pvs; now a wine to lay down 4-5 yrs. Led by cab (60%) with shiraz (27%) & merlot, it's concentrated with fine, dense tannins. 18 mths combo new/old Fr oak. **Pinotage** ★★★ **04** dark, extracted style; fleshy fruit/rhubarb, big tannins; not quite ready on release, need ±yr. Yr older Fr oak. **Chardonnay** ★★★ **04** inviting citrus, warm buttered toast aromas, poised yet lively. Yr 5th fill Fr casks. No follow-up vintages tasted. — *CR*

■ **Klompzicht** see Freedom Hill

■ *Kloofzicht Estate see* Alter Ego Wines

Kloovenburg Vineyards

*Swartland ▪ Est 1704 ▪ 1stB 1998 ▪ Tasting & sales Mon-Fri 9-4.30 Sat 9-2 ▪ Fee for groups R10 ▪ Closed Christian holidays ▪ Tours during tasting hours by appt ▪ BYO picnic ▪ Farm-grown olive products for tasting/sale ▪ Walks ▪ Conservation area ▪ Owner/winemaker Pieter du Toit ▪ Viti consultant Kobus van Graan (Jun 2000) ▪ 130 ha (cab, merlot, shiraz, chard, sauvignon) ▪ 6 000 cs own label 70% red 30% white ▪ PO Box 2 Riebeek-Kasteel 7307 ▪ info@kloovenburg. com ▪ www.kloovenburg.com ▪ **T 022·448·1635** ▪ F 022·448·1035*

In 1706 a pioneering settler from the Cape of Good Hope began a wine-farming tradition on the first farm in 'the place in the ravine' above the Riebeek Valley. Celebrating the farm's 300th anniversary, owner/winemaker Pieter du Toit last year introduced his maiden Eight Feet, a limited edition red blend named for the grape-pressing feet of his four children! Another new release in this festive year was the rose-tinted Kloovenburg White From Red Shiraz, in a style reminiscent of blanc de noir. And not to forget the Du Toits' delectable olive products — new is a pair of dipping and drizzling oils flavoured with herbs and spices (think basil, black pepper, chilli, oregano...)

★★★★☆ **Shiraz** Unflashy but consistently superb northern rhône-style red; **05** unready; last ed **04** ex-barrel showed a subtle white pepper undertone to the black-fruit, spice & nutmeg aromas, elegant tannins seamlessly integrated; alc less evident than similarly styled **03**, marked by well defined fruit flavours.

★★★★ **Chardonnay** New World styled, lavish oak character from new Fr barrel fermentation, ageing, but ripe fruit to match; **06** not ready for tasting. **05** mid-2005 showed toasty/smoky edges to grapefruit whiffs, good amplitude & succulence.

Cabernet Sauvignon Bottled version of pvs **04** (★★★★) sample lives up to expectations. Well crafted cassis, cedar & some leafiness following on to sleekly textured palate. Integrated oak (yr Fr barrels, 30% new) balanced by lively acidity, prolonged dark fruited farewell. Elegantly styled with gd potential. **03** (★★★★☆) was more sinewy, restrained. **Eight Feet** new ★★★★ Playful name belies a serious cab/merlot blend (60/40), 70% new Fr oaked, yr. **03**'s leaf, cassis & cedar nuances barely show through tight restraint of firm, sinewy tannins; lurking ripe fruit will need time to gain the exuberance of the Du Toit boys whose 8 feet helped crush the grapes. Only ex-cellar. **Merlot** ★★★ Ripe red/black fruit compote & bright acidity impart a juicy, lively mouthfeel in **05**; 14.5% alc balanced by subtle oak (as for Cab) & firm dry tannins. **White From Red Shiraz** new ★★ Coral pink **06** with soft, savoury & cranberry aromas and flavours. Dry, lightish textured & tangy, with savoury finish; makes a great alfresco picnic partner. **Sauvignon Blanc** ★★★ **06** similar cat's pee character to pvs, plus dusty buchu extra. Acidity more in balance than pvs, less edgy; appealing lemongrass lift for refreshing summer quaffing. 12% alc. — *MW*

Knorhoek Wines

*Stellenbosch ▪ Est 1827 ▪ 1stB 1997 ▪ Tasting & sales daily 9-5 ▪ Fee R10 ▪ Closed Dec 25 ▪ Restaurant/lapa Sep-May 12-4 ▪ Guest house (B&B) with conference, function, entertainment area (see Eat-out/Stay-over section) ▪ Facilities for children ▪ Tour groups ▪ Walks ▪ Conservation area ▪ Owners Hansie & James van Niekerk ▪ Winemaker/viticulturist Arno Albertyn (2005), advised by Wynand Hamman ▪ 105 ha (cabs s/f, merlot, pinotage, shiraz, chenin, sauvignon) ▪ 900 tons 10 000 cs own label 70% red 30% white ▪ Export label: Two Cubs ▪ PO Box 2 Koelenhof 7605 ▪ office@knorhoek.co.za ▪ www.knorhoek.co.za ▪ **T/F 021·865·2627***

The brothers Van Niekerk have been a-building — a new cellar, a new tasting venue opening on to a patio with a splendid view of the Simonsberg — upgrading, to top-notch standard, a slew of facilities for visitors. Production was up by 100 tons in what vini/viti man Arno Albertyn describes as 'a very good harvest' and, adding to the industry-wide chorus, 'particularly for whites, with no rot'.

★★★★ **Cabernet Sauvignon** Sleek & stylish **03** still available, showed its class last ed in concentrated cassis/roast tomato fruit, finely handled cedar tannins. Accessible, but deserved 6-7 yrs cellaring to evolve to its full potential. 2 yrs Fr oak, 48% new.

Two Cubs Cape Blend ☺ ★★★ **05** is merlot-dominant with generous helpings cab, shiraz, dab pinotage. Emphasis is on lively appeal, a dark-fruited juiciness that's quite moreish. **Two Cubs White Blend** ☺ ★★★ Perfect summer quaffer with lots of appetite appeal, **06** has nice appley fruit-salad flavours, clean, crisp finish. Chenin (50%), equal parts sauvignon & semillon. WO Coastal.

Pinotage ★★★☆ No new vintage. Last **01** had a bottle-age note adding interest & complexity to earthy mulberry/plum fruit. Yr oak, 40% new. **Syrah** ★★★☆ last tasted **03** in fruity New World mould. Generous prune & spice nose, creamy palate designed to please. Drink within ±2yrs. **Reserve** ★★★☆ Tightly wound four-way blend mainly cab (65%), shiraz, merlot, pinotage. Last ed **03** not revealing its true charm, shd with further 2-5 yrs cellaring. Elegant tannins wrapped around mulberry fruit. 2 yrs 100% new Fr oak. **Chenin Blanc** ★★★ Varietal definition already showing, melon & pear, but **06** still quiet on palate. Nicely rounded body. Ex-tank, same for next wine. **Sauvignon Blanc** ★★★☆ Taking no prisoners, **06** has pungent fynbos, green pepper, chopped herb styling. Invigorating acidity adds punch, mouthtingling freshness. **Two Cubs Rosé** NEW ★★☆ Mainly cab & some white grapes; **06** with fruit pastille nose, is light & pretty, for early drinking. WO Coastal for this, White, rest Smnsberg-Sbosch. — CR

■ *Koelenbosch* see Koelenhof Winery

Koelenhof Winery

Stellenbosch ▪ Est 1941 ▪ 1stB 1974 ▪ Tasting & sales Mon-Thu 9-5 Fri 9-4.30 Sat & pub hols 9-1 ▪ Closed Easter Fri, Ascension Day, Dec 25/26 & Jan 1 ▪ BYO picnic (excellent deli nearby) ▪ Play area for children ▪ Function venue ▪ Owners 75 shareholders ▪ Winemakers Wilhelm de Vries & Martin Stevens (Jan 2001/Oct 2003) ▪ Viticulturist Herman du Preez (Jan 2002) ▪ 14 000 tons 6 000 cs own label ±9m litres bulk 60% red 38% white 1% rosé 1% sparkling/grape juice ▪ HACCP certification in progress ▪ PO Box 1 Koelenhof 7605 ▪ koelwyn@mweb.co.za ▪ www.koelenhof.co.za ▪ T 021·865·2020/1 ▪ F021·865·2796

The open arms policy at this expanding 'service cellar' required an office space extension to accommodate wine-makers and -merchants who use its facilities. The KW lab is collaborating with Stellenbosch University and Nietvoorbij to research issues like phenolic ripeness, sugar balance and enzyme reactions.

Koelenbosch range

Shiraz NEW ★★★★ ✓ Well crafted (& priced) **04**, myriad interesting smells/tastes (incl new leather, charcuterie); juicy; already approachable with few yrs ahead. 18 mths new oak. 15.3% alc. **Chenin Blanc Wooded** ★★★ Steadily improving label; **05** subtler oaking (no new wood; 8 mths Fr) for freer fruit expression, lifted apricot/pine flavours courtesy of crackling acidity. New versions of following unready: **Merlot** ★★ Old-Cape dried-fruit character on **03**, with powerful tannins. Will have its followers. New oak, 20 mths. **Pinotage** ★★ 24 mths new oak for **03**, showing similar 'retro/nostalgic' quality as above in old-style acetone whiff, dry, fruit-shy profile. **Cabernet Sauvignon** ★★ Oaked as for Merlot, with similar effect: **03** very dry & lean, hints damp earth & dry leaves, begs a hearty country casserole. **Cape Blend** ★★ Equal merlot/pinotage partnership with 20% cab; oak as for Merlot (10% Am). **03** somewhat fruitier than range-mates, juicier tannins, wood not as obvious. **Sauvignon Blanc** ★★ **05** with downplayed fruit (early harvested); faint grass/asparagus suggestions, light-bodied casual quaffing.

Koelenhof range

Pinotage Rosé ☺ ★★ Appealing **06** shows balanced sweetness, sappy strawberry tones for easy sipping (not for quaffing, at 14% alc). **Koelnektar** ☺ ★★★ Ambrosial gewürz, (sample) **06** semi-sweet on paper but on palate delectably lively; delicately billows potpourri & litchi. Delightful.

Koelenkeur In abeyance. Only Hanepoot tasted this ed; other notes from pvs guide. **Shiraz** ★★★★ 02 dark fruits with touches fynbos & dried herbs, seamlessly oaked. Next is 04. **Chardonnay Wooded 05** unready for tasting. **Koelenhoffer** ★ Unpretentious semi-dry white a perennial brisk seller; **05** again from sauvignon, early picked, lightish & bracingly fresh. **Sauvignon Blanc Vin-sec** ★★★ Lightish, semi-dry carbonated sparkling with lots of friendly bubbles, slightly sweet tone & whiffs of pine & melon. **NV**, as is... **Pinotage Rosé Vin-sec** ★☆ Potpourri & dried-fruit bouquet, sweetish flavours without any grip, very undemanding. **Hanepoot** ★★★ Characterful fortified dessert returns to guide with **06**; lovely pure grapey wafts, clean spirity fillip (17% alc) warms the cockles. **White Jeripigo** ★ 04 with glow-inducing alc (17%); sweet grapey flavours from chenin. **Pino Porto** ★★ LBV-style (**NV**) port from pinotage, 2 yrs seasoned small oak. Traditional-style low fortification (16.4%), but what alc there is, is cheek-rougeingly active. — *CT*

Koelfontein

Ceres ▪ Est 1832 ▪ 1stB 2002 ▪ Visits by appt ▪ BYO picnic ▪ Farm produce, walks & other amenities ▪ Owners Handri & Zulch Conradie ▪ Vini consultant Dewaldt Heyns ▪ Viticulturist Zulch Conradie ▪ 19 ha (cab, merlot, shiraz, chard, colombard) ▪ 200 tons 2 000 cs own label + 110 000ℓ for customers ▪ 60% red 40% white ▪ PO Box 702 Ceres 6835 ▪ wine@koelfontein.com ▪ T 023·313·3130 ▪ F 023·313·4898

Brothers Handri and Zulch Conradie are so busy tending their vast Ceres fruit farm, producing 2 000 cases of own-wine and over 12 000 for clients under a variety of brands, they can easily be forgiven for stating they have 'no immediate plans'. They do believe, though, that shiraz can become their new flagship after the buzz sparked by the maiden 04 — especially because subsequent vintages look equally promising. The planned new visitor area in the farm's old cellar (a first for the area) offers atmospheric tasting and other facilities for visitors.

Shiraz new ★★★★ 04 smoulders with smoke & coffee; unobtrusively big alc (15.2%) but fruit-rich, red berry flavours have yet to incorporate showy new oak (16 mths, Fr). Shd gain equilibrium with yr/2's bottle-ageing. *Wine* ★★★★★. **Merlot** ★★★ Showy 02, with oak-boosted pungency, juicy plum flavours, still available, not retasted. **Chardonnay 04** (★★★★) ups ante on 03 (★★★★), which was rich & heavily oak-staved. 04 switches to barrels (9 mths new Fr), yielding more elegant, toasty wood character; fresh acidity (only 15% malo) invigorates vibrant lemon/lime tone. Delicious now & soon. — *CVZ*

■ **Kogmans Kloof** *see Zandvliet*
■ **Koningshof** *see Avondvrede*

Koningsrivier Wines

Robertson ▪ Est/1stB 2002 ▪ Visits by appt ▪ Owner SW Colyn ▪ Winemaker Niël Colyn ▪ Viti consultant Briaan Stipp ▪ 9 ha (cab) ▪ 435 cs 100% red ▪ PO Box 144 Robertson 6705 ▪ koningsrivier@barvallei.co.za ▪ T 023·625·1748/082·588·1262 ▪ F 023·625·1748

Events like the Wacky Wine Weekend have enticed an ever-increasing number of winelovers to the Robertson Valley, prompting Koningsrivier's rustic new tasting facility with its interesting display of antique winemaking and harvesting implements. But the real reason to visit is the wine — this is the only place you can sample Niël Colyn's full range: Cab (both the 03 and 04 available), 04 Shiraz and the non-vintage Cab-Merlot, none tasted this ed.

■ **Kosher** *see Backsberg, Eshkòl, Kleine Draken, Tempel*
■ **Kosie Möller** *see Klein Parys*

Kranskop Estate

Robertson ▪ Est/1stB 2001 ▪ Tasting & sales Mon-Fri 10-5; Sat 10-2 ▪ Closed Easter Sun, Dec 25 & Jan 1 ▪ Tours during tasting hours ▪ Light meals by appt ▪ Tour groups ▪ Facilities for children ▪ Walks ▪ Owner/winemaker/viticulturist Nakkie Smit ▪ 40 ha (cab, merlot, shiraz, chard) ▪ 500 tons 2 500 cs own label 90% red 10% white ▪ PO Box 18 Klaasvoogds 6707 ▪ kranskop@ myisp.co.za ▪ www.kranskopwines.co.za ▪ T/F 023·626·3200

It's all about an unhurried pace at this Robertson farm for Nakkie Smit, from hand-picking the grapes and operating the basket press to imparting his considerable knowledge to visitors during his cellar tours. The Shiraz and Cab 03 were both awarded silver at Veritas, welcome accolades for this boutique winery.

Cabernet Sauvignon ★★★ Cab character still subservient to oak in **04**; plums, red berries beginning to emerge; will show its worth over time but far from ready. Not harsh, just tight. 22 mths Fr, 20-30% new, as all the reds. **Merlot** ★★★ **04** dark fruit, choc, white pepper & oak that's currently in charge. Give another yr, drink over next ±4. **Shiraz** ★★★ Bold oaking to accompany the red fruit, gives **04** attractive vanilla spicing & a sold structure. Not for early drinking, this wine is built for 4+ yrs ageing. **Chardonnay** ★★★ Full bodied & firm-fleshed. **04**, tasted last ed, lifted by rush of acidity, good mineral finish . ±Yr Fr oak. All these WO Klaasvoogds. Discontinued **Merlot Reserve**, **Cabernet Sauvignon-Merlot**. — *CR*

▪ *Krone* see Twee Jonge Gezellen
▪ *Kuikenvlei* see Terroir Wines

Kumala/Constellation South Africa

Stellenbosch ▪ Est 1981 ▪ 1stB 1996 ▪ Closed to public ▪ Winemaker Ben Jordaan (Jul 2002) ▪ 25 ha (Journey's End: cab, shiraz, chard; Kumala Reserve: cab, merlot, pinotage, shiraz) ▪ 10 000 cs (Journey's End) + 3.1m cs (Kumala) + 750 000 cs (Zenith) ▪ 45% red 50% white 5% rosé ▪ PO Box 769 Stellenbosch 7599 ▪ ben.jordaan@cbrands.co.za or james.reid@cbrands. co.za ▪ www.kumala.com ▪ T 021·882·8177 ▪ F 021·882·8176

The hugely successful Kumala brand is distributed in 25 countries worldwide, including the US and UK, where it represents one in every three bottles of SA wine sold. Kumala is now part of the portfolio of US-based Constellation Brands, the world's biggest wine company, having been bought from Vincor in 2006. Constellation's US distribution network is set to provide a fillip for Kumala in that rapidly growing market.

Journey's End range

★★★★ **Cabernet Sauvignon** Grapes for range sourced from Journey's End farm in S/West. Classy, well-wooded **03** followed by much oakier **04** (★★★★ but Swiss gold), mid-2006 showing somewhat less of pvs's appealing fleshy ripe fruit. Might settle, fill out, given time. 50% new Fr barrels, rest 2nd/3rd fill Am. **Shiraz** Clear family resemblance between chunky & bold **03** (★★★☆) & hearty but more elegant **04** (★★★★); similar veldfire/wild scrub bouquet, rich, savoury but not overdone. Same big alc (14. 5%), tannins, but better behaved. 12-14 mths oak, 70% new Am, rest seasoned Fr. **Chardonnay** ★★★☆ **05** in customary full, well-upholstered style; ripe peach compote with vanilla whiff from new oak (50%, Fr, 9-12 mths). Sweetish this yr (4g/ℓ sugar), with contrasting hint astringency needing to settle. All above WO Sbosch; below W Cape unless noted.

Winemakers Selection

Shiraz-Cabernet Sauvignon ★★★★ Selected Paarl vyds, barrel-aged (20% new Am, rest older Fr). **03** 80/20 blend last ed well integrated & balanced, big fruity tannins matched by healthy ripe fruit. Serious wine — deserves few yrs to show its best.

Kumala Reserve range

Reds 20-50% Fr oak staved few mths. Following trio of reds not retasted: **Cabernet Sauvignon** ★★★★ Classically styled **04**, ripe cassis fruit checked by restrained dry tannins, well-applied oaking (incl some Am). WO Wllngtn, ditto… **Merlot** ★★☆ Minty whiffs on **04**, attractive sweet fruit but wood slightly apart initially, needed time to mesh. **Shiraz** ★★★ Ripe mulberry intro to **04**, touches choc & mocha, smooth & plump fruit held in place by supple tannins. **Pinotage** ★★★ More 'easy-drinker' than 'Rsv' in **05**, sweetish fruit & tannins give well padded tone/texture, conclusion is pleasantly dry. **Chardonnay** ★★★★ **04** last ed noted as showing attractive toasty oak, citrus flavours, smooth acidity for soft silky palate. 30% Fr/Am oak staved. **Sauvignon Blanc** ★★ **06**, light (some might say lean) dry white with sherbety texture & brisk acidity. 13% alc.

Kumala range

Intulo Red new ★★ **06** offers straightforward quaffability via jammy red-berry tone, easy tannins & suggestion of sweetness. From ruby cab & pinotage (80/20). **Cabernet Sauvignon-Shiraz** ★★★ Equal blend in **06**, good brambly fruit & ripe but quite sturdy tannins mid-2006, better with food. Partly oaked, as are all these reds. **Merlot-Pinotage** ★★ More pinotage (50%) this time, so **06** not unexpectedly firmer, with dry tannins. Still attractive, but more food-inclined than pvs. **Merlot-Ruby Cabernet** ★★ 50/50 assembly this yr; **06** not unpleasant green walnut whiffs, usual choc flavours & firm tannin base for food partnering. **Pinotage-Cinsault** ★★ Proportions switch to 50/50 for **06**, character changes too: côtes du rhône-like spiciness, juice, balanced tangy tannins. **Pinotage-Cabernet Sauvignon** new ★★ Fruity easy-drinker, **06** red fruit compote hint, comfortable tannins, mere suggestion of wood in the background. Breede Rvr grapes. **Pinotage-Shiraz** ★★★ **06** 60/40 mix a shade firmer than stablemates, as was pvs; whiffs bluegum & berry; good pizza/pasta wine. **Ruby Cabernet-Merlot** ★★★ Quaffable **05** again 80/20 blend, whiffs of ruby cab's signature grass/thatch, soft & smooth. Not restated. **Rosé** new ★★☆ Quartet of reds (incl pinotage) make up soft & refreshing, just-dry **06** pink. Summer-redolent crushed strawberry aromas/flavours to be enjoyed well chilled. **Chardonnay** ★★ **05** lively textured citrus fruit & subtle wood backdrop (20% oaked), soft finish. **Chardonnay-Semillon** ★★ Lightly oaked **05**, citrus & oak flavour profile, lively acidity; low 12% alc makes good lunchtime option. **Chenin Blanc-Chardonnay** ★★ **06** bit fatter than pvs, some creaminess from 50% chard, usual modest oak enhances appealing fruit salad tone. Swtland vyds. **Colombard-Chardonnay** ★★ Gd lightish everyday dry white; bit more chard (30%) in **06**, still bright tropical tone, soft fruity exit. Invisibly oaked. **Sauvignon Blanc-Semillon** ★★★ Pvs equal blend reprised in light-textured, summery **06**, fresh & appealing wintermelon tone. **Sauvignon Blanc-Colombard** ★★ **06** easy, light tropical-fruity 50/50 mix with smooth dry finish. All 06s above except Rosé tasted as samples.

Kumala Organic range

Pinotage-Shiraz ★★★ **04** pinotage dominant, taste-wise, in 60/40 blend. Ripe, plummy, brush of dry tannins on finish. Staves 2 mths. **Colombard-Chardonnay** ★★ **05** gentle dry white with zesty acidity, fresh & tasty, usual modest oak influence (Fr staves). Neither restated. — *CT/IvH*

■ *Kumkani* see The Company of Wine People

Kupferberger Auslese

Crowd pleasing, medium bodied white blend by Distell, refreshing & tangy despite semi-sweet 27g/ℓ sugar. Current **NV** ★★ predominantly chenin, with sauvignon & riesling. — *CvZ*

KWV Limited

Paarl ▪ Est 1918 ▪ KWV Wine Emporium daily tastings 9-4.30; fee R15 ▪ Sales 9-5 ▪ Tours Eng: 10, 10.30 & 14.15; Ger: 10.15 ▪ Tour groups ▪ Gifts (T 021·807·3007/8) ▪ KWV SA: chief winemaker Sterik de Wet ▪ Senior winemakers Bertus Fourie & Thys Loubser, with Nomonde Kubheka (reds) & Tania Joubert (whites) ▪ Senior viticulturist Cobus van Graan ▪ ±13 000 tons ▪ KWV International: PO Box 528 Paarl 7624 ▪ customer@kwv.co.za ▪ www.kwv.co.za ▪ T 021·807·3911 ▪ F 021·807·3349

KWV chose last year's Cape Wine show to unveil its Masterbrand strategy, elements of which are a new logo, new corporate colours and the separation of its products into three categories. The 'masterbrand' category includes the KWV Cathedral Cellar, KWV Reserve, KWV Roodeberg and KWV Classic ranges, all of which will be extended. Next is a category of 'endorsable' wines, yet to be named at press time, and finally there are 'independent' brands like Perold, Robert's Rock, Pearly Bay and Laborie. A hierarchy of winemakers has been put in place to implement the new vision: under chief vinifier Sterik de Wet are senior winemakers Thys Loubser, an incumbent, and newcomer Bertus Fourie (ex Diemersfontein), charged with producing innovative, experimental wines and with overseeing Dave Boyes, recently appointed winemaker for Laborie.

Cathedral Cellar range

★★★★★ **Cabernet Sauvignon** Expensively, carefully made cab. **02** more accessible than pvs; polished tannin, juicy flavours; freshening acidity contrasts rich fruit & firm structure. New oak 26 mths. Age 4-6 yrs, or drink while waiting for **01**'s elegantly layered structure to unfurl. Neither retasted this ed.

★★★★☆ **Merlot** Refined & elegant. **03** (★★★★) complex woodsmoke/venison aromas, spiced red berry mouthful, good vinous grip in tail. Well judged oak (as for Cab) provides foundation for 4/5 yrs ageing.

★★★★ **Pinotage** Pvs ed noted well-fruited **02** — redcurrants, cherries — given cinnamon/ sweet spicing with plenty of oak. Generous, with lovely balance; ripe, finishing dry enough for drinking solo or at table. WO Bosch. 18 mths new. Winemakers Choice.

★★★★☆ **Shiraz** Complex, silky & elegant. **02** combines Old World & New, with compelling savoury tones: prosciutto & white pepper on a brambleberry base, reflecting the marriage of fruit & 2 yrs equal new Fr/Am oak. Not revisited this ed.

★★★★ **Triptych** Blend cab, merlot, shiraz — near equal partnership in **01** (★★★★★) unfolding beautifully when tasted last yr; shimmering cassis, crushed berries, savoury balsamic/ meat extract notes, rich & deep. Impressive oak (26 mths new Fr) not dominant. 'Iron fist in a velvet glove', with framework for 6+ yrs ageing. 15% alc.

★★★★ **Chardonnay** Showy & powerful. **04** had wealth of flavours on review for pvs ed, from intense ripe fruit to generous oaking. House-style silky texture makes for irresistible drinkability. Winemakers Choice; **03** *Decanter* trophy. Fermented/8 mths new Fr oak.

Sauvignon Blanc ★★★★ **05** underlying minerality to bristling nettle edge; usual svelte sophistication undone by imposing 15.5 % alc. This range WO Coastal/W Cape unless noted.

KWV Reserve range

★★★★ **Cabernet Sauvignon** Impressive fruit purity & depth; cedar-infusing 16 mths new Fr oak. **03** elegant; blackcurrant/forest-floor fruits in tense tannic frame mid-2006, powder-fine tannins good for 5-6 yr cellaring. Moderate 13.5% alc.

★★★★ **Merlot** Seductive dark tones; black plums, bitter choc & mocha spicing; **03** with herbaceous glints. Medium bodied — carries 14.5% alc well. Oak as above.

★★★★ **Chardonnay 04** notch up on **03** (★★★☆), but same styling. Overt peach & citrus-pith, with extra fruit/wood dimensions of nutty crème brulée. Impression of rich concentration, but lime-fruit twist lifts the finish. 6 mths new Fr oak; single vyd. Not retasted.

★★★★ **Sauvignon Blanc** Beautifully balanced **05** offers grassy spine around which riper tropical fruits add flesh, breadth & complexity. Attractively dry; amenable alc.

Shiraz Loads of character in **03** (★★★★), back on ripe track after more herby/fynbos toned **02** (★★★☆). Latest offers plump cherry fruit intermingled with white pepper & musky spice, tobacco/leather interest. 16 mths new Am oak. 14% alc. This range WO Sbosch.

KWV Classic range

Roodeberg ★★★☆ A Cape institution: admirable quality given large quantities. Blend usually cab, shiraz & merlot. **03** lively red fruit, gently spiced, sweetly ripe palate, no hard edges — just juicy drinkability. Yr seasoned oak. Also in 1.5ℓ, 3ℓ, 5ℓ. This & reds below not retasted this ed. **Cabernet Sauvignon** ★★★☆ **03** built to please, has layers of interest: savoury nuances to cassis, plum core; approachable yet firm. Yr Fr oak. **Merlot** ★★★ **03** lighter than pvs, but still red berry flavour appeal, toasty oak. **Pinotage** ★★★☆ **03** attractive vibrant raspberry/brambleberry fruit layered in wood-spice; juicy, yet with fine-grained tannins. **Shiraz** ★★★ **03** carpaccio, wild berries & white pepper; gentler structure than pvs, enjoyable in youth. **Cape Blush** ★★ Blanc de noir **05**, fruit pastille flavours filled out by 8g/ℓ sugar. **Chardonnay** ★★★ Lighter oaking, just-dry; **05** trademark butterscotch, sweet-fruited send-off with hint of orange. **Sauvignon Blanc** ★★★ Figgy, herbaceous **06** approachable in light-textured, nicely balanced package. 12% alc. **Steen** ★★☆ 'Old-Cape' name for bone-dry version of chenin, tad sterner than sibling below. **06** grassy, refreshingly dry. **Chenin Blanc** ★★☆ **06** candyfloss cut by frisky acidity, rounded 6g/ℓ sugar, friendly 12% alc. **Val du Chêne** ★★★ Lightly wooded chenin. **04** crunchy fruit salad flavours, tangy lemon-biscuit finish. Not retasted. *Wine* ★★★★. **Cape Riesling** ★★ Restrained, mown hay of crouchen; **06** a touch leafy. **Late Vintage** ★★★ Pvsly noted as discontinued, makes a comeback with **05**: grapey, yet 23g/ℓ sugar nicely balanced, really doesn't cloy. **Mousseux Blanc Cuvée Brut** ★★ **NV** crowd-pleaser; lightly fruited, finishes dry & gentle (11.5% alc). **Mousseux Blanc Demi-Sec** ★★ Friendly quaffer; **NV**; developed musk-sweets flavours, medium-sweet finish. This range WO W Cape.

Robert's Rock range

Reds to follow not retasted for this ed: **Cabernet Sauvignon-Merlot** ★★★ **04**, near-equal blend, unshowy; cassis base toned down by dried herbs, touch stalky. Gently oaked, as is… **Cinsaut-Ruby Cabernet** ★★★ **04** track record of drinkability: exuberantly fruity, currants & cherries; juicy, goes down easily. **Merlot-Cinsaut** ★★★ **02** was last tasted. **Pinotage-Pinot Noir** ★★★★ Unusual & successful ±60/40 blend: early drinking **04** with cherry/red berry flavours, dab of cedar from yr oak. **Shiraz-Malbec** ★★★★ Compatible **03** partnership noted mid-2004, ex-barrel, as delivering good flavours, balance. **Shiraz-Cabernet Sauvignon** ★★★ **04** upfront Fortris flavour & smoky spice; soft, ripe & effortless. Not for keeping. **Cinsaut-Chenin Blanc** ★★★ Vibrant, cerise coloured **04**; red berry/fruit gum tastes, off-dry appeal. Unoaked 60/40 blend. **Chardonnay-Semillon** ★★★★ Lively, flavoursome. **05** pear & citrus melded with broad vanilla. Light 12.7% alc. **Chenin Blanc-Chardonnay** ★★★ **05** tropical tones filled out by off-dry finish. **Chardonnay** ★★★ **04** was easy, uncomplicated & quaffable when last tasted mid-2004. All WO W Cape.

Golden Kaan Reserve range

★★★★ **Winemaker's Reserve Cabernet Sauvignon** Cassis/raspberry fruit depth & concentration of **03** allow serious oaking (new Fr, 26 mths), contributing lovely cigar-box tone, & providing for 6+ yrs cellaring — tannins need time to become supple, integrate.

All to follow ★★★★: **Reserve Selection Cabernet Sauvignon** Well balanced **03**; oak well integrated with creamy red fruit, smoky/cedar spicing. Manicured structure. Yr Fr barrels, half new, as for… **Reserve Selection Shiraz** Harmonious, accessible **03** has fruit as the main focus (plum jam, cherry); deep & rich, with savoury hints, herbs & oak support. **Winemaker's Reserve Chardonnay** Bold New World style **03**: crystallised lemon rind, roast nuts, dried peaches with a big dollop oak (8 mths new Fr) — a well-rounded body. Chardonnay du Monde, SAA accolades. **Reserve Selection Sauvignon Blanc 05** interesting lemonade & fennel features; quiet grassiness followed by mouthfilling vibrant freshness, long finish escorts friendly 12% alc home. Concours Mondial gold. No new vintages, hence none of this range reviewed for this ed.

Golden Kaan range

Sauvignon Blanc ★★★ Muted pear-drop/lime character, simple refreshment in easy, off-dry **05**. All following ★★★, all **04** except Rosé, none revisited this ed. **Cabernet Sauvignon** Ripe & generous; cassis-infused, approachable. Oaking (9 mths seasoned Fr) only apparent in dry finish. **Merlot** Plenty to like: cassis/raspberries, light oak dusting, medium weight with just enough tannin for food. Oak as above. **Shiraz** Biggest selling member of range, in fruit-focused style: luscious straw-/red-berries, sweetly spiced. 9 mths used Am oak in support. **Pinotage** Fruit-dominant, basket of rhubarb-toned berries & plums, touch of oak (Fr/Am 9 mths) adds interest. **Pinotage Rosé 05** pretty colour, fruit pastille nose, juicy off-dry friendliness. **Chardonnay** Satisfying, elegant peach/citrus flavours perked up by brisk acidity, light wooding. All WO W Cape.

Bonne Esperance range

Dry Red ★★ This, below, **NV**, in 1ℓ screwcap, sold internationally; in SA only for KWV staff. Blend varies: usually cinsaut, ruby cab, smattering pinotage. Softly friendly; baked plum flavours, unwooded, 12.5% alc. **Dry White** ★★ Easy-going; summery, tasty grape flavours. Light 12.1% alc.

Pearly Bay range

> **Cape Red** ☺ ★★★ Vivid hues, flavoursome chewy fruit in lively palate; light-hearted, unwooded, 12.5% alc. **NV**, WO W Cape like siblings in range.

Cape White ★★ Crunchy freshness, grassy spine, tart tail. Just 11.8% alc. **Celebration** ★★ Cheerful semi-sweet bubbly from muscat d'A; low 8% alc.

KWV Fortified range

★★★★ **Millennium Port** Pvs eds noted graceful ageing **99**; cinsaut/tinta; 19.5% alc, 110g/ℓ RS; huge grape-tannin structure for keeping. Unwooded.

★★★★ **Tawny Port** Long maturation (5-8 yrs old oak), expert cellar handling, give consistent character yr after yr, at high level. Latest **NV** light mahogany with smoking-room allure: nuts, spiced dried meat, cigars… Sensual texture. Equal tinta/souzão. 19.3% alc. 120g/ℓ sugar.

★★★★ **Vintage Red Muscadel** From selected Rbtson vyds; Muscadel Award for rich, sophisticated **75**; pvs eds showed notable complexity: tealeaf, nutty oiliness, brandy-soaked raisins; long sweet/savoury finish. Large oak 8 yrs. 17.3% alc, 150g/ℓ sugar.

★★★★ **White Muscadel NV** golden patina alerts you to delights to come: unfettered by oak, a full expression of the glorious richness of fully ripe muscadel. Layered complexity: concentrated sultana, toffee — rich & savoury, beautifully balanced. 17.5% alc. WO Breede Rvr Vlly.

★★★★ **Red Muscadel** Current **NV** in same footprints as pvs but better: honeyed raisins, candied citrus peel, luscious & full bodied. Eminently drinkable because of the freshening acidity, livening spirit. 8 yrs large oak. 17.6% alc.

Ruby Port ★★★★ Current **NV** not retasted this ed; pvsly we rated it notch higher than pvs. Like drinking Xmas cake rich in brandy-soused dried fruit. 2 yrs large oak. From tinta/souzão. 19.3% alc. All these WO W Cape unless noted. *—DS/CR*

■ *La Beryl* see Fairview
■ *La Bon Vigne* see The Marais Family

Laborie Cellar   ⚲ 🍷 ☕ ♿

*Paarl ▪ Est 1691 ▪ Tasting & sales daily 9-5 (Nov-Apr) Mon-Sat 9-5 (May-Oct) ▪ Fee R10 for 5 wines; tour & tasting R20 ▪ Closed all Christian pub hols ▪ Tours for groups 10+ by appt ▪ Laborie Restaurant open daily 10-5 (T 021·807·3095) ▪ Owner KWV International ▪ Winemaker/viticulturist Dave Boyes ▪ 39 ha (cab, merlot, pinot, pinotage, shiraz, chard, sauvignon, viognier) ▪ 550 tons 40 000 cs ▪ PO Box 528 Suider-Paarl 7624 ▪ wolhuter@kwv.co.za ▪ www.kwv-international.com ▪ **T 021·807·3390/3196** ▪ F 021·863·1955*

Winemaker Dave Boyes has been hearing corks popping, both at this historic Paarl property, where a wedding venue and a restaurant are among the attractions; and in Champagne, to where the Cap Classique Challenge prize-winnings (for the 00 Blanc de Blanc), afforded Boyes a look-and-learn trip. Back home, with the focus on upgrading the cellar and tweaking the range, he's been experimenting with oak percentages; the Chardonnay's doing so well on the market that further vineyards were planted; and the red wine quality, he believes, 'is up there'.

★★★★ **Jean Taillefert** A bold New World shiraz flagship. Sultry **03** loaded with black berries & coffee, toned by tropical/toffee characters. Densely structured, not accessible in youth as was lighter but no less impressive, JCWCA-applauded **02**. Unfiltered, as are other reds.

★★★★ **Blanc de Blanc Brut** All-chard MCC, ±3 yrs on lees in bottle. **00** noted pvs ed as bone-dry & irresistible, with marmalade-spread brioche flavours. *Wine* ★★★★★, Winemakers Choice.

★★★★ **Pineau de Laborie** Luxurious, unique dessert from pinotage, mostly unfermented, matured 18 mths in used barriques, fortified with Laborie pinotage potstill brandy to ±17.5% alc. ±90g/ℓ sugar comfortable for solo sipping or with dessert/cheese. **02** last yr was deeply spiced plum-pudding character with enough spirituous bite amidst rich fruitiness to offset the sweetness. WO Paarl. 375ml.

Cabernet Sauvignon ★★★☆ Unshowy, reliable. **03** nutty edge to red berry features, accessible pleasure in youth, as with lighter textured, restrained **02**. Yr 300ℓ Fr barrels. **Merlot** ★★★★ **03** medium coloured/bodied, spice lifts plummy fruits; open yet refined. Oak of this & next as for Cab. **Merlot-Cabernet Sauvignon** ★★★★ Elegance with enough fruit concentration for interest; **03** pliable late grip. 60/40 blend. **Pinotage** ★★★☆ **03** vivid strawberry fruit touched with almond & clove, sufficient grip for table; enjoy in youth. 8 mths Fr casks. **Shiraz** ★★★ Leathery, more rustic style, medium fullness; **03** for early drinking. **Blanc de Noir** ★★★ Dry sparkler from pinot, dash other reds. Last tasted **00** noted as bottle-mature. **Chardonnay** ★★★ **05** in showy style, simple butterscotch fruit cut with citrus peel. 30% oaked 6 mths. **Sauvignon Blanc** ★★★ **05** characterised by cool fruit, nettles & grapefruit mid-2005, not revisited this yr. All WO Coastal unless noted. — *DS*

La Bourgogne Farm ○ ♀ ⌂ new

Franschhoek ▪ Est 1694 ▪ 1stB 2005 ▪ Visits by appt ▪ Self-catering cottages ▪ Owner La Bourgogne Farm (Pty) Ltd ▪ Vini adviser Justin Hoy (Aug 2004) ▪ Viti adviser Paul Wallace (Aug 2004) ▪ 5.5 ha (mainly semillon) ▪ 25 tons 100% white ▪ PO Box 96 Franschhoek 7690 ▪ george@cpsa.co.za ▪ www.labourgogne.co.za ▪ T 021·876·2115 ▪ F 021·876·2567

Having enjoyed wine since childhood, George Mayer finds it only natural to be producing from the 20 year old semillon on the farm. With his first vintage bottled, the bug has bitten: plantings of a further 3ha of red and white varieties are underway, and a cellar is planned. A flagship barrel-fermented semillon, unwooded chardonnay and white and red blends are envisaged, as is a basketful of other produce including export plums, olive oil, and plum and pear liqueurs.

★★★★ **Progeny Semillon** Sweet waxy, lanolin aromas, with spicy vanilla hint on **05**. Finely textured palate, slightly creamy with crisp, food-friendly greengage finish. Modest 13.1% alc; technically off-dry, but sweetness not obvious. Fermented/±8 mths oak. — *MF*

La Bri ♀

Franschhoek ▪ Tasting & sales Mon-Fri 10-12.30 Oct-Apr or by appt ▪ Fee R12 ▪ Closed pub hols ▪ Owner Robin Hamilton ▪ 18 ha (cabs s/f, merlot, petit v, shiraz, chard, viognier) ▪ 3 500 cs own label 85% red 15% white ▪ Ranges for customers: Helgerson Wines (US), Makro (SA) ▪ PO Box 180 Franschhoek 7690 ▪ info@labri.co.za ▪ www.la-bri.co.za ▪ T 021·876·2593 ▪ F 021·876·3197

Manager Johan Haasbroek can look back with satisfaction on almost a decade of replanting and raising the bar wine-wise. It's now time for tweaking — revamping the label, for example, for a 'new, bright look' — and for rationalisation. That process puts Affinity, a bordeaux-style blend, at the head of the fleet; the second-tier range is the Limited Release, extended by a maiden Shiraz-Viognier and a reintroduced Chardonnay.

Affinity ★★★★ Dollops petit v, cab f added to cab & merlot (68/22) in barrique aged (±20 mths) flagship blend; fuller (15.4% alc), better fleshed/fruited than maiden **03**, so quite approachable at early stage; but fine structure bodes well — pity not to allow **04** to achieve its potential. Note: only this, Shiraz-Viognier & Chard tasted this ed.

Reserve range

★★★★ **Cabernet-Merlot Reserve** 94% cab in **02**, yet more approachably 'New World' than pvs, thanks to succulent cassis fruit. 20 mths Fr oak, third new.

Merlot ★★★★ Ripe plum flavours, fine almost silky tannins, **02** sweet, floral end. Ready, maybe not for keeping. 20 mths Fr oak, some new.

Limited Release range

★★★★ **Shiraz-Viognier** new Red & white (10%) grapes co-fermented, yr older Fr/Am oak for appealing spicy/floral effect; also gutsy wood tannin on **05** but enough scrubby redfruit substance to cushion both tannin & high kicking 15.6% alc. Shd keep well.

Cabernet Sauvignon ★★★☆ **03** characteristic tobacco leaf/spice nose; fruity core on palate; supple, drinks well now. **Merlot** ★★★ **03** tightly wound, with fresh acidity, firm tannin, toasty plum fruit flavours. Structure for improvement. **Chardonnay** ★★★☆ Citrus freshness offsets richness of new Fr oak (fermented/yr aged), weight of ±15% alc, in **05**; lengthy, rounded white peach flavours enjoyable now & for next yr/2. — *DH*

■ *La Cave* see Wamakersvallei

La Chataigne

Franschhoek ▪ *Est 1972* ▪ *1stB 2003* ▪ *Visits by appt* ▪ *3 guest cottages* ▪ *Owners Parkfelt family* ▪ *Vini consultant Gerda Willers (2002)* ▪ *Viti adviser Pietie Le Roux (1996)* ▪ *15 ha (merlot, pinotage, shiraz, chenin, sauvignon, semillon)* ▪ *150 tons 1 000 cs own label 25% red 45% white 30% rosé* ▪ *PO Box 7 La Motte 7691* ▪ *richard@solvit.co.za* ▪ *www.lachat.co.za* ▪ *T/F 021·876·3220*

Owner Richard Parkfelt hails from Sweden, which he visited last year in response to an invitation from a group of hoteliers. He also spent time in Stockholm, where his wines are listed, and Gothenburg, and returned optimistic about export growth. Back on the farm in Franschhoek, a trio of guest cottages and a tasting room have been completed, the latter with a small open kitchen for Julie P, an experienced demo chef. 'The idea is to make it interactive,' explains her spouse, 'and to use what we grow and what's seasonal.'

Marron ★★★ Improved **04** same wooding (9 mths, older), same grapes, different proportions: merlot upped to 60%, pinotage down to 20%, same cab. Soft, well fleshed, v pleasant & easy-going. **Rosé** ★★ **04** last ed a friendly picnic companion from merlot; refreshing entry courtesy two blancs (chenin, sauvignon, 25% each); slightly sweet conclusion. **Sauvignon Blanc** ★★★★ Much improved this yr; **05** quite boldly flavoured, striking tropical bouquet of pineapple & passionfruit, juicy yet light — 12.7% alc good for lunchtime quaffing. Incl 15% bushvine semillon. **Kastanje** ★★★ **05** semi-dry charmer from mainly chenin; rounded, full flavours plumped by dash semillon (also incl 7% sauvignon); ripe-fruit finish. — *IvH*

La Chaumiere Estate new

Franschhoek ▪ *Est 2001* ▪ *1stB 2003* ▪ *Tasting & tours by appt (sales only from local outlets)* ▪ *Owners Ian & Margaret Slack* ▪ *Winemaker Justin Hoy (Dec 2004)* ▪ *3.6 ha (shiraz, chard)* ▪ *12 tons 600 cs* ▪ *PO Box 601 Franschhoek 7690* ▪ *slacki@telkomsa.net* ▪ *T 021·876·2135*

A first in 2006 for Ian and Margaret Slack: the maiden release of their second label, Slacki's Shiraz. 'We used young vines to produce a light, peppery, everyday wine, made in oak,' comments Ian S (aka 'Slacki'), 'with a slightly jokey label and priced for the value-market.' To follow: the maiden red in their premier range, the La Chimere Shiraz. Adding to the year's busyness was a push to finish the walled gardens around the winery, a final touch for a picturesque Franschhoek setting.

Slacki's Shiraz new ★★★★ ✓ Undimmed by 18 mths oak or exuberant tannins, **04** crackles with characterful dark spice, savoury persistence. Light texture, freshness, moderate alc provide most attractive early drinking. **La Chimere Chardonnay** ★★★ Butterscotch/lees aromas, freshening citrus zest flavour on **04**. Pleasantly moderate 12.5% alc. Fr oak, third new. — *AL*

■ *La Chimere* see La Chaumiere
■ *La Cotte* see Franschhoek Vineyards

La Couronne Estate

Franschhoek ▪ *Est/1stB 1999* ▪ *Tasting & sales Mon-Fri 10-4 Sat 9-1* ▪ *Fee R15* ▪ *Tours by appt (R10 p/p)* ▪ *Closed pub hols* ▪ *Weddings & conferences* ▪ *Facilities for children* ▪ *Tour groups* ▪ *Owners The Austrian Trust* ▪ *Winemaker Dirk Husselmann advised by Jean Daneel (Jul 2005)* ▪ *21 ha (cabs s/f, malbec, merlot, petit v, shiraz, chard, sauvignon)* ▪ *60-90 tons ±13 000 cs 60% red 40% white* ▪ *PO Box 459 Franschhoek 7690* ▪ *ninette@lacouronne.co.za* ▪ *www. lacouronne.co.za* ▪ *T 021·876·3939/2110* ▪ *F 021·876·4168*

With a splitting of assets on the ground — the hotel has been taken over by Mont Rochelle and now shares the name — the focus here at 'The Crown' is firmly on the winery. Open for visits, it boasts a spacious tasting area (with right royal views) as well as conference facilities, an outdoors bar and children's playground. Consultant Jean Daneel's brief is to develop a range of what marketing man Mike Moore describes as 'iconic wines'. Assisting is Dirk Husselmann, who was much involved in setting up the owners' second Franschhoek wine farm, Normandy.

★★★★ **Cabernet Sauvignon** Excellent vintage lifted the bar: **03** classically styled with deep ruby hues, ripe cassis palate, finessed oak tannins (18 mths, 30% new). Accessible, & a bright future. Mbury grapes (therefore NE). Step up on russet-edged **01** (★★★). No **02**, **04**; **05** not ready for review.

★★★★ **Shiraz** Showy & bold **03** has rampant warm-climate fruit (14% alc), lots of varietal pyrotechnics (smoke, wild scrub etc) kept in shape by ripely firm tannins & well judged oak (20 mths oak, 20% new, 20% Am). Mbury fruit/NE. Not retasted; **04** not ready.

★★★★ **Chardonnay Wooded 05** (★★★), 2nd vintage of this label similarly vinified to **04** but less successful, misses something of pvs's generosity, concentration & liveliness; oak unmelded mid-2006, whereas **04** was elegantly wooded & harmonious in youth. 20-30% new barrels, all Fr, 9-10 mths.

Merlot ★★★★ **03** most friendly of the reds: succulent red fruit (partly via dashes cab, shiraz), well structured & balanced; clean dry tannins. For now & few yrs. Mbury grapes, 18-22 mths Fr oak, 1st-3rd fill. **04** not ready. **Ménage à Trois** ★★★ **01** arrives out of vintage sequence (**03** tasted last ed, **04** unready); equal partnership cabs s & f, merlot; medium bodied, savoury, with pleasing grip & brisk finish. Fr oak. **Chardonnay Unwooded** ★★★★ **05** pure, unadulterated chard; last ed extroverted & zesty, oozed ripe peach & citrus; lovely balanced fruit-acid. **06** not ready.

'277' range

Exodus Dry Red new ★★★ Early drinking bdx blend led by cab (65%), dollops merlot, cab f & malbec. Plump & plummy, rounded & supple despite robust 24 mths Fr/Am oaking. **NV**. **Etienne Chenin Blanc** new ★★ **05** spicy melon fruit, slight lifted/oxidized character to nose, balanced acidity. **Sauvignon Blanc** ★★ **06** early harvested & showing bracing acidity, low fruit & (a plus) light 11.5% alc. **Cevennes Blanc** ★★★ Three-way blend sauvignon, chard & chenin; food-friendly **05** vibrant, ripe/green tones jostle with firm grapefruit finish. **06** not ready. Above widely sourced, so various WOs. Discontinued: **Mereaux Red**. — *IvH*

■ *Ladismith Wine & Brandy Cellar see* Southern Cape Vineyards
■ *Lady Anne Barnard see* African Pride

Lady Auret Wines   ◊ ♀ new

Paarl · Est/1stB 2002 · Tasting by appt · Owners Corius & Gina Swart · Winemaker Corius Swart (Jan 2002) · 2 200 btls 100% red · 14 Auret Str Paarl 7646 · ladyauret@polka.co.za · T 082·773·7059 / 082·377·2661

The Lady hails from Auret Street in Paarl and yes, she's available. A vintage 02 Shiraz (with 8% viognier for aroma and fruit), she's been matured in oak for 29 months. Fashionably late for review this ed, she's described by proud Corius Swart — who cites Eben Sadie (Sadie Family) and Willie de Waal (Scali) as his winemaking inspiration — as 'spicy, intensely fruity and downright exuberant.'

Laibach Vineyards   ◊ ♀

Stellenbosch · Est 1994 · 1stB 1997 · Tasting & sales Mon-Fri 10-5 Sat 10-1 (Nov-Apr only) Pub hols 10-1 · Closed Easter Fri/Sun, Dec 25 & Jan 1 · Fee R10 refunded on purchase · Tours by appt · Owners Laibach family · Winemakers Francois van Zyl & Stefan Dorst (Jan 2000/Jan 1997) · MD/Viticulturist Michael Malherbe (Jun 1994) · 42 ha (cabs s/f, malbec, merlot, petit v, pinotage, chard, viognier) · 300 tons 24 000 cs own label · 600 cs for Woolworths · 70% red 30% white · PO Box 7109 Stellenbosch 7599 · info@laibach.co.za · www.laibachwines.com · T 021·884·4511 · F 021·884·4848

Five years of experimentation with cab produced, in 2005, what Francois van Zyl calls 'a standout wine', an opinion validated that year by Young Wine Show judges. From a block that yields exceptional fruit and bottled without filtration or fining, it is 'a true reflection of what the farm can produce'. It's labelled The Widows Block, after the spouse of a previous proprietor who told the new owners, in 1994, that they should abandon their plans to plant shiraz in this particular site: 'This is cab country,' were her wise words. A third of the farm is now certified organic.

★★★★ **Friedrich Laibach** Rigorously selected bdx-style blend; farm's flagship. **03** cab, merlot, cab f, petit v quartet (64/16/13/7) sumptuous, imposing; skilfully tailored, shows off intricate mocha, mulberry features. Potential potential over good few yrs. 100% new Fr oak, 16 mths, half as blend. Not retasted.

★★★★ **The Widows Block** new From oldest cab parcel on farm, officially a 'single vyd'. Eager, youthful **05** liberal choc/mocha tones, ripe black fruits; behind enthusiasm lies persuasive, beautifully proportioned/toned future classic. Carefully handled for most burnished of tannins, purity of fruit. 100% new Fr oak, 16 mths. SAYWS champion.

★★★★ **Merlot** ✓ FvZ's favourite grape, among SA's most characterful; fast seller, **05** still closed, promises usual compact elegance, bitter choc, dark plum qualities. Careful tannin extraction, oaking, add to overall quality, distinction. Fr oak, soupçon new. SAA. **04** sold before we cld taste. **03** Wine ★★★★★; Winemakers' Choice. Smnsberg-Sbosch WO, as are following 4 reds.

★★★★ **Pinotage** Old dryland bushvines produce agreeably modern **05**. Riper elements comfortably offset by mineral freshness; expressive raspberry/spice fruits, well meshed tannins for current drinking & few yrs ageing. SAYWS gold. Frequent ABSA Top Ten. Fr barrels, 75% new, 13 mths.

★★★★ **Cabernet Sauvignon 04** offers savoury satisfaction rather than overt fruit. Agreeably fresh, with supple muscular feel, well melded tannins, whisper new oak. Claret-like **03** (★★★★) SAYWS champ.

The Dogleg ★★★★ Bdx-style blend cab/merlot/petit v/cab f (60/25/10/5); gently handled **04**'s straightforward flavours in fresh/ripe balance; for current-ish drinking. Fr oak, 40% new. **The Ladybird** ★★★★ Organically grown bdx-style blend. **05** subtle, homogenous mix merlot, cabs s/f. Light, supple texture; approachable minerally tannins incorporating fresh, sweet fruit. Balanced 25% new Fr oak, 13 mths. Unfiltered/fined. **Chardonnay** ★★★★ Quietly satisfying youthful **04**; last ed balanced oatmeal/citrus freshness, broadening dash oak. Juicy, well weighted; roundly dry. Good aperitif or with variety of foods. Half barrel fermented/yr new Fr oak. **Chenin Blanc** ★★★ **06** happily partnered with 5% viognier. Gentle floral notes, easy going richness; honeyed spice lift in fruity tail. Attractive quaffer. Pdberg/Bottlry Hills vyds. **Sauvignon Blanc** ★★★ **06** cool, crisp & refreshingly medium bodied. Easy but satisfying 'sauvage' minerals, gooseberries with lingering follow through. **Natural Sweet** ★★★★ **05** from chenin, partly new oak fermented, with low alc (7%). Still available. Balanced 9g/ℓ acid, 165g/ℓ sugar. 375ml. —AL

Lammershoek Winery

Swartland ▪ Est/1stB 1999 ▪ Tasting, sales & tours Mon-Fri 9-5; Sat/Sun & pub hols by appt ▪ Tours Mon-Fri 9-5 by appt ▪ Special house platter (R60 p/p) Mon-Fri 9-5 by appt; or BYO picnic ▪ Walks ▪ Conservation area ▪ Mountain biking ▪ Owners Paul & Anna Kretzel, Stephan family ▪ Winemaker Albert Ahrens (Jun 2002) ▪ Viticulturists Paul Kretzel & Albert Ahrens ▪ 130 ha (12 varieties, r/w) ▪ 200 tons 10 000 cs own label 75% red 25% white ▪ PO Box 597 Malmesbury 7299 ▪ info@lammershoek.co.za ▪ www.lammershoek.co.za ▪ T/F 022·482·2835

Things are growing apace here, with winemaker Albert Ahrens and wife Heidi celebrating the arrival of their first extension to the team — baby Lisa. Other additions include expanded space for barrel fermentation and maturation. Last year saw the first-time fermentation of shiraz in 500ℓ casks, and a once-off release of Cape Vintage Zinfandel. Says Albert A: 'There are no other vintages in the making but there might be in future…'

★★★★ **Roulette** The flagship red, a spicy Rhône-inspired blend shiraz, carignan, grenache, viognier — 74/14/10/2 proportions in winning **04**, chacteristically Pdberg with its scrubby, dried herb (incl lavender) bouquet, effortless fine-tannined balance. Sweet fruit, dry finish, fresh. Big 14.5% alc balanced. 16 mths mixed-age barrels.

★★★★ **Syrah 04** also expressive of this part of Swtland, with smoked meat, herby overtones. Savoury & ripe, full & powerful, yet some delicacy; clean mineral core. Oak a touch excessive in youth (16 mths 1st/2nd fill Fr/Am), but a gd overall balance. Like above, shd grow with few yrs.

★★★★ **Zinfandel-Syrah** Delicious, savoury **03** (tasted last ed) augmented by splashes cab, carignan, striking, individual & unusually refined given zin's boisterousness. Ready, but no hurry. Fr oak, portion new, 14 mths.

★★★★ **Roulette Blanc 05** shows appealingly & impressively as fine part of emerging Swtland tradition of chenin-led blends, here with 24% chard, 16% viognier. Powerful, rich (approaching off-dry), with nice phenolic touch & some obvious oak (fermented/10 mths, some new) which shd integrate in beneficial yr/2, add to emerging complexity.

★★★★ **Chenin Blanc Barrique** Unusual **04** with attractive oxidative complexity. Bold, showy **05** (★★★★) in fashionable oaky-sweet style (7.1g/ℓ RS; fermented/10 mths wood). Floral/tropical notes too, but 'green' acidity adds sweet-sour element to richness, in rather uneasy balance with big 14.5% alc.

★★★★ **Viognier Barrique** Last tasted was **04**. Big & rich; varietal aromas quietened by 14% hárslevelü; apricot/floral concentration on silky palate. Fermented/10 mths Fr oak, some new.

Pinotage Barrique ★★★★ **03** was last sampled: modern, elegant, dry, with fine vibrant tannins. Yr Fr oak, 33% new. **Tinta Barocca Barrique** ★★★★ After finely balanced, supple **02**, next will be **05**. **Straw Wine** ★★★★ Last was **04**; latest is elegantly packaged (375ml) **NV**. From sun-dried hárslevelü; citrus zest & peachy verve; satisfying balance, with 122g/ℓ sugar, 12.5% alc given dryish, grippy nett effect. Fresh, lingering. **Cape Vintage Zinfandel** ★★★ **01** branded as a 'Ruby'; **02**, confusingly, both as 'Vintage' (on front label) & 'LBV' (in winemaker's notes) — not very convincing as either — though unusualness granted! Boiled sweets, medicinal notes; sweet, not much grip. New Am oak 10 mths, 32 mths older Fr. Coastal WO. **Pinodoux** ★★★ Pinotage sweetened with grape juice to 102g/ℓ, fortified; yr older oak. Last tasted **03** smooth, rich; red fruits, toffee. Unheavy 16% alc.

Aprilskloof range

Red-Red Wine ★★★ Last tasted **04** mainly cab with pinotage, zinfandel, merlot, grenache, designed for wide appeal. Full of vitality, juicy ripe red fruits, bouncy tannins, lightly oaked. **Rosé** ★★ Last was oaked, full bodied grenache/syrah/chenin **NV** blend. Follow-up not certain. **Sauvignon Blanc** After particularly good **05** (★★★★), **06** (★★★★) pleasingly fresh, lively & dry; full 'green' lemon-drop flavours, with tropical hints. Moreish 13% alc. Coastal WO.

La Motte   ◊♀⚲🍷🏔🏛

Franschhoek · Est 1984 · Tasting & sales Mon-Fri 9-4.30 Sat 10-3 · Fee R15 · Closed Easter Fri/Sun, Dec 25 · Seasonal Food & Wine Experiences · Monthly classical concerts · Owner Hanneli Koegelenberg · Winemaker Edmund Terblanche (Dec 2001), with Werner Geldenhuys (Jun 2003) · Viticulturist Pietie le Roux (May 1986) · 108 ha (cabs s/f, merlot, shiraz, chard, sauvignon) · 900 tons 32 000 cs own label 53% red 47% white · Exported as Schoone Gevel · ISO 14001 certified · PO Box 685 Franschhoek 7690 · cellar@la-motte.co.za · www.la-motte.com · T 021·876·3119 · F 021·876·3446

Owned by acclaimed mezzo-soprano Hanneli Koegelenberg (née Rupert), it's hardly surprising that these cellars are described as 'ateliers' where nature, science and art are blended. There's also the tasting room, adorned with tapestries, and the classical concerts performed monthly. Not to mention the disa orchids cultivated here (Fleurs de la Motte) and the ethereal oils produced at the property's own extraction plant (Arômes de la Motte). And last but not least are the wines, graced by the Pierneef Collection, a tribute to SA artist JH Pierneef whose works illuminate the labels.

Pierneef Collection

★★★★ **Shiraz-Viognier** Darling-area shiraz fragranced with 11% of the aromatic white variety ex-Fhoek. Impressive **03** debut followed by still more delicious **04** (★★★★★); both with dark choc, smoked beef, black cherry bouquet; blackberry fleshiness cosseting a dry mineral core, fine focused tannins leading to spicy, lifted finish. 2nd/3rd fill Fr oak, 15 mths.

Sauvignon Blanc Tenderly crafted **06** (★★★★☆) a big step up. Pointedly assertive, it has a fine, cool 'wet stone' mineral core, expansive green fig aromas/flavours, rapier acidity & tangy grapefruit finish with hint of white pepper – all testimony to its maritime provenance. Arresting & different now, shd improve further over next few yrs. Great with something savoury like prosciutto. Own organically grown W Bay vyds. Maiden **05** (★★★☆ but Concours Mondial gold).

La Motte range

★★★★ **Shiraz 04** (★★★★★) lifts the bar with sensuous bouquet of smoked bacon, lilies & cranberries, luscious fruit, supple tannins & responsibly moderate alc (13.6%). Intense, not overpowering; long & refreshing. Beautiful now, has structure to improve ±5 yrs. Selected Coastal vyds. 16 mths oak, 30% new, mainly Fr. **03**, ex-barrel, had savoury flavours, a tannic backbone & lingering dry finish. MIWA DG, Santé Classic gold.

★★★★ **Millennium 03** back on track after vintage-impacted **02** (★★★★). Incl more merlot, less cab f & malbec & splash petit v. Classic bdx notes of cassis, violet & lead pencil. Classically structured too: restrained tannins, elegant chocolaty oak, poised & lengthy finish. Shd benefit ±5 yrs cellaring. 24 mths Fr oak, third new.

Cabernet Sauvignon ★★★★ Eucalyptus whiffs mingle with black fruit in **04**, also shows house-style cedar coolness, dark choc richness. Juicy plum palate v lightly gripped by firm tannins, almost too soft & accessible for cab. 17 mths Fr oak, 30% new. **Chardonnay** Sophisticated **05** (★★★★) perfectly groomed: spice, citrus & cream merge seamlessly, as do crisp acidity, firm tannin, judicious oak details. Partly fermented/±yr Fr/Hngrian oak, 50% new. Should improve over 2-3 yrs. **04** (★★★☆) more understated & reticent in youth. **Sauvignon Blanc** ★★★★ Just-bottled **06** still shy; more grass/hay than pvs passionfruit/tropical. Interest ensured by tangy sweet-sour acidity, slight tannin tug in tail. – *CvZ*

Landau du Val

Franschhoek • Tasting by appt • Sales at La Cotte Wine Sales, Franschhoek • Owners Basil & Jane Landau • Winemakers Anina Guelpa (Anatu Wines); Jean Daneel (2004 vintage) • Viticulturist Jaco Schwenke • **T 082·410·1130** *• F 021·876·3369*

Basil and Jane Landau have decided to specialise in semillon. Their gnarly bushvines, planted in 1905, still yield consistently excellent fruit, as was highlighted when LdV Semillon won its category in the 2006 Trophy Show and finished first in *Wine* magazine's line-up of 22 examples. The team, now including winemaker Anina Guelpa of Anatu Wines, deserve all the recognition for their expertise and efforts, the Landaus acknowledge.

★★★★ **Semillon** Handsome, warm-butter/brioche character flirts with opulence (as does 14% alc) but flash of lemon-toned acidity adds vigour to **04**, not retasted. Fr oak-fermented/aged 5-6 mths, seasoned barrels.

Discontinued: **Sauvignon Blanc Private Selection**. – *DS*

■ *Landsdowne* see Arlington

Landskroon Wines

Paarl • Est 1874 • 1stB 1974 • Tasting & sales Mon-Fri 8.30-5 Sat 9-1 • Fee R3 p/p for groups • Closed Easter Fri, Dec 25 & Jan 1 • Tours by appt • Picnics in summer by appt or BYO • Self-catering cottage (see Stay-over section) • Play area for children • Tour groups • Gifts • Walks by appt • Permanent display of Stone Age artefacts • Winemaker Paul de Villiers, with Fanie Geyser (Jan 1980/Dec 2002) • Viticulturist Hugo de Villiers Jnr (1995) • 270 ha (14 varieties r/w) • 1 100 tons 86% red 11% white 3% port • PO Box 519 Suider-Paarl 7624 • huguette@landskroonwines.com • www.landskroonwines.com • T 021·863·1039 • F 021·863·2810

This historic farm has witnessed extensive renovations over the past few years. During their second vintage in the new barrel maturation cellar, their state-of-the-art filling and labelling facilities were put to good use with the latest revamp: new labels. 'The design seems to have introduced a breath of fresh air into our wines,' says marketing manager Huguette van der Merwe. No surprise then that their 04 breezed in as joint winner of the *Wine* Value for Money Pinotage Award.

★★★★ **Paul de Villiers Cabernet Sauvignon** ✓ The flagship; selected parcels on home-farm, seriously oaked (all new Fr) for longevity. Current **02**, reported 'not made' last ed, very much alive, if still tight, v dry, lots of wood evident, but generous cassis core waiting to develop; similar youthful introversion noted for **03**, featured last ed.

★★★★ **Cabernet Sauvignon** ✓ Recent releases somewhat lighter toned, earlier approachable, still satisfying. **04** warm & welcoming; medium bodied but ripe; tasty flavours all the way through. Bit more substance, pleasure, than plummy **03** (★★★★, but *Decanter* ★★★★). Barrique aged.

★★★★ **Paul de Villiers Shiraz** More concentrated, showy than version below; partially barrique fermented/aged ±18 mths (Am/Hngrian wood). **04** (★★★★) aromatically well endowed, as pvs, whiffs *garrigue*, smoke & sweet spice; but more obvious, sweeter (3.5 RS), less serious than **03**, which big & gutsy, with gd potential.

★★★★ **Port** ✓ Usual approachable medley of tintas b/r, souzão, in attractive **01**, plus touriga in roughly equal proportions. Previewed last ed, now creamy, ripe & ready for drinking. Aged 300/500ℓ barrels 44 mths. ±100g/ℓ sugar, ±18% alc. **97** still available ex-tasting room.

Pinotage Blanc de Noir Off-Dry ☺ ★★★ **06** continues successful house style: 7.2g/ℓ sugar adds body curves, pinotage lends bright, red berry fruitiness & enough acidity for juicy, lively drinking. **Chenin Blanc Dry** ☺ ★★ Bone-dry, uncomplicatedly quaffable **06** offers Golden Delicious apple crispness, acid vibrancy & low 12% alc.

Paul de Villiers Reserve ★★★★ Unusual, characterful red, for immediate enjoyment or cellaring a while. Full bodied **04** attractively confected, warm, generous spiced fruit flavours. Shiraz, merlot, touriga (40/33/10), with dash cab, separately vinified/matured (new Fr/Am oak). **Cinsaut** ★★★ **05** light hearted braai/outdoor red; soft berry fruit, easy tannins; chillable in summer. Incl 14% cab f. Unwooded. **Merlot** ★★★ **04** again light textured, elegantly ripe cherry/red berry fruit flavours, for earlier drinking. Seasoned barriques. **Pinotage** ★★★ Slightly less affable this yr; **04** fairly generous beetroot & wild berry flavours but firm, dry tannins too, better in yr/2. *Wine* value pick. **Shiraz** ★★★ **04** repeats pvs full-ripe style, rich red fruit, vanilla spice, broad texture. Uncomplex but will please many. **Cabernet Franc-Merlot** ★★★★ ✓ **05** similar proportions as pvs (49/37, plus dash cab) but firmer, oak/tannins slightly astringent, herbaceous fruit tone; needs yr/2 to marry. Seasoned Fr oak, as pvs. **Cinsaut-Shiraz** ★★★ Smooth & engaging everyday wine. **05** compatible 45/40 marriage (plus dollops cab, touriga); shiraz adds weight, structure & savouriness to cinsaut's straightforward fruitiness. Fr oak staves. **Chardonnay** ★★ Unwooded. Gentle, softly rounded, uncomplicated **06**, medium bodied with peachy fruit salad flavours. **Sauvignon Blanc** ★★★ Easy, peardrop toned **06**, soft, honest flavours from selected W Cape vyds. **Chenin Blanc Off-Dry** ★★★ **06** light (12.5% alc) & friendly as always; just off-dry, with lively honeydew melon succulence. Better fruited than last yr. **Morio Muscat Jerepico** ★★★★ ✓ Intensely sweet but lively fortified dessert with beguiling perfume. **06** the essence of 'grape'; truly delicious, sugar richness (196g/ℓ) lifted by zingy acidity & alc (17.5%). Delicious lightly chilled. — CR

Landzicht GWK Wines

Jacobsdal (see Northern Cape & Free State map) ▪ Est 1976 ▪ 1stB ca 1980 ▪ Tasting & sales Mon-Fri 8-1; 2-5 Sat 8-11 ▪ Tasting fee on application ▪ Closed pub hols ▪ Tours by appt ▪ Meals/refreshments by appt, or BYO picnic ▪ Farm produce sold ▪ Play area for children ▪ Tour groups ▪ Conferences ▪ Owner GWK Ltd ▪ Winemaker Chrisna Botha ▪ Viti consultant Stefan Gerber ▪ 300 ha (cab, merlot, pinotage, shiraz, chard, chenin, colombard, muscadels r/w) ▪ ±2 200 tons 40 000 cs own label 20% red 40% white 20% rosé 20% fortified ▪ PO Box 94 Jacobsdal 8710 ▪ landzicht@kby.gwk.co.za ▪ **T** 053·591·0164 ▪ F 053·591·0145

After 22 years of taming the terroir of this summer-rainfall area ('Like going to war, you need certain weapons to attack the seasons — there's no chance for mistakes'), veteran winemaker Ian Sieg left on a high note, with a half-dozen Veritas awards, the first barrelled red wines ready for bottling, and a maiden port in the wings. Sieg's seeking new challenges (see Goudveld and Loopspruit), and his assistant, Chrisna Botha, now leads the squad.

Chardonnay ★ Light body (11% alc) & high acidity (5.9 g/l) give **06** a lean, rather austere feel; flavours are modest. **Chenin Blanc** ★★ **06** summer tipple; tropical/fruit gum flavours, softly rounded off-dry style, very easy to drink. **Blanc de Blanc** ★★ **06** tropical fruit tones, incl peach, in this light, uncomplicated quaffer. Following wines tasted last ed, no new vintages: **Cabernet Sauvignon** ★ Brawny **04** rather enthusiastically Fr oak chipped (as elsewhere in range), leaving sweetish red berry fruit somewhat overwhelmed. **Merlot** ★★ **04** touch of sour plum, dry astringent finish. **Pinotage** Huge **04**, wood driven & touch porty. 15% alc. **Shiraz** ★★ Rustically characterful **04**, sweet-sour plum flavours, some fruit cushioning from the dry tannins. **Gewürztraminer** ★★★ Tsunami of rosepetals & Turkish Delight. Wow! **04** well-rounded, off-dry on taste (though much higher 30g/ℓ sugar), soft. **Blümchen** ★★ Natural Sweet white from colombard & hanepoot; soft, guava-toned easy-drinker with low 8% alc. **NV**, as is... **Rosenblümchen** ★★ Natural Sweet rosé, cab gives the coral pink glints, otherwise identical to white version. **Vin Doux** Latest bottling of low-alc semi-sweet carbonated sparkling not tasted. **Sweet Hanepoot** ★★★ One of their better renderings, **04** enlivened by spirituous bite, lemony tang. **Red Jerepigo** ★★ Good winter warmer; **04** youngberry jam & molasses; glow-inducing finish (16% alc). **Red Muscadel** ★ Coral-tinted **04**, curiously acidic & distinctly warming. **White Muscadel** ★★★ **04** ultra-sweet & honeyed, 16.5% alc overpowered by soft muscat grapiness. All WO N Cape. — *CR*

■ *Land's End* see Hidden Valley
■ *Langkloof Vineyards* see Schoonberg

Langverwacht Cellar

*Robertson ▪ Est 1956 ▪ Tasting & sales Mon-Fri 8-12.30; 1.30-5 ▪ Closed pub hols ▪ Tours by appt ▪ Owners 30 members ▪ Manager/winemaker Johan Gerber, with Theunis Botha (Dec 1986, Dec 2005) ▪ Viti consultant Willem Botha (2005) ▪ ±600 ha (ruby cab, shiraz, colombard, sauvignon) ▪ ±9 800 tons ±9 000 cs own label 60% red 31% white 9% rosé ▪ PO Box 87 Bonnievale 6730 ▪ langverwacht@lando.co.za ▪ **T 023·616·2815** ▪ F 023·616·3059*

'Langverwacht' ('long awaited') is exactly what it must have felt like for winemaker Johan Gerber who — after sorting out a daunting amount of red tape — finally threw open the doors to their new tasting facility late last year. A quiet 2006 on all other fronts — yield was significantly reduced by heavy hail, so no new products in the pipeline; just gentle preparations for what will hopefully be a full recovery and a bumper 2007 harvest.

Shiraz ★★★ **04** warm, ripe fruit with wild scrub hint, amenable tannins & slightly sweet exit paint an easy picture. Following pair not retasted: **Cabernet Sauvignon** ★★★ **03** stewed currants, hints of lead pencil & bluegum, slightly jammy & green. **Ruby Cabernet** ★★★ **04**, like pvs, with black plum & thatch nuances, succulent plum/choc flavours; softly dry, with savoury twist. **Chardonnay** ★★★ Well judged oaking melds neatly with dried-fruit flavours on **06** sample, lovely long aftertaste with crisp clean finish. **Chenin Blanc** ★★ Again a muted expression of the variety; some spiced melon notes on **06**, light in body (12.5% alc) & flavour. **Colombar** ★★★ Back to its bouncy self in **06**, sample shows loads of juicy guava fruit in a light, zesty dry frame. **Colombar-Chardonnay** ★★★ **06** unready; **05** on tasting last ed was fruity & fun, sappy & light. — *DH*

Lanzerac Wines

*Stellenbosch ▪ Est 1991 ▪ 1stB 1995 ▪ Tasting & sales Mon-Thu 8.30-5; Fri & pub hols 9-4; Sat 10-2; Sun 11-3 ▪ Fee R15 (incl tasting glass) ▪ Tours Mon-Fri & pub hols 11 & 3 ▪ Closed Easter Fri, Dec 25 & Jan 1 ▪ Five-star Lanzerac Hotel for stay-overs; also Governor's Hall Restaurant & Craven Lounge (T 021·887·1132) ▪ Tour groups ▪ Gifts ▪ Conferences (T 021·887·1132) ▪ Walks ▪ Winemaker Wynand Lategan (Nov 2004) ▪ Viticulturist Tommie Corbett (Aug 2002) ▪ 50 ha (cabs s/f, malbec, merlot, petit v, pinotage, shiraz, chard, sauvignon) ▪ 500 tons 30 000 cs 80% red 20% white ▪ ISO 14000 & HACCP certification in progress ▪ PO Box 6233 Uniedal 7612 ▪ winesales@lanzerac.co. za ▪ www.lanzeracwines.co.za ▪ **T 021·886·5641** ▪ F 021·887·6998*

Wynand Lategan, who stepped over to Lanzerac from sister property Lourensford (where Lanzerac wines are bottled), is delighted with the relaunch of the Rosé, a national favourite for many years, in its original 'teardrop' bottle. Other recent highlights include their 04 being rated Best SA Merlot in Sweden, the Classic blend's class-winning performance at the 2006 IWSC, and the granting of membership to the historic farm by the Biodiversity Wine Initiative. Looking forward, the intention is to focus on strengths such as the Chardonnay, Merlot, Pinotage, Cab and red blend. New strategic alliances in the UK and Europe should help keep the flag flying high.

★★★★ **Chardonnay** Generously oaked style. Pale gold **05** (★★★★) bodes well initially, citrus & spiced peach aromas bolstered by appealing oak (11 mths Fr); palate delivers rather lightweight though pleasurable fruit, with fine acidity throughout. **04** good yr for variety; *Wine* ★★★★.

Cabernet Sauvignon ★★★★ **00** still current, last ed offered layered berry & spice; 24 mths oaking, third new, promised potential over serval yrs. **Merlot** ★★★ Cedar & subtle plum aromas suggest elegance in **04**, yet stalky tannins keep flavours in abeyance; sharp acidity, bitter-choc finish challenge harmony. 18 mths Fr oak. **Pinotage** ★★★★ Modern styling now for this pioneer pinotage label (**59** vintage was Cape's first), with lithe structure, firm dry tannins. Pvsly tasted lively, spicy **02** & **01** still available. **Shiraz** ★★★★ Stylish, delicious **03** still available; deep black fruit, whiffs smoke, savoury spice, underbrush. Judicious oaking (yr Fr, touch Am, third new) allows tasty accessibility. **Rosé** Returns to guide after extended hiatus with **06**, in original curvaceous bottle. Sample not available at press time. **Classic** ★★★★ Approachable bdx style blend, merlot dominant at 50%. Current **02** has stylish berry compote, cigarbox character from 18 mths new 300ℓ Allier oak. WOM selection, IWSC gold; not retasted. **Sauvignon Blanc** ★★★★ Unshowy, attractive **05** has decent breadth, with more delicate tropical fruit flavours carried along by zingy acidity. — *IM/CR*

La Petite Ferme

Franschhoek ▪ Est/1stB 1996 ▪ Wines below available in the restaurant or from the cellar 12-4 daily ▪ French country-style lunches daily; luxury guest suites (see Eat-out/Stay-over sections) ▪ Gifts ▪ Owners Dendy Young family ▪ Winemaker Mark Dendy Young (Jan 1996) ▪ Viticulturist John Dendy Young ▪ 8 ha (merlot, shiraz, chard, sauvignon) ▪ 6 000 cs 40% red 60% white ▪ PO Box 55 Franschhoek 7690 ▪ info@lapetiteferme.co.za ▪ T 021·876·3016 ▪ F 021·876·3624

It's remarkable that these wines leave the premises at all, so well do they complement the cuisine at La Petite Ferme's French country-style restaurant. The food-friendly Semillon has been discontinued: 'This vineyard was extremely successful but sometimes the old has to sometimes make way for the new — in this instance viognier,' explains winemaker Mark Dendy Young. There is also no unwooded Chardonnay 'due to an early harvest by baboons!' But good news is the launch of Maison Blanc and Maison Rouge, 'house wines which deliver way beyond expectations'.

Maison Rouge new ★★ Vivid sweet-fruitedness will please widely; **05** decidedly amicable cab, dollop shiraz, unwooded; 6g/ℓ sugar makes for slippery, effortless glassful. Samples tasted of following 4 wines: **Shiraz** ★★★ **05** chimes with vintage: ripe, quite powerful (though not alcoholic), spicy; lingering bluegum toned farewell. Some Am oak this yr. **Barrel Fermented Chardonnay** Single high Fhoek vyd accorded VIP treatment, incl 100% wood vinification (50% new Fr), full malo, partial native yeast ferment; **05** (★★★★) delicious buttery mouthfeel, full-ripe marmalade fruit with wood well melded, just shy of impressive concentration shown by restrained, classy **04** (★★★★). **Sauvignon Blanc** ★★★ **06** similar to pvs: austere with brisk acidity, restrained pear-drop fruit; moderate alc (13%). **Blanc Fumé** ★★★ Passionfruit-toned **06**, slightly bigger wooded component this yr (25%) but fruit's the focus; light, racy, fresh. Great with their smoked rainbow trout. **Maison Blanc** new ★★ Super little easy-drinker from colombard, dribs chard, chenin; **05** light, fresh summery feel, hints dried grass & green veggies. Low 12.5% alc. This, Rouge above, WO W Cape. No new vintages tasted for following: **Cabernet Sauvignon** ★★★★ Vanilla-accented **03**, well defined Ribena flavours, firm but fine tannin, well-balanced wood (Fr/Am). **Merlot** ★★★★ **04** dry, firm & spicy; keep few yrs or (following MDY's advice) try with casseroles & spicy sausage. Combo new/older Fr oak. **Bush Vine Pinotage** ★★★ **04** from organic fruit (though uncertified), big (15% alc), well padded, creamy; structured to improve over several yrs. 14 mths Fr oak. **Semillon** ★★★ **04** well fleshed, potential to develop into something really attractive; partly barrelled. **Chardonnay Unwooded** discontinued. — CT

La Providence

*Franschhoek ▪ Est 2001 ▪ 1stB 2002 ▪ Tasting & tours: see intro ▪ Luxury self-catering guest cottage (see Stay-over section) ▪ Owners Andy & Ana Higgins ▪ Vini consultants Justin Hoy & Anton Beukes (Nov 2004/Jan 2002) ▪ Viti consultant Pietie le Roux (May 2005) ▪ 2.2 ha (cab) ▪ 9.5 tons 5 510ℓ 100% red ▪ PO Box 363 Franschhoek 7690 ▪ info@laprovidence.co.za ▪ www.laprovidence.co.za ▪ **T** 021·876·4790 ▪ F 021·876·4898*

Owners Andy and Ana Higgins are moving step by step along the path to a fully fledged, bells-and-whistles winery. Next move will be to offer tastings on the Franschhoek farm, once their pending application for a liquor licence has been approved.

Cabernet Sauvignon ★★★ Comprehensively oaked **02** last yr showed caramel overtones to cab's signature blackcurrant, ultra-ripe flavours well concealed 14.4% alc. — MF

■ **La Siesta** see Signal Hill
■ **Lategan Family** see Bergsig

Lateganskop Winery

*Worcester ▪ Est 1969 ▪ 1stB 2004 ▪ Tastings & sales Mon-Fri 8-12.30; 1.30-5 ▪ Tours by appt ▪ Owners 5 members ▪ Winemaker Vlam Fourie, with J Manewick (Aug/Dec 1990) ▪ 238 ha (cab, cinsaut, merlot, pinotage, ruby cab, chenin, colombard, hanepoot, riesling, sauvignon, semillon, viognier) ▪ 650 cs + 2.2m litres bulk ▪ 50% red 50% white ▪ PO Box 44 Breërivier 6858 ▪ lateganskop@mweb.co.za ▪ **T/F (023) 355·1719***

'Let's try while we're still young,' quips winemaker Vlam Fourie, talking of the Lategan family co-op's venture into chardonnay — some 7ha were planted last year. Just released are two newcomers in the Twin Peaks range, a Hanepoot Jerepigo and a pinotage/cinsaut blend. The latter was class winner at the regional 2006 Young Wine Show; after a year on wood it's ready for the adult world. Neither wine was ready for tasting at press time, nor stablemates Lion's Drift Cabernet Sauvignon and Ruby Cabernet, or Twin's Peak Sauvignon Blanc.

L'Auberge du Paysan

*Stellenbosch (see Helderberg map) ▪ Est 1995 ▪ 1stB 1998 ▪ Tasting & sales during restaurant hours ▪ Closed Easter Fri-Mon, Dec 26, Jan 1 ▪ Art gallery ▪ Owners Frederick Thermann & Michael Kovensky ▪ Winemaker/viticulturist Tjuks Roos, with Ricardo Adams ▪ 3.8 ha (merlot, pinotage) ▪ 14 tons ±1 250 cs 100% red ▪ PO Box 315 Somerset West 7129 ▪ **T/F 021·842·2008***

The pinotage vineyard last year yielded a relatively small but excellent-quality crop, says Frederick Thermann, chef patron of this popular French-flavoured country restaurant. The young merlot vines produced an even smaller harvest, but this year's output should be of sufficient quantity for a maiden bottling.

Pinotage 05 unrated sample, halfway through yr oaking, lively strawberry fruit, savoury overtone, hints green banana & dark choc. **04** (★★★★) was elegant & amenable, with firm, silky, pinot-like tannins. Both 2nd fill oak, 15% Am. — CT

L'Avenir Estate

*Stellenbosch ▪ Est/1stB 1992 ▪ Tasting & sales Mon-Fri 9-5 Sat 10-4 ▪ Fee R15 ▪ Closed Easter Fri, Dec 25 & Jan 1 ▪ Tours by appt ▪ Picnic hampers available ▪ Luxury B&B guest house (see Stay-over section) ▪ Tour groups ▪ Farm-grown olives & olive products ▪ Owner Michel Laroche ▪ Winemaker Tinus Els, with Stephan du Toit ▪ Viti adviser Johan Pienaar ▪ 53 ha (7 varieties r/w) ▪ 380-400 tons ▪ 25 000 cs 50% red 43% white 7% rosé ▪ PO Box 7267 Stellenbosch 7599 ▪ info@lavenir.co.za ▪ www.lavenir.co.za ▪ **T** 021·889·5001 ▪ F 021·889·5258*

Shortly after publication of last years guide, L'Avenir became the latest Cape property to attract a famous French name: Chablis royalty Michel Laroche, whose eponymous domaine includes an extensive 100ha landholding and grand crus in Blanchot. Laroche brings his family's 150-year winemaking heritage, 12 years in southern France and five in Chile to bear on his latest venture. L'Avenir's reputation for benchmark pinotage and chenin will be burnished by Tinus Els (with extensive local and international experience as a 'flying winemaker'), succeeding semi-retired Francois Naudé (still consulting), assisted by incumbent Stephan du Toit. Refurbishments include a new irrigation system, own bottling line, sundry winery equipment and new-look luxury accommodation.

★★★★☆ **Grand Vin Pinotage** Replaces 'Black Label Reserve' as flagship offering. Concordant with name, **04** concentrated & flamboyant with powerful, long-haul tannins, effusive berry fruit & intense oak coffee & mocha. Behind the fireworks & drama, impressively pure & focused winemaking; truly deserves long maturation to achieve its potential. 12 mths new Fr barrels.

★★★★ **Pinotage** As always from this property, textbook pinotage: **05** banana, strawberry scents & some high-toned whiffs precede berried, tarry palate with green olive hint. Tannins very fine but persistent, need few yrs to soften, mesh with abundant fruit. 14.5%. VDG & SAA laurels for **04**, similar but with friendlier tannins. 13 mths Fr oak, 30% new.

★★★★☆ **Stellenbosch Classic** <u>new</u> Bdx-style blend with drop pinotage (9%) in **04** – which winemaker Els intends 'excluding from future blends'. Very satisfying, with plush red fruits & supple tannins, weighty yet balanced palate. Oak currently touch obvious on finish but structure/fruit shd absorb, given a few yrs. 12 mths older Fr barriques.

★★★★ **Cabernet Sauvignon** None since perfectly proportioned **03**, last ed showed opulent cassis & cedar matched by firm cab tannins & freshness. 18 mths Fr oak, 33% new, rest 2nd fill.

★★★★ **Chenin Blanc** One of first success stories in the Cape chenin renaissance. **06** (★★★☆) attractive thatch & floral notes, long, tangy farewell; 5% oaked portion adds mid-palate weight. Bit 'blunt' & unfocused mid-2006, might settle & reach heights of classy **05**.

★★★★ **Cape Vintage** From cab, irresistible if unclassic. None since **03** (★★★☆), which succeeded delicious **99**. Low 85g/ℓ sugar; beefy 19% alc followed Portuguese lead. Last tasted mid-2005.

Rosé de Pinotage <u>new</u>★★★ Replaces 'Maison' offerings below. **06** attractive salmon hue, dusty strawberry nose & flavoursome palate with a gentle tannin grip. Low 12.5% alc great for lunchtimes. **Chardonnay** ★★★ Despite a string of Chardonnay-du-Monde medals for this consistent white, new chablis styling focuses on fruit: only 15% (Fr) oak fermented, so **06** wood character much subtler, more supportive. Promising. No **05**. Charming if slightly warming **04** won gold at Santé Classic 2005. **Sauvignon Blanc** Full-flavoured & vibrant **06** (★★★★) lifts the bar with 'drink me' granadilla & ruby grapefruit, 'keep me' minerality & balance. **05** (★★★☆) had a more subtle mineral character, needing bottle-ageing to fill out. **Vin de Meurveur** ★★★☆ Intermittently produced golden dessert. Tasted pvs ed **04**, from colombard, was a 'Sweet Natural' due to dearth of botrytis. No new vintages of the following made, possibly will be discontinued: **L'Ami Simon** ★★ Honest country red blend of cabs f & s, merlot & pinotage in **03**. Herbaceous lifted nose; lots of chunky sweet fruit. **Merlot** ★★★☆ **01** was first & to date only bottled vintage. **Rosé Maison Dry** ★★★ Old-time Cape favourites clairette & cinsaut with cab & pinotage in appealing **04**; soft summer fruits/flowers, fresh body. **Rosé Maison** ★★★☆ The original, off-dry house pink, from pinotage. **05** had coppery tint, juicy red berry fruits. **Vin d'Erstelle** ★★★ Off-dry white from colombard, riesling (53/39) & splash crouchen. **05** showed spicy fruit salad scents, juicy kick, finished drier than 6.4g/ℓ RS suggested. — *CvZ*

■ *Lavida* see Overhex

Walker Bay ▪ Est 1997 ▪ 1stB 2006 ▪ Visits Mon-Fri 9-5 Sat 9-1 ▪ Closed Easter Sun/Mon, Dec 25/26 & Jan 1 ▪ The Champagne Veranda open daily 10-8 in season (see Eat-out section) ▪

Tour groups by appt • Permanent art exhibition • Owners Babylon Wines (Pty) Ltd & Viking Pony Properties 355 (Pty) Ltd • Winemaker Marc van Halderen (Jun 2005) • Viti adviser Andrew Teubes (Jul 2005) • 34 ha (pinot, sangiovese, shiraz, chard, sauvignon) • 100 tons 40% red 25% white 35% MCC • PO Box 1580 Hermanus 7200 • info@lavierge.co.za • www. lavierge.co.za • T 028·313·0130 • F 028·312·1388

A name ('The Virgin') fitting for land that's never borne vineyards, an innovative winery in the Hemel-en-Aarde valley and, adds young winemaker Marc van Halderen, 'We're new in a valley of giants in the industry.' Newcomers with enormous energy, however – a rewarding maiden harvest has come and gone, the sunken barrel cellar, champagne veranda and rooftop restaurant are completed, the tasting room now has a deli section and recently appointed GM Christian Voarick brings to the table 18 years' experience of winefarming in Burgundy.

★★★★ **Sauvignon Blanc** new Finely fruited maiden **06** (tank sample; rating provisional) from low-yielding W Bay vyds. Dense nettley aromas, herbaceous textures, ample weight & length, evident cool-climate freshness – & cool 13.1% alc. 3% barrel fermented. – *MF*

■ *La Vinette see Olsen Wines*

Lazanou Organic Vineyards　　　　　　　　　new

Wellington • Est/1stB 2006 • Closed to public • Owners Jo Lazarus & Candice Stephanou • Winemaker Corlea Fourie (Jan 2006) • Viti adviser Johan Wiese • 5.3 ha (mourvèdre, shiraz, chard, chenin, viognier) • 5 tons 100 cs own label 100% white • PO Box 834 Wellington 7654 • lazarus@iafrica.com • T 083·265·6341 • F 086·670·9213

Lazanou is a partnership between owners Jo Lazarus and Candice Stephanou, who in 2002 purchased a tiny but quite varied vineyard in Wellington from which they produce their 100 cases of wine. Although the maiden 2006 vintage comprised only chenin, this year promises wooded and unwooded chardonnays and a shiraz from young vines. They take care to ensure that all blocks are farmed strictly according to international organic standards, stresses Lazarus.

Chenin Blanc ★★★ Soft, delicate floral notes with quince & lemongrass on **06**, firm, almost steely acidity allied to taut structure make a super food wine. **Wooded Chenin Blanc 06** lovely complex vanilla & cinnamon spice with buttery baked apple overlay. Creamy texture, rich leesy, brioche notes. Succulent style with lively thread of acidity. 10 mths new Fr oak. Early sample tasted, potential ★★★☆. – *MM*

■ *Lazy Bay see Baarsma*
■ *Leatherwood see Prospect 1870*

Le Bonheur Estate

Stellenbosch • Tasting & sales Mon-Fri 9-5 Sat 10-4 • Fee R10 • Special tastings on request • Functions & conferences by appt • Owner Lusan Holdings • Winemaker Sakkie Kotzé (1993) • Viticulturist Eben Archer • Vineyard manager Louis Tshamba • 435 tons ±31 000 cs • PO Box 104 Stellenbosch 7599 • info@lebonheur.co.za • www.lebonheur.co.za • T 021·875·5478 • F 021·875·5624

Le Bonheur boasts a handsome manor house and a similarly traditional, hands-on winemaker in Sakkie Kotzé, whose scrutiny extends to every hand-selected bunch of grapes. 'If the best French châteaux can take the trouble to sort their grapes, so can we,' he says. The palette of soils, altitudes and aspects supports a compact selection of wines: two whites and two reds. A new cellar door strategy to increase visitor numbers includes special barrel tastings (by appointment) and limited releases available only on the farm.

★★★★ **Prima** Enduring merlot-led (±75%) blend with cab firmly on track after less focused & probably earlier-maturing **00** (★★★★). No **02**. **03** refined carmine robes, soft plum & floral scents; gorgeous velvety persistence; supple tannins give gentle underpinning for gd few yrs cellaring. Now only Fr oak, 50% new, ±18 mths.

Cabernet Sauvignon ★★★★ Well flavoured perennial; **03** lithe & integrated; red-fruit aromas/flavours daubed with eucalyptus, some beefy notes, Fr oak spice on finish (±18 mths). **Chardonnay** ★★★☆ **05** step-up on pvs; delicate white peach, tangerine & creamy vanilla notes; crisp acidity, well-knit oak, rounded & restrained flavours equally delicious solo or with food. 40% Fr barrel fermented. **Sauvignon Blanc** ★★★ Water-white **06** tropical melange on nose, shy-ish on palate; grassier than pvs with balanced tangy farewell. — *CvZ*

▪ *Lee & Jones* see Breeland
▪ *Leef op Hoop* see Le Riche
▪ *Leeurivier* see Terroir Wines

Le Grand Chasseur Estate

Robertson ▪ Est 1881 ▪ 1stB 1999 ▪ Tasting & sales Mon-Thu 8.30-5 Fri 8-5.30 Sat 9-5 ▪ Closed Easter Fri/Sun/Mon, Dec 25/26 & Jan 1 ▪ Tours by appt ▪ Deli & gifts ▪ Guest accommodation by appt (see below) ▪ Owner Albertus de Wet ▪ Winemaker Albertus de Wet, with Wickus Erasmus (Jan 2001) ▪ Viti consultant Francois Viljoen (Jan 1998) ▪ 275 ha (cab, merlot, pinotage, ruby cab, shiraz, chard, chenin, colombard, sauvignon) ▪ 3 100 tons 8 000 cs own label 37% red 60% white 3% rosé ▪ PO Box 439 Robertson 6705 ▪ cellar@lgc.co.za ▪ www. lgc.co.za ▪ T/F 023·626·1048 (cellar) ▪ T/F 023·626·5781 (tasting room)

In their chase for quality, the LGC team have installed bottling facilities on the premises, and harvested the first sauvignon from the coolest slopes of the farm. The resulting grassier flavours complement the more tropical tones of the established vineyards, says Wickus Erasmus, who's introduced another tweak by completing part of the first fermentation for their MCC in French oak. The new Grand Chasseur Cottage is a good base from which to stalk (with binoculars) the 'great hunter' which gives the estate its name: the regal African Fish Eagle.

Most of these carry prefix '1881'. **Cabernet Sauvignon** ★★★ **03** more straightforward than pvs; appears v ripe on nose, entry, but lacks fruit stuffing; glowing tail from ±15% alc. 2 yrs Fr oak. **Pinotage** ★★ **05** lightish & uncomplicated; savoury salad of smoked bacon & red berry, fleeting finish. Yr Fr oak. **Shiraz** ★★ **03** decidedly ripe, jammy & soft; some organic whiffs; needs to be drunk soon. Fr oak, 16 mths. **LGC Red** ★★★ Still stocked **02** succulent red berry, plum & greenpepper mix; juicy rounded tannin. Equal ruby cab, cab, 8 mths Fr/Am oak. Not retasted; nor was… **Rosé** ★★★ Pinotage's candied aromas on **NV** (03), with just enough honeyed development to be attractive; drink up. **Chardonnay** ★★☆ Agreeably fresh & summery quaffer; **06** gd varietal character, lengthy ripe peach & pear tones, ending crisply dry. Oak fermented. **Sauvignon Blanc** ★★ Somewhat too bracing for solo this yr; **06** early-picked (12.5% alc), correspondingly light guava flavours, sherbety texture. No newer releases tasted for following trio: **Sauvignon Blanc-Chardonnay** ★★★ Replaces 'LGC White'; 60/40 blend, lightly oaked; **05** green top notes from sauvignon, rounded mouthfeel from chard; equally good solo or with food. **Sparkling** ★★★ **NV** from pinotage; bursts with sweet red-berry flavour & excited bubbles. **Cap Classique** ★★★ 'Brut MCC' pvs ed. Last was **NV** from chardonnay; firm mouthfilling mousse with mushroom hint on bone-dry finish. — *JN/DH*

Leidersburg Vineyards

Paarl ▪ Est 1996 ▪ 1stB 1997 ▪ Visits by appt ▪ Owners Jan du Preez & Brian Craddock ▪ Winemaker Jan du Preez, with Jacques du Preez ▪ Viticulturist Jacques du Preez ▪ 6 ha ▪ 2 000 cs 100% red ▪ PO Box 7210 Stellenbosch 7599 ▪ leidersburgwines@intekom.co.za ▪ www. leidersburgwines.co.za ▪ T/F 021·886·251

It's been a year of re-setting priorities for Jan and Jacques du Preez. Having added small quantities of a stylefully packaged muscadel and port-style wine to their range (the latter not ready for tasting), the focus is on increasing total production to 12 000 bottles of each over the next five years. Generally, the father-and-son team are concentrating on building their brand and strengthening their presence in the US market.

Cabernet Sauvignon ★★★★ Well-knit & smooth **03**, last ed noted as classically toned with black fruit, fennel, smoke & mocha, refreshing & brisk cab acidity. **Sauvignon Blanc** ★★★ From W Bay vyds. **05** food-friendly; intense stonefruit & green pea character, gd mineral core. Aged *sur lie* 6

mths. A different **05** bottling, from Sbosch fruit, tasted last yr & rated ★★★★. **Red Muscadel** new
★★ Unctuous fortified dessert with ripe sugar (230g/ℓ), relatively low 16% alc & treacle/currant
flavours make for pudding in a glass – which slips down easily! WO Rbtsn.

Serengeti range

> **Pinotage Rosé** ☺ ★★★ **06** has tart & tangy red-berried appeal; balanced & juicy; some
> savoury nuances, refreshingly dry finish. Super aperitif.

Pinotage ★★★★ ✓ **05** upfront varietal spiced plum character, appealingly modern, fruity &
medium bodied, with supportive dry savoury tannins. **Shiraz** ★★★★ ✓ Loads of spicy dark fruit on
05, ripe, accessible, slightly smoky tannins with savoury note, juicy & very drinkable. **Cabernet
Sauvignon-Merlot** ★★★★ ✓ Cab's attractive leafy, cassis, cedar interplay on **05**, firm dry tannins
around a black fruit core, sustained flavour-filled finish. Accessible now, with legs for 2/3 yrs. **Sauvignon Blanc** ★★★ **06** light-styled, with racy acidity & distinct tart grapefruit flavour & finish. Sea-
food-friendly. All WO Coastal. — *MW*

Le Manoir de Brendel

*Franschhoek • Est/1stB 2003 • Tasting & sales Mon-Sat 11-4 Sun 11-3 • Fee R25 • Lunches
daily 12-3 • Luxury accommodation & other amenities/facilities • Owner Christian Brendel • 26
ha (cab, merlot, shiraz, chardonnay, chenin, sauvignon, semillon) • Export brand: Wine 4U •
PO Box 117 La Motte 7691 • lemanoir@brendel.co.za • www.le-manoir-de-brendel.com • T
021·876·4525 • F 021·876·4524*
At this 5-star establishment in Franschhoek, wine is one of many attractions. See the Eat-out
and Stay-over sections for details.
Cabernet Sauvignon new ★★ Elegant herbaceous overtones & undercurrents of black
fruit, unadorned by wood; **04** slight build (12% alc) with sweet-sour farewell. **Merlot** ★★
05 lighter fruited than pvs but fairly full bodied, still settling when tasted mid-2006. Yr Fr
oak. **Pinotage** ★★ Typical pinotage banana/strawberry, brisk acidity on **03**; last ed had
prominent tannins which might have softened by now. **Shiraz** ★★★ Tad less ebullient this
vintage, though **04** still pleasant, rounded; quickish clove-spiked flavours. 14 mths Fr oak.
Sauvignon Blanc ★ **06** again very light, with understated varietal character. — *JN*

Lemberg Estate

*Tulbagh • Tasting, sales & tours Mon-Sat 8-5 Sun 10-5 • Fee R5 • Gourmet lunches (book 2
days ahead) • Luxury guest cottage (see Stay-over section) • Walks/hikes • Owner/
winemaker/viticulturist Klaus Schindler • 4 ha (pinot, pinotage, sauvignon) • 50/50 red/white •
PO Box 317 Tulbagh 6820 • schindler@lando.co.za • www.kapstadt.de/lemberg • T
023·230·0659/083·270·3449 • F 023·230·0661*
German forestry scientist Klaus Schindler turned to winemaking after settling with partner
Uschi on this small Tulbagh property in 1994. Wines (not tasted for this ed) include a sauvignon (night-harvested and natural-yeast-fermented), a pinot and a pinot-pinotage blend.
Their varietal pinotage is named 'Phases of the Moon', illustrating KS's interest in
biodynamics: work in vineyards and cellar is done according to lunar cycles. When not in the
winery, professional hunter Schindler can be tracked down in the Karoo (or further afield)
where he leads hunting trips.

■ *L'Emigré* see De Morgenzon

Leopard Frog Vineyards

*Stellenbosch • 1stB 2003 • Closed to public • Owner Brookwood Capital Corporation • Winemaker
David John Bate • 1 000 cs 100% red • 8 Royal Ascot Lane, Sandown, Sandton 2196 • firstfrog@
leopard-frog.com • www.leopard-frog.com • T 011·884·3304 • F 011·883·0426*
After starting up with the help of seasoned Hempies du Toit, Canadian David John Bate is flying solo. The birth of his and wife Joanne's first daughter, Jordan, inspired LF's second red,

Tantra, named 'in honour of the spirit in which she was conceived'. Its success in his home country has inspired him to create at least one more blend. 'Who knows, we may release a new wine for each child – and we plan to have at least seven.'

Tantra 〔new〕 ★★★★ Tight, tannic, serious bdx-inspired blend cabs f/s & petit v (44/32/24); **04** well extracted blackcurrant fruit; gd wood management (18 mths Fr, some new), satisfying dusty-dry finish. Decant if opening now; if abstaining, gd maturation prospects. **Kiss & Tell Reserve** ★★★ **04** brings malbec into equal mix merlot & shiraz plus 12% mourvèdre; similar feel to above: attractively taut; touch green walnut, dash cinnamon spice; deserves time to show its best; needs gd aeration now. — *CT*

Leopard's Leap Wines

Franschhoek ▪ *Est 2000* ▪ *Closed to public* ▪ *Owner Leopard's Leap Wines (Pty) Ltd* ▪ *Winemaker Eugene van Zyl (Nov 2002)* ▪ *Viti adviser Francois Viljoen* ▪ *250 000 cs 60% red 40% white* ▪ *ISO 1400 certified* ▪ *PO Box 685 Franschhoek 7690* ▪ *Hs.marketing@ leopardsleap.co.za* ▪ *www.leopards-leap.com* ▪ ***T** 021·876·8002* ▪ *F 021·876·4156*

This everyday-drinking-with-style range is part of the Rupert Family Vineyards portfolio. Launched in 2000, the wines are intended to 'over-deliver on quality and packaging'. Vinified by the very experienced Eugene van Zyl, they are available locally and exported to North America, Europe and other markets.

No new vintages ready for tasting this ed. **Cabernet Sauvignon** ★★ **04** light, approachable with savoury fruit, mocha finish. **Shiraz** ★★★ Easy-drinking **04**, spicy red fruit melange, balanced, modest 13.5% alc. **Cabernet Sauvignon-Merlot** ★★★ 50/50 blend in **04**, undemanding, brims with berry fruit, for early enjoyment. Combo staves/micro-oxygenation (same for most of the reds). **Sangiovese-Pinotage-Cabernet Sauvignon** ★★★★ Spicy & wild shiraz-like aromas in attractive & different **03**; sweet-fruited suppleness aided by touch sugar. Equal blend. **Pinotage-Shiraz** ★★★ **03**, as pvs, 50/50 blend neatly balancing approachability & structure. **The Lookout Cape Mountain Red** ★★★ Jumble of 5 varieties (incl nebbiolo) in **03**; plums, berries & spice; firmish tannins cushioned by smidgen sugar (3.3g/ℓ). **The Lookout Rosé** ★ Candyfloss nose & palate, 14% alc gives warm lift to tail. From pinotage. **Chardonnay** ★★★ Appealing poolside quaffer. Crisp & refreshing **05**, pear/citrus notes, zesty acidity. **Chenin Blanc** ★★★ **05** friendly & fruity, Granny Smith apple flavours/crunch. Well balanced. **Sauvignon Blanc** ★★★ **05** leaner than pvs; still lively, light. **The Lookout Cape Mountain White** ★★★ Sprightly, light (12% alc) everyday white from chenin, sauvignon, chardonnay. **05** tasty if somewhat muted lemon-lime tones. **Chenin Blanc-Viognier** ★★★ Quaffable **04** loaded with tropical fruit & citrus, plumply round from touch sugar (±4g/ℓ). **Semillon-Chardonnay** ★★★ Changes to unoaked in **04** equal blend; attractively light & supple with the usual gentle acidity. **Chenin Blanc Semi Sweet** ★ Demure aromas & flavours on light bodied **04**, only a hint of sweetness (though 15g/ℓ sugar). All WO W Cape. — *JN/DH*

■ *Le Pavillon* see Boschendal
■ *Le Pommier Fine Wines* see Zorgvliet

Le Riche Wines

Stellenbosch ▪ *Est 1996* ▪ *1stB 1997* ▪ *Tasting & sales Mon-Fri 10-12.30 2-4.30 Sat & pub hols by appt* ▪ *Self-contained B&B (T 021·887·8958)* ▪ *Owner Etienne le Riche* ▪ *Winemaker Etienne le Riche, with Mark Daniels (1998)* ▪ *5 000 cs* ▪ *PO Box 6295 Stellenbosch 7612* ▪ *wine@leriche.co.za* ▪ *www.leriche.co.za* ▪ ***T/F** 021·887·0789*

The first Le Riche wines were produced a decade ago, so this is a gala year for owner and winemaker (with Mark Daniels) Etienne le R. Anniversary celebrations on the Jonkershoek farm need white wine as well as the winemaker's speciality, cab, and what more appropriate than a maiden vintage Chardonnay, sourced from two Stellenbosch vineyards? Now available is the Le Riche Bergerac Grand Vin de Terroir 03, produced by himself near Bordeaux, where he consults.

★★★★★ **Cabernet Sauvignon Reserve** Grand, unshowy Cape classic, composed with Etienne le R's signature light touch. **03** beguilingly gentle yet persuasive in both fragrance, structure. Ripe, dry, exudes a completeness sometimes lacking in unblended cabs. 45% new Fr oak, 2 yrs. 100% Jnkrshoek Vlly vyds.

★★★★☆ **CWG Auction Reserve Cabernet Sauvignon 03** repeat lot on 2006 Auction. Last yr we noted tightly wound blackcurrant fruit, plush texture; tasting great mid-2005; harbinger of rare pleasure from 2010 onwards; 100% cab, 100% new Fr oak, 18 mths.

★★★★☆ **Cabernet Sauvignon 02** (★★★★) formed with careful attention to difficult vintage; oaking, calm tannins, (just) under-control acid, all judged to complement lightish but sweet fruit. Sbosch fruit, 18 mths barrelled, mostly older. **01** SAA.

★★★★ **'Blend'** Unnamed at press time, replaces pvs 'Cab-Merlot', components to vary according to vintage/best available variety; still cab-led, as in previewed **04**, with merlot, shiraz & pinotage (26/14/13). Quiet red-wine character; medium bodied with fresh juicy acid, sweet fruit; concludes with tweak of pinotage's astringency. Too young to rate conclusively. 18 mths used Fr oak. **03** classic yet accessible 65/35 blend.

Leef op Hoop Merlot ★★★ Soft, accessible **04** still selling. Last yr's comments recorded rich meaty mouthful, frame enhanced by yr in older oak.

Chardonnay new First LeR white, **06** (ex-cask) shows usual unforced approach; freshness, delicacy woven into rich texture; clean, dry & long. Unrated but promising. Fermented/4 mths 100% new Fr oak. — *AL*

■ *Le Roux* see Vendôme
■ *Les Pleurs* see Avondale

Libertas

For selected export markets, these easy/early drinking wines fill a value-priced slot in the Distell portfolio.

Cabernet Sauvignon ★★★ Grape's characteristic blackcurrant aromas on **05**, pleasantly astringent fruit tannins, firm backbone lifted by sweet impression on finish, dusty hints from 9 mths Fr staves. **Merlot** ★★★ **05** ingratiating, rich & ripe, with hints of plum, bacon & sage. Warming alc (14.5%) & gruffish tannins provide rustic finish. **Pinotage** ★★★ **05** friendly tannins from combo barrels/staves & unoaked portion; juicy strawberry fruit makes this slip down easily, despite generous 14.7% alc. **Chardonnay** ★★★ **05** abounds with white peach & tangerine aromas, some lime/lemon flavours. Palate given grip by partial oaking/lees-ageing. Brisk acidity suggests better with food than solo. **Chenin Blanc** ★★★ Quaffable **06** shows bright green-apple flavours, crisp acidity. Ends touch lean & short, lacks usual mineral notes. **Sauvignon Blanc** ★★★. Crunchy, fresh, light bodied (11.5% alc) **06** lifts bar with pleasing array of nettle, gooseberry, grass aromas & flavours. All WO W Cape. — *CvZ*

Lievland Estate

*Stellenbosch • Est 1982 • Tasting & sales Mon-Fri 9-5 Sat & Sun 10-4 • Fee R10 • Closed Good Fri & Dec 25 • Tours by appt • Light meals/picnics by appt • Owner Susan Colley • Winemaker Kowie du Toit (Jan 2004) • 50 ha (cabs s/f, merlot, mourvèdre, roobernet, petit v, riesling, shiraz, viognier) • 250 tons 15 000 cs 50/50 red/white • PO Box 66 Klapmuts 7625 • lievland@ icon.co.za • www.lievland.co.za • **T 021-875-5226** • F 021-875-5213*

It's difficult to pin Susan Colley down — if she's not in the vineyard admiring her new shiraz rows (planted in 2003, it looks like the fruit will be good enough to vinify this year), she's busy in the cellar or personally conducting wine tastings. While shiraz remains the flagship, Susan C and winemaker Kowie du Toit are also working on improving the estate's red blends — to this end they have ripped out some 30ha, most of which will be replanted with cab.

Shiraz ★★★★ Last ed **03** showed renewed vigour & form. Classic savoury/wild berry aromas, supportive fruit, structure to improve over 3-5 yrs. Oak, 14 mths Fr/30% new, well integrated. **Lievlander** ★★★ Perfect barbeque fare. Now cab/shiraz blend, **03** in meaty, savoury mode, with peppery, toasty addition from harmonious oaking. **Chardonnay 05** (sample pvs ed) too unknit to rate. Muted lemon-drop/lime character; hint of oak gave structure & flavour. Staved 3 mths. **Sauvignon Blanc** ★★★ Last tasted **05** raised bar on pvs with better balance, fresher finish. Granny Smith apple/nuts, powerful fruit intensity. **Weisser Riesling ★★★** As per pvs ed, **04** had ethereal pineapple & tropical fruit fragrances/flavours; quaffably light, refreshing, off-dry. **Natural Sweet** Last tasted **04** was unrated; from riesling; very light; modest floral aromas; peachy flavours with hint quince on unexpectedly dry finish; partly barrel fermented; 12% alc. Above Smnsberg-Sbosch WOs. Discontinued **Cabernet Sauvignon-Shiraz, Chéandrie.** — *CR*

■ *Lifestyle* see Simonsvlei

L'illa   ♀ new

Robertson ▪ Est/1stB 2005 ▪ Tasting & sales by appt ▪ Owners/winemaker Nadia Cilliers & Gordon Newton Johnson ▪ Viticulturist AA Cilliers ▪ 1 ton 600 btls (375ml) 100% white ▪ PO Box 225 Hermanus 7200 ▪ gordon@newtonjohnson.com ▪ T 028·312·3862 ▪ F 028·312·3867

Winemaker Nadia Cilliers, who recently joined Newton Johnson Winery, and cellarmaster Gordon NJ have also teamed up on the Cilliers' family farm in the Eilandia area. The focus here: a 35 year old chenin vineyard which they turn to liquid gold in the form of the sweet wine below — with a little help from naturally low production, consistent botrytis and high-pH soils. Bunch pressing and minimal cellar intervention keep the L'illa (pronounced *leeya*) nectar natural.

Noble Late Harvest ★★★★ Charming & delightful dessert, its whimsical 'desert island' label (& the brand's name) a play on the WO, 'Eilandia'. **05** fragrant dried apricot, creamy vanilla & wet wool nuances; sweetness well freshened by brisk, tangy acidity. Older Fr oak fermented/matured. Delicious now & over next ±4 yrs. The ultimate desert island wine? — *CvZ*

■ *Lime Road* see Havana Hills
■ *Lindenhof* see Boland Kelder

Linde Vineyards   ♀♀🍾

Tulbagh ▪ Est 1998 ▪ 1stB 2001 ▪ Visits by appt ▪ Walks ▪ Owners Olof Gregor & Sylvia Linde ▪ Winemaker Sylvia Linde ▪ Viticulturist Jean Kotze ▪ 14 ha (cab, merlot, shiraz, chard) ▪ 80 tons 100% red ▪ PO Box 146 Tulbagh 6820 ▪ diggershome@mweb.co.za ▪ T 023·230·0742 ▪ F·023·230·2838

Hemisphere-hopping couple Olof Gregor and Sylvia Linde spend part of the year in California, with 6 ha in Geyserville, where the local Italian community put their handmade *vino* on the *tavola*; the rest in Tulbagh, where the vines are managed by Jean Kotze.

Cabernet Sauvignon ★★★★ 04 modern, concentrated, voluptuous but with dry finish. **Shiraz ★★★** Characterful & accessible **04**; rounded, smooth tannins, savoury finish. Both wines tasted last ed. — *CR*

Lindhorst Wines   ♀♀🍽⌂🍴🏃♿

Paarl ▪ Est 1996 ▪ 1stB 2002 ▪ Tasting daily 10-5 ▪ Fee R20 (incl tasting & snacks, redeemable against purchase of 6 btls) ▪ Cellar tours by appt ▪ Closed Easter Sun, Dec 25 & Jan 1 ▪ Lunches Wed-Sun year round (see Eat-out section) ▪ Functions by arrangement ▪ Self-catering Vineyard Cottage (see Stay-over section) ▪ Facilities for children ▪ Gifts ▪ Farm produce ▪ Owners Mark & Belinda Lindhorst ▪ Vini consultant Cathy Marshall (Nov 2002), with Ernie Wilken ▪ Viti consultant Kevin Watt (Jan 2001) ▪ 18 ha (cab, merlot, pinotage, shiraz) ▪ 60 tons 6 300 cs 90% red ▪ PO Box 1398 Suider-Paarl 7624 ▪ belinda@lindhorstwines.com ▪ www. lindhorstwines.com ▪ T 021·863·0199 ▪ F 021·863·3694

Lindhorst boasts one of the 'coolest' restaurants in the winelands — and that's not just because the 'outdoor aircon' is provided by mist sprays. Named The Terrace @ Lindhorst Wines, it's an empowerment venture outsourced to a group of enterprising women coached by Belinda Lindhorst, 'with Jamie Oliver's influence'. And it's flourishing. So is the wine business. Every 03 bottling achieved a local or international accolade, and the red created as a once-off to honour Mark L's late father proved so popular it's become an ongoing line: Max's

Tribute. Their head-turning roadside mannequins, Brad and Janet, may have the authorities in a tizz but provide a not-easy-to-miss landmark.

Cabernet Sauvignon ★★★★ Cab's signature cassis & cedar follow through with ripe but supple tannins, providing structure to medium bodied **04**; richly fruited, smooth, accessible & balanced; has potential for few yrs development. 21 mths Fr oak, ±half new. **Merlot ★★★★ 04** earthy dark fruit & choc aromas followed by leafier, less generous palate with sweet/sour black cherry nuances; flavours masked mid-2006 by firm, dry, cedary tannins; time needed for more harmony for develop. 22 mths Fr oak. **Shiraz** Notch-up **04** (★★★★) soft, spicy white pepper & cedar intro; palate richly embroidered with New World fruit & ripe supple tannins; oaking (22 mths Fr oak, 74% new) keeps components in check. Promising but youthful, needs time to develop. **03** (★★★☆) a spicy, elegant food wine. **Max's Tribute ★★★** Success of once-off 'Max's Shiraz' prompts this permanent addition to range; **04** a smoothly textured, juicy blend cab/shiraz (75/25), redolent with generous dark & red fruits, supple ripe tannins & bright acidity. Medium bodied. WO Coastal. **Statement ★★★★ 04** similar blend shiraz (74%) & merlot to pvs, serious wooding (as for Merlot) adding structure, depth, to ample red/black berried fruit profile. Smoothly textured & balanced, accessible but will reward few yrs cellaring. Great winter warmer & food partner. **03** Santé Classic gold. **Pinotage ★★★** Lively acidity with tangy sweet/sour red fruits & taut tannins on **05**, unheavy despite 14.4% alc, gd partner for Italian styled foods. **Sauvignon Blanc ★★★** new Dbnvlle fruit imparts signature dusty, herbaceous & minerally notes on **06**; racy acidity, passionfruit & lime on palate, where 10% wood fermented portion adds leesy breadth. Food or solo. — *MW*

Lindiwe Wines

*Paarl ▪ 1stB 2003 ▪ Closed to public ▪ Winemaker Chris Jansen (Oct 2003) ▪ Viticulturists Chris Albertyn & Cobus van Graan ▪ 20 000 cs 50% red 50% white ▪ ISO 9001 certified ▪ Suite 170 Postnet, Pvt Bag X3036, Paarl 7620 ▪ info@lindiwewines.com ▪ **T 021·949·6013/4** ▪ F 021·949·6036*

Lindiwe ('The One We Have Been Waiting For') is owned by Reinvest, a black economic empowerment company. The wines are made at KWV's Vinnova contract cellar, the latter company providing important initial guidance. Listings with four national retail chains, availability in the UK, and imminent entry to the north American market are cause for uncorking the newest addition to the range: a bubbly named Chazaa – township vernacular for 'sparkling wine'.

Cabernet Sauvignon ★★★ Seasoned oak gives creamy texture, sweet vanilla tones to generously berried **03**, an easy-drinker with hint of mint. **Merlot ★★★★ 02** was plummy & ready last yr; light textured despite big 14.5% alc. Yr Fr oak. **Shiraz ★★ 03** charry wood whiffs, soft ripe fruit, amenable tannins & alc for pleasant drinking now & for yr/2. 8-12 mths older oak. **Pinotage ★★** Tasted pvs ed, lightly wooded **02** fairly rustic, old-style estery whiff & big tannins. **Chenin Blanc ★★ 05** shy hay aromas, mellowing but still lively apple flavours, gd solo or with food. **Chardonnay ★★** Butter & cream notes on partly barrel fermented/matured **04**, gains extra smoothness, body, from touch sugar. **Sauvignon Blanc ★★** Easy-going **05**, lightish, unaggressive, with just a hint of nettle. **Chazaa** new ★★ Frothy, semi-sweet sparkling from chenin, with happy gingerbeer flavour. Carbonated, **NV**. All WO W Cape. — *CvZ*

Linton Park Wines

*Wellington ▪ Est 1995 ▪ 1stB 1998 ▪ Tasting & sales Mon-Fri 8-5 by appt ▪ Tours by appt Mon-Fri 9-4; also guided cellar/vineyard tours by appt (incl barrel tasting) ▪ Light lunches/picnics for small groups by appt Mon-Fri 9-4 ▪ Owner Linton Park plc ▪ Winemaker Hennie Huskisson, with Danie Stevens (Jan 2001/Oct 1999) ▪ Viticulturist Arnold Hugo ▪ 89 ha (cab, merlot, shiraz, chard, sauvignon) ▪ ±750 tons 20 000 cs 75% red 25% white ▪ Export brand: De Groene Heuwel ▪ PO Box 1234 Wellington 7654 ▪ lpexport@lantic.net ▪ www.lintonparkwines.co.za ▪ **T 021·873·1625** ▪ F 021·873·0851*

The Linton Park team has many reasons to smile, Marketing and sales manager Liezl Williams says. Firstly, their new on-site storage and bottling facility is being put to good use, so ensuring better stock control and giving quality a lift. Then, their popular Capell's Court Shiraz has attracted some 'five-star' attention — it is now available at the London Hilton. And finally, a new distribution chain in Johannesburg and healthy prospects in Asia and Africa provide even more reasons for good cheer.

Reserve range

★★★★ **Shiraz** Same 'Summer Hill' vyd as std version, different wooding — yr Am, followed by extra yr Fr. Still available **01** brazenly New World but not a fruit bomb, has some seriousness, structure, for maturation.

★★★★ **Cabernet Sauvignon** Same block ('Bush Vine') as version below, more extensively barrelled (yr new Fr, further yr 4th fill). **01** shows house's ripe-fruited styling yet still fairly easy to drink, spicy oak bit more evident. Neither above wines retasted.

★★★★ **Merlot** Selection of best barrels, oaked as per Rsv Cab. Current **03** impressively concentrated & deep-flavoured, hints mint & dark choc to attractive wild berry tone; ripe but tight tannins need time or decanting if opening now. 15% alc. WO Paarl.

Linton Park range

★★★★ **Shiraz** Softer & lighter than Rsv. **02** sweet brambly fruit, hints of flowers & fynbos. Yr Am oak.

Cabernet Sauvignon ★★★☆ **02** a well-behaved extrovert. Bright bramble aromas; plump & juicy fruit with hint cigarbox from new Fr oak, yr. **Merlot** ★★★ Ex-River Garden vyd; **02** light-hued; red plum jam nose, light, simple jammy fruit. Yr Fr oak, none new. Above trio not retasted. **Chardonnay** ★★★☆ **03** another expansive, opulent wine (15% alc); lemon zest & lime with marked toastiness from 50% new wood. Yr oak. **Reserve Port** ★ Limited release fortified dessert, 3 yrs oak; pvs was quirky but appealing; preview of current **NV** from cab, overripe, with distinct alc glow (21%).

Capell's Court range

These unwooded unless mentioned. **Cabernet Sauvignon 05** (★★★☆) was a waddling fatty, thanks to low acid. **06** also wide-girthed (14.5% alc), sweet, earthy; previewed sample too young to rate. **Merlot** ★★★ **05**'s luscious Peppermint Crisp character coupled with ripe-fruit succulence will seduce even hard-core classicists. **Shiraz** ★★ More envelope pushing here: usual teaspoon sugar now a ladle: 12g/ℓ! **06** touch more herbaceous than pvs, but retains crowd pleasing fleshiness, fruity succulence. **Chardonnay** ★★☆ Honest fresh drinkability with signature low alc (13%); **06** tank sample sweet entry, fat & leesy, amenable textured melon & citrus flavours. **Sauvignon Blanc** ★★ **06** even earlier picked than usual, so v light (11.5% alc), green toned (peas & asparagus) with pleasing acidic bite. — *CT*

■ *Lions Drift* see Lateganskop
■ *Lion's Gate* see Origin Wine
■ *Liquor Boys* see Oranjerivier Wine Cellars

Liquor World

See Selected wine shops section for store details ▪ *Enquiries Keith Simms* ▪ *ksimms@metro. co.za* ▪ *za* ▪ **T** *011·490·2300* ▪ **F** *011·689·2560*

The Cherry Hill wines below are selected and marketed exclusively by the Metcash Africa group through its Liquor World outlets nationwide.

Cherry Hill range   `new`

Merlot ★★★ **04** delivers mulberry, rhubarb whiffs, then light but harmonious & persistent fruit on palate with evident tannin. **Cabernet Sauvignon-Merlot** ★★★ Herbal notes along with light cherry & plum aromas on **04**, grainy-textured mid-weight body (±14% alc, like abv). **Pinotage** ★★ **03** gamey & vegetal notes pretty well conceal variety's typical varnishy tones; light tannins & gd length of flavour make for easy drinking. All these well priced wines WO Coastal. — *MF*

■ *Little River* see De Meye
■ *Live-A-Little* see Stellar Winery
■ *Livingstone* see Cape First

Lomond

Cape Agulhas ▪ Est 1999 ▪ 1stB 2005 ▪ Closed to public ▪ Winemakers Kobus Gerber (white) & Justin Corrans (red) ▪ Viticulturists Wayne Gabb & Johan Wiid ▪ 105 ha (merlot, shiraz, sauvignon, nouvelle, semillon, viognier) ▪ 750 tons ▪ ISO 9002 certified ▪ PO Box 1269 Gansbaai 7220 ▪ T 028·388·0095 ▪ F 028·388·0130

A member of the Biodiversity & Wine Initiative, Lomond also falls within the Walker Bay Fynbos Conservancy and has 200ha of pristine fynbos set aside for conservation. Each of the half-dozen single-vineyards is named after the region's unique flora, so the white wines bear such names as Pincushion and Sugarbush; the first single-vineyard reds, due soon, will follow suit (exact naming not available at press time). A black economic empowerment deal saw Distell and Lomond buy neighboring property Uylenkraal, now a company of which farm workers own a significant portion.

The following all tasted as pre-bottling samples (as were two 'pre-named' sauvignons last ed); any ratings provisional. **Pincushion Sauvignon Blanc** (Was 'Block 3'.) **06** like other sauvignons here: grassy savour, fig & flint, austerely rich & serious, tautly structured with fine integrated acidity, some real grip. Likely ★★★★; perhaps even more for... **'Estate' Sauvignon Blanc** Steely, full bodied & flavoursome, mineral core, some ripe tropical hints; **06** big & forthright but with cool-origin elegance, fine, harmonious balance. **Sugarbush Sauvignon Blanc ★★★★** ('Block 5' pvs ed.) The tropical-fruited cousin, this, but **06** also a lemongrass finish, & a tight core — in fact, powerful acidity threatens to subdue fruit. **05** IWC gold. The following **05** reds all too unformed to rate at all: **'Estate' Merlot** Chocolatey, ripely scented; still unknit but with plenty of fruit & structure on offer. **Syrah** Still very spicy-woody ex-barrel, but shows Fr-style notes of lilies & minerality. — *TJ*

Longbarn Winery   ◊ ♀ new

Wellington ▪ Est 2006 ▪ Visits by appt ▪ Owner/winemaker David Power, advised by Marais de Villiers ▪ 7 ha (cab, pinot, sauvignon) ▪ 10 tons 110 cs 100% white ▪ PO Box 1295 Wellington 7654 ▪ davidpower@kingsley.co.za ▪ T 021·873·6396 ▪ F 021·873·7059

Last year, retired paediatrician David Power and wife Sue vinified sauvignon from their 20 year old vines on Groenberg's northern slopes in the renovated 'longbarn'. Once a working cellar on their historic farm Boplaas, it was recently re-equipped by micro-winery supplier and Main Street Wines vintner Marais de Villiers. Their pinot, also from two decade old vines, is also flagged for own-vinification. Grubbed-up merlot and some cab may be replaced by more sauvignon, pinot, and perhaps viognier.

Sauvignon Blanc ★★ 06, from one Wllngtn vyd, herbal capsicum aromas announce a crisp, bone-dry palate with welcomely moderate 12.8% alc, but rather tart finish. — *MF*

Long Beach

Mediterranean inspired range by Robertson Winery for Vinimark, pitched at SA's 'ever-burgeoning café society'. Attractively presented with twist-off caps.

Chardonnay ★★★★ Particularly flavoursome this vintage; **06** packed with citrus fruit; layer of toasty oak for lively, characterful quaffing. **Sauvignon Blanc ★★★** Top sauvignon vintage lends zinging freshness to **06**; no spiky acids, just crisp roundness with greenpepper & green grass to taste. Low 12.5% alc. — *DH*

Long Mountain Wine Company

Stellenbosch ▪ Est/1stB 1994 ▪ Closed to public ▪ Owner Pernod-Ricard SA ▪ Winemaker/viticulturist Eben Rademeyer (Jun 2004) ▪ 50% red 49% white 1% MCC ▪ PO Box 1324 Stellenbosch 7599 ▪ vanda.davies@pernod-ricard-southafrica.com ▪ jaco.boonzaaier@pernod-ricard-southafrica.com ▪ www.longmountain.co.za ▪ T 021·880·8800 ▪ F 021·880·8860

Sourcing fruit from various Western Cape appellations, notably the Breede River Valley, Long Mountain's viticultural programme with growers (now in its fourth year) enables winemaking within various price-points, to meet growing consumer demand (particularly in the UK, Russia and potentially China). The tiered trio is headed by new premium range, Bushbuck Ridge, aimed at the on-consumption and specialist retail trade. The overall style — integrated fruit and soft tannins — sets out to woo modern consumers, avers export manager Jaco Boonzaaier.

Bushbuck Ridge range

Cabernet Sauvignon ★★ Fairly robust styling in **04**, (mildly) gripping tannins, leafy tone to wild berry fruit; won't be intimidated by hearty foods. **Shiraz ★★** Undemanding & pleasant **03**, full & sweet-fruited flavours in a sound commercial package. **Chardonnay ★★** Textbook chard citrus touched with minerals & buttery lees; v appealing, though **05** just a shade too light, unintense for higher rating. **Sauvignon Blanc ★★** Light, green tinged **06**, off Rwsnvlle vyds, attractive asparagus & green pea hints, a little sugar filling out mid-palate.

Gecko Ridge Reserve range

Cabernet Sauvignon ★★★ 03 last ed showed vintage's ripeness, generosity; lovely balanced red-berried drinkability. **Chardonnay ★★** Another atypical **05**: slatey mineral tautness with savoury/earthy notes; dry finish; strange contrast with appealingly soft & rounded pvs.

Long Mountain range

Cabernet Sauvignon ★★★ Scaled down but not dumbed down cab; **04** distinctive varietal cassis tempered by firm, dry, but balanced tannin. Honest, flavoursome wine with structure to drink/keep few yrs. **Pinotage ★★** Last reviewed was undemanding **03**, combo peppery & creamy red berry aromas, generous red fruit flavours. **Merlot-Shiraz ★★★ 05**, like pvs, tad fuller, more robust & dry than range-mates — which makes these gd BBQ partners. **Ruby Cabernet ★★** Hot & difficult vintage **05** leaves mark here, too, in atypical savoury chunkiness, ungushy fruit profile. **Shiraz-Cabernet Sauvignon ★★★☆** Step above pvs, yet **04** last ed noted as retaining hallmark seamless accessibility, generous red berried fruit. **Chardonnay** Invariably a tasty mouthful, though **06** a pre-bottling sample when reviewed, so hard to rate. Possibly ★★? ±30% oaked. **Chenin Blanc ★★ 06** vastly different to pvs delightful, super-frisky version. Latest is demure, sinewy & light, with hint of winter melon. **Sauvignon Blanc ★★★** Notes of capsicum & dust on **06**, light, firm, with grapefruit pith tang. **Semillon-Chardonnay ★★★** These have some staying power, but best young; **04** last ed had pleasant lime/lees tones, flourish of flavour in finish. **Chardonnay-Pinot Noir Cap Classique ★★★** Brut-style sparkling, carefully made (incl barrel fermentation/6 mths ageing of base wine, yr *sur lie*). Latest **NV** shade lighter, less refined than standout pvs; busy inelegant bubbles; fruity, with Marie Biscuit background note. — *CT*

Longridge

Stellenbosch • Owner Winecorp • Winemakers/viticulturists: see Winecorp • 40 ha • 13 000 cs 75% red 25% white • ISO 9001 certified • PO Box 99 Lynedoch 7600 • info@longridge.co.za • www.longridge.co.za • T 021·881·3690 • F 021·881·3699

Part of Stellenbosch-based Winecorp's portfolio (together with Spier and Savanha), Longridge occupies the position of 'ultra premium boutique'. Fruit for the Longridge range is exclusively off top-performing Helderberg mountain vineyards. Quantities have been curtailed, further upping the ante on quality. The award winning range now includes a Sauvignon, released as the guide went to press. An early accolade for this wine is a gold medal at the 2006 National Young Wine Show.

★★★★ Cabernet Sauvignon Serious & delicious **04** more savoury than pure-fruited **03**; smoky beef-extract tones with prune, blackberry fruit at core. Polished tannins already accessible, but as with all these reds, shd unfold to true potential over next 5+ yrs. Fr/ Am barrels, some 1st fill, 12–16 mths; similar oaking for remaining reds. These frequently gonged, lately by IWSC — gold for **02**. Coastal WO, as are other reds in range.

★★★★ **Merlot** Standout **03** (★★★★★) showed potential of SA merlot. Though no hard edges, **04** still tight, needs time. Already showing dark fruit, bitter choc, white pepper, but promises further delights over 6+ yrs.

★★★★ **Pinotage** Modern, stylish & much awarded rendition of the variety. A lesson in appetite appeal, **04**'s charms include cranberries, hedgerow fruit, beautifully judged oak holding everything in place, adding savoury layers, promising a 5+ yr future. Complex, concentrated **03** featured among ABSA Top Ten.

★★★★★ **Chardonnay 05** (★★★★) broader, more open than pvs, in process lost some definition. Still has wonderful appetite appeal: roasted nut boldness, oodles of citrus peel, underlying peach, but shorter finish than expected. Fermented/11 mths Fr oak, 60% new. **04**'s complexity, sophistication also recognised by *Wine*: ★★★★.

★★★★ **Sauvignon Blanc** new Purity of fruit in **06** (sample) speaks of careful handling: a tangy lime & gooseberry compote, vibrating with freshness, youthful energy. Classy & delicious.

★★★★ **Brut** MCC from chard, pinot; 9 mths on lees before 2 yr bottle fermentation/ageing. Skip from brioche-redolent **01** to **03**, which successfully — delightfully! — balances lemon freshness & creamier biscuit notes from extended lees ageing. Sleekly built, lively mousse, gd length. Modest 12.3% alc. 52/48 blend. No **02**.

Bay View range

Export only; WO W Cape/Coastal; reds 11 mths oak; no newer vintages tasted, notes from last ed. **Shiraz** ★★★★ Bold, flavourful **03**; black cherry, scrub, roasted spice; ripe tannins. Drink or keep 3+ yrs. **Merlot** ★★★★ **04** offered good typicity, flavour, supported by amenable tannins. Essentially light structured. **Pinotage** ★★★ Ripe, opulent **04**, dark plums, bananas & cream masking the hefty 15.2% alc. Ready, drink within ±3 yrs. Discontinued: **Cabernet Sauvignon, Chenin Blanc, Sauvignon Blanc.** — *CR*

■ *Longwood* see Dominion

Loopspruit Winery

Mpumalanga ▪ Tastings, sales & tours by appt ▪ Restaurant lapa or picnic baskets available ▪ Conferences ▪ Owner Mpumalanga Agricultural Development Corporation ▪ Winemaker Matthew Sibanyoni, advised by Ian Sieg ▪ Viti adviser Ian Sieg ▪ ±19 ha (cabs s/f, ruby cab, shiraz, chard, chenin, colombard, hanepoot, raisin blanc) ▪ ±150 tons ±10 000 ▪ PO Box 855 Bronkhorstspruit 1020 ▪ manie@madc.co.za ▪ www.madc.co.za ▪ T 013·930·7025 ▪ F 013·935·8020

This upcountry winery, which has the distinction of being Vergelegen super-heavyweight André van Rensburg's first winemaking gig, now has an equally large personality about its halls: consultant Ian Sieg, veteran of nearly 30 summer rainfall vintages (22 at Landzicht, six in Zimbabwe). Working closely with resident winemaker Matthew Sibanyoni, Sieg's upgrading the thatch-roofed cellar with its small tanks and copper potstill ('mampoer available'), and training vineyard personnel. 'It's a nice set-up with a replica of an Ndbele village, 150-seater restaurant and conference centre,' Sieg says. 'Now all it needs is accommodation facilities. Interested parties should contact me on 082·783·8272…'

Lord's Wines new

McGregor (see Robertson map) ▪ Est/1stB 2006 ▪ Visits by appt (T 082·378·3987) ▪ BYO picnic ▪ Walks ▪ Conservation area ▪ 4×4 trail by appt ▪ Tour groups ▪ Owners 12 shareholders ▪ Winemaker Newald Marais ▪ Viti adviser Briaan Stipp ▪ 12 ha (pinot, shiraz, chard, sauvignon) ▪ 27 tons 1 400 cs 50% red 50% white ▪ PO Box 165 McGregor 6708 ▪ groottoren@telkomsa. net ▪ T/F 023·625·1265

Surrounded by proteas and perched high on the mountains outside McGregor, this winery's tiny maiden production has already found its way to the demanding UK market. While the vineyards are only two years old and much of the focus is on producing organic wines, plans are already afoot to expand the range to include pinot, shiraz and chardonnay. Spanking new facilities and excellent views make a visit (by appointment) to this, Robertson Valley's highest cellar, a treat.

Both these **06** wines tasted ex-tank (some CO_2 still evident on first); both provisionally ★★★. **Sauvignon Blanc** Flinty capsicum hints & fresh finish. Moderate ±13% alc; bone-dry, as is… **Sauvignon Blanc Organic** Shows greenpepper & green fig aromas, with food-friendly alc (12.4%), length & crispness. — *MF*

L'Ormarins Private Cellar ○♀ℭ

Franschhoek ▪ Est 1965 ▪ 1stB 1982 ▪ Tastings Mon-Fri 9–4.30 Sat 10–3 Booking essential, ditto for vintage car museum visits Tue–Sun 9–4.30 ▪ Closed Easter Fri/Sun, Dec 25 & Jan 1 ▪ Owner Johann Rupert ▪ Terra Del Capo cellar: Winemaker Neil Patterson with Christo Hamerse ▪ L'Ormarins cellar: Thierry Haberer with Dawie Botha ▪ Viticulturist Rosa Kruger ▪ ISO 14001 certified ▪ PO Box 435 Franschhoek Valley 7690 ▪ tasting@lormarins.co.za ▪ www. lormarins.com & www.terradelcapo.com ▪ T 021·874·9000

As executive chairman of Swiss-based luxury group Richemont, Johann Rupert is surrounded with fine things, but few can be as beautiful as this Franschhoek property in the Drakenstein foothills. Extensive improvements have been made here over the past three years, in keeping with the plans of Rupert's late brother, Antonij. For starters there are new tasting room facilities and two state of the art cellars: the L'Ormarins Cellar for red wines; the Terra Del Capo Cellar for the property's Italian range and white wines. Then there's the vintage car museum. But the main focus continues to be the vineyards, with new blocks being planted on higher slopes, while lesser terroir gives way to paddocks for the stud farm.

★★★★ **Optima** Bdx-style cab/merlot blend to be discontinued, as is whole range, once **03** (untasted) sells out. Pvs showed refined New World ripeness; disciplined Fr oaking.

★★★★ **Cabernet Sauvignon 03** not tasted, small quantities might still be available. Pvs **02** classic cassis & cigarbox bouquet, light but ripe & elegant. 15 mths Fr oak; 60% new.

★★★★ **Sauvignon Blanc 06** last under this label. Not tasted. Pvs **05** quite austere, bone-dry with good weight, moderate food-friendly 12.5% alc.

Late Bottled Vintage ★★★ Still available; last ed we noted that **92** is as ready as this port style should be, dryish 75g/ℓ sugar, clean if lightweight. 5 yrs in cask. 17% alc. WO Fhoek. **Merlot, Barrique Select Merlot, Chardonnay** & **Blanc Fumé** discontinued.

Terra del Capo range

Sangiovese ★★★ Latest **04** not as convincing as **03**. Some sour cherry varietal notes, but usual focus, penetrating freshness dimmed by sweet oak vanilla. Softish, dry; pleasantly medium bodied for early summer drinking. 12.3% alc. 15 mths Fr oak, 30% new. **Pinot Grigio** ★★★☆ Plenty of pizzazz in drink-early **06**, smoke/green apple hints; medium bodied, refreshing, flavours extended by 4.5g/ℓ sugar. Both ranges WO Coastal unless noted. — *AL*

■ **Lorna Hughes** see Stonehill

Lorraine Private Cellar ♀🍇ℭ

Goudini (see Worcester/Breedekloof map) ▪ Est 1875 ▪ 1stB 2002 ▪ Visits by appt ▪ Tasting fee R15 (incl glass) ▪ BYO picnic ▪ Conservation area ▪ Owners Lorraine Trust (Johann & Lori Ann de Wet) ▪ Winemaker Johan de Wet ▪ Viti adviser Leon Dippenaar (2003) ▪ 150 ha (cab f, merlot, petit v, pinotage, ruby cab, shiraz, chard, chenin, sauvignon, viognier) ▪ 2 000 tons total 50t/±4 200 cs own label ▪ 75% red 25% white ▪ PO Box 2 Rawsonville 6845 ▪ info@lorraine.co.za ▪ www.lorraine.co.za www.lorraine-wines.com ▪ T/F 023·349·1224

Johan de Wet's family has been 'loving wine since 1875' and neither a tougher market nor a warmer, drier run-up to the 2006 vintage have dulled his enthusiasm: 'Our Sauvignon is straight fruit salad… so fruity and floral on the nose!' He's applied for membership of his Du Toitskloof mountainside property to the Biodiversity & Wine Initiative, and building conference and wedding facilities. 'One must have other income streams,' he remarks.

Cape Harmony ★★★ Shiraz enters this serious minded red blend in **04**, with roughly equal (30%) cab & pinotage, plus merlot; presently inharmonious, somewhat herbaceous & ungenerous, needs time to knit, develop; 2 yrs Fr/Am oak. Following pair not retasted: **Shiraz** ★★★ Modern, international style **03**, fragrant aromas generously decorated with wood; dense, heavy mouthfeel with roughish aftertaste. **Chardonnay** ★★★ Bright lemon-butter colour, aromas, smooth mouthfilling flavours in **03** crowd pleaser. **Sauvignon Blanc** ★★ Aromatic **06**; generous passion-fruit/tropical aromas not quite matched by rather light, unlingering flavours. — *JN*

■ *Lost Horizons* see Du Toitskloof

Louiesenhof Wines

Stellenbosch • Est/1stB 1992 • Tasting & sales daily 9-5 (summer) Mon-Sat 10-3 (winter) • Fee R10 • Closed Christian holidays • Light picnic meals in summer • Play area for children • Function facilities • Farm produce • Walks • Conservation area • Owner WS Smit Watergang Trust • Winemaker Jos le Roux • Viti consultant Gawie Kriel (2000) • 130 ha (cab, merlot, pinotage, tinta, chard, chenin, sauvignon) • 1 000 tons 2 000 cs own label 70% red 28% white 2% rosé • PO Box 2013 Stellenbosch 7601 • lhofwine@iafrica.com • www.louiesenhof.co.za • T 021·865·2632 • F 021·865·2613

It's all about making wines in concert with nature at Louiesenhof, which now boasts around 50ha of proclaimed fynbos nature reserve along the Bottelary Hills. This year it's business as usual, says winemaker Jos le Roux. 'Our plans are to bottle our listed wines… and to sell lots!' Not forgetting the Marbonne brandy, distilled in a German still 'unique in its construction and size', or the Perrouquet Cape Tawny, bottled in a traditional German 'krug'.

Cabernet Sauvignon-Cabernet Franc new ★★★★ Well crafted, harmonious equal blend, carefully manicured in oak (Fr, 2nd fill, yr), **05** attractively full & rounded flavours of wild berries & leaves. **Sweet Red** new ★★ Individual fortified dessert from cellar known for characterful bottlings; **NV** needs to be tried to be appreciated. Following **06**s new but not ready for tasting: **Pinotage Rosé Secco** & **Pinot Gris**. No newer vintages of the following tasted: **Pinotage** ★★★ Unwooded 'lifestyle wine'; **04** rich plum & black berry notes, soft ripe tannins, finishes fairly dry, touch dusty. **Tinta Barocca** ★★★ **02** Mediterranean-style food-friendly red with dried fruit on nose; hint choc on finish. Briefly oaked. **Pinotage Blanc de Noir** ★★★ Bone-dry **03** coral glints, sappy strawberry fruit with creamy touch. **Chardonnay Unwooded** ★★★ **04** shy pear/green melon on nose; minerally & restrained, good foil for seafood. **Sauvignon Blanc** ★★★ Water-white **05** liberal tropical aromas; brisk dusty finish. **Perroquet Cape Tawny** ★★★★ Rustic glow-inducer from tinta, off very old vyd; fortified with brandy, aged 5 yrs in barrels; **NV**; 19% alc. Last ed fairly developed character with savoury touches. — *CT*

Louisvale Wines

Stellenbosch • Est/1stB 1989 • Tasting & sales by appt only Mon-Fri 9.30-4.30 • Fee R10 • Closed Easter Fri-Mon, Dec 25/26 & Jan 1 • Tours by appt • Owners Michael A Johnston, Hendrik Kotzé & Martin Delaney • Winemaker/viticulturist Simon Smith (Jul 1997) • 23 ha (cab, merlot, shiraz, chard) • 200 tons 15 000 cs 20% red 80% white • PO Box 542 Stellenbosch 7599 • winery@louisvale.com • www.louisvale.com • T 021·865·2422 • F 021·865·2633

This Devon Valley chardonnay specialist is reaping the rewards of good ratings. Having been accorded scores between 86-89 pts by US authority Robert Parker, sales in America are soaring. Since first vintage in 89, no fewer than 11 successive bottlings have been selected for the Nederburg Auction - an unsurpassed record for chardonnay. Support for Chavant sees a donation made to breast cancer research.

★★★★ **Dominique 01** still available at press time, was firm when tasted, with claret grip, though this shd have loosened by now. **02** (★★★) somewhat austere, in line with lesser vintage & higher proportion cab f (23%, with cab, merlot 40/37); some gd dark fruit given fine oak treatment (yr Fr, 25% new) but not for keeping.

★★★★ **Chardonnay 04** back on form with ripe lemon, lime & slatey, cool cellar notes for extra interest, poised acidity & lengthy finish. Happily, released when nicely mature, but with time in hand — these can keep 5+ yrs. 6 mths Fr oak, 50% new. Oakier **03** (★★★★) was less arresting than usual.

Chavant Chardonnay ★★★★ ✓ **05** gorgeous bouquet ripe yellow peach, enhanced by modest oaking. Juicy & seductively curvaceous with more peaches & cream to taste; smooth acidity, lingering finish. Fermented/4 mths Fr oak. Grapes ex-home farm & Wllngtn, as for... **Chardonnay Unwooded** ★★★ Style established: **06**'s youthful floral & white peach aromas translate easily onto palate — fleshy & well endowed, creamy texture, good bouncy acidity. Just off-dry. — *IvH*

Lourensford

Stellenbosch (see Helderberg map) ▪ Est 1999 ▪ 1stB 2003 ▪ Tasting & sales Mon-Fri 8.30-5 Sat 10-2 Sun 11-3 Pub hols 9-4 ▪ Fee R15 ▪ Closed Easter Fri, Dec 25 & Jan 1 ▪ Tours Mon-Fri 11 & 3 ▪ Conferencing ▪ Fly-fishing ▪ Annual SAA Cape Town Flower Show ▪ Polo ▪ Cheesery ▪ Cellarmaster Philip Costandius ▪ Oenologist Hannes Nel (Dec 2002) ▪ Winemaker Adéle Louw ▪ Viticulturists Barry Humby, Ben de Villiers & Ronel Bester ▪ 285 ha (cab, merlot, pinotage, shiraz, sauvignon, viognier) ▪ 1 300 tons 80 000 cs 80% red 20% white ▪ ISO 14000 certification in progress ▪ PO Box 16 Somerset West 7129 ▪ winetastings@lourensford.co.za ▪ www. lourensford.com ▪ T 021·847·2300 ▪ F 021·847·0910

A snail-paced 2006 harvest but there's nothing slow about cellarmaster Philip Costandius and his team. Movers and shakers in the whites department (the Viognier was recently selected for the Blue Train), they harvested the first sauvignon from a new development high up in the Hottentots Holland mountains. They now boast three different bottlings of the variety — from sites named Peace & Hope, Sun City and Bluegum — and more sauvignon is in the planning. A new Chardonnay's in the bottle, and for the reds, whole-berry fermentation has been upped to fill out the fruit and enhance mouthfeel.

★★★★ **Viognier** Careful winemaking in **05** captures variety's floral perfume yet retains a satisfying palate weight, richness, to reward the drinker. Peach pip & biscuit flavours linger long after last drop. Third Fr oaked.

★★★★ **Semillon Noble Late Harvest** Distinctive, original, hedonistic. Previewed **05** reaches new heights; already a silky opulence, never-ending sweet-savoury flavours, riveting apricot/barley sugar perfume. Potential ★★★★★. **04** showed lavender scent, citrus freshness on long, silky finish. Partially oaked. 500ml.

Cabernet Sauvignon ★★★ **03** last ed noted as one to watch: dark fruit, smoked beef & fynbos nuances; finely honed tannins. Yr Fr oak. **Seventeen Hundred** Named for date of property's establishment: blend cab, merlot, shiraz; some own fruit. **04** (★★★★) a class act: lush fruit, mulberries/blackberries, draw you in to the serious yet svelte structure which can only come from masterly oaking. Still an infant, will show full potential over next 6+ yrs. 17 mths Fr barrels, half new. **03** (★★★★, MIWA DG) was bold & forceful, needed time. **Sauvignon Blanc** ★★★★ Unfinished sample **06** already showing well: asparagus/lime intensity, hints of nettles which come to fore on palate. Livened by racy acidity (7.5 g/ℓ), begging for food accompaniment.

Eden Crest range

Merlot ★★★ Last tasted was unwooded **04**; minted red berries with herbaceous/peppery tones adding lift & freshness. **Merlot-Shiraz** ★★★ Vintage blend; lively berry aromas alert you to 76% merlot dominance this yr (incl 5% mourvèdre) but **05** more than a pretty face: 6 mths oaking adds stiffening, yr/2 ageing potential. **Shiraz** new ★★★ **05** unwooded to allow brambleberry fruit centre stage, with grape tannins providing palate definition. Bold 15.5% alc. Following trio all new: **Sauvignon Blanc-Chardonnay-Chenin Blanc** ★★★ Replaces Chardonnay-Chenin Blanc. In **04** sauvignon (58%) fleshed out by equal partners & touch sugar. Built on sleek lines (12.7% alc), has dried fig, apple, slightly savoury character. **Chardonnay** ★★★ Light oaking & soupçon semillon in **06** add interest to a crisp, melon/citrus toned summer quaffer. Screwcapped, as is... **Sauvignon Blanc** ★★★ **06** perky, dry, gooseberry/pear melange with arresting, food friendly acidity (7.6g/ℓ). **Cape Blend** discontinued.

Five Heirs range

Unless noted, all screwcapped. **Cabernet Sauvignon** ★★★☆ Last tasted **04** has fruit as main focus, firm vein of oak tannin ensured food compatibility, few yrs ageing potential. **Cabernet Franc** ★★★★ Serious yet unintimidating. **03** continues to please with vibrant red fruit partnering variety's trademark green walnuts. Already accessible, but will reward 2-3 yrs cellaring. 15 mths Fr oak. Cork-closed. **Merlot** ★★★★ **05** a charmer: piquant red berries, white pepper-nuanced from yr Fr oak sojourn. Juicy palate shows enough tannin firmness for yr/2 ageing. Incl dab cab f. **Pinotage** ★★★☆ **04** last available, retained signature fruit purity with eminently drinkable juiciness. **Shiraz** ★★★☆ A lesson in varietal purity, **05** shows herbaceous brambleberries, woodsmoke aromas, flavours. Light texture, already appealing; judiciously managed oak, 10 mths. **Shiraz Mourvèdre** new ★★★★ Impressive debut in **05**, one to watch as vines get older. Ripe dark fruit, strong pepper presence coming together in juicy, flavourful 86/14 blend. Mix Fr/Am oak. **Rosé** ★★★ Uncomplicated alfresco lunch companion. Last tasted **03**, tasty, appealing fruit pastille tones. **Chardonnay** ★★★ **05** quarter oaked but 14% viognier addition points to where true heart lies: fruity/floral styling in a crisply fresh package. **Chardonnay-Viognier** new ★★★ Perfumed by 10% viognier, partial oaking, **05** is chard in summer clothes. Dab sauvignon adds freshness. 30% wooded, Fr. **Chenin Blanc** ★★★ Last tasted **04** had pear-drop & melon typicity, refreshing finish. **Sauvignon Blanc** ★★★ **06** quality boost showcases gooseberry purity, racy acidity. Just right for long lunches with friends. Touch semillon. — *CR*

■ *Lourens River Valley* see Morgenster
■ *Luca & Ingrid Bein* see Bein Wine

Luddite Wines

Bot River (see Walker Bay map) ▪ *Est 2000* ▪ *Tastings by appt* ▪ *Owners Niels Verburg & Hillie Meyer* ▪ *Winemaker Niels Verburg* ▪ *Viticulturist Penny Verburg* ▪ *5.5 ha (shiraz, mourvèdre, cab)* ▪ *2 500 cs 100% red* ▪ *Export brands: Niels Verburg & Mudge Point* ▪ *Ranges for customers: Barton, Elgin Vintners & Iona* ▪ *PO Box 656 Bot River 7185* ▪ *luddite@telkomsa.net* ▪ ***T 028·284·9308/083·444·3537*** ▪ *F 028·284·9045*

The 2006 vintage was made from up to 40% home fruit - 'very exciting' for Niels and Penny Verburg, who are gradually working towards their goal of 100% own grapes. 'We're plodding along happily,' says Niels V, citing steadily increasing exports to the US and new markets like Canada as proof that the tortoise approach works for them. As their choice of brand name suggests, the Verburgs are staunch advocates of traditional methods, and their pointed riposte to interventionist winemakers is: 'Remember, wine is made from grapes!'

★★★★☆ **Shiraz** Pure-fruited & classically styled, unshowy yet intense. **04** more peppery, silkier & more concentrated than **03**, but in same seamless mould. Fairly moderate alc (14.2%) & wood regime (yr, 80/20 Fr/Am, 25% new). Idiosyncratically — & successfully — draws on vyds from Mbury, via Sbosch to Bot R.

★★★★ **CWG Auction Reserve Shiraz 04** selection for 2006 Auction shows more peppery, black fruit notes, with oak tannins dominant mid-2006 — though fine, sweet berry fruit emerges silkily on the finish. — *MF*

Lusan Premium Wines

Stellenbosch ▪ *Closed to public* ▪ *info@neethlingshof.co.za* ▪ ***T 021883·8988*** ▪ *F 021·883·8941*
Umbrella organisation for Alto, Flat Roof Manor, Hill & Dale, Le Bonheur, Neethlingshof, Stellenzicht and Uitkyk. Wines from these farms, totalling some 800 ha of prime Stellenbosch vineyards, marketed by Cape Legends. See individual entries.

Lushof Estate

Stellenbosch (see Helderberg map) ▪ *Est 1997* ▪ *1stB 2000* ▪ *Tasting & sales Mon-Fri 10-4 Sat by appt* ▪ *Closed pub hols* ▪ *Tours by appt* ▪ *Owners Hennie & Linda Steyn* ▪ *Winemakers/viticulturists Petré Morkel (Dec 2005) & Hennie Steyn, advised by Bruwer Raats* ▪ *12.5 ha (cab, merlot, shiraz, chard, sauvignon)* • *70 tons 3 500 cs 75% red 25% white* • *PO Box 899 Stellenbosch 7599* • *info@ lushof.co.za* • *www.lushof.co.za* • *T 021·855·3134* • *F 0866·189·154*

Fresh from his oenology finals at the end of 2005, Petré Morkel stepped into the breach at this boutique cellar, acting winemaker Erika van Zyl having left some months earlier, and shouldered the challenge of what owners Hennie and Linda Steyn adjudged 'an exceptional vintage'. Performance was more than satisfactory on the sales side too, with the full range on export to Europe and Ireland. As Hennie S says: 'The frequency of repeat orders tells its own story…'

★★★★ **Sauvignon Blanc** Combo tropical & green notes are hallmarks of this well crafted offering. **06** true to type, some asparagus & green pea extras, persistent zesty flavours, moderate 13.5% alc.

Cabernet Sauvignon ★★★ **03** last ed showed restrained style; leafy, minty choc whiffs, usual fine tannin, suave oak (14 mths, 30% new). **Merlot** ★★★ **04** less fruit-rich & tailored than pvs; leafy/stalky flavours with abrasive tannins & beefy 15% alc. Yr oak, 50% new; similar regimen for… **Shiraz** ★★★ Sweet porty aromas, chunky savoury flavours & big spicy tannins in **04**; unexpected contrast to pvs, which was balanced & delightfully fresh. **Signet Red** ★★★★ Attractive cab-led blend with 30% shiraz, 5% merlot, judiciously oaked. **04** mineral & earthy; refined mulberry & plum fruit well harmonised with tannins & oak. Shd improve further with ±3 yrs cellaring. **Chardonnay** ★★ Partly oaked **05** genteel & innocuous; sweetish fruit tone unrefreshed by v soft acidity. — *CT*

Lutzville Cape Diamond Vineyards

Lutzville Valley (see Olifants River map) • *Est 1961* • *1stB 1980* • *Tasting & sales Mon-Fri 8-5 Sat & non-Christian hols 10-2* • *Tours by appt* • *'Café Wijne' coffee shop, picnic baskets by appt* • *Function/conference venue* • *Tour groups* • *Gifts* • *Farm-style produce* • *Owners 109 shareholders* • *Senior winemaker Gideon Theron (Nov 2005)* • *Winemaker Albie Rust, with Christiaan Visser (Jan 1999/Dec 2003)* • *Viticulturists Jaco Lategan (Dec 2002)* • *2 100 ha (cab, merlot, pinotage, ruby cab, shiraz, chard, chenin, colombard, sauvignon)* • *47 500 tons* • *40 000 cs own label 10% red 87% white 1% rosé 2% fortified/sparkling* • *PO Box 50 Lutzville 8165* • *info@lutzvillevineyards.com* • *www.lutzvillevineyards.com* • *T 027·217·1516* • *F 027·217·1435*

Experienced winemaker Gideon Theron joined this, SA's second-largest cellar, in time to oversee their second-biggest crop to date (sauvignon and chenin yields were particularly bountiful), coinciding serendipitously with a renewed focus on developing and marketing new brands, and continuing to expand their bottled-wine sales. Some excellent fruit from top-performing blocks, and good varietal typicity generally boosted their efforts to select and vinify wines for the premium end of the spectrum.

Cape Diamond range

Following reds unwooded: **Cabernet Sauvignon** ★★ Shows some of variety's sterner qualities in **05**; tobacco/tea-leaf aromas, leanish fruit, dry food-seeking tannins. **Merlot** ★★★ Friendlier than pvs, **04** last ed noted as firm but balanced, with dark, spicy notes & pleasant dusty whiff. **Pinotage** ★★ SAYWS gold medallist **05** floral hints to spicy/smoky fruit; swiggably light & undemanding. **Shiraz** ★★ **05** easy, ripe, midweight red fruit flavours, spicy touch & savoury tail. **Rosé** new ★★ Appealing, smoothly dry sunset sipper; **05** Turkish Delight flavours & savoury hint; ruby cab, with pinotage. **Chardonnay** ★☆ Touch sugar imparts roundness to **06**, light texture with usual pretty ripe-pear aromas, clean finish. **Sauvignon Blanc** ★ Pale, early picked **06**, lightish, as usual, with racy tropical fruit salad flavours. **Chenin Blanc** ★★ **06** straightforward quaffer offering fresh, light, semi-dry kiwifruit flavours. **Muscadel** ★★★ Honeysuckle-scented white dessert; **06** intensely sweet yet light-tripping thanks to well judged alc & acid.

Bat's Rock range

Ruby Cabernet ★★★ Unwooded **05** ripe & balanced, red-fruit confit tone, glides easily on usual lubricating dollop sugar. Real crowd pleaser. **Rosé** ★ Light-bodied **05**, as pvs, from pinotage & colombard; like liquid Turkish Delight, with tart twist in tail. **Chenin Blanc** ★★ **06** similar to Cape D version; zesty, semi-dry with attractively crisp finish. **Bouquet Blanc** new ★ Passionfruit-toned sweetie from colombard, morio muscat & chenin; **05** very light bodied & easy.

Friends range

Uncertified/vintage dated, in 500ml. **Ruby Sunset** ★★ Spicy, unchallenging dry red; shiraz leads 3-way unwooded blend. **Misty Morning** ★★ Colombard & chenin in equal measure; light, dry no-frills swigger with unusual custard hint. **Sunny Day** ★★ Aptly named semi-sweet from colombard, with dash hanepoot adding summery perfumes. — *MM*

Lyngrove

Stellenbosch (see Helderberg map) • 1stB 2000 • Tasting & sales by appt (T 021·842·2116) • Five-star Lyngrove Country House • Owner Baarsma's Holding B.V. • Winemaker Hannes Louw, with Danielle du Toit (June 2006) • Vineyard manager John Fullard • 76 ha (cab, merlot, shiraz, petit v, pinot, pinotage, chard, chenin, sauvignon) • 50 000 cs 80% red 20% white • PO Box 7275 Stellenbosch 7599 • info@lyngrove.co.za • www.lyngrove.co.za • T 021·880· 1221 • F 021·880·0851

Danielle du Toit, ex-Sentinel Vineyards, now partners winemaker Hannes Louw at this Helderberg winery, part of the 1m-cases-a-year Baarsma Wine Group. On the property is Lyngrove Country House, a luxury stay-over and conference venue in a quiet vineyard setting.

Platinum range

★★★★ **Pinotage** Barrique matured **03** very obviously pinotage but well behaved; generous fruity flavour in spicy vanilla toned package. Good lifted finish. Yr Am oak; unfiltered. **Shiraz** ★★★★ Aussie-style **03** quite a mouthful; zero finesse but loads of interest, extract, alc (14. 3%). Yr oak, 80% Am, none new. **Cabernet Sauvignon-Merlot** ★★★☆ European profile; **03** herbal hint to clean cassis; medium body, fine minerally structure. Yr Fr oak. **Chardonnay** ★★★☆ Classically styled **04**, attractive lemon-butter/citrus character throughout, some leesy girth, well handled new Fr oak (40%, 11 mths). WO Sbosch for above, none retasted.

Reserve range

Coastal & Sbosch WOs. **Cabernet Sauvignon-Merlot** ★★★ Same 60/40 ratio, but more concentration/extract noted last ed on **03** than pvs; fruity warmth & ripeness lifted by sweet-sour fillip; yr Fr oak. **Shiraz-Pinotage** ★★★ Pinotage ascendant (though only 30%) in appealing **04**, overt banana/spice character & variety's combo sweet fruit/dry tannins. Yr Am/Fr (60/40). **Chardonnay** ★★★★ Pleasing melding of buttery lushness & crisp minerality on **05**, well integrated wood (50% barrel fermented/aged Fr oak, some new, rest vinified with chips). **Pinotage** discontinued.

Lyngrove Collection

These mainly Sbosch WO. **Cabernet Sauvignon** ★★★ Sample **04** more ripeness, satisfaction than pvs; sweet mint-choc fruit, round, ready. 10 mths Fr oak. Newer versions of next 2 reds not ready: **Merlot** ★★ Light hued **03**, eucalyptus whiffs precede greenish, fairly tart sour plum palate. Needs hearty stew or pepper steak. **Shiraz** ★★ **03** stalky/spicy mulberry fruit & pronounced acidity. Fr/Am oak. **Pinotage** ★★★ Sweet-ripe style, soft & ingratiating; **05** polished red-berry/banana flavours & hint vanilla from 9 mths oak (equal Fr/Am). **Chardonnay** ★★★ Wooded in **05**, but subtly so: fruit's the focus (citrus, ripe pear); easy, light; to enjoy young. **Sauvignon Blanc** ★★★ **05** lighter toned than pvs; soft, sweet-fruited quaffer, with hints tinned asparagus & green pea. **Brut** ★★★ Characterful carbonated sparkling; last tasted was **04** from chenin (80%), chard. — *CT*

Lynx Wines

Franschhoek • Est/1stB 2002 • Tasting & sales Mon-Fri 11-5 Sat 10-1, otherwise by appt • Self-catering cottages • Owner Vista Hermosa (Pty) Ltd • Winemaker Dieter Sellmeyer (2002) • Viti adviser Kevin Watt (Apr 2002) • 11 ha (cabs s/f, grenache, merlot, mourvèdre, petit v, shiraz, viognier) • 1 500 cs 80% red 20% white/blanc de noir • PO Box 566 Franschhoek 7690 • winemaker@lynxwines.co.za • www.lynxwines.co.za • T 021·867·0406 • F 021·867·0397

Expansion has been the theme at Lynx, where Dieter Sellmeyer reports 50% production growth and three new varieties planted — petit verdot, grenache and mourvèdre. Persuasive importers convinced the owner/winemaker to export for the first time, to the US, Germany and Greece, among other destinations. Back at the winery the new tasting room has proved popular, and Sellmeyer says his greatest pride and joy has been the new concrete fermentation tanks, perfect for long cold-soaks and punch-downs for the grapes, 'provided you can keep your balance'.

★★★★ Xanache Supple, sweet-fruited bdx-style red; merlot portion slightly upped to 50% in **05**, equal cab plus dollop cab f; v attractive ripe brambleberry tone, slight grassiness; polished, fleet-footed despite ±15% alc. Yr Fr oak, 40% new.

★★★★ Cabernet Sauvignon Most recent versions show not unattractive herbal quality: Swiss gold winner **04** at relatively modest ±14% alc, but **05** (**★★★☆**) a lusty 15%, the alc lending a creamy denseness to the minty fruit. Yr Fr oak, increased to 50% new.

Shiraz ★★★☆ Super-ripe & showy; **05** cauldron of smoke, liquorice, vanilla & pulpy dark fruit; gd varietal character; enough firmness for brief ageing. Yr barrelled, third new, 25% Am. **04** Swiss gold. **Vino Tinto ★★★** Fleshy & characterful winter warmer (15% alc will keep juices flowing); **05** ushers shiraz into mix (11%, with pvs cab, merlot, cab f) for meatier, savoury edge to dark plum fruit. Yr Fr oak, 12% new. Screwcap. **Blanc de Noir ★★★** Summer veranda wine, dry, twist-off closure for easy drinking. **06** again from merlot; partridge-eye pink, restrained red fruits flavour — just enough for food/solo versatility. All above EW.— *CR*

■ *M23* see Bottelary Hills Wines
■ *Maankloof* see Mountain River Wines

Maiden Wine Cellars

*Gordon's Bay ▪ Est 1995 ▪ 1stB 1999 ▪ Tasting/tours by appt; also tailor-made wine tours (max 6 people) ▪ Owner Danie Hattingh ▪ 1 000 cs 100% red ▪ PO Box 185 Gordon's Bay 7151 ▪ mwines@mweb.co.za ▪ www.maidenwines.com ▪ **T 021·856·3052 / 082·554·9395 ▪** F 021·856·5085*

Shipments to Malaysia have more than doubled (reduced duties sweetening the success), and arrangements are being made to export to China, says MD Danie Hattingh. The only wine currently available is the Private Reserve 04, a shiraz, cab and merlot blend (not tasted this ed) from grapes sourced in the Olifants River region.

Main Street Winery

*Paarl ▪ Est/1stB 1999 ▪ Tasting & tours by appt ▪ Owner/winemaker Marais de Villiers ▪ 700 cs 50% red 50% white ▪ PO Box 2709 Paarl 7620 ▪ mainstreet@mweb.co.za ▪ **T/F 021·872·3006***

A busy year for Marais de Villiers, who provides *garagistes* with an ingenious DIY vinification system and uses cellar space on Paarl's Main Street, as he geared up five new micro-wineries, one as far-flung as Kakamas. In between bottling his own Chenin and Sauvignon (04 Merlot and Shiraz still in barrels), he's also commissioned a new 70-ton winery in the Helderberg, based on the same vinification principles as his mobile system.

Stoep range

Old-Cape labels a charming feature. Following all tasted last ed as samples; ratings provisional. **Shiraz 03** raises the bar with well-extracted savoury fruit, excellent varietal spice, properly dry finish; shows real elegance & grace. Possible **★★★★**. 26 mths 2nd fill Fr oak. **Merlot** Similar dramatic improvement: deep, densely layered mulberry-choc fruit; ripe dry tannins; already well-knit oak (as above). **03** more serious effort could rate **★★★★**. **Pinotage ★★☆** Last was tannin-rich **02**, with Bovril aroma & hint of prune. **Dry Red ★★★** No new version of amiable **NV** 4-way blend with hint of ruby cab's thatch. **Chardonnay ★★★** Plenty of character & flavour coaxed from **05** Tradouw Valley grapes. Lively & pure unwooded fruit, refreshing lemony tang. **Chenin Blanc ★★★** Lighter styled easy-drinker from Swtlnd fruit; **05** apple & pear flavours, zippy acidity. **Sauvignon Blanc ★★★** **05** much improved this yr; Dbnville grapes vinified to show their dusty fig character, cool-area freshness.— *JN*

Major's Hill Estate ☺🍷⚘🏃

Robertson ▪ 1stB 2002 ▪ Tasting & sales Mon-Fri 9.30-1; 2-5 Sat 10-4 ▪ Closed Good Fri, Dec 25/26 ▪ Tours by appt ▪ Facilities for children ▪ Owners Dewald, Johan & Anton Louw ▪ Winemaker Alkie van der Merwe, with Nico Renoster (both Jan 2003) ▪ Viticulturist Dewald Louw ▪ 52 ha (cab, merlot, pinotage, shiraz, chard, sauvignon) ▪ 15 000 cs own label + 15 000 cs for customers + 100 000ℓ bulk ▪ 60% red 40% white ▪ PO Box 561 Robertson 6705 ▪ info@ majorshill.co.za ▪ www.majorshill.co.za ▪ T 023·626·6093 ▪ F 023·626·6096

In an ever-more competitive market, the Louw brothers are clearly thrilled with the past year's progress. They've doubled production of own-label wines to 15 000 cases and bottled a further 15 000 under other livery, bringing their bulk wine output down by 20 000ℓ off their 52 ha of replanted vineyards. Following work on a tasting room in the restored original farm cellar (once home to South African pop-icon brandy 'Klipdrift', now the place to try their rare pinotage-based Port), they'll start on a restaurant.

★★★★ **Merlot 03**, which displayed admirable vinous qualities, potential, followed by swashbuckling **05** (★★★). Boldly ripe, touch porty, overtly sweet-toned from combo Am oak (30%, 18 mths), soft fruit & 15% alc. Extravagant styling will have its adherents. **04** sold out before we could taste.

Cabernet Sauvignon ★★★ **04** repeats roasted nut, fresh corn-on-cob aromatics of pvs, yet more abundant jammy fruit, perhaps not enough tannins to shore up the ripeness. Oak as for Cab. **Shiraz** ★★★ House penchant for extended hang-time evident here too (15% alc), yet **04** shows more controlled ripeness, thanks to fine spicy-dry tannins & slightly more Fr oak (80%, otherwise as for Cab). **Pinotage** ★★★ Control & restraint noted on Shiraz evident here, too; **04** no shortage of ripe fruit (plum/raspberry/prune), but managed by firm tannin, textured oak (100% Fr, yr). **Chardonnay** ★★★ Attractive, easy drinking **06**; riper-spectrum aromas of melon & peach; full body/flavour, with enough acid to refresh. 4 mths Fr oak. **Chardonnay Inner Circle Selection** new ★★★★ Only 1 200 btls of this barrel fermented version, its 9g/ℓ RS hailed by AvdM as adding to 'an unprecedented experience'; **05** opulently rich, coconutty & sweet; great foil for Thai curries. Fr oak, 6 mths. **Sauvignon Blanc** ★★★ Refreshing aperitif-style **06** copy of pvs, incl racy acidity revving up the grassy green hints. For earliest consumption. **Pinotage Port** ★★ Carefully made maiden **03** to be succeeded by a Tawny. — *JN*

■ *Makana* see Cape First

Makro

See Selected wine shops section for contact details ▪ Enquiries Carolyn Barton ▪ cbarton@ makro.co.za ▪ www.makro.co.za ▪ T 011·797·0503 ▪ F 011·797·0366

Makro remains one of the top retail destinations for wine lovers, offering a wide selection, from affordable lines to limited releases and auction wines. The 12-store chain was again among the top five buyers at the 2006 Nederburg Auction. Look out for lots of in-store wine events and tastings, plus a monthly newsletter. Buyer Carolyn Barton stresses the focus remains on securing the best possible wines in each category by keeping up with the latest offerings. The wines below are Makro exclusives.

Private Reserve range
★★★★ **La Bri Cabernet Sauvignon Reserve 02** pvsly noted as well stocked with ripe plummy fruit, sappy oak (30% new Fr, 18 mths), but not for long keeping. WO Fhoek.

★★★★★ **Overgaauw Touriga Nacional-Cabernet Sauvignon** Still-in-stock **03** last ed showed perfumed elegance & class; chunky tannins shd now be softening. 60/40 blend, ±18 mths oak, Sbosch fruit.

★★★★ **Yellowwood Ridge Merlot-Cabernet Sauvignon** By Vergelegen's André v Rensburg; 60/30 blend plus soupçons cab f, shiraz; **03** last ed was delicious, claret-like & elegant despite 14.5% alc. 21 mths Fr barriques, 30% new. WO Stbosch.

★★★★ **De Toren Diversity Shiraz** new ✓ Seamless & elegant **04**, spicily rich & ripe; hint liquorice to the protracted savoury flavours. Yr oak, Burgundian barrels, some ex-Hospice de Beaune.

★★★★ **Landskroon Merlot-Cabernet Franc** Still-available **03** (★★★★), 65/35 mix; pvsly noted as obvious but delicious; Xmas pud flavours with cinnamon dusting. **02** sophisticated wine which improved in bottle. Paarl WOs.

★★★★ **Boplaas Cape Vintage Port Private Bin** ✓ Ex-30 yr old touriga (50%), plus tinta (35%) & introducing splash souzão in **01**, with drier, more mineral profile than pvs. Still seriously delicious; maple syrup flavours; great now & for many yrs. These ±18% alc, ±18 mths 500ℓ Portuguese barrels; well-priced magnums (1.5ℓ). WO Cdorp.

Leef op Hoop Merlot new ★★★★ By Etienne le Riche (Le Riche Wines); **04** classically restrained styling, typical of EleR, tad unyielding still, needs time to allow minty plum fruit to flower. Sbosch bushvines; yr 2nd fill Fr oak. **Porcupine Ridge Collection Syrah-Cabernet Sauvignon** new ★★★★ Attractive, v ripe **02**, creamy bramble palate packed with spicy tannins; touch portiness in farewell invites early enjoyment. 73/25 shiraz/cab ex Wllngtn/Fhoek, dash own (Boekenhoutskloof) cab f; 27 mths Fr oak, some new. **Vriesenhof Vineyards Pinot Noir** ★★★★ Elegant, earthy red from pinotphile Jan Coetzee; **02** full bodied/flavoured, with long smoky finish. 14 mths 2nd fill barrels. WO Sbosch. Not retasted, like... **Villiera Cape Blend Merlot-Pinotage** ★★★ **02** unusually (for this cellar) firm & punchy (14.6% alc), yet attractive. WO Sbosch, like... **Truter's Reserve** ★★★★ From Beyerskloof's Beyers T. **04** usual blend cab & merlot, but more dimension/flavour this yr; ripe fruit core which shd emerge from tannin grip given few yrs. Shorter oaked: 4-6 mths, Fr, no new. **Flagstone Strata Series Cape Blend** ★★★★ Still sufficient stocks left to enjoy **02**'s lavender-scented silkiness. Mix shiraz, pinotage & merlot, aged 8-10 mths in 70% Am oak, 10% new. WO W Cape. **Diemersfontein Shiraz-Mourvèdre** ★★★ Old World style **04**, medium bodied with green leaf & mint bouquet; savoury-dry, food-inclined tannins. Seasoned with dollop pinotage; 14 mths oak, some new. **Morgenhof Estate Private Bin 44 Chardonnay** ★★★ Crowd pleasing **04** last yr showed generous toast & vanilla tones from fermentation/8 mths in oak, 1st-2nd fill. WO Sbosch. **The Field Day** new ★★★★ Mainly pinot blanc (84%), a sprinkle of 5 others in delightful **05**, nothing pretentious, just layers of floral, fruity notes to admire while you enjoy the shapely, refreshingly tangy drinking experience. **Misty Mountain** ★★ **06**, ex-Bon Courage; light off-dry chenin/colombard, offering value & uncloying quaffability. 1ℓ bottle.

Babbling Brook range

Cabernet Sauvignon ★★ Ex-Kanu (WO Sbosch); **01** slightly stern, thus better with food. 14 mths new Fr oak. **Merlot** ★★ Lightly oaked **04** (incl dollop petit v) soft & easy, good picnic red. By Franschhoek Vineyards. Neither retasted.

Mont d'Or range

All ★★, ±11.5% alc. **NV** carbonated sparklings by Van Loveren, none retasted. **Brut** Festive party fizz with touch pineapple; easy, gently dry. **Vin Sec** Slightly sweeter version from riesling, muscadel, with latter's enticing floral tone. **Vin Doux** Fully sweet & very soft crowd pleaser, wafting muscat & raisin.

Thomas Kipling range

One-off value offerings; range currently in abeyance.—*CT/CR*

■ *Malan de Versailles* see Versailles

Malan Family Vintners

Range of easy-drinkers by the Malan brothers of Simonsig, now trimmed to a pair of non-vintage blends.

Cape Rouge ★★★ Bottling tasted last ed had more definition than pvs. Pinotage, merlot, cab (49/31/20). Exuberantly fruity, raspberries/mulberries; grippy tannins to match food, promise few yrs ageing. **Cape Blanc** ★★★ Lightish, appealingly aromatic blend colombard, semillon, riesling & morio muscat; softly rounded. Not retasted. Both WO Sbosch. **Pinotage**, **Cabernet Sauvignon-Merlot**, **Chardonnay**, **Sauvignon Blanc** & **Sauvignon Blanc-Semillon** discontinued. — *CR*

■ *Mankazana* see Ross Gower Wines

Manley Private Cellar

Tulbagh ▪ Est/1stB 2002 ▪ Tasting & sales daily 10-4 Sat/Sun 10-12 ▪ Fee R5/wine ▪ Cellar tours by appt ▪ Closed Good Fri & Dec 25 ▪ Luxury B&B ▪ Gifts ▪ Walks ▪ Owner/winemaker/viticulturist David Manley Jordan ▪ 8 ha (cabs s/f, merlot, mourvèdre, pinotage, shiraz) ▪ Target: 5 000 cs ▪ PO Box 318 Tulbagh 6820 ▪ info@manleywines.co.za ▪ www.manleywines.co.za ▪ T 023·230·0582 ▪ F 023 230·0057

Sailor-turned-landowner, vinegrower and winemaker David Manley Jordan is pleased that his Pinotage is starting to show the same good form as the flagship Shiraz, as evidenced by the 04 vintage featuring in the 2005 ABSA Pinotage Top 10. Grapes not vinified for the own range are channelled to Flagstone.

★★★★ **Shiraz** In same mould, **05** preview offers opulent fruit in aroma & texture; mulberry, blueberry, occasional glimpses lavender, violet. Tannins are sheathed, the hidden structure that will hold the wine into its 3-4 yr future, but with such velvety accessibility, there'll probably be none left to age. 16 mths Fr, mix new/used.

Cabernet Sauvignon Still early but a beauty in the making; barrel sample **05**'s exuberant blackcurrant, black cherry richness hardly show the oak assimilation taking place, which speaks of barrel quality & expert winemaking. All Fr, 57% new, 16 mths. Potential ★★★★. Seems a notch up on hugely ripe **04** (★★★☆). **Merlot** ★★★★ No shortage of fruit in **05**, a veritable berry orchard, gloriously ripe. Still in development but has the hallmarks of a fine drinking wine: polished tannins, elegance, balancing acidity. 16 mths Fr oak, half new. **Pinotage** ★★★★ With the cellar's trademark plummy fruit, ex-barrel **05** has an intriguing salty liquorice overlay; admirable oak balance allows variety's juicy personality through. 16 mths barrel matured, combo Fr/Am, 60% new. Thoughtfully made, one to watch. **Sauvignon Blanc** discontinued. — *CR*

■ *Manor House* see Nederburg

MAN Vintners

Paarl ▪ Est/1stB 2001 ▪ Tasting & sales by appt ▪ Owners: see below ▪ Winemaker Tyrrel Myburgh ▪ 100 000 cs 70% red 30% white ▪ PO Box 389 Stellenbosch 7599 ▪ info@manvintners.co.za ▪ www.manvintners.co.za ▪ T 021·886·7532 ▪ F 021·887·4340

Thanks to Fairview's Western Cape distribution network, locals can now enjoy the affordable, easy drinking wines of MAN Vintners, initially conceived as an export line and already a presence in nine overseas markets (listed in UK *Wine Report's* Top 10 Up & Coming SA Wineries). Innovators José Conde (Stark-Condé), Tyrrel Myburgh (Joostenberg) and Fairview partner Charles Back promise consumers won't be disappointed with the fruits of these low-yielding Perdeberg vines (Perdeberg Co-op a shareholder), packaged in signature African style.

Sénga range
Shiraz ★★★☆ **04** will please for few yrs; aromatic smoked meat nose, forceful but restrained flavours supported by succulent acidity, gentle tannic grip. **Merlot-Cabernet Sauvignon** ★★★ Friendly & forthcoming **04** notes of choc, plummy fruit; fresh, but alc power (these both 14.5%) asserts itself on palate. Both Muldersvlei grapes; yr mostly Fr oak. No newer vintages tasted this ed.

Standard range
Cabernet Sauvignon ★★★ Juicy, fresh blackcurrant on **05**, complemented by grape tannin grip; well made, with splash merlot & refreshing acidity throughout. As all this range, simple, honest value, from Prdberg vyds (though labelled origin W Cape). Oak staves & micro-oxygenation impart youthful drinkability. **Shiraz** ★★★ **05** smoky bacon aromas, ripe plum & blackberry flavours, gentle tannins & sweet-savoury finish. **Pinotage** ★★ Less beguiling than pvs, **05** appealing fresh cherry aromas but little weight & thin finish. **Chardonnay** ★★★ **05** tasted last ed, generous, warm nutty citrus, dried peach flavours; full bodied, but fresh & eminently drinkable. Dash sauvignon. **Chenin Blanc** ★★★ Abundant tropical fruit aromas in **06**, delicious, concentrated fresh pineapple & melon flavours, balancing acidity provides lively, dry finish. **Sauvignon Blanc** ★★★ Dusty, grassy, lightweight **06**; mouthwatering acidity & quince flavours, agreeably low alc for lunchtime quaffing. — *IM/TJ*

■ *Marcel de Reuck* see Crows Nest

Marianne Estate   ♦ ⏲ 🍷 new

*Paarl ▪ Est/1stB 2004 ▪ Tasting & sales Mon-Fri 9-4.30 Sat 9-1 ▪ Fee R10 ▪ Closed Easter Fri, Dec 25 & Jan 1 ▪ Tours by appt ▪ Four-star B&B guest apartments (see Stay-over section) ▪ Owners Dauriac family ▪ Winemaker Pierre Casenave (2004) ▪ Viticulturist André van den Berg (Jan 2004) ▪ 17 ha (cab, merlot, pinotage, shiraz, sauvignon) ▪ 86 tons 90% red 10% white ▪ PO Box 7300 Stellenbosch 7599 ▪ info@mariannewinefarm.co.za ▪ www.mariannewinefarm. co.za ▪ **T** 021·875·5040/5672 ▪ **F** 021·875·5036*

Named for the Phrygian-hatted Marianne who symbolises post-revolutionary France, this estate belongs to the Dauriac family, owners of wine properties in Bordeaux. They've invested in more than vineyards and equipment: their new cellar, built a stone's throw away from the existing four-star guest apartments, came into use in 2005 (cellars were 'borrowed' for the maiden vintage of 2004). Pierre Casenave spends half the year vinifying here and the rest *chez* Dauriac.

Merlot ★★★★ **04** vintage (like all these reds), soft-fruited, with mulberry leaf hints, fine tannins & good length of flavour – but marred by big alc (15.1%) evident on finish. Restrained oaking – 20% new. **Shiraz** ★★★★ Barossa-style – all-new Fr oak, alc power. Nutmeg, vanilla, raspberry notes dominating, but dollops of texture & spice, with gd grip to finish. **Pinotage** ★★★★ Speaks clearly of variety in rather old-fashioned way, with varnishy herbal notes; earthy, rustic on the palate. But food-friendly, despite big alc (all these reds over 15%). 18 mths wooding (none new). **Cabernet Sauvignon** ★★★ There's chunky black fruit on offer, finishing sweetly spicy; robustly built, with ample grip. 30% new oak, as has… **Floreal** ★★★ Equal blend merlot, cab, shiraz mingles red/ black fruit (raspberry, black cherry) & plenty of spice; elegantly textured, but alc adds to sweetness of finish. **Desirade** ★★★ Two thirds merlot, rest cab, gives soft mulberry, blackcurrant aromas. Dense textures, very evident oak (but just 20% new). **Sauvignon Blanc** ★★ **05**'s tropical notes lead on to soft, unconcentrated palate flaunting its 14.5% alc. All WO Coastal. – *MF*

■ *Marimba* see Cru Wines, Southern Sky & Overhex

Marklew Family Wines   ♦ ⏲ 🍷

*Stellenbosch ▪ 1stB 2003 ▪ Visits by appt ▪ Tour groups (max 20) ▪ Pvt/business functions for small groups ▪ Walks ▪ Mountain biking ▪ Conservation area ▪ Owners Marklew family (Edward Dudley, Edward William, Lyn & Haidee) ▪ Winemaker Duan Brits, with Haidee Marklew (both Jan 2003) ▪ Viticulturists Billy Marklew & Duan Brits (Jun 2001/Jan 2003), advised by Cobus van Graan ▪ 45 ha (cabs/f, merlot, pinotage, shiraz, chard, sauvignon) ▪ ±300 tons 2 700 cs own label 70% red 30% white ▪ PO Box 17 Elsenburg 7607 ▪ wine@marklew.co.za ▪ www. marklew.co.za ▪ **T/F** 021·884·4412*

Brother-and-sister team Billy and Haidee Marklew seem to know no bounds, cheered on by retired parents Dudley and Lyn in the background. Some well executed moves saw dressage aficionado Haidee and cycling enthusiast Billy complete their latest winemaking round (in partnership with winemaker/viticulturist Duan Brits, a keen hunter/fisherman) to applause from SAA, *Wine* and Wine of the Month Club. Despite the small production, expect to see these wines far afield with exports to eight markets.

★★★★ **Capensis Reserve** Pinotage a minor partner in this 'Cape blend'; maiden **03** just 7% (with cab/merlot – 62/31), **04** (★★★★) 10%, but presence felt in tart red-fruit tones, assertive dry tannins somewhat cushioned by flesh, sweet cassis/mint flavours from cab, merlot, shiraz (45/32/12.5) & generous oak. Best monitored carefully. 18 mths new oak.

Cabernet Sauvignon 04 (★★★★) last ed showed more refined oomph than pvs. Same identifiable Smnsberg well toned muscularity as in **03** (★★★★). Yr Fr/Am oak, 40% new. **Merlot** ★★★★ **04** combines power, elegance & harmony, fresh ripe plum/dark choc tones. Better structure, fruit intensity than before. Third new barrels, Fr/Am; not retasted. **Chardonnay** ★★★ **05** unshowy, carefully oaked, medium bodied, for current drinking pleasure. Roast hazelnut & citrus tones with creamy texture. All above WO Smnsberg-Sbosch. – *AL*

Maske Wines 🍷 new

Wellington ▪ Est 1987 ▪ 1stB 2000 ▪ Tasting & sales by appt ▪ Owner/viticulturist Erich Maske ▪ Vini consultant Hein Hesebeck (2004) ▪ 5 ha (cab, merlot, chenin) ▪ 10-15 tons 500 cs ▪ PO Box 206 Wellington 7654 ▪ maske@iafrica.com or laureat@iafrica.com ▪ T 021·873·3407 ▪ F 021·873·3408

When Janine and Erich Maske bought Klein Waterval farm in 1987, it had nothing but a refuse dump and 'some scrappy old vineyards' on it, one of which was a 52 year old block of chenin. This was retained for a future 'special wine' and the rest replanted with merlot and cab. Their grapes were used by neighbouring Upland until 2000, when they made their first own-label Merlot. This and the 04 (made by Hein Hesebeck) are available; other vintages will be released when the Maskes feel their quality warrants.

Merlot ★★★★ 04 plummy, with rich dark choc textures, charry caramel & spice; 14% alc shows on the dry finish. Effectively oaked in new Rmnian barrels. — *MF*

◼ *Mason's Hill see* The Mason's Winery
◼ *Matuba see* Cape Coastal Vintners

Matzikama Organic Cellar 🍶

Olifants River ▪ Est 1999 ▪ 1stB 2001 ▪ Closed to public ▪ Owner/winemaker/viticulturist Klaas Coetzee ▪ 4 ha (shiraz) ▪ 180 cs 100% red ▪ PO Box 440 Vredendal 8160 ▪ info@ matzikamawyn.co.za ▪ www.matzikamawyn.co.za ▪ T 082·801·3737

No update from this producer; contact details from previous edition.

McGregor Wines 🍷♿

McGregor (see Robertson map) ▪ Est 1948 ▪ 1stB 1978 ▪ Tasting & sales Mon-Fri 8-5 Sat 10-3 ▪ Closed Easter Fri-Mon, May 2, Dec 16/25/26 ▪ Owners 42 members ▪ Manager/winemaker Jacques du Toit (Aug 2002) ▪ Winemaker André Scriven (Dec 2005) ▪ Viticulturist Anton Laas (Dec 2000) ▪ 700 ha ▪ 11 000 tons 25% red 75% white ▪ PO Box 519 McGregor 6708 ▪ mcg@ intekom.co.za ▪ www.mcgregorwinery.co.za ▪ T 023·625·1741/1109 ▪ F 023·625·1829

Things are moving apace with a new winemaker, André Scriven (ex-Ashton Winery), new international markets opening and — great news for those not living in the Western Cape — national distribution now in place. McGregor Wines also hosted a Mini Arts Festival in tandem with Robertson's Wacky Wine Weekend last year; this was such a success that it will now be an annual event — the first weekend in June is the one to earmark.

Winemaker's Reserve range
Cabernet Sauvignon ★★★ Handsomely packaged & seriously structured **03**; spicy tobacco whiffs, ripe black fruit flavours, supple dry finish. ±14 mths Fr barrelled. **Chardonnay ★★★ 05** billows ripe citrus zest; crisp & juicy; brief Fr oaking gives attractive nutty hint. Above pair tasted as samples last ed, not revisited. **Sauvignon Blanc ★★ 06** partly wood fermented; sample shows hint of straw; light texture & flavour; undemanding, dry.

McGregor range

Colombard ☺ **★★★** Perfect picnic wine. Guava & dried pear notes on **06**, usual flavourful light body, really refreshing just-not-dry finish.

Following trio still selling, not retasted: **Pinotage ★★★ 04** honest & well crafted, everything in position, looking/tasting gd (sample last yr); poised 13.5% alc. Small Fr oak, 6 mths: **Ruby Cabernet ★★★** Appealing & versatile quaffer (13.5% alc). **03** had pristine fruit, some grassy notes, quite firm, tangy. **Shiraz ★★★** Engaging & decidedly drinkable **04**, showed sweet-spicy brioche tones, well judged oak (6 mths Fr/Am), properly dry. **Cabernet Sauvignon-Merlot ★★ 04** more assertive vintage; stalky flavours, again slightly nutty tannins; might benefit from ageing yr/2. Merlot fraction oaked 4 mths. **Chardonnay ★★★** Uncomplicated but tasty **06** (sample), note of melba toast (though unwooded), well balanced for summer refreshment. **Chenin Blanc ★★ 06** guava, dry grass & melon whiffs; balanced crispness, light & easy to drink. **Sauvignon Blanc** ★★★ Light bodied, for early consumption. **06** appealing 'sweet' aroma of green fig preserve; ripe flavours; usual juicy-dry finish. **Colombar-Chardonnay** ★★ **06** lively if hasty tropical flavours, cheerful, undemanding & quaffable. **Late Harvest Bouquet** ★ **03** sold out. **White Muscadel** ★★★ Enticing sun ripened grape lead-in to **06**, palate also sun-sweet, touch heavy despite higher alc (17%) than last bottling. **Red Muscadel** ★★★ Light strawberry hues on **06**; usual scented bouquet of Turkish Delight & toffee, suggestion of tannin gives backbone, mouthfeel. **Cape Ruby** ★★★ **05** (sample) again from ruby cab but tastier, fleshier, than pvs; brandy pudding flavours, sweetish but clean finish. Barrique aged, yr. Also available, in 3ℓ packs, not tasted: **After Five Ruby Cabernet & After Five Chenin Blanc**. — *CT/MM*

MC Square

Est/1stB 1996 ▪ Closed to public ▪ Winemaker/viticulturist Jean-Luc Sweerts ▪ 300 cs 100% white ▪ PO Box 436 Somerset West 7129 ▪ mcsquare@iafrica.com ▪ T 083·303·5467 ▪ F 021·852·7740

In a departure from the non-sparkling whites which have appeared to date under his own label, Jean-Luc Sweerts is launching both a red and a méthode cap classique. Both are reminders of the past: J-LS, while at Avontuur, was a pioneer of the modern, earlier accessible Cape red, with his Avon Rouge; he was also the first to use the shortened 'MCC' on a label of local sparkling. This little protest (ask him to tell the story) is also the allusion in the name of his brand.

★★★★ **Cuvée Chardonnay** Subtitle — 'Méthode Classique' — sets tone for both vintages tasted to date: **00** fine honeyed patina to elegant marmalade/apricot tones. **01** fuller, richer, more youthfully citrus-fruited with attractive hints toast on nose/palate. Yr Fr barriques, ±20% new; bottle-aged extra yr. — *IvH*

■ *Meander see* Groot Eiland

Meerendal Estate

Durbanville ▪ Est 1702 ▪ 1stB 1969 ▪ Tasting & sales daily 8-5 ▪ Fee R10 per person, refunded on purchase of 6 btls ▪ Closed Easter Fri & Dec 25 ▪ Restaurant, bistro, deli & function venue (see Eat-out section) ▪ Owners HN Coertze, AF Swanepoel, JG Adriaanse, R Truter & CG Stride ▪ Cellarmaster Karl Lambour (Jul 2005) ▪ Viti adviser Kevin Watt (Jul 2005) ▪ Viticulturist Liza Goodwin (Apr 2006) ▪ 100 ha (cab, merlot, pinotage, shiraz, chard, chenin, gewürz, sauvignon) ▪ 650 tons 25 000 cs 80% red 20% white ▪ Private Bag X1702 Durbanville 7551 ▪ info@ meerendal.co.za ▪ www.meerendal.co.za ▪ T 021·975·1655 ▪ F 021·975·1657

Scaling down, trading up. That's this historic estate, re-invigorated by a syndicate not shy to invest in a viticulturally high-potential area. Kevin Watt is the new viti-advisor; former winemaker Liza Goodwin is the new viticulturist; cellarmaster Karl Lambour happily handles the scaled-down 650 tons off trimmed-down 100ha. The results include a Pinotage of a vineyard planted in 1955, a top-end Shiraz and a partly barrel fermented Chenin (some unready for tasting this ed). A 2006 Trophy Wine Show 'best merlot' citation is just the beginning, the team predicts. Fine dining plus alfresco alternatives make for a vibrant winelands experience.

★★★★ **Cabernet Sauvignon-Merlot** ✓ To be discontinued after still-available **03**; in bright, modern style. Yr Fr oak, 2nd/3rd fill. Not retasted.

★★★★ **Sauvignon Blanc Reserve 05** only ex-farm's restaurants/cellar door. Last ed noted Dbnville's classic cool ripeness & sleek concentration in this big but beautifully balanced single-vyd wine.

Cabernet Sauvignon ★★★★ **04**, sample last yr, pleasingly fresh, vigorous dry tannins to accompany lavish blackberry, cedar tones. Sensitively Fr oaked, third new. Promises greater complexity with time. Still available. **Merlot** ★★★★ Last yr we noted blockbuster with tightrope balance, harmony; very fresh core & polished oak recommended time to settle, which **04** did in time to take TWS trophy, maybe SAA selection. 15% alc. Fr oaked, third new. **Pinotage** ★★★★ Projected release of appealingly modern **04** early 2007. Mid-2005 we commented on generous raspberry/ cherry freshness, grippy but balanced tannins; careful oaking (Fr barrels, third new). **Shiraz** ★★★ Older style **03** still available. **04** untasted, due for release early 2007. **Chardonnay** ★★★★ Easy but satisfying **05**. Mineral, citrus aromatics followed by supple, broader though still zippy mouthfeel, as might be expected from only 50% barrel fermentation. **Sauvignon Blanc** ★★★☆ **06**, just post-bottling, good vigour, steely resolve with underlying fig richness. Agreeably medium bodied, dry. **Natural Sweet** ★★★★ **02** from gewürz sold out. Latest **06** from chenin unready. – AL

Meerhof Winery

Swartland • Est/1stB 2000 • Tasting & sales Mon-Fri 8.30-4.30 Sat 10-2 Pub hols 10-2 • Closed Easter Fri-Sun, Dec 25 & Jan 1 • Sunday lunch (T 022·482·2088); also BYO picnic • Functions for up to 100 by appt • Tours by appt • Owners C Kotze, Kotze Steyn Family Trust & private investors • Winemaker Emile Gentis (2005) • ±65 ha (cab, merlot, pinotage, shiraz, chard) • ±320 tons 90% red 10% white • PO Box 1229 Malmesbury 7299 • meerhof@ wcaccess.co.za • www.meerhof.co.za • T 022·487·2524 • F 0866·838·132

A flurry of changes have breathed new life into this growing Swartland cellar. The fresh energy can largely be attributed to newly appointed winemaker Emile Gentis (ex Villiera and Klein Constantia). Self-confessed Star Wars fan, EG says, 'what is the art of walking into a cellar with great accolades? I'd rather walk into a challenge which will keep us busy for the next 5 years and the force is strong in this one! It really is a winery with potential.'

Merlot new ★★ Ex low-yielding dryland bushvines; attractive **04** offers juicy rounded black-fruit flavours, dusty dry tannins from ageing with Fr staves. Sample tasted, ditto for… **Shiraz** ★★ **03** same vintage as last ed, different vinification (no new oak): still a biggie – 15% alc – but fruit overshadowed by spicy wood mid-2006. On current form, ★★. Incl dash cab. **Winemaker's Reserve Syrah** new ★★ New Fr oak for **03**, yet lighter (13. 9% alc), less 'Reserve'-like than above Shiraz, but well-fruited, for early enjoyment. Hand-applied wax seal. **Chardonnay Reserve** new Barrel fermented in Fr oak, preview **06** bit gawky, still quite oaky, clean if tad lean citrus fruit. ★★ on current showing; cld improve. 15% alc. **Chardonnay** ★ **05** partly oak-matured (same vintage listed last ed vinified without oak) seems to be past prime, offers some muted apple flavours. **Weisser Riesling** new ★★☆ **05/NV** (poss. to be marketed uncertified, with wax neck-seal & handwritten label); sample shows variety's delicate flowers & spice, less sweetness than 12g/ℓ would suggest. Yr lees-aged. New versions of following not ready: **Cabernet Sauvignon**, **Shiraz-Cabernet Sauvignon**, **Pinotage** & **Rosé**; **Dry Red** discontinued. – MM

■ *Meerland see Baarsma*

Meerlust Estate

Stellenbosch • Est 1693 • 1stB 1975 • Tasting & sales Mon-Fri 9-5 (9-4 May-Sep) Sat 10-2 • Fee R20 • Closed pub hols • Owner Hannes Myburgh • Cellarmaster Chris Williams (Jan 2004) • Viticulturist Roelie Joubert, advised by Paul Wallace (both 2001) • 110 ha (cabs s/f, merlot, pinot, chard) • 600 tons ±50 000 cs 90% red 10% white • PO Box 7121 Stellenbosch 7599 • info@meerlust.co.za • www.meerlust.co.za • T 021·843·3587 • F 021·843·3274

Winemaker Chris Williams is often asked: What makes Meerlust wines great, distinctive? His explanation begins, as it should, in the vineyard: clay subsoils, overlain by gravels, allowing excess water to drain, with just enough moisture retained to sustain the vines through the dry ripening season. Then there's the cooling influence of the Atlantic 5km southeast. And balanced vines through correct cropping and maintenance. Also vital is the Myburgh family's continuous ownership (250 years), promoting a natural, gradual progression of wine style, free from short-term demands. Williams's challenge? 'To better understand Meerlust's terroir.' Which involves separately managing small vineyard units, and vinifying (and initially maturing) single lots 'to preserve the purity and clarity of both site and variety'. Finally, he cites the luxury of time – four years bottle-maturation at the cellar for reds – 'the ultimate indulgence for a winegrower'.

★★★★★ **Rubicon** Iconic claret-style red & one of SA's most famous wines. Longevity enhanced by major cab component; 69% in **03**; merlot, cab f (19/12) in usual cohort roles. Captures vintage charm: elegantly expressive blackberry/cassis fruit, smoky oak accompaniment with hint clove. Seems more approachable than usual but has spine, confident frame for interesting development over several yrs. Fr oak, 80% new, 20 mths. No **02**; **01** (Pichon Longueville trophy at 2006 IWSC) still available, as are Merlot & Pinot 01s.

★★★★ **Red** Essentially '2nd-label Rubicon': released when vintage doesn't permit flagship quality. Wallet-cordial at less than half the price. To date only three: **85**, **90** & still-available **02**. Similar blend as flagship, less intense, not as long lived; complementarily oaked, yr Fr. *Wine* ★★★★.

★★★★ **Merlot** Polished, modern classic, stiffened with ±10% cab. Classy oak spice married with dark plum minerality on **03**; elegant, with depth, length of fresh, intense flavours. Fine, ripe tannin will benefit from min 3-4 yrs softening; promises usual 9-10 yrs evolution. Fr oak, 80% new. No **02**. **01** Tri-Nations 2006 category winner.

★★★★ **Chardonnay 05** Chris Ws' debut in guide as cellar chief (**04** sold out during yr). Familiar roast hazelnut introduction with subtle lime/pebble extras. Elegantly vinous; graceful & supple, firm frame, appealing mineral length. Needs 2/3 yrs to fully grow. Fermented/yr Fr oak, 60% new; 50% native yeast. **03** 90 pts *WS*.

★★★★ **Pinot Noir** Since fuller style **95**, some charming & convincing versions. **00** (★★★★★) delicate, fleshy, with structured tannins needing yr/2 to unleash greater delights. **01** (★★★) last ed atypically sombre, sturdy & dense, with formidable dry tannins. 50/50 Burgundian clones/BK5. 15 mths Fr oak (heavy-toast, tight-grain Allier). 14% alc. No **02**. — *AL*

Meinert Wines ɮ♀

Stellenbosch (see Helderberg map) ▪ *Est 1987* ▪ *1stB 1997* ▪ *Tasting & sales at 96 Winery Road Restaurant (see Eat-out section)* ▪ *Owner Martin Meinert* ▪ *Winemaker Martin Meinert, with Allison Adams* ▪ *Vineyard/farm manager Henk Marconi* ▪ *13.5 ha (cabs s/f, merlot, petit v, pinotage)* ▪ *90 tons 6 500 cs 100% red* ▪ *PO Box 7221 Stellenbosch 7599* ▪ *info@ meinertwines.com* ▪ *www.meinert.co.za* ▪ *T 021·865·2363* ▪ *F 021·865·2414*

There's been little change here over the past year. 'A sign of stability or conservatism?' wonders Martin Meinert, owner of this premium Devon Valley cellar. Our bet is on consistency – of the quality kind. Why change a formula that works so well? And with sterling assistance from Allison Adams in the cellar and Henk Marconi in the vineyards, Meinert (alongside his involvements at Ken Forrester Wines and Eagles Nest) has more time to spread the word about his 'wines with personality' in the winery's growing export markets: the United States and the UK.

★★★★★ **Synchronicity** The standard-bearer, but nothing 'standard' about this sexy, modern blend. **04** deeply fruited, simmers with tension as spiced vanilla berries held captive by fine-grained tannins (until at least 2010). Barrel-selected cab & merlot (60:30) with just the right proportion pinotage for harmony. 2 yrs new Fr oak.

★★★★ **Devon Crest** Bdx red bears moniker of home-farm with confidence. **04** (★★★★★) masterly display of power & elegance in parallel; ripe cherry/berry fruits knitted into cab-dominated lattice, a velvety beauty. Brambly tones & firm vinosity of **03** restored form after lighter but still excellent **02**. Cool s-facing vyds 10-15 yrs old. 81/19 cab/ merlot blend (pvs 69/31), yr new Fr oak solo, further 6 mths as combo.

★★★★ **Merlot** Urbane table companion, laden with panache. **04** minty edge to sleek black & red berry fruit, melded into plush, upholstered frame; understated without austerity. Dash pinotage, cab. 18 mths used Fr oak. — *DS*

Mellasat ɮ♀

Paarl ▪ *Est 1996* ▪ *1stB 1999* ▪ *Visits by appt, but encouraged* ▪ *Owner/winemaker/viticulturist Stephen Richardson, with Poena Malherbe* ▪ *8 ha (cab, pinotage, shiraz, tempranillo, chenin)* ▪ *50 tons 2 500 cs 85% red 15% white* ▪ *PO Box 7169 Paarl ⑦623* ▪ *mellasat@mweb.co.za* ▪ *www.mellasat.com* ▪ *T/F 021·862·4525*

Stephen Richardson has the advantage, in looking to export markets, of having family in Norfolk; a newly appointed marketer will operate from there, developing niche and top-end customer bases in the UK. Back home in SA, Stephen R has been concentrating on a new flagship blend – the 03 was released late last year, complete with new label – and on rationalising both premium and entry-level ranges. He explains: 'This allows for a "project" wine, such as a dessert wine, to be made in some years.'

Mellasat 'M' new ★★★ Flagship blend shiraz (64%), pinotage & cab; **03** attractively dry & chalky, medium-bodied; cedar & bluegum whiffs amid the oak (Fr/Am, 20% new, 18-22 mths), which dominates mid-2006. **Cabernet Sauvignon** ★★★ Chunky **03** not retasted; savoury & coffee/choc notes, lots of tannins last yr but sufficient fruit to balance. 15 mths Fr oak, none new. **Pinotage** ★★★ **03** of this, following wine (both listed as samples pvs ed), diverted into 'M' above. Current **02** full-bodied, floral; polished tannins but warming glow from obvious alc (14.4%). Yr Fr oak, 14% new. **Shiraz 02** work-in-progress last ed noted as showing improved tannin managament, provisionally rated ★★★★. **Tuin Wyn** ☆ 'Garden Wine' — chenin grapes air-dried on racks under the oaks; previewed **03** barrel-fermented/aged 30 mths, Am oak, reveals highly indvidual styling.

Dekker's Valley range

Revelation ★★★ Cab by another name; last tasted was attractive & different **02**; unfiltered; 15 mths oak, 50/50 Fr/Am. **Chenin Blanc** ☆ **06** light-bodied, austere version of pvs easy drinker; sweet-sour tone & bracing acidity. — *MM/DH*

■ **Merwespont Winery** see Bonnievale Wine Cellar
■ **Merwida** see Riverstone Vineyards

Metzer Wines ♀♂ new

Cape Town • Est/1stB 2004 • Tasting by appt • Owner/winemaker Wade Metzer • 5 tons 300 cs 100% red • 3 Village Close, Drama Str, Somerset West 7130 • metzerwines@telkomsa.net • T 084·340·8278 • F 021·851·8245

There are many perks to inner-city winemaking: for example, you can scooter off your wines to hospitality-trade clients by Vespa — which is the preferred mode of delivery for the own-brand wines of Wade Metzer. Full-time assistant at Signal Hill, Metzer says he managed to squeeze in some time last season for his own label in the midst of moving the SH cellar from the old Culemborg station to its ritzy new location in Mandela Rhodes Place, adding wryly that Church Street had to be blocked off for 30 minutes while his grapes were unloaded...

★★★★ **The Kitchen Sink Syrah** Evocative, individual **05** indeed crammed full of everything incl the proverbial...; altogether delicious. Burly; rumbles with demonstrative woodsmoke, spice, meat depths; but also amazingly fine, gentle, no ungainly hint of 15% alc. Definitely no 'KS' vinification: natural yeasts, unfined/filtered, only older Fr oak, 15 mths. Hldrberg/Firgrove vyds, WO Bosch. — *AL*

M'hudi Wines ♀♂

Stellenbosch • Est/1stB 2003 • Visits as for Villiera (see entry) • Owners Rangaka family • Winemakers Jeff Grier & Anton Smal, with Tseliso Rangaka (all 2004) • Viticulturist Simon Grier (2004) • 3 000 cs 33% red 67% white • PO Box 66 Koelenhof 7605 • wine@villiera.com • www.villiera.com • T 021·865·2002/3 • F 021·865·2314

Former Johannesburg advertising copywriter Tseliso Rangaka is the assistant viticulturist/ winemaker (with Jeff Grier of Villiera), marketer and self-confessed general Jack of all trades at M'hudi ('Harvester' in Setswana). 'True to the meaning of our name, we seek to source fruit from areas best known for a particular variety,' he explains. The 06 Sauvignon was vinified from Elgin grapes, for example, while a new addition to the family, a Merlot, grew up in the Koelenhof area.

Neither of the above available for review at press time. Following notes from previous ed. All samples, all likely ★★★. **Pinotage** Big, cheerful **04** bruiser with nicely dry finish, but sweet ripe fruitiness jolted by powerful acidity. Yr in mix Am/Fr oak. This, following wine, WO Sbosch. **Chenin Blanc** Forward tropical fruit notes, hints honey & interesting earthiness. **05** rounded & fresh, but with rather hard acidity, big 14.8% alc. **Sauvignon Blanc 05** characterful, pleasant aromas/flavours of passionfruit, melon; bone-dry & zippily balanced, 13.5% alc. WO Elim. — *TJ*

■ *Mia Bella Wines* see Mia Cara

Mia Cara Wines [new]

Closed to public • Owner Mia Cara (Pty) Ltd • Winemaker Hein Hesebeck (Rose Garden Vineyards) • PO Box 4560 Tyger Valley 7536 • miacara.wines@incapetown.com • www. incapetown.com/miacarawines • T/F 021·982·2200/082·571·4157

Vivian Kleynhans, MD of Mia Cara Wines which, in partnership with Rose Garden Vineyards, aims to become one of SA's largest black female-owned wine companies, cites company goals like setting 'measurable targets towards social responsibilities', working towards an 'anti-alcohol-abuse society' and being 'highly profitable'. But Mia Cara is not just about socio-economic transformation and empowerment: 'Our wines hold a romantic secret that will be discovered once they have been tasted,' promises Kleynhans.

Shiraz Reserve ★★★★ 03 like all in this range. Rich raspberry/black berry aromas with barnyard notes lead to amply fruited & well textured palate with enough tannins, big 14.6% alc. 10 mths in Fr oak. **Best Red ★★★** Blend ruby cab (70%) & shiraz offers cherry, white pepper, blackcurrant aromas. Nicely dry easy-drinker, despite some chunky tannins. **Pinotage ★★☆** Plum, cardamom whiffs with gamey edge; palate marked by dry, tannic finish. These all WO Paarl.

Mia Bella range

Pinotage-Shiraz ☺ ★★★ This range all **05**. Smoky, slightly varnishy aromas & full, sweet raspberry spice offer plenty of tasty, easy-drinking (if unlingering) pleasure. **Chenin Blanc-Colombard ☺ ★★★** Zesty tropical-fruited aromas featuring colombard's signature guava notes; mouthfilling fruit lingers happily on dry finish; moderate 13% alc just adds to quaffability.

Sauvignon Blanc ★★ Light & slightly fizzy, with whiffs of greenpepper, crisply tart finish. Bone-dryness & low 12% alc underscore the green elements here. WO W Cape, like all in this range. — *MF*

Micu Narunsky Wines [new]

Cape Town • Est 2005 • 1stB 2006 • Closed to public • Owner/winemaker Micu Narunsky • ±120 cases 80% red 15% white 5% rosé • PO Box 30994 Tokai 7966 • nmicu@hotmail.com • T 021 713·3163/073·600·3031

Professional jazz pianist Micu Narunsky was living in Paris when the wine bug bit: 'I travelled a lot to Bordeaux and became friendly with the winemaker at Ch Phélan-Ségur.' After studying winemaking at Bordeaux University and working the 2003 Languedoc harvest, Micu N visited the Cape. Returning to settle, he assisted at Nabygelegen and L'Avenir. Now solo, and using Stellekaya's facilities, he's particularly excited about the prospect of making a crisp, dry Rosé using Portuguese varieties. 'They ripen relatively early, resulting in wines that have freshness and relatively low alcohol.'

Touriga Nacional-Tinta Barocca ★★★ Rare pairing of these Portuguese varieties in an (unfortified) dry red will be welcomed by adventurous imbibers. Maiden **05** has surprising concentration of plummy fruit given the modest 12.8% alc; friendly tannins, pleasant funghi/forest floor nuance to tail. 85/15 blend, ±10 mths Fr oak. WO Coastal. — *CR*

Middelvlei Estate

Stellenbosch • Est 1919 • 1stB 1973 • Tasting & sales Mon-Sat 10-4.30 • Fee R15 • Closed Easter Fri & Dec 25 • Combo cellar tour/barrel tasting Mon-Fri 11 & 3 • Small conference facility • Walks • Owners Momberg family • Winemaker Tinnie Momberg (Jan 1992) • Viticulturist Ben Momberg (Jan 1992) • 130 ha (cab, merlot, pinotage, shiraz, tinta, chard, sauvignon) • 1 000 tons 35 000 cs own labels 95% red 5% white • Export brand: Hagelsberg • PO Box 66 Stellenbosch 7599 • info@middelvlei.co.za • www.middelvlei.co.za • T 021·883·2565 • F 021·883·9546

A cellar which has seen this many crushes occasionally needs some tender loving care — in an ongoing revamp, Tinnie Momberg has replaced some tanks, modified others and given the open cement tanks a spruce-up. It's all about staying in touch with trends and keeping the cellar workable. A restaurant featuring 'outdoor cuisine' in true SA tradition will add a new dimension to this family estate. A new label design punctuates the move, bearing the 'M' motif and designed for maximum eye-appeal.

★★★★ **Shiraz 03** skipped but **04** worth the wait: signature earth-after-rain aroma with white pepper tickle; polished plum & dark cherry flavours well complemented by oak (12–16 mths, mainly Fr). 'Playfully enchanting,' reckons Tinnie M.

Cabernet Sauvignon ★★★★ Shorter barrelling (14 mths, Fr, vs 26) for **04**, combines class & early approachability in a juicy, harmonious package. **Pinotage** ★★★ Pinotage in pinstripes: neat & well behaved but not dull. Step-up **04** appealing blackcurrant-jam tone with sweet-sour twist, fine tannins, moderate 13% alc. 12-14 mths oak, mostly Fr.

Pinotage-Merlot ★★★★ Understandably popular equal blend; **05** less oak/savoury character, so warm & juicy plum fruit shines through. Nice. 16 mths 2nd fill oak, 15% Am.

Chardonnay ★★★ As before, **06** modestly wooded (30%); combo dried pear & spiced peach flavours, trimmer than pvs but still pleasing. NE. – *IvH*

Migliarina Wines

Stellenbosch • Est/1stB 2002 • Closed to public • Owner/winemaker Carsten Migliarina • 500 cs 100% red • PO Box 673 Stellenbosch 7599 • carsten@migliarina.co.za • www.migliarina. co.za • T 072·233·4138

'Sold out' is the notice every winemaker wants to pin to his or her barrels, and a pleased Carsten Migliarina did just that last year when he waved goodbye to his last bottle of 04. The 05 – a tricky harvest – was released after the guide went to bed. No matter, it's the 06 ('already showing soft yet bold tannins and stunning fruit') that's got CM champing at the bit.

Shiraz ★★★ **04** last ed showed gentle ripe tannins, opulent berry fruit & marked freshness. – *IvH*

■ *Migration-Serengeti* see Leidersburg

Mike's Kitchen

Head office: 298 Main Rd, Bryanston Ext 1, Sandton • www.mikeskitchen.co.za • T 011·463·9269 • F 011·463·9300

Exclusive, easy-drinking range for the Gauteng-based restaurant chain, by Old Vines Cellars.

Reserve Red ★★★ Easy-drinking, lightly wooded **04** from merlot. Plush berry fruits & tannins, generously flavoured but still refreshing. Mix staves/oak. **Classic White** ★★★★ Food-friendly **06** mainly chenin (75%), showing creamy floral/wet wool scents, zesty layered flavours & racy acidity; no haste to open: there's enough structure to hold yr/2. **Stein Select** ★★★ Quick-quaff from chenin; **NV** ample butterscotch & brioche aromas, honeycomb flavours, soft sweetish finish (14g/ℓ sugar). All WO Coastal. – *CvZ*

Miles Mossop Wines

Stellenbosch • Est/1stB 2004 • Closed to public • Owner/winemaker Miles Mossop • 10 tons 700 cs 72% red 28% white • PO Box 7339 Stellenbosch 7599 • miles@tokara.com T 082·413·4335 • F 021·808·5911

Producing a mere 700 cases of 'truly handcrafted' wine under his own label, Tokara winemaker Miles Mossop aims to have these regarded as some of the finest from SA. The newly released bordeaux blend, named after his son Max (who in turn was named Maximilian Anthony after his two grandfathers), joins older sister's namesake wine, Saskia, in winging its way to the UK, US and Sweden.

★★★★ **Max** ('Bordeaux Blend' last yr, when tasted ex barrel) Precocious **04** (TWS gold on 1st outing) now fleshier, more fruit-rich, still exemplifies elegance in svelte bdx build. Dash petit v (21%) lends violets fragrance to classic cab/merlot scents (58/21). Beautiful oaking (20 mths Fr, 40% new). Merlot ex-Paarl; balance Sbosch.

★★★★ **Saskia** Sassy chenin (70%), viognier partnership, latter providing full bloom honey-suckle, apricot aromatic fireworks in **05**. Generous, powerful; rich rather than sweet; subtle savoury extras via natural ferment; some botrytis intrigue. Barrelled 10 mths, 25% new. Chenin 28 yr old Sbosch vyd; viognier ex-Pdberg. **04** Wine ★★★★. — AL

■ *Millberg* see Franschhoek Vineyards
■ *Millbrook* see Arlington

Millstream

Range by DGB for export chiefly to the UK, Ireland and the Netherlands.
Pinotage ★★★ Balanced easy-drinker; **03** attractive earthy touch; plump, dry savoury flavours. **Cinsault-Ruby Cabernet** ★★ Ripely appealing 50/50 melange in **04**, brambly/smoky whiffs, seamless carry-through to red-fruit palate. **Rosé** ★★ **05** strawberry & toffee apple whiffs, lively, uncomplex, lower alc (13.2%) than last. **Chardonnay** ★★★ **05** not tasted. **03** appealed widely with peaches & cream aromas, perky lemon-peach fruit. **Chenin Blanc** ★★★ Lightish **05**, casual-quaffing dry white, some melon fruit, not-too-dry finish. All WO W Cape; none retasted for this ed. — DH

■ *Milton Grove* see African Terroir

Minke Wines

Stellenbosch ▪ Closed to public ▪ Owner Henry Davel ▪ T 083·273·4561
A medical doctor, Cape Wine Master and burgundy fanatic, avuncular Henry Davel is excused for sweating every detail of his beloved Pinot, named after his granddaughter. Gauteng-based, Henry D makes wine the way they perform some surgery these days — by remote control. His virtual hands are the Muratie cellar team; Vriesenhof farm his viticultural Petri dish; Dijon clone 777 a *sine qua non*. Fine fruit, elegance and finesse are the aims, and he's well-satisfied with maiden 04. Now the fine-tuning begins...
Pinot Noir ★★★★ Characterful & ageworthy **04** opens in glass to classic pinot fragrance (earth/sour cherry), silky mocha, choc ebb & flow. Fine tannins give focus, grip. Two versions, differently wax-sealed: White cap: yr 100% new oak; earthier, finer tannins. Red: bit less new oak yet slightly more wood showing. ±13% alc. — CvZ

Miravel   🍷 🛏 new

Stellenbosch (see Helderberg map) ▪ Est 2002 ▪ 1stB 2005 ▪ Visits by appt ▪ Self-catering Fynbos Cottage ▪ Owner Miravel (Pty) Ltd/Maarten van Beuningen ▪ Winemaker Bartho Eksteen (Hermanuspietersfontein) ▪ Viti adviser Paul Wallace (Jun 2004) ▪ 32 ha (cab, cinsaut, merlot, petit v, pinotage, tinta b, chenin, sauvignon) ▪ 242 tons 225 cs own label ▪ PO Box 5144 Helderberg 7135 ▪ miravel@adept.co.za ▪ www.miravel.co.za ▪ T 072·212·4668 ▪ F 021·842·2456
Maarten van Beuningen grew fruit in Zimbabwe before starting a new life down south on this subdivision of the Dellrust property. He currently sells most of his grapes but started bottling a sauvignon made by Bartho Eksteen under his own label in 2005. The cool sea breezes the location enjoys are whispering 'white' in MvB's ear, and replanting will bring the red/white ratio closer to half each from its present 70/30. He is using his strong Dutch connections to take Miravel into the Netherlands.
Merlot ★★★ **03** mulberry & herbal aromas; dark choc throws some heavy hints; robust tannins enter to dominate the finish. Sbosch fruit; 18 mths oak. **Sauvignon Blanc** ★★★ Leafy capsicum whiffs on **05** prelude to thatchy green palate with a fine citrus-toned & lingering finish. Moderate 13% alc adds to drinkability. WO Coastal. — MF

Mischa Estate   🍷🛏🍴🚶

Wellington ▪ Est/1stB 1999 ▪ Tasting, sales & tours (incl vine nurseries in summer) by appt ▪ Fee R250, waived if 6+ btls purchased ▪ Closed pub hols ▪ Snacks & meals by appt ▪ Walks ▪ Mountain biking ▪ Owners JH & JA Barns ▪ Winemaker Andrew Barns (Jan 1999) ▪ Viticulturist Ruiter Smit (Jun 1960) ▪ 40 ha (cab, merlot, shiraz) ▪ 60 tons 3 000 cs own label 100% red ▪ PO

*Box 163 Wellington 7654 ▪ wines@mischa.co.za ▪ www.mischa.co.za ▪ **T 021·864·1016/ 19/20** ▪ F 021·864·2312*

Keeping only the pick of the crop, winemaker Andrew Barns is revelling in the success of his wines with an accumulation of awards and ever-growing export demand from markets as diverse as the US, Kenya and Hong Kong. Although established as a vine nursery 30 years ago, this estate on the foothills of the Groenberg now sells some 60% of its production to some of the industry's leaders. A broadened palette sees the release of their first Sauvignon.

★★★★ **Mischa Shiraz 04** lowers the alc power (to 14%), ups the subtlety without forfeiting generosity of spicy red fruit or aromatic peppery attractions. Ripe yet firm & supple tannin, lithe, sleek texture with long chalky dry finish. Deserves 3-4 yrs to show its best. MIWA DG. Yr Fr oak.

Cabernet Sauvignon Pvsly tasted 03 (★★★★☆) characteristic blueberry signature of poised Wllngtn cab, admirable elegance & balance. Scented **02** (★★★☆) had notes of currant & satsuma plum jam, pointing to great ripeness. **Merlot** ★★★☆ **03** last ed was more exciting than pvs, showed exotic minerally, spicy red fruit with hints of olive.

Eventide range

No new vintages of following trio tasted: **Cabernet Sauvignon 03** (★★★★) a 'lunchtime cab' with moderate 13.5% alc, sweet luscious fruit & attractive floral bouquet. **Merlot** ★★★ **03** sour cherry flavours & racy freshness; light textured/bodied at just 12.6 alc. **Syrah** ★★★☆ ('Shiraz' last ed.) **03** vanilla dominated, with simple red fruit flavours, some spice & leather. **Sauvignon Blanc** new **06** ★★★★ Shy herbaceous aromas develop into lively, zesty, lemon barley palate; bright acidity with hints of minerality, tart limy twist on farewell. Excellent food wine. **Viognier** ★★★★ Caresses with ethereal delicacy (despite ±14% alc): lovely notes of dried peach, incense & rosepetal; **06** balances lightness with alluring intensity & persistence; integrated barrel fermentation in 4th fill oak. *— MW*

■ *Misty Point see Southern Cape Vineyards*

Mitre's Edge   ♂♀ ℱ new

*Paarl ▪ Est 1999 ▪ 1stB 2004 ▪ Visits by appt ▪ Small tasting fee, refunded on purchase ▪ Farm produce ▪ Owners Bernard & Lola Nicholls ▪ Winemaker Lola Nicholls (2004), with Bernard Nicholls (Feb 2006) ▪ Viti consultant Paul Wallace (1999) ▪ 18 ha (cabs s/f, malbec, merlot, petit v, shiraz) ▪ 95% red 5% rosé ▪ PO Box 12290 Die Boord 7613 ▪ bernlola@iafrica.com ▪ www.mitres-edge.co.za ▪ **T 021·875·5960** ▪ F 021·875·5965*

Lola Nicholls worked at next-door Warwick for 6 years before husband Bernard, seeing which way the wind was blowing, gave up his engineering career to their start-up wine venture after taking over father Martin Hunting's farm, Mitre's Edge, in 1999. They replanted the entire property with the full complement of red bordeaux varieties, plus shiraz, but it's early days yet — so far only the latter has been bottled (unfortunately not ready for review by press time).

Monis Wines

*Paarl ▪ Est 1906 ▪ Closed to public ▪ Owner Distell ▪ Winemaker Dirkie Christowitz (Aug 1979) ▪ 22 000 cs 100% fortifieds ▪ PO Box 266 Paarl 7620 ▪ dchristowitz@distell.co.za ▪ www.distell. co.za ▪ **T 021·860·1601** ▪ F 021·872·2790*

This veteran of the fortified wine business has branched out, building a new port cellar with a 47-vat capacity. Expect a muscadel, wood matured for five years, annually from here on, and in 2008 we're promised a special treat: a Vintage Port.

★★★★★ **Muscadel** ✓ **00** continues path trodden by exalted forebears. Amber glints, inviting scents of raisined fruit, toffee, coffee & mulled-wine spices, followed by languid, silky flavours. Shd improve, hold, decade+. **92** garnered as many admirers as show gongs (incl Muscats of the World gold, Best Muscat trophy at TWS).

★★★★ **Tawny Port** Competition hero (Veritas, Peter Schultz, TWS et al). Among handful of dated tawnies. Gorgeous **96** (current release) noted last ed as sweeter than pvs, also longer in oak (109g/ℓ RS; ±8 yrs, Fr). Paarlberg tinta & cinsaut. Only 1 500 cs made.—*CvZ*

Mons Ruber Estate

Little Karoo ▪ *Est ca 1850* ▪ *Tasting & sales Mon-Fri 9-5 Sat 9-1* ▪ *Closed Easter Sun & Dec 25* ▪ *Self-catering overnight accommodation* ▪ *Estate produce for sale* ▪ *Hiking trail in proclaimed conservation area* ▪ *Owners Radé & Erhard Meyer* ▪ *Winemaker Radé Meyer* ▪ *Viti consultant J Mellet* ▪ *38 ha (cab, muscadels r/w, chard, chenin, hanepoot, palomino)* ▪ *±500 tons 10 000 cs own label 50% red 50% white* ▪ *PO Box 1585 Oudtshoorn 6620* ▪ *monsruber@lantic.net* ▪ *www.geocities.com/monsr_za* ▪ ***T/F 044·251·6550***

A wet run-up didn't prevent a difficult harvest 2006. 'The vines had an insatiable thirst,' recounts Radé Meyer, but they pulled through, producing grapes with high sugars, resulting in 'excellent muscadels, our forte' He and brother Erhard are nursing new cab vines and, having increased the area under chardonnay, are focusing on replanting red muscadel: 'Demand for fortified wines is growing as people rediscover their unique flavour and appeal,' they explain.

Conari ☺ ★★★ **05** easy-drinking unoaked cab with cheery plum & berry notes, party-friendly 13% alc. **Cabernet Sauvignon Jerepigo** ☺ ★★★ Aka 'Elegantia'. Can a fortified dessert be a superquaffer? This can. Unique in concept & character, **06**'s dried herb nose gives no hint of succulent sweetness to come; mouthcoating prune & tealeaf flavours; syrupy but irresistible.

Chardonnay ★★ Unfinished **06** full of melon & honey aromas/flavours. Modest 12.4% alc ideal for summer sipping. **White Muscadel Jerepigo** ★★★★ ✓ Flavour-packed fortified dessert with pretty floral notes accompanying its citrus peel/sultana richness. **06** sweet & full bodied, & really delicious – a big step up on pvs. 220g/ℓ RS; 17.8% alc. **Muscadel Liqueur** ★★★★ One of the idiosyncratic, long-matured fortifieds gleaned from the depths of Radé Meyer's cellar (last was Elusivo 89). **97**, unfinished sample last ed, is one of a kind; somewhat like old sherry, except for sweetness (240g/ℓ) you could practically eat with a spoon. Preserved clementine, savoury oak the dominant flavours. 9 yrs oaked, only 400 × 375ml btls made. 21.8% alc. No new vintages tasted for following: **Cabernet Sauvignon** ★★★ Unoaked, soft & plummy **00** was last. **Vino** ★★ NV (03) from chard, last ed showed bottle-age honey & peach whiffs, toasted nut flavours. **Regalis** ★★★ Current bottling (**NV**, 03) of fortified white muscadel sweeter, more syrupy than version above, with caramel & tealeaf nuances. **Hanepoot Jerepigo** ★★★ **04** ripe & grapey, with harmonious acid & spirit. Also bottled as Bonitas. **Sultana Jerepigo** ★★ **04** first in guide since '99, nutty character infused with hints honey & anise, silky & proudly sweet. **Red Muscadel Jerepigo** ★★★ Velvet smooth fortified dessert. **02** waxy & floral notes share the stage with bright muscat aromas. **Port** ★★★ Gentle tawny style **NV**, drier than most Cape ports; from cab. Mature looking russet-ruby, stewed fruit & mocha hints.—*CR*

Montagu Wine Cellar

Little Karoo ▪ *Est 1941* ▪ *1stB 1975* ▪ *Tasting & sales Mon-Fri 8-5 Sat 9-12* ▪ *Closed pub hols* ▪ *Tours during harvest by appt (call Marguerite van der Merwe)* ▪ *BYO picnic* ▪ *Owners 68 members* ▪ *Manager/winemaker Eben Rademeyer, with Collin Wright (2006/1990)* ▪ *Viti consultant Johannes Mellet* ▪ *660 ha (11 varieties r/w)* ▪ *12 500 tons 5 500 cs own label* ▪ *20% red 40% white 40% muscadel* ▪ *PO Box 29 Montagu 6720* ▪ *mkwmarketing@lando.co.za* ▪ ***T 023·614·1125*** ▪ *F 023·614·1793*

Under stewardship of newly appointed manager/winemaker Eben Rademeyer (Sonnie Malan retired after 34 years), Montagu Wine Cellar, traditionally home to fortified desserts (40% of bottlings are muscadel) is upping the ante on variety, visibility and quality. A Cab-Shiraz joins the range, and new labels feature Fort Sidney (circa 1899), manned by volunteer Gordon Highlanders during the Anglo-Boer war to guard the Cogmanskloof tunnel and pass.

Cabernet Sauvignon-Shiraz Reserve ᴺᴱᵂ ★★★ Full-ripe red berries & slight savoury note on attractive **05**, light textured, for earlier drinking. **Merlot-Ruby Cabernet** ★★ Unwooded **05**, uncomplicated warm ripe fruit, some plums & liquorice, rounded, goes down easily. **Chenin Blanc ★ 06** restrained & simple pear-drop & guava flavours, light fresh finish. **Colombard ★☆** Off-dry **06** quaffer with floral/sherbet notes, offering softly rounded drinkability. **Late Harvest ★★** Floral, fruity, softly sweet **NV**, easy to drink, helped by fairly gentle 12.8% alc. **Vin Doux Sparking Wine ★★☆** Sweet grapey bubbles with some minty muscat notes, appealing & lively, will have many fans. **NV**. **Red Muscadel ★★★★** A beauty, **05** unashamedly rich & sweet but there's an underlying structure holding it together, making you enjoy a 2nd glass. **White Muscadel ★★ 06** the closest thing to drinking liquidised raisins you'll ever find, very sweet & syrupy but delicious. Also available but not tasted: **Chardonnay**; **Mont Rouge**; in 500ml: **Mont Rosé** & **Mont Blanc** (semi-sweet). Mostly W Cape WOs. — *CR*

Mont Destin

Paarl ▪ Est/1stB 1998 ▪ Visits by appt ▪ Owners Ernest & Samantha Bürgin ▪ Winemaker Samantha Bürgin, advised by Bruwer Raats (Jan 2002/Jan 2003) ▪ Viticulturist André van den Berg (Jan 2000), advised by Johan Wiese ▪ 7 ha (cab, cinsaut, grenache, mourvèdre, shiraz, viognier) ▪ 15 tons 1 000 cs 80% red 20% white ▪ PO Box 1237 Stellenbosch 7599 ▪ info@ montdestin.co.za ▪ www.montdestin.co.za ▪ T 083·288·4985 ▪ F 021·875·5870

Ernest and Samantha Bürgin are satisfied with their decision a few years ago to downsize their property, which has enabled them to focus on making wine. The integrated cellar-cum-homestead (interleading through a fantastically pink door) inspired by Mexican architect Luis Barragan, with an added African flavour, is in itself well worth a visit. Their latest vintage had the benefit of their eagerly awaited, well-designed micro-cellar and new basket press which, in the case of the sought-after, artisanal Destiny Shiraz, is eschewed for feet.

★★★★ 1482 Name change underway for this flagship red, usually cab, shiraz & merlot in proportions guided by vintage. **04** blend 52/24/24, seriously styled with opaque core & appealing plum & mocha oak. Youthful, compact dark fruit & firm tannins not yet integrated in newly bottled sample. WO Sbosch, as is Chenin.

Destiny Shiraz Strikingly packaged, handmade limited release. Gutsy **03 (★★★★)** last ed noted as artisanal & personality packed. 20 mths new Fr/Am oak. Relatively plentiful 800 btls. **02 (★★★★** but *Wine* **★★★★)**. **Chenin Blanc ★★★★** Herbaceous aromas dominate **06** (sample), lees-ageing adds dimension. Fresh pineapple, guava flavours sustained by lean minerality & crisp acidity. **05** *Wine* **★★★★**. — *IM*

■ Mont d'Or *see Makro*

Mont du Bleu [new]

Stellenbosch ▪ Est 2005 ▪ Closed to public ▪ Owner Chilled 24/7 (Pty) Ltd ▪ Wine sourcing Johann Strauss ▪ 300 000ℓ own label 30% red 70% white ▪ PO Box 12429 Die Boord 7613 ▪ chilled247@yebo.co.za ▪ T 021·880·1722 ▪ F 021·880·0152

Here's an innovative way to market a wine brand and please by-the-glass customers — quality wine on tap, chilled as it flows through a specially designed dispenser and served at just the right temperature. Pleasing to clients too — there's no fridge space taken up, no storing or serving of yesterday's opened bottle, in fact no bottles to open at all. Orchestrated by Johann Strauss and developed by Rian Kerkhof, takers already include several major restaurant franchises, casinos and independent eateries.

Cabernet-Sauvignon-Merlot ☺ ★★★ Judiciously oaked **04** pleasantly plump with loads of pruney fruit, low tannins, generous 14.2% alc. 50/40 blend, smidgen cab f.

Dry Rosé ★★ Undemanding **06** a brilliant coral hue, lightly fruity & distinctly floral. From chenin, with dollops cabs/f & merlot. Enjoy this summer. **Rosé Semi Sweet 06** from colombard with reds as above, too unformed to rate. **Chenin Blanc ★★★** Soft & juicy **06** mixes marzipan & wild flowers on the nose, finishes with a sweet impression thanks to 13.7% alc.

Colombard ★★ **06** subtle floral scents, mellow sweetness from 25g/ℓ RS. Needs chilling & early drinking. All WO Wllngtn. — *IvH*

Mont du Toit Kelder

Wellington • Est 1996 • 1stB 1998 • Tasting & sales by appt • Owner Stephan du Toit • Winemaker/viticulturist Pieter-Niel Rossouw (Jan 2000), advised by Bernd Philippi (1997) • 26 ha (alicante bouschet, cabs s/f, merlot, petit v, tintas b & r(a), shiraz & mourvèdre) • ±130 tons ±10 000 cs 100% red • PO Box 704 Wellington 7654 • kelder@montdutoit.co.za • www. montdutoit.co.za • T 021·873·7745 • F 021·864·2737

'The impenetrable ways of officialdom!' sighs owner Stephan du Toit. What was planted, in good faith, as 'tempranillo' was then pronounced 'tinta roriz' and has recently been declared 'tinta amarela'. (Nonetheless, he's firm on last year's new planting — tinta barocca, bringing to nine the red varieties on the farm.) Perhaps not impenetrable but certainly 'tough as ever' is the international market, where governmental support for producers is evident, 'contrasted with the lack of support here and the ineptitude of trade negotiations in the past'.

★★★★☆ **Le Sommet** Ambitious blend (composition kept dark). **03** (★★★★) not fully open, accessible mid-2006. Less presence than magisterial **02** but still dignified, controlled. Concentrated mulberry fruit, notes of roast beef, oak char; very dry, verging on austere, with some gruffness to tannins. Shd reward cellaring 5-7 yrs.

★★★★ **Mont du Toit** Blend varies — usually cab, merlot, shiraz, cab f, but coyness rules! Plush black velvet texture on **03**, evidencing cab in big-boned, warm-climate, generous mode; balanced tannic grip, shd unfold with ease. 2 yrs oak (±30% new) imparts loads of spice. Deserves 4-6 yr wait.

Les Coteaux ★★★☆ Positioned pricewise between Hawequas & the summits. Cab/merlot blend **05**, tasted ex-barrel, has pleasing fullness, in muscular style with family resemblance to cellarmates, but slight bitterness mars finish. **Hawequas** ★★★ Last tasted **03** (**04** sold out before we had the chance) from cab/merlot (without shiraz sneaking in as sometimes) took on new seriousness. Gd oak (16 mths) showing, with cassis; ripe tannins but a touch bitter on long finish. All these Wllngtn/Kmuts fruit; WO Coastal. — *IvH*

Monterosso Estate

Stellenbosch • Est/1stB 2000 • Tasting & sales Mon-Sat 8.30-12.30; 1.30-5 • Closed Easter Fri/Mon, Apr 27, May 1, Jun 16, Dec 25 & Jan 1 • Tours by appt • Owners Socrate, Orneglio & Francesco De Franchi • Winemaker Orneglio De Franchi (Jan 2000) • Viticulturist Francesco De Franchi • 68 ha (cab, merlot, pinotage, sangiovese, shiraz, chard, chenin, sauvignon, semillon) • 6 600 cs own label 80% red 20% white • PO Box 5 Stellenbosch 7599 • monterosso@mweb.co.za • T/F 021·889·5021

From baby steps to large strides in 2006 for the De Franchi *fratelli*: the Cab-Merlot and Sangiovese having sold out, they increased production by over 300%, upping quantities of the Sauvignon and Chenin. Exports to Denmark, Sweden and the US are growing, while closer to home the wines have been launched in selected Western Cape restaurants. Markets have also been opened in Gauteng and Namibia.

Sauvignon Blanc ☺ ★★☆ **06** cheerful, zesty everyday dry white with hints cat's pee & honey.

Cabernet Sauvignon-Merlot ★★★ Attractively rustic red retains its handcrafted feel in **03**; improbably compatible flavours of steak tartare, iron & plum; balanced savoury tannins provide length & food-partiality. Fermented/matured 14 mths Fr oak (mix old/new). **Sangiovese Socrate** ★★★ Honours the De F paterfamilias. **04** has Italianate dryness, tannic ring, bitter-cherry flavour spectrum; quite woody still, needs time to settle. Italian yeasts; 14-16 mths 2nd fill oak. **Old Bush Vine Chenin Blanc** Unoaked, assertive but unaggressive **06** (★★★★ √) seems perfectly poised — refreshing acidity, rich mid-palate, marathon farewell. Dried pear, thatch flavours complemented by mineral notes. Bargain priced. **05** (★★★★) had similar gd qualities in slightly reduced form. — *CvZ*

■ *Montestell* see Boland Kelder

Montpellier

Tulbagh • Est ca 1950 • 1stB ca 1968 • Tasting, sales & tours Mon-Fri 9-12; 2-5 Sat 9-12 • BYO picnic • Restaurant, farm-style guest house, conferences & many other attractions • Facilities for children • Tour groups • Owner Lucas J van Tonder • Winemaker Anton Krynauw (Jan 2003) • Viti consultant Gawie Kriel (Apr 2003) • 50 ha (11 varieties, mainly white) • 300 tons 10 000 cs 30% red 70% white • PO Box 79 Tulbagh 6820 • montpellierwine@tiscali.co.za • www.montpellier.co.za • T 023·230·0656 / 082·300·6777 • F 023·230·1574

Johannesburg advocate Lucas van Tonder continues with the overhaul of this historic French Huguenot property (circa 1714). Old vines have been uprooted and virgin soil planted with chardonnay and viognier. Future extensions may include grenache, malbec and nebbiolo. Additions to the Old Cape Dutch Guesthouse include the atmospheric restaurant Forty's. Also on the menu of attractions are self-catering units, horse riding, quad-biking, water sports, camping and picnicking.

Cabernet Sauvignon ★★☆ Unpretentious braai buddy **04**, last yr was a generous cassis/choc mouthful, with gently firm dry tannins. **Shiraz** new ★ Big & burly **05** has 15.5% alc & tight, herbaceous fruit tannins (unwooded) demanding bottle-maturation. **Blanc de Noir** ★★ Soft, pale strawberry looks & tastes last yr; **05** bled from pinot juice & vinified as white. **Chardonnay** ★ Unwooded **05** off-dry & very ripe, with notes of straw & grass, bountiful 15.5% alc. **Chenin Blanc** ★☆ Simple, straightforward quaffing style, **05** with hint of guava. **Private Reserve** ★★★ Perfumed **02** from gewürz, colombard, clairette. When last tasted wafted rosepetals, showed gd balance in a light, soft body. **Méthode Cap Classique** ★★ Dry, explosively foamy **03** from semillon with dollops chenin & sauvignon; interesting flavour combo of fresh pineapple & dried fruits. **Port** ★ More correctly named 'sweet fortified pinotage'; unwooded, raisined & unctuous **05**. — *CT*

■ *Montpellier du Sud* see Constantia de Tulbagh

Mont Rochelle Hotel & Mountain Vineyards

Franschhoek • 1stB 1996 • Tasting & sales daily 10-6 • Fee R15 • Tours 11, 12.30 & 3 • Five-star hotel & restaurant (see Eat-out/Stay-over section) • Cheese platters; picnics & gourmet tastings by appt • Functions & events • Farm produce • Art gallery • Owner Mont Rochelle Mountain Vineyard Ltd • Winemaker Anneke du Plessis • Viti consultant Danie Botha • Farm manager Pieter Botha • 19 ha (cab, merlot, shiraz, chard, sauvignon) • 15 000 cs own label 50% red 50% white • ISO 14001 certified • PO Box 334 Franschhoek 7690 • info@montrochelle.co.za • www.montrochelle.co.za • T 021·876·3000 • F 021·876·2362

The luxury hotel previously known as La Couronne, gutted by fire, has been restored to its former opulence (including a French-toned restaurant, Mange Tout) and incorporated into the Mont Rochelle farming business, hence the name change to 'Mont Rochelle Hotel & Mountain Vineyards'. (La Couronne Winery continues as an autonomous operation and is listed separately.) In the boutique Mont Rochelle cellar everything, bar pressing, is done by hand: 'I don't want a machine to make the wine,' says Anneke du Plessis. Her hands-on approach extends to selecting of rows and indeed grapes for the Sauvignon Reserve; it shows in the 06, she reckons (and we concur) — this from an area not generally noted for sauvignon, she points out.

★★★★ **Barrel Fermented Chardonnay** ('Oak-Matured' pvs ed.) Last rated was richly textured **02**; **03** & **04** sold out before we tasted; **05** sample too young to call but shows gd supporting fruit & weight; prominent toasty wood just needs time to marry. 10 mths Fr oak, 15% new.

Syrah Elegantly hedonistic **03** (★★★★), last ed noted as having rich black cherry fruit layered with cinnamon & woodsmoke. More deliciously smooth & fine-grained than **02** (★★★☆), with a more savoury character. 20 mths Fr oak. Both ex-Paarl. **Cabernet**

Sauvignon ★★★☆ 03 too embryonic to rate last ed, now fully formed & attreactively herbaceous though still tight, needing yr/2 to show its best. 20% new Fr oak, 18 mths & WO W Cape, as is… **Artemis** ★★★☆ (Pvsly 'Alchemy'.) Varietal reshuffle with **03** to merlot, cab, pinotage, shiraz (40/30/20/10); winemaker aiming for velvety easy-drinker with light tannins — which achieved: minty, juicy, amenable but not frivolous. **Merlot** ★★☆ 03 stern & unyielding last ed, nothing like plump & velvety pvs; oak as for Syrah. **Merlot-Cabernet Sauvignon** ★★★☆ Debut **03**, previewed last ed, has developed well (& plenty in hand); ripe tannins & rich choc-laced fruit easily accommodate beefy 15% alc, for neatly tailored effect. **Natural Chardonnay** ★★☆ Unwooded version; **06** uncharacteristically subdued; hints of tropical fruit on quiet, softly dry palate. **Sauvignon Blanc Reserve** Quality jump from easy to drink **05** (★★★) to weighty & structured **06** (★★★★), packed with ripe fig fruit. Impressive concentration achieved without sacrificing drinkability or moderate 13.5% alc. **Sauvignon Blanc** ★★★☆ 06 again from Wllngtn grapes but much more interesting, pleasurable than pvs; slightly fuller too (13.5% alc), fresh & tangy kiwifruit & gooseberry flavours. — *CR*

■ *Mooiberge see* African Terroir

Mooi Bly Winery

Paarl • Est/1stB 2003 • 'Vine to wine tour' by appt • Self-catering cottages • Owner Wouters family • Winemakers Erik Schouteden & Theunis van Zyl • Viticulturists Erik Schouteden & Theunis van Zyl • 19 ha (cabs s/f, malbec, petit v, tannat, chard, chenin) • 2 300 cs own label + 40 000ℓ bulk • 35% red 65% white • PO Box 801 Huguenot 7645 • info@mooibly.com • www.mooibly.com • **T 021·868·2808/082·371·2299** *• F 021·868·2808*

By the time last season started all the 05 wines (the first from the farm's own cellar) were sold out, says farm manager Erik Schouteden with satisfaction. He hopes for a repeat performance for the next vintage, given that Mooi Bly has penetrated the Netherlands market. 'Last year we had the opportunity to introduce our wines to the Belgian crown prince,' says Erik S of a royal visit to SA. 'As we are originally a Belgian family it was quite an achievement… and publicity, of course!'

> **Chardonnay** ☺ ★★★ 06 creamy, pleasantly weighty from well judged 13.5% alc & 4 mths on lees; fruity core pierced by zesty acidity.

Cabernet Sauvignon [new] ★★☆ 05 a gracious Old World maiden; dry tealeaf character, gentle black fruit & tight savoury tannins. Yr in oak, some new, 15% unwooded. **Chenin Blanc** ★★ 06 crisp & refreshing, with bone-dry finish (1.6g/ℓ sugar); lots of dried peach, pear & a slice of pineapple. — *CT*

Mooiplaas Estate

Stellenbosch • Est 1963 • 1stB 1995 • Tasting & sales Mon-Fri 9-4 Sat & pub hols 10-2 • Closed Easter Fri-Mon, Dec 25/26 & Jan 1 • Fee R10 refundable with purchase • BYO picnic • Conservation area • Owner Mooiplaas Trust • Winemaker Louis Roos (1983) • Viticulturist Tielman Roos (1980) • ±120 ha • 750 tons 8 000 cs own label 57% red 43% white • PO Box 104 Koelenhof 7605 • info@mooiplaas.co.za • www.mooiplaas.co.za • **T 021·903·6273** *• F 021·903·3474*

A 2006 celebratory vertical tasting of the Roos brothers' Cabernet marked a decade of own-bottling here, and showcased the quality and consistency of their mature (1970/80s) Bottelary hillside vineyards. New in the portfolio is a limited-release flagship red, featuring top-performing cab franc. A 50ha area of rare renosterveld has been declared a nature reserve and is now accessible to visitors through a 5km hiking trail. Mooiplaas is also the first member of the Biodiversity & Wine Initiative.

★★★★ **Cabernet Sauvignon** Always released after a few yrs — a boon for those tired of youthful flavours. All-cab **02** departs from pvs additions of other varieties (**01** dashes merlot, shiraz). Beautifully proportioned, rich with cassis, spice & oak vanilla; svelte tannins, concentrated. Will reward ±10 yrs keeping. 21 mths oak, 75% Fr, 30% new.

★★★★ **Pinotage** ✓ Approachability a hallmark here. **03** delicious melange heavily spiced dark fruits & banana, agile tannins. Takes in 15% oaked cab (01 vintage) to add complexity, structure; otherwise unoaked. Shd improve 3-5 yrs. Slightly less charming **02** (★★★★) reflected difficult vintage.

★★★★ **'Blend'** new **03** unnamed at press time, led by cab f, with cab, merlot & shiraz (35/6/4); a selection of the best barrels (9, as it happened) from entire estate production. Fruit-rich & full yet gracefully balanced, lithe. 2 yrs Fr barriques. 300 cs.

Merlot ★★★☆ **03** similar to pvs, incl addition of 10% cab: touch severe in youth with ample tobacco, choc-plum notes, big dry tannins. 22 mths oak, 20% new. **Shiraz** ★★★★ **03** revels in well judged, supportive oak (22 mths seasoned Fr). More elegant than pvs, but still resplendently fruited with cherries, red berries & anise. **Chenin Blanc** new ★★★☆ ✓ From 30 yr old bushvines (+ dash semillon). **05**'s tropical fruit backed by creamy lees character. Impressive mouthfeel & lingering melon/tangerine flavours. 25% botrytised grapes add weight, complexity. **Sauvignon Blanc** ★★★☆ **05** sample tasted last ed, promised usual freshness, satisfying sharp green elements. —*DH*

Mooiuitsig Wine Cellars

Robertson ▪ Est 1947 ▪ Sales Mon-Thu 8-5 Fri 8-2 ▪ Tours by appt ▪ Stay-overs at De Rust Lodge (info@outdoorarena.co.za; T 023·616·2444) ▪ Owners Jonker & Claassen families ▪ Winemaker Christiaan van Tonder, with Nico van der Westhuizen (Dec 2002/Feb 2003) ▪ Viticulturist Casper Matthee ▪ 2 500 tons ▪ PO Box 15 Bonnievale 6730 ▪ info@mooiuitsig.co.za ▪ www.mooiuitsig.co.za ▪ T 023·616·2143 ▪ F 023·616·2675

A new warehouse in Port Elizabeth improved distribution last year for this extensive family owned drinks company. Also good for business was the appointment of experienced new MD, Paul de Villiers, who comes from a banking background. The 2006 harvest was smaller due to hail damage but no complaints about quality. There's a new Sauvignon, bottled under the Rusthof range, and last but not least: a toast to 'master blender' Oom Boet Jonker who turned 80 last year and still shows no sign of retiring!

African Wine Adventure range

Red ★★★ Light, dusty-dry equal blend cab/merlot, with treacle-like hints. **Chardonnay** new ★★★ Replaces pvs ed's 'White'. Quaffably light, dry & fruity; pleasant peachy tone & vanilla softness from Fr oak chip fermentation. WO W Cape. Both **NV**.

Mooiuitzicht range

Overberger ★★ Charmingly subtitled 'Opwindende Witwyn' ('Exciting White Wine'); last tasted was **05**, with lively acidity to offset the 9g/ℓ sugar. No newer released tasted for following carbonated sparklings from sauvignon: **Vin Brut** ★ Light bodied & bone-dry. **Vin Doux** ★★ Spritzy rather than fizzy, tropical flavours & gentle sweetness. Following fortified desserts all **NV**, fortified to ±17.5% alc. **Marsala** ★ Similar blend & analysis to following wine but with cherry tone, seems simpler & more spirituous. **Nagmaalwyn** (Sacramental Wine) ★★ Blend of 4 fortified red/white muscadels & jerepikos; almost cloyingly sweet, redeemed by spirited fortification. **Sweet Hanepoot** ★★ Sunshine-yellow dessert with grapey/floral varietal loveliness, sweet flavours, tangy dried apricot conclusion. **Old Tawny Port** ★★ 5 yrs Fr oak, traditional SA style low alc; latest bottling shows drying pruny/malty fruit; coming off the boil – drink up. **Bonwin Ruby Dessert Wine** ★ Similar to Marsala.

Oude Rust range

Certified desserts, fortified to 17.5% alc. **Red Muscadel** ★★ Unlike sprightly pvs, **04** mature tealeaf character & cranberry twist; tiring somewhat – enjoy soon. **Sweet Hanepoot** ★★★ Raises bar on pvs; **05** rich & warm gooseberry preserve aromas, matching hearty flavours yet a silk texture, gently ruffled by spirit. **White Muscadel** ★★★ Early-drinking style; lovely floral/apricot scents, **06** lusciously sweet & full bodied yet twinkle-toed thanks to deft fortification.

Rusthof range

These cork-closed wines **NV** unless mentioned. **Oulap Se Rooi** ★★ Quirkily packaged, lightly oaked equal blend cab, merlot, pinotage; styled for traditional potjiekos partnering. Latest touch less convivial, more rustic, savoury. Also as **Dry Red** in more conventional attire. **Rosé** ★ Light, uncomplicated pink from pinotage; slight cherry tone, not overly sweet. **Sauvignon Blanc** new ★★ Light, crisp & just-dry quick-quaff, **06** with hints of tropical fruit & gooseberry. **Potjie Effe Droog** ★★ Light bodied thirst-quencher from sauvignon, chardonnay, & chenin; fresh, clean dryish finish. 500ml screwtop. No new versions of following tasted: **Premier Grand Cru** ★★★ Light, flinty thirst-quencher from chardonnay, sauvignon, chenin, with brisk racy finish. **Blanc de Blanc** ★★ Slightly sweeter version of PGC. **Late Harvest** ★★ Light semi-sweet with subtle caramel tone, varieties as for BdB. All ranges from mainly from own, Breede Rvr Vlly vyds.
— JN/DH/MM

■ *Moonlight Organics* see Stellar Winery

Môreson

Franschhoek • Est 1986 • 1stB 1994 • Tasting & sales daily 11-5 • Fee R10 • Closed Dec 25 • Tours by appt • Bread & Wine Restaurant, farm grocer & other amenities (see Eat-out section) • Owner Richard Friedman • Winemaker Jacques Wentzel (2003) • General manager/viticulturist Anton Beukes (1994) • 18 ha (chard, chenin, sauvignon) • 300 tons 18 000 cs 40% red 55% white 1% rosé 4% MCC • Export brands: Pinecrest & MorningSide • ISO 14000 & Eurogap certified • PO Box 114 Franschhoek 7690 • sales@moreson.co.za • www.moreson.co.za • T 021·876·3055 • F 021·876·2348

Last year the Friedmans celebrated 20 years at Môreson — once part of La Motte, the farm was named 'Morning Sun' because of the beauty of the rays which wake the vineyards from their nightly slumber. The short 2006 harvest — smaller, due to the dry conditions — delivered healthy, aromatic and densely flavoured grapes which promise wines that age well. Always worth visiting, not least for their (weather permitting) alfresco lunches, Môreson's new Farm Grocer adds to the allure.

★★★★ **Magia** Gorgeous bdx-style red; **03** sleek, classic, manicured; vivid cedar/tealeaf bouquet; already seamless & balanced, gd prospects. With infusion Paarl fruit to pvs's Sbosch-only; cabs s/f, merlot (60/16/24), 14-18 mths oak, new for cab. Wine named by unidentified Bulgarian at international wine show, who declared the as yet unlabeled **98** 'magia!' (magical).

★★★★ **Pinotage** Suave & supple **03** achieved ABSA Top Ten, SAA listing. By contrast, **05** (★★★) burly & unsophisticated; meaty, tannin-laced dark plum fruit, distinct radiance from active 14.7% alc. Yr Fr oak, Sbosch vyds. **04** VDG sold out before we could taste.

★★★★ **Premium Chardonnay** Chard du Monde gold for **04**, which maintained quicker pace set by pvs vintage. **05** equally generous dimensions (14.2% alc), flavours, yet also elegant; lovely white peach fragrance, nutty butterscotch creaminess, more (but well judged) new oak (60%) than pvs. Fruit from La Motte area.

Cabernet Sauvignon These need yr/2 from release to settle, show their worth. **04** follows style with sweet-ripe, almost thick cab fruit lurking expectantly. Paarl vines, Fr oak, various coopers. Currently ★★★★, with potential. **Cabernet Franc** new ★★★ Team 'keeping winemaking interesting' by bottling this as single variety; **04** bold & ripe (14.5% alc) yet soft & slippery; raisined touch says 'drink early'. Paarl vyd, 24 mths 2nd & 3rd fill oak. **Merlot** ★★★★ **03** enthusiastically oaked, as pvs, also needs bit of time for wood (45% new F, 22 mths) to harmonise. Gd structure & ripeness, lovely cassis tones. **Chenin Blanc** ★★★★ Off vines old enough to remember being tended with horse-drawn plough; **06** fresh & floral, fragrant ripe melon/pear background note. Light & satisfying. **Sauvignon Blanc** ★★★ Recent earlier-picked, lighter textured releases not quite up to heights of pvs, though **06** well crafted, varietally true, attractively fresh & direct. Latest vintages of above mostly tasted as samples. Following pair of MCCs **NV**: **Blanc de Blancs** ★★★ Brut sparkling from chardonnay (90%), chenin. Latest reverts to riper 'New World' styling of earlier releases; fruity, generously fattened with lees, softly dry. **Cuvée Cape** ★★★★

Versatile standalone celebrator & food friend. Latest version something of a (pleasant) contradiction: 'brut' in analysis (6.5g/ℓ RS) yet sweetish on taste; unclassic varieties (pinotage & chenin 75/25) yet 'authentic' in character, convincing yeasty richness. Above WO Fhoek unless noted.

Pinehurst range

Cabernet Sauvignon ★★★ 04 robust, firm, quite a mouthful of ripe brambly fruit (& alc — 14.3%) but tasty, unaggressive; seasoned oak. **Merlot-Cabernet Sauvignon ★★★☆ ✓** Bigger merlot presence this yr (66%); **04** again attractively plump, rounded, fruity, comfortable tannins & protracted finish. 6 mths older wood. Paarl/Fhoek fruit. *Wine* value pick. **Pinotage ★★★☆** Sociable **05** (sample) a notch up; deliciously juicy & flavourful, balanced fruity tannins gently rounded in old oak, succulent choc/black cherry flavours. **Rosé Dry ★★** Easy summer quaffer. Preview **06** from pinotage, as usual; lovely coral-pink glints; fullish, juicy-dry pomegranate flavours. **Chardonnay** Unwooded. **06** preview too unformed to rate. **05 (★★★)** was lively, rounded, fruity & very soft. **Chenin Blanc ★★★☆ 06** invitingly fresh & aromatic, papaya & lemon hints, smooth, rounded unlingering flavours. **Sauvignon Blanc ★★** Perfectly pleasant **06** like pvs, doesn't shout the variety but shows balanced light bodied vinosity. This range WO Coastal unless noted. — *IvH*

Morewag

*Stellenbosch ▪ Est 1995 ▪ 1stB 2002 ▪ Closed to public ▪ Owners Michael & Ulrike Merkel ▪ Farm manager Charl Buys ▪ PO Box 290 Klapmuts 7625 ▪ morewag@mweb.co.za ▪ **T/F** 021·875·5626*

Lavender-and-grape farmers Ulrike and Michael Merkel leave the winemaking to Elsenburg vini/viti students: 'Our first wine, the Pinotage 02, was such a success that we've decided to continue this tradition ever since,' they say. The Merkels, after a programme of replanting, now have 30ha under vines, with 5ha of lavender on their adjacent property.

Pinotage ★★★ Sinewy, spicy & savoury **03** souped up by fresh acidity & sweet/sour fruit; unwooded. Last ed noted as drinking well (& for another 2-3 yrs) particularly with meaty dishes, where dried herbs/carpaccio notes should add interest. — *CR*

Morgenhof Estate

*Stellenbosch ▪ Est 1692 ▪ 1stB 1984 ▪ Tasting & sales Nov-Apr: Mon-Fri 9-5.30 Sat/Sun 10-5; May-Oct: Mon-Fri 9-4.30 Sat/Sun 10-3 ▪ Fee R10 ▪ Closed Easter Fri, Dec 25 & Jan 1 ▪ Light lunches/coffees & other amenities (see Eat-out section) ▪ Tour groups ▪ Owner Anne Cointreau ▪ Winemaker Jacques Cilliers (Dec 2004) ▪ Viticulturist Pieter Haasbroek (1998) ▪ 75 ha (cabs s/f, merlot, pinotage, touriga, chard, chenin, sauvignon) ▪ 30 000 cs 60% red 40% white ▪ PO Box 365 Stellenbosch 7599 ▪ info@morgenhof.com ▪ www.morgenhof.com ▪ **T** 021·889·5510 ▪ F 021·889·5266*

Morgenhof boasts an illustrious history dating back to 1692, but new heights were reached last year. First UK wine expert Steven Spurrier named the 01 Première Sélection as his best New World red wine; then owner Anne Cointreau was awarded the Chevalier de la Legion d'Honneur, France's highest civilian honour, for promoting French wine culture and, through Clearwater, her Relais & Châteux lodges in the Waterberg, 'l'art de vivre' in SA. A taste of the latter can also be had at Morgenhof's annual art exhibition; the wine awaits you all year round.

★★★★☆ Première Sélection Classically styled **01** from cab, merlot, cab f, malbec (60/25/9/ 6), concentrated, refined dark fruit with ripe sweetness, firm tannins but balanced, lengthy dry finish. 18 mths oak, 60% new. Like next two, not retasted.

★★★★☆ Cabernet Sauvignon Reserve Fine, deep, refined **01**. Lovely berry fruit, cool herbal touches. Magisterial, with an almost austere power. 18 mths new Fr oak.

★★★★☆ Merlot Reserve 00 (★★★★) had big tannin structure, **01** more seductive (but classy & serious), helped by less dominating oak (60% new Fr). Ripe, supple tannin integrating with warm, bright fruit, savoury acid.

★★★★ Merlot Last tasted was **01**. Now smoked beef, biltong, mint whiffs on **04 (★★★★)**, savoury theme continuing on palate, where fleshy, pleasurable side of merlot rules:

softish tannins, but some grip on finish, & very dry. 15% cab added for 'something extra', says Jacques C. 16 mths Fr oak, 30% new.

★★★★ **Chardonnay 05** will be last — one vyd uprooted, the other for Brut only. Pleasing yellow peach aromas, palate substantial & fleshy, but some elegance, slight sweetness on finish. Rich, creamy butterscotch notes from lees. 14.5% alc. 7 mths Fr oak, 20% new.

★★★★ **Chenin Blanc** From 30+ yr old vines, always impressive, barrel fermented/9 mths older oak. **05** plump & creamy, with variety's signature clean acidity for balance & excitement. Quality of fruit shows in lengthy finish, with the subtle spice often found in gd Cape chenin.

★★★★ **Brut Reserve 03** has depth & length. Tasted while still on lees, where it rests for 2 yrs before final dosage to balance. Shows fine creamy texture, crisp & dry with brisk bubble. Base wine fermented/9 mths used oak. Chard/pinot (60/40).

Cabernet Sauvignon ★★★★ 03 similar appealing qualities to pvs: cool cedar whiffs, ripely concentrated fruit with uplifting freshness, savoury appeal, fine dry finish. **Sauvignon Blanc ★★★** Juicy fruit revved up by racy acidity on **06**, more tropical than classic; bone-dry. None of following retasted this yr. **Noble Late Harvest ★★★★ 02** not oversweet at 105g/ℓ with balancing acidity, dry finish. Fermented/6 mths in oak. **Natural Sweet ★★★** Maiden barrel fermented **NV** had 90g/ℓ sugar, soft acidity, subtle oak on nose/palate. Lightish 12.6% alc. NE. **Cape LBV ★★★★** Very drinkable, flavourful port-style **01** from tinta, touriga, less sweet & rich than many; good acidity for lift; dry savoury finish. Touch more alc (this 17.6%) needed to complete modernisation of style. **Cape Vintage ★★★★** Last version of this port-style fortified was **00**, tinta/touriga in drier Portuguese mode. Above WO Smnsberg-Sbosch. **Pinotage** discontinued.

Fantail range

Pinotage ★★☆ Hearty, beefy **05** seems even riper than 13.5% alc suggests; some sweet red-berried fruitiness & soft, easy tannns, for early drinking. 10 mths oak. **Merlot ★★★** None since some smooth & supple **02**. **Vineyards Red ★★★ 04** plump & pleasing merlot-led all-sorts red, approachable & easy with some underlying seriousness; gd dry finish with brush of tannin. Up to 18 mths oak, some new. WO W Cape (others all Sbosch). **Rosé ★★★ 05** sweet plum & red cherry aromas/flavours, very dry, moderate 12.8 % alc. **Vineyards White ★★★ 06** blends chenin, sauvignon, chardonnay (44/42/14) for gentle peach & melon notes; rounded, juicy, with gd lingering fruity finish. — IvH

Morgenster Estate

Stellenbosch (see Helderberg map) ▪ *Est 1993* ▪ *1stB 1998* ▪ *Tasting & sales Mon-Fri 10-5 Weekends & pub hols 10-4* ▪ *Fee R10; additional R10 for estate grown olive oil & olive products* ▪ *Closed Good Fri & Dec 25* ▪ *Tours by appt* ▪ *Owner Giulio Bertrand* ▪ *Winemaker Marius Lategan, with Cornea Cilliers (Aug 1999, Jan 2004), advised by Pierre Lurton* ▪ *Vineyard/orchard manager Gerhard Bruwer, advised by Francois Viljoen* ▪ *40 ha (cabs s/f, merlot, petit v)* ▪ *200 tons 100% red* ▪ *PO Box 1616 Somerset West 7129* ▪ *wine@morgenster.co.za* ▪ *www. morgenster.co.za* ▪ **T 021·852·1738** ▪ F 021·852·0835

Giulio Bertrand, Italian modern architect of this historic property on the flanks of Schapenberg Hill, winemaker Marius Lategan and Bordeaux *conseillant* Pierre Lurton are achieving their vision of producing a range of world-class reds with their third offering, The Summer House. The name is an allusion to the summer retreat developed by the farm's original owner, 18th-century Cape governor Willem Adriaan van der Stel. Its elevation afforded first sight of provision-starved ships entering both False and Table Bays, giving the owner a trading advantage. Now it's giving Morgenster an edge. The same applies to the estate's internationally awarded extra-virgin olive oil, available for tasting at the wine cellar until a new 'olive oil educational centre' is completed.

★★★★★ **Morgenster** Classy & delicious Old-World-style flagship. A 'vyd' (as distinct from 'barrel') selection. Pvs **01** was merlot driven (51%); **03** dominated by cabs (sauv & franc — 70%). Last ed showed beguiling bouquet of herbs, cassis & eucalyptus with spice;

persistent flavours. Tannins, fruit, alc (14.3%) already well aligned yet deserving time to integrate fully & grow. 13 mths Fr oak, 90% new.

★★★★★ **Lourens River Valley** This more plentiful (& wallet friendly) '2nd' blend usually paces the flagship, though **03** (★★★★) just a tad less weighty, persistent than pvs. Cranberry, scrub & mushroom accents; fresh, leafy tannins; structure to improve good few yrs. 13 mths Fr oak. More merlot (68%), less cab s/f than **02**.

The Summer House ★★★★ ('Third Wine' last ed.) Fruit 'declassified' from 'Morgenster' above, vinified for suppleness, early drinking. Preview **04** mainly merlot (64%) with cab s/f, petit v & introducing sangiovese & nebbiolo; mix 1st/2nd/3rd fill Fr oak. Serious yet moreish. — *CvZ*

- ■ **Morkel** see Bellevue
- ■ **MorningSide** see Môreson

Morton Wines   ♀ new

*Stellenbosch ▪ Est 2003 ▪ Tasting & sales by appt ▪ Owners Aidan & Mandy Morton ▪ Viticulturist Aidan Morton ▪ Winemaker Miles Mossop ▪ 10 tons 700 cs 100% red ▪ PO Box 12242 Stellenbosch 7613 ▪ aidan@tokara.com ▪ www.mortonwines.co.za ▪ **T 082·564·2255** ▪ F 021·808·5971*

When Tokara viticulturist Aidan Morton (who also consults at neighbouring Thelema) and winemaker Miles Mossop were offered the opportunity to make their own labels, Morton's eyes naturally turned to the few small shiraz vineyards on some of the nearby properties he had helped develop. From what they believe are 'grapes from some of the best-managed sites in the country', they make some 700 cases, the second vintage of which Morton and wife Mandy are confident will sell as swiftly as the 03.

Shiraz ★★★★ High-tech harvesting (infrared scans determined picking time) followed by traditional vinification for **04**. Laid-back, fleshy; oaked to emphasise coffee/black pepper whiffs; some red fruit highlights on palate. Satisfying now & for a few yrs. Mainly Fr wood, 20% new, 18 mths. Unfiltered. — *AL*

Mostertsdrift Noble Wines   ♂♀🍶🦨

*Stellenbosch ▪ Est/1stB 2001 ▪ Visits & meals by appt ▪ Owners Anna-Mareè Mostert-Uys & André Mostert ▪ Winemaker Anna-Mareè Mostert-Uys (Jan 2001) ▪ Viticulturist Nico Mostert (Jan 2001) ▪ 7.5 ha (merlot, pinot, cab, chard, hanepoot) ▪ 29 tons 600-800 cs 70% red 30% white ▪ PO Box 2061 Dennesig Stellenbosch 7601 ▪ mostertsdrift@telkomsa.net ▪ **T 021·889·5344** ▪ F 021·887·1780*

Though the Mostert family maintain that the mid-harvest power outages aged them all, especially when it came to white-wine fermentation, the quality of the reds did much to keep them young. Their first bottle-fermented sparkling (only 200 bottles) was made with Belgian immigré Jean-Philippe Colmant at his new winery in Franschhoek.

Following 3 wines still selling, not retasted. **Cabernet Sauvignon** ★★ Bountiful red/black berry fruit, but initially v firm tannins on **04**; sensible 13% alc; 14 mths old oak/10 mths with new staves. **AnéRouge** ★★★ Usually a blend cinsaut/cab, though **04** incl splash merlot. Friendly strawberry/ plum flavours, smoky hint, supple & savoury. Sympathetically oaked, 14 mths seasoned barrels, merlot unwooded. **Sauvignon Blanc** ★★ **05** somewhat neutral in the aroma/flavour departments but zesty & refreshing. **Chardonnay** ★★★★ ✓ Unwooded but not lacking character, appeal; **06** (sample) generous tropical fruit flavours, hint lime; quite full, rich, leesy. **Chenin Blanc** ★ Honeyed **03**, noted as tired last ed. **Blanc de Blanc** ★★ **04**, 100% sauvignon from Fhoek, sold out, no newer release. — *CT/DH*

Mountain Oaks Winery   ♂♀🦨🏠🔑

Slanghoek (see Worcester/Breedekloof map) ▪ Est/1stB 2003 ▪ Visits Mon-Fri 10-4 Sat/Sun 10-2 ▪ Closed public hols ▪ Picnics by arrangement ▪ Guest cottage ▪ Organic farm produce ▪ Owners Stevens family ▪ Winemaker Christine Stevens (Jun 2003), advised by Ross Gower ▪ Viticulturists Christine & Mark Stevens ▪ 20 ha (cabs s/f, mourvèdre, pinotage, shiraz, chard, chenin, viognier) · 40-50 tons 2 000 cs 30% red 70% white · PO Box 68 Rawsonville 6845 · eikenbosch@iafrica.com · **T** 023·344·3107 · F 023·344·3688

The oaks which give this delightful property its name were planted in the late 1700s. Though the Stevens' have been there since 1999, the massive clean-up they deemed necessary delayed their first vintage until 2003. Ross Gower's expertise is called on less often as Christine's winemaking experience and confidence grows. She needs no help with the organically nurtured vines — her green fingers previously grew herbs for the restaurant trade. Ancient nut trees provide almonds which accompany tastings — a perfect match, say she & husband Mark, for their organic Chardonnay.

Pinotage Preview of characterful, deeply coloured **05** (potential ★★★★); tobacco & dark fruit; dense, ripe blackberry core supported by fine acidity & firm, seamless tannins. 16 mths older oak. **04** (★★★) similar but not as much presence. **Chardonnay** Hedonistic **05** (★★★★) limpid, weighty gold swirl in glass; butterscotch & almond precede rounded mouthful of rich melon & citrus fruit; creamy, luscious persistence & perfect balance/melding. Yr oaked. Enjoy now or keep few yrs; quantum leap up from **04** (★★★), with dominant oak. **Chenin Blanc Barrel Reserve** Ex-50 yr old vines; **05** (★★★★) limpid straw hue; perceptible oak mingles with lanolin & marzipan; fruit in confident balance with acid & oak; long, richly textured finish. **04** (★★★) closed when tasted, but with good length & texture. 9 mths 400ℓ wood. **Chenin Blanc** ★★★☆ **05** pear-drop aromas & lovely ripe fruit flavours balanced by ample acidity; moderate 13% alc contributes to elegance & perfect lunchtime wine. **Le Jardin** ★★☆ Tribute to the farm gardens. 60/40 unwooded chenin/oaked chard **05** offers simple but rich fruit flavours, pithy grapefruit core with oak backdrop. All organically grown, WO Slanghoek. — *IM*

Mountain Range

*Closed to public · Owners Belinda Traverso, Paul Finlayson & Paul de Waal · 1 000 cs · 67 Belmont Ave Oranjezicht 8001 · shelley@mountainrange.co.za · www.mountainrange.co.za · **T** 021·552·9251/073·225·6891 · F 021·555·4280*

Many wineries claim to market 'icon wines'; this merchant house sells its wines *in* an icon. Its Table Mountain-shaped bottles, filled with wines from a reputable Stellenbosch estate, fly off the shelves — and often fly home with tourists too. The distinctive bottles, available in miniature 50ml size as well, also hold local sherry, brandy and extra-virgin olive oil.

Table Red ★★★ Fruity, fun but not frivolous **03**, delicious berry aromas/flavours from cab, merlot, shiraz (45/35/20); vanilla/cedar notes from older oak, mix Am/Fr. **Table White** ★★ Zippy chardonnay, sauvignon, chenin blend; **04** herby bouquet & lime/orange flavour. Neither wine retasted this ed. — *CvZ*

Mountain Ridge Wines

*Wolseley (see Worcester map) · Est 1949 · 1stB 1976 · Tasting & sales Mon-Fri 8-5 Sat 10-1 · Closed Easter Fri-Sun, Dec 25/26, Jan 1 · Tours by appt · Tour groups · BYO picnic · Conference facilities · Owners 30 members · Winemaker Francois Agenbag (2002) · 500 ha (cab, chard, chenin, colombard) · 8 000 tons 5 000 cs own label 40% red 60% white · PO Box 108 Wolseley 6830 · sales@mountainridge.co.za · www.mountainridge.co.za · **T** 023·231·1070/80 · F 023·231·1102*

Previously 'Romansrivier Cellar', this winery has adopted its better-known wine brand name for both marketing and identity reasons, explains Francois Agenbag. He hopes more consumers will identify with the new moniker and help boost exports, which account for about 40% of production. The winemaker is excited about the new Dimension red blend — not meant for easy quaffing, he says. The 06 wines are all showing excellent potential, especially the Shiraz, he believes.

Cabernet Sauvignon Reserve ★★★ **04** revisited as finished wine shows easy drinkability with generous fruit & ripe tannins; shd smooth out further over next yr/2. ±13 mths new Fr/Am oak, as for... **Shiraz Reserve** ★★★☆ **04**, also retasted, spicy & savoury, smoked ham nuances; drink now with hearty stews or hold few yrs hoping big tannins will soften. Both above listed last ed without 'Rsv' tag, 14.5% alc, WO Breede Rvr Vlly; others

W Cape. **Pinotage** ★★★ **04** delightfully wild & scrubby with powerful tannins backing rampant berry fruit. *Wine* 'Best Value' ratings for this & above Shiraz. **Malbec-Pinotage** ★★ **04** unwooded campfire quaffer, riper & less fresh than pvs, with raisin & brazil nut character. **Chenin Blanc** new ★ Lightly wooded & medium bodied **06**, pretty light on aromas too. **Sauvignon Blanc** ★★ Crisp patio sipper; **06** light 11.8% alc, with soft, sweetish flick to tail (4g/ℓ sugar). **Chenin Blanc-Colombard** new ★★ **06** uncomplicated grassy/tropical toned summer quaffer, not quite dry. **Natural Sweet Rosé** new ★ NV's delectable strawberry notes shd win it some admirers. Discontinued: **Chardonnay Wooded**, **Chardonnay Unwooded, Colombard-Chardonnay**. — *CT*

Mountain River Wines

Paarl ▪ Est 1993 ▪ 1stB 1998 ▪ Closed to public ▪ Owner De Villiers Brits ▪ Winemaker De Villiers Brits with consultants ▪ 38 700 cs 60% red 40% white ▪ 146 Main Road Paarl 7646 ▪ dev@ mountainriverwines.co.za or mattie@mountainriverwines.co.za ▪ www.mountainriverwines. co.za ▪ T 021·872·3256/7 ▪ F 021·872·3255

Owner De Villiers Brits regards this as 'the make or break year for companies marketing wine internationally'. Preparing to do battle, the quality on all ranges has been upped and the labels revamped, already resulting in doubled exports of bottled wines and several international awards. Their focus remains on the establishment of brands which 'will build awareness and achieve staying power for the long haul'. To this end they work closely with selected cellars.

Pinotage-Cabernet Sauvignon new ★★ Uncomplicated quaffing style, **05** soft red fruit, some Aussie-style eucalyptus & pine scents. Following reds & Chard not retasted. **Cabernet Sauvignon-Merlot** ★★★★ Mellow cherry & strawberry notes precede sweet spice & slight savoury note on **01**, with light tannins. **Merlot** ★★ **02** classic flavours of mocha & plum, atypically powerful tannins last yr needed time to mesh with fruity core. **Pinotage-Shiraz** ★★★ Ripe, flavoursome **03** well rounded for everyday drinking. 70% new oak, Fr/Am. **Chardonnay** ★★★ Gently wooded **03** should be enjoyed soon. 6 mths 2nd fill oak, fruit ex-Bonnievale. **Estuary Sauvignon Blanc** ★★★★ Delicious **05** step up in quality; shows intensity than pvs, cool nettle & riper gooseberry nuances, delicate acid balance & crisp farewell.

Maankloof range

Shiraz ★★ Bold eucalyptus & spicy notes on **04**, some savoury extras but less complexity, concentration than pvs. **Chardonnay** new ★ **04** slight oxidative character heralds onset of maturity, invites drinking soon. No new vintages tasted for the following: **Cabernet Sauvignon** ★★★ **04** restrained but tasty, ripe fruit deftly supported by firm but not harsh tannins. **Pinotage** ★★★ Food-friendly **04** shows spicy fruit on bed of firm but ripe tannins. For early drinking, as are all these. **Rosé** ★★ **05**'s fresh berry flavours, savoury dry finish make for soft, rounded enjoyment. **Chenin Blanc** ★★★ Ripe, tropical toned, balanced **04**, light & pretty but not for keeping. **Sauvignon Blanc 04** untasted.

Rijckbosch range   new

Pinotage ★★ **05** a blend of Hldrberg & Olfnts Rvr grapes; green banana character with tight tannins, sweetish tail wag in (±5g/ℓ sugar). **Shiraz** ★★ **04** smooth & fruity quaffer marked by ultra-ripe berry nose with porty notes. **Pinotage Rosé** ★★ **06** with variety's beetroot aromas, unconcentrated plum flavours with firm acidity. **Chenin Blanc** ★★ Harmonious **06** notes of peach & savoury, crisp acidity a good match for seafood. **05** Concours Mondial gold.

Zaràfa range

Pinotage ★★ Soft & fruity **05** shows banana whiffs, dollop sugar designed to smooth slightly abrasive tannins. **Sauvignon Blanc** ★★ **06** cheerful easy-drinker with straw & grass flavours tickled by zesty acidity. All ranges WO W Cape unless noted. — *CT*

■ **Mountainside** see Fairseat Cellars, Ruitersvlei
■ **Mount Claire** see Cordoba

Mount Rozier Estate

Stellenbosch (see Helderberg map) • *Est/1stB 1997* • *Tasting, sales & tours by appt* • *Closed pub hols* • *Conservancy area* • *Owner Atlantic Wine Agencies, Inc* • *Winemaker Jacques Fourie (Sep 2001)* • *20 ha (cab, merlot, shiraz, sauvignon, semillon)* • *±1 500 cs own label 40% red 60% white* • *PO Box 1241 Somerset West 7129* • *wines@mountrozier.co.za* • *www. mountrozier.co.za* • **T 021·858·1130** • **F** *021·858·1131*

'We thought we had a premium wine estate — it turned out to be a gold mine,' exclaims estate manager Lindie Smith, referring to recent successes at the IWSC and *Decanter* World Wine Awards, for the Cab in particular. Deliberately lower yields characterised harvest 2006 for the estate wines, and another tweak saw the release of their debut red blend, a shift from the single-variety wine strategy. They're also giving serious consideration to joining the industry's Wine & Biodiversity Initiative.

★★★★ **Cabernet Sauvignon** Bold & beautiful **04** gaining complexity/gravitas as anticipated when previewed last ed; tad showy (so golds at IWC, *Decanter* World Wine Awards unsurprising) yet shows some restraint, balance despite 15+% alc. Off estate's Cuvée Burr vyd; Fr oak, 16 mths, 20% new. This, following 04 reds reviewed afresh for this ed.

★★★★ **Shiraz** New-World profile continues with **04** (★★★★) blockbuster; now billows ripe youngberry & smoky veld fire; athletic tannins for keeping; hot impression from 15.8% alc only detraction. 16 mths Fr oak, 20% new. **03** heralded loss of elegance but offered a sumptuous feast.

Merlot ★★★★ **04** retasted; all-new oak (Fr, 16 mths) still bit too powerful for delicate fynbos-scented fruit; tannins fine but dry; hopefully time will bring more harmony. **Sauvignon Blanc** ★★★ Last tasted was fresh & lively **05**, intense tropical notes; poised, well composed fruity finish.

Rozier Bay range

Range under construction. Only one wine assessed: **Sauvignon Blanc** ★★ **06** soft, easy, modestly flavoured version, dry & light (12% alc). Screwtop. WO Wrcstr. This, range below, NE.

Rozier Reef range

Shiraz ☺ ★★★ **05** good honest quaffer; lots of olfactory interest (incl smoked beef, black cherry), delicious balanced flavours, moderate 13.5% alc. Fr oak, 11 mths.

Pinotage ★★ Culling of this wine reported last ed apparently premature: **05** alive, well & undeniably pinotage; sweet vanilla veneer (Fr staves, 6 mths), youthful tannic grip. This, above red, from Wllngtn fruit. **Shiraz-Pinotage** ★★ [new] **05** blend somewhat inchoate mid-2006: sweetly ripe fruit from shiraz unmelded with v firm dry tannins; shd harmonise with time. 5-6 mths Fr staves. Wellngtn grapes. No new releases for following pair: **Chardonnay** ★★★ Friendly food-styled **05**; tropical notes, smooth acidity. Moderate 13.4% alc. **Chenin Blanc** ★★ **05**, with lovely green apple & pear hints, weightier than pvs at 13. 5% alc. **Sauvignon Blanc** ★★★ Light-bodied **06** similar to R Bay version but perhaps tad riper, so more flavour, interest. **Chenin Blanc-Chardonnay** ★★★ **06** rounded, fruity easy drinker; compatible blend from Wllngtn vyds. Low 12.5% alc. **Merlot**, **Ruby Cabernet** & **Ruby Cabernet-Merlot** discontinued. — *IvH*

Mount Vernon Farm

Paarl • *Est/1stB 2003* • *Visits by appt* • *Closed Easter Fri/Sun, Dec 25/26 & Jan 1* • *BYO picnic* • *Walks* • *Mountain biking* • *Owners David & Debbie Hooper* • *Winemaker Debbie Hooper, with Anele Mangena* • *Viticulturist Philip du Toit* • *28 ha (cab, malbec, merlot, petit v, pinotage, shiraz, chard)* • *205 tons 7 000ℓ* • *laurna@threepeakswine.co.za* • *PO Box 348 Klapmuts 7625* • **T/F** *021·875·5073*

'Whew!' describes 2006 for owners David and Debbie Hooper. Winemaker Debbie had to deal with a difficult harvest, though 'we just had the heat to contend with because we have water on the farm', slow ripening of the fruit at first and then a rush at the finish, an African odyssey during the winter and the weddings of both their children. However, it's destined to go down as a good year if you're confident, like the Hoopers, of the quality of your grapes.

Three Peaks range

Cabernet Sauvignon new ★★★ Opulent aromas of cassis, nutmeg & vanilla belie relative austerity of **04**. Concludes with warming glow thanks to 15% alc. 16 mths Fr oak. Smnsberg-Paarl WO, as is… **Cantata** new ★★★ 3 bdx grapes plus shiraz & pinotage in harmonious performance, lending fairly plush black fruited tone to **04**; acidity revives, but oak's still slightly off-pitch mid-2006, needs yr/2 to attune. Am/Fr oak for 16 mths. **Rosé** ★★★ Name change from 'Pinotage Rosé' for improved **06**, reflecting 36% chenin infusion. 'Better mid-palate & finish,' opines Debbie H — we concur; gd summer alfresco wine, with low 12% alc. Sample tasted, ditto for … **Chenin Blanc** ★★★ **06** weightier than pvs (14% alc) but not inelegant. Engaging fynbos/lemon-geranium scents, pithy quince flavours, lengthy farewell with hint of nut. — *CvZ*

■ *Mudge Point* see Luddite

Mulderbosch Vineyards

Stellenbosch ▪ Est 1989 ▪ 1stB 1991 ▪ *Sales: Mon-Fri 8-5; tasting by appt only* ▪ *Closed on pub hols* ▪ Owner Hydro Holdings ▪ Cellarmaster Mike Dobrovic (1991) ▪ *Winemaker Nic van Aarde* (Sep 2005) ▪ *Vyd manager Lionel Adams* ▪ 23 ha (cabs s/f, malbec, merlot, petit v, chard, sauvignon) ▪ 500 tons 30 000 cs 30% red 70% white ▪ PO Box 548 Stellenbosch 7599 ▪ info@ mulderbosch.co.za ▪ www.mulderbosch.co.za ▪ **T 021·865·2488** ▪ F 021·865·2351

High points of a complex, challenging season: surprisingly good sauvignon from high-lying, unirrigated blocks; a chardonnay vintage to remember; mellifluous merlot, malbec and petit verdot. Cellarmaster Mike Dobrovic (scientist, philosopher, winelands guru) typically commends his staff, plus the annual melange of maverick cellar-hands he attracts for Mulderbosch's achievements. Vintage 2006 welcomed Californian chardonnay specialist Katie Cochrane and Stellenbosch University viticulture/oenology graduate Nic van Aarde, now winemaker here. The latter's eclectic training (tasting guide at London's Vinopolis; cellar-rat in St Emilion, Sonoma, Margaret River, Marlborough; stints at Anwilka, Vrede en Lust) tailor-makes him for the job. Part-of-furniture Lionel Adams now manages the vineyards, Steen op Hout goes by a modified name, and a Cabernet Rosé has been released locally. Future plans? A botrytised sauvignon à la Sauternes and a balsamic vinegar from raisined roobernet.

★★★★ **Faithful Hound** Bdx quartet cab, merlot, malbec, cab f well meshed with drop shiraz in pvsly tasted **03**. Soft, cedar-edged red-wine aromas; creamily textured with cab's structural, seamless grip. Gd potential to 2009. 18 mths Fr oak 50% new. Earlier vintages 90 pts *WS*. **04** unready.

★★★★ **Beta Centauri 02** of this occasional 'stellar' offering still available. Plush cabs f/s merger with 12% petit v. More modern than 'Hound'; last yr we noted vibrant tannin would benefit from ageing. Harmonious 18 mths new Fr oak.

★★★★ **Chardonnay Barrel Fermented** Since first **97**, one of few to achieve symmetry between fruit & 100% new oak. Evidenced by **05** (★★★★), attractively poised melange buttered toast, lime & tropical fruit, though youthfully bracing acidity divorced from creamy texture, needs time to marry (& maybe integrate noticeable sugar — 7.6 g/ℓ). Native yeast fermented, Fr barrels, 9 mths, partial malo. **04** *Wine* ★★★★.

★★★★ **Chardonnay** Only partially barrel fermented (in contrast with above); combines elegance, depth of flavour. **04** lively build, in harmony with well-layered pickled lime/toast fruit; clean, persistent. 55% in Fr oak, 30% new. Partial native yeast ferment. *WS* favourite: **02**, **01** both 92 pts. **05** unready.

★★★★ **Chenin Blanc** Pvsly 'Steen-op-Hout', still oak-brushed to flatter chenin's pretty floral/honey features. **05** exhibits typical coy charm; just a whisper of extra breadth from wood; conclusion sustained by balanced 7g/ℓ sugar. From venerable, unirrigated hilltop bushvines; 7% in new Fr & 2nd fill Am oak, 4 mths.

★★★★★ **Sauvignon Blanc 06** reliable as always; usual mineral/steely features shot with equally distinctive greengage/gooseberry enticements. Well synchronised weighty fruit, energetic build to mouthwatering finish. Regular 90+ pts *WS*.

Shiraz Modern style **03** (★★★★) pure-fruited, lively, supple, with gentle tannin extraction. **04** (★★★★) dark-hued, expressive smoky/soft black berries but fairly straightforward; enlivened with 12% petit v. 100% new Fr oak well absorbed. Stanford/home vyds. **Cabernet Sauvignon Rosé** new ★★★★ **05** engaging, food friendly addition to this in-vogue style. True pink appeal; refreshing, clean; cab's classic berries, savouriness plus gentle grip to contrast fruity 5g/ℓ sugar.—*AL*

■ *Muldersvlei* see Westbridge

Muratie Estate

Stellenbosch ▪ Est 1685 ▪ 1stB ca 1920 ▪ Tasting & sales Mon-Fri 9-5 Sat & Sun 10-4 ▪ Fee R15, waived on purchase ▪ Closed Easter Fri, Dec 25 & Jan 1 ▪ Picnic baskets by appt ▪ Tours by appt ▪ Guest house ▪ Art gallery ▪ Owner Melck Family ▪ Winemaker Francois Conradie (Dec 2005) ▪ Viti consultant Paul Wallace (1998) ▪ 42 ha (cabs, merlot, pinot, shiraz, chard, hanepoot, port varieties) ▪ 210 tons 8 000 cs own label 85% red 15% white ▪ PO Box 133 Koelenhof 7605 ▪ info@muratie.co.za or sales@muratie.co.za ▪ www.muratie.co.za ▪ **T 021·865·2330** ▪ *F 021·865·2790*

'We have always strived to make honest, sincere, terroir driven wines,' says Rijk Melck, head of this centuries-old family owned estate, and custodian of one of the most charming and atmospheric old-Cape tasting venues in the winelands. 'Old' and 'new' are recurring themes here: in the viticultural realm, a venerable (30 years) shiraz block has been officially recognised, giving rise to an upcoming single-vineyard bottling – their first. New – that word again – winemaker Francois Conradie (ex-Boschendal) contributes youthful energy, as does his assistant, Dirkie Williams, who completed the SKOP 3 cellar training course at Elsenburg.

★★★★☆ **Ansela van de Caab** Classically built, subtle merlot/cab blend, **04** up there with the best, less overtly powerful than many. Fragrant dark mulberry, cigar smoke, fine oak spice; a sultry dark charmer, shows burgeoning complexity. 16 mths Fr oak, 35% new. Riper at 14% alc than **03**, Winemakers Choice, *Wine* ★★★★.

★★★★ **Cabernet Sauvignon** Latest **04** somewhat atypical (for Muratie) wild brambleberry & mint bouquet, palate lighter textured & savoury, moderate 13.4% alc. Dark-berried, tangy with dry, fine-grained tannins persisting in finish. **03** (★★★★) less successful: austere, dry, brittle tannins. Alc still lighter at 12.7%. These yr Fr oak, 35% new. Cellar 4-6 yrs. Like all major reds here, made in mix open fermenters/s steel.

★★★★ **Shiraz** After approachable **03**, warm & welcoming **04** (★★★★★); tasted pre-bottling last yr, now offers gorgeous whiffs toasty oak, roast beef, mocha, followed by ripe black-cherry flavours, supported by supple tannins. Rhône suggestions, but New World generosity. 28 yr old vines provided some fruit. Oaking 35% new, 18% Am. Cellar 3-5 yrs. TWS 2005 gold.

★★★★ **Isabella** Fine, bunch-pressed chard. Firmly woven **06** (sample) with pattern of ripe citrus fruit & lots of stylish oak forming very fabric of wine (40% fermented/6 mths, 20% new). Lively & creamy; long resonating finish. **05** not tasted, **04** also sampled ex-barrel.

★★★★ **Cape Vintage** Last-tasted **02** LBV in style; **04** more classically correct Vintage styling, so less approachable now – but great for fireside sipping in few yrs: firmly dense, black-hearted fruit, fine tannins & lengthy finish; gd spirit core at 19% alc; 87g/ℓ sugar. From single block, planted 1975: tintas b/r/f, souzão. 2+ yrs old oak.

Merlot ★★★☆ **03** in established mould: lead pencil, ripe cassis intro; developing minerally depth – savoury rather than dark choc, fine-grained tannins, classy dry finish. Well oaked, 28% new Fr. **Pinot Noir** ★★★☆ SA's first pinot vines planted here over 75 yrs ago. **04** shy; tangy redcurrants, firm-ish wood tannins (yr Fr oak, some new), distinctive earthiness on finish. Needs time to develop in the glass. **03** *Wine* ★★★★. **Melck's Red** ★★★ Stylish quaffer **04** shiraz/merlot (60/40); tasted last ed ripe pruney fruit, some meaty richness, enough tannin for interest. **Amber Forever** ★★★ Fortified muscat d'A, popular for over 75 yrs. As Rijk M says: 'a fun wine'. **06** (sample) gets 5 mths in used Fr casks to tame wilder edges of muscat. Less sweet-tasting than pvs, more style, with gd lively acidity.

Cape Ruby ★★★ Ever-popular **NV** from traditional port varieties, matured yr+ oak. Dark prune ripeness, richer & weightier than classic Ruby – & not too sweet. All above Smnsberg-Sbosch WOs. — *IvH*

Mvemve Raats ⚲ new

Stellenbosch • Est/1stB 2004 • Visits by appt • Owners/winemakers/viticulturists Mzokhona Mvemve & Bruwer Raats • 5 tons • 150 cs 100% red • PO Box 2068 Dennesig 7601 • braats@ mweb.co.za • T/F 021·881·3078

'It's a fantastic opportunity to make wine with à friend,' says Bruwer Raats (Raats Family Wines) of his collaboration with Mzokhona Mvemve (Sagila winemaker and taster for this guide), who gained initial experience as Raats' deputy at Delaire. The resultant *cuvée* is called De Compostella ('The Compilation of Stars') and they set out to make each of the five components able to stand as varietal wines. They then tasted these blind and constructed the blend in descending percentages, from the wine which rated highest to that in 5th place.

De Compostella ★★★☆ **04** harmoniously composed of sufficient of each of the five main bdx varieties to ensure none dominates. Welcoming black fruit aromas continue with persistent flavours accompanied by showy tannins, subtle oak (18 mths Fr, half new), non-intrusive big 14.5% alc. — *MF*

■ *My Best Friend* see Zandvliet

Mystery Wine Corporation

Cape Town • 1stB 2002 • Owner Saul Gorin • 4 000 cs 40% red 50% white 10% rosé • PO Box 281 Sea Point 8060 • gorin@isoft.co.za • www.mysterywines.co.za • T 083·628·5160 • F 021·686·5404

To minimise the possibility of spoiled wines, Saul Gorin has switched to top-of-the-range agglomerate closures (smaller pieces of cork bound together by an adhesive), with which he's had great success. While he'd prefer convenient twist-off caps, perceived lesser quality and other issues prevent this for now. But, we venture, he's unlikely to consider changing his ever-popular Rubenesque wine labels…

Dry Red ☺ ★★★ Approachable **05** has friendly tannins, juicy fruit, oak-brushed aromas of toffee, coffee & spice. Merlot, cab & shiraz, wood-staved, with dollop roobernet. **Dry White** ☺ ★★★ Easy summer drinking **06**, chenin-led (50%) with hearty dash chard & some sauvignon; bright & breezy, fatness from chard, granadilla from sauvignon.

Sauvignon Blanc ★ Still-selling **05** lightish (12% alc), faintly floral, zesty & short. **Tickled Pink** ★★ Rosé from merlot, smidgen shiraz; **06** billows ruby grapefruit, lively & fresh. **Melon** Sold out. — *MM*

My Wyn ♂♀

Franschhoek • Est/1stB 2001 • Tasting & sales at cellar door or by appt (T 021·876·3603) • Fee R15 • Closed pub hols • Owner/winemaker Jacoline Haasbroek • 200 cs • 75% red 25% white • PO Box 112 Franschhoek 7690 • envision@wine.co.za • T 021·876·2518/083·302·5556 • F 021·876·2518

Jacoline Haasbroek's tastings are becoming something of a magnet for locals and foreigners keen on a *garagiste*-style experience. (The Afrikaans winery name translates as 'My Wine'.) Not only because there is the thrill of dipping into such limited quantities (±700 bottles or fewer of each variety) but by-appointment tastings are hosted personally by the winemaker, who says she enjoys this one-on-one appreciation as much as making the wine.

Cabernet Sauvignon ★★★ **02** blackcurrant notes, ripe rounded tannins, well disguised 15% alc. 24 mths aged. Not retasted. **Cabernet Franc** new ★★ Sinewy **04**, good herbaceous varietal expression, dry gripping tannins need time/decanting. 18 mths 2nd fill Fr oak. **Petit Verdot** new ★★☆ Big (15.7% alc) **05**, inviting ripe mulberry aromas & strong, tight tannins, crying for further bottle maturation. Yr Fr oak, half new. **Sy Shiraz** ★★★☆ 'His Shiraz' — 'he' being JH's husband Johan, farm manager of La Bri, where the grapes are sourced. Aussie-style fireworks on **04**: smoke & bluegum whiffs, huge but well extracted & balanced flavours & tannins. 15% alc. 22 mths Fr oak, 2nd fill. Unfiltered, as are all these. **Viognier** ★★★ Ingratiating, fruit driven **06**; briefly wooded, unlike pvs; peach/melon notes on soft, full palate (15% alc). Best enjoyed early. — *CT*

Nabygelegen Private Cellar

Wellington • Est 1712 • 1stB 2002 • Tasting & sales Mon-Fri 10-5 Sat 10-1 • Closed Easter Fri/ Sun, Apr 27, May 1, Dec 25 & Jan 1 • Tours anytime by appt • BYO picnic • Walks • Owner James McKenzie • Winemaker Charles Stassen (Jan 2003) • Viti consultant Johan Wiese (May 2001) • 20 ha (cab, merlot, petit v, tempranillo, chenin, sauvignon) • 5 000 cs 60% red 40% white • PO Box 302 Wellington 7854 • avalonwines@icon.co.za • www.nabygelegen. co.za • T 021-873-7534 / 082-829-1189 • F 021-873-7534

This historic wine farm, given a gradual, thorough overhaul since 2001, is going from strength to strength, says owner James McKenzie. Upgrading of the vineyards continues with 20ha now under vine, including some 70-year-old veterans. Exports are up and 'achieving sold-out status'. Having restored the original buttressed cellar with its old concrete tanks, McKenzie is renovating the 1750s stables to house a tasting room and bakery. And the tasting fee, visitors will be pleased to learn, has been waived.

★★★★ **1712** Pvs ed noted more elegance & excitement in **04** incarnation of this characterful merlot-led bdx blend, thanks to beefed up portions cab & petit v (now 33% & 10%). Big mouthfeel; loads of fruit & serious structure supported by yr Fr oak. Unfiltered.

★★★★ **Scaramanga** ✓ After Francisco S, the Man with the Golden Gun, suave, sophisticated million-dollar-a-shot nemesis to James Bond. **05** (★★★★) a funky blend cab, malbec & tempranillo; wild, aromatic leather edges to tightly wound tannic core. 6 mths Fr oak toning; unfiltered. WO Coastal.

★★★★ **At The Limiet Natural Sweet** Joint venture with neighbour Graham Knox; moniker reflects the area's Limiet Mountains (extremity of the old Cape Colony) & boundary-pushing winemaking (grapes whipped off vines as winter rains begin; natural yeast barrel ferment). **03** last ed showed focused fruity persistence mellowed by 58g/ℓ sugar. From hárslevelü; ±yr *sur lie*. 500ml.

Chenin Blanc ★★★ **05** prominent oak (6 mths used Fr), almond, dried apple tints in rich finish. **Sauvignon Blanc** ★★★ **06** tropical fruit, green apple tones, refreshingly light 12. 5% alc. **Chenin Blanc-Sauvignon Blanc** ★★★ **06** not ready for review at press time. Last tasted **04** flew with Aeroflot, entertaining passengers with melon & peach tones to sauvignon grassiness. — *DS*

■ *Namaqua see* WestCorp

Napier Winery

Wellington • Est 1993 • 1stB 1994 • Tasting & sales Mon-Fri 9-5 Sat 10-4 Sun & pub hols by appt • Cellar tours by appt • Small conference facility • Self-catering cottage (sleeps 4) • Owners: Michael & Catherine Loubser, Leon Bester • Winemaker/viticulturist Leon Bester (Apr 2000) • 34 ha (five Bdx reds, shiraz, chard, chenin) • ±5 500 cs 30% red 70% white • PO Box 638 Wellington 7654 • sales@napierwinery.co.za • www.napierwinery.co.za • T 021-873-7829 • F 021-864-2728

A double coup for their Red Medallion: first the 01 vintage stole the 'Discovery of Show' trophy at the Trophy Wine Show 2005; then the 00 took a gold medal at the same competition — a year later! Another 'victory' at London's Vinopolis: the Greenstone Chenin is used exclusively for their How To Taste Wine seminars. Winemaker/viticulturist Leon Bester gets new petit verdot and malbec grapes to work with this season, and the first shiraz is in the bottle, awaiting release. Also available is Sir George, their 1999 vintage potstill brandy.

Red Medallion ★★★★ Bdx-inspired blend cabs s/f & merlot, interestingly released in reverse vintage order. **98** opens heady, touch volatile; ripe fruit compote lounges on mature tannins. **00** wowed 2006 TWS judges (gold). 18-24 mths Fr barrels, ±30% new. **Greenstone** ★★★☆

Unwooded chenin, 3 mths *sur lie*; **06** has real stone-fruit interest, glinting late acidity. Poised & elegant, with lunch-time 12% alc. Following not reviewed this ed: **Cabernet Sauvignon** ★★★ Limited release **03** savoury with cedar hint, touch herbaceous. 18 mths Fr oak, 30% new. **St Catherine** ★★★ Barrel-fermented/aged chardonnay, **03** balanced; tropical fruits & walnuts, well integrated 14% alc & 30% new Fr oak. — *DS*

Natte Valleij

Paarl (see Stellenbosch map) • Est 1715 • Visits by appt • B&B/self-catering accommodation (see Stay-over section) • Owner/winemaker Alexander Milner • 5 tons 200 cs 100% red • PO Box 4 Klapmuts 7625 • milner@intekom.co.za • www.nattevalleij.co.za • **T 021·875·5171 / 084·643·3600**

Natte Valleij is not a new winery, it's just been resting for the past 50 years,' says Alexander Milner (brother of Marcus M at De Meye), a Stellenbosch graduate freshly seasoned in the south of France. This historic farm was bought by the Milner family in the late 1960s, and vines replaced by post-and-rail fences in its makeover to a stud farm producing many champion racehorses. Wine was made again in 2005 in 'die melk stal' (old dairy), converted into a small cellar. Natte Valleij has no grapes of its own: unfortunately — or maybe fortunately? muses Milner, who sources fruit from the Wellington area.

Swallow Cabernet Sauvignon ★★ **05** shows berry, sun-dried tomato aromas; savoury palate, with 14% alc concealed behind quite herbal tannins. **Swallow Merlot** ★★ Herbaceous & mulberry whiffs on **05** & a limy finish. Tannins somewhat green, despite ripeness suggested by 14.5% alc (& some remaining sugar). Both these modestly priced wines open-fermented, aged yr in 2nd fill barrels. — *MF*

Naughton's Flight

Constantia • 1stB 2003 • Closed to public • Owner Francis Naughton • Vini consultant Ronell Wiid • 8 000 btls • 25 Willow Rd Constantia 7806 • naughts@mweb.co.za • **T 021·794·3928/ 082·571·3442** F 021·794·3928

After a successful first flight, Constantia-based Francis Naughton remains motivated by 'quality over profit'. He's delighted with Ronell Wiid as the winemaker chosen to deliver, more than satisfied with output — now up to 8 000 bottles, 1 200 of them a maiden Viognier (untasted by us). FN continues to build a solid foundation on the merging of his two beloved countries, SA and Ireland, to which he enjoys regular trips that combine visiting his mother and presentations to customers.

★★★★ **Shiraz** Not a jot of the blarney in describing FN's **04** as remarkably elegant & sophisticated. Appealingly fresh; complex minerals, spice aromas, resonant deeper smoked-meat flavour; fine, polished tannins, mainly from skilfully applied oak (14 mths, 80/20 Fr/Am, 50% new). Good now; better in a few yrs. WO Paarl. — *AL*

Nederburg Wines

Paarl • Est 1792 • 1stB ca 1940 • Tasting & sales Mon-Fri 8.30-5; Sat 10-2 (Apr-Oct); Sat 10-4 & Sun 11-4 (Nov-Mar) • Informal tasting fee dependent on wine; tasting & tour: R25 • Closed Easter Fri, Dec 25 & Jan 1 • Tours in Afrikaans, English, French & German by appt • Picnic lunches by appt Mon-Sun Nov-Mar • Corporate & private lunches/dinners by appt • 'Incredible Journey of Tastes' food & wine matching, by appt • Tour groups • Gifts • Conferences • Conservation area • Owner Distell • Cellarmaster Razvan Macici (Jan 2001) • Red-wine maker Elunda Basson (Jan 2000), with Wim Truter (Nov 2005) • White-wine maker Tariro Masayiti (Aug 2005), with Pieter Badenhorst (Mar 2001) • Viticulturists Hannes van Rensburg & Drikus Heyns • 18 000 tons • 1.1m cs • Private Bag X3006 Paarl 7620 • nedwines@distell.co.za • www.nederburg.co.za • **T 021·862·3104** • F 021·862·4887

Managing a vast portfolio, including a new range of blends and a special selection for the annual Nederburg Auction (a showcase for some of the Cape's leading labels), tireless cellarmaster Razvan Macici still brings innovation and experimentation to a stalwart brand: testing locally uncommon varieties such as mourvèdre, and creating blends with sangiovese, barbera and nebbiolo. He's also trialling natural-yeast ferments of chardonnay and chenin, and maturing wines in larger barrels (500ℓ) for subtler effect. Able assistance comes from ex-Fleur du Cap white-wine specialist Tariro Masayiti and red-wine maker Elunda Basson. Visitor attractions include special-release wines, vintage-wine tastings, food-and-wine pairings, brunches, summer picnics and classical concerts.

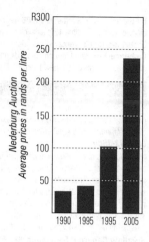

Private Bin wines for Nederburg Auction

The famous Nederburg Auction, now in its 33rd yr, is SA's biggest. It's open to any producer whose wine passes the selection process (Nederburg also subject to the screening). The Nederburg wines below are made in small quantities, usually from special vyd blocks, offered in lots of ±500 cs. Originally labelled under a meaningless Bin number, prefaced by a letter (R=dry red, D dry white, S dessert, C Cap Classique), they now also carry the variety/blend.

★★★★ **Cabernet Sauvignon Private Bin R163** Striking **04** from Papkuilsfontein (Darling) grapes. Fresh cedar, less herbaceous than some pvs; compact, concentrated dark-berried allure, tannin still taut. Shd easily last 10 yrs. These auction reds have 10% juice bled off after crushing to concentrate wine; mix open fermenters, steel tanks; 18 mths in new 300ℓ Fr oak barrels.

★★★★ **Cabernet Sauvignon-Merlot Private Bin R109** Classic aromas/flavours noted on **03** last yr – cassis, lead pencil, choc truffle with cab leading the way in 58/42 blend, giving frame for merlot's gentler attractions. Midweight, elegant; more approachable than R163. **04** unready.

★★★★ **Cabernet Sauvignon-Shiraz Private Bin R103** After taut, compact **03**, particularly fine **04** (★★★★★) with its concentrated black-berried fruit & notes of toast & tar. Firmly structured, gd tannic backbone; still youthful, needing few yrs to unravel. 60/40 blend, converse below.

★★★★ **Shiraz-Cabernet Sauvignon Private Bin R115** Warm-hearted shiraz leads **04**, with fleshy plums, black cherries. Cab's tannic structure significant armature for stylish fruit, but softer, more relaxed than above (both ex-Darling/Dbnvlle; both big ±14.7% alcs).

★★★★ **Merlot Private Bin R181** Fruit-forward rather than wood-led as always, there's ripe cassis, ripe meatiness on rounded **04**, though oak adds fragrant cinnamon. Juicy, dense fruit, plus fine tannins, long finish with sprig of mint. Ex-Darling. This, Pinotage below a touch less dry than others in range at ±4.1g/ℓ RS.

★★★★ **Pinotage Private Bin R172 04** hints at variety's unruly persona in whiff of wild brambleberry, tangy morello cherry & touch of tar. Well groomed in oak, has emerged suave & stylish, with gd varietal character, but will benefit from 5-7 yrs. Darling/Dbnville fruit.

★★★★ **Shiraz Private Bin R121** Savoury, compact, dense **04** takes time to open in glass & reveal subtle black cherry, choc, smoke; elegantly styled with taut tannins needing at least 3-6 yrs. Darling/Philadelphia grapes.

★★★★ **Sauvignon Blanc** Two distinct sources & styles. **Private Bin D215** Showy, in lush tropical style; **06** (WO Paarl) exotically flavoured with passionfruit, pomelo, with burst of lime; explodes & grows on palate. Big, fleshy & ripe at 14.6% alc. **Private Bin D234** Coolly classic **06** (WO Groeneklf) boasts nettles, dusty capsicum, delicate black-currant leaf; tender green aromas/flavours, minerally nuances, assertive, but only marginally less ripe than other version, at 14.3% alc.

★★★★ **Chardonnay Private Bin D270 05** (★★★★★) already shows extraordinary, with lots in hand. Generous, bold ripe fruit not overplayed, subtle minerally undertones & firm acid, with oak adding another dimension: fermented (half native yeast) then yr in new

Fr oak; 4.6g/ℓ sugar not obvious. Dbnvlle, Sbosch grapes. **04** repeated lime, citrus style of pvs, with minerally, stony notes.

★★★★ **Edelkeur** The botrytised chenin that gave rise to SA's NLH industry. **05** wafts orange zest, marmalade: ultra-rich but uncloying – intense, luscious orange, apricot flavours, rapier acidity ensures poise & tautness. The essence & soul of chenin. Heavily botrytised & very sweet at 283g/ℓ ('The sweetest I've ever made', says Macici proudly.) Superb **04** (★★★★★, IWSC gold, *Wine* ★★★★★).

★★★★ **Eminence** NLH, but in future will be labelled Natural Sweet – Macici believes it overshadowed by heavily botrytised versions in competitions. **05**'s spice, jasmine tea & camomile flowers suggest hand of master perfumier. Less sweet, more lithe & nimble, at mere 115g/ℓ RS than **04**'s 218, shows lively clean-cut citrus flavours to perfection after weight loss. From muscat de F. WO Paarl, like Edelkeur.

Malbec Private Bin R101 ★★★☆ Black plum, smoked beef, mocha aromas in **04**. Loads of berries crowd palate, jostle with toasty oak. Very dry, with youthful austerity on finish.

There are various Private Bin Auction wines made only when suitable grapes are available. The following were rated in earlier eds & may re-emerge in future vintages. **Sangiovese-Barbera-Nebbiolo Private Bin, Petit Verdot Private Bin R104, Cabernet Franc, Sauvignon Blanc-Chardonnay Private Bin D253, Sauvignon Blanc-Semillon Private Bin D252, Semillon-Viognier Private Bin D224, Semillon Private Bin D266, Gewürztraminer Private Bin D259, Semillon Noble Late Harvest, Weisser Riesling Noble Late Harvest Private Bin S316, Viognier**.

Private Bin wines (no numbers)

These more readily available than Auction versions. **Private Bin Cabernet Sauvignon 03** (★★★☆, but *Wine* ★★★★★) had gorgeous touches; latest **04** (★★★★☆) very special & seductive: ripe mulberry, warm oak spice, subtle vanilla of classy oak leads to warm ripe fruit-filled palate, with lengthy dry finish. 18 mths new oak. This range being phased out in emerging new strategy. Pvsly tasted have included **Shiraz, Sauvignon Blanc, Chardonnay**.

Manor House range [new]

★★★★ **Shiraz** Shapely & accessible **04** first offers choc, coffee bean, touch leather – appealing from first sniff; then comes richness laced with fine-grained tannins. Philadelphia, Darling fruit. 18 mths Am/European oak.

★★★★ **Sauvignon Blanc** Tropical toned **06** has layers of aroma & flavour, with passionfruit, kiwi, greengage tussling complexly with green fig, nettles. Full bodied, ripe & tangy, with thrilling acid/fruit balance. WO Coastal.

These available internationally or from Nederburg tasting room. **Cabernet Sauvignon** ★★★☆ **04** quieter than some above, more reserved, lighter texture; cool cedary notes, sprig mint; tightly woven, classically oriented. Yr oak, most new. WO Coastal.

Classic range

★★★★ **Edelrood** ✓ Distinctly, classically toned **04** with loads of blackcurrant, hints of lead pencil in long dry finish. Cab/merlot 60/40, intelligently oaked: yr mixed-age/origin. Quality improves as sales of looser-knit Baronne overtake it, opines Macici.

★★★★ **Noble Late Harvest** Seductive bouquet in latest **05** – tangerine, orange zest, glacé apricot with dusting of talc; stylish & serene sweetness subtly balanced by freshening acidity – altogether fragrant & charming. Mostly chenin, with muscat & a drop of semillon. 375ml **04** (★★★★★) brilliantly successful: TWS trophy, high Tri Nations placing, Mondial & IWSC golds.

> **Premier Grand Cru** ☺ ★★★ Not your usual bleak dry white: latest **NV** bottling chenin/chard (60/40) has ripeness & shapely build, crisp acidity. Both tangy & fleshy – & famously bone-dry.

Baronne ★★★ ✓ Hugely successful blend; smooth & velvety. **04**, meaty, hint of leather from shiraz (40%) which partners cab; dry almost brittle tannic grip to savoury smoked beef palate. Yr mixed oak, as for other reds in range. **Cabernet Sauvignon** ★★★☆ Cassis, cedar on **04**; gorgeous berry concentration, grippy tannins assert the variety, with long finish. 4.5g/ℓ sugar no doubt subtly seductive. **Merlot** new ★★★ **04** no shrinking violet, very ripe — showing plum rather than berry fruit. Still in firm tannic grip mid-2006, not showing much varietal grace, fleshiness. **Shiraz** ★★★ Flies out of the cellar, so two vintages tasted. Easy approachability the key, as **05** sample epitomises: dark-berried charmer, softer & easier than more concentrated **04** with lovely black cherries, hints of leather, good dry finish with brush of tannin; but both amiable, welcoming. **Pinotage** ★★★ **04** meaty & savoury, with varietal exuberance held in check by oak. Tangy freshness & gd fruit concentration; long dry finish. **Rosé** ★★★ Bang on form with cinsaut-dominated **06**, delicious pink ultra-soft sweetie (20g/ℓ RS), delicate cherry pink with flavours to match. **Sauvignon Blanc** ★★★★ **06** less tropical than pvs, now with greenpepper, green fig aromas; limy, citrusy flavours with touch flintiness — gd concentration, packed with flavour supported by crisp tangy acidity. **Sauvignon Blanc-Chardonnay** ★★★ **06** a revival of Prelude. Warmly ripe, juicy style but dry, with touches of yellow peach, hay, some real interest here. Chard portion oaked. **Rhine Riesling** Following delicately spiced **05** (★★★★), change in style with **06** (★★★★ ✓): now pure riesling & dry (just); fragrant, spicy with orange blossom & nutmeg, very individual. Terrific balance & lengthy, lime-tinged finish. **Paarl Riesling** ★★ Ever-popular tipple from crouchen. **06** less bold & assertive than some pvs, strangely soft & easy; modest 11.5% alc, bone-dry. **Chardonnay** ★★★ Aromas of dried peach, nut on **06**; very ripe with softish acidity & slight sweetness on finish. 30% fermented/6 mths new oak. **Stein** ★★★ Deservedly popular semi-sweet; **06** melon & honey flavours to gentle sweetness balanced by fresh acidity. 60% chenin with various others, incl some vinified as SLH. **Special Late Harvest** ★★★★ Fragrant sweetie, mainly chenin with gewürz, muscat, riesling. Gorgeous rosebud fragrance, crisp & lively flavours on **06**. If not your drinking style, put a dab behind each ear!

Lifestyle range

> **Lyric** ☺ ★★★ Loads of flavour on **06**, & more weight than pvs, but still crisp, off-dry blend led by sauvignon with chenin, chard.

Duet ★★★ From **06** no longer pinot/cab, but (as the int. version calls it) 'Shiraz-Pinotage' — either way a 60/40 blend, whiff wild brambleberry; chunky & robust, & only just dry. Like next, just a light oak influence (3 mths staves, with micro-oxygenation). **Shiraz-Viognier** new Like next, mostly for int. sales. **06** ★★★ Intended for easy, early drinking: succeeds admirably. Soft berry fruit & telltale leather hint; modestly tannined, a little sugar, & juicy. Like next, from tasting room only. **Chardonnay-Viognier** new ★★★★ ✓ **06** successful blend, with 10% viognier filling out, giving extra interest. Crisp, lively, with pleasing fullness. **Cuvée Brut** ★★★ Ever reliable carbonated **NV** threaded with fragrant citrus & not all that dry — but it's not about the flavours, it's about the bubbles.— *IvH*

Neethlingshof Estate

*Stellenbosch ▪ Tasting & sales daily 9-5 (open till 7pm Dec 1-Jan 31) ▪ Fee R25 (R30 incl cellar tour) ▪ Closed Easter Fri & Dec 25 ▪ Tours by appointment ▪ Lord Neethling Restaurant, Palm Terrace ▪ Play area for children ▪ Tour groups ▪ Conferences ▪ Owner Lusan Premium Wines ▪ Winemaker DeWet Viljoen ▪ Vineyard managers Hannes van Zyl & Arne Erasmus ▪ Viticulturist Eben Archer ▪ 210 ha ▪ 50 000 cs 60% red 40% white ▪ PO Box 104 Stellenbosch 7599 ▪ info@ neethlingshof.co.za ▪ www.neethlingshof.co.za ▪ **T** 021·883·8988 ▪ **F** 021·883·8941*

This estate's grand, kilometre-long avenue of stone pines once led to the home of a rather plebian Neethling, so given to airs and graces he was nicknamed 'Lord'. The stately approach these days leads to a warm welcome, with popular restaurants, children's play area, estate tours and, of course winetasting. Talking of which, DeWet Viljoen continues to rustle up new vinous offerings, most recently a single-vineyard Sauvignon Blanc for export and a once-off Lord Neethling Shiraz, untasted at press time.

Lord Neethling range

★★★★☆ **Laurentius** Refreshingly understated flagship red showing balance, refinement & length. **01**, still available, cab dominated (70%) with cab f, merlot & shiraz. Yr oak, Fr:Am 90:10, 70% new. Gold medals for this (Swiss) & **99** (IWC).

★★★★ **Cabernet Sauvignon** Still-current **00** (★★★) very dry with pronounced acidity. ±16 mths Fr oak. Harks back to the more severe tones of **98**, which needed some yrs to open.

★★★★ **Cabernet Franc 03** last ed returned to form after vintage-impacted **02** (★★★). Floral bouquet with generous dark fruits & serious structure, fine tannins. 14 mths Fr oak.

★★★★ **Pinotage 03** keeps on same track as exuberant **02**. Deep extract & youthful magenta rim; earthy, slightly medicinal cherry/tobacco aromas promise richness, delivered in style with plushly textured tannins, concentrated fruit & fine acidity. Enjoy now or keep a few yrs. Quieter **01** (★★★ but *Wine* ★★★★).

★★★★☆ **Chardonnay** Last tasted was showstopper **02**. Barrel-fermented/aged 7 mths new Fr oak.

★★★★☆ **Weisser Riesling Noble Late Harvest** Striking amber-tinted **05** emits typical botrytis apricot, honey aromas; acidity neatly lifts sweet marmalade flavours & 137g/ℓ sugar, & persists to vibrant, clean finish. Low 9.5% alc gives more classic profile. **04** IWSC gold.

Neethlingshof range

★★★★ **Cabernet Sauvignon 03** joins **02** in raising the bar with seriously styled textbook cab; spicy blackcurrant aromas & ripe blackberry, maraschino flavours held in by supple tannins & fine acid spine. 16 mths Fr, 10% Am oak, almost half new.

★★★★ **Shiraz** Brooding, introverted **01** needed time to develop & harmonise. **02** (★★★), though big & mouth-filling, with plentiful bold ripe flavours, last ed noted as more extracted, less fresh, with some awkward tannins.

★★★★ **Cape Blend** Mostly for export, though some available from estate. Last tasted was youthfully tannic **01**; mainly unwooded blend cabs s/f, pinotage (40/28/22) with dash cab.

★★★★ **Gewürztraminer 06** as distinctly honeysuckle & Turkish Delight as **05**. Limpid gold hues, off-dry, spicy litchi flavours persisting to zippy finish. Less sweet at 6g/ℓ RS. **04** *Wine* ★★★★.

Merlot ★★★★ Agreeably balanced food wine. Savoury plum & tealeaf aromas hint at elegant styling of **02**, firm tannins from yr oak, some new, still evident. **Pinotage** ★★ **03** step down from pvs with same hefty alc (15%), ripe mulberry aromas & bitter choc flavours; surprisingly aggressive, unknit, given conducive vintage. 43% new Fr/Am oak. **Cabernet Sauvignon-Merlot** ★★★★ **03** still available. Restrained, with prominent tannins, blackcurrant/black plum flavours, moderate 13% alc. 8 mths Fr oak. **Blanc de Noir** new ★★★ Pale rose-pink **06** (sample), sweet entry (7g/ℓ RS), characterful redcurrant flavours, with some structure & gd balance. **Chardonnay Wooded** new ★★★★ Preview **06** wooded version shows oak evident but fairly restrained; nutty oatmeal aromas with citrus & sweet-fruit finish. 50% oaked, Fr, 4 mths. **Chardonnay Unwooded** ★★★★ Pre-bottling look at **06** finds versatile food partner with bright peach, pineapple aromas & flavours, & citrus finish. **Sauvignon Blanc** ★★★★ Herbaceous capsicum on **06** preview, from cooler vyds; pineapple flavours in perfect balance with fresh acidity, tangy lime conclusion.—*IM*

Neil Ellis Meyer-Näkel ☿

Stellenbosch • Est/1stB 1998 • Tasting/sales at Neil Ellis Wines (see entry) • Owner Neil Ellis Meyer-Näkel (Pty) Ltd • Winemakers Neil Ellis & Werner Näkel • Viticulturist Pieter Smit • 10 ha • 3 500 cs 100% red • PO Box 917 Stellenbosch 7599 • info@neilellis.com • T 021·887·0649 • F 021·887·0647

A joint venture, principally between Werner Näkel, known as the 'king of red wine' in his native Germany, and Neil Ellis of Neil Ellis Wines. Näkel, whose main emphasis back home is pinot, here switches focus to cab and merlot under the banner Zwalu, meaning 'new beginnings'.

Z Previewed **04** (★★★★) friendly yet confidently built merlot. Delicious ripe red plum scents; quite plump but plenty enlivening freshness too; Fr oak, 16 mths, none new, for rounded drinkability. **03** (★★★☆) affable merlot/cab, uncomplicated but with good presence. 14% alc. **Zwalu** ★★★☆ **03** traditionally-styled cab; balanced, not obviously big; persistent. No **04**. — *AL*

Neil Ellis Wines   ⚲ ♗

*Stellenbosch ▪ 1stB 1984 ▪ Tasting & sales Mon-Fri 9.30-4.30 Sat & pub hols 10-2 ▪ Fee R15 p/ p, waived on purchase ▪ Closed Easter Fri, Dec 25/26 & Jan 1 ▪ Owner Neil Ellis Wines (Pty) Ltd ▪ Winemaker Neil Ellis, with Abraham de Klerk (Oct 2004) ▪ 40 000 cs ▪ 50% red 50% white ▪ PO Box 917 Stellenbosch 7599 ▪ info@neilellis.com ▪ www.neilellis.com ▪ **T 021·887·0649** ▪ F 021·887·0647*

When we catch up with Neil Ellis — who last year stated he'd had enough of travelling — he's in Atlanta. 'Not exactly winning on that score,' he says, 'if anything, it's worse.' Ellis cites the competitive environment, where mergers and acquisitions mean that bigger volumes are controlled by fewer people, as a key issue. 'Marketing is increasingly time-consuming. You have to carve a niche for yourself, then remain focused, because before you know it, things have changed again.' He's spent the past three years exploring the US, a market he likes because it's so untapped. He intends taking a fresh look at his stable with a view to possibly doing some pruning. 'But this is not an easy decision to take and it won't happen overnight...'

Vineyard Selection range
These single-vyd 'reserves' now more widely sourced (pvsly off home vines).

★★★★☆ **Cabernet Sauvignon** Splendid **04** (★★★★★), just pre-bottling, trademark Neil E elegance (abetted by svelte vintage) yet touch more power than usual courtesy fully ripe fruit, fine insistent tannins & richness of 100% new Fr oak (22 mths). Youthfully expressive, but will repay contemplation, patience. Many gongs, incl **03** *Wine* ★★★★; **01** 90 pts *WS*. WO Jnkrshoek Vlly.

★★★★★ **Syrah 04** same Grnekloof source as Premium wine below, more richness, smoky warmth without any loss of delicacy; secured by fine thread savoury acid, dry finish. Vibrant tannins will benefit from yr/2 softening; shd peak around 2010. New Fr oak 15 mths, unobtrusive 14% alc. Drink before bigger, richer **03**.

★★★★★ **Sauvignon Blanc 04** from same vyd as Premium version. Sophisticated, food-orientated style. 30% Fr oak fermented/matured 8 mths. No **05**.

Premium range

★★★★★ **Stellenbosch Cabernet Sauvignon** Like other reds, preview **04** (★★★★) engagingly modern, demonstrative but not showy cab aromas; quite tight, minerally structure in harmony with more delicate fruit. Spicy note from beautifully absorbed 22 mths Fr oak. **03** classic from wonderful vintage; promises impressive maturity around 2011/13.

★★★★ **Stellenbosch Pinotage 03** was refined, full flavoured, structured for longevity. **04** (★★★☆) slightly less so, but in Neil E's skilled hands, still delicious glassful. Pure, light, juicy flavours; clear ruby sheen; unaggressive savoury tail. Balanced 14.5% alc, 15 mths Fr oak.

★★★★ **Shiraz** (Pvsly 'Stellenbosch Shiraz'.) **04** provenance switches to 7 yr old Grnekloof vyd (pvsly Sbosch). Highlights variety's elegance; well-defined aromas, supple texture, pliable tannins for well-textured drinking over next ±3-4 yrs. Unobtrusive oak, Fr, 15 mths.

★★★★ **Stellenbosch Cabernet Sauvignon-Merlot** Unmistakeable cab cassis/blackberry scents announce dominant partner in **04** sample; 21% merlot adds breadth, richness to usual sleek, elegant blend. Probably less long-lived than **03** (★★★★★), but carefully composed to offer few yrs characterful, balanced drinking. Fr oak, 18 mths.

★★★★ **Stellenbosch Chardonnay** From home vyds. **05** lighter, more open vintage sympathetically vinified: only partial malo & oaking helps ensure elegant result, provides pleasantly taut structure for 2/3 yrs unfurling. 80% fermented/aged Fr barrels, 7 mths.

★★★★ **Elgin Chardonnay** Mirroring Sbosch partner, **05** youthfully uninhibited. Defined pickled lime, hazelnut aromas echoed on palate; touch softer, more juicy than usual but doesn't lack freshness, flavoursome length. Good 2/3 yrs drinking. Fr barrel fermented, shorter maturation (7 cf usual 10 mths) for vg oak assimilation.

★★★★ **Aenigma** Occasional label introduced for experimental wines. First/only **03** chardonnay, barrel-fermented with native yeasts, matured 10 mths. Small qty still available. Complex vinosity, rich burgundy-like savoury decadence rather than New World fruitiness. Good potential.

★★★★☆ **Groenekloof Sauvignon Blanc** ✓ More steely verve than aromatic fireworks in **06**, but harmonious, balanced as ever. Lightish, elegant, with typical vivid fruity acids; mouthwatering dryness, length. Screwcapped. — *AL*

Nelson Estate

*Paarl ▪ Est/1stB 1993 ▪ Tasting & sales Mon-Fri 9-5 Sat 9-2 Sun by appt ▪ Wine & vineyard tour R20 p/p ▪ Closed Easter Fri/Sun, Dec 25 & Jan 1 ▪ Tours Mon-Sat 10; Sun by appt ▪ Meals/refreshments by appt ▪ Facilities for children ▪ Tour groups ▪ Gifts ▪ Walks ▪ Conference/function/lapa venue ▪ Conservation area ▪ Owner Alan Nelson ▪ Winemaker Jean van Rooyen (Dec 2003) ▪ Viticulturists Daniel Nelson (Apr 2005) ▪ 60 ha (cab, merlot, pinotage, shiraz, chard, sauvignon) ▪ 340 tons 20 000 cs own label 65% red 30% white 5% rosé ▪ PO Box 2009 Windmeul 7630 ▪ info@ nelsonscreek.co.za ▪ www.nelsonscreek.co.za ▪ **T 021·869·8453** ▪ F 021·869·8424*

Last year saw the launch of the Pearl's Gate association, which proposed Windmeul be declared a standalone appellation within Paarl. 'The objective was to highlight the incredible achievements of the region, producing the grapes for the shiraz and cab wines that won best in the world in 2001 and 2003 at Vinexpo,' explains driving force Alan Nelson, whose California-seasoned daughter Lisha N is pursuing a MSc in Oenology at Stellenbosch University. They're especially proud of cellar assistant Solly Hendriks, chosen for a harvest in Burgundy as part of his Vineyard Academy training.

Nelson Estate range

★★★★ **Cabernet Sauvignon-Merlot** Stylish **02**, 81/19 blend, all Fr oak, 18 mths, 80% new. Classic cassis/cigarbox tones; firm, slightly grainy tannins; deftly applied wood.

★★★★ **Pinotage 02** settled down with extra yr in bottle; rich mocha/smoked meat character — appealingly showy. 18 mths Fr oak.

★★★★ **Chardonnay** After forceful, creamily concentrated **04**, current **05** (★★★★☆) touch lighter (though moderate ±13% alc welcome), firmer; honeyed lemon-butter tone tensioned by racy acidity. Native yeasts; fermented/aged new Fr barrels, 10 mths.

Shiraz ★★★☆ **02** full-bodied/flavoured (14.8% alc) but not overpowering; well layered with peppery red fruit, warm toast & coffee tones. VDG. Only Chardonnay retasted for this ed.

Nelson's Creek range

No newer releases tasted for following four reds: **Merlot** ★★★ Lead pencils & cassis announce **03**, clean ripe fruit, very big dry wood tannins from yr 2nd/3rd fill Fr oak. **Pinotage** ★★★ Switches to wooded (9 mths Fr) for **03**, different to silky pvs; this savoury & rustic, ±15% alc shows in hot finish. **Cabernet Sauvignon** ★★★ **02**, with dash merlot, similar to pvs; meaty whiffs, dry, savoury, slightly earthy flavours, firm tannins. 8 mths new Fr staves. **Shiraz** ★★★☆ Step-up **02** suave & supple; appetising dark choc/black cherry flavours; fine pervasive smokiness. From single 'Stony Hill' vyd; 2nd-4th fill oak, 10% Am. **Albenet** ★★ Mercurial blend; changes into merlot-led unwooded quintet in **03** (sample); earthy mulberry flavours & somewhat rustic dry tannins. **Cabernet Sauvignon-Merlot Rosé** ★★ Vermillion-hued **05**, decidedly (& attractively) dry this yr, dried-fruit flavours, tug spicy tannin for food cordiality. **Chardonnay** ★★★ **04** no-frills version; nice lime flavours, sharpish acidity. 'Great with garlic prawns' said Jean vR last ed. 4 mths Fr staves. **Sauvignon Blanc** ★★★☆ **06** (sample) usual sugar slick (±4g/ℓ) but zingier than pvs; flinty/herbaceous tone with capsicum nip, tingly acidity. **Triple Creek** Same varieties as pvs, but chard's in lead (70%, with chenin, semillon) in **06**; sample too unformed to rate. **Marguerite** ★★ Scented blend chenin, muscat d'A (84/16); **06** litchi notes, finishes crisply despite generous dollop sugar. — *CT*

New Beginnings Wines

*Paarl ▪ Tasting & sales Mon-Fri 9-5 ▪ Fee R20 for groups ▪ Vineyard tours by appointment ▪ Owner Klein Begin Farming Association ▪ Winemaker Sollie Hendriks, assisted by Jean van Rooyen (Nelson Estate) since 2003 ▪ 13 000 cs 60% white 40% red ▪ PO Box 2009 Windmeul 7630 ▪ victor@nelsonscreek.co.za ▪ **T 869·8453** ▪ F 869·8424*

No update from this pioneering empowerment winery. Contact details from the previous edition. Their Cabernet Sauvignon, Pinotage and Chardonnay last tasted in 2004.

New Cape Wines

*Worcester ▪ Est/1stB 2000 ▪ Tasting, sales & tours Mon-Fri 8-4.30 Sat 10-3 ▪ Owner/winemaker Christiaan Groenewald ▪ 80 ha ▪ 40% red 60% white ▪ PO Box 898 Worcester 6849 ▪ christiaan@ncw.co.za ▪ www.newcapewines.co.za ▪ **T 023·340·4112** ▪ F 023·340·4132*

'You must come to this side of the mountain to find out what's going on!' says Christiaan Groenewald of his plantings of rare-in-Cape-red tannat. Another new variety in his vineyard is nouvelle, a little of which he harvested and used in blends in 2006 but which he'll bottle as a single variety this year. Taking shape at press time were a restaurant and, across the valley from the winery, a 'weekend getaway' guesthouse so that visitors can enjoy to the full the farm's trails and dam.

Dwyka Hills Shiraz ★★★ When last tasted was lightly oaked **03**; well behaved, shy plum tones, fairly open texture, anise hints on sweetish finish.

Eagle's Cliff Reserve range

Shiraz ☺ ★★★ **03**, retasted, plummy fruit & oak in harmony, smooth textured for immediate enjoyment plus sufficient backbone for ±2 yrs cellaring.

Cabernet Sauvignon ★★★ Smoky **02** last ed had well-meshed oak cosseting cassis aromas, plump & juicy black fruit. **Chardonnay** ★★★ For those who like big & bold chards. **05**, yr on, oak still a strong presence yet more knit with peachy aromas & flavours. **Sauvignon Blanc** ★★★★ ✓ Cool-fruited (greengage, leaves) **06**, more Old World than New; restrained, an attractive mineral seam pierces its core. **Viognier** ★★★★ ✓ Revisit of **05** sample reveals mellowing nectarine, apricot & floral tones; palate overlain with savoury nuances from gentle wooding.

Eagle's Cliff range

Pinotage new ☺ ★★★ Good appetite appeal on **05**. Fleshiness ensures it slips down easily; brambleberry & banana make the trip enjoyable. W Cape WO. **Shiraz Rosé** ☺ ★★★ Light quaffing fare; **06** just off-dry, 7.2g/ℓ sugar giving plumpness to the palate. **Chenin Blanc** ☺ ★★★ **06** fresh & fruity quaffability, appealing pear & guava tones. **Sauvignon Blanc** ☺ ★★★ **06** has all of sauvignon's freshness plus gentle leafy minerality. Ideal lunchtime fare at 11.8% alc. **Viognier** new ☺ ★★★ **06** charms with floral, aromatic perfume, peach pip flavours. Characterful, but retains a delicate touch.

No new vintages of following duo, both 70/30 blends: **Merlot-Cabernet Sauvignon** ★★★ **03** reticent, with hints smoky stewed prunes, sweet-sour flavours. **Shiraz-Pinotage** ★★★ Plummy **02** was sweet fruited, plump & silky. **Chardonnay** ★★ **06** softly rounded, gentle peach aromas/flavours; uncomplicated summer sipper. Lap it up. Both ranges WO Wrcstr unless noted. — *CR*

Newton Johnson Wines

Hemel-en-Aarde (see Walker Bay map) ▪ Est 1996 ▪ 1stB 1997 ▪ Tasting & sales Mon-Fri 9-4 Sat 10-12.30 (Sep 22-Apr 29 only, otherwise by appt) ▪ Closed pub hols ▪ Heaven Restaurant ▪ Owners Dave & Felicity Newton Johnson ▪ Cellarmaster Gordon Newton Johnson (Jan 2001) ▪ Winemaker Nadia Cilliers (Aug 2006) ▪ Viticulturist Christopher Cloete (Jul 2005) ▪ 11 ha (pinot, shiraz, chard, sauvignon) • *120 tons 7 000 cs 44% red 48% white 8% rosé* • *PO Box 225 Hermanus 7200* • *wine@newtonjohnson.com* • *www.newtonjohnson.com* • *T 028·312·3862* • *F 028·312·3867*

The Newton Johnson family have completed their new cellar high up in the Hemel-en-Aarde Valley, offering spectacular views from their tasting area and instant hit eatery, Heaven. Cellarmaster Gordon NJ is delighted by the pinpointing of vineyard character afforded by the new gravity-flow system. Vine planting (set for completion at the end of this year) is done with typical care: potentially four different trellising methods are used, dependent on soil type' ('a nightmare' for viti man Chris Cloete, but a challenge he relishes). And there's a strong focus on ensuring material going into the soil is virus-free. Nadia Cilliers has joined to focus on the wines and 'accentuate the relationship between vineyard and cellar'. Vintage 06 promises 'sleeping giant' reds, particularly another 'superb' Pinot.

★★★★ **Pinot Noir** Historically a softer pinot. **05** (★★★☆) has lifted cranberry scents, choc/mocha oak mingling with gentle red berries on palate; sour cherry acidity & grainy tannins. Similar to, but lighter than **04**, which had lovely varietal attributes seamed with mineral acidity. Alcs now under 14% from solid 14.4% in **03**. 9-10 mths Burgundian oak, 35-40% new. Elgin, W Bay vyds.

★★★★ **Syrah-Mourvèdre** Bold & modern rhône-style blend off W Bay, Dbnvlle vyds; tight **05** needs airing to show best: spicy plums, tarry oak, mineral nuances; 93% shiraz delivers exemplary depth of flavour, lemony acidity, taut tannins; 14.8% alc glows on the finish. Structure to gain extra complexity over ±5 yrs. 12-13 mths Burgundy barrels, 36% new.

★★★★ **Pour Mes Amis** Occasional label; last was harmonious & zesty **05**, mainly sauvignon (75%), with dash semillon ex-W Bay to flesh out mid-palate. 3 mths new Fr barriques. Wine ★★★★.

★★★★ **Chardonnay** Strives to showcase flinty citric profile of reputed Vllrsdorp-area single vyd 'Kaaimansgat' ('Crocodile's Lair'); tight mineral core preserved by partial malo. Lipsmacking **05**'s bountiful ripe fruit cosseted by smart Burgundian oak (as for Pinot), lees-stirring gives creamy mouthfeel leavened by clean mineral tang. WO Ovrberg.

★★★★ **Sauvignon Blanc** From H-en-A Vlly & Elgin fruit, plus few drops oaked semillon ex-Bot Rvr. White asparagus & earth nuances to predominantly mineral character of standout **06** (★★★★★), marked by arresting tension between fruit ripeness & restrained nervous structure, harbouring gd maturation prospects. Greater gravitas than richly fruited, minerally **05**. Modest ±13% alc.

Felicité ★★★★ Sophisticated, food-friendly, lightish (±13% alc) dry rosé. **06** vibrant blend shiraz/sauvignon (61/39); raspberry & hay notes throughout, delightful zippy styling. **Cabernet Sauvignon** discontinued.— *CvZ*

■ *New World* see The Winery of Good Hope
■ *Nicholas L Jonker Estate* see Jonkheer

Nick & Forti's Wines

Est/1stB 2004 • *Closed to public* • *Owners Fortunato Mazzone & Saronsberg* • *Winemaker Dewaldt Heyns (2004)* • *200 cs 100% red* • *PO Box 25032 Monument Park Pretoria 0105* • *ritrovo@mweb.co.za* • *T 012·460·4367* • *F 012·460·5173*

Collaboration between Nick van Huyssteen of Saronsberg and Forti Mazzone, chef and co-owner of acclaimed Ritrovo Ristorante in Pretoria, celebrating 'life, friendship and superb wine'.

Both **04**, tasted pvs ed. **Shiraz** ★★★★ Spice, wild scrub & lavender whiffs; shiraz's breadth & roundness given heft by dollops malbec, petit v & cab. Friendly tannins, subtle oak (yr Fr, 40% new). Juicy early-drinker; as is… **Epicentre** ★★★★ Food-friendly bdx blend cab, merlot, petit v, malbec with suitably ritchenesque sniffs of tomato & black fruit, fine tannins (yr Fr, some new). TWS gold. Widely sourced grapes (Coastal origin).— *CvZ*

Nico van der Merwe Wines

Stellenbosch • *Est/1st 1999* • *Closed to public* • *Owners Nico & Petra van der Merwe* • *Winemaker Nico van der Merwe* • *45 tons 3 500 cs 85% red 15% white* • *PO Box 12200*

*Stellenbosch 7613 ▪ wilhelmshof@xsinet.co.za ▪ **T** 021·903·9507 / 083 26 52 167 / 084 29 49 296 ▪ F 021·903·9507*

At time of going to print, Nico van der Merwe was looking forward to the construction of a small wine cellar on his new Polkadraai Road domaine. The property (Amani and Jacobsdal are neighbours, and it's 'the last within the Stellenbosch municipal boundary', adds the proud owner) will be home to NvdM's wines and 'only a half-hectare of sauvignon'.

★★★★★ **Mas Nicolas** Nico vdM believes shiraz/cab is *the* 'Cape blend', hence his focus. **03** joins classy ranks with black cherry fruit, deeply veined tannins, liquorice notes, dried herbs. Elegant, supple, but still tightly held, deserving of more time. Blended after maturation, 14 mths, cab in new oak, shiraz 2nd fill, all Fr. Same vyds since first 99 — Kuils Rvr shiraz, Smnsberg cab.

Robert Alexander range

Merlot ★★★ **04** charms with generous berry fruit, juicy drinkability, well judged, integrated palate (yr combo Fr/Am). Drink at youthful best. **Shiraz** ★★★★ Complex, layered **05** impresses with red berries, white pepper/campfire notes, creamy fruit palate. Yr oaking, equal Fr/Am, dab new, provides ample support for next 2-3 yrs. This, range below, WO W Cape.

Nicolas van der Merwe range

Merlot-Shiraz-Cabernet Sauvignon ★★★★ Intended both for maturation & to while away time waiting for Mas N above. Fruit ex-Mas N vyd. Well constructed **04** already accessible, but built to last few yrs. Appealing choc-mint, cassis, reflecting bdx varieties' two-thirds pre-eminence. Yr equal Fr/Am oak, some new. **Sauvignon Blanc-Semillon** ★★★★ Pvs ed a sample, **05** loads of interest: richly fruited peach, Bosch pears, nicely rounded body, sure-handed gentle oaking. Perfect food partner & delicious solo. 50/50 blend. — *CR*

Nico Vermeulen Wines

*Paarl ▪ Est/1stB 2003 ▪ Closed to public ▪ Owner/viticulturist Nico Vermeulen ▪ Winemaker Nico Vermeulen, with Judy & Izelle Vermeulen ▪ 1 000 cs ▪ 3 Pieter Hugo Str Courtrai Suider-Paarl ▪ 13657631@sun.ac.za ▪ **T/F** 021·863·2048*

Havana Hills winemaker Nico Vermeulen wants these affordable own-label wines to be 'new and young in spirit' and 'have people dancing with excitement'.

The Right Two Reds ★★★★ **04** cassis nuanced by violets/venison characters, supple palate braced with tannins for food, cellaring. 15 mths in Fr oak, 30% new. **The Right Two Whites** ★★★★ Aptly named 3:1 sauvignon/semillon alliance, latter oaked. **06** leads with scrub-like aromas & grassy flavours, waxy fruits under wraps for now. Both tasted as samples. — *DS*

Niel Joubert Estate

*Paarl ▪ Est 1898 ▪ 1stB 1996 ▪ Visits by appt ▪ Walks ▪ Owner Joubert family ▪ Winemaker Ernst Leicht (May 2000) ▪ Viticulturist Daan Joubert ▪ 305 ha (cab, merlot, pinotage, shiraz, chard, chenin, sauvignon, viognier) ▪ 2 000 tons 40 000 cs own label 40% red 60% white ▪ PO Box 17 Klapmuts 7625 ▪ wine@nieljoubert.co.za ▪ www.nieljoubert.co.za ▪ **T/F** 021·875·5936*

Despite tough trading conditions, 2006 was 'kind', with good growth in their two main export markets, Ireland and the UK, and on the SA front. Niel Joubert Snr recalls being told by his father of the difficult times in the early 1900s, when there was a surplus of wine on the market. History's lesson heeded, they had the foresight to begin focusing on the local market some years ago, well ahead of the current wave, with a simple but effective policy: 'Keep your eye on the ball and the scoreboard will take care of itself…'

Christine-Marie ★★★★ Inadvertently omitted last yr (as was Shiraz, so both wines **new** to guide); stylish, well constructed & already harmonious **03**; full mulberry ripeness textured with cool mint, long complex flavours. Worthy flagship; 52/48 cab/merlot blend, Fr oaked. **Cabernet Sauvignon** ★★★ 75% unwooded but not unserious; Paarl sourced fruit for **05**, honest, well made; indisputably cab; nice cedary twist from the yr-oaked portion.

Merlot ★★ 04 an action replay of pvs's firm tannin, subdued fruit, herbaceous tone; same 14.5% alc, 70% Fr oaking. Might soften with few yrs cellaring. **Pinotage ★★ 04** trimmer than pvs, very dry & astringent, needs (more than complements) the pastas & pizzas Erni L recommends. Only 12% oaked. **Shiraz ★★★ 04** ex-Paarl, 18 mths Fr/Am/Hngrian oak; appears to be holding back mid-2006, fruit shyish but ripe, interesting, aromatic. Give yr/2 & see what happens. **Shiraz Rosé** new **★★** Uncomplicated **05**, softly dry tipple with lunchtime-light 12.8% alc, fairly firm savoury mouthfeel. **Chardonnay ★★** Almost invisibly wooded **06**, soft, quaffable, with muted boiled sweet tone. **Chenin Blanc ★★ 06** easy-flowing (& different) flavours of peach kernel & wild scrub; v soft, effortless quaffer. **Sauvignon Blanc ★★ 06** soft floral white, with more than just the usual suggestion of sweetness (5.5g/ℓ sugar). **Viognier ★★ 05** plump, perfumed sweetie; complex if tentative incense, peach & stone fruit bouquet; tad too little freshness for ±7g/ℓ sugar. 45% oaked. — *IvH/DH*

▪ *Niels Verburg see* Luddite

Nietvoorbij Wine Cellar

*Stellenbosch ▪ Est 1963 ▪ 1stB 1992 ▪ Tasting & sales Mon-Fri 9-4; phone ahead on Sat ▪ Fee R1/wine ▪ Closed pub hols ▪ Conferencing ▪ Owner Agricultural Research Council ▪ Winemaker Neil Strydom (2005) ▪ Viticulturist Guillaume Kotzè (Apr 2002) ▪ 32 ha (cab, malbec, merlot, pinotage, shiraz, chard, sauvignon) ▪ 150 tons 6 000 cs own label 74% red 24% white 1% port ▪ Private Bag X5026 Stellenbosch 7599 ▪ bosmand@arc.agric.za ▪ www.heritagegarden.co.za; www.heritagegarden-stellenbosch.com; www.arc.agric.za ▪ **T 021·809·3084/3091** ▪ F 021·809·3202/3064*

Owned by the Agricultural Research Council, this experimental wine cellar has access to the most advanced developments available. Last year the sauvignon grapes and pinotage for the rosé were mechanically harvested at night 'for better juice'; six new 3 000ℓ stainless steel tanks and a 10-ton press were also installed. Alchemical batches like this small should cost their weight in gold but Nietvoorbij offers exceptional value across the range.

Merlot ★★★ Full-ripe blackberries & plums on **04**, plenty of vanilla & spice, richness rescued by dry tannic thread. 13 mths Fr wood, 2nd fill. **Pinotage ★★★★** Dark fruited **03** enriched by liquorice notes; palate well supported by oaking, giving firm dry finish. Accessible, but can also age few yrs. **Rosé ★★★** Natural Sweet-style **06** from pinotage; forthcoming fruit pastille notes; super, cloy-free flavours & concluding tanginess will be a big hit this summer. **Sauvignon Blanc ★★★ 06** nicely structured for summer drinking (12.5% alc); lovely freshness, concentrated greengage & guava tones add to appeal. Screwcapped. **Port ★★★** Spiced plum pudding & brandy intro to **04** — can you resist? Full-sweet, lots of spice, with savoury hint to keep going back to. Yr older oak. All WO Smnsberg-Sbosch. — *CR*

Nieuwedrift Vineyards

*Swartland ▪ Est 1996 ▪ 1stB 2003 ▪ Visits Mon-Fri 9-12.30; 2-5 Sat 9-1 Otherwise by appt (phone mobile no. below) ▪ Light/buffet meals for groups of 5-74 by appt ▪ B&B guesthouse ▪ Facilities for children ▪ Tour groups ▪ Conferences & weddings ▪ Walks ▪ Owners Johan & Teubes Mostert ▪ Winemaker Johan Mostert, advised by Marais de Villiers ▪ Viti consultant Juliana Booysen ▪ 29 ha (shiraz, chard, chenin, colombard) ▪ ±7 tons 35% red 65% white ▪ PO Box 492 Piketberg 7320 ▪ nieuwedrift@telkomsa.net ▪ **T 022·913·1966/082·824·8104** ▪ F 021·913·1966*

The 7th-generation Mostert on the family farm, Johan, has made it a hat-trick — last year he was named Swartland winner of VinPro's Vineyard Practice competition for the third year running, this time for his shiraz. Time-out is mostly spent travelling Namibia (where wife Karin finds inspiration for her art) and, back home, providing expansive hospitality for as many as 60 in the farm's tasting venue, Wijnhuis. The Mosterts' tiny cellar ('with the emphasis on *tiny*,' says JM), handles seven (select) tons; the 400 excess are sold off.

Shiraz ★★★ Wood-driven styling. **04** step up on pvs; bit fleshier but still fairly light-fruited (& -bodied this time: 13% alc), big dry tannins from combo staves/3rd fill Fr wood, yr. **Chenin Blanc** ★★★ **06** (sample) balanced, flavourful summer tipple. Usual green-apple whiffs, clean & fresh acidity. — *MM*

Nitida Cellars

Durbanville ▪ Est 1992 ▪ 1stB 1995 ▪ Tasting & sales Mon-Fri 9-5 Sat 9.30-1 ▪ Closed Easter Fri/ Sun, Dec 25/26 & Jan 1 ▪ Tours by appt ▪ Owners Veller family ▪ Winemaker/viticulturist Bernhard Veller with Jacus Marais (1995/1999), advised by Eugene van Zyl & Johan Wiese ▪ 15 ha (cab s/f, merlot, pinotage, shiraz, sauvignon, semillon) ▪ 140 tons 7 500 cs own label 45% red 55% white ▪ PO Box 1423 Durbanville 7551 ▪ nitida@mweb.co.za ▪ www.nitida.co. za ▪ T 021·976·1467 ▪ F 021·976·5631

New here are facilities to host open-air concerts. 'We kicked off last year with [local icon] Chris Chameleon,' says marketing assistant Henriëtte Minnaar. 'It was a huge success, proving to us that Cape Town's northern suburbs are crying out for places for families to go on a Sunday afternoon.' Concerts are held every month from September to March, and Henriëtte M recommends bringing along a picnic and washing it down with — unsurprisingly — a glass of Nitida — perhaps the Sparkling Shiraz 'which has already stolen many hearts'.

★★★★ **Cabernet Sauvignon** Last tasted was elegant **03**, with light & lingering palate. Quintessential cool-climate cab, modest 12.9% alc, serious wooding: 18 mths Fr oak, 40% new.

★★★★ **Calligraphy** From merlot, cab f & s; 18 mths Fr oak, 30% new. **04** cleverly balanced to be unchallenging but not trivial or short-lived: just smooth-tannined, ripe, pleasing, with choc notes to fruitcake flavours.

★★★★ **Sauvignon Blanc** Typical exuberant capsicum, green apple aromas/flavours, with tropical perfume and limy finish on **06**. Modest 12.5% alc adds to fresh drinkability. Includes a drop of semillon.

★★★★☆ **Sauvignon Blanc Club Select** Largely sharing make-up & essential character, but more intense & more restrained than above: **06** less pungently aggressive, rounder texture, more tinned pea notes adding interest. Shd develop interestingly over few yrs.

★★★★ **Semillon** Silky texture shot through with shimmering acidity one of many exciting charms of **05**, along with notes of wet wool, honey, wax. Successfully integrated 50% portion ex-oak, half new. 5% sauvignon just adds to freshness, won't harm few yrs' ageability.

Syrah (Formerly 'Shiraz') Spicy, fruity **04** (★★★★) made for early satisfaction; broad, smooth & soft, ripe tannins in background. Yr Fr oak. Last under pvs name was poised & sharp **03** (★★★★). **Pinotage** ★★★★ **05** with sweet dark cherries, plush textured & lush fruited, for those who like chewy softness. Doesn't flaunt its 15% alc or yr Fr oak. **Sparkling Shiraz** NEW ★★★ **04** MCC in cellar's soft ripe style for reds: fine-bubbled, fresh & simply fruity with some tannic grip, dryish. Unusual but very drinkable, even fun. **Chardonnay** ★★★☆ Last tasted was oak-dominated **03**. — *TJ*

▪ *Noble Cape* see Origin Wine
▪ *No Name* see Pick 'n Pay
▪ *Nordale Winery* Bonnievale Wine Cellar
▪ *Nuwehoop* see Groot Eiland

Nuy Wine Cellar

Nuy (see Worcester map) ▪ Est 1963 ▪ 1stB 1967 ▪ Tasting & sales Mon-Fri 8.30-4.30 Sat 8. 30-12.30 ▪ Fee R15 for groups of 10+ ▪ Closed Easter Fri/Sun, Dec 25 & Jan 1 ▪ Braai facilities ▪ Owners 23 members ▪ Manager/winemaker Christo Pienaar, with Juan Slabbert (Sep/Oct 2003) ▪ Viti consultant Newald Marais (Oct 2002) ▪ 9 500 tons ▪ 9% red 79% white 12% muscadel ▪ PO Box 5225 Worcester 6849 ▪ wines@nuywinery.co.za ▪ www.nuywinery.co.za ▪ T 023·347·0272 ▪ F 023·347·4994

fine cultivars deserve nurturing.

With variable settings for red or white wine, electronic temperature control and UV Protection, the Samsung Wine Chiller is the contemporary solution to the classic art of wine.

www.samsung.co.za

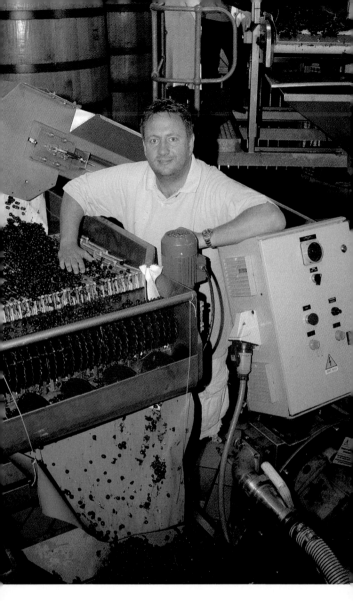

Making the best even better is a preoccupation of **Marc Kent**, much lauded Boekenhoutskloof winemaker and recipient of multiple five-star ratings in this guide. Which is why he and colleagues are helping to develop the ultra-selective French system in the picture, designed to remove fine stems and any other vine material to ensure only healthy grape berries – and nothing besides – make it into the fermentation vessel.

A pink parasol, a herd of pachyderms and a property in the newly declared winegrowing district of Plettenberg Bay all come together in this charming harvest-time image. The umbrella belongs to **Manon**, sister of **Bram**, who together give their name to the family sparkling-wine brand **Bramon**, owned by parents **Caroline** and **Peter Thorpe**. As for the incongruous elephants, they belong to neighbouring farm Elephant Sanctuary.

We keep good company.

Wine Cellar is passionate about identifying, acquiring and cellaring South African wines with investment potential. For more information on our current and back vintages of South Africa's

A property with one of the most famous views in the world, De Grendel crushed the first harvest in its brand-new 600-ton winery in 2006 'with huge excitement and anticipation'. With vineyards almost dipping their toes in the cool Atlantic, and conducive aspects and elevations, owner **David Graaff** (right), cellarmaster **Charles Hopkins** (back), general manager **Johnnie de Flamingh** (left) and vineyard manager **Granville Klerk** understandably believe they have 'The Key' to something special.

VISIT MAKRO FOR THE
FINEST WINE SELECTION!

Find great quality and incredible value in the vast range of wines available at your nearest Makro liquor store.

Award winners, auction wines, large formats, great gifts and special bottlings are all on offer alongside super wines for everyday enjoyment, all at great case prices.

Our wines advisors can assist you to locate the perfect wines to meet your requirements. Subscribe to our newsletter and enjoy news of new releases and upcoming in-store events.

Bringing Italian verve and passion to the Voor Paardeberg area are **Michela** and **Attilio Dalpiaz**, who, with friends and family back home, have taken ownership of part of the old Slent property, planted with vines and deciduous fruit. **Morné Kruger** (right) looks after the farm while Perdeberg Winery, a short hop away, makes the wines. Perdeberg Mountain in the background is home to a leopard which, the owners hope, one day will reveal itself.

Glass is 100% pure and totally natural.
That's why every fine vintage makes glass
its home for years and years.

Consol
GLASS

IT'S GOOD. IT'S IN GLASS

If you judge a book by its cover, then new-look Nuy is readying itself to hit the bestseller list. To match the elegant re-designed labels launched last year, the team are also hoping to shift perceptions of the brand, hitherto (with the exception of the Muscadels) more readily associated with easy-drinkers, by bottling their first Barrel Selection — last year only six casks made the grade; this year the range will be augmented with a Cab.

★★★★ **Red Muscadel** ✓ Deeply delicious fortified dessert, perfect to sip on a rainy day. **05** last ed was concentrated, muscat scented; silky, powerful but also elegant & lively with harmonious 16.5% alc. Stellar **03** (★★★★★) was deep flavoured, showed more potential than usual (these age very well). **04** Muscadel Awards gold.

★★★★ **White Muscadel** ✓ The wine that made cellar's name; golden-hued **05** rich & raisined as always, mid-2004 with lovely varietal notes of mint & cold tea. Tempting, luscious, not over-heavy. Will improve over many yrs. Lightly chilled, a summer delicacy. **02** Muscadel Awards gold.

Rosé new ☺ ★★★ **06** gently sweet blend red muscadel & white hanepoot. Honeysuckle & rosepetal nuances set out to enchant, & they do. **Chant de Nuit** ☺ ★★★ **NV** from Ferdinand de Lesseps table grape, pineapple scents its hallmark. Always lightish (±12% alc) &, despite 'sweet' aromas, ends brisk & dry. **Chardonnay** ☺ ★★★ **06** great advertisement for this cellar's consumer-friendly styling. Delicious stonefruit profile with mere suggestion vanilla oak (chips/staves). **Chenin Blanc** ☺ ★★★ Delightful quaffer, **06** unoaked but briefly aged on lees for zesty, mouthfilling fun. **Colombar Dry** ☺ ★★★ **06** billows guava, passionfruit & honeysuckle, lively acidity ups the refreshment. To be enjoyed young, as all these whites. **Sauvignon Blanc** ☺ ★★★ Hint of fynbos on bright **06**, fresh citrusy wag in its tail. **Colombar Semi-Sweet** ☺ ★★★ **06** delightfully poised, with gentle sweetness rounding out the palate, keeping the tropical finish alive. Friendly 11.8% alc. **Sauvignon Blanc Sparkling Vin Sec** ☺ ★★★ Well made, refreshing carbonated bubbly with gooseberry/greenpepper spilling out of the glass in **06**; not overly sweet; best young & well chilled.

Barrel Selection Syrah new ★★★ Attractive maiden from stringent barrel selection process; attractively lighter styled. **04** has smoke mingling with lilies & spicy scents. Fruity flavours very capable of absorbing the oaking & firm fruit tannins. Balanced 14% alc; 20 mths new oak, mix Fr/Am. Will reward 3-5 yrs patience. Following trio not retasted: **Cabernet Sauvignon** ★★★ **03** showed satisfying fruity substance; solid, rounded dry persistence. Some Fr oak. **Rouge de Nuy** ★★ Cab/merlot blend. **03** shy, bit lean, with drying tannins. Lightly oaked. **Noble Late Harvest** Botrytised chenin & hanepoot. **04** with apricot toned fruit, slight citrus touch in tail. 10.8% alc. **Fernão Pires** discontinued. — DH

Oaklands Wine Exporters

Est 2002 ▪ 1stB 2003 ▪ Closed to public ▪ Owner Danie Zeeman ▪ PO Box 12398 Die Board 7613 ▪ info@oaklandswines.com ▪ www.deza.co.za ▪ T 021·886·9626 ▪ F 021·887·0441

Widely experienced Danie Zeeman sources wines locally for clients in Europe to market under their own brands, and in some cases creates special blends to suit clients' requirements. Deza is his own label, and it flies to America, Switzerland and Singapore.

Deza Collection

Reserve Shiraz ★★★☆ **02** modern, ripe but not over-extracted, lots of toasty wood noted last ed (combo Fr/Am barrels, 80/20). **03** unready. **Shiraz-Pinotage** ★★ 60/40 mix, fruit again ex-Wllngtn, unoaked; **04** not as convincing as pvs: dry leaves/damp earth tone, rustic, sharpish finish. **Chardonnay** ★★★ Last was food-friendly **04** (sample); fresh & balanced, weighty, with lime marmalade aromas & flavours. **Sauvignon Blanc** ★★★ **06** not ready. **05** riper, more mouth-filling & grainier than pvs; melon/pineapple on nose/palate, bone-dry exit.

Afrikaanse Plesier range   new

Merlot ★★ Pleasantly nutty **05**, mulberry flavours & firm but friendly tannins, fullish body. **Shiraz Rosé** ★★★ Tasty, dry alfresco quaffer; strawberry-red **06** cherries on nose/palate, slight grip of tannins, pert cherry bite on finish. **Chenin Blanc ★★★ 06** well-crafted, harmonious easy-drinker with soft apple flavours, persistent acidity & ripe fruit. All WO W Cape. — *CT*

■ *Oak Lane* see Beau Joubert
■ *Oak Ridge* see Shoprite Checkers

Oak Valley Wines

Elgin · Est 1898 · 1stB 2003 · Tasting & sales Mon-Fri 9-5, otherwise by appt · Closed Easter Fri-Mon, Dec 25/26 & Jan 1 · Conservation area · Owner AG Rawbone-Viljoen Trust · Winemaker Pieter Visser · Viticulturist Pieter Visser, advised by Kevin Watt · 35 ha (cabs s/f, merlot, pinot, chard, sauvignon) · 6 700 cs white 2 300 cs red · PO Box 30 Elgin 7180 · wines@oak-valley.co.za · www.oakvalleywines.com · **T** *021·859·4110* · F *021·859·3405*
Vintage 2006 was a steep learning curve for this quality driven Elgin farm. An unseasonal gale-force northwester tore into the sauvignon on already viticulturally challenging 520m mountain slopes, culling the crop to just one ton/ha. Commercially disappointing but quality-wise exceptional, and 4th-generation grower Anthony Rawbone-Viljoen (also producer of premium apples, pears, prime beef, cut flowers — and grapes for other big names such as Rupert & Rothschild and Flagstone) can take further comfort in an excellent first Pinot, developing beautifully in the bottle, and a lovely maiden Chardonnay. It's early days, says winemaker Pieter Visser of the recently released reds — but having sampled the wines, we think he's being too modest.

★★★★ **The Oak Valley Blend** Mostly merlot in **04** (9% cab f, dollop cab s). Choc, burnt fruit-cake notes, with spicy vanilla. Big & self-assured, quite heavily extracted, with good succulent tannic structure. Herbaceous twist in the tail pleasantly stresses cool-climate origins, while 14.5% alc testifies to ripeness.

★★★★ **Pinot Noir** Interesting, forward aromas of forest floor, earth-covered strawberries on youthful **05**. Fruit concentration evidenced in un-obviousness of oak influence — yet 9 mths new Fr. Subtle tannins, but fine acidity more significant as structuring element. Shd develop well.

★★★★☆ **Mountain Reserve Sauvignon Blanc** new (as are above pair, Chard below) From a single vyd block at 520m altitude, maiden **05** is compelling, thrilling & still immensely drinkable. Quantitative difference from (vg) standard version becomes qualitative: more powerful & pungent, fuller & richer yet more steely & mineral, more concentrated — altogether more complete. Good (if rare?) case for argument that sauvignon can attain complexity.

★★★★☆ **Sauvignon Blanc** Delicately herbaceous as usual, **05**'s subtle passionfruit, gooseberry & dried grass made more interesting by mineral vein, tight structure. More elegant than showy, but substantial, balanced, confident. *Decanter* trophy.

★★★★☆ **Chardonnay** Creamy palate the best of many good features of **05**, along with overall classy restraint. Perfectly complementary 13.5% alc in harmonious whole; only oakiness slightly apart in youth (two thirds naturally fermented/8 mths new Fr oak, rest tanks), but shd integrate with the few yrs' deserved bottle maturation. — *TJ*

Obikwa

Value-priced Distell brand, exported to North & South America, Europe and the Far East.
Cabernet Sauvignon ★★★ 05 hearty & bold; dollop blackcurrant/blackberry fruit spiced up with 9 mths Fr staves. Dusty finish with sweet hint. **Merlot ★★★ 05** richer than pvs, riper plum aromas, chunkier tannins (9 mths staves), more obvious alcohol (14.5%). Similar savoury notes, persistent tea-leaf finish. **Pinotage ★★★** Earthy, strawberry-toned **05** easy drinking, thanks to friendly tannins from combo barrels/staves & unoaked portion. Noticeable 14.65% alc. **Shiraz ★★★** Muscled **05** flaunts a 'six-pack' of bacon, oregano & spicy fruit. Finishes smoother than Cab, despite similar oaking. **Chardonnay ★★★ 05** full-bodied, fairly rich; careful oaking/lees-ageing gives full expression to white peach/tangerine aromas; spiky acidity invites food. **Chenin Blanc ★★★** Usually a treat, with mineral notes. **06** has appealing green-apple bounce, sherbety texture but tad lean & short on finish. **Sauvignon Blanc ★★★ 06** nettle, blackcurrant & gooseberry complexity. Fresh, crunchy, light bodied (11.5% alc); more satisfying than pvs. All WO W Cape. — *CvZ*

■ *Oddbins* see Shoprite Checkers

Oewerzicht Private Cellar

Greyton • Est/1stB 2002 • Tasting & sales Mon-Fri 8-5 & by appt • Luxury guest cottages & tents • Wedding, conference & function facilities • Mountain biking/hiking trails • Owner/viticulturist/winemaker Kootjie Viljoen • 3 ha (cab) • 1 000 cs 100% red • PO Box 18 Greyton 7233 • oewerzicht@telkomsa.net • T 028·254·9831 F 028·254·9968

'Our best yet!' exults winemaker Kootjie Viljoen of this Greyton cellar's fifth vintage, which reaped the benefits of considerable vineyard input during the preceding winter. Opening of the cellar's new tasting room is the first in moves to expand, including additional sauvignon and merlot vineyards, and eventually relocating the cellar into a renovated building nearby.

Cabernet Sauvignon ★★★★ Quality leap for **03** noted pvs ed; showed softer side of this often austere-in-youth variety, thanks to gentle vinification & oaking. Ripe & accessible tannins, juicy finish. Yr Fr oak. Modest 13% alc. WO Ovrberg. — *IvH*

Old Bridge Wines

Closed to public • Owner Paulinas Dal Farm Holdings (Pty) Ltd • 20 000 cs 60% red 40% white • PO Box 557 St Francis Bay 6312 • rickety@iafrica.com • T 082·777·1519

Export-focused producer and negociant sourcing wines for a variety of brands, including private labels for specialised corporate clients. The wines, untasted, include limited-edition African Gold Collection: Cabernet-Merlot, Shiraz, Merlot mainly for US, Europe and Far East; Big Six Collection: boxed sets of Cabernet, Merlot, Shiraz, Pinotage, Sauvignon, Chenin for local game lodges/retreats and for export; and Old Bridge: Cabernet, Merlot, Shiraz, Pinotage, Sauvignon & Chenin.

■ *Old Brown* see Sedgwick's
■ *Old Chapel* see Robertson Winery

Old Vines Cellars

Cape Town • Est/1stB 1995 • Closed to public • Owners Irina von Holdt & Françoise Botha • Winemaker Irina von Holdt with Jan van Rooyen • 12 500 cs own label + 2 500 cs for pvt clients • 35% red 65% white • 50 Liesbeek Rd, Rosebank 7700 • fran@oldvines.co.za • www.oldvines.co.za • T 021·685·6428 • F 021·685·6446

Infiltration into the previously all-female camp increases with Fran Botha's marriage to Jurgen Potgieter, whom mother-in-law Irina von Holdt, a taster for this guide, is training to take over production; and new assistant winemaker Jan van Rooyen. The late Baron von Holdt, IvH's father, in tribute to whom she accepted her Cape Wine Master qualification in her maiden name, lived to see his name honoured on the red bordeaux-style blend he greatly approved of. It has proved a runaway success, as has the 04 Chenin Reserve (now served at Michelin-rated Alain Ducasse's restaurant in Mauritius; it also received the highest bid for a chenin at the Nederburg Auction). With their wines selected five times in almost as many months by Wine of the Month Club they are, as they modestly put it, 'doing something right'.

★★★★ **Baron von Holdt** Contemplative bdx-style blend, elegant rather than powerful. **04** ex-barrel, awaiting final tweaks, promises usual refinement, with plentiful cassis & sugared plum, reined-in tannins. 2 yrs new/old Fr oak.

★★★★ **Chenin Blanc** ✓ An unwooded standout — found in some of UK's poshest hotels & restaurants, says IvH. **05** silky & round, vibrant freshness leavening honeyed aromas & bruised apple flavours. Crafted to gain complexity with 4-7 yrs cellaring, as was notably elegant **04** (★★★★★).

★★★★ **Barrel Reserve Chenin Blanc 04**, tasted mid-2005, had ample creamy elderflower bouquet, elegant lemon & mineral flavours. Tad drier than **03** (2.3g/ℓ), longer in oak (10 mths Fr casks), 10% new wood (pvs none). These should age well.

★★★★ **Vintage Brut** Unusually for style, from chenin, made with help from Villiera's Jeff Grier; grapes ex-Sbosch bushvines. **01** degorged/bottled on demand – tasted mid-2004 was friendly, no brut-ish severity.

Blue White ★★★ Reticent **06** shows subtle floral, hay tones; gd acidity, hint sweetness (6.5g/ℓ) on finish. This, below, WO Coastal.

Spring Valley range

Chenin Blanc-Sauvignon Blanc ☺ ★★★ Zingy everyday white. **06** (75% chenin) creamy floral/wet wool aromas; layered flavours, crisp acidity. **Stein Select** ☺ ★★★ **NV** from chenin; appealing butterscotch & bready aromas, honey palate ends softly sweet (14g/ℓ sugar).

Shiraz-Merlot ★★★ Lightly wooded **05** (sample), nible & comfortable ±equal blend, with generous berry fruit, some pepper, lily & meaty hints. **Sauvignon Blanc** ★★★★ Tasted last ed, **05** spicy & floral; refreshing grapefruit palate & persistent soft finish. — *CvZ*

Olsen Wines

Paarl ▪ Est/1stB 2002 ▪ Visits by appt ▪ Fee R10 ▪ Home-style light meals for groups of ±10 by appt ▪ Farm-style jams ▪ Owner Greg Olsen ▪ Winemaker Helene van der Westhuizen (2005) ▪ Viticulturist Armand Botha (2000) ▪ 30 ha ▪ 500 cs 90% red 10% white ▪ Eurepgap registered ▪ PO Box 9052 Huguenot 7645 ▪ olsenwines@mweb.co.za ▪ T 021·862·3653 ▪ F 021·862·2589

SA can lay part-claim to another space explorer: American Dr Greg Olsen, owner of 30ha of Du Toitskloof Mountain vineyards, succeeded Mark Shuttleworth as the world's third 'private' astronaut in 2005. Greg O's honorary SA citizenship is cemented by his choice of pinotage as his favourite variety. This was the only wine bottled under the Olsen label in 2006 (for release in 2008), and it will be joined by a Chenin in due course. Wines are vinified the old-fashioned way in the farm's modern cellar.

★★★★ **Cabernet Sauvignon** Ripe & well balanced **03**; fine, firm, slightly herbal tannins give structure to sweet finish; elegant despite 14% alc.

Cabernet Sauvignon-Shiraz ★★ Herbaceous green-fruit aromas on **05**, intrusive tannins softened by well managed sweet fruit. 11.4% alc. **Pinotage** ★★★ Easy drinking **03**, attractive banana/black-fruit whiffs spiced with nutmeg; surprisingly soft tannins for variety. From high-yielding (15t/ha) vyd; 9 mths Fr oak. **Chardonnay** ★★ **05** tropical/marzipan aromas, fleeting flavours, curiously low alc (11.9%) for ripe Paarl fruit. No new vintages of above ready for tasting; notes from pvs ed. — *MF*

Olyvenbosch Vineyards

Wellington ▪ Est 1990 ▪ 1stB 2003 ▪ Closed to public ▪ Owner/winemaker Otto G Schmidtke ▪ 20 ha (cab, merlot) ▪ 110 tons 572 cs own label 100% red ▪ PO Box 235 Wellington 7654 ▪ ogschmidtke@telkomsa.net ▪ T/F 021·864·1195

Sometimes the stars align and the right wine falls into your lap…' is what US *Wine* magazine said about the 03 Otto's Bin Cab. And what better to serve it with than beef Wellington? Retired from a successful clothing and textile career in the Far East, Otto and Dagi Schmidtke have chosen Wellington as their home (son Oliver S, based in Boston, handles marketing in America). Most of the 110-ton production is bought up but a small parcel is kept back and hand-made into these boutique wines.

★★★★ **Cabernet Sauvignon** Revisited **03** (sample last ed) has integrated, improved; ripe, supple blackcurrant flavour delivered with style & finesse; healthy tannins & extended finish augur well for development. 13 mths new Fr oak. Unobtrusive 14% alc.

Otto's Bin range
Cabernet Sauvignon ★★★☆ Appealing, food-cordial **04**, dark cassis fruit in generous quantity, hints mint & bluegum in firm finish. Yr new Fr oak; same for… **Merlot** ★★★ **04** retasted; very ripe, even slightly raisined berry notes, tannins appear firmer than last time, possibly in unsettled phase. 14.5% alc not obvious. All above EW. — *IvH*

■ **Omnia Wines** see The Company of Wine People

Onderkloof

Stellenbosch (see Helderberg map) • Est 1998 • 1stB 1999 • Tasting Mon-Fri by appt • Sales & tours by appt • Private functions (lunch/dinner) by appt • Member of Schapenberg-Sir Lowry's Conservancy • Owners Daniël Truter & Beat Musfeld • Winemaker/viticulturist Daniël Truter, with Truter Willemse (May 2003) • 25 ha (cab, pinotage, shiraz, chenin, crouchen, muscat d'A, sauvignon) • 100 tons 4 000 cs own label 30% red 70% white • PO Box 90 Sir Lowry's Pass 7133 • wine@onderkloofwines.co.za • www.onderkloofwines.co.za • **T 021·858·1538** • F 021·858·1536

Named after the original pass over the Hottentots Holland mountain range, Onderkloof is located on the slopes of the Schapenberg where Cape governor Willem Adriaan van der Stel's sheep once grazed. But this is now recognised as prime vineyard territory, so winemaker/viticulturist/co-owner Daniël Truter is extremely proud that all the varietal wines from the 06 vintage are registered as 'single vineyard' Schapenberg.

★★★★ **Chardonnay 05** sleekly muscular, boldly oaked, with savoury centre to citrus fruit. **06** (★★★), only 50% barrelled (seasoned oak, rest tank-vinified), for lighter, still attractive feel. Unfiltered. Note: tasted as sample; ratings provisional; ditto for all new releases below.

Cabernet Sauvignon Concentrated, attractive **02** (★★★★) succeeded by more restrained, unfleshy **03**, showing rather more freshness & oak (14 mths Fr). Pre-bottling, rates ★★. **Pinotage** ★★★★ Satisfyingly ripe & juicy **04** billows rich mocha aromas, oozes creamy fruit. Bold, with no-nonsense tannins, but pleasing. Oak as for Cab; ditto for... **Shiraz** Pvs were brazenly New World in style, though **04** shade less fruit-rich & open textured; dusty sweet-sour flavours, which depart fairly hastily. Possible ★★★. **Floreal Rouge** ★★★ Interesting & unusual unwooded red, 'easy drinking for everyday' the intended style. **05** was malbec/merlot mix with brambly flavours, light & refreshing. Unready **06** shiraz/cab. **Chenin Blanc** ★★★ Well-applied oak chips again add some dimension, texture to **06**; taut mineral flavours & brisk acidity might fill out once bottled. Unfiltered, as is... **Sauvignon Blanc** ★★★★ **06** notch above pvs; broad tropical fruit flavours deftly tweaked with bright, clean acidity. Gd solo drink (lowish 13.5% alc a bonus). Ex-vyd est 1989. **Floreal Blanc de Blanc** ★★★★ Gorgeous semi-dry aperitif from chenin, muscat de A, crouchen. **06** not ready; **05** chenin a mere delivery platform for pure hanepoot fragrance, scented gewürz-like finish. — *MM*

■ **Onyx** see Darling Cellars

Oom Tas

With 2m-plus cases sold each year, all in returnable glass, this a contender for title of SA's biggest-selling budget-priced brand. By Distell. Tiger's eye hue & spicy muscat nose suggest a sweet wine, but it is always lean. **NV** ★ Latest sherry-like, oxidised. — *CvZ*

■ **Oorsprong Organic** see Origin Wine
■ **Open Sky** see Premium Cape Wines

Opstal Estate

Slanghoek (see Worcester map) • Est 1950 • 1stB 1978 • Tasting & sales Mon-Fri 9-5 Sat 10-2 • Closed Christian holidays • Tours by appt • Restaurant Wed-Sun 10-3 • Conference/function centre • Owner Stanley Louw • Winemaker Stanley Louw, with Jaco Theron (Jan 1999) • 103 ha (13 varieties, r/w) • 1 500 tons 10 000 cs own label 35% red 65% white • PO Box 27 Rawsonville 6845 • wine@opstal.co.za • www.opstal.co.za • **T 023·344·3001** • F 023·344·3002

After a flurry of activity, the Louws of Opstal took stock... and then decided that tasting should happen separately from eating — theirs is a popular restaurant — so are building a new tasting room. Much involved with tourism in this scenic valley, winemaker/owner Stanley L welcomes the recent gazetting of the Breedekloof district (divided into the Slanghoek and Goudini wards) within the Breede River region, and intends to market the new brand actively.

Cabernet Sauvignon ★★★ Characterful, lightish **02**, red berry flavours & plentiful dry tannins. ±Yr Fr oak. **Chardonnay** ★★★ Lightish **03** tropical fruit tones & fairly obvious vanilla from oak staving. **Hanepoot** ★★★ **03** warming, appealingly smooth & fragrant. Only following wine in this range retasted: **Chenin Blanc** ★★ 'Serious wine' says Stanley L, though to us **05** is light-hearted, fruity & ready for early enjoyment.

Carl Everson range

Classic Red makes way for… **Cabernet Sauvignon-Shiraz** ★★★ More traditional – not unappealing – style. **03** last ed a melange of black/green pepper, pronounced dry oak, full body but light texture. **Sauvignon Blanc** ★★☆ **05** dry, slightly dusty white; light & crisply refreshing. – *CT/DH*

Oracle

Distell export brand launched July 2002, initially into the UK retail market; the name an allusion to the 'ancient wisdom of Africa'.

Cabernet Sauvignon ★★★★ **05** supple, smooth, sexy red, off Paarl/Sbosch vyds. Blackcurrant mingles with forest floor, cigar box; touch sugar (6.4g/ℓ) mutes tannins. Yr Fr oak staves/casks. **Pinotage** ★★★☆ Puts variety's best foot forward with Dbnvlle/Hldrberg fruit. Luscious strawberry jam notes & pulpy, long flavours on **05**. Firm tannin, pleasantly sweetish end (4.8g/ℓ sugar). Combo barrels/Fr staves/unwooded. **Shiraz** ★★★★ **05** has old-fashioned smoky/leather nose, ripe fruit, mild tannins further mollified by dollop sugar (5g/ℓ) & soft oak (9 mths Fr/Am staves). **Chardonnay** ★★★ **05** pleases with acid/fruit balance & judicious oaking (chips, 6 mths), letting lime/orange/mango aromas & flavours dominate. **Sauvignon Blanc 06** vibrant scents of gooseberry, fresh-cut grass; layered, with fig, wet stone, earth notes. Light in alc (11.8%), not in presence or satisfaction. Classy sample provisionally rates ★★★★. All WO W Cape. – *CvZ*

Oranjerivier Wine Cellars   👁♟&

Lower Orange (see Northern Cape map) ▪ Est 1965 ▪ 1stB 1968 ▪ Tasting Mon-Fri 8-4.30 Sat 9-11.30 ▪ Fee R5 for 1-5 wines; R10 for 5+ wines ▪ Sales Mon-Fri 8-5 Sat 8.30-12 ▪ Closed pub hols ▪ Tours Mon-Fri 9, 11 & 3 Jan-Mar ▪ Owners ±930 shareholders ▪ Winemakers Johan Esterhuizen (Upington cellar), Jan Steenkamp (Grootdrink), Chris Venter (Groblershoop), Deon Truter (Keimoes) & Bolla Louw (Kakamas), with (in same cellar order) Jopie Faul/Philani Gumede, George Kruger/Tinus Kotze, Ferdi Laubscher, Christo Smit/Riaan Liebenberg & Johan Dippenaar/André Smit ▪ Senior viticulturist Henning Burger (2005) ▪ Viticulturist Nic Smit ▪ 332 837 ha (pinotage, ruby cab, chenin, colombard) ▪ ±150 000 tons ▪ Export labels: River's Tale ▪ Ranges for customers: Vine Collection & Liquor Boys (Liquor City); Country Cellars & Carnival (Spar) ▪ HACCP certification in progress ▪ PO Box 544 Upington 8800 ▪ marketing@owk.co.za ▪ www.owk.co.za ▪ T 054·337·8800 ▪ F 054·332·4408

Having completed a two-year, R20m-plus cellar upgrade, further increased bottling capacity and implemented a R1.8m upgrade to the casked wine line, this mega-operation has appointed agents in the UK and US to better cater for international demand. Local growth continues apace, including housewines for Spar and Liquor City retail outlets. All this activity has resulted in a second range, River's Tale, and the promise of more single-vineyard bottlings. Newly appointed head viticulturist Nic Smit oversees some 900 growers and experimental plantings of petit verdot, tannat, viognier, malbec and other rare-to-the-Cape grapes, to test their performance on hillier Orange River-flanking sites.

All below have moderate alcs (12-13.5% unless noted), & are for earliest possible consumption. Reds mainly unwooded. Only 05s & 06s tasted this ed; notes for all other vintages & NVs from pvs ed. **Cabernet Sauvignon** ★★★ Step above pvs; **04** fairly richly fruited, pleasant dry balanced tannin, easy to drink. **Pinotage** ★★☆ Good everyday red, comfortable & well flavoured. **Ruby Cabernet** ★ Surprisingly ungenerous **05**, hints red jam & thatch overwhelmed by demanding freshness & dry tannins. **Shiraz** ★★★ Good undemanding quaffer, lightly & well oaked. Appealing white pepper sniff on **04**, juicy tannins. **Rouge** ★★☆ From cab; smoky/savoury tone, hint oak (staves), berry fruit & undemanding dry tannins. **Rosé** ★ Shy, earthy semi-sweet pink from colombard, pinotage. **Blanc de Noir** ★★ Ruby cab does the business. Savoury last time; rounded & dryish despite ±17g/ℓ sugar. **Chardonnay** ★★ 04 bit honeyed & tired last ed; reminder that these have evanescent charms. **Chenin Blanc** ★★ 06 riper, with better balanced acidity than pvs; ripe apple & pineapple on taste. **Colombard** ★★ Again semi-dry in 06 but more manageably fresh, suitable as an aperitif. **Grand Cru** ★ Water-white & bracingly dry, as expected. From colombard. **Blanc de Blanc** ★★ Three whites led by colombard; soft, fruity, pleasant summer quaffer. **Nouveau Blanc** ★★ Popular semi-sweet from chenin; 06 uncloying, gentle ripe apple & tropical fruit flavours. **Light** ★ Very ordinary off-dry from chenin; austere, fruit-free. 8% alc. **Stein** ★★ Pleasant & inoffensive, lots of sweetness to mask otherwise austere profile. Varieties as for next wine. **Late Harvest** ★ Colombard, chenin with very little to offer beyond sweetness. **Special Late Harvest** ★★ Delicately perfumed 04, clean, with hint of fruit; varieties as for Late Harvest. **Sparkling Brut** ★★★ Sprightly carbonated dry bubbly with fine bead; clean, fresh & patently colombard. **Sparkling Doux** ★★ Big, bouncy bubbles; light & not too sweet. **White Jerepiko** ★★ Sultana stars in what tastes like liquidised raisins, with warm spirituous fruit. **Sweet Hanepoot** ★★★ Foursquare version with pineapple/tropical fruit hint, clean spirit edge. **Red Jerepigo** ★★ Invariably from ruby cab; 05's jammy blackcurrant fruit & big alc yet to mesh mid-2006. **White Muscadel** ★★★ 05 very sweet on entry but clean spirit quickly cuts any cloy; barley sugar & tangerine to enjoy over crushed ice. **Red Muscadel** ★★ 05 offers expected perfume counter attractions but also more unusual spirituous bite & overt sweetness, which might harmonise with time. **Red Port** ★★ Traditional-style fortified from ruby cab, with variety's fruit lushness evident in notch-up 05, blackcurrant jam & liquorice, higher than usual fortification (18%) gives drier, lifted effect.

River's Tale range

Shiraz-Cabernet Sauvignon new ★★★ Balanced, easy 05, well fruited 80/20 mix with juicy sour-plum flavour & hint rooibos tea, gentle tannin grip; lightly chill in summer. **Classic Red** ★★★ 02 was last tasted; smoky/savoury blend cab, shiraz, pinotage, ruby cab, 6 mths oak-staved; light, slightly grainy dry flavours. **Chenin Blanc-Chardonnay** new ★★ Appealing quaffing style: 05 fresh, fragrant & crisp, with touches pear & apple. Incl splash colombard. N Cape & Lower Orange WOs for both ranges. — MW

■ *Oranje Straat* see Rooiberg Winery

Org de Rac Domain   👤👃📖

Swartland ▪ Est 2004 ▪ 1stB 2005 ▪ Visits Mon-Fri 9-5 Sat 9-1 ▪ Closed Easter Fri/Sun/Mon, Dec 16/25/26 & Jan 1 ▪ Tour groups ▪ Conferences ▪ Owner Pieter Vercuiel ▪ Winemaker Hugo Lambrechts (Nov 2004) ▪ Viticulturist to be appointed ▪ 42.5 ha (cab, merlot, shiraz) ▪ 340 tons 17 000 cs 100% red ▪ HACCP certification in progress ▪ PO Box 268 Piketberg 7320 ▪ orgderac@mweb.co.za ▪ www.orgderac.com ▪ T 022·913·2397/3924 ▪ F 022·913·3162

This imposing establishment – its name meaning 'Organic on the Shelf' – found its feet last year. A marked improvement in the quality of the harvest (according to winemaker Hugo Lambrechts, a result of his vines starting to mature) coincided with the advent of new marketing director, Brian Smit, to help put the brand on the map. The focus is now squarely on reds, with Org de Rac Family Reserve the new flagship.

Family Reserve range

Cabernet Sauvignon, Merlot & Shiraz, slated for launch in 2006, at press time unfinished & so not rated.

Org de Rac range

★★★★ **Merlot** Generous maiden 05; rich & round, abundant berry aromas/flavours & wafts choc-mocha, plum & vanilla; succulent tannins allow access now, give potential to improve over next few yrs.

Cabernet Sauvignon ★★ In contrast to above red, this is firm & v dry, unsoftened by berried, slightly earthy fruit. **Shiraz** ★★★ Big & bold but supple wine, well handled tannins. Complex scents & tastes – plum, smoked meat, black cherry, spice – make an impressive debut. **Rosé** ★★ Demure first outing: light on fruit, v dry & savoury, touch earthy. All above **05**, certified organic & new to the guide. — *DH*

Origin Wine ⚱

Stellenbosch • Est/1stB 2002 • Closed to public • Owner Bernard Fontannaz • Winemakers Alain Cajeux & Theresa Bedeker (both Dec 2004), with Quintin van der Westhuizen & David Smit • 4 million cs • 55% red 40% white 5% rosé • Export brands: African Horizon, Cape 1652, Cape Original, Fair Hills, Noble Cape, Rocktail Bay, Stellenbosch Drive & ranges below • PO Box 7177 Stellenbosch 7599 • reception@originwine.co.za • T 0861 ORIGIN • F 021-865-2348

After extensive investments and expansions, everything is in place and running smoothly' at one of the Cape's largest (albeit low-key) wineries, says CEO Bernard Fontannaz. A major exporter of bottled and casked wine, Origin reports steady sales growth, especially due to new markets, notably China, Russia and Eastern Europe. Emphasis is now on local community development via the Fairhills project, a collaboration with Du Toitskloof Winery, certified by Fairtrade. Proceeds of wine sales (chiefly to Finland and the UK) benefit some 800 people.

Stellenbosch Drive range   new

Red Blend ★★★ Juicy, full bodied **05** bdx (cab, 50%) & rhône (shiraz/mourvèdre) partnership; latter contributes spice, red cherry flavour, former, pleasing firm mouthfeel. Partly barrel fermented, as is... **White Blend** ★★★ **06** mainly chenin & chard; drop viognier evident in delicate apricot waft; dry but creamy, balanced, for easy/early enjoyment.

Rocktail Bay range   new

Merlot-Cabernet Sauvignon ★★ **05** titivated by dollop sugar, but remains rather foursquare, with mild cranberry flavours for casual tippling. **Rosé** ★★ Similar to Cape 1652 version below, though this **06** mite drier on analysis (4.5g/ℓ) sugar.

African Horizon range

Pinotage-Shiraz ☺ ★★★ Skippered by pinotage this yr (60%), beneficially so: **05** easier, fruitier than pvs, whiffs spice & smoky bacon to fleshy fruit.

Cinsaut-Pinotage new ★★★ Uncomplicated, friendly & juicy 80/20 blend; **05** appealing youngberry jam character, medium body, chillable in summer. Following 7 wines, all **05**, not retasted: **Pinotage** ★ Touch ruby cab blended in; mainly banana character & puckering dryness. **Shiraz** ★★★ Robust, slightly smoky winter red; lacks charm & varietal character of pvs, but does a good warming job. **Pinotage-Ruby Cab-Cinsaut** ★ Very little of cinsaut's fruity juiciness apparent, faint raisin notes & challenging dry tannins. **Cabernet-Pinotage-Ruby Cabernet** ★★ Forthcoming cassis/vanilla notes, fruit restrained by dry tannins; drink with food or cellar yr/2. **Dry Red** ★★ Mainly pinotage — obvious from pleasant dried banana/wild berry sniffs; muted tannins make for comfortable anytime red. **Rosé** ★★ Delicate dry pink from pinotage; subdued but easy strawberry flavours. **Chardonnay** ★★ Bring back pvs vintage! Retiring **05** insubstantial & unmemorable. **Chardonnay-Viognier** ★★★ Soft, plump, peachy **05**, off Rbtson vyds, pleasant lightish quaffer, with spicy/floral nuance from the viognier. Stave fermented. **Colombard-Chardonnay** ★★ Chard portion oaked, adds vanilla touch to lime fruit; **06** more nervous acidity than pvs, better with food. Following trio of **05**s not retasted: **Chenin Blanc** ★ Has varietal character (Golden Delicious apple) in slender, lightish package. **Chenin Blanc-Colombard** ★★ Crisp, dry, hints guava & other tropical fruits; subtly flavoured 70/30 blend. **White** ★★ Cheerful chenin, colombard, muscat mix with delicate fruit salad aroma, light body.

Oorsprong Organic

'Cape Nature Organic' last ed. **Cabernet Sauvignon** ★★ Herbaceous profile with leaves & damp earth; **05** matching unfruity flavours/tannins. Not retasted. **Merlot** ★★★ **05** has filled out since tasted as sample last ed, though still bit unforthcoming; clean-cut red/ black berry fruit, touch dusty tannin. **Shiraz** ★★★ Lovely youthful purple colour noted last ed; **05** hint new leather, softly spicy flavour. **Colombard** ★★ Appealing alfresco wine; **06** crisply dry, fresh, light-bodied, with variety's signature guava tone.

Cape 1652 range

Pinotage-Cabernet Sauvignon ★★ No follow-up yet to **05** 70/30 blend, spicy/stalky red with earthy hint, food-friendly dry finish. **Cabernet Sauvignon-Shiraz** new ★★★ **05** fairly rich, juicy-fruity bouquet followed by more restrained, firmish, food-inviting palate. **Merlot-Cabernet Sauvignon** new ★★ **05** 60/40 bdx blend with attractively obvious red fruit flavours; soft & well pitched for unceremonious quaffing. **Pinotage-Shiraz** new ★☆ Spicy dry red with red cherry flavours; fruity, medium bodied, uncomplex but not unsatisfying **05**. **Rosé** ★★ Again from pinotage; **06** refreshing & dry picnic basket filler; light, with fresh strawberry flavours & touch savoury. **Chenin Blanc-Chardonnay** ★★ Your basic dry white — straightforward, light, crisp, **06** with a hint of apple.

Fairhills range

Approved/certified by the Fairtrade Labelling Organisation (FLO). **Cabernet Sauvignon** new ★★★ Comfortable & open-textured **05**, friendliness enhanced by smoothing grain sugar; enough padding to cope with dry oak tannins. **Shiraz** new ★★★ Quaffable **05**, gd everyday red with savoury-dry flavours, balanced spicy tannins. **Cabernet Sauvignon-Shiraz** new ★★★ Well-structured 80/20 blend with legs to run yr/3. **05** ripe blueberry tone, spicy grape tannins & fair smack dusty oak (ex-chips), latter a hallmark of all Origin reds. **Merlot-Shiraz** ★★ Successor to Starbucks-special **05** unready; mocha coffee & spice, lively flavours, youthful but balanced tannins. 10% oaked. **Shiraz-Cinsaut** new ★★★ 20% fruity cinsaut adds welcome padding to **05**'s dry wood & spicy shiraz tannins, which some will find too high for solo drinking. **Chardonnay** new ★★★ Stave fermented **05** unfleshy but balanced, flavourful; clean stone-fruit tone, attractively lively & dry. **Sauvignon Blanc** new ★★★ Fruit ex-Rwsnvlle; light bodied but full flavoured **06**, fresh, balanced, liberal gooseberry fruit. **Chenin Blanc-Chardonnay** new ★★★ Vinification with oak staves noticeable on **06**, unlingering pear/green-fruit flavours, dusty note on finish. **Colombard-Chardonnay** ★★ Last tasted was **05**, 80/20 split, small portion oaked. Early-evening aperitif with crisp, clean peach & apricot flavours. **Colombard-Sauvignon Blanc** new ★★ Light, crisp & compact 80/20 blend, **06** v straightforward & inoffensive. **Sauvignon Blanc-Colombar** new ★★ Case where parts are more than the whole: light textured **06** tad drier, leaner, less vibey than varietal Sauvignon above. **Semillon-Chardonnay** new ★★★ 80% semillon lends weight, waxy impression to **06**; some dusty oak whiffs (stave fermented) to quiet grapefruit palate.

Kaap Hollands range

This, following 5 ranges, still selling, not retasted for current ed. **Pinotage-Shiraz** ★☆ Undemanding & cheerful red, **05** jammy wild berry flavours, generous but balanced tannins. **Chenin Blanc-Chardonnay** ★★ Fruity easy-drinker, **05** apricot & orange zest aromas, clean — if quick — finish. 10% Fr oaked.

Evolution range

Merlot ★★ Incl 10% ruby cab in **05**, less engaging than pvs; stalky flavours, big dry tannins. 10% oaked. **Sauvignon Blanc** ★★★ **05** again light bodied, gooseberry intro; some flinty hints; lively acidity. **Semillon-Chardonnay** ★★ **05** crisp, dry & minerally; light bodied, for early enjoyment. Lower proportion (10%) Fr oaked. **Pinotage** ★★★ Partly wooded **04** mingle of red fruits, gentle tannins for easy drinking. **Shiraz** ★★★ Peppery touch to **04**, palate padded by touch sugar ±4g/ℓ. 20% Am oaked. **Rosé** ★★★ From pinotage; **04** plummy red berry character, crisp & refreshing, satisfyingly dry. **Merlot-Ruby Cabernet** ★★★ **04** rhubarb tartness to plum & choc flavours; firmish tannins; appealing; 15% Fr oaked. **Chardonnay** ★★☆ Portion wood-aged; **04** peaches & cream aromas, vanilla whiff, crisp liveliness. **Colombard** ★★★ **04** tropical fruit aromas, crunchy, boiled-sweet aftertaste.

Lion's Gate range

Both **05**. **Dry Red** ★★ Enough robust berry flavours & tannins to match your favourite BBQ meat or full flavoured Mediterranean food. 10% lightly oaked. **Dry White** ★★ As label says: dry, crisp, for no-frills party quaffing. Light bodied; mainly chenin, with colombard & muscat.

Noble Cape

All **05**. **Pinotage-Shiraz** ★★ For BBQ/outdoor days; well padded with strawberry flavour, tannins won't be bullied by a greasy chop; portion lightly oaked. **Chenin Blanc-Chardonnay** ★★ Effortless casual quaff, with light pineapple & dried peach flavours. 5% Fr oaked. **Vonkel Wijn** ★★ Explosion of straw-toned bubbles in hugely festive brut-style sparkling; perfect for party animals on a budget.

Pier 42 range

All **05**. **Merlot** ★ Sappy, stalky, green tone only partly offset by dash fruity ruby cab. 10% oaked, as is… **Chardonnay** ★★ Restrained, lightly buttery notes; dry & fresh, fairly soft flavours for comfortable quaffing. **Sauvignon Blanc** ★ More 'crisp dry white' than varietal hero; some wet wool character & racy acidity.

South Point range

Pinotage ★★ Rustic **05** wild strawberry fruit & fairly severe tannins; decant if drinking early. **Sauvignon Blanc** ★★ **05** greener-toned & lightish, crisp, dry, with hint of asparagus. Following both **04**: **Dry Red** ★★☆ Pleasant alfresco wine, smoothed by 4.5g/ℓ sugar. Mainly pinotage & shiraz, with dash ruby cab. **Chenin Blanc** ★★☆ Gentle, fresh tasting guava flavours, styled for undemanding quaffability. All ranges WO W Cape. — *JN*

Ormonde Private Cellar

Darling (see Durbanville/Darling map) • 1stB 1999 • Tasting & sales Mon-Fri 9-4 Sat & pub hols 9-1 • Closed Easter Fri, Dec 25/26 & Jan 1 • Vineyard tours by appt • Picnic baskets by appt or BYO • Function hall • Facilities for children • Farm produce • Walks • Owners Basson family • Winemaker Michiel du Toit • Viticulturist Theo Basson • ±400 ha (cabs s/f, merlot, mourvèdre, petit v, shiraz, chard, chenin, sauvignon, semillon) • 2 000 tons 35 000 cs own label 40% red 60% white • PO Box 201 Darling 7345 • info@ormonde.co.za • www.ormonde.co.za • T 022-492-3540 • F 022-492-3470

Starting off as grape growers in this cool-climate area, then subsequently deciding to keep the best fruit and try their hand at winemaking, the Ormonde team built and used their very own cellar for the first time last year. 'It's just outside Darling and it has a 1 000-ton capacity,' says proud director Theo Basson, who believes in using traditional techniques but modern equipment to make the premium Ormonde range, as well as the fruit-driven Alexanderfontein wines, 'for everyday enjoyment'.

Alexanderfontein range

★★★★ **Sauvignon Blanc** ✓ Darling's characteristic dusty, mineral & lime aromas give way to an explosion of tropical fruit & lipsmacking core of zesty acidity. **06** vivacious, fresh, with a sustained, long dry, mineral farewell. Delicious solo or with food. Moderate 13.5% alc; exceptionally well priced ex-cellar (plentiful, too: 10 000 cs). **05** *Wine* ★★★★ showed the same vim, appealing tropicality.

> **Chenin Blanc** ☺ ★★★ Lively, lighter styled **06** attractively mixes herbaceous notes, riper apple flavours & freshness, making the perfect summer picnic wine. Bonus 13% alc.

Cabernet Sauvignon ★★★☆ Opulent black berry fruit follows shyer aromas on **05**. Smooth, creamy texture, supportive oaking; supple, ripe tannic structure. Attractive dark choc & freshly ground coffee nuance on finish. 9 mths Fr, 25% new, micro-oxygenation during ferment. WO Coastal. **Merlot** ★★★★ None tasted since Marmite & dark choc toned **04**, with minty hints. **Chardonnay** ★★★★ ✓ Appetising, easy but serious **05**, bigger portion oaked (50%, Fr wood), which adds spicy breadth to rich, nutty, lime & buttered toast palate. Vibrant fruit & acidity in harmony with lingering lime marmalade aftertaste.

Ormonde range

Cabernet Sauvignon-Merlot ★★★★ Last we reviewed classically formulated **03**, 45/45 cab/merlot remainder cab f & petit v, with delightful breakfast nose of bacon & mushrooms, salty liquorice tang. **Chardonnay** ★★★ **04** limy acidity & spicy vanilla oak mid-

2006 vie for centre stage with core of dried fruit; honey & lime wait in the wings. Food wine, shd develop over 2-3 yrs. Fermented/8 mths new Fr oak. **Sauvignon Blanc** ★★★ **06** not ready for tasting. **04** last ed noted as fading into inoffensive drinkability. — *MW*

■ *Otto's Bin* see Olyvenbosch

Oubenheim Estate

*Olifants River ▪ Est/1stB 2002 ▪ Closed to public ▪ Owners DW Viljoen & Philip Viljoen ▪ Winemaker Philip Viljoen ▪ Merlot, pinotage, shiraz, chenin, sauvignon ▪ 800 cs 100% red ▪ PO Box 52 Vredendal 8160 ▪ oubenheim@telkomsa.net ▪ **T 083·509·9885** ▪ F 027 213·5624*

As the first registered 'estate' in the Olifants River region, Philip Viljoen's main focus continues to be the overseas market. 'We export about 85%,' he says of the top-end reds he makes for the hotel, restaurant and catering trade (none tasted this ed). However, there should be more for the rest of us to sample when he introduces a mid-tier range this year.

Oude Compagnies Post

*Tulbagh ▪ Est 1699 ▪ 1stB 2003 ▪ Tasting only by appt ▪ Owner Jerry Swanepoel Family Trust (Jerry & Henriette Swanepoel) ▪ Winemaker Jerry Swanepoel ▪ Viti adviser Hanno van Schalkwyk ▪ 18 ha (cab, merlot, pinotage, ruby cab, shiraz, chard, sauvignon) ▪ 80 tons 3 000 cs 100% red ▪ PO Box 11 Tulbagh 6820 ▪ swanepoel@intekom.co.za ▪ **T 023·230·1578/ 082·829·8404** F 023-230·0840*

High on the slopes of the Obiekwaberg, this farm boasts a wine pedigree dating back to 1850. But as early as 1699, its views across Tulbagh's Witzenberg Valley made it an obvious choice for an outpost of the Dutch East India Company — an historical connection which finds echoes in the 'VOC' insignia on the bottles and the allusions to the 'Compagnie' in the branding. Modern-day custodians Jerry and Henriette Swanepoel have rebuilt the old stone cellar and converted the manor house into a maturation cellar, and welcome visitors — only by appointment — to their special corner of the old Cape.

Compagnies Wijn range

★★★★ **Merlot** Pleasantly approachable, fresh **04** last ed had smooth, forceful tannins in good balance. 14 mths Fr oak not overwhelming. **05** diverted to Caap Ensemble.

Cabernet Sauvignon ★★★★ **05** looks promising beneath wood (sampled ex-barrel), with plenty of good fruit. ±15 mths Fr oak, as is… **Cabernet Sauvignon-Pinotage** ★★★★ 80/ 20 blend in bold, forthright **03** (not retasted) gd fruit albeit hollow-centred, firm structure. **Caap Ensemble** new Maiden **NV** blend merlot, cab (from Kuils Rvr), 10% pinotage, promises loads of dark-fruit flavour, chunky substantiality, savoury richness. Sample tasted; might attain ★★★★ in bottle. **Pinotage** ★★★★ **05** offers soft, sweetly charming fruit (berries & bananas), then wham! in come the big, drying tannins… 14 mths Am oak. **Shiraz** ★★★★ Roasted spice on **05** a prelude to pleasant red fruit, with herbaceous edge; some chewy dry tannin to conclude. 18 mths Fr oak. — *TJ*

Oude Denneboom

*Paarl ▪ 1stB 2003 ▪ Visits by appt ▪ Owner Daniel de Waal ▪ Winemaker/viticulturist Hannes Aucamp ▪ ±41 ha (cab, mourvèdre, pinotage, shiraz, nouvelle, viognier) ▪ 400 tons 150 cs 85% red 15% white ▪ PO Box 2087 Windmeul 7630 ▪ hannesaucamp@mweb.co.za ▪ **T/F 021·869·8073***

Hannes Aucamp, to date focused on making the perfect shiraz ('a balanced wine with berry fruit and spicy flavours, supple and structured') is diversifying into white: last year he planted nouvelle and harvested the first viognier; this year he hopes to experiment with a white blend, possibly a chenin-viognier. Meanwhile the Agter-Paarl farm has been opened to visitors by appointment.

Shiraz ★★★ **04**, tasted last ed, balanced, with a sweet impression thanks to 14.5% alc. Spicy/savoury flavours & bluegum aromas; drop viognier for perfume. More restrained, less concentrated & complex than pvs. 100 cs. — *CT*

Oude Kaap

Range by DGB for export mainly to Germany, Scandinavia and the Low Countries.

Cabernet Sauvignon ★★★ Fairly evolved aromas of roast meat & dried red fruit on **03**; soft, potpourri-scented palate. **Pinotage** ★★★ Meaty/savoury edge to **03**'s sweet-berry fruit, comfortable dry tannins. **Cabernet Sauvignon-Merlot** ★★★ Tasty, harmonious equal partnership in **03**; bramble/game notes with food-cordial savoury finish. **Ruby Cabernet** ★★ **04** lighter style BBQ partner with strawberry flavour, touch of variety's stalkiness, some astringency. **Klassiek Rood** ★★★ **04** good everyday red, mainly ruby cab & cinsaut; lively, rounded & juicy; enjoy young. **Blanc de Noir** ★★ Blue-tinged **05** again from pinotage, with variety's signature mulberry aromas, sweetish slightly grainy finish. **Chardonnay** ★★ Styled for the pop palate, though **04** will appeal more to lovers of an oaky style. **Chenin Blanc** ★★★ Lightish, softly dry **05** gorgeous white peach aroma, lively fresh flavours, good anytime glassful. **Elegant Wit** ★★ **04** equal chenin, colombard mix; shy, light, drier taste than 18g/ℓ RS would suggest. **Klassiek Wit** ★ 10% muscat de A fails to lift this light, foursquare dry white, redeemed by some zestiness on finish. **NV**. All above WO W Cape, none retasted this ed. — *DH*

Oudekloof Private Cellar

Tulbagh ▪ Est 1752 ▪ 1stB 2000 ▪ Closed to public ▪ Owners Francois Rozon, Lyndsay Webster-Rozon, Paul & Lucille O'Riordan ▪ Winemaker TBA ▪ GM/viticulturist Bernardt Krüger ▪ 22 ha (cab, shiraz, chard, chenin) ▪ 1 000 cs ▪ 25% red 75% white ▪ PO Box 191, Oudekloof Farm, Tulbagh 6820 ▪ oudekloof@mweb.co.za ▪ T (023) 230·1925 ▪ F 856·4595

No update from this winery; contact details from previous edition.

■ **Oude Rust** see Mooiuitsig

Oude Wellington Estate

Wellington ▪ Visits by appt ▪ Tasting fee R15 ▪ Closed Dec 25 ▪ A la carte restaurant ▪ Guest house & self-catering cottages ▪ Tour groups ▪ Facilities for children ▪ Conferencing ▪ Owners/ viticulturists Rolf & Vanessa Schumacher ▪ Winemaker Vanessa Schumacher (Jul 1995) ▪ 13 ha (cab, ruby cab, shiraz, chard, chenin) ▪ 80 tons ±2 500 cs own label 60% red 20% white 20% rosé ▪ PO Box 622 Wellington 7654 ▪ info@kapwein.com ▪ www.kapwein.com or http:// estate.kapwein.com ▪ T 021·873·2262 ▪ F 088021·873·4639

Ruby cab remains Vanessa Schumacher's first love, and, though she concedes it's not the most popular grape, she's not giving up on it. A good 2006 harvest at this German-toned *weingut* adds to the upbeat mood, as do gratifyingly brisk sales — achieved without bowing to fashion dictates: 'We please ourselves first and hope other people will share our sentiments.'

Cabernet Sauvignon ★ Lengthy barrel aging for **00** shows in volatile hints, austere tannins, mouth-puckering dryness. **Shiraz** ★★ Attractively ripe & rustic **04**, yr since tasted as sample still tannic, slightly volatile. 13 mths combo Fr/Russian oak. **Currant Abbey** ★★ Unwooded ruby cab (its name is an anagram). **05** very ripe-fruited; amarone-like volatile elements & alc (14.9%); uncomplex but balanced finish. No new vintages of the following tasted: **Ruby Cabernet** ★★★ **98** woody/earthy tones, nice dry tannins. **Blanc de Noir** ★ From... yes, ruby cab: **04** coppery, light fruit & zinging acidity. **Chardonnay Barrique** ★★ **02** pleasantly honeyed, shows balanced wooding (Am oak, 8 mths, 2nd fill). **Chardonnay Unwooded** ★★ **04** understated peach & citrus tones, losing freshness. **Gewürztraminer** ★★★ Rose-scented **03** tastes dryish thanks to brisk acidity despite 6g/ℓ sugar; modest 12% alc. — *IvH*

■ **Our Founders** see Bellingham
■ **Out of Africa** see African Terroir

Overgaauw Estate

Stellenbosch ▪ Est 1905 ▪ 1stB 1971 ▪ Tasting & sales Mon-Fri 9-5 Sat & pub hols 10–12.30 ▪ Closed Mar 21, Easter Fri-Mon, Dec 25/26 & Jan 1 ▪ Fee R10 ▪ Tours by appt ▪ Owner Braam van Velden • Winemaker Chris Joubert (1990), with David van Velden Jnr (Nov 2002) • Viti consultant Johan Pienaar • 75 ha (11 varieties) • 60% red 40% white • PO Box 3 Vlottenburg 7604 • info@overgaauw.co.za • www.overgaauw.co.za • **T** *021·881·3815 •* F *021·881·3436*

'Some winemakers are real winemakers, others are mechanics – and you can taste the difference,' Braam van Velden once told a reporter, and after a century of this family honing the craft here in the Stellenbosch Kloof, he should know. The third-generation farmer says winemaking requires patience – something his eldest son, David vV, will surely learn as his mentorship continues under well seasoned Chris Joubert. Meanwhile BvV still 'holds his land in trust' for his offspring – the rest of whom are involved elsewhere in the business.

★★★★☆ **Tria Corda** Early 'Cape claret' & still a benchmark. Compendium of pure cassis scents & more earthy forest-floor interest in **04**; ripe fruits swaddled in trademark extra-fine tannins. *Wine* ★★★★. Superb, if perhaps not quite as emphatic as **03**, which celebrated van Velden's centenary on the estate. Cab, merlot. cab f (85/32/3), 18 mths new Fr oak.

★★★★☆ **Cabernet Sauvignon** Always strapping, with 18 mths in Fr oak (now less new – 60%). Pre-bottling glimpse at **04** (★★★★) elegance personified; brambly berries cosseted by ripe tannins, yet not as lavish as vintage-boosted **03**. Both gd maturation prospects.

★★★★☆ **Merlot** First Cape bottling of this variety (82); seriously styled & needing a few yrs cellaring. Sample **04** (★★★★) in usual, savoury, elegant form but slightly less structure, oomph, than long-keeper **03**. 18 mths used oak.

★★★★ **Chardonnay** Doing the family business for yrs, now with less new oak to highlight fruit concentration. Sample **06** shows crisp lemons & limes, more freshness than pvs. Gentle 12.5% alc.

★★★★★ **Cape Vintage** ✓ Van Veldens pioneers of using Portuguese varieties locally, adherents to classic style (incl lower sugar, higher alc). Both **97** & **91** (★★★★) still available. Tannic in youth, in true vintage style; they show great balance, intensity & grip, for long development. Blend touriga with tintas b/f/r, souzão & cornifesto. 2½ yrs 1 300ℓ casks. Neither retasted this ed.

Shiraz-Cabernet Sauvignon ★★★★ Cellar's attractive Old World styling also evident here; **04** shiraz's choc-mocha/blackberry fruits layered on 20% cab backbone. 18 mths seasoned oak. **Sauvignon Blanc** ★★★★ **06** bright tropical tints, lovely balance, racy tail-up finish with temperate 12% alc. **Sylvaner** ★★★★ Sole varietal bottling in Cape, since 71. **06** individual; melon allure to supple spice, refreshing finish. 11.5% alc. – DS

Overhex Wines International

Worcester • Est 2006 • Owners Overhex Private Cellar & Waboomsrivier Co-op • Cellarmaster/ production Kobus Rossouw, with JC Martin • Viticulturist Pierre Snyman • 71 Stockenstrom Str, Worcester, 6849 • overhex@intekom.co.za • www.overhex.com • **T** *023·347·6838 •* F *023·347·6837*

Overhex Cellar: • Tasting & sales Mon-Fri 8-5 • Closed pub hols • Tours by appt • BYO picnic • Farm produce • Winemakers Johan Rossouw, with Natalie van Rooyen, Seugnet Rossouw & Willie Malan • Viticulturist Pierre Snyman • 10 000 tons • HACCP, BRC & ISO 9000 certification in progress • **T** 023·347·**5012** • F 023·347·1057

Waboomsrivier Cellar: Tasting & sales Mon-Fri 8–12.30; 1.30–5 Sat 8–10 • Closed pub hols • Cellar tours by appt • BYO picnic • Winemaker Bennie Wannenburg, with Wim Viljoen & Paul Burger • ±15 500 tons • wabooms@mweb.co.za • **T** 023·355·**1730** • F·023·355·1731

Worcester wineries Overhex Private Cellar and Waboomsrivier Co-op have pooled their resources under the banner of Overhex Wines International, and now jointly produce wines for their own brands, including Balance, Beacon Trail, Kaya, Lavida, Soulo and Yammé, and for customers Cape Mist, Country Cellars and Thorntree. The two cellars continue to welcome winelovers as before, during the above opening hours.

Soulo range

Cabernet Sauvignon new ★★ **05** appealing bouquet of mint, earth & choc; nutty flavours & big dry tannins to tame a char-grilled steak. Yr 2nd fill Fr oak; similar oaking (plus 3rd fill portion) for... **Shiraz** ★★★ **05**, grapes ex-Sbosch, well-textured, dry; amenable leathery tannins with spicy touch. **Sauvignon Blanc** ★★ Brisk, clean **06** early harvested for zing, lightness; ends lemon-dry. Following fortified desserts not re-tasted: **White Muscadel** ★★ Powerfully sweet & muscatty **04**, with touch of lemon. Reserve champ at SAYWS. **Red Muscadel** ★★★ **04** lauded by Muscadel Assoc, SAYWS; well-balanced despite high alc (18.5%) & daunting sweetness (239g/ℓ RS); earthy touch, long, lifted finish. Block since registered as single vyd. **Chardonnay** discontinued.

Balance range

Merlot-Cabernet Sauvignon ★★★ Last tasted was juicily quaffable **04**, generous berry fruit balanced by gently effective cab tannins. 4 mths oaked. **Pinotage-Shiraz** ★★ Fruit-driven, easy casual quaff; **05**'s suppleness boosted by ±6g/ℓ sugar, light brush of oak. **Shiraz-Merlot** ★★ Crowd pleasing formula: softness, balance, gd spread of varietal flavours incl plum, berry & pepper. **05** again equal blend, 5 mths oaked. **Pink** ★★ Off-dry **05** last ed had ripe plum nose, berry flavours with touch banana, smooth & easy-drinking. **Chenin Blanc-Colombard** ★★ Just-dry this yr, **06** muted guava hint, brisk no-frills white. **Colombard-Chardonnay** ★ **06** 70/30 partnership; light, simple, dry acidic finish. **Sauvignon Blanc-Semillon** ★★ **06** light, cheery tropical fruit tones, slightly less sugar this vintage (±9.5g/ℓ) for cloy-free pleasure. **Muscat d'Alexandrie** ★★ Light semi-sweet sipper with delicate grapey muscat bouquet; **NV** (06) better balanced, more satisfying than pvs. Following still selling; notes from last ed: **Vin Sec** ★★ **04** pleasantly fresh & lively, light, with suggestion of fruit. **Vin Doux** ★★★ Foaming fun for the sweeter-toothed. **04** fresh citrus blossom bouquet, light & sweet muscatty flavours.

Lavida range

Cape Red ★★ Bright, red-fruited quaffer; firmish & dry, unpretentious. **04** from mainly shiraz, plus merlot & pinotage, briefly oaked. **Cape White** ★★ Early drinking **05** from chenin, 40% colombard; rounded & pleasantly dry. Neither revisited for current ed. All ranges WO W Cape.— *CT*

Overmeer Cellars

Since 1996, no-frills quaffing range in 5ℓ packs, ex-Western Cape vyds. By Distell.

Following all **NV**. **Selected Red** ★★ Delightfully unpretentious & moreish. From unoaked pinotage, ruby cab & cinsaut, it's ripe, properly dry & has a tugging tannin grip. **Grand Cru** ★★ Pear/apple-toned sipper, delicate aromas & flavours. Touch higher alc than stable mates (11.8% vs ±11%). **Stein** ★★ Whispered lemon aromas & flavours, inoffensive sweetness. **Late Harvest** ★★ Tad sweeter, fuller than above, with pineapple/melon palate.— *CvZ*

■ **Overvaal** *see* Hartswater
■ **Paarl Heights** *see* False Bay Vineyards

Paarl Wine Company

Paarl ▪ Closed to public ▪ 9 Zuidmeer Str Huguenot Paarl 7646 ▪ izak.v@pwcwines.co.za ▪ **T 021·862·0616** *▪* **F** *021·862·6400*

Wine wholesalers and owners of the Fairbridge range.

Paddagang Wines

Tulbagh ▪ Est 1987 ▪ Tasting & sales daily 9-4 ▪ Fee R5 ▪ Paddagang Restaurant daily 8.30-4.30 ▪ Closed Easter Fri, Dec 25 & Jan 1 ▪ Guest house, gifts & other attractions (see intro) ▪ Owners Paddagang Vignerons ▪ Production manager Carl Allen (Aug 2002) ▪ Winemaker Elsabé Roux (Dec 2002) ▪ Viticulturist Callie Coetzee (Dec 2002) ▪ 5 300 cs 52% red 21% white 27% other ▪ PO Box 303 Tulbagh 6820 ▪ paddagang@mweb.co.za ▪ www.tulbagh.net ▪ **T 023·230·0394** *▪* **F** *023·230·0433*

A fresh new look for this wittily branded range of wines, sherries and brandies, made for a group of local vignerons. The familiar cartoon frog on the front label strikes a variety new of vinous poses, including as a delightfully wacky Napoleon, astride rampant steed Marengo, brandishing a glass of Paddapoleon brandy! Also spruced up is the historic wine shop where the brand is sold, now offering tastings and sales of olive products and cheeses, and local produce for your shopping basket.

All **NV. Paddarotti** ★★☆ Latest bottling is mainly cab (plus 8% shiraz) with variety's food-friendly firm tannins, berried fruit & an unlingering finish. Shiraz portion oaked. No new vintages tasted of the following: **Paddajolyt** ★★★ Easy unwooded *vin ordinaire* from pinotage & ruby cab (50/50); lightish, tangy dried-fruit finish. **Paddadundee** ★★ From chard, with fragrant passionfruit hints; creamy-dry finish. **Paddasang** ★★ Lightish sauvignon, its apple/pear tones last yr tinged with bottle-age. **Paddapoot** ★★★ Deliciously aromatic & fresh hanepoot, very soft & sweet. **Brulpadda** ★★★ Old-style Cape port from ruby cab & pinotage; soft, sweet, quite silky. Low 16.5% alc. — *DH*

■ **Pangolin** *see* MAN Vintners
■ **Panorama** *see* Du Toitskloof
■ **Papillon** *see* Van Loveren
■ **Papkuilsfontein** *see* Distell, Tukulu
■ **Paradyskloof** *see* Vriesenhof
■ **Patrys** *see* Assegai

Paul Cluver Estate

Elgin • Est 1859 • 1stB 1997 • Tasting & sales Mon-Thu 9-5, Fri 9-4, Sat & pub hols 9-3 (Sep-Apr), 10-2 (May-Aug) • Fee R10 for groups of 8-12 • Closed Easter Fri/Mon, Dec 25 & Jan 1 • BYO picnic • Guest house • Summer sunset concerts in amphitheatre • Conservation area • Owners Cluver family • Winemaker Andries Burger (Nov 1996) • Viticulturist Christiaan Cloete, advised by Kevin Watt (Feb 2005/Mar 2003) • 100 ha (cab, merlot, pinot, chard, gewürz, riesling, sauvignon) • 300 tons 20 000 cs 50% red 50% white • PO Box 48 Grabouw 7160 • info@cluver.co.za • www.cluver.com • T 021·844·0605 • F 021·844·0150

The cellar (again) went polyglot last year, with a trio of interns from three different countries (France, Germany and SA) working the harvest, and Bordeaux-trained Marianne Bodin back here to stay, as assistant winemaker, after helping out in 2005. Cellar chief Andries Burger put another notch in his belt this year, with a second consecutive win of the *Decanter* trophy for Noble Late Harvest. An in-tune-with-the-times development is the Slowine brand: it's a collaborative effort by PC, Beaumont, Luddite and Villiersdorp, catching the slow food and slow living wave.

★★★★ **Cabernet Sauvignon** After difficulties of **02** (★★★★), **03**'s inviting, cedary black fruit most welcome. Seriously structured & full-flavoured, savoury, nicely dry-finishing; best matured a few yrs yet. Usual ±18 mths Fr oak, 60% new.

★★★★ **Pinot Noir** Has generally been a good advertisement for cool Elgin over the yrs. **04**'s aromas mingle strawberry, forest floor, mocha toastiness, with slightly floral perfume. Hedonistic edge to taut tannin-acid structure, silky texture: inveigling balance of austerity & sensuality.

★★★★☆ **Chardonnay** As usual (though **04** not tasted), **05** reveals cool climate in green limy notes & mineral thread, though some richness checks austerity, & toasty oak element adds to complexity (partly natural ferment in oak; 9 mths on lees). Fresh acidity to help ensure good development.

★★★★☆ **Gewürztraminer** ✓ Lovely, expressive **05**, with rosepetal & honeysuckle notes, cleanly lingering flavours. A little sugar (6.9g/ℓ) but effectively dry, moderate alc, generous fruit — all finely, convincingly balanced, promising many yrs of pleasure. Superb alone or with spicy food.

★★★★ **Weisser Riesling 05** again delivers the thrill of this great variety purely & elegantly expressed. Typical peach/floral character, bright acidity focusing & controlling the counterbalancing sweet element. Surprisingly versatile food partner.

★★★★★ **Weisser Riesling Noble Late Harvest** Another in splendid series of botrytised desserts deploying riesling's tense, exciting balance of sweetness & racy natural acidity, swathing sumptuous fruit. Honey, dried peach, spicy pepper all part of **05**'s developing complexity & fascination, concentrated gorgeousness & clean, refined lines. Partly matured 8 mths in older oak. **03**, **04** (★★★★★) *Decanter* trophies, **03** *WS* 91 pts.

The Elgin Blend ★★★★ **04** blends home cab & bought-in Elgin merlot. Ripe, very appealing even in youth – though shd improve few yrs. Rather thick but smooth texture, substantial but soft tannins, intelligent supportive oaking, plenty of flavour. NE. **Sauvignon Blanc** ★★★★ Following fresh, balanced **04**, latest **05** (★★★★) subtly melds tropicality & cool greenpepper, plus a mineral note. Fresh, & showing estate's usual restrained refinement; well balanced, rounded but focused, tingling & dry. — *TJ*

Paul Wallace Wines

Elgin • Est 2004 • Closed to public • Vini adviser Inus Muller • 3 tons • 200 cs 100% red • PO Box 141 Elgin 7180 • wallovale@mweb.co.za • **T/F 021·848·9744**

In his 27 years as a roving viticulturist, Paul Wallace has identified many a vineyard of interest and quality, among them a parcel of malbec grapes which were the first he vinified himself. Such was the interest generated that when he and wife Nicky began planting their 25ha Elgin farm Wallovale, malbec claimed a place, together with sauvignon and pinot, with shiraz in the pipeline. The 05 and 06 Malbec from bought-in grapes awaiting release, Wallovale's maiden vintage from own vineyards takes place this year.

★★★★ **Malbec** Densely fruited yet elegantly polished **04**, last yr had blackcurrant & cedar notes, rich soft tannins, persistent spicy finish. Paarl grapes, yr oak. — *MF*

Pax Verbatim Vineyards

Stellenbosch • Est 2004 • Closed to public • Owner/winemaker Richard Hilton • 100 cs 100% red • 21 Topaz Street, Heldervue, Somerset West 7130 • info@paxverbatim.co.za • www.paxverbatim.co.za • **T/F 021·855·5244**

'Less bluster and power; more finesse and elegance' is how Richard Hilton describes his current approach. Grapes come from Groenekloof, 'a beautiful vineyard with 16 year old vines growing in deep, granite based soil', and less new oak creates a more classic Rhône style. Literally 'True Peace', Richard H says the name of his brand is emblematic of the tranquillity and joy he feels when making wine.

Blazing Hill Syrah ★★★ Last tasted was 2nd vintage **04**; sweet/sour cranberry flavours, unflamboyant but gd sinew & flesh. As with pvs, needs few yrs to start showing its best. 35% new Fr oak 16–18 mths. — *MM*

■ *Peacock Ridge* see Waterkloof
■ *Pearl Springs* see Cape Vineyards
■ *Pearly Bay* see KWV Ltd
■ *Pecan Stream* see Waterford

Pella Wines

Stellenbosch • Est/1stB 2004 • Closed to public • Owner Ingrid de Waal • Winemakers Ingrid & Daniël de Waal • Viticulturist Daniël de Waal • 100 cs • 100% red • PO Box 89 Vlottenburg 7604 • Pella@adept.co.za • **T 082·829·7509/021·881·3026** *• F 021·881·3026*

Ingrid de Waal and husband Daniël (one of DeWaal Wines's oeno-brothers) are passionate about red wine. Having fallen for a complex Circion in Rioja, 'the most perfect wine we had ever tasted', they returned home determined to recreate a similarly 'peppery, spicy, smoky' flavour. The resulting Pella wine is named after Ingrid dW's home town. At press time, the 05 was still in barrel.

Hoogland Shiraz ★★★★ Striking **04** with peppery whiffs, earthy mineral notes; last yr concentrated & well extracted, with evident though integrated tannins. 15 mths Fr oak, 20% new. — *MF*

■ *Pendoorn* see Virgin Earth

Perdeberg Winery

*Paarl • Est 1941 • Tasting & sales Mon-Fri 8-5 Sat 9-1 • Closed Easter Fri/Sat, Dec 25 & Jan 1 • Tours by appt during tasting hours • Owners 40 members • Winemakers Kobus de Kock, Ewald Kellerman & Pieter Carstens (1989/1997/2004) • Viticulturist Stephan Joubert (2001) • 3 100 ha • 21 500 tons 60% red 40% white • PO Box 214 Paarl 7620 • info@perdeberg.co.za • www. perdeberg.co.za • **T 021·869·8244/8112** • F 021·869·8245*

Think Perdeberg, think chenin. It's their first wine in many ways, being produced as long ago as 1942. But this tradition doesn't preclude innovation – the winery has moved to screwcaps, streamlined its wine portfolio, and generally started marketing itself seriously (having historically supplied third parties). They're rightly proud of their British Retail Consortium accreditation and biodiversity credentials: conserving 1ha of indigenous veld for every 3ha of vineyard – good news for the area's beautiful and endangered Geometric Tortoise.

Reserve Range

★★★★ Pinotage From old bushvine vyd. Pvs was **01**, with evident but soft tannins – but they're rather threatening & dry on latest **04** (★★★★), assailing luscious fruit presaged by attractive, forward varietal aromas. 14 mths Fr/Am oak.

Shiraz ★★★★ Exciting spicy-peppery aromas & some perfume on **05**; serious structure, yr in Fr/Am oak, supporting sweet red fruit. A touch tart. **Chenin Blanc** ★★★★ ✓ Softly rich (just-dry) but fresh & lively **06** oak fermented/aged 5 mths – spicy wood shows esp as aroma, well integrated on palate. 14.5% alc a touch hot on finish. **Sauvignon Blanc** ★★★★ ✓ Dbnvlle grapes show typical grassy, greenpepper liveliness on flavourful **06**, with some real substance & rich, dry concentration. **Viognier** ★★★★ ✓ **05** (tasted last ed) bold, aromatic (incl signature apricot), fat & rich; well integrated 5 mths oak. Discontinued: **Chardonnay, Merlot, Cabernet Sauvignon** (last 2 making way for a bdx style blend released end 2006).

Perdeberg range

Shiraz ☺ ★★★ Fresh, characterful, good-drinking **05** with ripe, baked aromas; nicely built, with savoury dry tannins; clean, forward fruit, well done stave-oaking. **Soft Smooth Red** ☺ ★★★ Indeed it's just that, this **NV** allsorts blend – & definitely off-dry, though decently structured. Apparently a big UK hit. **Cabernet Sauvignon-Merlot** ☺ ★★★ **05** fresh & juicy, straightforwardly simple rather than trivial – in fact, big tannins along with loads of (slightly sweet) flavour. Modest oaking. **Chenin Blanc Dry** ☺ ★★★ Deliciously straightforward **06**, with masses of tropical fruit flavour, dry, crisp balance. Unbeatable value?

Cinsaut ★★★ Bright & light textured **03** with succulent cherry tone. Not retasted, nor were next 2 reds. **Cinsaut-Shiraz** ★★★ **03** lively, quaffable 70/30 blend, lightish feel despite 14% alc; good value, super braai wine. **Pinotage** ★★★★ ✓ A benchmark for the unwooded style. Cherry-fruited **05**'s stern tannins needing yr/2 to relax. **Chenin Blanc Semi-Sweet** ★★★ As always, **05** (tasted last ed) not all that sweet on analysis or taste (12g/ℓ sugar); otherwise similar to dry version. **Cinsaut Liqueur Wine** ★★★ Fortified dessert with lush cherry/strawberry tone; **05** a little spirituous & sweet (125g/ℓ sugar; 18% alc). 375ml. **Cabernet Sauvignon** discontinued. – *TJ/JN*

■ *Perold* see KWV Ltd

Peter Bayly

*Calitzdorp (see Little Karoo map) • Est 2002 • 1stB 2004 • Visits by appt • Conservation area • Owners Peter & Yvonne Bayly • Winemaker Peter Bayly • 1.2 ha (tinta, touriga, souzão) • 700 cs 100% port • PO Box 187 Calitzdorp, 6660 • info@baylys.co.za • **T 044 213·3702** F 044·213·3702*

'No developments lately; not much has happened,' say the Baylys modestly, eventually conceding that a high point last year was a visit by Paul Symington of the celebrated port family, who stayed for dinner and 'raved about the 05, saying it was as good as the best he'd tasted and would compare with anything Symingtons was producing in Portugal'. Clearly Peter B's dream of making 'a truly great Portuguese-style port' is being realised. He's planning to put another hectare under vines but hasn't yet decided on the variety/ies.

★★★★ **Cape Vintage Port** From foot-trodden touriga, tinta, souzão, resampled maiden **04** (last ed's pre-bottling) now better, fresher: pruney, mocha aromas, richly satisfying, dryish finish – but more tannic grip would reassure about development & match classical build (20% alc, 95g/ℓ RS). EW. Undeniably delicious now, though, in charming skittle-shaped 500ml bottle adorned with flying pig. – *TJ*

Philip Jordaan Wines

*Rawsonville ▪ Est/1stB 1998 ▪ Closed to public ▪ Owner/winemaker Philip Jordaan ▪ Viti consultant Leon Dippenaar ▪ 1 ha ▪ 500 cs 100% red ▪ PO Box 55 Rawsonville 6845 ▪ philipjordaan@intekom.co.za ▪ **T 023·349·1601** ▪ F 023·349·1581*

Philip Jordaan, by day cellarmaster at Du Toitskloof, makes a small quantity of fine Cab Franc for his own label. No new vintage received for review.

PicardiRebel

*Est 1994 ▪ PO Box 18130 Wynberg 7800 ▪ mark.no@picardirebel.co.za ▪ **T 021·700·5500** ▪ F 021·700·5515*

Mark Norrish, wine-division head of this well-established national drinks chain, has been sniffing out new wineries/wines, training staff and 'micro-marketing': he's grouped the 90+ stores into niched 'clusters', increased shelf space for certain categories and introduced new ones like 'organic', all aimed at an enhanced consumer experience. Consultant Colin Frith has a nose for good value easy-drinkers, which are channelled into the cork-closed range 'Naked Truth'. The PicardiRebel 5ℓ casks are filled by Robertson Winery, while the occasional label, 'Coast' , is sourced by Norrish.

Pick 'n Pay

*Enquiries Elsa Gray ▪ Bahrain Drive Extension, Airport Industria, 7490 ▪ egray@pnp.co.za ▪ www.picknpay.co.za ▪ **T 021·936·8400** ▪ F 021·934·6355*

This national chain of supermarkets and hyperstores offers its 'No Name' house-brand wines in 3ℓ and 5ℓ casks. All are made by Robertson Winery, and commendably light in alcohol (±10–12.5%).

'No Name' range

Dry Red ☺ ★★ Appealingly smooth & round, well padded with plum & berry fruit; versatile – could even be chilled in summer.

Dry White ★★ Bright, lively everyday white with balanced tropical tone. **Dry White Light** ★★ Juicy, tasty, gd flavour & balance for this genre. **Stein** ★★ Our sample fresher, less honeyed than pvs; light, fruity & comfortably sweet. **Late Harvest** ★★ Soft, perky, not over-sweet, with tropical fruit flavours. **Semi-Sweet Rosé** new ★★ Pleasant light-textured 'pink' with tropical notes; balanced, not too sweet. – *DH*

Pick's Pick

*Owner Alan Pick ▪ thebutchershop@mweb.co.za ▪ **T 011·7848676/7** ▪ F 011·784·8674*

Stylish housewines of the ever-packed Butcher Shop & Grill on Nelson Mandela Square, Sandton, vinified to the owner's specs by various reputed wineries.

★★★★ **Late Bottled Vintage** new By accomplished port house JP Bredell; **02** has all correct qualities for style: ripe & accessible fruit (fruitcake & raisins); measured structure; dry, warm, firm, almost stately finish with persistent spiciness. Quite delectable. 20% alc.

Cabernet Sauvignon ★★★ **05** ex-Elgin, with cool-area raciness etched into red fruit; subtly but powerfully structured; latent class deserves (but presumably won't get) few yrs bottle-ageing. By Paul Cluver. Following all [new]: **Merlot** ★★★ First of three offerings by Jordan Winery; **04** with food-inviting dry tannins, leafy/'green walnut' character & jammy fruit. 16 mths Fr oak, some new. **Shiraz** ★★★ Meaty/savoury styling appropriate for carnivorous clientele; **04** easy, approachable, with soft spicy tannins. By Zevenwacht. **Cabernet Sauvignon-Shiraz-Merlot** ★★★★ From the Guardian Peak/Ernie Els stable; near equal portions cab/shiraz (47/41) in **04**, harmonious, pleasantly gripping; inviting vanilla essence aromas repeated on blackberry palate. **Chenin Blanc-Viognier-Chardonnay** ★★★★ By Rudera's Teddy Hall. **06** delightfully aromatic 60/33/7 blend, crafted with drinking pleasure in mind. Touch body-plumping sugar, balancing crisp acidity, to ensure food compatibility. Screwcapped. **Chardonnay** ★★★★ Delicious **04** full buttery/leesy style freshened with tangy lemon & marmalade. Still-active acid backbone provides pleasing firmness. By Jordan Winery; barrel fermented/9 mths Fr oak, 50% new. **Sauvignon Blanc** ★★★ **05** by Jordan Winery; appears few shades lighter than regular Jordan version. Dried grass/straw with hint gooseberry, crisp & dry. Also a **Pinotage Reserve** by Beyerskloof, unready for tasting. — *CT/CR*

■ *Pier 42 see* Goedverwacht, Origin Wine
■ *Pierre Jourdan see* Càbriere
■ *Pinecrest/Pinehurst see* Môreson

Plaisir de Merle   ◌♉♌

Simondium (see Franschhoek map) ▪ Est 1993 ▪ 1stB 1994 ▪ Tasting & sales Mon-Fri 8.30-5 Sat 10-4 (Nov-Mar) 10-2 (Apr-Oct) ▪ Fee R20 (informal), R30 (tasting & tour) ▪ Closed Christian hols ▪ Tours by appt during tasting hours ▪ Tour groups ▪ Day conferencing for small groups (15 max) ▪ Owner Distell ▪ Winemaker Niel Bester (Jan 1993) ▪ Viticulturist Hannes van Rensburg ▪ ±400 ha (cab, merlot, shiraz, chard, sauvignon) ▪ 800 tons 40 000 cs own label 80% red 20% white ▪ PO Box 121 Simondium 7670 ▪ nbester@distell.co.za or plaisirdemerletours@distell.co.za ▪ www.plaisirdemerle.co.za ▪ T 021·874·1071 ▪ F 021·874·1689 (sales) ▪ F 021·874·1488 (cellar)

'It was quite a boring year,' says cellarmaster Niel Bester of 2005/6. Enlivened, however, by another personal best for this action man: the Oudtshoorn Marathon last year was his fastest ever, a 3h:10 run. The Simondium spread has added another dimension to its historical charm in becoming a member of the Biodiversity & Wine Initiative. Its 500ha of conserved land on the Simonsberg encompasses endangered Boland Granite Fynbos, Kogelberg Sandstone Fynbos and a variety of fauna. As part of an empowerment drive, a trout farming project was initiated by the workers living on the property.

★★★★★ **Cabernet Franc** Elegant & fragrant expression of the grape; In standout **03**, showed extraordinary perfumes & a sense of mystery which shared by **04** (★★★★). Latest is carmine cloaked, scented with intriguing tomato- & tea-leaf, refreshed by brisk acidity. Balanced, if touch too lightweight this cooler vintage for higher rating. From a young (5 yrs) single vyd. 15 mths new Fr oak.

★★★★ **Merlot** Pvs featured splashes shiraz, cab or petit v; since **02** a monovarietal. **03** textbook merlot — opulent, rich & round, oozes luscious black plums & berries, integrated oak & alc (14.5%); fleshy tannins give a gentle grip to finish. Great now & over ±5 yrs. 11-17 mths Fr oak, 1st-3rd fill.

★★★★ **Shiraz** Modern but unflashy **03** ripe & fleshy, velvet textured with floral & savoury nuances, toasty vanilla & refreshing acidity. Judicious oaking (60% new Am/Fr, 12-16 mths) paves the way for fine maturation. Matches quality of hedonistic **01**; **02** (★★★★) was lighter, in line with vintage, & needed time to settle.

★★★★ **Grand Plaisir** Most focused of the reds; **03** loses **02**'s soupçon shiraz & becomes 'straight' bdx assembly cab, malbec & petit v (35/33/32). Resplendent ripe black fruits with intricate violets, iodine & spicy oak detailing. Opens to fruit-rich yet zesty palate with powdery tannins in balance. Impressive & delicious, deserves contemplation (& ageing ±5 yrs). 16 mths new Fr oak.

★★★★ Sauvignon Blanc 06 lifts the bar on **05 (★★★)** with exuberant & pungent green asparagus & nettle. Poised, juicy, persistent; for solo sipping or the dinner table. Shd improve over next few yrs. Grapes ex Paarl, West Coast & Elim, 4 mths lees-aged.
Cabernet Sauvignon Friendly but also quite serious dinner companion **03 (★★★★)**. Supple tannins, abundant cassis fruit & delightfully moderate alc (13.7%), with slight sweet/sour twist for interest. **02 (★★★★)** was also elegant though not especially intense. Fr oak ± 14 mths. **Chardonnay ★★★★** Excellent wooding gives enchanting spicy brioche character to **05**'s citrus fruit; creamy mouthfeel, balanced, persistent, with a pithy tug to its tail. Mainly WO Smnsberg-Paarl. — *CvZ*

■ **Podium** see Baarsma
■ **Poker Hill** see Somerbosch

Pongrácz

Popular and critically acclaimed brut-style cap classiques, named after the late Desiderius Pongrácz (pronounced Pon-*grats*), nobleman and refugee from the Hungarian uprising, who helped revitalise viticulture in the Cape. By Distell. Enquiries: sdekker@distell.co.za ▪ **T 021·809·8159.**

Desiderius ★★★★ Classic 60/40 chard/pinot sparkler, elegantly packaged & released in minuscule quantities. **99** softly vibrant mousse with hints strawberries & cream & bruised apple, honey-drizzled lemon meringue flavours; fine intensity & grip from 70 mths ageing on lees. Lightish 11.5% alc makes it even more delicious. **98** *Wine* **★★★★**. **Pongrácz ★★★★** Chard contribution (with pinot) to this evergreen sparkling upped to 75% for latest **NV** bottling, also much longer on lees (45 mths vs 24), giving extra breadth to palate. Lovely bright, busy bubbles, refreshing, long & crisp Granny Smith apple flavours. For drinking, not keeping. Both off Sbosch vyds. — *CvZ*

■ **Porcupine Ridge** see Boekenhoutskloof
■ **Porter Mill Station** see Tulbagh Wineries Co-op
■ **Porterville Cellars** see Tulbagh Wineries Co-op

Post House Cellar

Stellenbosch (see Helderberg map) ▪ *Est/1stB 1997* ▪ *Tasting & sales Mon-Fri 8.30-5 Sat by appt 8.30-1* ▪ *Closed Easter Fri/Sun/Mon, Dec 25/26 & Jan 1* ▪ *Owner/winemaker Nicholas Gebers* ▪ *40 ha (cab, merlot, petit v, pinotage, shiraz, chenin)* ▪ *±200 tons 4 500 cs own label* ▪ *PO Box 5635 Helderberg 7135* ▪ *nick@posthousewines.co.za* ▪ *www.posthousewines.co.za* ▪ *T/F 021·842·2409*

Blueish Black, Nick Gebers' new entry-level 'Cape blend', has the merest touch of blue (it's the pinotage that does it, he says) but the point is that it extends the postage stamp theme started with Penny Black, 'blueish black' being a colourist's tint. Next up, says NG, will be a chenin-based Blueish White in the same range. (Go figure!) His bonsai garden is an added attraction for visitors to the delightful little cellar where he conducts hands-on tastings surrounded by tanks, barrels and the corking machine. In a year or two, he hopes to have opened an art gallery: 'Painting was my first love and I've taken it up again.'

★★★★ Penny Black Sleek & supple red led by merlot, shiraz (equal third), cab & dab petit v. Raising the bar, **04 (★★★★★)** is a beauty: svelte, multi-layered, carefully made. The memory of violets, dark berries, Belgian choc lingers long after glass is empty. 18 mths Fr barriques, 35% new. **03** was lush with merlot's black fruits, cab backbone, shiraz/merlot opulence. Both structured to age gracefully.
★★★★★ Chenin Blanc Small crop from 23 yr old vines; native yeasts used. More Old World than New. Individual **05** already sold out ex-cellar & no wonder: baked apple, almonds, savoury citrus thread throughout, punctuated by a racy finish. Wld age beautifully if you cld still find some. 9 mths Fr/Am oak, 14% new.
Blueish Black new **★★★★ 05** unusual blend nearly equal shiraz, pinotage, merlot, with 13% cab, tailored for earlier drinking. Lavish fruit is the focus – a veritable berry orchard,

structured with lipsmacking juiciness. Quarter oaked. **Merlot** ★★★☆ Already accessible, **03** has lots of charm: blueberry, violet & mocha notes, integrated tannins. 24 mths oak, third new, gives it the backbone to age 3-4 yrs. *Wine* ★★★★. Following duo not revisited: **Cabernet Sauvignon** ★★★☆ Middleweight, dark-fruited **02** probably for drinking soon; lighter-textured than 14.3% alc suggests. Balanced oak (35% new, 20 mths). *Wine* ★★★★. **Shiraz 03** with red-fruit lushness, white pepper/lily fragrance. Oak (16% new) rampant when previewed mid-2004; shd have mellowed by now. Potential ★★★★. — *CR*

Premium Cape Wines

Stellenbosch • Est 2003 • Closed to public • Owner Premium Trust • PO Box 12149 Die Boord 7613 • ansgar@gravitywine.com • T/F 886·8515

No update from this young negociant company; contact details as per last edition. Brands have included Open Sky, Imvelo, De Sonnenberg and Uhambo.

■ *Private Collection* see Saxenburg, Spier

Prospect1870

Robertson • Est 1990 • 1stB 1998 • Closed to public (tasting at The Wine Boutique, Main Rd, Ashton) • Owners Louis, Nic & Chris de Wet • Winemakers Philip Louw & Johan van Wyk • 65 ha (cab, merlot, pinotage, shiraz, chard, sauvignon, viognier) • 5 000 cs own label 80% red 20% white • PO Box 141 Ashton 6715 • office@prospectwines.com • www.prospectwines. com • T 082·878·2884

The name of this 5th-generation family farm refers to its year of founding. The De Wets concentrate primarily on the US market, where Nic dW operates their own import company, Vineyard Varieties, and handles distribution in 11 states. Their current line-up (not tasted) includes a Cabernet Sauvignon 02 and Chardonnay 06 under the Prospect1870 label and, under the Leatherwood brand, a Cabernet Sauvignon 04 and Sauvignon Blanc 06.

■ *Provin* see Douglas Wine Cellar

Pulpit Rock Winery

Swartland • 1stB 2003 • Tasting & sales Mon-Fri 8-5 Sat 9-2 • Closed Easter Fri-Mon, Dec 25 & Jan 1 • BYO picnic • Tours by appt • Tour groups • Walks • Conservation area • Owner Brinkshof Wines (Pty) Ltd • Winemaker Piet Kleinhans (Dec 2003) • Viti consultant Koos van der Merwe (Aug 2005) • 400 ha (cab, merlot, petit v, pinotage, roobernet, shiraz, chard, chenin, sauvignon) • 1 000 tons 60% red 40% white • PO Box 1 Riebeek West 7306 • info@pulpitrock.co.za • T/F 022·461·2025

Seems winemaker Piet Kleinhans's tongue-in-cheek mention in last year's guide of 'no new toys' in the cellar paid off: additional tanks materialised and boosted capacity to 1 000 tons. Some 50ha of vineyards were planted with chenin, malbec, pinotage and shiraz, under the watchful eye of new viti consultant Koos van der Merwe. A new range, Brink Family, primarily aimed at the export market, was released after the guide's deadline.

The reds retasted (samples last yr). **Cabernet Sauvignon** ★★★ **04** a brooding giant, loaded with luscious mulberry fruit, supple tannins – & cellar's standard ±15% alc. Slight savoury hint invites early consumption. Oak ± as for... **Merlot** ★★★ Idiosyncratic & chunky **04** beginning to knit but full harmony's few yrs away. Beneath the bold wood tannins (13 mths new Fr oak), coffee-toned fruit lies in wait. **Pinotage** ★★★★ **04** packed with ripe plum, banana & sweet spice; super follow-through into palate with supportive floral oak, richness from 15.5 % alc augurs well for development. VDG, *Wine* ★★★★. **Shiraz** ★★★ **04** balanced & appealing. House's dry tannins here matched by savoury-touched plum fruit, for smoother, easier mouthfeel. 14 mths new oak, 30% Am. SAYWS gold. **Chardonnay** ★★★★ **04** when last tasted showed chunky peach fruit, beefy 14.8% alc & perhaps too low acid from partial malo. Fermented/8 mths Fr oak. MIWA DG.

Cape Haven range

Cabernet Sauvignon Balanced, drinks easily. **05** (sample) liberal berry fruit, controlled wooding (only 15-20% oaked, here & below), full but undaunting 14.5% alc. Potential ★★★. **Merlot** ★★ **05** similar ripe plummy intro as pvs; fat prune-like flavour with savoury middle, but also bold 15% alc, gravelly tannin. **Shiraz** ★★ Bit of a roughneck; **05** robust & raspy tannins send fruit scuttling, leaving dry smoky/savoury aftertaste. **Pinotage** ★★ Restrainedly fruited **05** has some astringent tannins, inviting hearty food. **Chardonnay** ★★★★ **05**, retasted, flavoursome & concentrated, with clear citrus & stonefruit notes, spicy effect from 6 mths barrelling. Delicious now & for another yr/ 3. **Chenin Blanc 06** sample fundamentally sound but too unknit to rate; light bodied, with tropical tone. — DH

■ *Quagga Ridge* see Horse Mountain

Quando

Robertson ▪ Est/1stB 2001 ▪ Visits by appt ▪ Owner Irene Bruwer Family Trust ▪ Winemaker Fanus Bruwer ▪ Viticulturist Martin Bruwer ▪ 80 ha ▪ 15 tons 1 600 cs own label 100% white ▪ EurepGAP certified ▪ PO Box 82 Bonnievale 6730 ▪ info@quando.co.za ▪ www.quando.co.za ▪ **T/F 023·616·2752**

A severe hailstorm hit the Bruwers' farm in November 2005, shattering windows, collapsing roofs under its weight and stripping trees and vines, resulting in the smallest harvest in 40 years. 'Apart from that, it was a very good year for sauvignon, and exports are booming to the UK and US,' reports phlegmatic Fanus B.

★★★★ **Sauvignon Blanc** ✓ Customary punch of passionfruit on decent, forthright **06**, with ticklings of asparagus. Greenly fresh lipsmacking balance, not too pungent. These can mature nicely a few yrs. — TJ

■ *Quantum* see Du Toitskloof
■ *Quiriga Reserve* see Rietrivier
■ *Queen of Sheba* see Eshkol

Quoin Rock Winery

Stellenbosch ▪ Est 2000 ▪ 1stB 2001 ▪ Tasting & sales Mon-Fri 10-5 Sat 10-3 Sun 10-3 (Dec-Feb) ▪ Fee R15, negated on purchase ▪ Closed Easter Fri, Dec 25 & Jan 1 ▪ Platters of fine cured meats & cheeses ▪ Tours by appt ▪ Owner Metlika Trading ▪ Winemaker Carl van der Merwe (Jan 2002) ▪ Viticulturists Doug Murdoch & Rossouw Theart ▪ 60 ha (cab, merlot, pinot, shiraz, chard, sauvignon) ▪ 180 tons 5 000 cs own label 70% red 30% white ▪ PO Box 1193 Stellenbosch 7599 ▪ wine@quoinrock.co.za ▪ www.quoinrock.com ▪ **T 021·888·4740** ▪ **F 021·888·4744**

Making the most of the very diverse conditions in their Stellenbosch and Cape Agulhas vineyards, Carl van der Merwe and his viticultural team commit themselves to producing grapes as organically as possible to best reflect site and vintage. A strongly holistic focus in both vineyards and winery extends to development of human potential through training and mentoring. You can test their theory that intent and authenticity can be recognised in the glass with a tasting which can now be enjoyed with platters of fine-cured meat and cheese — and impressive views from the slopes of the Simonsberg — throughout the week.

★★★★★ **Syrah** Warming, classy youngster with distinctive varietal expression. **04** depth of colour matched by intense savoury/spicy aromas; similar assertive flavours layered on supple mouthcoating texture. Current tannin vibrancy needs 2/3 yrs. 19 mths Fr oak, 30% new. **03** *Decanter* ★★★★. This, Oculus below, WO Smnsberg-Sbosch.

★★★★★ **Merlot** Last yr we noted **03**'s impressive structure, power & elegance; good freshness to alleviate 14.5% alc. Shd see 2010 in great shape. Smart Fr oaking (50% new). Smnsberg/Agulhas vyds (so WO W Cape). **02** (★★★★, also *Decanter* ★★★★), **01** still available.

★★★★ **Oculus** Site/vintage-driven dry white flagship; unnamed varieties sourced from same Smnsberg locations each yr. Still tight **04** vigorous minerality, piquant tangerine peel tone. Impressive vinosity, layered textures suggest excellent maturation potential. Food style par excellence. Fermented/yr Fr oak, 25% new.

★★★★ **Chardonnay** As with following wine, cool Agulhas vyds reflected in lime/lemon fruit purity, delicacy. **03** (not re-assessed) offers richness, freshening acid spine; for few yrs ageing. Fermented/aged yr Fr oak, 80% new.

★★★★ **Sauvignon Blanc** Sample **06** infused with steely, minerally precision. Lovely viscosity, fruit weight brightened by fine, savoury acid; moderate 13% alc. Lovely illustration of cool-provenance sophistication.

Glenhurst range

Red Blend ★★★★ 'Cape Blend' in pvs ed, where we noted still-available **01** (1st release) as pleasantly mellow & winey, with chewy savouriness. Shiraz, merlot, pinotage (41/31/28); Fr/Am oak, 50% new. WO W Cape. **Sauvignon Blanc-Viognier** ★★★☆ **06** 80/20 blend not ready for tasting. **05** compatible 78/22 partnership; figs/apricots nose; flavoursome, full bodied but balanced. Fr oak fermented/matured 4 mths. WO Smnsberg, as is… **Vine Dried Sauvignon Blanc** ★★★★ 'Natural Sweet' last ed. **04** as elegant as its tapered 500ml bottle. Pure, intense yet delicate orange blossom tone (no botrytis influence); softish, clean though slightly short. Used-oak fermented. Uncloying 130g/ℓ sugar. — AL

▪ **R62** see Joubert-Tradauw

Raats Family Wines   ♀

Stellenbosch ▪ Est/1stB 2000 ▪ Visits by appt ▪ Owners Bruwer & Jasper Raats Jnr ▪ Winemaker Bruwer Raats ▪ Viticulturist Jasper Raats Snr (2003) ▪ 20 ha (cab f, chenin) ▪ 4 500 cs 15% red 85% white ▪ PO Box 2068 Stellenbosch 7601 ▪ braats@mweb.co.za ▪ www.raats. co.za ▪ T/F 021·881·3078

Brothers Bruwer and Jasper Raats started this winery in 2000 while holding down full-time jobs elsewhere. Jasper subsequently moved to Marlboro, New Zealand, where he and winemaker wife Sally now produce their own-label Koru wines. But the family business has Bruwer's full attention since he moved on from Zorgvliet — good news for fans of their Chenin, the only SA version to have twice received 90+ points in US *Wine Spectator*. More cheer: Bruwer R believes 2006 was an 'exceptional year' for the variety.

★★★★☆ **Cabernet Franc** Run of standout vintages secures higher general rating for this beautifully crafted & multifaceted red. Alluring perfumed clove & floral aromas infuse **04** nose, palate; rich, velvety texture toned by supple fruit tannins. Lighter oaking (only 20% new vs 50% for **03**, both ±19 mths) provides seamless support.

★★★★ **Chenin Blanc** This wooded rendition widely & regularly saluted, lately by *Wine* (★★★★ for **04** & **03**), & *WS* (91 pts for **04**). Zesty, lithe & balanced **05** set to maintain Family tradition: intricate notes of spice, honey, ripe quince & nuts; rich, buttery palate alive with a finely judged fruit & acid tension. Brilliant oaking (only third barrelled & just 10% new, 6 mths Fr) adds verve, appeal.

★★★★ **Original Chenin Blanc** The unwooded version. **06** clean, spicy apple & quince flavours threaded with almond & freshened by lively acidity. Mid-2006 understated, perhaps shade less focused, but on past form shd perk up after short spell in bottle. Incl some Paarl fruit. — MW

▪ **Radford Dale** see The Winery of Good Hope
▪ **Rainbow Nation Wines** see The Shosholoza Collection

Rainbow's End Estate   ♀♀

Stellenbosch ▪ Est 1978 ▪ 1stB 2002 ▪ Visits by appt ▪ Fee R15 refundable on purchase of 4+ btls ▪ Owners Jacques, Anton & Francois Malan ▪ Winemaker Anton Malan, with Francois Malan ▪ Viticulturist Francois Malan, with Anton Malan ▪ 23 ha (cabs s/f, malbec, merlot, petit v, shiraz) ▪ 100 tons total 10 tons/850 cs own label 100% red ▪ PO Box 2253 Dennesig 7601 ▪

info@rainbowsend.co.za ▪ www.rainbowsend.co.za ▪ **T** 083·411·0170 / 082·413·7285 / 082·404·1085 / 021·885·1719 ▪ F 021·885·1722

This family-run estate has increased its focus on single-vineyard and -variety wines. Winemaker Anton Malan, who has won several accolades for his Shiraz, is upbeat about the single-block version, just released, and believes their maiden Cab and Cab Franc show similar form. Viticulturist brother Francois is equally enthusiastic about the latest cab franc and shiraz clones. To keep abreast of other news and developments, say the Malans, see their new website.

Cabernet Sauvignon new ★★★ High-toned, herbaceous **05**, cedar & tobacco whiffs; v firm tannins; big alc (14.5%) tad warming. New Fr/Hngrian oak, unfiltered/fined; same for… **Cabernet Franc** new ★★★☆ Has a distinct personality, plenty of aromatic appeal; **05** clean, rounded, juicy fruit; lovely lifted fynbos character, which helps offset 15% alc for surprisingly classically best. **Shiraz** ★★★☆ Elegant expression of extrovert modernity. **05** more fruity-spicy than savoury; hearty but balanced flavours, textures (15% alc), lingering cedar-fragrant farewell. Ex-single vyd; combo new Am/Fr oak. **Complexité** ★★★★ Aptly named bdx blend cab, merlot, cab f (39/31/30). **04** last ed showed refined yet ripe berry flavours, plenty of cab's firmer tannins; harmonious; potential for ±5 yrs. — IvH

Raka 👓🍷🍴🎵

Klein River (see Walker Bay map) ▪ Est/1stB 2002 ▪ Tasting & sales Mon-Fri 9-5 Sat 10-3 during peak season otherwise by appt ▪ Fee R10 for 4 wines ▪ Closed Dec 25 ▪ Tours by appt ▪ BYO picnic ▪ Walks ▪ Nature conservancy ▪ Owner/viticulturist Piet Dreyer ▪ Winemaker Danelle van Rensburg (2005) ▪ 62 ha (five Bdx reds, mourvèdre, pinotage, sangiovese, shiraz, sauvignon, viognier) ▪ 15 000 cs 75% red 17% white 8% rosé ▪ PO Box 124 Caledon 7230 ▪ rakawine@ telkomsa.net ▪ www.rakawine.co.za ▪ **T/F** 028·341·0676

Burly Piet Dreyer, a former commercial fisherman bringing a seaman's no-holds-barred attitude to the rarified wine world, was delighted by their 2006 Trophy Wine Show win: the Biography Shiraz 04 was voted best in its class *and* best red. (Our own five-star rating for the wine no doubt elicited a celebratory X-rated word or two.) But he's even more excited about the follow-up 05: 100% home-grown grapes, proudly labelled WO Klein River (a recent Overberg ward), polished by new winemaker Danelle van Rensburg (ex-Stellenzicht and Amani). A maiden Sangiovese honours Francisco di Santo, Italian POW and former owner of the farm, who urged the establishment of a vineyard.

★★★★☆ **Figurehead Cape Blend** 14% pinotage joins Bdx quintet to add Cape flavour without distracting from finely tuned ensemble. Maiden **04**, revisited, opulent plum/game tints with bramble fruits & pulpy red berries worked into incredibly fine tannic structure. Demands cellaring gd few yrs. MIWA DG. Yr 90% Fr oak, rest Am, mix new/used.

★★★★ **Quinary** Less overt cousin of above (no pinotage) carries cellar's stamp. **04** lush, sappy fruit rides on ribs of austere tannins hoping to emulate mineral **03**'s development — & trophy cupboard: MIWA Grand D'Or, SAA, VDG. Cabs s/f, merlot with dashes malbec, petit v. 14.5% alc.

★★★★ **Barrel Select Merlot** ('Best Barrique' pvs ed.) August selection of best Fr casks. **05** brooding youth, but enormously promising; buchu-spiked game meat flavours, massive tannins shield its delights for now; check from ±2010. Own vyds.

★★★★ **Biography Shiraz** Taking the shows by storm, **04** (★★★★★) topped all with TWS trophy. Astounding colour, swirling vanilla spice, dense fruit seamlessly integrated with & tethered by powder-fine tannins. Neither classic nor for the faint hearted, no shortage of character, alc (14.7%) either. Retasted, a sample last ed. VDG, SAA, SAYWS. Yr mix new/seasoned Fr/Am (70/30) oak. **03** also seamless, though sweetish finish.

★★★★ **Sauvignon Blanc** Striking, individual option from cool Stanford: quintessential sauvignon but with focus, character. **06** teems with herby canned pea features held in shape by extended racy structure.

Pinotage ★★★★ **05** secures sweet fruit in puckering tannic frame, needs time to allow softer plum features to emerge. **Spliced** ★★★ 88% merlot dominance racks up clever blend with cab, ruby cab in **04**; succulent, meaty fullness within open-weave frame. **Sangiovese** new ★★★ **05** characteristic food-friendly tannins, but in lighter, leaner style. **Rosé** ★★★ **05** slightly baked cinsaut fruit, nice dry finish. **Shannonea** ★★★★ Sauvignon (76%) joined by viognier & chard from **05**: perfumed, grippy lingering finish. Discontinued: **Cabernet Sauvignon-Merlot**, **Red**, **Semillon-Sauvignon Blanc**. — *DS*

■ **R & de R-Fredericksburg** *see* Rupert & Rothschild
■ **R & R** *see* Rupert & Rothschild

Ravenswood

Budget wines made by Robertson Winery for Vinimark. In 5ℓ packs; comfortably light-bodied (±10-12.5% alc); all **NV**.

Dry Red ☺ ★★ Versatile & appealing easy-drinker with plum & berry fruit padding, smooth & round — ok to chill in summer.

Rosé ★★ Balanced, not too sweet 'pink' with tropical notes, pleasantly light texture. **Grand Cru** ★★ Kinder version of this sometimes abrasive genre; bright tropical tone, balanced freshness & fruit. **White Light** ★★ Particularly gd flavour & balance for this style. **Stein** ★★ Light, fruity & manageably sweet. **Late Harvest** ★★ Soft & sweet tropical fruit flavours with perky finish. **Johannisberger** ★★ Delicate, sweet & light, according to style, easy tropical tones brightened by acidity. — *DH*

■ **Rawson's** *see* Cape Vineyards
■ **Ready Steady** *see* Southern Sky
■ **Red Wolf** *see* Wolvendrift

Remhoogte Estate   🍷 🍽 ⌂

Stellenbosch • Est 1994 • 1stB 1995 • Tasting & sales Mon-Fri 9-4 Sep-Apr, otherwise by appt • Tours anytime by appt • Olives & olive oil for sale • Conservation area • Exhibition of SA hunting trophies • Game camp • Owner Murray Boustred Trust • Cellarmaster Murray Boustred, assisted by Chris Boustred & advised by Michel Rolland • Viticulturist Jacques du Toit, advised by Johan Pienaar (Aug 2005/1994) • 30 ha (cab, merlot, pinotage, shiraz, chenin) • ±180 tons 6 500 cs own label 100% red • PO Box 2032 Dennesig 7601 • remhoogte@adept.co.za • T 889·5005 • F 021·889·6907

The zebra, bontebok, springbok and gnu at Remhoogte's new game reserve only add to its African feel — and belie the fact that this is a Franco-SA joint venture involving none other than Michel Rolland, the world's most famous wine consultant. (Then again, he sealed his partnership with former Johannesburg construction engineer and property developer Murray Boustred on a bushveld safari!) While it was the Merlot that first impressed him, Rolland has pushed for the production of three 'Cape blends' featuring pinotage. And while Rolland manages to visit four times a year, the day-to-day running of the cellar is now in the hands of Boustred's son, Chris, who recently completed his winemaking studies at the University of Stellenbosch.

★★★★ **Bonne Nouvelle** Rigorously structured **03** (not retasted) blends cab, merlot, pinotage (46:35:19), for classically styled but sumptuously fruited red; tannins evident but ripe.

★★★★ **Estate Wine** Merlot dominated blend with pinotage. Well wooded **04** more restrained & classic than 15% alc suggests, pleasingly savoury rather than simply fruity, with suavity tempered by firm, dryly tannic grip; but alc noticeable on warm finish. Shd mature good few yrs.

★★★★ **Cabernet Sauvignon** No new release since classic & restrained **01**; with 12% merlot. 18 mths oak, third new, same as for...

★★★☆ **Merlot 01** (★★★★) still available, not retasted. Savoury plum/mulberry notes, dense dry finish, herbal whiffs. Incl 15% cab. **00** gold at IWC 2003.

Aigle Noir ★★★ 04 has 44% pinotage (with merlot, cab); juicy, chewy, brawny (15% alc), with lots of red berries, sensibly modest oaking, savoury tannin structure. Some will notice bitter finish — our only reservation. Smnsberg-Sbosch WOs. — *TJ*

■ *Renosterbos* see Hofstraat

Reyneke Wines

Stellenbosch ▪ Est 1863 ▪ 1stB 1998 ▪ Tasting & sales by appt ▪ Uitzicht B&B ▪ Owners Reyneke family ▪ Winemaker Johan Reyneke (2005/6) ▪ Viticulturist Johan Reyneke (1992) ▪ 20 ha (cab, merlot, pinotage, shiraz, sauvignon) ▪ 1 250 cs own label 70% red 30% white ▪ PO Box 61 Vlottenburg 7604 ▪ wine@reynekewines.co.za ▪ www.reynekewines.co.za ▪ **T 021·881·3517/083·659·1826** *▪ F 021·881·3451*

Having converted the rest of his farm to biodynamic viticulture, environmental ethics graduate Johan Reyneke is now busy exporting the method to some neighbouring properties. His soils, he says, (and theirs) have shown dramatic improvement and, with only wild yeast cultures in use, the wines 'are definitely taking on a uniqueness they didn't have before'. He's slowly overcoming his resistance towards seeking biodynamic certification but hasn't yet decided which of the two international organisations to approach. A Stellenbosch University entomology student is doing a biodiversity count in a comparative assessment of the bug life on his farm and adjoining non-biodynamic properties.

★★★★ **Reyneke Reserve** 100% biodynamic flagship wine; 100% shiraz. Step-up **04** (ex-barrel, provisional ★★★★★), ringer rhône style with notable elegance & pure blackberry fruit; silky, balanced, already integrated oak (2nd fill Fr) complementing ripe fruit. **03**, with splash merlot, showed explosive 'Guy Fawkes' nose, big tannins well handled. Non-interventionist approach in winery for all wines: native yeasts, no additives, unfined.

Pinotage From farm's 1st biodynamic vyd, named 'Persephone'; **05** still in 2nd fill Fr oak, provisionally ★★★★, perhaps more — shd be recognised for particularly elegant, pure brambly fruit, deliciously vibrant, fruit filled palate; fine acidity provides thrilling backbone through to sappy finish. **04** (★★★★) attractive as always, if more demure than pvs. **Cornerstone ★★★★** Sales of this 60/40 cab/merlot blend help pay housing loans & tertiary education for farmworkers' families. Youthful magenta **05** (sample), freshness, grippy cab tannins, maintaining elegance & balance. Biodynamic vyds, new & 2nd fill oak. **Sauvignon Blanc 06** bunch pressed & still fermenting in barrel (so not rated) shows attractive, concentrated, zesty greengage flavours. **Blanc Fumé** Not retasted for this ed; fermented in 2nd fill barrels; **05** idiosyncratic character with greengage dominant. Last provisionally rated ★★★. — *IM*

Rhebokskloof Private Cellar

Paarl ▪ 1stB 1989 ▪ Tasting & sales daily 9-5 ▪ Fee R25 (informal, incl bite-size foods); R45 (formal, booking essential); R75 (sunset tasting, booking required) ▪ Tours by appt ▪ Restaurant (see Eat-out section) ▪ Play area for children ▪ Tour groups ▪ Gifts ▪ Conferences ▪ Conservation area ▪ Owner Rhebokskloof Wines ▪ Winemaker Daniël Langenhoven (May 1998) ▪ Viticulturist Magnus Joubert (Oct 2004) ▪ ±84 ha (cab, merlot, chard) ▪ 420 tons 28 000 cs 60% red 40% white ▪ PO Box 2637 Paarl 7620 ▪ info@rhebokskloof.co.za ▪ www.rhebokskloof.co.za ▪ **T 021·869·8386** *▪ F 021·869·8504*

Winemaker Daniël Langenhoven is pleased that his quest for quality is being taken seriously by the new owners of this Paarl winery. Business partners from the Mother City, they have great aspirations for Rhebokskloof including a vineyard update and changes to the cellar. A sound base already in place, positive reports are bound to follow.

★★★★ **Cabernet Sauvignon** The flagship, grown in two vyds ±17 yrs old; only Fr oak, 20% new, 14 mths. Still-listed **00** luxuriously upholstered, round, full & mellow, with, when last tasted, enough tannin to continue improving.

★★★★ Chardonnay Grande Reserve More obvious wood than version below, thanks to barrel fermentation/±11 mths in new Fr oak. **04** last ed suffused with vanilla/butterscotch & spice, rounded fruit still evolving.

Merlot ★★ 03 gawky mid-2006: oak looms, as does 15% alc, giving 'hot', unmelded impression. 70% wooded, 16 mths Fr, 30% new. **Pinotage ★★★** Step-up **05** delightful bouquet of rosewater & plum; full, fruit-sweet flavours buttressed by serious, long-term tannins; cld do with yr/2 to settle, grow. 20% new oak, 14 mths. **Shiraz ★★★ 03** not retasted; leathery, with fleeting mulberry whiff, savoury dry finish. 14 mths oak, 25% new, 10% Am. **Chardonnay Sur Lie/Barrel Selection ★★★★** Recently more elegant restraint than New World flamboyance. **05** appealing core of pure lime marmalade; oak timed (9 mths Fr, only 30% new, no malo); mid-weight, even, satisfying. **Weisser Riesling ★★ 05** last yr noted as same earthy/spicy profile as pvs, bone-dry ultra-crisp finish. **Tamay Sparkling** Fragrant not-quite-brut fizz; latest NV (06) from chardonnay, riesling & introducing viognier; too unformed to rate; pvs was **★★**. **Weisser Riesling Special Late Harvest ★★★ 05** from well-aged block (1988), last ed showed racy acidity, some lemon/lime richness, lovely up-tempo spicy finish. 375ml. **MCC ★★ 03** house's first; from chard, 18 mths lees-aged; intended as 'light, Fr style'; certainly is light bodied, gently effervescent, with delicate green-apple finish.

Rhebok range

Cabernet Sauvignon-Merlot ★★★ 04 mineral tinged black fruit with earthy hint; ripe, lively & juicy; volatile touch only quibble. Usual regime of 9 mths Fr oak, 10% new. **Dry Red ★★★** Tangy, herby blend pinotage, gamay, merlot; full bodied **03** characterful & tasty; savoury, with notes of coffee & choc. **Chardonnay ★★** Unwooded **05** shows maturing honey/marmalade veneer – still appealing but needs drinking soon; light 13% alc. **Sauvignon Blanc ★★★ 06** ex-Rbtsn; early harvested (12.5% alc) but enough fruit to balance the acid for fresh, tropical toned drinkability. **Chardonnay-Sauvignon Blanc ★★** Soupçon viognier sparks aromatic excitement in early harvested **06**; flowers & apricots on nose; v soft, slightly nutty flavours. **Bouquet Blanc ★★** Bouquet of Golden Delicious apple on **06** sample, from chenin; fresh & clean; tart acidity keeps sweetness well in check for semi-dry effect. **Dry White ★★ 06** now 4-way combo fronted by chard; light, fresh & fruity, to be enjoyed young. **Chenin Blanc** discontinued after brief revival. – *MM*

Rickety Bridge Winery

Franschhoek ▪ Tasting & sales Mon-Fri 8-5 Sat & pub hols 9-5 ▪ Closed Easter Fri, Dec 25/26 & Jan 1 ▪ Fee R10 refundable on purchase ▪ Cellar tours by appt ▪ BYO picnic ▪ Accommodation & other attractions (see intro) ▪ Owner DS Sarnia (Pty) Ltd ▪ Winemaker Wilhelm van Rooyen, with Dawid Gqirana (Jan 2001/Jun 1998) ▪ Viticulturist Wilhelm van Rooyen ▪ 16 ha (cab, merlot, shiraz, chard, chenin, semillon) ▪ 120 tons 5 000 cs own label 65% red 35% white ▪ PO Box 455 Franschhoek 7690 ▪ sales@ricketybridgewinery.com ▪ www.ricketybridgewinery. com ▪ T 021·876·2129/3669 ▪ F 021·876·3486

'Visitors welcome' is the message from this Franschhoek winery, having refurbished their tasting room and achieved that 'home-from-home' feel in their luxury stay-over, Rickety Bridge Country House. And for those looking for a vineyard venue to celebrate their vows, the wedding and function facilities (including a luxury loft lounge) has opened its doors and offers romantic views of the Franschhoek and Wemmershoek mountains.

★★★★☆ Shiraz Cellar's polished signature. Hallmarks are concentrated black fruit, well controlled by spicy oak. **03** last ed was less extrovert than pvs but still v fine; rich, spicy/savoury palate, pleasantly chewy tannins. 20-24 mths Fr barrels, 20% new.

★★★★ Paulinas Reserve Limited release barrel selections honouring farm's founder, Paulina de Villiers. **03 (★★★)** sampled last ed continued bdx formula (cab-merlot, 68/32), though lacked pvs's elegant generosity; Fr oak, 36% new. **02** (66/34) showed claret-like grip & feel.

Cabernet Sauvignon ★★★★ Attractive & harmonious **02**, more savoury, less overt berry character than pvs, but food-friendly; 30 mths Fr oak, 25% new. Following reds not retasted: **Merlot ★★★** More body than fruit on **03**, tautish tannins, mint/mocha aromas with meaty hint. 2 yrs Fr oak, 25% new. **Duncan's Creek Classic Red ★★★** Appealing, lightish & juicy **04**, shiraz (57%) with cab & dollop malbec. Gd fireside red or, lightly chilled, summer picnic partner; ±13% alc. **Chardonnay ★★★ 05**, like pvs, sinewy, elegant with good marmalade-toned fruit, smooth finish. 9 mths barrelled. **Chenin Blanc ★★ 06** dry white with quick vegetal flavours. **Sauvignon Blanc ★★★ 06** easy-drinker total contrast to beefy pvs: light (12.7% alc), almost delicate, with unusual rose-petal hint. **Semillon ★★★** Recent releases less weighty/serious; **05** strongly barrels influenced (9 mths Fr) — roasted nut overlay to variety's lanolin character, demure lemony finish. All these WO Fhoek or Coastal. — *MM*

Rico Suter Estate

Worcester ▪ Est 2004 ▪ 1stB 2006 ▪ Visits by appt only ▪ Accommodation (see intro) ▪ BYO picnic ▪ Table olives ▪ Walks ▪ Facilities for children ▪ Owner Rico Suter Family Trust ▪ Winemaker Carlo Suter, with Rico Suter (both Feb 2004) ▪ Viticulturists Bruno & Carlo Suter ▪ 60 ha (cab, cinsaut, merlot, petit v, pinotage, shiraz, tannat, sauvignon) ▪ 600 tons ±2 500 cs own label 100% red ▪ PO Box 38 Breerivier 6858 ▪ richsut@lantic.net ▪ T 023-355-1822/ 082-783-9157 ▪ F 023-355-1822

This is a family affair, father Rico assisting winemaker son Carlo in the cellar, viticulturist son Bruno in the vineyards, and Bruno's wife Erika in the process of establishing a small guest house. The Suters bought part of the farm back in 1993, clearing and then gradually replanting the vineyards. The adjacent property was added in 2002, reuniting the original farm which had been divided between two Du Toit brothers. Most grapes go to Waboomsrivier Co-op but the best are vinified in small quantities for the own-brand.

Cabernet Sauvignon ★★★ Restrained, Old-World style; **03** lightish hues, leafy damp-earth notes, dry but smoothly ripe tannins for easy drinking now & over next 2-3 yrs. **Cabernet Sauvignon-Petit Verdot ★★★★** Contrast to above: **04** hugely ripe (15.3% alc) 60/40 blend, gobs berry fruit & mineral/lead-pencil oak, blockbusterish tannins insist on decanting now or cellaring good few yrs. **Shiraz ★★★** (Even) bigger than blend (15.7% alc) but lighter textured, more amenable tannins; pleasing & soft blueberry flavours **04**. Incl 15% petit v. — *CT*

Ridder's Creek

Wellington ▪ Est 2002 ▪ Tasting by appt ▪ Owners George de Ridder & Jean Frick ▪ Vini consultant Jeff Wedgwood ▪ PO Box 72 Wellington 7654 ▪ ridders@iafrica.com ▪ www.ridderscreek.co.za ▪ T/F 021-873-7746

Wines and blending components for this negociant house are sourced from various regions and assembled under the experienced eye of Jeff Wedgwood. The team also does bottling for clients as well as local and international bulk-wine trading. Limited-release corporate gift packs are another speciality.

Pinotage new ★☆ Lean **04** with resin & bluegum aromas; taut tannins need time to mesh with fruit. **Shiraz ★★★ 04** last ed was approachable despite firm tannins & 14.5% alc. Black pepper, brambleberry aromas & flavours. **Cape Red ★★** New World styling evident in **05**'s sweetish entry & finish (5.6g/ℓ RS), chunky tannins & soft, ripe fruit. Sample tasted, same for next two. **Sauvignon Blanc ★☆ 06** has tropical fruit hints but too much freshness, giving a lean, austere feel. **Cape White ★★ 06** appealing summer quaffer with pineapple fruit & leafy tones, gentle touch of sweetness. **Cabernet Sauvignon** & **Chardonnay** discontinued. — *CT*

Ridgeback Wines

Paarl ▪ Est 1997 ▪ 1stB 2001 ▪ Tasting & sales Mon-Sat 10-5 (also Sun during peak season) ▪ Fee R15 for 5 wines ▪ Closed Easter Fri, Dec 25/26 & Jan 1 ▪ Deli-style meals ▪ Accommodation: see intro ▪ Tours by appt ▪ Owners Kilimanjaro Investments ▪ Winemaker Cathy Marshall (Jun 2000) ▪ Viti consultant Phil Freese ▪ 35 ha (cabs/f, grenache, merlot, mourvèdre, petit v, shiraz, chenin, sauvignon, viognier) ▪ 200 tons ▪ 16 000 cs own label 70% red 30% white ▪ Eurogap certified ▪ PO Box 2076 Windmeul 7630 ▪ ridgebacksales@mwebbiz.co.za or ridgetasting@mweb.co.za or ridgeback@mweb.co.za ▪ www.ridgebackwines.co.za ▪ T/F 869-8068/082-376-8498 ▪ F 794-1070

It's a time of consolidation: completion of the extensive vineyard make-over and the launch of additional labels Vansha and His Master's Choice following the first bottling in 2001, this Agter-Paarl farm is settling comfortably into its own skin. Now Jackie Rabe takes over as marketing manager in time for the opening of the guesthouse and deli-style lunchtime restaurant alongside the tasting room. With their new Sunday licence, the tasting room is now open seven days a week in the high season.

★★★★★ **Shiraz** ✓ Laudably consistent since maiden **01**. Latest **04** expansive but unshowy intensity; pure smoked meat, black pepper; red fruits hint; emphasis on rich yet fresh, sensual mouthfeel, savoury length. Delicious now, excellent potential. 16 mths Burgundian barrels, 20% new. Bejewelled **03** golds at Concours Mondial, CWT; *Wine* ★★★★.

★★★★ **Merlot-Cabernet Franc** ✓ Merlot leads this time (62/38), hence name change from pvs ed's 'Cab F-Merlot'. More stuffing, spice than Merlot below. And **04** more sumptuous, bigger than leafy, elegant **03**, though agreeably moderate 13.5% alc. Nascent dark plum/cinnamon complexity; properly dry; long, savoury. Sensitively Fr oaked, 10% new.

★★★★ **Merlot 04** quieter, more refined than pvs. Needs good aeration to energise suave dark plum, mocha tones, fill out sleek, fine tannined structure. Medium bodied, satisfyingly dry, for earlier enjoyment. Fr oak, 80% new, 14 mths. **03** Winemakers' Choice.

★★★★ **Viognier** Many fans of full-tilt, blazing-guns styling (full-ripe picking, 100% new oak fermentation, maturation) of this aromatic grape. **05** (★★★★) similar to sumptuous maiden **03**; assertive wood, 15.5% alc vie with ultra-ripe apricot tones. Demanding, sweetish mouthful; best young.

Cabernet Sauvignon ★★★★ Sturdy **04** with distinctive steak tartare/iron character; forceful dry tannins. Well absorbed 90% new Fr oak (incl malo). **His Master's Choice** ★★★★ Maiden **04** still selling. Shiraz with active 6% viognier, latter dominant mid-2005, needed time for delicate fruit to emerge from dense tannins. 16 mths 85% new Fr oak. **Vansha Dry Red** ★★★ **06** newly bottled, thus unsettled — yet friendly; chunky shiraz input provides satisfying everyday drinking. Unoaked, with 25% cab, moderate 13.2% alc. **Sauvignon Blanc** ★★★ Vigorous, 'sauvage' **06**; intense greengage/gooseberry aromatic enticements diminished by penetrating acid, lean mouthfeel. May pull together with brief spell in bottle. **Vansha Dry White** ★★★★ ✓ More exciting than name suggests — soupçon barrelled viognier adds va-va-voom to usual chenin-sauvignon mix in **06**. Enough concentration, persistence for enjoyable, balanced drinking. **'Sweet Viognier'** new At press time unnamed/certified/rated dessert; preview **06** vivacious & delicious mix apricot/peach, bright fruity acids, refreshing acid/sugar contrast & lowish 11.5% alc. *—AL*

■ *Ridgemor* see Weening & Barge

Riebeek Cellars

*Swartland ▪ Est/1stB 1941 ▪ Tasting & sales Mon-Fri 8-5 Sat 9-2 ▪ Closed Easter Fri/Sun, Dec 25 & Jan 1 ▪ Tours strictly by appt ▪ BYO picnic ▪ Farm produce ▪ Owners 60 shareholders ▪ Winemakers Zakkie Bester, Eric Saayman & Alecia Hamman (Dec 1999/Jan 1997/Dec 2004) ▪ Viticulturist Hanno van Schalkwyk (Sep 2000) ▪ 1 400 ha (cab, merlot, pinotage, shiraz, chard, chenin, colombard, sauvignon) ▪ 15 500 tons 45 000 cs own labels + 40 000 cs for customers, incl Rocheburg & Broken Rock (both UK) ▪ 35% red 60% white 5% rosé ▪ HACCP certification in progress ▪ PO Box 13 Riebeek Kasteel 7307 ▪ info@riebeekcellars.co.za ▪ www. riebeekcellars.com ▪ **T** 022·448·1213 ▪ F 022·448·1281*

Still reaping the fruits of their vine replanting programme, the Riebeek team is enthused by promising young blocks of viognier, tinta roriz, cab franc and malbec. Besides making appearances in blends, the quartet may take centre stage as varietal wines. With an eye on the international market, they're in the process of meeting HACCP standards and registering for Fairtrade. Partnership Vineyards, their farmworker empowerment project, is set to expand by a planned 45ha, including cab.

Reserve Selection

Shiraz-Cabernet Sauvignon ★★★☆ Warm, smoky, spicy fruit reveals shiraz dominance (60%) on **02**, quarter cab supplies the stiffening for 4-5 yrs ageing; meaty, beefy flavours & firm dry tannins suggest the style of food which suits. Incl dollops petit v & merlot; intricately oaked. **Pinotage** `new` ★★★★ Fine rhubarb & mulberry typicity with savoury nuance, **05** full of flavour & enough dry tannins for few yrs ageing. Nicely judged combo barrels & oak chips. **Shiraz** ★★★★ **04** chewy dark plum fruit with notes of smoke & black pepper; ambitious oaking a touch too obvious still, needs yr/2 to settle. Seriousness wine, nudges the next level. 18-24 mths Fr/Am wood, some new. **Chardonnay** ★★★ 100% Fr oak fermented, lees-aged; **04** delivers gd crisp drinkability, variety's lemons & limes upfront, wood supportive, dry food-style finish. **Chenin Blanc** ★★☆ New Fr oak fermented; **05** reticent mid-2006, shows some pleasant melon tones but not much varietal character; might need time; Swiss 2006 judges thought otherwise & awarded gold.

Limited Releases `new`

Pinotage ★★★★ **05** a big whack of wood greets you with sweet spice & vanilla, then ripe fruit asserts itself attractively for bold but balanced appeal. Has legs for 3/4 yrs. Barrels only for these — here 2nd/3rd fill, 10 mths, a more protracted 24 mths for next wine. **Tinta Barocca** ★★★☆ Appealing wildness to characterful **02**, touches pepper, game meat & savoury, typical tinta robustness; 2nd fill oak provides suitably sturdy backbone for future development.

A Few Good Men range

These from selected vyds, their owners/growers being the eponymous Few Good Men. **Cabernet Sauvignon** ★★★ Yr Fr oak, some new, for these. **04** obviously treated seriously with ageing in mind, hence firm dry tannins still holding fruit captive, needing few yrs. **Merlot** ★★★ Just-ripe plum character with white pepper on **04**, elegant & restrained mid-2006, seems to be holding back. Usual 9 mths 2nd fill oak. **Shiraz** ★★★☆ Portion new Am oak (30%, ±9 mths) distinguishes these; carefully handled **04** is rhône-inclined with layers of interest incl hedgerow, violet & roasted spice; oak supportive. Enjoy in aromatic youth. **Chardonnay** Noteworthy success in **05** (★★★★ ✓); lovely ripe citrus with biscuit nuance; textured & full flavoured; long & deliciously fresh. Regulation 100% barrel-fermentation/6 mths, Fr/Am oak (50/50). Danie du Toit's the Good Man. Notch above **04** (★★★★), with deliciously ripe lime fruit.

Riebeek Collection

Chenin Blanc ☺ ★★☆ Engagingly fresh & crisp melon & guava fruit, **06** forthcoming & optimistic, light textured for solo or to enjoy with alfresco foods.

Cabernet Sauvignon ★★☆ Herbaceous **05** (sample) underpinned by liquorice-toned black fruit, firm but melded tannins, well applied oak chips. An amenable food style. **Merlot** ★★ Usual astringency unleavened by fruit in tight, shy, savoury **05**, usual banana whiffs, fleshy fruit & variety-true flavours with oak-chipping well done. Coastal WO, as are most in range. **Shiraz** `new` ★★ Porty whiffs & liquorice on **04**, subdued fruit with 14% alc showing. **Redneck** ★★★ Mainly for export. Vibrant Mediterranean-style red, partly-oaked equal mix shiraz, malbec; savoury-dry **03** not retasted. **Shiraz-Cinsaut** ★★★ Replaces 'Cinsaut-Pinotage'. **05** (sample) tasty early-drinker with food-inviting combo dried herbs, sweet fruit & firm texture. Oak-chipped. **Pinotage Rosé** ★★★ Charming alfresco drink with redcurrant flavours in **06**; plump, accessible & just off-dry. **05** Winemakers Choice. **Chardonnay** ★★ Partly & subtly oaked **05**, last ed was pale & light, some elegance in friendly, undemanding package. **Sauvignon Blanc** ★★ **06** green fig & crunchy apple with a lot of freshness; leafier/greener styling goes well with food. **Stein** ★★ Grapey, rounded & sweet, slips down comfortably. Light-bodied **NV** from chenin, white muscadel. **Montino Petillant Light** ★★ Fresh, spritzy **NV** white with gentle grapey allures, from muscadel; chill well for summer refreshment. Light 8.5% alc. **Pieter Cruythoff Pinot2 Brut** ★★ **NV** carbonated sparkler, name hinting at duo of pinots (blanc 60%, noir) in blend; easy, briskly dry refreshment, with apricot nuance. **Red Jerepiko** ★★ Full-sweet winter warmer from tinta. Latest bottling powerfully ripe & sweet, like drinking blackberry jam! **NV**. **Cape Ruby**

★★★ Returns to deliciously drinkable, juicy-fruit mode with latest bottling; controlled sweetness & spirit for uncloying effect. **NV** blend tinta, souzão (80/20), 50% small-oaked 24 mths; 19.8% alc.

Cape Table range

NV range of lowish-alc 1ℓ packs; untasted; **Cellar Red, Cellar Rosé Semi-Sweet, Natural Sweet Rosé, Cellar White, Cellar Gold Late Harvest, Natural Sweet Low Alcohol White** & **Cellar Lite**. — *CR*

Rietrivier Winery

Montagu (see Little Karoo map) ▪ *Est 1965* ▪ *1stB 1990* ▪ *Tasting, sales & light meals Mon-Thu 8.30-4.30 Fri 8.30-3 Sat 9-1; or BYO picnic* ▪ *Closed pub hols* ▪ *Tours by appt* ▪ *Facilities for children* ▪ *Owners 46 members* ▪ *Manager/winemaker Chris-Willem de Bod, with Petrus Bothma (Oct 1999/Jan 1994)* ▪ *Viti consultant Johannes Mellet (Aug 2005)* ▪ *300 ha (merlot, shiraz, chard)* ▪ *5 000 tons 10 000 cs own label + 4m litres bulk 20% red 80% white* ▪ *PO Box 144 Montagu 6720* ▪ *rietrivier@lando.co.za* ▪ *www.rietrivier.co.za* ▪ **T/F 023·614·1705**

Upgraded tasting and sales facilities make this an attractive stop on Route 62 – and with far more visitors, wine sales have already increased. There's an eatery serving breakfasts and light meals, a farmstall stocked with jams and other country produce, a play area for children and a fireplace to warm your toes next to in winter. You can even fill up on petrol or diesel before you continue your journey through the scenic Little Karoo.

Quiriga Reserve range

Merlot ★★★ **04** local Young Wine Show class winner; supportively new-oaked (18 mths Fr) to make most of succulent red berry fruit; drinks well now, legs for another few yrs. **Shiraz** ★★★ Accessible, not-for-keeping **03**, last yr showed some pepper & mint touches, rich warm fruit. Oak as above.

Rietrivier range

Merlot ★★ **05** promise of clean berried nose unfulfilled by fairly lean, dry palate. 6 mths Fr staves. Following pair not retasted: **Pinotage** ★★ **04** cherry fruit, lightish tannins, medium body; 6 mths staves after fermentation. **Shiraz** ★★★ **04** yard better than pvs; dark cherry, spice & char aromas/flavours, dry finish, integrated 14% alc. **Petite Rouge** ★★ Rustic, light bodied quick-quaff from equal parts pinotage & ruby cab; unwooded, **NV**, 500ml. **Route 62 Red** ★★ High-octane unwooded mix pinotage, merlot (90/10), over-ripe mulberry fruit on last tasted **03**. **Rosé** ★ Natural Sweet style **NV** from pinotage, soft, sweet, with barely vinous red berry taste. **Blanc de Noir** new ★ Unsubtle **05** from red muscadel; eye-popping orange colour; sweet, soft, with flavours of orange jelly. **Sauvignon Blanc** ★ Semi-dry summer sipper; **06** v light & modestly fruited. **Colombar-Chardonnay** ★★ **04** last yr was tropically toned, fruity, smooth & ripe. **Petite Blanc** ★★ Crisp, fruity, light bodied off-dry white; **NV**, equal dollops colombard, chardonnay, sauvignon. 500ml screwcap. **Late Harvest** ★ Soft, sweet, straightforward chenin; **NV**; also in 500ml. **Sparkling Vin Doux** ★ Light & sweet fizz in red & white versions, both **NV**. **Montagu Red Muscadel** ★★★ Montagu-area speciality, here made jerepiko-style (no fermentation), fortified to ±17.5%. Lower ratings for recent releases prompted by cloying sweetness, as in latest **05**, with weighty raisined richness which the lovely, well fused spirit can't quite enliven. Also in 250 & 500ml. **Montagu White Muscadel** ★★ Barley sugar flavours, penetrating sweetness on **05**, 17.5% alc bit apart; perhaps needs time. **Montagu Hanepoot** ★★ **05** plump, distinctly sweet fortified with lemon zest flavours. 'Very popular,' advises Chris dB. **Montagu Ruby Port** ★★ From pinotage, **03** last yr noted as idiosyncratic, with mulled wine character, touch tannin to finish. — *IvH/JN/CR*

Rietvallei Estate

Robertson ▪ *Est 1864* ▪ *1stB 1975* ▪ *Tasting & sales Mon-Fri 8.30-5 Sat 9.30-1* ▪ *Closed Easter Fri-Mon, Sep 24, Dec 25/26 & Jan 1* ▪ *Light lunches or BYO picnic* ▪ *Facilities for children* ▪ *Tour groups* ▪ *Owner Johnny Burger* ▪ *Winemakers Johnny & Kobus Burger (1973/2001)* ▪ *Viti consultant Briaan Stipp (2000)* ▪ *137 ha (10 varieties r/w)* ▪ *2 040 tons ±36 000 cs own label 40% red 45% white*

*15% fortified ▪ Export brands: Wild Rush & Rushdale ▪ PO Box 386 Robertson 6705 ▪ info@ rietvallei.co.za ▪ www.rietvallei.co.za ▪ **T** 023·626·3596/4422 ▪ F 023·626·4514*

The 1908 block of bushvines which produced the maiden Red Muscadel bearing the estate's name — the 75 vintage, launched in 1976 — is still going strong and the wine remains an award-winner. The 30th anniversary of that release finds Rietvallei with a much broader portfolio and still wider horizons: 6th-generation scion-in-charge Kobus Burger notes almost 50% growth in local and export sales this past year. A new tasting room is open, and this well loved picnic spot will be serving light lunches as well.

Special Select range

★★★★☆ **Cabernet Sauvignon** new ★★★☆ Fruit-bomb **04** portiness precedes ripe blackberry jam aromas; acid cuts deftly through rich fruit. Unsurprising 15% alc & 20 mths new Fr oak. **Shiraz** new ★★★☆ Robust, ripe, modern **04** will be popular. Lush blackberry fruit toned down by firm acidity & integrated 20 mths new Fr/Am oak. Warm, showy finish from 15.5% alc. **Chardonnay** ★★★☆ Fresh, vibrantly fruity **06** appealing gum sweet/ citrus flavours & well-integrated oak (3 mths 100% new Fr). **Sauvignon Blanc** ★★★☆ **06** from Rbtson grapes (pvs ex-Elim), mix herbaceous & tropical characters with gd concentration, thread minerality & firm flavourful finish.

Rietvallei range

★★★★ **Red Muscadel** ✓ A fortified classic. **05** appealing raisined fruit & rooibos tea aromas (& colour); unctuously rich but avoids any cloying sweetness. 16% alc, 195g/ℓ RS. Enjoy lightly chilled on its own.

★★★★☆ **Muscadel 1908** From what's thought to be SA's oldest red muscadel vyd (tiny-yielding bushvines planted 1908). **03** lighter & drier (15% alc, 209g/ℓ RS) than **02**. Same opulent raisiny nose, cooked apricot jam flavours with excellent complexity & concentration. Tasted mid-2005. Gold at Muscats du Monde.

★★★★☆ **Cabernet Sauvignon** ★★★☆ **05** preview fresh blackcurrant, notes of tar & tealeaf hinting at more elegant style; grippy tannins lend dryness to raspberry fruit. Fr oak, yr, 10% 1st fill. **Shiraz** ★★★ Full bodied **05** needs time to integrate spicy oak with very ripe, sweet blackberry fruit. Yr Fr/Am wood, 10% 1st fill. **Juanita Cabernet Sauvignon Rosé** ★★★ Pale cherry red **05** (sample) offers mouthwatering sweet-sour cherry flavours & some structure. **Chardonnay** ★★★☆ ✓ **06** (sample) rich peach & vanilla aromas, stone fruit flavours; finishes dry thanks to vibrant acidity. 50% wood fermented/3 mths, rest tank. **Natural Chardonnay** ★★★ Unoaked, joyful, zesty **06**, sweet entry, lively acidity ensures dry finish, excellent drinkability. **Sauvignon Blanc** ★★★ Simple, fresh, grassy **06**, green apple flavours, friendly 12.5% alc. **Rhine Riesling** ★★★ Water-pale **06**, spicy white peach aromas, sweetness balanced crisp acidity; simple, light anytime wine. Low 11% alc.

John B range

Cabernet Sauvignon-Tinta Barocca ★★☆ **05** commercial style easy-drinker; 70:30 blend with raspberry fruit & oak flavours from staving. **Sauvignon Blanc-Colombar** ★★☆ **06** fresh 60:40 blend, intending to be a light, low alc wine (12.5%); perfect lunchtime quaffer. — *IM*

■ *Rijckbosch* see Mountain River Wines

Rijk's Private Cellar

*Tulbagh ▪ Est 1996 ▪ 1stB 2000 ▪ Tasting & sales Mon-Fri 10-4 Sat 10-2 ▪ Fee R5/wine ▪ Closed Easter Fri-Mon, Dec 25 & Jan 1 ▪ Tours during tasting hours ▪ Country Hotel T 023·230·1006 ▪ BYO picnic ▪ Tour groups ▪ Conferencing ▪ Walks ▪ Owner Neville Dorrington ▪ Winemaker Pierre Wahl (Jan 2002) ▪ Viti consultant Johan Wiese (Mar 1996) ▪ 28 ha (cab, merlot, pinotage, shiraz, chard, chenin, sauvignon, semillon) ▪ ±180 tons 11 000 cs own label 70% red 30% white ▪ PO Box 400 Tulbagh 6820 ▪ wine@rijks.co.za ▪ www.rijks.co.za ▪ **T** 023·230·1622 ▪ F 023·230·1650*

'I am entrusted with gently guiding the wine into the bottle,' is how Pierre Wahl describes his job at this 'dream cellar'. But getting his entry-level wines *out* of the bottle is now a simple matter of twisting and pouring, after the introduction of screwcaps for the Iceberg White and Red. 'We're still testing the market,' says the lanky winemaker. 'We're in no rush, as consumers have yet to make up their minds about the desirability of non-traditional closures.' Meanwhile, the tasting room has been extended, with racks added to showcase older vintages.

★★★★ **Bravado** Cab, shiraz, merlot blend (45/30/25); **02** improvement on maiden **01** (★★★) & admirable effort in difficult vintage. Elegant aromatic melange, choc/subtle mint highlights. Gd fleshy concentration, savoury minerality, balanced firm frame. Oaking complementary & refined (23 mths, 70% new Fr oak). **01** Winemakers' Choice .

★★★★ **Cabernet Sauvignon** Cab doesn't come much bigger than these (from area once touted as white-wine country!); **03** with usual tannin fortress, ±15% alc, though ultra-ripe beefy/pruny fruit lacks focused thrill of **02** (★★★★★). Successful show entrant (TWS 2005 gold, Decanter ★★★★. *Wine* ★★★★, Winemakers Choice for **02**) though no track record to judge longevity. 18 mths Fr oak, 70% new.

★★★★ **Cabernet Sauvignon-Merlot** Mouth-filling **02**, with excellent intensity from ripe fruited 65/35 blend, still available. 14.8% alc. Swiss gold. 20 mths Fr oak, 40% new.

★★★★☆ **Shiraz 02** last ed described as concentrated, broad, with explosive fruit, liquid fynbos flavours, slippery tannins. 16 mths Fr/Am oak, 30% new. *Wine* ★★★★.

★★★★ **Chenin Blanc 05** continues in impressive **04**'s footsteps. Personality plus in dainty floral, citrus, honey arrangement; remarkable lightness of touch (for 14.5% alc), fruit concentration aided by poised acid/sugar contrast (7g/ℓ; 8.3g/ℓ). Lovely mellowing potential. 70% barrel fermented, 11 mths mix Hngrian/Fr barrels, 20% new. Portion natural ferment.

★★★★ **Semillon** Sunshine filled style; redolent lanolin, beeswax, honeycomb seduction with squeeze lemony lift. **04** still youthfully fresh with hints oak sweetness, though 3.4g/ℓ sugar tech. dry; incipient silky viscosity, mellow savouriness. Shd be a stunner around 2008. Fermented/yr Fr oak, 20% new.

Pinotage ★★★☆ Show circuit favourite. Latest **03** more simple red-wine flavours than overt varietal character, also generous coconut oak. Nicely tamed tannins; fresh, balanced. **02** Pinotage Top Ten 2003, VDG, IWC gold. 16 mths largely new Am/Fr oak. **Merlot** ★★★ Characteristic minty thumbprint on **02**; sweet, simple fruit struggles against roughish dry tannins, alc. Drink up. 20 mths 60% new Fr oak. **Iceberg Red** new ★★★ More warming than name suggests. Medley ripe dark fruits, firm tannin brace, hint 14.8% alc glow in tail. **03** shiraz (52%) with cabs s/f, merlot; Fr oak, none new, 14 mths. Winemakers' Choice. This, White below, screwcapped. **Chardonnay** ★★★ Sturdy, country style **04**; strong oak & alc alleviated by slight creamy lift. Fermented/yr Fr oak, 70% new. *Wine* ★★★★. **03** Michelangelo DG. **Sauvignon Blanc** ★★★ **05** unusually retiring cool gooseberry/lemongrass notes, medium body highlights piquant acid. Drink up. 12. 4% alc. 80% fruit ex-Mbury, so WO Coastal. **Iceberg White** new ★★★ Everyday sauvignon, chardonnay, semillon blend; **04** attractive honeyed bottle-age/freshness aromatics, rather disjointed acid less palate-pleasing. — *AL*

■ *Rising River* see Cru Wines
■ *River Grandeur* see Viljoensdrift
■ *River's Edge* see Weltevrede
■ *River's Tale* see Oranjerivier

Riverstone Vineyards   ◷♟⌂♿

Breedekloof (see Worcester/Breedekloof map) • Est 1963 • 1stB 1975 • Tasting & sales Mon-Fri 8-12.30; 1.30-5 Sat 9-1 • Fee R10 refunded on purchase • Closed Easter Fri-Mon, Dec 25 & Jan 1 • Merwida Country Lodge T 023·349·1435 • Owners Schalk & Pierre van der Merwe • Winemakers Magnus Kriel (Dec 2000), with Sarel van Staden (Aug 1982) • Viticulturist Magnus Kriel • 630 ha (cab, merlot, shiraz, chard, chenin, sauvignon, semillon, viognier) •

*10 000 tons 20 000 cs own label 40% red 60% white ▪ PO Box 4 Rawsonville 6845 ▪ wines@ merwida.com ▪ www.merwida.com ▪ **T** 023·349·1144 ▪ F 023·349·1953*

The Riverstone brand of family-owned Merwida farm is on the up, with value for money the key. The message is still easy-drinking but renewed focus on whites saw the release of the first wooded Chardonnay and the new vintage of the Family Reserve Viognier, now also lightly oaked. Ruby Cab is back following the success of the previous vintage, which proved 'extremely popular'. Bottling now takes place on-site, thanks to a mobile filling unit.

Family Reserve range

Barbera ★★★ **04** food-styled wine with blackberry fruit & hints tobacco & vanilla, supple tannins & variety's attractively crisp acidity. Yr 2nd fill Fr oak. **Viognier** Exceptional barrel fermented **06** (★★★★ ✓) has generous white peach & apricot, judicious dabs oak vanilla, &, unusually for variety, vibrant acidity. ±14% alc also far more appealing than 15% for unwooded **05** (★★★). Delectably dry finish. Sample tasted.

Riverstone range

★★★★ **Chardonnay** new ✓ Genteel, sensitively oaked **06** exudes quiet confidence; attractive tropical nuances mingle with butterscotch, generous citrus flavours. Harmonious 14% alc adds palate weight & roundness; long, leesy finish from partial barrel fermentation.

Cabernet Sauvignon ★★☆ Easy-drinking **04**, last ed a sample with soft & sweet baked-fruit tones. **Ruby Cabernet** ★★★ Reported discontinued last ed, but range's benign monster' (regular ±15% alcs) not only continues but is also (unusually for variety in SA) now barrel fermented; **05** lively, with typical thatch & red berry character, & BBQ-cordial tannins. **Shiraz** ★★★ Mouthfilling **04** (sample pvs ed) oozes wild berries, which are well meshed with supple tannins & smoky notes from 18 mths in seasoned Fr oak. **Sauvignon Blanc** ★★☆ **06** firm & crisp, for early drinking; pleasant gooseberry & tropical fruit tones. **Chardonnay-Viognier** ★★★ Only limited stocks available at press time of **05**, synergistic 60/40 partnership, unoaked, lightish & lively; not retasted, as for… **Muscadel** ★★★☆ **03** abundant honeysuckle & muscat scents, satiny entry, tangy farewell. **Cuvée Brut** ★★★ Carbonated dry bubbly from sauvignon; returns to form with frothy, refreshing **06**, showing exuberant varietal aromas & flavours. **Port 00** still selling, not tasted. Both ranges WO Goudini. Heron range discontinued. — *DH*

Robertson Wide River Export Company

Joint venture between Robertson Winery and Vinimark, handling all Robertson Winery exports under brand names such as Kaapdal, Kleindal (mainly for Germany & UK), Silver Sands (chiefly UK), Sinnya (mainly Germany & Canada), The Veldt (primarily Scotland) and Vruchtbaar (The Netherlands). See Vinimark for contact details.

Robertson Winery

*Robertson ▪ Est 1941 ▪ 1stB 1987 ▪ Tasting & sales Mon-Thu 8-5 Fri 8-5.30 Sat/Sun 9-3 ▪ Closed Easter Fri, Dec 25 & Jan 1 ▪ Tours by appt ▪ BYO picnic ▪ Gifts ▪ Tour groups by appt ▪ Small wine museum ▪ Owners 43 members ▪ Winemakers Bowen Botha, Lolly Louwrens, Francois Weich, Jacques Roux (Jan 1982/May 1995/Sep 1997/Jan 2000/Nov 2001) ▪ Viticulturist Briaan Stipp (Jan 2005) ▪ 1 900 ha (cab, merlot, pinot, pinotage, ruby cab, shiraz, chard, chenin, sauvignon, viognier) ▪ 29 000 tons ▪ 40% red 60% white ▪ No 1 Constitution Rd Robertson 6705 ▪ gaenor@vinimark.co.za ▪ www.robertsonwinery.co.za ▪ **T** 023·626·3059 ▪ F 023·626·2926*

Producing many different wines and ranges meant SA's third-largest producer needed a more visible brand identity across its portfolio, so all its labels now sport the initials 'RW' as a logo and a new look to reflect their 'superb quality at all price-points'. New, too, is the winery's first Viognier, from two vineyards near Ashton and McGregor, and maiden Pinot (untasted), from a single parcel on Prospect Hill farm (already familiar to those who enjoy the Cab). Other developments include a partnership with the Robertson Farmers Market, where local farmers sell their produce on the first Friday of every month.

Vineyard Selection range

★★★★☆ **No. 1 Constitution Road Shiraz** Cellar's flagship, named after their street address in Rtbson town. Spicy & abundantly fruited, packed with potential; previewed **04** similar deep-layered aromas & flavours as pvs (black cherry to Karoo scrub & white pepper), judicious oaking (±2 yrs new wood, now portion Am), mineral core lends freshness, verve, ageability. Wild yeast ferment. More this time: 34 barrels made.

★★★★ **Phanto Ridge Pinotage** Graceful & elegant rendering of the often unruly grape; **05** with signature plum/banana combo, cherry & wood-char extras; flavourful & supple. Yr new oak, 20% Am.

★★★★ **Wolfkloof Shiraz** Continues in hearty style with **04**, rotund berried mouthful spiced with all sorts of exotica incl anise, cinnamon; ripe but more elegant this vintage (14% alc vs 15% for **03**), generous but harmonious 18 mths new oak. Gd prospects.

★★★★ **Prospect Hill Cabernet Sauvignon** Warm-country cab showing generous dimensions, approachable young with growth potential. **04** cements higher general rating mooted by notch-up **03**; lovely spicy/herby complexity, abundant ripe tannins polished by 18 mths oak, 1st-3rd fill, 20% Am. Screwcapped, as is next wine.

★★★★ **Kings River Chardonnay** Vigorous new-barrel-fermented styling, lots of smoky-spicy oak character but enough ripe peachy fruit in **05** to ensure balanced, satisfying drinking now & for a few yrs. 50% natural yeasts; 8 mths oaked.

★★★★ **Retreat Sauvignon Blanc** Another steadily improving label; serious rather than showy — though vintage-boosted **06** (★★★★☆) a real head-turner; usual ripe flint-toned tropical fruit but more weight, concentration, unaggressive freshness than before. Delicious now & for next 2/3 yrs. **05** *Wine* ★★★★.

★★★★ **Almond Grove Weisser Riesling Noble Late Harvest** The original NLH in this line-up, from the eponymous farm, **06** tasted newly bottled & only hinting at future form; genteel, understated as pvs; again beautiful sugar/acid balance underpinning the tangy apricot fruit; ±10.5% alc as before. Unwooded.

★★★★★ **Wide River Reserve Noble Late Harvest** Tour de force took this Vyd Selection range to the next level with **01**, deep golden nectar of remarkable richness, concentration. From riesling; 9.5% alc. VDG. Not retasted.

Robertson range

> **Ruby Cabernet** ☺ ★★★ 'If you have a winning recipe, stick to it,' says Lolly L. **05** perfect quaffer: full-fruited, sappy, bags of character, moderate 13.6% alc. **Colombard** ☺ ★★☆ Regional speciality again showing verve in delightful semi-dry **06**, lively guava/jasmine appeal, light 12.3% alc. **Beaukett** ☺ ★★★ Invariably charming semi-sweet white; **06** brimful of fragrant fruit; rounded, pretty, perfect solo sipper with low ±10% alc. **Gewürztraminer Special Late Harvest** ☺ ★★★ Beguiling scented dessert, **06** billows jasmine, honeysuckle & rose; rounded & smooth rather than sweet; best in bloom of youth.

Cabernet Sauvignon ✓ ★★★★ **05** exactly as pvs: smooth, soft, approachable, some quite stylish red berry fruit & whiffs spice, vanilla from 7 mths Fr oaking. **Merlot** ★★★★ ✓ Refinement continues in **05** via more delicate oaking which buffs the ripe, medium bodied plum fruit; supple tannin support enables few yrs development. **Pinotage** ✓ ★★★★ Delightful **05** with plum/banana scents, ripe berry flavours. Trim, elegant & well behaved for this feisty grape. **Shiraz** ✓ ★★★★ **05** alive with herbs, black pepper & ripe berry fruit, toasty oak backup, rounded & supple enough to drink now or keep yr/2. **Cabernet Sauvignon-Shiraz** ★★★ **05** near-equal blend surprisingly rich, full flavoured for its station; spicy pepper-dusted plums; easy & rewarding now & for next 2/3 yrs. **Chardonnay** ★★★★ Even more bang for your buck than last yr. Screwcapped **06** loaded with citrus fruit, glossed with toasty oak for lively, characterful glassful. **Chenin Blanc** ★★★ **06** again satisfies with floral aromas, lightish rounded tropical flavours, fresh just-dry finish. **Sauvignon Blanc** ★★★ Night-harvested **06** has super-fresh feel with whiffs greenpepper & green grass; rounded yet crisp, usual commendably low 12.5% alc. **Viognier** new ★★★ Light coat of oak gives interesting notes of cinnamon & cashew to **06**'s peach/apricot fruit; full, rounded yet lively. Screwcapped. **Port** ★★★ Rich ruby hues announce **04**, dryish yet-undeveloped plum flavours with low but surprisingly active spirit (15.5%); needs time.

Old Chapel range

> **Red** ★★☆ ☺ Juicy everyday glassful; supple, lively, lots of substance & flavour. **Natural Sweet Rosé** ☺ ★★★ Strawberry-toned sweetie with clean, lively acidity & low ±8% alc. **Semi-Sweet White** new ☺ ★★★ Bright, bouncy, uncloying tropical tones made extra-tasty by just the right amount of sugar.

White ★★★ Tropical-toned quaffer with pretty flower garden scents; lightish, crisp & fruitily dry. All **NV**, also in 1.5ℓ bottles.

Natural Light range

> **Rosé** ☺ ★★★ Pastel pink hues, tropical fruit salad flavours; fresh, zippy & drier than ±70g/ℓ RS wld suggest.

These low-alc wines (7.5-9.8%) all **NV**, mainly Natural Sweets. **Red** ★★ Gd combo ripe berries, fresh acidity & tart tannins. **White** ★★ Delicate, light & easy tropical tones, gd acid balance ensures there's no cloy. **Dry Light** ★★ Attractive easy-drinker with tropical fruit tone, fresh & not too dry.

Two-litre Certified Cask range

> **Ruby Cabernet** ☺ ★★★ Epitome of an easy-swigger; **05** bags of fruity character, sappy, super-smooth thanks to few grams sugar; moderate 13.6% alc.

Cabernet Sauvignon ★★★☆ ✓ **05** rounded & approachable red berry fruit, quite classy whiffs of spice & vanilla from 7 mths Fr oaking. **Merlot** ★★★★ ✓ Quite a serious (but undaunting) merlot, given the budget packaging; **05** delicate oak veneer for ripe plum fruit, medium body, supple tannins. **Shiraz** ✓ ★★★★ As with Merlot, great value in **05**; crackles with black pepper, ripe berries & toasty oak; quite 'serious' but easy to drink now or keep yr/2. **Chardonnay** ★★ Broader build than other whites via brief Fr-oak staving; still-listed **05** last ed has rounded & gentle citrus flavours. **Chenin Blanc** ★★★ floral aromas on **06**, lightish but satisfying rounded tropical flavours, fresh just-dry finish. **Sauvignon Blanc** ★★★ Zingy **06** rounded yet fresh, lovely 'clean green' feel from whiffs greenpepper & green grass amid gooseberry ripeness; low 12.5% alc.

Three-litre Certified Cask range   new
These similar to versions above: **Cabernet Sauvignon**, **Shiraz**, **Chardonnay** & **Chenin Blanc**.

Three-litre Cask range   new
Cheerful **NV** quaffers with colourful packaging to match. **Smooth Dry Red**, **Crisp Dry White**, **Extra Light**, **Johannisberger Semi-Sweet Red** & **Johannisberger Semi-Sweet White** all similar in character to versions below.

Vinipak range

> **Smooth Dry Red** ☺ ★★ Gratifyingly smooth & round, fully stocked with plum & berry; versatile – could be chilled in summer.

Good value anytime wines in 500ml, 1ℓ packaging. All **NV**, with low alcs (±7-12%). **Dry White** ★★ Lively, zesty easy-drinker with appealing tropical notes. **Extra Light White** ★★ Feather-light (5.6% alc) & juicy, tasty, with milder acidity than many of this genre. **Stein** ★★ Light & fruity with pleasing sweetness. **Late Harvest** ★★ As usual, drier than expected from this style, quaffable tropical tones, fresh acidity. **Sweet Red** ★★ Skilfully uses crisp acidity & tangy tannins to curtail the sweetness, showcase ripe berry fruit. **Natural Sweet Rosé** ★★ Pretty & floral, appealing full-ripe fruit & balanced sweetness. **Natural Sweet White** ★★ Easy tropical tones, delicate & light, bright acidity keeps the sweetness under control. — *DH*

■ *Robert's Rock* see KWV Ltd
■ *Robusto* see Rudera
■ *Rocco Bay* see Bottelary Winery
■ *Rocheburg* see Arlington, Riebeek Cellars
■ *Rockfield* see Du Preez Estate
■ *Rock Rabbit* see International Wine Services
■ *Rocktail Bay* see Origin
■ *Rodini* see Goudini
■ *Roland's Reserve* see Seidelberg
■ *Romansrivier Cellar* see Mountain Ridge Wines

Romond Vineyards

Stellenbosch • Est 1993 • 1stB 2003 • Visits by appt • Walks • Owners André & Rhona Liebenberg • Winemaker André Liebenberg, advised by Marais de Villiers & Inus Muller (Jan 2003) • Viticulturist De Wet Theron (Oct 2002) • 50 tons 3 000 cs • 100% red • PO Box 5634 Helderberg 7135 • romondwine@iafrica.com • T 021·855·4566/082·455·8838 • F 021·855·0428

The new cellar is up and running at this Helderberg property, and though it wasn't exactly in time for the 2006 harvest, André Liebenberg says he's 'pleased as punch' with the result. With their custom-designed equipment now in place and seven years of continuous development behind them, the team — now also advised by Marais de Villiers — are looking forward to concentrate fully on the wines.

Rebus ★★★ Blend cab f (56%) & cab s. Quality grapes show in nicely concentrated flavours on youthfully vigorous **03**, oak integrated well (20 mths staves) though over-fresh finish noted last yr. — *IvH*

■ *Rondebosch Cellar* see Alvi's Drift Private Cellar
■ *Roodeberg* see KWV Ltd

Roodezandt Wines & Vineyards

Robertson • Est 1953 • Tasting & sales Mon-Fri 8-5.30 Sat 9-12.30 • Closed Easter Fri-Mon, May 1, Dec 25/36 & Jan 1 • Tours by appt • Owners 54 members • Winemakers Christie Steytler & Elmo du Plessis, with Tiaan Blom (May 1980/Oct 1999/Oct 2005) • Viticulturist Anton Laas (Dec 2000) • 1 500 ha (cab, merlot, pinotage, ruby cab, shiraz, chard, chenin, colombard, sauvignon) • 23 000 tons • PO Box 164 Robertson 6705 • roodez@intekom.co.za • www.roodezandt.co.za • T 023·626·1160 • F 023·626·5074

The folk at Roodezandt fell in with the theme of last year's Robertson wine weekend: 'wacky' it was titled and wacky they were, with a pool of cab for a swim with a difference. Chairman of the members' committee, Ben Kriel, manager Abie Rossouw and production manager Christie Steytler 'christened' the event, with 150 visitors taking a dip during the day. 'It was a bit chilly,' says Christie S, 'but we were fine after a shower — next year we'll rig up a sauvignon blanc one!'

Syrah ☺ ★★★ Hard to resist **05**'s textured plum/blackcurrant fruit, enticing wafts of sweet spice. Luscious to drink, & not overdone at 13.5% alc. Fermented with Am/Fr wood. **Special Late Harvest** ☺ ★★★ **05** (sample) fragrant, with plenty of sweetness refreshed by racy acidity; delicious Turkish Delight & lemon-drop flavours, & only 11% alc.

Balthazar Classic Cabernet Sauvignon ★★★☆ Limited release honouring winery's ex-chair, Baltus Kloppers. **01** rich & full flavoured, appetising; dark fruit & prunes, generous spicing from yr new Fr oak, which also provides stiffening for short-term cellaring. Lightly filtered, unstabilised. Modest ±13% alc. **Cabernet Sauvignon** ★★★★ **02** fleshy & rounded, like all cellar's reds; singular eucalyptus & smoked ham character; wood (yr older Fr) gives definition on finish, backbone for 2/3 yrs ageing. **Balthazar Wild Yeast Chardonnay** ★★★★ Confidently fills shoes of pvs flagship chard, 'Balthazar Classic'; **04** attractive & v tasty honey & dried peach, with intriguing meaty/savoury undercurrent; semi-dry styling (12.5 g/ℓ RS) part of a distinctive persona. Natural yeasts, unfiltered/stabilised. **Sauvignon Blanc** ★★★ Pear-drop tone on **06**, showing well textured drinkability, clean, fresh lines. **White Muscadel** Sold out. **Red Muscadel** ★★★ Nothing shy about **04**, which (pleasantly) assails you with full-frontal sweetness, prune & raisin richness flavour. Enjoy in effusive youth. Muscadel Awards gold.

Keizer's Creek range

> **The Red** ☺ ★★★ Attractively ripe, creamy plum fruit in full, satisfying mouthful. Unwooded equal blend ruby cab, cab, merlot.

The Rose new ★★ Charming, light rosé from pinotage; ripe berry fruit flavours, soft dry drinkability. **The White** ★★ Just off-dry, medium bodied poolside tipple from colombard, chenin, sauvignon; **06** with supple ripe-apple flavour. These NV; Red & Rose tasted as samples. — CR

Rooiberg Winery

*Robertson ▪ Est 1964 ▪ 1stB 1974 ▪ Tasting & sales Mon-Fri 8-5.30 Sat 9-3 ▪ Closed Easter Fri/Sun, Dec 25 & Jan 1 ▪ Tours by appt ▪ Restaurant (see intro); also BYO picnic ▪ Facilities for children ▪ Tour groups ▪ 4×4 trail ▪ Audio-visual on video/CD ▪ Owners 30 members ▪ Cellarmaster André van Dyk, winemaker Eduard Malherbe, vini consultant Newald Marais (all Oct 2002) ▪ Viti consultant Willem Botha (2004) ▪ 600 ha (cab, merlot, pinotage, ruby cab, shiraz, chard, chenin, colombard, sauvignon) ▪ 10 000 tons 75 000 cs own labels 20% red 70% white 10% rosé ▪ Export brands: African Collection, African Dawn, Amandalia, Goeie Tye, Oranje Straat, Signum, Tembana Valley & Zebra Collection ▪ PO Box 358 Robertson 6705 ▪ info@rooiberg.co.za ▪ www.rooiberg.co.za ▪ **T 023 626·1663** ▪ F 023·626·3295*

Hardly pausing to draw breath after a complete facelift of cellar and entertainment areas, this popular landmark on the R60 to Robertson — recently made more visible by their red 'roadside people', a head-turning installation entitled 'Gesprek' (Conversation) by landscape artist Strijdom van der Merwe — has just opened an eatery, Bodega de Vinho, serving light meals, a bakery-deli offering fresh breads and pastries, freshly roasted coffee, and a farmstall and curio shop.

Reserve range

Cabernet Sauvignon ★★★ **04** austere, slightly dried out character, very dry, earthy finish — fruit perhaps overwhelmed by wood? These Rsv reds all 18 mths new Fr oak; alcs 14-14.5%. **Pinotage** After rustic, jammy **03** (★★), big jump in quality with **04** (★★★★ ✓), bursting with lively, tangy flavours; fragrant & mouthwatering, layered flavours of plums, coffee bean; excellent balance fruit/tannin, attractive juicy fruit & dryness on finish — hint of VA not detracting. **Merlot** ★★★★ **04** touch camphor to plummy fruit on nose; rich black fruit flavour, soft tannins, gd dry finish. **Shiraz** ★★★★ **04** seductive black choc, mocha; well judged weight & properly dry. Slight gruffness in tannin dept the only detraction. **Chardonnay** ★★★ Warm dried peach aromas, touch of peach pip in **05**; big whack of vanilla oak (fermented/9 mths new Fr), very dry earthy finish; nicely moderate 13% alc.

Rooiberg range

★★★★ **Red Muscadel** ✓ **04** signalled move to lighter texture, more elegance but also less substance. Wafting Turkish Delight, incense aromas, but palate less convincing, though not due to lack of sugar at 268g/ℓ. 500ml. Muscadel Assn platinum. **05** (★★)

tasted out of sequence last ed lacked concentration, but gd-hearted. Gold at Muscats du Monde 2006.

Cabernet Sauvignon-Merlot (Roodewyn) ☺ ★★★ Reliable steakhouse-type red. Gd meaty, savoury fruit on **05**, with dry tannic grip — but very manageable. Yr older Fr oak. **Pinotage Rosé** ☺ ★★★ **06**'s fresh raspberry aromas presage lovely burst of tangy red-berried fruits, succulent & juicy, but bone-dry. Will show real presence for picnics or sunset sipping.

Cabernet Sauvignon ★★ Sample **05** shy, strangely lacking in varietal character; big tannins. Like Ghost of Cabernet Past. Yr 2nd-3rd fill oak, like all dry reds in this range. **Merlot 05** (sample) more amenable than pvs, rounded with soft silky tannins — likely ★★★ at least. **Pinotage** ★★★ **05** more approachable than pvs, sweet-berried with softish dry tannins to match, warm finish. **Shiraz** ★★★ Gd dark-berried intro to **05**, firm tannins balanced by solid fruit. Rather stylish & elegant; dry, not-enormous 13.9% alc. **Selected Red** ★★ **06** light textured, easy-going quaffer from a whole bundle of different varieties. **Chardonnay** ★★★ Sample **06** shows gentle dried pear notes; ripe flavours, with attractive fullness — a brush of oak from wood fermented portion adds interest. **Chenin Blanc** ★★ Melon & freshly cut grass on easy-drinking (just 12.3% alc) & bone-dry **06**. **Sauvignon Blanc** ★★ Fresh, lively **06** shows gd varietal grip, with attractive grass, nettle character — for drinking soon. **Classic White** ★★ **06** crisply off-dry quick-quaff: tropical-toned blend chenin/sauvignon. **Cape White** ★★ **06** from colombard — soft, easy & off-dry, welcome low 11.9% alc. **Brut Sparkling** ★★ Frothy carbonated **NV** (as is next) from sauvignon, with soft grassiness on light, dryish palate. **Vin Doux Sparkling** ★★ Usual bright grapey aromas/flavours in foaming sweetish glassful. **Natural Sweet Red** ★ **05** thin, ultra-soft acidity makes for sweet (48g/ℓ sugar) flabbiness. **Natural Sweet Rosé** ★ **05** mostly from red muscadel, lacks substance & real flavour. **Natural Sweet Blanc** ★ **05** grapey nose remains the best part of this rather insipid offering. **Vintage Port** ★★★ **03** (not retasted) had enough acid/tannin to prop up the sugar but no real 'Vintage' structure or potential — but many will enjoy. **Rhine Riesling**, **Flamingo Sparkling**, **Hanepoot**, **Red Jerepiko** all discontinued. — *IvH*

■ *Roothman Wines* see Jonkheer

Rose Garden Vineyards

Paarl ▪ Est 1976 ▪ 1stB 2003 ▪ Visits by appt ▪ Cheese platters by appt; or BYO picnic ▪ Winemaker/viticulturist Hein Hesebeck (Jan 2004) ▪ 15 ha (pinotage, merlot, ruby cab, shiraz, chenin) ▪ 100 tons 8 000 cs own label 80% red 15% white 5% rosé ▪ PO Box 151 Wellington 7654 ▪ epstein@polka.co.za ▪ www.rosegardenvineyards.com ▪ T 021·869·8211/ 084·440·9253 ▪ F 021·869·8211

Maturation cellar completed, owner Shalom Epstein now plans to build a new tasting area in an attractive setting beside the farm lake. He's a member of the Pearl's Gate association, lobbying for the demarcation of the Windmeul area as a standalone appellation within Paarl. The former Botswana-based liquor distributor's Pinot, Pinotage and Maya's Red have been well received at the Michelangelo and Swiss Air awards, and, via a partnership with Mia Cara Wines, he's helping to bring fresh players into the wine game.

Premium range

Cabernet Sauvignon Limited Release ★★ **NV** (blend 03/05) rustic & forthright, with porty tones & bold, tight tannins, bolstered by 2 yrs Fr oaking. **Merlot Limited Release** new Idiosyncratic **04** not a mainstream style. 18 mths Fr oak. **Pinotage Special Release** new ★★ **03** ripe & robust, organic whiffs & big dry tannins. 2 yrs oaked. **Shiraz Reserve** The new **04** version sadly not a patch on characterful **03**. 18 mths Fr oak. **Shiraz Limited Release** new ★★ Shalom E aiming for 'Italian coffee shop in liquid form'; **04** popular ultra-ripe styling with sweet fruit & hint portiness. 18 mths Fr oak.

Rose Garden range

Merlot ★★★ Approachable & friendly **03** braai sipper with green walnuts & ripe plummy fruit; soft & supple enough for early drinking. **Pinotage** ★★★ Full, ripe wild-berry flavours, coupled with strong tannins & bright acidity give **03** 3-5 yrs ageing potential. **Pinot Noir** ★★★ Perfumed **04** offers flavours of sweet strawberry jam & dried peaches to enjoy early. Note the 15% alc. **Shiraz** ★★ Easy-drinking **03** with nutty, brambly fruit, dry savoury finish. **Shiraz Rosé Natural Sweet** ★ **05** crowd pleaser with strawberry bouquet, high 12. 8% alc for the style. **Maya's Red** ★★★ **03** smooth, easy drinking ruby cab (81%) with splash shiraz. Attractive red cherry fruit, lowish fruit tannins & enticing spicy top note. 14. 5% alc goes unnoticed. **Chardonnay Reserve 03** sample last ed showed promising limy flavours, interesting oxidative notes; 14 mths on lees in Fr oak. Provisional ★★★. Only next wine in this range retasted. **Chenin Blanc** ★★ **06** light bodied with usual terpine/bottle-age combo & notes of apricots & dried peaches. Different, has personality. — *CT*

Ross Gower Wines   ◊♀🍷♬

Elgin ▪ Est 2003 ▪ 1stB 2004 ▪ Tasting & sales Mon-Fri 9-5 ▪ Weekends & pub hols by appt ▪ Tours by appt ▪ Meals & picnic baskets by appt ▪ Self-catering cottages (see Stay-over section) ▪ Nature conservancy ▪ Owners Gower family ▪ Winemakers/viticulturists Ross & Robert Gower (Jun 2003) ▪ ±7 ha (shiraz, sauvignon) ▪ 3 000 cs 40% red 45% white 15% MCC ▪ PO Box 161 Elgin 7180 ▪ rossgowerwines@worldonline.co.za ▪ T/F 021·844·0197

This family winery in emerging cool-climate Elgin ward by former Klein Constantia vintner Ross Gower had a satisfying 2006. Their recently completed 'rammed earth' cellar exceeded expectations for practicality and efficiency. Production, though small, doubled, and they released their first Cap Classique (100% Elgin pinot), declared 'real champagne' by a visiting French sommelier tasting eyes wide shut. Gower is particularly upbeat about the pureness of Elgin fruit, allowing concentration on single-variety wines.

★★★★ **Sauvignon Blanc** Trio of bottlings in pvs ed (Reserve, std & Mankazana) now consolidated into this offering — the cellar's signature. Pyrazines veritably gallop out glass of **06** (sample); ultra-cool, highly reductive racy mouthful already developing depth.

★★★★ **Pinot Noir Brut** new Elgin's first MCC, asserts Ross G. **05** deliberately 'slightly pink' (as opposed to 'rosé'), with finesse to match the delicate hues. Cherry, raspberry fruits all shored up in electric mousse, a steely mouthful ending refreshingly dry (1.3g/ℓ sugar). 12% alc.

Merlot new ★★★★ **05** dense colour/extract (but low alc) leavened by fragrant violets, red berry fruits tucked into fine tannins, promising development. 70% new Fr oak, yr. **Shiraz** ★★★★ Chunkier red sibling, **05** open & approachable. Yr seasoned Fr barrels. Highest alc (13.7%) of the clutch. — *DS*

■ *Rotsvast* see Baarsma
■ *Route 101* see Du Preez Estate, Thirty-Two Degrees South
■ *Route 303* see Ultra Liquors

Royle Family Vineyards

Paarl ▪ Est 2000 ▪ 1stB 2001 ▪ Closed to public ▪ Owner Noel Woods ▪ Vini consultant Ronell Wiid (2005) ▪ Viti consultant Paul Wallace (May 2000) ▪ 45 ha (cab, merlot, mourvèdre, pinotage, ruby cabernet, shiraz, viognier) ▪ 750 cs own label 100% ▪ PO Box 298 Klapmuts 7625 ▪ johansouthey@roylewines.com ▪ www.roylewines.com ▪ T/F 021·875·5363

With the completion of the second stage of the cellar, Noel Woods' wine venture is growing from strength to strength, and they were able to process the second harvest in their own facility with its new air-cooled maturation area and storeroom. A chip off the old block (we couldn't resist the pun), UK-based son James W imports and distributes the family's wines, as well as those from other family-run vineyards in the region.

Cabernet Sauvignon ★★★★ Delicious, unforced **04**, seriously oaked for the long haul yet more than enough fruit, creamy flavour, to satisfy now. 18 mths mainly Fr oak, restrained 13.5% alc. Fleshier than… **Syrah** ★★★ Dominated by oak mid-2006, needs time; **04** gd but fleeting leathery flavours & austere tannins, notably on finish. 11 mths mainly Fr oak. **Viognier** Elegant & attractive **06** (sample), gorgeous floral bouquet, overlay of biscuit from fermentation/ageing ±6 mths older Fr oak, which already harmonised with fruit. Livelier than many examples of this naturally low-acid grape. Potential ★★★★. — *CR*

Rozendal

Stellenbosch ▪ 1stB 1983 ▪ Tasting, sales & tours by appt ▪ Luxury auberge with restaurant & amenities (see Stay-over section) ▪ Conference facilities ▪ Walks ▪ Owners Kurt & Lyne Ammann ▪ Winemaker Kurt Ammann ▪ 6 ha (cabs s/f, merlot) ▪ 2-3 000 cs 100% red ▪ PO Box 160 Stellenbosch 7599 ▪ rozendal@mweb.co.za ▪ T 021·809·2621 ▪ F 021·809·2640

When Kurt Ammann released his first red blend over two decades ago, it became a cult classic; since then followers have had to exercise extreme patience as Kurt A — a firm believer in biodynamics who pegs his winemaking calendar to the movements of the planets — will not be hurried into releasing vintages. Last year, however, was cause for celebration — his 02 was deemed ready. Untasted, the wine is available from Kurt and wife Lyne A's Auberge Rozendal in Stellenbosch.

■ *Rozier Bay/Reef see* Mount Rozier

Rudera Wines

Stellenbosch ▪ Est 1999 ▪ 1stB 2001 ▪ Closed to public ▪ Owners Teddy & Riana Hall ▪ Winemaker/viticulturist Teddy Hall ▪ 18 ha (cab, shiraz, chenin) ▪ 3 400 cs 45% red 50% white 5% NLH ▪ PO Box 2868 Somerset West 7129 ▪ info@rudera.co.za ▪ www.rudera.co.za ▪ T/F 021·852·1380

Four-time winner of the annual Chenin Challenge, and Diners Club Winemaker of the Year for the variety in 2001, Teddy Hall's position in any SA Chenin Hall of Fame is assured. The cigar-toting weekend pilot is also recognised internationally: at every Rendez-Vous de Fontevraud in France (previously Rendez-Vous du Chenin), his wines have ranked among the best in the world. His aim is the same as it was 'one rainy evening in front of the fire' when Rudera was born: 'to produce the best wine possible, without cutting any corners at any time, regardless of the cost or effort.' The wines below are his premium, longer-lived offerings; see under Teddy Hall Wines for something delicious to enjoy every day.

★★★★☆ **Cabernet Sauvignon** Minuscule quantities (185 half-cs + a few 3ℓ btls) epitomising hand-crafting; **03** (★★★★★) a connoisseur's wine, not for early consumption: brooding depths of molten plums & cassis, savoury spice, cigarbox. Tannins are suave, if you can't wait, but the peak is decade+ away. Unfiltered. New Fr oak, 23 mths. *WS* 90 pts. No **02** (best barrels offered at CWG Auction). **01**, with sugared-violet nuances, also a beauty. Off leased/managed vyds in Sbosch, as are wines below.

★★★★☆ **CWG Auction Reserve Cabernet Sauvignon** Big, impressive wine, lots of depth, prospects, in last tasted **02**. Unfiltered; oak as for std Cab. Only ±60 cs. **04**, for 2006 Auction, not tasted.

★★★★ **Syrah** Dark & trimly handsome **04**, mainly savoury in character: tapenade, peppery spices, dark choc, with some hedgerow fruit peeping through. Already accessible but gd ageing potential. 11 mths Fr barriques, 20% new; modest 13% alc; unfiltered.

★★★★ **Chenin Blanc** This & next from old bushvines, yielding small crops. **05** has the tropical, citrus, savoury complexity & nervy acidity we've come to expect from Teddy H, but mid-2006 at a quiet stage; shd emerge, spread wings over mths & yrs to come & reach heights of **04** *Wine* ★★★★, **03** *Decanter* ★★★★★. These native yeasts; 8 mths seasoned Fr barriques.

★★★★☆ **Robusto Chenin Blanc** 'Robust' but controlled, multiply gilded — *Wine* ★★★★ in 2006 for **01** among many felicitations. Skipping from last tasted, noble-rot-touched **03** to unbotrytised **05** (★★★★★): sleeker, more polished & even better with food. Still off-dry but you hardly notice, given the freshening acidity. Gorgeous flavours: silky yellow peach & citrus peel, pinenut savouriness. Good future, 5+ yrs, as all these, but only 750 cs made, alas. **04** sold out untasted. Fr barriques, 8-12 mths, half new.

★★★★☆ **Chenin Blanc Noble Late Harvest** Hand-selected botrytised berries; 100% native yeast ferment in new Fr small-oak. Following in exalted footsteps of beautifully balanced, racy **03** (*WS* 92 pts), came **05**, tasted last ed, with deep syrupy richness; complex, complete & irresistible. 140g/ℓ sugar. 12% alc.

★★★★☆ **CWG Auction Reserve Chenin Blanc Noble Late Harvest** Same vinification as above for maiden **03**; pvs ed sumptuous aromas assailed the nose, mouthfilling honeyed sweetness was tempered by bracing acidity. Gd 5+ yr cellaring potential. 132g/ℓ sugar; 12.5% alc. — *CR*

Rudi Schultz Wines

Stellenbosch ▪ Est/1stB 2002 ▪ Closed to public ▪ Owner/winemaker Rudi Schultz ▪ Viticulturist Dirkie Morkel ▪ 800 cs 100% red ▪ rudi@thelema.co.za ▪ T 082·928·1841

Rudi Schultz, by day Thelema's co-winemaker, has carved a niche for himself with just 800 cases per vintage of his own consistently excellent Syrah. While most goes to the US via select New York wine shops (not surprising, given regular 90+ *Wine Spectator* ratings), the wine has found a strong following among regular visitors who buy here and ship it home. Exports now also include Germany, Sweden and Ireland. Great news is an even 'better Syrah' (21 months in 100% new French oak), untasted, which Rudi S intends to make available with the standard 05.

★★★★☆ **Syrah** Hand crafted, in rich but classical style. Previewed **05** cements this cult wine's rise in our 'general' star rating begun with sumptuous **04**. Thrilling white pepper nuance to fragrant, beautifully spiced mouthful; built for a decade. Fr oaking now up to 20 mths, 50% new. — *DS*

■ *Ruiters* see Fairseat Cellars

Ruitersvlei Wines

Paarl ▪ Est 1692 ▪ 1stB 1995 ▪ Tasting & sales Mon-Fri 9-5 Sat 9-3 Sun 11-3 ▪ Fee R10 (incl glass) ▪ Closed Easter Fri, Dec 25 & Jan 1 ▪ Tours by appt ▪ Farm produce ▪ Facilities for children ▪ Tour groups ▪ Gifts ▪ Reception/conference venue ▪ Conservation area ▪ Owner John Faure ▪ Winemaker Reino Kruger, with Jaco van Niekerk (Jan 2004/Dec 2004) ▪ Viticulturist Kobus Mostert (Nov 2001) ▪ 289 ha (cab, merlot, pinotage, shiraz, chard, chenin, sauvignon) ▪ 1 400 tons 50 000 cs own labels 70% red 29% white 1% rosé ▪ PO Box 532 Suider-Paarl 7624 ▪ Sales@ruitersvlei.co.za ▪ www.ruitersvlei.co.za ▪ T 021·863·1517 ▪ F 021·863·1443

'Having the best of both old and new would definitely be an advantage,' says winemaker Reino Kruger of a planned replanting programme. To stay are the shiraz and cab, as well as selected pinotage; to go are the old riesling and tinta; coming in will be Mediterranean varieties like mourvèdre. There's trying and testing ahead, not least for new marketing manager Hardie Basson (ex-Morgenster), but buoyed up by 'a great winemaking year', as Kruger describes 2006, he's feeling positive plus.

Reserve range

Cabernet Sauvignon ★★★ Bottled version of last ed's **04** sample reveals ultra-ripe (perhaps tad porty) cranberry fruit juxtaposed with big, firm tannins, sweet-sour acidity. **Merlot** ★★ **04**, sample last ed, has come off the boil; youthful herbal quality & racy acidity (7g/ℓ) now shade too prominent for comfort. Yr Fr oak, 2nd-3rd fill. **Shiraz** ★★★ Last previewed **04** starting showing some maturity; more savoury now, firmer, with sappy dry finish. Enjoy soon. 2nd-3rd fill Fr oak. **Cabernet Sauvignon-Merlot** ⬚ⁿᵉʷ ★★★ Cab leads on paper (70%) & on palate — rather forceful structure of tannin & fruit, so **04** will benefit from decanting if opened now (& has wherewithal for few yrs ageing). **Chardonnay** ★★★ **05**, revisited this ed, full-flavoured but elegant (only 13% alc); ripe, uncloying citrus fruit, toasty butterscotch overlay from well-melded 100% new oak (Fr, 5 mths). **Four Sisters MCC** ★★★ NV Brut sparkling from pinot, chard, briefly bottle-aged. Latest version unready. **John Faure Port** ★★★★ Fortified dessert, more LBV-style than the intended Ruby, **NV** but satisfying nonetheless. Raisened softness, well-integrated spirit, drier than many in SA at 88g/ℓ sugar.

Ruitersvlei range

Chenin Blanc ★★★ 06 amenably crisp & fruity summer refresher with stone fruit flavours, balanced semi-dry finish, light 12.5% alc.

Cabernet Sauvignon ★★★ Last ed showed some of variety's firm structure; **04** fleshy fruit, minty whiff; shd soften over next yr/2. 6 mths Fr staves. **Merlot** new **★★** Robust, campfire-compatible styling, though heartiness achieved at agreeably modest alc (13%); **05** unwooded, with eucalyptus hint. **Pinotage ★★★** 'Fruit-driven for early consumption' – Reino K's mantra reflected in **05**'s generous bramble/banana fruit, subtle oak (Am/Fr staves), youthful vibrancy. **Shiraz ★★★** Gd partner for sturdier foods, given **05**'s savoury/ meaty tone, balanced, juicy red-fruit flavours & full but comfortable body. Fr/Am staves, 6 mths. Following not retasted: **Cabernet Sauvignon-Merlot ★★★** Early-approachable 55/45 mix; cool cedar & meaty whiff; **04** balanced & satisfying. Unwooded. **Sauvignon Blanc ★★ 05** (sample) boiled sweet aroma, tangy, dry, light fruit/body (12.7% alc).

Mountainside range

Red ☺ **★★** Half-dozen red varieties in **05**, giving whole melange of red-fruit flavours, plus whiff bluegum, spicy-dry & easily quaffable. Unwooded.

Pink ★★ 05 last ed was light, sweet & soft, with boiled sweet flavours & fuchsia pink colour from pinotage. **White ★★** Usual colombard/sauvignon pairing for **06**, just-dry, light & delicately fruity. **Gold ★★ 05** similar to White but semi-sweet. Not retasted. – *CT*

Rupert & Rothschild Vignerons   ♀♙&

*Simondium (see Paarl map) ▪ Est 1997 ▪ 1stB 1998 ▪ Visits only by appt Mon-Fri 9-4.30 ▪ Fee R5/wine ▪ Closed Easter Fri-Sun, Dec 25 ▪ Owners Rupert family & Baron Benjamin de Rothschild ▪ Cellarmaster Schalk-Willem Joubert (Jun 1997) ▪ Winemaker Yvonne Schröder, with Clive Radloff (Sep 2001/Jun 1997) ▪ Viticulturist Renier Theron (Oct 2003) ▪ 90 ha (cab, merlot, chard) ▪ 500 tons 35 000 cs 95% red 5% white ▪ ISO 14001 certified; HACCP accreditation in progress ▪ PO Box 412 Franschhoek Valley 7690 ▪ info@rupert-rothschildvignerons. com ▪ www.rupert-rothschildvignerons.com ▪ **T 021·874·1648** ▪ F 021·874·1802*

With each passing vintage, this classy collaboration between French vinous aristocrat Baron Benjamin de Rothschild and Cape business titans the Ruperts (headed by Johann R) manages to further fine-tune the trio of wines from their prime Simonsberg mountain property. Young cellarmaster Schalk-Willem Joubert and his team chill the grapes to 15°C before destemming (done manually for the 'Baron Edmond'), hand-sort all red grapes and ferment in 500ℓ barrels. 'Precision viticulture' includes harvesting individual vines and vinifying small batches separately. In classic French tradition, winemaking 'remains simple and as natural as possible'.

★★★★☆ Baron Edmond After gravitas lacking **02** (★★★★), **03** massive & impressive 76:24 cab-merlot blend, from Smnsberg, Hldrberg, Darling grapes. Very ripe, bright fruit, heavily extracted for power & richness, savoury intensity. Big, luscious tannins, lots of showy oak (20 mths new Fr). 15.3% alc hardly graceful or easy drinking, but not unbalanced.

★★★★☆ Baroness Nadine Ever-elegant chard, from widely sourced fruit: Elgin, Stanford, Cape Pt for lighter, charming **04** (★★★★). Limy, buttery nose leads to very bright, creamily rich but not intense palate. Toasty oak evident, though just 20% new. Like **03**, maturation potential.

Classique ★★★★ Cab-merlot blend, **04** with ripely fruity aromas, but big tannin tends to dominate fruit & well balanced wood. Holds 15% alc well, though. WO W Cape. – *TJ*

■ *Rushdale* see Rietvallei

Rustenberg Wines

Stellenbosch • Est 1682 • 1stB 1892 • Tasting & sales Mon-Fri 9-4.30 Sat 10-1.30 Sat 10-3.30 (Dec/Jan) • Closed Easter Fri, Dec 25, Jan 1 • Owner Simon Barlow • Winemaker Adi Badenhorst, with Randolph Christians & Gareth le Grange (Dec 1999/Oct 1995/Jan 2003) • Viticulturist Nico Walters (Nov 1999) • 150 ha (cabs s/f, grenache, merlot, mourvèdre, petit v, shiraz, chard, roussanne, sauvignon, semillon, viognier) • 1 800 tons 130 000 cs 70% red 30% white • PO Box 33 Stellenbosch 7599 • wine@rustenberg.co.za • www.rustenberg.co.za • T 021·809·1200 • F 021·809·1219

Rustenberg continues to deliver the goods, as its many accolades attest, and keeps interest levels up with some unusual-for-SA plantings (and some recent bottlings) such as grenache, mourvèdre and roussanne, and updated packaging for both the Rustenberg and Brampton lines. Good news for fans is that a bigger warehouse has boosted service delivery, while new SA distributor DGB has already achieved better availability and more competitive pricing around the country, says Simon Barlow. Upcoming vintages could benefit from recent extensive travels by the winemaking team to top cellars in France and Spain, while sales trips to the US and Canada have them enthused about the huge potential there. An additional 25ha of sauvignon and chardonnay will be planted, and other future plans include a larger cellar for Brampton wines.

Schoongezicht White new Engagingly different grenache bl, viognier, roussanne blend; **06** (sample) enticing wild herbs/flowers, touch earth, uncluttered by oak but firm, full, dry finishing grip. Possible ★★★★.

Single Vineyard range

★★★★☆ **Peter Barlow** Legendary Cape cab (originally 'Rustenberg Cab') now from nearly 20 yr old Smnsberg vyd. Bright, bold **04** mid-2006 still a restless youth; ultra-ripe fruit swathed in protective tannin but freshening acid shd allow for lengthy, necessary slumber, eventual grand maturity. 15% alc. Traditionally vinified; incl native yeast, unfiltered. 20 mths Fr barrels, 70% new. Widely gonged: **03** *Wine* ★★★★, Winemakers' Choice; **02** *Decanter* ★★★★.

★★★★ **Five Soldiers** Striking, quintessentially New World chard, named for five Stone Pine sentinels in the vyd. Ripe fruit, new Fr oak marshalled with precision into distinctive **04**. All indicators in place for rich, flavoursome depths to gain complexity over next 3-4 yrs. Natural ferment, malo in 100% new Fr oak, 15 mths. **03** 91 pts *WS*.

Stellenbosch Regional range

★★★★★ **John X Merriman** Classy bdx-style red, blended according to vintage dictates; impressive **04** thoughtfully composed mix merlot with cabs s/f, petit v (46/36/9/9), assembled from 44 batches of fruit. Merlot's aromatic generosity, cab's staunch structure, seamless, refined whole. Traditionally vinified, ±20 mths Fr oak. Could easily scale heights of **03** Calyon trophy winner; *Decanter* ★★★★★; SAA.

★★★★ **Chardonnay** The more decadent of Rstnbrg's oaked chardonnays. Seductive lime/lees notes with extra earthy 'je ne sais quoi' from 100% native ferment in **05**. Almost chewy toffee texture but unflabby; suggestion of sweetness nipped by combo lime/tannin. Yr Fr oak, 40% new. **04** *Wine* ★★★★; **03** gold IWSC; *Decanter* ★★★★

★★★★☆ **The Last Straw** No follow-up yet to **03** (★★★★) from bought-in, straw-dried chenin; barrel fermented yr, native yeasts. Deep dried apricot, mango flavours. **02** was electrifying.

Roussanne ★★★☆ Together with viognier, northern Rhône white grape of note. **04** unrated sample last yr, an SA first, with striking white hedgerow flowers, viscous qualities. **05** floral perfumes slightly dumbed by oak (though only older Fr barrels for fermentation); gd weight, solid build more typical.

Brampton range

★★★★ **QF** Weighty NLH appears intermittently when nature affords good botrytis, which not since **00** (aka 'QF2'), TWS trophy, from sauvignon.

Cabernet Sauvignon ★★★★ Screwcapped **04** previewed in last ed proved David among Goliaths, taking trophy at 2006 TWS; *Decanter* ★★★★. Sample **05** exuberant mouthful crunchy cassis bolstered by Am oak. Modern, forward ripe fruit contrasted by more traditional cab structure, but needs lot of time to regroup, settle. Am oak, 80% new. **Shiraz** Previewed **05** going whole southern Rhône route: mourvèdre, grenache, viognier backing-group to peppery shiraz lead. Better structured, finer tannins, more complex than pvs; light texture emphasises multiple flavours. Possible ★★★★. 15 mths oak, 30% Am, 15% alc. **04** (★★★★ but IWC gold). **Old Vines Red** ★★★★ Invitingly fresh, flavoursome, with perky tannins in 'country red' style. Previewed **05** cab-led with merlot, shiraz, splashes pinotage, cab f from Sbosch, Paarl, Pdberg, Darling grapes. **Rosé** new ★★★ Fashionable dry newcomer, **06** a friendly United Nations of cabs s/f, merlot, shiraz, mourvèdre & pinotage. Genteel red winey nose, more emphatic flavours, alc nudge in dry tail. For leisurely summer (or even winter) picnics. **Unoaked Chardonnay** ★★★ **06** compelling example of this increasingly characterful genre. Fresh, steely citrus tang underpinned/broadened by lees richness. Incisively dry, long. Matured on/fined with pvs yr's Sbosch Chard lees. WO Coastal. **Sauvignon Blanc** ★★★★ Vigour knit with ripe, juicy fruit in bouncy **06** sample. Mouthwatering & dry. From pedigreed sauvignon areas, incl Elgin, Grabouw, Dbnvlle. **Viognier** ★★★ **06** brightly hued; more measured though characterful dried apricot/honeysuckle fragrance, reprised on finish. Full bodied, rich, balanced with well fused oak (all used Fr; fermented/matured 4 mths). Following not retasted: **Natural Sweet** ★★★★ **01** natural cask fermented sauvignon. **Port** ★★★ **NV** from Portuguese varieties; drier style still available. **Brut** MCC **NV** a one-off. — AL

Rust en Vrede Estate

Stellenbosch • Est 1694 • 1stB 1979 • Tasting & sales Mon-Fri 9-5 Sat: 9-5 Oct-Apr; 9-4 May-Sep; pub hols 9-4 • Closed Easter Fri, Dec 25 & Jan 1 • Gifts • Walks • Owner Jannie Engelbrecht Trust • Winemaker Ettienne Malan (2005) • Viticulturist Wessel Combrink (Jun 1998) • 50 ha (cab, merlot, shiraz) • ±350 tons 20 000 cs 100% red • PO Box 473 Stellenbosch 7599 • info@rustenvrede.com • www.rustenvrede.com • T 021·881·3881 • F 021·881·3000

A mini-tornado swept through this top red wine estate last year — a real one, unfortunately, not a creative way of describing MD and Springbok rugby legend Jannie Engelbrecht as he oversaw the construction of a new malolactic fermentation cellar, maturation cellar, bin store and tasting room facilities. 'It destroyed part of the 17th-century manor house and caused damage to 150+ year old oak trees,' says marketing manager Oliver Bauer. The good news is that the structure has been rebuilt and no vineyards were harmed, so it's business as usual — which is just as well, with new markets having been established in Canada and Austria, and a new agent driving UK sales.

★★★★ **Estate Wine** Most recent releases of this prestigious cab-led blend to us somewhat less lustrous than pvs (though **02** rated 90 pts by *WS*). Current **03** usual seamless ensemble (60/30/10 cab/shiraz/merlot) but quieter, more pointedly fresh, unusually dense, oaky sweetness & tannins. 23 mths Fr/Am barrels, mainly new. 14.7% alc.

★★★★★ **Shiraz** Closely associated with this Hldrberg estate since maiden 79. **02** (★★★★) last ed marked by strong game/mushroom aromas, well-managed tannins & noticeably sweet/sour finish. For current drinking, unlike fine, authoritative **01**, which shd improve till ±2010. 15 mths new Fr/Am.

★★★★★ **Cabernet Sauvignon 02** (★★★★) still available, not retasted. Quiet, truffly bouquet, open, sweetish palate. Drink early to capture most pleasant features of unfavourable cab yr & before compact yet supple **01**. 18 mths new 300ℓ Fr oak.

★★★★ **Merlot** Consistently offers admirable breadth of flavour & texture with stylish restraint. **04** sonorous dark choc/plum aromas, classy new-oak augmentation noted last ed. Similar ripe/fresh contrast as in elegant, velvety **03**. Shd sustain delicious drinkability for 5/6 yrs. — AL

■ *Rusthof see Mooiuitsig*

Rusticus Vintage Cellar

Robertson • Est 2001 • 1stB 2002 • Tasting & sales Tue-Fri 9-4 Sat 10-4 Mon by appt • Closed Easter Fri & Dec 25 • Tours on request • BYO picnic • Self-catering cottages & guest houses (see Stay-over section) • Tour groups • Conferences • Walks/hikes • Game drives & conserva-

tion area · 4×4 trail · Owner Pat Busch · Winemaker/viticulturist Stephan Busch · 200 tons total, max 2 000 cs own label · PO Box 579 Robertson 6705 · info@rusticus.co.za · www. rusticus.co.za · **T** 023·626·2033 F 023·626·1277

Vini/viti man Stephan Busch (son of owner Pat) has great expectations of his first white wine, produced last year from a ton of viognier and barrel-fermented in French oak. More to follow — SB got to thinking when he saw how well 30 year old chenin vines had weathered the drought of 2005, and decided to nurture rather than replace them. 'We're going to be making some investments here,' he says of plans to convert one of the antique cellars on the property into a restaurant and the other into a white wine-making facility.

Cabernet Sauvignon ★★★ Swashbuckling but well polished **03**; as pvs, displays portlike concentration of blackberry & choc flavours, masking the vast 16% alc. Combo Fr/Am wood. **Merlot** ★★★ Super-ripe **03** still in stock; massively fruited, intense plum character, expansive palate dominated by potent 15.5% alc. **Pinot Noir** ★★★ **03** cherry aromas & intense berry flavours; unobtrusive older oak only. **Pinotage** ★★★ **03** varietally atypical cassis aroma, sweet impression (from massive 15.8% alc) not quite cushioning big dusty tannins. **Ruby Cabernet** ★★ Robust **02**; gamey whiffs, chunky palate with 14.3% alc. **Shiraz** ★ **03** similar porty/jammy notes as pvs, rustic & unrefined, whereas … **Shiraz Limited Release** ★★★ Shows some sophistication & typicity; **04** smoky bramble notes, full-ripe flavours, supple tannins; potential for development. 14 mths oak, mix new Fr, 2nd fill Am/Fr. **Tilled Earth 05** blend cab, merlot, shiraz (50/20/20) & dash pinot 'for the ladies', not ready. All these WO Klaasvoogds, none retasted. — DH

Sadie Family ◊8

Swartland · Est 1999 · 1stB 2000 · Tasting & sales by appt · Owners: the Sadie family · Winemakers/viticulturists Eben & Niko Sadie · 10 ha (grenache, mourvèdre, shiraz) · 850 cs 90% red 10% white · PO Box 1019 Malmesbury 7299 · sadiefamily@mail.com · **T** 021·869·8349 · F 021·869·8101

'Waste time, and you're wasting what you need to make wines better. Waste energy and you're wasting what you need for creativity.' So says Eben Sadie, revelling in two time-conserving changes to his life: a new cellar where he'll vinify for the family label and for Sequillo (see entry), and the return to SA after 10 years in Italy of sister Delana, who's helping to manage the business. The cellar's not complete ('We'll put in more storage facilities, and some of the things we want to do don't even exist in this country') but it's ready enough for vintage 2007: 'I'd rather spend money on barrels than fountains and flags.' Like the Griers of Villiera and Tom Lubbe of The Observatory, Eben S has vineyards offshore, in Priorat in Spain — there's more in the offing.

★★★★☆ **Columella** Extraordinary to suddenly realise the concentrated power, the tense structural strength informing the graceful ease of **04**! As always, shiraz with 20% mourvèdre. Darkly ripe fruit, lightly perfumed, nutmeg spice, hints of blackcurrant, in emerging complexity; the usual savoury, subtle, supple tannins. Native yeast ferment in open casks; 2 yrs scarcely toasted Fr oak, 80% new. Balance, concentration enhances gd maturation potential. **03** Wine ★★★★.

★★★★★ **Palladius** Pioneering Swtland blend, ±40% viognier, with chenin, chard, grenache bl. **05** most elegant yet, still rich & succulent, with mineral & tannic elements, lingering finish. Flourishes of peach/apricot, citrus over earthy bass-notes. Powerful, but big alc in satin-textured balance, with 3.7g/ℓ sugar imperceptible in savoury acidity; 18 mths Fr oak, 40% new. Like fine **04** (★★★★★), should mature few yrs at least. Sadie wines unfined/filtered. — TJ

Sagila Wines · · new

Stellenbosch · Est 2004 · 1stB 2005 · Closed to public · Owner/winemaker Mzokhona Mvemve · 13 tons 600 cs 100% white · PO Box 524 Stellenbosch 7599 · mgasela@iafrica. com · **T** 082·502·4562 · F 021·979·1719

'Establishing Sagila is about having one thing I can call mine in the true sense of the word,' says Mzokhona Mvemve, taster for this guide and winemaker for Cape Classics, joint-venture

Mvemve-Raats and now his own-brand Sagila (the name's a reference to the traditional mace his grandfather carried). Much of Sagila's output wings its way to Sweden and Germany but some features on the winelists of top local restaurants and wine shops.

Both **05**, both ★★★. **Chenin Blanc** Rich apricot/melon aromas a prelude to gd fruit weight on the palate, though acidity a little exposed on the finish, despite a touch plumping from sugar (3.5g/ℓ). **Sauvignon Blanc** Nettly capsicum & spanspek melon notes, with herbaceous quality to lingering flavours. Crisply food-friendly, especially given moderate 12.5% alc. — MF

Saltare

Stellenbosch • Est/1stB 2003 • Closed to public • Owners Christoff & Carla Pauw • Winemaker Carla Pauw • 15 tons • 250 cs • 50% red 30% white 20% MCC • PO Box 2290 Dennesig, Stellenbosch 7601 • ccpauw@gmail.com • T 021·883·9568

Carla Pauw now dances to three different tunes: during office hours she cellar-masters at Anura in Paarl; after five she light-trips with new partner-in-wine Agnes de Vos, owner of vineyards in the Joostenberg area, with whom she's made a chenin and a bordeaux-style blend under the Racetrack label; and, on the Saltare stage, she partners husband Christoff P on a debut chenin and the shiraz and bottle-matured sparkling below.

★★★★ **Cap Classique Brut 03** from chard (60%) & pinot. Last ed was full flavoured/bodied, rich & yeasty, with lively, lingering dry flavours of Marmite & spicy baked apple. Old-oak barrel fermented. WO Smnsberg-Paarl, like Syrah below. **05** is next.

Syrah ★★★★ Only 25 cs of **04**. Ultra-ripe, fruity & slightly porty aromas/flavours; 15% alc big but not brash, bright acidity & lovely smooth tannins. Fermented old oak; 18 mths 2nd fill Fr. **Agnes de Vos Damarakkloof Chenin Blanc** new Powerful concentration of ripe Paarl fruit on **06** preview; orange marmalade fruit & notes of almond; acid very soft; hard to rate mid-2006: potential ★★★? — IvH

Sanctum Wines

Stellenbosch • Est/1stB 2002 • Closed to public • Owners Mike & Alice Dobrovic • Winemaker Mike Dobrovic • 3.2 tons 240 cs 100% red • PO Box 11 Koelenhof 7605 • info@sanctumwines.com • www.sanctumwines.com • T 021·865·2483/082·882·2488 • F 021·865·2302

Having debuted with a shiraz (from bought-in grapes) carrying the moniker of their descriptively named family place of future retirement in the Elgin hills, Mulderbosch veteran winemaker Mike Dobrovic and wife Alice ('manager, bookkeeper, salesperson, bottlewasher') found 2006 'all very exciting'. They started pulling up apple trees and liming soils in preparation for their first hectare of sauvignon (vines on order). Space (0.6ha) is also being made for chardonnay. The site and the winemaker's skill, plus good karma, augur great things.

★★★★ **Shiraz** Elegant **04** most characterful to date. Evocative scented scrub, lifted white spice scents; light, supple texture, freshening savoury acid; recurring spicy kick in tail. Delightful cool-climate influence; portion from Stanford vyds, rest Sbosch. Unintrusive 100% new Fr oak, 18 mths. **03** 91 pts WS. WO W Cape. — AL

■ *Sandy River* see Zandvliet

Saronsberg Cellar

Tulbagh • Est 2002 • 1stB 2004 • Tasting & sales Mon-Fri 8.30-5 Sat 10-2 • Closed Easter Fri-Mon, Dec 25/26 & Jan 1 • BYO picnic • Tours by appt • Owner Saronsberg Cellar (Pty) Ltd • Winemaker Dewaldt Heyns (Oct 2003) • Viticulturist JP Dippenaar • 37 ha (cabs s/f, grenache, malbec, merlot, mourvèdre, petit v, shiraz, viognier, chard, sauvignon) • 65% red 35% white • PO Box 361 Tulbagh 6820 • info@saronsberg.com • www.saronsberg.com • T 023·30·0707 • F 023·230·0709

Top Veritas, Michelangelo and Winemaker's Choice awards for their 04 shiraz-based reds rewarded the Saronsberg team, who rejuvenated this former fruit and vine farm after a devastating 2002 fire. Exhaustive studies identified excellent vineyard potential: ancient shale-soil sites, soon to extend up the Saronsberg slopes for more shiraz, grenache and viognier. Nature's bounty is nurtured in the cathedral-like cement-and-stone cellar featuring grape chillers, sorting tables (hand-selecting bunches, then berries), and a gravity-fed tank system. New cab franc vines should soon enrich the bordeaux-style blend.

★★★★ **Full Circle** Powerful rhône-style blend driven by shiraz, with dollops mourvèdre & viognier (14/5%). **04** pvs ed showed amazing complexity: black pepper, lavender, lilies, smoked bacon; fruit concentration masked 15% alc, serious tannins provided structure for cellaring ±5-7 yrs. 16 mths 100% Fr oak.

★★★★ **Shiraz** Well oaked, delightfully fresh **04** last yr had juicy red berry & black plum tones spiced up by dashes (5%) mourvèdre, malbec, viognier. Plenty of gravitas despite its approachability. Mainly Fr oak, large % Burgundian barrels.

★★★★ **Sauvignon Blanc** Serious wine, deserving ±yr/2 to develop. **06** full-flavoured, with myriad tropical & green notes, yet athletic & light on its feet (12.3% alc).

Seismic ★★★★ Claret-style red powered by cab. **04** tasted mid-2005 displayed rich cassis/red berry fruit, whiffs lead pencil & Mochacino; tight, focused tannins needing probably 2 yrs to properly mesh. Charry touch from new Fr barriques. **Chardonnay** Elegant **05** (★★★★) has delicious silk & cream textures, hints nuts, lime & lemon, freshness assured by suppressed malo portion. Fermented/9 mths new Fr oak. **04** (★★★☆) also poised & tasty, with similar buttery & creamy mouthfeel. **Muscat de Frontignan** ★★★★ Fortified dessert with powerful muscat/nut character, lively floral & apricot notes. Tasted pvs ed, **05** very sweet (209g/ℓ) but not unctuous. — *CvZ*

Savanha

1stB 1997 ▪ Tasting, sales & tours at Spier ▪ Owner Winecorp ▪ Winemakers/viticulturists: see Winecorp ▪ 300 000 cs 75% red 25% white ▪ ISO 9001 certified ▪ PO Box 99 Lynedoch 7600 ▪ winecorp@iafrica.com ▪ www.winecorp.co.za ▪ T 021·881·3690 ▪ F 021·881·3699

This brand belongs to Winecorp, which also owns Longridge and Spier (where Savanha wines are made from fruit grown across the Western Cape). Says Winecorp group winemaker Frans Smit: 'Our goal with Savanha is to capture the invigorating energy of the abundant SA sun, paramount for producing grapes with powerful colour and intensity of flavour.' An export success of some years' standing, the brand is marketed under a Premium label (now available locally) and as a Special Reserve collection.

Naledi Cabernet Sauvignon, Sejana Merlot in temporary abeyance.

Special Reserve range

WO Coastal unless noted; reds all **05**. **Cabernet Sauvignon** ★★★☆ Perky, fruit driven but not simple; cassis/raspberries with underlying oak-spice, savoury firmness. Fr/Am barrel selection; ageing ability 1-2 yrs for all reds. **Merlot** ★★★☆ Abounds with voluptuous charms – black cherries, violets – but oak supplies underlying seriousness. Bold 15% alc, as has... **Shiraz** ★★★ Spiced red berries/plum compote ripeness fleshes out the firm frame. Paarl, Darling vyds. **Sauvignon Blanc** ★★★☆ Previewed **06** is higher end of the drinking scale: whiffs grapefruit on passionfruit base; nervy palate (7.6g/ℓ acid), slender at 12.5% alc but shapely, delicious. Great food partner.

Premium range

Merlot ★★★★ Winning combo in **05** for drinking enjoyment: opulent dark fruit in an accessible, smoothly rounded structure. Lightly oaked, as are other reds; all in range WO W Cape. **Cabernet Sauvignon** ★★★ Textbook **05** shows grassy/mint notes on bed of blackcurrants. Juicy, appealing; enough stiffening for yr/2's enjoyment. Incl 10% cab f. **Shiraz** ★★★ Smoothly accessible **05**, designed for earlier drinking, is herbaceous with appealing hedgerow fruit. Touch cab. **Chardonnay** ★★★ Flavourful, partially oaked **05** appeals with tropical fruit & biscuit quaffability. **Sauvignon Blanc** ★★★ Perfect summertime fare; **05** (sample) sparks with gooseberry/green fig liveliness, finishes crisply dry. — *CR*

■ **Savisa** see African Terroir
■ **Saw Edge Peak** see Conradie Family

Saxenburg 🍷🍸🍴🐓

Stellenbosch ▪ Est 1693 ▪ 1stB 1990 ▪ Tasting & sales Mon-Fri 9-5 Sat 9-4 Sun 10-4 (closed Sun-Tue in winter) Pub hols 10-4 (closed Easter Fri, Dec 25 & Jan 1) ▪ Fee R3-6 ▪ Guinea Fowl Restaurant & 'Lapa' (see Eat-out section) ▪ Farm produce ▪ Conferencing ▪ Miniature game park ▪ Owners Adrian & Birgit Bührer ▪ Winemaker Nico van der Merwe, with Edwin Grace (Nov 1990/Jan 2005) ▪ Viticulturist Len Coetzee (Jun 2001) ▪ 85 ha (cab, merlot, pinotage, shiraz, chard, chenin, sauvignon) ▪ 440 tons 50 000 cs 80% red 20% white ▪ Export brand: Bosman's Hill ▪ PO Box 171 Kuils River 7580 ▪ info@saxenburg.com ▪ www.saxenburg.com ▪ **T 021·903·6113** ▪ *F 021·903·3129*

Producing constant quality is Nico van der Merwe's aim, and the reason behind subtle tweaks to the recently released 03 vintage. These include limiting quantities of the Private Collection Pinotage to only 500 cases; vinifying only the very best blocks of shiraz; and bottling the PC Merlot unblended — the usual dollop of cab was not required. A continuing source of pleasure and pride for the ever-upbeat winemaker are the 'nice echoes' received from an appreciative market, including applause for the new label design and excellent sales of the Guinea Fowl duo. One suspects two further 'echoes' will also be well received: the Shiraz Challenge trophy for the 03 PC bottling, and our own five-star rating for the SSS.

Saxenberg Limited Release

★★★★☆ **Saxenburg Shiraz Select** Pricey showpiece deserving many yrs bottle-ageing. Careful block selection, only free-run juice, best barrels chosen after maturation. Deep, dark **03** (★★★★★) assails the senses with cocoa bean, liquorice richness, cream textured body, fully integrated tannins. Not big (despite 14.5% alc) but curvaceous, seductively delicious. Soupçons cab, merlot. 2 yrs all new wood, equal Fr/Am.

Private Collection

★★★★ **Cabernet Sauvignon** Handsome, dark fruited, cassis toned **03**, influenced by the vintage: still tight, all ingredients in place but long way off peak. No hard edges; suave tannins, drink now if you must, but will reward 8+ yrs cellaring. Yr Am/Fr 70/30, third new. IWSC gold.

★★★★ **Merlot** After accessible, 'feminine' **02**, latest **03** a keeper: lovely dark fruit, creamy choc layers but brusque tannins not fully melded. Give another yr, shd hold for 4+ more. Yr Fr casks, 40% new.

★★★★ **Pinotage** Back on track, elegant, well-crafted **03** seduces with array of berries, roasted spice, fine-grained tannins. Yr oak, 60/40 Am/Fr, 30% new. Only 500 cs, so hurry! Savoury, beefy **02** (★★★☆) showed signs of lesser red-wine vintage.

★★★★★ **Shiraz** Consistently & famously excellent. **03** back on track after **02** dip, transports you straight to the Rhône: violets, scrub, wild berries. Nico advises 'long maturation' but with such supple tannins, you won't listen! A beauty. 70/30 Am/Fr oak, third new. Shiraz Challenge trophy; *Wine* ★★★★☆. **02** (★★★☆) from difficult vintage: good fruit marred by awkward tannins.

★★★★ **Sauvignon Blanc** Clever combo riper style & early picked fruit in **06**, due to vyd/clonal selections; gooseberry & fresh apple aromas; palate is pure leafy, capsicum freshness. Will appeal widely.

Chardonnay ★★★★ Deservedly popular, always sells out. Bold **05** goes more for overt appeal than structure: citrus peel & butterscotch tones, broad texture, shapely drinkability. Yr Fr oak, 20% new. No new releases tasted of following **NV**s: **Le Phantom Brut Cap Classique** ★★★ 60/40 pinot/chard blend. **Le Rêve de Saxenbourg Natural Sweet** ★★★ Dusty, light textured dessert from sauvignon, chenin.

Guinea Fowl range

Red ★★★ Near equal merlot, shiraz, cab blend for early drinking. Latest **04**'s dry tannins underpinning mulberry fruit make it food compatible, gd for yr/2's ageing. Yr used Fr/Am. Own fruit. **White** ★★★ Chenin (78%) & Wllngtn viognier. **06** shows just how well blend works: floral toned, plenty of juicy vibrancy, just-off-dry perky freshness. WO Coastal.

Selection Famille

Named after Bührer children; only available from farm. Not retasted this ed: **Gwendolyn 01** 60/40 shiraz/cab blend with warm spicy choc notes. **Manuel** ★★★☆ Gear-up **00** united cab (65%) & merlot: minty cassis, firm tannins. Both ★★★★. Also wines ex-Ch Capion (Fr), so never tasted: **Appollonia** (white blend), **Fiona** & **Adrianus** (both red).

Concept range

Grand Vin Rouge ★★★ From 6 varieties, half blend ex-Capion; attractively different: creamy dark fruit, violets, in slender, approachable, lightly oaked structure. Uncertified because of Fr fruit. **Grand Vin Blanc** ★★☆ Light, 'cool fruit' style: leafy, herbaceous aromas, subdued minerality. Equal sauvignon, chenin, own fruit & Wllngtn: Both NV. — *CR*

Scali

Paarl ▪ Est/1st 1999 ▪ Visits by appt ▪ Olive oil ▪ B&B guest accommodation ▪ Owners/winemakers Willie & Tania de Waal ▪ Viticulturist Willie de Waal ▪ 70 ha (cab, merlot, pinotage, shiraz, chardonnay, chenin, sauvignon, viognier) 910 cs 100% red ▪ PO Box 7143 Noorder-Paarl 7623 ▪ info@ scali.co.za ▪ www.scali.co.za ▪ T 021-869-8340 ▪ F 021-869-8383

'My adventurous streak? Blame my great-great-grandfather who traded a diamond he'd discovered in Kimberley for the farm,' laughs Willie de Waal. He and wife Tania took a chance with their new chenin blend by fermenting it on the skins and following up with *pigeage*. This 'punching down' of the floating skins is usually for reds, to extract more colour, flavour and tannin. But the trick worked and the mere five barrels were snapped up fast. Equally thrilling: 2006 saw them once again joining the ranks of the 'Top 100 Wineries' at London's International Wine & Spirits Fair.

★★★★ **Pinotage** While **03** included cab, **04** (partly from 32 yr old vines) has 13% shiraz adding a delicate lift to red berry aromas & augmenting the lovely sweet fruit, which balances serious tannins & 14.7% alc. Sympathetic 2 yrs Fr oaking.

★★★★ **Syrah** Attractive shiraz perfume accompanies spicy oak aromas on **04** — lots of slightly drying wood apparent too on palate, with herbs & plentiful fresh red fruit. Strong, lithe tannins. Native yeast ferment; 2 yrs Fr oak. **03** (★★★★★) a standout.

★★★★ **Blanc** new Impressive, powerful **05** blend of 75% chenin, chard & a little viognier sold out overnight. Appealing notes of citrus, dried grass, but rich texture shot though with fine acid may be strongest point. Big in lingering flavour & structure — 14.8% alc. Clean, dry focus. Oxidative styling, with yr in old oak. All WO Voor Pdberg. — *TJ*

■ **Scarborough** see Cape Point Vineyards

Schalkenbosch Wines

Tulbagh ▪ Est 1792 ▪ 1stB 2002 ▪ Tasting & sales daily 9.30-4.30 ▪ Closed Dec 25/26 & Jan 1 ▪ Tours, meals & accommodation (B&B or self-catering) by appt ▪ Tour groups ▪ Walks ▪ Conservation area ▪ Mountain biking ▪ Owner Platinum Mile Investments ▪ Winemaker Johan Delport (Jan 2005) ▪ Viti consultants Johan Wiese & Andrew Teubes ▪ 35 ha (cab s/f, merlot, mourvèdre, petit v, shiraz, chard, sauvignon, viognier) ▪ 100 tons 7 500 cs 80% red 20% white ▪ PO Box 95 Tulbagh 6820 ▪ info@schalkenbosch.co.za ▪ www.schalkenbosch.co.za ▪ Office: T 023-230-0654; F 023-230-0422 Cellar: T/F 023-230-1488

The Biodiversity & Wine Initiative (BWI) is drawing ever more members, this Tulbagh spread among them. There's a moral responsibility, explains winemaker Johan Delport, referring to a renosterveld conservation and alien eradication programme in the pipeline, as well as the marketing value attached to 'greenness'. The 2006 vintage was his best ever but no 'sold out' signs, he promises — expansion in the cellar has ensured locals will be able to buy Edenhof and Isis (note the name change from Ibis).

Edenhof range

Cabernet Sauvignon ★★☆ Too unknit to rate pvs ed, **04** now better integrated but oak still dominating (yr, 50% new Fr). Ample vanilla, spice, fleshed out by juicy berries. **Bin 409** ★★★ ('Rhône-style Blend' pvs ed.) Debut **04** well composed of mainly grenache &

shiraz (43/33), smatterings mourvèdre, cinsaut & cab. Spicy/fruity notes deftly dusted by 6 mths 2nd fill Fr oak. Racy acidity ideal to lift rich, hearty dishes. **Cabernet Sauvignon-Merlot** ★★★ Cab-led (79%) **04**, quite plush with sugared plums & creamy sweet oak. Refreshing cab acidity lifts the finale. Yr 2nd fill wood, 50/50 Am/Fr. **Cabernet Sauvignon-Shiraz** new ★★ Alluring sweet plum, berry & vanilla notes, friendly tannins, but less attractive firm acidity. Combo Fr/Am oak. **Glen Rosa** ★★★ Generous merlot, cab f, cab (64/26/10) mix with plum & red berry whiffs, well integrated oak, moderate tannin grip. 15% alc evident. 50% new Fr oak, rest combo older Am/Fr. **Viognier** new ★★★ Promising **06** with typical viognier bouquet of ripe apricots & spice; misses some of variety's generous mid-palate. **Blanc de Blanc** ★★★ Back in range thanks to German following; charming patio sipper from two blancs, sauvignon & chenin (47/46) & hint muscat d'A. Floral, muscatty; bright acidity & note of greenpepper. Following tasted last yr: **Shiraz** ★★★ **04** differs from pvs rosé-like quaffers: shows stronger blackberry & savoury concentration, empathetic oaking (yr 2nd fill Fr) allows fruit to shine; tail touch warm (14.4% alc) but dry. **Sauvignon Blanc** ★★★ **05** same tropical notes as pvs, but acid more prominent. Both ranges WO W Cape.

Isis range
These in 1ℓ bottles. **Dry Red** ★★ **04** features dollops ruby cab & merlot plus 40% cinsaut. Unwooded, lightly coloured & flavoured with firm tannin. A fast mover in Sweden as is... **Dry White** ★★ **06** light bodied sauvignon (88%) with dashes colombard & muscat d'A. Uncomplex sweaty-armpit bouquet & racy acidity. **Rosé** ★★ **05** tart pink tipple from juice bled off cab. Intriguing tomato & white asparagus scents, demure flavours. Slimmer-friendly low 1.6g/ℓ RS. — *CvZ*

■ *Scholtzenhof* see Ken Forrester

Schoonberg

*Upper Langkloof · Est 1999 · 1stB 2002 · Visits by appt · Walks · Mountain biking · 4×4 trail · Owner Morné Jonker · 17 ha (cab) · 200 cs 100% red · PO Box 689 Oudtshoorn 6620 · morné@schoonberg.co.za · www.schoonberg.co.za · **T 044·888·1707** · F 044·203·3715*
No update available on this winery; contact details from previous edition.

■ *Schoone Gevel* see La Motte
■ *Sebeko* see Daschbosch

Sedgwick's Old Brown Sherry

An original, launched in 1886 & still the fisherman's friend (portion of sales go to long-running WWF-SA Fish Tagging Project). A Distell brand. **NV** ★★★ Blend jerepiko & dry sherry, from two muscats & chenin. Latest bottling as warm, sweet & welcoming as bread & butter pudding. 16.8% alc. WO W Cape. — *CvZ*

Seidelberg Estate

*Paarl · Est 1692 · 1stB 1989 · Tasting & sales Mon-Fri 9-6 Sat/Sun & pub hols 10-6 · Fee R12 · Closed Dec 25 · Tours daily (by appt for groups of 5+) · De Leuwen Jagt Restaurant · Play area for children · Farm produce · Events/functions · Tour groups · Gifts · Walks · Hiking trail · Conservation area · Tractor rides · Bronze-casting studio, glass blowing studio & artists lounge (with live demonstrations) · Owner Roland Seidel · Winemaker Cerina de Jongh (Jun 2002) · Viticulturist Ian de Lange (Apr 2006) · 110 ha (cabs s/f, malbec merlot, mourvèdre, pinotage, shiraz, chard, chenin, sauvignon, viognier) · +500 tons · 40 000 cs 70% red 20% white 10% rosé · PO Box 505 Suider-Paarl 7624 · info@seidelberg.co.za · www.seidelberg.co.za · **T 021·863·5200** · F 021·863·3797*
Wine tourism and winemaking in SA are in 'a stage of awakening', believes owner Roland Seidel, who maintains they're 'still polishing this gem'. Nothing unpolished about the company they keep — a tea lounge and art gallery joins the glass-blowing and bronze-casting studios, a combination

which had Seidelberg voted the best 'Art & Culture' experience in the winelands by the Great Wine Capitals Global Network. Meanwhile, the first mourvèdre and malbec grapes came in last year, and a new sorting table helps weed out the less-than-best grapes before the crush.

Roland's Reserve range

★★★★ Merlot 04 (★★★★) similar traits as pvs, incl broad build, ripe minty fruit, all in lower key; might simply be in subdued phase, having undergone more rigorous oaking — 50% 1st fill, vs seasoned wood only for precociously charming & accessible **03** (both ±16 mths, Fr).

★★★★ Pinotage Perfectly proportioned extrovert **03** succeeded by subdued & inward **04** (★★★), showing rather too much of variety's tannins & acidity; funky whiff invites early drinking.

Cabernet Sauvignon 03 (★★★★) a sample last ed, but misreported as '04', has grown in stature, appeal. Classic varietal signature of cassis in harmony with gorgeous lead pencil oak (Fr, 18 mths). *Decanter* ★★★★. Notch more serious & crafted than firmly muscled **02** (★★★★). **Syrah ★★★** Less serious/structured styling continues with **04**; more 'fruit driven red' than varietal icon, but flavourful & appealing. 18 mths Fr/Am oak, none new.

Seidelberg range

★★★★ Un Deux Trois Still a one-two-three part bdx-style red, but merlot leads cab & cab f (51/40/9) in **03**; more sophisticated than pvs 'characterful rustics', touch more serious, extracted. Approachable, but better in few yrs. Yr 3rd fill oak, 75% Fr.

Following reds mainly Fr oak-staved: **Cabernet Sauvignon ★★★ 03** less refined than pvs; over-ripe raisin tone with hot (14% alc), dry savoury finish. Incl 5% 04 merlot. Not retasted; ditto... **Cabernet Sauvignon-Merlot ★★★** Unwooded 53/47 blend, **03** cassis fruit & dry leaf hint; big pressy tannins invite food rather than standalone drinking. **Merlot ★★★** Combo staves/barrels for **04**, fairly restrained, herbaceous tinge to mulberry fruit, gd with richer food. **Pinotage ★★★ 05** back to modern fruit filled style after detour through 'old Cape'. Spiked with sharpish tannins, needing food. Partly oaked. **Shiraz ★★★ 04** more sedate compared with pvs swashbucklers; still v ripe but quieter on nose, easy unflamboyant flavours. **Rosé ★★** Softly dry, light **06**, wafts of fresh petals & potpourri, texturing dried-fruit tang ups the sippability. **Chardonnay ★★★** No barrels this yr, leaving **05** to age 8 mths on staves only, so less serious but still satisfying, lightish & eminently drinkable. **Chenin Blanc ★★★** Off oldest producing vyd on estate; **05** medium bodied; Granny Smith apple tone; last ed showed taut acidity. **Sauvignon Blanc ★★** Again incl super-early-picked fraction (18°B), **06** therefore light & austere; lemongrass whiff; crisp & bone-dry. WO W Cape. **Viognier ★★★** Fat, opulent & sweet-fruited **06**; harvested very ripe (26°B) for max flavour (lovely peach/tropical melon), but acidity in pre-bottling sample tad too low for richness & 15% alc; bunch-pressed.

De Leeuwen Jagt range

Reds mainly unwooded. **Cabernet Sauvignon ★★★** Lighter bodied, trimmer fruited **04** a departure from pvs hearty versions; dry chalky tannins add to leaner silhouette. Following two reds untasted this ed: **Merlot ★★ 04** repeats the usual leafy character on nose, palate much more wiry than pvs; demands (rather than invites) food. **Cabernet Franc-Merlot ★★★** Less exuberant partnership in **04**, cab f's stalky minerality upfront, sturdy long-term tannins. **Pinotage ★★★** A more savoury vintage, medium-full body & flavours, **05** undemanding & food-compatible. Mainly Hngrian staves. **Shiraz ★★ 04** shows the sunnier side of Paarl; raisined spiciness on nose, over-ripe vapidity on palate. Not for keeping. **Leuwenrood ★★★** Switches to shiraz (58%), merlot blend in **04**; full & fruity; v agreeable wild berry conclusion. **Rosé ★★ 06** quaffable semi-dry pink with dried peach aromas, light watermelon flavours. Following pair not retasted: **Chardonnay ★★** Unwooded **05** shy on nose yet quite effusive on palate; ripe fruit zested with clean lemon acidity. **Leuwenblanc ★★** Chenin from Rawsonville. **05** cheerful pineapple flavour; satisfying pre-lunch glassful. **Nuance ★★ 06** fragrant semi-dry white tipple from crouchen & muscadel, light, fresh, with rosepetal aroma. **Stein ★★** Last ed a light, charming white; **04** muscat, honey & raisin fragrances, creamy off-dry flavours. **Red Muscadel ★★★ NV** fortified dessert with fresh, grapey bouquet, balanced sweetness & alc (17% alc). MIWA DG. Some in this range WO W Cape. **Sauvignon Blanc-Chenin Blanc** discontinued. — *CT*

■ **Semaya** see Jonkheer
■ **Sénga** see MAN Vintners

Sentinel

Cape Town • Est/1stB 1995 • Closed to public • 20 000 cs 75% red 25% white • PO Box 30 Constantia 7848 • wine@sentinel.co.za

A new era for this established and critically acclaimed brand. It's now in the hands of Converge, holding company for leading mail-order club Wine of the Month, and with such experience at the helm, the future looks bright. Immediate plans were fluid at press time, but the vision is to develop a flagship Reserve range 'capable of winning double-gold Veritas and international awards'.

Sequillo Cellars   ♂♀

Swartland • Est/1stB 2003 • Visits/amenities by appt only • Owners Eben Sadie & Cornel Spies • Winemakers Eben & Niko Sadie • 4 000 cs 100% red • PO Box 1019 Malmesbury 7299 • info@sequillo.com • www.sequillo.com • T 021·869·8349 • F 021·869·8101

Eben Sadie is a passionate advocate of terroir, so much so that he believes grapes from one appellation shouldn't be vinified in another. He's even more passionate about the Swartland. Double delight, then, that Sequillo's grapes, from the Swartland, will now be vinified in the Sadie Family cellar tucked away in the Aprilskloof, where the Paardeberg foothills fold one on another. The why and wherefore? Eben S is now partnered in Sequillo by old friend and Cape Wine Master Cornel Spies, who bought Tymen Bouma's share when the latter decided to focus more keenly on Anura, where Sequillo production took place in the past. Another change is from red-only production — look forward to a white blend, due for release this year.

Sequillo Inspired by southern Rhône, expressive of Swtland, maiden **03** (★★★★) blended 63% shiraz, 30% mourvèdre, 7% grenache. Much the same in lightly rich **04** (★★★★), which at peak of fresh ripeness; suave but warmly generous, with velvet tannins, firm acid, sweet red fruit (tinged with lavender), all in balance. 2 yrs 2nd fill oak. — *TJ*

■ **Serengeti** see Leidersburg

Ses'Fikile   ♂♀ new

Stellenbosch (see Helderberg map) • Est 2004 • 1stB 2006 • Tastings at Flagstone (see entry) • Owner Indlezane Investments • Winemaker Bruce Jack, with Wilhelm Coetzee • Viticulturist Bruce Jack • 5 500 cs 70% red 30% white • PO Box 120 Guguletu 7750 • indlezane@mweb. co.za • sesfikile@gmail.com • www.sesfikile.co.za • T 021·694·9840/021·852·5052 • F 021·694·9840/021·852·5085

Four black women (three are school teachers) from Langa in Cape Town have launched a promising wine company in conjunction with Flagstone's Bruce Jack. Spokeswoman Nondumiso Pikashe says the dynamism, energy, challenges, fast pace and history of the wine industry are what attracted her and Jackie Mayo, Nomvuyo Xaliphi and Phelela Mgudlwa. Aptly, their venture's name means: 'We have arrived... in style!' The aim: capturing the emerging aspirational black middle-class with top-drawer, great value wines. Says Jack, who assists with sourcing and vinification: 'We are dealing with a new market which allows us to push the boat out style-wise. We intend to make this the most exciting empowerment brand ever.'

Cabernet Sauvignon-Merlot Reserve ★★★★ 04 a lot of well managed concentration & ripeness here; 2 yr Am oak treatment to anchor full-ripe red fruit, ensure longevity (±5 yrs); appealing vanilla spicing, fleeting glimpses of scrub, white pepper. Watch bold 15. 5% alc. **Pinotage ★★★** Plummy fruit given centre stage in previewed **05**: juicy, lively & friendly. Some light oaking. **Shiraz Reserve ★★★★ 04** is light yrs from version below in styling: raspberry compote with heaps of sweet spice, vanilla. Absorbs the 15.6% alc & 24 mths Am oak in its voluptuous structure. Cellaring potential 3-4 yrs. **Shiraz ★★★★ 05** (sample) more Old World than New: wild berries, underbrush/dried herb nuances & a silky, liquorice toned structure. Lightly oaked, delicious. Drink soon. **Chardonnay** ★★ Unwooded **06** (sample) has full-ripe dried peach aromas, flavours, but misses some mid-palate definition, structure. Bold 15% alc. **Chenin Blanc** ★★★ Peardrop & melon typicity in **06**, attractive food-friendly minerality on the finish. **Sauvignon Blanc** ★★★ **06** shows restrained leafy, capsicum styling; nicely fresh (6.8 g/ℓ acidity) & light textured (12.5% alc). Cld open up, reveal more once bottled. W Cape & Swtland WOs.— *CR*

■ *Seven Falls* see Southern Cape Vineyards

Seven Oaks

Worcester • Est 2003 • 1stB 2004 • Closed to public • Owner Farm Acres 27 (Pty) Ltd • Vini consultant Francois Agenbag (Mountain Ridge) • 27.5 ha (cab, cinsaut, pinotage, ruby cab, shiraz, chenin, sauvignon) • 345 tons total 574 cs own label • Brands for customers: Villa Verde & United Bulk • PO Box 11 Breerivier 6858 • jacqui@sevenoaks.co.za • www.sevenoaks.co.za • **T 083·639·0405**

This relatively new boutique winery gained invaluable exposure after receiving a number of awards for its maiden vintage (04). The Pols family have since added another hectare of cinsaut and nine of white varieties, and believe 2006 vintage quality to be higher for both the Chenin and Cab-Shiraz. A new Merlot-Cab (grapes for which were sourced from the family's SGS-certified organic farm, Rotenberg am Breede in Eilandia just outside Robertson) also shows potential. Exclusivity remains the aim but at affordable prices, they say.

Cabernet Sauvignon-Shiraz '6+1' ★★★ **05** honest & appealing 66/34 blend with gd tannins, hefty 14.9% alc buffered by touch sweetness, savoury/meaty notes. Not for keeping. Yr Fr/Am oak, portion new. **04** 'Rsv' Swiss gold. **Cabernet Sauvignon-Shiraz** ★★★ Spicy-fruited easy-drinker style; **06** unready; not retasted **04** oak chipped, so wooding not as fine as above, but who's quibbling? **Padre Rednose Merlot-Cabernet-Sauvignon** new ★★★ Food-inviting **05**, 70/30 partnership with dry tannins, low fruit & big wood presence from new Fr/Am oak, yr. **Chenin Blanc** ★★★ Sample **06** a super end-of-day glassful; eminently sippable, with melon, pear & fynbos flavours. All WO Breede Rvr Vlly.— *IvH*

■ *Shamwari* see The Company of Wine People
■ *Shatot* see Slaley
■ *Shepherd's Creek* see Clos Malverne
■ *Shibula* see Freedom Hill

Ship Sherry

Not 'sherry', but a jerepiko-style fortified from two muscats & chenin. **NV** ★★ Slips down warmly, evoking plump raisins, mulled wine & dry scrub through to its gently gripping conclusion (16.8% alc). By Distell. — *CvZ*

Shoprite Checkers

Enquiries: Stephanus Eksteen • 30 000 cs own labels 60% red 35% white 5% rosé • PO Box 215 Brackenfell 7561 • seksteen@shoprite.co.za • www.shoprite.co.za • **T 021·980·4000** • F 021·980·4012

Stephanus Eksteen, national wine-buyer for nationwide retail chains Shoprite and Checkers, was recently named as one of the most influential figures in SA wine. Aside from overseeing the selection of third-party brands for sale through nearly 350 super/hypermarkets (co-merchandising of wine and cheese a strong feature of the strategy), Stephanus E also convenes a panel of winemakers, wine experts and consumers who meet regularly to select the well priced in-house ranges below. Most are marketed under an anonymous 'bin number'. 'Like Agatha Christie,' SE explains, 'we hold a few secrets to keep consumers guessing and add to the fun.'

Oak Ridge range

Following vintages still selling, not retasted. **Cabernet Sauvignon ★★★ 03** lightish bodied but when last tasted showed variety's sturdy structure & tannins, mellowed somewhat by vanilla oak. **Merlot ★★★ 02** jovial, with roly-poly profile matched by sweet ripe tannins. Shd hold another yr/2. Following samples too unformed to rate last time: **Cabernet Sauvignon-Merlot-Cabernet Franc 03** austere & tight, green walnut whiffs & powerful tannins. **Pinotage 04** robust, rustic & tannic. **Shiraz ★★★** Honest to goodness *vin rouge*; **03** effortlessly drinkable, with mulberry fruit & balanced spicy tannins.

Oddbins range

Limited editions sourced directly from estates & private cellars; bin numbers change as batches are replaced by new lots.

> **Pinotage Bin 195** ☺ **★★★** Comfortable quaffing style with bright currant & plum fruit, **04** is midweight, with pleasantly low tannins & oak.

Cabernet Sauvignon Bin 219 ★★★★ ✓ 05 quite rich & full but ready & easy to drink, no need to mature this cab any further. Incl smatterings of merlot, cab f & petit v, aged yr in Fr oak, some new. Off Coastal vyds. **Cabernet Sauvignon-Merlot Bin 214 ★★★ 05** (sample) accessible, easy-drinking equal blend, partly oaked. Offers red berries, plums & a bit of choc, smooth & tasty with enough substance for another few yrs. Ex-Darling. **Shiraz Bin 201 ★★★★ ✓** Satisfying & supple **04**, plenty of sweet cherry/berry fruit wrapped in ripe tannins, just enough oak to highlight the hints of anise & herb. Enough structure, padding, for another 4-6 yrs. **Chenin Blanc Bin 211 ★★★** Off Darling vyds **06** is loaded with tropical fruit, has notes of pineapple & passionfruit in a fresh, zesty, lightish body. Both ranges WO Stbosch unless noted. — *DH*

Signal Hill　　　🍂🍷🍵

Cape Town · Est/1stB 1997 · Open Mon-Sat 10-7 (also Sun in season) · Luncheon restaurant · Owners Ridon Family Vineyards · Winemaker Jean-Vincent Ridon (1997), with Khulekani Laurence Buthelezi & Wade Metzer (1998/2005) · Viticulturist Marietjie Marais (1997) · 5 ha (cab, shiraz, pinot, muscat d'A) · 45 tons ±3 000 cs · 70% red 27% white 3% rosé · 23 Church Str, Cape Town 8000 · info@winery.co.za · www.winery.co.za · T 021·422·5206 · F 021·422·5238

Jean-Vincent Ridon is the urban 'vineyards with a view' man: he has vines below Table Mountain, on Kalk Bay slopes and now at the foot of the Twelve Apostles peaks; also in France, in St Paul (next door to the Griers of Villiera's new vineholding), wines from which are to be bottled under the Le Signal label and made available locally. Last year was varied and busy: the maiden cab franc was brought in, the first rows planted in Camps Bay, and stylish new glass-fronted premises in the heart of Cape Town readied for opening. 'Experimentation will continue at Signal Hill,' promises the winemaker, 'with clairette blanche and sweet reds to join the mix.'

★★★★☆　**Clos d'Oranje 05**, from tiny shiraz vyd in Oranjezicht, J-V Ridon's long-gestated tribute to SA wine's origins in the centre of Cape Town. Persuasive varietal scents of lilies, red fruits & spice delivered with Fr-style restraint. Youthfully coy, needs yr/2 for flavours to grow into underlying supple, graceful mouthfeel. WO Coastal ('WO Cape Town is still being discussed').

★★★★　**Petit Verdot 03** mentioned in last ed, not yet bottled. Mid-2005 showed a seductive bouquet; tight, firm structure; potential to improve gd few yrs.

★★★★　**Malbec** *Vive la Difference!* exclaims front-label, accurately. **04** had an exotic incense bouquet followed by lush cherry flavour, persistent finish. WO Smnsberg-Paarl. **05** not ready for tasting.

★★★★　**Malwenn** Pinotage, off Paarl, Smnsberg vyds; **02** was quintessence of the grape, with potent mulberry fruit. Next tasted **04** (**★★★★**) had pinot-like earthy tones, balanced tannins & alc. **05** mid-2006 still in cask, untasted. Yr Fr oak, 20% new.

★★★★　**Antica MM** From cab, made with minimal intervention to express the essence of mature Smnsberg bushvine fruit. **00** to be followed by **06**, not reviewed.

★★★★★ **Eszencia** new Ageless, restorative, impossibly delicious elixir extracted drop by drop from 2ha of furmint, chenin & sauvignon. Mere 120ℓ made & ushered — gingerly — into 375ml bottles, which priced at extreme R1 500 each — among highest ever for SA wine. But what sublime nectar! Vastly sweet & rich, flavours of apricot & orange marmalade electrified by nervy acid. Extreme stats too: 480g/ℓ sugar, 16g/ℓ acid, ultra-low 5.1% alc, latter recognised for wine in EU but not (yet) in SA. Uncertified/**NV** (02).

★★★★ **Vin de l'Empereur** NLH-style dessert from muscat d'A vyd on Smnsberg. **05** ±25% botrytised portion softens, introduces dimensions of cinnamon & baked apple to variety's vivid grapey tones. Smooth, velvety, yet fresh & very clean. WO Paarl.

★★★★ **Crème de Tête Muscat d'Alexandrie NLH** None since hedonistic **03**, succeeding warm vintages prompting winemaker to sigh: 'Oh dear, botrytis, we miss you!' Fortunately there's **06**, but will have to wait till next ed: these barrel fermented & yr *sur lie*.

★★★★ **Vin de Glacière 07** promised follow-up to **00** extraordinary 'assisted icewine' from muscat d'A, 'once deep freezer installed at winery' advises Ridon.

★★★★ **Mathilde Aszú 6 Puttonyos** Characterful Tokaji lookalike from botrytised Swtland furmint & Smnsberg sauvignon, a Cape first. None since maiden **02**, remarkable for its brilliant sugar/acid balance. Will **07** be next?

Cabernet Franc new Another ground-breaker from J-VR. **06** maiden crop from Kalk Bay single-vyd. Ex-barrel, too young to rate but sends good spicy/leafy signals, fine tannins, balanced acid. Most promising. WO Coastal. **Pinot Noir** ★★★★ Previewed in last ed, **05**'s pure ruby colour mirrored in clear, forthcoming cherry/forest floor fragrance. Lively tannins, lovely light texture. Will benefit from further yr/2. Matured in older oak. WO Sbosch. **Syrah** new ★★★★ **05** very fresh, tight, with fine, chalky tannins. Structure mirrored in focused mint-edged spice. Needs time to settle, relax. Hldrberg grapes. **Rosé de Saignée** ★★★★ Sunny, warm pink hue matches conditions conducive to sipping **05**, partnered by Mediterranean dishes. Dry, firm with savoury vinosity; wonderfully food-friendly. 30% fermented in older barrels. Mainly shiraz with 10% each pinot/cab. **Viognier** ★★★ **05**, last ed a sample, now shows more restraint than many. Fresh, minerally, dry, with dainty apricot tones; already suggestion bottle-age, so best enjoyed soon. 80/20 tank/Fr oak fermented. A one-off. No new vintages of the following tasted: **Constantia** ★★★★ (Pvsly 'Grand Rouge de Constance') Constantia tinta & soupçon cab f in still-available winter warming **02**, aged 18 mths in older 500ℓ vats. **Tête Blanche** ★★★★ 'My style of mature chenin,' notes Ridon; partly-oaked **03** still on market; melon & lemon fruit, cleansing lemon acidity. Off selected low-yield Smnsberg, Polkadraai vyds. **Straw Wine** ★★★★ Unknown field blend (possibly chard, chenin, riesling), air-dried on straw mats as traditional *vin de paille* style demands. **01** still selling. Pvs notes incl nutty, sherry-like tones. Arduous two yr fermentation, yielding just 10% alc. **04** next, not ready for tasting. **Climat de Corsaire Chardonnay; Argile Rouge** discontinued.

La Siesta range

★★★★ **Grenache Blanc** Rhône variety in vogue for white blends; this among SA's first varietal bottlings. **05** unready; last yr we sampled **04** which mirrored dusty lemon blossom nose, juicy almond & peach palate of **03**.

Grenache ★★★★ Southern Fr-style **03** still selling. Not retasted but last yr we noted its spicy red berry fruit, friendly tannins & refreshing dry acidity. Fermented, aged in 20% new Fr wood. — *AL*

■ *Signature Reserve* see Stettyn

■ *Signature Series* see Jean Daneel

■ *Signatures* see Doolhof Estate

■ *Signum* see Rooiberg

■ *Silver Myn* see Zorgvliet

■ *Silver Sands* see Robertson Wide River, Vinimark

Silverthorn Wines new

*Robertson • Est 1998 • 1stB 2004 • Closed to public • Owners John & Karen Loubser •
Winemaker/viticulturist John Loubser (1998) • 4 ha (cab, shiraz, chard) • 50 tons 225 cs 100%
white • PO Box 381 Robertson 6705 • john@silverthornwines.co.za • www.silverthornwines.
co.za • T 021·712·7239/082·891·0461*

From a farm he calls 'a little paradise on the banks of the Breede River', John Loubser and his
wife Karen truck their chardonnay grapes to Steenberg in Constantia (where he is cellarmaster), and there he turns them into cap classique. Loubser has no interest in diversifying
his style: 'MCC is my mission and my passion'. He calls his wine 'The Green Man' after the
mythical figure — an expression of his love of the soil and respect for nature.

★★★★ **The Green Man Blanc de Blancs NV** MCC from chard, from well-versed-in-bubbly
John L's own Rbtson vyds. **04**, pale silvery green, languid streams pin-prick bubbles;
roundly 'brut'. Still unevolved, though hinting at toasty development to come. Very
fine; great potential. Portion barrel fermented. 11.5% alc. As cork advises, it will 'delight your senses'. — *AL*

■ *Simonay see Simonsvlei International*

Simonsig Estate

*Stellenbosch • Est 1953 • 1stB 1968 • Tasting & sales Mon-Fri 8.30-5 Sat 8.30-4 (T
021·888·4915) • Fee R15/R25 (incl glass) • Closed Easter Fri, Dec 25 & Jan 1 • Tours Mon-Fri
10 & 3; Sat 10 (min 5; booking essential for groups) • Cheese platters (R35) or BYO picnic •
Play area for children • Tour groups by appt • Walking trail • Labyrinth vineyard • Owners Malan
brothers • Winemaker Johan Malan (1981), with Van Zyl du Toit & Debbie Burden (Dec 97/
Nov 99) • Viticulturist Francois Malan (1980), with Ludwig Uys & Martin Farao, advised by
Johan Pienaar • 205 ha (cab, merlot, pinotage, shiraz, chard, chenin, sauvignon) • 2 000 tons
57% red 25% white 18% MCC • PO Box 6 Koelenhof 7605 • wine@simonsig.co.za • www.
simonsig.co.za • T 021·888·4900 • F 021·888·4909*

A change of designation (back to 'Estate') notwithstanding, this remains a solidly family farm,
with Pieter Malan now handling international sales. More accolades came brother (and
winemaker) Johan M's way in 2005, when Simonsig topped the list of gold-winning natural
wines at Veritas. In fact, since 1981, when cellar wizard JM began working his magic, he's
won more yellow metal at the show than any other producer. It's been back to the future in
the vineyards (brother Francois's domain), with the first chenin in 20 years, and in the cellar,
with the return of a Rosé sparkling, last produced in the mid-90s. Development-wise, state-
of-the-art automated bottling and disgorging lines (the latter specifically to keep up with the
demand for Kaapse Vonkel) have led the way.

★★★★ **Frans Malan** Tribute to the visionary patriarch. Vigorous & ageworthy 'Cape blend',
led in **04** by pinotage (65%), with cab (31%) & dash merlot. Mulberry/plums mingle
with campfire smoke; opulent fruit cossets taut tannins; ripe (±15% alc), structured to
mature decade+. 16 mths Am/Fr barrels, 58/42. New oak component scaled back to
60% from 80% for multi-gonged **03**, which had equal pinotage & cab, smattering merlot. *Wine* ★★★★, VDG.

★★★★ **Tiara** Top-notch bdx-style blend, make-up varies each yr. Big boned **04** has ripe & generous cassis fruit but equally assertive oak & tannins will need time to mesh. Fine spiciness from mainly Fr oak, though high new-wood portion (±80%), extended barrelling
(21 mths), add to serious grip. Cab leads, plummy merlot supports (59/32), cab f & petit v add herbal high notes. Shd improve & hold gd few yrs. NE.

★★★★☆ **Merindol Syrah** Widely awarded shiraz from single vyd 'Rooigrond' on poor sandy-
loam soils. **04**'s alluring red-fruit, smoked beef bouquet ushers in poised palate refreshed by crisp acidity; tight, focused tannins, fruit concentration mask 15% alc. Delicious now, shd further improve with cellaring. Numerous awards incl TWS, IWSC &
Shiraz Challenge. 16 mths new Fr oak.

★★★★☆ **CWG Auction Reserve Shiraz** Elegant, with sheathed power, needs plenty of time to mesh, develop. **04** echoes **03**'s lovely perfumes, ripe red fruit wrapped around mineral core, entwined with broad, supple tannins. 15.4% alc warms the farewell. 17 mths equal Fr/Am, all new. NE.

★★★★☆ **Redhill Pinotage** From 40+ yr old bushvine vyd 'Rooibult'. Standout **04** demonstrates just how stately the variety can be when handled carefully. Elegance personified, restrained blackberry/mulberry bouquet; fine, well-knit tannins. Layered, intense & persistent; impressive now, has structure & fruit concentration to improve over many yrs. ±18 mths new oak, mainly Fr. *Wine* ★★★★ for this & show-stopping **03**, VDG, IWSC gold, SAA, Winemakers' Choice, Pinotage Top 10.

★★★★ **Chardonnay Reserve** new to the guide (but **03** SAA). Highly unusually, closed with a crown cap to keep it as 'fresh & lively as the day it was bottled'. You have to appreciate the style to enjoy opulent & silky **04**. Concentrated lime, lemon, tangerine notes mesh with nut, spice & pear; long, flavoursome farewell, zesty acidity lifts, refreshes. Fermented/matured 14 mths new Fr oak. Moderate 13.3% alc.

★★★★ **CWG Auction Reserve Valentine Viognier** Name inspired by pressing date — 14 February. Maiden **04**, pre-bottling last ed, lush peachy fruit, acacia flower fragrance, voluptuous textured richness aided by 7g/ℓ sugar, yet finishes fresh. Native yeasts; yr Fr barrels. WO Coastal.

★★★★ **Chenin Avec Chêne** Impressive example of judiciously oaked chenin retaining its personality. **05** confirms high standard set by debut **04** (sample last ed). Latest version is round (6g/ℓ sugar) but lifted by variety's mouth-juicing acidity, gorgeous wet-thatch, quince & elderflower notes, to which seamless oaking adds spice & cream. NE. **04** *Wine* ★★★★. Yr Fr barrels, half new.

★★★★ **Gewürztraminer** ✓ Special Late Harvest (not labelled as such) rings a welcome change from the usual bdx, burgundy & loire whites. Delicate & poised **06** a gorgeous perfumery of roses & limes; fresh, long, aromatic flavours; simply delicious. Light ±11% alc. Regular WOM, *Wine* 'best value' selection. NE.

★★★★ **Cuvée Royale** Prestige MCC sparkling made only in exceptional yrs. **96** (50/50 chard/pinot) proved ageability of good bubbly. **99** (★★★★★) mainly unwooded chard (91%), rich & enticing; sugar-dusted croissants on nose, on taste cinnamon-spiced apple compôte, luxurious texture from 7 yrs lees-ageing. Fine, racy beads add to sense of occasion.

★★★★ **Kaapse Vonkel** ✓ SA's first bottle-fermented bubbly, over 30 yrs back. Chard/pinot (55/42), splash rare pinot meunier; small oaked portion adds complexity. **05** in same classy mould as predecessors: chalky lemon-drop, apple pie & biscuit, honeyed touch; vibrant mousse & zesty acidity, appley farewell. Also in 1.5ℓ, 3ℓ, 9ℓ. NE.

★★★★ **Encore** ✓ Sec-style MCC, varieties as above in similar configuration but no oak. **00** was first; current **98** debuts out of vintage sequence, showing some highly attractive bottle maturity: honey-brushed brioche & candy apple characters; intense citrus acidity & explosive mousse deliver tighter, drier finish than 17g/ℓ sugar suggests.

★★★★☆ **Vin de Liza** Elegantly presented NLH honouring family matriarch. 62% semillon, 38% sauvignon in **05**, fiery Tiger's Eye hues; dried peach, apricot & almond kernel tussle for dominance in arresting tangy bouquet; richness, subtle spice imparted by well judged 10 mths oak; harmonious & velvet-textured; sweeter at 95g/ℓ sugar than pvs but still irresistible. NE.

Cabernet Sauvignon ★★★★ **03** vibrant cassis, black berry fruit, sweet vanilla/coconut oak tones, tannins fine & accessible; drink now & over ±5 yrs. 22 mths mainly Fr oak, some Am. **Pinotage** ★★★★ Resolutely unwooded version a steady performer. Last tasted **03** had rhubarb & brambleberry typicity, arresting fruit-dominant body, long tasty finish, & 14. 9% alc. **Shiraz** ★★★★ Friendly tannins, sweet vanilla richness from Am oak on fruit-plush **03** make it accessible, as does less daunting 14.3% alc (pvs 15.1%). 22 mths Fr/Am oak, some new. **Adelberg** ★★★ Exported as 'Cabernet Sauvignon-Merlot'. **04** tempts with plush berry, plum & forest floor fruit, deft touch spicy oak. Bottled under screwcap for spontaneous enjoyment. **Cabernet Sauvignon-Shiraz** ★★★ Export only. **05** underlying mulberry/red-berry fruit battles gamely with austere tannins. Lightly oaked, not for keeping. **Chardonnay** ★★★☆ Reliably satisfying barrel fermented/matured version (10 mths). Peach/citrus & buttered toast on **05**; rounded & balanced; concludes with enough acidic verve to pair with richer food. NE, as are next trio: **Chenin Blanc** ★★★ Dependably tasty rendition. **06** more reticent than pvs but well integrated, no sharp edges, appeal 'sweetened' by 7.5g/ℓ sugar. **05** Winemakers Choice; relatively senior **02** VDG in 2005. **Sauvignon Blanc** ★★★ **06** maintains house's generous easy-drinking style; tropical melange with green fig/summer meadow notes, zesty flavours just right for lunchtime food pairing. **Vin Fumé** ★★★ One of SA's first wooded sauvignons, still going strong. **05** admirably vinous with pungent herb/grass notes gently stroked by oak-spice. Incl soupçon semillon. **Adelblanc** ★★★ Exported as 'Sauvignon Blanc-Semillon'. **05** fresh & tropical; zesty, with some pithy cheek. If this was a girl, she'd ask you to dance. **Mustique** ★★☆ Comfortingly sweet end-of-a-hard-day sipper; **05** blend changes to colombard, riesling, muscat d'Ottonel; floral & soft, undemanding (±10g/ℓ sugar, ±12% alc). **Franciskaner** ★★★ Aromatic summer quaffer from chenin, morio muscat & colombard. **05**'s chenin very ripe, touch botrytised. Floral, spicy & semi-sweet, with light alc (37g/ℓ RS, 10.8%). **Brut Rosé** ★★★☆ Charming MCC sparkler from pinotage (88%), pinot returns to guide after extended hiatus. Creamy raspberry aromas meet with 'wake-up' acidity on palate, ensuring you're ready for the next sip. Light, dry, slips down easily (11.7% alc, 5.5g/ℓ sugar). — *CvZ*

Simonsvlei International 🍴🍷🐄🎣🏃♿

Paarl • Est/1stB 1947 • Tasting & sales: Mon-Fri 8-5 Sat 8.30-4.30 Sun 11-3 • Fee R15 for 5 tastings • Closed Easter Fri & Dec 25 • Tours by appt • Amenities & attractions see intro • Owners 65 shareholders • Cellarmaster Francois van Zyl (2000) • Winemaker Rolanie Lotz (2002) • Viticulturist Jannie Underhay (2002) • 1 200 ha (cab, shiraz, chard, chenin) • 10 000 tons 220 000 cs own labels + 300 000 cs for customers • 50% red 50% white • PO Box 584 Suider-Paarl 7624 • info@simonsvlei.co.za • www.simonsvlei.co.za • T 021·863·3040 • F 021·863·1240

Though it turns 60 this year, this winery beside the busy N1 and R101 roads keeps pace with the latest trends, offering visitors a more engaging cellar-door experience via the R101 Restaurant, function and conference facilities, gift and farm produce shop, and play area for children. Another attraction is their N1 Paragon Theatre where popular SA entertainers regularly perform (closed during harvest when space is at a premium). Consumer-friendly wines have made Simonsvlei a Woolworths Supplier of the Year and one of the fastest-growing wine brands in the country.

Hercules Paragon range

Cabernet Sauvignon ★★★☆ **03** classic cassis with dark choc & mint extras; variety's tannins provide solid backbone for ripe flavours. 12-13 mths on oak; ditto... **Shiraz** ★★★ **03** combines early/flavourful drinkability with good varietal character & enough structure for few yrs maturation. **04** Paarl Shiraz Challenge 2006 winner. **Sauvignon Blanc** ★★★☆ Seldom disappoints; **05** again from Dbnvlle, with signature dusty nettle aromas, ripe fruit, crisp acidic grip. None above retasted.

Classic range

Following reds 6-9 mths on Eur oak: **Cabernet Sauvignon** ★★★ **05** better & more approachable than pvs; classic cassis/tealeaf character, gd frame of fruit & tannin; yr/3 to go. **Pinotage** ★★★ Midweight, as pvs, but **05** a tad less easy on the palate now; subtler fruit, firmer tannins — but a good match for hearty food. **Shiraz** ★★★ **04** a less robust personality than pvs, shows restraint; 'European' cherry whiffs & fine, dry, food-invoking tannins. **Cabernet Sauvignon-Merlot** ★★★☆ Seamless, sensitively extracted red; minty **04** last ed repeated successful 50/50 formula, tweaked for approachability, plus scope for few yrs cellaring. **Rosé** ★★ Uncomplicated quick-quaff. Lightish semi-sweet **05** mainly chenin, with pinotage; latter lends fresh pomegranate flavour. **Chardonnay** ★★☆ **05** similar to pvs: dusty wood whiffs (from brief oak-chipping); full, ripe, lemony character, pleasing freshness. **Premier Chenin Blanc** ★★★ Appealing, honest & well made **06**, softly dry quaffer showing pleasing varietal character & freshness. **Sauvignon Blanc**

★★★ Lightish **06** softer, fleshier than pvs; grassy suggestion & grapefruit twang in tail. **Premier Bukettraube** ★★★ Characterful & full flavoured Late Harvest style **06**; again pale but tasty, fragrant, soft, uncloying. Following pair of fortifieds **NV: Humbro Hanepoot** ★★★ Jerepiko style dessert with rich colours, fragrances; lush, fruity palate glides to tangy marmalade conclusion. **Humbro Red Jerepigo** ★★★ Winter warmer from muscadel; lovely rosy blush, unusual watermelon preserve aroma, shade too sweet for some despite fairly generous alc enlivenment (±17%).

Lifestyle range

NV unless noted, unwooded. **Cabernet Sauvignon** ★★★ **05**, like most in range, carefully made, satisfying; tannins carefully massaged to enjoy now or in a yr/2. **Merlot** ★★★ More serious & introverted **05**, shows similar ripe red fruit profile, nutty hint, as pvs, but quieter, with drier tannins. **Pinotage** ★★★ **05** dry, smoky flavours & savoury, pleasantly bitter tannins make a gd foil for Italian & similar food. **Shiraz** ★★★ **05** same Aussie-style fruit density & juiciness as pvs, plus exotic coriander whiff & warming tail, courtesy of 14.7% alc. **Simonsrood** ★★★ Big selling four-way blend fronted by cinsaut has gained some heft & gravitas since we last met: affable jammy character replaced with sterner, drier savouriness, leaning more towards food. Also in 1.5ℓ. **Charming Red** ★★ Reports of culling in pvs ed premature. Same blend as Smnsrd but fattened (if perhaps not flattered) with extra ±6g/ℓ sugar. Distinctly sweet, confected, perfect for *glühwein* or with pudding. **Blanc de Blanc** ★★ From chenin; lightish, foursquare, with hint of pear, firm acidic finish. **Extra Light** ★ Latest is low in alc (±9%), bone-dry, vinous rather than fruity — the slimmer's choice. From crouchen, hanepoot. **Simonsblanc** ★★ Balanced, light, easy-drinking off-dry chenin showing some gd varietal character (Golden Delicious apple, quince). **Stein** ★★ No-frills, moderately sweet chenin; light bodied with ripe pear tone. **Natural Sweet Rosé** new ★★ Same varieties as Classic version above but softer, fleshier, not overtly 'sweet'; with ripe cranberry tone; only 5.9% alc.

Simonay range

3 & 5ℓ casks; all **NV**, most with moderate alc (11.5-13.5%). **Classic Red** ★★ Casual-quaffing quartet led by fruity cinsaut, with spicy touches (though unwooded) & beefy 14.8% alc. **Blanc de Blanc** ★★ Chenin, colombard, crouchen, semillon mix (same blend for most of these), refreshingly clean & dry, well made. **Stein** ★★ Very soft, fruity crowd-pleaser with balanced sweetness. **Late Harvest** ★★ Latest a notch up; balanced fruit salad flavours, bright, not over-sweet. **Johannisberger** ★★ Floral-toned chenin with white muscadel & hanepoot, pleasantly sweet & light summer quaffer. All ranges WO W Cape. — *JN*

■ *Simply Red/White* see Hippo Creek
■ *Sinnya* see Robertson Wide River
■ *Six Generations* see Rietvallei

Siyabonga ♂

Wellington • Est 1998 • 1stB 1999 • Closed to public • Owners H Investments #121 (Pty) Ltd/ Graham Knox • Winemaker Koos Bosman • Viticulturist Theo Brink (2003) • 15 ha (cabs s/f, merlot, pinotage, chenin, semillon, viognier) • 3 000 cs own label • PO Box 1209 Wellington 7654 • doolhof@mweb.co.za • T 021·864·3155 • F 021·864·1744

These vineyards are a treasure chest of aged vines, now tended by a group of viticulturists and winemakers intent on returning them to vigorous growth and rich fruitfulness. New to the team is consultant viticulturist Theo Brink, whose first project is to isolate red-skinned semillon from green-, in a block indiscriminately mixed, re-establish a block of pure redskins and propagate them. Historically, the redskins — just 750 vines in all — have contributed a mere half a barrel of juice: 'We had a score of 92 from *Wine & Spirits* with only a 6% contribution from the red-skinned grapes,' explains owner Graham Knox, 'and I'd like to see what we get with more than that.'

★★★★ **Cabernet Sauvignon-Merlot** Stylish, firm composition. **03** dusky echoes to tarry tones; concentrated blackcurrant fruits under ripe-tannin wraps. Young home vyd. 15 mths Fr oak. Neither this, red below, retasted for this ed.

★★★★ **Pinotage** Classical (Fr oak led) handling of sometimes trenchant grape gets boost of added finesse in **03**: unmistakably pinotage with plummy fruit, but dusty tannin keeps the opulence at bay. Low yielding own vyd. Yr Fr barriques.

★★★★ **Severney** 60/40 chenin/semillon blend, portion of former fermented in used casks. **04** (★★★) showing age at mid-2006 review; ready to drink. — *DS*

Skilpadvlei Wines

Stellenbosch ▪ Est 2004 ▪ Wine tasting, sales & restaurant hours daily 8-6 ▪ Tasting fee R10 ▪ Country produce, gifts, facilities for children & other amenities (see intro) ▪ Tour groups ▪ Closed Dec 25/26 & Jan 1 ▪ Owner/winemaker WD Joubert ▪ Viticulturist JW Joubert (1998) ▪ 62 ha (cab, merlot, pinotage, shiraz, chard, chenin, sauvignon) ▪ 652 tons 6 000 cs own label 65% red 30% white 5% rosé ▪ Skilpadvlei, Vlottenburg 7604 ▪ info@skilpadvlei.co.za ▪ www. skilpadvlei.co.za ▪ T 021·881·3237 ▪ F 021·881·3538

The name of the game here: quality, approachability and affordability, says Willie Joubert. So it's no surprise that the grapes from this Vlottenburg family farm are vinified by Stellenbosch Hills (known for their attractive price/quality ratio), a small percentage specifically for the Skilpadvlei label. The focus is on premium varieties, predominantly red. Creature comforts offered include a restaurant serving traditional dishes (and their wines), and six self-catering guest cottages. A conference centre and a function hall (popular for weddings) complete the package.

Cabernet Sauvignon-Shiraz ★★★ Spicy blackcurrant, plum-pudding notes on **04**'s 60/40 blend. Gentle oaking (4 mths, mostly Fr), soft tannins & light, dry finish make for easy approachability now, with 14.5% alc not obtrusive. **Cabernet Sauvignon-Merlot** ★★☆ Equal blend from difficult **02** vintage shows herbal, gamey bouquet, with hints of cassis; some mouth-puckering tannins mark the dry palate. 18 mths Fr oak. **Sauvignon Blanc** ★★☆ **06** has mixed herbaceous/tropical notes, with leesy hints & crisp, limy aftertaste. Food-friendliness augmented by reasonable 12.9% alc.

Skilpaddop range

Dry Red ★★★ **05** blends 71% merlot with pinotage — native variety's sweet estery character lifting the dominant herbal notes. Oak influence definitely there, though in wood just 4 mths. **Rosé** ★★ Off-dry **06** from unwooded pinotage has mulberry notes & slight varnishy spice; sweetness helps to conceal 14% alc. WO W Cape, as is… **Dry White** ★★ Fresh, easy-drinking **06** less sweet, though just off-dry, with dominant colombard (65%) guava character, while sauvignon gives green fruit freshness to the finish. — *MF*

Slaley Estate

Stellenbosch ▪ Est 1957 ▪ 1stB 1997 ▪ Tasting & sales Mon-Sat & pub hols 10-4 ▪ Fee R20 refunded with purchase ▪ Closed Easter Fri, Dec 25/26 & Jan 1 ▪ Tours by appt ▪ Farm produce ▪ Owners Hunting family ▪ Winemaker/viticulturist — Marius Malan (Oct 2005) ▪ 70 ha (cab, merlot, pinotage, shiraz, chard, sauvignon) ▪ 350 tons 12-15 000 cs own label 90% red 9% white 1% rosé ▪ EurepGAP certified ▪ PO Box 119 Koelenhof 7605 ▪ info@slaley.co.za ▪ www. slaley.co.za ▪ T 021·865·2123 ▪ F 021·865·2798

A new winemaker has led to new ideas at this Simonsberg estate, with Marius Malan (ex-Uva Mira) replacing Shaun Turnbull (now at Stone Hill Winery in the US). Large stainless steel tanks have given way to small-batch open fermenters, which the Slaley team expect will help boost wine quality on the range of classical wines and provide more scope for 'adventurous experimentation'. A three-year plan to develop a section of the estate without compromising vineyards or olive groves came to fruition with the launch of Slaley Agricultural Estate, comprising nine own-title residences.

Hunting Family range

★★★★ **Merlot** After big, softly ripe **02**, **03** (★★★★) has lower alc (13.7% vs pvs 14.8); dark choc, black cherry welcome; elegant blackcurrant fruit, firm tannins. Highish acid gives lean touch to fruit, but still some elegance. 18 mths new Fr oak. No pre-2006 wines in this range tasted this yr.

★★★★ **Pinotage** From 50 yr old vyd. **03** had supple ripe tannins, sweet berry/plum flavours, better fruit-acid balance than cellarmates. Gorgeous oak integration (yr Fr/Am, 50% new). Very manageable 12.8% alc (14.6% in **02**). Cellar 5-7 yrs.

★★★★ **Shiraz** Youthful **03** last ed showed components for maturing 3-7 yrs. Subtle spice to meaty fruit; muscular & trim, with fine-textured dry tannins on long, resonating finish. 18 mths Fr/Am oak, 50% new.

Cabernet Sauvignon-Merlot ★★★☆ **03** 80/20 blend with light texture & flavour — & modest 12.3% alc; tart, dry fruit, dry tannins, but good oak integration. Long finish with tang of acid. **Chardonnay** ★★★☆ Vanilla backdrop to juicy yellow peach in **05** (sample). Luscious, generous fruit, firm acid & oaking (11 mths used Fr). **Chardonnay Noble Late Harvest** new **06** (barrel sample) from vine-dried grapes, rich & unctuous, whiff lemon marmalade, 98g/ℓ sugar balanced by firm acidity. Mid-2006 seems to be mopping up new oak with ease. Possible ★★★★.

Broken Stone range

Shiraz ★★★☆ **04** notch up on pvs: robust & savoury, well balanced. Quite muscular, with baked plum, smoked beef aromas/flavours, tangy acid, dry finish. Yr Fr/Am oak, now 25% new. **Cabernet Sauvignon** ★★★ Mint & cool cedar intro to honest, dark-fruited maiden **03**; dry tannins, tart acidity, light body. Matured in oak. This & next 2 reds not retasted. **Cabernet Sauvignon-Shiraz** ★★★☆ **03** with 10% pinotage infusing attractive sweet plum character. Supple tannins, whiff vanilla; smooth juicy fruit; shows charm, grace. **Pinotage** ★★★ **03** savoury yeast-extract whiffs, savoury & dry, with firm tannins. **Sauvignon Blanc** ★★★ Sample **06** hints at green fig & grass, with pleasing fruitiness — & moderate 12.5% alc. Gd varietal character.

Shatot range

These all tasted last yr. **Lindsay's Whimsy** ★★☆ Thoroughly accessible **03** blend pinotage/cab, shows generosity of home variety; plump & pleasing, some warm plummy notes, nicely dry; ideal for a braai. **Planque** ★★ No-frills, everyday **03** blend cab/pinotage has modest fruit, dusty tannins; very dry. **Plinque** ★★★ Blue-ish pink from pinotage; **04** (sample tasted) full bodied yet fresh & lively. — *IvH*

Slanghoek Winery

Slanghoek (see Worcester map) · Est 1951 · Tasting & sales Mon-Fri 8-12.30; 1.30-5 Sat 10-1 · Closed pub hols · Picnic baskets by appt or BYO · Tours 11 & 3 by appt · Tour groups · Audio-visual presentation · Gifts · Conferencing · Walks · Conservation area · Owners 25 members · Cellarmaster Pieter Carstens (Aug 2002) · Senior winemaker Nicolaas Rust, with Nico Grundling, Johan Jordaan & Jacques de Goede (Oct 2003/Dec 2002/Nov 2003/Dec 2001) · Viticulturist Hennie Visser · 1 830 ha (17 varieties, r/w) · 40 000 cs own label + 14m litres bulk 20% red 60% white 10% rosé 10% fortified · Export brand: Zonneweelde · PO Box 75 Rawsonville 6845 · info@slanghoek.co.za · www.slanghoek.co.za · T 023·344·3026/7/8 · F 023·344·3157

Volumes were up in 2006, says Nicolaas Rust, 'and quality too'. A big plus was being able to swing into operation with a new 1000-barrel maturation cellar; the older underground cellar is now being used for the winery's Private Selection range. The Vinays have been given a tweak or two — 'a brighter colour, a longer label that fits the bottle better' — with the younger consumer in mind; new to market is a Crême de Chenin, a natural sweet wine. There's a new face to the 'viticulturist' label — Hennie Visser, ex Ashton, has replaced Francois Nel.

Cabernet Sauvignon ☺ ★★★ Refined cassis & damp earth bouquet & firm tannins take **04** up a quality level. Integrated 13.5% alc, ±14 mths 2nd fill Fr oak. **Special Late Harvest** ☺ ★★★ From muscat d'A; always delivers gd sugar-acid tension for effortless lightish sipping. **06** potpourri of rose, pineapple & nectarine.

Merlot ★★ **05** less brawny than pvs (14%), leafier, not for keeping. Less new oak, too: only 20%, Fr, yr. *Wine* 'Best Value' award. **Pinotage** ★★★ Distinctive acetone hints, strawberry fruit on **04**, appealingly typical of variety; savoury, well judged oak tannins (14 mths Fr wood, 30% new), warming 14% alc. **Shiraz** ★★★ Smoky **04** has hints nutmeg, dry leaves & meat, gripping tannins. Drink with food within yr. Following **NV** duo not retasted: **Vinay Red** ★★ Fruity & drinkable four-way blend, red berry flavours/aromas, brush of oak. **Vinay Rosé** ★★ From muscadel; delicate rosepetal waft, sweetish, but fresh acidic lift. All the Vinays in 1 000ml bottles. **Chardonnay** ★★★ 40% oak fermented in **05**, last ed showed as engaging dusty backing to zesty fruit; big alc (14.3%) encourages sipping, not swigging. **Chenin Blanc** ★★ Improved **06** almost back to super-quaffing style with tropical fruit tone, bright acidity. **Sauvignon Blanc** ★ **06** elusive aromas & flavours; dry & crisp but lacking fruity verve. **Semillon** ★★ **05** showing signs of oxidation in deep yellow hue, intense lanolin nose; 'oily' palate needs food. Following two sparklers carbonated, **NV**. **Cuvée Brut** For export only, untasted. **Vin Doux** ★★★ From hanepoot; reviewed last ed had energetic mousse, delicate scents, was not too sweet. **Vinay White** ★★ Supple, lightish off-dry **NV** quaffing blend, not tasted for few yrs now. **Crème de Chenin** new ★★★ Natural Sweet dessert from botrytised 90% chenin with dollop hanepoot; **05** classic noble rot characteristics of dried apricots & honey. Finishes sweeter than 97g/ℓ sugar suggests; not as vibrant as pvs. 500ml. **Noble Late Harvest** ★★★ Nicely proportioned **04** flourishes bright pineapple tones, with nutty & vanilla hints from 6 mths Fr oak. Mainly chenin, dollop hanepoot; roughly 7g/ℓ acid, 140g/ℓ sugar, 12% alc. 375ml. **Red Jerepiko** ★★★ Decidedly sweet fortified dessert from pinotage; soft, grapey **04** not retasted. **Sweet Hanepoot** ★★★ **05** pleasing marriage of poised acidity, grapey sweetness; hearty flavours supporting 16.5% alc. **Red Muscadel** ★★★ **05** more muscat character than pvs, well adjusted acidity & spirit for fleet-footed effect. *Wine* 'Value' award. Not retasted, nor was... **Cape Ruby** ★★★ **04** mainly touriga, smidgen malbec; full, rich red berry & plum flavour, earthy undertone. Traditional low 17.6% alc; 6 mths oak. **Camerca**, **Riesling-Semillon** discontinued. — *CT*

Slowine 🍷 new

Overberg ▪ Est 2005 ▪ 1stB 1997 ▪ Tasting & sales at Villiersdorp Cellar (see entry) ▪ Winemaker WS Visagie ▪ PO Box 48 Grabouw 7160 ▪ info@slowine.co.za ▪ www.cluver.com ▪ T 021·844·0605 ▪ F 021·844·0150

This range of 'happily affordable' and very drinkable wines is a joint venture between producers around the Groenland Mountain (where the first Wine & Biodiversity Route has been proclaimed). The producers — Paul Cluver, Beaumont, Luddite and Villiersdorp Cellar — all wish to celebrate a well lived life. We'll down tools and raise a glass to that!

Cabernet Sauvignon ★★★ Lightly structured **04** has decent varietal character (cedar, blackcurrant), but fruit a little fugitive. Sweetness more apparent than below, but 14.5% alc less so. Lightly wooded, like... **Merlot** ★★★ Very ripe & juicy **04**, with mocha, red berries. Gently easy, but some soft tannins & alc power alongside fruity geniality. **Rosé** ★★★ From pinot, **06** straightforward lunchtime pleasantness, roundness & touch sweetness from sugar, but balancing acidity, & even a little tannic grip. **Chenin Blanc-Sauvignon Blanc** ★★★ Charming enough **05**, with dominant sauvignon notes — grass, gooseberry, passionfruit, & chenin broadness tempering green bite; fresh 12.5% alc. — *TJ*

■ **Smook Wines** *see* Anthony Smook
■ **Soek die Geluk** *see* Goedverwacht

SoetKaroo

Prince Albert • Est 2000 • 1stB 2004 • Visits Mon-Sat 8-6 • Closed Easter Sun, Dec 25 & Jan 1 •
Self-catering cottage • Owners Herman & Susan Perold • Vini consultant Flip Smith • Viticultur-
ist Herman Perold • 0.6 ha (petit v, red muscat d'A, red muscat de F, touriga) • 3.4 tons 340 cs
(375/750ml) 100% fortified • 56 Church Str Prince Albert 6930 • perold@netactive.co.za •
www.soetkaroo.co.za • T 023·541·1768

Choosing a favourite from the first three vintages of this Prince Albert boutique winery's
critically hailed Red Muscat d'Alexandrie is like comparing three sisters: 'You can never
say which is better because you never experience them at the same age at the same
time,' chuckles co-owner Susan Perold. At press time the as yet unbottled 06 was 'blushing softly' but promised to fill out as it matured. 'Such is the nature of wine,' Susan P phi-
losophises, 'it keeps changing.' Flip Smith, cellarmaster at Kango Winery, is the
winemaker.

Red Muscat d'Alexandrie ★★★★ **05** tasted, but inadvertently not noted, as work-in-
progress last ed. Has since benefited from acid adjustment. Charms with incense & Turkish Delight perfumes, sappy dried-currant flavours. Incl dollops red muscat de F & touriga,
separately vinified/fortified. In 'piquant' 375ml bottles & individually numbered French-
made glass carafes. — *IvH*

Solms-Delta

Franschhoek • Est 1690 • 1stB 2004 • Visits daily 9-5 • Closed Dec 25 & Jan 1 • Picnics & selec-
tion of cheeses during opening hours • Tour groups • Guest houses • Gifts • Walks • Cultural
museum & archaeological sites • Owner 'Family trust' • Winemaker Hilko Hegewisch (Mar
2003) • Viti adviser Paul Wallace (Apr 2002) • 12 ha (mourvèdre, shiraz, viognier) • 5 000 cs •
43% red 43% white 14% rosé • PO Box 123 Groot Drakenstein 7680 • info@solms-delta.co.za
• www.solms-delta.com • T 021·874·3937 • F 021·874·1852

Three adjoining farms — the Solms family's Delta, the Astors' Lubeck, and Deltameer, which
belongs to a trust representing previously disadvantaged employees — are being integrated
to create a one-third empowerment-owned spread with 40ha under vines. This formalises
the multiple ties which have connected these properties since the late 1600s. Owner and internationally reputed neuro-specialist Mark Solms links the family farm ever more firmly to
the past: the early 20th-century dam in the forest has been restored and various historical
buildings soon will be; the 316-year-old English oak in front of the manor house has been declared a National Champion Tree, and the Museum van de Caab is expanding to include a
local heritage research centre.

Solms-Wijn de Caab range

★★★★ **Hiervandaan** Southern rhône style red led by shiraz, with mourvèdre, grenache,
carignan, viognier; portion desiccated on the vine (see Photo Gallery section). **05** satisfies with its medium body, engaging personality. Tad more emphatic spice, minerals
than debut **04** but still harmonious. Oak (13 mths mainly new Fr) a pleasing backdrop.
Swtland/Cdrberg/Paarl/home vyds.

★★★★ **Lekkerwijn** One of the best & most characterful dry Cape rosés. Finely tuned **05** echoes **04**'s pink/gold glints, touch more spiced apricot/peach enticement; presence
without showiness; firm, dry & exceptionally long. Viognier, mourvèdre, grenache fer-
mented/rounded in used Fr barrels, 10 mths; malo. Widely sourced fruit.

★★★★ **Amalie** Authoritative, sleek & supple dry white from viognier, seamlessly intertwined
with 19% desiccated grenache blanc; **05** realises promise suggested in last yr's sample. Remarkably refined; intriguing floral, mineral, earthy hints; fascinating ginger
twist. Delicious, with few yrs potential. 6 mths 100% new Fr oak. Elegant & classic, as
is whole range.

Solms-Hegewisch range   `new`

★★★★ **Africana** Ignore bland-sounding 'Shiraz' on label: amarone-inspired contents much
more exciting & flavoursome. **05**, from 100% desiccated berries (ex-Kuils Rvr), remarkable feat of balance; brilliant ruby clarity, subtle perfumes of wild strawberry &

spice. Invisible new Fr oak (16 mths). Extraordinary analysis (16% alc, 8.5g/ℓ sugar, 6. 9g/ℓ acid) part of wine's engaging personality.

Koloni Dry, oaked blend elegantly aromatic muscats d'A & F, riesling; viscous but with trademark light tread, purity. **06** sample, unrated. All above WO W Cape. — *AL*

Somerbosch Wines ♙♒♓♘♿♿

Stellenbosch (see Helderberg map) ▪ Est 1950 ▪ 1stB 1995 ▪ Tasting & sales Mon-Sat 9-5 Sun 10-3 in season, otherwise Mon-Fri 9-5 Sat/Sun 10-3 ▪ Fee R10 refundable with purchase of any 6 btls ▪ Closed Easter Fri, Dec 25/26 & Jan 1 ▪ Tours by appt ▪ 'Die Fonteine' Bistro daily 10-3 ▪ Facilities for children ▪ Owners Roux family ▪ Winemakers/viticulturists Marius, Japie & Wrensch Roux (1987/1995/2005) ▪ 80 ha (cab, merlot, pinotage, shiraz, cinsaut, chard, chenin, sauvignon, semillon) ▪ 70% red 30% white ▪ PO Box 12181 Die Boord 7613 ▪ enquiries@ somerbosch.co.za ▪ www.somerbosch.co.za ▪ T 021·855·3615 ▪ F 021·855·4457

A trio of winemakers and viticulturists, the brothers Roux are determined that their winery will live up to the 'summer' implied in its name: the season's celebrated in February with a harvest festival, so successful first time round in 2006 that it's to become an annual event; strawberries are on sale from spring through to midsummer; and summer picnic baskets are now available (orders, please!). Yet another reason to visit at whim: it's been decided to open the bistro every day.

Kylix ★★★★ Serious & harmonious **02**, mainly cab lifted by 13% shiraz & by clever oaking (1st fill Fr, 18 mths); last ed showed a classy mineral character, ripe, elegant tannin, structure to reward few yrs cellaring. **Cabernet Sauvignon ★★★ 04** notch up on pvs: smoother, fruitier, tannins well meshed with fruit. Similar oak regimen (Fr/Am, 2nd-4th fill, yr) gives support for 2/3 yrs ageing. **Merlot ★★★** These usually firmly built, needing yr/2 to soften; last ed **03** noted as having less fruity richness than pvs, leaner, drier, more food-styled. **Shiraz ★★★ 03** balanced easy-drinker still selling; smoky/meaty whiffs, oak (as for Cab) a pleasant background to soft berries. **Chardonnay ★★★ 05** unwooded; last yr had lemon zest on nose; crisp winey (rather than varietal) flavours, clean fresh send-off. **Chenin Blanc ★★** Food-styled this vintage, with salivating sherbetty acidity, compact fruit & hint of pineapple on **06**. **Sauvignon Blanc ★★★★ ✓ 06**, just bottled, continues upward trend with delicious mouthful of 'green' fruit (nettles & grass), plus riper figs & tropical fruit; fresh, dry, & well priced. **Pinotage**, **Chenin Blanc Barrel Fermented** & **Late Bottled Vintage Port** sold out.

Poker Hill range

Replaces 'Seugnet' range. **Shiraz-Merlot ★★ 04** fruit driven equal blend offering soft drinkability, ripe berry flavours, well disguised spicy tannins. Portion barrelled. **Semillon-Chenin Blanc ★★★** Crisp, pleasantly unpretentious **05**, honey hint to sweet straw toned fruit; refreshing everyday white. — *CT*

■ **Somerlust** see Viljoensdrift
■ **Sonop Organic** see African Terroir
■ **Soulo** see Overhex
■ **South African Premium Wines** see Cape Coastal Vintners

Southern Cape Vineyards ♙♒♓

Little Karoo ▪ Barrydale cellar: Est 1940 ▪ 1stB 1976 ▪ Tasting & sales Mon-Fri 8-5 Sat & pub hols 9-3 ▪ Closed Easter Fri-Mon, Dec 25 & Jan 1 ▪ Book ahead for tours ▪ BYO picnic ▪ Heritage garden ▪ Owners 25 members ▪ Winemaker Riaan Marais, with Ferdie Smit (Jan 1999/May 1985) ▪ Viti consultant Willem Botha (2000) ▪ 152 ha (cab, merlot, ruby cab, shiraz, chard, colombard, sauvignon) ▪ 2 000 tons 50% red 35% white 5% other ▪ Range for customer: Decent Red ▪ PO Box 59 Barrydale 6750 ▪ sales@scv.co.za ▪ www.scv.co.za ▪ T 028·572·1012 ▪ F 028·572·1541

Ladismith cellar: Est 1939 ▪ 1stB 1988 ▪ Tasting & sales Mon-Fri 8-5 ▪ Closed all pub hols except Easter Sat ▪ BYO picnic ▪ Tours by appt ▪ Conferencing ▪ Owners 75 members ▪ Winemaker Emile Schoch (2005) ▪ Viti consultant Johannes Mellet (Aug 2006) ▪ 600 ha (ruby cab, chard) ▪ *8 000 tons 4 200 cs own label + 3.2m litres bulk* ▪ *PO Box 56 Ladismith 6655* ▪ *info@scv.co.za* ▪ *www.scv.co.za* ▪ **T** *028·551·1042* ▪ *F 028·551·1930*

Though they fall under the corporate and management umbrella of Southern Cape Vineyards, Barrydale and Ladismith cellars retain their respective identities, wine brands — and charms — as stops along the visitor friendly Route 62 (see www.route62.co.za). Their first viognier has appeared (under the Towerkop label, unready at press time), the various ranges continue to target pocket pleasing prices, and the potstill brandies, of which Barrydale is the country's largest independent producer, continue to accumulate awards and fans.

Barrydale range

Decent Red ☺ ★★★ Ripe-fruited unoaked blend ruby cab, merlot, pinotage; choc, plums & mulberries, friendly tannins. **Decent White** ☺ ★★★ Cheerful everyday tipple with tropical notes, zippy acidity, satisfying mouthfeel. From chenin, chard, gewürz. Both **NV**, WO W Cape, as is following range.

Misty Point range

None retasted this ed. **Pinotage** ★★★ Gently grippy, soft fruited **02** an unchallenging drink-me-quick. **Red** ★★★ **02** very gulpable (a few yrs back…) union of ruby cab & merlot. **White** ★★ Pleasant semi-dry **03** from chenin, chard, gewürz.

Seven Falls range

Chardonnay-Sauvignon Blanc, **Shiraz-Cabernet Sauvignon** untasted. Range to be discontinued when current stocks sell out.

Towerkop range

Reds unoaked; all W Cape origin. **Pinotage** ★★★ Last tried was Regional Young Wine Show winner **03**. **Ruby Cabernet** ★★ Lively & juicy, very quaffable **05** (modest 12.2% alc helps), mulberry & thatch tones, long fruity finish. **Shiraz** new ★★★ Easy-drinking plum- & floral-tinged version. **05** midweight (13% alc) & well flavoured, with supple tannin. **Rosé** ★ Semi-sweet **NV** from pinotage, chard. Honeyed, shy, shd be drunk soon. **Chardonnay-Sauvignon Blanc** new ★★ Not-for-keeping **05** shows some honeyed bottle-age, along with notes of tropical fruit & lime; fair acidity. None of following retasted: **Blanc de Blanc** ★★ Uncomplicated **04** dry white from chard, sauvignon, with notably light alc (±11%). **Stein** ★★ **NV** supple, lightish summer tipple with soft acidity; dry for this style. **Amalienstein Muscadel** ★★★★ Powerfully scented **02** red fortified dessert with flavours of tangerine liqueur. **Towersoet** ★★★★ Fortified hanepoot, literally 'Magic Sweet', which it is. When last tasted **03** had enchanting muscat & Oriental market smells & fresh acidity.

Tradouw range

Following trio not retasted: **Cabernet Sauvignon** ★★★ Satisfying **02** firm, sweet-fruited; blackberries & minty whiffs; judicious wooding (new/2nd fill barrels). **Merlot** ★★★★ **03** was definite step up with layered rich black cherry fruit, gd body & almost opulent flavours. **Pinot Noir** ★★★ **03** less ripe than pvs; mid-2005 showed soft raspberry & cherry tones, friendly tannins, restrained alc. **Shiraz** ★★ **04** shows similar soft spicy profile of pvs; round & ripe; pleasant berry fruit, low tannins. **Chardonnay** ★★★ **04** half-notch up; still delicate & restrained but has greater fruit concentration & more poised acidity than pvs. **Sauvignon Blanc** ★★★ Zesty **06** filled with guava & pineapple fruit, dollop sugar for mouthfeel, touch of citrus for flair. Jolly gd drinking. — *DH*

■ *Southern Lights* see Bonnievale Wine Cellar

Southern Right   ◔♀🦪

Hemel-en-Aarde Valley (see Walker Bay map) ▪ *Est 1994* ▪ *1stB 1995* ▪ *Tasting & sales Mon 9-5 Sat 9-1* ▪ *Closed Easter Fri/Sun, Dec 25/26 & Jan 1* ▪ *BYO picnic by appt* ▪ *Tours by appt* ▪ *Owners Mark Willcox, Mikki Xayiya & Anthony Hamilton Russell* ▪ *Winemaker Hannes Storm* ▪ *Viticulturist Johan Montgomery* ▪ *21 ha (pinotage, sauvignon)* ▪ *225 tons 17 000 cs 40% red 60% white* ▪ *PO Box 158 Hermanus 7200* ▪ *hrv@hermanus.co.za* ▪ **T** *028·312·3595* ▪ *F 028·312·1797*

Not only is Anthony Hamilton Russell 'redefining pinotage' here; he's redefining Southern Right itself by establishing a new home for it. Concerned (from a viticultural and conservation aspect) that 448-ha Patryskloof farm on Hamilton Russell Vineyards' western border would be sub-divided and over-developed, he brokered a purchasing deal with friend Mark Willcox and equity partner Mikki Xayiya. Plans include 50ha of vines on a virgin northeast slope; a 350-ton cellar by 2008 (preceded by a tasting room); and a pressing facility for extra-virgin olive oil from 56ha of existing trees. Until established, Southern Right will still source fruit from Walker Bay, including Hamilton Russell's other farm, renamed Ashbourne (see separate entry), on HRV's eastern boundary.

★★★★☆ **Pinotage** As with **04**, immediate, forthcoming varietal character on **05** (★★★★); lots of ripe, sweet fruit on fresh palate, but not jammy, & well restrained by substantial, rather dry tannins. 55% new Fr oak. Shd develop over 5+ yrs.

★★★★ **Sauvignon Blanc 06** exuberantly billowing passionfruit aromas, with pungent greenpepper edge to full flavour, plus mineral hint. Big, luscious acidity, slight tannic edge. These both WO W Bay. — *TJ*

Southern Sky Wines ♀

*Paarl ▪ Est 2002 ▪ Tasting & sales at I Love Wine (see entry) ▪ Owner Andrew Milne ▪ 10 000 cs ▪ 80% red 20% white ▪ 40A Main Street Paarl 7646 ▪ sales@southernskywines.com ▪ www. southernskywines.com ▪ **T** 021·871·1437/082·876·8878 ▪ F 021·863·0444*

Andrew Milne's export eye has been firmly fixed on SE Asia but Africa is coming into focus: last year, the process of getting NAFDAC registration for Nigeria was underway. Still sourcing select parcels of bulk wines for certain customers, he's expanded his bottling services for clients' own labels. Last year was a happy one for Andrew M and his new fiancée, Elizma Hanekom, who handles tasting and sales at Ridgeback Wines; this year promises even more joy, with a winelands wedding in the offing.

Tara Hill range

Cabernet Sauvignon ★★★☆ Suave dinner companion, **03** last ed showed notes of sandalwood & cedar; slight nutty/leafy notes to succulent plum flavours. 16–18 mths Fr oak. **Sauvignon Blanc** sells out before we get to taste it.

Marimba range

Cabernet Sauvignon ★★★☆ ✓ Delicious & quite serious **03**'s sweet-fruited bouquet & rich palate supported by forest floor & tobacco notes, subtle oak nuances. **Pinotage** ★★★☆ ✓ Has interesting combo banana, cherry & blackberry on nose, plus woodsmoke on **03**, savoury fruit flavours & rounded tannins for easy but satisfying drinkability. **Shiraz** ★★★☆ ✓ **03** intricate toast, anise, choc-mocha array, all in addition to sweet fruit. Palate a little sweet but finishes satisfactorily dry. Super now, potential to develop few yrs. Above trio **new**. **Sauvignon Blanc** ★★ **05** tasted last ed; tropical aperitif with teasing flint & pepper notes. Following blends discontinued: **Merlot-Cabernet Sauvignon**, **Shiraz-Merlot**, **Chenin Blanc-Colombard**, **Sauvignon Blanc-Semillon**.

Ready Steady range

Both **NV**s for enjoying in youth. **Cape Red** ☺ ★★★ Anytime/anywhere rouge, with varietal character beside the point; plenty of spiced flavour, with red berries, plums, even a floral hint, plus a savoury touch. **Cape White** ☺ ★★★ Lively & attractive quaffer from chenin, oodles of fruit-salad aromas/flavours, & an energetic finish. All above widely sourced, various WOs. — *DH*

South Hill Vineyards ♀ 🍷 🏨 ⚘ new

Elgin ▪ Est 2001 ▪ 1stB 2006 ▪ Visits by appt ▪ Displays of original artworks ▪ Guest house & function venue for conferences & weddings ▪ BYO picnic ▪ Conservation area ▪ Owner South Hill Vineyards (Pty) Ltd ▪ Winemaker Sean Skibbe (Jun 2005) ▪ Viti consultant Andrew Teubes

(Mar 2006) ▪ *25 ha (cab, shiraz, chard, sauvignon, semillon)* ▪ *37 tons 800 cs 50% red 50% white* ▪ *PO Box 120 Elgin 7180* ▪ *info@southhill.co.za* ▪ *www.southhill.co.za* ▪ *T 021·844·0888* ▪ *F 021·844·0959*

Since its purchase in 2001 (a decision fuelled more by the love of wine than sound business principles, the owners happily admit), this neglected apple and pear farm has been planted mostly with sauvignon, as one would expect in Elgin, but with red varieties also getting a look in. 'Most noble varieties benefit from cooler conditions in order to achieve ripe flavours at respectable alcohol levels,' explains manager/winemaker Sean Skibbe, who intends catering for consumers 'tiring of fighting their way through alcohol and wood'.

★★★★ **Sauvignon Blanc** Promising debut from young (3 yrs) but low-yielding vines on windswept southerly slope. **04** intense greenpepper & fig bouquet with sweaty suggestion, generous passionfruit & ruby grapefruit flavours; pithy grip (2 mths on lees), back-palate weight heightened by small barrelled portion (1st fill Fr, 2½ mths). Bodes well for future as vines mature. — *CvZ*

■ *South Point* see Origin Wine
■ *Soweto* see Crossroads Wines

Spar SA

Est 1963 ▪ *PO Box 1589 Pinetown 3600* ▪ *ray.edwards@spar.co.za; livingworld@mweb.co.za* ▪ *T 031·719·1900/1844* or *012·998·4737* ▪ *F 031·719·1991* or *012·998·4738*

This group (the world's biggest in the supermarket category) casts its capacious net wide, and its local wine operation is no exception, tapping myriad vineyards and wineries around the winelands. Much emphasis is placed on blends, says wine consultant Tinus van Niekerk. 'Consumers globally are going for blends in a big way, they're by far our best sellers, and we as a team have an affinity for them because they allow for more complexity and, so, more enjoyment.' In this vein a 'pinnacle' blend is to make its debut — a bordeaux-style red made at Spier from vineyards managed by that winery. The ultimate goal, TvN reveals, is an 'icon' blend. The group's private-label wines, Country Cellars and Carnival, are listed separately.

■ *Spencer Bay* see WestCorp

Spice Route Wine Company ♀

Swartland ▪ *Est/1stB 1998* ▪ *Tasting & sales at Fairview (see entry)* ▪ *Owner Charles Back* ▪ *Winemaker Charl du Plessis (Dec 2001)* ▪ *Farm manager Freddie Truter (Dec 2004)* ▪ *Viti adviser Andrew Teubes* ▪ *107 ha (shiraz, mourvèdre)* ▪ *700 tons ±12 000 cs 60% red 40% white* ▪ *PO Box 645 Malmesbury 7299* ▪ *spiceroute@iafrica.com* ▪ *T 021·863·2450 (office); 022·485·7139 (cellar)* ▪ *F 021·485·7169*

Much happening at this always-in-ferment cellar in 2006: the first time all 107ha of vineyard were in production (700 tons handled in a 500-ton winery — luckily, expansions will see capacity increased to 1 000 tons); the first intake of fruit (mainly sauvignon and semillon) from a new Darling farm; and two barrels of maiden tannat (a Cape rarity). Owned by Fairview's dynamic grower Charles Back (who lauds SR winemaker Charl du Plessis for his 'rare combination of passion and precision'), this property is a hotbed of viticultural innovation: look out for sangiovese, barbera, grenache, carignan, tempranillo and primitivo (zinfandel) in future blends and varietal bottlings.

★★★★★ **Malabar** Flagship blend, components dependent on vintage. **03** last ed was spicy & perfumed, thanks to elegant peppery contribution of shiraz (72%), here with pinotage (11%), mourvèdre (11%) & dashes grenache, viognier. Effusive rhône-like aromas cloak 15.1% alc. All fruit hand-picked/selected, Fr oak matured. *Wine* ★★★★. Tad less striking than Santé Classic trophy winning maiden **02**.

★★★★ **Flagship Syrah** Super-ripe New World style, substantially wooded. **03** still available mid-2006; sweet & silk-tannined; notes of raspberry & almond; seamlessly managed oak (45% new all Fr); alc (15.3%) evident but not gauche. *WS* 90 pts. Probably just a shade finer than **02** with savoury meaty notes layering dense tannins. *Wine* ★★★★. Unfiltered.

★★★★ **Shiraz** new From Swtland bushvines, unfiltered. **05** enthrals with multi-facetted personality: combo Old & New World smoke, tar, blackberries, even white pepper & spearmint. 18 mths Fr, 30% new. Bold 14.9% alc integrated by fruit, oak.

★★★★ **Merlot** Mega-ripe, almost raisin/caramel notes, massive vinosity characterises **02**, last ed already fully accessible though tannins/alc still evident, 16 mths Fr oak soaked up by sumptuous fruit.

★★★★ **Pinotage** Back to the full-ripe side of the pinotage divide (14.9% alc) & as a result **05** (★★★★) loses some mid-palate definition. Trademark drinkability remains, dark fruit, banana tones, smooth texture, fully integrated oak (11 mths Am, 40% new). Concours Mondial gold. **04** was high toned with beautifully concealed tannins, elegance-enhancing 'lower' 14.4% alc.

★★★★★ **Chenin Blanc** Impressively handled chenin with 100% barrel fermentation; highlights best of fully mature bushvines (27 yrs). **05** another standout: opulent peach & floral tones, richly concentrated, just-dry yet with remarkable palate lifting freshness. A perfect drinking companion with excellent maturation potential. Similarly sumptuous yet restrained **04** *Wine* ★★★★.

★★★★ **Viognier** Intriguing bouquet on **06**, goes beyond merely floral towards savoury, fresh almonds, lavender biscotti, but the flavours are pure luscious peach, lipsmacking & delicious. From low-yielding Swtland vyds; bunch pressed; fermented older Fr oak.

Mourvèdre ★★★★ More Rhône than SA, **05** has a tarry, earthy, wild berry character from minuscule 2.7t/ha Swtland crop. Succulent & accessible; despite Am oaking (yr used barriques), fruit remains the hero. **Sauvignon Blanc** ★★★★ **06** (sample) first vintage from new Darling farm. Limited cropping, reductive winemaking captures appealing gooseberry, grapefruit character, invigorating acidity. **05** *Wine* ★★★★. — *CR*

Spier

Stellenbosch • Est 1692 • Tasting & sales daily 9-4.30 at Wine Centre • Tasting fees: R10 (Spier), R18 (Winelands Select), R30 (Wine Experience) • Meals, refreshments & picnics, see Eat-out section • Luxury hotel & wide variety of attractions/amenities • Owner Winecorp • Winemakers/viticulturists: see Winecorp • 400 ha (cab, merlot, pinotage, shiraz, chard, chenin, sauvignon, viognier) • 300 000 cs 60% red 40% white • PO Box 1078 Stellenbosch 7599 • francoisvdw@spier.co.za winecorp@iafrica.com • www.spier.co.za www.winecorp.co.za • **T 021·809·1143** *• F 021·809·1144*

Historic Spier, HQ of Winecorp (also owner of the Longridge and Savanna brands), is showing exceptional growth. Vineyards have increased by 100ha, production by 100 000 cases and cellar tank capacity by 760 000ℓ. Additional support for group winemaker Frans Smit, whose stated objective is to 'create well-structured, fruit-driven wines and offer the wine lover consistent good quality and great value', came in the form of an inert gas circulation system installed to help prevent oxidation. This extensive range can be tasted at the Spier Wine Centre, one of many attractions which include a four-star hotel, golf course, amphitheatre, restaurants and close encounters with African wildlife.

Private Collection

★★★★ **Cabernet Sauvignon** Multi-faceted wine for keeping. Impressive fruit concentration at core of **04**, given further dimension by toasted spice, tantalising whiffs herbs. Sleekly muscular frame, will drink even better in ±yr, hold for gd few more. Elegant & charming **03** VG; *Wine* ★★★★. Selection from Fr/Am barrels, 12-16 mths — similar oaking for all reds in range.

★★★★ **Merlot** Following in **03**'s complex, well crafted footsteps, **04** layers mulberries, dark plums, white pepper, smoky tendrils. Lithe, with firm backbone, shd develop beautifully. These always tightly structured but **03** had flesh for current accessibility. *Wine* ★★★★.

★★★★ **Pinotage** Riper, fruitier **04** (★★★★) lacks impressive suppleness, complexity of internationally acclaimed **03**, though blackberry, roasted spice & mocha tones v appealing.

Taut tannins will show better in ±yr, drink rewardingly over shorter term. Standout **03** golds at IWSC, Concours Mondial & IWC.

★★★★ **Shiraz** Similar blend & styling to pvs, deep, multi-faceted **04**'s smooth, richly rounded structure accommodates the oaking & 14.9% alc. As with pvs, ready, but has gd prospects. WO Coastal. Variety-true, richly layered **03** gold at IWSC.

★★★★☆ **Chenin Blanc** Awesome concentration & complexity in **05** (★★★★★), from a tropical fruits array to substantial oaking which respects the grape, adding flavour & ageing potential, to hovering citrus thread throughout. Utterly delicious, full bodied, tangy mouthful. Will reward few yrs cellaring. Glittering **04** golds at Concours Mondial, Chard du Monde; Chenin Challenge trophy; *Wine* ★★★★☆. Fermented/15 mths Fr oak.

★★★★☆ **Sauvignon Blanc** Despite racy acidity, previewed **06** (★★★★) not showing usual palate punch, intensity, cld do so in finished wine. Riper this year, green fig, gooseberries, lime, still wonderfully attractive. **05** combined intensity, brisk acidity & approachable 12.6% alc — perfect food wine.

★★★★ **Viognier** Still with expected peach & summer garden floral notes, **05** (★★★★) drier & more subdued than pvs. Oaking gentle, in balance. Cld show better with time. Delicious **04** had alluring scents honeysuckle, jasmine & variety's peach pip note.

Malbec ★★★☆ Last tasted **03** ripe plum fruit; velvety texture for immediate pleasurable drinking, with few more yrs ahead. Unfiltered. **Noble Late Harvest** discontinued.

Classic range

Cabernet Sauvignon ★★★ Sweetly ripe plums & cassis in **05**, with creamy vanilla spicing. Already accessible but tannins can take it another few yrs. All these reds 10 mths Fr oak. **Merlot** ★★★☆ **05** abounds with red berries; oak provides mocha shading, palate firmness. Shd be even better in yr, good for ±3. **Pinotage** ★★★ Lively, with plenty appetite appeal, **05** good mulberry fruit, rhubarb nuances & enough backbone for ageing. **Shiraz** ★★★ Eminently drinkable **05** textbook smoky, sweet spice with wild berry backing. Includes soupçon mourvèdre. **Sauvignon Blanc** ★★★ Ideally structured for summer imbibing with modest 12.5% alc, **06** offers juicy green fig appeal. **Chenin Blanc** ★★★ Characterful **06** abounds with vitality, appley fruit salad freshness. Lightly oaked, giving more texture than flavour. **Chardonnay** ★★★ Drier than pvs but still with friendly gulpability, **05**'s lemon drop, peach slice character gets a slightly savoury note from partial oaking. **Bouquet Blanc** discontinued. All WO W Cape.

Vintage Selection

Malbec-Cabernet Franc-Petit Verdot 04 (★★★★) raises the bar: meaty, vanilla-layered, with deep, dark fruit speaking of ripeness & malbec dominance in 53/30/17 blend. Elegant, silky structure, harmoniously oaked, already delicious, shd age attractively. Coastal WO. **03** (★★★★ but VDG). **Shiraz-Mourvèdre-Viognier** ★★★★ Compatible marriage of Rhône varieties. **04** stays with winning style: café au lait, vanilla spiced intro unfolding into peppery red fruit; elegantly structured charmer. 66/31/3 blend; Fr/Am oak. Concours Mondial gold. **03** IWSC gold, *Wine* ★★★★. **Sauvignon Blanc** new ★★★☆ Export only. Reductively made **06** uncompromising sauvignon: greengage & capsicum with enough riveting acidity (7g/ℓ) to get the juices going. Bring on the food! **Sauvignon Blanc-Chardonnay-Viognier** ★★★★ Quieter than pvs, though same blend, **05**'s 48% sauvignon, equal chard/viognier, touch chenin, semillon results in floral/fruity character. 4 mths oaking gives savoury finish, but expected layering not yet revealed, cld do so with time. WO W Cape unless noted, as is next range.

Discover range

Merlot ★★★ This & next new, export only. Unwooded **05** attractively ripe plummy character; smooth, entry-level red, simple but tasty. **Pinotage-Shiraz** ★★★ Honest, interesting 70/30 blend; **05** is cut above usual quaffers, with piquant rhubarb & brambleberry aromas, flavours. Unwooded, as is... **Red** ★★★ Last tasted **05** smoothly accessible, characterful blend pinotage, shiraz (70/30). **Rosé** new ★★ **06** from pinotage, light-hearted & pretty, with 13g/ℓ sugar to make it even friendlier. **Chenin Blanc** ★★ This & next new, export only. **06** offers melon & tropical ripeness, softly rounded palate. Friendly quaffing style. **Sauvignon Blanc** ★★ Gentle varietal character in **06**, pear-drop base with whiffs lime, green fig. **White** ★★★ Early-drinking blend chenin & colombard: **06** shows just-picked apple/pear crunchy freshness. **Sweet** ★★★ **06** tasted pre-bottling but already showing well: peach & pineapple perfume, flavours & semi-sweet structure will find many fans. Mainly colombard, chenin, touch hanepoot. — *CR*

■ *Spitz* see Bellingham
■ *Splendour* see Villiersdorp Cellar

Springfield Estate

*Robertson • Est/1stB 1995 • Tasting & sales Mon-Fri 8-5 Sat 9-4 • Closed Easter Fri/Sun, Dec 25 & Jan 1 • BYO picnic • Owners Bruwer family • Winemaker/viticulturist Abrie Bruwer, with Johan van Zyl (Jun 2000) • 150 ha (cabs s/f, merlot, petit v, chard, sauvignon) • PO Box 770 Robertson 6705 • info@springfieldestate.com • www.springfieldestate.com • **T 023·626·3661** • F 021·626·3664*

Some think big, some think big *and* long. Abrie Bruwer's one of the latter, and he'd built a new warehouse-cum-garage (that's the big) to house the special 'narrow' tractors needed to work vineyard blocks planted a claustrophobic 8 000 vines to the hectare. The planting philosophy — applied to sauvignon and semillon thus far — is integral to a plan to make a white super-blend (that's the long of it). The Work of Time, his bordeaux-style red, was 12 years in the making, he reminds us; the new white, he hopes, will be 'only' seven. Then again, he might find other vines that he wants to include in the mix...

★★★★☆ **The Work of Time** Realisation of a 12 yr project to make a bdx-style red on the estate. And now... more time needed before **02** can be unveiled, decrees Abrie B, so fans must be patient. For consolation, there's always maiden **01**, marvellously concentrated, fleshy yet elegant blend cab f & merlot (40/40), with cab & soupçon petit v. 18 mths Fr oak, some new.

★★★★☆ **Méthode Ancienne Cabernet Sauvignon** Steep, rocky, thorn-strangled site cleared 23 yrs ago for this single-vyd, its fruit treated to 'ancient' winemaking methods (native yeast fermentation of whole berries in 100% new Fr oak; 2 yrs ageing on lees, min. 2 yrs in bottle; unfined/filtered). Purity, balance & suppleness the hallmarks of pvs **99** & current **01**; delicious on release, both have a great future. Decision pending on whether to release **00**.

★★★★☆ **Whole Berry Cabernet Sauvignon** Cellar's quest for gentlest possible extraction — via fermentation of uncrushed berries with native yeasts — also reflected here. Ripe cherry, blackberry & herby notes on **04**, melt-in-mouth softness underpinned by active fine tannins, ensuring customary gorgeousness on release plus potential over many yrs. Sensitive oaking: ±12 mths Fr oak, 33% new.

★★★★☆ **Méthode Ancienne Chardonnay** Extreme winemaking taken to the limit with this single-vyd version 'inspired by ancient Burgundy': native yeast ferment in Allier oak, 50-80% new; yr on lees without sulphur; bottled un-everything (-filtered, -fined, -stabilised). 03 was to be next but ended up in the vinegar barrels! Fortunately there's ultra-stylish **04**, beautifully poised & focused wine, utterly belies its 14% alc. Like pvs, 'made to last a lifetime'.

★★★★ **Wild Yeast Chardonnay** Unwooded, characterful version, off well-aged block (24 yrs); vinification mostly as above; 13 mths *sur lie*, 100% through malo, which shows in creamy rich texture of **04**, packed with array of tropical fruits; v full but lively; impressive surge of flavour on finish. Gd prospects, as has standout **03** (★★★★★), showing stunning concentration & persistence.

★★★★ **Life from Stone Sauvignon Blanc** Striking & individual wine from estate's stoniest soils. **06** reflects standout sauvignon yr in concentrated bellpepper/gunpowder pungency; exuberant freshness with squeaky acidic edge setting up sharp, clean flavours, plus some gentler tropical notes smoothing the zesty finish. Excellent now & over several yrs. Just 12.6% alc, as is...

★★★★ **Special Cuvée Sauvignon Blanc** From mature (±20 yrs) extra-cool riverine vyd. Muscular, & usually distinct from 'extra-flinty' version above, though step-up **05** had a distinct stony undertone. Show-stopping **06** (★★★★☆) probably their best ever sauvignon; billowing tropical bouquet; ripe, creamy fruit-salad flavours in a soft, almost airy texture, punctuated on finish by zinging acidity which brings the whole palate alive. Amazing! — *DH*

Springfontein

Walker Bay ▪ Est 1996 ▪ 1stB 2004 ▪ Visits by appt ▪ BYO picnic ▪ Facilities for children ▪ Walks ▪ 4 self-catering cottages (B&B by appt) ▪ Owners Weber family & friends ▪ Winemakers Clinton le Sueur & Anja Weber ▪ Viticulturist Clinton le Sueur, with André du Toit (1998) ▪ 25 ha (cab, merlot, mourvèdre, petit v, pinotage, shiraz, chard, chenin, sauvignon, semillon) ▪ 64 tons 3 500 cs ▪ 80% red 20% white ▪ PO Box 71 Stanford 7210 ▪ info@springfontein.co.za ▪ www. springfontein.co.za ▪ T 028·341·0651 ▪ F 028·341·0112

German couple Johst and Anja Weber, their friends back home and the new winemaker have embraced a multicultural mix at this promising Stanford winery, typified by last year's harvest being brought in to the sounds of everything from Norwegian rock to hip-hop, R & B and Mozart. Ex-Mulderbosch winemaker Clinton le Sueur probably needed the soothing tones of the latter to settle his nerves with production volumes tripled and some fermentation tanks having to stand outside because of the pressure on space. 'There is no way out but to extend the cellar for 2007 if we want to handle the 100 tons as planned,' he says.

★★★★☆ **Jil's Dune Chenin Blanc** Youngish W Bay vyd, strong maritime influence yielding sumptuous yet refined chenin (presumably the didjeridoo -serenading at each racking helps). **05** fermented/yr oak (30% new), bottled unfiltered; apricot, pineapple & peardrop notes on elegantly austere but enormously persistent palate, fine acidity; less showy (despite 13.5% alc, up 1%) than debut **04** where more viscous textures dominate.

★★★★ **Ikhalezi Chenin Blanc** Succulent, sumptuous **04** tasted last ed, NLH-style dessert (labelled 'Natural Sweet'); botrytis-touched honeysuckle & peach; fresh acid, moderate 11.6% alc balancing fruit richness & 167g/ℓ sugar.

Jonathan's Ridge Pinotage ★★★★ Earthy minerality on **05** ('wet & difficult season' requiring careful grape selection); with varnishy whiffs, subtle spice, sweet tannins, good length. Yr oak, 30% new. **Ulumbaza Shiraz** ★★★ Luscious & concentrated blockbuster **04** tasted last ed, with polished tone but noticeably big 15% alc. — *MF*

■ **Spring Grove** see Zorgvliet
■ **Spring Valley** see Old Vines Cellars
■ **Spruitdrift** see Westcorp

Stanford Hills Winery

Walker Bay ▪ Est/1stB 2002 ▪ Visits by appt ▪ 3 self-catering cottages ▪ Airstrip & flying school ▪ Owner Stanford Hills (Pty) Ltd ▪ Winemaker Niels Verburg (Luddite), with Peter Kastner (Jan 2002/Apr 2005) ▪ Viti consultant Schalk du Toit (Jan 2002) ▪ 8 ha (pinotage, chard, sauvignon) ▪ 30 tons 750 cs own label 100% red ▪ PO Box 1052 Stanford 7210 ▪ stanfordhills@maxitec. co.za ▪ T 028·341·0841 ▪ F 028·341·0286

New developments at this pocket sized Walker Bay vineyard (owned by Hermanus restaurateur Peter Kastner, wife Jami and business partners) include plantings of sauvignon and chardonnay, complementing existing pinotage; the appointment of Luddite winemaker Niels Verburg from nearby Bot River as consultant; and the selection of their Pinotage to represent Walker Bay at the Pinotage Association's annual 'new vintage' tasting. The current vintage still carries the name Jackson's after founder/previous owner Maurice Jackson.

★★★★ **Jacksons Pinotage** Distinctive, if not distinctly pinotage. **05** poised & lighttoned, as pvs, layered savoury, curry leaf, lavender bouquet with hint of cherry. Suggestion of bitterness but enough fruit to hide both it & very ripe 15% alc. 11 mths Fr oak, 2nd/3rd fill. — *CvZ*

Stark-Condé Wines

Stellenbosch ▪ Est/1stB 1998 ▪ Tasting & sales Fri 1–4.30 Sat 10–2 ▪ Owner Jonkershoek Cellars (Pty) Ltd ▪ Winemaker José Conde ▪ Viticulturist Pieter Smit ▪ 40 ha (cabs s/f, merlot, petit v, shiraz) ▪ 60 tons 3 000 cs 100% red ▪ PO Box 389 Stellenbosch 7599 ▪ info@stark-conde. co.za ▪ www.stark-conde.co.za ▪ T 021·887·3665 ▪ F 021·887·4340

You can see José Conde's graphic design credentials (New York, Tokyo, Stellenbosch) in the beautiful labels of both Stark-Condé wines and those of MAN Vintners, in which he is a partner. But he has also taken to making wines which have swiftly established an enviable reputation – now more widely available locally, thanks to a new distribution network in the Western Cape. Presently, he is excited to have planted 2ha of cab and shiraz at 580m, vying for the title of highest red-wine vineyard in Stellenbosch.

Condé range

★★★★☆ **Cabernet Sauvignon** After massive **03**, 90 pts *WS*, alc down (at 14.5%) on subtle but ripe **04**, with lovely high toned aromas, compact structure: structuring but supple unobtrusive tannins & succulent, savoury acidity well balanced – as is oaking (22 mths, 75% new). Approachable now, but shd develop over 5+ yrs. Like below, from single Jnkrshoek vyd.

★★★★ **Syrah** Black-pepper delicacy, not overt power, of variety exploited in fine **04** (★★★★☆), though harmonious intensity not lacking. Silky texture, ripely smooth tannin. Intelligently restrained oaking (22 mths, 15% new) highlights fruit purity. 14.3% alc, following balance-tipping 15.5% of **03**, 90 pts *WS*, which incl 15% cab.

Stark range

★★★★ **Cabernet Sauvignon** Supple & chewy **03** had 5% merlot & dash shiraz; **04** (★★★☆) just the merlot. Fresh, light fruit with herbaceous & herbal notes. Smoothly chunky, ripe tannins; satiny texture a pleasure. 22 mths oak, 40% new.

★★★★ **Syrah 04** most satisfying: easily approached already, thanks to clear fruit, rich texture, softly integrated (but firmly structuring) tannins, gd fruit. 22 mths mostly 2nd fill oak. 14.3% alc down on pvs. Like Merlot, unfined/filtered.

Merlot ★★★★ Bright, soft, light-feeling (despite 14.5% alc) **04**, though rich enough & well built; pleasing fresh balance. 22 mths oak. Incl 10% cab. – *TJ*

■ *St Clements see* David Frost Estate

Steenberg Vineyards

Constantia ▪ Est 1990 ▪ 1stB 1996 ▪ Tasting & sales Mon–Fri 9–4.30 Sat & public holidays 9.30–1.30 ▪ Closed Easter Sun/Mon, Dec 25/26 & Jan 1 ▪ Fee R5 p/p for groups of 10+ ▪ Tours by appt Mon–Fri 10 & 3 Sat 10 ▪ Catharina's Restaurant; five-star Steenberg Hotel; championship golf course etc (see Stay-Over/Eat-out sections) ▪ Owner Graham Beck ▪ GM Herman Hanekom ▪ Cellarmaster John Loubser (Nov 2001) ▪ Winemaker Ruth Penfold (2003) ▪ Viticulturist Johann de Swardt (1990/1999) ▪ 63 ha (cabs s/f, merlot, nebbiolo, pinot, shiraz, chard, sauvignon, semillon) ▪ 450 tons 50 000 cs 40% red 60% white ▪ PO Box 224 Steenberg 7947 ▪ info@steenberg.co.za ▪ www.steenberg-vineyards.co.za ▪ T 021·713·2211 ▪ F 021·713·2201

Winemaker Ruth Penfold is relieved at not having to face the challenge of the previous year's fires during the 2006 vintage – by contrast a cool, slow season with lower than usual tonnage and excellent fruit, particularly favouring the hallmark herbaceous sauvignons. Biodiversity has been a focus in the vineyards, and they're in the process of becoming members of the Biodiversity & Wine Initiative. During cellar renovations, wine tasting will take place in the Cape-colonial surrounds of Catharina's Restaurant.

★★★★ **Catharina** Flagship red, after farm founder Catharina Ras. Quintet of grapes varying with vintage, but headed by merlot; shiraz near-equal partner in **04**, with cabs s/f, (38/37/17/5), seasoned with nebbiolo. More harmonious, no variety dominant; complex sweet/savoury richness; fine integrated tannins; lovely balance, persistence. 20 mths new Fr barriques. **03** Top Red Blend at inaugural Terroir Awards.

★★★★★ **Merlot** Serious red with trademark minty, red berry elegance. **05** unready. **04** had greater nuance, depth than pvs. Velvety, rich, with fresh acid backing; polished by 15 mths new Fr oak. Delicious; probably even better around 2009.

★★★★ **Cabernet Sauvignon** new to guide, but **03** *Wine* ★★★★★. **05** fresh, touch mint to cassis intensity, revealing cool climate origins. Compact support to sweet ripe fruit; bristling dry tannins invite 2/3 yrs ageing. Wears 14.5% alc lightly. 12–14 mths new Fr oak. WO W Cape.

★★★★ **Nebbiolo** One of handful of varietal bottlings in SA; track record for honest individuality. **05** (★★★★) big, dry yr, tad less distinctive; usual fruit delicacy diminished by ultra ripeness; early drinkable, thanks to a little sweetness, but lacks **04**'s grip, concentration, ageability. Yr used Fr oak.

★★★★ **Shiraz** White spice, brush of mint plus whiff exotic nutmeg add liveliness to very ripe **05**. Gently handled tannins, oak & supple texture encourage current drinking; probably best over next yr/2. Yr new barrels, 60/40 Fr/Am. 15% alc.

★★★★★ **Sauvignon Blanc Reserve** Among long established leaders in Cape sauvignon hierarchy. **06** (★★★★★) also serious, ageworthy, sophisticated. Exhilarating steely precision to usual breadth, richness, distinctive dried grass resonance. Lots still to give. **05** *Wine* ★★★★; **04** *Wine* ★★★★★. **05**, **03** IWSC golds. Ex-single vyd/clone, 20 yrs old, on farm's propitious 'golden acre'.

★★★★ **Sauvignon Blanc** Quality as consistent as its popularity. Intoxicating cool climate scents on **06**; well fleshed yet agile, concentrated fruity acids carry through to explosive, sustained finish. Bold, but not too aggressive or showy. Lower than usual alc (13. 2%). Incl usual important ±6% semillon. WO W Cape.

★★★★ **CWG Auction Reserve Barrel Fermented Sauvignon Blanc** Last was **05**, more austere & tense than either above; great concentration & expanse of trademark dried grass, mineral, citrus flamboyance. Used Fr oak fermented/aged 4 wks.

★★★★★ **Semillon** Usually rivetting, though in notably cool **06** (★★★★☆) ripening problematic. Aromatically less dramatic, but trademark suavity, textured richness achieved via larger than usual sauvignon injection (15% vs ±5%), subtle wooding. Expect foodfriendly development over yr/2. **05** *Wine* ★★★★; Winemaker's Choice trophy. Fermented/4 wks new Fr oak.

★★★★★ **CWG Auction Reserve Barrel Fermented Sauvignon Blanc-Semillon** To date the **05**, showing focused, clean lines; sophisticated fresh citrus peel/honey complexity; silky viscosity. 60/40 blend, fermented/aged 4 wks seasoned Fr barrels before blending.

★★★★ **Steenberg 1682 Brut** Chard-based MCC, splash pinot (13%) evident in ripe straw hue, delicate raspberry hint on latest **NV** (05). Lightish (11.8% alc) but quite rich, biscuity; creamy mousse. Dainty enough for aperitif, also sufficient substance for seafood & poultry. Small portion barrel fermented; 18 mths on lees.

Unwooded Chardonnay ★★★★ No **06**, all limited crop went to MCC above. **05** food friendly, clean & bone-dry. Two 'entry' wines, **Cabernet Sauvignon** and **Sauvignon Blanc** (distinguished by round labels), WO W Cape, mainly for export to Europe/US, not tasted. — *AL*

Stellar Winery   ◊ ♡

*Olifants River ▪ Est 1998 ▪ 1stB 2001 ▪ Tasting & sales Mon-Fri 8-5 ▪ Closed Easter Fri/Sun & Dec 25 ▪ Tours by appt ▪ Tour groups by appt ▪ Owner Stellar Winery (Pty) Ltd ▪ Winemaker Dudley Wilson (Jan 2002), with Berty Jones (2000) ▪ Viticulturist Dudley Wilson ▪ 100 ha (merlot, pinotage, shiraz, chenin, colombard, sauvignon, muscat d'A) ▪ 2 500 tons (organic) + 5m litres bulk (non-organic) + 10 000 cs for clients, incl Peter Riegel (Ger), Lovian (Hol), Triton Export Exchange (USA), Masuda Co (Japan), Les Caves de la Riviera (Côte d'Ivoire), Ehrmanns (UK) ▪ 80% red 17% white 2% rosé 1% other (incl sulphur-free) ▪ Fairtrade, Control Union (organic) & Eurepgap accredited; HACCP in progress ▪ PO Box 4 Klawer 8145 ▪ info@ stellarorganics.com ▪ www.stellarorganics.com ▪ **T** 027-216-1310 ▪ F 027-216-1537*

A welcome addition for sulphur-intolerant imbibers is organic-certified Stellar's range of SO2-free wines, available through Woolworths retail outlets under their Organic label (a sell-by date helping to ensure freshness). Stellar's own zero-sulphur wines are now also stocked by specialist outlets in the UK and US, such as organic chain Wholefoods. Listings with Sainsbury and Carlsberg for their regular ranges (also low in sulphur) are further evidence of growing consumer awareness and demand. Plans are afoot to extend their presence in the UK, Scandinavia and Asia, and, on the social awareness front, support for Fairtrade objectives is gaining ground via the establishment of several new worker trusts on farms supplying the winery.

The Sensory Collection

No new vintages tasted. **Cabernet Sauvignon ★★★ 03** oak dominated in youth, sufficient black fruit to counter, help it soften with yr/2 cellaring. **Merlot ★★★ 03** sweet tempered & shy, hint of mulberry fruit, youthful balanced tannins. **Shiraz ★★★** Swiss gold for **03**, black cherry & dark choc whiffs; flavourful & poised despite huge 15.4% alc, supportively oaked. **Pinotage ★★** Full-bore wooding the norm here: **03**'s soft plum fruit struggles with great whack of vanilla oak, powerful wood tannins.

Stellar range

Cabernet Sauvignon ★★ 04 shy, with some volatile elements, lovely balanced finish. **Merlot ★★ 04** similarly taut & ungenerous as pvs; sufficient sweet/sour fruit to sustain alc frame (14.6%); aggressive tannins, hint volatility. **Pinotage ★★ 03**, not retasted, quite a beefy number (14.5% alc), muted plum notes, strident tannins need food/time. **Shiraz ★★ 04** savoury & red fruited, firm dry tannins ideal match for pasta/pizza. **Chardonnay Reserve** new **★★★** Oxidative fermentation with Fr oak for **06** gives pleasant citrus & lime aromas & flavours but active 14% alc dulls the finish. **Colombar** Last was **02**. **Sauvignon Blanc Reserve** new **★★★** Generous gooseberry, grass & curry leaf notes on **06**; pleasing texture & weight, finishes a bit short. **Sauvignon Blanc ★★ 06** quietish bouquet & palate with hints of orange marmalade, fresh but lacks varietal verve. **Colombard-Sauvignon Blanc ★★** Very light flavour & body in **06**, some dusty notes from Fr oak chips, quite developed already. **Heaven on Earth Vin de Paille** None since **03**, sample provisionally rated **★★★★★**. **No-Sulphur-Added Merlot Reserve** new & **No-Sulphur-Added Chenin Blanc** exclusively for Woolworths, see that entry.

Live-A-Little range

Really Ravishing Red ★ Unoaked shiraz; **04** hot fruited (13.9%) & hollow centred, with gruff exit. **Rather Revealing Rosé ★★ 06** from shiraz; light, dryish & gentle, appealing rosepetal hues & scents. **Wildly Wicked White ★★ 06** predominantly chenin (84%) with splash sauvignon; grapefruit toned, 'wicked' acidity, needs taming influence of a creamy pasta.

Juhantha range

Cabernet Sauvignon new **★★★** Made & bottled for a customer, fruit from non-organic Koekenaap vyds. **03** shy tobacco leaf nose, touch of red fruit on the palate, gentle tannin. For drinking rather than keeping. All ranges WO W Cape. *– MM*

■ *Stellcape Vineyards* see Stellenrust

Stellekaya Winery

Stellenbosch ▪ Est/1stB 1999 ▪ Tasting Mon-Fri 10-4 Sat 11-3 ▪ Fee R10 (incl glass) ▪ Sales Mon-Sat 9-4 ▪ Closed pub hols ▪ Meals by appt ▪ Facilities for small tour groups ▪ Owner Dave & Jane Lello ▪ Winemaker Nontsikelelo Biyela, advised by Mark Carmichael-Green (2004/ 2005) ▪ 100 tons 100% red ▪ PO Box 12426 Die Board 7613 ▪ info@stellekaya.co.za ▪ www. stellekaya.com ▪ T 021·883·3873 ▪ F 021·883·2536

Stellekaya recently sent their staff packing – to France! Winemaker Nontsikelelo Biyela and marketer Anna Vlok went to broaden their horizons and 'spy' on the competition. They returned feeling that SA wines 'are better than we think they are'. Travels apart, 'Ntsiki' B (as she's known) has another reason to celebrate: 2006 saw the release of the 04 wines, the very first she helped produce from beginning to end. Bucolic foot-crushing has meanwhile become a harvest-time tradition at Bosman's Crossing, the upscale 'community village' which Stellekaya anchors.

★★★★☆ **Orion** Classically styled flagship, bdx blend cab, merlot, cab f (60/30/10) in clean-lined elegant **04**; vibrant, complex black fruit aromas, herb & spice tones complementing sinewy fruit; taut tannins & acid backbone provide structure for cellaring gd few yrs. Like maiden **03**, 2 yrs in barrel.

★★★★ **Cabernet Sauvignon** Ruby-garnet rim of **04** suggests an early maturer; layered spice & tobacco aromas, redcurrant fruit in balance with dry tannins; drinks well now, best enjoyed soon. **03**, somewhat overwhelmed by wood mid-2005, went on to win gold at 2006 IWC.

★★★★ **Hercules** ⬚new⬚ Achieves intended Tuscan feel with classic sangiovese tones of tar & rose, some tealeaf peeping through on **05**; lovely sappy elegance, fresh acidity drives the flavours — no tutti-frutti here — made for food, Italian style. Will keep few yrs, though delicious now. Incl merlot & cab (27/23).

Merlot 04 (★★★★) plum & blackcurrant flavours & gd ripe tannins; already shows some maturity, so best enjoyed soon. JCWCA 'first'/gold. Ripe **03** (★★★★) in higher league. **Cape Cross** ★★★☆ Lean, earthy blend merlot, pinotage, cab (50/30/20) made for food; **04** raspberry fruit & slightly stalky tannins in balance, notable acid backbone. 20 mths Fr oak. **Boschetto Rosso Red** ★★★★ Consummate pizza wine with inclusion of juicy sangiovese, with cab, merlot & shiraz; previously reviewed **04** still available. — *IM*

■ *Stellenbosch Drive* see Origin

Stellenbosch Hills   🍷 ☕

Stellenbosch • Est 1945 • 1stB 1972 • Tasting & sales Mon-Fri 8-5 Sat 9-12.30 • Fee R10; R35 wine & biltong/nuts tasting • Closed Easter Fri, Dec 25 & Jan 1 • Food & wine evenings • Owners 20 members • Winemaker PG Slabbert, with Suzanne Miller (Jan 1997/Nov 2003) • Viticulturist PG Slabbert (Jan 1997), advised by Johan Pienaar • ±1 000 ha (cab, merlot, pinotage, shiraz, chard, chenin, sauvignon, muscat de H) • 8 000 tons 20 000 cs own label 65% red 35% white • PO Box 40 Vlottenburg 7604 • info@stellenbosch-hills.co.za • www. stellenbosch-hills.co.za • T 021·881·3828/9 • F 021·881·3357

Their penchant for good wines at competitive prices has already attracted a loyal following (and critical acclaim from the likes of *Wine*'s Value Awards), now their facelifted tasting area offers further appeal in the form of a Wine & Biltong Adventure, a truly SA pairing of wines with different dried meats or, for a vegetarian option, Nuts About Wine. Food and wine evenings during winter feature the cellar's best bottlings partnered with hearty chill-banishers like bredies.

★★★★ **1707 Reserve** Flagship bdx-style blend from equal cab & merlot. **01** was stylish & showy; problem-vintage **02** (★★★★), though elegant, is subdued & restrained, aromas/flavours must be coaxed from glass. Slight hints blackberry, spice & cedar mesh well with firm backbone.

★★★★ **Cabernet Sauvignon 04** (★★★★) last ed called for 3+ yrs to soften its puckering tannins. Leaner, more alcoholic (13.9%) than savoury **02**. 16 mths Fr oak, 30% new.

★★★★ **Merlot 03** (★★★) mid-2005 was fruit-shy, lacking flesh to smooth rasping tannins. Classically styled **02** did well in a difficult vintage.

★★★★ **Muscat de Hambourg** ✓ Fortified, jerepiko-style & attractive example of unusual variety. Pleasing & refined **05** tasted last ed; 210g/ℓ sugar countered by fresh acidity, effective 16.5% alc. Nice rosy finish. 375ml.

Chenin Blanc ★★★ **06** mouthwatering tropical fruit salad given extra zip, flavour, by fresh acidity. Lightish 12% alc begs place on patio table. Enjoy young. **Sauvignon Blanc** ★★★ Generously flavoured **06** impresses with granadilla tones & fresh citrus finish. **Blanc de Blanc** ★★ Latest **NV**'s muted aromas & flavours given needed oomph by zesty lemon freshness. This & next in 1 000ml screwcapped flagon. No new vintages of the following tasted: **Rouge** ★★ **NV**; unwooded & unpretentious blend pinotage & merlot with choc, game & blueberry aromas, fresh, but tad bitter on finish. **Pinotage** ★★★ **02** short on flesh

& fruit; muted blueberry & cherry notes, touch green. Yr older Fr oak. **Shiraz ★★★** Medium bodied **02** with sweet finish thanks to dominating Am oak (16 mths Fr/Am, 50% new) but enticing cassis/Xmas cake aromas. **Chardonnay ★★★★ 05** (sample) delightfully ripe aromas & flavours with vibrant acidity. — *DH*

■ *Stellenbosch Vineyards see* The Company of Wine People

Stellenbosch Wine & Country Estate

Stellenbosch • Est 2004 • 1stB 2005 • Closed to public • Owner Stellenbosch Wine & Country Estate (Pty) Ltd • Winemaker Wynand Pienaar (Feb 2004), with Boschendal (James Farquharson) & Justin Hoy • Viticulturist Wynand Pienaar • 29.8 ha (cinsaut, pinotage, shiraz, chenin) • 31 tons 1 450 cs • 80% red 20% white • PO Box 158 Elsenburg 7607 • wynlpers@ iafrica.com • T 083·305·7332 • F 021·982·7925

His second vintage behind him, vini/viti man Wynand Pienaar is concentrating on a vineyard rejuvenation programme: the Muldersvlei property he and his partners bought three years ago boasts 30 year old chenin and shiraz that's almost as old, and the intention is to help them give of their venerable best. No release date for the maiden Pinotage and Shiraz has yet been confirmed: 'The winemakers and I are still arguing over whether they're ready for bottling!' he says.

Chenin Blanc ★★★ 05, ex-barrel last ed, robust, big-boned, oxidative style with sweet-ripe peach & prominent alc. Fr barriques, 6 mths. WO Smnsberg-Sbosch. — *IvH*

Stellendrift

Stellenbosch • Est/1stB 1995 • Sales via phone or from Hudsons on Vredenheim farm daily 9-5 (see separate entry) • Closed Dec 25 • Owner/winemaker/viticulturist Fanie Cilliers (SHZ Cilliers/Kuün Wines) • 12 ha (cab, merlot, pinotage, shiraz) • ±5 000 cs 90% red 10% white • PO Box 6340 Uniedal 7612 • fcilliers@wam.co.za • T 021·887·6561/082·372·5180 • F 021·887·6561

Improvements to Vredenheim's cellar, where full-time winemaker Fanie Cilliers also vinifies his Stellendrift own-range, have eased the pressures of wearing two hats come harvest. Sales continue apace, particularly the Cab-Merlot; hopes are that his maiden Shiraz will meet with equal enthusiasm. The place to taste and buy both ranges is Hudson's Coffee Shop at Vredenheim; not only does it offer crystal-clear views of the mountains but eland and bontebok graze 50 metres from your table.

Cabernet Sauvignon ★★★ 03 well-made lighter-style cab showing attractive ripe berry fruit & firm grip. Incl dash merlot; ±8 mths Fr/Am oak. **Cilliers Cellars Cabernet Sauvignon ★★★** Returned to guide with **03**, approachable choc flavours, soft, easy & characterful. **Merlot ★★ 03** *Wine* Best Value award, but to us very retiring compared with ripe, plummy **02**; some dry savoury tones, usual sweet-sour finish. 2nd fill oak. **Pinotage ★★** First under Stellendrift brand; **03** hints mulberry fruit & booming dry tannins. 4 mths 1st/2nd fill oak. **Cabernet Sauvignon-Merlot ★★★ 04** ripe-fruited 70/30 blend, yr Fr oak; ripe red berry fruit, firm but balanced tannins & acidity, approachable but better in yr/2. **Merlot-Pinotage ★★★ 'A** fluke,' avers Fanie C, amazed **04** turned out so well; 70/30 mix with ingrained food cordiality via lively acidity, dry savoury finish. **Special Select Dry Red ★★ 03** affable, undemanding; mainly cab, slugs pinotage, merlot, drizzled with soft vanilla oak (3rd fill Fr). **Cape White ★★** Rara avis in this red-wine portfolio; **NV** 80/20 chenin, chardonnay, unwooded, oxidative style, some lemon barley hints, medium body. None above retasted this ed. — *DH*

StellenHills Wines

Stellenbosch • Est/1stB 2001 • Visits by appt • Owner/winemaker Johann Slazus • ±700 cs 36% red 64% white • PO Box 415 Stellenbosch 7599 • orders@stellenhills.co.za • www. stellenhills.co.za • T 083·252·2020 • F 021·887·7745

Ophthalmic surgeon and chardonnay specialist Johann Slazus produces two complementary styles of his chosen variety, plus a dry red.

Charade ★★★★ From shiraz (60%) & cab, fermented in open wooden vats, aged yr in new Fr oak. **01** soft & plump with meaty/plummy notes, powdery but harmonious tannins; modest 13% alc. No new vintages tasted of this, wines below. **Barriques Nouveau** ★★★★ Barrel fermented/aged chard, new Fr oak; from single Sbosch vyd. Toasty oak & vanilla aromas on **04**, marmalade & nutty flavours; intense & weighty but lively finish. **Chardonnay** ★★★★ Older oak for this version, 11 mths; vibrant & crisp **04** a melange of orange peel, Golden Delicious apple & lemongrass; succulent, elegant. — *MM*

Stellenrust   ♻♲♨🍇🍷

*Stellenbosch • 1stB 1928 • Tasting, sales & tours Mon-Sat 10-5 • Fee R20 for 7 wines (incl appetisers) • Closed most pub hols • Farm-style platters; or BYO picnic • Grape 'stompings' • Conferences/functions for 200+ • Art gallery • Owners Tertius Boshoff (winemaker) & Kobie van der Westhuizen (viticulturist) • 200 ha (cab, merlot, pinotage, shiraz, chard, chenin, sauvignon) • 1 700 tons total 150 tons/10 000 cs own label 80% red 20% white • PO Box 26 Koelenhof 7605 • info@stellenrust.co.za or jjwines@mail.com • **T 021·880·2283** • F 021·880·2284/021·865·2010*

Listed in the guide last year as Stellcape, the wines below now appear under the banner of the family farm Stellenrust, founded in 1928. (The Stellcape brand will be used as a marketing vehicle by farmworkers and their families, who have also gained a section of land under a black empowerment deal.) At the Stellenrust helm are Tertius Boshoff and Kobie van der Westhuizen, who have registered the limited release JJ Handmade Wines brand as an international trademark — and, gratifyingly, sold the entire European allocation within a fortnight of release. The wines are now made in what was an old milk-shed, converted into a boutique cellar conducive to the production of 'handmade wines'. Newly built conference facilities can accommodate 300 delegates.

Timeless ★★★★ (Pvsly 'Cabernet Sauvignon-Merlot'.) Last ed's flamboyant **04** barrel sample has since toned down, but is still showy & dense, & to us yr/2 from showing its best (though admired by Wine & Spirit Asia judges, WineX show-goers & others). 60/40 blend, 16 mths Fr oak, mostly new. Rest of range new: **Simplicity** ★★★★ ✓ Supple, harmonious mix merlot, shiraz, cab (40/37/23); **05** dark berry/choc creaminess matched by elegant tannins. Yr Fr oak + 2 mths Am 'cubes' in barrel. **Chenin Blanc** ★★ Alfresco quaffer, **06** with appealing tart green apple/fig notes, upbeat just-dry finish. **Sauvignon Blanc** ★★★ Satisfying summertime drink; **06** veritable 'bowl of tropical fruit' aromas, balanced acidity, pleasant nip in tail. Above listed under Stellcape banner last ed.

JJ Handmade Wines

'No machinery involved' say owners; free-run juice only, natural ferments; 14 mths Fr oak. Following revisited (pvsly samples): **Cabernet Sauvignon** ★★ **04** 'hot', volatile first impression; pvsly noted tannins still tight, gripping. **Merlot** ★★★★ Attractive red-berry character on **04**, succulent ripe fruit, herbaceous touch, ends dry with sweet-sour tang. **Shiraz** ★★★ **04** long, elegant red-fruit flavours with hint white pepper, good dry tannins. — *MM/CvZ*

■ *Stellenvale* see Ultra Liquors

Stellenzicht Vineyards   ♻♲

*Stellenbosch • Tasting & sales Mon-Fri 9-5 Sat/Sun & pub hols 10-4 • Fee R25 • Owner Lusan Holdings • Winemaker Guy Webber, with Ilse van Dijk • Vineyard manager Johan Mong • Viticulturist Eben Archer • 70% red 30% white • PO Box 104 Stellenbosch 7599 • info@stellenzicht.co.za • www.stellenzicht.co.za • **T 021·880·1103** • F 021·880·1107*

The new Cellarmasters Releases from these mountain slopes in Stellenbosch's 'Golden Triangle' give winemaker Guy Webber and his team the opportunity to identify small parcels of wines of exceptional quality, usually no more than 5000ℓ, and bottle these separately. The Cab and Shiraz under this new label join the pocket-friendly Hill & Dale bottlings, listed separately, the mid-priced Golden Triangle and the Stellenzicht label, positioned at the apex.

★★★★☆ **Syrah** Set Cape shiraz benchmark with dramatic **94**; quality level sustained with current **02**, last yr noted as deserving cellaring another 3-4 yrs to allow deliciously ripe, smoky fruit to emerge from tannin sheath. IWC 2004 & TWS 2006 golds for **01**. These & **00** still available. Yet untasted **03** *Wine* ★★★★.

★★★★ **Stellenzicht** Classic cab-dominated (±50%), médoc-style blend with merlot (30%), equal parts cab f, malbec. None since still-available **00**, with polished structure.

★★★★☆ **Semillon Reserve 03** (★★★☆), to us somewhat less striking when reviewed mid-2004, went on to impress *Decanter* (Best Regional White 2005) & SAA judges; **02** achieved admirable complexity in a lesser yr. Both vintages still available. **01** *Wine* ★★★★ in 2006.

Rhapsody ★★★☆ Densely fruited 50/50 shiraz/pinotage blend; **04** has similar earthy touch as last reviewed **02**. Similar wooding too: 16 mths mainly new oak, Fr/Am/Hngrian. Unsampled **03** lauded at Winemakers Choice awards.

Cellarmaster's Release range   new

★★★★ **Cabernet Sauvignon** Pronounced minty, blackcurrant & cedar aromas on **04**; spot-on for varietal typicity; well balanced, fruit driven, plushly textured wine, enjoyable now but enough supple tannins for few yrs. 100% new Fr oak, 16 mths.

★★★★ **Shiraz** Forthright oak & black pepper aromas on **04**, showy, lush, perfectly ripe blackberry fruit well integrated with oak (mix Fr/Am/Hngrian). Gd ageing potential.

Golden Triangle range

Cabernet Sauvignon ★★★☆ **01** textbook cassis & spearmint; approachable nutty tannins; ripe red fruit, warm finish from 14.4% alc; still available, not retasted. **Merlot 03** sampled from barrel (mix Fr, Am, Hngrian) mid-2006: deep extract, sour plum aromas; wood masks fruit, components yet to integrate; provisional ★★★★. **Pinotage** ★★★ Youthful & ripe crowd-pleaser; **04** plump, slightly sweet fruit, contrasting bitter twist on warm finish (14.3% alc). 16 mths oak, Fr/Am/ Hngrian, some new). Laurels at Winemakers Choice, Pinotage Top Ten for step-up **03** (★★★★). **Shiraz** ★★★ **04**'s very ripe mulberry aromas & blackberry flavours lead to unexpectedly fresh acidity. 16 mths mainly Fr wood. **Chardonnay** ★★★ Not available for tasting for this ed. Barrel fermented/matured **03** creamy, spicy & savoury; sweet-sour tang on finish. **Sauvignon Blanc** ★★★ Previewed **06** sweet, slightly confected pineapple aromas & flavours contained by crisp acidity. — IM

Sterhuis

Stellenbosch ▪ Est 1980 ▪ 1stB 2002 ▪ Visits by appt ▪ Closed Christian holidays ▪ Facilities for children ▪ Conservation area ▪ Owners Kruger family ▪ Winemaker Johan Kruger ▪ Viticulturist Hendrik de Beer ▪ 48 ha ▪ 300 tons 4 000 cs own label 25% red 75% white ▪ PO Box 131 Koelenhof 7605 ▪ sterhuis@intekom.co.za ▪ T 021·906·1195/083·411·0757 ▪ F 021·906·1196

'Awesome' is the description of the 2006 vintage: ripe fruit at lower sugar levels and thus lower alcohol. More good news: the bemedalled Sauvignon and Chenin are now also available under screwcap. New among the reds: a Cab and the merlot-cab blend. Johan Kruger (2005 Diners Young Winemaker of the Year) has left Diemersdal to focus on the family wines full-time. On the horizon: vineyard expansion and perhaps even their own cellar.

★★★★ **Cabernet Sauvignon** new Kruger motto might be 'no easy journey from earth to the stars', but this serious & impressive red makes it look positively effortless. **04** packed with ripe cassis fruit & extract, yet balanced by cool minty edge, fine structure, elegantly austere finish. Moderate 13.5% alc. 20 mths all new Fr oak well integrated.

★★★★☆ **Barrel Selection Chardonnay** Reflects house style: generous yet pacy, elegant. **05** (★★★★) delicious buttered fruit & toasty oak character. Accorded gold by Swiss judges, but to us inch off stellar form of **04**, *Wine* ★★★★★, Diners Club Young Winemaker of Yr.

Merlot ★★★☆ Densely coloured **04**, opulent mulberry/pastille fruits, again — somehow — restrained by tense structure in refined send-off. 15% alc hidden under dry tannins. Half new Fr oak, 16 mths. **Sterhuis Red** new **04** not tasted/rated. **Sauvignon Blanc** ★★★☆

06 sets off in overweight, tropical style but finishes nicely balanced; passionfruit ripeness contained within mineral core. Modest 13% alc. **05** SAA; it & **04** both *Wine* ★★★★. **Chenin Blanc** new ★★★★ Naturally fermented/matured seasoned oak, 6 mths; **05** complex marzipan, marmalade fruit breadth reined in by brisk acidity. — *DS*

Stettyn Winery

Worcester · Est 1964 · 1stB ca 1984 · Tasting Mon-Fri 8-5 Sat 10-1 · Closed pub hols · Tours by appt · BYO picnic · Owners 11 shareholders · Winemaker Albie Treurnicht (Nov 2000) · Viti consultant Pierre Snyman (VinPro) · 310 ha (12 varieties r/w) · ±4 600 tons 3 000 cs own label + 3.6m litres bulk · 20% red 80% white · Export brand: FirstCape · PO Box 1520 Worcester 6849 · stettyncellar@telkomsa.net · www.stettyncellar.co.za · T/F 023·340·4220/4101

Big volumes flow overseas with Stettyn signed up as supplier to FirstCape — the fastest-growing SA brand in the UK, with sales of 9ℓ cases expected to touch the 1-million mark this year. Visit their charming new tasting room, decorated with original paintings by Dale Elliott, father-in-law to one of the 7th-generation Botha sons, taste their own-label wines, and drink in the views of a beautiful winegrowing area — still largely undiscovered, and all the more special for it.

Signature Reserve range

Cabernet Sauvignon new ★★★★ ✓ Elegant & well-structured **03**; clean, pure cab flavours with cedar fragrance from deft, sympathetic oaking (2 yrs, 3rd fill Fr). Maturing gracefully. **Shiraz-Cabernet Sauvignon** ★★★ Shiraz 60% as before, but **02**'s bigger, bolder than pvs, with sweet tone from 14.8% alc; attractive cassis fruit spiced with cardamom. Wood as above. **Chardonnay** new ★★★ Powerful, oaky **05**, 100% barrel fermented (mainly Fr wood); deep golden hues matched by buttery richness & toasted nut overlay. Ready, & best enjoyed soon. **Vin de Paille** ★★★ Characterful dessert from air-dried muscat d'A; **NV**; botrytis whiff enlivening marmalade & apricot richness. Barrel fermented/2 yrs Fr/Am oak. 15% alc. Not retasted.

Millstone range

Millstone Pinotage ★★★ Last tasted was **01**, offering satisfying ripe plum/red cherry flavours; charry touch to long fruity tannins. 14 mths 3rd fill oak. **Chenin Blanc** new ★★ Ex-25 yr old vyd block; restrained, zesty, food inviting styling; **06** with hint of Granny Smith apple. Screwcapped, as is... **Sauvignon Blanc** ★★★ Appealing **06** expressive & intense citrus aromas/flavours, though usual light body (±12% alc). Clean, summery wine. Both ranges Wrcstr & W Cape WOs. **Semillon-Chardonnay** discontinued. — *MM*

- ■ *Steytler* see Kaapzicht
- ■ *Stoep* see Main Street Winery
- ■ *Stonebuck* see Middelvlei
- ■ *Stonecross* see Deetlefs

Stonehill

Stellenbosch · Est 1990 · 1stB 2003 · Open by appt · Vini consultant Mark Carmichael-Green (2003) · Viticulturist Lorna Hughes · 3.2 ha (cab, shiraz) · 100% red · PO Box 612 Stellenbosch 7599 · llhughes@telkomsa.net · T 073·420·3300 · F 021·865·2740

Lorna Hughes has dispensed with the eponymous name for her Stellenbosch wine business, opting instead to build her Stonehill brand. Joining the Bristle (no, not named for whiskered husband Dave H, a taster for this guide, but for her dog, 'a cross between a jackal and a farm bicycle') is a Rosé, with a serious, long-wooded Cab to come this year. A new tasting room was a-building as we went to print.

Bristle Red ★★★★ Equal blend of gnarled-vine shiraz & younger cab. **05** bit more structured than last, fuller, more tannins; again well integrated wood (only 50% oaked, yr); slightly 'wild', savoury flavours, with note of spicy smoked meat. **Dry Cabernet Sauvignon Rosé** new ★★★★ Piquant addition to increasingly popular dry pinks category; refreshing sweet-sour tang on **06**, potpourri bouquet, fleshy berry flavours with meaty/savoury hints — the whole picnic basket in a bottle, conveniently screwcapped. — *CT*

Stonewall Wines

Stellenbosch (see Helderberg map) • *Est 1828* • *1stB 1997* • *Visits by appt Mon-Fri 9-5 Sat 9-1* • *Closed Easter Fri/Sun, Dec 25/26 & Jan 1* • *Conferencing* • *Owner/viticulturist De Waal Koch* • *Vini consultant Ronell Wiid (May 2000)* • *75 ha (cabs s/f, merlot, pinotage, shiraz, chard, sauvignon)* • *2 500 cs own label 90% red 10% white* • *PO Box 5145 Helderberg 7135* • *stonewall@mweb.co.za* • *T 021·855·3675* • *F 021·855·2206*

'I'm one year older,' is De Waal Koch's impish response when asked about 2006 milestones. But then no news is good news when you're as happy with your cellar as he is. New plantings are now trellised to fine-tune yields — though he's quick to add that he doesn't let them bear too heavily — and he bottled 200 magnums of 04 Cab for his German fans who, together with Denmark and UK, account for 95% of his sales. Who needs change?

★★★★ **Cabernet Sauvignon** Serious cab, raised in new Fr oak, off low-cropped (4-6 t/ha) mature bushvines. **04** back up to speed with fruitier profile; still elegant, classic cassis, earthy sniffs; ripe berry flavours, same dusty-dry exit as **03** (★★★☆) but more padding. 18 mths oak. 14% alc.

★★★★ **Rubér** Fruit-forward New World styling for this bdx blend, since **03** (★★★☆) touch more merlot than cab. Well-made **04**, plush berry fragrance with lead pencil, gd dusty finish & porty nuance suggesting this an earlier bloomer. 18 mths Fr oak, cab portion new.

Chardonnay ★★★ Barrel fermented **05**, very soft, rich, buttery this yr. Fruit pastille-like aromas, sweet entry (3.6g/ℓ sugar), well-wielded wood (50% new oak 6 mths) but misses zinging freshness of pvs. — *CT*

Stoney Croft

Stellenbosch • *Est 2000* • *1stB 2001* • *Visits by appt* • *Owner Excelebrate (Pty) Ltd* • *Winemaker Danie Steytler, with Charl Coetzee (Jan 2001/Mar 2003)* • *Viticulturist George Steytler (Mar 2000)* • *3 ha (shiraz)* • *25 tons 2 000 cs 100% red* • *PO Box 239 Koelenhof 7605* • *margie@excelebrate.co.za* • *T/F 021·865·2360/083·447·0899*

A flurry of activity after a quiet period of consolidation: a five-year contract to export wine to the US has just been concluded — part of the deal is to extend the range with at least three new varietal wines — and further negotiations are underway in Europe.

★★★★ **Shiraz** Piquant bouquet of cassis & spearmint on **03** (★★★), an underlying smokiness & notes of leather; light bodied (12.7% alc) compared with pvs, with drying tannins. Best enjoyed early. Yr Fr oak, 35% new. Small quantities of **01** (★★★★☆) & **02** (subtitled 'Jenny's Legacy'), also available at press time. — *CR*

Stony Brook

Franschhoek • *Est 1995* • *1stB 1996* • *Tasting & sales Sep-Mar: Mon-Fri 10-3 Sat 10-1; Apr-Aug Mon-Sat 10-1 or by appt* • *Closed Easter Fri/Sun/Mon, Dec 25/26, Jan 1* • *Fee R20 (refunded on purchase of 6 btls/taster)* • *Owners Nigel & Joy McNaught* • *Winemaker Nigel McNaught* • *Viti consultant Paul Wallace* • *14 ha* • *80 tons 5 500 cs 60% red 40% white* • *ISO 14001 certified* • *PO Box 22 Franschhoek 7690* • *info@stonybrook.co.za or mcnaught@iafrica.com* • *T/F 021·876·2182*

The McNaughts' farm is just five minutes from Franschhoek town yet a million miles away — that's the sense you get when you're sitting on the new covered patio with its wrap-around views of the vineyards, enjoying the personal attention Joy and Nigel give wine-tasting guests. Nigel, the winemaker, made a 'wrap-around selection', from throughout the winelands, when buying in for his new Cap Classique, a pinot/chardonnay blend due for release next year, after two years on the lees.

★★★★ **Ghost Gum** Premium label named for 150 yr old sentinel tree that sheds its bark & shimmers, eerily white in the full moon, each Jan. Cab with small dashes merlot & petit v. **03** (★★★★★) intense blackcurrant concentration & fine-grained oak support, elegance to raise goose bumps. 30 mths Fr oak, unfiltered. **02** *Wine* ★★★★☆. Long-aged shiraz may join the GG brand in time.

Stony Brook Vineyards range

★★★★ **Reserve** Blend mainly cab, merlot, soupçons petit v, malbec, cab f in early approachable **03**. Attractive mulberry, lead pencil intro, neat classic build, delicate tannins not overwhelming, clean dry finish. 20 mths oak, 70% new.

★★★★ **Cabernet Sauvignon Reserve** Distinctive eucalyptus to dense dark-berried **03** fruit; plush texture ruffled by house's signature firm tannins. Needs gd few yrs before opening. 22 mths Fr oak, 80% new.

★★★★ **Shiraz Reserve 03**'s power discreetly cloaked in oak, super concentration of dark meaty flavours; ripe tannins, touch earthiness on finish. **02** (★★★★★) had exceptional concentration & balance. From Mbury, Fhoek fruit. 14 mths oak. Reds in range not re-tasted this ed.

Semillon Tangy, mouthwatering food wine. **05** (★★★★) deep flavour folded into waxy texture, sharpened by exciting fruit-acid tension. Yr new oak, mostly Fr with Am & Hngrian. 50% native yeasts. Tangy **04** (★★★★, but *Wine* ★★★★).

Stony Brook range

Rosé new ★★★ Dry rosé from cab & merlot (55/45); **06** buffed copper colour; sultry berry flavours in tangy tail. **Sauvignon Blanc** ★★★★ **05** exemplar of balance: spiky grass with tropical flesh, breadth of fruit with acid seam. Super length, moderate 12.7% alc. Below still available & not revisited: **Camissa** ★★★★ Maiden **03** blend merlot & cab with 10% shiraz. Ripe black berries noted mid-2004 as firmly encased in sweet tannin & oak (Fr/Am oak, ±yr). **Cabernet Sauvignon** ★★★ **03** flavours & dark-berried fruit all present & correct – with forbidding tannins: needs 5/7 yrs. 20 mths mixed oak. **Merlot** ★★★★ **03** firmer, with more oak than pvs, unyielding mid-2005. 20 mths mostly new Fr wood. **Shiraz** ★★★★ **03** less ripe than pvs, more meaty, savoury, with twist of black cherry fruit to finish. 14 mths older oak. **Chardonnay** ★★★★ **04**'s delicate peach aromas lead to firm, juicy flavours, with refinement. Bunch-pressed, fermented/4 mths oak. **Annie's Wine** ★★★ Uncertified NLH-style dessert; **02** 80% sauvignon plus semillon. Orange marmalade character; lightly textured, doesn't cloy. 2 yrs new Fr oak. Discontinued: **Pinotage**. — *DS*

Stormhoek

Owner Orbital Wines ▪ 13 Chapter Street, Pimlico, London SW1P 4NY ▪ nick@orbitalwines. co.uk ▪ www.stormhoek.com ▪ T +44·020·7802·5415 ▪ F +44 020·7976·5376 ▪ Vineyards & winery (Wellington): graham@stormhoek.co.za ▪ T 021·864·3155 ▪ F 021·864·1744

Here's a case study of how a small winery gained an outsized international voice. Using the latest internet-based marketing (viral marketing, web 'blogging') and a catchy slogan, 'Freshness matters', the Stormhoek brand owners in under three years have secured 3 000 listings in the UK in the premium price sector, and 2 500 listings at similar price-points in the US. Superlatives abound: Stormhoek claims more web exposure than any other wine globally, and the highest Google hits per day of any SA wine. 'But,' says local point man Graham Knox, 'Stormhoek has substance too, as evidenced by the Best Pinotage trophy for the 05 vintage at the 2006 IWSC.'

Cabernet Sauvignon-Shiraz ★★★★ **03** bearer of the 'freshness' standard: last ed richer, softer, more refined than cellarmates below. Ripe cassis, measured fruit/acid verve. Tank fermented, 50% yr Fr oak. **Pinotage** new ★★★ **05** took the shelves by storm – and 2006 IWSC trophy for variety. Purple & plummy, very ripe fruits in chunky texture. Fermented on Fr/Am oak staves. **Shiraz** ★★★ **05** hot flush to ripe, confected character; fruit-pulp finish. Oak staves. **Cabernet Sauvignon 04**, **03** not tasted/rated. **Rosé** ★★★ **05** copper-toned & aromatic; berry fruitiness retained in reductive style. From shiraz. **16-Barrel Semillon** ★★★★ ('Reserve' pvs ed.) **05** golden patina, sultry oak; lanolin/litchi combo with character. 14.5% alc. Grapes off 35 yr old Wllngtn vyd; half new Fr barrels 8 mths. **16-Barrel Chenin Blanc** ★★★★ ('Reserve' in pvs ed.) **05** shows toasty oak, ripe cling-peaches-in-cream width to finish. 15% alc. Own & Paarl grapes. 11 mths Fr casks. **African Storm Chenin Blanc** new ★★★ Floral chenin with aromatic muscat (10%) & splash wooded viognier. **05** fruity, with oak breadth. **Pinot Grigio** ★★★ **05** novel herbal interest to medium/full body, nettle-like finish noted pvs ed. **Sauvignon Blanc** ★★★ **06** ripe gooseberry flesh cut by zesty citrus, fresh acid tail. Low 11.5% alc. All WO W Cape. Discontinued: **The Storm Sangiovese-Merlot**. — *DS*

■ *Stormy Cape* see Thelema

Stoumann's Wines

Vredendal (see Olifants River map) · *Est 1997* · *1stB 1998* · *Tasting & sales Mon-Fri 8-12; 2-5 Sat 9-11* · *Fee R10* · *Closed Easter Fri-Mon, Dec 25 & Jan 1* · *Owners Stoumann & Sons* · *Winemaker/viticulturist Napoleon Stoumann* · *112 ha (cab, merlot, shiraz, chard)* · *±1 900 tons ±300 cs own label 96% red 2% white 2% rosé* · *PO Box 307 Vredendal 8160* · *stoutmans@kingsley.co.za* · **T/F 027·213·2323**

To avoid any confusion with a similarly named Robertson winery (Excelsior), 'Excelsious' has been dropped in favour of 'Stoumann's' and the family identity is to come to the fore. The striking labels (depicting the endangered Namaqualand geometric tortoise) make the wines of this small Vredendal cellar easily identifiable. Their flagship is titled 'Vin de la Tortue' (tortoise) – a fittingly French signature for Napoleon Stoumann, the proud winemaker. No new vintages available for review.

■ *Strandveld* see Agulhas Wines
■ *Strata Series* see Flagstone
■ *Suikerbosch* see Zidela

Sumaridge Wines

Hemel-en-Aarde Valley (see Walker Bay map) · *1stB 2001* · *Tasting & sales daily 10-3* · *Fee R10* · *Closed Easter Fri/Sun & Dec 25* · *Light lunches daily 12-2.30* · *Self-catering guest house (up to 6 people)* · *Conferencing* · *Walks* · *Owner Brenda Harcourt-Cook* · *Winemaker/viticulturist Gavin Patterson* · *±25 ha (merlot, pinot, pinotage, shiraz, chard, sauvignon)* · *120 tons 6 000 cs own label 50% white 40% red 10% rosé* · *PO Box 1413 Hermanus 7200* · *sumaridge@itec.co.za* · *www.sumaridge.co.za* · **T 028·312·1097** · F 028·312·2824

Zimbabweans Gavin and Sharon Patterson, now happily ensconced in the Hemel-en-Aarde Valley, report a 'fabulous' 2006 harvest. While Gavin P is kept busy expanding vineyards and restructuring the cellar layout, Sharon heads up sales and marketing, and holds ownership of the estate restaurant, Rhotalia's. Plans include horseback trails through the vineyards and the re-launch of their vine basket sculpture venture begun in Zim. Their wine vision: 'Earthly expression portrayed to heavenly effect.'

★★★★ **Syrah 04** (★★★★) vibrant & refreshing with racy acidity, cranberry flavours & sobriety-promoting 13% alc. Not quite the intensity, complexity of **03** which, on release, needed bottle-ageing to harmonise. 16 mths Fr oak, half new; partial native yeast ferment.

★★★★ **Merlot 04** last ed achieved spicy richness & power at moderate alc (13.6%). 16 mths Fr oak, 40% new. **03** *Wine* ★★★★.

★★★★☆ **Chardonnay 05** heralded new confidence & seriousness for this label; rich, toasty butterscotch flavours with popcorn-butter richness. 100% fermented/aged 11 mths in small Fr oak, 40% new. **06** barrel sample too unformed to rate. **04** Winemakers Choice.

★★★★ **Sauvignon Blanc 06** (★★★★) valiant effort from wind-reduced crop (requiring 50% Bonnievale/W Bay fruit supplement). Maintains 'cool/green' house style in capsicum whiffs, racy blackcurrant flavour. **05** notch up on pvs; fresh, generous, with asparagus & fig intensity.

Pinot Noir Old-style SA pinot with savoury note. Crop ravaged by birds in **05** (★★), showing unstained flavours & astringent woody tannins. 11 mths Fr oak, 40% new. **04** (★★★★) widely lauded: SAA, Swiss gold, *Wine* ★★★★. **Pinotage** ★★★ **05** smoky first impression, mulberry flavours seasoned with obvious oak (10 mths Fr, 35% new), aloe lift to finish. **Dry Rosé** ★★ From merlot; **06** slightly herbaceous & earthy, refreshing & light (13% alc). – *CvZ*

■ *Sunay* see Wandsbeck
■ *Swallow* see Natte Valleij

■ *Swartberg Reserve* see Kango Winery

Swartland Winery

Swartland • Est 1948 • Tasting & sales Mon-Fri 8-5 Sat 9-2 • Closed Mar 21, Easter Fri/Sun, Dec 25/26 & Jan 1 • Tours during tasting hours by appt • BYO picnic • Play area for children • Tour groups • Gifts • Farm produce • Conferences • 60 producers • Cellarmaster Andries Blake • Winemakers Andries Eygelaar, Sean Nieuwoudt, Sunèl Malherbe & Corrien Geleijnse • Viticulturist Klaas Coetzee (Jun 2006) • 3 200 ha (cab, merlot, pinotage, shiraz, tinta, chenin, chard, sauvignon) • 21 000 tons • 50% white 47% red 3% rosé • BRC, ISO 9001 & WIETA certified, IFS & SANS in progress • PO Box 95 Malmesbury 7299 • mkotze@swwines.co.za • www. swwines.co.za • T 022·482·1134/5/6 • F 022·482·1750

As they begin lining up celebratory sparkling for their 60th anniversary next year, the Swartland team have capped the process of transforming from old-style co-operative to dynamic new-Cape contender by formally adopting the identity and structure of a 'wine company'. As 'Swartland Winery', the management team and 60 owner-producers believe they will be able to 'produce market-driven wines in the future'. A strengthened vineyard team, headed by new full-time viticulturist Klaas Coetzee provides improved support to the growers and ensures full control from soil to cellar. In addition, the members of the winemaking team are dedicated to particular ranges, in conjunction with the in-house laboratory. Bottling also takes place on-site. Social responsibility is not neglected, as evidenced by their accreditation with the Wine Industry Ethical Trade Association.

Idelia new Serious (& seriously wooded) flagship; four-way blend (cab, shiraz, merlot, pinotage; 1st/2nd fill Fr/Am oak 24 mths). **04** preview big & powerful; whiffs of pinotage's banana, vanilla & cassis; mid-2006 still very youthful, unyielding, but shows plenty of character. Potential ★★★☆.

Indalo range

Cabernet Sauvignon ★★★★ **04** doesn't shout the variety but good juicy fruit & enough complexity to maintain interest. Oak as for next wine. **Shiraz** ★★★★ Off selected bushvine blocks, Fr/Am barrels 9-12 mths. **04** steps up with gd concentration, multi-faceted flavours. Balanced, & sufficiently stocked with savoury tannins to keep few yrs. **Pinotage** Fr-oaked **05** robust & chunky; barrel sample too unformed to rate mid-2006. **Chenin Blanc** ★★★ **06** another biggie: abundant chewy peach, prickly pear & lees richness, cut by variety's brisk acid. 15% alc. **Sauvignon Blanc** ★★★ Change from ripely round pvs to racy **06**, light textured with crisp dry tropical flavour & sherbety acidity.

Reserve range

Known as 'Eagle Crest' in overseas markets. **Cabernet Sauvignon-Merlot** ★★★★ ✓ **05** reprises pvs's laudable varietal definition, harmony, satisfying flavour; well extracted tannins for food partnering. Combo barrels/staves/chips for this, following wine. **Shiraz-Cabernet Sauvignon** ★★★☆ ✓ Fruit driven & riper styled but elegant; 70/30 assembly in **05**, scented with bluegum; fine spicy tannins, full bodied but balanced. **Chenin Blanc-Sauvignon Blanc-Chardonnay** new ★★☆ Appealing food/solo white, **06** soft & ripe fruited with peachy hint & mouthwatering acidity on finish. **Chenin Blanc** & **Chenin Blanc-Chardonnay** discontinued.

Swartland range

> **Merlot** ☺ ★★★ Latest version juicier, more fun to drink; **05** full, ripe, rounded mulberry mouthful, fresh & lively to the end.

Reds unwooded unless noted. **Cabernet Sauvignon** ★★★ Where pvs allowed standalone enjoyment, **05**'s gruffish green-leaf tone probably better with proverbial fatty chop. **Pinotage** ★★ **05** last ed was richer & less sprightly than pvs; soft, slightly raisined character with 14% alc evident. **Shiraz** ★★★ Grassiness of pvs replaced with riper tone on **05**, spicy brambles plus hints soot & anise; full flavoured, well balanced tannins. **Tinta Barocca** ★★★ Retasted **05** chunkily ripe, as always, with firm nutty tannins needing decanting (& allowing yr/2's keeping). **Cabernet Sauvignon Merlot ★★★** Small-oaked (4-6 mths) **05**, vanilla patina to good berry fruit, still hemmed in by tannins; give yr/2 to develop. **Shiraz-Malbec ★★** Zingy-sounding combo but, like pvs, **05** not a pulse racer; faint stalky whiffs, robust plum tastes, spicy-dry exit. **Dry Red ★★** Seldom fails to appeal/satisfy; smoothly dry all-sorts red, **NV**, lowish 13.5% alc adding to its cheerful quaffability. **Rosé ★★** Light (12% alc), sweetish summer swigger from pinotage, **06** with potpourri scents & soft round finish. **Blanc de Noir ★★★** Bushvine pinotage, worked into easy, uncloying drinkability; **06** interesting balsamic note, imparting sweet-sour bite. **Chardonnay ★★** Now (briefly) oaked; **06** quieter than pvs but still easy to quaff, with hints of peach & lemon. **Chenin Blanc ★★** Soft, light, happy little quaffer; **06** smooth, easy white peach/melon flavours. **Sauvignon Blanc ★★** Somewhat simpler, more reticent this yr; **06** soft, light textured with grassy hint. ±13% alc. **Premier Grand Cru ★★** Mildly fruity **NV**, dry but bit rounder, fleshier, more characterful than most in genre. 13% alc. **Fernão Pires/Light ★★** Good lunchtime tipple with low ±8% alc (but, dieters note, ±8g/ℓ sugar). **NV** ripe pineapple aromas, light leafy flavours. **Bukettraube ★★** Gentle, light bodied **06**, hints toffee apple & candyfloss, unctuously sweet. **Hanepoot ★★★** Enduring favourite & one of the great fortified bargains; latest **NV** rich confectionery aromas, grapey flavours; vibrant acidity & alc (17.5%) ideal for winter cuddling or pouring over ice in summer. **White Jerepiko ★★** From chenin. Latest **NV** very sweet & raisined. **Red Jerepiko ★★ NV** from pinotage. Current bottling seems prematurely tired; some thatchy/smoky whiffs & green-leaf molasses flavours. **Port ★ NV** from tinta; latest shows earthy/vegetal aromas & unintegrated spirit (though 18.5% alc is low for style). **Vintage Port ★★★ 04** again tinta, shiraz & cab, fortified with brandy spirit — 20% alc amply apparent on nose, palate; big dry finish. May become better knit with bottle-age.

Sparkling range

Cuvée Brut ☺ ★★★ Latest version delightfully light & fresh, clean apple & pear flavours — &, as always, not as dry as name suggests. From sauvignon.

Demi Sec ★★ Appealing apricot-toned fizz for the sweeter-toothed; latest is light bodied but full of Late Harvest-like sunny fruit flavours. From chenin & buket. Both budget-priced carbonated sparklers are **NV**.

D'Vine range

Untasted this ed; 500ml, 750ℓ glass, 2, 3 & 5ℓ casks, all **NV. Dry Red**, **Rosé**, **Dry White**, **Johannisberger/Semi Sweet** & **Light**.

Cask range

2, 3 & 5ℓ packs not reviewed; **Shiraz-Cabernet**, **Grand Cru**, **Blanc de Blanc**, **Stein** & **Late Harvest**, all **NV**. — *CT*

■ *Sweetwell* see Terroir Wines

SylvanVale Vineyards

Stellenbosch ▪ Est 1997 ▪ 1stB 1998 ▪ Tasting & sales daily 11-7 ▪ Fee R15 refundable with any purchase ▪ Open pub hols ▪ Tours by appt ▪ Flavours Restaurant, Vineyard Terrace & Cedarwood Lounge (see Eat-out section) ▪ Picnics by appt ▪ Luxury 38-room hotel (see Stay-over section) ▪ Conferences ▪ Tour groups ▪ Play area for children ▪ Walks ▪ Owners LGI Hotels & Vineyards ▪ Vini consultant Mark Carmichael-Green (2002) ▪ Viti consultant Lorna Hughes (1997) ▪ 10 ha ▪ 4 600 cs 80% red 10% white 10% rosé ▪ PO Box 68 Stellenbosch 7599 ▪ info@sylvanvale.com ▪ www.sylvanvale.co.za ▪ T 021·865·2012 ▪ F 021·865·2610

Winelands hospitality knows no bounds here: the landmark Devon Valley Hotel, situated in one of the most beautiful vinous valleys in Stellenbosch, has been recognised by the Great Wine Capitals Global Network, scooping a Best of Wine Tourism award for accommodation. The surrounding vineyards, tended by Lorna Hughes (wife of Dave H, taster for this guide), are now also producing grapes for a recently launched second label, Ghost Tree, named after the elder trees on the vineyard terrace.

★★★★ **Pinotage Reserve** Wild herb & mint overtones characterise these modern, partly new oak matured examples. Full-bodied **04** (★★★★) quite opulent though variety's insistent tannin/nip of bitterness evident in sweet-fruited finish. Yr Fr wood, 70% new. Notch down on **03**, which displayed unblemished fruity lushness & fine tannin grip.

★★★★ **Jewel of the Valley** Unctuous dessert from desiccated chenin berries; **02** good winey feel despite low 9% alc, though finishes a little tamely. 14 mths new Fr oak. ±30 yr old vines.

★★★★ **Vine Dried Pinotage** Broodingly dark dessert from ultra-ripe grapes, fermented with native yeasts; **00** buchu/spice-rack bouquet; smooth, balanced 16% alc. 18 mths in older Fr oak. 375ml.

All bove, following pair, still available, not re-tasted. **Cabernet Sauvignon** ★★★☆ Uncomplicated & approachable **04**; nicely harmonised fruit/oak; well-managed tannin; simple yet tasty sweet mulberry/strawberry flavours. Fr oaked, 75% new. **Ghost Tree Rosé** ★★★ For the sweeter-toothed. **05** generous ripe strawberry/raspberry aromas, flavours. Pleasant, if little short on verve. Cab with chenin. **Devon Valley Cape Blend** ★★★☆ Pinotage-led **04** last ed had house's wild herb/mint thumbprint; cab, shiraz (57/29/14) added extra spice/flesh, tame lead variety's more assertive tannins. Harmonised by yr 100% new Fr oak. **Devon Valley Red** new ★★ **05** mainly pinotage with cab & shiraz; fairly extracted, dense, with hints dried herbs & food-inviting dry tannins. **Shiraz** ★★☆ **05** similar qualities to pvs but quieter, lighter textured; unshowy sweet red cherry fruit with eucalytus hint, pliant tannins; new Fr oak (40%) an understated backdrop. **Dry Cabernet Sauvignon Rosé** ★★★ Single vyd specially groomed for this wine; sample **06** food-friendly as usual, attractive savoury hint; unusually plump, fleshy; bold 14% alc. 20% barrel-fermented. **Chenin Blanc** ★★★ Off 38 yr old vines; incl 40% barrel-fermented portion, which already v well woven with juicy greengage/melon fruit in sample **06**. As pvs, plump, satisfying, gently rounded for early, enjoyable drinking. All above Devon Vlly vyds. — *IvH/AL*

■ *Table Bay* see Ultra Liquors

Table Mountain

Distell range initially targeted at the Japanese market, now also available in the UK and Denmark.

Cabernet Sauvignon ★★★ **05** full-blown blackcurrant/blackberry fruit, firm backbone, sweet impression on finish, dusty hint from 9 mths ageing with Fr staves. **Merlot** ★★★ **05** rich, ripe & savoury with abundant plum fruit, warming alc (14.5%). Chunky tannic tail (similar oak to Cab). **Chardonnay** ★★★ Food-friendly **05**, white peach & tangerine aromas/flavours complemented by careful oaking/lees-ageing. Brisk acidity readies palate for another sip. **Chenin Blanc** ★★★ **06** lean & short; sherbety; green-apple flavours charming but lack usual mineral zing. Light 11.5% alc. **Sauvignon Blanc** ★★★ **06** more complex than pvs; layered with nettle, blackcurrant-leaf & gooseberry flavours. None above for keeping. All WO W Cape. — *CvZ*

■ *Talana Hill* see Vriesenhof

Tall Horse

DGB's slightly higher priced version of the 'critter brands' (Yellowtail, Little Penguin) flying off US supermarket and cash 'n carry shelves. Colourful and awarded packaging features a stylised giraffe.

Flattering dollops sugar a feature throughout this range, not revisited this edition. **Cabernet Sauvignon** ★★☆ **03** has some varietal character & structure propping up the sweetness (10.5g/ℓ RS) for overall balanced appeal. **Merlot** ★★☆ Underlying tannins rescue **03** from being a Slush Puppy. Sugar (10.7g/ℓ) lifts fruit, masks the astringency. **Shiraz** ★★☆ Ingratiating **03** offers marzipan & Demerara sugar flavours; rich & rotund, unctuous texture heightened by Am sweet-oak. Bound to be a pop hit. **Chardonnay ★★** Quaffable & friendly **04**, creamy mouthfeel, ripe toffee-toned fruit. Perversely, driest (RS 7g/ℓ) of all these. WO W Cape all. — *DH*

■ *Tamboerskloof see* Kleinood

Tanagra Private Cellar

Owners Christoph Reinhold & Felicia von der Schulenburg • PO Box 92 McGregor 6708 • ffvdscar@lando.co.za • **T 023·625·1780** *• F 023·625·1847*

After 10 years of wine farming, this self-described 'family circus', with their troupe of dogs, cats, birds and fish, are putting their property on the market and moving to the Lowveld (architect Christoph Reinhold has been assigned to manage the building of the 2010 Soccer World Cup stadium in Nelspruit). A highlight was the 05 wines, which Felicia von der Schulenburg feels are the best they produced in their time here.

Taking a cue from mentor Abrie Bruwer, these all whole berry, native yeast fermented. **Heavenly Chaos ★★ 05** switches to claret style red (cab 47%, with merlot & cab f); intended as everyday drink though some might find the stalky tannins need food. **Felicity ★★★** Another bdx blend, also driven by cab, with merlot & cab f (33/10). **05** ripe, dark-fruited, with somewhat more structure & flesh than the above. Fr oaked. **Carah ★★ 05** equal cab/shiraz mix, like pvs, has a savoury raisined character, plus tart dry finish. **Rosé** Last was **05**, an unrated preview. **Chardonnay** Sample **06** too young & unformed to rate. — *MM*

■ *Tara Hill see* Southern Sky
■ *Tarentaal see* Assegai
■ *Tarentaal Farm see* Terroir Wines

Tassenberg

Dry red affectionately known as 'Tassies'. By Distell. Launched 1936, blend has varied over the years. Latest **NV ★★** from cab & cinsaut; affable with supple red fruit flavours, fruit-tannin tug (no oak) & moderate 12.5% alc. W Cape vyds. — *CvZ*

Taverna Rouge

Big-selling, off-dry (8g/ℓ sugar), budget-priced red blend from Distell. Latest **NV ★★** from cinsaut, cab, ruby cab; cherry bouquet & flavours, affable 12% alc. W Cape vyds. — *CvZ*

Teddy Hall Wines

SA's Sultan of Chenin, Teddy Hall, vinifies a variety of top-end versions for his own Rudera brand (see separate entry) and for clients. The release below, under an eponymous label (and screwcap) is the one you'd most often find on Hall's table, accompanying lunch in the garden.

Chenin Blanc ★★★ Stylistic change in **06**, less tropical & more citrus, but the drinkability is never in question: a lively, tangy dryness. WS 'top value' pick. Sbosch fruit. — *CR*

■ *Tembana Valley see* Rooiberg

Tempel Wines

Paarl • Est 2000 • 1stB 2003 • Closed to public • Owner Tuan Marais • Vini consultant Neil Schnoor (2000) • Viti consultant DeWet Theron (2000) • 3 ha (pinotage) • 11.8 tons 700 cs 100% red • PO Box 7295 Noorder-Paarl 7623 • tempelwines@lantic.net • www.tempelwines. co.za • **T 021·872·4065** *F 021·872·3883*

The unlikely cultural blend behind this kosher Pinotage – Tuan Marais suspects he's the only English speaking Catholic Afrikaner to produce one – is soon to broaden even more. Daughter-in-law Lara M, proficient in various European languages, has joined as sales and marketing representative, and New York distribution under the aegis of an Indian friend from Marais's textile days is on the cards.

Pinotage ★★★★ Unique & rather good — & unmistakably pinotage: **04** starts fruitily with red/black pastille succulence, concludes firmly dry. Sympathetically oaked: 8 mths Fr, some new. Low sulphur a benefit of flash pasteurisation used in the kosher vinification, says Tuan M. — CR

■ **Terra del Capo** see L'Ormarins

Terroir Wines of SA

Stellenbosch • Est 2002 • 1stB 2003 • Closed to public • Owners/viticulturists Inus Muller & Bennie Diedericks • Winemaker Inus Muller (2002) • 8 tons 600 cs 100% red • PO Box 5435 Helderberg 7135 • inusmuller@absamail.co.za or bennad@telkomsa.net • **T 082·825·9001/082·452·7263** • F 021·842·2373

This is a one-stop winegrowing advisory service owned and run by Inus Muller and Bennie Diedericks, providing assistance to a new generation of artisan winemakers. Clients include Kelsey Farm, Kuikenvlei, Leeurivier Wines & Olives, Paul Wallace Wines, Romond, Sweetwell and Tarentaal Farm, some listed separately. Muller and Diedericks also make small quantities of wine for their own account under the brand name Karmosyn.

Sweetwell Cabernet Sauvignon ★★★★ Appealing & well-made **03**, classic cab flavours with fine herbaceous note; soft & ripe tannins; classy, gd prospects. Hldrberg fruit, 2 yrs in oak. **Karmosyn Shiraz** ★★★ Extroverted smoky/meaty varietal character on **03**, big-boned (14.5%) but unintimidating. Hldrberg & Paarl vyds; 16 mths oaked. **JWL Shiraz** ★★★ **03** scented vin ordinaire with freshness & flavour, lightly gripping tannins. Hldrberg fruit, 2 yrs barrelled. None revisited this ed. — CT

Teubes Family Wines

Olifants River • Est/1stB 2003 • Visits by appt (9-5.30 during wildflower season — Aug/Sep) • Closed public holidays • Self-catering/B&B guest house • Tour groups • Walking trails • Owners Johan & Ella Teubes • Winemaker Helene van der Westhuizen (Jan 2004) • Viticulturist Johan Teubes • 2 400 cs own label 100% red • Also exported as Houmoed • PO Box 791 Vredendal 8160 • ella@teubeswines.co.za • www.teubeswines.co.za • **T 083·274·4832/(027) 213·2377** • F (027) 213·3773

No update received from this producer, owner of extensive organically cultivated vineyards. Contact details from the previous edition.

Text

DGB-owned range launched late 2003 in packaging calculated to appeal to 'fashion conscious trendsetters in the 25 to 35 age group'.

Ruby Cabernet-Merlot ★★ 50/50 blend, similar to pvs with hint of mulberries; fruity entry to palate but the finish is lean, dry with slight tannic grip. **Chenin Blanc** ★★ Latest not as sexy, more assertive alc (13.5%). Faint deciduous fruit flavours, dry, uncomplex. Both **NV**, WO W Cape; neither retasted this ed. — DH

■ **Thabana Li Meli** see Bartinney Cellars

Thabani Wines

Stellenbosch • Closed to public • PO Box 1381 Stellenbosch 7599 • thabani@iafrica.com • www.thabani.co.za • **T 021·412·9302** • F 021·412·9305

Jabulani Ntshangase remains thabani ('joyful') about his and partner Trevor Steyn's venture, the first wholly black-owned wine company in SA. Always fast-forward, JN decelerates long enough to shepherd groups of black oenology students though the system, and serve on the tasting team for this guide. Current Thabani releases, not reviewed, are the Shiraz, Merlot and Cab-Merlot from the 03 vintage, and the Sauvignon 06.

■ **Thandi Wines** see The Company of Wine People
■ **The Auction Crossing** see Hex River Crossing

■ *The Beach House* see Douglas Green
■ *The Berrio* see Flagstone
■ *The Blends* see Bellingham

The Cheviot Winery   ◊ 🖰 [new]

*Stellenbosch ▪ Est/1stB 2004 ▪ Tasting & sales by appt Mon-Fri 9-12 ▪ Fee R20 p/p, refundable on purchase ▪ Closed pub hols & Christian religious days ▪ Owners/winemakers Elmari Swart & Jaap Scholten ▪ Viticulturist John Arnold (2005) ▪ 100 cs 100% red ▪ PO Box 5 Green Point 8051 ▪ winesales@cheviot-wines.com ▪ www.cheviot-wines.com ▪ **T 082·553·4771/ 082·698·4315** ▪ F 021·434·7249*

It's amazing what a good bottle of bubbly can do. Partner Jaap Scholten had faith in housemate Elmari Swart's ability to make a great shiraz and so, over a glass of sparkling, a plan was hatched for a *garagiste* winery. Producing from Helderberg grapes and using Stellenbosch cellar space, the dream came true. Friends lend a helping hand and word-of-mouth referrals support sales.

★★★★ **Syrah** Handcrafted styling: open-top ferment, bottled unfined/filtered. **04**'s white pepper, plum & raspberry notes lead on to harmonious, finely spiced blend of elegant mid-weight fruit, moderate 13.5% alc, discreet oak (2nd fill only) though with coconut/vanilla whiffs from 50% Am component; persistent flavours. – *MF*

The Company of Wine People   ◊ 🖰 🍷 ⚐ 🚶 ♿

*Stellenbosch (see Stellenbosch & Helderberg maps) ▪ Est 2004 ▪ Tasting at two venues: Helderberg Winery Mon-Fri 9-5.30 Sat 9-5; Welmoed Winery Mon-Fri 9-5.30 Sat & pub hols 9-5 Sun 10-4 ▪ Both venues closed Easter Fri, Dec 25 & Jan 1 ▪ Meals: Helderberg Restaurant Mon-Sat during tasting hours (T 021·842·2012); Welmoed: Duck Pond Restaurant daily during tasting hours (T 021·881·3310) ▪ Both restaurants available for after-hours functions by appt ▪ Play areas for children ▪ Tour groups ▪ Owners: more than 200 shareholders ▪ Winemakers Nicky Versfeld, Morné van Rooyen, Stephan Smit & Danie van Tonder ▪ Viticulturists Francois de Villiers & PD Koegelenberg ▪ 15 000 tons 2.5m cs 60% red 40% white ▪ ISO 9001, BRC, HACCP & WIETA certified ▪ PO Box 465 Stellenbosch 7599 ▪ info@thecompanyofwinepeople.co.za ▪ www. thecompanyofwinepeople.co.za ▪ **T 021·881·3870** ▪ F 021·881·3102*

The former Omnia Wines, a union between Vinfruco (whose core business was exporting fruit to the northern hemisphere's hungry grocery chains) and Stellenbosch Vineyards, has re-named itself 'the company of wine people' – the lowercase notation underscoring its commitment to a human dimension despite being among the top five wine exporters by volume. Large and successful brands like Arniston Bay cohabit in its portfolio with terroir wines like the single-vineyard Kumkani Lanner Hill and the innovative VVS blend. TCOWP owns no vineyards, but sources grapes from Stellenbosch, Paarl, Elgin, Durbanville and Robertson, and has similarly dispersed wineries or partner cellars. The company owns a significant stake in Thandi, SA's leading black economic empowerment wine company, and is the first wine brand in the world to be Fairtrade accredited.

Kumkani range

★★★★ **Shiraz** Well made, inviting **03** followed by boldly New World-styled **04** (provisional ★★★★; sample tasted), showy oak-spice & vanilla, sweet-ripe fruit; though wood's upfront, there's enough flesh to make an appealing drink; will have lots of fans. 15 mths Fr/Am oak (70/30). For early enjoyment.

★★★★★ **Triple J Shiraz 04** easily manages difficult challenge of concentration & elegance. Tailored lines, well judged tannins, delectably ripe berry fruit touched with spice; shows admirable restraint. Last yr's advice bears repeating: try not to drink it all now, gd for another 5+ yrs. Yr oaked. 13.5% alc.

★★★★★ **Pinotage** ✓ Multi-layered complexity confirmed class of **04**, opulent, spicy, with velvety texture; previewed **05** (★★★★) banana & dark fruit character; carefully oaked, as always, to make most of lesser vintage. 14 mths wood, 30% new.

★★★★ **Shiraz-Viognier** new ✓ Lush-fruited & fragrant **04**, lithe, lively, almost athletic, its unheavy character enhanced by low 13% alc; already remarkably accessible yet a sense of more to come, so cellar some (tannins allow) for heightened enjoyment on maturity few yrs hence. Co-fermented, aged 14 mths Fr/Am oak.

★★★★☆ **Chardonnay-Viognier** new ✓ Utterly delicious **05** beckons with intriguing bouquet of peach, lavender & impressively restrained oak (only 35% barrelled, 8 mths); radiates beautiful clean freshness from nose to creamy, flavour crammed finish. A tour de force.

★★★★☆ **Sauvignon Blanc** ✓ Successive standout vintages usher in higher general rating for this sophisticated food wine, dazzling combo racy green freshness & concentrated, succulent fruit. **06** (sample), like **05**, layered, delicious kiwifruit, nettle, green fig array; fine mineral thread adds tension, lift. Moderate ±13% alc. WO Coastal.

★★★★☆ **Lanner Hill Sauvignon Blanc** From single Groenekloof vyd. Powerhouse maiden **05** has bulging trophy cabinet incl VDG, SAA trophy, *Wine* ★★★★. To follow, a riper, slightly less bracing but still irresistible **06** (★★★★); gooseberry & lime suaveness, delicious in lighter textured vein. Sample tasted.

★★★★ **VVS** Innovative blend viognier, verdelho, sauvignon, with viognier's aromatic charms dominant; **05** (★★★★) warmer/riper vintage, hence less definition, verve, yet still attractive, flavourful; tropical/peachy fruit. 9 mths 300ℓ Fr oak. **04** 61/29/10 mix, beautifully balanced, crisp, weighty. *Wine* ★★★★.

Shiraz-Cabernet Sauvignon ★★★☆ Inviting spiced plum pudding tone on **04**, appealingly ripe & drinkable now, with enough polished tannins to carry few yrs. Yr Fr oak. **Chenin Blanc** new ★★★★ Attractive & friendly **05**, tropical roundness rather than chenin's pointed freshness; drinkability abetted by waxiness on nose, palate. WO Coastal. **Viognier** Unlike VVS above, **05** (★★★★) shrugs off harvest heat – apparent in 14.8% alc – with zinging freshness & vibrancy, excellent concentration & persistence of fruit; gorgeous summer flower garden scents. Half unoaked, 4 mths on lees; rest short period new Fr oak. **04** (★★★★ but TWS gold).

Thandi range

Cabernet Sauvignon ★★★☆ Work in progress already promises well, **04**'s luscious red fruit provides gd foundation for serious oaking (2 yr Fr). Winemaker clearly understood wine's potential: longest-lived of all the reds, 4+ yrs. Elgin fruit here, below, unless noted. **Pinot Noir** ★★★ Noteworthy just-picked raspberry fruit purity on **04**, with sweet spice, whiffs violets on nose, palate more retrained, austere than expected. For drinking soon. 10 mths barrelled. Following trio WO W Cape. **Merlot-Cabernet Sauvignon** ★★★☆ **04** good partnership, giving lush, ripe berry fruit, yet enough stiffening for ±2 yrs ageing. Appealing, elegant structure, juicy accessibility. Older Fr oak, 14 mths. **Cabernet Sauvignon-Merlot** ★★★★ **05** judiciously oaked, so fruit has centre stage: plums, cherries; firm but ripe tannins ensure 3-4 yr cellaring future. 8 mths Fr, portion new. **Shiraz-Cabernet Sauvignon** new ★★★ Showing more shiraz than cab in its personality, attractively so, **04**'s tones are savoury, smoky, dark fruit. Harmoniously oaked, combo barrels/chips, made for earlier drinking. **Chardonnay** ★★★★ Using lemony cool fruit characteristics as base, **05**'s oaking is well judged, a nutty overlay. Result is tasty, confidently made wine. Fermented/matured 9 mths Fr oak, 30% new. **Sauvignon Blanc-Semillon** ★★★ 75/25 blend in **06** sample, sauvignon dictating leafy, capsicum styling, with semillon adding some palate weight. Nice freshness, drinkability. W Cape vyds.

Arniston Bay range

Rosé ☺ ★★☆ Exuberant, dry **06**, red berry fruit from top to tail, lightish, crisp & lipsmacking.

Shiraz ★★★ Usually friendly & quaffable, though **05** has some dry tannins which gd with food; added interest from hedgerow fruit & hint of scrub. Portion oaked this yr. **Ruby Cabernet-Merlot** ★★★ Liquorice-spiked, dark-fruited **05**. Smooth & generous, veined with just enough grape tannin to enjoy solo or with food. Unwooded. **Shiraz-Merlot ★★★ 05** again softly savoury, with merlot's portion adding juice & flesh to shiraz's spicy tones. Delicious; not wooded. **The Shore Red** new ★★★ Smooth textured **05**, mini bdx blend merlot, cab; mulberry & plum attractions, uncomplex but quaffable. **Chenin Blanc-Chardonnay ★★** Among biggest SA brands in Britain. **06** apple, pear freshness throughout; vibrant, juicy crowd pleaser. 80/20 blend ex-Pdberg, Rbtson. **The Shore White** new ★★ **06** light bodied chenin, semillon, colombard mix, tasty-ripe summer fruits on offer, modest 12% alc ideal for quaffing. **Méthode Cap Classique ★★★** Latest version of **NV** bottle fermented sparkling bursts with freshness & lemon/kiwifruit flavour; full, creamy, more 'brut' than 15g/ℓ sugar would suggest. 'Traditional varieties', 36 mths on lees. No new versions of following tasted: **Merlot Reserve, Chardonnay-Semillon & Pinotage-Merlot.** W Cape, Coastal WOs.

Versus range

Red ★★☆ 04, allsorts quaffer, lighter textured than pvs, dash oak adds firmness, flavour, food cordiality. **Rosé ★★★** Pinotage, shiraz combo in **06**, tad sweeter than pvs (±15 g/ℓ sugar) but still highly drinkable, attractive fruit-pastille character, friendly 13.5% alc. **White ★★★** Perfect drinking companion; **06** exuberantly fruity, perky & light, undemanding (on pocket & palate). 100 000 (!) fun-filled cases. All in 1ℓ & 500ml bottles; WO W Cape.

Welmoed range

Rosé new ☺ ★★☆ Delightful addition to the dry pinks genre; **06** crackles with just-picked berry freshness; medium bodied pinotage/shiraz blend (60/40), pretty in every way.

Cabernet Sauvignon ★★★ 05 continues in friendly, versatile mode; open textured blackcurrants & plums to taste, accessible despite partial oaking (yr Fr). **Merlot ★★★** Quieter, less fleshy this yr; **05** minty/herbaceous seam; Fr oaking gives firm, dry, food inviting finish; enjoy in prime of youth. **Pinotage ★★★** Partially oaked **05** shares pvs's food-inviting tautness; varietally typical rhubarb, mulberry flavours, attractive 'cool fruit' feel. **Shiraz ★★★ 05** savoury, hints leather & black pepper; lively red-fruit flavours, not too full bodied, warmth of 14.5% alc on finish. **Chardonnay ★★★☆ ✓** Only 50% oaked (Fr, 6 mths), cleverly capturing **05**'s lovely tropical fruit character, adding biscuity layer to juicy, fresh palate. Delicious now & soon. **Sauvignon Blanc ★★★ 06** harvested early-ish yet has riper-spectrum gooseberry flavours; quiet but fresh, satisfying, won't overwhelm food. **Chenin Blanc ★★☆** After exuberant pvs, **06** more demure yet still appealingly fresh, light textured green-apple/pear flavours drink easily.

Infiniti range

Brut ★★★ Classic cap classique from chard, pinot; **03** trademark toasty intro, brioche & lemon peel flavours; warm & ripe, with some attractive honeyed development peeping through.

Shamwari Merlot-Cabernet Sauvignon, Shiraz & Chardonnay all discontinued, as are **Credo CWG Auction Reserve Groenekloof Sauvignon Blanc, Stellenbosch Cabernet Sauvignon, Stellenbosch Shiraz & Groenekloof Sauvignon Blanc.** — *CR/MW*

The Foundry   ♂♀

Stellenbosch ▪ Est 2000 ▪ 1stB 2001 ▪ Visits by appt ▪ Owners Chris Williams & James Reid ▪ Winemaker/viticulturist Chris Williams, with selected growers ▪ 20 tons 1 000 cs 90% red 10% white ▪ PO Box 12423 Die Board Stellenbosch 7613 ▪ thefoundry@mweb.co.za ▪ www.thefoundry.co.za ▪ T 082·577·0491 ▪ F 021·843·3274

'The last two years have really been about refining the quality of our wine. And it's been a deeper understanding of our vineyard sites that has led us to more complex and profound wines. More and more we try to let the reins go and let the truth of each site shine through,' avers Chris Williams, resident winemaker at Meerlust, who's afforded the freedom to follow his own-wine dreams too. With partner James Reid and selected growers, he makes small quantities of Syrah and Viognier hailed by critics and cognoscenti around the world, including Australia ('believe it!') and soon ('most gratifyingly of all') Paris, France.

★★★★☆ **Syrah** Much admired for refinement, subtlety. **04** being held back for further yr, not tasted. **03** incl dash 04 viognier, sold out. Profound yet delicate spicy/floral aromas. Rich with structure, length; agreeably understated oak. Possible peak ±2013. 17 mths Burgundian oak, 10% new; unfiltered. 20% screwcap closure. Sbosch, Paarl, Wllngtn vyds. 91 pts *WS*.

★★★★ **Viognier** Subtly expressive realisation of this fashionable variety. **06** (sample) refined, complex; native yeast fermented portion adds intricate earthy extras to dried apricot/ spice allure. Rich, rounded, classically dry & confidently structured. Older Fr oak fermented/4 mths. Coastal WO (Wllngtn vyd). — *AL*

The Goats do Roam Wine Company ♀

Paarl ▪ Est/1stB 1998 ▪ 72% red 20% white 8% Rosé ▪ See Fairview for tasting/sales information
Welcome to three new members of Charles Back of Fairview's caprine-themed Goats do Roam brand, a registered trademark in Britain, Ireland and SA, the irreverent humour behind which belies internationally recognised quality (*Wine Spectator* Top 100 listing for GdR in Villages Red). Meet Goat Door, Bored Doe and Goatfather, latter featuring Italian varieties barbera, primitivo and whatever else takes herd leader Don Goatti's fancy…

★★★★ **Goat-Roti** Shiraz plus seasoning white grape viognier calculated to deliver spicy tones of northern Rhône. Yr later, **04** (tasted pre-bottling last ed) has shed any awkwardness, gained complexity: violets, smoky dark fruit, peppery nuances. Assimilates 15% alc in its smoothly rounded structure. 14 mths Fr/Am oak, some new. Concours Mondial, *Decanter* golds.

★★★★ **The Goatfather** new The name already alerts you, **05** is individual, powerful. More Old World than New (unsurprisingly), mixes shiraz, cab, merlot, barbera, primitivo for a dark-toned, scrub/white pepper-nuanced experience. Accessible, cd age few yrs. Yr oak, some new. Share with those you trust…

★★★★ **Bored Doe** new Classic bdx blend (naturally!), merlot dominant (48%), rest cab, malbec, petit v. Nothing boring or frivolous about **04**: cedar-veined cassis, choc mint; suave, integrated tannins for current accessibility or further few yrs development. Used Fr wood, 12 mths.

★★★★ **Goats do Roam in Villages Red** Serious blend shiraz, pinotage, mourvèdre & seasoning viognier. **04** (★★★★☆) still available: lighter, easier drinking, with brisk acidity. **03** homogeneous & well assembled. Yr Fr/Am oak, none new.

Goats do Roam White ☺ ★★★ Varying blend, usually chenin, crouchen, clairette base, with focus on tasty quaffability. **06** gains from viognier's floral addition, semillon's weight.

Goats do Roam Red ★★★☆ Côtes-du-Rhône-style red featuring Mediterranean varieties herded by shiraz; pinotage adds local dimension. **05** captures an intriguing foreignness; hedgerow fruit, savoury/peppery, scrub, but the lightly oaked palate is juicy, seamless drinking vinosity. Top selling SA wine in America, & no wonder. **Goats do Roam Rosé** ★★★★ **06** gorgeous from top to toe; cerise hued, bright fruited multi blend; dry & food-perfect. Transports you to the Côte d'Azure. **Goats do Roam in Villages White** ★★★☆ Created for enjoyment rather than show; now viognier, grenache (50/30), rest chard, chenin; **05** nicely balances aromatic appeal with light textured, rejuvenating freshness. Partially oaked. **Goat Door Chardonnay** new ★★★☆ More than just a witty name & label, **05** delivers textbook chard styling (citrus peel, lightly buttered toast), but doesn't take itself too seriously; the oaking is partial, body shapely, likeability infectious. All Goats WO W Cape/ Coastal; GdRs now under screwcap, except Bored Doe. — *CR*

The High Road new

Stellenbosch ▪ Est/1stB 2003 ▪ Closed to public ▪ Owner Les Sweidan & Mike Church ▪ Winemaker Nontsikelelo Biyela (2004), advised by Mark Carmichael-Green (2005) ▪ 16 tons 1

*000 cs 100% red • PO Box 4721 Cape Town 8000 • les@thehighroad.co.za • www. thehighroad.co.za • **T** 021·425·4209 • F 021·418·2660*

This boutique venture specialising in bordeaux-style reds is underpinned by a friendship built on a passion for wine, good food and sport. 'We enjoy our product so much, we might only sell what we don't consume ourselves,' joke owners Les Sweidan and Mike Church. They use only premium grapes from Stellenbosch's 'Golden Triangle' and what they call 'high road' winemaking practices. After the first vintage at Yonder Hill, vinification moved to Stellekaya. The wines are available at selected restaurants but mostly sold privately.

★★★★ **Reserve** Sleekly stylish bdx blend (60/30/10 cab, merlot, cab f), well groomed from its mint-touched blackcurrant fruit, finely grained tannins, to long dry finish. **03** accessible, but built for long haul – will reward cellaring gd few yrs. 16 mths Fr barriques, 60% new. Also in magnum (1.5ℓ).

Classic Blend ★★★★ Similar to above, touch more merlot, less cab f; 50% new wood; **04** wears heart on sleeve: effusive cassis & sweet spice; elegant, juicy flavours well harmonised with oak; delicious earlier drinking. *– CR*

■ *The Juno Wine Company* see Juno Wine Company

Thelema Mountain Vineyards

*Stellenbosch • Est 1983 • 1stB 1988 • Tasting & sales Mon-Fri 9-5 Sat/Sun 10-3 (Nov-Feb) 10-1 (Mar-Oct) • Closed pub hols • BYO picnic • Tour groups by appt • Owners McLean & Webb Family Trusts • Winemakers Gyles Webb & Rudi Schultz (1983, Dec 2000) • Viti consultants Aidan Morton & Phil Freese • 70 ha (cab, merlot, shiraz, chard, sauvignon, riesling) • 30 000 cs 40% red 60% white • Export brand: Stormy Cape • PO Box 2234 Stellenbosch 7601 • wines@ thelema.co.za • www.thelema.co.za • **T** 021·885·1924 • F 021·885·1800*

Much pleasure is being derived by this stellar Stellenbosch team from their venture in new cool climate hot spot Elgin. The second crop of sauvignon from their Sutherland farm is 'looking fantastic', says marketer Thomas Webb. They've picked some excellent shiraz and planted pinot. Back home on the Simonsberg, Webb Jnr can't resist mentioning two IWC golds (one for the maiden 'Mint'). Dad Gyles Webb is notoriously sceptical about wine shows – he prefers pleasing his *customers*' palates (vindicated by twice being runner-up in the 'best winery in SA' category of *Wine*'s annual reader poll). Ever professional, they invested in a generator to guarantee quality during a harvest plagued by regional power outages. With equally characteristic humour, they cursed the noise levels: 'It sounded like a Boeing landing in the vineyards!'

★★★★★ **Cabernet Sauvignon** From **04**, farm's classy flagship red sails without signature minty clone (see The Mint below) yet retains distinctive & delicious 'modern classic' styling: refined, rich, dark-berry/mocha tones, medium body (more so than other 04 reds), ample freshness & grip to balance creamy mouthfeel. Fr barriques, 50% new, 20 mths. **03** 91 pts WS, *Wine* ★★★★.

★★★★★ **The Mint Cabernet Sauvignon** new From original 1985 cab vyd, single clone with distinctive mintiness long associated with this farm. **04**, inevitably dubbed 'The Full Minty', obliges with striking ripe cassis/menthol scents, plus spicy oak. If fruit tone is modern (love it or hate it), structure is pure cab: tight & fresh, bracing tannin & length to promote good few yrs maturation. 20 mths new Fr oak. IWC gold.

★★★★★ **Cabernet Sauvignon CWG Auction Reserve** None since rich & perfectly proportioned **03**, barrel selection best cab; 20 mths 100% new Fr oak. Decade+ potential.

★★★★ **Merlot** Blackcurrant/herb thumbprint elaborated on **04** with unusual density. Suave, creamy & rich, with fine, lively tannin; very long, savoury & dry. All belie 15% alc, but Webb avers: 'It appears gentle, but packs a punch.' Probably best before punch predominates (±2008?). 20 mths Fr oak, 30% new. 90 pts WS.

★★★★★ **Merlot Reserve** After show stopper **03** (★★★★★), **04** more youthfully introverted but still seriously hedonistic; pedigreed blackcurrant/fennel/coffee aromas; same creamy texture as regular bottling with extra viscosity, flavour intensity. 100% new oak, lofty 15.5% alc, both brilliantly assimilated. Probably less long lived than **03**, which has decade+ potential. 20 mths 100% new Fr oak.

★★★★ **Shiraz** Honest shiraz fruit the focus here. **04** particularly characterful; plentiful nuanced dark berries & spice; rounded, fleshy; spice reprised in savoury farewell. Well contained 14.6% alc. Drinks well now & for a few yrs. Fr/Am oak (80/20), 30% new. **03** 91 pts *WS*.

★★★★ **Arumdale Shiraz** From Webb's Elgin neighbour; ref to Thelema on back-label only. **04** (★★★★) simpler, less intense than maiden **03**; smidgen sugar & spicy tail lift straightforward red fruits, cover drama of 14.8% alc. For earlier drinking. 18 mths Fr/Am oak (90/10), none new.

★★★★ **Chardonnay** 'Why don't people want to buy it anymore? Beats me,' Webb laments about this proven 'prince of dry white wines'. Beats us, too. Spirited **05** delicate hazelnut/lime intro, ends with more expansive flourish. Big but not over-rich or heavy. Usual sound potential. Tighter **04** IWC gold. Fermented/11 mths Fr oak, 33% new.

★★★★ **Ed's Reserve** Demure ref to variety (chardonnay) on back label; similar unshowy front-label childhood pic of materfamilias, Edna McLean (who ensures visitors leave tasting room with cases of wine, happy memories). Though less pungent than pvs, **05** has distinctive grapey, lemon-cream tone, great flavour purity & freshness. 50% new Fr oak.

★★★★ **Sauvignon Blanc** A perennial favourite in this increasingly populous & competitive category. **06** jot more rapier-like intensity, concentration to gorgeous white peach, greengage, gooseberry elegance. Sleek; brims with minerally vigour; moreish ripe-fruit conclusion.

★★★★ **Sutherland Sauvignon Blanc** From highland Elgin site, yielding cooler, more ethereal quality than Thelema's own elevated Sbosch vyds. **06** delicate yet concentrated; mouthwatering fruity acids; memorably long. Not a question of 'either or' with this, above, wine – there's the right mood/food for both.

★★★★ **Rhine Riesling 05** (★★★★) with usual spicy/limy attractions, though tad riper, less racy than pvs. Shd mellow, develop drier profile with maturation, peak around 2010. **04** & pvs were bone-dry, nervous, balanced, suggesting ±decade improvement.

Muscat de Frontignan ☺ ★★★ Delightful, different quaffer. **06** exudes lime/kiwifruit/grape allure. Touch fuller, drier than pvs (9g/ℓ sugar), but in balance with vivacious freshness.

Arumdale Cabernet Sauvignon new ★★★★ **04** first crop from Elgin vyds. Claret-like; satisfying if uncomplex. Quiet rare meat, iron, herb aromas; trim, firm fruit; gentle minerally enlivenment. 20 mths Fr oak, half new. **Pinotage** ★★★★ Friendly & juicy, for medium-term enjoyment. **04** modest dark plum/blackcurrant nose; rounded succulence with firm underbelly; savoury tail. 18 mths Fr oak, 20% new. Coastal WO (fruit ex-Paarl). **Muscadel** ★★★★ Warming & luscious dessert; **98** sold out – fans will have to wait yr/2 for next release. *—AL*

The Marais Family

Robertson ▪ Est ca 1884 ▪ Tasting & sales Mon-Fri 8.30-6 Sat 8.30-1 ▪ Tour groups ▪ Conference & picnic facilities, 4×4 trail & other attractions ▪ Owner Paul René Marais ▪ Winemaker Stefan Bruwer (2002) ▪ Viticulturist Gert Visser, advised by Anton Laas (Jan 1997/Jan 2005) ▪ 240 ha (cab, merlot, pinotage, ruby cab, shiraz, chard, chenin, sauvignon, viognier) ▪ 5 500 tons 3 000 cs own label ▪ 10% red 80% white 1% rosé 9% fortified ▪ PO Box 4 Robertson 6705 ▪ law@lando.co.za ▪ ***T 023·626·2212*** *▪ F 023·626·2669*

Nostalgia in dollops here: the old cellar has become a tasting room, with stairs leading around a tree to a deck and what was an old loft where Italian prisoners-of-war, used as farmhands, once bedded down. Grandfather Eksteen Marais hosted parties and get-togethers there; its new incarnation is as a conference and function venue. Most sparkling of post-launch functions was Monica Marais' marriage last December to Henk van Niekerk. 'He has no wine connection,' says the bride-to-be, 'except that he certainly knows how to enjoy it!'

Merlot new ★★★ **05** pleasant & light textured despite 14% alc; elegant nutmeg & oak-spice nuances; ready, & not for keeping. **La Bonne Vigne Sauvignon Blanc** ★★★ 'The

Good Vyd' picked in stages (half early, half late), flavour enhanced by lees-ageing. **06** crisp & bracing with zesty fruit backbone & freshly cut grass bouquet. **Wonderfontein Red Muscadel** new ★★★ Hedonistic sweet fortified; **06** gentle perfumes, slight raisined character; at 229g/ℓ sugar, a dessert in a glass. — *CT*

■ *The Mask* see Baarsma

The Mason's Winery   ♂ ♀

*Paarl ▪ Est/1stB 2001 ▪ Visits by appt; tasting/sales also at I Love Wine (see entry) ▪ Owner Mason's Hill Wines (Pty) Ltd ▪ Winemaker Derek Clift ▪ 10 tons 700 cs 100% red ▪ PO Box 515 Suider-Paarl 7624 ▪ dehoop@mweb.co.za ▪ **T 083·228·7855** ▪ F 021·863·1601*

For Derek Clift, it's all about shiraz, and he is intent on getting the focus and timing just right. Experimentation with different clones and sites, and allowing his wines to mature a little in bottle before release, are among recent tweaks. Vintage 2006 shows great potential, says he.

★★★★ **Shiraz** Barossa-style flamboyance & power (14+% alc) the hallmarks. No shortage of fruit or winemaking confidence in **04**; deeply rich cherries, raspberries, voluptuous body given 22 mths oak treatment, assimilated with ease. Already lots to reward the drinker, but wine at early stage of evolutionary cycle, has 5+ yrs ahead.

★★★★ **Centenary Reserve Shiraz** More elegant & svelte version of above, **03** tasted last ed, similar creamy fruit, appealing sleekness; probably better prospects than std version but this so seductive, prognostications almost irrelevant. — *CR*

The Observatory Cellars   ♂ ♀

*Cape Town ▪ 1stB 2000 ▪ Tasting by appt ▪ Owners Tom, Catherine, Elizabeth & André Lubbe ▪ Winemaker/viticulturist Tom Lubbe, with Catherine Lubbe (Jan 2000/Jun 2002) ▪ 15 ha (pinotage, shiraz, chard, chenin) ▪ 17 tons 700 cs 60% red 40% white ▪ PO Box 1098 Malmesbury 7299 ▪ syrah@netactive.co.za ▪ **T/F 022·487·3023***

The Lubbe family's long-awaited winemaking move from a facility in central Cape Town to their Paardeberg farm, Boschgaasfontein, is finally happening. 'We can't wait for everything to be in one place,' says Elizabeth L. It hasn't been easy getting everything shipshape – and for these proponents of biodynamics, that has included the re-vegetation of the dilapidated property. 'The proud boast of the previous owner was the destruction of all indigenous trees, bar one old wild olive which refused to die – even after they tried to blow it up!'

★★★★☆ **Syrah** Low-yielding, granitic Pdberg vyd gives lovely, perfumed, nervy purity on **04**. No swaggering power but persistent flavour, with refined fruit & minerality, subtle tannins, all in satisfying, eminently drinkable balance. Fine wine. 2 yrs 2nd fill oak. 13.5% alc.

★★★★ **Carignan-Syrah** Serious **03** (★★★★☆) reversed name, with 79% shiraz, but **04** has 67% carignan, 22% syrah, 11% cab. A pure-fruited terroir wine, miles from blockbusterism, delightful herbal, blackcurrant aromas. As before, lowish 12.5% alc in light (over-light?), harmonious elegance.

★★★★ **Pinotage-Syrah** Elegantly exuberant **04** not re-tried: scrub, herbs, mineral, with bright, sweetly cheerful fruit. Charming expression of pinotage (57%; biodynamically farmed), supple well balanced tannins.

★★★★ **Chenin Blanc-Chardonnay 05** offers dry fynbos aromas, with lemon, fennel & more in 50/50 blend. Light 12.5% alc, with some tannin adding to substance, big vibrant acidity, bone dry. Yr in older wood. Unusual but exciting; excellent food partner; shd mature well for few yrs. — *TJ*

■ *The Ruins* see Bon Cap
■ *The Sadie Family* see Sadie Family

The Saints

Enduring range of easy drinkers by DGB. Quantities now top 300 000 cases a year, 60% white, rest equal portions red and rosé.

St Raphael ★★★ Muted black fruit aromas, smoky/mocha notes in salt-of-the-earth cinsaut, ruby cab (50/50) blend; light textured, soft & dry for every day drinking. **St Celine** ★★ Same blend as St R. Uncomplicated quaffing, bit jammy & sweet (13g/ℓ sugar). Both reds lightly Fr oak chipped. **St Claire** ★★ Appealing Natural Sweet rosé with low alc (8%); honeysuckle wafts, fresh & balanced sweetness. **St Vincent** ★★ Last-tasted bottling was sauvignon dominated but only just (40%), with equal portions chenin & colombard. Tropical aromas & flavours, refreshing & light bodied but uncomplex. **St Morand** ★★ Aromatic blend chenin, colombard & hanepoot; technically semi-sweet, though bottling sampled mid-2005 tasted dryish & was a tad tired, but still pleasant. **St Anna** ★★ Perfumed Natural Sweet white, with low alc (±8%). Delicate fruit salad flavours, honeysuckle aromas, invariably a lovely blend of perfumed varieties including gewürz. All **NV**, WO W Cape. No new vintages ready for review this ed. — DH

■ *The Sensory Collection* see Stellar Winery

The Shosholoza Collection [new]

*Cape Town ▪ Closed to public ▪ Owner: Rainbow Nation Wines ▪ PO Box 44852 Claremont 7735 ▪ info@rainbownationwines.com ▪ www.rainbownationwines.com ▪ **T** 021·674·7227 ▪ F 021·671·6036*

Taking 'Shosholoza', SA's rallying cry at sporting events worldwide, into the wine arena, this young company sources from several boutique to medium-sized wineries, including Boplaas, JP Bredell, Heron Ridge, Napier Winery, Rudera and Viljoensdrift, for its three-tiered 'collections' destined for the overseas market. At press time a range was about to be released in SA too.

The Stables 🍷🍴☕🎻

*KwaZulu-Natal ▪ Est 2004 ▪ 1stB 2005 ▪ Tasting, sales & tours Mon-Thu by appt; Fri/Sat/Sun 10-6 (Oct-Apr) 10-4 (May-Sep) ▪ Fee R20 ▪ Closed Dec 25 & Jan 1 ▪ Gourmet picnics in heated lapa or the herb garden ▪ Farm-style produce ▪ Harvest & jazz festivals (see website) ▪ Tour groups ▪ Owners/winemakers/viticulturists Tiny & Judy van Niekerk ▪ 5 ha (pinot, pinotage, shiraz, chard, nouvelle, riesling, viognier) ▪ 30 tons 5 000 cs 50% red 50% white ▪ PO Box 159 Nottingham Road 3280 ▪ info@stableswine.co.za ▪ www.stableswine.co.za ▪ **T** 033·266·6781/082·441·3701 F 033·266·6252*

A feature on the popular Midlands Meander, KwaZulu-Natal's first registered wine estate is pleasantly surprising skeptics. Telephonic support from Cape consultant Marius Malan talked winemakers Tiny and Judy van Niekerk through any hiccups during the 2006 harvest, when increased production had them on the trot for 36 hours at a time. Now the vNs, bolstered by a Swiss Awards 'Seal of Approval' for the Shiraz, are looking forward to vinifying grapes from their own vineyards next year.

★★★★ **Reserve 1.618 Perfectly Proportioned** [new] Original by name & nature. From KZN fruit, **05** shiraz-led (81%) blend with with merlot & cab; layers smoked bacon, lush red berries, savoury spices & dark wet earth. Powerful bouquet & flavours, with integrated & supple tannins, modest 13% alc. 15 mths new Fr oak.

Nottingham Road range [new]

Pinotage ★★★★ **05** enticing & accessible, flush with ripe plums & cherries; flexible tannins, & gd oak support from seasoned barrels. **Shiraz** ★★★★ Well muscled **05** balances 13.5% alc with flexible yet gripping tannins, robust fruit & healthy sprinkling spices. Aged older oak, shd improve ±3 yrs. **Chardonnay** ★★★ **05** as inviting as a bakery with oven-fresh croissants… Plus white peach & citrus nuances, delicate vanilla oak tones (fermented/11 mths older Fr). But advanced for its age, don't keep. Also available but not tasted: **Chenin Blanc 06, Sauvignon Blanc 06, Drakensberg Tawny**. All in range Sbosch fruit, so WO W Cape.

KwaZulu-Natal range

Pinotage ★★★ **05**'s dense cranberry fruit, gentle wood flavours (ripe fruit has absorbed/melded with 14 mths new Fr oak) & agile tannins make for delightful easy drinker. Friendly

13% alc. Like next, new, awaiting WO KZN certification. **Pinotage Clariet ★★☆** Made blanc de noir style: brief skin contact, then free-run juice bled to old barrels for fermentation. Pale coral hue with blue tinge; drying – & decidedly oaky – tannins; lively acidity & cherry flavours. Following tasted last ed. **Sauvignon Blanc ★** Early-drinking **05** with developed golden hues thanks to minimal sulphuring. **06** not ready for tasting. **Blanc Fumé ★ 05** similar tints to above, sweets & almonds aromas, firm finish. – *DH*

Theuniskraal Estate

Tulbagh ▪ Est 1705 ▪ 1stB 1947 ▪ Tasting & sales Mon-Fri 9-12; 1–4 Sat 10-1 ▪ Fee R5 refundable on purchase ▪ Closed Easter Fri/Sun, Dec 25 & Jan 1 ▪ BYO picnic ▪ Tour groups ▪ Owners Rennie & Kobus Jordaan ▪ Winemaker Andries Jordaan (1991) ▪ Viticulturists Jordaan brothers ▪ 140 ha (13 varieties, r/w) ▪ ±1 600 tons ±35 000 cs own label 10% red 90% white ▪ PO Box 34 Tulbagh 6820 ▪ tkraal@lando.co.za ▪ www.theuniskraal.co.za ▪ **T 023·230·0687/88/ 89/90** ▪ F 023·230·1504

Last year saw the release of this historic estate's first Rosé, adding a fashionably rosy hue to the predominantly white range – the enduring Riesling, launched more than 50 years ago, still its cornerstone. Ixia, after the indigenous flower found on the farm, is a new export brand.

> **Bouquet Blanc Natural Sweet** ☺ **★★★** Effusive gewürz/buket blend (60/40); **05** roses & lime bouquet, palate; unctuous entry yet restrained & uncloying finish.

Prestige ★★★ Stable's lone red. **04** same blend as pvs (ruby cab/cab, 67/33). Last ed burst with strawberry/raspberry flavour, tannic twitch from cab. **Rosé** new **★★** Tangy **06** has dusky looks, easy flavours, for sunset quaffing. Mainly muscat ottonel, equal dollops cab/shiraz. **Riesling ★★** From crouchen, aka Cape riesling. **06** low-key aromas/flavours, racy acidity not dissimilar to Loire's seafood hero, muscadet. **Semillon-Chardonnay ★★★** Charming, well-knit, unwooded **06**, 56/44 blend. Delicate aromas; some lemon/lime richness, semillon freshening & chardonnay fattening. Tasty now & for ±2 yrs. – *CvZ*

■ *The Veldt see* Robertson Wide River

The Winery of Good Hope

Stellenbosch (see Helderberg map) ▪ Est/1stB 1998 ▪ Open by appt ▪ Owners Alex Dale, Edouard Labeye, Ben Radford, Heather Whitman, Stephen Ludlam, Andrew Openshaw & Craig Smith ▪ Winemakers Ben Radford, Edouard Labeye, Guillaume Nell (2006) & Gus Dale, with Tubby May (Feb 2003) ▪ Viticulturist Guillaume Nell ▪ ±120 ha (cab, carignan, grenache, merlot, mourvèdre, pinot noir, shiraz, chard, chenin, sauvignon, viognier) ▪ ±850 tons 40 000 cs own label 50/50 red/white ▪ Postnet Suite 124 Private Bag X15 Somerset West 7129 ▪ thewineryofgoodhope@thewineryofgoodhope.co.za ▪ www.thewineryofgoodhope.com ▪ **T 021·855·5528** ▪ F 021·855·5529

Final consolidation of four production sites and a ±1 000-barrel maturation cellar by the end of this year will constitute the 'transformation' (says MD Alex Dale) of this quality Helderberg wine business. Joining the team is internationally schooled viticulturist/winemaker Guillaume Nell. A 'strategic focus on individual or unique blends, uncommon vineyard areas and unusual styles' in 2006 (including an old-vine Riesling and a Shiraz from Aussie partner Ben Radford's Eden Valley estate) raised the global profile. This continues with introductions of a premium Pinot, Viognier, (yet untasted) Viognier dessert wine and first-time Pinotage. A no-discount policy in a tough market has worked, with sales up a third, boosted by 'instant bestseller', the newer Winery of Good Hope range. As the guide went to press, an elated team prepared to announce a partnership with a major international wine family...

Radford Dale range

★★★★☆ Gravity Name derives from gentle, machinery-eschewing vinification. **03** seamlessly combined merlot, shiraz, cab, impressed with pure savoury vinosity in soft frame; **04** just bottled when tasted last ed, provisional **★★★★**; shd gain depth, complexity &

intensity with time; clean, well defined flavours, promising. Partly barrel fermented, ±14 mths in wood.

★★★★ **Merlot** With Old World leanings, previewed **05** has lovely wild herb, violet, white pepper nuances, subtle, silky elegance. 18 mths Fr/Am oak. Elgin fruit. Merlot for grownups.

★★★★ **Shiraz 05** sashays back to the New World after glorious rhône-toned **04** (★★★★☆). Latest has plenty of ripe dark fruit, an array of oak spices & smoky liquorice tones. Admirable definition achieved in warm vintage, but a wine for drinking rather than keeping.

★★★★ **Shiraz-Viognier** Co-fermented, which accounts for complete integration, harmony of **05**, previewed last ed, now finished wine. Brambleberries, white pepper, earthy notes, with a hovering fragrant lift from viognier. 14 mths mainly Fr oak, 40% new. Unfined/filtered. 15% alc well assimilated.

★★★★☆ **Chardonnay** Meticulous vyd selection & cellar care shows in **05**'s sleek, thoroughbred lines. Quite burgundian (not surprising, given Alex D's background) in its restraint, minerality, deep-seated peach & citrus flavouring. Yr Fr oak, portion new.

★★★★ **Viognier** [new] Always the unexpected from this team, ex-barrel **06** has more lavender, candied violet shadings than normal peach aromatics of variety. Ripe (15% alc) but not overblown, it offers exotic drinkability. Fermented new/2nd fill Fr oak.

Pinot Noir 05 sample last ed, provisional ★★★☆; medicinal & slightly astringent, delicate redcurrant flavours; plenty of elegance; Fr oak, none new. Dijon clone, Elgin & Sbosch fruit.

Black Rock range

★★★★☆ **Red Blend** Range named after Swtland, source of bushvine fruit. Southern Rhône-inspired exotic blend, individual & compelling. **05** has different moods, aspects: lavender, scrub, blueberry; a salty liquorice & prosciutto explosion of flavour, long ultrasmooth finish. Mainly shiraz, carignan (60/23), rest grenache, mourvèdre, viognier. Two-thirds oaked, mainly Fr, some new.

★★★★ **White Blend** Distinctive assemblage dominated by 40 yr old bushvine chenin. Beautifully integrated & fragrant **05** shows deeply rich citrus, tropical fruit, yet a persistent minerality that refreshes, is food compatible. Fr barrel fermented, 15 mths matured. Qtr chard, dab viognier.

Vinum range

★★★★ **Chenin Blanc** From old Hldrberg bushvines; **06** work in progress mid-2006 but already showing expected class, concentration: tropical fruit, some citrus; curvaceous body & variety's appetising acidic bite. **05** sample showed honey & apricot with generous acidity, nascent complexity.

Cabernet Sauvignon 04 (★★★★) previewed last ed, now sleek & polished; cassis, dark choc, vanilla spicing & a satin textured accessibility, despite the underlying structure. Yr 70/30 Fr/Am oak. Elegant **03** (★★★☆) sleek, mouthwatering, harmonious.

The Winery of Good Hope range

Cabernet Sauvignon-Merlot ★★★ Unashamedly fruit-driven **06** sample has perfectly ripe red berries, juicy structure, soft tannins, lovely drinkability. Equal blend. Following pair of samples [new]: **Pinotage** Ripe dark fruit at core of **06** given a savoury shading by oak. Tannins busy integrating, difficult to rate mid-2006 — ★★★? **Pinot Noir** ★★★☆ Though work in progress, **06** already textbook styling: elegant structure, piquant red berries, underbrush, hints of other nuances to come. Elgin vyds. **Chardonnay** ★★★ **06** is that rare creature, unoaked chard with character: peach/tropical tones, rounded fresh-fruity mouthfeel. This & next screwcapped. **Chenin** ★★★ Just-bottled **06** shows crunchy apple/ pear freshness in a light, food-friendly format. Bone-dry, with perky 7.1g/ℓ acidity.

New World range

No new vintages tasted for this ed. **Shiraz** ★★★ **05** boiled sweets & smoky 'matchstick' nose/palate, meaty hint. In same uncomplicated vein as pvs. This, next, a sample last yr. **Sauvignon Blanc** ★★★ **05** hot-climate sauvignon with slight topical pineapple & lunchtime pleasing 12% alc. **Cabernet Sauvignon-Merlot** ★★★ **03** medium bodied 60/40 blend, smoothed for readiness by wild strawberry/plum fruity sweetness. **Shiraz-Pinotage ★★★ 04** peppy, easy-going 60/40 partnership. Substantial, expressive flavour richness, warmingly long. Unoaked. **Semillon-Chardonnay ★★★** Satiny **04** unwooded 60/40 mix; flavoursome waxy lemon intensity, gd zippy length. WO W Cape. — *CR*

■ *Thierry's Wine Services see* Cape Grace

Third World Wines

*Est 2001 • MD Jonathan van Blerk • Vini consultant Kosie Möller • The Stables, Westcot, Wantage, OX12 9QA UK • wineorders@3rdworld.co.uk wineorders@gatsbyhotels.com • www.3rdworld.co.uk www.gatsbyhotels.com • **T 0944·779·191·3044** • F 0944·123·575·1755*

No update available on this winery; contact details from previous edition.

■ *33 Degrees South see* Wamakersvallei

32 South Ltd

*Est 1998 • Closed to public • 100 000 cs 55% red 45% white • UK office: Millennium Harbour, 202 Pierpoint Building, Westferry Rd, London E14 8NQ • T 0944·0208 985·9700 • F 0944·0870 487·5747 • 32south@btconnect.com • **T/F 887·9112***

No update from this merchant house, whose ranges have included 32 South and Isabelo. Contact details are from the previous edition.

Thokozani Wines   Ò♀ new

*Wellington • Est/1stB 2005 • Tasting & sales at Diemersfontein (see entry) • Owners Diemersfontein employees, external investors & Diemersfontein Wines • 1 000 cs 40% red 40% white 20% rosé • PO Box 41 Wellington 7654 • info@thokozani.co.za • **T 021·864·5050** • F 021·864·2095*

There's an infant in the Diemersfontein family: Thokozani (appropriately, it translates as 'celebrate') is a partnership between the Wellington winery, its staff and outside black economic empowerment investors. Barely two years old, the venture uses Diemersfontein grapes, winemakers, production facilities and tasting room, but the plan is to source more widely as the fledgling grows into independence.

All **★★★**. **Shiraz-Mourvèdre 04** full-ripe, prunes & berry preserve, with liquorice, sweet spice layers. Dry yet ultra-friendly, rounded, for early drinking. 16 mths combo Fr/Am, barrels & staves. **Rosé 06** vivid cerise-coloured off-dry charmer showing off the attributes of its blending partners: strawberry/mulberry from pinotage, shiraz; herbal touch from mourvèdre; juicy drinkability from them all. **SCV** Named for its blend, semillon, chenin, viognier (55/30/15), **05** has a savoury, dried peach, almost bready perfume, floral fruit coming to the fore on palate. Tasty, food-friendly, helped by fresh 6.5g/ℓ acidity. Coastal fruit. — *CR*

■ *Thomas Kipling see* Makro
■ *Thornhill see* Veenwouden

Thorntree Wines

*Est/1stB 2001 • Closed to public • Owner/winemaker André Badenhorst • 70 000 cs 50/50 red/white • Export brands: Cape Mist, Witteboomen • Suite 310 Private Bag X16 Constantia 7848 • andrebad@iafrica.com • www.thorntreewines.co.za • **T 021·786·2487** • F 021·786·1476*

Selling well across nine states in the US, Thorntree is now one of the 10 top SA wine producers exporting to this challenging growth market. Owner/winemaker André Badenhorst also developed a new brand in conjunction with one of the biggest US distributors last year and expected market penetration to extend to 17 states. Badenhorst is upbeat about SA expansion in the US, and believes producers should pool resources and cooperate more marketing-wise while reducing the number of entry-level brands competing for shelf space.

Merlot ★★ **05** as sturdy as pvs but with sweeter finish (6.2g/ℓ sugar); needs bit of time for red berry fruit, oak tannins to mesh. 50% oaked. **Shiraz** ★★★ **05** robust fireside sipper, as 14% alc attests. Older-style smoke & meat aromas/flavours dominate. Again, some sugar sweetness apparent. **Chardonnay** ★★☆ Lightly flavoured **06**, softly oaked to not obscure gentle lemon-butter nuances. Orange-peel hints, creamy finish. Third wooded. **Sauvignon Blanc** ★★ **06** bright & zesty, rounded by sprinkle sugar; lowish 11.7% alc adding to easygoing quaffability. All WO W-Cape. Discontinued: **Cabernet Sauvignon, Pinotage, Chenin Blanc**. — *CT*

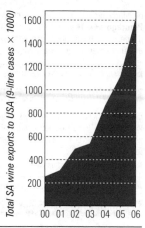

Total SA wine exports to USA (9-litre cases × 1000)

(y-axis: 200, 400, 600, 800, 1000, 1200, 1400, 1600)

(x-axis: 00 01 02 03 04 05 06)

■ *Three Anchor Bay see* Cape First
■ *Three Gables see* The Winery of Good Hope
■ *Three Peaks see* Mount Vernon
■ *Three Rivers see* Bon Courage
■ *Thys Drift see* Goedverwacht

Tierhoek

*Citrusdal ▪ Est 2001 ▪ 1stB 2003 ▪ Closed to public ▪ Owner Tony Sandell ▪ Winemaker Ian Nieuwoudt ▪ Viticulturist Johan Viljoen ▪ ±15 ha (chard, chenin, sauvignon) ▪ ±2 000 cs 5% red 95% white ▪ PO Box 53372 Kenilworth 7745 ▪ ssandell@iafrica.com ▪ **T 021·674·2468 / 082·536·7132** ▪ F 021·674·2468*

Now typical of a Sandveld homestead of the 19th-century, the restored farmhouse on this upland Citrusdal spread awaits its equine elements: period stables, horse mill and saddlery. Upgrading of the vineyards has coincided with the building work: another 9ha of white vines went into the soil last year, with selected reds still to come.

★★★★ **Wooded Chenin Blanc** Food-friendly, poised **05**, now dry; thatch, spice, honey threads from bouquet to finish; stylish oaking adds nuance & grip; no malo, so acidity's firm. Fermented/5 mths new Fr oak. Midweight (12.5% alc) compared with **04** (★★★★) which was solid yet refreshing. Both should improve with few yrs age.

Grenache ★★★ **05** ups ante for this unusual (in SA) varietal bottling. Abundant dark fruit — enough to stand up to, if not (yet) tame, powerful oak (15 mths new Fr), dry tannins; refreshing tangy acidity. **Unwooded Chenin Blanc** `new` ★★★★ **05** debuts in subdued fashion; light, elegant floral/thatch scents & flavours with mineral core, long farewell. Cld age few yrs. **Sauvignon Blanc** ★★★★ **06** unready; last tasted **04** was promising; litchi & gooseberry charms, emphatic 'wet pebble' finish. All EW, WO Piekenierskloof. — *CvZ*

■ *Timbili see* Ernst & Co
■ *Tin Mine see* Zevenwacht
■ *Todo see* Helderkruin

Tokara

Stellenbosch ▪ Est/1stB 2000 ▪ Tasting & sales 9-5 Sat, Sun & pub hols 10-3 ▪ Tokara Restaurant for lunch & dinner Tue-Sat (T 021·808·5959) ▪ Farm-grown varietal olive oils from The Olive Shed ▪ Art exhibits (enquiries: Julia Meintjes ▪ T 083·675·1825) ▪ Owner GT Ferreira ▪ Winemaker Miles Mossop (Jan 2000), with Dumisani Mathonsi (Jan 2004) ▪ Viticulturist Aidan Morton (Nov 2000) ▪ 110 ha (cabs s/f, grenache, malbec, merlot, mourvèdre, petit v, shiraz, chard, chenin, sauvignon, semillon) ▪ *700 tons 50 000 cs* ▪ *60% red 40% white* ▪ *PO Box 662 Stellenbosch 7599* ▪ *wine@ tokara.com* ▪ *www.tokara.com* ▪ **T** *021·808·5900* ▪ F *021·808·5911*

Release of the flagship range from big-businessman GT Ferreira's classy property atop Stellenbosch's Helshoogte just after we put last year's guide to bed, made an immediate splash with acclaim pouring in from around the wine world. One suspects it's just the beginning. Talented young Miles Mossop predicts 'powerful reds' from 2006. Promising first crops of sauvignon and chardonnay from Tokara's Elgin and Hemel-en-Aarde properties may warrant stand-alone bottlings akin to the Walker Bay Sauvignon. Bought-in Stellenbosch fruit supplies Zondernaam until own vineyards reach full production around 2012. New chenin vines will feed the recently launched 5 Year Old Potstill Brandy. Don't miss the cellar's Wine Made Art exhibitions, demonstrating the beverage's untapped capabilities...

★★★★☆ **Red** Critically acclaimed flagship (VDG, *Wine/Decanter* ★★★★, Calyon Top Ten, 90 pts *WS*); **04** bigger, richer than maiden **03**, complex array black/red berries, mocha tones. Cream textured, dry & long. Will need yr/2 to absorb youthful tannin; like pvs, possibly best within first 5 yrs. Cab with merlot, petit v & introducing cab f (69/14/11/6); sensitively oaked (Fr, 78% new, 20 mths).

★★★★☆ **White** Distinctive – & scintillating evidence that sauvignon is not a one-horse grape. **05** as fine as maiden **04**, more Bdx (riper, richer) than Loire. Deep gooseberry, granadilla sophistication; firm build, fruit richness harnessed by nip polished tannin. Barrelled for extra dimension, longevity (potential until ±2010). Fr oak fermented/6 mths, 13% new. **04** *Decanter* ★★★★.

★★★★ **Chardonnay 05** mirrors cool minerality of maiden **04**. Modern but unshowy toasty/ nutty notes, more pickled lime substance on palate; oaked to harmonise, increase vinosity. Sleek, ultra-clean finish. Fermented/11 mths Burgundy barrels, 40% new. Partial malo. **04** 90 pts *WS*.

★★★★ **Sauvignon Blanc** From GTF's sea-breezed Hemel & Aarde Valley vyd. Cool provenance evidenced in pure, intense fig/gooseberry fragrance, clean lines. **06** cushioned mouthfeel suavely contrasted by crisp fruity acids. Very moreish.

Zondernaam range

★★★★ **Cabernet Sauvignon** After difficult **02** (★★★★), **03** returns to top form with classy, expensive profile. Claret-like vivid cassis, violets & mineral notes, spicy new-oak overlay. Compact, firm but not intimidating. Properly dry, lingering. Incl effective splashes cab f, petit v. 40% new Fr barriques, 18 mths. 70% Sbosch-area vyds.

★★★★ **Shiraz 04** elegant kaleidoscope white/dark spice, red fruits fragrance plus mocha resonance. Comfortably medium bodied with fruit-lifting savoury acid; fluid but still quite pushy tannins need yr/2. **03** (★★★★★) beguiling red fruits/lilies fragrance. Shd peak around 2009/10; worth the wait. 18 mths Fr/Am casks, 30% new. WO Coastal.

★★★★ **Sauvignon Blanc** ✓ Styled for wide appeal. Striking **06** tad more assertive than pvs. Keen, stimulating greengage, gooseberry scents; medium bodied with mouthwatering fruity acids, enthusiastic finishing zest. Sbosch, S/West & home vyds.

Chardonnay ★★★★ **04** with maturing echoes of roast hazelnuts & hints of ripe cheese. Pleasing lime/mineral thread enlivens richness, creamy lees. Drink over next yr. Mainly Fr oak fermented/10 mths, 23% new. Home vyds. **Chenin Blanc** ★★★★ **04** tasted last yr, bold, juicy with alc kick in sweetish tail. Sold out; **05** all sold before we could taste; **06** not ready. Bought-in Sbosch grapes; natural ferment in barrel, partially new oak. **04** *Wine* ★★★★☆, VDG. **05** *Wine* ★★★★. – *AL*

■ *Tokolosh* see International Wine Services
■ *Tom Lubbe Wines* see The Observatory

Topaz Wine

Somerset West ▪ *Est/1stB 2000* ▪ *Visits by appt* ▪ *Owners/winemakers Clive Torr & Tanja Beutler* ▪ *Viticulturists Tanja Beutler, Francis Yeatman, Willie de Waal, James Downes & Clive Torr* ▪ *0.04 ha 450 cs 100% red* ▪ *26 Topaz Str, Heldervue, Somerset West 7130* ▪ *topazwines @mweb.co.za* ▪ **T** *021·855·4275 / 082·557·0826* ▪ F *021·855·5086*

'The wine is horns!' quips Clive Torr, Cape Wine Master and taster for this guide, summing up the excitement over the first crop from his and partner Tanja Beutler's 'garden vineyard' in suburban Somerset West. Their garagiste is winery slowly going biodynamic: racking for the Pinot, for example, was timed to coincide with the crescent moon. The hand-crafted Shiraz, now including grapes from a new Elgin vineyard 'to spice up the old faithful Stellenbosch fruit', is their other labour of love.

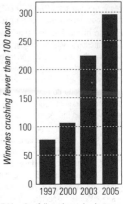

★★★★ **Pinot Noir** Off Elgin vines, **05** (★★★★) ripe red berries & varietal perfumes more forthcoming on nose than restrained palate mid-2006. 'Feminine' fruit barred behind firm savoury/gamey tannic structure & tight acidity. Needs time to evolve (& rate higher), show more charm. **04** last ed had Burgundian barnyard hints in tight tannin jacket.

★★★★ **Syrah** Elegant & poised **05**, black pepper, ripe wild berries & lingering spicy incense; palate enhanced by savoury smoked meat nuances & svelte creamy texture. Some cooler Elgin fruit adds pure clean-fruited dimension in this hot vintage. **04** (★★★★) more Rutherglen, less Rhône (& shade less stunning) than outstanding **03** (★★★★★). One-third new Fr oak. — MW

- ■ **Towerkop** see Southern Cape Vineyards
- ■ **Tradouw** see Southern Cape Vineyards
- ■ **Tribal** see African Terroir
- ■ **Tricolore** see Weltevrede
- ■ **Trini Cella** see Rooiberg

Tukulu

Groenekloof • Est 1998 • Tasting & sales by appt at Bergkelder (see entry) • Owners Distell, Leopont 98 Properties, Maluti Groenekloof Community Trust • Winemaker Adian Fry (2003) • Viticulturist Hannes van Rensburg (1998) • 245 ha (cab, pinotage, sangiovese, shiraz, chard, chenin, sauvignon, viognier) • 4 500 cs own label • 60% red 40% white • PO Box 184 Stellenbosch 7599 • info@tukulu.co.za • www.tukulu.co.za • T 021·809·7000 • F 021·882·9575

This is the original black empowerment brand in the Distell stable, its continuing success over nearly a decade due in no small measure to the quality of its fruit source: the Papkuilsfontein vineyards near Darling. These also supply other Distell-owned brands, but in 2005 the 'truly excellent' quality of the shiraz prompted a portion to be held back for a maiden bottling under the Tukulu label. Enthused winemaker Adian Fry believes the newcomer might even top the widely lauded Pinotage. Also new is a chardonnay from an organically farmed block which, Fry says, also holds great promise.

★★★★ **Pinotage** Latest **04** back to form after quiet **03** (★★★★). Shy at first, but all there on palate, richly crammed with blackberry, tangy plum flavours. Plump jammy fruit, controlled by softish tannins; slight sweetness on finish. 14 mths new oak, mostly Fr, 30% Am.

★★★★ **Shiraz** new **05**, with gorgeous black cherry, dried scrub, veldfire & toast, combines ripe sweet fruit with firm dry tannins. Concentrated, but supple, lithe & balanced. 14 mths mixed-origin oak, 70% new. Best give 2-3 yrs to harmonise/develop.

★★★★ **Chenin Blanc** In recent yrs tasted only pre-bottling, incl **06** (★★★) with bruised apple, wild scrub aromas: softer, gentler & possibly less definition & authority than **05**. 4.7g/ℓ sugar revealed on sweetish finish. A third new-oaked. — IvH

Tulbagh Mountain Vineyards

Tulbagh ▪ Est 2000 ▪ 1stB 2003 ▪ Tasting, sales & tours by appt ▪ Owners Jason Scott & George Austin ▪ Winemaker/viticulturist Chris Mullineux (Dec 2002) ▪ 16 ha (cab, mourvèdre, shiraz) ▪ 88 tons 90% red 6% white 4b% straw wine ▪ PO Box 19 Tulbagh 6820 ▪ info@tmv.co.za ▪ www.tmv.co.za ▪ T 023·231·1118 ▪ F 023·231·1002

This rising star can boast a year of good reviews; a widening distribution network; a maiden white blend and straw wine; and a developing style of winemaking which is being tracked with satisfaction by co-owners George Austin and Jason Scott. They're champions of the Swartland, the source of grapes for their negociant wine: 'It'll emerge as a flagship region for SA, particularly in its expression of shiraz and shiraz blends.' Their focus is now firmly on the wine, 'not the story or the personalities behind it', as Jason S (himself one of those personalities – see their website) would have it. But we simply can't resist: winemaker Chris Mullineux and assistant winemaker Andrea Kozlowski are officially engaged!

★★★★ **Syrah-Mourvèdre** Youthfully tight, powerful **04** dominated by taut minerality & spicy Fr oak (22 mths, third new), lily & spice character announcing majority shiraz (85%), & strong, rather dry tannins hopefully softening into the lurking sweet fruit. Like Theta, certified organic; like all from this cellar, native yeast fermentation.

Theta ★★★★ Ambitious, dark, ripe-fruited **03** (not retasted) from shiraz – with spicy-tobacco oak (22 mths Fr, 50% new) & touch of volatility. One to watch. No **04**.

TMV range

★★★★☆ **Swartland Syrah** 2nd vintage of this elegantly generous, immensely engaging wine, with Swtland's scrubby, herbal notes to shiraz's lilies. Smoothly firm, refined tannins, excellent natural acidity, succulent fruit & a balance reinforced by subtle Fr oak (11 mths, 11% new). Unobtrusive 14.6% alc. Lovely young, but will repay keeping few yrs.

★★★★ **Viktoria** Half shiraz, with mourvèdre, cinsaut, cab. Notably ripe, forward fruit, richly flavourful & mouthfilling; robust but restrained structure. Integrated oak – largely as above; also unfined/filtered.

★★★★ **White** new (Replaces Chenin Blanc.) Herbs & spices, mineral aromas, mingling with understated floral, peachy perfume of viognier (4%, with 6% clairette) on dominant chenin character. Richly round but elegantly focused & dry. Clever, restrained oaking again: here 11 mths older Fr.

★★★★☆ **Vin Pi One** new **(NV**, no. to change each vintage) Name puns on vin de paille – chenin grapes dried outdoors, then naturally fermented in old oak. Solera system for fractional blending (here across 3 vintages), allowing some slow oxidation. Unusual, but gorgeous: baked apple, burnt toffee elements to its classy deliciousness. V sweet (298g/ℓ sugar), but uncloying given fine balance with fresh acidity & light 11% alc.

Above from, or include, bought-in grapes. WO W Cape, **05** unless noted. **Cabernet Sauvignon-Merlot, Syrah-Cabernet Sauvignon** discontinued. – *TJ*

Tulbagh Wineries Co-op

Tulbagh/Swartland ▪ Est 1906/2006 ▪ Owners 126 members ▪ Production manager Carl Allen (Aug 2002) ▪ Cellarmaster André Oberholzer (Porterville, Dec 1996) ▪ Winemakers Elsabé le Roux (Tulbagh, Dec 2002) & Dico du Toit (Sep 2004) ▪ Viticulturists Jan-Carel 'Callie' Coetzee (Tulbagh 2002) & Juliana Boysen (Porterville, 2005) ▪ 1 930 ha ▪ 20 000 tons 20% red 70% white 10% other ▪ Ranges for customers: Kumala, Porter Mill Station & Paddagang ▪ Tulbagh cellar: Tasting & sales Mon-Fri 8-5 Sat 9-1 ▪ Closed pub hols except Easter Sat, May 1 & Sep 24 ▪ Gift shop ▪ PO Box 85 Tulbagh 6820 ▪ tkw@tulbaghwine.co.za ▪ www.tulbaghwine.co.za ▪ T 023·230·1001 ▪ F 023·230·1358 ▪ Porterville cellar: Tasting & sales Mon-Fri 8-5 Sat 9-1 ▪ Closed Easter Fri-Mon, Dec 25/26, Jan 1 ▪ Tours by appt ▪ Picnics/light meals by appt or BYO ▪ Tour groups ▪ PO Box 52 Porterville 6810 ▪ info@portwines.co.za ▪ www.portervillecellars.co.za ▪ T 022·931·2170 ▪ F 022·931·2171

Last year saw SA's oldest co-op reach its centenary and simultaneously take on a new identity after merging with Porterville Cellars of Swartland. Production has risen to roughly 20 000 tons (largely white), and the combined teams have been able to strengthen their strategic position on local and international markets. Production manager is Tulbagh stalwart Carl Allen while the new cellarmaster is André Oberholzer of Porterville. A poignant farewell, however, to Jack Marasi who shared 50 of Tulbagh's 100 years — an achievement which few will ever match.

Tulbagh range

Shiraz ☺ ★★☆ Vibrant quaffer with well defined red berry notes & oak/acid balance on **05**, vanilla nuances adding sweetness, touch of complexity. **Sauvignon Blanc** ☺ ★★☆ Cheerful, light **06** from early picked grapes. Intense tropical notes, flashes lemongrass, crisp acidity. WO Coastal.

Unfortified reds in range lightly wood-chipped. **Cabernet Sauvignon** ★★ **04** ideal BBQ wine given outdoorsy aromas of damp earth & autumn leaves; but fruity, well muscled tannins, nicely dry. **Merlot** ★★ Timid varietal characters play hide & seek on **05**; gripping, less easy-drinking than pvs. **Pinotage** ★★ Eminently quaffable **05** has plum aromas/flavours set off by friendly tannins. **Chardonnay** ★★ Unwooded **06** a hiccup in track record, with scanty peach scents, lacklustre presence. **Chenin Blanc** ★★ **05** tasted pvs ed; spicy notes, compact & racy. **06** unready. **Port** ★★★ **NV** last ed stylistically hovered between old & new styles; dusty/earthy, not over-sweet, lowish alc (18.4%) but higher than pvs. From pinotage & ruby cab.

Klein Tulbagh Reserve range

Still selling, none retasted; unfortified reds barrel aged 9-12 mths. **Cabernet Sauvignon** ★★★ Classically styled **03** rung above austere pvs; appealing redcurrant & green olive flavours, supple tannins. **Merlot** ★★★ Massively ripe, unsubtle style; **03** deeper coloured than pvs, more extracted; stewed plums & dried fruit, grainy tannins. **Pinotage** ★★★ **03** mulberry aromas & vanilla suggestion (from 47% Am oak); ripe, more satisfying than above wines. Pinotage Top Ten 2005. **Shiraz** ★★★ **03** shy strawberry nose, woodsmoke sniffs; soft & quaffable. **Vintage Port** ★★★ From pinotage; **02** older-style with lower alc, highish sweetness — but delicious; packed with succulent fruitcake flavour.

Village Collection

Classic Red ☺ ★★★ Unwooded, plummy & dry, with charming balance & vinosity. Latest from cab (50%), with pinotage & shiraz, all putting their fruits together delightfully.

All in range **NV**, sold in 750ml screwtops & 3ℓ packs. **Natural Sweet Rosé** ★★ Gently sweet, light (8.2% alc) & round; touch of cab gives nice hint of tannin. **Crispy White** ★★ Tangy, light, appley blend of mostly sauvignon with a quarter colombard. **Extra Light** ★ Latest (unlike pvs) less crisp than Crispy, but still pretty light (9.8% alc) & bone-dry. Blend fernão pires plus 4 other whites. **Simply Sweet** ★★ Spicy, bouncy semi-sweet from quartet of grapes incl hanepoot.

Porterville Unfiltered Reserve range

Cabernet Sauvignon ★★★ **04** soft, fruity & fairly easy red; hints dried leaves, distinct dry tannins. Yr Fr barrels, same for most following reds. **Pinotage** ★★ Medium bodied **04**, savoury tone with pleasant sweet-sour twist, muted fruit & some astringency. **Shiraz** ★★★ **04** light bodied (12.5) with restrained fruit & muted varietal character. **Visage** ★★★ Interesting blend shiraz (42%), pinotage, cab, grenache noir, merlot; **03** showed soft wild berry fruit &, in youth, this range's vibrant tannin structure. Modest 13% alc. **Chardonnay** ★★★ Wooded **03** plumply forceful, enough stuffing, alc (14.7%), to stand up to full-flavoured food. **Chenin Blanc Unfiltered** ★★★ Wood-fermented **03** lanolin & lime marmalade tone, suggestion butterscotch/caramel; full-bodied & balanced. **Chenin Blanc-Chardonnay-Grenache Blanc** ★★ (Pvsly 'Chanaché') **05** appealing peachy notes, gd fresh mouthful of sweet fruit, open & accessible. Fr oak chips/barrels 7 mths. W Cape, Coastal & Swtlnd WOs for these. None in this, range below, retasted this ed.

Porter Mill Station range

'Friendly & fruity drinking wines' is the goal for this eye-catching line-up. **Cabernet Sauvignon** ★★★ **04** hints wet earth & wild berries; softer, more accessible character than stable mates. Yr Fr barrels, same for most following reds. **Pinotage** ★★ **04** similar sweet-sour zing, understated savoury/strawberry tone & dense tannin. **Shiraz** ★★★ **04** smoky wild berries & bluegum whiff; leanish body with restrained fruit, pressy dry tannins. **Chardonnay** ★★ Pleasant dry white, crisp & light (12.5%). **Chenin Blanc** ★★ **05** lightly fruity dry white with hint of winter melon. **Chenin Blanc-Chardonnay-Grenache Blanc** ★★ **05** appealing summer-evening drink; light (13% alc), undemanding, crisply dry. Lightly wooded. **Sauvignon Blanc** ★★ **05** grilled seafood partner; taut, wiry frame, firm acid backbone; asparagus & cut grass whiffs. W Cape & Swtlnd WOs for these. Disa range discontinued. — *DH*

■ **Tulbagh Winery** *see* Tulbagh Wineries Co-op
■ **Tutuka** *see* Buthelezi Wines

Twee Jonge Gezellen Estate   ♂♀

Tulbagh ▪ Est 1710 ▪ 1stB 1937 ▪ Tasting & sales Mon-Fri 9-4 Sat & pub hols 10-2 ▪ Casual tasting: no charge; formal tasting: fee on request ▪ Tours Mon-Fri 11 & 3; Sat & pub hols 11 ▪ Closed Easter Fri-Mon, Dec 25-26 & Jan 1 ▪ Owner/winemaker Nicky Krone ▪ 100 ha (petit v, pinot, muscat de F, chard, chenin, riesling, sauvignon, semillon, viognier) ▪ 800 tons 8% red 80% white 12% rosé ▪ PO Box 16 Tulbagh 6820 ▪ tjg@mweb.co.za ▪ www.tjwines.co.za ▪ T 023 230·0680 ▪ F 023 230·0686

Two decades on and a dream's come true — the flagship sparkling range, 'The House of Krone', is set to sail! First on board was the 87 vintage, launched in 91, of Mary and Nicky K's Krone Borealis Cuvée Brut, with successors lauded and awarded. Second in what's destined to be a range of MCCs was released late last year: the Rosé Brut. As tradition demands, the new sparkler is a pinot/chardonnay blend; again, tradition on the Krone family farm is that picking for the Rosé was done by hand, at night or in the cool of the early morning. Both the old and the new have been issued smart new livery.

Krone range

★★★★ **Borealis Brut** MCC in well established, acclaimed line, from chard/pinot; latest **00** shows slightly more weight than pvs (within fine-boned TJ context); sweet red-berried pinot flavours dominating in youth, with attractive vinosity. Lightish alc (11.5%), & dryer profile these days, at 7–8g/ℓ sugar.

★★★★ **Rosé Brut Cuvée** new Exciting **00** pink MCC bubbly, fragrant with lovely fresh strawberries, delicate & refined. In the accomplished Krone style, poised & elegantly balanced. Dry, lightly fruity, with ribbons of the finest bubbles, after impressive 4.5 yrs on the lees. The ultimate St Valentine's charmer (& any other time…).

Syrah ★★★★ **02** attractive dusty berry & dried prune quality, dry earthy tannins; ripe fruit sweetness; easily carries 14.5% alc. No new samples tasted of this & next 2. **Balm of the Night** ★★★ Fortified muscat de F; **99** was last. **Engeltjipipi** ★★★ Delicate botrytised **01** from semillon, chenin, riesling, firm acidity, balanced sweetness.

TJ range

The Rose ☺ ★★★ Still a hit, still a bargain. Carbonated **NV**, deep rose-pink; meaty & assertive like a red wine, with refreshing lazy bubble. Chill well, & tuck into picnic basket. Blend chard, chenin, pinot, shiraz. **Light** ☺ ★★★ Ideal lunchtime wine, low 8.5% alc. Wafting muscat still a signature: **06** sprinkling perfumed talc, delicate dry palate comes as delightful surprise. **Schanderl** ☺ ★★★ Fragrant honeysuckle on off-dry, zesty & assertive **06** from muscat de F. These can age pleasantly, developing tangy grapefruit tones. Easy-going tipple at 12% alc. No **04**, **05**.

Thirty Nine ★★ Riesling-dominated blend (39 = clone number), with sauvignon, chenin. **06** like pvs with modest aroma; some baked notes; delicate, light, very soft. **Night Nectar Natural Sweet** ★★★ **04** blend chenin, some viognier. Graceful uncloying sweetie (59g/ℓ RS), with delicate acidity. Not retasted; no **05**. — *IvH*

▪ **Twin's Peak** *see* Lateganskop
▪ **Two Cubs** *see* Knorhoek

Two Oceans

Good value range by Distell mainly for export, though the Cab-Merlot and Sauvignon are distributed locally and available for tasting at Bergkelder Wine Centre (see entry).

Pinotage ★★ Barrel/chips combo meshes pleasantly with **05**'s plum/mulberry flavours. Tad bitter finish. For early drinking, as are most of these. **Shiraz** ★★★ Fruit-shy **05** more smoke/tar than flowers/berries on nose; big, bold tannins from 3 mth sojourn in new Fr oak (pvsly Fr staves/chips). **Cabernet Sauvignon-Merlot** ★★★★ **05**'s 60/40 blend an inviting melange of black cherries, mocha, choc. Abundant fruit, malleable tannins, dry tea-leaf finish. **Merlot-Shiraz** ★★★ Lushness of merlot (65%) constrained by tannins mid-2006; shd relax, fill out, with bit of time. **05** mix staves/barrels, ±9 mths. **Soft & Fruity Red** ★★★ (Pvsly Cape Red.) Fireside (& poolside?) sipper with touch oak. Cab, pinotage, ruby cab as usual in **05**, with dollop shiraz upping red berry aromas/flavours. Smooth & fresh-finishing. **Rosé** ★★★ Sip-me-soon **05** adds pinot & cab to usual mix pinotage & carignan. Strawberry flavours; technically off-dry but freshened by lemon acidity. **Chardonnay** ★★★ **05** shows ripe mandarin tone of pvs, none of its plush oak. Now vinified with chips & staves — all contributing to dusty tail. **Chenin Blanc-Chardonnay** ★★★ **05** lively, medium-bodied 70/30 blend with subtle lemon flavours; spice (from oak chips) but no creaminess. **Sauvignon Blanc** ★★★ Nettly **06** crafted for summertime quaffing. Fresh as eponymous ocean breeze. **Semillon-Chardonnay** ★★ **05** minimally oaked 70/30 blend, quaffability upped by clever marriage of acid & waxy fruit. **Fresh & Fruity White** ★★★ (Pvsly Cape White.) Pretty & floral **05**, chenin (85%), colombard combo; perky acidity balances 11g/ℓ sugar. All WO W Cape. Depending on country, available in 750ml/1.5ℓ bottles & 3ℓ casks. — *CvZ*

▪ **Tygerberg** *see* Altydgedacht
▪ **Ubuntu** *see* Umkhulu, Vukani
▪ **Uhambo** *see* Premium Cape Wines
▪ **Uiterwyk Estate** *see* DeWaal Wines

Uitkyk Estate

Stellenbosch ▪ Tasting & sales Mon-Fri 9-5 Sat/Sun 10-4 ▪ Fee R20-R25 incl glass ▪ Picnics in summer ▪ Owner Lusan Holdings ▪ Estate manager Rudi Buys ▪ Winemaker Estelle Lourens (2000) ▪ Viticulturist Eben Archer ▪ ±870 tons ▪ 20 000 cs ▪ PO Box 104 Stellenbosch 7599 ▪ info@uitkyk.co.za ▪ www.uitkyk.co.za ▪ T 021·884·4416 ▪ F 021·884·4717

The long-time favourite wine from this estate had its name 'Carlonet' dropped for a while, but winemaker Estelle Lourens (neé Swart) has now succumbed to local demand, and all Uitkyk's cab production now emerges under that moniker (a combination of one-time owner Baron von Carlowitz's name and the cab grapes he used in the wines). The estate brandy will soon appear in revamped packaging. With its serene Georgian architecture and many amenities, Uitkyk remains a popular day out.

Carlonet ★★★★ (Pvs ed 'Cabernet Sauvignon'.) Returns to original name with **01**, & regains some of the pizzazz associated with Smnsberg cab. Big in all respects, incl heady 15% alc, still-stern tannin. But has freshness, concentration, for yr/3 further aging. 18 to 21 mths oak, mainly Fr, 57% new. Swiss gold; VG. **Shiraz Reserve** ★★★★ **03**, heralding demise of 28-yr-old vyd, still available. Last ed greeted with lilies, black pepper & red fruit; yielding tannins & moderate alc (13.4%). Fr oak with Am, some Hungarian, 60% new. Probably not for keeping. **Cabernet Sauvignon-Shiraz** ★★★★ In difficult cab yr, satisfying **02** (with 50% shiraz) agreeable pure ripe black berry fruit throughout. Tasty, sweet & fresh; melded tannins, sensitive oaking for current drinking. 14–18 mths oak, mainly Fr, 66% new. **Chardonnay** ★★★ Mellowing yellow-gold shades on **04**. Bold wooding shows in assertive buttered toast/lime marmalade bouquet; sprinkle citrus zest cuts leesy richness. 13% alc. 9 mths oak, mainly Fr, 42% new. **Sauvignon Blanc Special Release** ᴺᴱᵂ ★★★★ Green pea/passionfruit/dried grass intensity set **05** apart from bottling below. Concentration balanced by rich mouthfeel; 14% alc adds intrusive glow to sweet-fruited length. VG. **Sauvignon Blanc** Possible ★★★★ rating for work-in-progress **06**; forthcoming ripe fig/tropical fruit aromas invigorated by greengage/greenpepper zest. Big mouthful, assertiveness cushioned by juicy sweetness. — AL

Uitvlucht Wines

Montagu (see Little Karoo map) • *Est 1941* • *Tasting & sales Mon-Fri 8-5.30 Sat 9-1.30 Sun 11-2 during high season* • *Light meals* • *Tour groups welcome* • *Functions* • *Owners 41 members* • *Winemaker/viticulturist Alwyn Liebenberg (Aug 2006), with Johannes Mellet* • *325 ha* • *5 000 tons 12 000 cs 36% red 22% white 28% muscadel 14% sparkling* • *PO Box 332 Montagu 6720* • *info@uitvlucht-wines.co.za or riette@lantic.net* • **T 023·614·1340/ 082·374·9981** • *F 023·614·2113*

This cellar in Montagu, the heartland of SA's fortified dessert wines, muscadel, is being revitalised by a new team: GM Jacques Jordaan, winemaker Alwyn Liebenberg (ex-Boplaas) and marketer Riëtte Coetzee. Together they're helping revive the Montagu Muscadel Festival and, buoyed by three golds at the Muscadel Awards for their Muscat de Frontignan Red (matured for three years in French oak) and White Muscadel, are re-introducing wine lovers to muscadel's versatility: as a winter drink, dessert wine, summer spritzer, sundowner… the options are endless.

Cabernet Sauvignon 03 unready for tasting. **Merlot** ★★★ Last we tasted juicy & approachable **03**, with modest but appealing red-berry fruit. **Pinotage** ★★★ Ripe banana aromas on **04**, smoothly dry, firm but friendly for current & early-ish enjoyment. **Shiraz** ★★ Lighter style **04**, last ed showed gd smoky red berry fruit in fairly compact package. **Derde Heuvel Rood** ★★★ Still available **02**; spicy, light textured red with plum pudding character, toasty dry finish. **Rosé** ★★ Follow-up to light hearted, friendly, sweetish **05** not ready for tasting. **Chardonnay** Sold out. **Chenin Blanc** ★★ **06** again offers Granny Smith apple & fruit salad flavours, crisply dry & fresh. **Blanc de Blanc 05** from colombard, chenin, not ready for tasting. Following bubblies carbonated, **NV**, from chenin: **Vin Sec Sparkling** ★★ Delicately foaming, semi-dry, anytime quaffer, with hints of apple & fresh crusty bread. **Vin Doux Sparkling** ★★ Light, fresh, floral, with summer-sweet flavours, soft pear-toned bubbles. Muscadel Awards 2006 for following trio of fortified desserts, none retasted: **White Muscadel** ★★★ **04** flavours of honey-drizzled sultana, correspondingly syrupy texture. **Red Muscadel** ★★★ Winter warming **05** cloyingly sweet, with fruit pastille/jellied sweet aromas. **Muscat de Frontignan** ★★★ Lusciously sweet **01**; raisin & tealeaf aromas, dried apricot flavours & enlivening savoury acidity. **Port** ★ Workmanlike **04**, last ed showed dusty liquorice hints, drier flavours than expected. — JN

Ultra Liquors

Leading independent discount liquor chain, sourcing value for money wines for its exclusive labels which include: Table Bay (Red, White and Rosé), Stellenvale (Cabernet Sauvignon, Merlot, Pinotage, Shiraz, Chardonnay and Sauvignon Blanc), Route 303 (Red and White) and Beaufort (5ℓ cask range). See Specialist wine shops section for store locations and contact details.

■ **Umculi** *see Rooiberg*
■ **Umfiki** *see Goudini*

Umkhulu Wines

Stellenbosch ▪ Est/1stB 2000 ▪ Closed to public ▪ Owner Fiona Phillips ▪ 20 000 cs 80% red 20% white ▪ PO Box 132 Simondium 7670 ▪ info@umkhulu.co.za or fiona@cybercellar.co.za ▪ www.umkhulu.com ▪ T/F 021·874·2106

More US success for Umkhulu, reports Fiona Phillips, thanks to recent listings with the Holland America Line's five-star fleet substantially lifting sales. Still an export-only brand, Umkhulu is also selling well across newer markets in Europe, notably Spain.

★★★★ **Tian** Bdx-style blend led by cab, with cab f, merlot, malbec, petit v. After extracted, modern **02**, **03** (★★★★) last yr rather shy, light feel & texture; subtle dark berries held in check by firm tannins; stylishly oaked (yr Fr, 50% new), not excessive 13.4% alc. **04** unready.

★★★★★ **Pinotage** Stylish, bright & modern **04** continues accessible trend: soft, plush black fruit, usual wafting vanilla spice of new Am oak (30%, yr). Slight sweetness to fruit hauled back by firmish oak tannins which add needed texture, dryness. Drink now & over next 2-3 yrs.

Ubuntu ★★★☆ Pleasingly plump 'Cape blend' of pinotage & 17% each petit v, malbec; 2nd vintage **04** repeats pvs's velvety softness, not incongruous sweetness from pinotage. Good glassful, quietly satisfies. Yr 100% new Fr oak. **Malbec** ★★★ **04** a replica of pvs, complete with pungent mint overtone, graceful cassis fruit, soft tannins for early drinking, very dry finish. Yr Am oak, 30% new. **Shiraz** ★★★★ Strikingly deep coloured **04** (sample), minty hint – the house signature – good oak; sweet black cherry, rich & cordial-like, tannins again worked to early drinkability. Yr Fr oak, 50% new. **Akira** ★★★☆ Blend cab, pinotage, petit v (49/34/17), pinotage sweetness adds generosity & plumpness to **03**; retasted, now has more elegant tannins than last yr, same untrammeled approachability. Yr Fr/Am oak, 25% new. **Njalo** ★★★ Same varieties (merlot, shiraz, pinotage), different proportions (60/20/20), different outcome: **05** angular & a tad green, bold tannins need time/food. **Dry Red** ★★ Last tasted was frisky unwooded blend cab, pinotage, petit v. **03** sample showed whiffs mulberry, plum; clean-cut flavours. **Sauvignon Blanc** ★★★ Last tasted was **05**, capsicum/green fig character in lower key; firm acidity, bone-dry. **Dry White** ★☆ Soft, dry, quaffable **04** was the last vintage reviewed. **Chardonnay** discontinued. — *IvH*

Under Oaks

Paarl ▪ 1stB 2003 ▪ Visits by appt ▪ Fee R20 ▪ Owners Hans & Theresa Britz ▪ Winemaker Theresa Britz ▪ Viticulturist Hans Britz ▪ 30 ha (cab, chard, chenin, viognier) ▪ 2 000 cs 50% red 50% white ▪ PO Box 641 Wellington 7654 ▪ info@underoaks.co.za ▪ www.underoaks.co.za ▪ T 021·872 6070 ▪ F 021·872·5575

Three years after Hans and Theresa Britz purchased the neglected Paarl farm, Oaklands, with the intention to extensively restore and replant, they're on the home run with new blocks of cab and chardonnay as well as a small parcel of viognier taking root. It's a time-consuming business starting from scratch but if their prowess in the kitchen is anything to go by, the promise of the Britz partnership is poised for take off.

Cabernet Sauvignon ★★ **04** not ready. Well-balanced **03** last ed showed black fruit, forest floor flavours & aromas, firm ripe tannins. Yr Fr/Am barrels, 70% new. **Chenin Blanc** ★★ **05** powerful, 15.3% alc dominated nose & palate mid-2005, remarkably viscous, blowsy for this variety. **Limited Release Sauvignon Blanc** ★★★ Friendly, bright, summery **06**, balanced freshness & flavour, with grassy grapefruit tone. For early enjoyment. — *MM*

■ **Unity** see African Terroir
■ **Upington** see Oranjerivier Wine Cellars

Upland Estate

Wellington ▪ Est/1stB 1998 ▪ Visits by appt ▪ Self-catering cottages (see Stay-over section) ▪ Distillery ▪ Farm-grown/made olives & tapenade ▪ Owners Edmund & Elsie Oettlé ▪

*Winemaker/viticulturist Edmund Oettlé • 12 ha (cab, chenin, crouchen) • 30 tons 500 cs 100%
red •* PO Box 152 Wellington 7654 *• edmund@oettle.com •* http://oettle.com *•*
T 082·731·4774 *•* F 021·873·5724

The inventive Edmund Oettlé has ventured into the making of port — 'the only truly organic estate bottling in SA, with our organic brandy used in fortification'. The Wellington farm's organic cultivation, now officially certified but dating back nine years, has led to what the
winemaker and co-owner describes as 'a dramatic improvement in soil and crop quality, and
a significant reduction in soil erosion'. Other fruits of the farm are red wine, brandy, Italian-
style grappa, olives, almonds and tangerines.

Cabernet Sauvignon ★★★☆ Authentic 'bio wine' from low-cropped organic vyds; barrel
matured ± yr. **02** last ed noted as ripe & curvaceous, even fleshy, soft tannins, showing a particularly amiable side of cab. **Pheasant Haven Cabernet Sauvignon** new ★★★☆ The 'second
label'. Moniker underscores eco-credentials of this producer; from what is now officially recognised organic single vyd (as is Port). **03** more elegant than above; admirable 'claret' tone, supple
fruit, spicy tannins; will cellar well. Barrel matured 2 yrs, seasoned Fr oak. **Merlot** See under
Maske Wines. **Equinox Port** new ★★★ Previewed mid-2006, still somewhat spirituous but brims
with character, ripe berry fruit succulence, satisfying dry finish. NV. — *DH/lvH*

Urbane Wines

This easy-drinking range made and bottled for export to the US by Porterville Cellars/Tulbagh
Wineries Co-op, now discontinued.

Usana

*Stellenbosch • Est/1stB 2003 • Tasting by appt • Owner Joubert Family Trust • Vini consultant Mike
Dobrovic (Mar 2003) • Viticulturists Joubert brothers • PO Box 7087 Stellenbosch 7599 • usana@
xsinet.co.za • www.usana.co.za • **T** 082·896·3437/083·625·2301 • F 021·865·2441*

A trio of well regarded areas from which to source grapes (Stellenboschkloof, Devon Valley
and Elgin); a top winemaker, Mike Dobrovic (Mulderbosch); a go-ahead marketing duo,
Jennie and Naomi Joubert — this family venture has all the right credentials, and a social con-
science, too: a portion of the proceeds from these wines goes to a group of children in
Stellenbosch affected by Aids.

★★★★ **Cabernet Sauvignon** ✓ Smartly oaked & attractive **04** has all the bounce, energy &
style of a debutante; ripe berry/cherry fruit with touches choc & char from new oak
(40%, yr); all well knit with youthful but pliable tannins. Shd reward gd few yrs cellaring. This & Merlot new. All WO Sbosch.

Merlot ★★★★ Easy-drinker but no pushover; **04** big on fruit & character, choc/vanilla mingle with mellow berries, mint & herbs; 13.7% alc adds pleasant glow. Wooding as for Cab.
Sauvignon Blanc 05's (★★★★✓) delicate, water-white appearance belies admirable
depth & concentration; aromatic capsicum & sun-dried hay; delicious now yet worth
keeping yr/2 to develop further. Continues upwards trend set by **04** (★★★☆). — *DH*

Uva Mira Vineyards

*Stellenbosch • Est 1997 • 1stB 1998 • Tasting & sales Mon-Fri 8:30-4.30 Sat 9.30-1 • Closed Chris-
tian holidays • Owner Denise Weedon • Winemaker/viticulturist Matthew van Heerden (May
2003), advised by Kevin Watt • 30 ha • 5 000 cs 60% red 40% white • info@uvamira.co.za • www.
uvamira.co.za • PO Box 1511 Stellenbosch 7599 • **T** 021·880·1683 • F 021·880·1682*

The Helderberg may be better known for red wines but Uva Mira boasts some of the highest
sauvignon blocks in Stellenbosch. 'The maiden release of our Single Vineyard Chardonnay
also gives the wine drinker a true reflection of our unique high-altitude positioning,' says
winemaker/GM Matthew van Heerden. Gorgeous 360-degree views incorporating Table
Mountain, the Atlantic and Indian oceans, 'with Cape Point and Robben Island thrown in for
good measure', can now be experienced at a recently completed tasting facility. 'We
guarantee not to disappoint.'

Vineyard Selection

★★★★☆ **Chardonnay** A contemporary classic & star of this cellar. From highest single chard vyd on Hldrberg, **05** beckons with toast, mandarin orange, grilled hazelnuts. Understated flavours grow on palate – lime, peach interplay with discreet oak adding tannin hint. Fermented/11 mths new Fr oak; all through malo. A complete wine. Equally superb & harmonious **04** won IWSC gold, TWS trophy.

★★★★ **Uva Mira** Maiden **04** now bottled, cab-led blend with 18% merlot, 6% shiraz, 4% cab f. Fine bouquet cassis, tealeaf, lead pencil; dense & compact, in classic mould, tightly bound by fine-grained tannins: starting to relax, but 5-7 yrs to go (drink blend below while waiting). 18 mths Fr oak, 30% new.

Cellar Selection

Merlot-Cabernet Sauvignon ★★★☆ Still youthful **04** has merlot dominating with 74%; berries/ roast beef intro, taut tannins, lighter texture than version above, but cld develop 3-5 yrs. Oaked 15 mths Fr, 25% new. **Sauvignon Blanc** ★★★☆ **06** aromas of passionfruit, gooseberry & ripe capsicum; then a soft curvaceousness – lipsmacking & luscious. **05** SAA. – *IvH*

■ *Vals Baai see* False Bay Vineyards

Van Loveren Private Cellar

Robertson ▪ Est 1937 ▪ Tasting & sales Mon-Fri 8.30-5 Sat 9.30-1 ▪ Closed Easter Fri/Sun, Dec 25 & Jan 1 ▪ Tours on request ▪ Sweetcorn fritters available Sat 9.30-1 ▪ Tour groups ▪ Conference/function venue ▪ Walks ▪ Owners Nico, Wynand, Phillip, Hennie, Bussell & Neil Retief ▪ Winemaker Bussell Retief ▪ Viticulturists Neil & Hennie Retief ▪ 220 ha (cab, red muscadel, sauvignon) ▪ 3 900 tons 300 000 cs 33% red 33% white 34% rosé ▪ PO Box 19 Klaasvoogds 6707 ▪ info@vanloveren. co.za ▪ www.vanloveren.co.za ▪ T 023·615·1505 ▪ F 023·615·1336

The family Retief last year celebrated the silver anniversary of their wines – brothers Wynand and Nico launched with 500 cases; 25 years on, their 300 000 gives Van Loveren the rank of 'largest privately owned brand in SA'. What better way to mark the occasion than with an empowerment deal? The Retiefs have bought a farm in the Goree district, given an employees' trust a major shareholding and signed a long-term grape supply contract with it, which will make the venture profitable from year one. Most of the grapes will be used in the new Big Five range destined for national parks, game reserves and tourist destinations.

Signature Series Limited Releases

Cabernet Sauvignon Big, bold & rich with ripe cassis & red berry fruit; tannins unexpectedly gruff on **05** sample, shd smooth out with yr's bottle-age. Possible ★★★★. **Shiraz** ★★★ **04** tasted pvs ed, oozed Am oak vanilla & coconut, slipped smoothly down but lacked extract of pvs. Ex-single vyd. Yr oak, 70/30 Fr/Am. **Chardonnay** ★★ **06** (sample) firmer & less charming than pvs, with pear-drop & smoky nuances from new Fr oak (fermented/5 mths); misses luscious lemon-butter appeal of **05**. **Noble Late Harvest** ★★★ Botrytised dessert from riesling, unwooded. **03** is new but appears to be maturing fast: advanced orange/gold colour, hints dried apricot & caramel, dry finish for style (70 g/ℓ RS). 11% alc. Not for keeping.

Van Loveren range

> **Merlot** ☺ ★★★ **05** quintessential merlot, brimming with choc & plum, coffee & floral nuances; firm ripe tannins, light oak flavours (from 6 mths on staves). Attractive early-drinker, as is… **Pinotage** ☺ ★★★ Varietally true **05** has high-toned bouquet & ripe strawberry flavours cushioning some taut tannins. Oak as for merlot. **Cabernet Sauvignon-Shiraz** ☺ ★★★ Most satisfying of the reds, unoaked. Cab (70%) leads **05** with black berries, firm core; shiraz adds flesh, breadth; gd dry finish.

River Red ★★★ **05** last ed was a sassy, spicy quaffer unfettered by oak or tannin. Shiraz, merlot, ruby cab (50/30/20) blend; also in 500ml under screwcap. **Blanc de Noir Shiraz** ★☆ Stumbles in **06**; lacks flavour, vinosity & *joie de vivre* of pvs. **Blanc de Noir Red Muscadel** ★★ Attractive & undemanding pink quaffer for the sweeter toothed; **06** light, muscat scented, finishes fairly crisply. **Chardonnay** ★★ Lightly wooded for early accessibility. **06** clean & light citrus/tropical tones, some nutty nuances. **Cape Riesling** ★★ **06** touch leaner, more austere than pvs; still bone-dry with tangy tail. **Colombard** ★★ Fruit-lifting dollop sugar (13g/ℓ) gives boost to fresh tropical flavours on **06**. Comfortably rounded & easy to drink. **Fernão Pires** ★★ Sample **06** technically off-dry but crisp, with shy pear-drop & boiled sweets aromas tickling the nose. **Pinot Grigio** ★★ Vinous rather than fruity (which makes it food-friendly) **06**, pleasantly dry & savoury. **Sauvignon Blanc** ★★ **06** more tropical-toned than green-fruited. Bright & breezy, begs shellfish. **Blanc de Blanc** ★★ Perky **06** ideal for lazy days on picnic blankets; dry, from colombard & sauvignon. Also appears as **Vino Blanc** in 500ml under screwcap. **Colombar-Chardonnay** ★★★ Sound version of area's trademark blend. **06** (sample) white peach notes, lively acidity, long, lipsmacking lemony farewell. **Semillon** Replaced with next wine. **Light White** new ★ Light by name & nature (9% alc); with semillon's muted lemon/wax notes on drink-young **06**. **Special Late Harvest Gewürztraminer** ★★★ **06** sample too unformed to rate. **05** was pure, unshowy & delicate; 40g/ℓ sugar enlivened by bright acidity. **Red Muscadel** ★★★★ ✓ Fortified dessert from muscadel; **05** perfumed by honeysuckle & rosepetal; unctuously sweet (200g/ℓ RS) but lifted on finish by well judged spirit & acidity. **Ruby Port** ★★★ NV (blend of 03 & 04). Brilliant hues introduce delicious choc-laced prunes & berries, hints of mocha coffee; tastes drier than 150g/ℓ sugar suggests.

Four Cousins range

All **NV**, uncertified handy party-size 1.5ℓ bottles. **Dry Red** ★★★ Visited pvs ed, chummy, uncomplicated melange of shiraz, merlot & ruby cab; styled for anytime, anywhere quaffability. **Sweet Rosé** ★★ From various muscats giving strawberry aromas, soft flavours & low alc (7.5%) to chill well & quaff this summer. **Dry River White** ★★ Undemanding, guava-scented dry colombard/sauvignon partnership, with Granny Smith apple zip.

Four Cousins Natural Sweet range

Red ☺ ★★ Wonderful juicy berry & plum character, perfect quaffing for sweet teeth (&, dare we say, a natural choice for Glühwein — just add spices!)

These all **NV**, uncertified, with low alcs (8–9%); variously available in 500ml, 750ml & 1. 5ℓ. **Rosé** ★★ Subdued wild strawberry & cream flavours, best enjoyed young & well chilled. **White** ★★ Eminently sippable, sun-sweet muscadel/chenin with generous mouthfeel.

Five's Reserve range   new

Name refers to Big 5 game featured on this BEE range's labels; some screwcapped. **Cabernet Sauvignon-Merlot** ★★ Cab has 55% of blend in **05**, chunky winter night's warmer with 14% alc, firm tannins & sweet fruit. Yr on Fr oak staves; only 8 mths for... **Pinotage** ★★ **05** undemanding outdoor sipper; supple fruit & tannin, plummy banana notes. **Merlot Rosé** ★★ **06** light, more blanc de noir in style with subdued berry/candyfloss bouquet, very dry finish demanding food. **Chenin Blanc** ★★ Fruit-shy **06** relies on sweetness (12g/ℓ sugar) & acidity for its character, poise.

Papillon sparkling range

Demi-Sec ☺ ★★★ White muscadel delivers the foaming goods: creamy & sweetish (36g/ℓ RS) but there's sufficient fruit & acid to perk up any palate.

These are wallet-friendly, lowish alc (11–11.5%) **NV** carbonated bubblies; colour-coded butterfly labels depict style. **Brut** ★★ Pick-me-up from colombar & sauvignon; gleeful bubbles usher in bright tropical notes. **Vin Doux** ★★ Party-pink muscat de F with spicy whiffs, almost cloying sweetness despite the sparkling lift. — DH

■ *Vansha* see Ridgeback

Van Zylshof Estate

*Robertson ▪ Est 1993 ▪ 1stB 1994 ▪ Tasting & sales Mon-Fri 9-5 Sat 9-1 ▪ Closed Easter Fri & Dec 25 ▪ Tours by appt ▪ Owner Van Zylshof Trust ▪ Winemaker/viticulturist Andri van Zyl ▪ 32 ha (cab, merlot, chard, chenin, sauvignon) ▪ 10 000 cs 10% red 90% white ▪ PO Box 64 Bonnievale 6730 ▪ vanzylshof@lando.co.za ▪ **T 023·616·2401** ▪ F 023·616·3503*

Last year was a huge relief after the trials and tribulations of the 2005 harvest: 'It was fantastic, the best I've ever had,' enthuses cellar/vineyard man Andri van Zyl. 'Quality-wise, the grapes were unbelievably healthy.' The arrival of a harvester and consequent full mechanisation of the picking process helped. With two Veritas golds for his Chardonnay under his belt, the Van Zyl family's winemaker has high hopes for the latest vintage.

Chenin Blanc ☺ ★★★ **06** cheery guava-toned quaffer; soft, light (12.1% alc) & ideal for alfresco occasions.

Cabernet Sauvignon-Merlot ★★★ Revisited **04**, appealing easy-drinker with earthy/nutty hints & cedary whiff from well applied Fr oak (6 mths). 70/30 blend. **Chardonnay** ★★★ Modicum Fr oak adds character, hint marmalade, to lemon rind notes on **05**. Plump & juicy; for early enjoyment. **Chardonnay Riverain** Unwooded Rbtson chardonnay; **06** preview shows usual crisp lime minerality, hint of lemon; potential ★★★. **Sauvignon Blanc** ★★ Previewed **06**, light bodied/textured with tart acidity. — *CT*

■ *Van Zylskloof* see Johan van Zyl Wines

Vaughan Johnson's Wine & Cigar Shop

*Cape Town (V&A Waterfront Pierhead Cape Town) ▪ Est/1stB 1985 ▪ Sales Mon-Fri 9-6 Sat 9-5 Sun 10-5 ▪ Open pub hols ▪ Gifts, souvenirs, spirits & beer available ▪ Owner Vaughan Johnson ▪ PO Box 50012 Waterfront 8002 ▪ vjohnson@mweb.co.za ▪ www.vaughanjohnson.com ▪ **T 021·419·2121** ▪ F 021·419·0040*

Events at Cape Town International Convention Centre are bringing more feet through the door at this high-profile wine shop strategically located in Cape Town's Waterfront. Bonhomous owner Vaughan Johnson welcomes visitors from all over the world, and is a good source of insider-info regarding wine retailing trends. He reports that sauvignon, cab and shiraz continue to sell well. A slowdown in demand for wines (especially unknown brands) over R150 has, however, been noted. High-alcohol wines are not well received either.

Sunday Best Red ☺ ★★★ Name honours V-J's hard-won Sunday trading licence; happy plums & prunes, sage & marjoram notes on 60/40 blend cab/merlot. Oodles fruit, zippy acidity; firm tannic goodbye. **Good Everyday Cape Red** ☺ ★★★ NV red-grape cocktail a best-seller locally & in Ireland thanks to supple tannins, winsome fruit. **Sunday Best White** ☺ ★★★ Colombard & sauvignon lend floral & citrus charms to this easy summer sipper. Both ranges **NV**, mainly ex-Paarl vyds; all for current consumption.

Good Everyday Cape White ★★ Their fastest seller. Mid-2005 showed subdued pear-drop aromas, unobtrusively dry finish; pleasant if quick.

Waterfront Collection

Captain's Claret ☺ ★★★ Everyday red enjoyed in Antartica & on round-the-world solo voyages, says V-J. 100% shiraz; chipper red fruit, firm tannins softened by dash sugar (4. 2g/ℓ).

Nautical labels distinguish this value-priced, quaffable duo. **Great White** ★★ Uncomplicated fun, usually from chenin; current bottling mid-2005 had inviting floral nose & fruity sherbet finish. — *CvZ*

■ *Veelplesier* see Baarsma
■ *Veelverjaaght* see Beau Joubert

Veenwouden Private Cellar   ◯♀

Paarl ▪ Est 1989 ▪ 1stB 1993 ▪ Sales Mon-Fri 9-4.30 ▪ Tasting by appt Mon-Fri 9-4.30 ▪ Fee R100/btl if no purchase made ▪ Closed pub hols ▪ Tours by appt ▪ Owner Deon van der Walt Trust ▪ Winemaker Marcel van der Walt, with Faried Williams (Jan 1994/1995) ▪ Viticulturist Marcel van der Walt, with Sias Louw (Jan 1994/1995) ▪ 14 ha (cabs s/f, malbec, merlot) ▪ ±100 tons 5 500 cs own labels 99% red 1% white ▪ PO Box 7086 Northern Paarl 7623 ▪ admin@veenwouden.com ▪ www.veenwouden.com ▪ T 021·872·6806 ▪ F 021·872·1384

Tributes poured in from around the world following the family tragedy in which Veenwouden owner Deon van der Walt, one of the world's leading tenors, and his father, estate manager Charles, both died. His singing may no longer fill the intimate music theatre here but the wine business continues as before under brother Marcel. The personal touch also remains, with private sit-down tastings and tours by appointment. New wines to try are the two Thornhill blends, featuring fruit from the eponymous nearby farm (also the winemaker's long-time home), vinified and readied at Veenwouden.

★★★★☆ **Merlot** Introduced with fanfare & still prized a decade on: **03** fresh off the bottling line pvs ed, enormously promising: beautiful flesh resting in sumptuous folds of powdery tannin, fine-toned structure reverberates with finesse. Fuller than pvs. Single low yielding vyd on home farm, with 10% cab. 2 yrs 70% new Fr oak. Note: vintages above, below, still available, none revisited.

★★★★☆ **Classic** Acclaimed bdx-style red more retiring & intricate than above. **03** striking Belgian-lace delicacy to the composition, a sleeper when reviewed last ed. Cabs s/f, merlot &, latterly, soupçon malbec. Oaking as above.

★★★★ **Vivat Bacchus** More understated blend than above – & eminently delicious on release. **03** cassis fruits mingle in firm yet pliable frame, finessed lingering exit. 60% merlot, with malbec, cabs f/s. 50% new Fr oak, 2 yrs.

★★★★☆ **Chardonnay Special Reserve** Comes with a big swing ticket (only cellar door); worth it for its rarity (just 30 cs) – & individuality. Neither merely opulent nor just elegant: rather special: **04** Meursault-like apple pie with a tangerine twist. New Fr oak fermented, *sur lie* ageing now 9 mths. Moderate 13% alc.

Thornhill range

★★★★ **Shiraz** Stylish, bold & dramatic, **04** secures rating upgrade with new style: more perfumed & spicy, less chunky – beautifully balanced – than **03**. 14 mths seasoned Fr oak, 8% unwooded viognier replaces cab of pvs.

Tempranillo-Cabernet Sauvignon NEW ★★★☆ Pre-bottling sample **05** in lighter, tangy style, boosted by 40% cab. 14 mths used Fr wood. **Viognier-Chenin Blanc** NEW ★★★☆ Unwooded – just as well: no space for anything more in **06**! Bulges with peach-pip/apricot cream fullness, tropical fruit braced by acid. 13% alc. – DS

Vendôme   ◯♀♋&

Paarl ▪ Est 1692 ▪ 1stB 1999 ▪ Tasting & sales Mon-Fri 9.30-1 Sat 9.30-12.30 ▪ Fee R5 refunded on purchase ▪ Closed pub hols ▪ Tours on request ▪ Conferencing/functions for up to 60 ▪ Owner/viticulturist Jannie le Roux Snr ▪ Winemaker/viticulturist Jannie le Roux Jnr ▪ 40 ha (cabs s/f, merlot, shiraz, chard, chenin, colombard, sauvignon, semillon) ▪ 20 tons 1 400 cs own label 70% red 30% white ▪ PO Box 36 Paarl 7645 ▪ lerouxjg@icon.co.za ▪ www.vendome.co.za ▪ T 021·863·3905 ▪ F 021·863·0094

Jannie le Roux Jnr, whose eye is on the top end of the market, has been experimenting with cab and merlot ratios to create new wooded blends (including the version below), as well as an unwooded sauvignon-chardonnay which earned him third place in the Diners Club Young Winemaker of the Year competition. Le Roux says he was most inspired by his sojourn in Bordeaux: 'They do nothing fancy; no adding or subtracting; no 'plastic'. Just simple, honest winemaking.'

Classique new ★★★☆ 'Classically New World' red from merlot, cabs s&f; **03** deep layers of fruit & brisk acidity, giving athletic, pleasantly firm mouthfeel with touches mineral & savoury. Yr oak, 10% Am; natural yeasts; unfiltered. Promising. **Sans Barrique** new ★★★☆ Unwooded, food-accommodating sauvignon (56%), chard blend; **05** lightish, attractively mellow vinous character; still fresh thanks to limy acidity but shd be enjoyed soon. **Cabernet Sauvignon**, **Le Roux Merlot-Cabernet Sauvignon** & **Chardonnay** discontinued. — *MM*

■ *Vera Cruz Estate* see Delheim

Vergelegen

Stellenbosch (see Helderberg map) ▪ *Est 1700* ▪ *1stB 1992* ▪ *Tasting daily 9.30-4.30 (sales close at 5)* ▪ *Entrance fee R10 p/p* ▪ *Closed Dec 25, May 1 & Easter Fri* ▪ *Lady Phillips Restaurant: à la carte lunches daily; Rose Terrace: alfresco restaurant Nov-Apr; picnics Nov-Apr* ▪ *Guided winery tours daily 10.15, 11.30 & 3 Fee R2-R10/wine* ▪ *'Interpretive Centre' depicting farm's history; also self-guided tour to the homestead* ▪ *Gifts* ▪ *Tour groups* ▪ *Owner Anglo American plc* ▪ *Winemaker André van Rensburg (Jan 1998)* ▪ *Viticulturist Niel Rossouw, with Petrie Dippenaar & Dwayne Lottering* ▪ *112 ha (cabs s/f, merlot, shiraz, chard, sauvignon, semillon)* ▪ *47 000 cs 60% red 40% white* ▪ *ISO 9001/140001 & BRC certified* ▪ *PO Box 17 Somerset West 7129* ▪ *vergelegen@vergelegen.co.za* ▪ *www.vergelegen.co.za* ▪ *T 021·847·1334* ▪ *F 021·847·1608*

The Cape's 18th-century Dutch governor Willem Adriaan van der Stel, conceptualiser of Vergelegen as an international 'model estate', must be turning in his grave… with glee! Amid the torrent of awards and accolades in 2006, none satisfied MD Don Tooth, marketer Eddie Turner and cellarmaster André van Rensburg more than New York-based *Wine Enthusiast*'s selection of Vergelegen as its 2005 New World Winery of the Year, in recognition of 'outstanding contributions to the world of wine and spirits'. Critics and connoisseurs clearly concur: see, once again, our five-star rating this year; Trophy Show awards; *Wine*'s annual reader poll… Yet, shining like a light amid the gala dinners, manicured vineyards, hi-tech winery facilities, sophisticated management and marketing style, uncompromising commitment to 'be the best', is pure love of the fruit of the vine, most openly expressed by ebullient Van Rensburg, invariably manning the buzziest stand at any given public tasting.

★★★★★ **Vergelegen V** Luxury priced, cult-style wine. **01** was first release; **03** (★★★★☆, not re-tasted) also single-vyd cab, also with ±10% merlot, dash cab f. Impressive, enormous & dramatic in its youth, needing yrs for concentrated sweet fruit to emerge from sombrely tannic, oak-dominated shell (2 yrs new barrels) — but already vibrant, deep & long.

★★★★★ **Vergelegen** Now established Cape bdx-style blend showing its class in immaculate fruit, alluring texture, suave tannins. Mainly cab from relatively warmer Rondekop vyd, with 18% merlot & drop cab f in superb **03** (tasted last ed); beguiling, incipiently complex; showy oak (2 yrs new) shd integrate, if given the time deserved. IWSC gold. **00**, **01** Calyon Top Tens, **01** IWSC gold, *Decanter* ★★★★★.

★★★★★ **Vergelegen CWG Auction Reserve** Barrel selection of the above, **02** (not re-tasted) powerful & lingering, for long development.

★★★★★ **Cabernet Sauvignon** Pencil shavings & cassis announce variety on modern, yet classically minded & subtle **04**. Savoury tannins control fruit till firm finish, & good balance shd ensure long harmonious development — though fresh & lively drinkability already. Like **03** (SAA, IWSC gold), with 8% cab f, 7% merlot. 2 yrs oak, 70% new, well carried. **01** *WS* 90 pts.

★★★★★ **Merlot** Showy, lipsmacking **04**, with 15% cab f adding fragrance, has serious, slightly dry tannins supporting rich, luscious fruit; choc-mint, blackcurrant tones in savoury whole. Beautifully managed oaking (20 mths, 50% new), apparent in youth but will integrate. Shd grow over gd few yrs.

★★★★★ **Shiraz** As usual sweet-fruited, luscious & ingratiating even in youth; **04** with aromas of pepper, spice, herbs, mocha, & pure, rich flavours — but fairly refined rather than blockbusterish, despite not too obvious 15% alc. Firm, balanced structure; supportive oaking (9 mths, new then into older barrels).

★★★★★ **Vergelegen White** Much-praised blend, with proven possibilities for maturing well over 5+ yrs. **05**, our Wine of the Year this ed, youthfully tight, quiet, but great, elegant intensity, & long finish recalling lemon & tropical aspects — ripe sauvignon prominent mid-2006, though only 33% (20% in **04** SAA, *Decanter* ★★★★). Impressive already in its austere, subtly oaked opulence, promising harmonious development. Both varieties bunch-pressed, fermented/10 mths in barrels, half new. **01** Best Museum Class White Blend at 2006 TWS.

★★★★☆ **CWG Auction Reserve White 04** was barrel selection of above: silky, elegant & thrilling.

★★★★☆ **Chardonnay Lower Schaapenberg** Formerly 'Reserve', name now reflects official single vyd status of **05**. More elegant than spectacular, though assertive, long-lingering; with the powerful delicacy of rich silk. Lightly spicy, with nutty notes, long mineral finish — all promising more complexity to come. Well balanced 13% alc. Excellent, subtle wooding (natural ferment & 13 mths in Fr oak, half new).

★★★★ **Chardonnay** Immediately beguiling **05**, outgoing notes of spice, toasted oak, hazelnut, but nothing too obvious: a thoughtful, well bred wine, silky but not over-rich, fresh, dry & refined. Should start showing its best from mid-2007. Fermented/±9 mths oak, 40% new; partial malo.

★★★★☆ **Sauvignon Blanc Schaapenberg** Pvsly 'Reserve'; AvR's favoured, wind-swept Schaapenberg site now registered as single vyd origin for what is now his undisputed top sauvignon. **05**'s fine acidity focuses richer (yet almost austere), deeper element of intense, ripe fruit — its clean, fresh purity expressed with hints of fynbos, lemongrass, stone. Some skin contact, then with lees for 7 mths.

★★★★ **Sauvignon Blanc** Last-tasted **05** had customary uplift of ±10% semillon. Showed ripe passionfruit, melon, with mineral undertone. Light-feeling, tightly textured, with finely balanced acidity, dry finish. Small proportion fermented in oak. SAA; Best Unwooded White Blend at 2006 TWS. WO W Cape. **06** not ready for tasting.

★★★★ **Semillon 04** last ed had subtle honey, citrus, blossom aromas, incipient waxiness; 10 mths in oak lending richness to fine, acid-shot texture.

★★★★ **Weisser Riesling Noble Late Harvest** new Lashings of pineapple & marmalade, some honey & raisins on **05**. Good German-style balance, with low 10% alc & high acidity invigorating 160g/ℓ sugar sweetness. Delectably lingering.

Mill Race Red Savoury **03** (★★★★) followed by an **04** (★★★★) from merlot, cabs s & f, attractively mingling fruit aromas with tobacco & spice; less fruit on palate, touch of herbaceous leanness, strong dry tannic grip. 22 mths oak, 20% new. **Vin de Florence** ★★★☆ ✓ Always charming chenin-based blend, with semillon & riesling in winning **06**. Some fleshy sweetness, well offset by intriguing limyness & vibrant acidity. WO W Cape. **Schaapenberg Reserve Sauvignon Blanc** discontinued. — *TJ*

Vergenoegd Estate

Stellenbosch ▪ Est 1773 ▪ 1stB 1972 ▪ Tasting & sales Mon-Fri 8.30-5 Sat 9.30–12.30; tasting also during restaurant hours: Tue-Sat lunch & (booking essential) dinner; Sun & pub hols lunch only; breakfast for groups by appt only ▪ Tours by appt ▪ Owner Vergenoegd Trust ▪ Winemaker John Faure (1984) ▪ Vineyard manager Chris van Niekerk (May 2003), advised by Drikus van der Westhuizen ▪ 90 ha (cabs s/f, merlot, shiraz) ▪ 500 tons 10 000 cs own label 95% red 5% port ▪ PO Box 1 Faure 7131 ▪ enquiries@vergenoegd.co.za ▪ www.vergenoegd.co.za ▪ T 021·843·3248 ▪ F 021·843·3118

The homestead on the Faure farm (now sole-owned by the family trust) has taken centre stage: it houses a new restaurant as well as the relocated sales and tasting facility. Linger after lunch and you'll see John Faure's 300-strong flock of Indian Runners waddling home after doing snail duty in the vineyards. John F is more than a maker of classic reds and fine ports; he's the duck man behind 'Best on Show' title holders at the annual Worcester Poultry Show.

★★★★☆ **Vergenoegd** Imposing médoc styled blend; cab-dominated **03** mid-2006 offers complex barnyard, medicinal, red fruit aromas; sturdy tannins balance concentrated dark berry flavours & firm acidity; long, savoury finish. Grape tannins & 18+ mths in 95% new barrels require few yrs to soften – keep ±10. (Most vintages listed still available; none below revisited.)

★★★★ **Cabernet Sauvignon** Rich, robustly built wine. **03** aromatic whiffs red berry & mint, last ed still very youthful, needing time to unmask underlying rich cassis flavours. Spiciness from combo Fr, Russ & Am oak. Best broached in few yrs, shd keep ±decade.

★★★★ **Shiraz** 'Masculine' style **03** with splash cab; leathery, smoky notes; plushly textured, though acidity bites before juicy, dark plum fruit pushes through. Burly 14.7% alc evident throughout. 65% new Fr oak provides structure for 5-6 yrs.

★★★★ **Old Cape Colony Vintage Port** Classically profiled – around 85g/ℓ sugar, 20% alc; fermented in open *kuipe*, old wood matured 18 mths. Now 66% tinta, with touriga. **01** (★★★★★) particularly good: refined, complex. **02** (★★★) lighter-seeming, though same stats. **00** exclusively tinta, well balanced & firmly structured.

Merlot ★★★★ **03**'s wooding (Fr, half new, 22 mths) stood out last yr, alongside chocmint, green-edged notes – otherwise nicely balanced & dry. **Terrace Bay** ★★★★ Serious minded, modestly wooded 'second label', **03** blends farm's 6 varieties into an austere, savoury style. Drink soon. – *IM/TJ*

Versailles

Wellington ▪ Est 2003 ▪ 1stB 2004 ▪ Visits by appt ▪ Conservation area ▪ Owners Tienie Malan & Annareen de Reuck ▪ Winemakers: see below ▪ Viticulturists of Wellington Cellar ▪ 116 ha (cab, merlot, shiraz, chenin) ▪ 1 200 tons 2 240 cs own label 100% red ▪ Export brand: Malan de Versailles ▪ PO Box 597 Wellington 7654 ▪ adereuck@ezinet.co.za ▪ T 082·898·9314 ▪ F 021·873·2608

The Malans have farmed Versailles since 1864, and, following the untimely death of her brother Jannie, sixth-generation Annareen de Reuck (née Malan) has taken it upon herself to maintain the family heritage by growing wine under the farm name. Displeased with previous agents' performance, she's ready to 'pack her basket and head to the markets' herself to sell her 'sleeping beauty' Shiraz, made by Stefan Smit (Louiesenhof) in conjunction with Loftie Ellis (Elsenburg), and matured on the Versailles property near Wellington.

Malan de Versailles Shiraz ★★ **03** plum/raspberry bouquet, with soft tannins & sweetfruited finish making for easy-going drinking – though 14.5% alc does show itself. – *MF*

■ *Versus* see The Company of Wine People
■ *Vertex* see Bonnievale

Vilafonté

Stellenbosch ▪ Est 1996 ▪ 1stB 2003 ▪ From Mar 2007: tasting & sales daily 10-7 (later, on demand) ▪ Closed Dec 25 & Easter ▪ Italian bistro serving light meals; Lavazza coffee shop ▪ Retail gift shop ▪ Local produce ▪ Wine & Cigar Experience ▪ Cellar tours & tour groups by appt ▪ Function room for special occasions ▪ Owners Mike Ratcliffe, Zelma Long & Phil Freese ▪ Winemaker Zelma Long, with Bernard Du Pré le Roux ▪ Viticulturist Phil Freese ▪ 15 ha (cabs s/f, malbec, merlot) ▪ ±80 tons 3 000 cs 100% red ▪ PO Box 64 Elsenburg 7607 ▪ mike@vilafonte.com ▪ www.vilafonte.com www.vilafonte.blogspot.com ▪ T 082·853·8737 ▪ F 0866·81·7557

Things are literally smoking at Vilafonté with the launch of the Series X Cuban cigar, a fragrant enhancement to their wine portfolio. The members of this US-SA venture (winemaker Zelma Long and viticulturist husband Phil Freese, Warwick's Mike Ratcliffe and US distributor Bartholomew Broadbent), have also been clocking up 'some serious frequent flyer miles' with an international launch tour covering seven European countries and 20 US states. This is already paying dividends: distribution has been vastly extended and more target markets are in the pipeline. Amid euphoria over the many accolades for their wines (including nomination, in their first year, for New World Winery of the Year by *Wine Enthusiast*), at press time they prepared to unveil their new cellar and visitor centre at Bosman's Crossing in the heart of Stellenbosch.

★★★★☆ **Series C** Clearly cab led (52%), which name implies: more austere, imposing than M below, though influential 35% merlot adds sweet-fruited mid-palate flesh; **04** serious tannin grip but also verve, freshness to balance riper style, ensure ageing potential.

Seasoned with cab f, malbec (9/4%). Seamlessly polished by 19 mths ±70% new barriques. **03** *Wine* ★★★★, IWC gold.

★★★★★ **Series M** Though style rather than variety determines blend, the two 'Ms' — supple, luxurious merlot & minerally malbec — are major influences here. **04** marginally more accessible than 'C', though both need min 5 yrs. Sophisticated composition cab, merlot, malbec, cab f (36/31/25/8); ripe, velvety with dense tannin, focussed freshness. Fr oak, 37% new, 19 mths. Both WO Paarl. — *AL*

Viljoensdrift Wines ⬡♟♨🍸

Robertson · Est/1stB 1998 · Tasting & sales Mon-Fri 8.30-5 (cellar); Sat 10-2 & 1st Sun of month 11-2 (riverside); every Sun in Dec · Closed Easter Fri, Jun 16 & Dec 25 · Breede River cruises Wed, Sat & 1st Sun of month 12 noon, weather permitting; booking essential; additional weekday trips for groups of 15+ by appt · Create your own picnic from the deli · Tours by appt · Owners Fred & Manie Viljoen · Winemaker Fred Viljoen · Viticulturist Manie Viljoen · 120 ha (cab, pinotage, shiraz, chard, chenin, sauvignon) · 1 200 tons ±80 000 cs 50% red 48% white 2% rosé · Export brands: Die Rivierkloof, Elandsberg, Keurfontein, Somerlust & River Grandeur · PO Box 653 Robertson 6705 · viljoensdrift@lando.co.za · www.viljoensdrift. co.za · T·023·615·1901 · F 023·615·3417

Making the most of their position on the Breede River, the Viljoens are planning to build a bigger tasting room on the river bank, venue for fireside wine tastings and a deli with foods for a DIY picnic meal — best enjoyed aboard Uncle Ben, their river cruiser. Also on the drawing board is a conference hall with old-fashioned bioscope armchairs, seating for visitors watching videos of the farm and its environs. In keeping with the riverside theme is the new Wine on the Water Rosé, a farm first on two counts in that it's semi-sweet and screwcapped. And to celebrate it, another first: their upcoming maiden MCC.

River Grandeur range

★★★★ **Cabernet Sauvignon 04** (★★★½) complex cassis, mint, herby, meaty flavours enlivened by cab's fine tannins. 14% alc well hidden but finish slightly greener/drier than on fruit- & oak-sweet **03**. Will reward cellaring ±3-5 yrs. Like next, yr Fr oak. Open fermenters for all reds in range, none retasted this ed.

★★★★ **Pinotage 04** had a spicier profile than firm **03** (★★★★) & long savoury finish thanks to change from mostly Am oak to mainly Fr. Charming scents strawberry, floral, smoke & bacon; well-knit palate with bright acidity/fruit, supple tannins.

★★★★ **Shiraz** Hedonistic **04** (★★★★) lavish with lily, lavender & opulent red fruit. Tannins & alc (14.5%) brusque in youth, shd mellow ±3 yrs. **03** had been more approachable in youth. Yr 50/50 Fr/Am oak.

Chardonnay Last tasted **04** (★★★) was rich — & zippy despite touch sugar. Appealed to the panels: MIWA DG, *Wine* ★★★★★; **06** sample (not ready to rate) rather more reticent: soft citrus, white stonefruit brushed with vanilla oak (30% fermented/3 mths new Fr). **Chenin Blanc** ★★★ **06** shows little of floral notes of pvs: it's shy & unforthcoming, lacking concentration & complexity. **05** flew SAA. **Sauvignon Blanc** ★★★ Delicate **06** offers cut grass & floral aromas/flavours, moderate ±12.5% alc & 4.4g/ℓ sugar for palate roundness.

Viljoensdrift range

★★★★ **Serenity** Classy bdx-style blend cab, merlot, cab f, petit v (40/30/20/10). Last tasted **03** refined yet concentrated, with fruit, tannin, alc in harmony; gd in youth, but structured to improve over 5-7 yrs. Grapes fermented, matured separately 24 mths new Fr oak. Calyon Top Ten placing.

Merlot-Shiraz ★★★ Merlot-led (62%) **04** delicious mid-2005: meaty/mineral aromas, tomato & plum flavours, persistent dry tealeaf finish, benefiting from 12% petit v. Yr Fr oak. **Rosé** ★★★ Last ed, **04** vibrant & dry with gentle grip courtesy of fruit tannins; raspberry/blackberry notes. From juice 'bled' off shiraz. Sweet **NV** version, 'Wine on the Water Sweet Rosé', from pinotage & muscadel, not ready for tasting. **Colombar-Chenin Blanc** ★★ Friendly, zesty **06** blend (69:31) for summer quaffing, though aromas/flavours somewhat reticent. **Cape Vintage Reserve** ★★★★ Classically styled but very ripe **03** relatively high alc (±18%) & dry (79g/ℓ RS); from souzão/tinta (65/35). Bold choc, cherry, caramel aromas/flavours. *—DH*

■ *Village Collection see* Tulbagh Wineries Co-op

Villiera Wines

Stellenbosch • Est/1stB 1983 • Tasting & sales Mon-Fri 8.30-5 Sat 8.30-1 • R7.50 p/p for groups • Closed Easter Fri/Sun, Dec 25, Jan 1 • Self-guided tours anytime during tasting hours; guided tours by appt • Annual St Vincent's Day dinner (closest Sat to Jan 22) • BYO picnic in summer • Owners Grier family • Winemakers Jeff Grier, with Anton Smal (Oct 1992) • Viticulturist Simon Grier • 260 ha (13 varieties, r/w) • 2 000 tons 110 000 cs own label + 16 000 cs for Woolworths + 8 000 for Marks & Spencer (UK) • 38% white 33% red 4% rosé 25% sparkling • PO Box 66 Koelenhof 7605 • wine@villiera.com • www.villiera.com • T 021·865·2002/3 • F 021·865·2314

The energetic and enterprising Grier family have purchased a vineyard in southern France – 22ha near St Paul in the Agly Valley, Roussillon, where old grenache, shiraz, carignan and some macabeo are rooted in good black schistous soils. Vine tending is by the former owner, assisted by neighbour Jean-Louis Denois, long-time Grier family friend and champagne-maker who helped Villiera become a premier producer of *méthode champenoise* bubbly. Back home, *Wine's* annual reader poll 'best-value winery' has increased its cap classique production, installed new cellar equipment, introduced an exclusive new supermarket range, and agreed to vinify Elgin Vintners' Sauvignon in exchange for fruit from this promising cool upland.

★★★★ **Monro** Varying blend merlot/cab successfully & stylishly straddles conservative/modern divide. **03** retains merlot dominance but shows the best of both: complex array of violets, mixed red fruit, herbal nuances, with fine-grained tannins busy working their magic. Accessible now but has 6+ yr future, as all these. Up to 2 yrs mostly new Fr oak.

★★★★ **Traditional Bush Vine Sauvignon Blanc** Officially recognised single-vyd wine. As elegant & steely as **05**, with cool fruit styling, **06** impresses with taut minerality, gunflint, nettles, invigorating palate freshness (7.4g/ℓ acidity). More Loire than New World, very stylish. Modest 12.2% alc.

★★★★ **Inspiration** NLH from hand-selected botrytised chenin. **05** previewed last ed, retasted, hasn't lost a jot in interim: tangy, unfolding peach/apricot tones, decadently delicious texture, flavours. 176g/ℓ sugar, 13.9% alc – but excellent vibrant acidity. These fermented/±9 mths Fr oak. Already delicious, will keep/develop well. 375ml.

★★★★ **Tradition Rosé Brut** Uncertified salmon pink **NV** MCC. Colour from ripe pinotage (majority) added to pinot, chard juice. Latest has ripe strawberry entry juxtaposed with earthy palate austerity; finishes crisply dry. A sophisticated, grown-up bubbly. 56/24/20 blend. *Wine* ★★★★.

★★★★ **Monro Brut** Pale colour presages mature baked apple & yeasty biscuit bouquet on last-tasted **00**. Richly, silkily elegant blend of barrel-fermented/matured chard (55%) & pinot, disgorged after 5 yrs on lees. Lingering savoury dry finish – low 7.5g/ℓ sugar. WO Paarl. Fine, well matured **99** *Wine* ★★★★.

★★★★★ **Brut Natural** ✓ Notably dry & refined MCC from chard – no dosage, no sulphur or other additives apart from sugar, yeast for 2nd, bubble-forming fermentation. **03** last ed had decadent ripe-apple, brioche, spice bouquet/flavours, & usual creamy, bone-dry richness. These, including standout **01** (★★★★★), need more careful storage than sulphur-protected wines if matured more than yr/2.

> **Sonnet** ☺ ★★★ Label & blend change, sample **06** now 100% muscat ottonel in all its aromatic, grapey glory. Off-dry, light (12.5% alc) & perfectly charming.

Cabernet Sauvignon ★★★ ✓ Brilliantly reliable wine, textbook varietal expression, well structured, honest & good. **04** doesn't disappoint: cassis-infused, yet with underlying savoury oak that confirms the 3+ yr ageability. Supported by yr Fr/Am wood (like

Pinotage, Shiraz). **Pinotage** ★★★ For drinking rather than keeping, **04** shows good typicity, rhubarb & dark fruit, all nicely wrapped in a lively, juicy package. **Shiraz** ★★★☆ Hard to resist, delicious **04** has high-toned fruit, brambleberries, mulberries shot through with roasted sweet spice; shows all the fleshy richness that good vyd care brings. **Merlot** ★★★ **04** in lightly spiced blackberry & herbal house-style, going for youthful, crisp drinkability rather than opulence. Yr Fr oak, qtr new. **Merlot-Shiraz-Pinotage** 𝗇𝖾𝗐 ★★★ Designed to drink rather than impress, **04** has dark plum tones, minimal oaking & fresh-fruity, lively flavours. Highly quaffable. Touch gamay. **Chenin Blanc** ★★★☆ ✓ Another fine bargain. **06** freshly sliced melon & pear, showing joyful youth, verve, yet structural credentials for 2-3 yrs ageing. Gains texture from partial barrel ferment. **Sauvignon Blanc** ★★★☆ **06** non-aggressive, satisfying ripe, fruity style delivering expected palate zest for food matching, solo drinking. Dab semillon. **Sauvignon Blanc-Chenin Blanc** 𝗇𝖾𝗐 ★★★ Previewed **06**'s sauvignon dominance (62%) dictates style: pear-rich fruit salad, light textured & refreshing, perfect for alfresco joining. With near-equal chenin/chard. **Rhine Riesling** ★★★☆ ✓ Glacé pineapple, tantalising spiciness & honeysuckle are part of **06**'s appeal. Slender but well formed, a lovely food wine. **Gewürztraminer** ★★★☆ ✓ Graceful, appealing **06** has textbook rosepetal perfume & flavour in a gently rounded off-dry package. **Tradition Brut** ★★★☆ Ever-reliable uncertified **NV** MCC from chard, pinot, pinotage, with splash of pinot meunier. Latest appeals with tiny exuberant bubbles, refreshingly flavourful styling, well crafted drinkability (incl 12.5% alc). 51/28/16/5 blend. Also in 1.5ℓ & 375ml. **Brut Special Dosage** 𝗇𝖾𝗐 ★★★☆ Friendly **NV** MCC with dosage to brut limit, touch muscat to enhance fruitiness. Rest of blend & winemaking similar to Tradition. Warm, ripe character, attractive plumpness, with bubbles supplying celebratory lift. **Fired Earth** ★★★☆ ✓ In LBV port style, last available **01** from 48% shiraz with touriga, pinotage, tinta. Deliciously ready (but will keep ages), with mocha, pruney spicy notes; grip more from acid than tannin. 3 yrs in older oak. 85g/ℓ sugar; 20% alc. WO Coastal.

Cellar Door range

★★★★ **Merlot** C-D prefix indicates made in best years only. This from 'Robin's Block' vineyard. Quietly elegant aromas mocha, dark fruit on last available **03**, perfumed spice. Still youthful, prominent acidity, well integrated oak — yr mostly new. Trifle 'hot' on finish from 14.6% alc.

★★★★ **Chenin Blanc** Characterful example fermented/matured on lees in mostly new Fr oak ±6 mths; good ageing potential, as all these. **05** peach perfume, flavours, with fruit richness contributing to voluptuous mouthfeel, long finish.

★★★★ **Rhine Riesling Noble Late Harvest** Probably a one-off, says Grier — 'a high level of botrytis caught us by surprise in **05**'; last ed showed lingering tinned pineapple & marmalade notes & integrated acidity on light, fine richness. 103g/ℓ sugar, 13.2% alc. 500ml.

Down to Earth range

White ☺ ★★★ Reliably tasty fresh quaffer; sauvignon-based blend with chenin, semillon. **06** sample in same winning style: exuberant summer fruits, crisply dry finish.

Red ★★★ 5 varieties consort in safe, pleasant **05**, tasted last ed. Toasty baked aromas, warmly friendly palate. Yr oaked; 14% alc. **Rosé** ★★★ Completing the trio, still-available dry **05**, mostly pinotage (plus gamay, shiraz); earth & red berry flavours — all very satisfying. — CR

Villiersdorp Cellar

Worcester ▪ Est 1922 ▪ 1stB 1980 ▪ Tasting & sales Mon-Sat 8-5 ▪ Fee R10 for groups of 7+ ▪ Closed Easter Fri & Dec 25 ▪ Fully licensed restaurant, farm stall, wine boutique & gift shop (hours as above + Sun & pub hols 9-3) ▪ Owners 55 growers ▪ Winemaker WS Visagie ▪ Viticulturist Ryan Puttick ▪ 500 ha ▪ 5 600 tons 10 000 cs own label 20% red 60% white 6% rosé 14% fortified ▪ PO Box 14 Villiersdorp 6848 ▪ info@vilko.co.za ▪ www.vilko.co.za ▪ T 028·840·1151 ▪ F 028·840·0957

Now also the 'House of Slowine' (see separate entry), Villiersdorp Cellar is the production site for this joint-venture label (with partners Paul Cluver, Beaumont and Luddite) on the pioneering Green Mountain Eco Route, which shows off the area's rare natural heritage through wine-tinted glasses. Slowine and Splendour, another new brand from Villiersdorp Cellar, can be sampled in the Kelkiewyn Farmstall & Restaurant, which doubles as the tasting centre. GM Ben Klindt says these new ranges reflect the energy and capital which has been channelled into the cellar in recent years.

Cabernet Sauvignon ★★ Shows same lusty oaking as sibling **05** reds (here, only Fr); hint of cocoa & black fruit, but mostly wood character & dry dusty tannins. Will need plenty of time. **Merlot** new ★★★ **05** chunky (from active 14.5% alc, strong tannins) yet fairly slender fruit. Serious intent (yr Fr oak), so perhaps just needs cellaring. **Shiraz** new ★★ Am oak lines up behind Fr in putsch on **05**'s timid fruit; wood (yr) has upper hand mid-2006, but might relent with enough time. **Rosé** new ★★ Onion-skin-hued **05** has muscadel's endearing perfume (here with chenin, shiraz); slender build; Natural Sweet-style sugar (80 g/ℓ) needs chilling, even if you're sweeter-toothed. **Chardonnay** ★★★ Citrus & tropical fruit in **04**, last ed was still fresh, with whistle-clean dry finish. Unwooded. **Chenin Blanc** ★★★ **06** (sample) light, fresh passionfruit taste; smoothly dry, easy, with interesting spicy undertone. Ovrberg WO, as is... **Sauvignon Blanc** ★★★ **06** attractive spread of green flavours/aromas, with dusty figleaf note; lively light texture & poised acidity. Enjoy in yr of vintage. **Late Vintage** ('Bouquet Blanc' pvs ed; unrated.) **06** untasted. **Hanepoot Jerepigo** ★★★ Full-sweet fortified dessert, **06** fresh-grape/muscat loveliness; fuller than pvs, sweeter flavours of barley sugar. Gd over crushed ice. **Port** ★★★ Pvs were traditional Cape-style fortifieds with fruity/jammy character; **06** from tinta & pontac too unformed to rate. Both ranges WO W Cape unless mentioned.

Splendour range   new

> **Classic Red** ☺ ★★★ Classic quaffing combo ripe berry fruit, lively texture, light brush of oak on **05**; full, generous, slightly toasty equal cab/merlot blend. **Blanc de Blanc** ☺ ★★★ Eminently quaffable colombard/chenin medley; latter grape's green-apple tone adds freshness, zing to **06**, balanced & clean-finishing. Both in 1000ml. — *MM*

- ■ *Vine Collection* see Oranjerivier Wine Cellars
- ■ *Vineyard Selection* see Blaauwklippen, Kleine Zalze, Neil Ellis, Robertson Winery
- ■ *Vinfruco* see The Company of Wine People

Vinimark

*Stellenbosch • Closed to public • Directors Tim Rands, Cindy Jordaan, Geoff Harvey & Gys Naudé • PO Box 441 Stellenbosch 7599 • Exports: Brad Gold bradg@vinimark.co.za • www. vinimark.co.za • **T 021·883·8043/4** • F 021·886·4708*

Wine merchants marketing, selling and distributing various ranges with local partners, including Jonkerskloof, Kleindal, Long Beach, Ravenswood, Silver Sands and Zomerlust, listed separately.

Vins D'Orrance   ☿♀

*Constantia • Est/1stB 2001 • Tastings by appt 8.30–4.30 • Closed Easter Sun, Dec 25 & Jan 1 • Owner/winemaker Christophe Durand • 840 cs 70% red 30% white • 10 Squirrels Way, Newlands 7735 • christophe@vinum.co.za • **T 021·683·7479** • F 021·683·7489*

Here's a positive perspective on a solo show, conducted in the High Constantia cellar by Frenchman Christophe Durand: 'Being a small producer is a pure pleasure and a permanent challenge,' he tells us. 'There is no place for error.' He even enjoys the associated stress, experiencing each harvest as unique. As the guide went to press, he bottled the third wine in his range, a varietal Viognier.

★★★★ **Syrah Cuvée Ameena** After dramatic, 100% new-oaked **03**, **04** revisits more elegant style where wood (Fr, 80% new) supports plentiful spicy/savoury excitement.

Youthful edginess needs yr/2 to yield to richly layered, supple texture. Shd age with distinction. 15% alc. WO Sbosch.

★★★★ **Chardonnay Cuvée Anaïs 05** more yielding than youthfully tight **04**. Roast nut, lime, mineral complexity but exudes classic chic. Remarkably light feel for flavour concentration, 14% alc. Promises delicious maturity around 2009. Barrel fermented/matured, 100% new Fr. —AL

Vintage International Brands

PO Box 19049 Wynberg 7824 ▪ info@vib.co.za ▪ **T** *021·762·5975 ▪ F 021·761·8536*
Independent producing-wholesaler based in Cape Town, importing wines and spirits for the retail trade and producing their own-label wines, Hippo Creek and Simply Red & White (see Hippo Creek).

■ *Vintage Selection* see Spier
■ *Vinum* see The Winery of Good Hope

Vinus Via

Stellenbosch ▪ Est/1stB 2004 ▪ Closed to public ▪ 10 000 cs (projected) 50/50 red/white ▪ 21 Topaz Street, Heldervue, Somerset West 7130 ▪ info@vinusvia.co.za ▪ www.vinusvia.co.za ▪ **T/F 021·855·5244**
Made from a combination of wines sourced from various wineries, Vinus Via is more of a blending and marketing exercise for Richard Hilton (who satisfies his desire for 'real' winemaking with his Pax Verbatim label, listed separately). The idea is to make good quality wines which cater for the commercial price category — probably the toughest arena to crack. But three years on, Hilton is making inroads.

Red Bishop Cabernet Sauvignon ★★★ Agreeable dinner companion with ripe plum jam tone, brisk acidity. **04** for early drinking. **Shaka Zulu Shiraz** ★★★ Lighter, more accessible style. **04** crushed black pepper, spice & savoury notes. Round soft tannins, versatile, quaffable. **Wild Lily Chardonnay** ★★★ Juicy & delicious **05**, crisp marmalade aromas & flavours. **African Jack Chenin Blanc** ★★ Easy-drinking, sherbety, with hints of lemon; low 12.4% alc. No new versions of above tasted; unwooded.—MM

Vin-X-Port South Africa

Paarl ▪ Est 2001 ▪ Closed to public ▪ Directors Hennie van der Merwe & Maretha Waso ▪ 191 Main Rd Paarl 7646 ▪ marketing@x-port.co.za ▪ www.x-port.co.za ▪ **T** *872·0850 ▪ F 872·0849*
Negociant house specialising in procuring, producing and shipping quality wines, and in creating and marketing new brands. Its extensive portfolio includes African Treasure, Cape Circle and BunduStar, exported to various countries.

Virgin Earth

Little Karoo ▪ Tasting by appt ▪ Postnet Suite 57, Private Bag X18, Milnerton 7435 ▪ sales@havanahills.co.za ▪ **T/F** *021·972·1110/05*
On a 13 000ha farm in the rugged Langeberg, given over mainly to ranging eland, black wildebeest, gemsbok and springbok, Havana Hills owner Kobus du Plessis is letting his creativity similarly run free. Once they are filled in the rustic sandstone cellar, he lowers his red wine barrels into a dam for up to a year of underwater maturation — a unique technique, not least in adding scuba equipment to the list of cellar expenses. More conventionally, he is extending plantings with chenin and pinotage.

High 5ive ★★★★ **05** attractive creamy berry fruit amongst scrubby spice, nicely judged tannins. Cabs s & f, merlot, shiraz & petit v; now all ex-L Karoo. Yr oak, 30% new. Following reds **new**: **Terroir** ★★★ Third each cab, merlot & shiraz, **04** smoky red/black fruits temper rough tannins. L Karoo/Philadelphia fruit, partly barrelled, yr. **Pinotage** ★★★ Unequivocal estery 'Duco' tint to sweet plum lines, **04** further fleshed out by oak (yr all Fr, 30% new). Pdberg grapes. **Sauvignon Blanc** ★★★ Characteristic smooth texture a counterpoint to fynbos features of **06**. Gentle 12.5% alc, same for… **Chenin Blanc** `new` ★★★ **06** spun-sugar nose, sweetly fruited mouthful with some fullness in the tail. — *DS*

Virginia

Enduring big-volume white, by Distell. **NV** ✩ Equal blend chenin/colombard; semi-dry, lightish (11% alc), slips down easily. In 2ℓ btls, 4.5ℓ flagons. W Cape vyds. — *CvZ*

■ **Vlottenburg Winery** *see* Stellenbosch Hills

■ **Volmaak** *see* Baarsma

■ **Vondeling** *see* Armajaro

Von Ortloff

Franschhoek ▪ *1stB 1994* ▪ *Tasting, sales & tours by appt* ▪ *Owners/winemakers Georg & Eve Schlichtmann* ▪ *Viticulturist Eduard du Toit (2005)* ▪ *13 ha (cab, merlot, shiraz, chard, sauvignon)* ▪ *5 000 cs own label 60% red 40% white* ▪ *PO Box 341 Franschhoek 7690* ▪ *vortloff@ mweb.co.za* ▪ *T 021·876·3432* ▪ *F 021·876·4313*

Last ed we had no update from husband and wife team Georg and Eve Schlichtmann. Turns out they were simply too busy, planting shiraz, installing smaller-scale vinification tanks, employing viticulturist Eduard du Toit (who's proved a dab hand in the cellar too), setting up a distribution facility in Germany, re-entering the US market; and — whew! — releasing their new flagship, Quintessence.

★★★★★ **Quintessence** `new` Cab-led (64%) blend with merlot, from a few select barrels, in classic Old World style. **00** has a core of pure, dark cassis fruit with beautifully woven cedary, cigarbox oak. Fine dry tannins & svelte, velvet texture. Commendably cellar-aged & released when ready, though enough structure & substance for gd few yrs. 19-24 mths Fr oak, 80% new.

★★★★ **Cabernet Sauvignon-Merlot** These have style & presence, showing attention to detail: only free-run juice, individual oaking for components. **01** blend 76% cab, 24% merlot; ripe cassis fruit, less taut, continues trend to easier accessibility. Cab 24-26 mths barriques, 60% new; merlot 24 mths, 50% new, all Fr. No newer vintage ready.

★★★★ **No. 7** From merlot. **04** rich fruit compote with cedar, sweet tobacco & dark choc overlay. Palate bursts with juicy dark fruit (rather than meaty nuance of **03**). Balanced, with bright acidity & ripe tannins; immensely drinkable. 9 mths Fr oak, 10% new.

★★★★ **Chardonnay** Elegant barrel fermented example since **93**. **03** more commercial (★★★★), misses some of the classic restraint of earlier vintages. Not retasted. **02** had a tangy palate & extraordinary length. 12-14 mths, all Fr, 70% new. No **04/05** of this or unwooded version below.

No. 5 ★★★✩ From sauvignon. **06** (sample) has bright kiwi and passionfruit aromas, similar mouthwatering flavours & lively, zesty acidity. Great summer quaffer with long tropical farewell. **No. 3** ★★★★ Preview **06** delicious example of chard untrammelled by oak. Redolent with ripe pear & yellow peach, clean, pure mid-palate & perky acidity. Ideal food partner & welcome option for oak-shy palates. — *IvH*

■ **Voorspoed** *see* Baarsma

Vooruitsig

Paarl ▪ *Est 1998* ▪ *1stB 2002* ▪ *Closed to public* ▪ *Owner Mozelle Holdings (Pty) Ltd* ▪ *Vini consultant Jean-Vincent Ridon (Signal Hill, 2002)* ▪ *3ha (merlot)* ▪ *500 cs 100% red* ▪ *PO Box 6080 Uniedal 7612* ▪ *www.prime-invest.co.za/vooruitsig.htm* ▪ *vooruitsig@prime-invest.co.za* ▪ *T 082·566·4700/082·564·3241* ▪ *F 021·855·3028*

This boutique winery adjoining prime property Veenwouden still produces only merlot, though the intention remains to establish cab, cab franc, malbec and shiraz under the oversight of adviser Jean-Vincent Ridon. The latest 'planting' is of a different nature: ex-Zimbabwean Larry Norton, realist wildlife artist of international repute, has set up his studio here.

Merlot Limited Release ★★★☆ These are brooding individuals, deserving further maturation. A lot of ripeness in **03**, pruney fruit, 15% alc, deep beefy layers, given serious oak attention (18 mths Fr). — *CR*

Vrede en Lust Wine Farm

*Paarl ▪ Est 1996 ▪ 1stB 2002 ▪ Tasting & sales daily 10-5 ▪ Closed Dec 25 & Jan 1 ▪ Tours 10-4 by appt ▪ Cotage Fromage Deli & Restaurant ▪ Guest accommodation in two cottages & manor house ▪ Play area for children ▪ Tour groups by appt (max 26 people) ▪ Gifts ▪ Farm produce ▪ Conferences & functions ▪ Owners Dana & Etienne Buys ▪ Winemaker Susanne Wessels ▪ Viticulturist Etienne Buys (Jun 1998) ▪ 42 ha (cab, malbec, merlot, petit v, shiraz, chard) ▪ 20 000 cs own label ▪ ISO 14001 certified ▪ PO Box 171 Groot Drakenstein 7680 ▪ info@vnl.co.za ▪ www.vnl.co.za ▪ **T 021 874·1611** ▪ F 021 874·1859*

The Buys brothers have involved their staff in the purchase of an 89-ha farm in Elgin, simultaneously fulfilling black economic empowerment (BEE) objectives and securing a source of premium sauvignon grapes to complement the predominantly red range, now made by exNeethlingshof deputy winemaker Susanne Wessels. Free tastings are part of a drive to develop a stronger wine culture, and, for the more wine-literate, there is the 'Wine Enthusiast' package, pairing V&L wines with a selection of cheeses, pâtés and chocolate. The Jacques de Savoy brand is being phased out, and wines previously under that banner continue as part of the 'classic' V&L range.

Reserve NEW ★★★★ From classic bdx varieties cab & merlot (50/38) with dollop petit v, dash malbec. **02** deeply rich, ripe plums & cassis, underbrush & cigarbox notes. Structured for the longer haul, as befits a Rsv. WO Coastal. **Classic** ★★★ Blend cab, merlot, malbec & petit v (65/26/5/4); **03**, yr on, tannins more amenable but still providing firm base for ±3/4 yrs development. Lead pencil, dark fruit, forest floor hints quite Old World in style. **Cara** ★★★ Robust fruit profile & strong tannins from blend cab, shiraz, merlot (39/37/24); **03** (not retasted) has less new oak than earlier versions (10% vs. ±25). **Simond** ★★★ The early-drinking version of above cab, merlot, shiraz; **04** fruity, with just enough oak presence to add definition. **Barbère** ★★☆ Dry rosé, make-up varies with vintage. Shiraz, cab & merlot in **05** gives unusual bready character to strawberry fruit; wld go well with food. WO Paarl. **Marguerite** ★★☆ From chard, bunch-pressed, Fr cask fermented/10 mths. **03** (sample) last ed was still woody, citrus/stonefruit core needed opportunity to unfold. **Karien** ★★★ Chenin with dash semillon, lees-aged. **06** more than just a fruity quaffer: has savoury leanings, making it food-compatible. All WO Smnsberg-Paarl unless stated. — *CR*

■ **Vredendal Winery** *see* Westcorp

Vredenheim Wines

*Stellenbosch ▪ Tasting & sales Mon-Fri 9-5 Sat 9.30-2 (Dec 9-5) ▪ Fee R2/tasting ▪ Closed Easter Fri, Dec 25 & Jan 1 ▪ Barrique Restaurant ▪ T 021·881·3001 ▪ Hudson's Coffee Shop ▪ T 021·881·3590 ▪ Other amenities: see intro ▪ Owners Bezuidenhout family ▪ Winemaker Elzabé Bezuidenhout, advised by Fanie Cilliers ▪ 80 ha ▪ 10 000 cs 60% red 40% white ▪ PO Box 369 Stellenbosch 7599 ▪ trendsetter@vredenheim.co.za ▪ www.vredenheim.co.za ▪ **T 021·881·3637** ▪ F 021·881·3296*

It's been 20 years since the Bezuidenhouts took over Vredenheim and it's clearly been a busy two decades, with a choice of dining venues now on offer, art exhibitions, a gift shop featuring local arts and crafts, and game drives to view their buck (an exciting new addition was an eland calf), wildebeest, zebras and ostriches up close. Last year saw a cellar upgrade and the launch of a new logo. No new vintages tasted for their Reserve 214 red blend, Shiraz, Pinotage, Rosé, Chenin Blanc, Angel's Natural Sweet dessert or Vredenvonkel demi-sec sparkling.

■ **Vreughvol** *see* Baarsma

Vriesenhof Vineyards

Stellenbosch ▪ Est 1980 ▪ 1stB 1981 ▪ Tasting Mon-Thu 10-4 Fri 10-3.30 Sat 10-2 (groups of 10+ by appt only) ▪ Tours & meals/refreshments by appt ▪ Owner Landgoed Vriesenhof (Pty) Ltd ▪

Winemaker Jan Coetzee, with Richard Phillips (2001) ▪ Viticulturist Hannes Coetzee ▪ 37 ha (cabs s/f, merlot, pinot, pinotage, chard) ▪ ±500 tons 85% red 15% white ▪ PO Box 155 Stellenbosch 7599 ▪ info@vriesenhof.co.za ▪ www.vriesenhof.co.za ▪ T 021·880·0284 ▪ F 021·880·1503

Veteran winegrower Jan Coetzee is enjoying his latter years. Having celebrated a quarter century on Vriesenhof in 2005, his next season (31st as a winemaker) confirmed his opinion that, since the 1960s, the Cape has not had such a run of great vintages. He's making the most of it, curtailing consultancies to concentrate on Vriesenhof, nestled in a Stellenbosch Mountain kloof. Despite a reputation for classic bordeaux-style reds, this burgundian at heart has often extolled the virtues of his patch's surprisingly cool climate, and the pinots he makes prove it.

Vriesenhof range

★★★★ **Enthopio** Pinotage stars in this charismatic blend, its Greek name meaning 'truly indigenous' (though soupçons non-'SA' shiraz, merlot & cab f incl for complexity). **03** usual marvellous generosity, muscular tannins eased by juicy, fruit-rich finish; already well-knit & poised to gain complexity with further ageing. **02** (★★★★★) a standout in difficult yr. Fermented in new oak then ±yr used barrels.

★★★★ **Pinot Noir 05** preview shows classic pinot perfumes & flavours, textured silkiness, in context of warmer vintage. Cooler yr **04** (★★★★★) was quintessential pinot: truffles & cherries, poised tannins, reviving freshness. These gd for 5± yrs; Dijon clones in varying soils, sympathetically oaked (seasoned barrels only, ±10 mths Fr); relatively slender ±13.5% alcs.

★★★★ **Cabernet Sauvignon** Returns (in magnum only) after a short hiatus with all classic Vriesenhof Cab characters (tight texture, underlying elegance, promise of ±decade's gradual unfolding) in a modern, juicier package; **03** & **02** tasted together, hints dry scrub & forest floor, fresh acidity, astringent tannins, all set for the long haul.

★★★★★ **Kallista** Flagship bdx-style red usually led by merlot though **03** has cab f (35%) just ahead, contributing leafy tones, & junior partner cab (31%) adding lemon-like freshness to merlot's rounded girth. Impressive tannins not overpowering. Generously oaked: 50% new Fr, ±18 mths for long keeping. ±13.5% alc.

Melelo [new] ★★★★ Aromatic before or after-dinner fortified from venerable red muscat d'A vines (50 yrs), dash touriga 'for gd colour'. **05** heady bouquet of spices, raisins & watermelon, very sweet (189g/ℓ sugar) but not cloying, nicely balanced by 15% alc. Name derived from the African 'mpumelelo' for prosperity.

Talana Hill range

★★★★ **Royale** Historically, a blend of cabs s/f & merlot, but **02** (★★★☆) switches to 67/32 merlot/cab f. Retasted as finished wine this yr, savoury biltong aromas & black plum & tarry oak notes. Firm tannins, astringent tealeaf farewell; 14% alc just raises its head. For earlier drinking. **01** initial oak-vanilla attack balanced by opulent black fruit. 8 mths Fr oak, new/2nd fill.

Chardonnay ★★★★ Bunch-fermented in barrel. Tasted mid-2005, **04**'s citrus zest cut buttered scone richness, alc tinge (13.5%) to finish.

Paradyskloof range

Pinotage ★★★ **03** tasted last yr was a robust step above easy-drinking pvs. Lanolin, raspberry, smoke aromas & slight acetone whiff; earthy/organic flavours. Modest 13% alc. **Pinot Noir** [new] ★★★ **04** winter warmer has cherry on colour, nose & aftertaste, plus lovely wet earth notes, refreshing acidity, drying tannins, manageable 13.4% alc. **Cabernet Sauvignon-Merlot** ★★★☆ **04** plush fruit with intriguing whiffs iron, tar & smoke. Fruit-sweet palate, gentle tannic embrace. 12-16 mths 2nd/3rd fill oak. **Chardonnay** ★★★ **04**, tasted last ed, notch up on pvs, delicate lemon/grape flavour with tangy finish. — *CvZ*

Vruchtbaar Boutique Winery ◊♟🍷📖

Robertson ▪ Est/1stB 2001 ▪ Visits by appt ▪ BYO picnic ▪ Tour groups ▪ Guest house ▪ Owners Alwyn & Francois Bruwer ▪ Winemaker Francois Bruwer ▪ Viti adviser Briaan Stipp (2005) ▪ 35 ha (cab, pinotage, merlot, ruby cab, chenin, chard, colombard, sauvignon) ▪ 400 tons 100 cs *own label • 75% red 25% white • PO Box 872 Robertson 6705 • vruchtbaar@mweb.co.za • **T** 023·626·2334 / 082·335·1152 / 082·447·4790 • F 023·626·4081*

If you stayed in their guesthouse or an establishment in the vicinity during Robertson's Wacky Wine Weekend, you would have received a free bottle of Vruchtbaar wine and a pamphlet about this young boutique winery. The Bruwer father-and-son team's marketing forays have extended into the Port Elizabeth area, netting listings in several restaurants and golf clubs, as well as good feedback. Now clearly signposted, the winery is open by appointment only.

★★★★ Cabernet Sauvignon ✓ **04** a stylish cross of two pvs vintages: the restrained fruit & fine tannins of **03**, sweet Am oak coconut tones of **02**. Poised & persistent, with subtle cassis & fresh herb bouquet. Will reward cellaring. From single block. 18 mths, 50/50 Fr/Am oak.

Island Red new ☺ **★★★** Instantly popular, light-hearted, early-ready red from young vines; 63% cab & 37% pinotage. **05** bursts with fruit & florals, friendly tannin, balanced acidity.

Sauvignon Blanc ★★★ 06 unready; sample **05** mid-2005 was super-fresh with green fig & greenpepper notes, racy lime/citrus palate, undaunting 13.5% alc. — *CvZ*

■ *Vruchtbaar* see Robertson Wide River

Vukani Wines   ♀ new

Est 2005 • Tasting/sales/winemakers as for Bramon Wines (see entry) • Fee R20 for 4 wines • ±1 400 cs 56% red 44% white • PO Box 1606 Plettenberg Bay 6600 • peter@vukaniwines. com or jonathan@vukaniwines.com • www.vukaniwines.com • T/F 044·534·8007

Vukani Wines is the vinous arm of Vukani-Ubuntu, a non-profit organisation empowering disadvantaged communities. According to trust member Peter Thorpe (of Bramon Wines), it embraces the unique selling points of black economic empowerment and Fairtrade. 'By supporting and enjoying Vukani Wines, the wine drinker is happy to imbibe, secure in the knowledge that a significant percentage of the price is going directly to the impoverished communities responsible for production — who have the innate potential to become part of the mainstream of the global wine production sector.'

Shiraz ★★★ Big though unshowy **04**. Pepper/spice, dark berries plus slight porty notes. Am oak sweetness lifts palate. Drink up before 15% alc dominates. **Shiraz-Cabernet Sauvignon ★★★** Straightforward but tasty **04**; melange choc, spice, red fruits smoothly meshed in 60/40 blend; savoury finish. Yr Fr/Am oak, none new. **Chardonnay ★★★ 05** unoaked, with straightforward tropical aromas. Juicy, smooth; fruit bolstered by 5g/ℓ sugar. **Sauvignon Blanc ★★★★** ✓ Delightfully fresh **05** captures variety's gooseberry/lemongrass purity. Medium bodied, dry; gentle yet well defined flavours. All above WO W Cape. — *AL*

Vuurberg Vineyards   ♀

Stellenbosch • Est 2000 • 1stB 2003 • Visits by appt • Owner Sebastiaan Klaassen • Winemaker Miles Mossop, with Sebastiaan Klaassen (both 2003) • Viti adviser Aidan Morton (2002) • 10 ha (cab s/f, malbec, merlot, petit v, chenin, grenache blanc, roussanne, viognier) • 1 500 cs 100% red • PO Box 449 Stellenbosch 7599 • vuurberg@mweb.co.za • www. vuurberg.com • T/F 021·885·2595

Delighted with their 05 Chenin, Sebastiaan Klaassen and Anna Poll last year upped the white count with chenin, viognier and sauvignon (destined for a blend). They also bought three new open-fermenters for greater extraction and concentration in the reds. Encouraging responses to their wines at Cape Wine 2006 prompted orders from the US, UK, Denmark and Holland (Klaassen's homeland). Wine stocks, previously kept offsite, are now held at their mountain-hugging cellar, and they say visitors are welcome to come and taste by appointment.

★★★★ **Vuurberg** Classy cab-merlot blend dominated by cab's fragrant cassis, hint lead pencil; **03** plush dark velvet texture, unobtrusive tannins, dry finish with fine tannins, lingering oak. **04** (★★★★), now bottled, has all above attractions in a touch more restrained, less concentrated form. Incl dollop petit v. 18 mths Fr oak, 30% new.

★★★★ **Vuurberg Reserve** new Selection of best barrels of above, 60% new oak component; Impressive **04** has merlot slightly ahead (50%), cab at 40% & smidgen petit v; rich, dense & warm fruit with meaty mocha overlay, subtle & disciplined oak; excellent balance & potential.

Chenin Blanc ★★★★ Ripe, chard-like **05**, sample last yr, now a luscious marmalade character with soft, sweetish, rounded profile courtesy of touch sugar & 14.5% alc. Oak 50% new. **Tridente** discontinued. *— IvH*

■ *Waboomsrivier Co-op* see Overhex Wines International

Wamakersvallei Winery

Wellington • Est 1941 • Tasting & sales Mon-Fri 8-5 Sat 8.30-12.30 • Closed pub hols except May 1 • Tours by appt • BYO picnic • Conferences • Owners 40 members • Cellarmaster Hugo Truter • Winemakers Hugo Truter & André Swanepoel • Viticulturist Koos van der Merwe • 1 400 ha • 55% red 45% white • PO Box 509 Wellington 7654 • sales@wamakers.co.za • www. wamakersvallei.co.za • T 021·873·1582 • F 021·873·3194

All change in the valley! First newcomer was viticulturist Koos van der Merwe, leaving Vredendal Winery after four years to return to his hometown. He'll divide his time between Wellington Cellar growers and Wamakers' members. Next to arrive was Hugo Truter, coming in as cellarmaster/winemaker, with experience of several local operations (most recently Swartland Winery) and Hugues de Beauvignac in Languedoc. Causing less of a stir but a matter for pride — the winery was recently accredited by the Wine Industry Ethical Trade Association.

La Cave range

Cabernet Sauvignon ★★★ **04** lauded by Winemakers' Choice judges; we find pronounced & appealing ripeness, dark fruit richness on nose, contrasting powerfully gripping tannins, inviting decanting if opening now. 15.5% alc. **Merlot** ★★★ Ripe, fruit-filled bouquet on **04**; flavours touch less effusive but pleasantly soft, easy to drink; tangy background freshens, avoids potential brawniness of 15.5% alc. **Pinotage** ★★★★ High-kicking/flying version: ABSA Top Ten, *Wine* ★★★★, Winemakers' Choice gongs for showy **04**, inviting caramel/strawberry shortcake aromas, well ripened fruit & refreshing acidity. Attractive wine, for earlier enjoyment. Benefits from less glow-inducing alc (14.5%) than pvs. **Shiraz** ★★★ Pvs blockbuster styling eschewed for sleeker & more sinewy **04**, with old leather whiffs, ripe but appealingly racy red fruit & strong spicy tannins. Welcome moderate 13.5% alc. New oak, 20-30% Am, 10-12 mths, for all above.

Bain's Way range

Cabernet Sauvignon ★★★ **04** convincing varietal notes plus nutty/earthy extras; attractively restrained herbaceous tone offsets weightiness of 15% alc. 9-12 mths seasoned oak; same for all these reds. **Merlot** ★★ Unpretentious **05** quite big, punchy; wild berry flavours & tangy acidity wld complement hearty stews. **Pinotage** ★★★ **04**, retasted, robust & fairly demanding. Contrast of light brambly fruit, racy acidity & taut dry tannins best enjoyed with food. **Shiraz** ★★★ Mega-ripe **04**'s raisined tone lacks spicy zing of pvs, but fans of the fruit-laden style will enjoy. **Chardonnay** ★★★ **06** unwooded, with juicy acidity, hints lemon & lime, big but invisible 14% alc. **Chenin Blanc** ★★ **06** fresh dry white with light flavours of Golden Delicious apple. **Sauvignon Blanc** ★★ **06** lighter bodied/toned than pvs; crisply dry; shows variety's greener tones. **Viognier** ★★★ Unwooded **06** hint of pvs's white peach; big, textured palate with low fruit; gd with lightly spiced food. **Sparkling Vin Sec** ★★★ Latest NV not tasted. Pvs were zesty, refreshing any-occasion bubblies. **Cinsaut** discontinued.

33 Degrees South range

All **NV**, for drinking soonest after purchase. **Dry Red** ★★ Latest version unready. Last was more robust pinotage/cinsaut blend with fairly firm tannins. **Rosé** new ★★ Light, summery semi-sweet pinotage with coral pink hues, fresh strawberry flavours. **Dry White** ★★ No new bottling ready; last again 100% chenin, dry, slightly oxidised. **Semi Sweet** new ★★ Cheerful, balanced quaffer from chenin; tropical fruit punch flavours, drier than name suggests.

Dessert range

Both **NV**, not retasted. **Fishermans Jerepigo** ★★★ Fortifying salty sea dogs since 1941; from hanepoot; very sweet & insinuating. **Jagters Port** ★★★ 'Hunter's Port', from cab. Suave rather than rustic & earthy; for trophy seekers who wear Gucci.— *CT*

Wandsbeck Wines

Robertson • Est 1965 • 1stB 1986 • Tasting & sales Mon-Fri 8-5 • Closed Easter Fri-Mon, May 1, Dec 25/26 & Jan 1 • Tours by appt • Owners 22 members • Winemaker Helmard Hanekom (Jan 1986) • Viti consultant Willem Botha • 448 ha (cab, cinsaut, merlot, pinotage, semillon) • 6 440 tons ±10 000 cs own label 50% red 50% white • PO Box 267 Robertson 6705 • wandsbeck@breede.co.za • T 023·626·1103 • F 023·626·3329

A few personnel changes: with Tiaan Blom now at Roodezandt, Zonia de Kok helped Helmard Hanekom out for the 2006 harvest; and Willem Botha of VinPro was recently appointed as their new viticulturist. A satisfying harvest was followed by good sales last year, particularly of their white wines. You can purchase these and the reds directly from the winery or La Verne wine shop in Robertson (T 023·626·4314).

Cabernet Sauvignon ★★ **02** BBQ-amenable quaffer with dark berry fruit, vanilla hint, low tannins & sensible 13.4% alc. Yr Fr oak; extra yr bottle-aged. **Ruby Cabernet** ★★ **04** cheery & distinctive thatch & plum whiffs; supple tannin. Rounded palate (via 6.7g/ℓ sugar) but dry finish thanks to combo brisk acidity & fruit tannins (unwooded). **Shiraz** ★ Powerful & unsubtle **04**, in youth 15% alc accentuated gruff tannins, giving harsh finish. **Chenin Blanc** ★ **05** tenuous tropical fruit flavours, zesty but short. **Sauvignon Blanc** ★★ **05** light (12.5% alc), with restrained lime & lemon aromas, crisp acidity. **Muskadel** ★★ Sweet fortified red, **04** pleasant muscat scent, syrupy finish — could do with splash more acidity. 17.5% alc big for style. None above retasted.— *DH*

Warwick Estate

Stellenbosch • Est 1964 • 1stB 1984 • Tasting & sales Mon-Fri 10-5 Sat/Sun 10-4 • Closed Easter Sun, Dec 25 & Jan 1 • Tours by appt • Mediterranean picnic baskets by appt, or BYO • 'Wedding Cup' demonstrations • Gifts • Walks/hikes • Owners Ratcliffe family • GM Mike Ratcliffe • Winemaker Louis Nel (Jun 2001) • Viticulturist Ronald Spies (Aug 2001), advised by Phil Freese • 65 ha (cabs s/f , merlot, pinotage, shiraz, chard, sauvignon) • 300 tons 23 000 cs 70% red 30% white • PO Box 2 Elsenburg 7607 • info@warwickwine.com • www.warwickwine.com www.warwickwine.blogspot.com • T 021·884·4410 • F 021·884·4025

Bank of England, House of Lords, Harrods and the Queen Mary II — what seems to be a who's who list is a tally of Warwick's most prestigious clientele. The team is celebrating in style as well: the listing of their wines at the exclusive Burj Al Arab hotel in Dubai was marked by opening a 27ℓ bottle of Trilogy for the 180 guests — 'one glass each!' On the local scene they're taking the wine to the people, too. Creative director and family head Norma Ratcliffe is driving the new Warwick Wine Club which aims to break through 'competition clutter' and connect directly with the customer. Honours went to winemaker Louis Nel with his election to the CWG — and the establishment of a Cape Viticulturist Guild to acknowledge their 'secret weapon' Ronald Spies would be welcomed.

★★★★☆ **Trilogy (Estate Reserve)** Singular flagship featuring two cabs, s/f, escorted by 10% merlot; generous new Fr oak buff — 80% in classy **04**. Expressive cassis/spice fragrance continues on palate. Very taut, svelte, dry; beautifully proportioned for 8-10 yrs cellaring. **03** *Decanter* ★★★★.

★★★★ **CWG Auction Reserve** [new] Louis N's first Auction offering, **04** a variation on the above: more cab s (67% cf 56%), evident plush new oak (100%). Some grandeur, opulence, though cab's dark berries still barricaded by youthful tannins. Shd become more expressive after further 3/4 yrs.

★★★★ **Three Cape Ladies** From **04** unofficially '*Four Cape Ladies*' — shiraz joining usual pinotage, cab, merlot trio (13/21/33/33) in homogenous, quite modern blend; well oaked, sumptuous; juicy red fruits underpinned by vibrant dry tannins. Promises usual enthusiastic reception. 2 yrs Fr oak, 20% new.

★★★★ **Cabernet Franc** An early leader in the Cape; distinctive **04** shd continue to show the way. Big, intense, but still with lifted leafy/spicy fragrance, typical filigree tannins, lovely savoury acidity. Shd evolve elegantly. 2 yrs Fr oak, 75% new, effortlessly absorbed.

★★★★ **Chardonnay** Nothing overdone or forced in creamy & flavoursome **05**. Refined pear/grapefruit tones; confident smooth structure, oak very much in supportive role. Usual Fr oak ferment, 25% new, 8 mths on lees.

Old Bush Vines Pinotage ★★★★ Vivid, tart red-fruit scents with mint/acetone embellishments are varietal giveaways on **05**. Tasty tangy/juicy contrast; concluding bitter nip no detraction to early drinking. Fr oak polished, 20% new. NE, Sbosch WO. **Professor Black Sauvignon Blanc** ★★★☆ **06** with focused though elegant varietal buzz. Plenty of bounce, concentration, minerally drive; in youth tastes somewhat sweeter than 3g/ℓ sugar suggests but may firm up over yr/2 (which structure allows). **05** IWC gold. **Stansfield** ★★★☆ One-off **03** cab named for late patriarch Stan Ratcliffe. Not re-assessed, nor yet released. Blackcurrant & spice tones with firm tannin, unexpected finishing sweetness. 2 yrs new Fr oak. ±5 yrs potential. NE. All above WO Smnsberg-Sbosch unless noted. — *AL*

Waterford Estate 👤🏵🍷♿

Stellenbosch • Est/1stB 1998 • Visits Mon-Fri 9-5 Sat 10-3 • Fee R20-35 • Closed Easter Fri, Dec 25 & Jan 1 • Wine & Chocolate Experience (bookings recommended) • Owners Jeremy & Leigh Ord, Kevin Arnold • Winemakers Kevin Arnold & Francois Haasbroek • Viticulturist Lombard Loubser • 45 ha (barbera, cabs s/f, malbec, merlot, mourvèdre, petit v, shiraz, chard, sauvignon) • 400 tons 30 000 cs 80% red 20% white • PO Box 635 Stellenbosch 7599 • info@ waterfordestate.co.za • www.waterfordestate.co.za • T 021·880·0496 • F 021·880·1007

There's been great excitement with the bottling of their first 'estate blend'. It's the culmination of many years experimentation with varieties new to the area, part of Kevin Arnold's goal 'to grow and blend a world-class wine which reflects the Stellenbosch/Helderberg terroir'. To this end grenache and tempranillo are also being planted on selected sites to increase future blending opportunities. An international standard bearer when it comes to warm and professional service, Waterford was recognised for Excellence in the Cellar Door Experience by the Great Wine Capitals Global Network. A visit to their stylish tasting room will no doubt have you succumb to what they've dubbed 'the Waterford way'.

★★★★ **Cabernet Sauvignon** Quintessential cab seasoned with soupçons cab f, merlot, malbec (total ±15%) in **03** (★★★★★). Last ed showed restrained power; nose & palate infused with spice/choc; taut tannins, mineral finish; for 5+ yrs ageing. Combo Fr/Am oak, mix new/old. **02** had cab f etc in smaller measure (10%), similar bouquet, oak regime; sensuous tannins. SAA.

★★★★☆ **Kevin Arnold Shiraz** Standout rhône style red; with dash mourvèdre (6%) in current **03**. Heady spice, lavender & leather scents; fine red-fruited palate reined in by tannins. Lowest Am oak fraction to date (30%). *Wine* ★★★★, 91 pts *WS*. **02** VDG, *Wine* ★★★★. Both shd improve several yrs.

★★★★☆ **CWG Auction Reserve** Red for 2006 Auction similar piquant varietal melange as pvs: mourvèdre, petit v, barbera (35/10/5) & shiraz, all vinified separately, matured 14 mths as blend. **04** aromatic, restrained lily/white pepper bouquet; polished tannins; persistent, markedly dry finish. More youthfully introverted than **03**, which an exotic mix of cab & 6 other bdx/rhône varieties. Both for long haul.

★★★★ Chardonnay Trademark vibrant fruit-acid a signature of **05** (★★★★★), provides zinging counterpoint to deliciously rich, oven-fresh croissant aromas & flavours. Poised & long, refreshingly understated. Fermented/3 mths Fr oak, ±65% new, no malo; incl tank-fermented portion. Enjoy 3–5 yrs from harvest. **04**, with dash chenin, was retiring last yr but had moreish tangerine/lime flavours; needed time.

★★★★ Heatherleigh Noble Late Harvest Replaces Natural Sweet 'Family Reserve Heatherleigh' of pvs eds. Opulent botrytised dessert from equal parts chard, hanepoot & semillon. Wafts apricots, almonds, clotted cream; complex, luxuriously sweet (95g/ℓ sugar) with cleansing acidity & pithy lift to tail. 50% barrel fermented/yr 2nd fill Fr. 15% alc. 375ml.

Sauvignon Blanc Restraint, nervosity the hallmark of these taut, minerally sauvignons; **05** (★★★★) somewhat muted initially; light bodied **06** (★★★★) more open, accessible fig flavours, usual 'wet pebble' tang. Gains bit of weight from 3 mths on lees.

Pecan Stream range

Stylish & well priced '2nd label'. **Cabernet Sauvignon-Shiraz** Savoury, lightly wooded blend; **04** (★★★★) raised bar with juicy fruitiness; **02** (★★★★ ✓), released out of vintage sequence, even better thanks to exceptional quality of fruit 'declassified' from 1st label. Bright acidity, length & complexity; melded tannin. For now, keeping few yrs. **Chenin Blanc** ★★★★ ✓ **06** calls out for seafood; floral/wax/thatch scents & layered flavours, gentle acidity. **05** flew SAA. **Sauvignon Blanc** new ★★★★ Classy addition to gourmet picnic basket. **06** tropical smells & tastes, lovely, textured grapefruit palate from 2 mths on lees. — *CvZ*

■ *Waterfront Collection* see Vaughan Johnson

Waterhof

Stellenbosch (see Helderberg map) • *Est 1997* • *1stB 2003* • *Visits by appt* • *Self-catering facilities* • *Owner SWF Farming (Pty) Ltd* • *12 ha (cab, shiraz)* • *140 tons 100% red* • *PO Box 1560 Somerset West 7129* • *info@waterhofestate.co.za* • *www.waterhofestate.co.za* • **T 842·3531** • *F 842·2858*
No update received from this producer. Contact details from previous editon.

Waterkloof
new

Stellenbosch/Helderberg • *Est 2004* • *1stB 2005* • *Closed to public* • *Owner False Bay Vineyards* • *Winemaker Werner Engelbrecht (Jun 2004)* • *Viticulturist Werner Engelbrecht, advised by Johan Pienaar* • *47 ha (cabs s/f, grenache, merlot, mourvèdre, shiraz, chard, sauvignon)* • *120–140 tons 11 000 cs 30% red 70% white* • *Other export brands: Circumstance & Peacock Ridge* • *P/a False Bay Vineyards, PO Box 1286, Wellington 7654* • *ceo@boutinotsa.co.za or wine@boutinotsa.co.za* • **T 021·873·2418/2639** • *F 021·873·7580*

'We believe Schapenberg to be the best cool-climate vineyard site in SA, if not in the New World,' says Waterkloof MD Jean du Toit, whose neighbours include acclaimed properties Vergelegen and Morgenster. Ocean proximity, altitude and soil variation are credited for the successful launch — and listings at various Michelin-rated restaurants — of the aptly named Peacock Ridge range (the brightly plumed birds conspicuous here), as well as traditional winemaking techniques which were shared with the team by winemaker Paul Boutinot, founder of the UK-based Boutinot Wine Group.

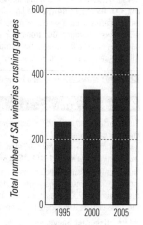

Total number of SA wineries crushing grapes

(bar chart showing values for 1995, 2000, 2005)

Following all new: **Waterkloof Sauvignon Blanc ★★★☆ 05** attractive debut for this fine, balanced, vibrant wine; clean dry finish preceded by fantail of delicious tropical granadilla & pineapple flavours. Potential to improve further. **Circumstance Mourvèdre Rosé ★★★** Delightful pale salmon hued **06**; fresh & fruity, with spicy top notes. Slight grip from 3 mths on lees; charming & lively despite big 14% alc. Paarl fruit.

Peacock Ridge range

★★★★ **Merlot** Quintessential merlot: rich & round with ripe plums, choc & violets, hint of coffee & charry oak; **05** juicy tannins & fruit surge on lively finish giving immediate pleasure, powerful 15% masked by flavour concentration. 10 mths Fr oak.

★★★★ **Chardonnay 05** cleverly wooded for gentle vanilla nuances, creamy texture; fine acid core lifts & focuses the white peach & citrus fruit melange. Opulent, persistent lemon-butter finish. Screwcapped; 30% barrel fermented, 100% matured old/new Fr oak, 10 mths.

Sauvignon Blanc ★★★☆ 05 similar genes to above version; widescreen tropical bouquet & palate, full-flavoured, with taut but juicy acidity ensuring length, balance & drinkability. Screwcapped. — *DH*

Waverley Hills Organic Wines   ♀

Tulbagh ▪ 1stB 2004 ▪ Visits by appt ▪ Owners Du Toit family ▪ Winemaker Theuns Botha, advised by Mark Carmichael-Green ▪ 22 ha ▪ Export brand: Dixon's Peak ▪ PO Box 71 Wolseley 6830 ▪ info@waverleyhills.co.za ▪ www.waverleyhills.co.za ▪ T 023·231·1060 ▪ F 023·231·0954

Once the home of internationally reputed wool blankets, a 22 ha vineyard was established here in 2000 and subsequently certified as organic. The first olive groves soon followed, and now olives and extra-virgin olive oil as well as natural products like grape seed extract are made on the property. The 2006 wines were made at the Mountain Ridge cellar by their first full-time vini man Theuns Botha, using their own equipment. An on-site cellar completed and opened to the public, the Du Toit family plans to open an organic food bistro.

This entry unintentionally omitted from last ed, so all following new to the guide. **Cabernet Sauvignon 05** (★★★★) big advance on pvs: more intense & complex fruit, tighter tannins, greater oak influence (now 30% new, Fr); fruit sufficiently ripe & juicy to balance oak flavours/textures; structure to improve 3-5 yrs. **04** (★★★) for youthful easy drinking. **Shiraz ★★★ 05** recalls **04** with its light fruit & spiciness, but latest a touch more complex, adding earthy, vanilla-wood flavours. 15% new oak, mix Fr/Am. **Semillon-Chardonnay new ★★★★** Charming **06**; tropical & stonefruit whiffs merge in litchi/nectarine array, daubs oak vanilla & butterscotch complete the picture. 10% chard 4 mths in new Fr oak. All SGS-certified organic, minimal chemical use in winemaking. — *DH*

■ *WaverleyTBS* see Cape Promise

Webersburg Wines   ♀ 📦

Stellenbosch ▪ Est/1stB 1996 ▪ Tasting & sales Mon-Fri 9-5 Sat 10-4 ▪ Closed pub hols ▪ Luxury guest house ▪ Owner Fred Weber ▪ Viticulturist Braam Steyn (Apr 1996) ▪ 22 ha (cabs, merlot) ▪ ±3 000 cs 100% red ▪ PO Box 3428 Somerset West 7129 ▪ weber@iafrica.com ▪ www.webersburg.co.za ▪ T 021·881·3636 ▪ F 021·881·3217

Now that the existing buildings have been restored — the 1786 homestead has been turned into a well-appointed guesthouse, and the original 1796 cellar into a maturation cellar and tasting venue — 2007 sees a new building on this historic property: a winery, in time to vinify the 2008 vintage. Until then, the wines will continue to be made at Meerlust.

★★★★ **Cabernet Sauvignon** Classicism & consistency are hallmarks, antithesis of market-driven jolly immediacy. Expresses place & vintage, needs time to unfurl. Still current **01** showed rich cassis fruit woven into plush frame when reviewed mid-2004. 18 mths Fr oak, 70% new.

★★★★ **Webersburg** Elegant, singular **02** bore standard with aplomb mid-2005; piquant savoury edges to sumptuous fruit, in all refined genre. 70% cab with merlot, 18 mths Fr wood, two thirds new. — *DS*

Wedderwill Estate Wines

Stellenbosch (see Helderberg map) • Est 1992 • 1stB 1997 • Visits incl tours by appt Mon-Sat 9-6 • BYO picnic • Walks/hikes • Game reserve • Owners Georg Ludwig von Loeper & Neil Ian Jowell • Winemaker Nico Vermeulen • Viticulturist Dawie le Roux • 42ha (cabs s/f, malbec, merlot, mourvèdre, petit v, shiraz, chard, chenin, semillon, viognier) • 40 tons 3 200 cs 80% red 20% white • PO Box 75 Sir Lowry's Pass 7133 • contact@wedderwill.co.za • www.wedderwill.co.za • T/F 021·858·1558

High on the Schapenberg slopes, this new wine-and-olive-oil cellar was once an old barn, now converted by the Von Loeper and Jowell families in charming Cape vernacular style, and surrounded by lavender beds and olive groves. At this 40-ton facility they're making a Shiraz, bordeaux-style blend and Sauvignon from their own fruit, with the assistance of Nico Vermeulen and Dawie le Roux. Hands-on manager Wolfgang von Loeper says two qualities are essential when it comes to making exceptional wine: precision and a favourable viticultural location. 'The latter,' he believes, 'is very evident in the farm's fruit.'

Shiraz new Powerful & richly fruited **04** (sample) brims with savoury, wet earth & spicy aromas/flavours, clean peppery farewell. Likely ★★★★ when bottled. **Sauvignon Blanc** new ★★★ Food-friendly **NV** (blend of 05 & 06), green varietal aromas, crisp acidity & sufficient weight & body to hold its own against rich seafood. — *CT*

Wederom

Robertson • Est 2002 • 1stB 2003 • Tasting & sales Mon-Fri 9-6 • Fee R10 pp for groups of 10+ • Closed Good Friday • Meals by appt during tasting hours • Facilities for children • Conference facilities • Hiking/biking trails • Guest house • Owners Philip & Almien du Toit • Vini consultant Newald Marais, with Philip du Toit • Viticulturist Philip du Toit • ±20 ha (merlot, shiraz, chenin) • ±120 tons 1 320 cs 100% red • PO Box 60 Robertson 6705 • wederom@myisp.co.za • www. wederom.co.za • T 023 626·4139 • F 023 626·3306

Wederom means 'see you again' in Dutch but 'arrividerci' might seem more appropriate for this boutique winery proudly flying the Italian flag. When fourth-generation owners Philip and Almien du Toit decided to restore the original cellar, they discovered a mural painted by Giovanni Salvadori, a prisoner-of-war who worked on the farm during WWII. In his honour and to acknowledge the largely uncelebrated role of the Italian POWs in SA history, they offer their Salvadori Shiraz.

Salvadori Vino Rosso Shiraz ★★★ **04** earthy/leathery intro, followed by tart, food-friendly cranberry flavours; dry & gripping, as you'd expect from an Italian-styled red. 18 mths oak. — *MW*

Weening & Barge Winery

Stellenbosch (see Helderberg map) • Est 2003 • 1stB 2005 • Tasting & sales Mon-Fri 10-4 • Discretionary tasting fee • Guest villa (see Stay-over section) • Owner Veronique Weening-Barge • Vini consultant Johan Joubert (2003) • Farm manager Ken Nicholson (2003) • 35.2 ha (cab f, pinot, sangiovese, shiraz, chenin, sauvignon) • 156 tons 16 000 cs own label • 77% red 12% white 11% rosé • PO Box 3625 Somerset West 7129 • info@weeningbarge.com • www.weeningbarge.com • T 021·842·2255 • F 021·842·3393

Veronique Weening-Barge has reason to be proud of the achievements here, as development continues apace on the farm and in the cellar. Besides new sangiovese vines and two new bottlings (including their first white), they've launched the Ridgemor second label (a range of blends), and opened a new tasting facility. Plans are also afoot to develop a picnic area near the farm dam and allow trout fishing.

★★★★ **Cuvée Lynette Pinot Noir** Earthy, wild strawberry aromas lead to **04**'s forceful but restrained palate, with some incipient complexity & fairly robust tannins. Gd support from 14 mths 2nd/3rd fill barrels.

★★★★ **Cuvée Quint Shiraz 04** has ripe nose of creamy, smoky toffee. Dense, flavourful, big (14.5% alc); a little unyielding in youth but plentiful sweet red fruit, gd tannic underpinning, balanced wood (14 mths older oak). Above reds not retasted.

Cuvée Twister Cabernet Franc new ★★☆ **05** shows house's predilection for ripeness & sweetness (5.2g/ℓ sugar), here juxtaposed with v dry, food-inviting tannins. Like rest of range, presented in curvaceous bottle. **Cuvée Terry Lynn Shiraz Rosé** ★★ Same deep onion-skin colour as pvs, but dry **06** much more demure, light, with vaguely savoury tone. **Cuvée Blondie** new ★★☆ Chenin, in cheery mode; **06** (sample) zesty white-peach tones smoothed by some sugar for easy summer quaffing.

Ridgemor range   new

Shiraz-Cabernet Franc ★★ 70/30 blend. Very ripe intro to **05**, leading to unexpectedly dry, dusty cab f palate (despite soupçon sugar); needs time to soften, fill out. **Pinot Noir-Shiraz-Cabernet Franc** ★★★ Roughly equal proportions; more approachable blend than above; **05** pleasing flavours of dark-berry compote, sappy, well integrated. Neither red oaked. **Chenin Blanc-Viognier** ★★★ Appealing, richly spicy **06**; 70/30 blend with ripe apricot/yellow peach aromas/flavours, decidedly sweet (±6g/ℓ sugar) & succulent. Above trio tasted as samples; ratings provisional. — *MM*

Welbedacht Wines

Wellington ▪ 1stB 2003 ▪ Tasting, sales & tours Mon-Fri 8.30-5 Sat 9-2 Sun by appt ▪ Fee R15 (incl glass) ▪ Closed Dec 25 & Jan 1 ▪ BYO picnic; also meals/refreshments for groups by appt ▪ Facilities for children ▪ Tour groups ▪ Conferences ▪ Mountain biking ▪ Owner Schalk Burger Family Trust ▪ Winemaker Matthew Copeland, with Franco Lourens (Sep 2004/Dec 2005) ▪ 140 ha (cabs s/f, cinsaut, merlot, mourvèdre, petit v, pinotage, shiraz, chard, chenin, sauvignon, viognier) ▪ 1 200 tons 100 tons/7 000 cs own label ▪ 75% red 25% white ▪ PO Box 51 Wellington 7654 ▪ wine@welbedacht.co.za ▪ www.welbedacht.co.za ▪ T 021·873·1877 ▪ F 021·873·2877

Owned by former rugby Springbok Schalk Burger, and Schalk Jnr currently playing for his country, you'd expect a fair amount of patriotism at Welbedacht. 'Our markets are focused in southern Africa, and we have enormous faith in claiming and maintaining chenin and pinotage as our own,' confirms winemaker Matthew Copeland, adding that a 'Cape blend' containing at least 30% pinotage is in the pipeline. Sibling Tiaan B is now responsible for marketing — and for the cricket pitch after which the bordeaux blend is named!

★★★★ **Cricket Pitch** Confident debut last ed for this merlot-cab blend (60/40), traditionally vinified (basket press, open fermenters et al). **03** raspberry fruit-sweetness checked by savoury dryness, tangy tannins. Mid-2005 pleaded few yrs to show best. 18 mths small oak, combo new-3rd fill.

Cabernet Sauvignon Barrique Select ★★★★ Rated provisionally last yr (ditto Merlot & Chard), **03** has benefited from bottle-ageing — well judged oak & fruit now better knit. Gd mineral core with notes of choc, coffee & black fruit; tail's still warm though (14.5% alc). **Merlot Barrique Select** ★★★ **03**'s full-ripe aromas & flavours refreshed by zesty acidity. Tannins which abrasive mid-2005, now friendlier, fruit ripeness & 14.5% alc still give sweet impression. **Meerkat Pinotage** new ★★★ Light hearted name (after the gregarious mongooses on the farm) for quite a serious wine; **05** subdued mulberry whiffs, satisfying flavour, balance & oak integration through judicious use of older barrels (16 mths). Same regime for… **Shiraz** new ★★★ Promising **05** brooding red/black fruit melange, ripe tannins & slightly salty farewell. Well hidden 14.5% alc packs a punch. **Chardonnay Barrel Fermented** ★★★ Understated **05**, shy lemon cream & pineapple whiffs, buttery flesh supported by spicy oak. Ends clean but hot (14% alc), with pithy bite. Fermented/7 mths *sur lie* in new oak (75/25 Hungarian/Fr), as for… **Bush Vine Chenin Blanc Barrel Fermented** ★★★ This, below, from 30 yr old bushvines. Honey & vanilla hints to apple compote ripeness on **05**, palate fattened by rich oak vanilla & leesy breadth yet manages a crisp finish. Like Chard, shd hold/improve few yrs. **Unwooded Chenin Blanc** new ★★★ 'Made to compete with cool-climate sauvignons',**06** does in fact lean towards a greenpepper, grassy character, delivered with some old-vines intensity & weight. But basically an easy-drinker, for current consumption. All WO W Cape. — *CvZ*

Welgegund Farm

Wellington ▪ Est 1800s ▪ 1stB 1997 ▪ Tasting & sales by appt ▪ B&B ▪ Owners Alex & Sheila Camerer ▪ Winemaker Corlea Fourie ▪ Viticulturist Johann Smit (Winecorp, 2004) ▪ 30 ha (cab, carignan, cinsaut, grenache, merlot, pinotage, shiraz, viognier) ▪ 100% red ▪ PO Box 683 Wellington 7655 ▪ alex.camerer@welgegund.co.za ▪ www.welgegund.co.za ▪ T 082·554·7871 ▪ F 021·873·2683

Enamoured of rhône-style wines, owner Alex Camerer, with winemaker Corlea Fourie, is re-positioning the farm as a producer of grapes and wines usually found in the south of France. Grenache and viognier have been planted, adding to existing shiraz, carignan and 34 year old cinsaut bushvines. The latter produced last year's 'most pleasant revelation', and was duly bottled separately. Says Alex C: 'We saved these from the chop a few years ago and now they're showing their mettle.'

Cabernet Sauvignon ★★★ 04 exuberant minty mulberry greeting, mint-choc flavour, firmly tannic finish despite 4.4g/ℓ sugar. Mix new/used oak. **Merlot ★★★** 04 voluminous dark-fruit nose with savoury edge; tight 'green leaf' tannins. **Carignan Rosé ★★** 04 light, raspberry-toned & properly dry, with hint tannin; ex-27 yr old bushvines. **Carignan ★★★★** Incl dash shiraz for extra heft. 03 light bodied, juicy lunchtime wine, serve lightly chilled. 04 slightly fuller, deeper coloured. Portion fruit ex-Swtland. No new releases tasted for above. **Cinsaut Noir [new]** Ex-recognised single vyd; 06 (sample) sweet-fruited & soft, very ripe (14.5% alc), some raisin hints & spice, gentle tannic grip. On current form ★★. 25% new Am oak, rest 2nd fill Fr. — *CT*

Welgeleë Vineyards

Paarl ▪ Est 1999 ▪ 1stB 2003 ▪ Visits daily 9-5 ▪ Picnics by appt ▪ Owners/viticulturists Liris Trust (Chris & Lidea Meyer) ▪ Winemaker Chris Meyer ▪ 3 ha (shiraz) ▪ 300 cs 100% red ▪ PO Box 439 Klapmuts 7625 ▪ welgelee@absamail.co.za ▪ T/F 021·875·5726

Asked for his job description these days, Chris Meyer's reply would be 'a bit of everything'. He's taken over full-time viti- and vinicultural duties from Morné Kemp, who consulted from the maiden (2003) vintage. He's completed a tasting room and sales venue, and now welcomes visitors seven days a week (picnics by appointment). In the pipeline are more shiraz, cab and chardonnay. Meanwhile, he and equally energetic wife Lidea parent a plenitude of pets.

Shiraz Reserve ★★★★ Elegant 03 nutmeg & cassia aromas, black berry flavours. Fine tannins, with good, unobtrusive support from 9 mths Fr oak. 04 (unrated preview last ed) promisingly spicy. **Cabernet Sauvignon ★★★** 04 ripe fruit tannins mid-2005 mingled with abundant blackcurrant fruit, mocha/coffee finish; needed ±2-4 yrs for dominant oak to knit with fruit. **Petlou Shiraz [new] ★★★★** NV tribute to 'the world's mothers' says Chris M. Balanced & refined; alluring choc-mocha & liquorice tones complement juicy fruit & black pepper flavours. — *IvH*

Welgemeend Estate

Paarl ▪ 1stB 1979 ▪ Tasting Wed 2-4 Sat 9-12.30 ▪ Sales during office hours only by appt ▪ Closed pub hols ▪ ±11 ha (cab s/f, grenache, malbec, merlot, 'petit mystery', pinotage, shiraz) ▪ 3 500 cs 100% red ▪ PO Box 1408 Suider-Paarl 7624 ▪ welgemeend@worldonline.co.za ▪ www.welgemeend.co.za ▪ T 021·875·5210 ▪ F 021·875·5239

It's the end of an era at Welgemeend, with the Hofmeyrs parting with their Paarl farm. Matriarch Ursula H, who put 32 years into managing the vineyards, is taking a well earned retirement. Daughter Louise H took over the reins from her late father Billy H, with whom she shared a passion for a classic, restrained style of winemaking, 19 years ago. The new owners plan to make the estate more tourist-friendly, with wine tasting just one of the items on offer.

★★★★☆ Estate Reserve The first Cape bdx blend — cab, merlot, cab f — with loyal following around the wine world for over 25 yrs. 02 (★★★★) mainly cab (85% s & f); well focused, lighter fruit reflecting vintage. 01 chiefly merlot, marked by signature elegance, finesse. Moderate ±13% alc throughout range. These oaked for the long haul (18 mths, 30% new); need time & patience to offer their best.

★★★★ **Douelle** A fragrant, alternative nod to bdx, mostly malbec with merlot, cab & soupçon cab f, 18 mths oaked. **02** quintessential Welgemeend stamp of tightly woven, supple tannins; sweet-fruit touch in well judged finish.

Amadé ★★★☆ Idiosyncratic Cape interpretation of rhône-style blend. **02** 40/30/30 shiraz, pinotage & grenache ensemble: smoky, earthy, baked pudding features. 18 mths used oak. **Soopjeshoogte** ★★★★ Cabs s/f with merlot; for earlier drinking than Reserve. **02** toffee/asphalt notes, lightly fruited, firm finish. Seasoned wood. Note: all 02s tasted as pre-bottling samples mid-2005 & not retasted for this ed. — *DS*

Welgevallen Wines   ⚲ new

Stellenbosch • Est/1stB 2000 • Visits Mon-Fri 10-2 • Closed pub & school holidays • Owner Paul Roos Gymnasium Old Boys Union • Vini consultant Wouter Pienaar (Jan 2001) • 10 tons 450 cs 100% red • oldboys@prg.wcape.school.za • www.paulroos.givengain.org • T/F 021·883·8627
The Old Boys Union of Paul Roos Gymnasium uses the University of Stellenbosch's cellar (both situated on the original Welgevallen farm granted to Steven Jantz Botma in 1689) to vinify 10 tons of cab each year — keeping old school ties strong, these are sourced from former PRG pupils in the area. Current pupils are introduced to the winemaking process, and proceeds from the resultant wine sales finance special projects and fund several underprivileged pupils' tuition.

Cabernet Sauvignon ★★★ Satisfying & well made **02**; wide spectrum of flavours — incl cherries, smoky oak, sweet spices — ripely firm tannins for accompanying food. Better in ±yr, will keep another few. Incl 14% merlot. 18 mths fr oak, 1st-3rd fill. WO Coastal. — *MM*

■ *Welgevonde* see Daschbosch

Wellington Cooperative Cellar   ⚲ ♿

Wellington • Est/1stB 1934 • Tasting & sales Mon-Fri 8-1; 2-5 • Owners 49 members • Winemakers Gert Boerssen, Koos Carstens & Chris Smit (1980/1990/2005) • Viticulturist Koos van der Merwe (Sep 2005) • 1 600 ha (cinsaut, pinotage, chard, chenin, sauvignon) • 12 000 tons ±6 500 cs own label • PO Box 520 Wellington 7654 • info@wellingtoncellars.co.za • www.wellingtoncellar.co.za • T 021·873·1163 • F 021·873·2423
A challenging first season for new viticulturist Koos van der Merwe, who's 'returned to his birthplace' after working at Vredendal Cellar: he had winter drought to contend with but fortunately no serious heatwaves. Overall, the grape quality was pleasing, particularly for the earlier varieties, and delivered the goods for new red-wine maker Chris Smit (ex-McGregor Wines; brother Stephan's winemaker at Welmoed).

Reserve range
Cabernet Sauvignon ★★ Exuberant wooding last yr obscured **03**'s attractive, rich cassis fruit, needed 2-3 yrs to integrate. Spent 14 mths in Fr oak, as did following duo. **Pinotage** ★★★ **03** emerges from rigorous oak regime with more accessible fruit than cellar mates, hints ripe plum & dark fruits; should knit within 2-3 yrs. **Shiraz** ★★ **03** oak a heavy influence; robust tannins & vanilla spice dominate ethereal ripe plum fruit. None in this range retasted; 04s of above on current price list, not received for review. **Chenin Blanc** ★★ Chunky **04** mid-2005 sheathed in wood character (3 mths); uncertain whether lurking fruit will emerge. This, range below, WO Paarl.

Wellington range

> **Chenin Blanc** ☺ ★★☆ **06** an easy-going addition to summer's pleasures; vibrant pear/apple aromas & flavours, pleasant dry finish.

Classic Cape Red new ★★★☆ Well balanced **04** a promising debut, very gulpable; gd fruit concentration, deft oaking (14 mths Fr). None of following retasted; notes from 2006 ed. **Cabernet Sauvignon** ★★★ **03** wood-powered style needs plenty of time to settle. 9 mths Fr oak, as for... **Merlot** ★★★ Friendly **03** had red & black berries, healthy acid/tannin backbone. **Pinotage** ★★ **04** gd varietal aromas of red berry & cherry, fruit on palate less ripe & gripped by stern tannins. 3 mths oak. **Shiraz** ★★★ **04** still middle-of-the-road style but lesser fruit concentration this vintage, 9 mths oak influence yet to integrate. **Cinsaut-Ruby Cabernet** ★★★ 75/25 combo, partly oaked. Light textured **03** easy-drinker chillable in summer. **Pinotage Rosé** ★★★ Scented semi-sweet with firming touch tannin; **04** noted as tasting dry despite 10g/ℓ sugar. **Chardonnay** ★★★ Lightly oaked **03**, full & lively, for early enjoyment. **Sauvignon Blanc** ★★★ Bouncy, lightish **04** with subtle gooseberry aromas/tastes, moderate 13% alc. **Late Harvest** ★★★ **04** semi-sweet chenin; pear tones & hint of tangerine, not too sweet; light 12% alc. **Hanepoot Jerepiko** ★★★ Fortified dessert with delicate & charming floral aromas, **05** unusual steely streak just doesn't match its cloying sweetness. **Port** ★★★ Last was ruby-style **02** from tinta, fruity & balanced, with traditionally low fortification (17.5% alc). — *IvH*

■ *Welmoed* see The Company of Wine People

Weltevrede Estate

Robertson • Est 1912 • 1stB 1975 • Tasting & sales Mon-Fri 8-5 Sat 9-3.30 • Tours by appt • Under the Vines Bistro for lunch Tue-Sat (closed Jun/Jul) or BYO picnic • Weltevrede Guest Cottage • Conservation area • Walks • 4×4 trail • Mountain biking • Owner Lourens Jonker • Winemaker Philip Jonker (1997) • Viticulturist Philip Jonker, advised by Francois Viljoen • 100 ha (cab, merlot, shiraz, chard, colombard, sauvignon) • 150 tons 25 000 cs own label 15% red 75% white 10% other • PO Box 6 Bonnievale 6730 • info@weltevrede.com • www. weltevrede.com • T 023-616-2141 • F 023-616-2460

Last harvest was blessed with 'perfect bunches of berries — not one needed to be discarded', and the cellar rang with the laughter of five Ugandan nuns who spent a month learning about winemaking. A candlelit tasting of site-specific wines in the underground cellar, followed by a tractor-drawn visit to the various vineyard blocks, is a special experience (booking essential, minimum 12 people). The vineyards themselves are special too: Oupa se Wingerd, the first to be awarded 'conservation-worthy' status by the Board for National Monuments, turned 80 last year. Philip Jonker, celebrating a decade as winemaker on this family farm, is building his MCC portfolio with a quartet of new cuvées, awaiting release.

★★★★☆ **Poet's Prayer Chardonnay** An oenological artwork born of attention to detail: wild yeast ferment (which can last full yr), 19 mths Fr oak, further yr in bottle — all lavished on a single barrel. **04** (★★★★) in familiar, complex mineral style of pvs, but whisper short of their finesse. **03** plush & rich, yet tight, elegantly structured.

★★★★ **Rusted Soil Chardonnay** While above expresses cellarmaster's personality, this & duo of chards below reflect the character of their terroir. Limestone origin of farm's oldest vyd site gives **04** lush tropical peach & pineapple flesh; a tangerine twist hauls it up just short of decadence. Fermented/10 mths Fr cask.

★★★★ **Place of Rocks Chardonnay** From shale soils, taut, less exuberant: **05** shines with flinty mineral seam, a foil for lemon/lime fruits tucked into concentrated palate. Excellent amongst already weighty peers. Barrel fermented/aged 10 mths.

★★★★ **The Travelling Stone Sauvignon Blanc** Hand-harvested *vine* selection from vyd on quartzite stone which originally 'rolled down the surrounding hills'. **06** proffers tropical fruit with herbaceous edge in youth, likely to develop stony mineral tones with age.

★★★★ **Rhine Riesling** Still current **01** was well developed when last tasted mid-2004; orange sheen, herbs & dried apricots on honeyed palate. *Wine* ★★★★.

Bedrock Black Syrah ★★★★ Leads the duo of reds in otherwise white wine territory; no shortage of cellar's commitment to expression of site. **04** bristles with white pepper aromas, plum/mulberry fruits laced with leather & spice; generous frame. All Fr oak. **Gewürztraminer** ★★★★ **05** aromatic rosepetal delicacy to litchi flesh, Turkish Delight viscosity in off-dry finish. Not retasted. **Ovation Rhine Riesling** ★★★ 'Natural Sweet' in crossover style: botrytis richness but drier than NLH. **99** well-developed at last review mid-2005. **Philip Jonker Brut** ★★★★ Critically acclaimed MCC from chard. **04** rich mouthfeel, fresh finish; enjoy on release. **00** *Wine* ★★★★. **Ouma se Wyn** ★★★ Single white muscat de F vyd; **05** grapey, full sweet, clean finish. 375ml. **Oupa Se Wyn** ★★★★ From red muscadel & muscat de H, partly ex-octogenarian bushvines. **05** fresh, concentrated grape flavours, certain gravitas to palate. Muscadel Awards 2006 platinum. 375ml.

River's Edge range

> **Chardonnay** ☺ ★★★ Fourth in Jonker's terroir studies, this from alluvial soils, unwooded.
> All-occasions **06** summer melon/banana allure, focused lemon freshness. 14.5% alc.

Sauvignon Blanc ★★ **06** perky poolside quaffer with fresh grapefruit tones. Discontinued: **Colombard**.

Tricolore range

Duo of three-way blends crafted 'for my friends'. **Red** ★★★ Merlot, cab & syrah – 'a blend with personality'. **04** black berry fullness, lipsmacking texture. 14 mths oak. **White** ★★★ **06** vibrant medley sauvignon, colombard fleshed out with semillon; fresh & grassy, a hit with consumers. – *DS*

Welvanpas ◊♀

Wellington • Tasting & sales Mon-Fri 9-12.15; 1-5 Sat 9-1 • Owners D Retief & Son Cellars • Winemaker/viticulturist Dan Retief Jnr • ±500 tons (15-30 tons for own range, 75% red 25% white) • PO Box 75 Wellington 7654 • welvanpas@xsinet.co.za • T 021·864·1238 / 082·498·5145 / 082·393·6268 • F 021·864·1239

This farm has been in the Retief family for three centuries and is steeped in history. If you can get Dan Retief Snr started on the subject, this spinner of colourful stories will have you mesmerised. Dan Jnr vinifies a small amount of selected grapes, and is delighted with the Veritas bronze and silver medals awarded to his 03 Cab and Pinotage.

Following pair ⟨new⟩: **De Krakeelhoek Rooi** ★ Equal shiraz/merlot blend seasoned with oak staves; straightforward, touch rustic, for early consumption. 15.2% alc. EW. **Revival Red** ★★ Chiefly merlot (62%) with cab, shiraz. Uncomplicated quaffer with fruit pastille flavours & grainy tannins. Following still available, not re-tasted: **Cabernet Sauvignon** ★ Artisinal **03** with smoky, oxidised & savoury aromas & flavours, chewy tannin. **Pinotage** ★ Rustic & reticent **03**, 15% alc gives a sweet impression to lifted finish. **Chenin Blanc** ★ **04** tropical tones, with caramel/oxidised notes. – *MM*

■ *Weskus* see Winkelshoek

Westbridge Vineyards ◊♀⌂♪

Stellenbosch • Est 1998 • 1stB 1999 • Tasting & sales Mon-Sat 8-6 (phone ahead T 083·631·2229) • B&B guest accommodation • Chapel/wedding venue • Owner JC Starke & Muldersvlei Estates • Winemaker Ian Starke • Viticulturist Julian Starke • 17 ha (cab, chenin) • 60 tons 4 000 cs 85% red 15% white • PO Box 66 Muldersvlei 7607 • wine@muldersvlei.co. za • T 021·884·4433/083·631·2229

The Starke family opted to sell their entire 2006 harvest to Koelenhof Winery, while the remaining 2004/05 bottled wines went overseas in response to increasing foreign interest. Happily, says Helen Starke, there are still stocks of older wines available, such as the 02 Shiraz and 03 Pinotage 'which have aged beautifully'. They have also retained a few cases of younger wines for cellar sales, tastings and functions.

★★★★ **Pinotage Reserve** Two vintages to date: **99** characterful & full-flavoured with pronounced savoury edge; **00** attractively rustic profile.

No new vintages tasted; above/following notes from a pvs ed. **Shiraz** ★★★ **02** characteristic shiraz spice, plus house's earthy touches, firm tannins. 3rd fill Fr oak. **Merlot 03** too young to rate but shows extraordinary concentration. **Pinotage** ★★★★ **03** individually styled, tropical fruit & whiffs tobacco/earth, tannins less daunting than pvs. Oak chip fermented/aged. **Juliette** Sparingly wooded blend changes with vintage; vinified/matured separately & blended just before bottling; **02** (★★★) cab, merlot, shiraz, appealingly round; **03** (★★★★) 22% pinotage injection, shows as fruitier, more satisfying. – *DH*

WestCorp International

Olifants River (see Vredendal Cellar on Olifants River map) • Est 2002 • Tasting & sales Mon-Fri 8-5 Sat 8.30-12 (sales close 30 mins later) • Closed pub hols • Tours at 10 & 3 during harvest • Light meals by appt or BYO picnic • Tour groups (±42 people) • Conferencing • Audio-visual presentation • Gifts • Owners 224 members • Winemakers Alwyn Maass, Pieter Verwey, Driaan van der Merwe & Len Knoetze (1997/1999/2000/2002), with Koos Thiart, Johan Weideman & Renier van Greenen (all Jan 2004) • Viticulturists Marina Bruwer & Hein Jansen van Rensburg (Jan 2004/Jan 2004) • 4 990 ha (cab, merlot, pinotage, ruby cab, shiraz, chard, chenin, colombard, sauvignon, hanepoot) • 86 000 tons 610 000 cs 30% red 70% white • www.westcorp.co.za • Vredendal Cellar: PO Box 75 Vredendal 8160 • info@westcorp.co.za • T 027·213·1080 • F 027·213·3476 • Spruitdrift Cellar: PO Box 129 Vredendal 8160 • T 027·213·3086 • F 027·213·2937

More clever marketing from this West Coast operation, which combines Vredendal and Spruitdrift cellars: it's secured the Heart Foundation's stamp of approval for its new Gôiya Shiraz (Weigh-Less endorses some of WestCorp's other low-alcohol wines). A second innovation is new one-litre and, more significantly, 250ml carton packaging for five products in the Namaqua range, a move set to secure its position locally, where Nielsen puts it at No 1, and in the UK, where it's the second-biggest SA seller, now with listings for Namaqua bottlings in Tesco.

Spencer Bay range

Special winemaker's selections; only in best vintages. Both new. **Merlot** ★★★ Coolly ripe fruit & fine acidity combine to make **03** special; lively, graceful & well behaved. **Shiraz** ★★★ Satisfying **03** well fruited with spiced plum & touch of savoury; lots of vigorous tannins with legs to carry 2/3 yrs.

Gôiya range

Pronounced 'Hoya', meaning 'First'. **Shiraz** new ★★★ 1st Heart Foundation approved red, de-alcoholised to a light 8% by vol. Spicy baked plums with earthy notes, very dry finish. **Merlot-Cabernet Sauvignon** ★★ Unretasted **03** was noted as stern last yr, with rustic tannins & savoury edge to choc-berry flavours. **Shiraz-Pinotage** ★★ Made in very large quantities. When last tasted, **04** offered shy game & smoked meat aromas, simple & obvious flavours. **Chardonnay-Sauvignon Blanc** ★★ Equal blend, as pvs, **06** semi-dry & uncomplicated everyday quaffer.

Gôiya D-Lite-Ful range

All **NV**, with low ±9% alc, approved by Weigh-Less. **Red** ★ Dry & lean blend shiraz, pinotage & ruby cab with baked fruit hint. **Rosé** ★ Very plain & dry, with jazzy orange tints from pinotage. **White** ★ Light & lean mix chenin, hanepoot; bone-dry. Following both new: **Rosé Sparkling** ★ Uncomplicated dry bubbles from mainly chenin, with pinotage supplying subtle red-wine aromas. **Brut** ★★★ Crisply dry sparkling with busy bubbles & slightly spicy finish.

Namaqua range

Following all **NV**, variously available in 250ml, 1, 3 & 5ℓ. **Dry Red** ★★ Soft, plummy shiraz, pinotage & ruby cab; at 14.5% alc, for sipping rather than glugging. **Rosé** ★ Simple & fairly dry-tasting (though 16g/ℓ sugar); pinotage supplies the colour. **Blanc de Blanc** ★★ (Pvsly 'Grand Cru'.) Light undemanding dry white with soft acid & hint of apple. **Stein** ★★ Well balanced & not as sweet as many in this genre; finishes crisp & clean. **Late Harvest** ★★★ Delightful semi-sweet with lovely ripe guava aroma, hints quince & honey; from chenin & colombard (as are most of the whites). **Extra Lite** ★ Weigh-Less approved for its low alc (9%), bone-dryness; subtle wet wool aromas & soft acidity. **Johannisberger** ★★ Pleasant, light bodied sweetie with flavours of sunripe grapes. **B4 Spumante** ★★ 'B4 you start an occasion you have to drink some' instructs label of this low-alc carbonated fizz from hanepoot, billowing muscat & passionfruit. **Johannisberger Red** ★★ Similar to pvs with firm tannins, so tastes off-dry rather than full-sweet. Merlot, pinotage & ruby cab.

Spruitdrift range

Shiraz ☺ ★★★ Pleasing fruitiness on **05** (sample), warm baked plum flavours, delightfully soft & easy tannins. WO W Cape. **Brut Sparkling** ★★★ Smoothly dry, fruity summer refresher from colombard; attractive ripe flavours, surprisingly refined mousse for its price (Charmat method); **NV**.

Cabernet Sauvignon ★★★ **04** last yr showed typical cassis with some leafy notes, house dryness though slightly fruitier than other reds. **Merlot** ★★ **04** smoked bacon & dried fruit on nose, lean & savoury, big dusty tannins. Not retasted; same for... **Pinotage** ★★ More savoury than fruity this vintage; **04** lots of puckering astringency. **Grand Cru** ★★ **NV** from chenin, colombard; light, lemony & fresh, with bone-dry finish as per style. **Sauvignon Blanc** ★★★ Crisply dry **06** with boiled sweet and lemon-drop character. **Johannisberger** ★★ Popular-styled sweet white with delectable fresh-off-the-vine muscat flavour, ultra-soft & inviting. **Vin Doux Sparkling** ★★ Again a pleasant, light, summery fizz with crisp bubbles controlling the sweetness. Carbonated **NV**. **Hanepoot Jerepigo** ★★★ Sweet, spirituous dessert with whiff of pine & unconcentrated flavour. **White Muscadel** ★★★ *Wine* value award for **NV** fortified dessert with notes of barley sugar & orange; sweet & workmanlike. **Red Muscadel** ★★★ Much improved: morello cherry & Turkish Delight beckon from glass, delightful red berry flavours follow, still bit unknit but hits the spot. **NV**. — *DH*

■ *Western Wines South Africa* see Kumala

Whalehaven Wines ♂🍷🏠

Hemel-en-Aarde Valley (see Walker Bay map) ▪ *Est/1stB 1995* ▪ *Tasting & sales Apr-Nov (incl) Mon-Fri 9.30-5 Sat & non-religious holidays 10.30-4.30; Dec-Mar (incl) Mon-Fri 9.30-5 Sat, Sun & non-religious hols 10.30-4.30* ▪ *Fee R10 for groups of 10+* ▪ *Closed Easter Fri/Sun, Dec 25 & Jan 1* ▪ *Tours by appt* ▪ *BYO picnic* ▪ *Owners Bottega family* ▪ *Winemaker Sydney Burke, with Reino Thiart (Oct/Jan 2005)* ▪ *Viticulturist Tim Clark (Feb 2001)* ▪ *80 tons 6 500 cs own label 70% red 25% white 5% rosé* ▪ *Private Bag X14 Hermanus 7200* ▪ *wine@ whalehavenwines.co.za* ▪ **T 028·316·1633** ▪ *F 028·316·1640*

It was a 'heads down, tails up' year after the recent success of Whalehaven wines in competitions and on the sales front. The Viognier-Chardonnay's popularity is growing steadily ('It's something different to the usual whites,' elucidates marketer Kath Simm), and Hermanus weekenders, in particular, are adopting Old Harbour Red as their table wine. The Bottega family plan to expand the winery to handle increased production and modernise the tasting room. Winemaker Sydney Burke (Paul Engelbrecht is now at Havana Hills) also devotes his attention to the family's well-received Idiom wines (see separate entry).

★★★★ **Pinot Noir** Elegant, restrained but succulent, well-wooded **00**, violets & delicate redberry fruit well synchronised with oak's vanilla & tannins. Low ±13% alc.

Note: no newer vintages of above, following, tasted this ed. **Cabernet Franc** ★★★★ **04** sappy, somewhat green, stern tannins mask savoury fruit. 50% new Fr oak. Sbosch grapes, ditto... **Merlot** ★★★ **04** mulberry, smoked bacon features soften otherwise tight, hard structure & 15% alc. 40% new Fr wood. **Bord de Mer** ★★★★ **03** merlot/cab-based composition with cab f, shiraz, pinotage & mourvèdre filling the palette. Sultry tar nuances to shy black berry fruits, nicely grained tannins will protect their development for a few yrs. WO W Cape. **Old Harbour Red** ★★★ Chunky **NV** blend merlot, cab & shiraz; earthy, tasty fullness to firm tannins. **Rosé** ★★★ **04** crisp edge lifts off-dry mouthful; enjoy in flush of youth. Sbosch cab f & merlot; pinotage adds colour, viognier fragrance. **Chardonnay** ★★★★ Big, bold styling to **04**; heavy oaking (80% new Fr) dominates tropical/citrus fruits. W Bay grapes. **Viognier-Chardonnay** ★★★ Quick selling 85/15 unoaked blend. **05**: aromatic jasmine, peach & pear angles to ripe mouthful; 16% alc unfettered in just-dry finish. Sbosch fruit. — *DS*

■ *White River* see Bergsig
■ *Wide River* see Robertson Winery

Wildekrans Estate

Walker Bay ▪ Est/1stB 1993 ▪ Tasting & sales: Farm cellar Mon-Fri 9-5 (closed pub hols unless gate is open); Wildekrans Wine Shop & Art Gallery at Orchard Farmstall, Grabouw (T/F 021·859·5587), daily (except Dec 25) 8.30-5.30 (Sep-May) 9.30-5.30 (May-Aug) ▪ Cellar tours on request ▪ Meals, snacks, gifts, farm produce at farmstall, or BYO picnic to farm by appt ▪ Accommodation at Wildekrans Country House ▪ Play area for children ▪ Conservation area ▪ Owner Eric Green ▪ Winemaker Bruce Elkin, with William Wilkinson (2001/2003) ▪ Viticulturist Bruce Elkin ▪ 40 ha (cabs s/f, merlot, pinotage, shiraz, chenin, sauvignon, semillon) ▪ 240 tons 10 000 cs own label 50% red 50% white ▪ PO Box 200 Elgin 7180 ▪ wines@ wildekrans.co.za ▪ www.wildekranswines.co.za ▪ T 028·284·9829 ▪ F 028·284·9902

It's an ill wind that doesn't please some farmer, somewhere: in summer 2006, while the rest of the region was being buffeted by the seasonal south-easter, it blew cooling cloud cover over Bot River Valley, giving the grapes beneficial extra days on the vine. Winemaker Bruce Elkin promises good vintages of both chenin and sauvignon. New to the team is fixed-wing pilot Melissa Nelsen, an Overberger born and bred, whose brief will be provincial sales and national promotions.

Cabernet Sauvignon ★★★ Firm-tannined, spicy & herbal. **05** features 10% merlot; shows usual reticent fruit, dry, slightly tarry tannins. 9 mths Fr oak, 80% 1st fill, attractively light 13.3% alc. **Pinotage Barrel Select** ★★★ Fragrant oak (1st fill Fr, 9 mths) still obvious on **04**, banana/mulberry fruit unevolved, needs time to settle & fill out. Tarry but ripe, supportive tannins should facilitate. **Shiraz** ★★★★ Step-up **05**, touch of the Old World: restrained fruitiness, dry, food accommodating spicy/savoury tannins; still quite astringent but potential to develop into something delicious. 70% new Fr oak, 9 mths. **Cabernet Franc-Merlot** ★★★ **05** lean-ish, earthy fruit in big dry frame of tannin, calls for hearty food or spell in the cellar. 89/11 blend, 9 mths 2nd/3rd fill Fr oak. **Chenin Blanc** ★★ **06** again v shy, light, rapier-fresh acidity, unrounded by brief oaking (3 mths used Fr barrels). **Sauvignon Blanc** ★★★ Cool climate nettly tone with hint of mineral, **06** mite fuller, bigger, trademark zinging freshness (7.7g/ℓ acid). No newer releases tasted for following: **Pinotage** ★★★★ **03**, only seasoned wood, more obviously fruity, juicy, appealing than version above. **Warrant** ★★★★ Educated & classy bdx-style blend, 40/40/20 cab, merlot, cab f; **01** dusty cedary fruit, sweet vanilla oak, grippy tannins. Mainly new Fr oak. **Chardonnay** ★★★★ **04** partly barrel fermented/3 mths seasoned oak; some toasty whiffs, orange rind & honey flavours; smooth, lively, thanks to generous acidity. **Semillon** ★★★★ Broad shouldered, mouthfilling, oaky; bracing seam of acidity (8g/ℓ!) adds welcome counterpoint on **04**; 3 mths 2nd/3rd fill oak. **Méthode Cap Classique** ★★ Characterful brut from chardonnay, 3 yrs on lees; **02** appley/lactic aromas, clean dry mousse.

Caresse Marine range

Cape Red Blend ★★★ Shiraz (45%) leads pinotage (39%) & merlot in punchy, characterful **05** red, with ripe savoury tannins. 20% new wood (9 mths, Fr) a pleasantly subtle backdrop. NE **Merlot** ★★ House's signature austerity again evident in 2nd vintage **05**, muted 'green walnut' fruit flavours; dusty, dry, food imploring tannins. Oak as above. **Dry White** ★★ Premier Grand Cru-style **05**, mainly chenin (95%), semillon, portion 3 mths wooded; light, taut, with bracing freshness. NE. **White** new ★★ **06** semi-sweet version from chenin. ±15g/ℓ sugar adds fatness, rounds off racy acidity. Oak as for White. — *CT/CR*

■ **Wildfire** *see* Cape Vineyards
■ **Wild Rush** *see* Rietvallei
■ **Wild Tales** *see* Baarsma
■ **Wilhelmshof** *see* Nico van der Merwe

William Everson Wines

Paarl ▪ Est/1stB 2001 ▪ Tasting, sales & tours by appt ▪ BYO picnic ▪ Owner/winemaker William Everson ▪ 300 cs 80% red 20% white ▪ 7 Prospect Street Somerset West 7130 ▪ we@ intekom.co.za ▪ T 082·554·6357 ▪ F 021·851·2205

Transport company MD William Everson has no intention of giving up his day job: sharing cellar space on Paarl's Main Street, he says his plans are 'to keep production limited and focus on quality'. He believes that procuring grapes from all over the Western Cape allows him to find 'the ideal terroir for every specific variety', and he then handles grapes 'under strict reductive protocols' to allow the lowest possible sulphur levels.

Shiraz ★★★★ Well controlled **04** from Paarl fruit; usual abundant varietal character & fruit underpinned by dense but ripe tannins, for gd few yrs cellaring; balanced 14% alc. Incl 15% mourvèdre. 2 yrs oak, 2nd fill. **Chardonnay ★★★** Barrel fermentation, yr 3rd fill oak impart touch caramel richness to **05**'s elegant, lively, compact fruit (13% alc); delightful now & over shorter term. Both unfiltered, tasted as samples, WO Coastal. — *JN/CT*

Windmeul Cooperative Cellar ♀ &

Paarl • Est 1944 • Tasting & sales Mon-Fri 8-5 Sat 9-1 • Closed pub hols • Tours during tasting hours by appt • Owners 48 members • Winemakers Danie Marais & Francois van Niekerk (Dec 1999/Dec 2004), with Pierre Vienings (Dec 2005) • Viticulturist Paul Malan (Dec 2001) • 1 700 ha (cab, merlot, shiraz, chard, chenin, sauvignon) • 11 013 tons 6 000 cs own label 55% red 45% white • PO Box 2013 Windmeul 7630 • windmeul@info.com • www.windmeulwinery. co.za • T 021·869·8043/8100 • F 021·869·8614

Windmeul is spreading its wings with its wines, sporting freshly re-designed labels, now distributed locally and in Gauteng. A new tasting room and conference facilities should also help boost sales, as no doubt will membership of the new Pearl's Gate marketing alliance. Winemaker Francois van Niekerk, who stepped into Danie Geldenhuys' boots (his filled by new arrival Pierre Vienings), is upbeat about the quality of the 2006 wines but modestly says he's always striving to improve to reach the highest possible standards.

★★★★ Cabernet Sauvignon Reserve Longer oaking distinguishes this from version below; no new vintage since **03** (**★★★**) — restrained; fruit on nose, less on palate; ripe tannins, crisp acidity. Structure suggests may fill out with time. Yr new Fr barriques. **02** (sample) was stylish, seductive.

> **Chenin Blanc ☺ ★★★** Lengthy lees-ageing gives **06** presence & weight; inviting tropical tones, crisp apple flavours & vibrant acid backbone. Cheerful summer sipper.

Merlot ★★ 04 not as friendly/charming as **03**. Latest faintly vegetal with stalky tannic grip, unripe flavours. Warmer 14% alc. This, reds below, yr Fr staves. **Pinotage ★★ 04** dusty & rustic; acetone notes, drying astringent tannins. **Shiraz ⁿᵉʷ ★★** Robust & rustic **04**; redcurrant-tangy tannins overlain with savoury notes. Touch unripe. **Cabernet Sauvignon-Merlot ★★** Casual quaffing 70/30 blend; **05** leafy aromas, sweet-fruit entry, palate lifted by clove & cinnamon nuances. Drink up (& watch hearty 14.5% alc). **Mill Red ★★** Typically shiraz, cinsaut, cab f blend, yielding smoky & savoury flavours. Latest **NV** untasted. **Sauvignon Blanc ★★** Consistent easy-drinking style. **06** with muted tropical aromas & flavours, zesty tail. **Mill White ★★★** Latest **NV** not tasted. Pvs had a melon/hay bouquet, brisk tropical palate. No new versions of the following reviewed: **Cabernet Sauvignon ★★ 03** less of a fruity crowd-pleaser than pvs; shy mineral & organic notes, sinewy palate. **Shiraz Reserve ★★★★ 03** offers creamy vanilla flavours, sweet/sour twist. Yr oak, 45% Am. **Port ★★★** Rich Xmas cake bouquet; **03** concentrated, sweet/sour flavours, perhaps touch too sweet (102g/ℓ sugar) for classicists, more so the variety: ruby cab. Yr older Fr barriques. WO Coastal, as are regular Cab & Pinotage; all others Paarl. **Late Harvest** discontinued. — *CT*

■ *Winds of Change* see African Terroir

Wine Concepts

Cape Town • Tasting & sales Mon-Fri 9-7 Sat 9-5 • Cardiff Castle, cnr Kildare & Main St, Newlands 7700 • sales@wineconcepts.co.za • www.wineconcepts.co.za • T 021·671·9030 • F 021·671·9031

The limited-release Cab made by Murray Giggins, partner (with Mike Bampfield-Duggan) in this fine-wine retailing and *garagiste* outfit, was about to be released at press time. It will be sold from their shops in Newlands and Gardens under the name Lalapalooza. See Specialist Wine Shops section for more store details.

Winecorp

Stellenbosch ▪ Closed to public ▪ Group winemaker Frans Smit ▪ Senior winemaker procurement Johan de Villiers ▪ Senior winemakers Kobie Viljoen (red) & Eleonor Visser (white) ▪ Winemakers Etienne le Roux, Anton Swarts, Jacques Erasmus & Nevin du Toit ▪ Senior viticulturist Johann Smit ▪ PO Box 99 Lynedoch 7603 ▪ winecorp@iafrica.com ▪ www.winecorp.co. za ▪ ISO 9001 & BRC certified ▪ T 021·881·3690 ▪ F 021·881·3699

Producer of the Longridge, Spier and Savanha brands, Winecorp recorded another successful year in 2006, with, among others, an international gold-medal run at the Concours Mondial, IWC and *Decanter* Awards, and return trips to the podium for Eleonor Visser, who became the first female winner of the Chenin Challenge, and, shortly afterwards, was named Woman Winemaker of the Year. The company's brands reflect selective wine production based on quality, site and price-point. Longridge concentrates on premium wines from prime Helderberg mountain slopes; Spier wines are mainly of Stellenbosch and Coastal origin, and Savanha of wide ranging Western Cape origin, both vinified at the Spier winery. See separate listings for these brands, which are distributed in the UK and Ireland by British partner PLB.

Dumisani range

Meaning 'Praise' in Xhosa. All WO W Cape. Streamlining sees **Pinotage**, **Ruby Cabernet-Merlot**, **Chardonnay** & **Chenin Blanc** discontinued. **Pinotage-Shiraz ★★☆** Early-drinking unoaked 70/30 blend. Tasty **05** shows lively fruit of pinotage perked up by savoury, dark toned layering of shiraz. **Pinotage Rosé ★★** Easy, uncomplicated drinking. Previewed sample **06** more restrained than pvs, but still charms with red fruitgum character, added roundness from touch sugar. **Chenin Blanc-Chardonnay ★★★** Lemon/pear character retained in **06** sample, as is 65/35 proportion, soupçon oak. Has appealing youthful freshness. Note: Fat Ladies range discontinued. — *CR*

■ *Wine 4U see Le Manoir de Brendell*

Wine of the Month Club

Est 1986 ▪ Founder Colin Collard ▪ MD Tai Collard ▪ 250 000 cs 50% red 49% white 1% sparkling ▪ Private Bag X2 Glosderry 7702 ▪ wineclub@wineofthemonth.co.za ▪ www.wineofthemonth.co.za ▪ T 021·657·8100 ▪ F 021·415·6385

SA's original and still leading wine mail-order club, handling some 250 000 cases a year. Besides wines selected by the club's panel for distribution to over 40 000 customers, WOM also supplies its own-label wines, none tasted for this edition.

■ *Winery of Good Hope see The Winery of Good Hope*
■ *Wines of Charles Back see Fairview, Goats do Roam, Spice Route, Western Wines*

Wine Village-Hermanus   ◌◌

Walker Bay ▪ Est 1998 ▪ 1stB 2004 ▪ Open Mon-Fri 9-6 Sat 9-5 Sun 10-3 ▪ Closed Easter Fri & Dec 25 ▪ Owners Paul & Cathy du Toit ▪ ±1 000 cs 50% red 50% white ▪ wine@hermanus.co.za winenews@hermanus.co.za ▪ www.wine-village.co.za ▪ T 028·316·3988 ▪ F 028·316·3989
The housewines of this delightful country wine-shop, owned and run by Paul and Cathy du Toit, are made back-stoep-style by the proprietors, some friends and enthusiastic staff members, and offered to wine lovers in a spirit of fun. Available are a Dry Red and Dry White, neither tasted.

Winkelshoek Wine Cellar   ◌◌◌◌

Piketberg (see Swartland map) ▪ Tasting & sales Mon-Fri 9-4 Sat 9-12 ▪ Fee R5 ▪ Gifts ▪ Owners Hennie Hanekom & Jurgens Brand ▪ Winemaker Hennie Hanekom (1984) ▪ PO Box 395 Piketberg 7320 ▪ info@winkelshoek.co.za ▪ T 022·913·1092 ▪ F 022·913·1095
This cellar's easy-drinkers are available for tasting and sale from the visitor centre at the intersection of the N7 and R44 roads near Piketberg. The wines, untasted for this edition,

include the Weskus Dry Red, Grand Cru, Blanc de Blanc and Late Harvest; and the Cap Vino Red (unwooded) and White (chenin).

Withington   new

*Paarl ▪ Est 1999 ▪ 1stB 2002 ▪ Tasting & sales by appt ▪ Closed pub hols ▪ Owners Withington family ▪ ±3 000 cs own label 67% red 33% white ▪ Export brand: Livingstone (UK) ▪ PO Box 625 Paarl 7624 ▪ mail@withington.co.za ▪ www.withington.co.za ▪ **T 021·872·8648** ▪ F 088·021·872·8648*

Father-and-daughter team Charles Withington and Vanessa Hall list as their greatest asset the people they work with at selected cellars. These tailor-make wines according to their guidelines, the culmination of Charles W's 30-something years of experience in the wine industry, combined with his daughter's marketing background. Their main export market is the UK.

Shiraz-Cabernet Sauvignon ☺ ★★★ Food-friendly, eminently quaffable (helped by moderate 13% alc); **04** has pepper, vanilla aromas & restrained but sweetly persistent black fruit. From Pdberg grapes. Yr Fr/Am oak.

Cabernet Sauvignon ★★★ **02** classic blackcurrant & lead pencil aromas lead on to austere but elegant flavours & dry, tannic finish. Grapes ex-Sbosch. 18 mths Fr oak. This, next, WOM selection. **Merlot** ★★★ Rich plum aromas & lovely choc notes on Paarl-originated **03**, with herbal/mulberry finish. 15 mths Fr oak. **Chardonnay** ★★★ **06** chalky citrus notes, limy sweet-fruited finish; seamless & long, with oak well integrated (fermented/4 mths Fr). Wllngtn fruit. — MF

Withoek 🏠

*Calitzdorp (see Little Karoo map) ▪ Est/1stB 1996 ▪ Tasting & sales Mon-Fri 9-4 ▪ Closed Mar 21, Easter Fri, Apr 27, May 1, Jun 16, Aug 9, Sep 24 ▪ Tours by appt ▪ Self-catering cottages ▪ Farm produce ▪ Walks ▪ Conservation area ▪ Owner/winemaker/viticulturist Koos Geyser, with Fanie Geyser (1996/2000) ▪ 20 ha (cab, petit v, ruby cab, shiraz, tinta, touriga, chenin, colombard, hanepoot, muscadel) ▪ ±300 tons 400 cs own label 50% red 50% fortified ▪ PO Box 181 Calitzdorp 6660 ▪ withoek@telkomsa.net or stabilpave@mweb.co.za ▪ **T/F (044) 213·3639***

No update available on this winery; contact details.

■ **Withof** *see Cru Wines*
■ **Witteboomen** *see Thorntree*
■ **Wolvenbosch** *see Jason's Hill*

Wolvendrift Private Cellar

*Robertson ▪ Est 1903 ▪ 1stB 2002 ▪ Tasting & sales Mon-Fri 9-4.30 Sat 10-1 ▪ Closed Easter Fri-Sun, Dec 25/26 & Jan 1 ▪ Tours by appt ▪ BYO picnic ▪ Farm produce ▪ Walks ▪ Owner Michael Klue ▪ Winemakers Michael & Jan Klue (Jan 1973/Jan 2003) ▪ Viticulturist Jan Swart (Jan 2000) ▪ 120 ha (cab, merlot, chard, chenin, colombard, sauvignon) ▪ 45% red 45% white 10% fortified ▪ PO Box 24 Robertson 6705 ▪ wolvendrift@lando.co.za ▪ www.wolvendriftwines.co.za ▪ **T 023·616·2890** ▪ F 023·616·2396*

Fourth-generation winemaker on this century old wine farm, Jan Klue experienced his 'best ever' harvest since joining dad Michael in 2003. No rot, no diseases, rain at the right time, grapes in exceptionally good condition made the increasing focus here on quality that much easier. A new 'serious' cab-merlot blend (18 months in French oak) was due to join the value-for-money version after the guide went to bed. A glass of their sauvignon on the Breede riverside winery's deck was the perfect ending to a memorable vintage, the Klues recall.

Cabernet-Sauvignon-Merlot ★★★ 60/40 blend aka 'Red Wolf'; still-selling **04** last ed was juicy, with red berry fruit touched by toasty oak (8 mths Fr), agreeably firm tannins. **Chardonnay** ★★★ **06** not ready, **05** flew overseas before we could get our hands on it, last tasted **04** unshowy early drinker with understated citrus character & delicate oak. **Riverstone Sauvignon Blanc** ★★★ Lifts the bar a notch; though still modest, **06** is bracingly fresh, green-fruited, pleasantly weighty thanks to 4 mths lees-ageing. **Muscadel** ★★★ Fortified *red* (it doesn't say so on the label) muscadel; **06** brims with incense, Turkish Delight & raisins, comfortingly sweet yet tangy; mellow 17% alc. — *IvH*

■ *Wonderfontein see* The Marais Family

Woodhill Wines `new`

Stellenbosch ▪ *PO Box 206 Stellenbosch 7599* ▪ *info@woodhillwines.com* ▪ ***T 021·855·3625*** ▪ *F 021·855·2143*

Made and marketed by Grangehurst Winery, this brand offers 'a good excuse to enjoy a glass of wine every day, especially with food'.

Cape Rosé ★★ Half pinotage, with merlot & shiraz; light berry & boiled sweet character on **05**. Lowish alc (12.2%), generally demure, dry. — *TJ*

Woolworths

Category manager William Fakude T 021·407·3683 ▪ *Technologist Warren Dam T 021·407·2714* ▪ *Wine trainee Eric Botha T 021·407·3107* ▪ *Selection manager Allan Mullins **T 021·407·2777** F 021·407·3847 AllanMullins@woolworths.co.za* ▪ *Buying manager Ivan Oertle T 021·407·2762 IvanOertle@woolworths.co.za*

The past year has been a busy one for this quality minded retail chain, with at least four new wines launched a month. Selection manager (and Cape Wine Master) Alan Mullins notes growing customer demand — to which they've responded, of course — in the sparkling and rosé categories, as well as the organic and sulphur-free sector. Consumer resistance to high alcohol is another focus, and the selection team makes a point of choosing easier, more food-compatible products. The Limited Release range has 'really taken off' and the What? wines have met with such a great response, Mullins & co have released a Sangiovese (joining the Pinot Grigio and Primitivo sourced in Italy). The team is also involved in a packaging and closure project, led by Ivan Oertle and Warren Dam, recently returned from a trip to Portugal.

Reserve range

★★★★ **Founder's Reserve Cabernet Sauvignon** Choice barrel selection from Diemersfontein, owned by Wlwrths' founding family. Last sampled was less showy **03** (★★★), with pleasant damp earth character, lively fruit/acid interaction, lighter oaking (60% new, 70/30 Fr/Am, 15 mths). No **02**. Impressive **01** was weighty & concentrated.

★★★★ **Groenekloof Shiraz** Extravagant version from Darling Cellars. **03** tasted mid-2005 had classic black pepper varietal character, appealing ripe juiciness & salty liquorice-toned mid-palate, powerful finish. ±14 mths Fr oak, 60% new.

★★★★ **Cabernet Sauvignon-Merlot** Reflects vintage variations through mirror of Neil Ellis' classicism. **03** serious, special occasions red, with 4-5+ yrs potential. **04** (★★★★) a shorter term wine; exaggerated farmyard bouquet with meaty hint; brooding black fruit flavours, supple but dry tannins. 15 mths Fr barrels, ±25% new.

★★★★★ **Chardonnay** `new` Lightly oaked **03** shows a gorgeous array of citrus aromas: lime, lemon, orange, tangerine; fresh acidity & gentle wood spices lift the palate, elongate the nutty finish. Single-vyd bottling by De Wetshof; EW.

★★★★ **Chardonnay** Since **97**, by Neil Ellis. **04** untasted, still available. **03** noted pvsly as boldly New World: tangy citrus peel & buttered toast, food-friendly acidity. Fermented/ 9 mths oak, 80% Fr, third new.

★★★★ **Barrel Chenin Blanc** From old bushvines. **05** (★★★★), tasted mid-2005, pineapple & peach entry, sweet-ripe fruit glazed with dollop sugar (5.3g/ℓ). Tasty, if commercial. Fermented/6-9 mths barrelled, 20% new Fr. By Ken Forrester. See for NLH below.

★★★★★ **Sauvignon Blanc** `new` Specially selected for Wlwrths — 'Only outstanding Groote Post tanks made it into our bottles,' says Mullins of impressive & refined **06**. Dusty nettles & fynbos cavort on nose, grapefruit & asparagus on palate; knife-edge balance, persistent mineral finish. Closed with Vino-lok glass stopper.

★★★★ **Noble Late Harvest Chenin Blanc Barrel Reserve** Previewed **06** sumptuous & complex, vibrant interplay between honey, apricot & lemon; shd attain heights of pvs once sweet fruit & tangy acidity have melded. **03** was deeply ripe, its sweetness tempered by racy acidity. Naturally fermented in barrel.

Cabernet Sauvignon-Shiraz ★★★★ Cab again leads in **04** (60%), same oaking as pvs (older Fr barrels, touch Am, 21 mths). Charry oak & black fruit mingle with pleasing & classic cab structure, grip; balanced, though tannins slightly herbaceous. From La Motte. **Pinotage** ★★★★ Off Bellevue vyds in Bottelary. While creamy Am oak (100%) swamps fruit mid-2006, **05**'s abundant macerated berry flavours shd integrate, come to fore with time. Yr small barrels, 50% new.

Limited Release range

★★★★ **Malbec** From Bellevue; pvsly in Classic range. **04** big & bold but polished. Turmeric, black pepper & red roses; mouthwatering fruit, strong yet sleek tannins. At 13% alc (vs 14%), more balanced than pvs. Yr new Fr oak.

★★★★ **Pinot Noir** Delicious offering from BWC Wines; garnet-hued **05** (★★★★) enchanting combo fruity cherry & darker funghi on nose; flavours tad lighter, tannins less supple & generous than **04**, with truffly hint & friendly firmness matching most serious food.

★★★★ **Shiraz-Grenache** new Crackerjack by Ken Forrester; grenache portion the last from 50 yr old Devon Vlly block. **03** fresh & juicy, fruit expertly buffed with oak (new/old Fr, some Am). Delicious now, shd improve over few yrs.

★★★★ **Chardonnay Sur Lie** Top-notch white aperitif, unwooded but brimful of character thanks to well judged lees-ageing. Viscous & concentrated **06** lushly fruited, creamy/nutty textures, downright delicious. By Jordan Winery.

★★★★★ **Sauvignon Blanc** ✓ Thoroughbred offering from Cape Point Vineyards. **06** a restrained & elegant beauty; taut & mineral with lipsmacking 'wet slate' character & hint white pepper; steely core swaddled with concentrated greenpepper & granadilla fruit. Great value, great future. **05** (★★★★) gooseberries & *petits pois* character; crisp, racily dry & refreshing.

★★★★ **Sauvignon Blanc** new Refined, focused & pure **06**, restrained but ripe gooseberry flavours, cool hint of nettle; floral note & mid-palate weight added by 5% semillon; lovely waxy persistence. By Nitida, who also made the next wine.

★★★★ **Semillon 04** (★★★★) sample light textured, subtle & poised, with crisp finish. More powerful & showy **05** had sauvignon-like nettle aroma & hints fruit pastille & pear. **06** unready for tasting.

★★★★★ **Gewürztraminer** new Fabulously aromatic **05** distinguished by perfect balance of elegant fruit, sweetness & acidity; textbook rosepetal intro followed by waves of mango, passionfruit, lime… complexity its middle name. Gentle sweetness (11.6 g/ℓ sugar) lifted by zesty acidity. By Paul Cluver; EW.

Cabernet Sauvignon-Merlot new ★★★★ **03** led by cab (85%), dollop merlot & dash petit v. Classic lead pencil, cassis & iodine-like aromas; concentrated flavours & focussed tannins. Finishes just a tad stalky. By De Wetshof; EW. **Merlot** Well crafted **04** (★★★★) lifts the bar with intense tealeaf & black plum fruit, broad fleshy palate enlivened by bright acidity, neatly knit tannins. Similar, but more defined than **03** (★★★★), with spicy tannins ideal for dinnertime cordiality. 16 mths new/old Fr barriques. By Jordan Winery. **Pinotage** ★★★★ **06** certainly no shrinking violet; wood-driven styling shows in flamboyant charry character, very noticeable yet nicely handled. Peeking from behind it all is deliciously ripe & succulent strawberry fruit. Ex-Diemersfontein, as is next wine. **Shiraz** Untasted. **Weisser Riesling** From Paul Cluver Estate (EW). Breath of fresh air in a market dominated by Fr varieties. Step-up **05** (★★★★) beautiful roses & limes, hint terpene; lithe & balanced, sprinkle sugar adds roundness & weight. Elegant **04** (★★★★) floral & flinty, gets palate grip from brisk acidity (7.8g/ℓ). **Springfield Wild Yeast Chardonnay** moves to Classic range.

Organic range

By Stellar Winery unless noted. **Cabernet Sauvignon** ★★★ Interesting & different combo meat, baked fruit & bread pudding on firmly tannic **06**. **Merlot** ★★★ **05** savoury bacon whiffs, prune & raisin flavours & warming 14.9% alc. For this, cab above, in-store sell-bydate regimen strictly enforced because no sulphur is added as a preservative. **Shiraz** ★★★ Unwooded **04** not retasted; last ed showed spicy & savoury-dry flavours, smoky & herbaceous notes. By African Terroir. **Chenin Blanc Sulphur Free** No new vintage. **Chardonnay** new ★★★ **06** refreshing lemon/lime flavours mingle with toasty notes, buttery aromas. Enjoyable, if big boned (14.3% alc). **Sauvignon Blanc** ★★★ **06** animated & flavourful; cool green nuances of capsicum, hay & grass, slight tannin grip on the tail. **The Fennel** renamed 'The Lady Bird' & moved to range below; ditto **Syrah Reserve**, which loses its Rsv tag.

Classic range

★★★★ **Cabernet Sauvignon** Shows Villiera's restrained generosity; **04** layered with sugared plum & cassis, distinct coconut note from Am oak portion; tannins supple & approachable yet firm. Yr Fr/Am oak.

★★★★★ **Cobblers Hill** new to the Wlwrths portfolio, & one of this guide's Wines of the Yr last ed; superb, classy cab-dominated bdx blend by Jordan Winery; **03** dark & brooding, concentrated & long, impeccably structured & balanced with magnificently managed tannins. Merlot 30%, petit v 15%. 23 mths Fr oak.

★★★★ **Nature in Concert** new Top-drawer pinot from De Wetshof. **05** intense farmyard/funghi whiffs & sour cherry hint mingle with wet earth; flavoursome, with elegant tealeaf finish, commendable balance & moderate 13.2% alc. Will reward 3-4 yrs ageing. Yr Fr barriques.

★★★★ **Chardonnay Lightly Wooded** (Simply 'Chardonnay' pvs ed.) **05** simultaneously rich, savoury & fruity; opulent lime, lemon-butter & lees characters, toasty new Fr oak, crisp conclusion. Fermented/9 mths Fr oak; incl 13% unwooded portion. Ex-Jordan Winery.

★★★★ **Limestone Hill Chardonnay** Unwooded styling by De Wetshof. **06** (★★★★) atypically subdued bouquet, flavours; steely length in which 14.9% alc noticeable. **04** lightish but invigorating, tangy lemon zest finish. EW.

★★★★ **Wild Yeast Chardonnay** Unwooded version by Springfield Estate moves here from Limited Release range. **04** classy, understated but delicious; rich & round flavours leavened by vibrant acidity, persistent apricot finish.

Merlot Steps up the focus, intensity & grip with **05** (★★★★). Riot of plummy fruit, spicy, well integrated tannins, flattering tealeaf top note. Yr Fr oak, none new. **04** (★★★★) full & ripe yet balanced. This bottling by La Motte; following by Villiera: **Merlot** ★★★ **04** similar mould to attractive, last-tasted **04**, Woolworths Wine of Yr in 2004. Generous, warm red-fruit compote sprinkled with confectionery sugar; v soft tannins, roundly accessible. Yr Fr oak, 25% new. No **03**. **Pinotage** new ★★★★ Organic offering from Bon Cap. **04** quintessential pinotage acetone/rubber & banana, strawberry flavours, slight bitter lift to finish. Yr oak. Also from Bon Cap: **Syrah** ★★★ Pvsly in Organic range as 'Syrah Reserve'. Powerful & super-ripe **04** not retasted. **Shiraz** ★★★ Ex-Rooiberg. **05** robust yet friendly red with cranberry nuance, gentle tannin nudge. Yr seasoned Fr oak. Following two reds from Diemersfontein: **Shiraz-Cabernet Sauvignon** ★★★★ **03** enticing cranberry & vanilla notes, palate flush with v ripe, almost raisined fruit, nicely focused tannins. For quiet contemplation… or exuberant sharing! 63% shiraz, 30% cab, smidgen petit v. Combo new/old Fr/Am oak, ±10 mths. **Goshawk Chant** new ★★★ Merlot the leader in this five-way blend with cabs s/f, shiraz & petit v, matured separately yr in Fr oak. Classic Diemersfontein expansiveness in **04**: sprawling ultra-ripe red & black fruits with tannins to match. **Grand Rouge** ★★★ Reliable bdx blend (cab, merlot, malbec) by La Motte. **05** earthy & raisined with black tea nuance, chunky tannins; tasty if somewhat inelegant. Partly oaked in barriques, 13 mths. **The Ladybird** 'The Fennel' pvs ed; relocates from the Organic range. Merlot-led blend with cabs f/s (50/30/20); **05** (★★★★) bursts with flavour, appeal; ultra-ripe plums & prunes with leafy tones adding dimension; combo long tannic farewell, big 14.5% alc, provide structure for further improvement. Yr Fr oak, 25% new. Last tasted **03** (★★★★) had appropriate liquorice whiff. Ex-Laibach. **Viognier** new ★★★★ Organically grown by Bon Cap, showing all of variety's charm & none of its blowsiness. Lightly oaked **06** has exotic apricot perfume & buttery texture. 14.5% alc is obvious but doesn't overwhelm fruit. Following pair from Cabrière: **Chardonnay-Pinot Noir** ★★★★

Flavourful & refreshing lunchtime wine with moderate 12.5% alc. **06** shows a strawberry blush, hint of lime, lovely silky finish courtesy of few grams sugar. EW. **Pierre Jourdan Tranquille** ★★★ Light summertime white from chard & pinot. Candyfloss & raspberry notes on **04**, gentle semi-dry flavours. 11.5% alc. **Rhine Riesling** ★★★★ ✓ **06** puts riesling's ethereal aromatics in the spotlight: flowers & limes in bouquet, tropical mangoes & papayas on taste, juicy off-dry finish. By Villiera. **Sauvignon Blanc Bush Vine** ★★★★ Ex-Darling Cellars. **06** reserved nose but explosive full-ripe fruity palate; zesty, moreish, especially at 11.7% alc. **Cabernet Sauvignon-Merlot**, **Shiraz** & **Gewürztraminer** discontinued. **Malbec** moves to Limited Release range.

House Wines

Red ☺ ★★★ **05** amicable cab, shiraz, cinsaut mix. Juicy black fruit, light spices (from 8 mths staving) & pleasantly gripping tannins. By Franschhoek Vineyards, same for White.

White ★★ **06** breezy unoaked semillon-led blend with zesty acidity, tropical & grassy nuances. **Bel Rosso Sweet Red** ★★ Medium bodied **05** from tinta & merlot. Sappy ripe plum fruit with peppery note, well balanced, surprisingly unsugary for ±37g/ℓ sugar. By Bergsig. **Late Harvest** ★★ Ex-Simonsvlei; **06** fresh pineapple, musk sweet aromas & flavours, light, not over-sweet.

What? range

Chardonnay ☺ ★★★ Style change for **06**: still unadorned by oak but now creamier, weightier thanks to few mths lees-ageing. By Weltevrede; EW.

These are attractive easy-drinkers 'representing their varieties as closely as possible'. Local examples joined by untasted Sangiovese, Primitivo & Pinot Grigio from Italy. **Cabernet Sauvignon** `new` ★★★ New World eucalyptus scents join classic cassis in **04**, firm tannin backbone & hint of spice from 18 mths ageing in older Fr barrels. By Neil Ellis Wines. **Merlot** ★★ **04** sourced via Groundworks; last ed very ripe crowd pleaser, with sweetish fruit slipping down easily. **Pinotage** ★★★★ Unwooded **05** showed savoury & spicy fruit, sweet banana whiffs noted last yr. By Ken Forrester, as for next wine. **Shiraz** `new` ★★**04** has lifted acetone notes, sappy red fruit, tannins & slightly bitter finish. Older oak 18-24 mths. **Chenin Blanc** ★★★ By Ken Forrester. Unwooded **06** a brisk everyday white, fruity & clean with floral tone, softly dry finish. **Sauvignon Blanc** ★★★ Cat's pee & 'sweaty' notes on **06**, zesty & just-dry, light (11.7% alc). Ex-Bergsig; EW.

Longmarket range

Merlot ☺ ★★★ Lightly oaked, friendly red for early drinking. **05** tealeaf aromas & plummy raisined tastes, pleasantly astringent tannins. From Simonsvlei. **Rosé** ☺ ★★★ **06** trio muscadel, pinotage & gamay has wide appeal; raisined muscat perfume with boiled sweet hint, usual soothing smidgen sugar. 12.5% alc. By Villiera.

Mid-priced cork-closed range; some also in 2ℓ 'Flexibles' line-up below. **Cabernet Sauvignon** ★★ **04** rustic dry everyday red, sourced via Groundworks. Tasted pvs ed, as was... **Merlot-Cabernet Franc** ★★★ **04** shy nose hinting at plums & wild berries, fruity on palate, spicy tannins. Shd be drunk soon. By Simonsvlei. **Pinotage** ★★ Popular, unobtrusively oaked version ex-Rooiberg. **05** juicy, with loads of friendly strawberry flavours & woodsmoke whiffs. **Blanc de Noir** ★★★ **05** light strawberry colour/flavour, attractive & persistent, balanced, quaffable. From Swartland Winery, not retasted. **Chardonnay** ★★★ Ex-Robertson Winery. Easy-drinking but shy **06** teases with fleeting melon & lime flavours. **Chenin Blanc** ★★★ From Rooiberg, another effortless quaffer; **06** floral, with boiled sweet hint; sweet-fruit tone again buoyed by good acid backbone. 12.5% alc. **Sauvignon Blanc** ★★★ **06** balanced & fresh, inviting capsicum & hay notes, crisp dry acidity. By Robertson Winery. **Wet Rocks Sauvignon Blanc** `new` ★★★ Another Bergsig contribution. **05** restrained gooseberry aromas

& flavours, lacks fruit concentration to carry moderate but active 12.6% alc. EW. **Chardonnay-Semillon** ★★★ Characterful & charming dry white for early drinking, from Delheim. **06** zesty lemons, waxy/buttery texture lifted by limy tang. Portion Fr oaked, 4–5 mths. **Sauvignon Blanc-Semillon** new ★★★ Drink-me-quick 50/50 blend from Winecorp. **05** lively musk & honey aromas, bright acidity, waistline-friendly bone-dry finish. **Blanc de Blanc** ★★☆ Vibrant appetite whetter from Villiera; **06** mainly sauvignon with chenin; gooseberry aromas/flavours, touch tannin adds food-friendliness to the menu. **Gewürztraminer** new ★★☆ Lightish everyday **05**; appealing if slightly confected roses & lime character, sweetish finish (7.7g/ℓ RS). Supplier is Bergsig. Also available, not tasted, a **Shiraz** by Swartland Winery and **Pinot Grigio** by Van Loveren. **Spicy** discontinued.

Lite range (pvsly Sweet & Lite)

Bianca Light ★★ Light but not lacking flavour, as low-alc wines can be. **06** subdued nose but satisfying & crisp palate. 9.5% alc. From Delheim. **Bel Rosso Sweet Red** moves to House range.

Zesties

> **Zesty White** ☺ ★★☆ **06** tropical exuberance, friendly ±12% alc & wake-up acidity perfect for summer refreshment. From chenin & colombard.

Juicy Red ★★ **05** spicy-dry tinta/merlot marriage with plum & marzipan fruit, slippery tannins. **Perky Pink** ★★ **06** affable quick-quaff; strawberry hue/aroma from tinta, sappy flavour care of chenin & a touch sugar; 12% alc. **Sassy Sweet** ★☆ **06** perfumed & sweetish three-way mix colombard, chard & hanepoot. These all by Bergsig. An Italian Juicy & Italian Zesty, untasted, complete the range.

Concept range (psly The Wilds)

From Franschhoek Vineyards. **Reckless Red** ★★ **05** suitably chunky & smoky campfire companion led by devil-may-care pinotage, with two red sidekicks. **Hint of Red Rosé** ★ From cab, with farmyard whiffs & definite tannins. **05** could be sipped solo, but more amenable with food. **Wild White** ★★ Like pvs, **06** 'untamed' in name only; rather: soft & balanced, light, with hints of hay & muscat. Crouchen, chenin & 4 other fruity whites.

Cap classique sparklers

★★★★ **Vintage Reserve Brut** By Villiera, as are all these. Distinguished pinot/chard (60/40) sparkler, traditionally made & matured ±6 yrs on lees, further 6–12 mths on cork. Luxurious **99** (★★★★☆) rich & creamy; brioche & honey accents to refined citrus/red berry fruit. Vibrant mousse, invigorating acidity.

★★★★ **Brut Zero** 'Zero' referring to lack of preservatives & absence of 2nd sugar *dosage*, giving ultra-dry profile (1.7g/ℓ RS). **03** last ed was classic & elegant with chalky lime fruit, fine mousse, rich, slightly toasty aftertaste. 100% chard; 2 yrs on cork.

Brut Rosé ★★★☆ ✓ Onion-skin-hued **NV**; pinotage (56%) plays greater role in latest bottling, near-equal dollops pinot & chard. Red berry bouquet with soft meaty nuances; enters fruit-sweet but finishes softly dry, long. Min. 18 mths on lees, 6 on cork, sugar as for Brut. **Blanc de Blanc Brut Chardonnay** ★★★☆ **04**'s opulent, leesy creaminess enlivened by lemony acidity, 'sweetened' by apple compote ripeness. Fine, melting bubbles, fresh finish. 8g/ℓ RS. **02** *Wine* ★★★★. **Brut** ★★★☆ ✓ Good-natured **NV** from chard (51%), two pinots (noir & meunier) plus pinotage, ±2 yrs on lees. Chalky, with lemon hints & enriching toasty notes, dry finish (9g/ℓ RS).

Basic sparklers

NV carbonated bubbles from Rooiberg. **Brut** ★★ Lightish (11% alc) semi-dry rather than 'brut'; fizzy & fresh but rather neutral sauvignon. **Spumante Rosé** ★★ Frothy, aromatic sweet pink predominantly from red muscadel; softer this yr with colombard replacing merlot in the blend. **Spumante** ★★ Sweet, lively & balanced; grapey muscat tone from white muscadel, here gently frothing with colombard.

Cask wines/'Flexibles'

These 1ℓ, 2ℓ 'flexibles' (certified), 3ℓ & 5ℓ casks, filled on demand for freshness. All made by Simonsvlei unless noted.

> **Dry Red** ☺ ★★★ Fruity quartet shiraz, pinotage, cinsaut & ruby cab ensures **05** bursts with berry flavour; light tug tannin invites a place around the braai. **Selected Cape Red** new ☺ ★★★ **05** gently tannic, brightly berried four-way blend, unwooded, round & long.

Merlot ★ Beef, berry & caramel diversity on **05**, raisiny flavours, slightly sweet finish (4. 4g/ℓ RS). **Cabernet Sauvignon-Merlot** ★★ Fresh, strawberry toned **05** has enough fruity grip to cope with heartier foods. **Chardonnay** ★★ **06** poolside companion; low on varietal character but quite long on vinosity & balance. From Robertson Winery, as is next wine. **Sauvignon Blanc** ★★ **06** unchallenging, dry & zesty picnic wine. Some grass, hay hints. **Blanc de Blanc** ★★ Down from quartet of varieties to fruity duo chenin & colombard. Floral whiffs mingle with apple tones in gluggable **06**. **Crisp White** ★★ **06** suitably brisk & refreshing, with appley aromas & flavours. Chenin leads colombard's tropical flourish in the 3ℓ cask; the 1ℓ version is 100% chenin, with shy floral hint, bright acidity tempered by ripe pineapple fruit. **Light White** ★★ Low-alc tipple, **06** 60/40 crouchen, semillon blend with demure aromas, hint of semillon waxiness. **Stein** ★★ **06** light bodied semi-sweet chenin, with fresh floral & honey tones. **Semi-Sweet** ★★ Late Harvest-style **06**, quite pronounced sweetness; floral, honey & hay notes, very soft acidity. Widely sourced, so many WOs. Following ranges discontinued: Signature Series, Art of Blending, Artisan & Selected. — *CvZ*

Worcester Winelands

Worcester ▪ Est/1stB 2005 ▪ Tasting & sales Mon-Fri 8-5 Sat 9-4 ▪ Fee R10 for 5 wines, waived on purchase ▪ Closed Easter Fri/Sun, Dec 25 & Jan 1 ▪ Restaurant & self-catering chalets & other amenities (see intro) ▪ 48% red 52% white ▪ PO Box 59 Worcester 6849 ▪ manager@ worcesterwinelands.co.za ▪ www.worcesterwinelands.co.za ▪ T 023·342·8710/20 ▪ F 021·342·2294

Head for the 'wine house' at Kleinplasie, home of the Worcester Wine Route, and sample this new range, recently listed with Woolworths. Aptly named '100% Worcester', the wines are blended by Nuy Wine Cellar's Christo Pienaar from components submitted by the route's nine member-cellars and selected by an independent panel. The adjacent open-air museum, which offers a glimpse of early Cape life, and a fascinating collection of steam trains and machinery, is worth a visit too.

100% Worcester range

> **Chenin Blanc** ☺ ★★★ **06** bone-dry yet fragrant quaffer, with apricot & guava aromas/flavours, soft texture & long finish.

Shiraz ★★★ Pleasantly easy-drinking **05** takes in 10% merlot & delivers notes of plum, vanilla, allspice & coconut — revealing some clever oak handling (yr with barrels & staves). Soft tannins & controlled 14.5% alc. **Sauvignon Blanc** ★★ Customary greenpepper notes on light-fruited & flinty **06**, from high yielding vyds. Modest 11.7% alc & crisp dryness suggest a gd summer lunchtime companion. — *MF*

■ *Yammé see Overhex*

Yonder Hill Wine Farm

Stellenbosch (see Helderberg map) ▪ Est 1989 ▪ 1stB 1993 ▪ Tasting, sales & tours Mon-Fri 9-4 ▪ Closed pub hols ▪ Owners Naudé family ▪ Winemaker/viticulturist David Lockley (Jul 1998) ▪ 10 ha (cabs s/f, merlot) ▪ 85 tons ±12 600 cs 100% red ▪ PO Box 914 Stellenbosch 7599 ▪ wines@yonderhill.co.za ▪ www.yonderhill.co.za ▪ T 021·855·1008 ▪ F 021·855·1006

It bemuses winemaker David Lockley that visitors always enquire about tons per hectare. 'I grow wine, not grapes! I'm only interested in "quality wine per hectare".' Quality merlot, to be precise, Lockley having uprooted a chardonnay vineyard planted on 'beautiful' soil in 2002 to make way for two different clones of his prized red variety. 'I love merlot — *real* merlot, *Old World* merlot.' He also planted three rows of petit verdot 'just to make things interesting' when it comes to Inanda, the bordeaux-style blend.

★★★★ **Merlot**, Small harvest (off tiny own Sbosch vyd) lavished with 100% new small Fr oak 18 mths. Confident & delicious **04**, bottled, fulfils promise of last ed's sample with lush dark fruit, silky rounded texture. 14.5% alc carried with grace & charm.

★★★★ **Inanda** Adds dash petit v to bdx array cab, cab f, merlot (63/20/14) in classy & complex **04** (★★★★☆). Oak-imparted savoury-dry notes to richly textured palate, brooding aromas, woven into firmly ripe tannic frame. Infanticide to open now — needs 3-5 yrs to develop, shd hold many more. Bigger % new oak (60) for cab, longer (14-15 mths) before blending. **03** ★★★★ had asphalt tones, herbaceous flintiness in athletic styling.

Cabernet Sauvignon ★★★ No successor yet to herbal **02**. **Shiraz-Merlot** None since emphatic & unambiguous **04** (★★★★) with bulging berry flavour, bristling tannins, power finish. Less intense **03** (★★★★ but *Wine* ★★★★). **Chardonnay** discontinued.

Y range

> **Merlot** ☺ ★★★ Our Superquaffer of the Yr. A warm hearted, solid citizen (complete with what passes for stylised SA flag on charming front-label!). **06** ripe & dark fruited; smoothly approachable with lively acidity & long spicy dry finish. Incl fruit from house-owned Rbtsn vyds; staves & older supportive oaking. *Wine* 'Best Value', as for next wine.

Shiraz ★★★ Oak adds a charry nuance to polished leather in **05**, sweet pipe-tobacco & red fruit; more aromatic & chunky than pvs, with firming tannins. Needs food & yr/ 2 to loosen, grow. Own Rbtsn fruit; 4 mths staved then 14 mths older barrels. **Muscadel** ★★★ **03** bottled sunshine in a 500ml bottle; moreish. **04** unready for tasting. — *MW*

Zandberg Farm

*Stellenbosch (see Helderberg map) • 1stB 2001 • Tasting & sales daily 10-6 • 96 Winery Road Restaurant (see Eat-out section) • 4-star guesthouse & other amenities • Owner Ernst Heusser • Winemaker Anton Bredell • Viti consultants Kobus van Graan & Johan Wiese • ±12 ha (cab & merlot) • 2 200 cs 100% red • PO Box 5431 Helderberg 7135 • wine@zandberg.co.za • www. zandberg.co.za • **T 082·323·6367** • F 021·842·1505*

No update available on this winery; contact details from previous edition.

Zanddrift Vineyards

*Paarl • Est 1995 • Closed to public • Owner Windsharp Trading 23 (Singapore) • PO Box 1302 Suider-Paarl 7624 • zanddrift@xsinet.co.za • **T 021·863·2076** • F 021·863·2081*

After a hiatus of several years during which the vineyards, decimated by 'black goo', were replanted in rehabilitated soils, this Paarl winery is again in production. Two wines, a Cab and a Shiraz (not tasted for this edition), will be bottled in June.

Zandvliet Estate

*Robertson • Est 1867 • 1stB 1975 • Tasting & sales Mon-Fri 9-5 Sat 10-2 • Closed Easter Fri, Dec 25 & Jan 1 • BYO picnic • Owners Paul & Dan de Wet • Winemaker Johan van Wyk (Apr 2000), advised by Paul de Wet • Viticulturist Dan de Wet, advised by Francois Viljoen • 150 ha (cab, shiraz, chard) • 1 350 tons 60 000 cs own label 50% red 45% white 5% rosé • Export brands: Enon, Cogmans/Kogmans Kloof, Cogmans River & Sandy River • PO Box 36 Ashton 6715 • info@zandvliet.co.za • www.zandvliet.co.za • **T 023·615·1146** • F 023 615·1327*

Encouraged by their success in establishing Zandvliet as a top SA shiraz brand, Paul and brother Dan de Wet are 'concentrating on offering our loyal customers more shiraz under the Zandvliet name, from entry level to iconic'. Speaking of the latter, last year was the 10th harvest of the meticulously groomed, chalk-rich Kalkveld vineyard, from which a 'pinnacle wine' will be released in the near future. Meanwhile, the new My Best Friend range has shown 'phenomenal' growth. The Astonvale reds, conversely, are gradually being phased out.

★★★★ **Kalkveld Shiraz French Oak Matured** Leader of the trio celebrating the 'Kalkveld' terroir – a 'holy trinity' of Jurassic Period limestone, gravel & clay – deemed perfect for shiraz. This version barrelled ±18 mths in new Fr wood. Persistence & seamlessness are keynotes of dense **01**, complex & refined, a compendium of pepper spice & fruit in tailored package.

★★★★ **Kalkveld Shiraz American Oak Matured** A further expression of the ancient hill-side vyd site, here all new Am oak (also ±18 mths) is the medium. Still current **01** more open, mellow, woody than Fr-oak version, though overt barrel characters offset by well-defined fruit & bottle-age. Delicious at a well-appointed table, should cellar for up to a further 3 yrs. Above reds not retasted.

★★★★ **Kalkveld 'Hill of Enon' Shiraz** Literally the pick of the crop: only smallest, most concentrated berries chosen for this vinification (thus ridiculously small yield: 2t/ha), matured new Am oak 14 mths; **03** was blooming into a rhône-like beauty last yr; oak vanilla set off fragrant allspice features, textured grip in mouth, concentrated mineral finish.

★★★★ **Shiraz** This less demanding version far from 'lesser' than siblings above; fruit focused yet refreshingly unflashy. **04** continues pacier trend set by **03**, trademark woodsmoke & white pepper features toned by tight tannins. No clashing cymbals, just tempered class. ±18 mths seasoned barrels.

★★★★ **Chardonnay** Unruffled integration of citrus fruit with high-society oak in fluid balance **05**; rounded fruit/oak girth freshened by mineral tang to rein in any potential opulence. 30% cask fermented/3 mths, laudably moderate 13% alc.

Cabernet Sauvignon-Shiraz ★★★ Promising **02** spiced berry fruit, easy finish, not retasted for this ed. Yr 2nd fill barrels for 80% cab, rest unoaked.

My Best Friend range

Cheerful trio of easy-drinkers, all under screwcap, NE & new. **Red** ☺ ★★★ **04** smoky interest to plump, chunky fruit, food-friendly tannins for pizza/pasta. **Shiraz Rosé** ☺ ★★★ **06** burnished copper glints; cherry-toned mouthful; undemanding 12.5% alc. **White** ☺ ★★★ **06** fresh melange chard, chenin & colombard: touch of sweetness in brisk tail. Just 13% alc.

Astonvale range

Sauvignon Blanc ☺ ★★★ **06** summery asparagus features with litchi, fresh cut-grass fillip to finish. Aperitif, lunchtime pick-me-up. **Crème** ☺ ★★★ **06** uncluttered poolside medley of fragrant colombard & tropical sauvignon. Both modest 12.5% alc.

Unwooded Chardonnay ★★★ **06** 'wild' individuality; herby edge to lime fruits, enjoy in flush of youth. All NE. Discontinued: **Shiraz** & **Ruby Cabernet**. – *DS*

- ■ *Zandwijk* see Kleine Draken
- ■ *Zantsi* see Darling Cellars
- ■ *Zaràfa* see Mountain River Wines
- ■ *Zebra Collection* see Rooiberg
- ■ *Zellerhof* see Huguenot Wine Farmers

Zevenwacht

Stellenbosch ▪ Est 1800 ▪ 1stB 1983 ▪ Tasting & sales Mon-Fri 8.30-5 Sat/Sun 9.30-5 ▪ Fee R17 ▪ Closed Dec 25 ▪ Cellar tours ▪ Restaurant & picnics daily (see Eat-out section) ▪ Luxury country inn, vineyard cottages & self-catering chalet (see Stay-over section) ▪ Conferences/banqueting ▪ Chef school ▪ Spa ▪ Tour groups ▪ Children's play park ▪ Farm produce ▪ Conservation area ▪ 4×4 trail ▪ Owner Harold Johnson ▪ Winemaker Jacques Viljoen (Jan 2002), with Pierre de Klerk & Riyaat Fanie (Sep 2004) ▪ Viti adviser Kevin Watt (Jan 2001) ▪ 200 ha (cab, merlot, pinotage, shiraz, che-

nin, sauvignon) ▪ ±1 000 tons 65 000 cs 50% red 50% white ▪ PO Box 387 Kuils River 7579 ▪ info@
zevenwacht.co.za ▪ www.zevenwacht.co.za ▪ **T** 021·903·5123 ▪ F 021·903·3373

Winemaker Jacques Viljoen sings the praises of his assistant, Pierre de Klerk, while also
enthusing about the 2006 harvest as 'close to perfect, a winemaker's dream', aided by a
new generator. The harvest featured the first viognier and mourvèdre, and with grenache
being planted as well, Viljoen promises further excitement. New to the line-up is their
first dessert wine, from semillon; also new is the Mangwanani African Day Spa, adding to
the myriad non-vinous attractions.

★★★★ **Primativo** 'A date at dusk with a Belgian beauty: curves, shadowy scarlet skies…'
Jacques V lyricises of this one-barrel wonder. **04** an Amazon: billowing brambles, generous palate laden with opulent fruits; firm tannins & now lesser alc (14.5 vs 16% for
03). Phew! Zinfandel, by another name (which also spelt 'primitivo'); Mbury fruit. All
new Am casks.

★★★★ **Merlot 04** (★★★) last ed noted as capricious hiccough in lineage of 'serious treatment, serious result' versions; less new oak (40%), & Am joins Fr in the confected fray:
scrub-like nature, sweet finish. Pvs **02** deftly integrated; fresh acid & 14% alc buffed by
dark-choc weight.

★★★★ **Syrah** Gentler, less oaky, more focused fruit expression in **04**: spice intensity honed by
2.3% viognier, fine tannins echoed in length of finish. 10% new Am, rest used Fr casks.

★★★★ **The Tin Mine White** Celebrates enterprise of early 20th century miners on the property. **05** (★★★★) full & foxy: 9% Fhoek viognier adds tangy interest to 51% chard (both
oaked 8 mths) but less complex than pvs. 40% unwooded sauvignon is the spine. Last
tasted **03** had herbaceous scrub characters balanced by ample scented fruits.

★★★★ **Gewürztraminer** Striking, premium priced package; alsace-style bone-dry elegance
on **05** (now bottled, pvs ed a preview), petals & litchi fruitiness, not as racy or riveting
as **03** (★★★★★), with gorgeous potpourri bouquet, great texture & structure. Barrel
fermented.

Zevenrood ☺ ★★★ **04** finer berry fruits, less chewy texture than pvs; a harbinger of
planned quality overhaul. For outings or at table. WO Coastal.

Cabernet Sauvignon ★★★☆ Still current leafy/vegetal **01** not retasted. Next will be **05**: not
ready for review. **Pinotage** ★★★☆ Pvs ed noted **04** as redolent of tropical groves; liquorice twist
to banana features, firm & tannic. Yr used Fr oak. **The Tin Mine Red** ★★★☆ Partner of white blend
above; shiraz driven with merlot, cab & now zin. **04** less gauche, more concentrated, better finish
than pvs. 70/30 Fr:Am oak. **Sauvignon Blanc** ★★★☆ **06** grassy & taut, mineral tints to terrific
crisp send-off. **Zevenblanc** ★★★ A duo of blancs, chenin & sauvignon; **06** peachy, with brisk tail.
Semillon Natural Sweet new ★★★★ Made in a straw-wine method but not officially registered
as such, so this dessert wine 'Natural Sweet' for now. **05** lighter styled, fruit cocktail pleasure.
136g/ℓ sugar, 11% alc. Following not retasted: **Chenin Blanc** ★★★ **05** ripe guava/fruit salad
mouthful fleshed out further with wood (25%, 4 mths). **Bouquet Blanc** ★★★ **05** off-dry charmer,
aromatic riesling & gewürz union with honeysuckle girth. — *DS*

Zidela Wines

Stellenbosch ▪ Est 2001 ▪ 1stB 2002 ▪ Closed to public ▪ Owners Danie Kritzinger, Herman Nell
& Jaco Kritzinger ▪ Winemaker: Jaco Kritzinger (May 2002) ▪ 80% red 15% white 5% rosé ▪
Other brands: Suikerbosch & Gordon's Bay ▪ PO Box 3021 Matieland 7602 ▪ gianni@
zidelawines.co.za ▪ www.zidelawines.co.za ▪ **T** 021·880·2936 ▪ F 021·880·2937

As one of the younger players in the industry, this wine services company, already active in the export market, is now making inroads into the local arena with their Zidela, Suikerbosch and
Gordon's Bay brands. At the wheel are Herman Nell, Danie Kritzinger and son Jaco Kritzinger.

Chenin Blanc new ☺ ★★★ Real character & appeal at a giveaway price; **06** light but
lively wintermelon fruit backed by fine, zesty acidity.

Merlot new ★★ Attractively 'untamed'; **04** funky whiffs, flavours of wild berry, lightish bodied for uncomplicated quaffing. **Shiraz** ★★★ Lasted tasted was **03**, which showed elegant allspice whiffs, raspberry fruit & lightly supportive tannins. **Cabernet Sauvignon-Merlot** ★★ Green leaf, plum notes noted last ed on 60/40 blend; **04** compact, with dry earthy finish. **Sauvignon Blanc** ★★★ Very lively, crisp, refreshing summer white; **06** light bodied with aromas of musk sweets & dusty figs. Dbnville fruit.

Gordon's Bay range

Sauvginon Blanc ★★★ **06** similar to Zidela bottling above. No follow-ups yet to: **Shiraz** ★★★ Youthful & vibrant **04** with zesty fruit, firm tannins & dry finish. **Chardonnay** ★★ **04** slight oxidative character & sweet-sour finish.

Suikerbosch range

> **Chenin Blanc** new ☺ ★★★ ('Kaapse Wit' pvs ed.) **06** similar to Zidela sibling; well-fruited & lively with satisfying mouthfeel.

Kaapse Rooi ★★ **05** no cab this time (just unwooded shiraz, merlot); very soft, slightly raisined flavours, medium bodied easy-drinker. **Rosé** new ★ From shiraz ex-Wcstr; **06** plain & simple yet with interesting pomegranate aroma. All above WO W Cape. **Perlé Rosé** discontinued. — CT

Ziggurat Vineyards   👂🍷📖

Paarl ▪ Est 1692 ▪ 1stB 2003 ▪ Tasting & sales Mon-Sat 9-5 (Oct to Apr); otherwise call ahead T 021·863·3494 ▪ Tours by appt ▪ B&B/self-catering cottage ▪ Owners Louw family ▪ Winemaker Anton Louw (Jan 2005) ▪ Viticulturist Dawid Gerstner (Jul 1999) ▪ 174 ha (cab, merlot, shiraz, chard, sauvignon) ▪ 1 080 tons total ▪ 11 tons/500 cs own label 65% red 35% white ▪ PO Box 2 Simondium 7670 ▪ ziggurat@mweb.co.za ▪ www.zigguratwines.co.za ▪ T 021·863·3494 ▪ F 021·863·1804

They had to contend with equipment failure, says 'winemaker etc' Anton Louw. 'Most disastrous was the hi-fi; I had to hum the whole harvest!' Electricity was a now-you-have-it-now-you-don't factor, so gravity was used as an alternative. Production's up (and in 2006 included a light rosé from cinsaut and shiraz) but is still just 11 tons. Anton L comments on the people-pleasure the newish tasting room affords the Ziggurat team — a mutual enjoyment, he believes, judging from sales.

★★★★ **Shiraz** Praiseworthy debut: judicious oaking allows bright fruit the centre stage. **04** abundant red-fruit melange, floral nuances from 5% viognier add gloss. Balanced, enduring fleshy flavours & polished tannins mask 14.5% alc. 18 mths 2nd fill Fr wood. Satisfying now, shd improve few yrs. This, all below, new.

Cabernet Sauvignon-Merlot ★★★★ Upbeat, early-drinking 50/50 blend reaching a heady but well hidden 15% alc in **04**. Tomato notes mingle with plum, char, mocha. Impressive fruit weight, supple tannins, vanilla finish. 18 mths combo new-4th fill Fr oak; **03** same blend, more savoury/meaty notes. **Rosé** ★★★★ ✓ **06** rather sophisticated despite its lurid hue; herb & red-fruit scents, zesty acidity, firm fruit tannins & bone-dry tail (1g/ℓ RS), food-cordial mid-palate bite from 2 mths on lees. **Wild Card Chardonnay** ★★★ Mid-2006, **05** certainly is 'wild' & unmeshed — needs time. Bouquet a riot of oak-influenced aromas (incl almonds, vanilla, acacia), palate thick with lime & ripe tangerine. Acidity cuts richness short on finish, then 14.5% alc glow kicks in. 6 mths 1st fill Fr oak. **Sauvignon Blanc 06** attractive freshly cut grass, tropical fruit & 'wet pebble' notes, racy yet flavoursome acidity on unfinished sample, possible ★★★★ on release. WO Smnsberg-Paarl. — CvZ

Zoetendal Wines   👂🍷🧀🍓

Elim (see Southern Cape map) ▪ Est/1stB 2004 ▪ Tasting, sales & tours Mon-Fri 9-5 Sat 9-1 ▪ Closed Easter Sun, Dec 25 & Jan 1 ▪ Meals for groups of 10+ by appt; BYO picnic ▪ Farm produce ▪ Walks ▪ Conservation area ▪ Owners Willem & Louise Loots, Johan & Elizan de Kock ▪

Winemaker Willem Loots • Viticulturists Willem Loots & Johan de Kock • 10 ha (shiraz, sauvignon) • 45 tons 6 300 cs 2% red 98% white • PO Box 22 Elim 7284 • zoetendal@telkomsa.net • T 028·482·1717 F 028·482·1720

Sustainable, creature-friendly, environment-aware. These are some of the guiding principles of Elim wine-partners Willem Loots (winemaker) and Johan de Kock (vinegrower), whose choice of the exquisite Pincushion Protea for their winery logo says it all. A short hop from Africa's southernmost tip, their aim is to capture their cool, wind-tossed maritime situation in the bottle. Though the power cuts last year had them temporarily worried, their grapes were so good that no acidification was necessary.

Shiraz ★★★☆ Dusty, spicy, perfumed aromas on **05**, fresh liveliness, firmly supportive tannic structure & subtle oak (14 mths mostly older Fr); marked by herbal & herbaceous notes. 13.5% alc much lower than pvs. **Sauvignon Blanc** ★★★★ Attractive **06** in variety's delicate rather than brash guise, revealing cool origins with grassy, asparagus notes; smooth-textured, good fresh bite, well balanced 12.5% alc. Both these pushing higher ratings.— *TJ*

■ *Zomerlust* see Vinimark
■ *Zondernaam* see Tokara

Zonnebloem

Stellenbosch • Owner Distell • Group cellar manager Callie van Niekerk (Dec 2005) • Cellar manager (Adam Tas facility) Michael Bucholz (Jan 2006) • Winemakers Hendrik de Villiers (reds, Jul 2006), with Bonny van Niekerk; Deon Boshoff (whites, Dec 2001), with Elize Wessels • Viticulturist Henk van Graan (Jan 1996) • 9 000 tons ±220 000 cs 59% red 41% white • PO Box 46 Stellenbosch 7599 • www.zonnebloem.co.za • T 021·808·7911 • F 021·883·2603

'An interesting harvest, compliments of Eskom,' comments Callie van Niekerk drily, referring to the power cuts which bedevilled production in 2006. He's now in the elevated position of group cellar manager for Distell, after 33 years' service; also climbing the ladder is erstwhile red-wine maker for Zonnebloem, Michael Bucholz, now cellar manager for the Adam Tas facility. Stepping onto the rungs are new red-wine maker Hendrik de Villiers and Elize Wessels, assisting Deon Boshoff in the white-wine cellar.

★★★★ **Lauréat** ✓ The flagship; more showy, generously oaked than rest of range. Internationally hailed **04** (IWC, IWSC golds) unites cab, merlot, shiraz, (55/30/5) with malbec, petit v, no variety dominating. Sumptuous, intense dark fruits/spice, mouthcoating tannins, balanced freshness augur well. 14 mths new/used Fr/Am/Hngrian/Rmnian oak.

★★★★ **Shiraz** Big, vibrant but well balanced **04** (★★★☆); peppery oomph & straightforward varietal savouriness. As with other reds, at best around 7 yrs from vintage. 50% in new/used small oak. **03** elegant yet substantial, persistent.

Premier Grand Cru ☺ ★★☆ Previewed **06** shares chenin/colombard in sound everyday white. Unshowy herby/tropical tones; bright acid balanced by juicy 4.5g/ℓ sugar. **Blanc de Blanc** ☺ ★★☆ Cool, fresh greengage/gooseberry array on **06** chenin/sauvignon blend. Lightish, stimulating, with agreeable fruity length.

Cabernet Sauvignon ★★★★ Pleasantly modern. **04** forthcoming, pure black berry/cassis flavours, fine, lively tannin; good harmony for current drinking. Fr oak barrels/staves. **Merlot** ★★★★ Elegance captured in **04**'s ruby clarity, gentle choc/plum fruit. Readied by basic, pure flavours, firm, rounded tannins. **Pinotage** ★★★ Contemporary, though readily recognisable style. Suggestion Am oak lifts fresh raspberry fruit on **04**. Medium bodied, light textured with rounded grip. **Chardonnay** ★★☆ **05** less characterful than pvs. Shy nut/citrus character; sturdy, with some creaminess; slightly sweet, short. Half barrel fermented. **Sauvignon Blanc** ★★★★ **06** more 'sauvage' than pvs, without over-aggression. Greenpepper/dust concentration emphasised by incisive dryness. Balance, persistence add to drinkability. All above WO W Cape.— *AL*

■ *Zonneweelde see* Slanghoek

Zorgvliet Wines

Stellenbosch ▪ Est/1stB 2000 ▪ Tasting & sales Nov-Apr: Mon-Thu 9-5 Fri 9-6 Sat 10-7 Sun 10-5 May-Oct: Mon-Fri 9-5 Sat/Sun 11-5 Pub hols Jan-Dec 10-3 ▪ Closed Easter Fri & Dec 25 ▪ Fee R15 p/p ▪ Herenhuis 1692 Restaurant Mon-Sat 12-9.30 Sun 12-3.30; Le Pommier Restaurant: daily 8am-9.30pm (see Eat-out section) ▪ Zorgvliet Deli: Tue-Sun 9-6 weather permitting ▪ Cellar tours by appt ▪ Facilities for children ▪ Gifts ▪ Conferencing ▪ Banhoek Vineyard Lodge (see Stay-over section) ▪ Owners Mac & Marietjie van der Merwe ▪ Winemaker Neil Moorhouse (Jan 2003) ▪ Viticulturist Rudolf Jansen van Vuuren, with Shaun McLeod (Jun 1999 / Jun 2004) ▪ Viti adviser Kevin Watt (Aug 2002) ▪ 57 ha (cabs s/f, merlot, shiraz, chard, sauvignon, semillon, viognier) ▪ 500 tons 25 000 cs own label 60% red 40% white ▪ PO Box 1595 Stellenbosch 7599 ▪ info@zorgvliet.com ▪ www.zorgvliet.com or www.zorgvlietwines.co.za ▪ T 021·885·1049 ▪ F 021·885·1290

The past year saw Zorgvliet usher their wines onto a broader stage, both literally and figuratively: increased international distribution and wine show appearances on the one hand; on the other, webcams in the cellar to let aficionados watch the crush, plus underwriting a one-man comedy by Frank Opperman, aimed at demystifying wine. Innovations include a flagship bordeaux-style blend, debuting late last year, and a shake-up of the Silver Myn range with the addition of a Pinot (untasted), Viognier and a white blend.

★★★★☆ **Richelle** new Top-of-the-range, intricate blend of cab (50%), petit v & 10% each cab f, merlot & malbec; equally complex oaking results in fragrant tobacco & cedar notes luring you into richly fruited palate, svelte & luxurious. **04** still firmly but elegantly restrained by minerality & dry, fine tannins with bright acids. Pure infanticide now: cellar 5-8 yrs to reveal its blue-blooded class. 20 mths in wood, 90% Fr, 10% Rssian; 80% 1st fill, bal. 2nd & 3rd.

★★★★ **Cabernet Sauvignon** Variety's signature cassis, herbaceous leafy & cedar tones on **04**; tight, chalky, dry tannins from fruit & hint Rssian/Hngrian oak (4% each, bal. Fr) rein in compact black fruit. Elegant core deserves cellaring 4-8 yrs to show full potential. Incl dashes merlot, cab f.

★★★★☆ **Sauvignon Blanc** Clean, fresh-fruited pleasure, drinks beautifully now. **06** nettles, citrus & passionfruit richly concentrated, mouthfilling. Zesty, lively acidity balances midweight palate, long ruby grapefruit finish.

Shiraz ★★★★ ('Syrah' pvs ed.) Restrained, with soft, smoky red-berried fruit & some spice on **04**. Brisk acidity, dry tannic finish & now all Fr oak (40% new) contribute to cooler, slower maturing profile, begging time to develop.

Silver Myn range

★★★★ **Cabernet Franc** Herbaceous & perfumed nuances evident but **05** fruit still subdued & tightly bound up in firm, dry, tannic structure. Oaking now includes 14% Hngrian, rest Fr (third 1st fill). Stylish & restrained, with long perfumed farewell, needs time to develop. **04** (★★★★) lacked intensity & exuberance of pvs.

★★★★ **Petit Verdot** 10% Rssian oak replaces Am component in **05**, usual touch merlot (14%) giving fragrant violet lift to mineral/inky nose & palate. Dry, fine tannins ensure tight form, well balanced with 15% alc not evident.

★★★★ **Chardonnay 05** rich leesy notes to ripe citrus flavour, excellent mouthfeel & length; moderate 13.5% alc last ed noted as suiting all occasions. WO Coastal.

No new vintages tasted for Chard or following four wines: **Merlot-Cabernet Franc** Step-up **04** (★★★★) more balanced & persistent than pvs; 65/35 mix; meaty/spicy notes to the berries; not for long keeping. Jammy **03** (★★★★ but VDG). **Cabernet Sauvignon** ★★★★ **04** better balanced than pvs; dark-fruit flavours well-knit, though last yr needed time for mid-palate to flesh out. **Shiraz** ★★★ Straightforward **04** sweet spicy nose, tutti-frutti palate. WO Coastal. **Sauvignon Blanc 05** (★★★★) attractive tropical fruit-punch tone & some richness, medium bodied, not for keeping. Same lingering finish as **04** (★★★★). **Dry Rosé** ★★★ Pinot enters mix in **05**, with lower alc (12%) making for a light, restrained & refreshing summer aperitif style, with cranberry piquancy & savoury nuance. **Viognier** new ★★★★ Alluring, perfumed **06**, jasmine & magnolia spiced with ripe peach &

apricot, all continue on delicious off-dry (10.2 g/ℓ) palate balanced by lime acidity; long aftertaste. Rich & generously fruited, it's a perfect partner for spiced Oriental cuisine. 50% wood fermented/5 mths, Fr. **White** new ★★★☆ **06** semillon & sauvignon (60/40) develop in glass into rich salad of passionfruit & lime. Sweetness (5.8g/ℓ) well balanced by zesty acidity. Brush oak (2 mths Fr, 80% new) lends creaminess to an appetising blend. WO Coastal.

Le Pommier range
Cabernet Sauvignon Reserve new ★★★★ Generously fruited palate follows subtle, classic aromas of pencil shavings & dark berries in **04**. 10% 1st fill oak (16 mths) adds vanilla & cedar notes, fine gripping tannins still in control. Nudges next rung up, esp. given time to show full potential. **Cabernet Sauvignon** ★★★★ Fruit-driven **04** last yr offered raspberries & some spice. 14 mths older oak. Touch less elegant than pvs. **Cab Franc** ★★★ Currently brooding & sullen, **04** earthy, savoury, firm fruit & tannins hold more benevolent aromatic characteristics to ransom mid-2006. Food wine. **Shiraz** ★★☆ **04** resinous hint to restrained fruit, wood dominant mid-2005 thanks to third new oak, 14 mths. **Sauvignon Blanc** ★★★★ Dollop semillon adds breadth to exuberantly fruity **06**, lively acidity with a long citrus & passionfruit farewell; perfect solo option. WO Coastal. All screwcapped. **Dry Rosé** & **Semillon** discontinued.

Spring Grove range
New vintages of these unready. **Cabernet Sauvignon** ★★★ **04** garnet robe, dense berried nose, cassis/sour cherries on palate, judicious wooding. **Shiraz** ★★★ **03** jelly-baby aromas, red fruit miscellany which ends quickly; lacks character of pvs. 14 mths oak, third new. — *MW*

■ *Zwalu* see Neil Ellis Meyer-Näkel

Introducing the tasters for this edition

ANGELA LLOYD

During her 23 years' professional involvement with wine, Angela has lectured and broadcast about and 'even made' wine. She's pursued her love of travel, exploring the world's winelands, on occasions as a judge, a role also regularly fulfilled in SA. As a wine writer, commissions come from local and international publications; she's also associate editor of *Grape*. Last and most significantly, this edition is her 21st as a taster and scribe for the guide.

CATHY VAN ZYL

Cathy van Zyl is SA's only resident Master of Wine. A relative newcomer to the wine industry, over the past few years she has judged at the Trophy Wine Show, Diner's Club Winemaker of the Year, for Grapeworx and has started judging internationally. She is a co-founder of *Grape*, and still a regular contributor. Cathy also lectures for the CWA on tasting. Her online wine diary, Cathy's Blog, is an SA pioneer of this increasingly popular genre.

CHRISTINE RUDMAN

Christine started out in FMCG marketing in Johannesburg. Accepting a job at SFW and needing to learn about wine, she enrolled with the CWA. Her Cape Wine Masters qualification was earned in 1988; she ran the CWA as principal for seven years, and has since been occupied with consultancy work, professional tastings, wine judging and writing three wine columns. She's travelled widely to the world's wine countries, tasted on international panels (including the International Wine Challenge in London as panel chairman); written two editions of *A Guide to the Winelands of the Cape*; and says there's no retirement in sight, she's 'having too much fun'.

CLIVE TORR

Clive first made wine in 1984 at Elsenburg College. In a blind tasting it won first place, inspiring him to study oenology and start various tasting clubs. Tasting subsequently became his passion, profession and hobby. He attained a wine judging certificate and his Cape Wine Masters in 1993. He's an inspirational, entertaining wine educator and hand-crafts wines both in the Cape and Burgundy. He is also a former principal of the CWA. Panels judged on include Wine, Wine of the Month Club, Diner's Club Winelist of the Year, Veritas, Swiss Air, Grapeworx, *Wynboer* and the Terroir Wine Awards.

DAVE SWINGLER

Dave earns his keep outside the drinks trade: indulging his hobbies of wine and words for the guide is 'sheer pleasure'. Having travelled the winelands of the world, he remains 'misguided enough to continue a pursuit of the vinous Holy Grail — affordable great red Burgundy'. Dave is co-author of *One Hundred Wines — An Insiders' Guide*, drinks contributor to *Posh Nosh* and an occasional columnist for *Wine* and other media. He brings a hearty consumer perspective to the guide.

DAVE HUGHES

Honorary Cape Wine Master Dave Hughes has judged in most of the world's big-name competitions — including the International Wine & Spirit Competition (IWSC) since 1975. He is the first ever non-British resident invited to join the Worshipful Company of Distillers. He was invested as Keeper of the Quaich in 2003 and is a member of the British Wine Guild, a Life Member of the International Wine and Food Society, and a founder of the Cape Wine Academy (CWA) and the Wine & Spirit Education Trust. He has also had several books published and, 'like a well-aged red, drinks very well'.